Ten Questions Prospective Franchisees Should Consider

1. Are you willing and able to take on the responsibilities of managing your own business?
2. Will you enjoy the franchise?
3 Are you willing to completely follow the franchisor's system?
4. Do you have a history of success in dealing and interacting with people?
5. Can you afford the franchise?
6. Have you carefully studied the legal documents?
7. Does the franchise you are considering have a track record of success?
8. Are the current franchisees generally happy and successful?
9. Do you like the franchisor's staff—those people with whom you will be working?
10. Do you have a supportive family and/or friends?

Source: Adapted by the authors from *Franchise Opportunities Guide* (Washington, D.C.: International Franchise Association, 1993), pp. 10-14.

Consumer Attitudes Toward Shopping

Statements on Shopping

% of Consumers Agreeing with the Statements

Store preference is based on selection.

Store preference is based on price.

Store preference is based on quality.

Store preference is based on location.

Familiar labels are important.

Value/comfort is preferred over fashion.

Store preference is based on service.

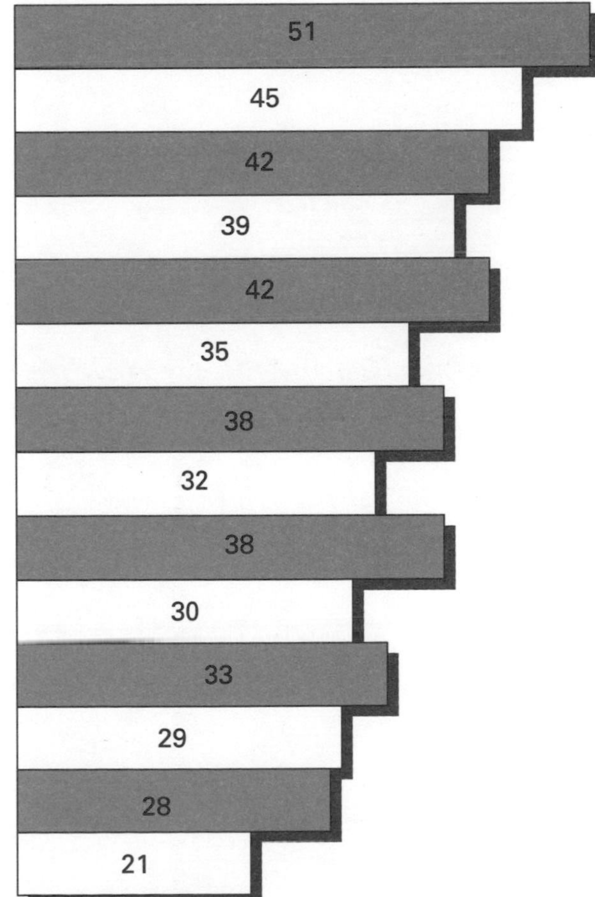

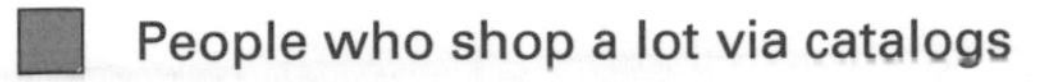

People who seldom shop via catalogs

Source: Adapted by the authors from Harvey D. Braun, "The Catalog Shopper of the '90s," *Direct Marketing* (March 1993), p. 17.

Retail Management

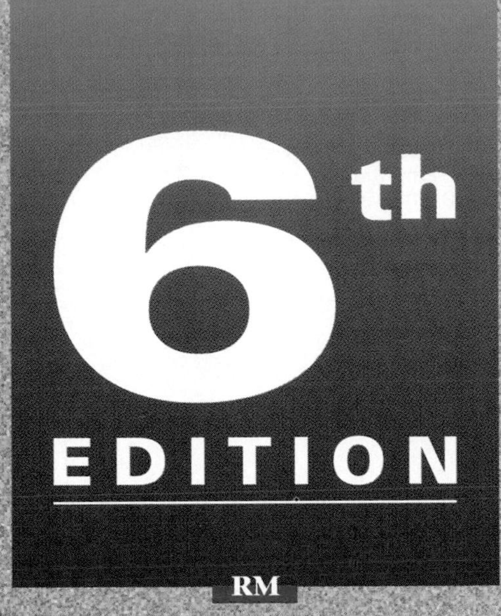

Retail Management

A Strategic Approach

Barry Berman
Hofstra University

Joel R. Evans
Hofstra University

Prentice Hall
Englewood Cliffs, NJ 07632

LIBRARY OF CONGRESS CATALOGING-IN-PUBLICATION DATA

Berman, Barry
Retail management : a strategic approach/
Barry Berman, Joel R. Evans.—6th ed.
p. cm.
Includes indexes.
ISBN 0-02-308661-0
1. Retail trade—Management. I. Evans, Joel R. II. Title.
HF5429.B45 1995
658.8′7—dc20 94-36424
CIP

Acquisitions Editor: David Borkowsky
Production Editor: Katherine Evancie
Managing Editor: Fran Russello
Interior/Cover Designer: A Good Thing, Inc.
Design Director: Pat Wosczyk
Copy Editor: J. Edward Neve
Buyer: Paul Smolenski
Assistant Editor: Melissa Steffens
Editorial Assistant: Aviva Rosenberg
Production Assistant: Renée Pelletier
Illustrations: A Good Thing, Inc.
Cover Photo: © Glenn Allison / Tony Stone Images, Inc.

A Simon & Schuster Company
Englewood Cliffs, New Jersey 07632

Printed in the United States of America

10 9 8 7 6 5 4 3 2 1

ISBN 0-02-308661-0

Prentice-Hall International (UK) Limited, *London*
Prentice-Hall of Australia Pty. Limited, *Sydney*
Prentice-Hall Canada Inc., *Toronto*
Prentice-Hall Hispanoamericana, S.A., *Mexico*
Prentice-Hall of India Private Limited, *New Delhi*
Prentice-Hall of Japan, Inc., *Tokyo*
Simon & Schuster Asia Pte. Ltd., *Singapore*
Editora Prentice-Hall do Brasil, Ltda., *Rio de Janeiro*

To Linda, Glenna, and Lisa

To Linda, Jennifer, and Stacey

Thank you for your enduring patience and understanding.

About the Authors

Barry Berman (Ph.D. in Business with majors in Marketing and Behavioral Science) is the Walter H. "Bud" Miller Distinguished Professor of Business and Professor of Marketing and International Business at Hofstra University. Previously, Dr. Berman was the associate dean of the Hofstra School of Business for seven years. He has served as a consultant to such organizations as Fortunoff, Associated Dry Goods, the State Education Department of New York, and professional and trade groups.

Dr. Berman is the author or editor of numerous books and articles and is active in various professional associations. He served as the associate editor of the *Marketing Review* for many years. At Hofstra, he has been honored as a faculty inductee in Beta Gamma Sigma honor society and received two Dean's Awards. In 1984, Dr. Berman was selected as Teacher of the Year by the Hofstra M.B.A. Association.

Joel R. Evans (Ph.D. in Business with majors in Marketing and Public Policy) is the RMI Distinguished Professor of Business and Professor of Marketing and International Business at Hofstra University. Previously, Dr. Evans was department chairperson for seven years. Before joining Hofstra, he worked for United Merchants and Manufacturers, owned a retail mail-order business, and taught at Bernard M. Baruch College and New York University. He has also served as a consultant for such diverse companies as PepsiCo, Nynex, and McCrory.

Dr. Evans is the author or editor of numerous books and articles and is active in various professional associations. At Hofstra, he has been honored as a faculty inductee in Beta Gamma Sigma honor society and received two Dean's Awards and the School of Business Faculty Distinguished Service Award. In 1988, Dr. Evans was selected as Teacher of the Year by the Hofstra M.B.A. Association.

Barry Berman and Joel R. Evans have worked together since 1976 and are the co-authors of several best-selling texts. At present, Drs. Berman and Evans are co-directors of the Retail Management Institute and the Business Research Institute at Hofstra University. In addition, they are co-chairs of the American Marketing Association's Special Interest Group in Retailing and Retail Management. Both regularly teach undergraduate and graduate courses to a wide range of students.

Brief Contents

Contents

Part 3: Targeting Customers and Gathering Information 185

Part 8: Planning for the Future 615

Appendixes A1

Preface

We are gratified by the continuing responses to this text, as evidenced by adoptions at over 500 colleges and universities around the world. In this sixth edition, we have set out to retain the material and features most desired by professors and students, add new material and features requested by professors and students, keep the book as current as possible, and maintain the length of prior editions.

As in earlier editions, the concepts of a strategic approach and a retail strategy form the foundation of *Retail Management: A Strategic Approach*, sixth edition. With a strategic approach, "the underlying principle is that a retail firm needs to plan for and adapt to a complex, changing environment. Both opportunities and constraints must be considered." A retail strategy is "the overall plan guiding a retail firm. It has an influence on the firm's business activities and its response to market forces." The major objectives of our text are to enable the reader to become a good retail planner and decision maker and to help focus on change and adaptation to change.

The book is designed as a one-semester text for a beginning student of retailing or retail management. In many cases, such a student will have already been introduced to marketing principles. We strongly believe that retailing should be viewed as one form of marketing and not distinct from it.

The Tradition Continues

These significant features have been retained from earlier editions of *Retail Management: A Strategic Approach*:

- Full coverage of all major retailing topics—including consumer behavior, marketing research, store location, operations, service retailing, the retail audit, retail institutions, franchising, human resource management, computerization in retailing, and retailing in a changing environment.
- A decision-making orientation, with many flowcharts, figures, tables, and photos.
- A real-world approach that focuses on both small and large retail firms. Among the well-known retailers discussed in the text are Dayton Hudson, Dillard's, Home Depot, Lands' End, The Limited, McDonald's, Merry-Go-Round, J.C. Penney, Toys "R" Us, Sears, and Wal-Mart.
- Part openers to introduce each section of the text.
- A "Retailing in Action" box in each chapter. These boxes further illustrate the concepts presented in the text by focusing on real firms and situations.
- A numbered summary keyed to chapter objectives, a key terms listing, and discussion questions at the end of each chapter.
- Thirty-six end-of-chapter cases involving a wide range of retailers and retail practices.
- Eight end-of-part comprehensive cases.
- Up-to-date information from such sources as *Advertising Age, Business Week, Chain Store Age Executive, Direct Marketing, Discount Store News, Dun & Bradstreet, Forbes, Fortune, Journal of Retailing, National Retail Federation, Progressive Grocer, Stores,* and *Wall Street Journal.*
- A convenient, one-semester format.
- "How to Solve a Case Study," following Chapter 1.
- An appendix on franchising, following Chapter 4.
- An appendix on direct marketing, following Chapter 5.
- A career orientation, with actual career ladders and a thorough discussion of ownership and employment alternatives.
- End-of-text appendixes on careers in retailing, firms with retailing positions for college graduates, and a glossary.
- Computer-based exercises.

New to the Sixth Edition

Since the first edition of *Retail Management: A Strategic Approach*, we have worked hard to be as contemporary and forward-looking as possible. We have continually strived to be proactive rather than defensive in our preparation of each edition. That is why we have always taken this adage of the late Sam Walton so seriously: "Commit to your business. Believe in it more than anybody else."

Thus, for the sixth edition, there are a number of changes in *Retail Management: A Strategic Approach*. We hope you like them:

1. The organization of the text has been revamped.
   a. There are 19 chapters (up from 18 in the fifth edition). The material on operations management is now covered in two chapters instead of one.
   b. To integrate the material better throughout the text, the changing environment of retailing has been moved to Chapter 3 (it was the last chapter in the fifth edition).

2. These substantive chapter revisions have been made:
   a. Chapter 1 (An Introduction to Retailing)—The beginning of the chapter has been made much more "reader friendly." There is a detailed discussion of Wal-Mart's evolution and why the firm is so successful. The total retail experience, customer service, and relationship retailing are described.
   b. Chapter 2 (Strategic Planning in Retailing: Owning or Managing a Business)—There is more emphasis on organizational mission and positioning.
   c. Chapter 3 (Strategic Planning in Retailing: Dealing with the Changing Environment)—Ethics and social responsibility are more fully examined. The international dimensions of retailing receive greater coverage.
   d. Chapters 4–5 (Part 2: Situation Analysis)—All data regarding retail institutions have been updated.
   e. Chapter 6 (Identifying and Understanding Consumers)—All data regarding consumer demographics have been updated.
   f. Chapter 7 (Information Gathering and Processing in Retailing)—The discussion of retail information systems has been expanded and now appears in the first half of the chapter; the retail research process comprises the second half of the chapter.
   g. Chapters 8–9 (Part 4: Choosing a Store Location)—The concept of geographic information systems (GIS) is introduced, accompanied by a multipage photo montage.
   h. Chapter 10 (Retail Organization and Human Resource Management)—The coverage of employee training has been revised.
   i. Chapter 11 (Operations Management: Financial Dimensions)—This chapter deals with profit planning, asset management, budgeting, and resource allocation.
   j. Chapter 12 (Operations Management: Operational Dimensions)—This chapter covers eleven different nonfinancial aspects of operations management.
   k. Chapters 13–15 (Part 6: Merchandise Management and Pricing)—There is enhanced coverage of private labels, merchandise sources, direct product profitability, and everyday low pricing.
   l. Chapters 16–17 (Part 7: Communicating with the Customer)—A broader view of retail communication is presented. The concept of a planogram is introduced. Frequent-shopper programs are now covered.
   m. Chapter 18 (Planning by a Service Retailer)—There are more examples. SERVQUAL is discussed.
   n. Chapter 19 (Integrating and Controlling the Retail Strategy)—The concept of a retail performance index is introduced.
   o. Appendix C (Retail Management Software)—In addition to 15 computer-based exercises that are denoted by a computer symbol throughout the text, *Retail Management: A Strategic Approach* is now also accompanied by a simulation exercise and a data-base exercise.

3. There is an all-new text design. The book is in a full four-color format, with plentiful art and photos throughout. Each chapter now begins with an attractive two-page spread.

4. The in-chapter boxed material—which is all new—has been made more topical and more focused. Every chapter contains a "Retailing in Action" box, a "Retailing Around the World" box, and an "Ethics in Retailing" box.

5. All of the chapter-opening vignettes are new.
6. To make them easier to find, footnotes now appear on the bottom of the pages in which citations have been made.
7. Almost all of the chapter-ending cases are new or substantially revised. Nineteen of these cases have a video component; they are denoted by a video symbol in the text.
8. All of the part-ending comprehensive cases are new.
9. Current data on retailing opportunities and an assortment of new career ladders appear in the text-ending Appendix A.
10. An interactive computerized study guide is bundled with the text. It is quite user friendly and facilitates student review and studying.

How the Text Is Organized

Retail Management: A Strategic Approach is divided into eight parts. Part 1 introduces the field of retailing, the basic principles of strategic planning, the decisions to be made in owning or managing a retail business, and the changing environment of retailing. In Part 2, retail institutions are examined on the basis of ownership types, as well as store-based, nonstore-based, and service versus goods strategy mixes. The wheel of retailing, scrambled merchandising, and the retail life cycle are also covered. Part 3 focuses on selecting a target market and information-gathering methods, including discussions of the consumer decision process and the retailing information system. Part 4 presents a four-step approach to location planning: trading-area analysis, choosing the most desirable type of location, selecting a general locale, and deciding on a specific site.

Part 5 discusses the elements involved in managing a retail business: the retail organization structure, human resource management, and operations management (both financial and operational). Part 6 deals with merchandise management (the buying and handling of merchandise, as well as the financial aspects of merchandising) and pricing. In Part 7, the ways of communicating with customers are analyzed, with special attention paid to store image, atmosphere, and promotion techniques. Part 8 covers service retailing, and integrating and controlling a retail strategy.

At the end of the text, Appendix A describes various careers in retailing, Appendix B presents a detailed listing of potential retail-related employers, Appendix C explains the computer materials keyed to the text, and Appendix D offers a comprehensive glossary.

Three student supplements are available to accompany *Retail Management: A Strategic Approach*, Sixth Edition:

- The interactive computerized study guide diskette that is bundled free with the text.
- A comprehensive companion text (*Applying Retail Management: A Strategic Approach*, Sixth Edition) that contains chapter objectives, key terms and concepts, readings and exercises on real-life companies and situations, chapter questions, and a complete appendix on retail mathematics (with dozens of problems to be solved).
- A *Retail Management Software* computer diskette, containing the programs noted in Appendix C in the text, that is available to schools adopting *Retail Management*. This user-friendly software brings more excitement to student learning of key retailing concepts and is PC-based.

A well-rounded teaching package is available for instructors. It includes a detailed instructor's manual, transparency masters, color transparencies, a large test bank, and a manual for the video lectures. All of the instructional materials have been developed or written by the authors (except for the videos, which we personally selected).

Please feel free to send us comments regarding any aspect of *Retail Management* or its package: Barry Berman or Joel R. Evans, Department of Marketing and International Business, Hofstra University, Hempstead, N.Y., 11550-1090. We promise to reply to any correspondence we receive.

B.B.
J.R.E.

About the Boxed Material in *Retail Management: A Strategic Approach*

As noted earlier in the preface, there are three applications boxes per chapter in the text: "Retailing in Action," "Retailing Around the World," and "Ethics in Retailing." Through these boxes, a wide variety of thought-provoking situations are presented. They are balanced by size of company, geographic coverage, and so on.

"Retailing in Action" Boxes

"Retailing Around the World" Boxes

"Ethics in Retailing" Boxes

About the Videos that Accompany *Retail Management: A Strategic Approach*

Retail Management: A Strategic Approach has two video supplements available: one for the 21 videos denoted by the symbol in the text and another that includes four separate video lectures.

Every chapter (except Chapter 1) has two end-of-chapter cases, 19 of which have optional video components. In addition, a video for Chapter 1, on Wal-Mart, augments the chapter discussion of that firm; and a career-oriented video can be used in conjunction with Appendix A.

These are the cases that have a video component:

Chapter	Case	Text Page Reference
1	Wal-Mart (extended in-chapter discussion)	15
2	2. Lands' End: A Large Firm's Retail Strategy	58
3	1. Foodland in Hawaii	91
4	2. Maaco: Evaluating Franchising Opportunities	123
5	1. Rewriting the Definition of Membership Clubs	165
	2. The Home Shopping Network: Behind the Scenes	167
6	1. Personal Cleansing: Cleaning Up on a Changing Category254	219
7	2. The Marsh Super Study	254
8	1. Arby's: The Use of Strategic Mapping Software	294
10	2. Supervalu: Performance Appraisal	364
12	1. Category Management: Soft Drink Sales and Profitability	418
	2. Sensormatic: Pilferage Control	420
13	1. Supervalu: Produce Power	460
	2. Lillian Vernon: Order Processing	462
15	1. Dahl's Fair Practices	534

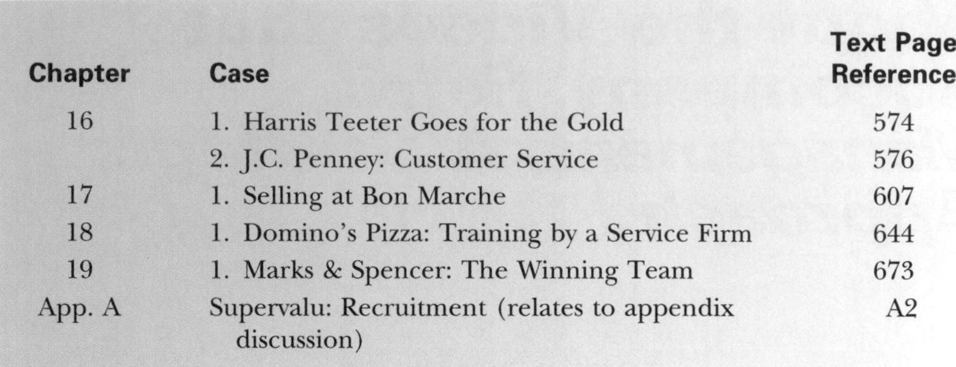

Chapter	Case	Text Page Reference
16	1. Harris Teeter Goes for the Gold	574
	2. J.C. Penney: Customer Service	576
17	1. Selling at Bon Marche	607
18	1. Domino's Pizza: Training by a Service Firm	644
19	1. Marks & Spencer: The Winning Team	673
App. A	Supervalu: Recruitment (relates to appendix discussion)	A2

In addition to the video cases, videos are available so that the professor can enhance his or her coverage of these retailing topics:

Video Number	Video Title	Length of Video
1	Franchising	24 minutes
2	Mass Merchandising	17 minutes
3	Retail Site Selection	17 minutes
4	Managing Merchandise Assortments	22 minutes

Full-length lecture notes accompany the preceding videos.

Acknowledgments

Many people have assisted us in the preparation of this book, and to them we extend our warmest appreciation.

We thank these individuals for contributing cases:

Bixby Cooper, *Michigan State University*
John I. Coppett, *University of Houston—Clear Lake*
Roger A. Dickinson, *University of Texas at Arlington*
Marvin A. Jolson, *University of Maryland*
Raymond A. Marquardt, *University of Nebraska—Lincoln*
William J. McDonald, *Hofstra University*
Ronald D. Michman, *Shippensburg University*
Nancy A. Oliver, *East Carolina University*
John L. Roman, *Rochester Institute of Technology*
Lynn Samsel, *University of Nebraska—Lincoln*
William A. Staples, *University of Houston—Clear Lake*
Ginger A. Woodard, *East Carolina University*

We thank these individuals for participating in a lengthy focus group session for this edition:

Betty J. Diener, *University of Massachusetts—Harbor Campus, Boston*
Frederick Langhrehr, *Valparaiso University*
Milton Shuch, *Simmons College*
Robert A. Swerdlow, *Lamar University*

We thank the following reviewers, who have reacted to this or earlier editions of the text. Each has provided us with perceptive comments that have helped us crystallize our thoughts:

Larry Audler, *University of New Orleans*
Ramon Avila, *Ball State University*
Stephen Batory, *Bloomsburg University*
Joseph Belonax, *Western Michigan University*
Ronald Bernard, *Diablo Valley College*
Charlane Bomrad, *Onondaga Community College*
David P. Brennan, *University of St. Thomas*
John J. Buckley, *Orange County Community College*
Joseph A. Davidson, *Cuyahoga Community College*
Peter T. Doukas, *Westchester Community College*
Jack D. Eure, Jr., *Southwest Texas State University*
Letty Fisher, *Westchester Community College*
Myron Gable, *Shippensburg University*
Linda L. Golden, *University of Texas at Austin*
James I. Gray, *Florida Atlantic University*

Mary Higby, *Eastern Michigan University*
Charles A. Ingene, *University of Washington*
Marvin A. Jolson, *University of Maryland*
Ruth Keyes, *SUNY College of Technology*
J. Ford Laumer, Jr., *Auburn University*
Richard C. Leventhal, *Metropolitan State College*
John Lloyd, *Monroe Community College*
Elizabeth L. Mariotz, *Philadelphia College of Textiles*
James O. McCann, *Henry Ford Community College*
Frank McDaniels, *Delaware County Community College*
Brian McNeeley, *University of Wisconsin—Parkside*
Michael Messina, *Gannon University*
Ronald Michman, *Shippensburg University*
James R. Ogden, *Kutztown University*
Howard C. Paul, *Mercyhurst College*
Roy B. Payne, *Purdue University*
Dawn Pysarchik, *Michigan State University*
Curtis Reierson, *Baylor University*
Steven J. Shaw, *University of South Carolina*
Gladys S. Sherdell, *Montgomery College*
John E. Swan, *University of Alabama in Birmingham*
Anthony Urbanisk, *Northern State University*
Lillian Werner, *University of Minnesota*
Kaylene Williams, *University of Delaware*
Terrell G. Williams, *Utah State University*

Special thanks and acknowledgment are due to the fine Prentice Hall people who have worked on this edition, in particular, our editor Dave Borkowksy. We also appreciate the efforts of John C. Galloway, Jr. for his computer work; Diane Schoenberg and Susan Parker for their editorial assistance; Linda Berman for compiling the indexes; and Linda Evans for her work on the video manual.

Barry Berman
Joel R. Evans
Hofstra University

A Tour of Berman/Evans

Retail Management: A Strategic Approach

SIXTH EDITION

A Brief Walking Tour

Over the next few pages, you will find an overview of many of the unique elements we have included in *Retail Management: A Strategic Approach*. Through these elements, we seek to present comprehensive coverage of retailing and retail management—and to do so in an appealing and contemporary way.

We've got the field of retailing covered—from the total retail experience and relationship retailing in Chapter 1 to the retail performance index in Chapter 19.

In *Retail Management: A Strategic Approach*, we introduce and integrate the key concepts of retailing, many of which have grown more important in recent years. The total retail experience, relationship retailing, geographic information systems (GIS), and SERVQUAL, are just four of the major concepts that are given extended coverage.

The Total Retail Experience

While one person may shop at a discount store, another at a neighborhood store, a third at a full-service store, and so on, these diverse shoppers have something crucial in common: They each encounter a total retail experience (including everything from parking to checkout counter) in making a purchase.

The ***total retail experience*** consists of all the elements in a retail offering that encourage or inhibit consumers during their contact with a given retailer. Many elements, like the number of salespeople on the floor, display windows, prices, the brands carried, and inventory on hand, are controllable by a retailer; others, like the adequacy of on-street parking, the timing of deliveries from suppliers, and sales taxes, are not. If some part of the total retail experience is unsatisfactory, consumers may not buy a given good or service—they may even decide not to patronize a retailer again.

We look at retailing from a broad perspective.

Throughout the text, there is a discussion about the technologies now available to assist retailers in their planning.

THE USE OF GEOGRAPHIC INFORMATION SYSTEMS IN TRADING-AREA DELINEATION AND ANALYSIS

Increasingly, retailers are using geographic information systems software in their trading-area delineation and analysis. ***Geographic information systems (GIS)*** combine digitized mapping with key locational data to graphically depict such trading-area characteristics as the demographic attributes of the population, data on customer purchases, and listings of current, proposed, and competitor locations. Thus, GIS software enables retailers to rather easily research the attractiveness of alternative locations and to present the findings on computer-screen maps.[6] Prior to GIS software, retailers often placed different color pins on paper-based maps to represent their current and proposed locales—as well as competitor sites—and typically had to do their own data collection and analysis.

Relationship Retailing

Today, good retailers realize that it is in their interest to engage in ***relationship retailing***, whereby they seek to establish and maintain long-term bonds with customers, rather than act as if each sales transaction is a completely new encounter with them. This means that the retailers must concentrate on the total retail experience, monitor shopper satisfaction with customer service, and stay in touch with customers.

To be effective with relationship retailing, a firm has to keep these two points in mind: First, because it is harder to lure new customers than to make existing ones happy, a "win-win" approach should be enacted. For the retailer to "win" in the long run (lure shoppers, make sales, earn profits, etc.), the customer must also "win" in the long run (receive a good value, be treated with respect, feel welcome at the store, etc.). Otherwise, the retailer loses (shoppers go to other stores) and customers lose (by having to spend time and money to learn about other retailers). Second, as a result of the advances in computer technology, it is now much easier to develop a customer data base—complete with data about people's attributes and past shopping behavior. Thus, ongoing customer contact can be better, more frequent, and more focused.

The long-term nature of retailer-customer relations is explored.

Answer YES or NO to each of these statements:	YES	NO
1. There is a clearly defined mission for the firm.	______	______
2. There are stated long-term and short-term goals.	______	______
3. Key environmental trends are studied on a regular basis.	______	______
4. A target market has been identified and its characteristics are known.	______	______
5. The unique dimensions of service retailing are understood, with regard to		
a. Intangibility.	______	______
b. Inseparability.	______	______
c. Perishability.	______	______
d. Variability.	______	______
6. The strategic plan takes into account each of the factors noted in item 5.	______	______
7. Employees understand their special relationship with customers.	______	______
8. Customer service is stressed.	______	______
9. There are ongoing efforts to communicate the firm's image.	______	______
10. The pricing approach is keyed to the target market and the services and positioning of the firm.	______	______
11. A service blueprint is used to maximize productivity.	______	______
12. a. High-caliber personnel are hired and trained.	______	______
b. Employee turnover is low.	______	______
13. Service value is properly conveyed to customers.	______	______
14. Customer referrals are encouraged and rewarded.	______	______
15. Complaints are promptly resolved—to the customer's satisfaction.	______	______
16. The actions of competitors are monitored.	______	______
17. New services are added, so the firm's offering does not become stale.	______	______
18. A significant amount of time is spent in planning.	______	______

NOTE: ANSWERING NO TO ANY OF THE STATEMENTS MEANS THE SERVICE RETAILER HAS A DEFICIENCY THAT NEEDS TO BE CORRECTED.

FIGURE 18–8
Assessing a Service Retailer's Performance

Emphasis is placed on assessing performance.

We want to provide you with the most useful book possible. That is why there are four end-of-text appendixes.

Careers in Retailing

A person looking for a career in retailing has two broad possibilities: owning a business or working for an employer. One alternative does not preclude the other. Many people open their own stores after getting experience as employees. A person can also choose franchising, which has elements of both entrepreneurship and managerial assistance. Franchising was discussed in Chapter 4.

Regardless of the specific retail career path chosen, it is important to note that recent college graduates often gain personnel and profit-and-loss responsibilities faster in retailing than in any other major industry. For instance, after an initial training program, an entry-level manager supervises personnel, works on in-store displays, interacts with customers, and reviews sales and other data on a regular basis. And an assistant buyer helps in planning merchandise assortments, interacting with suppliers, and outlining the promotion effort. Typically, new merchandise selections must be made at least once every four to six months.

Owning a retail establishment is quite popular, and many opportunities exist. About four-fifths of all retail outlets are sole proprietorships. In addition, many of today's retail giants started out as independents. J.C. Penney, R.H. Macy, Kmart, Filene's, Toys "R" Us, McDonald's, and Sears illustrate this point. The founders of Lands' End, Petrie Stores, Body Shop, Wal-Mart, Weis Markets, and The Limited are profiled in Table 1.[1]

Too often, people overlook the possibility of owning a retail business. In a number of cases, initial investments can be quite modest (several thousand dollars). For example, many mail-order, vending-machine, direct-selling, and service retailers require relatively low initial investments—as do various franchising opportunities. In addition, financing may be available from banks, manufacturers, store-fixture firms, and equipment companies. Chapter 2 contained an in-depth discussion of starting and operating a retail business.

[1] For profiles of other successful retailing entrepreneurs, see James Barron, "The New Millionaires: Making It in Tough Times," *New York Times* (August 15, 1993), pp. 1, 10.

We describe the various career options available in retailing.

Selected Firms Seeking College Graduates for Retail-Related Positions

Abraham & Straus
420 Fulton Street
Brooklyn, NY 11202
Department store chain
New York, New Jersey

Acme Markets, Inc.
75 Valley Stream Parkway
Malvern, PA 19355
Supermarket chain
East

Albertson's
250 Parkcenter Boulevard
Boise, ID 83726
Supermarket, superstore, and combination food/drug chains
West, South

American Stores Co.
P.O. Box 27447
Salt Lake City, UT 84127
Supermarket and drugstore chains
U.S.

Ames Department Stores
2418 Main Street
Rocky Hill, CT 06067
Discount department and variety store chains
Northeast, Mid-Atlantic

Associated Merchandising Corporation
1440 Broadway
New York, NY 10018
Affiliated with 30 department stores
Retail service organization
Northeast

J. Baker, Inc.
P.O. Box 231
Readville, MA 02136
Licensed shoe departments/shoe wholesaler and retailer
U.S.

Banana Republic
1 Harrison Street
San Francisco, CA 94107
Specialty clothing chain
U.S.

Banker's Note, Inc.
4900 Highlands Parkway
Smyrna, GA 30082
Specialty store chain
South

Barnes & Noble
120 Fifth Avenue, 5th Floor
New York, NY 10011
Bookstore chain
U.S.

W. Bell & Co., Inc.
12401 Twinbrook Parkway
Rockville, MD 20852
Showroom/warehouse/catalog chain
Washington, D.C.; Baltimore, Maryland; Chicago, Illinois

Best Products
1400 Best Plaza
Richmond, VA 23260
Catalog showroom and jewelry store chains
27 states

Big B, Inc.
P.O. Box 10168
Birmingham, AL 35202
Drugstore chain
South

Big V Supermarkets, Inc.
176 North Main Street
Florida, NY 10921
Supermarket chain
New York

Bloomingdale's
1000 Third Avenue
New York, NY 10022
Department store chain
8 states

Bon Marche
1601 Third Avenue
Seattle, WA 98101
Department store chain
Pacific Northwest, Rocky Mountain states

Boys Markets, Inc.
777 Harbor Boulevard
La Habra, CA 90631
Supermarket chain
California

Bradlees
1 Bradlees Circle
Braintree, MA 02184
Discount department store chain
Northeast

A listing of more than 200 potential retail employers is provided.

Retail Management Software

This appendix and an accompanying computer diskette let you engage in decision making under simulated conditions and apply many of the concepts studied during a course in retailing or retail management. The *Retail Management Software* diskette has three separate software packages: *Computer-Based Exercises in Retail Management*; *SUPERCO*, a retail simulation program; and *Appliance Data Base*, a customer and inventory data-base program for a small appliance-repair firm. Each of these packages is described in Appendix C.

The software is designed to run on a DOS-based PC and will work with a color or monochrome monitor. Although the overall quality of the graphics for these software [illegible]

General directions for copying the software onto a floppy disk or your hard drive are contained in the next section. Then, specific information on each package is presented.

Directions for Copying the Retail Management Software Diskette

To use the *Retail Management Software*, you need to purchase a blank computer diskette and make a personal copy of the master diskette that is available to your instructor.

These directions assume that your PC has two 3-1/2" high-density drives or one 3-1/2" high-density drive and a hard drive, and that you are using a version of DOS that is 5.0 or newer. If your computer system does not match this configuration, you will have to employ other procedures for copying your diskette. In that case, please refer to the DOS booklet that accompanies your computer system.

The following procedure creates three directories: EXERCISE, SUPERCO, and APPLDATA on your floppy disk or hard drive.

Using a Computer with Two Floppy Drives

If you are working with a two disk-drive computer with no hard drive, then follow these instructions. In this configuration, the floppy drives are known as drive "A" and drive "B."

To make your copy of the three software packages from the *Retail Management Software* master diskette, insert a disk operating system (DOS) diskette in drive A. Turn

Several different computer applications can help improve your decision-making skills.

Glossary

Addition to Retail Percentage Measures a price rise as a percentage of original price:

$$\text{Addition to retail percentage} = \frac{\text{New price} - \text{Original price}}{\text{Original price}}$$

Additional Markup An increase in retail price after—and in addition to—the original markup; it is used when demand is unexpectedly high or when costs are rising.

Additional Markup Percentage Looks at total dollar additional markups as a percentage of net sales:

$$\text{Additional markup percentage} = \frac{\text{Total dollar additional markups}}{\text{Net sales (in \$)}}$$

Administered Pricing Occurs when a retailer seeks consumer patronage on the basis of a distinctive retailing mix. If strong differentiation can be reached, a firm can control the prices it charges.

Advertising Any paid, nonpersonal communication transmitted through out-of-store mass media by an identified sponsor.

Affinity Exists when the various stores at a given location complement, blend, and cooperate with one another, and each benefits from the others' presence.

Agate Line Used in newspaper advertising; there are 14 agate lines to an inch of space, one column wide.

All-You-Can-Afford Method A promotional budgeting technique in which a retailer first allocates funds for every element of the retail strategy mix except promotion. Any funds left over are placed into a promotional budget.

Analog Model A computer site-selection tool in which potential sales are estimated based on existing store revenues in similar areas, the competition at the prospective location, expected market shares at that location, and the size and density of the location's primary trading area.

Ancillary Customer Services Extra elements that enhance a retail strategy mix. They do not have to be provided.

Application Blank Provides data on an applicant's education, experience, health, reasons for leaving previous jobs, organizational memberships, hobbies, and references.

Asset Turnover A performance measure based on a retailer's net sales and total assets. It is equal to net sales divided by total assets.

Assets Any items a retailer owns that have a monetary value.

[illegible] exhibits a wide range of merchandise for the customer. It may be open or closed.

Atmosphere The physical characteristics of a store that are used to develop an image and to draw customers.

Attitudes (Opinions) The positive, neutral, or negative feelings a person has about the economy, politics, goods, services, institutions, and so on.

Audit Form Lists the area(s) to be examined and the exact data required in evaluating each area.

Automatic Markdown Plan Controls the amount and timing of markdowns on the basis of the length of time merchandise remains in stock.

Automatic Reordering System Orders merchandise when stock-on-hand reaches a pre-determined reorder point. An automatic reorder can be generated by a computer on the basis of a perpetual inventory system and reorder point calculations.

Bait Advertising An illegal practice whereby a retailer lures a customer by advertising goods and services at very low prices; then, once the customer contacts the retailer, he or she is told the good/service of interest is out of stock or of inferior quality. A salesperson tries to convince the customer to purchase a better, more expensive substitute that is available. The retailer has no intention of selling the advertised item.

All of the key terms in the text are conveniently defined in the glossary.

A Brief Walking Tour

This edition of *Retail Management: A Strategic Approach* has a colorful new design to make it more visually attractive.

Retail Institutions by Strategy Mix

❖ Chapter Objectives

1. **To describe the wheel of retailing, scrambled merchandising, and the retail life cycle and show how they help explain the performance and evolution of retail strategy mixes**
2. **To examine the characteristics of a wide variety of retail institutions involved with store-based strategy mixes (divided into food-oriented and general merchandise groupings)**
3. **To look at the characteristics of the three major retail institutions involved with nonstore-based strategy mixes: vending machine, direct selling, and direct marketing**
4. **To contrast service-based retailing with goods-based retailing**

Because gas station owners are struggling with reduced profit margins from their sale of gasoline, they have been increasingly adding merchandise lines they feel are compatible with gasoline. This has led to some interesting approaches: gas stations that sell flowers, gas stations with dry cleaning services, and even gas stations that sell prepared foods such as tacos. Mobil Corporation, for example, is currently experimenting with a combined gas station and McDonald's in Naples, Florida, a combined gas station and Burger King in Chicago, and a combined gas station with Taco Bell and Pizza Hut at further locations. Other gas stations are even adding fax/copier centers, parcel drop-off services, and video rental units.

The rise in this form of scrambled merchandising is due to various factors: environmental regulations, competition from specialized car-service firms, and changes in consumer behavior. Recent environmental regulations have forced many gas stations to replace their storage tanks and pumping equipment to control fumes during pumping and to eliminate fuel spills. The cost of meeting these state and federal rules are so high that stations often need other product lines to supplement gasoline sales. A number of stations now have vacant service bays because they have lost customers to specialized oil change, tune-up, muffler replacement, and tire shops. Thus, their dormant service bays provide space for other retail uses. Last, consumers feel more comfortable buying unrelated products (even prepared foods) at gasoline stations than they did before.

One concern about the sales of nontraditional goods and services by gas stations is the blurring of the traditional image of the gasoline station as a place where cars are serviced and gasoline is sold. Another potential problem is that the sale of gasoline and some unrelated items may be in conflict with one another. For example, the sale of gasoline is generally maximized when payment dispensers (that accept credit cards directly at the gasoline pump) are used. Yet, because drivers do not have to leave their cars when payment dispensers are used, the sale of highly-profitable impulse goods such as soda, coffee, and cigarettes is minimized. Dispensers are particularly favored by women drivers with children in the car; but, this represents a key customer group for fill-in items such as milk, eggs, and snack foods for children.[1]

[1] Agis Salpukas, "Fill It Up? Send a Fax? Have a Taco?" *New York Times* (December 27, 1993), pp. D1, D3.

Reprinted by permission

132 133

From the beginning of every chapter

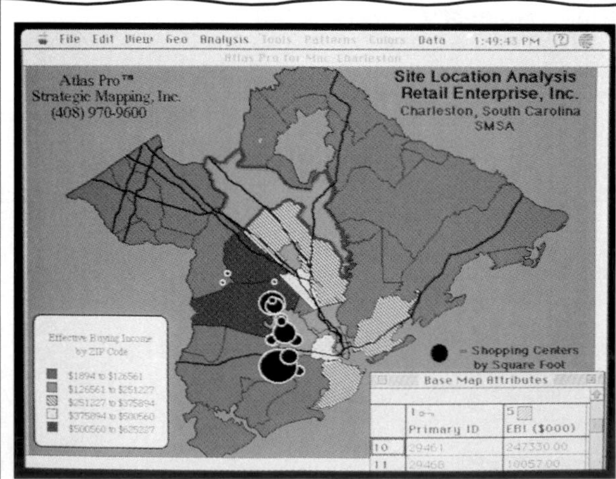

Figure 8–2 (Continued)
Strategic Mapping is well known for its GIS software. Among its retailing clients are Arby's, Circuit City, Citibank, Marriott, and May. The firm's most popular software is its Atlas series—which consists of Atlas GIS, Atlas Site Analyst (an add-on module for Atlas GIS), and Atlas Pro. Atlas Site Analyst and Atlas Pro are highlighted on this page. As Strategic Mapping states, "GIS offers the retailer numerous competitive advantages including the ability to: base decisions on both quantitative facts and geographic information; consider multiple alternatives through easy, interactive 'what if' and 'show me' analysis; produce and update maps and reports quickly and easily; and present conclusions in a clear and persuasive fashion with boardroom-quality maps and corresponding data-base reports."
Reprinted by permission of Strategic Mapping, Inc.

Through the figures contained therein, the field of retailing comes to life.

Retail Management: A Strategic Approach has three thought-provoking boxes in each chapter: "Retailing in Action," "Retailing Around the World," and "Ethics in Retailing." Each one presents a real-life situation.

Important managerial issues are raised.

RETAILING IN ACTION

Rolling on the River?

Retail customer service has certainly come a long way! For example, the Oak Park Price Less supermarket, located in Jeffersonville, Indiana, has been operating a river delivery service to boats on the Ohio River for more than 10 years. These deliveries now account for one-quarter of the supermarket's total annual sales.

This is how Oak Park Price Less' river delivery business operates: Boats fax their orders, which average $1,500, directly to the store. The orders are then picked by supermarket personnel and delivered directly to Oak Park Price Less' 32-foot cruiser. The supermarket makes ten cruiser deliveries in a typical week; and, despite the large order size—which usually includes a week's supply of food for a boat crew, orders are often filled within an hour.

To best serve its customers, Oak Park Price Less makes river deliveries on a 24-hour per day, year-round basis (including Christmas and New Year's Day). Deliveries are even made in poor weather conditions, such as 6-foot waves. Oak Park Price Less also delivers necessities for crew members that the store does not carry—such as prescription medicines, shoes, and washing machines.

According to Oak Park Price Less, "We take care of them [boat customers] just like we take care of customers that walk into the store."

Source: Based on material in Tom Chiat, "Rolling on the River," *Progressive Grocer* (October 1993), pp. 133–134.

Ethical issues are introduced that are consequential and provocative.

RETAILING AROUND THE WORLD

How Far Will People Travel to Shop?

Until recently, foreign shoppers represented a significant target market only for those U.S. retailers located in exclusive shopping areas such as Madison Avenue in New York City, the Magnificent Mile in Chicago, and Rodeo Drive in Beverly Hills. Now, shopping areas such as the Mall of America in Bloomington (outside Minneapolis-St. Paul), Sawgrass Mills in Ft. Lauderdale, and factory outlet stores in Fall River, Massachusetts, report that a growing proportion of their sales comes from tourists who live in Australia, Japan, and Western Europe.

For example, Sawgrass Mills, a factory outlet mall, finds that almost one-half of its 18 million annual visitors are foreign. The mall estimates that a foreign visitor spends an average of $500 to $1,000 on a shopping trip, compared to $200 for a typical local customer.

The increased patronage of foreign shoppers can be explained by four factors. One, some foreign travel agencies now organize shopping trips and promote these visits as part of organized U.S. tours. Two, some malls have begun to advertise overseas. Third, the prices of many items are considerably cheaper in the United States, due to both the competitive environment in this country and the low relative value of the U.S. dollar. Fourth, many U.S. retailers feature goods and services that are unavailable in foreign markets.

Source: Based on material in Barnaby J. Feder, "U.S. Malls Luring Foreign Shoppers," *New York Times* (December 13, 1993), pp. D1, D3.

An international perspective to retailing is presented

ETHICS IN RETAILING

Why Is Ben & Jerry Ahead of the Pack?

Unlike most firms, Ben & Jerry publishes two types of audits in its annual report: financial and social. The social audit, conducted by an outside firm, evaluates Ben & Jerry's performance in such areas as employee benefits, plant safety, ecology, community involvement, and customer service. Ben & Jerry's supplies the social-audit analysts with all employee and corporate documents; it also agrees to publish the report in an unedited format.

Past social audits of Ben & Jerry's have been quite candid. For example, in its 1992 audit, the social auditor chided Ben & Jerry's plant-safety record and cited the increase in plant accidents from 52 in 1991 to 75 in 1992. Lost days due to accidents also increased from 902 to 1,702, an amount in excess of sales and production growth. The report also questioned Ben & Jerry's strategy of paying its highest-paid employee no more than seven times the salary of its lowest-paid worker in light of the number of vacant executive positions.

Public relations analysts believe that Ben & Jerry's social audit enhances its credibility among institutional investors, stockholders, and consumers. Few firms, however, have added a social audit to their annual report. Given Ben & Jerry's strong financial performance, maybe more should.

Source: Based on material in Betsy Wiesendanger, "Ben & Jerry Scoop Up Credibility," *Public Relations Journal*, (August 1993), p. 20.

A Brief Walking Tour

Our goal is to reinforce the concepts in *Retail Management: A Strategic Approach* in a helpful and stimulating manner. Thus, we have all the in-text pedagogy you could want: part openers, chapter objectives, opening vignettes, chapter overviews, highlighted key terms, pertinent tables, photos and line art, summaries linked to the chapter objectives, review and discussion questions—and more!

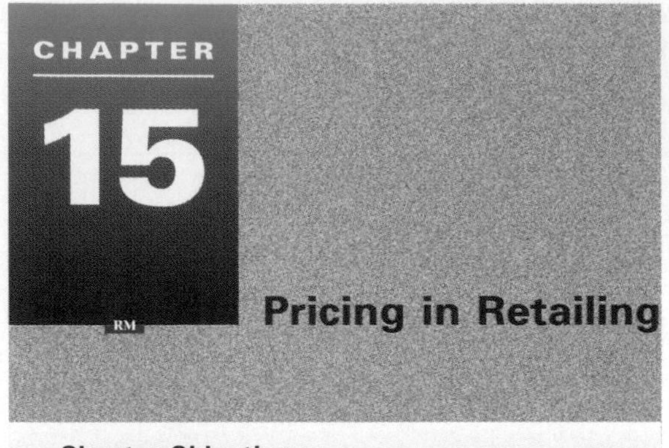
CHAPTER

15

RM

Pricing in Retailing

Chapter Objectives

1. To describe the role of pricing in a retail strategy and to show that pricing decisions must be made in an integrated and adaptive manner
2. To examine the impact of consumers; government; manufacturers, wholesalers, and other suppliers; and current and potential competitors on pricing decisions
3. To present a framework for developing a retail price strategy: objectives, broad policy, basic strategy, implementation, and adjustments

Reader-friendly objectives begin each chapter.

Summary

1. *To describe the role of pricing in a retail strategy and to show that pricing decisions must be made in an integrated and adaptive manner* Pricing is important to a retailer because of its interrelationship with overall objectives and the other components of the retail strategy mix. A price strategy must be well integrated and responsive.
2. *To examine the impact of consumers; government; manufacturers, wholesalers, and other suppliers; and current and potential competitors on pricing decisions* Before developing a price strategy, a retailer must study the factors affecting pricing. In some instances, these factors have only a minor effect on a retailer's pricing discretion; in others, they severely limit pricing options. nation, minimum prices, unit pricing, item price removal, and price advertising. Manufacturers, wholesalers, and other suppliers may be required to provide price guarantees (if they are in a position of weakness) and there may be conflicts about which party controls retail prices. The competitive environment may foster market pricing, which could lead to price wars, or administered pricing.
3. *To present a framework for developing a retail price strategy* Such a framework consists of five stages: objectives, broad price policy, price strategy, implementation of price strategy, and price adjustments.

   Retail pricing objectives can be chosen from among sales, dollar profits, return on investment, and/or early recovery of cash. After goals are chosen, broad

Overview

A retailer must price goods and services in a way that achieves profitability for the firm and satisfies customers, while adapting to various constraints.

Pricing is a crucial strategic variable for a retailer because of its direct relationship with a firm's goals and its interaction with other retailing-mix elements. A retailer's pricing strategy must be consistent with its overall sales, profit, and return-on-investment goals. For example, a retailer interested in an early recovery of its investment, due to expansion plans, might enact a mass-marketing strategy. That approach uses low prices.

The interaction of price with other retailing-mix elements can be shown through the following example. Tie Town is an off-price tie shop. Thus, its two partners have developed a broad strategy consisting of

- A target market of price-conscious men.
- Selling inexpensive ties (in the $9 to $12 range).
- A limited range of merchandise quality.
- Self-service.
- A downtown location.
- A deep assortment.
- Quantity purchases at discount from suppliers.
- An image of efficiency and variety.

This chapter divides retail pricing into two major sections: the external factors affecting a price strategy and developing a price strategy.

Chapter overviews introduce the material to be covered.

Key Terms

law of demand	market penetration	everyday low pricing (EDLP)
price elasticity of demand	market skimming	variable pricing
horizontal price fixing	multistage approach	one-price policy
vertical price fixing	demand-oriented pricing	flexible pricing
fair trade	cost-oriented pricing	odd pricing
Robinson-Patman Act	competition-oriented pricing	leader pricing
minimum-price laws	psychological pricing	multiple-unit pricing
predatory pricing	price-quality association	price lining
loss leaders	prestige pricing	price adjustments
unit pricing	markup pricing	markdown
item price removal	markup	additional markup
bait advertising (bait-and-switch advertising)	markup percentage	markdown percentage
	initial markup	off-retail markdown percentage

Questions for Discusssion

1. Why is it important for retailers to understand the concept of price elasticity even if they cannot compute it?
2. Comment on each of the following from the perspective of a small retailer:
   a. Horizontal price fixing.
   b. Vertical price fixing.
   c. Price discrimination.
   d. Minimum-price law.
   e. Item price removal.
3. Why do some retailers sell gray market goods?
4. Give an example of a price strategy that integrates demand, cost, and competitive criteria.
5. Explain why markups are usually computed as a percentage of selling price rather than of cost.
6. A floor tile retailer wants to receive a 40 per cent markup (at retail) for all merchandise. If one style of tile retails for $9 per tile, what is the maximum that the retailer would be pay for a tile?
7. A car dealer purchases multiple-disc for $175 each and desires a 40 per c (at retail). What retail price should b
8. A photo store charges $11.00 to proc slides; its cost is $6.50. What is the m centage (at cost and at retail)?
9. A retailer has planned operating exp $110,000, a profit goal of $52,000, ar reductions of $28,000 and expects ar to be $600,000. Compute the initial r centage.
10. At the end of the year, the retailer in determines that actual operating exp $120,000, actual profit is $42,000, an sales are $600,000. What is the main markup percentage? Explain the diff your answers to Questions 9 and 10.

Look at the end-of-chapter pedagogy:

- The numbered summaries are linked to beginning-of-chapter objectives.
- The key terms lists indicate the pages where terms are defined.
- The questions ask about concepts and applications.

Retail Management: A Strategic Approach has 36 new end-of-chapter cases and 8 new comprehensive end-of-part cases. They represent a range of organizations and scenarios. Many of the chapter cases have an optional video component.

CASE 2

Sensormatic: Pilferage Control†

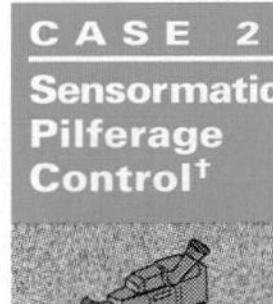

Sensormatic Electronics, with annual sales exceeding $500 million, has a 70 per cent U.S. market share for anti-pilferage equipment. Its major competitors are Knogo (with a 12 per cent market share) and Checkpoint Systems (with a 9 per cent market share). Sensormatic has an annual research and development budget of $15 million; as a result, three-quarters of its revenues come from products introduced over the past six years. In 1992, Sensormatic acquired ALP, Europe's largest distributor of anti-shoplifting equipment.

Although Sensormatic makes a variety of electronic article surveillance (EAS) products (such as an ink tag that marks the thief and damages stolen goods, sophisticated cameras that monitor stores and warehouses, and unobtrusive labels that can be hidden under a product's regular label), its most popular product is the Ultra-Max system.

The Ultra-Max system uses raised plastic tags that resemble chicklet gum in both size and shape. Unlike other products, Ultra-Max tags can be reactivated if customers return products to the store. Because Ultra-Max tags are clearly visible to the shopper, they are an active deterrent to theft. The Ultra-Max system is based upon acousto-magnetic technology. When an Ultra-Max tag that has not been deactivated enters a magnetic field located near a store's exit, the material inside the tag vibrates. This vibration sets off an alarm. Each Ultra-Max tag costs about six cents.

In contrast, the anti-shoplifting devices made by Checkpoint Systems and other major manufacturers are based on radio frequency technology. Unless these tags are deactivated at the checkout counter, an alarm is set off when the tags pass through an electrical field generated by two panels that are placed near store exits. Checkpoint tags costs 3 to 4 cents each. Unlike Ultra-Max tags, Checkpoint tags can be easily hidden under a product's price tag or inside a carton. These tags cannot be reused if packages are returned.

One of the most important emerging developments in pilferage control is source tagging, whereby manufacturers place anti-theft devices on products before shipment to retailers. At present, most EAS tags are attached to goods by retailers. However, source tagging relieves retailers of the labor expense of placing sensors on each product and increases sales of manufacturers' products. Without source tagging, many retailers would lock up small valuable products in glass cases that need to be opened by sales clerks. Although this practice results in lower pilferage costs, it also reduces revenues for both manufacturers and retailers.

The effectiveness of source tagging was recently proven in a four-month field experiment during which Target (the discount-department store chain) studied the impact of tagging on both sales and pilferage of calculators. One Target store displayed the calculators with a noticeable anti-theft tag in a self-service environment. A second Target store had a similar display, but with no noticeable anti-theft tag. At a third Target store, tagged calculators were placed in a glass case that required a sales clerk equipped with a key to open the display. According to Target's vice-president

† The material in this case is drawn from "Anti-Theft Tag Is Rejected," *New York Times* (November 12, 1993), p. D5; Pan Demetrakakes, "Packaging Can Offer Safety From Theft, Too," *Packaging* (October 1993), p. 25; Peter Nulty, "Sensormatic: Why Not to Kill Your Competitor," *Fortune* (May 3, 1993) pp. 71–72; and *Sensormatic 1993 Annual Report.*

Every chapter (beginning with Chapter 2) ends with two cases, 19 of which have an accompanying video and separate video questions.

PART 5 COMPREHENSIVE CASE

Growth Through Portfolio Retailing*

Introduction

Some retailers are growing robustly, drawing market share from all competitors in their path. Single-business firms—such as Home Depot, a fast-growing chain of home-improvement warehouse stores, and The Container Store, a small chain selling household storage and organization products—are among the winners. Other retailers are growing rapidly with multibusiness strategies. Examples include Toys "R" Us, which developed the Kids "R" Us apparel chain, and The Limited, Inc., which operates jewels such as Express and Victoria's Secret.

The idea of building a portfolio of retail businesses is not new. Indeed, diversification seems to be losing cachet, with the proportion of highly diversified U.S. corporations declining markedly in the 1980s. Yet, portfolio retailing is not just assembling a collection of firms: it blends the strategy of diversification with the strategy of focus. It is not diversification that is passé, but unfocused diversification. Focused diversification is an approach that many respected U.S. retailers are using to grow. Portfolio retailing, when executed properly and under the right conditions, lets a retail firm prosper in both troubled and good times.

Focusing on Competencies

Portfolio retailers leverage a common set of core competencies across multiple retail concepts targeted to fit the shopping preferences and buying patterns of specific market segments. They are best understood not by their formats—department store, specialty store, catalog, and so on—but by their core competencies, which are their integral capabilities. Core competencies are not resources like capital, facilities, or information systems, but rather the shared intellect that shapes their development.

The leveraging of core competencies provides the focus characteristic of successful portfolio retailers. Various businesses in a portfolio may appear unrelated when, in fact, they require a common set of core capabilities. Circuit City, America's largest home electronics chain, surprised many with its announcement that it planned to enter used-car retailing on a test basis. Yet, its customer-service skills, operating controls, and expertise in selling high-ticket durable goods on credit provide synergies with auto retailing.

There are three tests for identifying core competencies in a firm: They must provide access to various markets, contribute significantly to perceived customer benefits, and be hard for competitors to imitate. Core competencies are hard to imitate because they are intellectual or service activities. The more dispersed the critical knowledge and skills are in a firm, the harder it is for competitors to imitate them. Competitors may duplicate Wal-Mart's use of "people greeters," but few can match the efficiencies of its cutting-edge inventory management and distribution system. The former is one idea; the latter is the product of many ideas from many people.

Toys "R" Us, in operating its Kids "R" Us stores, passes the three tests. The large, clean, colorful stores—specializing in children's apparel and linked to the famous toy store—offer visible price and assortment benefits. Toys "R" Us' expertise in running supermarket-like stores gives it access to a children's clothing market via similarly-run stores. Toys "R" Us' knowledge of large-store operations, its vendor credibility and purchasing power, and its prowess in inventory management make competitive imitation difficult.

Portfolio retailers use their core competencies to meet customer demand innovatively. They are oriented toward satisfying customer preferences rather than to sustaining a particular retail concept. They test new retail concepts aggressively, push strong concepts hard, and reinvent or jettison faltering concepts. Internal response to external change is a constant.

In portfolio retailing, timing is critical—knowing when to push a new concept and when to redesign or let go of an existing one. Thus, America's best portfolio retailers are masters of using information technology to listen to the market. Executives know immediately what is selling and what is not, who is buying and who is not, and which concepts are working and which aren't.

Portfolio Retailing: Not for Everyone

Many retailers have no core competencies, no specific knowledge or skills that offer market access. These firms must first develop competencies to support their established business before diverting resources into new ones. Spreading mediocrity from one retail concept to multiple ones rarely makes sense.

Multiple concepts may also not make sense for a firm with a strong retail concept, limited geographic coverage, and modest growth resources. A Pea in the Pod, which sells fashionable maternity clothes for the profes-

* The material in this case was adapted by the authors from Leonard L. Berry and Kathleen Seiders, both of Texas A&M University, "Growing Through Portfolio Retailing," *Marketing Management,* Vol. 2 (Number 3, 1993), pp. 9–20. Reprinted by permission of the American Marketing Association.

Each end-of-part case covers material from the various chapters in its part and includes questions pertaining to those chapters.

Retail Management

An Overview of Strategic Retail Management

- In Part 1, the field of retailing, the basic principles of strategic planning, the decisions made in owning/managing a retail business, and the environment facing retailers are covered.
- Chapter 1 describes the framework of retailing, shows why retailing is an important field to study, and examines its special characteristics. The role of strategic planning is noted and applied to Wal-Mart. The elements of the retailing concept are presented, as well as the nature of the total retail experience, customer service, and relationship retailing. The focus and format of the text are detailed. At the end of the chapter, hints for solving case studies are offered.
- Chapter 2 shows the value of strategic planning for all kinds of retailers. Each aspect of the planning process is examined in depth: situation analysis, objectives, identifying consumers, overall strategy, specific activities, control, and feedback. The controllable and uncontrollable components of a retail strategy are highlighted. Strategic planning is viewed as a series of interrelated steps that are continuously reviewed.
- Chapter 3 looks at the changing environment that retailers face. Trends related to these particular topics are examined: consumer demographics, consumer life-styles, consumerism, ethics and social responsibility, technology, retail institutions, and the international dimensions of retailing. And the implications are discussed.

An Introduction to Retailing

❖ Chapter Objectives

1. To define retailing, consider it from various perspectives, demonstrate its importance, and note its special characteristics
2. To introduce the concept of strategic planning and apply it
3. To relate the marketing concept to retailing, with an emphasis on the total retail experience, customer service, and relationship retailing
4. To indicate the focus and format of the text

The field of retailing is both fascinating and appealing. In the United States alone, retailers—firms that sell goods and services to consumers for their personal or household use—employ millions of people and are approaching $2.5 trillion in annual sales (via store and nonstore transactions).

Through retailing, a person such as Leslie Wexner can begin with one small store and end up as the billionaire head of a chain like The Limited, Inc.; an individual can become the owner of a McDonald's, TCBY, Maaco, or some other firm's franchised outlet; an entrepreneur can start a business by placing a small ad in a magazine and shipping merchandise out of his or her garage; and a person can carve out a challenging career at a leading firm like Dillard's. Retailing opportunities are bounded only by one's imagination and vision.

However, along with the numerous opportunities, there are some risks. For instance, after years of record sales during the 1980s, the U.S. retailing industry has entered a tougher period. Due to the economic recession in the early 1990s, the overbuilding of stores in various locales, the intense competition among retailers, the harried life-styles of two-worker families (which make them less interested in shopping), and other factors, a number of firms have not performed up to their expectations—some have even gone out of business or been forced to file for bankruptcy.

So, in this setting, understanding and applying sound strategic retailing principles is more important than ever for a retail business to prosper. Here's a good example:

> Men's Wearhouse's customers do not have to pass up good service just because they're shopping at a discount retailer. Enter a company store and a salesperson will walk up to you and introduce himself/herself by name—and ask yours. Service is like a good restaurant's, usually unobtrusive until you need it. The stores offer a wide selection of suits, from well-known brands like Halston to private labels. Prices are 20 per cent to 30 per cent below those at department stores, which is what draws customers the first time. But, the firm sees a huge opportunity to delight customers with niceties like free pressing and realteration for the life of any suit bought in the store. CEO George Zimmer insists salespeople call 15 days after a suit is sold to make sure it fits right.[1]

[1] Rahul Jacob, "Beyond Quality & Value," *Fortune* (Autumn–Winter 1993), p. 11.

Reprinted by permission of Dillard's.

The Framework of Retailing

Retailing consists of those business activities involved in the sale of goods and services to consumers for their personal, family, or household use. It is the final stage in the distribution process.

To better understand retailing's role in the distribution process and the range of retailing options that are possible, let us look at it from several perspectives:

- Suppose we own a manufacturing firm that makes vacuum cleaners. How should we sell these vacuum cleaners to our customers? Our company could work with big chains like Circuit City electronics stores or neighborhood appliance stores or have a sales force that visits customers in their homes (as Electrolux does) or set up our own stores (if we have the ability and resources to do so).
- Suppose we come up with a new idea for a service business, such as a way to better teach pre-schoolers how to use computer software related to spelling and vocabulary. How should we market this service? Our firm could rent a store in a neighborhood shopping center and advertise in the local paper or rent after-school space in a local Y and rely on teacher referrals or do mailings to parents and visit children in their homes.
- Suppose, as consumers, that we are interested in purchasing apparel. What choices do we have? We could go to a department store or to a store that specializes in apparel. We could shop with a full-service retailer or buy from a discounter (even at a flea market). We could go to a shopping center to have a variety of stores to visit or order from a catalog to maximize our convenience. We could look to retailers that feature a broad assortment of clothing (if we like to buy complete outfits) or look to retailers that have a deep assortment of clothing in one category (if we like to buy items like shirts and outerwear at different stores).
- Suppose we want to open a retail business that features floral products. What choices do we have? Our store could locate in a neighborhood shopping center or in a big mall. We could concentrate on fresh flowers or a mix of fresh flowers and synthetic ones. We could rely on in-store customers or deliver. We could be open from 7:00 A.M. to 6:00 P.M. or 10:00 A.M. to 9:00 P.M. We could set above-average prices because of our first-quality flowers or set discount prices for average-quality flowers. We could advertise in the newspaper or rely on customer word of mouth.

There is a tendency to think of retailing as primarily including the sale of tangible (physical) goods. However, it is quite important to realize that retailing also encompasses the sale of services. A service may be the shopper's primary purchase (such as a haircut or airline travel) or it may be part of the shopper's purchase of a good (such as delivery or training).

Retailing does not have to involve the use of a store. Mail and telephone orders, direct selling to consumers in their homes and offices, and vending machines all fit within the scope of retailing. See Figure 1–1.

Lastly, retailing does not have to include a "retailer." Manufacturers, importers, nonprofit firms, and wholesalers are acting as retailers when they sell goods and/or services to final consumers. On the other hand, purchases made by manufacturers, wholesalers, and other organizations for their use in the organization or further resale are not part of retailing.

Reasons for Studying Retailing

Among the reasons for studying the field of retailing are its impact on the economy, its functions in distribution, and its relationship with firms that sell goods and services to retailers for their resale or use. These factors are discussed in this section. A fourth, and quite important, element for students of retailing is the broad range of career opportunities, which are described separately in Appendix A at the end of this book.

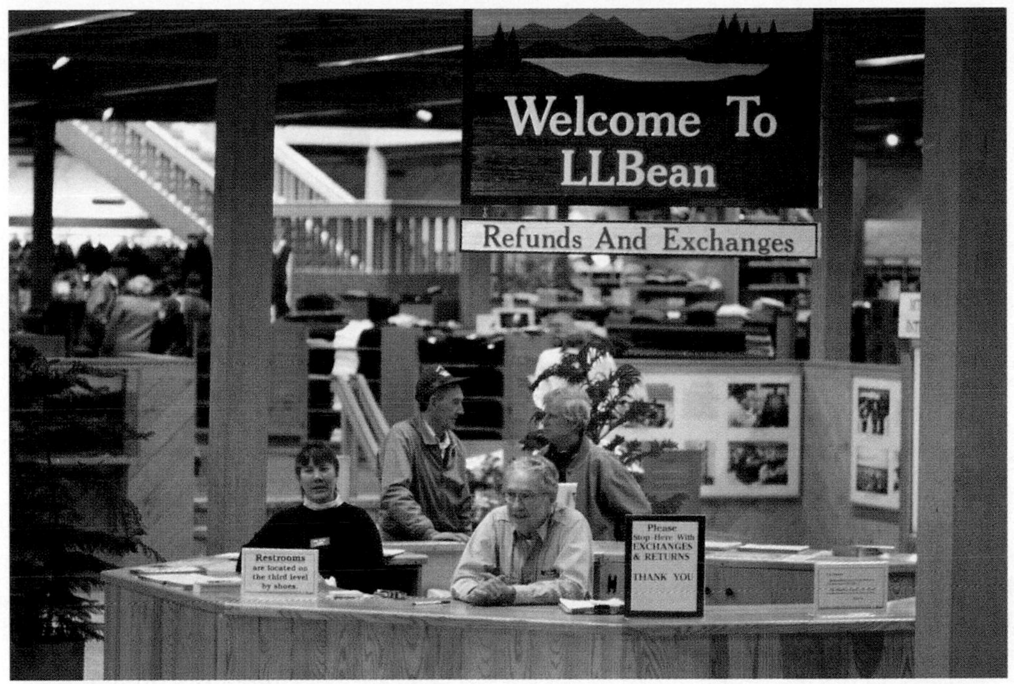

FIGURE 1–1
The Diverse Nature of Retailing
L.L. Bean is a leading mail-order retailer that also operates a large store in Freeport, Maine, attracting two million people per year.
Reprinted with permission.

The Impact of Retailing on the Economy

Retailing is a significant aspect of the U.S. and world economies. Retail sales and employment are both major contributors to the economy, and retail trends often mirror trends in a nation's overall economy.

According to the Department of Commerce, annual U.S. retail store sales (including some mail-order sales by store retailers) are well over $2 trillion. Telephone and mail-order sales by nonstore retailers, vending machines, and direct selling generate an additional $200 billion in yearly revenues. Furthermore, personal consumption expenditures on financial, medical, legal, educational, and other services account for another several hundred billion dollars in annual retail revenues. Outside the United States, retail sales are several trillion dollars per year.

U.S. retail store sales from 1984 to 1993 are presented in Table 1–1. Overall, sales rose by 62 per cent between 1984 and 1993. This increase was far above the level of inflation for the period, except during 1990–1991—when the United States (like the rest of the world) was in the midst of a large-scale recession. For the entire 1984–1993 time frame, the sales of durable goods stores increased at a rate that was somewhat higher than that for nondurable goods and service stores, mostly due to strong 1992–1993 sales and the performance of furniture and appliance stores. Because of changing shopping patterns and life-styles, family apparel stores, drugstores, and eating and drinking places had above-average sales growth through the decade. For the same reason, variety store sales fell and liquor store sales rose slowly. Gasoline service stations had erratic sales due to the ups and downs in petroleum prices. Some other nondurable goods stores had below-average growth as a result of intense competition and the resultant price cuts.

During 1992, the largest 100 retailers in the world generated over $1.1 trillion in revenues. These firms represented 15 different nations and a number of retail categories. Of the top 100, 38 were supermarket chains, 18 were diversified retailers, and 16 operated department stores; and these three categories accounted for 71 per cent of the top 100's revenues. Thirty of the largest 100 were based in the United States (including 4 of the top 10), 12 each were based in France and Great Britain, and 11 were based in Japan.[2]

[2] Daniel J. Sweeney, Linda L. Hyde, and Ira A. Kalish, *Retail World: Window of Opportunity* (Columbus, Ohio: Price Waterhouse/Management Horizons, 1994).

TABLE 1–1 U.S. Retail Store Sales by Kind of Business, 1984–1993 (Millions of Dollars)[a]

Type of Retailing	1984	1985	1986	1987	1988	1989	1990	1991	1992	1993	Average Yearly % Increase
All retail stores	1,286,914	1,375,027	1,449,636	1,541,299	1,657,594	1,762,165	1,849,792	1,865,477	1,962,423	2,084,409	5.5
Durable goods stores, total	454,481	498,125	540,688	575,863	629,626	658,472	671,032	653,900	705,096	782,120	6.3
Automotive group	273,320	303,199	326,138	342,896	371,715	384,113	384,627	368,943	398,067	447,506	5.8
Furniture and appliance group	61,432	68,287	75,714	78,072	86,673	94,230	96,295	98,612	105,844	117,131	7.5
Lumber, building materials, and hardware group	57,481	61,237	67,244	72,338	78,904	80,572	83,628	81,381	87,310	94,731	5.8
Nondurable goods/services stores, total	832,433	876,902	911,948	965,436	1,027,968	1,103,693	1,178,760	1,211,577	1,257,327	1,302,289	5.1
General merchandise group	150,283	158,636	169,397	181,970	192,746	206,851	216,501	228,473	247,354	265,378	6.5
Department stores (excluding leased dept.)	120,487	126,412	134,486	144,017	151,637	160,775	166,216	173,506	187,676	201,567	5.9
Variety stores	8,700	8,459	7,447	7,134	7,121	7,248	7,246	7,074	6,703	6,414	−3.3
Apparel group	64,341	70,195	75,626	79,322	85,330	92,357	95,835	97,464	104,994	106,945	5.8
Men's and boys' wear stores	8,206	8,458	8,646	9,017	9,513	9,836	9,411	9,043	9,143	8,966	1.1
Women's apparel, accessory stores	23,764	26,149	28,600	29,208	31,122	33,399	34,653	35,401	38,168	39,006	5.7
Family and other apparel stores	16,443	17,827	19,336	21,472	23,629	25,770	27,410	29,101	33,085	34,216	8.5
Shoe stores	12,306	13,054	13,947	14,594	15,457	17,320	18,091	17,591	17,672	17,253	3.9
Gasoline service stations	107,565	113,341	102,093	104,769	109,674	121,477	136,201	134,100	133,000	133,955	2.7
Eating and drinking places	121,321	127,949	139,415	153,461	168,226	178,349	190,990	196,875	201,866	212,676	6.5
Food group	271,909	285,062	297,019	309,461	325,947	347,995	369,839	376,892	384,013	393,486	4.2
Drug and proprietary stores	44,011	46,994	50,546	54,142	57,910	63,489	70,796	75,883	77,285	79,775	6.9
Liquor stores	18,273	19,532	19,929	19,826	20,026	20,876	22,938	23,990	25,619	24,363	3.3

[a] Includes some mail-order sales for the retail categories shown in the table.

Sources: Computed by the authors from *Current Business Reports* (Washington, D.C.: U.S. Department of Commerce), various issues.

TABLE 1–2 The 25 Largest Retailers in the United States, 1992

Rank	Company	Sales (Thousands)	After-Tax Earnings (Thousands)	Number of Stores
1	Wal-Mart	$55,483,771	$ 1,994,794	2,136
2	Kmart	37,724,000	941,000	4,792
3	Sears Roebuck	31,960,500	−1,508,500	1,995
4	Kroger	22,144,587	−5,943	2,214
5	American Stores	19,051,180	206,358	1,672
6	J.C. Penney	18,009,000	770,000	1,266
7	Dayton Hudson	17,927,000	383,000	834
8	Safeway Stores	15,151,900	43,500	1,103
9	May Department Stores	11,150,000	603,000	3,866
10	Great Atlantic & Pacific (A&P)	10,499,465	−189,501	1,193
11	Melville	10,432,843	133,429	8,213
12	Winn-Dixie	10,337,341	216,419	1,189
13	Albertson's	10,173,676	269,217	656
14	Woolworth	9,962,000	280,000	8,990
15	Southland	7,477,104	−131,449	6,395
16	Walgreen	7,474,961	220,628	1,736
17	Price Club[a]	7,320,187	129,112	81
18	Food Lion	7,195,923	178,005	1,012
19	Toys "R" Us	7,169,290	437,524	918
20	Home Depot	7,148,436	362,863	214
21	Federated Department Stores	7,079,941	113,009	217
22	The Limited	6,944,296	455,497	4,425
23	Publix	6,600,000	167,000	401
24	Costco[a]	6,500,193	113,295	89
25	R.H. Macy	6,449,000	−1,250,193	231

Note: McDonald's systemwide sales would place it among the top 25 firms; however, the majority of sales are made by franchised outlets.

[a] Price Club and Costco have since merged to become Price/Costco.

Source: David P. Schulz, "Top 100 Retailers," *Stores* (July 1993), pp. 30, 32, 41.

Table 1–2 shows the performance of the 25 largest retailers in the United States during 1992. These retailers accounted for over $357 billion in sales—about 18 per cent of total U.S. retail store sales—and operated almost 56,000 stores. Their after-tax earnings as a percentage of sales ranged from 6.6 per cent for McDonald's to −19.4 per cent for R.H. Macy (due to restructuring costs). Discount and traditional department stores (e.g., Wal-Mart, Kmart, Sears, J.C. Penney), supermarkets (e.g., Kroger, American Stores), variety stores (e.g., Woolworth), and specialty chains (e.g., Toys "R" Us) are among the wide range of retail types represented in the table.

Retailing is a major source of jobs. In the United States, Bureau of Labor Statistics' data show that about 20 million people are employed by traditional retailers. Yet, this figure understates the true number of people working in retailing because it does not include the several million persons employed by various service firms, seasonal employees, proprietors, and unreported workers in family businesses or partnerships.

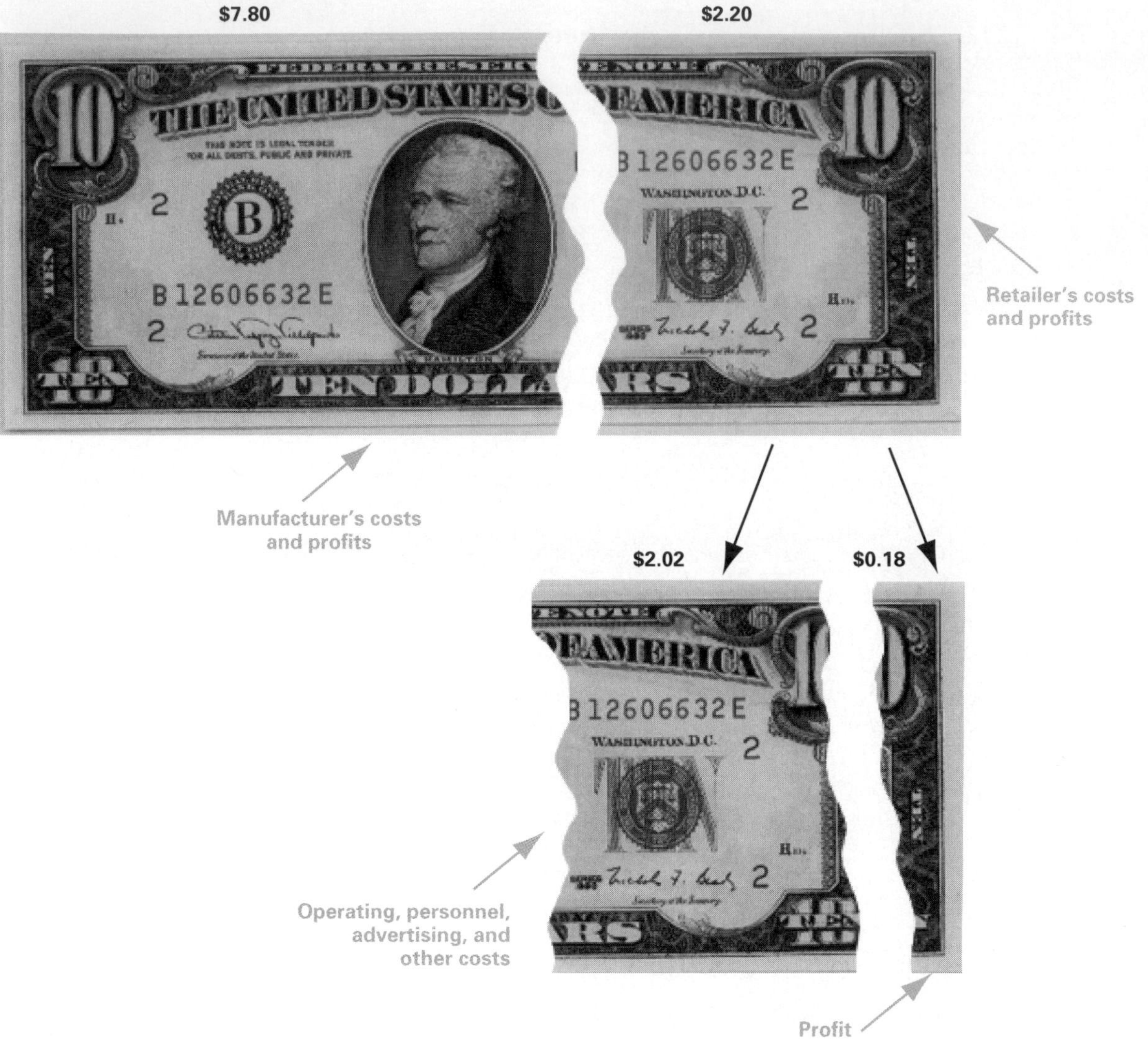

FIGURE 1–2 The High Costs and Low Profits of Retailing—Where the Typical $10 Spent in a Supermarket Goes

RETAILING AROUND THE WORLD

Can Pier 1 Succeed as a Global Retailer?

Pier 1, a U.S. retailer known for its imported home furnishings and accessories, has recently opened stores in Great Britain, Puerto Rico, and Mexico. By the year 2000, Pier 1 plans to open 250 stores outside the United States and Canada, and to have foreign operations generate 5 per cent of sales and 10 per cent of profits.

Pier 1 understands that foreign markets, while excellent vehicles for growth, can be especially challenging. For example, rents in Great Britain are high, Germany has very restrictive labor laws, and cultural differences abound. Pier 1 feels that its experience with carrying imported merchandise in its U.S. stores gives it a competitive edge. It realizes that it must learn what different cultures desire. For example, Pier 1 knows that Far East customers prefer Native American artifacts and posters of U.S. pop heroes, that furniture sold in Japan must be downsized to fit into small Japanese apartments, and that the scarcity of built-in closets in European countries makes freestanding closet wardrobes best-sellers there.

To lessen its risk and overcome resistance in foreign markets, Pier 1 intends to expand globally through joint ventures and licensing agreements with local companies in each market.

Sources: Based on material in Stephanie Anderson Forest and Ruth Golby, "A Pier 1 in Every Port?" *Business Week* (May 31, 1993), p. 88; and Allyson L. Stewart, "U.S. Puts Pier Pressure on Europe's Retailers," *Marketing News* (August 2, 1993), pp. 6–7.

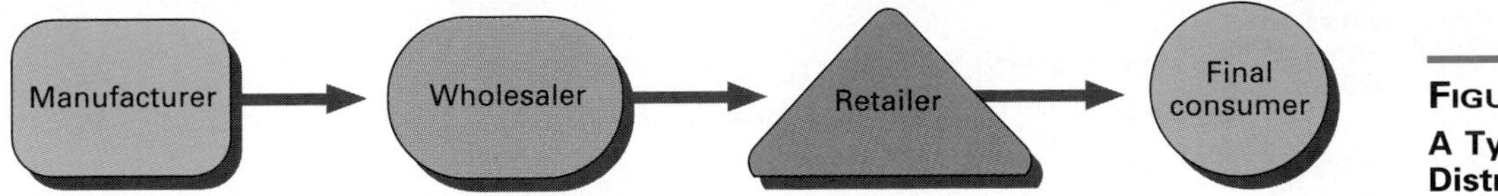

Figure 1–3
A Typical Channel of Distribution

Among the leading retail employers in the United States—and other countries, as well—are eating and drinking places, food stores, general merchandise stores, apparel and accessory stores, and furniture and home furnishings stores.

From another perspective—costs—retailing is a substantial field of study. In the United States, on average, 38 cents of every dollar spent in department stores, 42 cents of every dollar spent in specialty stores, and 22 cents of every dollar spent in supermarkets go to the retailers as payment for the operating costs they incur, the activities they perform, and the profits they earn. Costs include rent, in-store displays, personnel compensation, advertising, and store maintenance. Only a small portion of each sales dollar is actually profit for the retailer. In 1992, the pre-tax profits of the fifty largest U.S. retailers averaged under 2 per cent of sales.[3] Figure 1–2 shows the costs and profits of a typical supermarket. Thus, a change in retail efficiency would have a great impact on consumers and the economy. Price levels and product assortment are also affected by retailer competence.

Retail Functions in Distribution

Retailing is the last stage in a ***channel of distribution***, which comprises all of the businesses and people involved in the physical movement and transfer of ownership of goods and services from producer to consumer. A typical distribution channel is shown in Figure 1–3.

In a distribution channel, retailing plays an important role as an intermediary between manufacturers, wholesalers, and other suppliers and final consumers. The retailer collects an assortment of goods and services from various sources and offers them to customers. This procedure is called the ***sorting process***.[4] To maximize their efficiency, many manufacturers (suppliers) would like to make one basic type of item and sell the entire inventory to as few buyers as possible. Yet, many customers want to choose from a variety of goods and services and purchase a limited quantity. Through the sorting process, the retailer bridges the gap between manufacturers (suppliers) and final consumers. See Figure 1–4.

A retailer satisfies manufacturers (suppliers) by buying their limited range of products in large quantities. In this way, each manufacturer (supplier) becomes more efficient. A retailer satisfies customers by offering an assortment of goods and services, collected from a number of sources, and by selling them in small quantities. Wide retail assortments enable customers to undertake one-stop shopping; and consumers are able to choose and buy the product version and quantity that they desire. The word *retailing* is actually based on this breaking-bulk function. It is derived from the old French word *retailler*, which means "to cut up."

Another distribution function that retailers perform is to communicate with their customers and with their manufacturers and wholesalers. Via ads, sales personnel, and store displays, customers are informed about the availability and characteristics of goods and services, store hours, special sales, and so on. Manufacturers, wholesalers, and others are informed about sales forecasts, delays in shipping, customer complaints, defective products, inventory turnover (by style, color, and size), and so on. Many goods and services have been modified as a result of retailer feedback to suppliers.

For small manufacturers and wholesalers, retailers can provide valuable assistance by transporting, storing, marking, advertising, and pre-paying for merchandise. On

[3] "Retailing: Basic Analysis," *Standard & Poor's Industry Surveys* (May 13, 1993), p. R83; "60th Annual Report of the Grocery Industry," *Progressive Grocer* (April 1993), p. 80; and David P. Schulz, "Top 100 Retailers," *Stores* (July 1993), pp. 30, 32, 41.

[4] This concept was formally introduced by Wroe Alderson, *Marketing Behavior and Executive Action* (Homewood, Ill.: Richard D. Irwin, 1957), pp. 199–211.

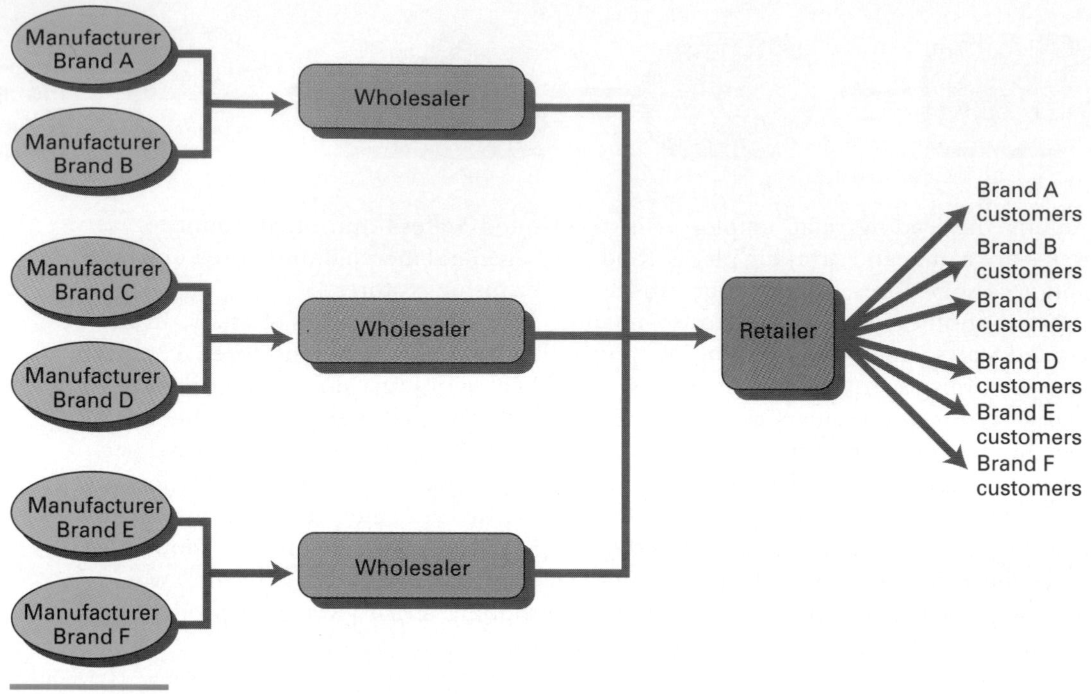

Figure 1–4
The Retailer's Role in the Sorting Process

the other hand, small retailers may need the same type of help from their suppliers. The number of functions performed by a retailer has a direct bearing on the percentage of each sales dollar that it needs to cover costs and profits.

Retailers also complete transactions with their customers. This means trying to fill orders promptly and accurately; it often involves processing customer credit through the retailer's or another charge plan. In addition, retailers frequently provide customer services such as gift wrapping, delivery, and installation.

For these reasons, in most cases, goods and services are sold via retail outlets not owned by a manufacturer. This enables the manufacturer to reach more customers, reduce expenditures, improve cash flow, increase sales more rapidly, and concentrate on its area of expertise.

Some manufacturers such as Sherwin-Williams and Liz Claiborne do operate their own retail facilities (besides selling through traditional retailers). When doing so, they need to complete the full range of retailing functions in order to compete with conventional retailers. They must consider how many final consumers will buy their products, how geographically dispersed those people are, what company resources are needed to fulfill retailing functions, what service will be required by consumers, and other factors. Even strong manufacturers can fail as retailers. As an illustration, in the 1980s, IBM opened a number of company-owned IBM Product Centers to sell IBM-brand PCs, typewriters, and accessories. But IBM encountered many problems: it offered too limited a product assortment and had an inadequate number of stores, unattractive decors, poor staffing, and a weak record-keeping system. In short, IBM really did not know how to be a good retailer. After a few disappointing years, IBM sold its stores and exited from retailing.

The Relationships Among Retailers and Their Suppliers

It is essential that the complex relationships among retailers and their suppliers be understood. On the one hand, retailers are part of a distribution channel; thus, manufacturers and wholesalers must be concerned about their retailers' coverage of the consumer market, the caliber of in-store displays, the level of customer services, store hours, and retailers' reliability as business partners. On the other hand, retailers are also major customers of such goods and services as items for resale, store fixtures, data-processing equipment, management consulting, and insurance.

Retailers and their suppliers may have divergent viewpoints, which need to be reconciled. Control over the distribution channel, the allocation of profits, the number of competing retailers handling the suppliers' goods and services, in-store display space and locations, advertising support, payment terms, and flexibility in operations are just a few of the issues over which retailers and suppliers have their own distinct priorities and goals. Because of the growing number of regional, national, and international retail chains, retailers have more power in the distribution channel than ever before.

Channel relations are generally smoothest when exclusive distribution is involved. With ***exclusive distribution***, suppliers enter into agreements with one or a few retailers that designate the latter as the only companies in specified geographic areas that are allowed to carry certain brands and/or product lines. This arrangement stimulates both parties to work together in maintaining an image, assigning shelf space, allotting profits and costs, advertising, and so on. Yet, it also usually requires that the retailer limit its assortment of goods/services in the product categories covered by the agreement; this means a retailer might have to pass up handling other suppliers' items. From a manufacturer's perspective, exclusive distribution may limit its long-run total sales potential.

Channel relations tend to be most volatile when intensive distribution is used. With ***intensive distribution***, suppliers sell through as many retailers as possible. This arrangement usually maximizes suppliers' sales; and it enables retailers to offer many different brands and product versions. As a result, competition among retailers selling the same items is high. In response, retailers may use tactics not beneficial to individual suppliers, as they are more interested in overall store sales than in the sales of any one brand. The retailer may allocate shelf space, set prices, and advertise in a way that adversely affects individual brands (by giving them poor shelf space, using them as sale items, and not advertising them).

With ***selective distribution***, suppliers sell through a moderate number of retailers. The approach combines aspects of both exclusive and intensive distribution. It allows suppliers to have higher sales than possible in exclusive distribution and lets retailers carry some competing brands. It encourages suppliers to provide advertising and other support, and encourages retailers to give adequate shelf space. However, this middle-ground approach generally has neither the channel cooperation found in exclusive distribution nor the sales potential of intensive distribution. See Figure 1–5.

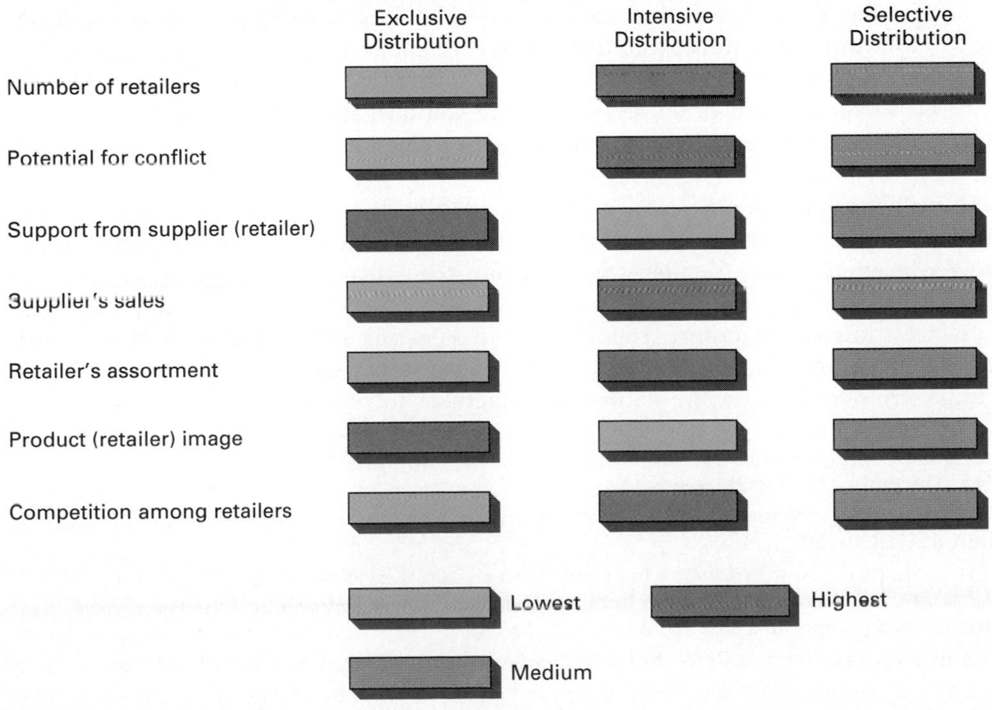

Exclusive Distribution
Intensive Distribution
Selective Distribution

Number of retailers
Potential for conflict
Support from supplier (retailer)
Supplier's sales
Retailer's assortment
Product (retailer) image
Competition among retailers

Lowest
Highest
Medium

FIGURE 1–5
Comparing Exclusive, Intensive, and Selective Distribution

Unless suppliers are aware of the attributes and needs of retailers, they cannot develop good rapport with them; and as long as there is a choice of suppliers, retailers will select those that best understand and react to their needs. The following illustrate several issues in retailer-supplier relations:

- Competition in the marketplace—"The folks at Totes Inc. thought up a pretty nifty product. They took a heavy pair of socks, stuck rubbery treads on them to provide traction on slippery floors, and called the result slipper socks. A year after introducing them, Totes was selling 14 million pairs a year. Kmart and Wal-Mart alone accounted for as many as 1.5 million pairs. But, not for long. Within two years, both giant discounters had found suppliers that made knockoff slipper socks for less. They dropped Totes—and lowered the price of their knockoffs 25 per cent or more, to under $3 a pair."[5]
- Product image—It took J.C. Penney more than six years to get Maidenform to let Penney sell its branded intimate apparel. Maidenform was concerned about its upscale image and the possible retaliation of other department stores (with regard to their dropping Maidenform products). For instance, when Levi Strauss began selling to Penney, Macy's dropped the Levi brand. Today, J.C. Penney is Levi's biggest customer. Since late 1990, Penney has been able to carry the Maidenform brand because "for our intents and purposes, Penney's is like a department store, and we felt we should be there with the other intimate apparel people."[6]
- Slotting allowances—Some large supermarket chains have been requiring manufacturers to pay slotting allowances in return for securing store shelf space. The chains feel the fees deter manufacturers from introducing "me-too" products, trying to keep shelf space from competitors, and using their shelves as testing labs for new products. However, manufacturers feel the fees are exorbitant, discourage new product introductions, and raise prices to consumers. Even mail-order firms sometimes charge slotting fees. Sharper Image asks suppliers to pay a monthly $750 fee per product the first time an item appears in its catalog and $250 each time thereafter.[7]
- Distribution rights—"Bausch & Lomb quietly rolled out an abridged version of what was supposed to be the contact lens marketer's largest consumer ad and promotion campaign ever. The original 'Teen Eye Deal,' an international effort targeted at 13-to-19-year-olds, was canceled just days before it was set to break on TV, following objections from doctors and retailers. Both were furious that Bausch & Lomb planned to advertise a specific price for the program, which offered a year's supply of lenses, a lens-care solution starter kit, and a wristwatch, all for $39. They were also angry about plans to mail lenses directly to consumers."[8]

Manufacturers of goods that are used in retail businesses should also have a working knowledge of retailing. For example, a fixture manufacturer has to understand the requirements of its retailers. Store layout, the linear feet of shelf space, the use of self-service merchandising, the routing of customer traffic, and storage specifications are some of the criteria retailers use in selecting store fixtures. Both a knowledge of basic retailing principles and the special factors relative to a given type of retailer are necessary for the fixture manufacturer to succeed.

[5] Zachary Schiller, Wendy Zellner, Ron Stodghill II, and Mark Maremont, "Clout!" *Business Week* (December 21, 1992), p. 66.

[6] Karyn Monget, "Penney's to Get Jockey, Warner's, and Maidenform," *Women's Wear Daily* (June 28, 1990), pp. 1, 3.

[7] Eben Shapiro, "New Products Clog Food Stores," *New York Times* (May 29, 1990), pp. D1, D17; and Christina Duff, "Nation's Retailers Ask Vendors to Help Share Expenses," *Wall Street Journal* (August 4, 1993), p. B4.

[8] Emily DeNitto, "Bausch Refocuses Deal," *Advertising Age* (November 1, 1993), p. 48.

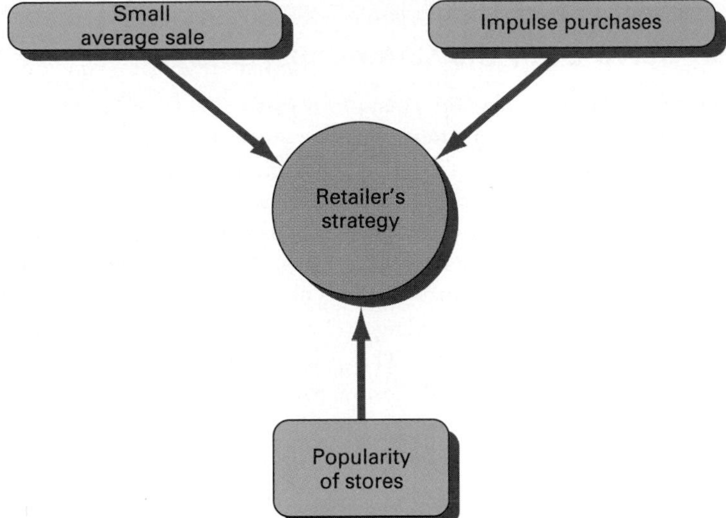

FIGURE 1–6
Special Characteristics Affecting Retailers

Similarly, firms that sell services, such as insurance, to retailers can benefit from a good understanding of retailing. Inventory valuation, employee job functions, construction costs, crime rates, and depreciation are some factors that must be examined. For example, how should merchandise that has been marked down in price be appraised if there is a fire? Or how much will fire insurance premiums be reduced if sprinklers are installed in a store?

SPECIAL CHARACTERISTICS OF RETAILING

Several special characteristics distinguish retailing from other types of business. Three of them are highlighted in Figure 1–6 and discussed here: The average size of a sales transaction for retailers is much less than for manufacturers. Final consumers make many unplanned purchases; those who buy for resale or for use in manufacturing products or running a business are more systematic and plan ahead. Most retail customers must be drawn to a store location; salespeople generally visit manufacturers, wholesalers, and other firms to initiate and consummate transactions. Each of these factors imposes unique requirements on retail firms.

Average sales transactions are about $35 for department stores, $34 for specialty stores, and $18 for chain supermarkets. These low average sales create a need to control tightly the costs associated with each transaction (such as credit verification, delivery, and bagging); to maximize the number of customers drawn to the store, which may place an emphasis on ads and special promotions; and to increase impulse sales by more aggressive in-store selling. However, low average sales and high costs cannot always be controlled by the retailer. For example, over the last decade, the average amount of a sales transaction in a specialty store has gone up by much less than the rate of inflation. And, despite their high costs, three-fifths of department store sales are on credit.[9]

Because of the many small sales transactions to a large number of different customers, inventory management is often difficult for retailers. As an illustration, the average chain supermarket had yearly sales of $11.5 million in 1992; it also had over 13,000 weekly transactions.[10] This makes it harder for retailers to determine the levels of existing stock and the popularity of various brands, sizes, and prices of merchandise. For that reason, retailers are expanding their use of computerized inventory systems.

9 "Retailing: Basic Analysis," p. R83; and "60th Annual Report of the Grocery Industry," p. 80.
10 "60th Annual Report of the Grocery Industry," pp. 49, 80.

ETHICS IN RETAILING

How Does Hanna Andersson Serve Both the Community and Its Bottom Line?

Hanna Andersson Corporation, a retailer of children's clothing, is often cited as a firm that has achieved strong performance in both its financial and social responsibility goals. The company started as a mail-order operation in 1983, as the result of Gun Denhart's dissatisfaction with the quality of clothing available for her first child. Today, it has three stores in addition to its mail-order operation, 300 employees, and revenues of over $40 million per year—an impressive financial performance.

Hanna Andersson's social-responsibility performance is equally superior. The firm pays half of the child-care costs for all of its employees (part- and full-time), allows paid days off so employees can care for sick children at home, and offers flex-time work schedules. Under its Hanna-downs Program, customers receive a 20 per cent credit (of an item's initial purchase price), when they return their children's outgrown Hanna garments to the retailer. Hanna Andersson then donates the used clothing to charities.

According to Gun Denhardt, "Hannadowns is a win-win situation." This program offers a substantial discount to the firm's customers, increased loyalty to the retailer, and the donation of badly-needed, high-quality used clothing for the poor.

Source: Based on material in "Retailer Entrepreneurs of the Year: Gun Denhart," *Chain Store Age Executive* (December 1993), pp. 24–25.

Often, retail sales involve unplanned or impulse purchases. For example, surveys have shown that a large percentage of grocery consumers ignore newspaper ads before shopping, do not prepare shopping lists in advance (or deviate from these lists once in a store), and make purchases that are completely unplanned. This signifies the value of point-of-purchase displays, attractive store layouts, well-organized stores, and store windows. Candy, cosmetics, snack foods, magazines, and other items can be sold as impulse goods if they are placed in visible, high–traffic locations in the store. Because consumers buy so many goods and services in an unplanned manner, the retailer's ability to forecast, budget, order merchandise, and have the proper number of personnel on the selling floor is made harder.

Retail customers normally visit a store, even though mail and telephone sales have increased dramatically in recent years. For instance, the large number of final consumers; the interest of many consumers in shopping in person and in comparison shopping among different brands and models; the small average sale size; the unplanned nature of purchases; and consumers' desire for privacy from in-home selling are just some of the reasons for the popularity of retail stores. And because consumers must be attracted to a particular store, the retailer needs to consider such factors as location, transportation facilities, store hours, proximity of competitors, merchandise assortment, parking, and advertising.

Developing and Applying a Retail Strategy

A ***retail strategy*** is the overall plan guiding a retail firm. It has an influence on the firm's business activities and its response to market forces, such as competition and the economy. Any retailer, regardless of size or type, can and should utilize these six steps in strategic planning:

1. The type of business is defined in terms of the goods or service category and the company's specific orientation (such as full-service or "no frills").
2. Long-run and short-run objectives are set with regard to sales and profit, market share, image, and so on.
3. The customer market to which to appeal is defined on the basis of its characteristics (such as gender and income level) and needs (such as product and brand preferences).

4. An overall, long-run plan is developed and gives general direction to the firm and its employees.
5. An integrated strategy, which combines such factors as store location, product assortment, pricing, and advertising and displays, is implemented to achieve objectives.
6. Performance is regularly evaluated, and weaknesses or problems are corrected as they are observed.

To illustrate these points, the background and strategy of Wal-Mart—the world's largest retailer—are presented. Then, the marketing concept is applied to retailing.

WAL-MART: FROM HUMBLE BEGINNINGS TO INDUSTRY GIANT[11]

Company Background

Wal-Mart, based in Bentonville, Arkansas, is now one of the world's great retail firms. It has grown impressively from very modest beginnings.

Shortly after World War II, Sam Walton began acquiring Ben Franklin five-and-dime (variety) stores. By the early 1960s, he owned 15 such stores in Arkansas, Kansas, Missouri, and Oklahoma. When Walton asked Ben Franklin's management about opening discount department stores in small rural markets, he was rebuffed; the conventional wisdom then was that a discount department store required a population base of 50,000 or more people.

So Sam Walton bade good-bye to Ben Franklin and opened his first Wal-Mart discount department store in Rogers, Arkansas. He built his overall retailing strategy around three basic concepts: discounting, small-town locations, and excellent employee relations.

Discounting was needed to attract consumers from as far as 50 miles away from each rural Wal-Mart store—and to deter people from shopping in larger metropolitan areas. Sam Walton felt a chain of discount department stores with small-town locales could have the same purchasing and distribution cost economies as chains based in large cities. These economies were necessary for his stores to be profitable.

Sam Walton knew small towns provided an ideal launching ground for a discount chain. They had been virtually ignored by such national retailers as Sears, Kmart, and May Department Stores. As such, the towns represented an important, but neglected, market segment. Wal-Mart's focus on small towns also allowed the chain to grow without direct competition from bigger firms. It gave rural consumers, who had previously done much of their shopping in metropolitan areas, access to a discounter located close to their homes.

Since its inception, Wal-Mart has enjoyed a special relationship with its managers and hourly employees. Every worker is called an associate, not an employee. Managers are given access to key information they would not receive if employed at other retailers. For example, they are privy to such data as freight costs, profit margins, and pilferage rates. Important decisions, like what items to display in high-traffic locations, are generally delegated to clerks on the sales floor.

Some Wal-Mart store managers earn over $100,000 per year from their salaries and profit-sharing distributions. Profit sharing extends down to the level of hourly em-

[11] The material in this discussion has been drawn from Wal-Mart company literature; *Wal-Mart Annual Report 1993*; Sam Walton and John Huey, *Made in America* (New York: Doubleday, 1992); "Global Expansion Targets Canada, Latin America," *Discount Store News* (June 7, 1993), pp. 63–64; Andrea Adelson, "Wal-Mart Entering Canada," *New York Times* (January 15, 1994), p. 39; Arthur Markowitz, "Weekly Reviews Help Keep Wal-Mart at Top," *Discount Store News* (September 30, 1993), p. 11; James F. Moore, "Predators and Prey: A New Ecology of Competition," *Harvard Business Review*, Vol. 71 (May–June 1993), pp. 82–83; Stephanie Strom, "Wal-Mart Reportedly in Kmart Deal," *New York Times* (November 2, 1993), p. D5; and "Wal-Mart Blazes Retail Trail as Other Discounters Follow," *Discount Store News* (June 7, 1993), pp. 41–48.

FIGURE 1–7
At Wal-Mart: People Make the Difference
From the "people greeter" at the front door of each Wal-Mart store to the firm's senior management, there is a strong motivation to please customers.
Reprinted by permission.

ployees. If the profit goal is exceeded for a store, hourly associates share part of that additional profit. Hourly employees are also eligible for an anti-pilferage bonus of up to $200. Thus, Wal-Mart's pilferage rate has been below the industry average. Under its profit-sharing plan, Wal-Mart contributes a percentage of eligible employees' wages (mostly in Wal-Mart stock). This enables some hourly associates to retire with as much as $150,000 in profit-sharing distributions. According to David D. Glass, Wal-Mart's chief executive officer, "We have no superstars at Wal-Mart. We have average people operating in an environment that encourages everyone to perform way above average." See Figure 1–7.

On Friday and Saturday mornings, senior executives meet with buyers and regional managers—and others by satellite TV—to discuss "everything" that affects Wal-Mart. Every week, corporate policies are studied and critiqued. Unlike the typical entrepreneur, Sam Walton was also smart enough to establish a strong management structure and a succession plan so that his company would prosper after he was no longer at the helm. Thus, although Sam Walton passed away in 1992, Wal-Mart is well positioned for the twenty-first century.

The Current Strategy

Building on the foundation just noted, these are some key elements of Wal-Mart's current retailing strategy: everyday low pricing, a "Buy American" program, the use of state-of-the-art technology in information management and ordering, emphasis on multiple store formats, geographic expansion into new markets, and a concern for the surrounding community.

Everyday low pricing was started in 1980 because the firm felt customers would prefer to pay everyday low prices throughout the year rather than have to wait for special sales. Everyday low pricing also lets Wal-Mart have lower advertising costs than competitors. It runs one or two newspaper circulars per month while competitors with weekly specials must run weekly freestanding inserts and ads. Everyday low pricing further enables Wal-Mart to have better control over out-of-stock situations as demand is more stable; and there is less labor needed to reprice merchandise and reset prices on displays.

Wal-Mart has been involved with its "Buy American" program since 1985. The program is a cooperative effort between Wal-Mart and domestic manufacturers. The goal is to help re-establish the competitive position of American-made goods. Wal-Mart places advance orders with U.S. manufacturers for specific quantities of items; this enables the manufacturers to use the orders as security when obtaining lines of credit from their banks and other financial institutions. There are several benefits of the "Buy American" program to Wal-Mart. One, many workers in jobs saved or created by Wal-Mart become loyal customers. Two, research findings suggest the "Buy American" campaign has increased sales to the general population. Three, the "Buy American" campaign may blunt criticism of Wal-Mart's foreign purchasing practices. Even with this campaign, between 25 and 30 per cent of Wal-Mart's goods are still imported, about double the percentage at Kmart. Though Wal-Mart has heavily promoted its "Buy American" theme, it is committed to buying American-made goods only if their price and quality match those for imported goods.

Wal-Mart uses state-of-the-art technology in information management and ordering. See Figure 1–8. It is a leader in the use of point-of-sale scanning equipment. A satellite system lets Wal-Mart send messages on TV monitors to all stores, gather store data for analysis in a master computer, handle credit approval, and track inventory. The computer system monitors sales and automatically reorders fast-moving items. Wal-Mart orders electronically from 2,000 vendors.

Wal-Mart has been at the forefront in terms of its experimentation with different store formats. It continually improves the merchandise assortment and presentation in its Wal-Mart discount department stores; and many other retailers have copied its use of people greeters to welcome customers to the stores. The firm has opened a number of Wal-Mart Supercenters that combine discount department stores and supermarkets under one roof. Sam's Wholesale Club is one of the leading membership

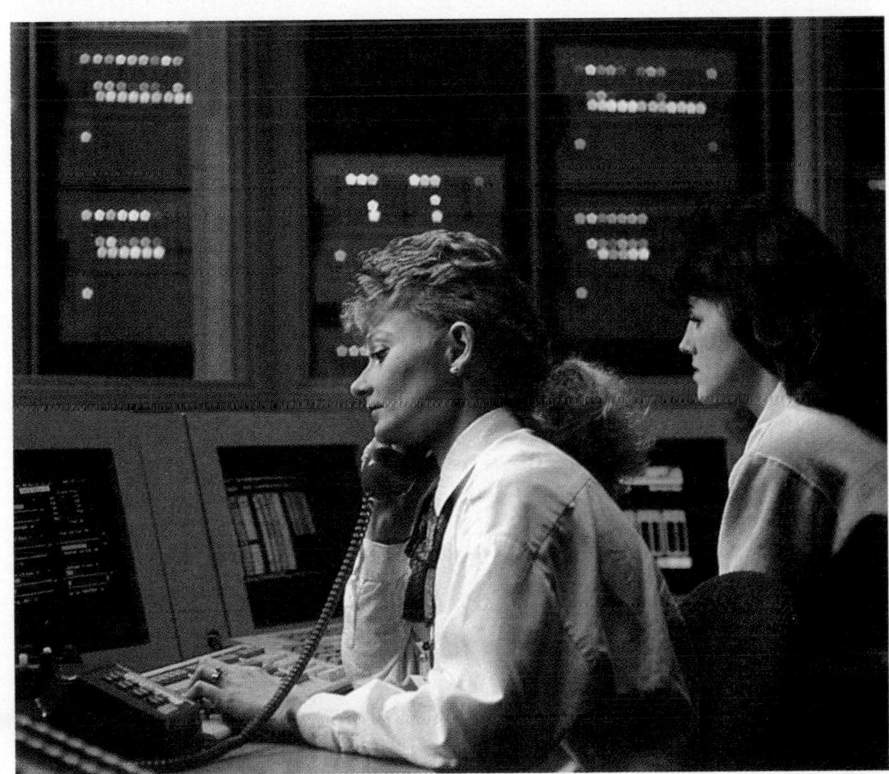

Figure 1–8
Wal-Mart's State-of-the-Art Technology
Wal-Mart has consistently been a leader in computerizing operations. This has helped to give it the lowest cost structure among major retailers, as well as make it one of the most efficient.
Reprinted by permission.

chains in the industry. Wal-Mart has also been testing "vendor stores," which have a more limited selection of brands; each vendor has a larger than usual display area for its brand(s) and they are allowed to select products and displays for the stores. Participating vendors include Gitano Group, Cannon, and Rubbermaid.

Wal-Mart has ambitious expansion plans. It already has Wal-Mart stores and Sam's Clubs from coast to coast in the United States; and Sam's Clubs has been enlarged by the purchase of 110 Pace Membership Warehouse stores from Kmart. Wal-Mart has entered Mexico via a joint venture and recently bought 120 Woolco stores in Canada from Woolworth. Overseas expansion still lies ahead.

For years, Wal-Mart has displayed a strong commitment to both the physical environment and the communities it serves. Since 1989, the firm has challenged manufacturers to improve their products and packaging, so they are better for the environment. Each Wal-Mart store has a Green Coordinator and community recycling bins are placed in store parking lots. The Wal-Mart Foundation contributes to such charities as the United Way and Children's Miracle Network Hospitals. Whenever a new Wal-Mart store or Sam's Club is opened, the company makes a donation to the local United Way.

Remembering "Mr. Sam"

In his 1992 memoirs, Sam Walton offered some sage advice, appropriate for anyone in retailing to keep in mind:

> Over my whole career, I have stuck by one abiding principle: The secret of successful retailing is to give your customers what they want. And really, if you think about it from your point of view as a customer, you want everything—a wide assortment of good quality merchandise; the lowest possible prices; guaranteed satisfaction with what you buy; friendly, knowledgeable service; convenient hours; free parking; a pleasant shopping experience. The next time some overeager, slightly eccentric shopkeeper opens up a business in your neck of the woods, before you write him or her off too quickly, remember that two codgers once gave me 60 days to last in my dime store down in Fayetteville, Arkansas.
>
> The bigger Wal-Mart gets, the more essential it is that we think small. Because that's exactly how we have become a huge company—by not acting like one. Above all, we are small-town merchants. Here are six of the more important ways we at Wal-Mart try to think small: Think one store at a time. Communicate, communicate, communicate [with customers, employees, and suppliers]. Keep your ear to the ground. Push responsibility—and authority—down the firm. Force ideas to bubble up [from associates and others]. Stay lean, fight bureaucracy.

The Marketing Concept Applied to Retailing

As just described, Wal-Mart has demonstrated a sincere long-term desire to please its customers. In addition, it utilizes a coordinated, companywide approach to strategy development and implementation and it has a clear goal orientation. Together, these principles form the marketing concept, a notion first introduced by General Electric (a leading U.S.-based manufacturer).

The marketing concept can be transformed into the retailing concept; and it should be understood and used by all retail firms. See Figure 1–9. The ***retailing concept*** has these elements:

1. Customer orientation—A retailer must determine the attributes and needs of its customers and must endeavor to satisfy these needs to the fullest.
2. Coordinated effort—A retailer must integrate all plans and activities to maximize efficiency.
3. Goal orientation—A retailer must set goals and then use its strategy to attain them.

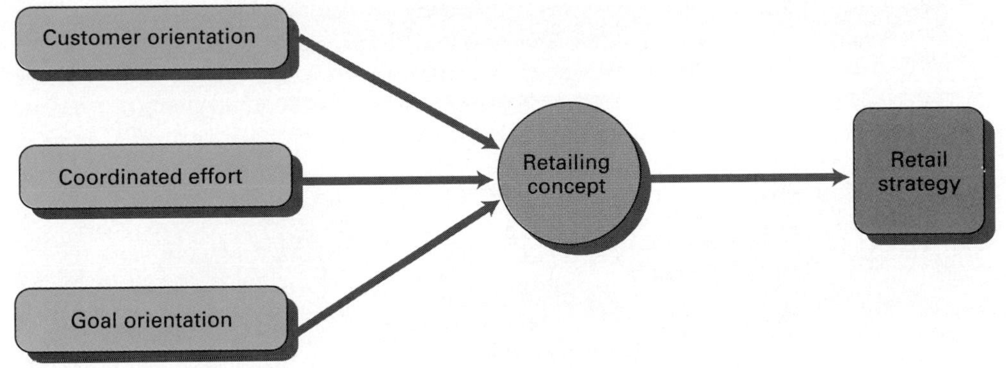

Figure 1–9
Applying the Retailing Concept

Unfortunately, the retailing concept is not understood and used by every retailer. Some are indifferent to customer needs, plan haphazardly, and have unclear goals. Too often, retailers are not receptive to change or new ideas, or they blindly follow strategy changes implemented by competitors. Some retailers do not research their customers or get feedback from them; they rely on the reports of their suppliers or their own past sales trends.

The retailing concept is fairly easy to adopt. It requires communicating with consumers and considering their desires as critical to the retailer's success, developing and enacting a consistent strategy (like having designer brands, plentiful sales personnel, attractive displays, and above-average prices in an upscale clothing boutique), and working to achieve meaningful, specific, and reachable goals. However, the retailing concept is only a guide to company strategy. It does not deal with a firm's internal capabilities or competitive advantages but offers a broad framework for planning.

Let's look at three issues that relate to a retailer's performance in terms of the retailing concept: the total retail experience, customer service, and relationship retailing.

The Total Retail Experience

While one person may shop at a discount store, another at a neighborhood store, a third at a full-service store, and so on, these diverse shoppers have something crucial in common: They each encounter a total retail experience (including everything from parking to checkout counter) in making a purchase.

The ***total retail experience*** consists of all the elements in a retail offering that encourage or inhibit consumers during their contact with a given retailer. Many elements, like the number of salespeople on the floor, display windows, prices, the brands carried, and inventory on hand, are controllable by a retailer; others, like the adequacy of on-street parking, the timing of deliveries from suppliers, and sales taxes, are not. If some part of the total retail experience is unsatisfactory, consumers may not buy a given good or service—they may even decide not to patronize a retailer again.

Thus, in planning and enacting a customer-oriented, integrated strategy, a retailer must ensure that all of its strategic elements are in place. For the shopper segment to which a particular retailer appeals, the total retail experience must be aimed at fulfilling customer expectations—and it must be consistent with those expectations. This means that a discount store should have ample stock on hand when it advertises sales, but not plush carpeting on the floor; a neighborhood store should be open late hours, but not have overly trendy products; and a full-service store should have knowledgeable personnel, but not have them perceived as too haughty by customers. See Figure 1–10.

Retailers certainly want to avoid situations like these:

> Lisa Deragon, a personal trainer in New York, loves music. But she hates music stores. She finds the cacophony [harsh sounds] of most chain-owned record stores irritating and their music inventory spotty. "They always seem to be out of

FIGURE 1–10 Gottschalks' Total Retail Experience

California's Gottschalks takes pride in combining quality merchandise priced to represent genuine value, electronic information reporting systems to maintain proper stock levels, and the human factor of personalized service to meet customers' needs.
Reprinted by permission.

> stock, and there's never any help on the floor," says the 27-year-old fan of the Grateful Dead, 10,000 Maniacs, and other groups. Recently, at a store owned by one chain, she got so frustrated waiting in line to pay that she dumped her goods and has never gone back. A growing number of music lovers seem to share Ms. Deragon's frustration. As many as 51 per cent of the people who enter music stores leave without buying—48 per cent because they couldn't locate music they wanted.[12]

Customer Service

Customer service refers to the identifiable, but sometimes intangible, activities undertaken by a retailer in conjunction with the basic goods and services it sells.[13] It has a strong impact on the total retail experience. Among the many factors that comprise a firm's customer service strategy are its store hours, parking access, the shopper-friendliness of the store layout, the acceptance of credit, the level and caliber of salespeople, such amenities as gift wrapping, the availability of rest rooms, employee politeness, the handling of special customer orders, delivery policies, the amount of time customers spend on checkout lines, and customer follow-up. This list is not all inclusive; and it differs in terms of the strategic approach taken—discount versus full service. Consumer satisfaction with a retailer's customer service performance is influenced by people's expectations (which relate to the type of retailer involved) and past experience. Furthermore,

> Consumer assessments of customer service depend on their perceptions—not necessarily reality. Different consumers may evaluate the same customer service

[12] Patrick M. Reilly, "Music Stores Grow Larger and Livelier, Adding Previewing Posts, Apparel, Pizza," *Wall Street Journal* (June 18, 1993), p. B1.

[13] Peter D. Bennett (Editor), *Dictionary of Marketing Terms* (Chicago: American Marketing Association, 1988), p. 51.

levels quite differently. The same consumer may even evaluate a retailer's service level quite differently at different times, although customer service remains constant.[14]

It is imperative that retailers view customer service as consisting of two components—expected services and augmented services:

> Expected services are those that customers want to receive from any retailer, such as basic employee courtesy. Yet, how many employees are trained to always say, "Hello, how may I help you?" and "Thank you for shopping at our store." Thank you seems to be disappearing from the retail vocabulary. Too often, augmented services—those that enhance the shopping experience and give retailers a competitive advantage—are stressed without enough attention placed on expected services.[15]

According to a study on mass merchandisers, consumers said these aspects of customer service would have a major impact on shopping behavior: having more employees on the selling floor, opening more checkout counters, improving store layout, having fewer items out of stock, and using more informative signs/shelf tags. And in a study on consumer satisfaction with supermarkets, people reported that congested aisles, spotty price labeling, missing sale items, and long waits at checkout lines each caused negative feelings.[16]

Nordstrom and Direct Tire Sales are among the many retailers that are acknowledged as outstanding in customer service. Recently, Nordstrom was rated first among 70 U.S. department store and discount store chains on a Retail Satisfaction Index, based on surveys with 2,000 shoppers. The firm was cited as best on such factors as pleasant shopping experience and most professional salespeople.[17]

Fortune magazine made these comments about Direct Tire Sales:

> Of course, Direct Tire Sales loans customers cars while theirs are being repaired. And fixes flats for free on all tires purchased. And guarantees linings and pads on brake jobs for the life of the car. But what excites customers about this independent tire dealer [with $6 million in annual sales] is the customer lounge. The room is spotless, a high-tech coffee pot burbles in one corner, and the magazine rack features publications like *Newsweek, Discover,* and *Cosmopolitan.* It even has an aquarium. And no girlie magazines featuring Miss Drive Train. Sales employees wear a tie as part of their uniform, and "Yes, sir" and "Yes, ma'am" customers with all the polish of a West Point cadet.[18]

Some retailers have found that customer service can be improved if they empower personnel. In ***employee empowerment***, workers have discretion to do what they believe is necessary—within reason—to satisfy the customer, even if this means bending some company rules. At Nordstrom, a salesperson may drop off a customer's package on the way home from work. At Direct Tire Sales, a salesperson may pay for a cab to get a stranded customer to his or her destination. Home Depot has even built employee empowerment into its daily way of doing business. Every employee on the selling floor gets a minimum of eight weeks training prior to meeting their first customer. They have wide latitude in making on-the-spot decisions. Thus, they can freely talk with individual customers and act as consultants and problem solvers.[19]

14 Barry Berman, "Developing and Implementing a Customer Service Strategy," *Retail Strategist* (Number 2, 1991), p. 10.

15 Joel R. Evans, "How LI's Retailers Can Stay Afloat," *Newsday* (March 24, 1992), p. 83.

16 "IMRA Study Details Best Customer Service Ideas," *Discount Store News* (June 21, 1993), pp. 26, 32; and "Survival Guide to the Supermarkets," *Consumer Reports* (September 1993), pp. 559–568.

17 Cyndee Miller, "Nordstrom Is Tops in Survey," *Marketing News* (February 15, 1993), pp. 12–13.

18 Rahul Jacob, "How to Retread Customers," *Fortune* (Autumn–Winter 1993), pp. 23–24.

19 "Retailers Adapt Home Depot Service to Their Business," *Discount Store News* (May 3, 1993), pp. 101–102.

Retailing in Action

Rolling on the River?

Retail customer service has certainly come a long way! For example, the Oak Park Price Less supermarket, located in Jeffersonville, Indiana, has been operating a river delivery service to boats on the Ohio River for more than 10 years. These deliveries now account for one-quarter of the supermarket's total annual sales.

This is how Oak Park Price Less' river delivery business operates: Boats fax their orders, which average $1,500, directly to the store. The orders are then picked by supermarket personnel and delivered directly to Oak Park Price Less' 32-foot cruiser. The supermarket makes ten cruiser deliveries in a typical week; and, despite the large order size—which usually includes a week's supply of food for a boat crew, orders are often filled within an hour.

To best serve its customers, Oak Park Price Less makes river deliveries on a 24-hour per day, year-round basis (including Christmas and New Year's Day). Deliveries are even made in poor weather conditions, such as 6-foot waves. Oak Park Price Less also delivers necessities for crew members that the store does not carry—such as prescription medicines, shoes, and washing machines.

According to Oak Park Price Less, "We take care of them [boat customers] just like we take care of customers that walk into the store."

Source: Based on material in Tom Chiat, "Rolling on the River," *Progressive Grocer* (October 1993), pp. 133–134.

Relationship Retailing

Today, good retailers realize that it is in their interest to engage in ***relationship retailing***, whereby they seek to establish and maintain long-term bonds with customers, rather than act as if each sales transaction is a completely new encounter with them. This means that the retailers must concentrate on the total retail experience, monitor shopper satisfaction with customer service, and stay in touch with customers.

To be effective with relationship retailing, a firm has to keep these two points in mind: First, because it is harder to lure new customers than to make existing ones happy, a "win-win" approach should be enacted. For the retailer to "win" in the long run (lure shoppers, make sales, earn profits, etc.), the customer must also "win" in the long run (receive a good value, be treated with respect, feel welcome at the store, etc.). Otherwise, the retailer loses (shoppers go to other stores) and customers lose (by having to spend time and money to learn about other retailers). Second, as a result of the advances in computer technology, it is now much easier to develop a customer data base—complete with data about people's attributes and past shopping behavior. Thus, ongoing customer contact can be better, more frequent, and more focused.

The Focus and Format of the Text

There are various approaches to the study of retailing: an institutional approach, which describes various types of retailing and their development; a functional approach, which concentrates on the activities that retailers must perform (such as buying, pricing, and personnel practices); and a strategic approach, which involves defining the retail business, setting objectives, appealing to an appropriate customer market, developing an overall plan, implementing an integrated strategy, and regularly reviewing operations.

We will study retail management from each of these perspectives, but focus on the ***strategic approach***. The underlying principle is that a retail firm needs to plan for and adapt to a complex, changing environment. Both opportunities and constraints must be considered. Strategic retail management constantly encourages a retailer to evaluate competitors, suppliers, economic factors, changes in consumers, marketplace trends, legal restrictions, and other elements. A firm will prosper when its competitive strengths are matched with the opportunities presented in the environment, weaknesses are eliminated or minimized, and plans look to the future, as well as the past.

This text is divided into eight parts. The balance of Part 1 presents strategic planning in retailing. Each step in the strategic planning process is covered in detail and the changing environment of retailing is examined.

Part 2 characterizes retailing institutions on the basis of ownership, store strategy mix, nonstore retailing, and service retailing. Part 3 deals with consumer behavior and information gathering in retailing.

Parts 4 to 7 discuss the specific elements of a retailing strategy: store location planning; managing a retail business; merchandise planning, handling, and pricing; and communicating with the customer.

Part 8 looks at the special characteristics of service retailing. It also shows how a retailing strategy may be integrated and controlled.

SUMMARY

In this and every chapter in the text, the summary is linked to the objectives stated at the beginning of the chapter.

1. *To define retailing, consider it from various perspectives, demonstrate its importance, and note its special characteristics* Retailing entails the business activities involved in selling goods and services to consumers for their personal, family, or household use. It may be viewed from the perspectives of manufacturers, service firms, consumers, and traditional retailers. It includes tangible and intangible items, does not have to use a store, and can be conducted by manufacturers and others—as well as by retail firms.

   Annual U.S. retail store sales exceed $2 trillion. In addition, telephone and mail-order retailing, vending machines, direct selling, and personal service providers account for hundreds of billions of dollars in revenues annually. The largest 100 retailers in the world generate more than $1.1 trillion in yearly revenues. About 20 million people in the United States work for traditional retailers, a number greatly understating the number of people actually employed in some retailing capacity. Retailers such as department and specialty stores receive up to 40 cents or more of every sales dollar as compensation for their operating costs, the functions they perform, and the profits they earn.

   Retailing is the last stage in a distribution channel, which contains the businesses and people involved in the physical movement and transfer of ownership of goods and services from producer to consumer. In a channel, retailers perform many valuable functions as the intermediaries between manufacturers, wholesalers, and other suppliers and final consumers. Via the sorting process, retailers collect an assortment of products from various suppliers and offer them to customers. Retailers communicate with customers and other channel members, such as manufacturers and wholesalers. Retailers may ship, store, mark, advertise, and prepay for items. They complete transactions with customers and often provide customer services.

   Retailers and their suppliers have complex relationships because the retailers serve two roles. They are part of a distribution channel aimed at the final consumer; and they are major customers for their suppliers. Thus, divergent viewpoints may occur, and they must be reconciled. Channel relations are smoothest with exclusive distribution; they are most volatile with intensive distribution. Selective distribution combines aspects of both in an attempt to balance sales goals and channel member cooperation.

   Retailing has several special characteristics. The average size of a sales transaction is small. Final consumers make many unplanned purchases. Most retail customers must be drawn to a store location.

2. *To introduce the concept of strategic planning and apply it* A retail strategy is the overall plan that guides the firm. It contains six basic steps: defining the business, setting objectives, defining the customer market, developing an overall plan, implementing an integrated strategy, and evaluating performance and making necessary modifications. Wal-Mart's strategy has been particularly well designed and carried out.

3. *To relate the marketing concept to retailing, with an emphasis on the total retail experience, customer service, and relationship retailing* The marketing concept (known as the retailing concept when applied to retailing situations) should be understood and used by all retailers. This concept requires a firm to have a customer orientation, use a coordinated effort, and be goal-oriented. Unfortunately, despite its ease of use, many firms do not adhere to one or more elements of the retailing concept.

   Three issues relate to a retailer's performance in terms of the retailing concept: the total retail experience, customer service, and relationship retailing. The total retail experience consists of all the elements in a retail offering that encourage or inhibit consumers during their contact with a given retailer. Some elements are controllable by a retailer; others are not. Customer service includes identifiable, but sometimes intangible, activities undertaken by a retailer in association with the basic goods and services sold. It has a strong impact on the total retail experience, and consists of two components—expected services and augmented services. With relationship retailing, a retailer seeks to establish and retain long-term bonds with customers, rather than act as if each sales transaction is a thoroughly new encounter with them.

4. *To indicate the focus and format of the text* Retailing may be studied by using an institutional approach, a functional approach, and a strategic approach. Although all three of these approaches are utilized in this text, the focus will be on the strategic approach. The underlying principle is that a retail firm needs to plan for and adapt to a complex, changing environment.

Key Terms

retailing (p. 4)
channel of distribution (p. 9)
sorting process (p. 9)
exclusive distribution (p. 11)
intensive distribution (p. 11)
selective distribution (p. 11)
retail strategy (p. 14)
retailing concept (p. 18)
total retail experience (p. 19)
customer service (p. 20)
employee empowerment (p. 21)
relationship retailing (p. 22)
strategic approach (p. 22)

Questions for Discussion

1. Which of these involve retailing? Explain your answers.
   a. Insurance company specializing in automobile insurance.
   b. College restaurant.
   c. Travel agency dealing with corporate accounts.
   d. Gift shop in a hospital.
2. According to Table 1–1, sales by women's apparel and accessory stores are nearly 4.5 times those of men's and boys' wear stores. As a prospective retailer, what would this mean to you?
3. Describe the sorting process from the manufacturer's perspective. From the retailer's perspective.
4. What kinds of information do retailers communicate to customers? To suppliers?
5. What are the pros and cons of a firm such as Liz Claiborne having its own retail facilities, as well as selling through traditional retailers?
6. Why would one retailer seek to be part of an exclusive distribution channel while another seeks to be part of an intensive distribution channel?
7. Describe how the special characteristics of retailing offer unique opportunities and problems for gasoline retailers.
8. What is a retail strategy? Could it be utilized by a small neighborhood dry cleaner? Why or why not?
9. On the basis of the chapter presentation on Wal-Mart, present five suggestions that a new retailer should consider.
10. Explain the retailing concept. Apply it to a hair salon chain.
11. Define the term "total retail experience." Then, describe a recent retail situation where you were dissatisfied and state why.
12. Differentiate between expected and augmented customer services. Relate your answer to the concept of employee empowerment.
13. How could a small retailer engage in relationship retailing?
14. Distinguish among these approaches to the study of retailing:
    a. Institutional.
    b. Functional.
    c. Strategic.

How to Solve a Case Study

The information contained in this section is intended to give you some insights into case-study analysis. A case study is a collection of facts and data based on a real or hypothetical problem-oriented business situation.

The objective of a case study is to develop one's ability to solve complex business problems, using a logical framework. The issues within a case are generally not unique to a specific individual, company, or industry, and they frequently deal with more than one element of a retail strategy. Sometimes, the material presented in a case can be in conflict. For example, two managers may disagree about a strategy; statistics may be contradictory; or there may be several interpretations of the same information.

In all case studies, you must analyze the material presented and state which specific actions best resolve the major issues. These actions must reflect the information in the case and the environment facing the firm.

Steps in Solving a Case Study

Retailing case studies revolve around the identification of key points and the enumeration and evaluation of proposed courses of action. Any analysis of a case study should include these sequential steps:

1. Presentation of the facts surrounding the case.
2. Identification of the key issue(s).
3. Listing of alternative courses of action that could be taken.
4. Evaluation of alternative courses of action.
5. Recommendation of the best course of action.

PRESENTATION OF THE FACTS SURROUNDING THE CASE

It is helpful to read the case several times until you are familiar with the information contained therein. Rereadings often are an aid to understanding facts, possible strategies, or questions that need clarification and were not apparent earlier. It is important to pay particular attention to exhibits, tables, charts, and diagrams. Data can often reveal vital information when translated into percentages or compared with prior years.

In analyzing the case, you should assume that you are a retail consultant hired by the company. Although facts and figures should be accepted as true, statements, judgments, and decisions made by the individuals in the case should be questioned, especially when not supported by facts or figures—or when one individual disagrees with another.

During the first and subsequent readings of the case, you should

- Underline important facts.
- Interpret all figures and charts.

- Question comments made by individuals.
- Judge the rationality of past and current decisions.
- Develop a list of questions whose answers would be useful in addressing the retailer's key issue(s).

Identification of the Key Issue(s)

Many times, the facts surrounding a case point out the key issue(s) facing a retailer, such as new opportunities, a changing environment, a decline in market share, poor profitability, and/or excess inventories. As a retail consultant, you must identify the characteristics and ramifications of the issue(s) and examine them, using the material contained in the case and in the text. In some instances, you must delve deeply because the key issue(s) and their characteristics may not be immediately obvious.

Listing of Alternative Courses of Action That Could Be Taken

Next, alternative courses of action pertaining to the key issue(s) in the case, identified in the previous step, are listed. These courses of action are considered based on their appropriateness to the firm and the situation. Thus, the advertising strategy for a small neighborhood stationery store would not be appropriate for a large gift store located in a major shopping center.

Proposed courses of action should take into account such factors as

- The business category.
- Objectives.
- The customer market.
- The overall strategy.
- The product assortment.
- Competition.
- Legal restrictions.
- Economic trends.
- Marketplace trends.
- Financial capabilities.
- Personnel capabilities.
- Sources of supply.

Evaluation of Alternative Courses of Action

Each potential course of action must be evaluated, according to the facts surrounding the case, the key issue(s), the retail strategy concepts discussed in the text, and the environment of the firm. Specific criteria should be used, and each alternative should be analyzed on the basis of these criteria. The ramifications and risks associated with each course of action should also be considered. Important information and statistics not included in the case should be mentioned.

Recommendation of the Best Course of Action

Be sure your case analysis is not just a summary of the case. The analysis will be critiqued by your professor on the basis of how well you identify the key issue(s) or problem(s), outline and assess the alternative courses of action, and reach realistic conclusions (that take the retailer's size, competition, image, and so on into consideration). It is most important that you show a good understanding of both the principles of strategic retail management and the dynamics of the case.

Be precise about which alternative is more desirable for the retailer in its current context. Remember that the objective of case study analysis is the learning of a logical reasoning process applied to retailing. A written report must demonstrate this process.

Note: The cases in this text have questions to guide you in your analysis. However, your analysis should not be limited by them.

Strategic Planning in Retailing: Owning or Managing a Business

❖ Chapter Objectives

1. To show the value of strategic planning for all types of retailers
2. To explain the steps in strategic planning for retailers: situation analysis, objectives, identification of consumers, overall strategy, specific activities, control, and feedback
3. To examine the individual controllable and uncontrollable elements of a retail strategy
4. To present strategic planning as a series of integrated steps

Recently, three founders of retail firms—Mervin Morris, Alan Gold, and Annye Camara—were asked to provide suggestions for entrepreneurs interested in operating a retail business. Mervin Morris started Mervyn's in 1949; the chain now is a division of Dayton Hudson and has annual sales exceeding $4 billion. Alan Gold began Accessory Lady in 1977; it was acquired by Melville in 1987 and now consists of 110+ stores. Annye Camara co-founded Books & Co. with her husband in 1978. Today, it is the largest bookstore retailer in Ohio.

Their suggestions may be used as a checklist for those seeking to start a new retail business or purchase an existing one:

- The odds of success are best if an entrepreneur has experience, confidence, and a passion for the retail business he or she is starting or acquiring.
- Every venture needs a clear and concise mission statement. It must be periodically re-evaluated and rewritten. It can be built around a distinct niche in the market and should be based on appealing to a specific target market, selling specialized merchandise, or having superb customer service.
- The firm's organizational culture should encompass innovation and experimentation. Opinions should be sought from all employees, especially those who are closest to the customer.
- The business plan should be tied to multiyear projections—with worst case, best case, and probable case scenarios. A plan that is set somewhere between the worst case and most probable case is recommended. Entrepreneurs must have adequate resources to operate for at least 24 to 36 months under the worst case projection.
- A list of strengths and weaknesses should be prepared, including all the reasons why the firm should succeed and everything that could go wrong. There must be an honest appraisal in this assessment.
- An adequate information system is critical to planning and control. Such a system should allow managers to access information at the product level and to integrate merchandising and operating information.
- Excellent employees make a real difference. Thus, managers need to seek out superior job candidates. And good training is essential; part of a manager's job should be to coach newer employees.
- Marketing research should be regularly conducted by questioning consumers about how the firm is doing, what additional goods and services are desired, and what could make the firm easier to patronize. Ideas should be solicited from both customers and employees.[1]

[1] Mervin Morris, Alan Gold, and Annye Camara, "Creating a Company," *Arthur Andersen Retailing Issues Letter* (March 1992), pp. 1–4.

Reprinted by permission of IBM.

Overview

As noted in Chapter 1, a ***retail strategy*** is an overall plan or framework of action that guides a retailer. Ideally, a plan will be at least one year in duration and will outline the mission, goals, consumer market, overall and specific activities, and control mechanisms of the retailer. Without a pre-defined and well-integrated strategy, the firm may flounder and be unable to cope with the environment that surrounds it.

The process of strategic retail planning has several attractive features. First, it provides a thorough analysis of the requirements of different types of retailing. Second, it outlines the objectives of the retailer. Third, a firm is shown how it can differentiate itself from competitors and develop an offering that appeals to a group of customers. Fourth, the retailer studies the legal, economic, and competitive environments. Fifth, the total efforts of the company are coordinated. Sixth, crises are anticipated and often avoided.

Strategic planning can be conducted by the owner of the firm, professional management, or a combination of the two. As a person moves up a retail career ladder, a key measure of performance and advancement potential is whether increased planning responsibility is undertaken and how well it is completed.

The steps in planning and enacting a retail strategy are interdependent; and a firm will often start with a general plan that becomes more specific as options and payoffs become clearer. In Chapter 2, we cover the development of a comprehensive, integrated retail strategy, as shown in Figure 2–1.[2] In Chapter 3, we look at the changing environment that retailers are facing as they conduct strategic planning.

Situation Analysis

Situation analysis is the candid evaluation of the opportunities and potential problems facing a prospective or existing retailer. It seeks to answer two general questions: What position or status is the firm in now? In which direction should it be heading? For a retailer, situation analysis means defining and adhering to an organizational mission, evaluating ownership and management options, and outlining the goods/service category to be sold.

During this stage, especially for a new retailer or one thinking about making a major strategy change, an honest, in-depth self-assessment is needed. It is all right for a person or company to be ambitious and aggressive; yet, dramatically overestimating one's abilities and prospects may be harmful—if the result is entry into the wrong retail business, inadequate resources, and underestimating the competition.

Organizational Mission

An ***organizational mission*** is a retailer's understanding of its role in the business system; it is reflected in the firm's attitudes to consumers, employees, competitors, government, and others. A clear organizational mission lets a firm gain a consumer following and distinguish itself from competitors.

These are a few examples:

> Vons is a premier retailer of foods and related categories, including goods and services associated with drugstores. We respond to needs and preferences of a

[2] For interesting articles on strategic planning, see Steve Weinstein, "How Retailers Set Goals—and Reach Them," *Progressive Grocer* (April 1990), pp. 155–160; David Carson and Stanley Cromie, "Marketing Planning in Small Enterprises: A Model and Some Empirical Evidence," *Journal of Consumer Marketing*, Vol. 7 (Summer 1990), pp. 5–18; Jeffrey S. Conant, Denise T. Smart, and Roberto Solano-Mendez, "Generic Retailing Types, Distinctive Marketing Competencies, and Competitive Advantage," *Journal of Retailing*, Vol. 69 (Fall 1993), pp. 254–279; and Paul J. H. Shoemaker and J. Edward Russo, "A Pyramid of Decision Approaches," *California Management Review*, Vol. 36 (Fall 1993), pp. 9–31.

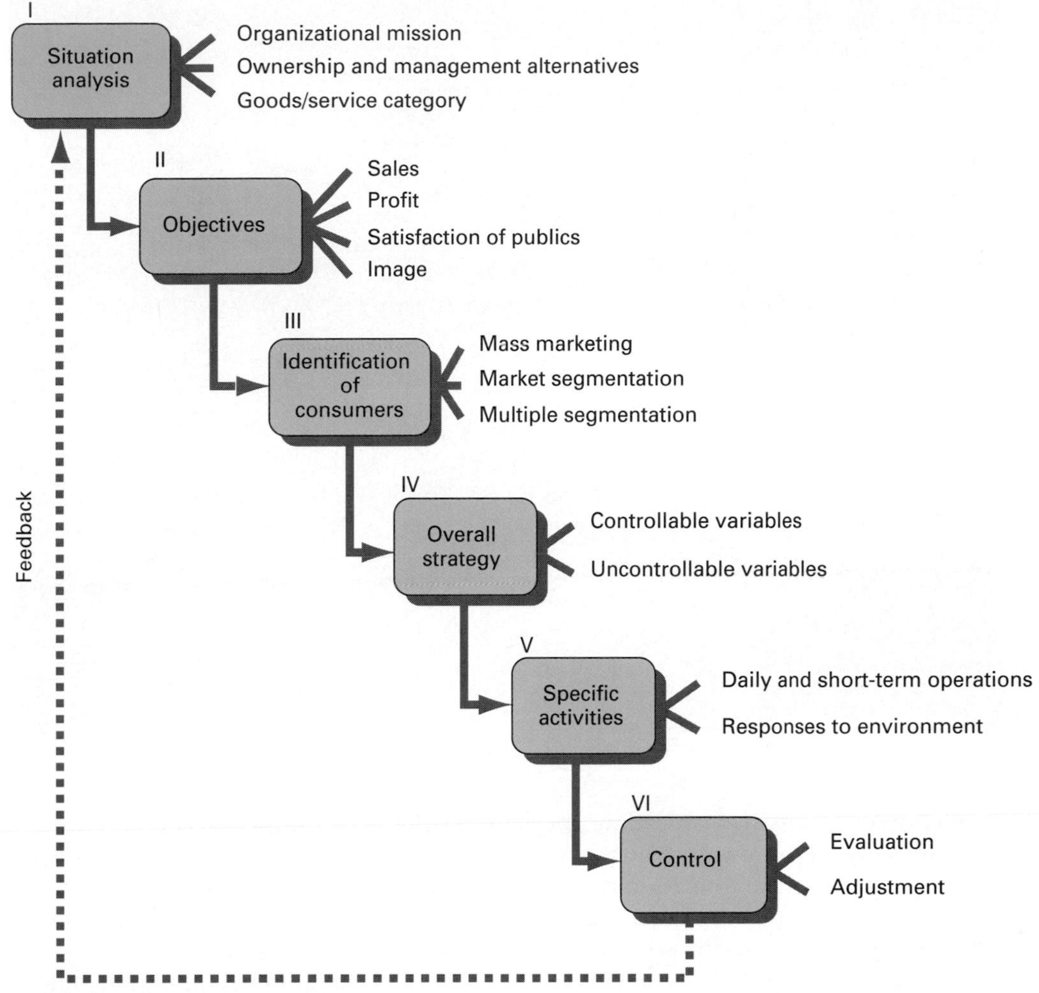

Figure 2–1
Elements of a Retail Strategy

wide spectrum of customer segments with a dense and growing state-of-the-art store network employing several names and store types. All are merchandised, staffed, and operated with the highest integrity—providing quality shopping experiences designed to create and keep customers. We are good corporate citizens of the communities in which we operate. We provide a rewarding work environment which attracts, develops, and retains quality people. In this manner, we grow our business in volume, share, and profits to maximize shareholder value.[3]

Spiegel, Inc. is the nation's dominant multichannel specialty retailer, marketing fashionable apparel and home furnishings to millions of American consumers via approximately 70 catalogs and more than 275 stores. Known for our trademark semiannual catalog and specialty catalogs, Spiegel, Inc. is also the parent company of Eddie Bauer, which serves men's and women's casual life-style needs through catalogs and specialty retail stores. The Spiegel businesses serve as an invaluable fashion and home furnishings resource for the value-conscious, discerning consumers of the 1990s.[4] [See Figure 2–2.]

[3] *The Vons Companies, Inc. 1992 Annual Report,* inside front cover.

[4] *Spiegel, Inc. 1992 Annual Report,* inside front cover.

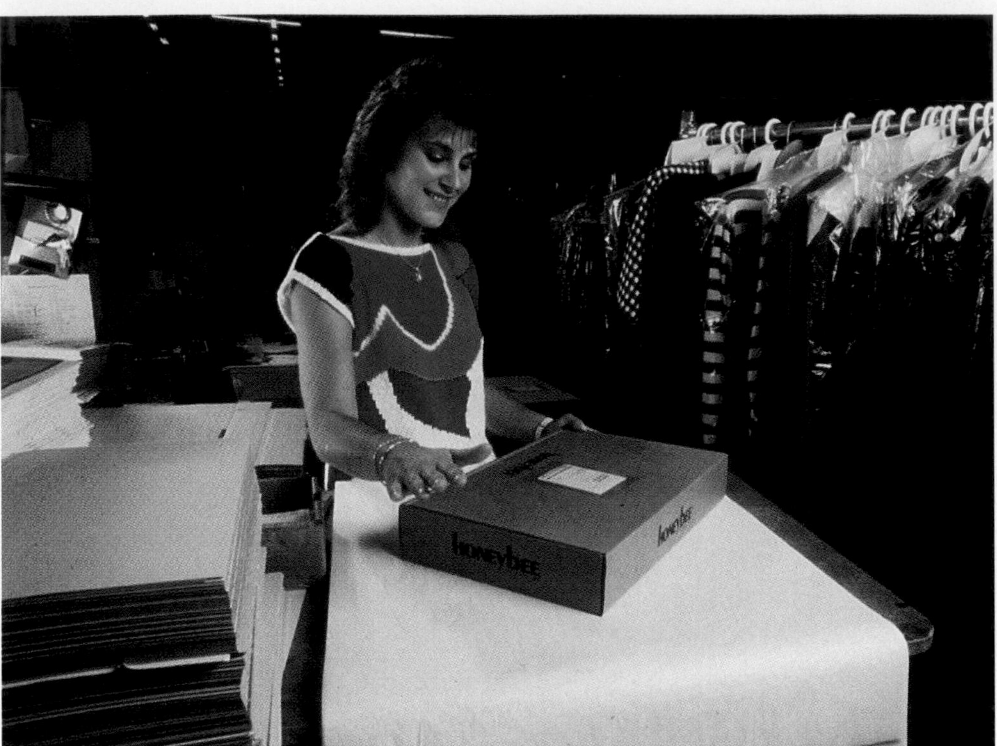

Figure 2–2
Spiegel's Honeybee
Among the 70 catalogs published by Spiegel are those featuring the Honeybee name.
Reprinted by permission.

> Hechinger Company is a leading specialty retailer providing goods and services for the care, repair, remodeling, and maintenance of the home and garden. The Company serves the home improvement industry through its three operating divisions: Hechinger Stores Company, located primarily in the Mid-Atlantic region; Home Quarters Warehouse, Inc., located primarily in New England, the Midwest, and Southern United States; and Triangle Building Centers, located in Mid-Eastern Pennsylvania.[5]

A firm's mission includes a long-term commitment to a type of business and a place in the market. One key decision a retailer must make is whether to base its business around the goods and services sold or around consumer needs. For example, a retailer entering the lumber business must decide if a line of bathroom vanities should be stocked, in addition to raw lumber products. A traditionalist retailer would probably decide not to carry the vanities since they seem unconnected to the perceived business. But, a retailer that views a lumberyard as a do-it-yourself home-improvement center sees the vanities as a logical part of its product mix. The latter firm would carry any merchandise that the consumer, not the storekeeper, desires. See Figure 2–3.

A second major decision for a retailer is whether it wants a place in the market as a leader or a follower. On the one hand, a retailer could seek to offer a unique strategy, such as Taco Bell becoming the first nationwide quick-serve Mexican food chain. On the other hand, a retailer could emulate the standard practices followed by competitors in its category but do a better job in executing them, such as a neighborhood fast-food hamburger restaurant having 5-minute guaranteed service and a cleanliness pledge.

A third important decision involves a retail firm's market scope. Although a large chain can seek a broad customer base (because of its resources and recognition), it is usually best for a small retailer—and most startups—to focus on a narrow customer base. By concentrating its efforts, a small company can usually compete quite effectively with larger firms; the latter tend not to adapt their strategies as well to local markets.

[5] *Hechinger Company 10K for the Fiscal Year Ending January 30, 1993.*

FIGURE 2–3
Home Depot's Customer-Oriented Philosophy of Business
Home Depot's chain of home centers offers a broad range of products for do-it-yourselfers. Each outlet carries 30,000 items, including lumber, lighting equipment, tools, and plumbing fixtures and supplies.
Reprinted by permission.

Although the development of an organizational mission is the first step in a retailer's planning process, the mission should be continually reviewed and adjusted to reflect changing company goals and a dynamic retail environment.

OWNERSHIP AND MANAGEMENT ALTERNATIVES

A very essential part of situation analysis is the assessment of ownership and management alternatives. Ownership decisions include whether to operate as a sole proprietorship, a partnership, or a corporation—as well as whether to start a new business, to buy an existing business, or to become a franchisee. Management alternatives include owner-manager versus professional manager and centralized versus decentralized structures.

A ***sole proprietorship*** is an unincorporated retail firm owned by one person. All benefits, profits, risks, and costs accrue to the single owner. A sole proprietorship is simple to form, fully controlled by the owner, operationally flexible, easy to dissolve, and subject to single taxation by the government. It does make the owner personally liable with regard to legal claims from suppliers, creditors, and others; and it may result in limited capital and limited expertise.

A ***partnership*** is an unincorporated retail firm owned by two or more persons, each of whom has a financial interest. Partners share benefits, profits, risks, and costs. A partnership allows responsibility and expertise to be divided among two or more owners, provides a greater capability for raising funds than a proprietorship, is simpler to form than a corporation, and is subject to single taxation by the government. It, too, makes owners personally liable as to legal claims from suppliers, creditors, and others; may be dissolved upon a partner's death or due to a disagreement; binds all partners to actions made by any individual partner acting on behalf of the firm; and usually has less ability to raise capital than a corporation.

A ***corporation*** is a retail firm that is formally incorporated under state law. It is a legal entity apart from its individual officers (or stockholders). A corporation allows funds to be raised via the sale of company stock, does not allow legal claims against individuals, makes ownership transfer relatively easy, is assured of long-term existence (even if a founder leaves, retires, or dies), has the most use of professional managers, and sets clear operating authority via corporate officers. It is subject to double taxation (company earnings and stockholder dividends), faces more government rules

NAME OF BUSINESS______________________________

A. SELF-ASSESSMENT AND BUSINESS CHOICE

1. Evaluate your strengths and weaknesses.
2. Commitment paragraph: Why should you be in business for yourself? Why open a new business rather than acquire an existing one or become a member of a franchise chain?
3. Describe the type of retail business that fits your strengths and desires. What will make it unique? What will the business offer for customers? How will you capitalize on the weaknesses of competitors?

B. OVERALL RETAIL PLAN

1. State your philosophy of business.
2. Choose an ownership form (sole proprietorship, partnership, or corporation).
3. State your long- and short-run goals.
4. Analyze your customers from their point of view.
5. Research your market size and store location.
6. Quantify the total retail sales of your goods/service category in your trading area.
7. Analyze your competition.
8. Quantify your potential market share.
9. Develop your retail strategy: store location and operations, merchandising, pricing, and store image and promotion.

C. FINANCIAL PLAN

1. What level of funds will you need to get started and to get through the first year? Where will they come from?
2. Determine the first year profit, return on investment, and salary that you need/want.
3. Project monthly cash flow and profit-and-loss statements for the first two years.
4. What sales will be needed to break-even during the first year? What will you do if these sales are not reached?

D. ORGANIZATIONAL DETAILS PLAN (ADMINISTRATIVE MANAGEMENT)

1. Describe your personnel plan (hats to wear), organizational plan, and policies.
2. List the jobs you like and want to do and those you dislike, cannot do, or do not want to do.
3. Outline your accounting and inventory systems.
4. Note your insurance plans.
5. Specify how day-to-day operations would be conducted for each aspect of your strategy.
6. Review the risks you face and how you plan to cope with them.

Figure 2–4
Selected Factors to Consider When Starting a New Retail Business
Source: Adapted by the authors from *Small Business Management Training Instructor's Guide: No. 109* (Washington, D.C.: U.S. Small Business Administration).

than other ownership forms, requires a complex and costly process when established, may be viewed as impersonal, and may separate ownership from management. A closed corporation is usually operated by a limited number of persons, who control ownership; stock is not available for public purchase. In an open corporation, stock is widely traded and available for public purchase.

Sole proprietorships account for 71 percent of all retail firms in the United States that file tax returns, partnerships for 5 percent, and corporations for 24 percent. In terms of sales volume, sole proprietorships account for 10 percent of total U.S. retail store sales, partnerships for 3 percent, and corporations for 87 percent.[6]

Starting a new business—being an entrepreneur—offers a retailer flexibility in location, operations, product lines, customer markets, and other factors; and it allows the strategy to be fully tailored to the owner's desires and strengths. It may also mean having construction or renovation costs, having a time lag until the business is ready to open and then until profits are earned, beginning with an unknown name and image, and having to establish supplier relationships and develop an inventory of goods. Figure 2–4 presents several factors to be considered when starting a new business.

[6] *Statistical Abstract of the United States 1993* (Washington, D.C.: U.S. Department of Commerce, 1993), p. 531.

Buying an existing business allows a retailer to acquire an established company name, a customer following, a good location, trained personnel, and standing facilities; to operate immediately; to generate ongoing sales and profits; and possibly to get good lease terms and/or financing (at favorable interest rates) from the seller. It also means fixtures may be older, there is less flexibility in developing and enacting a strategy tailored to the new owner's desires and strengths, and the growth potential of the business may be limited. Figure 2–5 provides a checklist of questions to consider when purchasing an existing retail business.

By becoming a franchisee, a retailer can combine independent ownership with franchisor management assistance, thorough strategic planning, a known company name and a loyal customer following, cooperative advertising and buying, and a regional or national (rather than local) image. It also means that a contractual agreement may specify rigid operations standards, limit the product lines to be sold, and restrict the choice of suppliers; the franchisor usually receives continuous payments (royalties); advertising fees may be required; and there is a possibility of termination by the franchisor if the agreement is not followed satisfactorily.

Strategically, the management format chosen has an additional impact on decision making. In an owner-manager system, planning tends to be less formal and more intuitive, and many tasks tend to be reserved for the owner-manager (such as employee supervision). With a professional manager system, planning tends to be more formal

NAME OF BUSINESS ______

These questions should be considered when purchasing an existing retail business:

1. Why is the seller placing the business up for sale?
2. How much are you paying for goodwill (the cost of the business above its tangible asset value)?
3. Have sales, inventory levels, and profit figures been confirmed by your accountant?
4. Will the seller introduce you to his/her customers and stay on during the transition period?
5. Will the seller sign a statement that he/she will not open a directly-competing business in the same trading area for a reasonable time period?
6. If sales are seasonal, are you purchasing the business at the right time of the year?
7. In the purchase of the business, are you assuming existing debts of the seller?
8. Who receives proceeds from transactions made prior to the sale of the business but not yet paid by creditors?
9. What is the length of the lease if property is rented?
10. If property is to be purchased along with the business, has it been inspected by a professional engineer?
11. How modern are the storefront and store fixtures?
12. Is inventory fresh? Does it contain a full merchandise assortment?
13. Are the advertising policy, customer service policy, and pricing policy of the past owner similar to yours? Can you continue old policies?
14. If the business is to be part of a chain, is the new unit compatible with existing units? How much trading-area overlap is there with existing stores?
15. Has a lawyer examined the proposed contract?
16. What effect will owning this business have on your life-style and on your family relationships?

FIGURE 2–5
A Checklist for Purchasing an Existing Retail Business

and systematic. However, the professional manager is usually more constrained in his or her authority than the owner-manager. In a centralized structure, decision-making authority is limited to top management or ownership; in a decentralized structure, managers in individual departments have major input into decisions. Regardless of management format, a retailer is best able to develop and enact a successful strategy only if there is ample information and communication.

A comprehensive discussion of independent retailers, chains, franchises, leased departments, vertical marketing systems, and consumer cooperatives appears in Chapter 4.

GOODS/SERVICE CATEGORY

Before a prospective retail firm can design a well-defined plan, it must select a ***goods/service category***—the line of business—in which to operate. Figure 2–6 shows the diversity of goods/service categories from which a retailer may choose. Chapter 5 examines the attributes of food-based and general merchandise store retailers, nonstore retailers, and the differences between goods and service retailing in detail. Chapter 18 looks at the special strategic features of service retailing.

At this stage of planning, it is advisable (for most retailers) to specify both a general goods/service category and a niche within that category. For example, Wendy's is an eating and drinking place that specializes in fast food, with a menu that emphasizes hamburgers. The Gap is an apparel chain that specializes in moderate-priced casual clothes. Motel 6 is a hotel chain that specializes in inexpensive rooms with few frills.

When selecting the goods/service category, the potential retail business owner should select a type of business that will allow him or her to match personal abilities, financial resources, and time availability with those required by the kind of business.

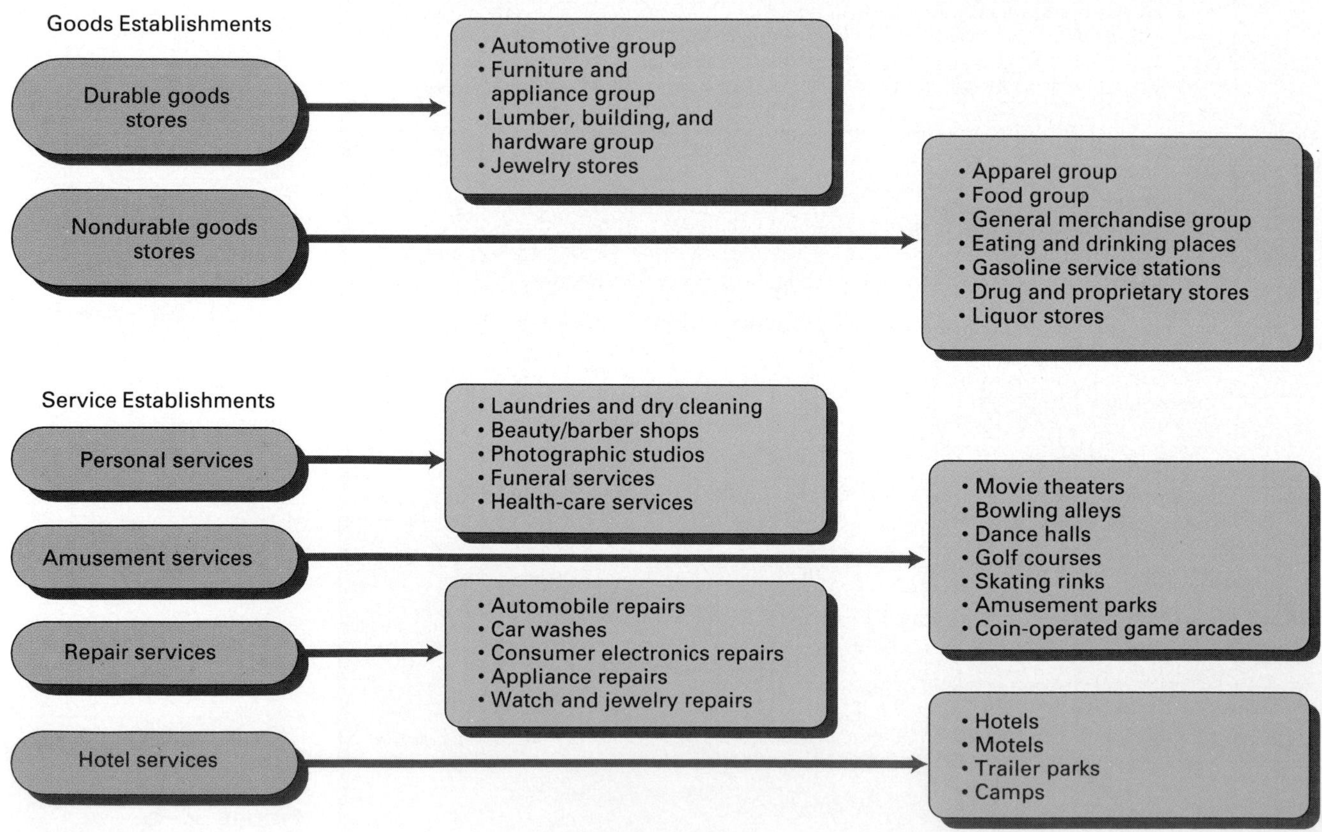

FIGURE 2–6
Selected Kinds of Retail Goods and Services Establishments

ETHICS IN RETAILING

How Can Retailers Regain Consumers' Trust?

According to an executive at a major marketing research firm, there has been a general erosion of trust for retailers by consumers. Although this can be viewed as a threat, it is also a major opportunity for those retailers that offer "genuine value to customers in a forthright, believable manner."

Retailers can gain—or regain—consumers' trust by selling goods and services that are well-suited for their intended use, by pricing goods and services fairly, and by promptly and adequately responding to customer complaints. Among the retailers that are commonly regarded as "fair players" to their customers are Lexus auto dealers and Hampton Inn hotels.

Lexus dealers take a proactive approach and initiate communication with customers to determine their satisfaction. Dealers routinely call customers shortly after the purchase of a new car and after each service call.

In contrast, Hampton Inn takes a reactive approach by guaranteeing to refund the full cost of a hotel room to any unsatisfied customer. This guarantee policy enables the chain to track customer complaints (by hotel unit and by cause), as well as to regain lost customer trust. Close to 90 per cent of customers that invoke the guarantee say that despite their complaints they will use a Hampton Inn again.

Source: Based on material in Leonard L. Berry, "Playing Fair in Retailing," *Arthur Andersen Retailing Issues Letter* (March 1993), pp. 1–5.

Personal Abilities

Personal abilities depend on an individual's aptitude—the preference for a type of business and the potential to do well; education—formal learning about retail practices and policies; and experience—practical learning about retail practices and policies.

A person should have an aptitude for the business to be entered. For example, an individual who wants to run a store, who likes to use initiative, and who has the ability to react quickly to competitive developments will be suited to a different type of situation from a person who depends on others for advice and does not like to make decisions. The first individual could be an independent operator, in a dynamic business like fashion; the second might seek partners or a franchise and a business that is stable, like a car wash. In addition, some people enjoy personal interaction with their customers; they would dislike the impersonality of a pure discount or self-service operation. Still others enjoy the impersonality of mail-order retailing.

In certain fields, education and experience requirements are specified and enforced by federal or state laws. Insurance brokers, stockbrokers, real-estate brokers, barbers, beauticians, certified public accountants, pharmacists, and opticians represent a cross-section of the kinds of retailers who must satisfy minimum educational and/or experience standards. They must demonstrate professional competency. For instance, real-estate brokers must be licensed. This involves an analysis of individuals' ethical character, as well as an examination of their knowledge of real-estate practice and law. (Yet, designation as a broker does not depend on the ability to sell, keep good financial records, or negotiate with buyers and sellers.)

Some skills can be learned through education and/or experience; other skills are inborn. Potential retailers must be able to examine their personal skills and match them with the requirements of a business. This is a hard process that involves insight into oneself and careful reflection. Strengths and weaknesses must be assessed and evaluated in this matching process. Partnerships may arise when two or more parties possess complementary skills: A person with extensive selling experience and ability may join someone having the operating skills needed to open a store. Each partner would have valued skills but may be unable to operate a store without the expertise of the other.

Financial Resources

A second major consideration in the selection of a goods/service category for a retail business is the level of ***financial resources*** required. Many enterprises, especially new,

Table 2–1 Some of the Typical Financial Investments for a New Retail Venture

Use of Funds	Source of Funds
• Land and building (lease or purchase)	• Personal savings, bank loan, commercial finance company
• Inventory	• Personal savings, manufacturer credit, commercial finance company, sales revenues
• Fixtures (including display cases, storage facilities, signs, lighting, carpeting, etc.)	• Personal savings, manufacturer, credit, bank loan, commercial finance company
• Equipment (including cash register, marking machine, office equipment, computers, etc.)	• Personal savings, manufacturer, credit, bank loan, commercial finance company
• Personnel (including salespeople, cashiers, stock-people, etc.)	• Personal savings, bank loan, sales revenues
• Promotion	• Personal savings, sales revenue
• Personal drawing account	• Personal savings, life insurance loan
• Miscellaneous: Equipment repair Credit sales (bad debts) Professional services Repayment of loans	• Personal savings, manufacturer and wholesaler credit, bank credit plan, bank loan, commercial finance company

Note: Collateral for a bank loan may be a building, fixtures, land, inventory, and/or a personal residence.

independent ones, fail because the owners do not correctly project the financial resources needed to succeed. Table 2–1 outlines some of the typical financial investments for a new retail venture.

New retailers frequently underestimate the need for a personal drawing account, cited in Table 2–1. This account is used for the daily, weekly, and monthly household expenses of the owner and his or her family over the early, unprofitable stage of a business. Housing, clothing, food, medical, and other personal expenses are paid from this account. Because few new retail ventures are immediately profitable, the budget must include personal expenditures.

The costs of renovating an existing facility are also often underestimated by new retailers. It is common for underfunded firms to invest initially in only essential renovations. Other improvements wait until the firms are prospering, and alteration costs are paid from profits. This practice reduces the initial investment, but it can give the retailer a poor image.

Merchandise width and depth of assortment, as well as the types of goods and services sold, have an impact on the financial outlay required of a new retailer. The use of a partnership, corporation, or franchise agreement will also have an effect on the initial investment.

Table 2–2 shows the financial requirements for a hypothetical used-car dealer. Table 2–3 shows inventory costs and revenues for this retailer.

The initial personal savings investment of $166,350 required to enter this type of business would force many potential retailers to rethink the choice of product category, as well as the intended format of the retail organization. First, the plans for a fifty-car inventory reflect the owner's desire to have a balanced product line. However, if the firm described in Tables 2–2 and 2–3 concentrates on subcompact, compact, and intermediate cars, it can be more specialized and significantly reduce inventory size. This would lead to lower investment costs. Second, an entering used-car dealer can also reduce the initial investment by seeking a location whose facilities do not have to be modified, like the site of a previous used-car dealer. Third, fewer of one person's financial resources are needed if he or she enters into a partnership or corporation with others, which allows costs—and profits—to be shared.

TABLE 2–2 Financial Requirements for a Used-Car Dealer

Total investments (first year)	
Lease (10 years, $55,000 per year)	$ 55,000
Beginning inventory (fifty cars, average cost of $5,300)	265,000
Replacement inventory (fifty cars, average cost of $5,300)[a]	265,000
Fixtures and equipment (includes painting, paneling, carpeting, lighting, signs, heating and air-conditioning system, electronic cash register, service bay)	50,000
Replacement parts	50,000
Personnel (one mechanic)	35,000
Promotion (brochures and newspaper advertising)	25,000
Drawing account (to cover owner's personal expenses for one year; all selling and operating functions except mechanical ones performed by the owner)	40,000
Accountant	9,000
Miscellaneous (including loan payments)	50,000
Profit (projected)	35,000
	$879,000
Source of funds	
Personal savings	$166,500
Bank loan	300,000
Sales revenues (based on expected sales of fifty cars, average price of $8,250)	412,500
	$879,000

[a] Assumes that fifty cars are sold during the year. As each type of car is sold, a replacement is bought by the dealer and placed in inventory. At the end of the year, inventory on hand remains at fifty units.

Time Demands

Time demands on retail owners (or managers) differ significantly by goods or service category. They are influenced both by consumer demand and needs and by the owners' or managers' ability to automate operations or delegate activities to others.

Firms such as major appliance stores must be open during weekends and evening hours—and even on holidays—because appliance purchases are usually made jointly by husbands and wives (those times are especially convenient for such customers). Convenience food stores sell their greatest volume when supermarkets are closed;

TABLE 2–3 Analysis of Beginning Inventory Costs and Expected First-Year Sales Revenues by Type of Car for a Used-Car Dealer

Type of Car	Number of Cars in Beginning Inventory	Average Cost	Average Selling Price	Total Cost of Beginning Inventory	Annual Total Revenue[a]
Subcompact	10	$3,848	$ 5,600	$ 38,480	$ 56,000
Compact	14	4,673	7,308	65,422	102,312
Intermediate	15	5,498	8,800	82,470	132,000
Full-size/luxury	6	7,973	12,808	47,838	76,848
Station wagon/van	5	6,158	9,068	30,790	45,340
	50	$5,300	$ 8,250	$265,000	$412,500

[a] Fifty cars are sold during the year. As each type of car is sold, a replacement is bought by the dealer and placed in inventory. At the end of the year, inventory on hand remains at fifty units.

thus, late evening and weekend hours must be kept. Gift shops, sporting goods stores, house painters, and others have extreme seasonal shifts in business and keep long hours during prime seasons. On the other hand, mail-order firms (which can process orders during any part of the day) have much more flexible hours.

The ability or inability of retailers to automate operations or delegate duties also affects the number of hours worked. Some types of businesses require rather low involvement by the owner. These include gasoline stations that offer no repair or maintenance services, coin-operated laundromats, movie theaters, and motels. The emphasis on automation, self-service, standardized goods and services, and financial controls lets these business owners minimize time investments. Other types of businesses require the active involvement of owners. Beauty parlors, television repair stores, butcher shops, restaurants, and jewelry stores are examples of time-consuming businesses.

Intensive owner participation can be caused by several factors. First, the owner may be the major worker, and consumers may be attracted by his or her skills (the major competitive advantage of the firm). In that case, delegating work to others will diminish consumer loyalty. Associated with this aspect is the personal service and expertise that only an owner can give to certain customers. Second, some types of retailing, such as personal services, are not easy to automate. In these cases, the time involvement of the retailer is needed to provide the services. Third, many smaller retailers are underfunded. Therefore, the owner and his or her family must operate all aspects of the business because there are insufficient funds to hire employees. According to one study, spouses work in 40 per cent of family-owned businesses and children work in 37 per cent of them.[7] Fourth, a business that operates on a cash basis and has weak financial controls requires the owner to be on the premises to avoid being cheated: In a small store with poor inventory procedures, it may be difficult to match sales with inventory levels. So, it may be easy for employees to pocket cash sales if not watched by the owner.

A common error is to assume that a person running a retail business works only when a store is open. But, off-hours activities are often necessary. A butcher must go to a meat wholesaler at least once a week to make purchases. (Meat wholesalers are usually busiest between 3 and 6 A.M.) In a restaurant, some foods must be prepared in advance of the posted hours for customers to dine. An antique dealer often spends nonstore hours hunting for goods. A small storekeeper cleans, stocks shelves, and does the books during the hours the store is closed.

A prospective retail business operator should also examine his or her own time preferences in terms of stability versus seasonality (some would rather work 40 hours per week for 48 weeks a year; others would rather work 80 hours per week for 24 weeks a year and relax the balance of the year); ideal working hours (days and times); and the level of personal involvement (absentee ownership or on-site management).

Objectives

After situation analysis, a firm's objectives are chosen. ***Objectives*** are the goals, long-run and short-run, that a retailer hopes to attain. The statement of clear objectives helps to mold a strategy and translate the company mission into action. A retailer may be concerned with one or more of these objectives: sales (including growth, stability, and market share); profit (including level, return on investment, and efficiency); satisfaction of publics (including stockholders and consumers); and image (including customer and industry perceptions). Each of these objectives is sought by many retailers. Some retailers attempt to fully achieve all of the objectives; others concentrate on a few and attempt to achieve these really well.

[7] Arthur Andersen & Co.'s Enterprise Group, "All in the Family," *Crain's New York Business* (May 24, 1993), p. 18.

SALES

Sales objectives are related to the volume of goods and services sold by a retailer. Growth, stability, and/or market share are the sales objectives most often sought by retailers.

Some retailers set sales growth as a top priority. Under this objective, a firm is interested in expanding operations and increasing sales. There is less emphasis on short-run profits. The assumption is that investments in the present will yield profits in the future. A small or large retailer that does well often becomes interested in opening new units and increasing sales volume. Yet, too active a pursuit of expansion can result in problems. Many retailers that are successful in their current business fail when they open new units. Management skills and the "personal touch" are sometimes lost with improper expansion. Sales growth is a legitimate goal for large and small retailers, but it should not be too fast or preclude considering other goals.

Stability in annual sales and profits is the objective of a wide range of retailers that place emphasis on maintaining their sales volume, market share, price lines, and so on. Small retailers are often interested in stable sales that will enable the owners to make a satisfactory living every year, without the pressure of downswings or upsurges. Other retailers develop a loyal following of consumers and are intent not on expanding but on maintaining the approach that attracted the original consumers.

Proper market share is another goal of many retailers. Market share is the percentage of total retail-category sales contributed by a firm. In retailing, it is often an objective only for large retailers or retail chains. The small retailer is more concerned with competition across the street or down the block than with total sales in a metropolitan area.

Sales objectives may be expressed in dollars and units. To achieve its dollar objectives, a retailer can employ a discount strategy (low prices and high unit sales), a moderate strategy (medium prices and medium unit sales), or a prestige strategy (high prices and low unit sales). In the long run, the use of sales units as an indicator of performance is important. Dollar sales over a several-year period may be difficult to compare because of changing retail prices and the rate of inflation; but, sales in units are relatively easy to compare from year to year. A company with dollar sales of $350,000 in 1985 and $500,000 in 1994 might assume that it is doing very well, until unit figures are computed: 10,000 in 1985 and 8,000 in 1994.

PROFIT

With ***profitability objectives***, retailers seek to attain at least a minimum level of profits during a designated time period, usually a year. Profits may be expressed in dollars or as a percentage of sales. For a firm having yearly sales of $5 million and total yearly costs of $4.2 million, pre-tax dollar profits are $800,000 and profits as a percentage of sales are 16 per cent. If the pre-tax profit goal of the firm is equal to or less than $800,000, or 16 per cent, it is satisfied. If the pre-tax profit goal is greater than $800,000, or 16 per cent, the firm has not attained the minimum desired level of profits and is dissatisfied.

Firms with large capital expenditures in land, buildings, and equipment often specify return on investment (ROI) as a goal. ROI is the relationship between company profits and investment in capital items. It is used in the same way as any profit statistic: A satisfactory rate of return is pre-defined by the company, and this rate is compared with the actual rate of return at the end of the year or other designated period. For a firm having annual sales of $5 million and expenditures (including monthly long-term payments for capital items) of $4 million, the yearly profit is $1 million. If the total price to the retailer for land, buildings, and equipment is $10 million, then ROI equals $1 million/$10 million, or 10 per cent per year. The company's ROI goal would have to be 10 per cent or less per year for it to be satisfied.

Increased efficiency in operations is an objective of many retailers. Efficiency may be expressed as 1 – (operating expenses/company sales). The larger this figure, the more efficient the firm. A retailer with sales of $2 million and operating expenses of $1 million has an efficiency rating of 50 per cent ([1 – ($1 million/$2 million)]). Fifty cents of every sales dollar go to cover such nonoperating costs as merchandise purchases and to profits, and fifty cents go for operating expenses. The retailer might set a goal for next year to increase operating efficiency to 60 per cent. On sales of $2 million, operating costs would have to drop to $800,000 ([1 – ($800,000/$2 million)]). Then, 60 cents of every sales dollar would go for nonoperating costs and profits; and 40 cents would go for operating expenses. The increased efficiency would lead to an overall profit increase. Nonetheless, a firm must be careful; if expenses are cut too much, customer service may decline—and this would probably lead to a sales decline and a resulting profit decrease.

SATISFACTION OF PUBLICS

A retailer may be interested in ***satisfaction of publics' objectives***. Publics include stockholders, consumers, suppliers, employees, and government.

Stockholder satisfaction is a vital goal for any retail firm that is publicly owned. It is up to top management to set and attain goals that are consistent with the wishes of stockholders. Many companies have policies that lead to small annual increases in sales and profits (because these goals can be sustained over the long run and indicate good management), rather than policies that introduce innovative ideas possibly leading to peaks and valleys in company sales and profits (indicating poor management). Stable earnings for firms lead to stable dividends for stockholders.

Consumer satisfaction with the total retail experience is a goal that most firms are working toward today, although some have acknowledged this only recently. It is crucial to satisfy consumers and not have a policy of caveat emptor ("Let the buyer beware"). Retailers must listen to criticism and adapt to the desires of consumers. They can accomplish this by gearing their overall mission and objectives to consumer needs. If consumers are satisfied, the other goals are more apt to be reached. Yet, despite the inclusion of consumer satisfaction as a stated objective of today's retailers, the importance of this goal ranks too low for many, large and small alike. For them, the other objectives cited rate higher in the list of priorities.

Good supplier relations are also a key goal. Retailers must understand and work with suppliers, such as manufacturers and wholesalers, if favorable purchase terms, new products, good return policies, prompt shipments, and cooperation are to be received. Because suppliers perform many functions for small retailers, good relations are particularly important for them.

Congenial employee relations are another major goal—and often basic to retailers' performance, whether they are small or large. Positive employee morale means less absenteeism, better performance, and lower turnover. Relations can be improved via effective selection, training, and motivation.

Because federal, state, and local governments can all impose regulations affecting retailing practices, a significant goal may be to understand and adapt to their policies. In some cases, retailers are able to influence government rules by acting singly or as members of large groups, such as trade associations or chambers of commerce.

IMAGE (POSITIONING)

A major goal for virtually any retailer is to create and maintain the image that firm feels is appropriate for the specific type of business involved. An ***image*** is how a given retailer is perceived by consumers and others. A firm may be seen as innovative or conservative, specialized or broad-based, discount-oriented or upscale. The key to a successful image is that consumers view the retailer in the manner the latter intends. See Figure 2–7.

Through ***positioning***, a retailer seeks to project an image relative to its retail category and its competitors, and to determine how consumers respond to that image.

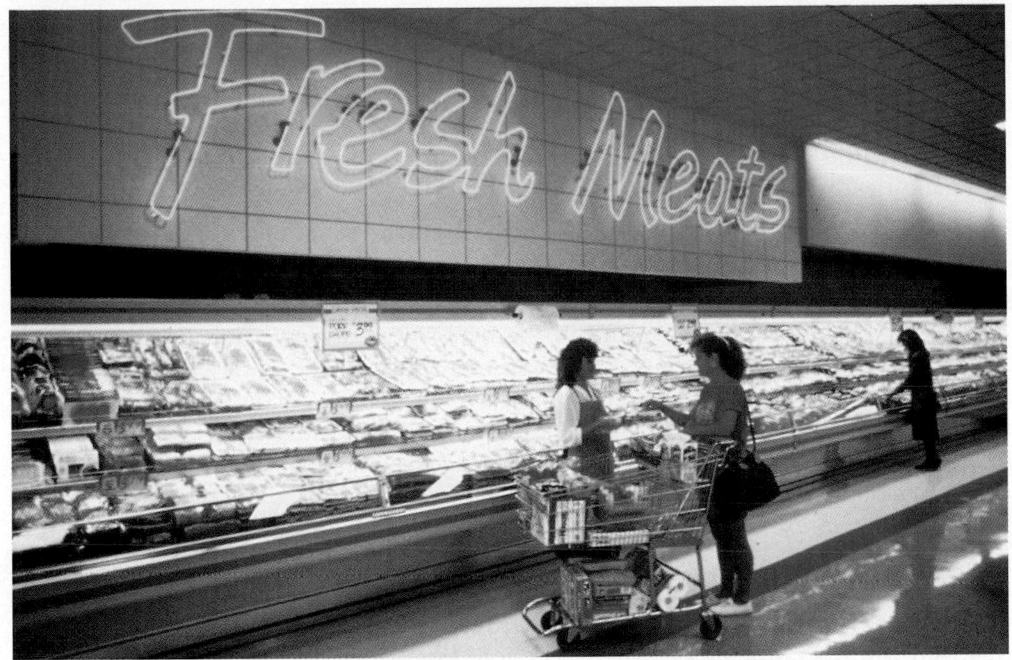

FIGURE 2–7
Kroger's Distinctive Positioning
Kroger has worked very hard to have customers perceive it as a nice place to shop. This means a large assortment of products, special departments, attractive displays, an emphasis on freshness, and time-saving store layouts.
Reprinted by permission.

For example, a retailer selling women's clothing could be generally positioned as an upscale specialty store, a mid-priced specialty store, a department store, a discount department store, or a discount specialty store, and it could be specifically positioned in relation to any nearby retailers selling women's clothing.

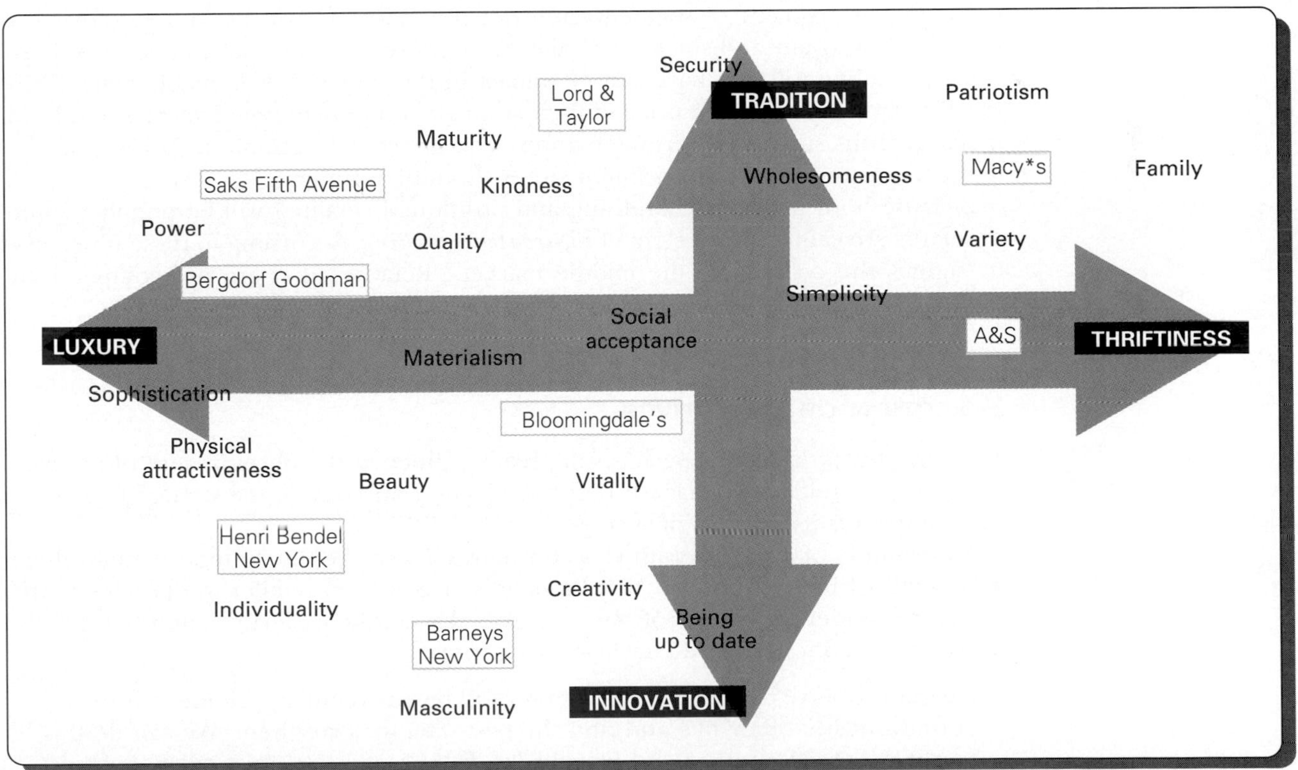

Please note: A&S (Abraham & Straus), Bergdorf Goodman, Bloomingdale's, Lord & Taylor, Macy's, and Saks Fifth Avenue are all department stores. Barneys New York and Henri Bendel are apparel stores.

FIGURE 2–8
Mapping a Store's Personality
Reprinted by permission of BBDO Worldwide and the New York Times. *Copyright 1993.*

The concept of positioning is illustrated in Figure 2–8, which is based on a research study of women living in Manhattan by BBDO Worldwide, a leading advertising agency:

> Shoppers' feelings about eight stores helped researchers place those stores on a "map" of perceptions. On this map, the vertical axis ranges from tradition to innovation; the horizontal from luxury to thriftiness. Other qualities shoppers associated with one or more stores appear near those stores, revealing shoppers' relative preferences.[8]

For some retailers, such as McDonald's, Hertz, or the market-leading drugstore chain in your region, industry leadership (which may be local) is an important objective. This leadership often results in two major benefits for a firm. First, company image may be improved because consumers are apt to place the leader on a higher plateau than its competitors. Second, other retailers may follow pricing and other strategies of the leader rather than develop their own innovative approaches; this form of imitation is the best kind of flattery. A subsidiary benefit is the internal satisfaction accompanying being "number one," and this encourages all to work harder.

Mass merchandising is a positioning approach involving retailers that present a discount or value-oriented image, handle several merchandise lines, and have large store facilities. The retailers want to appeal to a broad customer market, attract high levels of customer traffic, and generate high stock turnover. Because mass merchants have relatively low operating costs, achieve economies in operations, and appeal to value-conscious people, their continuing popularity is forecast. And, in the future, the sales of newer forms of mass merchandisers (like huge value-oriented specialty stores, factory outlet malls, and membership stores) are expected to rise a lot.

A counter positioning approach to mass merchandising is ***positioned retailing***, whereby retailers identify customer segments and develop unique strategies to address the desires of those segments. In positioned retailing, firms concentrate their efforts on a specific segment or segments and not the mass market. Positioning creates a high level of loyalty and shields a retailer from more conventional competitors. Positioned retailing will also have a large impact in the future. It will enable many firms to stress factors other than price in their strategies and encourage a more specialized focus by firms such as department stores. The growth of boutiques, specialty stores, and compartmentalized department stores should continue.

Because both mass merchandising and positioned retailing will be popular, some observers are calling this the era of ***bifurcated retailing***. According to these observers, it "signals the collapse of the middle market." Retailers that are not competitively priced nor particularly individualistic may have difficulty competing.[9]

Selection of Objectives

The objective(s) a retailer selects will greatly influence the development of an overall strategy. A retailer that clearly defines objectives and develops a strategy to achieve them improves its chances of success.

An example of a retailer with clear objectives and a proper strategy to attain them is Hannaford Bros., Northern New England's largest food retailer. It operates nearly 100 stores under the names of Shop 'n Save, Alexander's, Martin's, and Sun Foods. It also has six Shop 'n Save Pharmacy drugstores:

> We want to serve people so well that they will be our regular customers. We need to find out what they like and find the best ways to serve them. We can do this best if we work together enthusiastically. To succeed, we must satisfy our customers, our associates, our communities, and our shareholders. To achieve this,

[8] Stephanie Strom, "Image and Attitude Are Department Stores' Draw," *New York Times* (August 12, 1993), p. D1.

[9] "31 Major Trends Shaping the Future of American Business," *The Public Pulse*, Vol. 2, No. 1 (1988), p. 1.

we must practice the highest level of ethical, social, legal, and professional behavior. We must constantly anticipate the changing needs and desires of our customers and respond quickly and effectively to those needs and desires. We are committed to distributing the goods and services consumers want with prices and quality that represent superior value. We are committed to the growth of all our associates. To accomplish this, we need a growing business, a sharing of common goals, and an atmosphere of mutual trust, openness, and encouragement. We will support and participate in the efforts of local, state, and national organizations which best contribute to the quality of life. We will strive to earn, during any five-year period, an average Return on Equity in the upper quartile of companies in similar businesses. In the long run, we will best serve the interests of our shareholders by serving well our customers, associates, and communities.[10]

Identification of Consumer Characteristics and Needs

Next, the retailer or prospective retailer must identify the characteristics and needs of consumers. The customer group that a retailer seeks to attract and satisfy is called the ***target market.*** In selecting its target market, a retailer may use one of three techniques: selling goods and services to a broad spectrum of consumers, the ***mass market***; zeroing in on one specific group, a ***market segment***; or aiming at two or more distinct consumer groups, ***multiple segments,*** with different retailing approaches for each group.

Conventional supermarkets and drugstores and traditional shoe stores (such as Thom McAn) are examples of retailers that define their target markets broadly. They have a wide assortment of medium-quality items sold at popular prices. In contrast, a small upscale men's shoe store or a fruit-and-vegetable store exemplifies the retailer selecting a well-defined and specific consumer group and offering a narrow, deep product assortment at above-average prices (or in other cases, below-average prices). A retailer aiming at one segment does not try to appeal to everyone.

Department stores are among the retailers that seek multiple market segments. They cater to several groups of customers and provide unique goods and services for each. As an example, women's clothing may be sold in a number of distinctive boutiques scattered throughout the store. Also, large retail chains frequently have divisions that appeal to different market segments. Dayton Hudson Corporation operates Hudson's and Dayton's department stores for customers interested in full service and Target and Mervyn's discount stores for customers interested in low prices.

As shown in Table 2–4, the selection of a target market gives direction to a retailer's choice of a location, the goods and services mix, promotion efforts, and prices. It further enables a firm to stress its competitive advantages and allocate financial resources. In particular, the concept of ***competitive advantage***—the distinct competency of a retailer relative to its competitors—must not be overlooked. The choice of a target market and its satisfaction by a unique retail offering are necessary for a retailer's goals to be achieved. Some examples will demonstrate this

Neiman-Marcus defines its target market as upper-class, status-conscious consumers. Thus, it situates stores in prestigious shopping areas, offers prominent brands of high-quality products, uses finely drawn newspaper ads, has extensive customer services, and charges relatively high prices. Kmart describes its target market as middle-class, value-conscious consumers. Thus, it locates stores in mid-range shopping centers and districts, offers national brands and Kmart brands of medium-quality merchandise, features "good values" in its ads, maintains some customer services, and charges below-average to average prices. Off-price stores aim at extremely price-conscious consumers. Many locate in discount strip shopping centers or districts, offer national brands (sometimes manufacturers' overruns or merchandise not sold by other retailers) of average to below-average quality merchandise, emphasize low prices in ads,

[10] *Hannaford Bros. Co. 1993 Annual Report,* inside front cover.

Table 2–4 Methods for Selecting a Target Market and Their Strategic Implications

Strategic Implications	Target Market Selected: Mass Market	Market Segment	Multiple Segments
Retailer's Location	Near a large population base	Near a small or medium population base	Near a large population base
Goods and Services Mix	Wide assortment of medium-quality items	Deep assortment of high quality or low-quality items	Distinct goods/services aimed at each market segment
Promotion Efforts	Mass advertising	Direct mail, subscription	Different media and messages for each segment
Price Orientation	"Popular prices"	High or low	High, medium, and low—depending on market segment
Strategy	One general, "middle-of-the road" strategy directed at a large homogeneous (similar) group of consumers	One specific strategy directed at a specific, limited group of customers	Several specific strategies, each directed at different (heterogeneous) groups of consumers

offer few or no customer services, and set very low prices. The key to the success of each of these retailers lies in their ability to define their customers and cater to their needs in a distinctive manner.

A retailer is better able to select a target market and satisfy customer needs if it has a good understanding of consumer behavior. This topic is discussed in Chapter 6.

Overall Strategy

After completing a situation analysis, setting objectives, and selecting a target market, the retailer is ready to develop an in-depth overall strategy. This strategy involves two components: those aspects of business that the retailer can directly affect (such as store hours and sales personnel) and those to which the retailer must adapt (such as competition, the economy, and laws). The former are called ***controllable variables***, and the latter are called ***uncontrollable variables.*** See Figure 2–9.

A retail strategy must be developed with both kinds of variables in mind. And the ability of firms to grasp and predict the effects of controllable and uncontrollable vari-

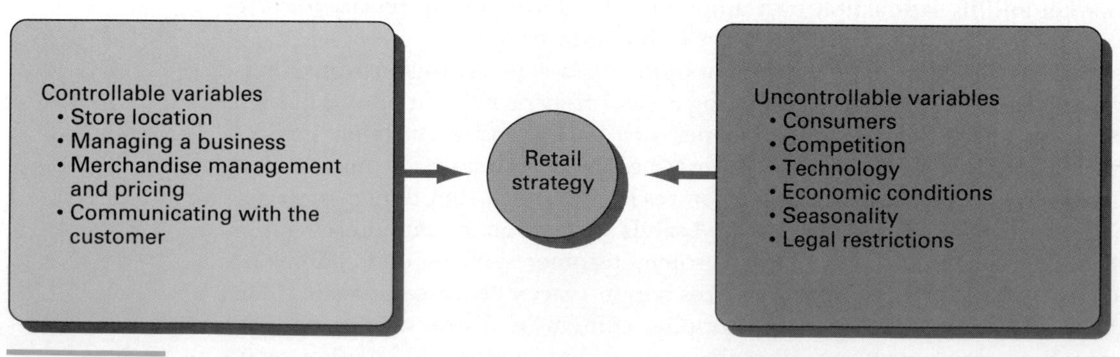

Figure 2–9
Developing an Overall Retail Strategy

RETAILING IN ACTION

Making Jewelry Sales Glitter?

Jewelers are increasingly relying on promotions, new merchandise, and educational advertising as ways of coping with competition from home shopping channels, discount jewelers, and buying clubs. Here's a sampling of strategies used by a cross-section of jewelers during one recent Christmas season.

Sharples Jewelers of Chinook, Montana, guaranteed a full refund on all Christmas gifts if it snowed three inches or more on Christmas Day. The promotion, which was covered by bad weather insurance, increased sales by 50 per cent (it didn't snow on Christmas). And, one West Chester, Pennsylvania, jeweler mailed out tiny shovels for customers to "dig" for jewels in the store's small "gold mine."

Some merchants increased revenues by offering less costly selections of jewelry. The Gordon division of Zale's, for example, offered lower-priced 10-karat jewelry. Even Tiffany's introduced a line of men's stainless steel accessories.

Other jewelers relied on consumer education programs to enable consumers to better understand a gem's value. An Oklahoma City jeweler, for instance, developed a checklist for consumers. It told them to examine all gems under a microscope and to have jewelry guaranteed by a retailer for both color and grade. That jeweler credited this program with a 20 per cent increase in sales.

Source: Based on material in Bob Ortega, "Jeweler's Bet Honest Image, Price Cuts Will Make Sales Glitter," *Wall Street Journal* (December 6, 1993), pp. B1, B10.

ables is greatly aided by the use of appropriate data. In Chapter 7, information gathering and processing in retailing are described.

CONTROLLABLE VARIABLES

The controllable parts of a retail strategy are broken down into the basic categories shown in Figure 2–9: choosing a store location, managing a business, merchandise management and pricing, and communicating with the customer. A good strategy integrates these areas so a unified plan is devised and followed. These elements are comprehensively covered in Chapters 8 to 18.

Choosing a Store Location

A retailer has several store location decisions to make. The initial one involves whether to utilize a store or a nonstore (e.g., mail-order) format. Next, for store-based retailers, a general location and a specific site must be determined. Competitors, transportation access, population density, the type of neighborhood, nearness to suppliers, pedestrian traffic, and store composition are among the factors to be considered in picking a location.

The terms of tenancy (such as rent, flexibility, and length of contract) must be evaluated; and a build, buy, or rent decision must be made. The location of multiple outlets, an increasing phenomenon today, must be considered if expansion is a goal of the firm. Each of these aspects of location can cause problems if inadequately defined in the strategy phase.

Managing a Business

The second area of strategic planning, managing a business, involves two major elements: the retail organization and human resource management, and operations management. Tasks, policies, resources, authority, responsibility, and rewards are outlined via a retail organization structure. Through human resource management, practices pertaining to employee hiring, training, compensation, supervision, and so on are established. Job descriptions and functions should be detailed and communicated, along with the authority and responsibility of all personnel and the chain of command.

Operations management entails efficiently and effectively performing the tasks and policies needed to satisfy the goals of customers, employees, and management. The financial dynamics of operations involve asset management, budgeting, and resource allocation. Other specific aspects of operations management include store format and size, space allocation, personnel use, store maintenance, energy management, inventory management, store security, insurance, credit management, computerization, and crisis management.

Merchandise Management and Pricing

The third aspect of strategic planning deals with merchandise management and pricing. In merchandise management, the general quality of the goods and/or services offered must be determined. Decisions are needed about the width of assortment (the number of different product categories carried) and the depth of assortment (the variety of products carried in a given category).

Policies are needed about how innovative the retailer is going to be when introducing new items. Criteria for buying decisions (how often, what terms, which suppliers, and so on) need to be set. Forecasting, budgeting, and retail accounting procedures must be outlined. The level of inventory has to be outlined for each type of merchandise carried. Finally, the retailer should devise procedures to assess the success or failure of each item sold.

With regard to pricing, a retailer would choose from among several pricing techniques (such as leading/following, cost-plus/demand-oriented, and so on). It would decide what level of prices to charge, consistent with the firm's image and the quality of goods and services offered. The number of prices within each product category would be determined, such as how many prices of candy to carry. Psychological pricing may also be used. Finally, the use of markdowns should be planned in advance.

Communicating with the Customer

The fourth area of planning involves establishing and maintaining a distinctive image, and using promotion techniques. As mentioned earlier, image is critical for retailers. Therefore, a distinctive and desirable (by the target market) image must be sought. This image can be created and sustained through the use of several techniques.

The physical attributes, or atmosphere, of a store and its surrounding area greatly influence the consumer's perception of a retailer. The impact of the storefront (the building's exterior) should not be undervalued, as it is the first part of the store seen by the customer. Inside the store, layouts and displays (the arrangement and positioning of merchandise), wall and floor colors, styles of lighting used, scents, music, and the kind of sales personnel also contribute to a store's image.

Customer services and community relations can generate a favorable image for the retailer. Customer services are such things as parking, gift wrapping, a liberal return policy, extended store hours during special seasons, layaway plans, alterations, credit, and phone and mail sales. Community relations are enhanced by involvement in civic activities, donations to charity, and so on.

The appropriate use of promotion techniques can enhance a retailer's sales performance. Techniques can range from inexpensive door-to-door flyers for a supermarket or take-out restaurant to an expensive national ad campaign for a franchise chain. Three forms of paid promotion are available: advertising, personal selling, and sales promotion. In addition, a retailer can obtain free publicity when stories about the firm are written, televised, or broadcast.

The preceding discussion has outlined the basic controllable portions of a retail strategy. Yet, uncontrollable variables must also be kept in mind when setting up a strategy. A discussion of these variables is next. In Chapter 3, the changing environment facing retailers is examined.

Uncontrollable Variables

The uncontrollable parts of a retailing strategy can be divided into the categories shown in Figure 2–9: consumers, competition, technology, economic conditions, seasonality, and legal restrictions. Retailers need to monitor the external environment and adapt the controllable parts of their strategies to take into account elements beyond their immediate control. The uncontrollable nature of these variables is explained next.

Consumers

Once a target market has been picked, a firm's strategy must be set accordingly. A good company knows it cannot alter demographic trends, change life-style patterns, impose tastes, or "force" goods and services on people. Rather, the firm needs to learn about its target market and develop an offering consistent with consumer trends and desires. Selecting a target market is within the control of a retailer, but the firm will be unable to sell goods or services that are beyond the price range of its customers, that are not wanted, or that are not displayed or advertised in the proper manner. The total retail effort must be geared to satisfying the target market.

Competition

After the type of business and store location are chosen, there is little most retailers can do to limit the entry of competitors. In fact, a retailer's success may encourage the entry of new firms or cause established competitors to modify their strategies to capitalize on the popularity of that retailer. An excessive increase in competition should lead a company to re-examine its strategy, including the definition of its target market and its merchandising focus, to ensure that it sustains a competitive advantage. An error too many retailers make is assuming that being first in a location is a sufficient advantage in fighting off new entrants. Yet, a continued willingness to satisfy the target market better than any other retailer is fundamental.

Technology

In today's world of retailing, technology is advancing rapidly. Complex computer systems are now available for inventory control and checkout operations. Electronic surveillance may be used to reduce shoplifting. The Universal Product Code (UPC), in growing use, is revolutionizing merchandise handling and inventory control. More efficient warehousing and transporting of merchandise have been developed. Toll-free 800 numbers are more popular than ever before for consumer ordering. Nonetheless, some advancements are expensive and may be beyond the reach of small retailers. For instance, although small firms may be able to use computerized checkouts, they will probably be unable to use fully automated inventory systems or toll-free 800 numbers. As a result, the efficiency of small firms may be less than that of their larger competitors. They must adapt by providing more personalized service (because prices may be above average to reflect operating costs).

Economic Conditions

Economic conditions are beyond the control of any retailer, no matter how large. Inflation, unemployment, interest rates, tax levels, and the annual Gross Domestic Product (GDP) are just some aspects of the economy with which a retailer must cope and which it cannot change. In delineating controllable aspects of its strategy, a retailer needs to consider and adapt to forecasts about international, national, state, and local economies.

Seasonality

Another constraint on certain types of retailers is the seasonality of goods and services and the possibility that unpredictable weather will play havoc with sales forecasts. For example, retailers involved with sports equipment, clothing, fresh food, travel services, amusement parks, and car rentals cannot control the seasonality of consumer demand or bad weather. A solution to this uncontrollable part of strategic planning may be for such retailers to diversify offerings. A goods/service mix containing items that are popular in each season of the year could be developed. For instance, a sporting-goods retailer can emphasize ski equipment and snowmobiles in the winter, baseball and golf equipment in the spring, scuba equipment and fishing gear in the summer, and basketball and football supplies in the fall. Thus, the impact of seasonality and weather are reduced by adapting the controllable part of the retail strategy.

Legal Restrictions

Finally, all retailers should be familiar with the legal restrictions placed on them. Table 2–5 shows how each of the four controllable aspects of a retail strategy are affected by the legal environment. A discussion of legislation at the different levels of U.S. government follows.

At the federal level, legislation began in 1890 with the Sherman Act, which was designed to reduce monopolies and restraints of trade. The Clayton Act was enacted in 1914 to strengthen the Sherman Act. Also in 1914, the Federal Trade Commission was established to deal with unfair trade practices and consumer complaints. In the 1930s, the Robinson-Patman Act (1936) and the Miller-Tydings Act (1937) were passed. These laws were aimed at protecting small retailers after the Depression. The Robinson-Patman Act was enacted because of the special discounts A&P was getting in the purchase of its products. The Miller-Tydings Act (fair trade) attempted to limit discounting on the part of some retailers by forcing all retailers to sell fair-traded items at the same prices. This law has now been removed in all states.

The Anti-Merger Act was passed in 1950 to limit mergers between large firms. The 1960s and 1970s saw a number of consumer protection acts in such areas as door-to-door sales, product labeling, product safety, packaging, consumer credit, and product warranties and guarantees. Although these acts are mostly oriented toward manufacturers, they affect retailers that use deceptive selling practices and/or sell private-label merchandise. The 1980s were a period of federal deregulation and self-regulation, allowing retailers greater freedom in their operations. The 1990s have seen somewhat more government activity with passage of the Telephone Consumer Protection Act and the Food and Drug Administration's new rules for food labeling.

At the state and local levels, retailers must deal with many restrictions. Zoning laws prohibit firms from operating at certain sites and demand that building specifications be met. Construction, fire, elevator, smoking, and other codes are imposed on retailers by the state and city. Minimum resale laws sometimes require that specified items cannot be sold for less than a floor price. Blue laws limit the days or hours during which retailers can conduct business. Other ordinances restrict direct selling practices. In addition, various licenses necessary for operation are under the jurisdiction of the state or city. And many states and municipalities are involved in consumer protection; they police retailers from this vantage point. Over the past decade or so, numerous states and cities have stepped up their efforts to restrict unfair or socially undesirable retailing practices.

A retailer voluntarily adhering to the spirit and letter of the law is one that will maintain a consumer following and be less likely to attract adverse government attention. A retailing strategy must be established in a manner satisfying all three levels of government. For further information, the reader should contact the Federal Trade Commission, state and local regulatory agencies, the National Retail Federation, the local Better Business Bureau, or a specialized group such as the Direct Marketing Association.

INTEGRATING OVERALL STRATEGY

At this point, a retailer has finished devising an overall strategy. It has chosen an organizational mission, an ownership and management style, and its goods/service category. Meaningful long-run and short-run goals have been set. A consumer market has been designated, and its attributes and needs have been studied. General decisions have been made about store location, managing the business, merchandise management and pricing, and customer communications. These elements must be coor-

TABLE 2–5 The Impact of the Legal Environment on Retailing[a]

Controllable Factor Affected	Selected Legal Constraints on Retailers
Store Location	Zoning laws—Restrict the potential choices for a location and the type of facilities that may be constructed. Blue laws—Restrict the days and hours during which retailers may operate. Environmental laws—Limit the retail uses of certain sites. Door-to-door (direct) selling laws—Limit the hours and manner of business to protect consumer privacy. Local ordinances—Involve fire, smoking, outside lighting, capacity, and other regulations. Leases and mortgages—Require parties to abide by the stipulations in tenancy documents.
Managing a Business	Licensing provisions—Mandate minimum education and/or experience requirements for personnel in certain retail businesses. Personnel laws—Involve the nondiscriminatory hiring, promoting, and firing of employees. Antitrust laws—Limit mergers and expansion. Franchise agreements—Require parties to abide by legal precedents with regard to purchase terms, customer service levels, etc. Business taxes—Include real-estate and income taxes. Recycling laws—Mandate that retailers participate in the recycling process for various containers and packaging materials. Delivery laws—Penalties for late deliveries are imposed in some states.
Merchandise Management and Pricing	Trademarks—Provide retailers with exclusive rights to the brand names they develop. Licensing agreements—Allow retailers to sell goods and services created by others in return for royalty payments. Merchandise restrictions—Forbid some retailers from carrying or selling specified goods or services. Product safety laws—Prohibit retailers from selling items that have been inadequately tested or that have been declared unsafe. Product liability—Allows retailers to be sued if they sell defective products. Warranties and guarantees—Must adhere to federal standards. Lemon laws—Specify consumer rights if products, such as autos, require continuing repairs. Sales taxes—In most states, consumers are required to pay state and/or local taxes on items, in addition to the prices set by retailers. Unit-pricing laws—Require price per unit to be displayed (most often applied to supermarkets). Correct marking laws—Specify that discounted and sale items must be marked properly. Dual pricing—Occurs when the same item has different prices on different containers (to reflect the higher prices of new goods). In some areas, this is not permitted. Collusion—Retailers not allowed to discuss selling prices with competitors under any circumstances. Sale prices—Defined as a reduction from the retailer's normal selling prices. Calling anything else a sale is illegal. Minimum-price and loss-leader laws—Require that certain items not be sold for less than their cost plus a markup to cover retail overhead costs. Price discrimination—Suppliers generally not allowed to offer unjustified discounts to large retailers that are unavailable to smaller ones. Item-price-removal laws—Mandate that prices be marked on each item, as well as on store shelves.
Communicating with the Customer	Truth-in-advertising and -selling laws—Require retailers to be honest and not omit key facts in ads or sales presentations. Truth-in-credit laws—Require that consumers be fully informed of all terms when buying on credit. Telemarketing laws—Intended to protect the privacy of consumers with regard to telephone sales transactions. Comparative advertising—Retailers expected to provide complete documentation when making claims about their offerings versus competitors (e.g., lower prices). Bait-and-switch laws—Make it illegal to lure shoppers into a store to buy low-priced items and then to aggressively try to switch them to higher-priced ones. Inventory laws—Mandate that retailers must have sufficient stock when running sales. Labeling laws—Require merchandise to be correctly labeled and displayed. Cooling-off laws—Allow customers to cancel completed orders, often made via in-home sales, within three days of a contract date. Other restrictions—Prohibit some goods and services from being advertised in certain media (e.g., no liquor ads on radio or television).

[a] This table is broad in nature and omits a law-by-law description. Many laws are state or locally oriented and apply only to certain areas; the laws in each locale differ widely. The intent here is to give the reader some understanding of the current legal environment as it affects retail management. For more specifics, contact the sources named in the chapter.

dinated to have a consistent, integrated strategy. And the uncontrollable variables affecting the firm (consumers, competition, technology, economic conditions, seasonality, and legal restrictions) must be systematically accounted for in the strategy and its components.

Now the retailer is ready to take on the specific activities necessary to carry out its strategy productively.

Specific Activities

Short-run decisions must be made and enacted for each controllable part of the retail strategy outlined in Figure 2–9. These actions are known as ***tactics*** and encompass a retailer's daily and short-term operations. They must be responsive to the uncontrollable environment. Here are some of the tactical decisions that a retailer needs to make and carry out:

- Store location—Trading-area analysis is necessary to gauge the geographic area from which a firm draws its customers. The level of saturation in a trading area should be studied regularly. Relationships with nearby retailers need to be optimized. Lease terms and provisions must be negotiated and fulfilled. A chain must carefully decide on the sites of new outlets. Facilities must actually be built or modified.
- Managing a business—A clear chain of command from senior executives to entry-level employees must be instituted. The appropriate organizational arrangement must be set into place. Personnel must be hired, trained, and supervised. Asset management must account for all assets and liabilities. The budget must be spent properly (and throughout the year). Systematic operating procedures should be used and adjusted as required.
- Merchandise management and pricing—The assortments within departments and the space allotted to each department require constant decision making. Innovative firms must look for new merchandise and be willing to clear out slow-moving items. Purchase terms may have to be negotiated often, and new suppliers sought. A retailer must be sure selling prices reflect its image and target market. Price alternatives can be used to offer consumers some choice. Adaptive actions may be needed to sell slow-moving items, respond to higher prices by suppliers, and react to competitors' changing their prices.

Retailing Around the World

How Is Russia's Leading Department Store Changing with the Times?

When Russia had a centrally planned economy, the GUM (pronounced "Goom") department store in Moscow was known for rude sales clerks, long lines, and prices that were set without regard for costs or demand. GUM's retail mix was set by government bureaucrats; and products that sold out faster than anticipated were restocked the following year, not immediately. Sales of foreign products were restricted to special customers.

Now, under privatization, about 60 per cent of the goods sold at GUM are foreign made. GUM contains boutiques from 30 Western companies—including Benetton apparel, Estée Lauder cosmetics, Samsonite luggage, and Botany 500 menswear—all of which are profitable. These firms have designed their own boutique shops in GUM, provide merchandise, and train managers; but, GUM managers operate each store (including reordering stock and setting prices) and all sales staff are GUM employees.

Despite privatization, some vestiges of Communism remain. For example, markups are generally low—in the 10 to 25 per cent range—as Russians are still especially critical of excessive profits. And, while a customer can see an item, pay for it, and receive the merchandise with one sales contact at a foreign boutique in GUM (as in the United States), in traditional GUM departments, customers face three separate lines (one for each function).

Source: Based on material in Ann Imse, "Across from Lenin's Tomb, A Monument to Capitalism," *New York Times* (September 19, 1993), Section 3, p. 5.

- Communicating with the customer—The storefront and display windows, store layout, and merchandise displays need constant attention. These elements can help a firm gain consumer enthusiasm, present a fresh look, introduce new product categories, or reflect changing seasons. Ads must be designed and then placed during the proper time and in the appropriate medium. The use of sales personnel varies by merchandise category and season.

Consumer demand, competitor actions, economic conditions, technological advances, seasonality, and legal restrictions especially need to be weighed when making tactical decisions. The essence of good retailing is building a sound strategy and "fine-tuning" it as the environment changes. A retailer that stands still is often moving backward. Tactical decision making is discussed in much greater detail in Chapters 8 through 18.

Control

As already noted, a firm's strategy and tactics should be evaluated and revised continuously. In the ***control*** phase, a semiannual or annual review of the company should take place (Step VI in Figure 2–1), with the strategy and tactics (Steps IV and V) that have been developed and implemented being evaluated against the business mission, objectives, and target market (Steps I, II, and III) of the firm. This procedure is called a retail audit, which is a systematic process for analyzing the performance of a retailer. The retail audit is covered in Chapter 19.

As a retailer's performance is assessed, its strengths and weaknesses are revealed. The aspects of a strategy that have gone well should stay in place; those that have gone poorly should be revised, consistent with the firm's mission, goals, and target market. If possible, minor adjustments should be made, because major changes in operations may confuse customers. The adjustments that are made should be evaluated in the next retail audit.

Feedback

During each stage in the development of a retail strategy, an observant management receives signals or cues as to the success of that part of the strategy. These signals or cues are known as ***feedback***. See Figure 2–1. Some forms of positive feedback are high sales, no problems with the government, and low employee turnover. Some forms of negative feedback are falling sales, government sanctions (like fines), and high employee turnover.

Retail executives should look for positive and negative feedback so they can determine the causes and capitalize on opportunities or rectify problems.

SUMMARY

1. *To show the value of strategic planning for all types of retailers* A retail strategy is the overall plan or framework of action that guides a firm. It consists of situation analysis, objectives, identification of a customer market, broad strategy, specific activities, control, and feedback. Without a well-conceived strategy, a retailer may stumble and/or be unable to cope with environmental factors.

2. *To explain the steps in strategic planning for retailers* Situation analysis is the candid evaluation of the opportunities and potential problems facing a retailer. It seeks to determine a retailer's current position and where it should be heading. This analysis consists of defining and adhering to an organizational mission, evaluating ownership and management alternatives, and outlining the goods/service category to be sold. An organizational mission is a long-term commitment to a type of business and a place in the market. Ownership and management alternatives are selected from a sole proprietorship, partnership, or corporation; starting a new business, buying an existing one, or being a franchisee; owner management or professional management; and being centralized or decentralized. The goods/

service category chosen depends on personal abilities, financial resources, and time resources.

Objectives are the long- and short-run goals of a retailer. A firm may pursue one or more of these objectives: sales (growth, stability, and market share), profit (level, return on investment, and efficiency), satisfaction of publics (stockholders, consumers, and others), and image/positioning (customer and industry perceptions).

Next, consumer characteristics and needs are determined, and a retailer selects a target market. A firm can sell to a broad spectrum of consumers (the mass market); zero in on one customer group (a market segment); or aim at two or more distinct groups of consumers (multiple segments), with separate retailing approaches for each.

Then, a broad strategy is formed. It involves controllable variables (the aspects of business a firm can directly affect) and uncontrollable variables (the factors a firm cannot control and to which it must adapt).

After a general strategy has been set, a firm has to make and implement short-run decisions (tactics) for each controllable part of that strategy. These actions must be forward-looking and responsive to the external environment.

Through a control process, a retail strategy and tactics should be evaluated and revised continuously. A retail audit systematically reviews a strategy and its execution on a regular basis. Strengths need to be emphasized and weaknesses minimized or eliminated.

A firm must also be alert for signals or cues, known as feedback, that indicate the level of performance at each step in the strategy.

3. *To examine the individual controllable and uncontrollable elements of a retail strategy* There are four major controllable factors in retail planning: store location, managing a business, merchandise management and pricing, and communicating with the customer. The principal uncontrollable variables affecting retail planning are consumers, competition, technology, economic conditions, seasonality, and legal restrictions.
4. *To present strategic planning as a series of integrated steps* Each of the stages in a retail strategy needs to be performed, undertaken sequentially, and coordinated in order to have a consistent, integrated, unified strategy.

KEY TERMS

retail strategy (p. 30)
situation analysis (p. 30)
organizational mission (p. 30)
sole proprietorship (p. 33)
partnership (p. 33)
corporation (p. 33)
goods/service category (p. 36)
personal abilities (p. 37)
financial resources (p. 37)
time demands (p. 39)
objectives (p. 40)
sales objectives (p. 41)
profitability objectives (p. 41)
satisfaction of publics' objectives (p. 42)
image (p. 42)
positioning (p. 42)
mass merchandising (p. 44)
positioned retailing (p. 44)
bifurcated retailing (p. 44)
target market (p. 45)
mass market (p. 45)
market segment (p. 45)
multiple segments (p. 45)
competitive advantage (p. 45)
controllable variables (p. 46)
uncontrollable variables (p. 46)
tactics (p. 52)
control (p. 53)
feedback (p. 53)

QUESTIONS FOR DISCUSSION

1. Why is it necessary to develop a thorough, well-integrated retail strategy? What could happen if a firm does not develop such a strategy?
2. How would situation analysis differ for a small retailer and a large retailer?
3. What are the pros and cons of starting a new business versus buying an existing one?
4. Develop a checklist that would help a prospective retailer to choose the proper goods/service category in which to operate. Include personal abilities, financial resources, and time demands in this checklist.
5. Why do retailers frequently underestimate the financial and time requirements of a business?
6. Draw and explain a positioning chart showing the kinds of retailers selling eye-care products.
7. Differentiate between mass merchandising and positioned retailing. Why will it be possible for both approaches to succeed?
8. Discuss local examples of a retailer appealing to a mass market, a retailer appealing to a market segment, and a retailer appealing to multiple segments.
9. Jill Watson is a buyer for a large computer soft-

ware chain. She has saved $75,000 and wants to open her own software store. Devise an overall strategy for Jill, including store location, managing the business, merchandise management and pricing, and communicating with the customer.

10. A competing retailer has a better store location than you do. It is in a modern shopping center with a lot of customer traffic. Your store is located in an older neighborhood and requires customers to travel a great distance to reach you. How could you use a merchandising, pricing, and communications strategy to overcome your disadvantageous location?

11. How could each of these minimize the effects of seasonality?
    a. Travel agent
    b. Gift store
    c. College bookstore

12. Describe how a retailer would use fine tuning in strategic planning.

13. How are the control and feedback phases of retail strategy planning interrelated?

14. Should a service-oriented retailer (such as a bank) use the strategic planning process differently from a goods-oriented retailer (such as a home appliance firm)? Why or why not?

CASE 1

Julie's Video Shoppe: A Small Firm's Retail Strategy*

Julie Burns has owned and operated Julie's Video Shoppe for seven years. The Video Shoppe is a full-service, independent video store that offers for rental and/or sale a good selection of prerecorded movies, music videos, and video games. It also sells blank VCR tapes, VCR cleaning supplies, and related items. Julie's Video Shoppe is located in a suburban shopping center. Its current competition consists mainly of a video rental department in a large supermarket located within two miles from Julie's on the same major road.

Over the years, Burns has done well, largely because of an integrated overall retail strategy:

- Realistic objectives—A steady yearly sales growth of 8 to 10 per cent, with a net after-tax profit of 5 to 7 per cent on sales (in addition to Burns' $35,000 annual salary), is sought. At present, Julie's annual sales are just over $320,000; and after-tax profit for the most recent year was $22,000.
- Full-service approach—While many video stores have a no-frills approach, the Video Shoppe provides several important customer amenities. For example, two salespeople are always out among the customers to give them advice. Personnel also phone customers that have reserved movies to confirm that they are now available. In the area of the store containing children's videos, there is a TV monitor showing cartoons; this entertains children and gives parents more time to browse. The store recently installed two personal computers with CD-ROM players. These players use Microsoft's Cinemania software—which includes summaries of 19,000 movies, 4,000 in-depth movie reviews, video and sound clips, and biographies of movie stars. Julie hopes customers will perceive this software as a valuable customer service and that the software will also increase rentals of older videos.
- Family/community orientation—The Video Shoppe has a warm, family-oriented image. It does not carry adult-rated movies. Two-day rentals are allowed to reduce customer inconvenience. Tapes on first aid and safe driving practices are available free-of-charge as a public service.
- Good store location—Julie's Video Shoppe is situated in a medium-sized shopping center anchored by a large branch outlet of a major pharmacy chain. The shopping center is off a heavily traveled highway in a middle-class residential community. Parking is plentiful.
- Selection of rental tapes—Four years ago, Julie acquired the lease on the store adjacent to hers in the shopping center. This allowed the Video Shoppe's total space to double to 5,000 square feet. As a result, the store now carries 12,000 movie tapes (including 4,000+ separate titles); the supermarket's video department carries 3,000 tapes in a 1,000-square-foot area. Since new releases account

* Julie's Video Shoppe is a composite video retailer based on the authors' research. For further information, see Glenn Snyder, "Video Rental: The 'Outsider' Approach," *Progressive Grocer* (January 1993), pp. 21–26; Glenn Snyder, "Covering All the Bases for Better Video Rental," *Progressive Grocer* (July 1993), pp. 17–25; and Mark Stevenson, "All of the Pleasure, None of the Pain," *Canadian Business* (November 1993), pp. 64–69.

for 50 per cent of revenues, the Video Shoppe carries up to 25 copies of these titles; the supermarket competitor typically carries only 5 to 10 copies. Although Julie's strategy effectively meets initial demand, it generally results in a surplus of a particular title over time. When the new release title is no longer "hot," Julie sells excess copies as used tapes for $5.00 to $10.00 each; but no title ever is completely removed from inventory.

- Promotion—The Video Shoppe actively promotes free membership in its Video Clubbe. Members receive a monthly newsletter with reviews of new releases involving both rental and for-sale tapes, discounts on blank tapes and supplies, and special events. The newsletter discounts and special events are only available to members. Recent specials were "all horror movies for 99 cents each" on Halloween, "buy a pizza, get a movie rental free" (a cooperative promotion with a local pizza parlor), and "rent two videos, get an extra day free." Burns estimates that over 75 per cent of her customers are Video Clubbe members.
- Appropriate prices—Because of the Video Shoppe's superior customer service level, including its higher inventory of new releases, the store is able to maintain movie rental prices that are 25 to 50 per cent higher than those at the supermarket. New releases are rented for $3.59; other titles are priced at $2.59.
- Regular evaluation of performance—Each three months, Julie does a complete analysis of revenues and costs by product category. Particular attention is paid to new releases and the redemption rate on newsletter coupons. Based on this analysis, new titles are ordered, additional copies of new releases are purchased, excess tapes are sold, and special promotions are designed.

Even though her business is successful, Julie is concerned about two possible competitive developments. One, it is rumored that Blockbuster is looking at a nearby site. The chain has 3,000+ video stores (some franchised), large stores with a huge selection of videos, and many tie-in promotions. Two, in the long run, Julie is worried that interactive video technology (enabling consumers to order movies by telephone for viewing at home) could have a vast impact on future sales when the technology becomes available. Interactive television would offer consumers the convenience of not having to leave home to pick up and return a video; they would also never have to reserve a video or find that a particular selection is unavailable. The selection of movies available on interactive television would be enormous.

Questions

1. Evaluate the goods/service category of Julie's Video in terms of personal abilities, financial resources, and time availability.
2. Develop a list of appropriate objectives for Julie's Video.
3. Evaluate Julie's strategy from the perspective of the controllable variables shown in Figure 2–9.
4. What types of feedback should Julie monitor? Explain your answer.

CASE 2
Lands' End: A Large Firm's Retail Strategy†

Gary Comer worked for an advertising agency for ten years, but his true vocation was sailing. So, in 1963, he left the agency and with his sailing partner, Dick Stearns, opened a catalog outlet store in Chicago specializing in sailing equipment and fittings. This let him combine business and pleasure.

After five years, and only moderate success, Gary Comer bought out his partner and began tinkering with the catalog. He added clothing, accessories, and luggage aimed at full-time and weekend sailors. In 1976, Comer decided to no longer carry sailing equipment; competition was too intense. Instead Lands' End focused on recreational and informal clothing, accessories, shoes, and soft-sided luggage—and broadened its customer market. Unlike many other apparel-based retailers, most Lands' End clothing is traditionally styled and has only slight seasonal variations. In 1986, Lands' End went public.

Today, annual revenues (via mail-order, toll-free phone transactions, 12 stores, and electronic shopping) exceed $800 million, the Lands' End customer base is almost 6.8 million people, and 15.6 million people are on the firm's mailing list. Headquarters, warehousing facilities, and customer-service operations are located in the quiet Wisconsin farming community of Dodgeville.

Lands' End's overall strategy includes these major elements:

- Growth-oriented objectives—It is directed to long-run growth. The sales growth goal is 10 to 15 per cent per year for the 1990s; the actual compound annual growth rate from 1985 through 1993 was above 15 per cent. To reach this goal, it will seek higher volume from existing customers and try to get more customers in its data base who have not bought in the last three years to do so. The firm also hopes to gain from a new British catalog operation.
- Appeal to a prime consumer market—It is very strong with 34- to 54-year-old baby boomer customers, most of whom have incomes of $50,000 and up, have attended college, and are professionals. The firm focuses on "the top 25 per cent of the income spectrum."
- Outstanding customer service—It prides itself on the level of customer service. Phone calls are answered within 1.5 rings, almost all merchandise is always available in stock, and the firm aims to ship orders within 24 hours of their being placed.
- Personalized company image—Unlike traditional mail-order retailers, which only show pictures of their products, present brief descriptions of them, and cite their prices, Lands' End adds a personal touch. For example, a typical entry for slacks may contain a story on "why the chino slacks may be the best 'hanging out' pants you'll ever put on." The catalog also includes short stories by such writers as David Mamet (author of *Glengarry Glen Ross*), William Least Heat-Moon (author of *Blue Highways*), and Edward Hoagland (author of 15 books). The Land's End full and unconditional guarantee, "Guaranteed. Period," is stated in each catalog, as is its toll-free 800 number. Customers who call Lands' End are likely to reach one of its full-time, year-round operators, who provide information, answer questions, and process orders.

† The material in this case is drawn from Kate Fitzgerald, "Catalogs Evolve into High-Tech Kiosks," *Advertising Age* (May 10, 1993), p. 47; *Lands' End 1993 Annual Report*; Kevin Goldman, "Lands' End Catalog Features Mamet Story," *Wall Street Journal* (February 23, 1994), p. B3; and "Prodigy Aids Catalogers," *Chain Store Age Executive* (January 1993), pp. 153, 156.

- Consistent promotion program—The firm mails a new catalog every few weeks. It also runs ads in *Fortune, Inc., New York Times Sunday Magazine, Wall Street Journal*, and *USA Today*. There are even specialty catalogs that appeal to a more narrowly defined target market—to reduce seasonality and to reduce total catalog production and mailing costs. These catalogs include *Kids Catalog* (launched in 1990), *Beyond Buttondowns* (a men's clothing catalog begun in 1990), *Coming Home* (a bed and bath catalog introduced in 1991), and *Textures* (a women's catalog begun in 1993).
- Commitment to electronic shopping—The firm is committed to new technology that can change the nature of the catalog business. It recently signed an agreement with the MicroMall electronic shopping system. This system lets customers order Lands' End merchandise from touch-screen terminals located in transit stations, office buildings, and hotel lobbies. Lands' End customers that have access to a computer and a modem can also shop at home using Prodigy.
- Efficient operations—Ordering, warehousing, and other operations are highly automated and computerized. The firm has outlet stores in Wisconsin, Illinois, and Iowa. These stores sell returned merchandise or items that have been overordered and must be cleared out.
- Responsiveness to unsatisfactory performance—Despite sizable growth in 1990, profits declined in that year to 2.4 per cent of sales, the lowest level in its history as a public company. Christmas orders were much greater than anticipated in 1990; so, Lands' End could not ship one-quarter of its orders on a same-day basis. Besides losing sales, this forced Lands' End to ship back orders at its expense. To remedy the situation, the firm now has higher inventory levels, new specialty catalogs (for home furnishings, and children's clothing), and a new vice-chairman and a new chief executive officer. As a result, since 1991, profits as a percentage of sales have been well above 4 per cent.

Lands' End is committed to its customers and to an ongoing, integrated strategic retailing plan. The firm has a distinct product offering, solid goals, a large and loyal customer base, and sound operating principles, as well as a system for implementing and improving its strategy.

QUESTIONS

1. Evaluate Lands' End's goods and services category mix.
2. Develop a positioning map for Lands' End and its major competitors. Explain the significance of this map in terms of Lands' End's strategy.
3. What uncontrollable variables can affect Lands' End? Why?
4. Do you feel Lands' End's overall retail strategy is integrated? Explain your answer.

VIDEO QUESTIONS ON LANDS' END

1. List Lands' End's principles of doing business.
2. Evaluate these principles.

CHAPTER

3

RM

Strategic Planning in Retailing: Dealing with the Changing Environment

❖ Chapter Objectives

1. To examine demographic, life-style, consumerism, and ethics and social responsibility trends—and consider the impact of them on retailing
2. To consider the effects of technological advances
3. To describe the ways in which retail institutions are, and will be, responding to environmental trends
4. To discuss the international dimension of retailing

For several reasons, the external environment facing McDonald's is a tough one. Its U.S. share of fast-food sales has hovered around 16 per cent for the past several years. The hamburger segment is growing more slowly than fast-food pizza and ethnic food segments. It is increasingly difficult for McDonald's to find acceptable conventional U.S. locations; in 1972, there were 2,800 Americans per fast-food outlet—but, by 1993, this number had declined to 1,400 Americans per fast-food outlet. Lastly, many consumers are concerned about McDonald's ethical responsibility as a fast-food retailer with a large proportion of children as customers. Let's see how McDonald's has responded to these environmental threats and opportunities.

Due to slow-growth prospects in the U.S. hamburger segment, McDonald's has aggressively sought sites in overseas markets. Two-thirds of its new outlets are planned for international markets that offer better growth opportunities. As of 1994, McDonald's had over 4,700 overseas stores, double the 1988 amount. Forty per cent of McDonald's sales are already from international markets; this is expected to increase significantly in the future.

McDonald's is using multiple formats, many of which would be considered nontraditional outlets—such as a small-town version, a drive-through version, and a satellite location version. These formats allow McDonald's to open units in areas that would have otherwise been unprofitable or to adapt a store to the unique configurations of a lot. The store version for small towns can be built for $400,000 less than a full-size McDonald's and needs $300,000 less in annual sales than a conventional store to meet profit goals. The drive-through store is designed specifically for off-premises consumption of food and beverages. Satellite sites are run as additional units by existing McDonald's franchisees looking to serve niche markets. Examples include a seasonal outlet in New York's Coney Island, an airport site in Manchester, New Hampshire, and more than 80 outlets inside Wal-Mart stores.

To address the questions about the healthfulness of fast food, McDonald's has produced an advertising campaign that encourages children aged 2 to 11 to eat healthy foods. The campaign differentiates between "sometimes foods" (such as cake, cookies, and potato chips) and "everyday foods" like rice, bananas, and carrots. No McDonald's foods have been mentioned in those ads.[1]

[1] Barnaby J. Feder, "McDonald's Finds There's Still Plenty of Room to Grow," *New York Times* (January 4, 1994), Section 3, p. 5; Jeanne Whalen, "McDonald's Caters to Drivers," *Advertising Age* (January 10, 1994), p. 2; and Laura Bird, "McDonald's Slates Nutrition-Advice Spots," *Wall Street Journal* (September 23, 1992), p. B6.

Reprinted by permission of McDonald's.

Overview

To attain and maintain long-run success, a retail firm's strategy must anticipate and plan for the changing environment. In particular, the firm should carefully identify the opportunities and threats that are evolving. ***Opportunities*** are the marketplace openings that exist because other retailers have not yet not capitalized on them. For example, Ikea has done well because it is the pioneer firm in offering a huge selection of furniture at discount prices. ***Threats*** are environmental and/or marketplace factors that can adversely affect retailers if they do not react to them. For example, single-screen movie theaters have virtually disappeared in some areas since they have been unable to fend off inroads made by multiscreen theaters.

A company needs to spot and adapt to trends early enough to satisfy its target market and stay ahead of competitors, yet not so early that the target market is unready for changes or that false trends are perceived. A late response to trends could mean that a firm might miss profitable opportunities but minimize its risks. Strategic planning must take into account the nature of environmental factors in terms of their certainty of occurrence and magnitude of change, their effect on the retailer's business, and the time required for the retailer to react properly.

Environmental factors vary with regard to their certainty of occurrence. For example, population size can be forecast more accurately than average household income because the former relies on birth rates and death rates (which can be estimated with relative precision), whereas the latter depends on the unemployment rate, labor productivity, the level of inflation, the amount of imports, and other factors (which are more difficult to predict). When forecasts are accurate, future planning is simplified; with uncertain forecasts, retailers need to be more careful in their strategies.

A retailer must plan for greater strategy modifications if a factor's magnitude of change is large. For instance, a beauty salon may have to enact significant strategy revisions to adjust to the large long-term increase in the number of working women. Hardware and other retailers must react to the rise in do-it-yourselfers.

The time a retailer requires to react to the changing environment depends on the aspect of its strategy needing modification. Merchandising-strategy shifts—like stocking an unexpectedly popular fad item—are much more quickly consummated than adjustments in a firm's overall locational, pricing, or promotion strategy. In addition, a new store can adapt to trends more readily than existing stores with set images, ongoing leases, and space limitations.

While other years are noted, this chapter looks at the anticipated changes in retailing's environment from now to 2000. Trends in consumer demographics, consumer life-styles, consumerism, ethics and social responsibility, technology, retail institutions, and the international dimensions of retailing are each discussed and related to strategic planning in retailing.

The period of the present to 2000 is emphasized because

- Relatively short forecasts are more accurate than longer ones.
- This time frame is lengthy enough to develop long-range retail plans and react to forecast changes.
- Much research data are available.

Demographic Trends[2]

Demographics are objective and quantifiable population data that are easily identifiable and measurable. U.S. trends involving population size and age, the number of households, population mobility, population location, working women, and income are noted in this section. Individually, these demographic factors have a great impact

[2] Unless otherwise indicated, the data in this section are drawn from U.S. Bureau of the Census, *Current Population Reports* and *Census of Population*.

on retailing; collectively, they should dominate a retailer's strategic planning for the future. Additional information on consumer demographics is presented in Chapter 6 ("Identifying and Understanding Consumers").

Population Size and Age Distribution

The U.S. population size will increase from 263 million in 1995 to 275 million in 2000. Although the overall rate of population growth will only be 1 per cent per year during this period, the United States will add about 12 million people. The population's median age will rise steadily, reaching 36 in 2000.

When studying U.S. population size and age trends, retailers also need to be aware of these factors:

- The average life expectancy for both males and females will continue to increase.
- Newborns will account for 1.5 per cent of the population, down from about 2.0 per cent during the 1960s. However, more births will involve firstborns, requiring parents to spend several thousand dollars in "tooling-up" costs for items such as baby furniture, clothing, and supplies.
- Couples will continue to get married at later ages than previously. They will also wait longer to have children and have fewer children.
- The fastest-growing age segments will be those 35 to 64 and 75 and over, particularly those 45 to 54. The under-35 segments will fall from a total of 51.2 per cent of the population in 1995 to 48.8 per cent in 2000.

Retailers must realize that although younger markets will always represent large segments of the population, their relative importance is declining in the United States; and firms should act accordingly. For example, the eating, shopping, recreational, and other habits of younger people are very different from those of their older counterparts. In addition, the one-quarter of the population ages 50 and older controls three-quarters of the financial assets in the United States.

Number of Households

Despite the slow rate of overall U.S. population growth, the number of households is forecast to rise significantly by the year 2000. As defined in Chapter 6, a household is comprised of a person or a group of persons occupying a dwelling unit, whether related or unrelated. In contrast, a family consists of two or more people residing together who are related.

U.S. households are expected to rise from 100 million in 1995 to 110 million by 2000. At the same time, the average size of a U.S. household will drop from 2.6 in 1995 to about 2.5 in 2000. The percentage of single-person households should remain steady at 25 per cent.

The decreasing size of U.S. households is due to three major factors: the larger number of older people who live apart from their grown children, the high divorce rate, and the later age at first marriage.

The trend has been for older people to increasingly live apart from their grown children. Two-thirds of the people over age 65 are now heads of separate households; and this percentage will continue to rise. In addition, due to widowhood, by 2000 there will be 11 million single-person households headed by people age 65 and older (three-quarters of whom will be women).

Not only the number but also the rate of U.S. divorces has gone up greatly over the past three decades. Between 1970 and 1980, the number of divorces rose by two-thirds, before stabilizing. The high number of divorces is expected to continue, while the rate per 1,000 marriages declines slightly.

Because many young adults are getting married at a later age, due to the desire to finish their education, advance in their careers, and other reasons, they are likely to live in smaller households (since they are apt to have fewer children). This is most true for persons who wait until their thirties to be married for the first time. Furthermore, 10 to 12 per cent of U.S. adults will never marry. On the other hand, to combat the high cost of living, many adults under the age of 25 are living at home longer.

These household trends have key implications for retailers. First, more decisions will be made by people functioning as both buyers and consumers; there will be more purchasing for self-use. Second, since each household requires furniture, housewares, and other goods and services, there will be opportunities for retailers in these areas. Third, smaller housing units, downsized appliances, and single-serving food packaging will be popular.

Population Mobility

The proportion of Americans who move each year is expected to continue to be about one-sixth of the overall population. The rate of mobility will vary widely by age group; it will be highest among households headed by adults under the age of 35. People will continue to migrate to Mountain, Pacific, South Atlantic, and Southwest states.

These are several retail implications of high mobility:

- Well-known chains and franchises will prosper.
- National and regional brands will sell well among mobile persons.
- Purchase levels, especially of clothing and home-related goods and services, will be high because many people discard items in moving to new environments (particularly if there are changes in climate or long-distance moves).
- Rentals become important.
- Shopping centers will be focal points for purchases.
- Use of a unified, nationwide credit system will ease purchase transactions.
- Large-scale advertising will be helpful in generating and maintaining a retailer's image.

Location of the Population

During the last decade, the number of people living in suburban communities has increased at a rate almost twice that of the total U.S. population. Over the same time period, the number of people living in big central cities has gone up only slightly. Similar trends are foreseen through 2000.

The average earnings of suburban families are higher than those of city families. It is estimated that the suburbs account for well over two-thirds of all personal income in metropolitan areas and an even higher proportion of discretionary income.

The growth of suburban markets has important implications for retailers:

- Firms may have to shift to suburban sites or add branch stores.
- Warehouses may have to be relocated to be near suburban store locations.
- Retail opportunities will exist relating to suburban home ownership and lifestyles for items such as furniture, lawn care, snow blowers, do-it-yourself projects, and major appliances.
- Planned shopping centers will maintain their strength.
- It may be time for chain stores to re-examine their use of central-city buying offices.

RETAILING IN ACTION

How Will Health Care Reform Affect Retailing?

A study conducted for the National Retail Federation estimates that, to comply with President Clinton's initial health-care reform proposal, retailers' health insurance costs would have to increase by two to three times. The proposal would require employers to pay 80 per cent of the cost of their employees' health insurance premiums.

A major concern for retailers is a clause that prorates the health insurance costs of part-time and seasonal workers. Many of these workers currently do not get health insurance benefits.

The proposal may benefit smaller retailers whose health insurance costs would be capped at between 3.5 per cent and 7.9 per cent of their total payroll. These retailers could also join regional health alliances to better negotiate premiums. Retailers with more than 50 employees would have costs limited to 7.9 per cent of their total payroll.

According to testimony before a House Subcommittee by a Kmart executive, the initial health-care reform proposal would increase its annual health care insurance costs between $150 million and $400 million. Dayton Hudson estimated that its costs would rise $65 million; and this might force the firm to fire up to 15,000 part-time employees. The National Retail Federation assumes that in total between 500,000 and one million retailing jobs would be at risk if retailers downsize to meet higher insurance costs.

Source: Based on material in "Health Care Reform: How Much Will it Cost You?" *Stores* (November 1993), pp. 22–26.

WORKING WOMEN

At present, over one-half of U.S. adult women (age 16 and older) are employed; by 2000, over 60 per cent of women will be working outside the home. During the 1990s, the size of the female work force will grow by 12 million persons, while the male work force will grow by 7.5 million persons. Women will represent about 47 per cent of all workers as of 2000.

The working woman's profile is also changing. In the past, the typical U.S. working woman was young and unmarried (including divorced and separated) or her husband was unable to provide for the family. Now, she is likely to be married (58 per cent of all working women) and somewhat older (median age of 36 years) and to have one or more children under the age of six in the home (three-fifths of those mothers). The trends toward working wives and mothers are expected to continue throughout the rest of the 1990s.

The rise in the number of females combining the roles of working woman, wife, and/or mother has these implications for retailers. Working women:

- Are apt to spend large amounts for major appliances and household equipment, especially when they are time-saving.
- Are more independent in their purchases, as they seek individualism and personal identity.
- Are prone to use leisure time for pleasure. This has a strong influence on the market for ready-made clothing, sporting goods, and car-rental agencies.
- May be unable to shop during regular retail hours. This is meaningful for direct marketers and retailers with extended hours.
- Have less time to prepare meals. Growing in importance are prepared foods, convenience foods, and quick-serve restaurants. Some experts are predicting limited growth in supermarket sales.
- Require services (such as repairs) to be offered during evenings and weekends.
- Increase family affluence, thus expanding the purchase of luxuries.
- Will be more responsive to advertising placed in evening time periods, particularly on television.

Income

In the early 1990s, an economic downturn held down incomes. Since then, ***real income***—household income after adjusting for inflation—has gone up slightly in the United States. On balance, from now to the year 2000, solid real-income gains (averaging 1–3 per cent per year) are projected. Although the pattern of real-income growth will not be consistent—due to fluctuations in the economy, there will be considerably more U.S. households with $50,000+ annual incomes by 2000.

The higher incomes suggest broadened markets for luxury goods and services. It can also be anticipated that the demand for high-quality goods and services, better customer services, and wider assortments will increase. At the same time, retailers need to consider the effects of unemployment, inflation, and resource shortages on consumer spending patterns and to plan accordingly. They should also keep in mind that there is (and will continue to be) a sizable group of consumers with low income levels who need to buy goods and services.

Figure 3–1 shows the distribution of U.S. household income by age of head of household. Note that the percentage of affluent households goes up with the age of the head of household and that the percentage of lower-income households falls and then rises again with the age of the head of household (due largely to early retirement).

Life-Style Trends

Besides analyzing demographic trends, it is necessary for a retailer to study the life-style trends of its target market. As defined in Chapter 6, ***life-styles*** represent the ways in which individual consumers and families (households) live and spend time and money. The trends regarding gender roles, consumer sophistication and confidence, the poverty of time, and self-fulfillment are examined next. These life-style trends must be interpreted by retailers and interrelated with demographic trends.

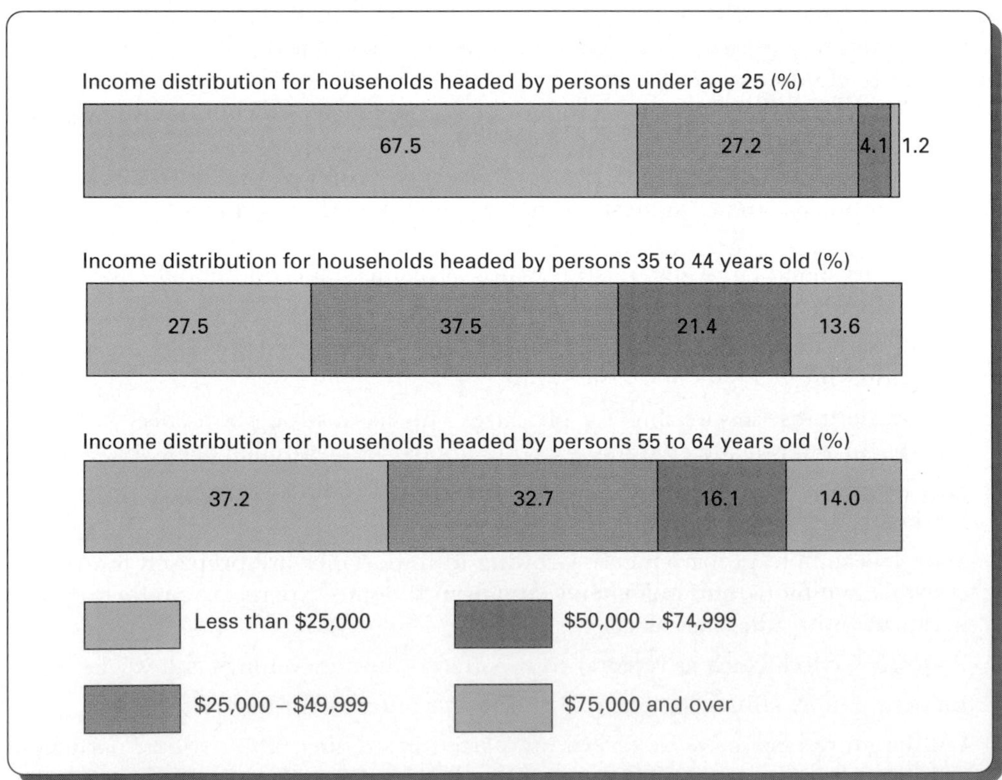

Figure 3–1
Household Income by Age of Head of Household
Source: U.S. Bureau of the Census, *Current Population Reports.*

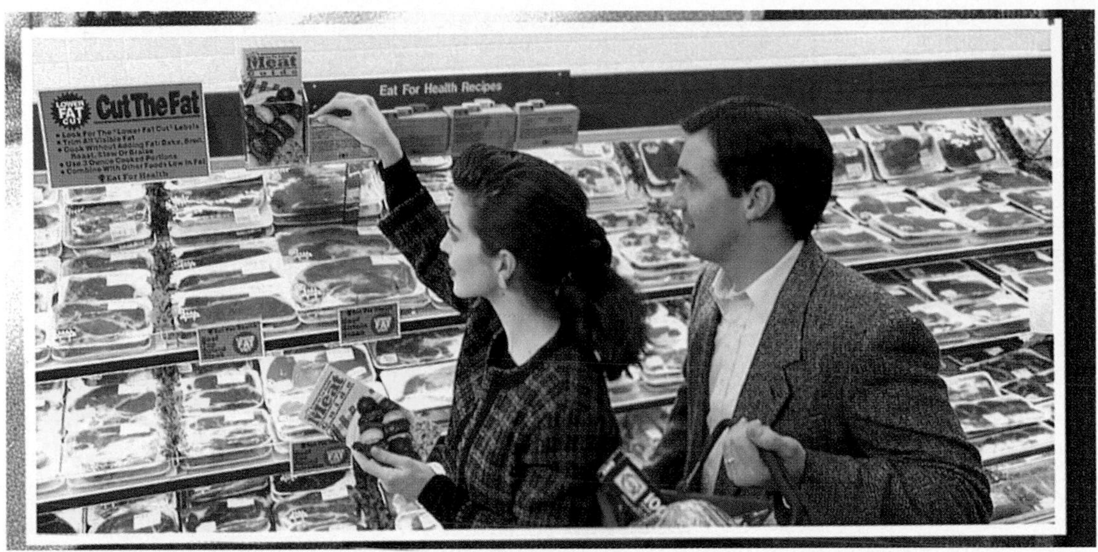

Figure 3–2
Blurring Gender Roles
Due to changing life-styles, more husbands and wives shop together.
Reprinted by permission of Giant Food.

Gender Roles

The increasing number of working women, who may put in an average of 60 to 70 hours (or more) each week between their job and home responsibilities, is altering life-styles significantly.

Compared to women who have not worked, working women tend to be more

- Self-confident and individualistic.
- Adept at handling their social environment.
- Concerned with the convenience and ease of performing household duties.
- Interested in sharing household and familial tasks with their husbands.
- Cosmopolitan in taste, and knowledgeable and demanding as consumers.
- Interested in leisure activities and travel.
- Concerned with improving themselves and their educational background.
- Appearance-conscious (concerned with the way they dress).
- Interested in maintaining a youthful posture.
- Interested in equal rights.
- Indifferent to small price differences among stores or merchandise.
- Uninterested in leisurely shopping trips.

Due to the trend toward more working women, the life-styles of American males are also changing. Large numbers of men now take care of children, shop for food, do laundry, wash dishes, cook for the family, vacuum the house, and clean the bathroom. For example, today, about 30 per cent of U.S. supermarket sales (in dollars) are accounted for by male shoppers.[3] See Figure 3–2.

[3] Robert Dietrich, "Tracking the Invisible Man," *Progressive Grocer* (November 1992), pp. 69–82.

The future will see still more changes in men's and women's roles (and in their conflicts over them). Furthermore, the authority and duties of husbands and wives will be shared with greater frequency than before. Retailers need to understand and adapt to this trend.

Consumer Sophistication and Confidence

Consumer life-styles will reflect increased levels of education. For example, by the year 2000, more than 45 per cent of all Americans 25 years of age and older will have completed at least 1 year of college; and one-quarter will have 4-year degrees. For younger adults, education levels will be even higher.

Thus, many U.S. consumers will be more knowledgeable and cosmopolitan; more aware of national and worldwide trends in tastes, styles, and goods and services; and more sophisticated. Furthermore, nonconforming behavior will be more widely accepted since increased education will lead to the self-assurance that shoppers require to reduce their need for conformity, while providing an appreciation of available choices. Confident shoppers depend less on brands and labels and are more willing to experiment, but more educated consumers also insist on detailed information about goods and services.

As two analysts note:

> Because today's consumers are well-educated and skeptical, they're also more apt to see through hollow claims.[4]
>
> Consumers will exhibit a sharply stronger demand for quality in goods and services. Retailers will be forced to use all means at their disposal to satisfy quality requirements: careful merchandise buying, visual assurances, service, store layout, amenities, and reliable follow-through on the promised benefits of patronage.[5]

Poverty of Time

For some households, the increased number of working women, the desire for personal fulfillment, the longer distances between the locations of work and home, and the greater number of people working at second jobs contribute to a ***poverty of time***. According to this concept, an interest in financial security may result in less rather than more free time since the alternatives competing for consumers' time rise considerably. Many customers are thus apt to place a high value on goods and services minimizing time expenditures.

There are various ways for retailers to respond to the poverty-of-time concept. They can

- Describe, label, and identify goods and services more clearly in advertising and displays. Popular brands also facilitate customer shopping.
- Carry pre-packaged products, which can be selected via self-service.
- Set up specialized departments by goods/service category within the store. For instance, firms can place all cookware and dinnerware items in one specific department, instead of scattering them through the store.
- Maintain adequate inventory to avoid running out of stock.
- Increase the number of branch stores to limit customer travel time.
- Have longer hours of operation, including evening and weekend openings.
- Add on-floor sales personnel.
- Reduce checkout time.
- Use mail-order and telephone selling.

[4] Bill Kelley, "The New Consumer Revealed," *Sales & Marketing Management* (May 1993), p. 51.

[5] "Retail Trend to Affect Quality of Goods, In-Store Service," *Marketing News* (February 15, 1988), p. 18.

For instance, L. Luria & Son—a 50-store Florida chain—is striving to make its operations as convenient and efficient as possible for consumers:

> Our south Miami prototype store represents a radical departure from our long-established catalog showroom strategy. It shows our commitment to specialty discount retailing, while shifting from a catalog showroom format over the next few years. At the prototype store, we've reduced our warehouse space and moved much of our merchandise onto the selling floor to increase customer convenience and encourage impulse purchases. Instead of waiting for an item to be delivered to a package pick-up area, customers can select products directly from well-stocked shelves, drop them in a shopping cart, and move quickly through the checkout counter. As we open new stores and renovate existing ones throughout Florida, we plan to introduce our prototype format to more Luria's customers.[6]

Self-Fulfillment

Of growing importance is the concept of ***self-fulfillment***, whereby

> consumer behavior is becoming more individualistic and less defined by reference to easily identified social groups. Americans are piecing together "component life-styles" for themselves, choosing goods and services that best express their growing sense of uniqueness.[7]
>
> The consumer of the 90s is likely to head to a discount chain store to get the best price on socks and T-shirts, move on to a deep-discount drugstore for shampoo and toothpaste, and then head to the supermarket to buy store-brand bread and cookies. But the last stop may be a small specialty shop where she [he] selects an expensive figurine of blown crystal to add to her [his] collection.[8]

These are some ways in which different consumers seek to fulfill themselves. They may

- Emphasize physical health, fitness, and exercise.
- Search for meaningful careers.
- Emphasize or de-emphasize material possessions and status symbols.
- Become more or less interested in romanticism.
- Turn to or away from life-style simplicity.
- Try for self-improvement.
- Attain individuality ("Do your own thing").

When reacting to consumer desires for self-fulfillment, retailers need to understand the motivations of their target markets, and they must present an appropriate value orientation:

> Value has many meanings. It is situational because it depends on the needs and perceptions of the customer. Assuming a fair price, white-collar consumers are most likely to shop department stores, specialty stores, and off-price retailers because *quality* and *fashion* dominate their perceptions of value. By contrast, blue-collar customers are more likely to shop mass merchandisers, discount stores, lower-priced specialty stores, and possibly off-price stores for the same kinds of

[6] *Luria's 1993 Annual Report*, pp. 3–4.

[7] "31 Major Trends Shaping the Future of American Business," *The Public Pulse*, Vol. 2, No. 1 (1988), p. 1.

[8] Michael J. McDermott, "Retailing," *Adweek* (September 11, 1989), p. 124.

goods because *price* tempers their perceptions of quality and price. Today's best retailers match the value perceptions of their customers. Value is as important for retailers as it is for consumers.[9]

Consumer interest in self-fulfillment will continue to expand in the future.

Consumerism

Consumerism involves the

activities of government, business, and independent organizations that are designed to protect individuals from practices that infringe upon their rights as consumers.[10]

This definition focuses on the fact that consumers have rights and that these rights should be protected by government, business, and independent organizations. As stated by President Kennedy in the early 1960s, consumers have the right to safety (protection against hazardous goods and services), the right to be informed (protection against fraudulent, deceptive, and incomplete information, advertising, and labeling), the right to choose (access to a variety of goods, services, and retailers), and the right to be heard (consumer feedback, both positive and negative, to the firm and to government agencies).

There are many reasons why retailers need to avoid potentially harmful and/or deceptive business practices, and why they should do all they can to understand and protect consumer rights. Here are some of them:

- Retailing is so competitive that people will be more apt to patronize firms perceived as "customer-oriented" and not to shop with ones seen as "greedy."
- Because consumers are more knowledgeable and selective than in the past, retailers must offer fair value, provide detailed information, and be prepared to handle questions and complaints.
- Consumers are becoming more price-conscious. The popularity of off-price retailing is also heightening consumer awareness of prices.
- Large retailers are sometimes viewed as indifferent to consumers. They may not provide enough personal attention for shoppers or may have inadequate control over employees (resulting in poor practices and a lack of uniformity from one branch outlet to the next).
- The use of self-service is increasing, and it can cause frustration for some shoppers.
- The rise in new technology is unsettling to many consumers, who must learn new shopping behavior (such as how to use automatic teller machines).
- Retailers are in direct contact with consumers, so they are frequently blamed for and asked to resolve problems actually caused by manufacturers (such as defective products and unclear operating instructions). Thus, retailers need to balance the interests of their suppliers and their customers. In addition, retailers can pass along safety, information, and other recommendations to their suppliers.

Accordingly, several retailers have developed and implemented programs to protect consumer rights without waiting for government or consumer pressure to do so. Following are examples of these actions.

J.C. Penney adopted the "Penney Idea" in 1913 and still adheres to its seven basic concepts:

[9] Max L. Densmore and Sylvia Kaufman, "How Leading Retailers Stay on Top," *Business*, Vol. 35 (April–June 1985), pp. 28–35.

[10] Peter D. Bennett (Editor), *Dictionary of Marketing Terms* (Chicago: American Marketing Association, 1988), p. 42.

> To serve the public, as nearly as we can, to its complete satisfaction; to expect for the service we render a fair remuneration and not all the profit the traffic will bear; to do all in our power to pack the customer dollar full of value, quality, and satisfaction; to continue to train ourselves and our associates so the service we give will be more and more intelligently performed; to improve constantly the human factor in our business; to reward men and women in our organization via participation in what the business produces; and to test our every policy, method, and act in this way—"Does it square with what is right and just?"[11]

In the 1970s, Giant Food—a leading supermarket chain—hired Esther Peterson (once President Johnson's special consumer-affairs assistant) at a rank equal to vice-president. The firm then developed a consumer bill of rights, based on President Kennedy's, which it follows today:

1. Right to safety—Giant's product safety standards, such as age-labeling toys, go far beyond those required by government agencies.
2. Right to be informed—Giant has a detailed labeling system and utilizes unit pricing, open dating, and nutritional labeling.
3. Right to choose—Consumers who want to purchase possibly harmful or hazardous products (like cigarettes and foods with additives) can do so.
4. Right to be heard—A continuing dialogue with reputable consumer groups has been established.
5. Rights to redress—There is a money-back guarantee policy on all products.
6. Right to service—Customers should receive good in-store service.[12]

Many retailers have voluntarily implemented their own product-testing programs, whereby merchandise is tested for such attributes as value, quality, misrepresentation of contents, safety, and durability before being placed for sale. Sears, J.C. Penney, A&P, Macy's, Target Stores, Montgomery Ward, and Giant Food are just a few of the firms involved in testing. See Figure 3–3.

Among the other consumerism activities undertaken by numerous retailers are setting clear procedures for handling customer complaints, reviewing advertising-message clarity, sponsoring consumer education programs, and training company personnel on how to interact properly with customers.

Consumer-oriented actions are not limited to large retail chains; small retailers can also be involved. For example, a local toy store can separate toys by age category. An independent supermarket can set up special displays featuring environmentally safe detergents. A neighborhood restaurant can cook foods in low-fat vegetable oil and emphasize menu items with reduced sodium content. A sporting-goods store can give away free equipment to area schools.

Ethics and Social Responsibility

In dealing with all of their constituencies (customers, the general public, employees, suppliers, competitors, and others), retailers have a moral obligation to act in an ethical and socially responsible manner. Furthermore, due to the heightened societal and media attention now paid to company behavior—and the high expectations that people have today, a company's failure to be responsive may very well lead to adverse publicity, law suits, the loss of customers, and a lack of self-respect among company employees. Each of these events happened to Sears when it was discovered that the firm was overcharging auto-repair customers because of the overzealous and deceptive sales practices being used by its employees.

[11] J.C. Penney.

[12] Giant Food.

Target's Responsibility

At Target, toys are an important part of our business. We want the toys you buy to meet Target's and the U.S. Government's high standards of quality, value, and safety. Therefore, we abide by all U.S. Consumer Product Safety Regulations. Target also utilizes an independent testing agency. They test samples of all toys we sell to help ensure your child's safe play.

All toys sold at Target are tested to be certain they are free from these dangers:

Sharp edges

Toys of brittle plastic or glass can be broken to expose cutting edges. Poorly made metal or wood toys may have sharp edges.

Small parts

Tiny toys and toys with removable parts can be swallowed or lodged in child's windpipe, ears, or nose.

Loud noises

Noise-making guns and other toys can produce sounds at noise levels that can damage hearing.

Sharp points

Broken toys can expose dangerous points. Stuffed toys can have barbed eyes or wired limbs that can cut.

Propelled objects

Projectiles and similar flying toys can injure eyes in particular. Arrows or darts should have protective soft tips.

Electrical shock

Electrically operated toys that are improperly constructed can shock or cause burns. Electric toys must meet mandatory safety requirements.

Wrong toys for the wrong age

Toys that may be safe for older children can be dangerous when played with by little ones.

FIGURE 3–3
Voluntary Product Testing at Target Stores
Courtesy Target Stores.

When a retailer has a sense of ***ethics***, it acts in a trustworthy, fair, honest, and respectful manner with each of its constituencies.[13] For this to occur, the firm's executives must clearly articulate to employees what kinds of behavior are acceptable and which are not—and how unacceptable behavior will be treated. Often, society may deem certain behavior to be unethical but laws may not forbid it. Most observers would agree that practices like these are unethical (and sometimes illegal, too):

- Raising prices on scarce products after a natural disaster such as a hurricane or earthquake.
- Not having adequate stock when a sale is advertised.
- Charging high prices in low-income neighborhoods because consumers there do not have the transportation mobility to shop out of their neighborhoods.
- Selling alcoholic and tobacco products to children.
- A salesperson posing as a market researcher when engaged in telemarketing.

The best way to avoid unethical acts is for firms to have written ethics codes, clearly communicate them to employees, monitor behavior, and punish poor behavior—and for top managers to be highly ethical in their own conduct.

[13] N. Craig Smith, "Ethics and the Marketing Manager" in N. Craig Smith and John A. Quelch, *Ethics in Marketing* (Homewood, Illinois: Irwin, 1993), pp. 3–34.

ETHICS IN RETAILING

Why Has Domino's Abandoned Its 30-Minute Delivery Pledge?

Responding to a 1993 jury award of $78 million to a woman who was hit and injured by a Domino's driver, Domino's Pizza has announced that it will no longer guarantee that its pizza will be delivered within 30 minutes of a phone order. Although this was only one of several delivery-related legal judgments against Domino's, it was the largest and most widely publicized. And, while the company never charged its deliverypeople for any late deliveries, many consumers perceived that the guarantee encouraged unsafe driving behavior.

Domino's 30-minute delivery guarantee, begun in 1984, was the major element in the firm's overall retail strategy. Until 1986, the pizza was free for those orders that arrived beyond the 30-minute wait. Beginning in 1986, customers who had to wait for more than 30 minutes received a $3 discount.

Domino's now plans to heavily promote a new product-satisfaction program that guarantees a new pizza or a full refund to any dissatisfied customers. Yet, some retail analysts question whether this approach will succeed. According to these analysts, Domino's reputation was based more on speed of delivery than on taste.

Sources: Based on material in Michael Janofsky, "Domino's Ends Fast-Pizza Pledge After Big Award to Crash Victim," *New York Times* (December 22, 1993), pp. A1, D15; and Krystal Miller and Richard Gibson, "Domino's Stops Promising Pizza in 30 Minutes," *Wall Street Journal* (December 22, 1993), pp. B1, B3.

Many trade associations promote ethics codes to member firms. For example, the Direct Marketing Association (DMA) has a code of ethics that members are encouraged to follow. Here are some of the articles covered in the DMA's code:

- Article 1—All offers should be clear, honest, and complete.
- Article 5—Disparagement of any person or group on grounds of race, color, religion, national origin, gender, marital status, or age is unacceptable.
- Article 7—Offers suitable for adults only should not be made to children.
- Article 17—Sweepstakes prizes should be advertised in a clear, honest, and complete way so the consumer may know the exact nature of the offer.
- Article 28—Merchandise should not be shipped without first having received the customer's permission.
- Article 38—Telemarketers should remove the name of any customer from their telephone lists when requested by the individual.
- Article 42—Direct marketers should adhere to Better Business Bureau standards and all applicable government laws.[14]

When a retailer exhibits ***social responsibility***, it acts in the best interests of society—as well as itself. The firm then strives to balance corporate citizenship with a fair level of profits (for stockholders, management, and employees). Here are two examples.

A growing number of retailers have embarked on recycling and conservation programs to protect the environment (since 3.5 pounds of trash a day per person is discarded in the United States). They include Wal-Mart, McDonald's, L.L. Bean, Mary Kay, and many others. For instance, Mary Kay recycles cartons and donates the proceeds from recycling programs or a percentage of profits to environmental groups of employees' choosing, such as the Texas Nature Conservancy.[15] Figure 3–4 highlights Hannaford's recycling efforts.

Dollar General, the general-merchandise chain serving low-, middle-, and fixed-income families, has a commitment to giving back to the community:

> We have a passion to honor our functionally illiterate founder, J. L. Turner, by doing whatever we can to meet the intractably imbedded literacy needs of our customers, the "J. L. Turners" of today.

[14] *Direct Marketing Association Guidelines for . . . Ethical Business Practices* (New York: Direct Marketing Association).

[15] Richard C. Bartlett and Liz Barrett, "A Retailer's Perspective on the Environmental Challenge, *Arthur Andersen Retailing Issues Letter* (June 1992), pp. 1–4.

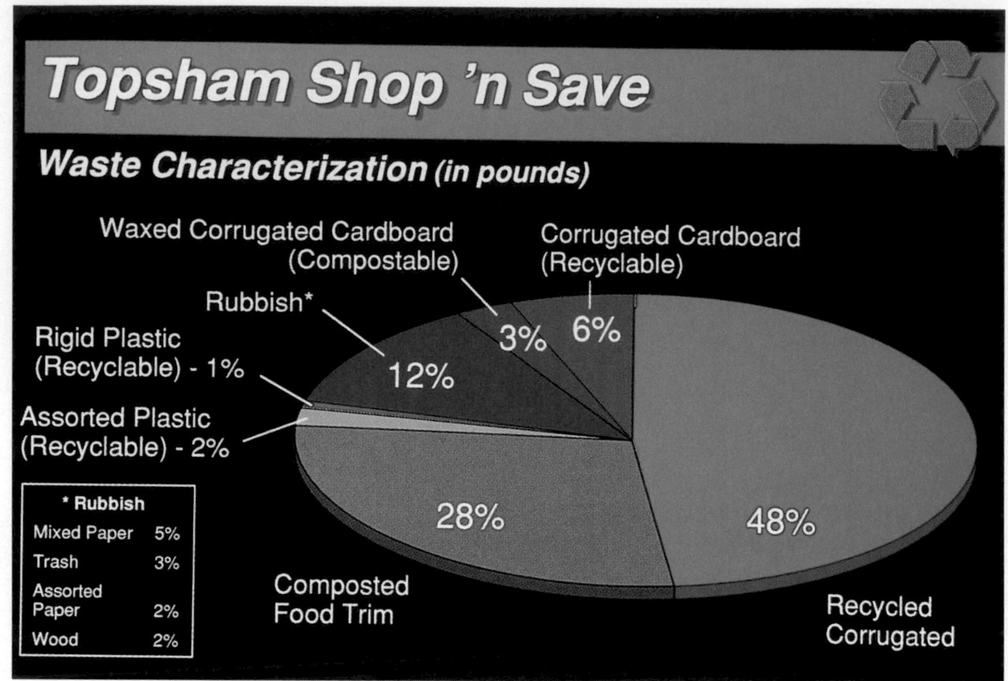

FIGURE 3–4
Hannaford's Recycling Efforts
Hannaford is very aggressive as a recycler. This figure (highlighting its Topsham, Maine, Shop 'n Save supermarket) indicates the in-depth analysis that the firm does.
Reprinted by permission.

- Our GED-Learn-to-Read program has helped more than 25,000 people take the first step toward getting their GED [general equivalency diploma] or learning to read.
- In a joint venture with Lindsey Wilson College of Columbia, Kentucky, we have created a satellite campus in Scottsville, Kentucky, which has the greatest concentration of our employees.
- Dollar General has established and continues to support Nashville Read, a new program which coordinates and enhances literacy efforts.

Having done this, the coming year will see us truly reaching out in a fearful exercise of faith. In partnership with local government, we are opening a one-of-a-kind Dollar General Store in the Sam Levy project homes of inner-city Nashville, Tennessee. This venture will provide literacy and employment training to a neighborhood that desperately needs these services. We will even provide child care so that single working parents can take advantage of these services. Businesses have fled this part of Nashville—until now. These people really need us and we have a lot at stake, as do the residents of Sam Levy Homes. We are hopeful about making this newest move another *right move.*[16]

Technology

Over the next several years, many technological advances that impact on retailers will continue. The emerging technology most affecting retailers will center on such developments as electronic banking, video-ordering systems, and computerization of operations.

[16] *Dollar General Corporation 1993 Annual Report*, p. 7. See also Mary Hance, "Nashville Challenge," *Stores* (January 1994), pp. 49–51.

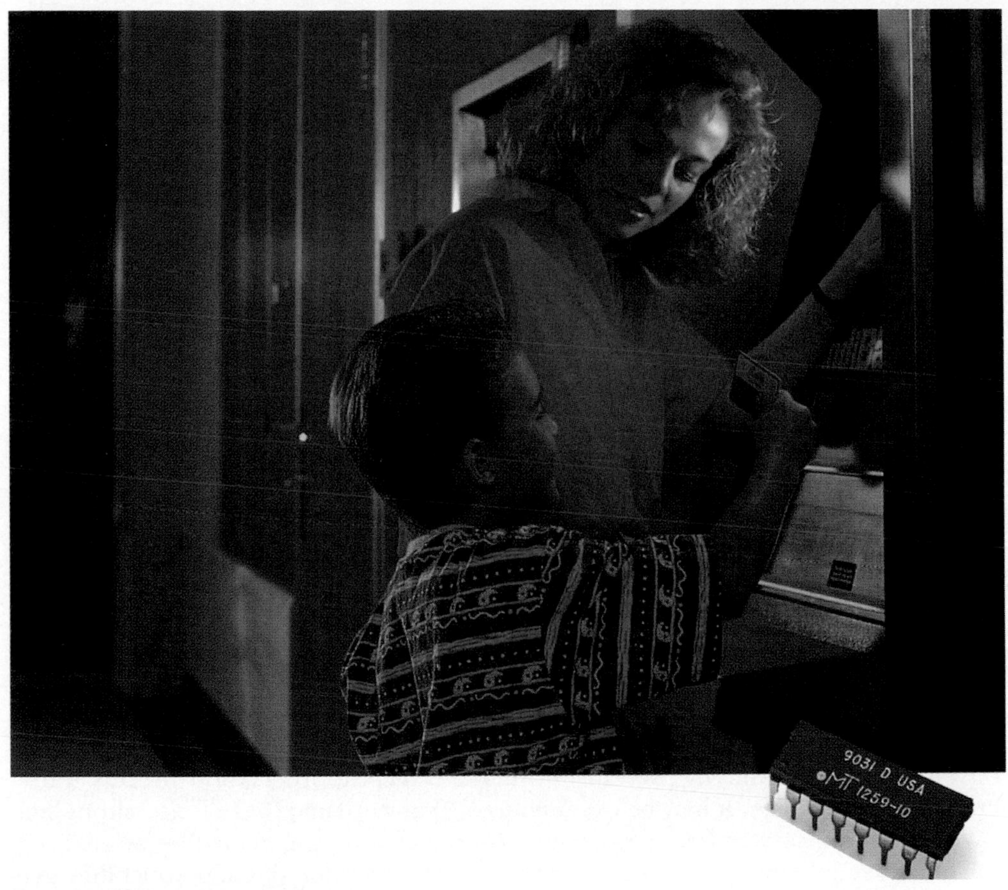

FIGURE 3–5
The Growing Role of Automatic Teller Machines
ATMs have become an indispensable part of more people's lives. Their many functions would not be possible without memory chips. ATMs use Micron's DRAM chips to help people withdraw and deposit money, inquire about balances, and transfer funds from account to account at any time.
Reprinted by permission of Micron Technology. Photographer Steve Welsh.

ELECTRONIC BANKING

Electronic banking involves the use of automatic teller machines (ATMs) and the instant processing of retail purchases. It allows centralized record keeping and enables customers to complete transactions 24 hours a day, 7 days a week at a variety of bank and nonbank locations. See Figure 3–5.

At present, there are 90,000 ATMs in use in the United States alone, a number that is expected to keep rising in the future. They are located in banks, shopping centers, department stores, supermarkets, convenience stores, hotel lobbies, and airports; on college campuses; and at various other sites. "Sharing systems" let consumers make transactions at ATMs outside their local banking areas. For instance, the Cirrus and Plus networks each enable consumers to have access to tens of thousands of ATMs worldwide.[17]

Besides its use for typical financial transactions (such as check cashing, deposits, withdrawals, and transfers), electronic banking will increasingly be used in retailing in the future. More banks and other retailers (especially those previously accepting only cash or check payments, such as supermarkets) will rely on some form of electronic debit payment plan, whereby the purchase price is immediately deducted from a consumer's bank account via computer and entered into a retailer's account. This is discussed further in Chapter 12.

The use of individual-retailer credit cards and accounts will drop by the year 2000 due to the enactment of a more centralized, nationwide credit and banking system (dominated by firms such as Visa and MasterCard). Yet, many retailers will still stress their own credit cards since they believe they may lose their identities if these cards are used less frequently by customers.

[17] *Statistical Abstract of the United States 1993* (Washington, D.C.: U.S. Bureau of the Census, 1993), p. 517; and Margaret Mannix, "Checks Made of Plastic," *U.S. News & World Report* (March 14, 1994), pp. 72–74.

These are some ramifications associated with the projected long-term growth in electronic banking:

- Consumers must be educated as to how to use electronic banking and the benefits of doing so.
- More retailers will have to accept national credit (debit) cards in addition to or rather than their own.
- Retail operating expenses will be reduced. Collections and bad debts will be issues handled by financial institutions rather than retailers.
- Customer loyalty will be reduced if credit (debit) cards are accepted by a number of retailers and not just by those originally issuing the cards.
- Financial transactions (like check deposits and cash withdrawals) will more often occur in nonbank settings, like supermarkets and department stores.
- The need for bank personnel will decline.
- Financial services will be available at all times during the week.
- Vending machines will be able to process transactions very easily because of their acceptance of debit cards.

VIDEO-ORDERING SYSTEMS

The spread of video-ordering systems will strongly affect the sales and promotional methods of various retailers. Through a ***video-ordering system***, a retailer can efficiently, conveniently, and promptly present information, receive orders, and process transactions with customers. It may be oriented toward in-store and/or in-home shopping.

With an in-store video-ordering system, a consumer orders merchandise by entering data into a self-prompting, computerized video-display monitor; often, product information (and sometimes pictures or animated presentations) is also available via a video display. The order is processed by the computer, and the consumer goes to a checkout area to pick up and pay for it. For example, at Service Merchandise, consumers can place orders via "Silent Sam," an in-store video-ordering system. See Figure 3–6.

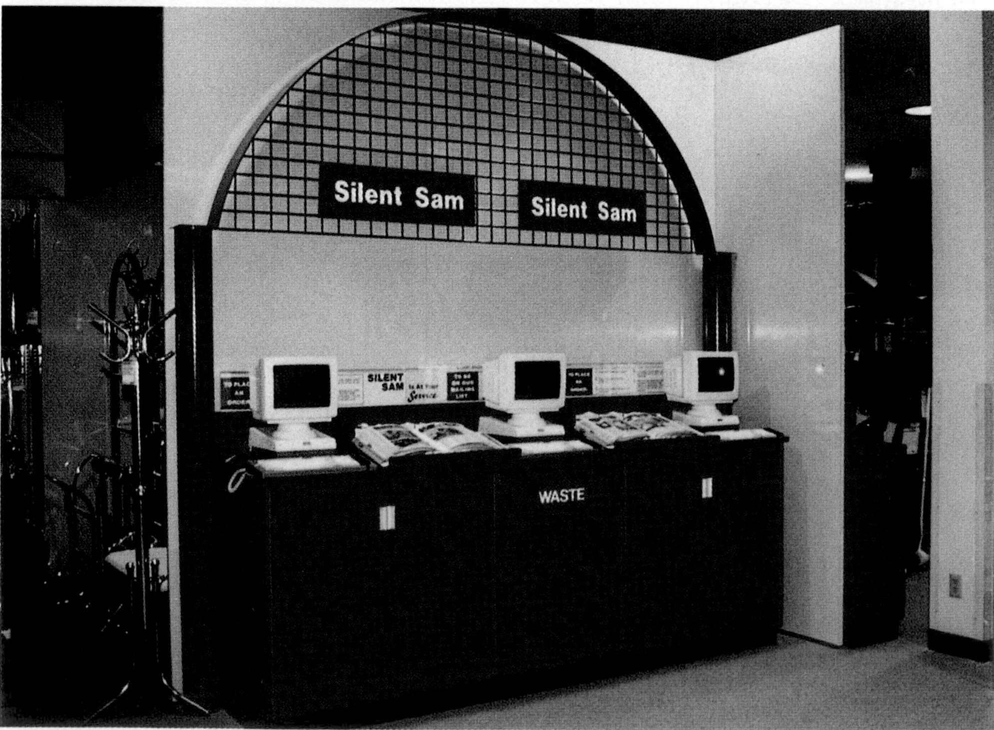

FIGURE 3–6
Silent Sam: A Video-Ordering System
Reprinted by permission of Service Merchandise.

An in-home video-ordering system may rely on one of three basic formats: television programming, interactive computer programming, and merchandise catalogs. With a television-based system, the consumer watches special programming that appears on commercial or cable television and places an order via a toll-free 800 telephone number. Home Shopping Network (which operates the Home Shopping Club) and QVC are the largest firms in this category—each with annual sales exceeding $1 billion. Industry-wide revenues are more than $3 billion per year.[18] In the future, it is expected that people will be able to shop interactively via their TV sets by placing remote-control activated orders or touch-tone phone orders (as people do now for pay-per-view shows).

With an interactive computer-based system, an in-home consumer uses a PC to view graphic or pictorial presentations of goods and services, accompanied by text descriptions and ordering procedures. The person orders by entering a product code number into the PC and indicating the quantity desired. Information is exchanged between the consumer and the retailer via a computer modem linked to the consumer's telephone. The retailer's computer records and interprets the order, schedules delivery, and posts transactions. To date, interactive systems have not generated the high consumer usage anticipated, mostly because of the relatively low number of U.S. households having PCs with modems and many consumers' discomfort with shopping by computer. Yet, Sears and other retailers have confidence that interactive systems will succeed over the next decade. Together with IBM, Sears invested more than $700 million to develop Prodigy, which was introduced in 1988 and had 2 million subscribers as of mid-1994. Forty retailers participate in Prodigy, whose leading competitor is CompuServe (with 1.7 million subscribers).[19]

For a merchandise video catalog, the retailer usually reproduces its printed shopping catalog on a videocassette or videodisc and sends the catalog to appropriate customers. In-home shoppers then watch the catalog on their television sets (via their VCRs or videodisc players) and telephone orders to the retailer. Spiegel has done this with its *Just For You* catalogs, targeted at large-size customers.

Many retailers will intensify their use of some form of video-ordering system for several reasons:

- Shoppers can conveniently place orders.
- Fewer personnel are needed.
- Investment costs can be reduced (such as the lesser need for elaborate in-store displays).
- Efforts can be targeted to specific groups.
- The geographic trading area can be expanded through in-home ordering.
- Inventory requirements may be lessened.
- Customer data bases can be developed.

Yet, despite the long-run potential of video-ordering systems, retailers should keep these points in mind:

- Numerous consumers will be relatively uninterested with in-home video shopping, preferring to go to stores.
- Expensive, complex items do not readily lend themselves to video shopping.
- Without personal selling, consumers may not trade up to higher-priced models or add options.
- Attractive in-store displays are usually more likely to generate impulse purchases.
- Image is harder to portray via graphic or pictorial representations.

[18] Don L. Boroughs, "Purchasing Power," *U.S. News & World Report* (January 31, 1994), pp. 56–59.

[19] "The Paperless Chase," *Advertising Age* (March 7, 1994), p. S–12; and Phaedra Hise, "Prodigy: Smart Sales Channel?" *Sales & Marketing Management* (February 1994), p. 77.

FIGURE 3–7
Pegman Space Management Software
Pegman is designed to optimize the use of in-store space. It lets retailers graphically depict products on-screen in sections or categories, linked to inventory and financial information. The retailers can set displays, assess them based on financial and aesthetic goals, and determine the impact on sales if changes are made.
Reprinted by permission of MarketWare.

COMPUTERIZATION OF OPERATIONS

More and more retailers will continue to computerize their operations, as a result of better technology, interest in productivity, and the affordability of new PCs and computer networks. In particular, they will rely more on computerized checkouts to process transactions, so as to be efficient and to improve inventory management and reordering. This is covered in greater detail in Chapter 12.

A variety of firms are developing computer software for retailers' use. For example, as shown in Figure 3–7, Pegman space management software by MarketWare assists in planning shelf displays and layouts. Business Modeling Techniques offers QuikTeller software, which enables retailers to customize automatic teller machines to their personal needs. GE Information Services has developed a GE Quick Response program to facilitate ordering and inventory control. Dataserv offers the Surpass software program for specialty stores; it supports multiple point-of-sale terminals and aids in inventory planning and control. The National Retail Federation has also published a directory listing various software packages. In addition, some retailers are devising their own customized software.

Retail Institutions

The trends in demographics, life-styles, consumerism, ethics and social responsibility, and technology will undoubtedly have an impact on the nature of retail institutions. In addition, many retailers believe profit margins will continue shrinking, due to intense competition and high costs. This decline will put pressure on retailers to tighten internal cost controls and to promote higher margin goods and services while eliminating unprofitable items.

For example, here's one view of the future:

> Until fairly recently, the retailing industry was characterized by lines of trade and retail formats that were easily distinguished because of their pricing and service strategies, but especially because they had distinctive product offers. Consumers went to drugstores for prescription drugs and supermarkets for food. Consumers' expectations about the nature of the shopping experience in each type of store were fairly standard.

> Today, the distinctions among retail sectors have blurred as retailers expand their offerings to meet customers' need for convenience, generate more traffic, and attempt to get a large share of customers' pocketbooks. We see increased competition for a number of product categories that once were the exclusive or primary domain of a particular store type. In the current slow-growth environment with increasing constraints on growth in the number of stores, retailers will continue to look for opportunities to sell more to the customers they already have. The need to gain a strong differential competitive advantage is greater than ever. Retailers must broaden their perception of who competitors are and act accordingly.[20]

Progressive retailers know their individual strategies must be modified as retail institutions evolve over time. Complacency is not desirable. As one leading futurist says, "Successful retailers of the future will make a habit of adaptation, based on an ever-deepening knowledge of their marketplace and their consumers, to whom they will listen, learn from, and respond."[21]

The use of a ***retailing effectiveness checklist***, which enables a firm to systematically assess its preparedness for the future, can be quite helpful in planning. An illustration of such a checklist is shown in Table 3–1. If a retailer answers no to any of the questions raised in the table, it needs to adapt its strategy to prosper in the future.

In the following sections, we examine how retailers will respond to the changing environment through mergers, diversification, and downsizing; risk-minimization retailing; and adaptation strategies.

MERGERS, DIVERSIFICATION, AND DOWNSIZING

Over the past two decades, some firms have used mergers and diversification to sustain sales growth in a highly competitive environment (or when the institutional category in which they operate matures). For stronger firms, this trend is expected to carry over into the future.

Mergers involve the combination of separately owned retail firms. Diversification mergers occur between retailers of different types, such as the one between H&R Block (the largest U.S. consumer tax preparer) and CompuServe (the computerized in-home shopping firm). Specialization mergers occur between similar types of retailers, such as two local banks or two supermarket chains. By merging, retailers hope to jointly maximize resources, enlarge their customer base, improve productivity and bargaining power, limit weaknesses, and gain competitive advantages. This is a way for resourceful retailers to grow more rapidly and for weaker ones to enhance their long-term prospects for survival (or gain some return on investment by selling assets).

With ***diversification***, retailers become active in businesses outside their normal operations—and add distinctly different goods and/or service categories. For example, by the early 1980s, Kmart believed it had reached a saturation point with its traditional full-line discount stores; so, to thrive in the long run, Kmart decided to diversify. It opened American Fare stores, experimented with fast-food facilities in selected Kmart stores, and devised a new image campaign featuring Martha Stewart, the lifestyle expert. It also acquired Waldenbooks, Builders Square, Pay Less (a discount-drug-store chain), Sports Authority, Pace Membership Warehouse, and other retailers.

Because of mergers and diversification, the size of many retail chains has grown dramatically. And they have not all done well with that approach. Thus, as in the manufacturing sector, even though stronger firms are expanding, we are also now witnessing ***downsizing***—whereby unprofitable stores are closed or divisions are sold off—

[20] Linda Hyde, "Cross Competition Escalates Battle for Market Share," *Chain Store Age Executive* (August 1993), pp. 11A–13A.

[21] Roger Seibert, "Retailing's Five Most Important Trends," *Arthur Andersen Retailing Issues Letter* (March 1991), p. 4.

TABLE 3–1 A Retailing Effectiveness Checklist

Answer yes or no to each of the following questions. For "no" answers, you should analyze your performance in these areas and determine how to improve efforts.

1. Is a clear long-term organizational mission articulated? ______
2. Is the current status of your firm taken into consideration when setting future plans? ______
3. Is your firm's role in the business system understood? ______
4. Are sustainable competitive advantages identified and pursued? ______
5. Are company weaknesses identified and minimized? ______
6. Is your management style compatible with the firm's way of doing business? ______
7. Is there a logical short-run and long-run approach to your firm's chosen goods/service category (line of business)? ______
8. Are there specific, realistic, and measurable short- and long-term goals? ______
9. Do these goals guide strategy development and resource allocation? ______
10. Are the characteristics and needs of your target market known? ______
11. Is the strategy tailored to the chosen target market? ______
12. Are systematic plans prepared for each element of your strategy mix?
    a. Location ______
    b. Managing the business ______
    c. Merchandise management and pricing ______
    d. Communicating with the customer ______
13. Are these uncontrollable factors monitored?
    a. Consumers ______
    b. Competition ______
    c. Technology ______
    d. Economic conditions ______
    e. Seasonality ______
    f. Legal restrictions ______
14. Is your overall strategy integrated? ______
15. Are short-, moderate-, and long-term plans compatible? ______
16. Does your firm know where each merchandise line, for-sale service, and business format stands in the marketplace? ______
17. Are tactics carried out in a manner consistent with the strategic plan? ______
18. Are your strategic plan and its elements adequately communicated? ______
19. Is unbiased feedback regularly sought for each aspect of the strategic plan? ______
20. Is information about new opportunities and threats sought out? ______
21. After a strategic plan is enacted, are company strengths and weaknesses, as well as successes and failures, studied on an ongoing basis? ______
22. Are results studied in a way that reduces your firm's chances of overreacting to a situation? ______
23. Are strategic modifications made when needed? ______
24. Are strategic plans modified before crises occur? ______
25. Does your firm avoid strategy flip-flops (which confuse customers, employees, suppliers, and others)? ______

Source: Adapted by the authors from Joel R. Evans, "Strategic Planning in Retailing: A Necessity in the 1990s," *Retail Strategist* (Number 2, 1991), p. 19.

on the part of retailers dissatisfied with their performance. As an illustration, the Kmart diversification strategy did not meet expectations, leading the firm to close or sell off some of its ventures, including American Fare, Pay Less, and Pace.

For several reasons, the interest in downsizing is expected to continue: One, various retailers have overextended themselves and do not have the resources or management talent to succeed without retrenching. Two, in their quest to open new stores, certain firms have chosen poor sites (because they have already saturated the best locations). Three, retailers like Barnes & Noble are becoming more interested in operating fewer, but much larger, stores. Four, companies such as Herman's Sporting Goods are finding that they can do better when they focus attention regionally rather than nationally. Five, diversified firms like Kmart have decided to return more to their roots.

As Woolworth's chief executive recently said: "[Downsizing] is consistent with our long-standing strategy to restructure, reformat, and revitalize businesses that can meet our financial objectives within a reasonable time span—and to redeploy assets away from those businesses which cannot. We expect this program, as well as other recent steps, will move the company closer to its goal of being a low-cost, customer-driven organization."[22]

What this means is that "Retailers have grown accustomed to shifts in what the consumer wants and are well acquainted with economic cycles. Even as they shutter unprofitable stores, both Woolworth and The Limited, Inc. are opening newer, profitable formats—such as Northern Reflections, World Foot Locker, and Structure—and are converting existing units to these formats."[23]

Risk-Minimization Retailing

In ***risk-minimization retailing***, firms strive to hold down both their initial investment costs and the ongoing costs of operations. In the future, a risk-minimization approach will be utilized by more retailers because of the intense competition from discounters, the need to control complicated chain or franchise operations, high land and construction costs, the volatility of the economic environment, and the interest in maximizing productivity.

It can be accomplished via one or more of these strategy-mix decisions:

- Standardizing operating procedures.
- Standardizing store layouts, size, and product offerings.
- Using secondary locations, freestanding units, and locations in older strip centers and by occupying sites abandoned by others (second-use locations).
- Locating in smaller communities where building regulations are less strict, labor costs are lower, and construction and operating costs are reduced.
- Using inexpensive construction materials, such as bare cinder-block walls and concrete floors.
- Using plain fixtures and lower-cost displays.
- Buying used equipment.
- Joining cooperative buying and advertising groups.
- Encouraging manufacturers to finance inventories.

At present, a number of retailers use a form of risk-minimization strategy in their small-town stores. These include Dollar General (discount variety stores), Bi-Lo (food stores), Pamida (discount department stores), KFC, and Wal-Mart.

[22] "Retailing: Current Analysis," *Standard & Poor's Industry Surveys* (January 27, 1994), p. 70.
[23] Ibid., p. 71.

ADAPTATION STRATEGIES

In response to the dynamic environment of the 1990s, many retailers will need to develop and enact adaptation strategies. One of the most important challenges for any store-based retailer will be to get people to perceive it as a ***destination store***, whereby consumers believe a particular retailer is worth a special shopping trip, and to hold on to this perception:

> The key for retailing entities in the 1990s—from mass merchandisers to specialty stores to entire malls—is to view, define, and position themselves as shopping destinations. They must strive to be destinations for consumers to consciously seek, rather than places for consumers to wander into. If a retailer stakes out and captures a consumer's "share of mind" in its chosen category, it has accomplished differentiation.[24]

A good example of a retailer with a destination store image is Home Depot, the fast-growing, industry-leading chain:

> In some cases we have 25,000 to 30,000 people walking through a store in a week, 50 per cent of whom are women. We could sell them anything. If we wanted to put panty hose up at the front register, we'd sell a fortune in panty hose. But we don't. We don't want the customer to think we're a discounter, a food store, a toy store, or anything else, because it would confuse her. The perception of the consumer always has to be, when they think of a do-it-yourself project, they think of Home Depot.[25]

As one retailing expert says, "Home Depot succeeds where other do-it-yourself chains stumble because it staffs stores with knowledgeable sales help, not the kid who can tell you only that sheetrock is in aisle seven. If a customer is thinking of putting up, say, a stockade fence in his yard, a Home Depot salesperson can explain how many sections to order, what kinds of posts are needed to reinforce the fence, and even what size nails to use."[26]

Here are illustrations of how various retailers are using adaptation strategies to prepare for the future.

Montgomery Ward has increased the use of leased departments on its premises. Among the well-known retail tenants are Toys "R" Us. By leasing out store space, Montgomery Ward is sharing its occupancy costs, allocating store space more productively, gaining added customer traffic, and providing merchandise offerings that would be expensive to develop internally.[27]

In Wheaton, Illinois, The Gap worked with a developer to build a new type of open-air shopping center, with the goal of having the stores located there be more accessible to consumers. Along with 50 other specialty stores, The Gap has outlets of its Gap, Banana Republic, and GapKids chains in a small "town square" mall arrangement; The Gap occupies 17,000 square feet of the shopping center's 180,000 square feet. This center has no large anchor stores and there is easy entry into all the shops. There is no "no-hassle" shopping.[28]

Ukrop's supermarkets in Richmond, Virginia, have a Ukrop's Cafe in about one-half of the firm's stores. These cafes are open for breakfast, lunch, and dinner—and serve such items as tarragon chicken salad, grilled salmon fillets, and New Orleans jambalaya: "After decades of standing by and letting the McDonald's of the world gobble

[24] Seibert, "Retailing's Five Most Important Trends," p. 4.

[25] Susan Caminiti, "The New Champs of Retailing," *Fortune* (September 24, 1990), pp. 86, 90.

[26] Ibid., p. 100.

[27] Gary Hoover, Alta Campbell, and Patrick Spain (Editors), *Hoover's Handbook of American Business 1994* (Austin, Texas: Reference Press, 1993), pp. 786–787.

[28] Adrienne Ward, "The Gap Opens Door to New Mall Concept," *Advertising Age* (January 21, 1991), p. 39.

RETAILING AROUND THE WORLD

How Do Retailers Cope in Canada's Tough Economy?

Despite a recent turnaround in Canada's economy, some retail analysts feel that the Canadian economy will not soon be restored to its pre-recession level. Consumer confidence remains rather low, unemployment is still high, and a recent 7 per cent goods and services tax (GST) has also hurt retail sales.

Canadian retailers have used a number of strategies to survive in the harsh economic situation there. Two common approaches are cost containment and the aggressive use of promotion.

For example, to reduce its costs, Woolworth Corporation has consolidated the operations of two Canadian subsidiaries: F.W. Woolworth Co. Ltd. and Kinney Canada. This has resulted in lower labor costs, streamlined operations, and reduced overhead costs.

In an effort to increase its base of customers, Sears Canada has more widely promoted the Sears Club. The Club lets customers earn points each time they shop at Sears; the points can be accumulated toward the purchase of products. The enrollment drive has increased Club membership by 700,000. Sears' research indicates that Club members spend more at Sears than the average customer.

Some Canadian retailers, such as Canadian Tire and Smitty's, have even expanded into the United States to be less dependent on the Canadian economy.

Sources: Based on material in "Canadian Recovery Spurs Store Growth," *Discount Store News* (August 2, 1993), p. 28; and Susan Reda, "Sears Canada Set to Rebound," *Stores* (March 1992), pp. 27–30.

up consumers' food dollars, supermarket operators like Ukrop's, are fighting back. They are strengthening deli departments, revamping menus, and devoting more space to showcase a wider selection of prepared foods. Some are installing food courts that bear a striking resemblance to ones found in shopping malls, with ample seating, separate checkout counters, and colorful signs."[29]

The International Environment of Retailing

The international environment of retailing encompasses both U.S. firms operating in foreign markets and foreign retailers operating in U.S. markets. In the future, more retailers will be international in scope, building on the robust recent trend in this direction:

> The world economy is shifting in ways that make retailing in the less-developed world increasingly lucrative and even necessary for firms based in the rich nations. Countries from such diverse regions as East Asia, Latin America, and Eastern Europe are providing a new opportunity for growth as their consumer sectors blossom. In addition, within the developed world, a consumer orientation is becoming more a part of economic growth in such regions as Western Europe and Japan. The United States, on the other hand, with a mature and saturated retail market, represents an increasingly difficult business environment for retail growth. It is not surprising, then, that many successful U.S. retailers are looking abroad for growth.
>
> Yet, retailers of The Americas continue to seriously lag behind the other trade blocs in their globalization efforts. Only 40 per cent of U.S.-based Top 100 retailers operate outside the United States, and only 20 percent have ventured outside The Americas trade bloc.[30]

When embarking on an international retailing strategy, firms should consider the factors shown in Figure 3–8.

[29] Eleena De Lisser, "Catering to Cooking-Phobic Customers, Supermarkets Stress Carryout, Add Cafes," *Wall Street Journal* (April 5, 1993), p. B1.

[30] Daniel J. Sweeney, Linda L. Hyde, and Ira A. Kalish, *Retail World: Window of Opportunity* (Columbus, Ohio: Price Waterhouse/Management Horizons, 1994), pp. 3, 14.

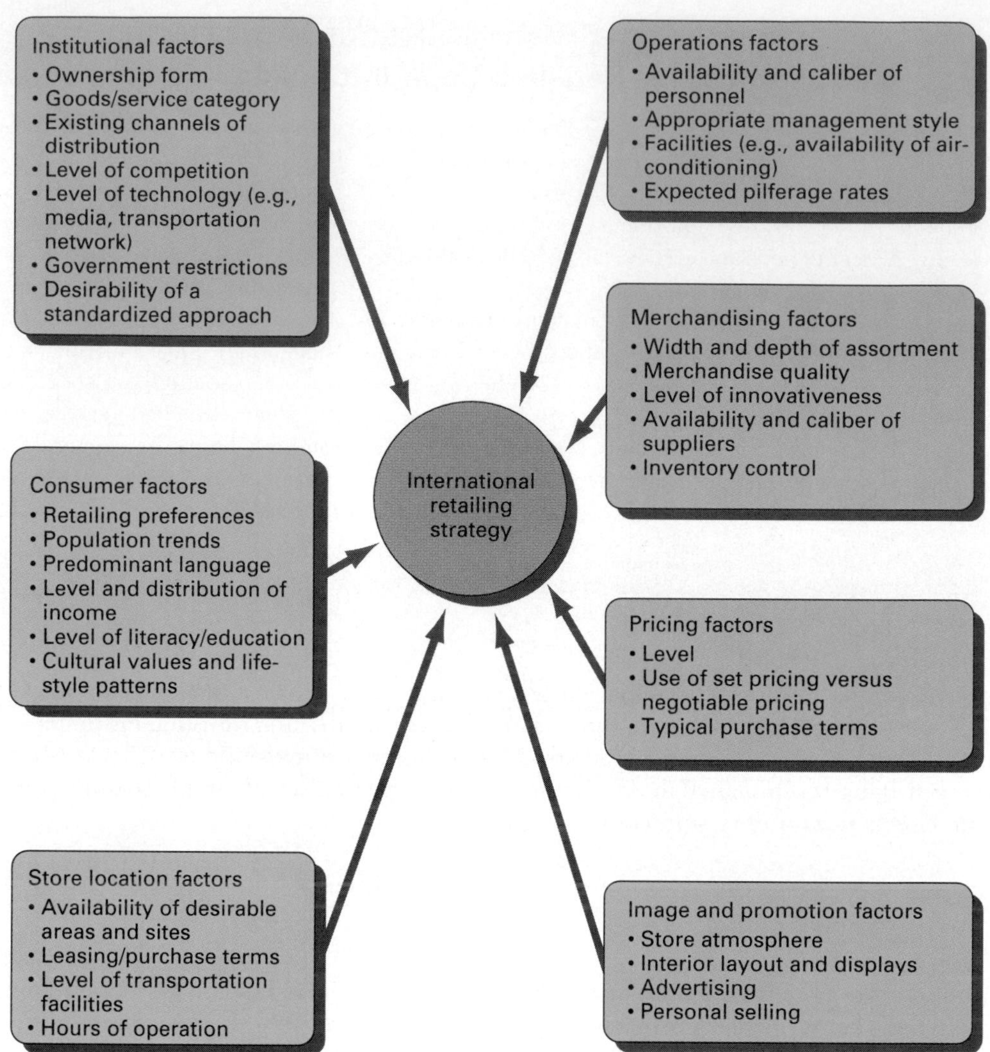

Figure 3–8
Factors to Consider When Engaging in International Retailing

Opportunities and Risks in International Retailing

For participating firms, there are wide-ranging opportunities and risks in international retailing.

Opportunities may exist for several reasons. One, foreign markets may represent better growth opportunities (because of population and other trends). Two, domestic markets may be saturated or stagnant. Three, a retailer may be able to offer goods, services, or technology not yet available in foreign markets. Four, competition may be less in foreign markets. Five, foreign markets may be used to supplement, not replace, domestic sales. Six, there may be tax or investment advantages in foreign markets. Seven, due to worldwide governmental and economic shifts, many countries are now more open to the entry of foreign firms.

Risks may also exist for several reasons. One, there may be cultural differences between domestic and foreign markets. Two, management styles may not be easily adaptable. Three, foreign governments may place restrictions on some operations. Four, personal income may be poorly distributed among consumers in foreign markets. Five, distribution systems and technology may be inadequate (for example, poor roads, lack of refrigeration, and a weak mail system). Six, institutional formats may vary greatly among countries.

When developing an international strategy, a retailer must pay particular attention to the concept of ***standardization***. Can the strategy followed in a firm's home market be standardized and directly applied to foreign markets, or do personnel, the

TABLE 3–2 Selected Retailing-Related Data by Country

Country	Average Weekly Hours of Operation	Employees' Minimum Number of Paid Vacation Days and Holidays	Level of Competition	Quality of Infrastructure	Entry Barriers	Urban Per-Capita Income
Canada	68	19	High	High	Moderate	High
France	51	36	High	High	High	High
Germany	58	40	High	Moderate	High	High
Great Britain	56	31	High	High	High	High
Italy	66	42	Moderate	Moderate	High	High
Japan	54	23	Moderate	High	High	High
Mexico	54	17	Low moderate	Low moderate	Moderate	Low
Netherlands	57	28	High	High	High moderate	High
Spain	66	44	High moderate	High moderate	High	Moderate
United States	72	15	High	High	Low	High

Sources: Adapted by the authors from *Going Global: International Opportunities for Retailers* (New York: Ernst & Young, 1993), various pages; and Coopers & Lybrand, "Retailing in the 21st Century: A Global Perspective," *Chain Store Age Executive* (1993), Special Issue, various pages.

physical structure of outlets, operations, advertising messages, product lines, and other factors have to be adapted to local conditions and needs?

For example,

> Compared to the 50 states [in the United States], with their principal language of English and overall federal law and tax systems, Europe is a jigsaw of cultures, languages, and nationalistic differences that will not be instantly diluted by the removal of internal trade barriers.
>
> This patchwork includes those who have a general suspicion of financial institutions and therefore a low use of credit (the French); a nation of families who wouldn't dream of driving out to breakfast on a Sunday morning (the British); a country with longer trading hours than the 10 A.M. to 10:00 P.M. of the United States, but where a majority of the shops close for three hours in the middle of the day (Spain); and the most economically powerful country in Europe whose citizens are notoriously price-conscious and do much of their food shopping in no-frills discount stores (Germany).[31]

Table 3–2 shows some of the retailing-related differences in various countries. Next are examples of how retailing is conducted by domestic firms in three nations: Japan, Poland, and India.

Until recently, traditional family-owned businesses (small mom-and-pop stores) virtually dominated the retailing environment in Japan. These 2+ million businesses were able to exert vast control over legislation with regard to operating hours and store size, thus preventing evening hours and keeping large stores from opening. The small store owners still sweep the streets in front of their stores, greet people returning home with the phrase "okaeri nasai" (welcome home), are hesitant to use sales promotions that could lead to price wars, and do not criticize competitors in ads. But changes in various laws have somewhat reduced the impact of these firms—and

[31] Ian Waddell, "Global Challenges Set the Scene for 1992," *Chain Store Age Executive* (May 1990), p. 190.

allowed the entry of foreign firms like Toys "R" Us. In addition, Japan is striving to improve an "antiquated and inefficient distribution system, in which wholesalers sometimes send a truck to deliver five boxes of detergent and the abacus [rather than the computer] reigns supreme."[32]

In post-communist Poland, the majority of stores in such cities as Warsaw are still government-owned (although there are a growing number of privately owned retail outlets). At government shops, "the floors are dirty and the attitude of employees toward customers ranges from indifference to resentment. Want a plastic bag? It's an extra cost. And most purchases cannot be concluded without that quintessential Polish ritual: the requirement that customers fish through every pocket to provide the necessary change. In Poland, the onus of making change is on the shopper rather than on the shopkeeper."[33]

India is a country with well over 850 million people. During the 21st century, it is expected to become the largest consumer market in the world. At present, the retailing system there is quite underdeveloped:

> India's fledgling retail industry is dominated by small family-owned shops and open-air booths serving neighborhoods. Each specializes in a single product category like textiles, shoes, utensils, or spices. Customer relationships and tradition play a very important role. These shops are usually family-run and passed down from generation to generation. This retail structure is now a necessity due to the large, poor, immobile rural population. Yet, the retail structure is becoming more international, sophisticated, and impersonal due to increases in geographic and economic mobility being fueled by an aggressive trade liberalization program.[34]

U.S. Retailers and Foreign Markets

Here are examples of U.S. retailers with high involvement in foreign markets.

Toys "R" Us has been active internationally for years, and now owns and operates more than 300 stores abroad (up from about 75 in 1990). Among the 20 or so countries in which it has stores are Australia, Canada, France, Germany, Great Britain, Japan, Malaysia, Singapore, and Spain. In 1994, it entered into its first foreign franchising agreements, thus entering Saudi Arabia, the United Arab Emirates, and other Mideast nations: "With cultural differences and various laws prohibiting complete ownership by foreign entities in many foreign nations, the franchising concept will allow us to get into countries and regions of the world we may never have considered.[35] See Figure 3–9.

Many of the world's leading mail-order retailers are U.S.-based, including American Express, Avon, Citicorp, Franklin Mint, and Reader's Digest. These firms are efficient and have a clear handle on customers and distribution methods. However, as of now, total worldwide mail-order sales (for both U.S. and foreign firms) outside the United States are only a fraction of those in the United States. Thus, there is great growth potential in foreign markets.

Executives are "masterminding an ambitious expansion that is transforming stodgy old J.C. Penney into a major international retailer." Stores are being built in Canada. It is adding 1-million square feet of retail space in Japan. It is looking into Chile

[32] David E. Sanger, "Japanese Give in Grudgingly on a New Way of Shopping," *New York Times* (November 12, 1990), pp. A1, D8.

[33] Stephen Engelberg, "A Treat for Night Owls in Poland," *New York Times* (August 21, 1990), pp. D1, D3.

[34] Coopers & Lybrand, "Retailing in the 21st Century: A Global Perspective," *Chain Store Age Executive* (1993), Special Issue, p. 41.

[35] "Toys 'R' Us Plans to Open 115 Stores During the Year," *New York Times* (January 12, 1994), p. D4; and Joseph Pereira, "Toys 'R' Us to Buy Stock for $1 Billion," *Wall Street Journal* (January 12, 1994), p. A3.

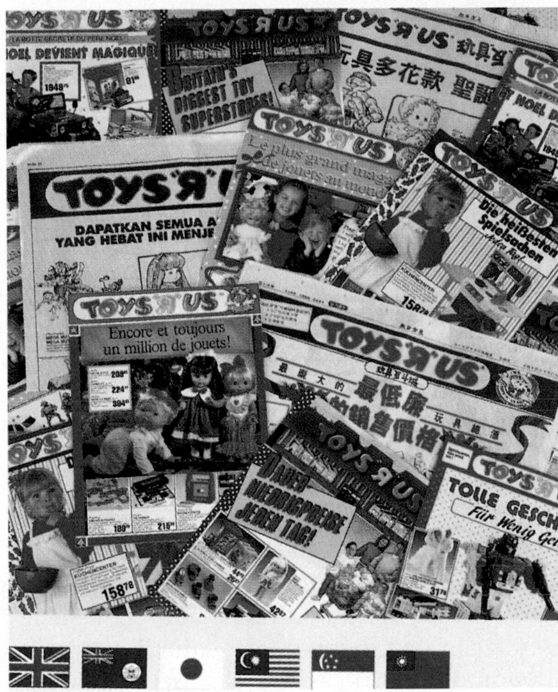

FIGURE 3–9
Toys "R" Us Around the World
Reprinted by permission.

because shoppers there are eager to buy U.S. goods. The firm has licensed stores in Portugal, Singapore, and other nations; and it has been negotiating for more in Greece. The company is considering anchoring a mall in Taiwan and also looking at Thailand and Indonesia. It has mail-order catalogs in Brazil, Russia, and Thailand; and it has translated a version of its U.S. catalog into Spanish to appeal to the Latin American market.[36]

For the past decade, the majority of McDonald's new restaurants have been located outside the United States. Today, foreign sales (from outlets in more than 65 nations) account for 40 per cent of total systemwide revenues. Besides having restaurants throughout the United States and Western Europe, McDonald's also has outlets in such countries as Argentina, Brazil, Brunei, Canada, Costa Rica, Czech Republic, Hungary, Japan, Mexico, New Zealand, Philippines, Poland, Russia, Venezuela, and Yugoslavia. The restaurant in Russia is the largest in the company. It has 700 inside seats, 200 outside seats, and 27 cash registers. In a single day, it has served more than 20,000 customers. A "Big Mac" costs the U.S. equivalent of $6.00. Although no breakfast items or children's "Happy Meals" are served, apple pie is extremely popular.[37]

Avon recognizes that in the United States and other developed industrial nations, its traditional direct-selling approach has been losing popularity: "We applied all the tried-and-true stimuli to our direct-selling system—changes in recruiting, incentives, commissions, brochures, and more. We had some success. But, we didn't stop the decline of customer purchasing activity. Research told us our problems were image and access." Thus, the firm is now quite active in developing nations across Latin America and the Pacific Rim where "the traditional Avon system works wonderfully"—which is why developing nations presently account for 27 per cent of company sales. For instance, "in China, women are so eager for Avon products that we sold a projected six-month inventory in only two weeks. Similarly, in Poland, we offer customers access to cosmetics and personal care items never before available to them."[38]

[36] Bob Ortega, "Penney Pushes Abroad in Unusually Big Way as It Pursues Growth," *Wall Street Journal* (February 1, 1994), pp. A1, A6.

[37] *McDonald's 1993 Annual Report,* various pages; and Rosemarie Boyle, "McDonald's Gives Soviets Something 'Worth Waiting For'," *Advertising Age* (March 19, 1990), p. 61.

[38] *Avon Products 1992 Annual Report,* pp. 2, 5.

FOREIGN RETAILERS AND THE U.S. MARKET

A large number of foreign retailers have entered the United States, so as to appeal to the world's most affluent mass market. Here are three examples.

Ikea is a Swedish-based home-furnishings retailer with stores in about 25 countries; in 1985, Ikea opened its first U.S. store in Pennsylvania. Since then, it has also opened stores in such areas as California, Maryland, New Jersey, New York, and Washington, D.C.—a total of 12 U.S. stores in all. The company features durable, stylish ready-to-assemble furniture at "rock-bottom prices." Because Ikea positions itself as a dominant furniture retailer, its stores are large and have enormous selections. For instance, the outlet in Elizabeth, New Jersey (the U.S. flagship store) occupies 270,000 square feet and has a playroom for children and other customer amenities. The firm generates annual sales of $350 million from its U.S. stores.[39]

Germany's Aldi is a supermarket chain that ranks among the world's top 20 retailers (in sales). There are about 400 Aldi stores in the United States, with more than $1.2 billion in yearly revenues. Most U.S. stores are in the west: "The stores don't advertise; they aren't even in the phone book. Stores are located away from costly real-estate such as strip malls. They generally measure 8,000, one-third the size of a typical grocery store. Aldi situates mostly in farm towns or blue-collar neighborhoods. It likes dealing with big working-class families that eat at home and eat heartily."[40]

The Body Shop is a British-based chain that specializes in natural cosmetics and lotions such as Peppermint Foot Lotion, Passion Fruit skin cleansers, and White Musk Shower Gel—"products that cleanse, beautify, and soothe the human form." There are well over 900 Body Shop stores in 41 countries, including the United States. As of mid-1993, the firm had 133 U.S. stores, a figure the company plans to increase by 50 per year. U.S. stores already contribute roughly 15 per cent of overall Body Shop sales.[41]

Besides extending their traditional businesses into the United States, a number of foreign firms have acquired major ownership interests in American retailers. According to the U.S. Department of Commerce, sales of U.S.-based retail stores owned by foreign companies are more than $20 billion annually. Foreign ownership in U.S. retailers is highest for general merchandise stores, food stores, and apparel and accessory stores. Some of the U.S. acquisitions made by foreign firms over the last two decades are shown in Table 3–3.

Both U.S. retailers operating in foreign markets and foreign firms operating in the U.S. market need to be careful in their approach:

> Being nimble is perhaps the most important of all managerial traits for global managers. Successful retail organizations need to be structured for nimbleness to respond appropriately and quickly to changes in the market. There are few retail markets that aren't changing. America is aging, and the "silver streakers" are changing the way we do business. Consumers have less time to shop, yet they want better, more personalized service. Information moves so quickly that fashion trends that once took months to travel from Paris to New York to Dallas now fly half way around the world overnight. A failure to spot changes that make old ideas worthless can be the management equivalent of putting on blinders, and almost always results in markdowns, unsold merchandise, or even business failure.[42]

[39] Richard W. Stevenson, "Ikea's New Realities: Recession and Aging Consumers," *New York Times* (April 25, 1993), Section 3, p. 4; and Sweeney, Hyde, and Kalish, *Retail World: Window of Opportunity*, p. 20.

[40] Marcia Berss, "Bag Your Own," *Forbes* (February 1, 1993), p. 70.

[41] Judith Valente, "Body Shop Has a Few Aches and Pains," *Wall Street Journal* (August 6, 1993), pp. B1–B2.

[42] Lou Grabowsky, "Globalization: Reshaping the Retail Marketplace," *Arthur Andersen Retailing Issues Letter* (November 1989), p. 5.

TABLE 3–3 Selected Acquisitions of U.S. Retailers by Foreign Firms

U.S. Retailer	Principal Business	Foreign Acquirer	Country of Acquirer
Burger King	Restaurants	Grand Metropolitan	Great Britain
Brooks Brothers	Apparel	Marks & Spencer	Great Britain
Carvel	Ice cream	Investcorp	Bahrain
Great Atlantic & Pacific (A&P)	Supermarkets	Tengelmann	Germany
International House of Pancakes (IHOP)	Restaurants	Wienerwald	Switzerland
Kay Jewelers	Jewelry	Ratners Group	Great Britain
Motel 6	Economy motels	Accor	France
Saks Fifth Avenue	Department stores	Investcorp	Bahrain
Spiegel	Mail-order and specialty stores	Otto Versand	Germany
7-Eleven (Southland)	Convenience stores	Ito-Yokado	Japan
Talbots	Apparel	Jusco Ltd.	Japan

SUMMARY

1. *To examine demographic, life-style, consumerism, and ethics and social responsibility trends—and consider the impact of them on retailing* To be successful in the long-term, retailers need to anticipate and plan for the changing environment, with its attendant opportunities and risks. Thus, far-sighted retailers will study the environment on a regular basis.

   U.S. demographic forecasts show a population increase of 12 million people between 1995 and 2000, a low growth rate (percentagewise), and an aging populace. Other important U.S. demographic trends include the high number of firstborn babies, later first marriages, the growing number of households (because of more one-person households), relatively high population mobility, the steady movement of the population to suburban communities, the large number of working women, and the rising number of higher-income families (although there will also be a high number of poor families).

   Life-style trends will include different and expanding roles for women and increased consumer sophistication and confidence. Many consumers will experience a poverty of time and will seek greater convenience in shopping. In addition, consumers will continue placing importance on self-fulfillment and a value orientation.

   Consumerism activities (those practices designed to protect consumers) involve government, business, and independent organizations. Four consumer rights are considered basic: the right to safety, the right to be informed, the right to choose, and the right to be heard. Many retailers have already implemented voluntary plans to aid consumers.

   Ethical retailers act in a trustworthy, fair, honest, and respectful manner with each of their constituencies (customers, the general public, employees, suppliers, competitors, and others). Firms are more likely to avoid unethical behavior if they have written ethics codes, communicate them to employees, monitor and punish poor behavior, and have ethical senior executives. Retailers perform in a socially responsible manner when they act in the best interests of society—as well as themselves. Many are doing this through recycling and conservation programs, and other efforts.

2. *To consider the effects of technological advances* The major technological trends affecting retailers will focus on electronic banking (transactions through some form of automatic teller machines, including those in stores), video-ordering systems (consumers' ordering goods and services in a store or

from their homes after seeing them listed or described on video-display monitors, television programs, PC monitors, or VCRs or videodisc players), and computerizing operations (via computerized checkouts and various software applications).

3. *To describe the ways in which retail institutions are, and will be, responding to environmental trends* Many retail institutional changes will occur because of the evolving environment. For individual firms, a retailing effectiveness checklist can aid in rating future preparedness.

   Each of these approaches will be popular for different firms, depending on their strengths, weaknesses, and goals: mergers—whereby separately owned retailers join together; diversification—whereby a retailer becomes active in businesses outside its normal operations; and downsizing—whereby unprofitable stores are closed or divisions are sold. Sometimes, single companies will use all three approaches.

   More firms will engage in risk-minimization retailing and strive to hold down initial investment costs, as well as operating costs. There are many ways to do this.

   A challenge for any store-based retailer will be to be perceived as a destination store, thereby worth a special shopping trip.

4. *To discuss the international dimension of retailing* International retailing, encompassing both U.S. firms in foreign markets and foreign firms in U.S. markets, will continue to rise substantially in the future.

   When entering a foreign market, a retailer must consider institutional, consumer, store location, operations, merchandising, pricing, and image and promotion factors. Opportunities and risks need to be evaluated, as well as the applicability of standardization: A retailer must decide how much of its domestic strategy should be modified to address foreign needs and legal requirements.

Key Terms

opportunities (p. 62)
threats (p. 62)
demographics (p. 62)
real income (p. 66)
life-styles (p. 66)
poverty of time (p. 68)
self-fulfillment (p. 69)
consumerism (p. 70)
ethics (p. 72)
social responsibility (p. 73)
electronic banking (p. 75)
video-ordering system (p. 76)
retailing effectiveness checklist (p. 79)
mergers (p. 79)
diversification (p. 79)
downsizing (p. 79)
risk-minimization retailing (p. 81)
destination store (p. 82)
standardization (p. 84)

Questions for Discussion

1. Comment on this statement: "Strategic planning must take into account the nature of environmental factors in terms of their certainty of occurrence and magnitude of change, their effect on the retailer's business, and the time required for the retailer to react properly."
2. What impact will the overall rate of U.S. population growth have on retailers?
3. How should supermarkets modify their strategies in response to the changing gender roles of U.S. males and females? What elements of their strategies should not be modified? Explain your answer.
4. How will consumer sophistication and confidence affect retailers? Will they affect all types of retailers? Explain your answer.
5. Differentiate between consumerism and social responsibility from the perspective of a retailer.
6. Describe three unethical, but legal, acts on the part of retailers that you have encountered. How have you reacted in each case?
7. What are the pros and cons of ATMs? As a retailer, would you want an ATM in your store? Why or why not?
8. Will the time come when most consumer purchases are made through some form of video-ordering system? Explain your answer.
9. What is a retailing effectiveness checklist? How could a small retailer use it? A large retailer?
10. Explain how a retailer could utilize all three of these approaches at the same time: mergers, diversification, and downsizing?
11. Describe the advantages and disadvantages of risk-minimization retailing.
12. What is a destination store? Why is it so important for a retailer to be perceived as one?
13. How could a standardized strategy on the part of a U.S. retailer fail when introduced into Canada, a country with many similarities to the United States?
14. What are the opportunities and risks facing a U.S. retailer that enters India?
15. Why do you think so many foreign-based firms have acquired U.S. retailers?

Case 1
Foodland in Hawaii*

Foodland Super Market, Hawaii's largest grocery chain, operates 29 stores on four of Hawaii's eight islands. Its 1993 sales were close to $350 million; and this comprised 31 per cent of Hawaii's total grocery sales. Foodland was started by Maurice Sullivan, a Buffalo, New York, resident stationed in Hawaii during World War II. Sullivan realized that, unlike in the mainland United States, Hawaii had no self-service supermarket. He returned after the war to start Foodland as an independent supermarket. Over time, it grew to be a chain.

The overall environment that Foodland encounters in Hawaii is a difficult one: The population is demographically diverse. Operating costs are high. The competitive environment is tough and intensifying. People are environmentally sensitive.

Hawaii's population is diverse. Fifty-eight per cent of the population is Asian or Pacific Islander, 31 per cent is white, 7 per cent is Hispanic, 2 per cent is African-American, and 2 per cent is comprised of other groups. Thus, Foodland caters to the special food preferences of ethnic groups with such offerings as guava cake; a fruit drink made of a mixture of passion fruit, orange, and guava; goat meat; and poke, bite-sized pieces of various types of fish. Foodland must not only appeal to these groups, but also understand the demographic differences that exist for each store location. As an example, customers of stores located near military bases have different demographic characteristics in terms of ethnic makeup, age distribution, and family size than stores having few military shoppers.

Foodland, like all Hawaiian supermarkets, has an expensive operating structure. There are high freight and handling costs for grocery products, fixtures, and supplies received from the mainland (Hawaii is 2,400 miles from San Francisco). The costs of transporting and handling goods among the four islands where Foodland has stores are high. Lastly, Hawaii has the highest electrical rates (based on cost per kilowatt hour) in the United States due to its reliance on oil as a fuel to power electric generators. Thus, Foodland's operating costs are 25 to 26 per cent of net sales revenue. The corresponding figure for a mainland U.S.-based supermarket chain is 20 per cent. To achieve its planned net profit goals, Foodland requires 27 to 28 per cent gross margins; this compares to 22 per cent for the average mainland-based chain.

Although Foodland's key competitors have been supermarket chains such as Safeway and independents, Wal-Mart, Sam's, Price/Costco, and Kmart have announced intentions of expanding into Hawaii. In an effort to retain its market share, Foodland has increased its emphasis on perishables, created its own Sack N Save warehouse store division, and developed a new advertising campaign. Perishables (meat, produce, floral, seafood, bakery, and deli items) now account for 45 per cent of Foodland's total sales; it estimates that this percentage will increase in the long run. The chain has expanded its bakery, deli, and produce operations in the belief that its new competitors cannot match its quality in these areas. In some cases, such as with the popular Maui onion, Foodland has developed long-term contracts with local farmers that enable the firm to secure virtually all of the farmer's produce. This strategy is effective in locking out competition for some locally-grown produce.

Foodland's Sack N Save warehouses feature a limited selection of goods, buying-club-sized stores, multipacks, and inexpensive fixtures. The role of the Sack N Save stores is to be an alternative format for those customers interested primarily in price. Foodland hopes that its Sack N Save stores (that do not require an annual membership fee) will pre-empt the growth of Sam's and Price/Costco, two of the buying clubs that have earmarked Hawaii for growth. The chain also feels that these competitors will have to charge higher prices in Hawaii than in the mainland United States due to higher operating costs. Although profit margins are lower in Sack N Save stores than in traditional Foodland units, the warehouse stores have a lower labor

* The material in this case is drawn from Murray and Neil Raphel, "The POGs Are Coming!" *Progressive Grocer* (October 1993), p. 15; and "Supermarket Recycles Food Waste," *Chain Store Age Executive* (August 1993), p. 76.

cost—due in part to groceries accounting for 50 per cent of Sack N Save's total sales versus 43 per cent in the average Foodland unit. The average transaction size is $19.00 for Sack N Save versus $16.75 for Foodland.

Foodland's new advertising campaign focuses on its being an island institution. One television commercial features Hawaiian music and shows Pacific-Islander workers enjoying their jobs at Foodland. The commercial ends with the lines: "We give you heart. You give us soul. Foodland: Doing Our Best For *You*." Since most of Foodland's sales are to islanders as opposed to tourists, the latter are not regarded as an important target market.

Foodland is environmentally sensitive. It is testing a recycling program in four stores. With this program, organic food from the produce, deli, and bakery departments is picked up and processed; the food is then recycled into fertilizer, animal feed, and electricity. Foodland estimates that recycling the waste from just one store will divert more than 84 tons of waste from city landfills each year. The program also saves Foodland money because recycling costs less than Foodland's dumping fees. For other programs, Foodland recycles meat, seafood, and produce scrap and waste into agricultural feed. It also recycles all corrugated cardboard and office paper.

QUESTIONS

1. Describe the opportunities and threats represented by Foodland's culturally diverse clientele.
2. How can Foodland reduce its high operating costs? Explain your answer.
3. Evaluate Foodland's strategy of developing the Sack N Save format to pre-empt competition.
4. Comment on Foodland's recycling programs.

VIDEO QUESTIONS ON FOODLAND IN HAWAII

1. Compare the performance of the average Foodland and Sack N Save store.
2. Evaluate Foodland's perishables strategy.

CASE 2

Hayes Appliance Store: Meeting New Forms of Competition†

Walter Hayes has operated Hayes Appliance Store in a similar manner since founding the store twelve years ago. Although the store is located in a small community of 75,000 people, it serves a trading area of some 200,000 people. Hayes' store sells a wide range of major appliances (such as refrigerators, dishwashers, and washing machines) and small appliances (such as blenders, electric frying pans, and microwave ovens). While the best-selling models and brands of each appliance are displayed in the store, customers seeking other models are shown manufacturers' catalogs. Hayes feels his limited inventory policy frees valuable showroom space, lowers inventory investment, and reduces the number of display models that eventually must be sold at discount prices.

Hayes prides himself on his store's reputation for fair dealing. Unlike some discounters with artificially high prices that are lowered for special sales events, Hayes charges the same prices throughout the year. Other appliance dealers advertise promotional goods (such as television sets without remote controls or washing machines without bleach dispensers) to generate store traffic and then trade customers up to more costly and more profitable merchandise. In contrast, Hayes consistently advertises middle-of-the-line and top-of-the-line models. And Hayes' prices always include delivery, hookup to existing plumbing lines and electrical outlets, and re-

† This case was prepared and written by Professor Ronald D. Michman, Shippensburg University.

moval and disposal of customers' old appliances. Other retailers charge between $35 and $100 for comparable services or do not even offer these services.

Hayes Appliance's yearly sales grew consistently at 5 to 7 per cent until two years ago. Annual revenues peaked at $2 million; they then declined to $1,800,000 last year and to $1,250,000 this year. As a member of the regional Independent Appliance Retailers Association, Walter Hayes has learned that other independents in his geographic area have faced similar circumstances. Even though the area had relatively few appliance discounters in the past, they are now beginning to target this geographic area.

Hayes attributes his revenue loss to the opening of two new stores in his trading area: Kmart and Discount City. Kmart has taken sales away from Hayes in the small appliance area. Discount City, an outlet of an eighteen-store regional chain, has taken sales away in both major appliances and small apliances. Although Hayes estimates that, on average, Kmart and Discount City underprice him by 10 per cent, Discount City's prices do not include delivery, hookup, and installation of new appliances or removal and disposal of old appliances. He also estimates that when Kmart advertises a small appliance, it could easily be 15 to 20 per cent less than Hayes' price.

Walter Hayes has prepared listings of the competitive advantages and disadvantages of each competitor versus Hayes Appliance—based on his own observations, conversations with noncompeting retailers, and discussions with a retailing professor at the local state college. He believes his listings accurately portray the competitive environment. See Tables 1 and 2.

Through additional research, Hayes knows that the ratio of customers walking out of his store compared to those making a purchase has increased this year to 12 to 1, in contrast to the 8 to 1 ratio last year. An analysis of the walk-out group revealed that the majority desired to learn more about the appliances and to comparison shop.

Table 1 Competitive Advantages and Disadvantages of Hayes Appliance Versus Kmart for Small Appliances

Competitive Advantages of Hayes Appliance

- Hayes has better trained and more knowledgeable sales personnel.
- Hayes personnel provide more personalized attention to each customer.
- Hayes has lower employee turnover; some customers are loyal to particular salespeople.
- Many shoppers prefer to buy from a local merchant.
- Kmart does not stock some exclusive brands and some high-end models.

Competitive Disadvantages of Hayes Appliance

- Kmart has a much more flexible return policy.
- Kmart can underprice Hayes by 10 to 20 per cent.
- Kmart offers a family-oriented, one-stop shopping environment.
- Kmart is open 7 days per week versus 6 days for Hayes; Kmart is also open longer hours.
- Kmart has a large and convenient parking area surrounding the store.
- Kmart appeals to those shoppers that like a self-service environment.
- Kmart has a lower cost structure than Hayes due to economies of scale.
- Kmart extensively advertises through the use of freestanding inserts in Sunday newspapers.

Table 2 Competitive Advantages and Disadvantages of Hayes Appliance Versus Discount City for Major Appliances

Competitive Advantages of Hayes Appliance

- Hayes has better trained and more knowledgeable sales personnel.
- Hayes personnel provide more personalized attention to each customer.
- Hayes has lower employee turnover; some customers are loyal to particular salespeople.
- Many shoppers prefer to buy from a local merchant.
- Discount City does not stock some exclusive brands and some high-end models.
- Hayes delivers and installs the new appliance, and removes and discards the old appliance as part of the purchase price.
- Hayes provides more flexible delivery services; for example, it can guarantee delivery after 5 P.M. for working couples.
- Hayes will deliver appliances based on telephone orders. This is important for people who are confined to their homes due to illness, lack of a car, etc.
- Hayes deliverers are trained to show consumers how to use appliances.

Competitive Disadvantages of Hayes Appliance

- Discount City can underprice Hayes by 10 per cent or more if consumers elect to deliver and install the appliance themselves.
- Discount City generates a substantial amount of store traffic from its advertising of promotional goods. It is able to convert much of this traffic into sales of higher-priced goods.
- Discount City generates high profit margins from its sales of extended warranties to consumers.
- Discount City is open 7 days per week versus 6 days for Hayes.
- Discount City has a lower cost structure than Hayes due to operating economies and its ability to buy manufacturer closeouts and end-of-season goods.

Questions

1. Develop three alternative strategies that Walter Hayes should consider in response to the new competitors.
2. Which of the strategies should Hayes select? Fully explain your choice.
3. How can Hayes adapt its strategy to better serve working women? Poverty of time life-styles?
4. Can Hayes Appliance become a destination store? Explain your answer.

PART 1 COMPREHENSIVE CASE

Retailing—The Global Mandate*

Introduction

Business Week features a cover story on companies setting up shop in China. The front page of the *Wall Street Journal* notes Lands' End's London opening. Toys "R" Us sets up shop in Japan, J.C. Penney in the Middle East, and Dillard's in Mexico. From the publicity, you might conclude that retailers have jumped in with both feet and are going global aggressively. The reality is less dramatic, however.

Having just returned from a year of travel around the world, I can report that while there is indeed an imperative to "go global," currently it's more talk than actual movement. During my travels, I observed the emerging trends and pitfalls that the wise retailer will heed. The retailers who will reap the most from the global market will be aggressive but prudent, carefully weighing diverse considerations.

My own travels stemmed from Arthur Andersen's ongoing project to study the best practices of some of the leading worldwide companies in eight industries. I led our retail industry initiative, where we studied 35 retailers in seven countries on four continents.

U.S. and Foreign Trends

In the United States, retailers are starting to demonstrate a significant interest in global markets. This is a healthy, important interest for several reasons. First, the U.S. market for retailing is mature—there is more retail space than customers. Retail square footage grew 58 per cent in the 1980s, growing far more than sales or the population. The result is that per-capita square footage rose from 13 in 1980 to 18 square feet today. Overstoring, coupled with the ongoing effects of a slow-growth economy, means American retailers who want to continue growing must look outside the U.S. market.

The non-U.S. retail environment is changing as significantly as the United States. There are trading blocks developing which will permanently change buying patterns. Although "EU 92" (the unification of Western Europe) has not proven the bonanza predicted by some, it has brought about change. The North American Free Trade Agreement (NAFTA) is now a reality, but even without formal legal sanction, the pace of trade between Mexico, the U.S., and Canada increased. Some Asian countries are also discussing the formation of new trading blocks.

Sometimes, U.S. companies behave as if the rest of the world waits on them. When I ask a U.S. audience how many of them have been to foreign countries to study retailers and to examine cultural differences, there are very few responses. Yet, it is a rare event that a retailer outside the United States has not thoroughly studied U.S. retailers. Outside the United States, many large retailers already operate beyond their borders.

To the world traveler, the United States is still the world's leader in retailing. Most exciting, innovative concepts are American-born. Yet, it would be a mistake to assume that globalization is as easy as opening the box and re-creating concepts already tested in the United States. The trick is to take advantage of the world's fascination with Western habits, while understanding that each market has its own unique cultural and economic environment.

The world is adopting "Westernized" as never before. As I travel and visit people in their homes, I see significant similarities to the U.S. consumer. This hasn't always been the case. Once, when I lived in Australia, there was a significant difference between Australia's standard of living and America's. That gap has closed. Today, an Australian home might have two VCRs and multiple televisions, and the family watches the same Hollywood fare I watch. Children in North Dallas look like children in Japan. Backward baseball caps with their favorite logos, untucked shirts, and fancy athletic shoes are *de rigueur*. A thousand years from now, historians will identify us as the culture that brought the world Levi's, Coca-Cola, and CNN.

The increasing taste for consumer goods in general—particularly all things Western—is a powerful lure for American companies. This, combined with changing economic and political conditions, as well as the mature United States market, present a unique set of circumstances—circumstances that spell opportunity, but require a challenging decision-making process. Indeed, these opportunities exist; but where does a retailer go? And how does a company approach the decision-making process?

If you step back, retailing is already international to some degree.

In Spain, for example, a decade ago, retailing was basically a mom-and-pop affair, owned locally. Today, more than half of Spain's retail sales are derived from stores that are not Spanish-owned.

* The material in this case was prepared and written by Larry R. Katzen, Managing Partner of the Arthur Andersen & Co. Worldwide Retail Industry Practice. It originally appeared in "Retailing—The Global Mandate," *Arthur Andersen Retailing Issues Letter* (Center for Retailing Studies, Texas A&M University: September 1993), pp. 1–5. Reprinted by permission.

Here in the United States, we already see names such as Ikea and Benetton. Moreover, 20 per cent of the food retailing in the United States is already owned by non-U.S. companies, and include such names as Food Lion, Loblaw, Ahold, Hannaford, Shaws, Aldi, and others. In New York, Country Road, an Australian specialty store, recently opened its first store—as did a posh Japanese store—Mitsukoshi.

U.S. retailers are also seeking new markets. Toys "R" Us expanded to Australia and Japan, as well as several countries in Europe and the Pacific Rim. Companies such as Price/Costco, Staples, T.J. Maxx, and Pier 1 imports are expanding to Great Britain. In addition, Kmart is pioneering in Eastern Europe and J.C. Penney is doing the same in the Middle East. Still, a global perspective shows that U.S. retailers have moved more slowly than those in other countries.

Why U.S. Retailers Have Not Been Global Enough

A study by Management Horizons (the retail consulting division of Price Waterhouse) examined the top 100 publicly-held retailers in the world in 1980 and again a decade later. It found that the U.S. market share decreased from 46 per cent of the world's sales to 35 per cent. I am puzzled when I examine these positions because I believe that U.S. retailing concepts still lead the world in innovation. Concepts such as warehouse clubs and the discount store originated in the United States. So what's holding us back?

I have asked retail executives the question, "What are you thinking about?" Many U.S. retailers articulated self-imposed barriers. Here are a few that I heard frequently:

- "It didn't work in the past." Pointing to past failures—of J.C. Penney in Europe or Sears in South America—becomes reason to fear to tread outside home territory.
- "It's too complex." Political, economic, and cultural differences, on top of the different business practices and the challenge of travel appear to reinforce the appeal of simple and manageable operations on the home turf.
- "There's still untapped market potential here." This appears in the annual reports of companies like The Limited. The argument goes, "Why squander precious financial and human resources elsewhere?"
- "It will dilute our management focus. American business schools have taught well the risks of distracting management."
- "Real estate is too expensive." This is also heard as "It's too expensive," or "It doesn't fit our economic model."

Having traveled broadly for the past two years, I now question the legitimacy of these concerns. Again, recall that few U.S. retailers have actually visited potential new markets in person or observed consumers and competing retailers. Yet, non-U.S. retailers are observing and studying daily in the United States. There is no more effective way to approach globalization than to study potential global markets first-hand. As you begin to understand cultural and economic differences, you can begin to tailor your concepts and skills to satisfy the needs of those markets. Would the best approach be a franchise, joint venture, or even a strategic alliance? How strong is your name? Will it be well-recognized in the new country?

The more one visits different countries and studies their retailers, the firmer the conclusion that each country is unique. Although Walter Wriston, former chairman of Citicorp, has said that sovereignty is obsolete, it would be more accurate to say that sovereignty is dissolving and the evolution of a world economy is not an accomplished fact. It is critical, at this point, to study and explore each country and not be unduly influenced by others.

With this as background, let me share with you my first-hand impressions of the significant opportunities that exist around the world for retailers that want to grow.

Opportunities Around the World

China

How can you ignore a country with one-quarter of the world's population? About 1.2 billion people live in China! Political changes are largely responsible for creating a climate more favorable to entrepreneurs and business investment. The result is increasing incomes and, as night follows day, increasing incomes create consumer demand. Newspapers report Chinese consumers spending on Rolex watches, TVs, VCRs, designer clothing, automobiles—whatever they can get their hands on.

Some ask how the Chinese can have excess disposable income when the average household income is only $2,000 a year. First, averages are misleading when you have a 1.2 billion base. It is estimated that only 1 per cent of the population is "affluent," but that translates into 12 million people! Second, China may give new meaning to the phrase "pent-up consumer demand." Moreover, it's not only the privileged few in China who represent a potential market. This is a country where housing costs for families are subsidized, and where most individuals pay no income tax. Basic consumer goods such as clothes, cooking utensils, fashion jewelry, and makeup are potentially within the grasp of many Chinese consumers.

For example, Hush Puppies have become a hot item, and the exporter who closed that deal was quoted saying happily to the *Detroit News*, "The Chinese have a great desire for branded products." It's a desire they can afford to indulge as the economy is booming—estimates are for a 7 per cent annual growth rate over the next decade. Airline passenger traffic is growing by 25 per cent annually. Motorola put together a low-cost plan to produce paging devices for the Asian market. It is selling the entire weekly output of 10,000 units in China alone; a pager with a year's service costs $200 (U.S.).

Australia

At the opposite end of the spectrum, Australia is the size of the United States, and has a population less than New York City! Approximately 80 per cent of the population is in two cities: Melbourne and Sydney. Population and economic growth are flat. I lived in Australia during the 1970s, and have visited periodically since then. Certainly, the two countries have similar tastes and interests. Within this environment, one lone retailer—Coles Myer Ltd.—has cornered 25 per cent of total retail sales, probably making it the most dominant retailer in any democracy in the world. Interestingly, a major U.S. retailer has minority investment interest in this company.

In Australia, global competition is a recent arrival. One of the Japanese companies participating in Arthur Andersen's Global Best Practices study opened a beautiful store just across from Myer's main store. The old saying that competition brings out the best in you is evident in Australia, where the dominant retailer is striving to become a *world-class* retailer, rather than a first-class *Australian* retailer. Despite its isolation from the rest of the world, the Australian retailing scene will see significant change. It is ripe for new retail concepts—such as warehouse clubs—which provide quality merchandise at lower prices.

An American company looking at the Australian market needs to expect a very different environment, however. Labor unions are quite strong and control the trading hours to the extent that even limited Sunday hours are a recent development. These attitudes will need to be modified if Australian retailers want to become globally competitive. Australian retailers will also need to take advantage of a worldwide trend to maximize the use of technology, streamline operations, get close to the customer, and lower costs.

Jim Manzi, of Lotus Development Corporation, says investment in technology and information is the "first essential, absolute rule for companies that want to succeed in the global marketplace." While you might expect to hear that from a top Lotus executive, there is a great differential across the world. Technology is certainly on the rise, but it is not universally at the same level as the United States. There is virtually no EDI (electronic data interchange) with or quick response order fulfillment from vendors. Yet, the advantages to implementing these in Australia must be placed in the framework of the labor situation and local cultural expectations. Thus, Australia presents an opportunity for retailers who want to pioneer concepts in a country that has Westernized tastes and values.

South Africa

South Africa is isolated for different reasons—more political than geographic or economic. It appears to present similar opportunities for retailers able to surmount the challenges of distance, and although the political situation has made great strides in recent years, a company moving into South Africa may still find the political instability discomfiting. Because of this, virtually all merchandise sold in South Africa is manufactured domestically. The South African rand (the unit of currency) has decreased significantly in value, making imports prohibitive. Yet, during a recent visit, retailers seemed to be doing very well with double-digit sales and profit gains.

The reason for this robust South African growth is that retailers are taking advantage of a significant increase in middle-income groups and catering to diverse populations. In the United States, practically everybody came from somewhere else, and we have adapted to diversity. If you consider this, the skills and creativity of American retailers should be transportable to South Africa. It is no surprise that Great Britain's Marks & Spencer has already created a strategic alliance with one leading South African retailer. This is a good example of a retailer making a foreign investment, but adopting new and creative techniques to adapt to the local market.

South African consumers have a passion for high-quality merchandise and services, similar to consumers in other parts of the world. South African retailers also adopt and utilize technology on a wide scale and have applied new retailing concepts, such as hypermarts (combined supermarket/discount department stores) and specialty stores. However, the stores do not offer the same breadth and depth of merchandise selections as you see in the United States. As an example, department stores might be less than half the size of a department store in the United States or Australia, and much smaller than a Japanese department store. Almost all merchandise offerings are from domestic sources and many new retailing concepts haven't arrived in South Africa. Thus, opportunities certainly exist in South Africa. The key is to take advantage of this market while minimizing the political and economic risks.

Mexico

This is the country most U.S. retailers think of first when thinking about global trends. Indeed, many leading American retailers did not wait for NAFTA. Companies such as Wal-Mart, Price/Costco, J.C. Penney, Dillard's, and Neiman-Marcus are already operating or have announced their intention of operating in Mexico. Some industry analysts are concerned, however. While Mexico has 90 million people, it may become overstored in the short run, if there is a rapid flow of new concepts and names.

Although incomes are relatively low in Mexico, 60 per cent of Mexico's citizens are under the age of 25 with many buying years ahead of them. According to Arthur Andersen's *International Trends in Retailing,* Mexico's growth is likely to outpace most developed countries, and the Mexican inflation rate has been dropping. Further, as inflation decreases, the buying power of consumers will increase in real terms. Foreign investment is welcomed, and the privatization of commercial banks was completed in 1992.

Mexico is *not* Texas moved south. The cultural differences between countries are significant. Mexico is an overwhelming 95 per cent Catholic with a strong, traditional, family orientation. One anecdote illustrates cultural differences as well: Mexico City has staffed its pollution enforcement squad entirely with women because, as officials explained, people are less likely to try to bribe women and more likely to treat them with respect.

Mexico's real value, in my opinion, is as a stepping stone for South America. Nations such as Chile and Argentina present exceptional opportunities for U.S. retailers. They are closer to home than nations on other continents, with many elements familiar to our own political and economic situation, and where retailing will be growing significantly. In fact, some individuals estimate that the retail market in Argentina, Chile, and Brazil is four times as great as that in Mexico.

Japan

This is a country built on the concept of trust. There is no diversity. Everyone in Japan has been born and raised there. How different from the United States! Japanese people aim to please, and their service level is unprecedented. There is no tipping. Communication is open. People are loyal—both to their employer and their family. Although much has been made of recent changes, these traditional characterizations of Japanese society still hold.

The concept of mystery shoppers (people who observe store operations in an unobstrusive way so their presence is unknown to store employees) is abhorrent in Japan. I wish I could illustrate this with pictures of executives' faces when, during our research, we asked Japanese retailers if they use mystery shoppers. They immediately felt that this was spying and espionage, which conflicts with their concept of trust.

Shrinkage (theft) is less than 0.5 per cent of sales, even in the huge department stores in our sample. Japanese are highly educated. It's not uncommon to meet merchants with degrees in law, economics, or literature. Education continues throughout their career. Our findings revealed that not only do Japanese retailers study the world, they also offer three to four times more training to their employees than other retailers around the world.

It's true that Japanese crave branded, high-quality merchandise, that they are suddenly becoming sensitive to cost, and that the Japanese have adopted Western dress and consumer goods wholeheartedly. They do have four selling seasons, not two, and two gift-giving seasons (similar to our Christmas gift-giving season). Japanese department stores are larger than any others in the world. Average sales per square foot approximate $2,500. One store alone may do over one billion dollars in sales! Yet, new retailing formats, common in the United States, have not made their way to Japan.

Rules for the Road

The initial reaction of a U.S. retailer may be, "Terrific, how soon can we start?" But not so fast. If you believe, as many leading retailers in our study did, that it is important for store personnel to mirror the consumer to the extent possible, are you prepared to deal with these cultural differences? How will you recruit, train, manage, and incorporate into your organization individuals with these backgrounds, skills, and interests?

There is very little employee turnover in Japan, and the government there believes in the concept of full employment funded by business. You see this in the elevator operator, pushing the buttons for each floor in the otherwise automatic elevator. It is estimated that there are more than a million surplus workers in Japan, all employed. How will you rationalize them—within your operations—to your national employees or your investors?

I am impressed that virtually every visionary who studies the world believes that those who think through global strategies will be the leaders in the future. My colleague in Global Best Practices, Stanley Marcus (formerly of Neiman-Marcus), made headlines with a prediction that 75 per cent of today's retailers would be gone at the turn of the century. He is sticking to that prediction. Lou Pritchett, retired Procter & Gamble executive, speaking at an Arthur Andersen advanced retailing seminar, commented that, "When the rate of change outside your company is greater than the rate of change inside your company, disaster is imminent."

I find many retailers are now *thinking* about expanding operations into new markets, but few are systematically surveying the opportunities and examining where there may be a fit and how best to exploit the opportunity. Instead, retailers are influenced by what their national competitors are doing, or they pick locations based on nonstrategic criteria such as, "They speak our language."

My advice for companies with global ambitions is to use a highly focused approach. Give consideration to assigning two or three individuals to visit and study areas of opportunity and emerging markets around the world. These people should have a combination of skills including strategic, financial, and real-estate expertise.

Look at the effort as an investment in research and development. The sole purpose of the effort is to research new markets and educate executive management about emerging opportunities. Where possible, the study team should also visit and learn from international companies—even if they are from a different industry—since retailers are newer to global expansion than many other businesses. Finally, this team should supplement its resources with outside financial and legal consultants who are familiar with local markets and customs. These consultants can be invaluable resources to the team by helping them network within each country.

It is important to develop a strategic plan that builds off your company's strengths. A good plan will demonstrate how to leverage those strengths to gain competitive advantage. The plan, therefore, should identify the best sectors of retailing for the company to pursue, as well as formats that best balance risks and related rewards. In some cases, new formats such as license agreements, joint ventures, or even wholesaling your private merchandise, may be considered.

Finally, the company will need to make detailed financial projections based on the recommended approach. These projections should be made over a minimum of a three-to-five-year period, since it may be at least that long before you achieve desired returns. Global expansion requires a longer-term perspective than national expansion. In some cases, expansion strategies might be piloted and fine-tuned before making significant investments and commitments. The benchmarking (standards) you employ will be different than the measures used in your own country, so it is strongly advised that you use local experts to help with the financial projections. In many cases, you will need to adjust your practices to recognize local market differences, rather than force your approach in another country.

In addition, since the income-tax consequences will now be more complex and will significantly affect the liquidity of your investments, an international tax strategy should be formed to support your overall business strategy. This can result in significant rewards as your international business grows.

Final Thoughts

In summary, I recommend that to expand abroad, you should use a dedicated team to study the global market in a highly-focused manner. A strategic business plan should then be developed for each country in which you want to pursue expansion opportunities. The strategic plan should be supported by a financial plan and global income tax strategy that support the overall business plan.

The most important advice, however, is to commit to some expansion in some market. Manzi, of Lotus, preaches that, "Globalization of markets is a very real, inevitable force." Stanley Marcus puts it bluntly: "By the year 2000, big retailers will either be global or they'll be gone." I see retailing as a high-growth industry for those who want to redefine their market and capitalize on their expertise around the world.

Questions

1. Why haven't more U.S. firms engaged in international retailing? Why should they?
2. With regard to the concept of the total retail experience, what points should a company that wants to operate stores in two different countries keep in mind?
3. In deciding *whether* to open a foreign store, what *company* factors should be considered?
4. In deciding *where* to open a foreign store, what *country* factors should be considered?
5. Based on your answer to question 4, rank the countries cited in this case from most to least attractive for U.S.-based retailers and explain why.
6. Present a five-step plan for a U.S.-based retailer to enter a foreign market.
7. Comment on this statement: "By the year 2000, big retailers will either be global or they'll be gone."

PART

2

Situation Analysis

❖ In Part 2, the organizational missions, ownership and management alternatives, goods/service categories, and objectives of a broad range of retail institutions are presented. By understanding the unique attributes of these institutions, prospective and ongoing retailers are better able to develop and adapt their own strategies.

❖ Chapter 4 examines the characteristics of retail institutions on the basis of ownership type: independent, chain, franchise, leased, vertical marketing, and consumer cooperative. The methods used by manufacturers, wholesalers, and retailers to obtain control in a distribution channel are also discussed. An end-of-chapter appendix offers additional information on franchising.

❖ Chapter 5 describes retail institutions on the basis of strategy mix. Three key concepts are introduced: the wheel of retailing, scrambled merchandising, and the retail life cycle. Then, a variety of store-based, nonstore-based, and service versus goods strategy mixes are examined in depth. An end-of-chapter appendix provides further information on direct marketing.

RM

Retail Institutions by Ownership

❖ Chapter Objectives

1. To show the ways in which retail institutions can be classified
2. To study retailers on the basis of ownership type and examine the characteristics of each
3. To explore the methods used by manufacturers, wholesalers, and retailers to obtain control in the distribution channel

Over the past thirty years, independent drugstores have faced growing competition for both prescription drugs and health-and-beauty-aid products from drugstore chains, full-line discount stores, supermarkets with pharmacy departments, mail-order pharmacy services, and even buying clubs. In addition, the proportion of prescriptions now keyed to third-party drug payment plans (such as health maintenance organizations, unions, and Medicaid plans) has grown to 41 per cent of all prescriptions. These plans generally ask for price discounts of as much as 20 per cent, as well as discounted fees for filling of prescriptions; as a result, drugstores have increased paperwork, lower profit margins, and must wait to receive full payment.

The various competitors of independent drugstores each have distinctive strengths. For example, Perry Drug Stores, a 210-store Michigan chain, uses its PerryLink computer system to link all of its drugstores and speed up reimbursement from third-party programs. Giant Foods, a Washington, D.C.-based supermarket chain, uses its computer system to check for possible side effects if a person has multiple prescriptions; and it notifies customers of possible interaction effects. Mail-order pharmacies generally compete on the basis of discount prescription prices; and customers are often provided with 800-toll-free phone numbers and personnel to answer questions.

To compete against these firms, many independent drugstores are employing such personal services as delivery to customers who are unable to come to the store, advice on when to take a pill (e.g., before meals), and advice on which over-the-counter drug is most suitable for a given ailment. A number have bought computer systems to track prescription usage by clients; some have satellite links with suppliers' and insurers'. Independent drugstores that purchase from McKesson Corporation, a major wholesaler, can automate the direct-reimbursement process and thereby learn what a person's insurance covers and electronically transmit bills to a centralized data-processing center for payment. Still other independents are seeking to increase their nonprescription business by selling exclusive lines of cosmetics not carried by chains and/or by employing full-time cosmeticians.

Independents are also hoping that the 37 million Americans who currently have no health insurance will provide additional prescription business if and when a national health plan becomes effective.[1]

[1] *Standard & Poor's Industry Surveys: Retailing* (May 13, 1993), pp. R94–R97; and Kate Fitzgerald, "Retailers Prescribe Pharmacies," *Advertising Age* (March 15, 1993), pp. 3, 51.

Reprinted by permission of Perry Drug.

Overview

The term ***retail institution*** refers to the basic format or structure of a business. In the United States, about two million different firms are defined as retailers by the Bureau of the Census, and these firms operate more than 2.4 million establishments.

An institutional study of retailers shows the relative sizes and diversity of different kinds of retailing; enables firms to better develop and enact their own strategies; and indicates how various types of retailers are affected by the external environment. In particular, institutional analysis is important in these phases of strategic planning: selecting an organizational mission, choosing an ownership alternative, defining the goods/service category, and setting objectives.

In this chapter and the next, retail institutions are examined from these perspectives: ownership (Chapter 4), store-based retail strategy mix (Chapter 5), nonstore-based retail strategy mix (Chapter 5), and service versus goods retail strategy mix (Chapter 5). Figure 4–1 contains a breakdown of each category. These classifications are all not mutually exclusive; that is, a retail institution may be correctly placed in more than one category. For example, a department store unit may be part of a chain, have a store-based strategy, accept mail-order sales, and sell services, as well as goods.

It is vital that the data in Chapters 4 and 5 be interpreted carefully. Since some institutional categories are not mutually exclusive, care should be taken in combining

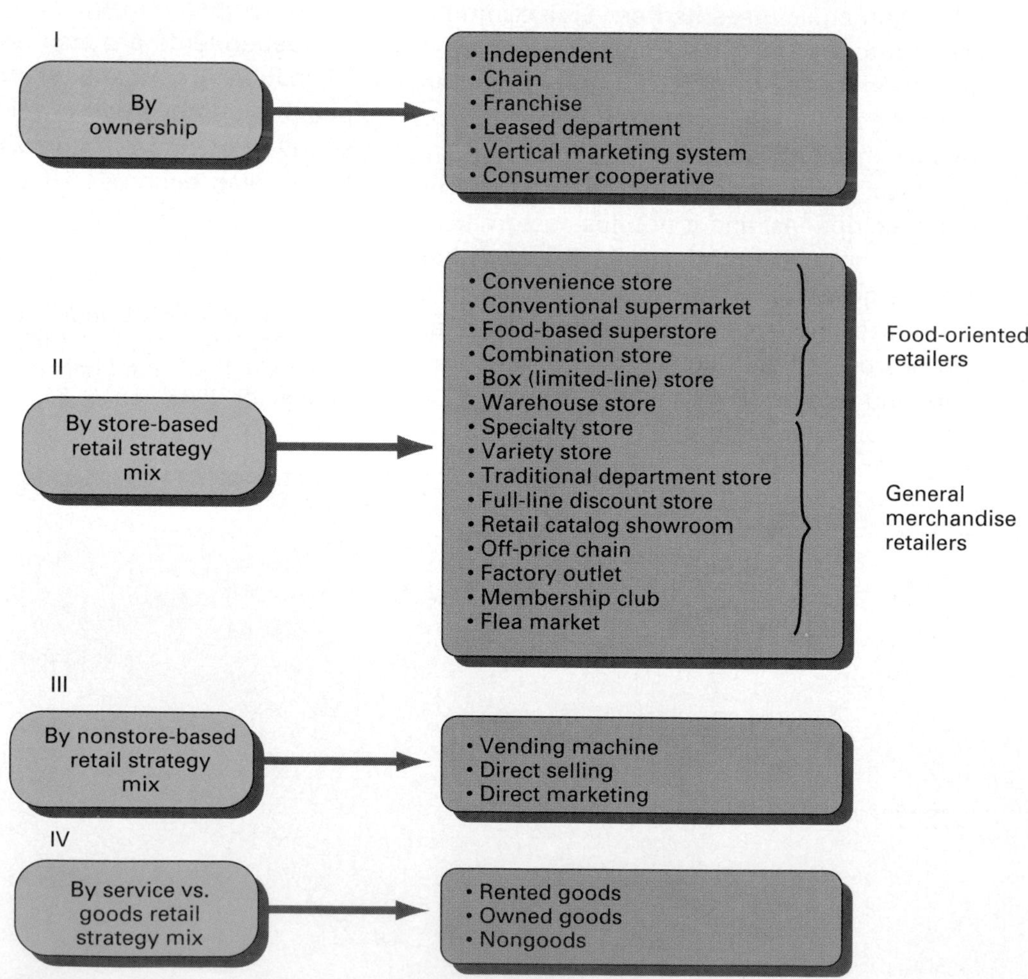

FIGURE 4–1 A Classification Method for Retail Institutions

statistics to aggregate data so that double counting does not occur. And while the data are as current as possible, not all information corresponds to a common date and (as of this writing) the last full published U.S. government retailing census is the *1987 Census of Retail Trade.*

Retail Institutions Characterized by Ownership

Retail firms may be independently owned, chain-owned, franchisee-operated, leased, owned by manufacturers or wholesalers, or consumer-owned.

Although retailers are primarily small (nearly 80 per cent of all retail stores are operated by firms with only one outlet and over one-half of all firms have two or fewer paid employees), there are also very large retailers. According to *Fortune,* the five leading U.S. retailers averaged nearly 315,000 employees and $35 billion in annual sales in 1992.

INDEPENDENT

An ***independent*** retailer owns only one retail unit. In the United States, there are 1.9 million independent retailers. They account for about 45 per cent of total U.S. store sales. Nearly one-half of all independents are run entirely by the owners and/or their families; these firms generate just 3 per cent of total U.S. store sales (averaging $65,000–$70,000 in annual revenues) and have no paid workers (there is no payroll).

The high number of independent retailers is associated with the ***ease of entry*** into the marketplace. Due to low capital requirements and no, or relatively simple, licensing provisions, entry for many kinds of small retail firms is easy. The investment per worker in retailing is usually much lower than for manufacturers. Retailer licensing, although somewhat more stringent in recent years, is still pretty routine. Each year, tens of thousands of new retail businesses, most independents, open in the United States.

The ease of entry into retailing is reflected in the low market shares of the leading firms in many goods/service categories as a percentage of total category sales. For example, in two retail categories where large chains are quite strong (drugstores and grocery stores), the five largest drugstore retailers and the five leading grocery retailers account for only about 26 and 20 per cent of sales in their respective categories.[2]

Since a great deal of competition is generated due to the relative ease of entry into retailing, it is undoubtedly an important factor in the high rate of retail business failures among newer firms. The Small Business Administration estimates that one-third of new U.S. retailers do not survive their first year and two-thirds do not continue beyond their third year. Most of these failures involve independents. Because the decade of the 1980s was relatively good economically for the United States, failure rates were comparatively low. However, in the early 1990s, failure rates were higher—as a result of the economic slowdown. When the economy recovered in 1993–1994, failure rates again fell.[3]

Competitive Advantages and Disadvantages of Independents

Independent retailers have a variety of advantages and disadvantages facing them. Among their advantages are flexibility, low investments, specialized offerings, direct control of strategy, image, consistency, independence, and entrepreneurial drive.

[2] *Standard & Poor's Industry Surveys: Retailing,* pp. R89–R96; and "The 50 Largest Retailing Companies," *Fortune* (May 31, 1993), pp. 220–221.

[3] Michael Selz, "Small-Business Survival Rate Expected to Rise in 1994," *Wall Street Journal* (February 18, 1994), p. B2.

RETAILING AROUND THE WORLD

How Can Small Toy Stores in Australia Compete with the Giants?

World 4 Kids (operated by Coles Myer, Australia's leading retail chain) and Toys "R" Us (based in the United States) are the first retailers entering the Australian toy market using megastore formats. World 4 Kids megastores have 12,000 different items in each store and Toys "R" Us megastores each carry 16,000 different items.

Both chains hope that their presence will increase overall toy purchases in Australia. Australians currently spend $59 per capita each year on toys versus $321 in the United States and $617 in Japan.

Existing Australian toy retailers operate 10,000 much smaller stores and they are aggressively fighting to hold on to their current market share. The 220-store Toyworld chain has developed an advertising slogan that reminds its shoppers that "we're not just a small neighborhood store—we are a big national chain." Its ads also tell consumers that it is Australian-owned. Toy Kingdom, a group of 110 independent toy stores that have joined together as a co-operative, is using ads that cite low prices for particular items. Unlike the megastores, that offer below-cost specials on popular toys to build store traffic, Toyworld and Toy Kingdom are focusing on selling specialized products (such as baby clothes and scooters) that are less common in megastores.

Sources: Based on material in Geoffrey Lee Martin, "Australian Toy Giants Worry Smaller Stores," *Advertising Age* (December 13, 1993), p. I-15; and Jennifer Porter, "Aussies Gird for Toys "R" Us Entry," *Advertising Age* (June 21, 1993), p. I-21.

There is a great deal of flexibility when choosing store locations and developing strategy. Because only one store location is involved, a detailed list of specifications can be derived for the best location and a thorough search undertaken. Uniform location standards are not needed, as they are for chain stores, and independents do not have to worry about being too close to other company stores. In setting strategy, independents have great latitude in selecting target markets. Because many independents have modest goals, small segments of the overall customer market may be selected rather than the mass market. Product assortments, prices, store hours, and other factors are then set consistently with the market.

Because independents run only one store, investment costs for leases, fixtures, employees, and merchandise can be held down. In addition, there is no duplication of stock or personnel functions. Responsibilities are also clearly delineated within the store.

Independents often operate as specialists and so develop skills in a niche of a particular goods/service category. These firms can then be more efficient and can attract customers interested in specialized retailers.

Independent retailers can exert strong control over their strategies since only one store must be managed, and the owner-operator is typically on the premises. Decision making is usually centralized, and the layers of management personnel are minimized.

There is a certain image attached to independents, particularly small ones, that chains find difficult to capture. This is the image of a friendly, personalized retailer that provides a comfortable atmosphere in which to shop.

Independents are able to sustain consistency in their efforts because only one geographic market is served and only one strategy (store hours, product assortment, prices, sales personnel, promotion, and so on) is carried out. For example, there cannot be problems due to two branch stores selling identical items at different prices.

Independent retailers have "independence." Owner-operators tend to be in full charge and do not have to worry about stockholders, board-of-directors meetings, and labor unrest. Independents are frequently free from union work rules and seniority regulations. This can greatly affect labor productivity.

As a last major advantage, owner-operators usually have a strong entrepreneurial drive. They have personal investments in their businesses, success or failure has substantial implications, and there is a high degree of ego involvement.

Among the disadvantages of independent retailing are limits in bargaining power, few economies of scale, labor intensiveness, reduced access to media, overdependence on the owner, and little time and few resources for planning.

When bargaining with suppliers, independents may not have much power since they often buy in small quantities. Thus, in some instances, independents may be bypassed by suppliers or limited in the selection of merchandise made available to them. Reordering may also be hard for independents if minimum order requirements are too high for them to qualify. To overcome this problem, a growing number of independents, like hardware stores, are forming buying groups to increase their power in dealing with suppliers.

Independents often cannot establish economies of scale (low per-unit costs due to the handling of many units at one time) in buying and maintaining inventory. Due to financial constraints, small assortments of items are bought several times per year rather than large orders once or twice per year. This means that transportation, ordering, and handling costs per unit are high.

Operations for many independents are very labor intensive, with little computerization. Ordering, taking inventory, marking merchandise, ringing up sales, and bookkeeping are generally done manually. Such procedures are less efficient than computer tabulations (which are expensive for small firms in terms of the initial investment in hardware and software—although these costs are falling rapidly). In many cases, owner-operators are unwilling to spend time learning how to set up and implement computerized procedures.

Because of the relatively high costs of television ads and the large geographic coverage of magazines and some newspapers (too large for firms with one outlet), independent retailers are limited in their access to advertising media and sometimes pay abnormally high fees per infrequent ad compared to regular users. Yet, creative independents have a number of promotion tools available (see Chapter 17).

A key problem for independents—particularly small, family-run ones—is an overdependence on the owner. In numerous cases, all decisions are made by this person, and no continuity of management is stipulated for the time the owner-boss is ill or on vacation or retires. According to a recent study of family-owned businesses, the leading concerns at those businesses involved the identification of successors, the roles of nonfamily employees, and management training for family members.[4] Long-run success and employee morale can be affected by overdependence on the owner.

Another serious problem for independent retailers is the limited amount of time and resources allocated to long-run planning. Since the owner is intimately involved in the daily operations of the firm, responsiveness to new legislation, new products, and/or new competitors often suffers.

CHAIN

A ***chain*** retailer operates multiple outlets (store units) under common ownership; it usually engages in some level of centralized (or coordinated) purchasing and decision making. In the United States, there are roughly 60,000 retail chains that own about 550,000 establishments.

The relative strength of chains is great and their popularity has been rising, even though the number of retailers operating as chains is small (about 3 per cent of all U.S. retail firms). Today, chains operate more than one-fifth of all retail establishments; and because stores in chains tend to be considerably larger than those run by independents, chains account for well over one-half of total store sales and employment.

While almost four-fifths of all retail chains have 4 or fewer outlets, the several hundred retailers having 100 or more outlets account for one-third of total U.S. retail store sales. There are even 40 or so U.S. retailers with at least 1,000 outlets each (not including franchise operators like McDonald's). See Figure 4–2.

[4] Arthur Andersen & Co.'s Enterprise Group, "Family Worries," *Crain's New York Business* (May 24, 1993), p. 19.

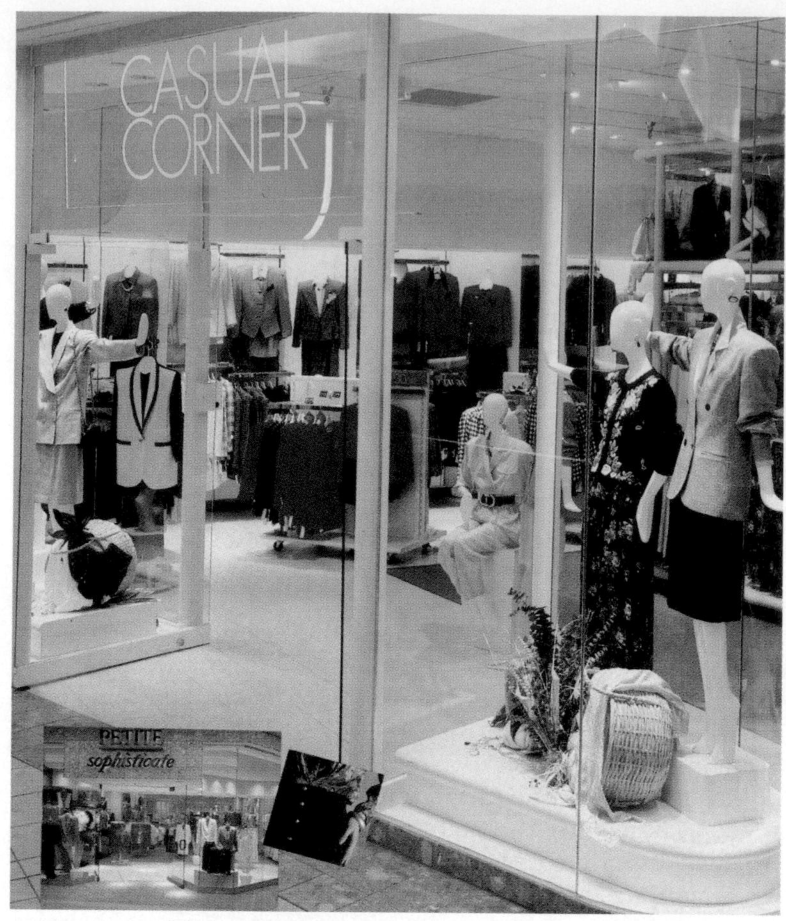

FIGURE 4–2
The Many Faces of U.S. Shoe
U.S. Shoe Corporation operates over 2,400 retail stores, including the Casual Corner, Petite Sophisticate, and LensCrafters chains.
Reprinted by permission.

The dominance of chains varies greatly by type of retailer. For example, in these categories, chains operating two or more outlets generate 75 per cent or more of total retail sales: department stores, variety stores, and grocery stores. On the other hand, stationery, beauty salon, furniture, and liquor store chains (with two or more outlets) generate far less than 50 per cent of total retail sales in their categories. Figure 4–3 shows selected data by retail store category for firms having 11 or more outlets.

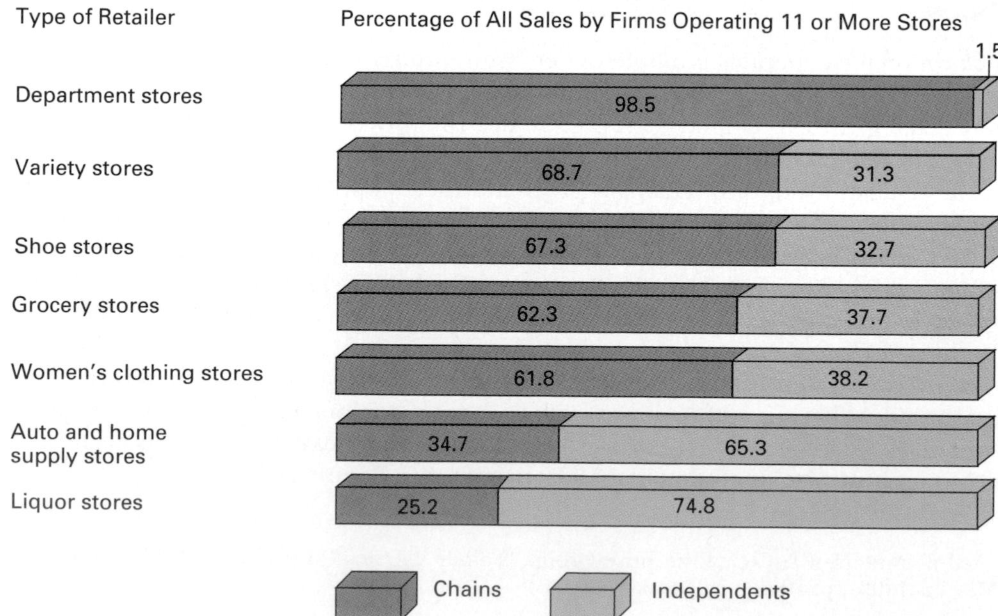

FIGURE 4–3
The Popularity of Chains for Selected Types of Retailer

Source: Computed by the authors from *Combined Annual and Revised Monthly Retail Trade: January 1983 Through December 1992* (Washington, D.C.: U.S. Department of Commerce, 1993), p. 36.

Competitive Advantages and Disadvantages of Chains

There are many competitive advantages for chain retailers: bargaining power, wholesale function efficiencies, multiple-store efficiencies, computerization, access to media, well-defined management, and long-range planning.

Many chains have bargaining power when dealing with suppliers because of the amount of the chains' annual purchases. As a result, these chains can receive new items as soon as they are introduced, have reorders promptly filled, get proper service and selling support from suppliers, and obtain the best prices possible. In addition, large chains may gain exclusive rights to selling certain items and may have suppliers make goods under the retailers' brands. For example, Kmart has exclusive selling rights for Jaclyn Smith clothing products, and Sears has manufacturers make appliances carrying the Sears' Kenmore brand name.

Chain retailers can achieve cost efficiencies by performing wholesaling functions themselves. Buying directly from suppliers and in large quantities, shipping and storing goods, and attending trade shows sponsored by suppliers to learn about new offerings are just some wholesaling activities that can be fulfilled by chains. By doing so, they can sometimes bypass wholesalers, and the result is lower supplier prices to the retailers. Thus, prices paid by chains are often less than those paid by independents, without violation of the Robinson-Patman Act.

Efficiency in multiple-store operations can be gained through shared warehousing facilities; volume purchases of standardized store fixtures, employee uniforms, and so on; centralized purchasing and decision making; and other factors. Chain retailers typically give headquarters executives broad authority for overall personnel policies—as well as for buying, pricing, and advertising decisions.

Chain retailers, because of their resources and number of transactions, are well able to use computers in ordering merchandise, taking inventory, forecasting, ringing up sales, and bookkeeping. This use of computers increases efficiency and reduces overall costs.

Chains, particularly national or regional ones, can take advantage of a variety of media, from television to magazines to traditional newspapers. Large sales volume and geographic coverage of the market allow chains to utilize all forms of media.

Most chains have well-defined management philosophies, whether centralized or decentralized. These tend to be solid overall strategies, and employee responsibilities are clearly outlined. In addition, continuity is usually ensured when managerial personnel are absent or retire because there are personnel to fill in and succession plans in place.

Finally, many chain retailers expend considerable time and resources in long-run planning. Frequently, specific personnel are assigned to long-term planning on a permanent basis. Opportunities and threats are also carefully monitored.

Chain retailers do have a number of disadvantages: inflexibility, high investments, reduced control, and limited independence.

Once chain retailers are well established, their flexibility is limited. Adequate, nonoverlapping store locations may be hard to find. Consistent strategies must be maintained throughout all branches—prices, promotions, and product assortments must be similar for each store. For chains that use centralized decision making, there may be difficulty in adapting to local needs, such as taking into account differences in life-styles among city, suburban, and rural customers.

Chains' investment costs may be high. Multiple-store leases, fixtures, product assortments, and employees are involved. The purchase of any merchandise may be costly because a number of store branches must be stocked.

Managerial control can be tough for chains, especially for those with geographically dispersed branches. Top management cannot maintain the control over each branch that independent owners have over their single outlets. Lack of communication and time delays in making and enacting decisions are two particular problems.

Personnel in large chains may have limited independence in their jobs. In many cases, there are several layers of management, unionized employees, stockholders, and boards of directors. Thus, some chain retailers are now empowering their personnel to give them more independence—so they can better address special customer needs as those needs arise.

RETAILING IN ACTION

What's Next for Burger King?

Burger King's market share of the U.S. fast-food hamburger business has recently dropped. Retail analysts partly attribute this decline to McDonald's renewed emphasis on customer service, product selection, and value; and to Wendy's successful advertising campaign—featuring its founder, Dave Thomas.

Thus, after an extensive operations review, Burger King has decided to reduce its costs, improve services, and place greater emphasis on its flame-broiled hamburger—the Whopper. The 7,100-restaurant franchisor plans to use a new advertising agency and bring back its "Have it Your Way" advertising slogan. Advertising will also feature the Whopper hamburger and the chain's use of "flame-broiling" (other chains fry their hamburgers).

An important part of Burger King's repositioning will be its continued improvement in franchisee relations. Recently, its parent company (Grand Metropolitan of Great Britain) added an ombudsman to review franchisee complaints. There are now plans to allocate a larger share of the overall marketing budget to local franchisees; these funds can be used by each franchisee at its discretion. Grand Metropolitan hopes this strategy will not only improve franchise relations but also better enable each franchisee to react to its local market.

Source: Based on material in Richard Gibson, "Burger King Overhaul Includes Refocus on Whopper," *Wall Street Journal* (December 15, 1993), p. B4.

FRANCHISING

Franchising involves a contractual arrangement between a franchisor (which may be a manufacturer, a wholesaler, or a service sponsor) and a retail franchisee, which allows the franchisee to conduct a given form of business under an established name and according to a given pattern of business. In a typical arrangement, the franchisee pays an initial fee and a monthly percentage of gross sales in exchange for the exclusive rights to sell goods and services in a specified geographic area. Franchising represents a retail organizational form in which small businesspeople can benefit by being part of a large, multiunit chain-type retail institution.

There are two broad types of franchising arrangements: product/trademark and business format. In ***product/trademark franchising***, franchised dealers acquire the identities of their suppliers by agreeing to sell the latter's products and/or operate under suppliers' names. Dealers operate relatively autonomously from suppliers. Although they must adhere to certain operating rules, they set store hours, choose locations, determine store facilities and displays, and otherwise run the stores. Product/trademark franchising represents about 70 per cent of all retail franchising sales. Examples are auto dealers and many gasoline service stations.

In ***business format franchising***, there is a more interactive relationship between the franchisor and the franchisee. The franchisee receives assistance on site location, quality control, accounting systems, startup practices, management training, and responding to problems—in addition to the right to sell goods and services. The use of prototype stores, standardized merchandise lines, and cooperative advertising enable these franchises to achieve a level of coordination previously found only in chains. During recent decades, the major growth in franchising has involved business format arrangements—which are common for restaurants and other food outlets, real estate, and service retailing. Due to the small size of many franchisees, business format franchising accounts for 75 per cent of all franchised outlets (though just 30 per cent of total sales).[5]

Though variations in franchising exist, McDonald's is a good example of a business-format franchise arrangement. The firm provides each new franchisee with intensive training at its "Hamburger U," a detailed operations manual (complete down to the most minute facets of running machinery), regular visits by field service managers, and repeat trips to Hamburger U for brush-up training. In return for a twenty-year franchising agreement with McDonald's, a conventional franchisee invests several hun-

[5] *Franchise Opportunities Guide* (Washington, D.C.: International Franchise Association, 1993), pp. 38–39.

TABLE 4–1 1992 Retail Franchise Sales[a]

Type of Retailer	Sales (billions)	Percentage of Total Sales
Auto and truck dealers	$375.0	51.5
Gasoline service stations	112.3	15.4
Restaurants (all types)	98.9	13.6
General merchandise stores	34.0	4.7
Hotels and motels	28.4	3.9
Automotive goods and services stores	17.3	2.4
Convenience stores	15.2	2.1
Other food stores	12.3	1.7
Rental services firms	8.4	1.2
Real-estate firms	8.2	1.1
Personal and household services firms	7.8	1.1
Recreation, entertainment, and travel businesses	5.5	0.7
Educational goods and services firms	2.4	0.3
Miscellaneous firms	2.6	0.3
Total	$728.3	100.0

[a] A small amount of nonretail sales may be included in some cases.

Source: Estimated by the authors from *Franchising in the Economy: 1989–1992* (Washington, D.C.: International Franchise Association Educational Foundation, Inc., and Arthur Andersen & Co., 1992), various pages; and 1992 data provided by the International Franchise Association.

dred thousand dollars (over 90 per cent of which goes to suppliers of kitchen equipment, signs, seating, and decor, and for pre-opening expenses) and pays royalty fees totaling at least 12 per cent of gross sales directly to McDonald's.[6]

Size and Structural Arrangements

Retail franchising began in the United States in 1851, when the Singer Sewing Machine Company first franchised dealers. It did not become popular until the early 1900s as underfinanced auto makers started using franchising to expand their distribution systems. Although auto and truck dealers still provide more than one-half of all U.S. retail franchise sales, there are few retail sectors that have not been affected by franchising's growth. There are now 3,000 U.S. retail franchisors. They accounted for 520,000 franchisee- and franchisor-owned U.S. outlets and generated nearly $730 billion in retail sales during 1992, well over one-third of total retail store sales.* In addition, several hundred U.S.-based franchisors currently have foreign operations, representing tens of thousands of outlets.[7] Table 4–1 shows 1992 U.S. retail franchise sales by goods/service category.

In the United States, about 85 per cent of franchising sales and 83 per cent of franchised outlets are from franchisee-owned units; the rest are from franchisor-owned outlets.[8] If franchisees operate only one outlet, they are classified as independents by

[6] *McDonald's Franchising.*

* Because the available data do not break down all the types of firms into retail and nonretail categories, a small amount of nonretail sales may be included here.

[7] Michael H. Seid, "Franchising Thrives in the '90s," *Stores* (May 1993), pp. 68–79; and Alan G. Gilman, "Franchising Opens Emerging Markets," *Chain Store Age Executive* (January 1994), p. 191.

[8] *Franchising in the Economy: 1989–1992* (Washington, D.C.: International Franchise Association Educational Foundation, Inc., and Arthur Andersen & Co., 1992), p. 22.

the U.S. Department of Commerce; franchisees that operate two or more outlets and franchisor-owned stores are classed as chains. Today, a large and growing number of franchisees operate as chains.

Three types of structural arrangements dominate retail franchising:

- Manufacturer-retailer—A manufacturer gives an independent businessperson the right to sell goods and related services (subject to conditions) through a licensing agreement.
- Wholesaler-retailer
  a. Voluntary—A wholesaler organizes a franchise system and grants franchises to individual retailers.
  b. Cooperative—A group of retailers sets up a franchise system and shares the ownership and operations of a wholesaling organization.
- Service sponsor-retailer—A service firm licenses individual retailers to let them offer specific service packages to consumers.

Figure 4–4 presents examples of each of these structural arrangements.

Competitive Advantages and Disadvantages of Franchising

Franchisees receive several benefits by investing in successful franchise operations. First, individual businesspeople can own and operate retail enterprises with relatively small capital investments. Second, franchisees acquire well-known names and goods/service lines. Third, standard operating procedures and management skills may

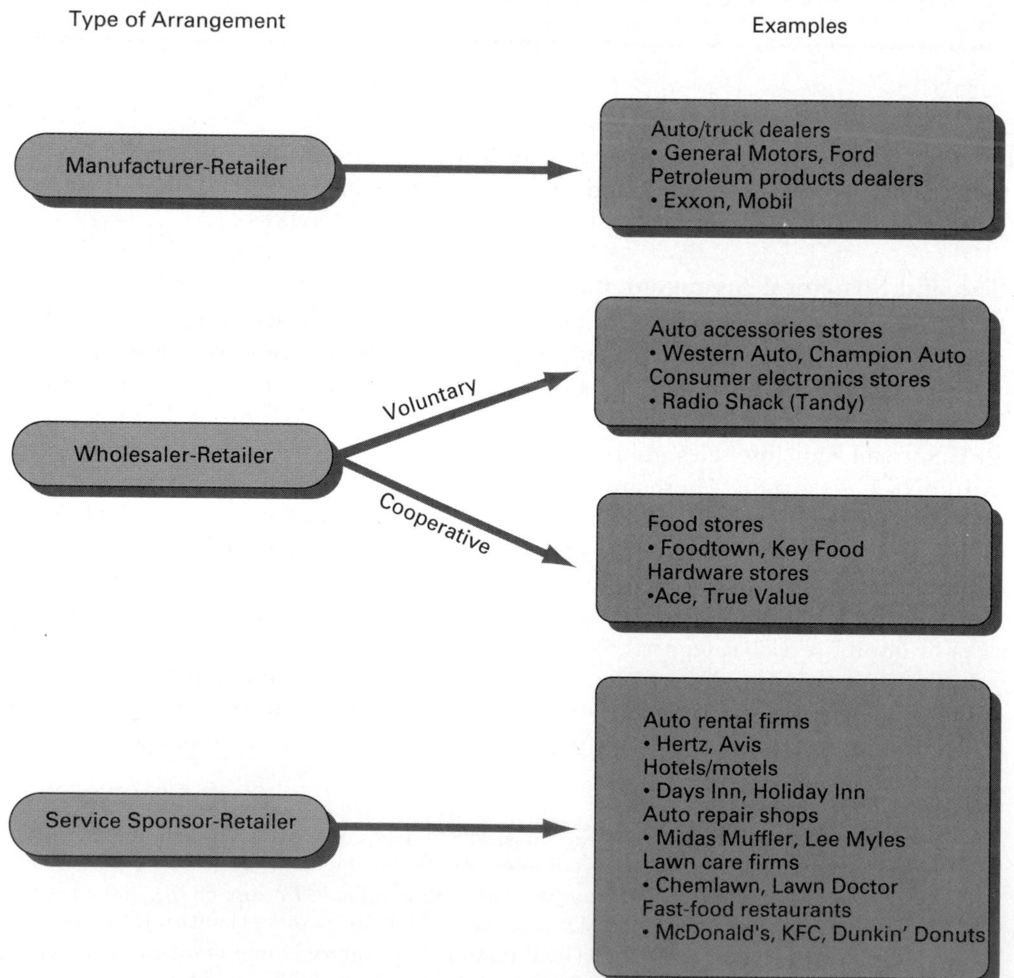

FIGURE 4–4
Structural Arrangements in Retail Franchising

be taught to the franchisees. Fourth, cooperative marketing programs are often employed (e.g., national advertising) that could not otherwise be afforded. Fifth, franchisees obtain exclusive selling rights for specified geographical territories. Sixth, franchisee purchases may be less expensive per unit due to the volume represented by the overall firms.

Some potential problems do exist for franchisees. First, oversaturation could occur if too many franchisees are located in one geographic area; the sales and profits of each unit would then be adversely affected. Second, because of overzealous selling by some franchisors, the income potential and required managerial ability, initiative, and investment of franchised units may be incorrectly stated. Third, franchisees may be locked into contract provisions whereby purchases must be made through franchisors or certain approved vendors. Fourth, cancellation provisions may give franchisors the right to void individual franchises if any provisions of franchise agreements are not met. Fifth, in some industries, franchise agreements are of short duration. Sixth, under most franchise contracts, royalties are a percentage of gross sales, regardless of franchisees' profits. These six factors contribute to ***constrained decision making***, whereby the franchisor can exclude franchisees from or limit their involvement in the strategic planning process.

To curb unfair franchisor sales practices, the Federal Trade Commission (FTC) has a "Disclosure Requirements and Business Opportunities" rule. It applies to all franchisors in the United States and is intended to provide potential franchisees with adequate information prior to making investments. Though the FTC does not regularly review disclosure statements, more than a dozen states do check them and may require corrections. Also, a number of states have fair practice laws stipulating that franchisors may not terminate, cancel, or fail to renew franchisees without sufficient cause. Arizona, California, Indiana, New Jersey, Virginia, Washington, and Wisconsin are among the states with fair practice laws. Furthermore, many states require that franchise offerings be registered.[9]

Franchisors accrue lots of benefits by selling to individual franchisees. First, a national presence can be developed more quickly and with smaller investments on the part of franchisors. Second, qualifications for franchise ownership can be set and enforced. Third, money is obtained when goods are delivered rather than when they are sold. Fourth, agreements can be drawn up that require the franchisees to abide by stringent regulations set by the franchisors. Fifth, because franchisees are owners and not employees, they have a greater incentive to work hard. Sixth, after franchisees have paid for their franchised outlets, the franchisors also receive royalties and/or sell products to the individual proprietors.

Franchisors also face potential problems. First, franchisees could harm a firm's overall image and reputation if they do not maintain company standards. Second, a lack of uniformity could adversely affect customer loyalty. Third, intrafranchise competition is not desirable. Fourth, the resale value of individual units is injured if franchisees perform poorly. Fifth, ineffective franchised units directly injure their franchisors' profitability from selling services, materials, or products to the franchisees and from royalty fees. Sixth, franchisees, in greater numbers, are seeking their independence from franchisor rules and regulations.

Additional information on franchising is contained in the appendix that follows the cases at the end of this chapter.

LEASED DEPARTMENT

A ***leased department*** is a department in a retail store—usually a department, discount, or specialty store—that is rented to an outside party. The proprietor of a leased

[9] Richard Gibson, "McDonald's Challenging Iowa's New Franchise Law," *Wall Street Journal* (May 14, 1992), p. B2; Jeffrey A. Tannenbaum, "Ruling Chills Franchisers' Use of Evictions as Leverage," *Wall Street Journal* (June 21, 1993), p. B2; and Jeffrey A. Tannenbaum, "New Rulings Cloak Franchisees with Sturdier Armor," *Wall Street Journal* (December 30, 1993), p. B2.

FIGURE 4–5
Meldisco: A Leader in Leased Departments
Reprinted by permission of Melville Corporation.

department is usually responsible for all aspects of its operations (including fixtures) and normally pays the store a percentage of sales as rent. The store imposes various requirements on the leased department to ensure overall consistency and coordination.

In most situations, leased departments are used by existing store-based retailers to broaden their merchandise or service offerings into product categories requiring highly specialized skills or knowledge not possessed by the retailers themselves. Thus, leased departments often operate in categories that tend to be on the fringe of the store's major product lines. Leased departments are most common for in-store beauty salons, photographic studios, and millinery, shoe, jewelry, cosmetics, watch repair, shoe repair, and sewing-machine departments. They account for about $12 billion to $15 billion in annual sales in department stores. Unfortunately, data on current overall leased department sales are not available.

Meldisco, a division of the Melville Corporation, is a leading operator of leased departments. Altogether, it has leased shoe departments in more than 2,600 stores and annual sales of $1.2 billion. Most of Meldisco's leased departments are in Kmart stores, as illustrated in Figure 4–5. In these departments, Meldisco owns the inventory and display fixtures, staffs and merchandises the departments, and pays fees for the space occupied. The stores in which Meldisco has its leased departments cover the costs of utilities, maintenance, advertising, and checkout services.[10]

[10] *Melville Annual Report 1992*, p. 22.

Competitive Advantages and Disadvantages of Leased Departments

From the stores' perspective, using leased departments has a number of benefits. Store personnel might otherwise lack the merchandising ability to handle and sell certain goods and services. The leased-department operators pay for inventory and personnel expenses, thus reducing store costs. The market can be enlarged by providing one-stop customer shopping. Personnel management, merchandise displays, the reordering of items, and so on are undertaken by the lessees. A percentage of revenues is received regularly.

There are also some potential disadvantages, from the stores' perspective. Leased departments may use operating procedures that conflict with those of the stores. Lessees may adversely affect stores' images. Customers may blame problems on the stores rather than on the lessees.

For leased department operators, there are these advantages: Existing stores are usually well known, have a large number of steady customers, and generate immediate sales for leased departments. Some expenses are reduced because of shared facilities, such as security equipment and outside display windows. There are economies of scale (volume savings) through pooled ads. Lessees' images are aided by their relationships with popular stores.

Lessees face these possible problems: There may be inflexibility as to the hours they must be open and the operating style they must utilize. The goods/service lines they are allowed to offer will usually be restricted. If lessees are successful, the stores may raise the rent or may not renew leases when they expire. The in-store locations may not generate the sales expected.

A leased department may be viewed from two perspectives: as an element in a shopping center and as a part of a franchise system. In the shopping-center context, a leased department operator is renting an area with a given traffic flow to conduct its business. The lessee must examine the character of the traffic flow and its relationship to the chosen target market; the lessor must examine the extent to which the leased department will either create added traffic or be a parasite and live off the traffic generated by other parts of the store. The franchise analogy relates to a leased department's ability to blend with the merchandise philosophy of another retailer and the need to set a broad policy for all departments, so an entire store's image is not injured by one operator.

An example of a successful long-term lease arrangement is one shared by the CPI Corporation and Sears. For 35 years, CPI has operated photo studios in Sears stores. In exchange for the use of 300 square feet of space in each of about 1,000 Sears stores, CPI pays Sears 15 per cent of its gross sales. CPI has annual sales per square foot that are much higher than Sears' overall average. CPI's agreement with Sears can be terminated by Sears on sixty days' notice. At present, CPI's yearly revenues via leased departments in Sears outlets exceed $325 million.[11]

VERTICAL MARKETING SYSTEM

A ***vertical marketing system*** consists of all the levels of independently owned businesses along a channel of distribution. Goods and services are normally distributed through one of these types of vertical marketing systems: independent, partially integrated, and fully integrated. See Figure 4–6.

In an ***independent vertical marketing system***, there are three levels of independently owned businesses: manufacturers, wholesalers, and retailers. Such a system is most often used if manufacturers and/or retailers are small, intensive distribution is sought, customers are widely dispersed, unit sales are high, company resources are low, channel members want to share costs and risks, and task specialization is desir-

[11] Julianne Slovak, "CPI Corp.," *Fortune* (March 13, 1989), p. 73; and Gary Slutsker, "Look at the Birdie and Say: 'Cash Flow'," *Forbes* (October 25, 1993), pp. 100, 102.

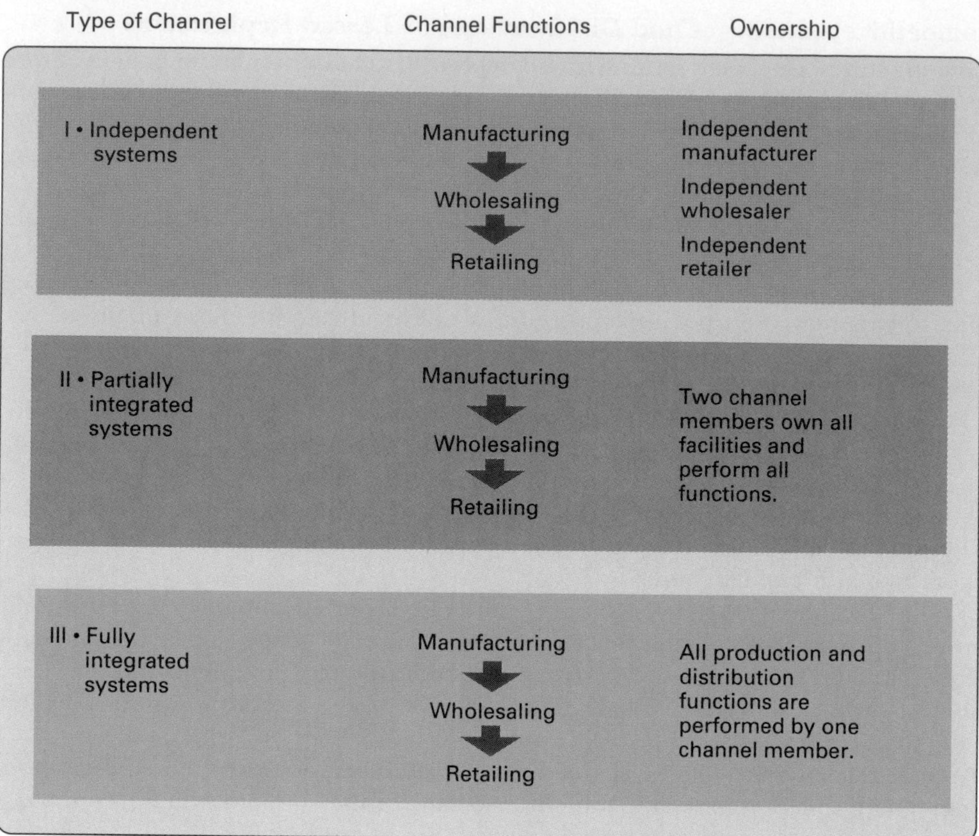

Figure 4–6
Vertical Marketing Systems: Functions and Ownership

able. Independent vertical marketing systems are used by many stationery stores, gift shops, hardware stores, food stores, drugstores, and a number of other businesses. They are the leading form of vertical marketing system.

With a ***partially integrated vertical marketing system***, two independently owned businesses along a channel perform all production and distribution functions without the aid of the third. The most common form of this system occurs when a manufacturer and a retailer complete transactions and shipping, storing, and other distribution functions in the absence of an independently owned wholesaler. A partially integrated system is most apt if manufacturers and/or retailers are large, selective or exclusive distribution is sought, unit sales are moderate, company resources are high, greater channel control is desired, and existing wholesalers are too expensive or unavailable. Partially integrated systems are often used by furniture stores, appliance stores, restaurants, computer retailers, and mail-order firms.

Through a ***fully integrated vertical marketing system***, a single firm performs all production and distribution functions without the aid of any other firms. In the past, this type of system was usually employed only by manufacturers, such as Avon, Goodyear, Sherwin-Williams, and major gasoline refiners. At Sherwin-Williams, the paint manufacturer, its 2,000 company-owned stores account for 61 per cent of company sales.[12] Today, more retailers are using fully integrated systems for at least some of their products. For example, Kroger (the food retailer) produces dairy items, baked goods, ice cream, and other items; and Sears has ownership shares in an appliance maker, a paint and detergent maker, an apparel maker, and others. See Figure 4–7.

A fully integrated vertical marketing system enables a firm to have total control over its strategy, to have direct contact with final consumers, to have higher retail markups without raising prices (by eliminating channel members), to be self-sufficient and not

[12] Gary Hoover, Alta Campbell, and Patrick J. Spain (Editors), *Hoover's Handbook of American Business 1994* (Austin, Texas: Reference Press, 1993), pp. 980–981.

Figure 4–7
Integrated Vertical Marketing at Kroger
Besides the supermarkets and convenience stores that it operates, Kroger acts as a food processor and wholesaler for more than 4,000 private-label products. It has 37 food-processing facilities.
Reprinted by permission.

rely on others, to have exclusivity over the goods and services offered, and to keep all profits within the company. For example, by making many of the products sold in its stores, Ben & Jerry's (the ice cream firm) maximizes product visibility, trains and supervises store personnel, has exclusivity over its brands, and controls retail ads and prices. However, there may be some difficulties associated with a fully integrated system, including high investment costs and a lack of expertise in both manufacturing and retailing.

Some firms (including many cited in this section) use a ***dual vertical marketing system***, whereby they are involved in more than one type of distribution arrangement. Thus, Sherwin-Williams has a fully integrated system for its Sherwin-Williams paints and sells them only at company-owned stores. Sherwin-Williams also sells its Dutch Boy paints in home improvement stores, full-line discount stores, hardware stores, and others via an independent vertical marketing system (which includes wholesalers). Thus, Sherwin-Williams can appeal to different consumers, increase revenues, share some of its costs, and maintain a good degree of control over its strategy. See Figure 4–8.

Besides partially or fully integrating a vertical marketing system, a firm can exert power in a distribution channel because of its economic, legal, or political strength; superior knowledge and abilities; customer loyalty; or other factors. ***Channel control*** occurs when one member of a distribution channel can dominate the decisions made in that channel via the power it possesses. Manufacturers, wholesalers, and retailers each have a combination of tools to improve their positions relative to one another.

Manufacturers can exert control through franchising, whereby franchisees' marketing programs come under close scrutiny; developing strong brand loyalty, wherein retailers are forced to stock merchandise because of consumer demand; pre-ticketing merchandise, thereby designating suggested list or selling prices; and exclusive distribution, whereby retailers voluntarily agree to adhere to given standards in exchange for sole distribution rights in given geographic areas.

Wholesalers have the ability to exert influence over manufacturers and retailers in these situations: If wholesalers are large, their businesses are important and they can put pressure on suppliers and buyers. They can introduce their own private brands and circumvent manufacturers. A franchise system and/or brand loyalty can be developed to control the distribution system. The wholesalers can become the most efficient members in the channel for the functions they perform, such as shipping and processing reorders.

FIGURE 4–8
Sherwin-Williams' Dual Vertical Marketing System

Retailers can exert clout with other channel members in the following instances: a large proportion of a supplier's output is sold to one retailer, private branding is employed, or economic power (large gross sales) exists.

When one retailer represents a large percentage of a manufacturer's sales volume, channel control may be applied. For example, there are a number of independent companies from which Sears purchases a large proportion of its output. One such company is Whirlpool Corporation, the manufacturer of major appliances, which produces Sears' Kenmore brand of appliances. As a result, Sears has a strong bargaining position.

Private brands (labels) or store brands can enable retailers to have channel control, improve competitive positioning, and raise profit margins. For instance, over one-half of the apparel purchased by national chains and about one-fifth of the apparel bought by specialty retailers involve private-label goods. In a typical supermarket,

ETHICS IN RETAILING

Whose Heart Is in San Francisco? Under One Roof!

Under One Roof, a California gift shop, is the first store in the United States that is exclusively dedicated to AIDS relief. Under One Roof is now a year-round operation, after its first six-week Christmas operation resulted in $173,000 in net income.

The store's objective is to return all of its sales revenues to local and regional AIDS groups. This requires corporate and private donations and unpaid volunteers for staffing. The store particularly appeals to institutions and individuals that wish to reach a group of AIDS organizations through one donation. Chevron, Miller Brewing, the *San Francisco Examiner*, The Gap, and Macy's are among the firms that have helped underwrite the store's activities. And, most personnel are unpaid volunteers.

The best-selling items in Under One Roof include a compact disc assembled by a New Age radio station, the *Project Open Hand Cookbook*, the San Francisco's AIDS Foundation's greeting cards, and homemade crafts (such as jewelry and Christmas tree ornaments).

The store's volunteer nine-member board includes a publicist, a merchandiser, a store designer, an information management specialist, a CPA, and an attorney. Many of these board members are also working with other AIDS groups to assist them in merchandising and product development.

Source: Based on material in Teresa Andreoli, "Under One Roof," *Stores* (September 1992), pp. 35–36.

private-label goods (including "no-name" generics) account for 15 to 20 per cent of purchases. At Sainsbury, a British-based supermarket chain, 65 per cent of the products it buys are private-label items.[13]

With private labeling, retailers may gain significant power over wholesalers and manufacturers by attaining brand loyalty for their own products, converting brand loyalty to store loyalty, and requiring merchandise to be made to specifications. Private labeling thus enables retailers to switch vendors (sellers) with no impact on their customer loyalty, as long as the same product specifications are followed. The threat of switching vendors (with no offsetting impact on private-brand sales) is often adequate action to get a supplier in line on a retailer's price, delivery, or terms request.

It is important to note that clearly established channel roles often have significant advantages for all parties. Long-term relationships allow for scheduling efficiencies and enable retailers to receive supplier financing and for vendors to obtain bank loans (due to pre-sold inventories). Some economies result because many activities are eliminated, simplified, or shared. For instance, advertising, financing, and billing are dramatically simplified, and many tasks, such as merchandise marking, can be performed by the manufacturer.

CONSUMER COOPERATIVE

A ***consumer cooperative*** is a retail firm owned by its customer members. In a cooperative arrangement, a group of consumers invests in the company, receives stock certificates, elects officers, manages operations, and shares the profits or savings that accrue. In the United States, there are several thousand consumer cooperatives, ranging from small buying clubs to Recreational Equipment Inc. (REI) with $310 million in annual sales. Consumer cooperatives have been most popular in food retailing. However, the 4,000 or so U.S. food cooperatives account for only a fraction of one per cent of total retail store sales (and less than one per cent of total grocery sales).

Consumer cooperatives exist for these basic reasons: Some consumers feel they can operate stores as well as or better than traditional retailers. They also believe that existing retailers are inadequately fulfilling customer needs with regard to healthful, environmentally safe products. They further believe that existing retailers often make excessive profits and that they can sell merchandise for lower prices.

This is how REI operates: It sells outdoor recreational equipment, such as backpacks and bicycles, to 1 million active members. It has 3,500 employees in about 36 stores; unlike other cooperatives, REI is operated by a professional staff that adheres to the policies set by the member-elected board. There is a small one-time membership fee, which entitles customers to shop at REI, elect people to the board of directors, and share in profits (based on the amount spent by each member). REI's goal is to distribute a 10 per cent dividend to members.[14]

Cooperatives have not grown beyond their current level since they involve a lot of consumer initiative and drive; consumers are usually not expert in buying, handling, and selling goods and services; cost savings and low selling prices have not been as expected in many cases; and consumer boredom in running or working for the cooperatives frequently sets in. Traditional retailers are also now doing a better a job of appealing to consumer niches in categories such as grocery products.

[13] Gretchen Mortgenson, "Back to Basics," *Forbes* (May 10, 1993), pp. 57–58; Bruce Fox, "Brand Erosion Potential," *Chain Store Age Executive* (February 1994), pp. 28, 37; and Steve Weinstein, "A Run for Their Money," *Progressive Grocer* (November 1993), pp. 67–76.

[14] REI; and Marianne Wilson, "Shoppers Climb the Wall at REI," *Chain Store Age Executive* (August 1993), pp. 72–73.

Summary

1. *To show the ways in which retail institutions can be classified* There are two million retail firms in the United States operating over 2.4 million establishments. They can be classified on the basis of ownership, store-based strategy mix, nonstore-based strategy mix, and service versus goods strategy mix. These categories are not mutually exclusive; many retailers can be placed in more than one category. This chapter deals with retail ownership. Chapter 5 examines the other classifications.

2. *To study retailers on the basis of ownership type and examine the characteristics of each* Eighty per cent of U.S. retail establishments are run as independents, with each operating only one store. This large number is mostly due to the ease of entry into retailing. Among the competitive advantages of independents are their flexibility, low investments, specialized offerings, direct control of strategy, image, consistency, independence, and entrepreneurial spirit. Disadvantages include limited bargaining power, few economies of scale, labor intensiveness, reduced media access, overdependence on the owner, and limited planning.

   Retail chains consist of multiple stores under common ownership, usually engaged in some centralized purchasing and decision making. They account for a fifth of retail establishments but over half of U.S. retail sales. Chains have these advantages: bargaining power, wholesale function efficiencies, multiple-store efficiencies, computerization, access to media, well-defined management, and long-range planning. They face these potential problems: inflexibility, high investments, reduced control, and limited independence.

   Franchising embodies contractual arrangements between franchisors (which may be manufacturers, wholesalers, or service sponsors) and retail franchisees that allow the franchisees to conduct given businesses under established names and according to specified rules. It accounts for over one-third of retail store sales. Franchisees have these benefits: small investments, well-known company names, standardized operating procedures and training, cooperative marketing efforts, exclusive selling rights, and volume purchases. They may also face constrained decision making via oversaturation, lower-than-promised profits, strict contract provisions, cancellation clauses, short-term contracts, and continuing royalty payments. Franchisors benefit by more quickly and cheaply developing large businesses, setting franchisee qualifications, improving cash flow, outlining strict operating procedures, gaining high franchisee motivation, and receiving ongoing royalties. They may suffer if individual franchisees hurt the company image, do not operate uniformly, compete with one another, lower resale values, and seek greater independence.

   Leased departments are in-store sites rented to outside parties. They usually exist in categories on the fringe of their stores' major product lines. Stores gain these advantages: expertise of lessees, reduced costs, greater traffic, merchandising support, and leasing revenues. Potential disadvantages are conflicts with lessees and adverse effects on store image. Benefits for lessees are well-known store names, steady customers, immediate sales, reduced expenses, economies of scale, and an image associated with the store. Potential problems are inflexibility, restrictions on items sold, lease nonrenewal, and poorer results than expected.

   Vertical marketing systems consist of all the levels of independently owned firms along a channel of distribution. In independent systems, there are separately owned manufacturers, wholesalers, and retailers. In partially integrated systems, two separately owned firms, usually manufacturers and retailers, perform all production and distribution functions without the aid of a third. In fully integrated systems, single firms perform all production and distribution functions. Some firms use dual vertical marketing systems, whereby they are involved in more than one type of system.

   Consumer cooperatives are retail firms owned by their customers, who invest, receive company stock, elect officers, manage operations, and share savings or profits. They account for a fraction of one per cent of retail store sales. Cooperatives are formed when consumers believe they can perform retailing functions, offerings of traditional retailers are inadequate, and traditional retailers' profits and prices are too high. They have not grown further because a lot of consumer initiative is required, expertise may be lacking, expectations have frequently not been met, and boredom occurs.

3. *To explore the methods used by manufacturers, wholesalers, and retailers to obtain control in the distribution channel* Even without an integrated vertical marketing system, channel control can be exerted by the most powerful firm(s) in the channel. Manufacturers, wholesalers, and retailers each have methods for increasing their impact in a channel. Retailers' influence is greatest when they represent a large percentage of their vendors' sales, private branding is used, and economic power due to order volume exists.

KEY TERMS

retail institution (p. 104)
independent (p. 105)
ease of entry (p. 105)
chain (p. 107)
franchising (p. 110)
product/trademark franchising (p. 110)
business format franchising (p. 110)
constrained decision making (p. 113)
leased department (p. 113)
vertical marketing system (p. 115)
independent vertical marketing system (p. 115)
partially integrated vertical marketing system (p. 116)
fully integrated vertical marketing system (p. 116)
dual vertical marketing system (p. 117)
channel control (p. 117)
consumer cooperative (p. 119)

QUESTIONS FOR DISCUSSION

1. What are the characteristics of each of the ownership forms discussed in this chapter?
2. How may a retailer be categorized by more than one ownership form? Give two examples.
3. Why does the concept of ease of entry usually have a greater impact on independent retailers than on chain retailers?
4. How can an independent retailer overcome the problem of overdependence on the owner?
5. What difficulties might an independent encounter if it tries to expand into a chain?
6. What competitive advantages and disadvantages do regional chains have in comparison with national chains?
7. Do you expect retail chains with 100 or more outlets to continue to increase their percentage of U.S. retail sales? Explain your answer.
8. What are the similarities and differences between chains and franchising?
9. From the franchisee's perspective, under what circumstances would product/trademark franchising be advantageous? When would business format franchising be better?
10. Why would a department store want to lease space to an outside operator rather than run a business, such as shoes, itself? What would be its risks in this approach?
11. What are the pros and cons of Avon's using a dual vertical marketing system?
12. At many retail apparel chains, store brands account for more than 50 per cent of sales. What are the pros and cons of this strategy from a channel control perspective?
13. How could a small independent gift store increase its channel control?
14. Why have consumer cooperatives not expanded much in recent years? What would you recommend to change this?

CASE 1
Book Superstores' Challenge to Independents*

Bookstore chains such as Barnes & Noble and Borders (a division of Kmart) have begun writing a new chapter in book retailing with their superstores. In comparison to both independent and chain-based bookstores, these superstores have economies of scale, lower advertising costs, a better selection, and a much improved ambiance.

Although there are slight variations on a store-by-store basis, most superstores are 12,000 to 37,000 square feet in size, stock between 80,000 and 100,000 different titles, employ discount pricing, have extended hours, and offer an atmosphere that favors browsing. For example, Barnes & Noble discounts hardcover books by 10 per cent, titles on the *New York Times* hardcover best-seller list by 30 per cent, and publishers' overstock by up to 80 per cent. Most of its superstores are open until 11 P.M. or even midnight, have coffee bars (with cappuccino, pastries, and sandwiches), and provide comfortable chairs and tables for reading and browsing. Some have in-

* The material in this case is drawn from Meg Cox, "Barnes & Noble's Boss Has Big Growth Plans That Booksellers Fear," *Wall Street Journal* (September 11, 1992), pp. A1, A9; Laura Liebeck, "Superstores Write New Chapter in Retailing," *Discount Store News* (May 3, 1993), pp. 27–28; Richard Phalon, "A Bold Gamble," *Forbes* (February 28, 1994), pp. 90–91; and Carol Steinberg, "Book Superstores Challenge Independents," *New York Times* (December 19, 1993), pp. 1, 16.

creased traffic by including events such as signings by well-known writers, food samplings, and story times for children. Some also have pads and pencils on tables to enable browsers to write down important facts or even copy recipes from cook books. Many managers position their superstores as "a library where you can purchase books;" others view their stores as "a kind of community center that makes people keenly aware of the pleasures of reading."

Even though superstores have been heralded by casual readers, as well as bibliophiles, their success has caused concern among independent booksellers. Many independents have already lost market share to membership clubs like Price/Costco (that sell books for the same prices that these booksellers typically buy them). They now worry that the buying power of large chains, the chains' ability to use advertising media that they cannot afford (such as TV and regional editions of magazines), and the superstores' higher sales per square foot give them real competitive advantages over the independents.

There are no definitive data on the sales volume or profitability of superstores, but some data are available from Barnes & Nobles and the American Booksellers Association. A Barnes & Noble prospectus says its superstores average more than $3.5 million in annual sales; and more than 80 per cent of superstores are profitable during their first full year of operation. However, retail analysts estimate that it takes about four years for a new superstore to achieve the profitability of older, smaller stores. The new superstores also require a $1.6 million investment per unit. And the president of the Dart Group, a 50 per cent owner of Crown Books (a competitor of Barnes & Noble) asserts that Barnes & Noble's superstores are only marginally profitable.

Research conducted by the American Booksellers Association has found that larger stores sell more books and keep customers browsing longer than smaller stores. Although there are no data on the number of independent bookstores that have closed as a result of superstores, there is some evidence to support the hardships of independents. For example, Words-Worth, a 2,000-square-foot store that has been in Holbrook, New York, for the past 20 years, has seen a drop in sales of 40 per cent due to the "double whammy" of competition from a nearby Price Club and a Borders store. This decline is in sharp contrast to the increase in retail book sales during the 1990s. Managers of superstores do not agree that their growth has been at the expense of smaller independents. They claim that the superstore has increased the number of new readers, and that this phenomenon has benefitted both small and large booksellers.

All is not rosy for the superstores: Some cut staff drastically after the heavy Christmas seasons, resulting in a drop-off in customer service at some superstores. In an effort to increase revenues, many chains have allowed store managers to adapt their book selections to better meet local interests. While this approach may lead to higher revenues at individual units, it has angered publishers that can no longer be guaranteed chainwide compliance with book promotions. Lastly, with so many booksellers adding superstores, there is some wariness about the saturation of markets. For example, Barnes & Noble's sales per square foot have actually fallen since 1990.

Independent bookstores hope to keep their customers by emphasizing their own superior customer service, capitalizing on long-established first-name relationships with regular customers, stocking selected titles that appeal to readers interested in niche markets, discount pricing, and frequent buyer programs. Some independents are also refocusing their merchandise to put greater emphasis on calendars, videos and toys, and sales of books to school libraries. The chairman of Western Publishing (the partner with Toys "R" Us of its Books "R" Us division) believes smaller stores may have an advantage over the superstores for casual readers and less-educated people who may find superstores too intimidating.

QUESTIONS

1. How can an independent bookseller avoid being overdependent on the owner?
2. Describe the competitive advantages and disadvantages of independents relative to chain superstores.
3. Develop three strategies for an independent to best compete with a new superstore located within three miles of its current store.
4. Assess the impact of the success of the book superstore on control in the channel of distribution.

CASE 2 Maaco: Evaluating Franchising Opportunities†

Maaco Auto Painting and Bodyworks was founded in 1972 by Anthony A. Martino, the man who had created Aamco Transmissions in the 1950s. After Martino sold his interest in Aamco in the 1960s, he observed that another segment of the auto after-market business was ripe for franchising: auto paint and collision repair. At that time, auto body and painting service businesses were fragmented—with thousands of small independent body shops, one national company that performed cheap jobs, and custom shops that specialized in restoring expensive vehicles.

As Martino saw it, the low- and high-priced ends of the market were saturated, while the huge middle market was underrepresented. So, he devised the methods, manuals, and systems for an auto painting and collision repair franchise business via a pilot shop he opened in Wilmington, Delaware. Today, there are over 450 independently owned and operated Maaco franchises in 43 states and Canada. Since its founding in 1972, Maaco franchisees have painted and repaired almost 7,000,000 vehicles—over 500,000 in 1993 alone.

Maaco is the only national firm in the $34-billion-a-year paint-and-collision business. It specializes in repainting cars aged three to seven years old, restoring rust-damaged cars, and repairing cars that have been involved in accidents. Although it offers paint jobs for as low as $199, Maaco specializes in the middle-market price range of $500 paint jobs. According to Anthony Martino, "Maaco's strategy of painting 40 cars a week at $500 per car is more profitable than painting three or four cars a week for $1,200." The success of Maaco is due to its positive image, the consistency and uniformity of operations, and the support programs provided to franchisees.

Maaco is the best-known U.S. auto paint and collision repair chain. Its strong reputation is built on the quality provided by local franchisees, fair dealing by local franchisees, and a nationally-accepted limited warranty (in case a car owner moves or a local franchisee is no longer in business). The image is reinforced via a national advertising program and public relations conducted by Maaco, as well as local ads and public relations by franchisees.

Maaco instills consistency and uniformity throughout all of its franchised locations. Each location uses the same manner of operation (that includes hand and machine sanding, chemical washing, proper masking, painting in a modern spray booth, and baking in a temperature-controlled oven), and the same caliber supplies. Every Maaco center offers free estimates on painting, body work, and rust restoration; accurate scheduling; and written warranties that are valid systemwide. Each franchisee—regardless of background, education, and experience—also receives several weeks of formal training at corporate headquarters and on-site training. Lastly, the

† The material in this case is drawn from *Maaco: The Franchise* (King of Prussia, PA: 1990); *The Maaco Story: 1972 to the Present*; and Greg Matusky, "The Bungee Principle," *Success* (September 1991).

use of prototype store designs (with specifications as to shop colors, office and waiting area size, the number of service bays, and the type and size of ovens) fosters uniformity.

Maaco assists franchisees with site selection, preparation of the chosen site, facilities installation, required weekly reports, and troubleshooting (both operations and marketing). Its customer support team consists of more than 125 employees. These men and women work with franchisees on financing assistance, site selection, installation of equipment, lease negotiations, placing ads for crews, crew training, and problem solving. During training, franchisees receive operations, sales, advertising, and promotional manuals; and they meet and discuss their store opening with department heads of each major support area. After store openings, Maaco provides ongoing support for sales and marketing, public relations, purchasing, operations, weekly reports, and quality control. Attendance at the annual five-day meeting is required of franchisees; the periodic local and regional one- to three-day sessions and the monthly newsletter ensure that Maaco's training process is an ongoing one.

Total costs for a Maaco franchise are about $170,000. This includes all equipment, an initial inventory of supplies, a $25,000 franchise fee, and take-home pay for the franchisee for his or her first year of business. In addition, franchisees pay a royalty fee of 8 per cent of sales to Maaco and are obligated to spend $750 per week in local advertising. Some franchisees pool their advertising budgets to advertise on television.

Maaco's objectives call for each franchised unit to have a net profit of $150,000 per year. While the costs (based on rents and local labor rates) and income (based upon the number of paint jobs, the per cent of insurance claim work, and the per cent of fleet business) differ by location, Maaco's profit expectations are based on the average franchise location repairing/painting 25 to 30 cars per week at a $300 to $350 gross profit per car. Maaco also assumes that each franchised outlet can convert 60 per cent of its estimates into completed business with an average price of $500 per car.

The average franchise has weekly sales of between $12,000 and $15,000 for all but the coldest winter months, when business in the northern climates is slower. Franchisees in these locations generally run special sales during the winter season to keep their full-time work crews busy.

QUESTIONS

1. What are the pros and cons of an individual opening a Maaco franchise rather than an independent auto paint and body shop?
2. Develop a checklist of factors a person should consider in evaluating a Maaco franchising opportunity.
3. What additional information, besides that provided in the case, should a prospective franchisee acquire before purchasing a Maaco franchise? Cite sources that he or she could use to acquire this information.
4. Evaluate the financial data provided in this case from the perspective of a potential franchisee.

VIDEO QUESTIONS ON MAACO

1. Explain the statement "franchisees are in business for themselves, but not by themselves."
2. Assess the video as a means of attracting potential franchisees.

Appendix on Franchising

This appendix is presented because of the high growth rate for franchising and the interest in it. For example, before Mail Boxes Etc. turned to franchising in 1981, it had 3 company-owned stores in Southern California that focused on mail services, including 24-hour postal boxes. Although the firm wanted to grow, "venture capitalists laughed us out of the office." So, to be able to expand aggressively, Mail Boxes Etc. decided to become a franchisor and fund expansion via franchisee investments. Today, the firm has 1 company-owned store and 2,100 franchisee-owned outlets (at a current franchisee investment of $85,000 to $100,000 per store). It has stores throughout the United States and in nations like Brazil and Australia; these outlets offer photocopying and fax services, electronic tax filing, money orders, passport photos, office supplies, and more—in addition to the core mail service business. Its rate of growth and level of success would not have been possible without franchising.[1]

In this appendix, we go beyond the discussion of franchising in Chapter 4. And we provide information on managerial issues in franchising and on the relationships between franchisors and franchisees.

Since 1980, annual U.S. retail franchising sales have far more than doubled. Today, 520,000 establishments in the United States are affiliated with 3,000 franchisors and employ 7.2 million full- and part-time workers (including the proprietors). Many large business format franchisors have at least 1,000 outlets. The U.S. Department of Commerce predicts that retail franchising will continue to grow sharply through the year 2000.

U.S. franchisors are now situated in over 50 countries worldwide, a number expected to rise rapidly in the near future. This trend is due to these factors: U.S. franchisors recognize the growth potential in foreign markets. Franchising is becoming accepted as a retailing format in more nations. Trade barriers among nations are being reduced due to such pacts as NAFTA—the North American Free Trade Agreement that is making it easier for U.S.-, Canada-, and Mexico-based firms to operate in the others' marketplaces.[2]

Managerial Issues in Franchising

Franchising appeals to many owners and potential owners (franchisees) of small businesses for a variety of reasons. Most franchisors have easy-to-learn, standardized operating methods they have perfected over the years. This means new franchisees will not have to learn via their own trial-and-error methods, which may be costly and time-consuming. Franchisors often have training facilities where franchisees are taught how to operate equipment, manage employees, maintain records, and improve customer relations; they usually follow up with field visits by a service staff.

[1] Jeffrey A. Tannenbaum, "Mail Boxes Etc. Delivers Profits But Not to Everyone," *Wall Street Journal* (October 13, 1993), p. B2.

[2] See Jeffrey A. Tannenbaum, "U.S. Franchisers Expect NAFTA to Boost Mexican Business," *Wall Street Journal* (November 13, 1993), p. B2; and Sandra M. Huszagh, Frederick W. Huszagh, and Faye S. McIntyre, "International Franchising in the Context of Competitive Strategy and the Theory of the Firm," *International Marketing Review*, Vol. 9 (Number 5, 1992), pp. 5–18

A new outlet of a nationally advertised franchise (such as Domino's Pizza, Fantastic Sam's hair salons, or True Value hardware stores) can develop a large customer following rather quickly and easily because of the reputation of the firm. And not only does franchising result in good initial sales and profits, it also reduces franchisees' risk of failure. According to one study, 97 per cent of franchisee-owned stores are still in business five years after they open; and 86 per cent of franchisee-owned stores are still operated by the original franchisee five years after they open.[3]

The investment and startup costs for a franchised outlet can be as low as a few thousand dollars for a personal service business and as high as several million dollars for a hotel. In return for its expenditures, any franchisee usually gets exclusive selling rights for a geographic area; a business format franchisee also gets training, store equipment and fixtures, and assistance in picking out a store site, negotiating with suppliers, advertising, and so on.

What kind of person is most interested in becoming a franchisee? This is what two franchisors believe:

> It used to be that the potential franchisees would be someone looking for a second income, or a husband and wife wanting to work together. But today the person coming to us is definitely more sophisticated. He or she has often worked in the corporate world and senses the nonsense and craziness and decides that he [she] doesn't need the aggravation any more.
>
> When someone buys a franchise, he [she] has a safety net—if there's a problem there's someone to catch you. If someone wants to start a new company in a business that he [she] already knows, then he [she] doesn't really need to become a franchisee. But if someone wants to start a business in which he [she] has no experience, it is better to buy a franchise. The ideal franchisee is intelligent, hard-working, has the necessary capital, is good with people, and wants to succeed.[4]

As a cautionary note, the International Franchise Association (IFA) says, "People who have difficulty following directions or working within a system will find franchising extremely frustrating."[5]

According to a study of more than 200 franchise companies, the typical franchisee has attended college (over 40 per cent have at least a bachelor's degree), is between the age of 35 and 50, and earns an annual income of $67,000+. More than one-third previously worked in professional or executive positions.[6] And recently a Gallup poll of retailing franchisees found that

- 94 per cent of the franchisees said they were very or somewhat successful.
- 75 per cent of the franchisees said their businesses met or exceeded their expectations.
- 63 per cent of the franchisees expressed greater satisfaction with their franchising experience than with their prior business experience.
- 79 per cent of the franchisees rated the relationship with their franchisors as good or excellent.
- 75 per cent of the franchisees said they would again buy an outlet from the same franchisor if they had the opportunity to do so.[7]

[3] *Franchising in the Economy: 1989–1992* (Washington, D.C.: International Franchise Association Educational Foundation, Inc., and Arthur Andersen & Co., 1992), p. 16.

[4] Jacquelyn Bivens, "Franchising Boom Makes Headway," *Chain Store Age Executive* (October 1986), pp. 19–20.

[5] *Franchise Opportunities Guide* (Washington, D.C.: International Franchise Association, 1993), p. 21.

[6] Dan Fost and Susan Mitchell, "Small Stores with Big Names," *American Demographics* (November 1992), pp. 52–58.

[7] Michael H. Seid, "Franchising Thrives in the '90s," *Stores* (May 1993), p. 74.

TABLE 1 Investment and Startup Costs for New Franchisees by Goods/Service Category[a]

Goods/Service Category	Median Total Investment	Median Startup Cash Needed	Median Single-Unit Franchise Fee
Hotels and motels	$1,500,000	$425,000	$20,000
Restaurants (all types)	$250,000	$80,000	$20,000
Convenience stores	$180,000	$46,500	$22,500
Rental services firms	$130,000–$150,000	$30,000–$40,000	$15,000–$25,000
General merchandise stores	$120,000	$50,000	$20,000
Other food stores	$115,000	$50,000	$20,000
Recreation, entertainment, and travel businesses	$100,000	$49,500	$22,500
Automotive goods and services stores	$100,000	$40,000	$24,500
Educational goods and services firms	$80,000	$25,000	$27,250
Personal and household services firms	$10,000–$150,000	$6,000–$50,000	$5,000–$16,500

[a] Data are not available for auto and truck dealers and gasoline service stations.

Sources: Adapted by the authors from *Franchising in the Economy: 1988–1990* (Washington, D.C.: International Franchise Association Educational Foundation, Inc., and Horwath International, 1990), various pages; and *Franchising in the Economy: 1989–1992* (Washington, D.C.: International Franchise Association Educational Foundation, Inc., and Arthur Andersen & Co., 1992), various pages.

An illustration of how inexpensive franchising can be is Rainbow International Carpet Dyeing & Cleaning, a Texas-based firm with over 2,000 franchise arrangements. A typical franchisee makes an initial payment of about $21,000 (including $5,800 for equipment and supplies) and ongoing royalty payments of about 7 per cent of sales. The franchisees engage in on-site carpet and furniture dyeing and cleaning.[8]

Table 1 shows the median investments, startup cash, and franchise fees required of new franchisees in a wide range of goods/service categories. At present, funding support is offered by almost 30 per cent of U.S. franchisors. In addition, through various programs, the U.S. Small Business Administration is one of the best financing options for prospective franchisees. And some banks offer special lower interest rates for franchisees affiliated with well-established franchise operators.[9]

Besides receiving fees and royalties for allowing franchisees to run one or more outlets, franchisors may sell goods and services to their franchisees. Sometimes, this is required; more often, for legal reasons, such purchases are at the franchisees' discretion (subject to franchisor specifications). Each year, franchisors sell billions of dollars worth of items to franchisees.

Franchisors can set detailed standards covering every aspect of the business, such as signs, product freshness, merchandise selection, the level of involvement expected of franchisees, and employee uniforms. About one-half of U.S. business-format franchisors require franchisees to be owner-operators and work full-time at the business.

[8] *Franchise Opportunities Guide*, p. 161.

[9] Ibid., pp. 32–33.

TABLE 2 Outlets and Sales of Franchisee-Owned and Franchisor-Owned Retail Businesses by Goods/Service Category

Goods/Service Category	Number of Franchisee-Owned Outlets as Percentage of Total	Number of Franchisor-Owned Outlets as Percentage of Total	Percentage of Annual Sales from Franchisee-Owned Outlets	Percentage of Annual Sales from Franchisor-Owned Outlets
Auto and truck dealers	100	0	100	0
Gasoline service stations	82	18	82	18
Restaurants (all types)	79	21	76	24
General merchandise stores	98	2	95	5
Hotels and motels	89	11	98	2
Automotive goods and services stores	84	16	82	18
Convenience stores	38	62	34	66
Other food stores	92	8	87	13
Rental services firms	76	24	48	52
Personal and household services firms	89	11	74	26
Recreation, entertainment, and travel businesses	99	1	99	1
Educational goods and services firms	95	5	65	35
Real-estate firms	99	1	99	1

Sources: Adapted by the authors from *Franchising in the Economy: 1988–1990* (Washington, D.C.: International Franchise Association Educational Foundation, Inc., and Horwath International, 1990), various pages; and *Franchising in the Economy: 1989–1992* (Washington, D.C.: International Franchise Association Educational Foundation, Inc., and Arthur Andersen & Co., 1992), various pages.

The franchisors' standards must be adhered to by franchisees. Thus, franchisor concerns about systemwide consistency and franchisee desires to conduct their own business sometimes lead to conflicts.

Franchised outlets can be purchased (leased) directly from franchisors, master franchisees, or existing franchisees. Franchisors sell either new locations or company-owned outlets (some of which may have been taken back from unsuccessful franchisees). Sometimes, they sell the rights to develop outlets in geographic regions or counties to master franchisees, which then deal with individual franchisees. Existing franchisees usually have the right to sell their units if they first offer them to their franchisor; if potential purchasers meet all financial and other criteria; and/or if purchasers undergo comprehensive training. Table 2 shows the percentages of outlets and sales from franchisee-owned and franchisor-owned outlets by goods/service category.

Figure 1 contains a checklist by which potential franchisees could assess opportunities. When using this checklist, franchisees should also obtain full prospectuses and financial reports from all franchisors under consideration; and they should talk to existing franchise operators and customers.

1.	What are the required franchisor fees: initial fee, advertising appropriations, and royalties?
2.	What degree of technical knowledge is required of the franchisee?
3.	What is the required investment in time by the franchisee? Does the franchisee have to be actively involved in the day-to-day operations of the franchise?
4.	What is the extent of control of a franchise by a franchisor in terms of materials purchased, sales quotas, space requirements, pricing, the range of goods to be sold, required inventory levels, and so on?
5.	Can the franchisee accept the regimentation and rules of the franchisor?
6.	Are the costs of required supplies and materials purchased from the franchisor at market value, above market value, or below market value?
7.	What degree of name recognition do consumers have of the franchise? Does the franchisor have a meaningful advertising program?
8.	What image does the franchise have among consumers and among current franchisees?
9.	What are the level and quality of services provided by the franchisor to franchisees: site selection, training, bookkeeping, human relations, equipment maintenance, and trouble-shooting?
10.	What is the franchisor policy in terminating franchisees? What are the conditions of franchise termination? What is the rate of franchise termination and nonrenewal?
11.	What is the franchisor's legal history?
12.	What is the length of the franchise agreement?
13.	What is the failure rate of existing franchises?
14.	What is the franchisor's policy with regard to company-owned and franchisee-owned outlets?
15.	What policy does the franchisor have in allowing franchisees to sell their business?
16.	What is the franchisor's policy with regard to territorial protection for existing franchisees? With regard to new franchisees and new company-owned establishments?
17.	What is the earning potential of the franchise during the first year? The first five years?

FIGURE 1
A Checklist for Prospective Franchisees to Evaluate Franchise Opportunities

Franchisor-Franchisee Relationships

Many franchisors and franchisees have good relationships because they share goals regarding company image, the way the business is operated and managed, the goods and/or services offered, cooperative advertising, and sales and profit growth. As one observer noted, "It is one of the fundamentals of successful franchising that the franchisor must support the franchisee throughout the life of their relationship."[10]

This two-way relationship is shown by the actions of Great Expectations Creative Management, a franchisor of video-dating services. As a result of the early 1990s U.S. economic downturn and increased competition, the firm agreed to reduce its royalty rate from 10 to 8 per cent and to pay $1.25 million for its first national advertising campaign (with decisions made by franchisees). Great Expectations' founder commented: "There's nothing in the franchise agreement that says I had to do anything about the recession. But I chose to respond to franchisees' concerns in ways that will make a difference."[11]

[10] "Letting Others Mind Your Business," *Management Today* (November 1992), p. 94.

[11] Jeffrey A. Tannenbaum, "Franchisors and Franchisees Make Some Concessions," *Wall Street Journal* (February 7, 1991), p. B2; and *Franchise Opportunities Guide*, p. 92.

Yet, for several reasons, tensions do exist between various franchisors and their franchisees. These are just some of the reasons:

- The franchisor-franchisee relationship is not one of employer to employee. Franchisor controls are often viewed as rigid.
- Many U.S. franchise agreements are considered too short in duration by franchisees. Forty-five per cent of agreements are ten years in duration or less (17 per cent are 5 years or less), usually at the franchisor's request.
- For the many franchisees that lease their outlets' property from their franchisors, the loss of a franchise license generally means eviction; and the franchisee receives nothing for "goodwill."
- Some franchisees believe their franchisors want to buy back their units because of higher profit potential.
- Some franchisors believe their franchisees do not reinvest enough in their outlets and that this results in a poor image for the firm.
- Franchisees may not be concerned enough about overall company image and the consistency of offerings from one outlet to another.
- Franchisors may not give adequate territorial protection to franchisees and may open new outlets near existing ones.
- Franchisees may refuse to participate in cooperative advertising programs.
- Franchisees may offer substandard service.
- Some franchisors use minor contract infractions to oust franchisees.
- Franchised outlets that are put up for sale must usually be offered first to franchisors, which also have approval of sales to third parties.
- Some franchisees believe franchisor support is low.
- Franchisees may be prohibited from operating competing businesses.
- Restrictions on purchases and suppliers may cause franchisees to pay higher prices and/or to have limited product assortments.
- Franchisees may band together to force changes in franchisor policies and exert pressure on franchisors.
- Sales and profit expectations may not be realized.

Tensions can lead to conflicts—even litigation. Potential negative franchisor actions include terminating agreements; reducing promotional and sales support; and adding unneeded red tape for orders, information requests, and warranty work. Potential negative franchisee actions include terminating agreements, adding competitors' product lines, refusing to promote goods and services, and not complying with franchisor information requests.

Each year, business format franchisors terminate the contracts of seven per cent of their franchisee-owned stores that opened within the prior five years; and the American Arbitration Association is asked to mediate hundreds of franchising disputes—at the request of both franchisors and franchisees. From 1989 through 1993, the Federal Trade Commission got 1,360+ franchisee complaints of poor business practices on the part of their franchisors.[12]

Although franchising has historically been characterized by franchisors' possessing more power than franchisees, this inequality has been reduced in several ways. First, a number of franchisees affiliated with specific franchisors have joined together to increase their power. For example, the National Coalition of Associations of 7-Eleven

[12] *Franchising in the Economy: 1989–1992,* p. 106; Barbara Marsh, "Arbitration Cases Soar in Franchising Industry," *Wall Street Journal* (July 25, 1990), p. B1; and Jeffrey A. Tannenbaum, "Senator Joins Campaign for a Franchisee's Right to Sue," *Wall Street Journal* (July 26, 1993), p. B2.

Franchisees represents 2,100 franchisees running 7-Eleven convenience stores. Second, a number of large umbrella organizations representing franchisees, like the California Franchise Council and the National Franchise Association Coalition, have been formed.

Third, many franchisees now operate more than one outlet, so they have greater clout. For instance, the major oil producers fear that multiunit gasoline stations can amass enough power to buy from independent suppliers. Fourth, there has been a substantial rise in litigation between franchisors and franchisees. As an example, an association representing franchisees that operated 3,100 KFC outlets filed suit against the franchisor after the latter sought to eliminate a clause in their franchise agreements stipulating that no new outlets could be built within 1.5 miles of existing ones.[13] Fifth, when dissatisfied, some franchisee groups have sought to purchase their franchisors. For instance, franchisee groups at Straw Hat Pizza and at Eastern Onion (a singing-telegram service) each acquired their franchisor.[14]

Improved communication and better cooperation will be necessary to resolve these issues. One innovative approach to doing so is used by Subway Sandwiches & Salads, a growing franchise chain with thousands of outlets. At Subway, a group of franchisees comprise a committee with full responsibility for the firm's multimillion dollar annual advertising budget (including hiring and firing ad agencies).[15]

Another progressive approach is the new code of ethics devised by the International Franchise Association. If the IFA's 800 franchisor members adhere to this voluntary code, the conflicts between franchisors and franchisees will decline substantially. These are some of the standards of conduct recommended in the IFA code:

- Franchisors' offering circulars shall be complete, accurate, and not misleading.
- Franchisors and franchisees shall deal with each other in an honest, ethical, and mutually respectful manner.
- Franchisors shall not prohibit franchisees from forming, joining, or participating in any franchisee association.
- Franchisee agreements may only be terminated for good cause. Franchisees shall be given a reasonable opportunity to remedy their shortcomings before they are actually terminated.
- Prior to opening new outlets, franchisors shall consider the potential impact of those outlets on existing franchisees if the new outlets would be in close proximity to them.[16]

As one observer has summed things up:

> To attract more-qualified franchisees, purchase arrangements must be more flexible. To increase franchisee satisfaction, a more balanced partnership between franchisor and franchisees is needed. To maximize the prospects for financial success for both parties, operating arrangements should take into account individual circumstances. Therefore, more franchisors will adopt, or at least experiment with, restructured franchise arrangements. This restructuring will affect both the terms of purchasing a franchise and the ongoing franchisor-franchisee relationship.[17]

[13] Scott Hume, "Franchisees to Sue KFC on Territory Rule," *Advertising Age* (May 21, 1990), p. 23.

[14] Gail DeGeorge, "Fed-Up Franchisees," *Business Week* (November 13, 1989), p. 85.

[15] John P. Cortez, "Subway Builds Its Way to No. 2," *Advertising Age* (July 5, 1993), p. 32.

[16] *Internal Franchise Association Code of Ethics* (Washington, D.C.: International Franchise Association, 1992).

[17] Bruce J. Walker, "Retail Franchising in the 1990s," *Arthur Andersen Retailing Issues Letter* (January 1991), p. 4.

Retail Institutions by Strategy Mix

❖ Chapter Objectives

1. To describe the wheel of retailing, scrambled merchandising, and the retail life cycle and show how they help explain the performance and evolution of retail strategy mixes
2. To examine the characteristics of a wide variety of retail institutions involved with store-based strategy mixes (divided into food-oriented and general merchandise groupings)
3. To look at the characteristics of the three major retail institutions involved with nonstore-based strategy mixes: vending machine, direct selling, and direct marketing
4. To contrast service-based retailing with goods-based retailing

Because gas station owners are struggling with reduced profit margins from their sale of gasoline, they have been increasingly adding merchandise lines they feel are compatible with gasoline. This has led to some interesting approaches: gas stations that sell flowers, gas stations with dry cleaning services, and even gas stations that sell prepared foods such as tacos. Mobil Corporation, for example, is currently experimenting with a combined gas station and McDonald's in Naples, Florida, a combined gas station and Burger King in Chicago, and a combined gas station with Taco Bell and Pizza Hut at further locations. Other gas stations are even adding fax/copier centers, parcel drop-off services, and video rental units.

The rise in this form of scrambled merchandising is due to various factors: environmental regulations, competition from specialized car-service firms, and changes in consumer behavior. Recent environmental regulations have forced many gas stations to replace their storage tanks and pumping equipment to control fumes during pumping and to eliminate fuel spills. The cost of meeting these state and federal rules are so high that stations often need other product lines to supplement gasoline sales. A number of stations now have vacant service bays because they have lost customers to specialized oil change, tune-up, muffler replacement, and tire shops. Thus, their dormant service bays provide space for other retail uses. Last, consumers feel more comfortable buying unrelated products (even prepared foods) at gasoline stations than they did before.

One concern about the sales of nontraditional goods and services by gas stations is the blurring of the traditional image of the gasoline station as a place where cars are serviced and gasoline is sold. Another potential problem is that the sale of gasoline and some unrelated items may be in conflict with one another. For example, the sale of gasoline is generally maximized when payment dispensers (that accept credit cards directly at the gasoline pump) are used. Yet, because drivers do not have to leave their cars when payment dispensers are used, the sale of highly-profitable impulse goods such as soda, coffee, and cigarettes is minimized. Dispensers are particularly favored by women drivers with children in the car; but, this represents a key customer group for fill-in items such as milk, eggs, and snack foods for children.[1]

[1] Agis Salpukas, "Fill It Up? Send a Fax? Have a Taco?" *New York Times* (December 27, 1993), pp. D1, D3.

Reprinted by permission.

Overview

In Chapter 4, retail institutions were described by type of ownership arrangement. In this chapter, we discuss three key considerations in planning retail strategy mixes: the wheel of retailing, scrambled merchandising, and the retail life cycle. We then view retail institutions from diverse strategic perspectives: store-based, nonstore-based, and service versus goods retailing.

Considerations in Planning a Retail Strategy Mix

A retailer may be classified by its ***strategy mix.*** This mix is a firm's particular combination of these factors: store location, operating procedures, goods/services offered, pricing tactics, store atmosphere and customer services, and promotional methods.

Store location refers to the use of a store or nonstore format, placement in a geographic area, and the kind of site (such as a shopping center versus an isolated store). Operating procedures include the kinds of personnel employed, management style, store hours, and other factors. The goods/services offered may encompass several product categories or just one; and quality may be low, medium, or high. Pricing refers to a retailer's comparative strategy: prestige pricing (creating a quality image via high prices); competitive pricing (setting prices at the level of rivals); or penetration pricing (underpricing other retailers to attract value-conscious consumers). Store atmosphere and customer services are reflected by a firm's physical facilities and the level of personal attention provided, credit, return policies, delivery, and other factors. Promotion involves the retailer's activities in such areas as advertising, displays, personal selling, and sales promotion. By combining these elements, a retailer can develop a unique strategy.

To succeed in today's environment, a retailer should strive to be dominant in some aspect of its strategy. The firm may then be able to reach ***power retailer*** status—whereby consumers view the company as distinctive enough to become loyal to it and go out of their way to shop there. We tend to link "dominant" with "large." Yet, both small and large retailers can dominate in their own way. There are several ways to be a power retailer:

1. Be price-oriented and cost-efficient to appeal to price-sensitive shoppers.
2. Be upscale to appeal to full-service, status-conscious consumers.
3. Be convenience-oriented to appeal to consumers interested in shopping ease, nearby locations, or long store hours.
4. Offer a dominant assortment with an extensive selection in the product lines carried to appeal to consumers interested in variety and in-store shopping comparisons.
5. Be customer service-oriented to appeal to people who are frustrated by the decline in retail service—as they perceive it.
6. Be innovative or exclusive and provide a unique method of operations (such as videodisc kiosks at airports) or carry products/brands not stocked by other firms to appeal to customers who are innovators, bored, or looking for items not in the "me too" mold.

Combining two or more of these approaches can yield even greater power.[2]

Before we examine specific retail strategy mixes, three important concepts that help explain the performance and evolution of these mixes should be understood: the wheel of retailing, scrambled merchandising, and the retail life cycle. These concepts

[2] Joel R. Evans, "U.S. Retailing in the 1990s: Back to the Future," *Retail Strategist,* Vol. 1 (Number 1, 1991), p. 7.

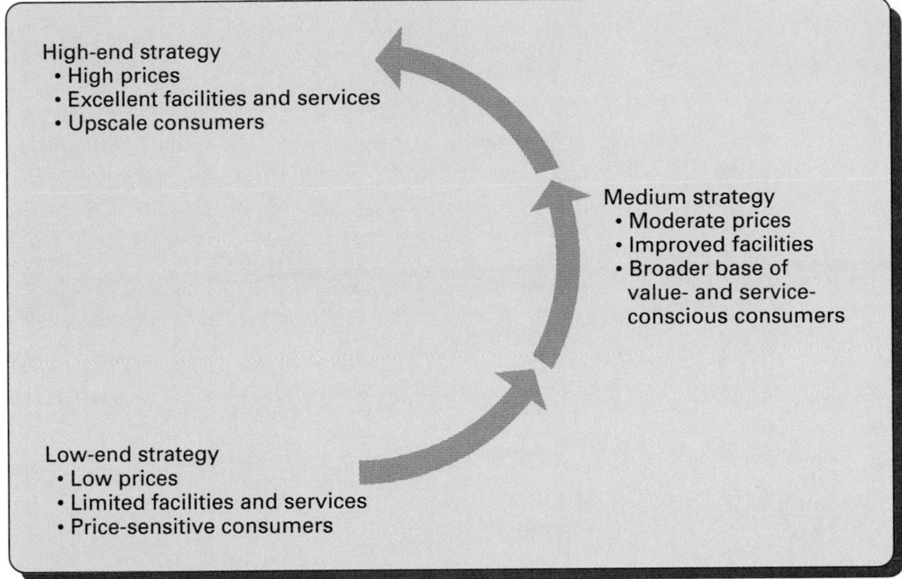

FIGURE 5–1
The Wheel of Retailing
As a low-end retailer upgrades its strategy, to increase sales and profit margins, a new form of discounter takes its place.

are particularly useful in describing the performance of existing retailers, predicting new retail institutions, determining the impact of new institutions on existing retailers, and forecasting how existing retailers are likely to respond to change.

THE WHEEL OF RETAILING

According to the ***wheel-of-retailing*** theory, retail innovators often first appear as low-price operators with a low-cost structure and low profit-margin requirements. Over time, these innovators upgrade the products they carry and improve store facilities and customer services (by adding better-quality items, locating in higher-rent sites, accepting exchanges and allowing refunds, providing credit and delivery, and so on), and prices rise. As the innovators mature, they become vulnerable to new discounters with lower cost structures; hence, the wheel of retailing.[3] See Figure 5–1.

The wheel of retailing is based on four basic premises:

1. There are many price-sensitive shoppers willing to trade customer services, wide selections, and convenient locations for lower prices.
2. Price-sensitive shoppers are often not store-loyal and are willing to switch to retailers offering lower prices. Other, prestige-sensitive customers like to shop at stores with high-end strategies.
3. New institutions are frequently able to implement lower operating costs than existing institutions.
4. When retailers move up the wheel, they typically do so to increase sales, broaden the target market, and improve store image.

For example, in the 1950s and again in the 1970s, traditional department store prices rose to levels that spurred the growth of two new institutional forms: the full-line discount store and the retail catalog showroom. These firms could stress low prices

[3] The pioneering works on the wheel of retailing are Malcolm P. McNair, "Significant Trends and Developments in the Postwar Period," in A. B. Smith (Editor), *Competitive Distribution in a Free High Level Economy and Its Implications for the University* (Pittsburgh: University of Pittsburgh Press, 1958), pp. 17–18; and Stanley Hollander, "The Wheel of Retailing," *Journal of Marketing*, Vol. 25 (July 1960), pp. 37–42. For a more recent analysis of the concept, see Stephen Brown, "The Wheel of Retailing: Past and Future," *Journal of Retailing*, Vol. 66 (Summer 1990), pp. 143–149.

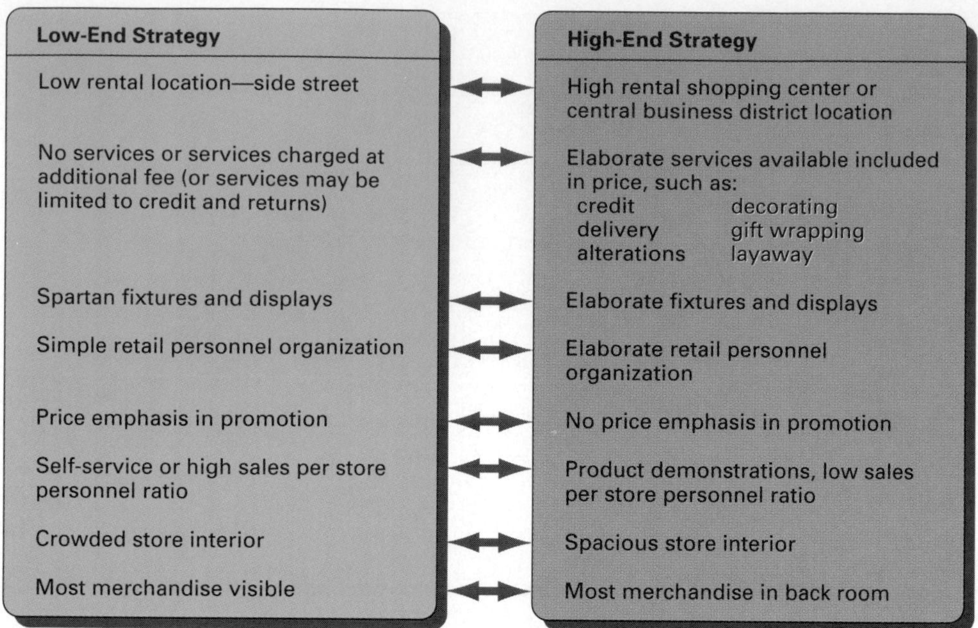

Low-End Strategy
Low rental location—side street
No services or services charged at additional fee (or services may be limited to credit and returns)
Spartan fixtures and displays
Simple retail personnel organization
Price emphasis in promotion
Self-service or high sales per store personnel ratio
Crowded store interior
Most merchandise visible
High-End Strategy
High rental shopping center or central business district location
Elaborate services available included in price, such as:
credit
decorating
delivery
gift wrapping
alterations
layaway
Elaborate fixtures and displays
Elaborate retail personnel organization
No price emphasis in promotion
Product demonstrations, low sales per store personnel ratio
Spacious store interior
Most merchandise in back room

Figure 5–2
Retail Strategy Alternatives

because of such cost-cutting techniques as having a small sales force, situating in lower-rent store locations, using inexpensive fixtures, emphasizing high stock turnover, and accepting only cash or check payments for goods.

As full-line discount stores and retail catalog showrooms succeeded, they typically sought to move up along the wheel. This meant enlarging the sales force, improving locations, upgrading fixtures, carrying lower-turnover merchandise, and granting credit. These improvements led to higher costs, which, in turn, led to higher prices. In the 1980s, the wheel of retailing again functioned as newer types of discounters, such as off-price chains, factory outlets, and flea markets, expanded to satisfy the needs of the price-conscious consumer. Today, an emerging retail institution known as the "category killer" store (a large discount-oriented outlet specializing in one or a few product categories) is appealing to consumers who are interested in low prices and a large selection in the product line(s) carried. The category killer store's size lets it both buy merchandise and operate very efficiently.

As indicated in Figure 5–1, the wheel of retailing reveals three basic strategic positions: low end, medium, and high end. The medium strategy may have some difficulties if retailers in this position are not perceived as distinctive by consumers. Figure 5–2 shows the opposing alternatives a retailer faces when considering a strategy mix. Through this dichotomy, one can differentiate between the two extreme cases of strategic emphasis: low end and high end. The wheel of retailing suggests that established retailers should be cautious in adding services or in converting their strategy from low end to high end. Because price-conscious shoppers are not usually store-loyal, they are likely to switch to lower-priced firms. Furthermore, retailers may be eliminating the competitive advantages that have led to profitability.

Scrambled Merchandising

Whereas the wheel of retailing focuses on strategy changes based on product quality, prices, and customer service, scrambled merchandising involves a retailer's increasing its width of assortment (the number of different product lines carried). ***Scrambled merchandising*** occurs when a retailer adds goods and services that are unrelated to each other and to the firm's original business. See Figure 5–3.

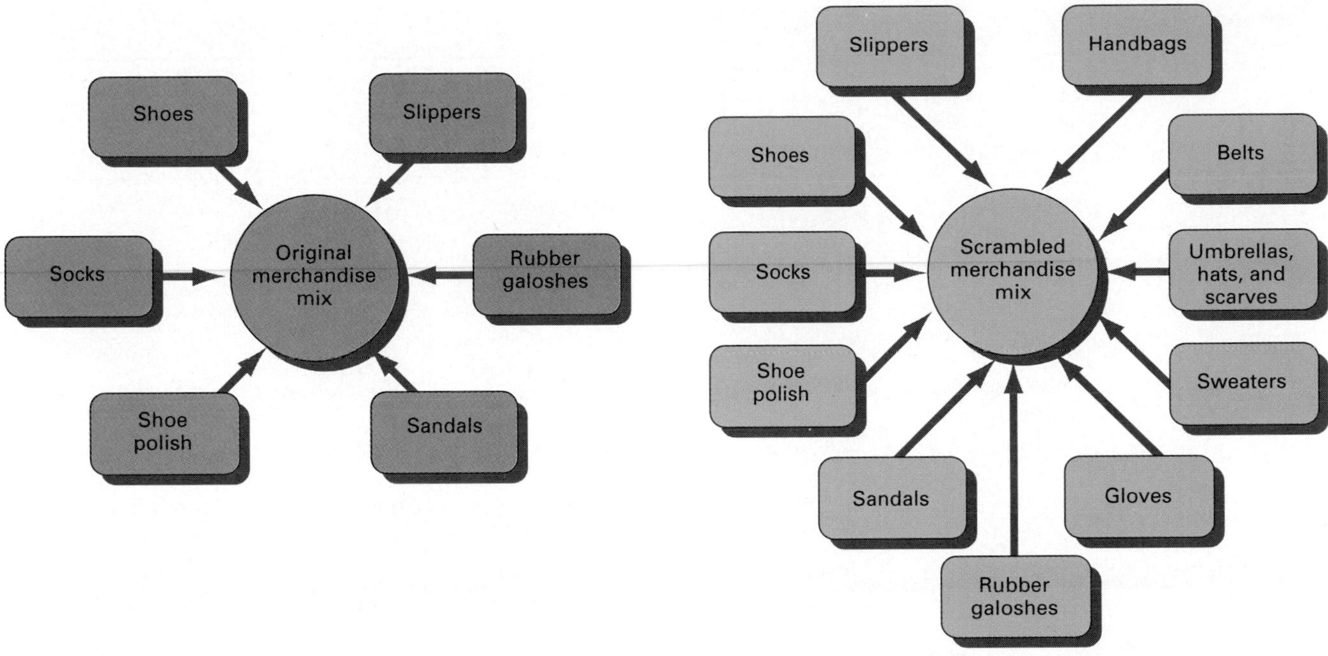

FIGURE 5–3 Scrambled Merchandising by a Shoe Store

The great popularity of scrambled merchandising in recent years is due to a number of factors: retailers are interested in increasing overall sales volume; goods and services that are fast-selling and have high profit margins are usually the ones added; consumers may make more impulse purchases; consumers are attracted to one-stop shopping; different target markets may be reached; and the effects of seasonality and competition may be reduced.

It is important to note the contagious nature of scrambled merchandising. For example, drugstores, bookstores, florists, and photo-developing firms are all affected by scrambled merchandising on the part of supermarkets. About 10 per cent of total U.S. supermarket sales are from general merchandise, health and beauty aids, and other nongrocery items, such as pharmacy products, books and magazines, flowers, and seasonal merchandise.[4] In response, these retailers are compelled to use scrambled merchandising to fill the void in their sales caused by the supermarkets. They have added unrelated items, such as toys and gift items, greeting cards, batteries, and cameras. This then creates a void for other retailers, which are also forced to scramble.

The growth in scrambled merchandising means that competition among different types of retailers is increasing and that distribution costs for manufacturers are rising as sales are dispersed over more retailers. There are other limitations to scrambled merchandising, such as the lack of retailer expertise in buying, selling, and servicing items with which they are unfamiliar; the costs associated with a broader product assortment (including lower inventory turnover); and the potential damage to a retailer's image if it performs poorly.

THE RETAIL LIFE CYCLE

A third useful concept in understanding the performance and evolution of different retail strategy mixes is the ***retail life cycle***. This theory asserts that retail institutions—like the goods and services they sell—pass through identifiable life cycles with four

[4] "1993 Non-Foods Sales Manual," *Progressive Grocer* (August 1993), p. 43.

TABLE 5–1 The Retail Life Cycle

	Area or Subject of Concern	Stage in the Life Cycle: Innovation	Accelerated Development	Maturity	Decline
Market characteristics	Number of competitors	Very few	Moderate	Many direct competitors; moderate indirect competition	Moderate direct competition; many indirect competitors
	Rate of sales growth	Very rapid	Rapid	Moderate to slow	Slow or negative
	Level of profitability	Low to moderate	High	Moderate	Very low
	Duration of stage	3–5 years	5–8 years	Indefinite	Indefinite
Appropriate retailer actions	Investment/ growth/risk decisions	Investment minimization; high risks accepted	High level of investment to sustain growth	Tightly controlled growth in untapped markets	Marginal capital expenditures and only when essential
	Central management concerns	Concept refinement through adjustment and experimenting	Establishing a pre-emptive market position	Excess capacity and "overstoring"; prolonging maturity and revising the business concept	Engaging in a "run-out" strategy
	Use of management-control techniques	Minimal	Moderate	Extensive	Moderate
	Most successful management style	Entrepreneurial	Centralized	"Professional"	Caretaker

Source: Adapted by the authors from an exhibit in William R. Davidson, Albert D. Bates, and Stephen J. Bass, "The Retail Life Cycle," *Harvard Business Review*, Vol. 54 (November–December 1976), p. 92. Reprinted with permission of the *Harvard Business Review*. Copyright 1976 by the President and Fellows of Harvard College; all rights reserved.

stages: innovation, accelerated development, maturity, and decline.[5] The direction and speed of institutional changes can be interpreted from this theory. Table 5–1 summarizes the stages of the retail life cycle.

From an industrywide perspective, in the United States:

> The first life cycle focused on merchandise. Money was made when the goods were bought. Stores were located in the inner city. Market reach was limited and

[5] William R. Davidson, Albert D. Bates, and Stephen J. Bass, "The Retail Life Cycle," *Harvard Business Review*, Vol. 54 (November–December 1976), pp. 89–96. See also Stanley C. Hollander and Glenn S. Omura, "Chain Store Developments and Their Political, Strategic, and Social Interdependencies," *Journal of Retailing*, Vol. 65 (Fall 1989), pp. 299–325; Ronald Savitt, "Looking Back to See Ahead: Writing the History of American Retailing," *Journal of Retailing*, Vol. 65 (Fall 1989), pp. 326–355; and Albert D. Bates, "The Extended Specialty Store: A Strategic Opportunity for the 1990s," *Journal of Retailing*, Vol. 65 (Fall 1989), pp. 379–388.

FIGURE 5–4
Carrefour's Now-Defunct Hypermarket in Pennsylvania
Reprinted by permission of Carrefour.

local. Advertising was mostly by word of mouth or in the local media. This life cycle of retailing came to an end with the Great Depression.

The second wave began to hit its growth phase in the post-World War II era. This wave was expansion-oriented. Opening new stores was the focus of management. Money was made when the goods were sold. Stores followed their customers to the suburbs and the regional mall was born. Market reach was now national, as was advertising. The beginning of the end for this life cycle was the 1987 stock market crash and the collapse of Campeau [then owner of Federated Department Stores].

The new life cycle in retail development reflects the informationalization of the industry. This cycle represents a shift in management focus from market expansion to information intensification, from geography to communication-focused technologies, from return on investment to return on customers, from sales growth to profit growth, from increasing individual transactions to establishing long-term customer relationships. Third-wave retailers share these characteristics: global focus, obsession with technology, and organizational restructuring around the customer.[6]

Let us now study the individual stages of the retail life cycle and show specific examples. During the first stage of the cycle (innovation), there is a strong departure from the strategy mixes of existing retail institutions. A firm in this stage significantly alters at least one element of the strategy mix from that of traditional competitors. Sales and then profits often rise sharply for the first firms in a category. Yet, there are risks that new institutions will not be accepted by consumers, and there may be large initial losses due to heavy investments. At this stage, long-run success is not clear.

An example of an institution that never made it past the innovation stage in the United States was the hypermarket—a huge (200,000+ square feet) combination economy supermarket and discount department store. It sought people interested in low prices and one-stop shopping. Although popular in Europe for over 40 years, due to the otherwise small stores there, it only recently came to the United States. These were among the problems hypermarkets encountered during their U.S. introduction: per-unit sales for most stores were not large enough to earn reasonable profits; revenues were too great for low-margin food items and too low for higher-margin general merchandise; the high amount of customer traffic needed to break even was not attained; and American consumers found the initial stores to be too large and, thus, too inconvenient to shop in quickly. Noted one analyst: "The stores were somewhat cumbersome. They were too big for U.S. consumers."[7] In 1993, the leading European hypermarket retailer—France's Carrefour—announced it was exiting the U.S. market and closing its two Philadelphia-area stores. See Figure 5–4.

[6] Carl Steidmann, "Third-Wave Retailers Find New Way to Do Business," *Chain Store Age Executive* (August 1993), p. 9A.

[7] Emily DeNitto, "Hypermarkets Seem to Be Big Flop in U.S.," *Advertising Age* (October 4, 1993), p. 20.

Ethics in Retailing

Is Selling Used CDs OK?

Although the sales of used compact discs account for only 1 to 2 per cent of the $9-billion U.S. recorded music industry, major recording industry firms are very much concerned about this segment:

- Unlike records, compact discs do not deteriorate with use.
- In the past, the sales of used discs were confined to small retailers; now, large chains have begun to sell used CDs.
- Used CDs sell for about one-half the price of new releases and, thus, reduce the sales of new CDs.

In response to the threat of used CDs, Sony, Warner Music, Capitol-EMI, and MCA—firms representing three-fourths of recording industry sales—stopped sending cooperative advertising payments to retailers stocking used CDs. These payments equaled tens of millions of dollars in marketing support. EMI even went one step further: it would not accept CDs for credit if the security seal was broken—this included defective products.

Retailers that sell used CDs argue that all durable products have a used market. Furthermore, much of their used disc inventory comes from consumers who receive CDs as incentives to join record clubs. Several of these clubs are owned by firms such as Sony and Warner.

Sources: Based on material in Larry Armstrong, "What's Wrong with Selling Used CDs?" *Business Week* (July 26, 1993), p. 38; and Lisa Gubernick and Kate Bohner, "Garth's Barbecue," *Forbes* (August 2, 1993), p. 120.

In the second stage (accelerated development), both the sales and profits of a retail institution exhibit rapid growth. Progressive firms expand their geographic bases of operations, and newer companies of the same type enter the marketplace. Toward the end of accelerated development, cost pressures (to cover a larger staff, a more complex inventory system, and extensive controls) may begin to affect profits.

The videodisc kiosk—a freestanding interactive computer terminal that displays products and related information on a video screen, enables the consumer to place an order, and then completes the transaction (usually with a credit card) and arranges for the product to be shipped—is an institution in the innovation stage. Such kiosks can be situated virtually anywhere (from the lobby of a college dormitory to an airport), require little or no personnel besides maintenance workers, and can be an entertaining and easy way for people to shop. As of 1994, about a decade after the concept's introduction, there were 87,000 videodisc kiosks generating hundreds of millions of dollars in yearly U.S. sales. It is predicted that by the end of 1997 there could be as many as 500,000 kiosks, with sales rising accordingly.[8]

The third stage (maturity) is characterized by a slowdown in total sales growth for the institutional type. This means that even though overall sales may continue to rise, that rise will be at a much slower rate than during the introduction and growth stages. It also means profit margins may have to be reduced in order to stimulate purchases. Maturity is brought on by saturation of the market due to a high number of retailers operating in the institutional format, competition from newer types of institutions, and management skills that may be inadequate to direct larger firms. Once maturity is reached, the goal is to sustain it as long as possible and not fall into decline.

The liquor store, a form of specialty store, is an institution currently in the maturity stage of the retail life cycle; sales are continuing to rise, but very slowly compared to earlier years. As noted in Chapter 1, U.S. liquor store sales went up by only 3.3 per cent from 1984 through 1993; that was far less than the overall sales growth rate for all U.S. retailers. The slowdown in sales growth has been due to competition from other retail institutions, such as membership clubs, mail-order wine retailers, and supermarkets (in states allowing wine and/or liquor sales by supermarkets); changing American life-styles and attitudes with regard to liquor; the lifting of the drinking age from 18 to 21 in all fifty states; and the limitations on the nonalcoholic items that liquor stores are permitted to sell in some areas.

[8] Jeffrey A. Trachtenberg, "Interactive Kiosks May Be High-Tech, But They Underwhelm U.S. Consumers," *Wall Street Journal* (March 14, 1994), pp. B1, B8.

The final stage in the retail life cycle is decline. During this stage, industrywide sales and profits for the retail format fall off, many firms abandon the institutional format, and newer formats attract consumers previously committed to that retailer type. In some cases, a decline may be hard or almost impossible to reverse. In others, the decline may be avoided or postponed by repositioning the institution.

For example, U.S. variety store sales reached a peak of $8.7 billion in 1984; now, annual sales are more than $2 billion less. And the future does not look promising, especially after industry leader Woolworth's decision to close 400 more of its variety stores. As an institution, variety stores are limited in the items they sell, have a "nickel and dime" image, and have struggled against competition from low-end discounters. On the other hand, conventional supermarkets have slowed their decline by locating new units in suburban shopping centers, redesigning interiors, lengthening store hours, maintaining low prices, expanding the use of scrambled merchandising, closing unprofitable smaller units, and/or converting to larger outlets.

In general, the retail life-cycle concept is helpful in indicating how retailers should respond as their institutions evolve. Expansion should be the focus in the initial stages, administrative skills and operations become critical in maturity, and adaptation is essential at the end of the cycle:

> No matter how successful an organization has been in the past, that is no guarantee of future success. If anything, past greatness creates a barrier to future change. For retailers that understand the changes which are taking place in their business environment, the future represents an unprecedented landscape of opportunity.[9]

Retail Institutions Categorized by Store-Based Strategy Mix

Selected aspects of the strategy mixes of 15 store-based retail institutions are presented in this section and highlighted in Table 5–2. These strategy mixes are divided into food-oriented and general merchandise groupings. Though not all-inclusive, the strategy mixes do provide a fairly comprehensive overview of store-based retailing strategies.

FOOD-ORIENTED RETAILERS

Six key strategy mixes are used by food-oriented retailers: convenience store, conventional supermarket, food-based superstore, combination store, box (limited-line) store, and warehouse store. Each is discussed in the following subsections.

Convenience Store

A ***convenience store*** is usually a food-oriented retailer that is well located, is open long hours, and carries a moderate number of items. This type of retailer is small (only a fraction of the size of a conventional supermarket), has average to above-average prices, and average atmosphere and customer services. The ease of shopping at convenience stores and the impersonal nature of many large supermarkets make convenience stores particularly appealing to their customers, many of whom are male.

Forty years ago, there were 500 convenience stores and industry sales were under $200 million. As of 1992, there were 70,000 convenience stores (excluding the thousands of stores where food was a very small fraction of revenues); and total annual sales were $75 billion (including gasoline). Today, U.S. convenience stores account for 7 per cent of retail grocery sales, 5 per cent of fast-food sales, and 20 per cent of gasoline sales.[10]

[9] Steidmann, "Third-Wave Retailers Find New Way to Do Business," p. 11A.

[10] *1993 State of the Industry Report* (Alexandria, Virginia: National Association of Convenience Stores, 1993); and authors' estimates.

TABLE 5–2 Selected Aspects of Store-Based Retail Strategy Mixes

Type of Retailer	Location	Merchandise
Food-Oriented		
Convenience store	Neighborhood	Medium width and low depth of assortment; average quality
Conventional supermarket	Neighborhood	Extensive width and depth of assortment; average quality; national, private, and generic brands
Food-based superstore	Community shopping center or isolated site	Full assortment of supermarket items, plus health and beauty aids and general merchandise
Combination store	Community shopping center or isolated site	Full selection of supermarket and drugstore items or supermarket and general merchandise; average quality
Box (limited-line) store	Neighborhood	Low width and depth of assortment; few perishables; few national brands
Warehouse store	Secondary site, often in industrial area	Moderate width and low depth; emphasis on national brands purchased at discounts
General Merchandise		
Specialty store	Business district or shopping center	Very narrow width of assortment; extensive depth of assortment; average to good quality
Variety store	Business district, shopping center, or isolated store	Good width and depth of assortment; below-average to average quality
Traditional department store	Business district, shopping center, or isolated store	Extensive width and depth of assortment; average to good quality
Full-line discount store	Business district, shopping center, or isolated store	Extensive width and depth of assortment; average to good quality
Retail catalog showroom	Business district, shopping center, or isolated store	Good width and depth of assortment; average to good quality
Off-price chain	Business district, suburban shopping strip, or isolated store	Moderate width, but poor depth of assortment; average to good quality; low continuity
Factory outlet	Out-of-the-way site or discount mall	Moderate width, but poor depth of assortment; some irregular merchandise; low continuity
Membership club	Isolated store or secondary site (industrial park)	Moderate width, but poor depth of assortment; low continuity
Flea market	Isolated site, racetrack, arena, or parking lot	Extensive width, but poor depth of assortment; variable quality; low continuity

Items such as milk, eggs, and bread once represented the major portion of sales; now, sandwiches, tobacco products, snack foods, soft drinks, newspapers and magazines, beer and wine, video rentals, lottery tickets, and a car wash are also often key items. In addition, gasoline generates 20 to 40 per cent or more of total sales at many stores; at one time, virtually no convenience stores carried gasoline. A number of convenience stores have even installed automatic teller machines and expanded nonfood offerings to remain attractive to shoppers.

TABLE 5–2 (*Continued*)

Prices	Atmosphere and Services	Promotion
Average to above average	Average	Moderate
Competitive	Average	Heavy use of newspapers, flyers, and coupons; self-service
Competitive	Average	Heavy use of newspapers and flyers; self-service
Competitive	Average	Heavy use of newspapers and flyers; self-service
Very low	Low	Little or none
Very low	Low	Little or none
Competitive to above average	Average to excellent	Heavy use of displays; extensive sales force
Average	Below average	Heavy use of newspapers; self-service
Average to above average	Good to excellent	Heavy use of ads; catalogs; direct mail; personal selling
Competitive	Slightly below average to average	Heavy use of newspapers; price-oriented; moderate sales force
Competitive	Below average	Heavy use of catalogs; little advertising; self-service
Low	Below average	Use of newspapers; brands not advertised; limited sales force
Very low	Very low	Little; self-service
Very low	Very low	Little; some direct mail; limited sales force
Very low	Very low	Limited; self-service

7-Eleven, Circle K, Dairy Mart, and National Convenience Stores are four of the largest food-based convenience store chains in the United States, with 7-Eleven alone having 6,200 outlets. Texaco's Food Mart and Amoco's Food Shops are among the convenience store chains operated by oil companies at their gas station locations.

The convenience store's natural market advantages are its usefulness for fill-in merchandise when a consumer does not want to travel to or spend time shopping at a supermarket, the ability of customers to buy gas and fill-in merchandise at the same time, the use of drive-through windows, and the long store hours. Most of the items sold by a convenience store are used within thirty minutes of purchase. Many customers shop there at least two or three times a week; and the average sales transaction is small. Due to limited shelf space, stores receive multiple weekly deliveries; and prices reflect the small sale amounts and the high handling costs. Because customers are less price-sensitive than those shopping at other food-oriented retailers, gross margins are much higher than those of conventional supermarkets.

Lately, the industry has faced various problems: some areas are saturated with stores; supermarkets are providing more competition due to longer hours and better stocking of nonfood items; a number of stores have become too big, making shopping less expeditious; the traditional target market (35-year-old blue-collar workers) has been shrinking; and several chains have had financial difficulties, including 7-Eleven, Circle K, and National Convenience Stores.

Conventional Supermarket

The Food Marketing Institute defines a ***supermarket*** as a self-service food store with grocery, meat, and produce departments and minimum annual sales of $2 million. Included in the definition are conventional supermarkets, food-based superstores, combination stores, box (limited-line) stores, and warehouse stores.

A ***conventional supermarket*** is a departmentalized food store that emphasizes a wide range of food and related products; sales of general merchandise are rather limited. This institution started in the 1930s when it was recognized that only a large-scale operation would enable a retailer to combine volume sales, self-service, and low prices. The self-service concept allowed supermarkets to cut costs, as well as to increase volume. Personnel costs were reduced, and impulse buying increased. The car and the refrigerator contributed to the supermarket's success by lowering travel costs and adding to the life span of perishable items. Easy parking and lower prices (for consumers buying in bulk) were marketing strategies used by the supermarket to exploit these inventions.

Since the early 1960s, overall supermarket sales have stabilized at about 72 to 75 per cent of total U.S. grocery sales, with conventional supermarkets now responsible for just under one-half of total supermarket sales. In 1992, there were almost 20,000 conventional supermarkets, with sales amounting to $141 billion.[11] Chains account for the majority of sales. Leading chains are Kroger, American Stores, Safeway, A&P, and Winn-Dixie. Most independent supermarkets are affiliated with cooperative or voluntary organizations, such as IGA and Supervalu.

Conventional supermarkets have generally relied on high inventory turnover (volume sales). Their profit margins are low. In general, average gross margins (selling prices less merchandise costs) are 22 per cent or so of sales and net profits are 1 to 2 per cent of sales.

Conventional supermarkets are facing intense competition from other types of food stores: convenience stores offer greater customer convenience; food-based superstores and combination stores have more product lines and greater variety within them—as well as better gross margins; and box and warehouse stores have lower operating costs and prices. Membership clubs (discussed later in this chapter), with their discount prices, also provide considerable competition—especially now that they have aggressively expanded their food lines. Thus, over the last 15 years, thousands of conventional supermarkets have closed; and many others have changed their strategy mix to another format. Variations of the conventional supermarket are covered next.

Food-Based Superstore

A ***food-based superstore*** is larger and more diversified than a conventional supermarket but usually smaller and less diversified than a combination store. This format originated in the 1970s as supermarkets sought to erode sales declines by expanding

[11] "60th Annual Report of the Grocery Industry," *Progressive Grocer* (April 1993), p. 49.

store size and the number of nonfood items carried. Some supermarkets merged with drugstores or general merchandise stores, but more grew into food-based superstores. In 1992, there were 5,550 food-based superstores in the United States, with sales of $84 billion.[12]

The typical food-based superstore occupies 25,000 to 50,000 square feet of total space and obtains 20 to 25 per cent of revenues from general merchandise items, such as garden supplies, flowers, small household appliances, wine, and film developing. It caters to consumers' complete grocery needs and offers them the ability to buy fill-in general merchandise.

Like combination stores, food-based superstores are efficient, offer people a degree of one-stop shopping, stimulate impulse purchases, and feature high-profit general merchandise. But they also offer other advantages: It is easier and less costly to redesign and convert supermarkets into food-based superstores than into combination stores. Many consumers feel more comfortable shopping in true food stores than in huge combination stores. Management expertise is better focused in food-based superstores.

Over the last decade, all of the leading U.S. supermarket chains have turned more to food-based superstores. They have expanded and remodeled existing supermarkets and built numerous new stores. Many independent supermarkets have also converted facilities to food-based superstores.

Combination Store

A ***combination store*** combines supermarket and general merchandise sales in one facility, with general merchandise typically accounting for 25 to 40 per cent of total store sales. The introduction of food-based combination stores can be traced to the late 1960s and early 1970s, when common checkout areas were developed for independently owned supermarkets and drugstores or supermarkets and general merchandise stores. A natural offshoot of this was to fully integrate the two operations under one management. As of 1992, over 1,200 combination stores (including supercenters) were in the U.S. marketplace and annual sales reached $22 billion.[13]

Combination stores are popular for the following reasons. They are very large, from 30,000 up to 100,000 or more square feet. This leads to operating efficiencies and cost savings. Consumers like one-stop shopping and will travel further to get to the store. Impulse sales are high. Many general merchandise items have better gross margins than traditional supermarket items. Supermarkets and drugstores have many commonalities in the customers served and the kinds of low-price, high-turnover items sold. Drugstore and general merchandise customers are drawn to the store more frequently than they would be otherwise.

A ***supercenter*** is a special type of combination store that blends an economy supermarket with a discount department store. It is the U.S. version of the hypermarket (the European institution that did not succeed in the United States). At least 40 per cent of supercenter sales are from nonfood items. These stores usually range from 75,000 to 150,000 square feet in size and they stock up to 50,000 and more items, much more than the 30,000 or so items carried by other combination stores.[14]

Among the firms operating combination stores are Meijer, Fred Meyer, Wal Mart, Kmart, Albertson's, and Bigg's.

Box (Limited-Line) Store

The ***box (limited-line) store*** is a food-based discounter that focuses on a small selection of items, moderate hours of operation (compared to supermarkets), few services, and limited national brands. There are usually less than 1,500 items, little or no

[12] Estimated by the authors from "60th Annual Report of the Grocery Industry," p. 49.

[13] Ibid.

[14] See Michael Sansolo, "After the Wake-Up Call," *Progressive Grocer* (September 1993), pp. 54–58; and Christina Duff, "Adding Groceries, Super Kmarts Try to Be More Things to More People," *Wall Street Journal* (June 7, 1993), pp. B1, B6.

refrigerated perishables, and few sizes and brands per item. Price marking is on the shelf or on overhead signs. Items are displayed in cut cases. Customers do their own bagging. Checks are usually not accepted. Box stores depend on aggressively priced private-label brands. They aim to price merchandise 20 to 30 per cent below supermarkets.

The box-store concept originated in Europe around 1970 and was exported to the United States in the mid-1970s. The growth of these stores has not been as anticipated, although sales have gone up a lot in the 1990s. Other food stores, in some cases, have matched box-store prices. Many people are loyal to national brands, and box stores cannot fulfill one-stop shopping needs.

There were 700 box stores in the United States in 1992, with sales of $2.1 billion.[15] Among the leading box operators are Aldi and Save-A-Lot.

Warehouse Store

A ***warehouse store*** is a food-based discounter offering a moderate number of food items in a no-frills setting. Unlike box stores, warehouse stores appeal to one-stop food shoppers. These stores concentrate on special purchases of national brands. They use cut-case displays, provide little service, post prices on shelves, and locate in secondary sites (like industrial districts).

Warehouse stores began in the late 1970s. As of 1992, there were about 3,000 stores with $38 billion in sales.[16] There are three warehouse store formats in terms of size: from 15,000 to 25,000 square feet, from 25,000 to 35,000 square feet, and from 50,000 to 65,000 square feet.

The largest store is known as a super warehouse. There are 350 of them in the United States. They have annual sales exceeding $20 million each and contain a variety of departments, including produce. High ceilings are used to accommodate pallet loads of groceries. Shipments are made directly to the store. Customers pack their own groceries. Super warehouses can be profitable at gross margins that are far lower than those for conventional supermarkets. Major super warehouse chains include Food 4 Less (Fleming Companies), Sun Food Market (A&P), and Cub Foods (Supervalu).

A potential problem, which may limit the growth of warehouse stores, is the lack of brand continuity. Because products are bought by the stores when special deals are available, brands may be temporarily or permanently out of stock. In addition, many consumers do not like shopping in warehouse settings.

Table 5–3 provides selected operating data for convenience stores, conventional supermarkets, food-based superstores, combination stores, box stores, and warehouse stores.

GENERAL MERCHANDISE RETAILERS

There are nine store-based general merchandise retail strategy mixes shown in Table 5–2; each is covered in the following subsections: specialty store, variety store, traditional department store, full-line discount store, retail catalog showroom, off-price chain, factory outlet, membership club, and flea market.

Specialty Store

A ***specialty store*** concentrates on selling one goods or service line, such as apparel and its accessories, toys, furniture, or muffler repair. In contrast to a mass-marketing approach, specialty stores usually carry a narrow, but deep, assortment of goods or services in their chosen goods/service category and tailor their strategy to selective

[15] Estimated by the authors from "60th Annual Report of the Grocery Industry," p. 49; and Stephen Bennett, "Right for the Times," *Progressive Grocer* (November 1993), pp. 57–60.

[16] Estimated by the authors from "60th Annual Report of the Grocery Industry," p. 49.

TABLE 5–3 Selected Typical Operating Data for Food-Oriented Retailers, 1992

Factor	Convenience Store[a]	Conventional Supermarket	Food-Based Superstore	Combination Store[a]	Box (Limited-Line) Store	Warehouse Store
Number of stores	70,000	19,920	5,550	1,230	700	3,000
Total annual sales	$75 billion	$141 billion	$84 billion	$22 billion	$2.1 billion	$38 billion
Average annual sales per store	$1.1 million	$7.1 million	$15.1 million	$17.9 million	$3 million	$12.7 million
Average store selling area (sq. ft.)	3,500 or less	15,000–20,000	25,000–50,000	30,000–100,000+	5,000–9,000	15,000+
Number of checkouts per store	1–3	6–10	10+	10+	3–5	5+
Gross margin	25–30%	18–22%	20–25%	25%	10–12%	12–15%
Number of items stocked per store	3,000–4,000	12,000–17,000	20,000+	30,000+	Under 1,500	2,500+
Major emphasis	Daily fill-in needs; dairy, sandwiches, tobacco, gas, beverages, magazines	Food; only 5% of sales from general merchandise	Positioned between supermarket and combo store; 20–25% of sales from general merchandise	One-stop shopping; general merchandise is 25–40% of sales	Low prices; few or no perishables	Low prices; variable assortments; may or may not stock perishables

[a] Convenience store data include some outlets owned by oil companies and gas stations (where nongasoline sales represent a major part of the business). Combination store data include supercenters.

Sources: "60th Annual Report of the Grocery Industry," *Progressive Grocer* (April 1993); and authors' estimates.

market segments. This enables specialty stores to maintain better selections and sales expertise than their competitors, which are often department stores. It also allows them to control investments and exercise a certain amount of flexibility.

Consumers often shop at specialty stores because of the knowledgeable sales personnel, the variety of choices within the goods/service category, the customer service policies, the intimate store size and atmosphere (although this is not true of the category killer store), the lack of crowds (also not true of category killer stores), and the absence of aisles of merchandise unrelated to their purchase intentions—they will not have to pass through several departments looking for the desired merchandise. While some specialty stores have elaborate fixtures and upscale merchandise for affluent consumers, others have a discount orientation and aim at price-conscious consumers.

Total specialty store sales are difficult to estimate because they sell almost all kinds of goods and services, and aggregate specialty store data are not compiled by the U.S. Department of Commerce. However, annual specialty store sales in the United States are hundreds of billions of dollars. During 1992, the top 50 specialty store chains had sales of $85 billion and operated 58,500 outlets. Among the top 50 chains, 18 were involved with apparel, 6 with shoes, and 5 with consumer electronics. The leaders included Toys "R" Us (toys), The Limited, Inc. (apparel), and Melville (shoes/apparel).[17]

[17] Computed by the authors from David P. Schulz, "Top 100 Specialty Stores," *Stores* (August 1993), pp. 21–33.

Retailing in Action

Who Will Win the Consumer Electronics Retailing Battle?

The two leading U.S. consumer electronics and major appliance retailers, Circuit City and Best Buy, are now invading each other's territory. Circuit City, for instance, recently opened 18 stores in Chicago, the largest market for Best Buy; and, Best Buy is expanding into Atlanta and Phoenix, major markets that have long been dominated by Circuit City.

Each chain has a different retail strategy: Circuit City provides high levels of customer service and pays its staff on a commission basis. Yet, it holds down costs via a highly automated inventory tracking and distribution system. In comparison, Best Buy relies on more self-service and pays sales help on a salary basis. According to Best Buy's president, sales clerks are "there to assist the customer and not to manipulate the customer."

Although Best Buy's overhead expenses are lower than Circuit City's, its high use of self-service makes it harder to sell such highly-profitable items as extended warranties. In contrast, these warranties are a key component of Circuit City's sales. One analyst has computed that extended warranties account for about 75 per cent of Circuit City's profits and give it a large cushion that enables it to lower retail prices.

Sources: Based on material in Marcia Berss, "High Noon," *Forbes* (December 20, 1993), pp. 44–45; and Gregory A. Patterson, "Best Buy Rides High with Low-Key Sales Approach," *Wall Street Journal* (December 17, 1993), p. B4.

As noted earlier in the chapter, a new type of specialty store—the category killer—is now gaining strength. A ***category killer store*** is an especially large specialty store. It features an enormous selection in its product category and relatively low prices; and consumers are drawn from wide geographic areas. Toys "R" Us, The Limited, The Gap, Sam Goody, and Barnes & Noble are among the many specialty store chains that are opening new category killer stores to complement existing stores. Blockbuster, Sports Authority, Home Depot, and Staples are among the specialty store chains fully based on the category-killer store concept. For example, Toys "R" Us accounts for 25 per cent of all U.S. toy sales. As its chief executive says, "We achieved these results by having the best merchandise selection, stocked in-depth, and being even more competitive by further reducing our everyday low prices. We have reinforced our price selection and inventory image with the consumer, which has enhanced our ability to achieve longer-term growth objectives."[18]

Nonetheless, smaller specialty stores can prosper as long as they are focused, offer strong customer service, and avoid being imitations of larger firms. An illustration is Leg Room—a fast-growing, New York-based specialty store chain that sells pantyhose, socks, and a "smattering" of intimate apparel. Its stores are located in business areas—to capitalize on the pedestrian traffic of professional women going to and from work. The stores occupy just 400 to 1,000 square feet each and average $1,350 of sales per square foot. Leg Room's founder says, "Our mission from the beginning was to operate a well-situated, well-edited store that concentrates its efforts on saving its customers time. My customer doesn't have time to trek to the nearest department store, rifle through a sea of packages, and hope to find what she needs. They don't have time for that aggravation."[19]

Any size specialty store can be adversely affected by seasonality or a decline in the popularity of its product category because its offering is so focused. This type of store may also fail to attract consumers interested in one-stop shopping for multiple product categories. In addition, the category killer store may not appeal to consumers interested in a small-store setting and uncrowded aisles.

Table 5–4 shows selected 1992 operating data for four kinds of specialty stores.

Variety Store

A ***variety store*** handles a wide assortment of inexpensive and popularly priced goods and services, such as stationery, gift items, women's accessories, health and beauty

[18] *Standard & Poor's Industry Surveys: Retailing* (May 13, 1993), p. R83.

[19] Susan Reda, "Store Sells Time, Hosiery Too," *Stores* (August 1993), pp. 64–65.

TABLE 5–4 Selected Operating Results for Various Types of Specialty Stores, 1992

Specialty Store Category	Average Annual Sales Per Store	Annual Sales Per Gross Square Foot	Annual Operating Income Per Gross Square Foot	Operating Income as a Per Cent of Sales
Apparel stores	$ 1,588,049	$237	$18.87	7.7
Drugstores	2,936,295	292	12.83	4.3
Hard lines stores	2,114,789	226	18.01	7.2
Home improvement stores	16,659,610	213	12.04	5.1

Note: Operating income = Sales – Cost of goods sold – Selling, general, and administrative expenses (including depreciation and amortization).

Source: Management Horizons, "Apparel Stores Most Efficient at Turning Sales into Operating Profits," *Chain Store Age Executive* (August 1993), p. 12A.

aids, light hardware, toys, housewares, confectionary items, and shoe repair. Transactions are often on a cash basis. There are open displays and few salespeople. Variety stores do not carry full product lines, may not be departmentalized, and do not deliver products.

In 1993, variety store sales were $6.4 billion, about 0.3 per cent of total U.S. retail store sales. McCrory, with 700 variety stores, and Woolworth, with 450 outlets (after the closings mentioned earlier in this chapter), are the leading firms in this store category.

Over the past fifteen years, variety stores have shown the poorest performance of any retail store category. This trend is due to the heavy competition from specialty stores and discounters, the older facilities of many stores, the low profit margins associated with some of the items carried, and the decision of firms such as Woolworth to diversify. One retailing analyst even says that "I'd not be surprised if within a few years, Woolworth will not have a single variety store."[20] At one time, Woolworth had 1,200 variety stores—whose annual sales reached $2 billion. See Figure 5–5.

One interesting spin-off of the conventional variety store is now taking place. Dollar discount stores and closeout chains are becoming more prevalent. These stores frequently sell similar kinds of merchandise as traditional variety stores, but do so in plainer surroundings and at much lower prices. Family Dollar and Dollar General are leading dollar-discount store chains and Consolidated Stores and Pic 'N' Save are two major closeout chains.

Traditional Department Store

A ***department store*** is a large retail unit with an extensive assortment (width and depth) of goods and services that is organized into separate departments for purposes of buying, promotion, customer service, and control. It has the greatest selection of any general merchandise retailer, often serves as the anchor store in a shopping center or district, has strong credit-card penetration, and is usually part of a chain. To be defined as a department store by the U.S. Bureau of the Census, a store has to meet four criteria. First, it must employ at least fifty people. Second, apparel and soft goods (nondurables) must account for at least 20 per cent of total sales. Third, the merchandise assortment must include some items in each of these lines: furniture, home furnishings, appliances, and radio and TV sets; a general line of apparel for the

[20] Andrea Adelson, "Woolworth to Shutter 970 Stores," *New York Times* (October 14, 1993), pp. D1, D6.

FIGURE 5–5
Away from Variety Stores and into Specialty Stores
Although it was the leader for decades, Woolworth has been turning away from the no-longer-popular variety-store format and emphasizing specialty-store chains, such as Foot Locker and World Foot Locker.
Reprinted by permission.

family; and household linens and dry goods. Fourth, if annual sales are under $10 million, no more than 80 per cent can be from any one line. If sales are at least $10 million, there is no limitation on the percentage from a line, as long as combined sales of the smallest two lines are at least $1 million.

Two types of retailers satisfy the Bureau of Census definition: the traditional department store (introduced by Macy's, Wanamaker, and others in the 1860s) and the full-line discount store (introduced by firms such as Kmart, Target, and Wal-Mart in 1962). Together, they accounted for $202 billion in sales in 1993—excluding leased departments. This was almost 10 per cent of U.S. retail store sales. The traditional department store is discussed here; the full-line discount store is examined in the following subsection.

At a ***traditional department store***, merchandise quality ranges from average to quite good. Pricing is moderate to above average. Customer service ranges from medium levels of sales help, credit, delivery, etc. to high levels of each. For example, Macy's strategy is aimed at middle-class shoppers interested in a wide assortment and moderate prices, whereas Bloomingdale's aims at upscale consumers through more trendy merchandise and higher prices. Some traditional department stores (such as Dayton's and Rich's) sell textile products, family wearing apparel, and furniture and appliances. Others (such as Nordstrom and Saks Fifth Avenue) place greater emphasis on apparel and do not carry major appliances.

Over their history, this form of retailer has been responsible for many innovations, such as advertising prices, implementing a one-price policy (whereby all consumers pay the same price for the same good or service), developing computerized checkout facilities, offering money-back guarantees, adding branch stores, decentralizing management, and moving into suburban shopping centers.

During the last several years, the industrywide sales growth of traditional department stores has lagged behind that of full-line discount stores; and long-time chains such as Gimbels and B. Altman have gone out of business, leading various observers to ask "will the traditional department store survive?" Today, traditional department store sales, $92 billion in 1993, represent less than one-half of total department store sales. These are some reasons for this institution's difficulties:

- They no longer have brand exclusivity for a lot of the items they sell; manufacturers' brands are available at specialty and discount outlets.
- Many firms have been too passive with private-label goods. Instead of creating their own brands, they have signed exclusive licensing agreements with fashion designers to use the latter's names. This perpetuates customer loyalty to the designer and not the store.
- There are more price-conscious consumers than ever before, and they are attracted to discount retailers.
- The popularity of shopping malls has aided specialty stores since consumers can accomplish one-stop shopping via several specialty stores in the same mall or shopping center.
- The number of large specialty chains has steadily increased, so they have strong supplier relations and extensive advertising campaigns; department stores do not dominate the smaller stores around them as they once did.
- Many discounters, which did not previously, now accept credit cards.
- Customer service has deteriorated; and store personnel are not as loyal, helpful, or knowledgeable as before.
- Some stores are too large and have too much unproductive selling space and low-turnover merchandise.
- The scrambled merchandising of food retailers has drawn away sales.
- Unlike specialty stores, many department stores have had a weak focus on customer market segments and a fuzzy image. Too often, departments have been organized by supplier brand name rather than according to customer needs.
- Such chains as Sears have repeatedly changed their strategic orientation, confusing consumers as to their company image. (Is Sears a traditional department store chain or a full-line discount store chain?)
- Chain management has sometimes been too decentralized; thus, there have been different merchandising strategies in branch stores (which blur image).
- Some companies are not as innovative in their merchandise decisions as they were; they react to suppliers rather than make suggestions to them.
- Specialty stores often have better assortments in the product categories they carry. For example, no department store has the toy selection of Toys "R" Us or the sporting-goods assortment of Sports Authority.
- Leveraged buyouts have saddled several chains with significant debt, causing a poor cash flow; limited funds for store renovations, advertising, and (in some cases) adequate merchandise assortments; and adverse publicity.

To overcome these difficulties, traditional department stores need to clarify their niche in the marketplace (store positioning); place greater emphasis on customer service and sales personnel; present more exciting, better-organized store interiors and displays—and change them frequently; use space better by downsizing stores and eliminating slow-selling, space-consuming items (such as J.C. Penney dropping consumer electronics products); and open outlets in smaller, underdeveloped towns and cities (as Sears has been doing). They can also centralize more buying and promotion functions, do better research, and reach customers more efficiently (via such tools as targeted mailing pieces). As one expert recently noted,

TABLE 5–5 Selected Operating Results for Traditional Department Stores, 1992

Average annual sales per store	$21,952,658
Annual sales per gross square foot	$167
Annual operating income per gross square foot	$9.13
Operating income as a per cent of sales	6.1

Note: Operating income = Sales − Cost of goods sold − Selling, general, and administrative expenses (including depreciation and amortization).

Source: Management Horizons, "Apparel Stores Most Efficient at Turning Sales into Operating Profits," *Chain Store Age Executive* (August 1993), p. 12A.

Traditional department stores, all but written off for dead a couple of years ago, have been showing signs of life lately. They have moved forcefully to clean up their acts. They have dropped money-losing lines and adopted the purchasing and inventory practices that help make discounters successful. Furthermore, many department-store chains have strengthened their balance sheets. Sloppy financial management—especially ill-conceived leveraged buyouts—played as big a role in triggering problems as did weak operating results. These factors are helping traditional department stores to recapture market share, especially from specialty apparel stores.[21]

Table 5–5 shows selected 1992 operating results for traditional department stores. The data in this table can be compared with those in Table 5–4 (operating results for various specialty stores). For example, traditional department stores had higher per-store sales but lower sales per square foot.

Full-Line Discount Store

A ***full-line discount store*** is a type of department store with these features:

- It conveys the image of a high-volume, low-cost, fast-turnover outlet selling a broad merchandise assortment for less than conventional prices.
- Centralized checkout service is provided.
- Customer service is not usually provided within store departments. Products are normally sold via self-service with minimal assistance in any single department.
- A catalog order service is generally not available.
- The nondurable (soft) goods carried are typically private brands, whereas the durable (hard) goods are well-known manufacturer brands.
- Hard goods often account for up to 60 per cent of sales. There is greater emphasis on such items as auto accessories, gardening equipment, and housewares than in traditional department stores. Less fashion-sensitive merchandise is carried.
- Buildings, equipment, and fixtures are less inexpensive; and operating costs are lower than for traditional department stores and specialty stores.
- There is somewhat less emphasis on credit sales than in full-service stores.

During 1993, full-line discount stores had revenues of $102 billion (excluding supercenters), well over 50 per cent of all U.S. department store sales. Together, three

[21] Gregory A. Patterson, "Department Stores, Seemingly Outmoded, Are Perking Up Again," *Wall Street Journal* (January 4, 1994), pp. A1, A6.

TABLE 5–6 Selected Operating Results for Full-Line Discount Stores, 1993

Product Category	Total Industry Sales (billions)	Average Per Cent of Store Sales	Average Annual Sales per Square Foot	Average Annual Stock Turns	Percentage Initial Markup	Percentage Gross Margin
Apparel	$32.0	28.7	$142	3.0 times	42.6	28.1
Health and beauty aids	7.9	7.0	351	3.9	20.7	12.0
Housewares	6.6	5.9	279	3.0	39.1	29.7
Domestics	6.1	5.4	179	2.5	44.3	32.5
Consumer electronics	6.0	5.4	247	2.9	28.8	16.4
Hardware	5.4	4.8	264	1.9	38.6	29.4
Food	5.2	4.7	262	7.2	21.9	19.1
Toys	5.0	4.5	167	2.5	34.9	25.4
Automotives	4.2	3.8	212	3.7	30.2	20.8
Sporting goods	4.2	3.8	223	2.1	37.6	25.9
Pharmacy	3.9	3.5	NA	NA	23.2	22.1
Photography	3.4	3.0	744	4.7	20.1	13.1
Lawn/garden	3.2	2.9	149	3.3	34.1	21.2
Household cleaners	2.4	2.2	135	4.3	27.4	15.7
Jewelry/watches	2.4	2.2	399	1.3	65.4	36.0

Source: "Full-Line Discount Store Productivity: 1993," *Discount Store News* (August 2, 1993), p. 34. Reprinted by permission. © Copyright Lebhar-Friedman, Inc., 425 Park Avenue, N.Y., N.Y., 10022.

chains (Wal-Mart, Kmart, and Target) operated almost 5,000 full-line discount stores that accounted for almost $70 billion in sales during that year. Overall, about a dozen full-line discount chains had sales of at least $1 billion in 1993.[22]

The success of full-line discount stores is due to a variety of factors. They have a clear customer focus: middle-class and lower-middle-class shoppers looking for good value. The stores feature popular brands of average- to good-quality merchandise at competitive prices. They have been aggressive in adding new goods and service categories and are beginning to have their own, well-advertised brands. Firms have worked hard to improve their image and have made more customer services available. The average outlet tends to be smaller than a traditional department store, which improves productivity. Sales per square foot are often higher than in traditional department stores. A number of full-line discount stores are located in small towns, where competition is reduced. The chains have been very well managed, with standardized branch outlets and good employee relations. And full-line discount store facilities are newer than those of many traditional department stores.

The greatest challenges facing full-line discount stores are the strong competition from other retailers (particularly lower-priced discounters and new store formats, such as category killers), too rapid expansion of some chains, and the saturation of prime locations. As a result, the industry has had a number of consolidations, bankruptcies, and liquidations involving such chains as Zayre, Ames, Bradlees, Lechmere, S.E. Nichols, and Heck's. Some of these firms have since reorganized and recovered.

Table 5–6 shows selected operating results for full-line discount stores by product category. Note the high overall sales from apparel and health and beauty aids, and the high sales per square foot from photography and jewelry.

[22] *Monthly Retail Trade: Sales and Inventories* (Washington, D.C.: U.S. Department of Commerce, December 1993), p. 4; and authors' estimates.

Retail Catalog Showroom

With a ***retail catalog showroom***, consumers select merchandise from a catalog and shop in a warehouse-style setting. Sometimes, shoppers not only select merchandise by number but also write up sales orders. Some goods are stored out of the shoppers' reach; the closed inventory areas may encompass up to two-thirds of the outlet's space.

The merchandise mix is a key part of a showroom's overall strategy. A handful of categories (jewelry, electronics, housewares, gifts, and watches) account for the bulk of overall sales, with jewelry typically providing a quarter or more of all revenues. Showrooms do not normally stock soft goods such as apparel. Although gross profit margins on many products are 10 to 20 per cent of revenues, profit margins on jewelry are close to 50 per cent.

The strategy of a catalog showroom is tied to its ability to offer competitive prices due to operating costs below those of other types of retailers: Payroll expenses are low because there are few salespeople; products are not demonstrated; customers write up orders; and products are not assembled or delivered. Shoplifting losses are low because many goods are kept in a stockroom. Store decoration costs are low because most floor space is in the warehouse area. By avoiding clothing and other high-fashion items, the complexities of sizing and style changes are eliminated, so reordering is easier. Inasmuch as many customers pre-shop in catalogs at home, there is less need for displays and sales assistance. Catalogs generally cost $2 to $5 each to print and distribute. Catalogs and flyers are the key advertising expenses.

In the United States, retail catalog showrooms had sales of $7 billion during 1993. The leading catalog chain, Service Merchandise, accounted for more than one-half of industry sales and operated a total of about 375 stores during that year.[23]

The retail catalog showroom's popularity peaked in the mid-1980s; since then, annual sales have declined or been relatively stagnant. This has occurred for several reasons: Many other retailers are aggressively cutting costs and prices; showrooms are no longer low-price leaders. Showrooms have a difficult time reacting both to price rises by suppliers and price cuts by competitors because catalogs must be printed so far in advance. Many consumer electronics and other stores will "beat any advertised price," so consumers take their catalogs to these stores to receive better prices. Because of the need to reach more consumers, advertising expenses have increased. Too many of the items sold are slow-sellers and/or have low profit margins. Some consumers find catalog showrooms to be too crowded and dislike writing up orders; and the lack of displays reduces browsing time. The lack of apparel goods has also held down sales volume.

Off-Price Chain

An ***off-price chain*** features brand-name (sometimes designer label) apparel and accessories, footwear (primarily women's and family), linens, fabrics, cosmetics, and/or housewares and sells them at everyday low prices in an efficient, limited-service environment. It frequently has community dressing rooms, centralized checkout counters, no gift wrapping, and extra charges for alterations. Merchandise is bought opportunistically, when special deals occur. Other retailers' canceled orders, manufacturers' irregulars and overruns, and end-of-season merchandise are often purchased for a fraction of their original wholesale prices.

Off-price chains usually aim at the same type of shoppers as traditional department stores, but at prices up to 40 to 50 per cent lower. As a T.J. Maxx executive once noted, "We're going after department store shoppers. That's where we're going to get market share."[24] In addition, various off-price shopping centers now appeal to these consumers' interest in one-stop shopping.

[23] "Jewelry/Hard Lines Sales Lag Behind Discount Industry," *Discount Store News* (July 5, 1993), p. 70.

[24] Alison Fahey, "Off-Price Chains Strike Back at Price Cutters," *Advertising Age* (July 16, 1990), p. 28.

The most crucial aspect of the strategy of off-price chains involves buying merchandise and establishing long-term relationships with suppliers. To succeed, the chains must secure large quantities of merchandise at reduced wholesale prices and have a regular flow of goods into the stores. Their stock turnover is far higher than that of department stores.

Sometimes, manufacturers seek out off-price chains to sell samples and products that have not done well (this generally occurs three to four weeks after the beginning of a season) and/or merchandise remaining on hand near the end of a season. In this way, manufacturers have access to quick cash, obtain a market for closeouts and discontinued items, and have a relationship with retailers that promise not to mention brand names or prices in ads (to not alienate department store or specialty store clients). Also, off-price chains are usually less demanding than department stores in terms of the advertising allowances requested from suppliers, do not return products, and pay promptly.

Other times, off-price chains employ a more active buying strategy. Instead of waiting for closeouts and canceled orders, they convince manufacturers to make merchandise such as garments during off-seasons and pay cash for items before they are produced (or delivered).

In 1993, the total sales of U.S. off-price apparel stores were $16 billion; and the four leading chains had sales of $8 billion and operated almost 1,400 stores.[25] The leaders are Marshalls, T.J. Maxx, Ross, and Burlington Coat.

Off-price chains do face some marketplace pressures because of growing competition from other institutional formats (such as department stores running special sales throughout the year), the discontinuity of their merchandise, poor management at some firms, insufficient customer service for some upscale shoppers, and the shakeout of some underfinanced companies.

Factory Outlet

A ***factory outlet*** is a manufacturer-owned store that sells the manufacturer's closeouts, discontinued merchandise, irregulars, canceled orders, and, sometimes, in-season, first-quality merchandise. Manufacturers' interest in outlet stores has increased for four basic reasons. First, a manufacturer can control where its discounted merchandise is sold. By placing outlets in out-of-the-way locations, depressed areas, or areas with low sales penetration of the firm's brands, factory outlet revenues are unlikely to affect a manufacturer's key customers (which may be specialty and department stores). Second, these outlets can be profitable despite prices up to 60 per cent less than customary retail prices. This is due to low operating costs—as a result of few services, low rent, limited displays, and plain store fixtures. In addition, the manufacturer does not have to pay wholesalers and/or retailers. Third, through factory outlets, manufacturers can decide upon store visibility, set promotion policies, remove labels, and be sure that discontinued items and irregulars are disposed of properly. Fourth, since many specialty and department stores are increasing their use of private labels, manufacturers may need revenue from outlet stores to sustain their own growth.

In recent years, more factory outlet stores have been locating in clusters or in outlet malls to expand customer traffic and use cooperative ads. Large outlet malls are in Connecticut, Florida, Georgia, New York, Pennsylvania, Tennessee, and many other states. In 1993, there were 10,000 factory outlet stores in the United States—many in the 340 outlet malls nationwide; and they accounted for $10 billion in sales.[26] Examples of manufacturers with factory outlets are Warnaco (maker of Hathaway shirts,

[25] "Off-Price Apparel Booming in a Recovery Year," *Discount Store News* (July 5, 1993), p. 74; and authors' estimates.

[26] Kerry J. Smith, "Getting into the Outlets," *Promo* (December 1993), pp. 69–71.

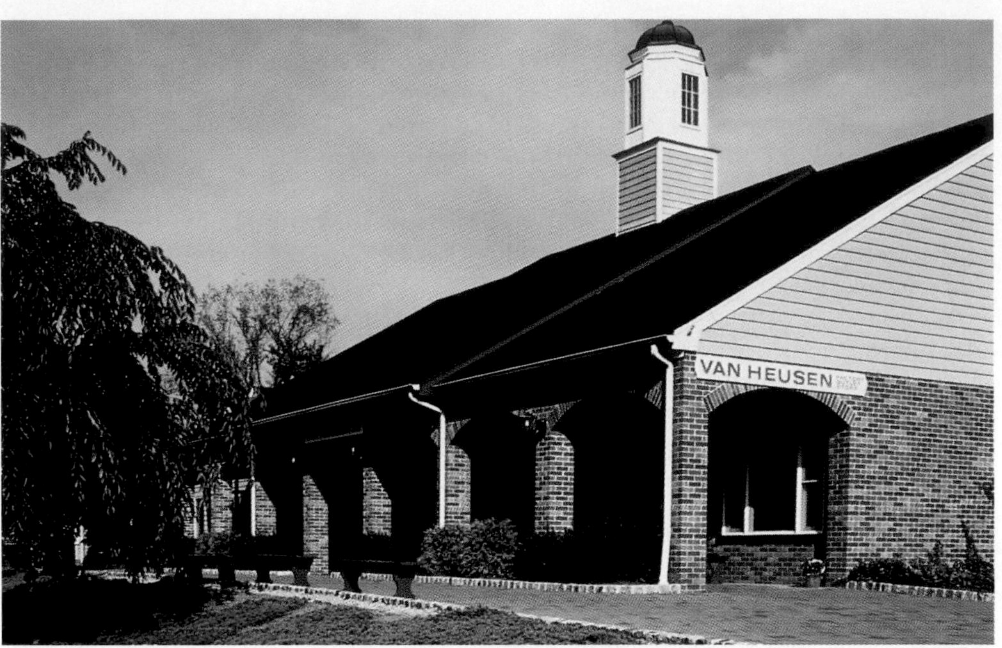

FIGURE 5–6
Factory Outlets: The Phillips-Van Heusen Way
Phillips-Van Heusen is a manufacturer that is a big believer in factory outlet stores as a way to sell overruns, out-of-season merchandise, and irregulars. It has a number of such stores around the United States.
Reprinted by permission.

White Stag sportswear, and Warner's lingerie), Phillips-Van Heusen, Palm Beach (maker of Evan Picone and Gant sportswear), U.S. Shoe Corp. (with its Bannister Shoe stores), Hamilton Clock, and Health-Tex (Kids Port USA). See Figure 5–6.

When determining whether to enter into or expand factory outlets, manufacturers need to be cautious. They must evaluate their expertise in retailing, the dollar investment costs, the impact on existing retailers that buy from them, and the response of final customers. Certainly, manufacturers will not want to jeopardize their products' sales at full retail prices.

Membership Club

A ***membership club*** appeals to price-conscious consumers, who must be members to shop there. It straddles the line between wholesaling and retailing. Some members of a typical club are small business owners and employees who pay a nominal annual fee (such as $25 to $35 each) and buy merchandise at wholesale prices; these customers make purchases for use in operating their firms and/or for personal use. They represent 60 per cent of total club sales. The bulk of members are final consumers who purchase exclusively for their own use; they represent 40 per cent of overall club sales. These consumers also usually pay a nominal membership fee and must belong to a union, be municipal employees, work for educational institutions, or belong to other specified groups to become members (in reality, eligibility is often defined so broadly as to exclude few consumers). In some cases, they are charged prices slightly higher than those paid by business customers.

The membership club is a derivative of the membership-based discount retailer popular in the 1950s and 1960s in the United States and the giant European warehouse outlet catering to small food and drugstore retailers. The operating strategy of the current membership club began in the mid-1970s and centers on large store facilities (up to 100,000 or more square feet), inexpensive isolated or industrial-park locations, opportunistic buying (with no continuity of merchandise), one-tenth the number of items stocked by full-line discount stores, little or no advertising, plain fixtures, wide aisles (to allow forklift trucks to have access to shelves), concrete floors, no delivery, little or no credit, merchandise sent directly from manufacturers to stores, and very low prices.

A membership club sells three kinds of goods: general merchandise, such as appliances, computers, housewares, consumer electronics, tires, and apparel (35 to 60 per cent of sales); food (20 to 35 per cent of sales); and sundries, like health and beauty aids, tobacco, liquor, and candy (15 to 30 per cent of sales). Its stock turnover rate is several times that of a department store.

In 1993, there were more than 900 membership clubs. The retail aspect of these clubs accounted for sales of $15 billion to $20 billion, up from $2.5 billion in 1985. Together, the two leading firms, Price/Costco and Sam's, now generate well over 85 per cent of industry sales.[27]

The major retailing challenges faced by membership clubs are the limited size of their final consumer market segment, the allocation of efforts between business and final consumer accounts (without antagonizing one group or the other, and without presenting a blurred store image), the lack of interest by many consumers in shopping in warehouse-type stores, the power of the two industry leaders, and the potential for saturation caused by overexpansion.

Flea Market

A ***flea market*** has many retail vendors offering a range of products at discount prices in plain surroundings. It is rooted in the centuries-old tradition of street selling—shoppers touch, sample, and haggle over the prices of items. Once, flea market vendors sold only antiques, bric-a-brac, and assorted used merchandise. Today, they also frequently sell new goods, such as clothing, cosmetics, watches, consumer electronics, housewares, and gift items. Many flea markets are located in nontraditional sites not normally associated with retailing: racetracks, stadiums, arenas, and drive-in movie parking lots. Others are at sites abandoned by supermarkets and department stores. They may be indoor or outdoor.

At a flea market, individual retailers rent space on a daily, weekly, or seasonal basis. For example, a large flea market might rent twenty-foot by forty-foot spaces for $30 to $50 or more per day, depending on the location. Some flea markets impose a parking fee or admission charge on consumers shopping there.

There are a few hundred major flea markets in the United States—such as the Rose Bowl Flea Market in Pasadena, California—but overall sales data are not available. The improved credibility of a number of flea markets (which have been operating for a long time and are open throughout the year), consumer interest in bargaining, the rising interest in Sunday shopping, the broadened product mix, the availability of some brand-name merchandise, and consumers' heightened price sensitivity have all contributed to the growth of this retail institution. For example, the U.S. No. 1 Flea Market and Antiques in New Brunswick, New Jersey, has 500 vendors and attracts 30,000 shoppers on a typical Friday, Saturday, or Sunday. Haggling over prices is encouraged, and many vendors gain their first real experience as retail entrepreneurs: "It's an easy way to get started in business."[28]

Some traditional retailers are not happy about flea markets. They believe flea markets represent an unfair method of competition because the quality of merchandise may be misrepresented or overstated, consumers may purchase items at flea markets and then return them to other retailers for refunds that are higher than the prices paid, suppliers are often unaware their products are sold there, state and federal taxes can be easily avoided, and operating costs are quite low. Furthermore, flea markets may cause traffic congestion.

The high total sales volume generated by off-price chains, factory outlets, membership clubs, and flea markets can be explained by the wheel of retailing. All of these institutions are low-cost operators that appeal to price-conscious consumers who are not satisfied with other retail formats—which have upgraded their merchandise and customer services, raised prices, and moved along the wheel.

[27] "Price, Costco Merge; Has Club Growth Peaked?" *Discount Store News* (July 5, 1993), p. 70; Stephanie Strom, "Wal-Mart to Buy PACE Warehouse Clubs," *New York Times* (November 3, 1993), p. D5; and Bob Ortega, "Warehouse-Club War Leaves Few Standing, And They Are Bruised," *Wall Street Journal* (November 18, 1993), pp. A1, A15.

[28] "Here, Doubtful Shoppers Are Advised to Pounce," *New York Times* (February 25, 1990), p. 46.

Retail Institutions Categorized by Nonstore-Based Strategy Mix

Firms are engaged in ***nonstore retailing*** when they use strategy mixes that are not store-based to reach consumers and complete transactions. Nonstore retailing is conducted through vending machines, direct selling, and direct marketing. Some retailers, such as J.C. Penney and L.L. Bean, combine both store and nonstore activities to expand their customer markets and sales potential. Others, such as Mary Kay and QVC, concentrate on nonstore retailing to better target their market segments and keep down operating costs. Overall nonstore retailing sales are more than $200 billion annually. A discussion of each of the three nonstore-based strategy mixes is next.

VENDING MACHINE

A ***vending machine*** is a retailing format that involves the coin- or card-operated dispensing of goods (such as beverages) and services (such as life insurance sales at airports). It eliminates the use of sales personnel and allows for around-the-clock sales. Machines can be placed wherever they are most convenient for consumers—inside or outside a store, in a motel corridor, at a train station, or on a street corner.

Although many attempts have been made to "vend" clothing, magazines, and other general merchandise, 97 per cent of the $27 billion in 1993 U.S. vending machine sales involved hot and cold beverages, food items, and cigarettes. Because of various health-related issues, between 1979 and 1993, cigarettes' share of vending machine sales fell from 25 per cent to under 10 per cent. With the heavy concentration of vending-machine revenues in beverages and foods, the greatest sales volume is achieved in factory, office, and school lunchrooms and refreshment areas; public places such as service stations are also popular sites for machines. Newspapers on street corners and sidewalks, various machines in hotels and motels, and cigarette machines in restaurants and at train stations are highly visible aspects of vending, but they account for less than 30 per cent of U.S. vending-machine sales.[29] Two of the leading vending-machine operators are Canteen Corporation and ARA Services.

Items priced above $1.50 have not sold well in vending machines because too many coins are required for each transaction, and fewer than one-quarter of U.S. vending machines are equipped with dollar bill changers. Furthermore, many consumers have been reluctant to purchase more expensive items that they cannot see displayed or have explained. However, consumers' expanded access to and use of debit cards (whereby customer bank balances are immediately reduced to reflect purchases) are expected to have a major impact on resolving the payment issue; and the new video-kiosk type of vending machine lets people see product displays and get detailed information (and then place a credit- or debit-card order). Well-known brands and standardized nonfood items are best suited to increasing sales via vending machines.

To improve productivity and customer relations, vending-machine operators are enacting a variety of innovations. For instance, machine malfunctions have been reduced by the application of electronic mechanisms to coin-handling and dispensing controls. Microprocessors are being utilized to track consumer preferences, trace malfunctions, and record receipts. Some machines even have voice synthesizers that are programmed to say such phrases as "Thank you, come again" or "Your change is 15 cents."

Operators must still deal with these issues: theft, vandalism, stockouts, above-average prices, and the perceptions of a great many consumers that vending machines should be patronized only for fill-in convenience items.

DIRECT SELLING

Direct selling includes both personal contact with consumers in their homes (and other nonstore locations such as offices) and telephone solicitations that are initiated

[29] *Vending Times Census of the Industry* (1993); and authors' estimates.

RETAILING AROUND THE WORLD

Avon Calling: In China and Brazil?

Although its domestic sales are flat, Avon has been racking up high sales growth in some foreign markets. Among its key foreign successes are China and Brazil.

Avon's direct-selling system gives the firm a significant competitive advantage in China due to the close ties among family members and friends. Direct selling also enables Avon to easily distribute its products in China: Sales representatives pick up products at one of the company's 10 branch offices and deliver them to their customers. Manufacturers that rely upon store-based methods of distribution are at a disadvantage due to poor roads and uneven store coverage. Avon predicts that its sales in China will increase by 50 per cent per year.

Avon's strong performance in Latin America is based on its ability to adapt to local conditions. For example, in some small mining towns, Avon sales representatives accept eggs or gold powder as payment for cosmetics. The salespeople also facilitate transactions by offering credit for customers. Unlike in the United States, where Avon assumes that salespeople understand the basics of makeup application, it has had to instruct some Latin American Avon ladies as to how to use makeup and deodorant themselves. Latin America now accounts for 35 per cent of Avon's total sales.

Sources: Based on material in Nancy Arnott, "Avon Calling in China," *Sales & Marketing Management* (November 1993), p. 16; and Jack Epstein, "Avon Calling Near the Amazon," *Fortune* (October 25, 1992), pp. 16–17.

by a retailer. Cosmetics, household goods and services (such as carpet cleaning and lawn care), vacuum cleaners, encyclopedias, dairy products, and magazines and newspapers are among the items sometimes sold in this manner. In 1993, direct selling accounted for $14 billion in U.S. sales and employed more than five million people (most on a part-time basis).[30]

The strategy mix for direct selling emphasizes convenience in shopping and a personal touch. Many times, detailed demonstrations can be made. Consumers are often more relaxed in their homes than in stores. They are also likely to be attentive and are not exposed to competing brands (as they are in stores). For some shoppers, such as older consumers and parents with young children, in-store shopping is difficult to undertake because of limited mobility. For the retailer, direct selling has lower overhead costs because store locations and fixtures are not necessary.

Nonetheless, direct-selling revenues in the United States have risen relatively slowly over the last several years. Here are some reasons why:

- More women are now working; therefore, they may not be interested in or available for in-home purchases.
- Improved job opportunities in other fields and the interest in full-time career-oriented positions have reduced the number of people interested in direct-selling jobs.
- A firm's market coverage is limited by the size of its sales force. Many firms are able to reach fewer than one-half of potential customers.
- Sales productivity is low because the average transaction is small and most consumers are unreceptive to this type of selling—many will not open their doors to salespeople or talk to telephone sales representatives.
- Sales-force turnover is high. The bulk of employees are poorly supervised part-timers.
- To stimulate sales personnel, compensation is usually 25 to 50 per cent of the revenues they generate. This means average to above-average prices.
- Various legal restrictions are in effect due to deceptive or high-pressure sales tactics.
- A poor image is associated with the term *door-to-door*; hence, the industry preference for the term *direct selling*.

[30] Direct Selling Education Foundation.

FIGURE 5–7
Spiegel: A Leading Specialty Direct Marketer
Spiegel's direct-marketing apparel sales are over $1 billion, mostly via its specialty catalogs. Customers may place mail orders or talk to well-trained telephone operators (who are represented here).
Reprinted by permission.

Firms are responding to these issues in various ways. For example, Avon is placing greater emphasis on workplace sales—which today account for 30 per cent of its total direct-selling revenues; is offering free training to sales personnel (it used to charge a fee); is rewarding the best workers with better territories; and is rapidly expanding internationally. Mary Kay and Tupperware use community residents as salespeople and have a party atmosphere rather than a strict door-to-door cold-canvassing approach; this requires networks of family, friends, and neighbors. Inasmuch as Fuller Brush salespeople reach about two-thirds of U.S. households, it uses mail-order catalogs to reach the other one-third. It also advertises for sales positions in the catalogs. Kirby salespeople make more evening in-home presentations to contact working women.

Among the leaders in direct selling are Avon and Mary Kay (cosmetics), Amway (household supplies), Tupperware (plastic food containers), Shaklee (vitamins and health foods), Fuller Brush (small household products), Kirby (vacuum cleaners), and Encyclopedia Britannica. Some department stores, such as J.C. Penney, also use direct selling. Penney's decorator consultants sell a complete line of furnishings, not available in its stores, to consumers in their homes.

DIRECT MARKETING

Direct marketing is a form of retailing in which a customer is first exposed to a good or service through a nonpersonal medium (such as direct mail, conventional or cable television, radio, magazine, or newspaper) and then orders by mail or telephone (usually through a toll-free 800 number)—sometimes, by computer. Annual U.S. sales to final consumers are over $160 billion (including charitable contributions), and over 100 million people make one or more direct-marketing purchases during a typical year. Among the products bought most frequently are gift items, apparel, magazines, books and records/CDs, sports equipment, home accessories, and insurance.[31]

Direct marketers can be divided into two broad categories: general and specialty. General direct-marketing firms offer a full line of products and sell everything from clothing to housewares. J.C. Penney (via its mail-order business) and QVC are examples of general direct marketers. Specialty firms focus on more narrow product lines, like their specialty store counterparts. Spiegel, L.L. Bean, Publishers Clearinghouse, and Franklin Mint are among the thousands of U.S. specialty direct marketers. See Figure 5–7.

[31] *Direct Marketing* (January 1994), p. 4; *1991/92 Statistical Fact Book* (New York: Direct Marketing Association, 1992); and authors' estimates.

Direct marketing has a number of strategic business advantages:

- Many costs are reduced—startup costs are rather low; reduced inventory levels can be maintained; no fixtures or displays are needed; a prime site is unnecessary; regular store hours do not have to be kept; a personal sales force is not needed; and a firm may be operated out of a garage or basement.
- It is possible for a firm to offer lower prices (due to reduced costs) than store retailers selling the same items. A very large geographic area can be covered inexpensively and efficiently.
- Customers are given a convenient method of shopping; there are no crowds, parking congestion, or lines at cash registers.
- Specific consumer segments can be pinpointed through mailings.
- Sometimes, consumers can legally avoid paying sales tax by purchasing from direct marketers not operating retail facilities in the consumer's state (however, a number of states are interested in eliminating this loophole).
- A store-based retailer can use direct marketing to supplement its regular business and expand its geographic trading area (even becoming a national or international retailer) without adding outlets.

There are some limitations to direct marketing, but they are not as critical as the problems that face direct-selling firms. First, products cannot be examined prior to their purchase by a consumer. Thus, the range of items sold via direct marketing is usually more limited than that sold in stores. Direct marketers also need liberal return policies to attract and maintain customers. Second, prospective retailers may underestimate entry costs. Catalogs can be costly: for glossy catalogs, printing and mailing costs are easily several dollars per catalog. A computer system may be required to track shipments, monitor purchases and returns, and keep mailing lists current. A 24-hour telephone staff may be necessary.

Third, since most catalogs are delivered by third-class mail, the profitability of direct marketers is highly sensitive to postal rates and to the costs of paper stock. In 1991, the U.S. Postal Service raised the rates charged for third-class mail by an average of 25 per cent; and increases occur with some regularity. Fourth, even the most successful catalogs draw purchases from less than 10 per cent of recipients. The high costs and relatively low response rates have caused some merchants to charge for their catalogs (with the fee usually reimbursed after the first order is placed) or to limit catalogs to customers previously meeting minimum purchase amounts. Fifth, direct marketing clutter exists. In 1993, about 14 billion catalogs were mailed—55 apiece for every man, woman, and child in the United States. Sixth, some unscrupulous direct marketers have given the industry a poor image because of delays in delivery and the shipment of damaged goods. Seventh, because catalogs are prepared several months to a year in advance, prices and styles may be difficult to plan.

The "30-day rule" is a U.S. federal regulation that greatly affects direct marketers. This rule requires that mail-order firms ship orders within 30 days after their receipt or notify customers of delays. If an order cannot be shipped within 60 days, the customer must be given a specific delivery date and offered the option of canceling the order and obtaining a refund or continuing to wait for the order to be filled. In early 1994, this rule was extended to include consumers shopping by telephone, fax, and computer.[32]

Despite the limitations it faces, long-run growth for direct marketing is projected for several reasons. Consumer interest in convenience and the difficulty in setting aside time for shopping are expected to continue. More direct marketers will be operating 24-hour service for orders. Product standardization and the prominence of well-known brands will reduce consumer perceptions of risk when buying on the basis of a catalog or other nonpersonal description. Direct marketers have rapidly improved

[32] Rita Rubin, Margaret Mannix, and Andrea Wright, "News You Can Use," *U.S. News & World Report* (February 28, 1994), p. 69.

their skills and efficiency; they are much more effective than ever before. Technological breakthroughs and new direct-marketing approaches, like in-home computerized ordering systems, are expected to encourage more consumer shopping.

Because direct marketing represents such a large, expanding, and dynamic aspect of retailing, further information is provided in the appendix at the end of this chapter, following the cases.

Retail Institutions Categorized by Service Versus Goods Strategy Mix

Service retailing involves transactions between companies or individuals and final consumers where the consumers do not purchase or acquire ownership of tangible products. ***Goods retailing*** focuses on the sale of tangible (physical) products. Some retailers are engaged in either service retailing (such as travel agencies) or goods retailing (such as hardware stores); others offer some combination of the two (such as video stores that rent, as well as sell movie tapes). As noted in Chapter 1, total U.S. service-retailing sales are several hundred billion dollars annually. Service retailing involves such diverse businesses as hotels and motels, personal services, auto repair and rental, and amusement and recreational services.[33] There are three kinds of service retailing: ***rented-goods services***, in which consumers lease and use goods for specified periods of time; ***owned-goods services***, in which goods owned by consumers are repaired, improved, or maintained; and ***nongoods services***, in which intangible personal services (rather than goods) are offered to consumers—who experience the services rather than possess them.

Some examples of rented-goods service retailing are Hertz car rentals, carpet cleaner rentals from a supermarket, and videocassette rentals at a 7-Eleven. In each case, a tangible good is leased for a fee for a fixed time duration. The consumer may enjoy the use of the item, but ownership is not obtained and the good must be returned when the rental period is up.

Owned-goods service retailing illustrations include repair of a watch mainspring, lawn care to eliminate weeds, and an annual air-conditioner tune-up to maintain performance. In this category, the retailer providing the service never owns the good involved.

In nongoods service retailing, personal services, involving the use of the owner's or an employee's time in return for a fee, are offered; tangible goods are not involved. Some examples are stock brokers, tutors, travel agents, real-estate brokers, and babysitters. In each case, the seller offers personal expertise for a specified time period.

The characteristics of services differ significantly from those of goods, as shown by the following list:

- The buyer is often called a *client*—not a *customer.*
- Surpluses cannot be inventoried; thus, some services can be very perishable.
- Standards are not precise because many services cannot be mass produced.
- Service performance may vary from one customer to another and from one experience to another.
- Service prices are sometimes expressed as rates, fees, admissions, charges, tuition, and so on.
- It may be hard to apply the economic concepts of supply and demand, and costs are also difficult to assign because of the intangible nature of services.
- Few service chains have existed (but this is changing rapidly—examples are Century 21 for real estate and H&R Block for tax services), and the concentration of firms in the service sector is relatively small.

[33] See *Current Business Reports: Service Annual Survey* (Washington, D.C.: U.S. Department of Commerce, annual).

- Many service retailers do not understand that their services must be promoted; being available does not guarantee business.
- Symbolism derives from how well a service is performed rather than from the ownership of a good.
- Many services are performed in a professional or formal manner.
- In some cases, consumers may decide to bypass retailers and complete services themselves.
- Some service firms (like the public library) are nonprofit in nature.

It should be noted that although several services have not been commonly considered a part of retailing (such as medical, dental, legal, and educational services), they should be when they entail a transaction with a final consumer.

Chapter 18 presents a detailed discussion of strategic planning concepts as they apply to service retailing.

SUMMARY

1. *To describe the wheel of retailing, scrambled merchandising, and the retail life cycle and show how they help explain the performance and evolution of retail strategy mixes* In Chapter 4, retail institutions were examined by type of ownership. This chapter views retailing from three strategy perspectives: store-based, nonstore-based, and service versus goods. A retail strategy mix involves a combination of factors: location, operations, goods/services offered, pricing, atmosphere and customer services, and promotion. To flourish, a firm should strive to be dominant in some aspect of its strategy and thus reach power retailer status.

   Three important concepts help explain the performance and evolution of various retail strategy mixes. According to the wheel of retailing, retail innovators often first appear as low-price operators with a low-cost structure and low profit-margin requirements. Over time, these firms upgrade their offerings and customer services and raise prices accordingly. They then become vulnerable to new discounters with lower-cost structures who take their place along the wheel. Scrambled merchandising occurs when a retailer adds goods and services that are unrelated to each other and the firm's original business to increase overall sales and profit margins. Scrambled merchandising is contagious, and retailers often use it in self-defense. The retail life cycle assumes that retail institutions pass through identifiable stages of innovation, development, maturity, and decline. Attributes and strategies change as institutions mature.

2. *To examine the characteristics of a wide variety of retail institutions involved with store-based strategy mixes* Retail institutions may be classed by store based strategy mix and divided into food-oriented and general merchandise groupings. In all, 15 store-based strategy mixes are covered in the chapter.

   These are the food-oriented store-based retailers: A convenience store is well located, is open long hours, and offers a moderate number of fill-in items at average to above-average prices. A conventional supermarket is departmentalized and carries a wide range of food and related items; little general merchandise is stocked; and prices are competitive. A food-based superstore is larger and more diversified than a conventional supermarket but smaller and less diversified than a combination store. A combination store unites supermarket and general merchandise sales in a large facility and sets competitive prices; the supercenter is a type of combination store. The box (limited-line) store is a discounter focusing on a small product selection, moderate hours, few services, and few national brands. A warehouse store is a discounter offering a moderate number of food items in a no-frills setting that can be quite large (for a super warehouse).

   These are the general-merchandise store-based retailers: A specialty store concentrates on one goods or service line and has a tailored strategy; the category killer is a special kind of specialty store. A variety store has an assortment of inexpensive and popularly priced items in a simple setting. A department store is a large retailer that carries an extensive assortment of goods and services. The traditional one has a range of customer services and charges average to above-average prices. A full-line discount store is the form of department store with a low-cost, low-price strategy. A retail catalog showroom is a discounter at which customers select merchandise from catalogs and shop in a warehouse-style store. An off-price chain features brand-name items and sells them at low prices in an austere environment. A factory outlet is manufacturer-owned and sells that firm's closeouts, discontinued merchandise, and irregulars at very low prices. A membership club appeals to price-conscious shoppers, who are required to be members to be eligible to shop there. A flea market has many retail vendors that offer a range of goods at discount prices in non-traditional store settings.

3. *To look at the characteristics of the three major retail institutions involved with nonstore-based strategy mixes: vending machine, direct selling, and direct marketing* Firms are engaged in nonstore retailing when they use strategy mixes that are not store-based to reach customers and complete transactions. A vending machine is a format that involves the coin- or card-operated dispensing of goods and services; it may be placed at any site that is convenient for consumers. Direct selling includes both personal contact with consumers in their homes and telephone solicitations by the seller. In direct marketing, a consumer is first exposed to a good or service through a nonpersonal medium and then orders by mail or phone.

4. *To contrast service-based retailing with goods-based retailing* Service retailing involves transactions between companies or individuals and final consumers where the consumers do not purchase or acquire ownership of tangible products. Goods retailing focuses on sales of tangible (physical) products. A retailer may engage in one format or the other, or combine the two. There are three kinds of service retailing: rented goods, owned goods, and nongoods. Strategic planning for service retailers is examined in Chapter 18.

KEY TERMS

strategy mix (p. 134)
power retailer (p. 134)
wheel of retailing (p. 135)
scrambled merchandising (p. 136)
retail life cycle (p. 137)
convenience store (p. 141)
supermarket (p. 144)
conventional supermarket (p. 144)
food-based superstore (p. 144)
combination store (p. 145)
supercenter (p. 145)
box (limited-line) store (p. 145)
warehouse store (p. 146)
specialty store (p. 146)
category killer store (p. 148)
variety store (p. 148)
department store (p. 149)
traditional department store (p. 150)
full-line discount store (p. 152)
retail catalog showroom (p. 154)
off-price chain (p. 154)
factory outlet (p. 155)
membership club (p. 156)
flea market (p. 157)
nonstore retailing (p. 158)
vending machine (p. 158)
direct selling (p. 158)
direct marketing (p. 160)
service retailing (p. 162)
goods retailing (p. 162)
rented-goods services (p. 162)
owned-goods services (p. 162)
nongoods services (p. 162)

QUESTIONS FOR DISCUSSION

1. Describe how a small firm could be a power retailer.
2. Explain the wheel of retailing. Is this theory applicable today? Why or why not?
3. Develop a low-end retail strategy mix for a cosmetics store. Include location, operating procedures, goods/services offered, pricing tactics, and promotion methods.
4. The cosmetics store in Question 3 wants to upgrade to a high-end strategy. Outline the changes that must be made in the firm's strategy mix. What are the risks facing the retailer?
5. How could these retailers best apply scrambled merchandising? Explain your answers.
   a. Bookstore.
   b. Lawn-care service company.
   c. Movie theater.
   d. Restaurant.
6. Contrast the strategy emphasis that should be followed by institutions in the innovation and growth stages of the retail life cycle with the emphasis by institutions in the maturity stage.
7. What alternative approaches are there for institutions that are in the decline phase of the retail life cycle?
8. Contrast the strategy mixes of convenience stores, conventional supermarkets, food-based superstores, and warehouse stores. Is there room for each in the marketplace? Explain your answer.
9. Do you think that supercenters will succeed in the long-run? Why or why not?
10. Contrast the strategy mixes of specialty stores, traditional department stores, and full-line discount stores.
11. What must the off-price chain do to succeed in the future?
12. Do you agree that nonstore retailing will continue to grow? Explain your answer.
13. Differentiate between direct selling and direct marketing. What are the strengths and weaknesses of each?
14. One retailer sells cars; another firm rents them. Develop a strategy mix for each, and compare these mixes.

CASE 1
Rewriting the Definition of Membership Clubs*

Supermarkets feel especially threatened by the success of membership clubs due to their impact on supermarket sales and the cost advantages of the clubs. Although estimates vary, at least one-half of total membership club sales are from supermarket items. Data compiled by Nielsen Household Services also indicate that nine of the twelve best-selling items at membership clubs are among the twelve best-sellers at supermarkets. See Table 1. This overlap is particularly disturbing to supermarkets since they frequently advertise specials on best-sellers to generate store traffic.

Table 1 Best-Selling Items in Supermarkets and Membership Clubs

Rank	Supermarkets	Membership Clubs
1	Carbonated beverages	Tobacco and accessories
2	Tobacco and accessories	Paper products
3	Milk	Detergents
4	Cereal	Snacks
5	Bread and baked goods	Carbonated beverages
6	Packaged meats	Electronics/records/tapes
7	Frozen prepared foods	Shelf-stable juices/drinks
8	Shelf-stable juices/drinks	Refrigerated juices/drinks
9	Snacks	Cereal
10	Pet foods	Candy
11	Refrigerated juices/drinks	Packaged meats
12	Paper products	Frozen prepared foods

Source: Nielsen Household Services.

The greatest anxiety among supermarket operators involves the relative cost advantage of clubs. A recent study sponsored by the Food Marketing Institute found that membership clubs are able to sell grocery products for 26 per cent less than conventional supermarkets. Fifty per cent of the cost differences is due to the operating efficiencies of the clubs, 42 per cent is due to large product sizes and "other discounts," and 8 per cent is due to membership fees helping to subsidize prices. The study also examined mass merchants and drug chains; but the cost differences were greatest between membership clubs and conventional supermarkets.

Membership clubs' operating expenses average 7.5 per cent of sales as compared with 20 per cent for conventional supermarkets. Membership fees not only provide two-thirds of the typical club's operating profits; they discourage the presence of shoplifters (who cannot enter the club without a membership card). The larger pack-

* The material in this case is drawn from Alice Bredin, "The Fight Begins," *Stores* (September 1993), pp. 23–26; "60th Annual Report of the Grocery Industry," *Progressive Grocer* (April 1993), p. 49; Howard Schlossberg, "Grocers, Club Owners Battle for Territory," *Marketing News* (September 13, 1993), pp. 11, 16; Howard Schlossberg, "Warehouse Club Owners Hope to Sign Up Everybody Eventually," *Marketing News* (September 13, 1993), pp. 1, 10; and Eric Wieffering, "Who Shops the Clubs?" *American Demographics* (October 1993), pp. 25–26.

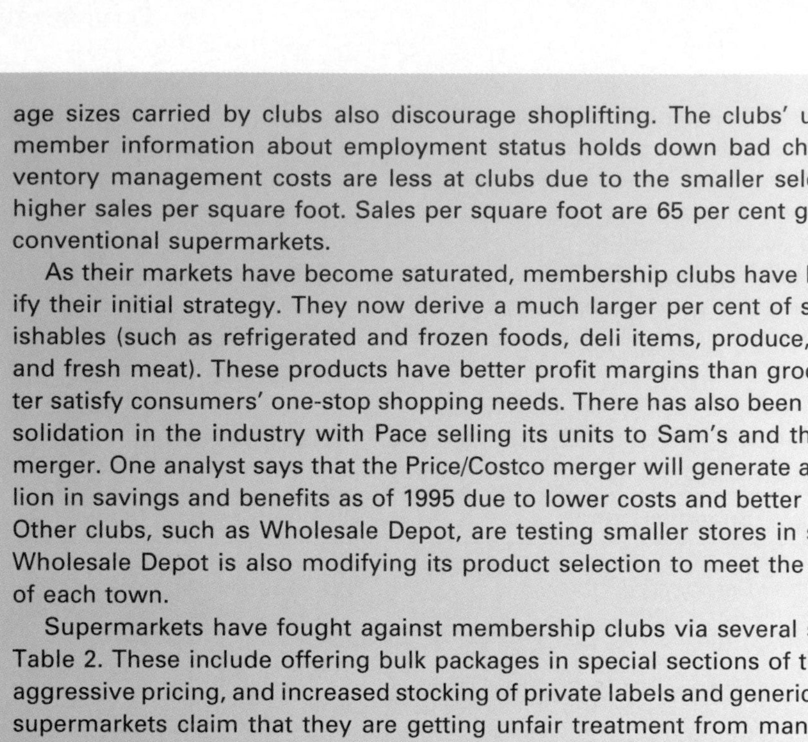

age sizes carried by clubs also discourage shoplifting. The clubs' use of detailed member information about employment status holds down bad check losses. Inventory management costs are less at clubs due to the smaller selection and the higher sales per square foot. Sales per square foot are 65 per cent greater than for conventional supermarkets.

As their markets have become saturated, membership clubs have begun to modify their initial strategy. They now derive a much larger per cent of sales from perishables (such as refrigerated and frozen foods, deli items, produce, baked goods, and fresh meat). These products have better profit margins than groceries and better satisfy consumers' one-stop shopping needs. There has also been increased consolidation in the industry with Pace selling its units to Sam's and the Price/Costco merger. One analyst says that the Price/Costco merger will generate about $110 million in savings and benefits as of 1995 due to lower costs and better buying power. Other clubs, such as Wholesale Depot, are testing smaller stores in smaller towns. Wholesale Depot is also modifying its product selection to meet the varying needs of each town.

Supermarkets have fought against membership clubs via several strategies. See Table 2. These include offering bulk packages in special sections of the store, more aggressive pricing, and increased stocking of private labels and generic brands. Some supermarkets claim that they are getting unfair treatment from manufacturers and have threatened legal action. Yet, experts suggest that supermarkets compete against the clubs by becoming "the best supermarkets in town"—with the best service, quality, and appearance.

Table 2 10 Ways Supermarkets Can Win Market Share back from Membership Clubs

1. Don't panic. Remember that clubs have narrow assortments, limited services, and long waiting lines. Clubs only gain limited market penetration.
2. Continue to do what you do best. For example, if your specialty is produce, stay with it.
3. Promote your competitive advantages such as location, service, quality perishables, and selection.
4. Conduct market research. Determine who club customers are, do price checks, and monitor their selections. Carefully observe the effects of the club's bakery, produce, meat, and paper goods sales on your business.
5. Feature a value-pack section for customers who favor low prices and large sizes. Use only best-selling brands for these value packs.
6. Negotiate hard with vendors to secure the best possible prices and terms. Do not allow manufacturers to give better terms to membership clubs that cannot be cost justified.
7. Watch your operating costs carefully.
8. Develop your own no-fee membership club that offers special prices to members on selected items.
9. Emphasize items that clubs do not stock such as cheeses, imported foods, ethnic specialties, catering, salad bars, etc.
10. Consider special services such as delivery and the acceptance of credit cards.

Source: Points 1 to 6 have been adapted by the authors from Robert E. O'Neill, "Close-Up Clubs," (May 1992), *Progressive Grocer* (May 1992), p. 64.

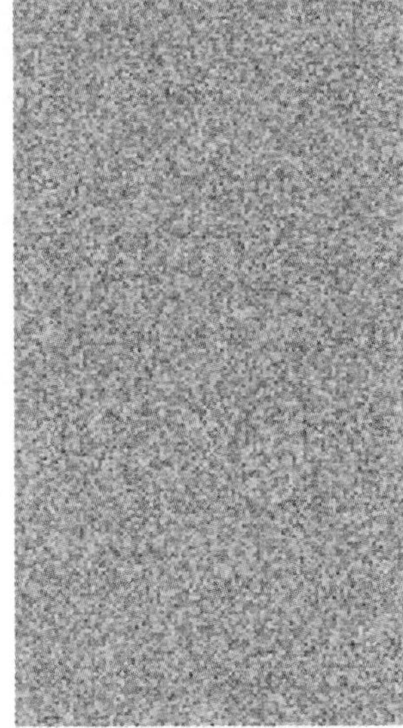

Questions

1. What are the overall strengths and weaknesses of membership clubs as compared with supermarkets?
2. Cite additional implications of the Price/Costco merger beyond operating cost savings and buying power.
3. Discuss the impact of the high overlap among best-selling items between supermarkets and membership clubs from the supermarkets' perspective.
4. Present your own recommendations as to how supermarkets can fight back to win market share. Expand on the items in Table 2.

Video Questions on the Membership Club Explosion

1. Evaluate the data describing the growth of membership clubs as compared with supermarkets.
2. Describe how clubs have responded to consumer demand since their inception.

Case 2

The Home Shopping Network: Behind the Scenes†

TV-based home shopping is a multibillion dollar business that is growing 20 per cent annually. Only 5 per cent of U.S. consumers bought goods via TV shopping programs in 1988; about twice as many are doing so today. The popularity of TV-based home shopping is expected to rise at an even faster pace as the number of channels increases and as interactive shopping technology (which enables people to browse through channels and ask for information and advice) becomes available.

Once regarded as a medium primarily for shut-ins and the lower middle class, the typical TV-based shopper is now younger, more fashion-conscious, and as apt to be from a high-income household as the overall U.S. population. See Table 1. Convenience and low prices are the major advantages of TV-based shopping to customers. Shoppers encounter no crowds or parking difficulties and can order twenty-four hours per day. And prices may be lower than traditional merchants. According to one retail analyst, "It's a low-cost distribution system. You don't need thousands of stores, and you don't need thousands of pieces of inventory in each location."

The TV-based home-shopping industry is dominated by two companies: Home Shopping Network (HSN) and QVC. HSN reaches 60 million households, one-half through cable channels and one-half through broadcast channels. QVC reaches 47 million households, all of whom are cable subscribers. Annual revenues of HSN and QVC each exceed $1 billion. Together, the firms reach over two-thirds of all U.S. television households.

The strategies of HSN and QVC are similar. Both firms feature jewelry and women's clothing, and do not generally sell nationally-recognized brands. Most items must be purchased from HSN and QVC during the limited time the products are advertised. This practice encourages consumers to act immediately; but it also forces some consumers to watch programs for long hours in the hope that specials are repeated. Although HSN and QVC provide detailed hour-by-hour schedules, the schedules are only available to members. QVC has also recently launched a major advertising campaign that tells viewers the exact times particular products will be shown

† The material in this case is drawn from J. Douglas Eldridge, "Nonstore Retailing: Planning for a Big Future," *Chain Store Age Executive* (August 1993), pp. 34A–35A; "Our Reporter Rates the TV Shopping Shows," *Money* (August 1993), p. 20; Patrick M. Reilly, "TV Shopping Hooks High-Toned Viewers," *Wall Street Journal* (November 16, 1993), pp. B1, B10; and Laura Zinn, Gail De George, Rochelle Shoretz, Dori Jones Yang, and Stephanie Anderson Forest, "Retailing Will Never Be the Same," *Business Week* (July 26, 1993), pp. 54–60.

Table 1 Selected Attributes of TV-Based Shoppers and Typical U.S. Store-Based Shoppers

Attributes	TV Shoppers	Store Shoppers
Age		
Per cent 25 to 34	26	24
Per cent 65-plus	11	16
Gender		
Per cent female	52	53
Per cent male	48	47
Highest education completed		
Per cent high school graduate	34	31
Per cent some college	27	30
Income		
Average household income	$34,900	$38,000
Per cent of households earning more than $75,000	8	9
Fashion consciousness		
Per cent open to new styles and trends	26	16
Per cent preferring traditional things	29	33
Per cent choosing value and comfort over fashion	29	35

Source: Laura Zinn, Gail De George, Rochelle Shoretz, Dori Jones Yang, and Stephanie Anderson Forest, "Retailing Will Never Be the Same," *Business Week* (July 26, 1993), p. 56.

on its programs. HSN and QVC both have money-back guarantees—their rates of return average 20 per cent overall, but can exceed 40 to 50 per cent on some items. Both add shipping and handling and state taxes (that are applicable in the buyer's home state). Shoppers who return items to either firm must pay return postage and insurance costs.

In contrast to QVC, HSN personalizes its merchandise presentation. It encourages past customers and current ones to call in and have their comments aired. Typically, callers state their first names, their home cities, and their overall satisfaction with the product being advertised on the screen. HSN calls its voice-response computer "Tootie" and toots a horn for callers. It offers club members merchandise credits on birthdays and anniversaries. HSN has also signed a letter of intent to fill orders and provide customer service for Macy's when it starts its own 24-hour television shopping channel. QVC began selling a private-label clothing line for Saks Fifth Avenue in May 1993.

Retail executives and analysts have mixed opinions as to the impact of TV-based home shopping on traditional store-based retailing. Many feel home shopping will not replace the social dimensions of store shopping, such as parent-child bonding or bonding among teenagers. They also believe consumers may be uncomfortable buying items like shoes without trying them on or buying a pair of slacks without feeling the fabric. Others are equally adamant that it will hurt traditional retailing because it offers a low-cost distribution system for similar goods and the resultant competition means fewer dollars available for spending in other outlets. And, according to a study by Roper Starch Worldwide, TV-based shopping has resulted in fewer consumers using mail-order catalogs and department store catalogs.

Analysts generally agree that HSN and QVC need to shift their focus away from cheap jewelry and unknown brands. A study by Deloitte & Touche found that TV-based shoppers want more travel packages, children's clothing, men's clothing, major appliances, and furniture advertised.

Questions

1. Evaluate the overall strengths and weaknesses of TV-based home shopping as compared to traditional department stores.
2. Discuss the implications of the data in Table 1 with regard to the overall retail strategy of Home Shopping Network.
3. Comment on the similarities and differences in the retail strategies of Home Shopping Network and QVC.
4. What problems and opportunities can HSN encounter if it adds such goods and services as travel packages, branded appliances, and furniture?

Video Questions on Home Shopping Network

1. Describe the use of technology by the Home Shopping Network.
2. Evaluate the overall retail strategy of Home Shopping Network.

Appendix on Direct Marketing

Although direct marketing is one of the largest and fastest-growing retail institutions in the United States, it is also one of the most misunderstood. According to one expert, "It used to be easy to spot direct marketers. We were the ones who used to put all those envelopes and catalogs in the mail. But yesterday's mavens of direct mail are now becoming masters of multimedia, as we access a large and rapidly expanding arsenal of technological tools."[1] Nonetheless, direct marketing is quite different from store-based retailing: "In the retail store business, you buy an inventory and sell it off. In the direct-marketing business, you create a demand and fill it." And "traditional retailers tend to be burdened by real estate."[2]

Therefore, an appendix on direct marketing can give the reader further insights into this important, evolving, and challenging retail institution. We will discuss the domain of direct marketing, emerging trends, the steps in a direct-marketing strategy, and key issues facing direct marketers.

What Is Direct Marketing?

As defined in Chapter 5, direct marketing is a type of retailing in which a consumer is exposed to a good or service through a nonpersonal medium and then orders by mail or phone—or computer. It may also be viewed in this manner:

> Direct marketing is an interactive system of retailing which uses one or more advertising media to effect a measurable response and/or transaction at any location. It requires the existence and maintenance of a data base to record names of customers, expires,* and prospects; to provide a vehicle for storing, then measuring, results of advertising, usually direct response advertising; to provide a vehicle for storing, then measuring, purchasing performance; and to provide a vehicle for ongoing direct communication.[3]
>
> In talking about direct marketing, direct marketers speak of it in terms of a way of doing business, a methodology or approach as opposed to a collection of specific pursuits. Just as general retailing encompasses a wide range of techniques in its pursuit of reaching the customer, so, too, direct marketing is seen as a specific way of thinking about retailing.[4]

Accordingly, we *do* include these as forms of direct marketing: any catalog; mail, television, radio, magazine, newspaper, telephone directory, or other advertisement; or other nonpersonal contact that stimulates customers to place orders via the mail, the telephone, or the computer.

[1] Howard C. Kraft, "The Destiny of Direct: A New Perspective on the Future of Direct Marketing," *Journal of Direct Marketing*, Vol. 7 (Autumn 1993), p. 65.

[2] Holly Klokis, "Catalog Options: Mail-Order or Store Traffic?" *Chain Store Age Executive* (May 1985), p. 31; and Susan Reda, "Formula for the Future," *Stores* (October 1993), p. 74.

* Expires are those prospects who have been or shortly will be dropped from a data base.

[3] Adapted by the authors from *Direct Marketing*. A condensed version of this definition appears in every issue of this monthly magazine.

[4] Adapted by the authors from *Direct Marketing in the Year 2000* (New York: Yankelovich, Skelly and White/Clancy, Shulman, Inc. 1987), p. 14.

We *do not* include these as forms of direct marketing:

- Traditional vending machines—Consumers are exposed to nonpersonal media but do not usually complete transactions via mail or phone. These people do not really interact with the firm, and a data base cannot be generated and kept.
- Direct selling—Consumers are solicited through in-home (and in-office) personal selling efforts or seller-originated telephone calls. In both cases, the company uses personal, rather than nonpersonal, communication to initiate contact with consumers.

Direct marketing *is* involved in many videodisc kiosk transactions; when items are mailed to consumers, there is interaction between the firm and the customer, and a data base can be formed. It is also involved when consumers originate telephone calls, based on catalogs or ads they have seen.

Emerging Trends

Several emerging trends are relevant to direct marketing: changing consumer life-styles, the increased competition among firms, the greater use of dual distribution channels, newer roles for catalogs, technological advances, and mounting interest in international direct marketing.

CHANGING CONSUMER LIFE-STYLES

From a direct-marketing perspective, the life-styles of American consumers have shifted dramatically over the last two decades, mostly because of the large number of women who are now in the labor force and the longer commuting time to and from work for suburban residents. Currently, many consumers do not have the time and/or the inclination to shop at retail stores. They are attracted by the convenience and ease of purchases through direct marketing.

Because consumers are now more satisfied with their direct marketing experiences than in the past (owing to improved company performance), sales should continue to be strong. These are some of the factors consumers consider when selecting a direct marketing firm with which to deal:

- Company reputation (image).
- Types of goods/services offered.
- Assortment.
- Brand names carried.
- Availability of a toll-free telephone number for ordering.
- Credit-card acceptance
- Promised delivery time.
- Comparable store prices.
- Satisfaction with past purchases.

INCREASED COMPETITION AMONG FIRMS

As direct marketing sales have increased, so have the number of firms in the industry. Although there are a number of large direct marketers, such as J.C. Penney and Spiegel, there are also thousands of small companies. For example, according to the Direct Marketing Association, there are now over 10,000 U.S. mail-order companies.

The high level of competition has occurred because entry into direct marketing is far easier and less costly than entry into store retailing. A direct marketer does not need a store location, can function with a limited staff, and can place inexpensive, one-inch ads in the back of leading magazines or send out brochures to targeted customer groups. It can keep minimal inventory on hand and place orders with suppliers after customers have paid for items (as long as the direct marketer abides by the 30-day rule of the Federal Trade Commission).

The "Marketplace" advertising section of *Runner's World* magazine (with several hundred thousand subscribers) can be used to further illustrate the ease of entry into direct marketing. In 1994, it cost $525 for a one-inch ad. Among the mail-order items advertised in that section are running shoes, rowing machines, sports watches, contact lenses, sports apparel, and heart rate monitors.[5]

Because direct marketing lures many small firms whose owners may inadequately define their market niche, offer nondistinctive goods and services, have limited experience, underestimate the effort required, have trouble keeping supplier continuity, and receive a large share of consumer complaints, it is estimated that one out of every two new direct-marketing companies fails. According to one survey, about one-half of mail-order shoppers say they have had problems with an order.[6]

Greater Use of Dual Distribution Channels

Another contributor to the intense competition among direct marketers is the expanding use of dual distribution channels by store-based retailers. In the past, most store retailers used advertising to draw customers into their stores. But today, many of them are supplementing in-store revenues by utilizing ads, brochures, and catalogs to generate mail-order and telephone sales. They recognize that direct marketing is efficient, can focus on specific consumer segments, appeals to people who might not otherwise patronize them, and requires a lower investment to reach new geographic markets than opening branch outlets.

Bloomingdale's and Nordstrom are examples of two store-based retailers that have entered into direct marketing relatively recently. Bloomingdale's by Mail was established in 1982 and has seen sales grow rapidly since then. Annually, it issues dozens of catalogs and has sales of $100 million. Nordstrom's The Catalog was started in 1994. It capitalizes on the firm's legendary reputation for customer service: toll-free 24-hour shopping, same-day shipments for orders placed before 11:00 A.M., second-day air delivery via Federal Express, and complementary gift boxes.[7]

These comments sum up the appeal of direct marketing to store-based retailers:

> The two sales mediums are clearly complementary to each other, rather than competitive. The synergy of store-based retailing and direct marketing is a way to expand in two very competitive markets.
>
> I don't know anyone who buys everything by mail. People who buy by mail and phone also buy a lot in our stores.
>
> In terms of growth potential, we can grow faster than the three years it takes to build a new store.
>
> Any time we go into a new area and open a store, we already have a whole set of customers there from the catalog.[8]

[5] "Marketplace," *Runner's World* (April 1994), pp. 108–113.

[6] "Tough Choice for Catalogs: Mail or Mall?" *Chain Store Age Executive* (October 1990), p. 35; and Judith Waldrop, "Catalog Complaints Cut Sales by Mail," *American Demographics* (February 1993), p. 12.

[7] *Federated Department Stores Annual Report 1993*; and Cyndee Miller, "Catalogs Alive, Thriving," *Marketing News* (February 28, 1994), p. 9.

[8] Cara S. Trager, "Retailers, Catalogers Cross Channels," *Advertising Age* (October 26, 1987), pp. S-9–S-10.

Newer Roles for Catalogs

Direct marketers are recasting the ways in which they use their catalogs in three basic areas. First, many firms are now printing "specialogs" in addition to (or instead of) the annual catalog that features all of a company's offerings. For example, yearly, Spiegel, L.L. Bean, and Talbots send out dozens of catalogs in all, including separate specialogs for petite women, gifts, shoes, intimate apparel, and other goods. By using specialogs, firms can cater to the specific needs of customer segments, emphasize a limited number of items, and reduce their catalog production and postage costs (as a specialog may be eight to fifty pages in length, compared to hundreds of pages for a general catalog). As a Lands' End spokesperson noted, "We found that specialty catalogs fetch a better response. The bigger the book, the less productive it is."[9]

Second, to help defray catalog costs, some companies are now accepting advertising from noncompeting firms that are compatible with the direct marketers' images. For instance, Bloomingdale's by Mail has had ads for cognac, Lincoln Continental, and Club Med. Overall, catalog ads provide several million dollars in revenues for direct marketers.

Third, both to stimulate sales and to defray costs, some catalogs are now being sold in bookstores, supermarkets, and airports. Thus, thousands of stores carry an assortment of the catalogs made available to them; the Waldenbooks chain alone sells tens of thousands of catalogs per month. The percentage of consumers buying a catalog who actually make a product purchase is many times higher than that for those who get catalogs sent via the mail.

Technological Advances

Direct marketing is in the midst of a technological revolution that is improving operating efficiency and offering enhanced sales opportunities. These are just a few of the advances taking place:

- Companies can inexpensively use computers to enter customer orders when they are received by mail or telephone, arrange for merchandise shipments, monitor inventory on hand, and maintain data bases of prospective consumers.
- Customers can dial toll-free 800 telephone numbers to place orders and get information. The cost per call for the direct marketer is quite low.
- Videodisc kiosks are a convenient and interactive method for consumers to purchase goods and services.
- Videocassette catalogs enable consumers to view detailed, animated descriptions of merchandise in the privacy of their own homes.
- Special cable-television programming allows consumers to view 24-hour shopping channels and place telephone or mail orders.
- In-home computerized shopping transactions can be completed by consumers who have personal computers and modems (to interface with the seller).
- It is now relatively easy for direct marketers to set up and maintain computerized data bases.

Mounting Interest in International Direct Marketing

More U.S. firms have become involved with international direct marketing over the last several years because of the opportunities in foreign markets. Among the rising number of U.S. direct marketers with a significant international presence are Hanna Anderson, Eddie Bauer, Sharper Image, and Williams-Sonoma.

[9] Sunita Wadekar Bhargava, Stephanie Anderson Forest, and Lois Therrien, "After the Big Book, The Big Race," *Business Week* (September 20, 1993), p. 106.

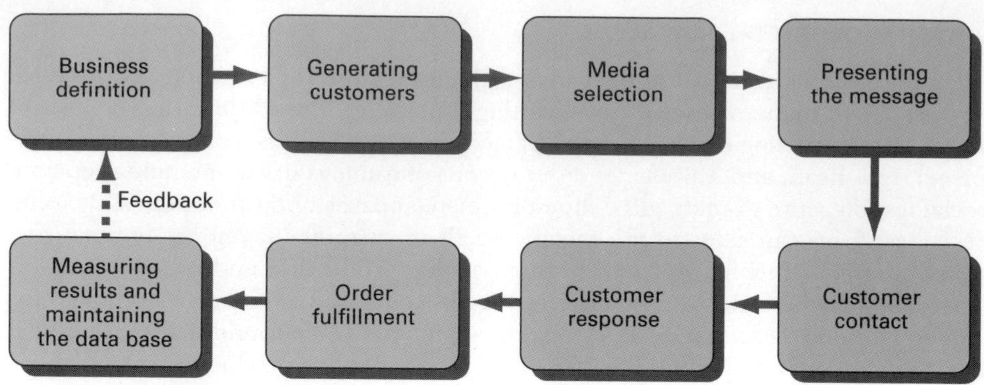

FIGURE 1
Executing a Direct Marketing Strategy

Annual mail-order sales outside the United States (by domestic and foreign firms) from transactions with final consumers already exceed $50 billion. German consumers account for nearly a third of total non-U.S. spending.[10]

In general,

> It seems that direct marketers' constant pursuit of strategic windows of opportunity have led many of them to seek and serve new markets with new goods, new services, and new delivery systems. As U.S. direct marketers face saturated domestic markets with higher levels of competition—including the arrival of foreign competitors who are attempting to globalize their programs—they will consider other means of increasing their business. These pressures have forced some U.S. direct marketers to move ahead and enter other markets. Also, it appears that many of the recent geopolitical changes and technological advances will act as a catalyst to spur companies to seek new foreign opportunities.
>
> However, there are still many problems to overcome before success can be achieved. Restrictions on consumer privacy, barriers of culture, language and monetary systems, and various other regulations and customers are impediments to expansion and foster considerable apprehension among many direct marketers.[11]

The Steps in a Direct-Marketing Strategy

A direct marketing strategy consists of eight stages: business definition, generating customers, media selection, presenting the message, customer contact, customer response, order fulfillment, and measuring results and maintaining the data base. See Figure 1.

BUSINESS DEFINITION

First, a firm must make these two decisions regarding its business definition:

- Is the company going to be a pure direct marketer or is it going to engage in a dual distribution channel (involving both store-based and direct marketing)? If the company chooses the latter, it must clarify the role of direct marketing in its overall retail strategy.
- Is the company going to be a general direct marketer and carry a broad product assortment, or is it going to specialize in one goods/service category? Either way, a merchandising approach needs to be conceived.

[10] Arnold Fishman, "International Mail Order Review," *Direct Marketing* (October 1992), pp. 28–32.

[11] Martin T. Topol and Elaine Sherman, "Trends and Challenges of Expanding Internationally Via Direct Marketing," *Journal of Direct Marketing* (Winter 1994), p. 39.

GENERATING CUSTOMERS

Next, a mechanism for generating customers must be devised. Several options are available. A direct marketer can

- Purchase a mailing list from an established list broker. For a single mailing, such a list usually costs from $50 to $100 or more per 1,000 consumer names and addresses; it is supplied in mailing-label format. Annually, mailing-list suppliers rent or sell billions of consumer names and/or addresses to direct marketers—which can buy broad lists or ones broken down by gender, location, occupation, and so on. When purchasing a mailing list, the direct marketer should be assured of its currency.
- Send out a blind mailing to all the residents in a particular area. This method can be expensive and may receive a very low response rate.
- Advertise in a newspaper, magazine, or other medium and ask customers to order by mail or call a telephone number.
- Contact consumers who have previously purchased from the firm or requested information. For example, over the years, J.C. Penney has been able to generate and maintain a multimillion name customer data base. This is the most efficient means, but it takes a while to develop a data base. And if a company wants to grow, it cannot rely solely on these consumers.

MEDIA SELECTION

Several media are available to direct marketers. They include

- Printed catalogs.
- Direct-mail ads and brochures.
- Inserts with monthly credit-card and other bills ("statement stuffers").
- Freestanding displays with coupons, brochures, or catalogs (such as magazine subscription cards at the supermarket checkout counter).
- Ads or programs in the mass media: newspapers, magazines, radio, television.
- Videodisc kiosks.
- On-line computer services.
- Video catalogs.

When choosing among these alternatives, the direct marketer would consider costs, ease of distribution, lead time required, and other factors.

PRESENTING THE MESSAGE

At this point, the firm needs to develop and present its message in a manner that engenders consumer interest, creates (or maintains) the appropriate image, points out compelling reasons for a purchase, and provides information about the goods or services offered (such as prices, sizes, and colors). The message must also contain complete ordering instructions, including the method of payment, how to designate the items purchased, shipping charges, and the address/telephone number of the firm.

The direct marketer should plan its message and the medium in which it is presented in the same way a traditional retailer plans a store. The latter uses a storefront, lighting, carpeting, the store layout, and displays to foster a particular atmosphere and image. In direct marketing, the headlines, message content, use of color, paper quality, personalization of letters to customers, space devoted to each item, and order in which items are presented are among the elements affecting a firm's shopping atmosphere and image.

CUSTOMER CONTACT

Direct marketers must decide whether to contact all customers in their data bases or seek out specific market segments (with different messages and/or media aimed at each). They can classify prospective customers as regulars (those having bought from the firm on a continuous basis); nonregulars (those having bought from the firm on an infrequent basis); new contacts (those having never been sought before by the firm); and nonrespondents (those having been contacted before but never making a purchase).

Regulars and nonregulars are the most likely to respond to any future offerings of a company. Furthermore, a direct marketer can better target its efforts to these customers because it has purchase histories on them. For example, customers who have bought clothing in the past are prime prospects for specialized apparel catalogs.

New contacts probably know little about the firm. Messages to them must create interest, accurately portray the firm, and present meaningful reasons for consumers to purchase. This group is important if growth is sought.

Nonrespondents who have been contacted repeatedly by a firm without making any purchases are highly unlikely to buy in the future. Unless a firm can present a message in a vastly different format, it will be inefficient to continue seeking this group. Nonetheless, companies such as Publishers Clearing House annually send millions of mailings to people who have never made a purchase; in their case, this is appropriate because they are selling inexpensive impulse items and need only a small response rate to succeed.

CUSTOMER RESPONSE

Customers can respond to direct marketers in one of three ways: They can buy via mail or telephone; request further information, like a catalog; or ignore the message. In general, purchases are made by no more than 2–3 per cent of the people contacted. This rate is higher for specialogs, mail-order clubs (e.g., for books or music), and firms concentrating on repeat customers.

Table 1 shows the items that consumers have the greatest and least interest in purchasing via direct marketing.

ORDER FULFILLMENT

The firm needs a system to process orders. If they are received by mail, the company must sort them, determine if payment is enclosed, check whether the requested product is in stock, mail the proper announcement to customers if items cannot be sent on time, coordinate shipments, and replenish inventory. If orders are placed by telephone, the company must have a trained sales staff available during the hours in which customers may call. The sales staff answer questions, make suggestions, enter the orders, note the method of payment, check whether the items are in stock, coordinate shipments, and replenish inventory. In both cases, customer names, addresses, and purchase information are added to the data base for future reference.

During peak seasons, additional warehouse, shipping, and sales personnel will be necessary to supplement regular employees. Direct marketers that are highly regarded by consumers fill orders promptly (usually within two weeks), have knowledgeable and courteous personnel, do not misrepresent product quality, and provide liberal return policies.

MEASURING RESULTS AND MAINTAINING THE DATA BASE

The last step in a direct-marketing strategy is to analyze results and maintain the data base. Most forms of direct marketing yield clearly measurable results, such as these:

- Overall response rate—It can be determined what number and/or percentage of the people reached by a particular brochure, catalog, and so on actually make a purchase.

TABLE 1 Consumer Interest in Direct Marketing by Product Category

Product Category	Percentage Who Prefer Buying Via Direct Marketing	Percentage Who Would Never Buy Via Direct Marketing
Books, records, tapes	33	29
Casual clothing	20	46
Underwear, intimate apparel	19	48
Sports equipment	16	45
Small kitchen appliances	16	48
Home tools	15	45
Children's clothing	12	48
Cosmetics	11	55
Costume jewelry	11	60
Cameras	10	62
Shoes	7	68
Gourmet food	6	65
Woman's/man's suits	6	71
Major appliances	6	71
Expensive dresses	5	72
Children's shoes	4	62
Expensive jewelry	3	84

Source: *Direct Marketing in the Year 2000* (New York: Yankelovich, Skelly and White/Clancy, Shulman, Inc., 1987), p. 43. Reprinted by permission.

- Average purchase amount—This can be analyzed by customer location, gender, and so on.
- Sales volume by product category—Sales can be related to the space allocated to each product in brochures, catalogs, and so on.
- Value of list brokers—The revenues generated by various mailing lists can be compared.

After measuring results, the direct marketer should review its customer data base and make sure that new shoppers are entered, that address changes have been noted for existing customers, that purchase and customer background information is current and available in various segmentation categories, and that nonrespondents are purged from the data base (when feasible).

This stage provides valuable feedback for the direct marketer each time a new campaign is planned.

Key Issues Facing Direct Marketers

In planning and implementing their strategies, direct marketers need to keep these and other key issues in mind.

A large number of U.S. households still dislike some aspect of direct marketing. The greatest levels of consumer dissatisfaction deal with late or nondelivery, deceptive claims, items broken or damaged in transit, the wrong items being delivered, and the lack of information provided. Yet, in most cases, the leading direct marketers are highly rated by consumers.

Most U.S. households report that they open all direct mail; but many would like to receive less of it. Since the average American adult and child is sent 55 catalogs a year, besides hundreds of other direct-mail pieces, firms must be concerned about the marketplace clutter. It is hard to be distinctive in this kind of environment and to increase customer response rates.

Some consumers are concerned that their names and background information are being sold by list brokers; they believe the practice is an invasion of privacy. To counteract this, the industry will remove names of consumers from mailing-list circulation if they make a request to the Direct Marketing Association. As two experts note,

> Consumer privacy has become a key issue to direct marketers who use data bases to organize and share information on customers and prospects. Descriptions and allegations of privacy infringements have become a popular topic for articles in news media; state and national legislatures have begun to pass stricter laws dictating what direct marketers can and cannot do; and many direct marketing service companies have changed their own policies due to pressures from what might be called "privacy advocates."[12]

Dual distribution retailers need to sustain a consistent image for their store-based and direct-marketing efforts. They must also recognize both the similarities and the differences in the strategies for each approach. As one observer says, "One is centralized and one is decentralized. Catalog is a case of you shout to the guy in the next cubicle to solve a problem. With retail, you have to go 200 miles down the Amtrak line to talk to people. Of the catalogs that have gone into retail, I'd guess less than 50 per cent have been successful."[13]

The steady increase in postal rates has made the mailing of catalogs, brochures, and other promotional materials quite expensive for some firms. As a result, the president of the Direct Marketing Association feels "industry growth is going to slow. Cost-conscious companies aren't going to give up direct marketing, but they are going to take a cautious approach." As a result, many direct marketers are turning more to newspapers, magazines, and cable television.[14]

Finally, direct marketers must carefully monitor the legal environment. In particular, they must be aware that, in the future, more states will probably require their residents to pay sales tax on out-of-state direct-marketing purchases; the companies would have to remit these tax payments to the affected state.

[12] Paul Wang and Lisa A. Petrison, "Direct Marketing Activities and Personal Privacy," *Journal of Direct Marketing*, Vol. 7 (Winter 1993), p. 8.

[13] N. R. Kleinfield, "Even for J. Crew, the Mail-Order Boom Days Are Over," *New York Times* (September 2, 1990), Section 3, p. 5.

[14] Kin Foltz, "Postal Rise May Cancel a Direct-Marketing Edge," *New York Times* (February 19, 1991), p. D11.

PART 2 COMPREHENSIVE CASE

How Small Firms Are Competing with Wal-Mart*

Introduction

Gediman's Appliance Store occupies a sagging storefront on Centre Street in Bath, a town on the Maine coast. Gediman's opened in 1931 and kept selling right through the depression—a dollar down, a dollar a week. The store was passed down through two generations of the Gediman family and then sold to Jayne Palmer and husband Russell. The Palmers put in long hours so Gediman's could stay in business, affirming the human connection that has given their store life. People wander in to sit in easy chairs and watch the large-screen TVs, as if they were settling in over morning coffee in the Palmers' kitchen. Gediman's offers easy terms and a quaint sort of accountability.

A block down Centre Street is Burgess' Market, which opened in 1942. It fills 7,000 square feet of space, yet carries almost everything a much larger supermarket does. There are brimming aisles, with hand-lettered signs signaling specials. A butcher's case and a bakery in the rear of the store accent the service and familiarity that pervade Burgess'.

Charlie senior gave the business to Charlie junior, who worked 14-hour days until a heart attack slowed him down; then, his son Craig stepped in to help. Craig also runs a computer store in Bath, a convenience store one town over, and a tax-planning and financial-planning business off his desktop.

On Bath's main shopping street, Front Street, sits Renys Department Store, with high ceilings and fluorescent lighting. A creaky staircase at the store's center descends into a basement filled with bargains. Renys buys odd lots and displays with quality brand-name goods at low prices. Halcyon Blake, owner of Halcyon Yarn, a mail-order firm in Bath, says Renys is more bazaar than department store: "You go there and you never know what you're going to find, whether it's shirts at 80 per cent off or some other incredible deal. At Renys there's always an element of surprise."

Bob Reny has 15 such stores across Maine in small towns like Bath. He has been in business for years, working with his sons Bob junior and John, and when he describes his retailing methods, it is clear Reny revels in surprise: "We do crazy things around here. You never know what tomorrow's deal is going to be, because we don't know." Dave Morse, who publishes seven small papers along the coast, says Reny "gives his customers incredible value."

What Happens When Wal-Mart Comes to Town

Bath has 100 merchants. Many are small-town shopkeepers working in comfortable proximity to—if not in solidarity with—one another. In a place like Maine, cooperation often takes a back seat to independence, resourcefulness, and stubbornness. But, those attitudes shifted when the merchants of Bath first heard that a different sort of business was coming to town: Wal-Mart.

Wal-Mart started out in a small town not unlike Bath. It thrived by placing stores in rural areas, where people were traditionally underserved. They were willing to drive 30 miles not just to shop but to indulge, as well, in the experience of walking into a huge store, stacked with consumer goods.

In a 1992 poll of corporate executives, Wal-Mart was selected as one of the three most admired U.S. corporations. Yet, others view the company as a ravenous force that has altered forever the pattern and tempo of commercial life in small-town America. As Wal-Mart rolled out its stores, it sucked commerce off Main Streets, destroying traditional retailers that had served their communities for generations. But, in the face of the abundance Wal-Mart produced in the form of more jobs, consumer savings, and expanded trade, the loss of Main Street life seemed an incidental price to pay.

During the mid-1980s, Ken Stone—an Iowa State University professor— started hearing from small-town Iowa retailers whose downtowns were dying. He gathered sales-tax data and concluded in 1988 that Iowa towns within a 20-mile radius of 14 Wal-Mart stores saw total retail sales drop by 25.4 per cent after five years. Even towns outside that radius felt Wal-Mart's pull; their retail sales fell by 17.6 per cent after five years.

Stone also found that small specialty stores' sales dropped substantially. Eight years after Wal-Mart's Iowa entry, department stores—led by Wal-Mart—had a 20.2 per cent gain in market share, while clothing, drug, jewelry, auto-parts, hardware, variety, and grocery stores lost market share ranging from 2 per cent to 44 per cent.

* The material in this case was adapted by the authors from Edward O. Welles, "When Wal-Mart Comes to Town," *Inc.* (July 1993), pp. 76–88. Reprinted by permission. Copyright © 1993 Goldhirsh Group, Inc., 38 Commercial Wharf, Boston, MA 02110.

Wal-Mart's strategy relies on developing overwhelming critical mass. It often simultaneously opens stores of 90,000 square feet and up, putting them so close together that they compete with one another. The firm has 230 stores in Texas alone.

The more Stone observed Wal-Mart, the more he felt that small merchants had to niche around it. That meant improving customer service, tailoring selection to customer needs, and not competing directly with Wal-Mart's product lines: "There are a lot of voids and niches to be filled by specialty retailers—and that's the only hope. Wal-Mart has a distribution system that is the best in the world. Its costs are lower than anyone else's because it ties the manufacturer right into its stores."

Stone notes that Wal-Mart won't tolerate inventory losses—not keeping an eye on such losses is a way for store managers "to get fired real fast." Thus, its inventory shortages are around 1 per cent, while other retailers often settle for 3 to 5 per cent. Similarly, Wal-Mart, which relies on word-of-mouth promotion, spends 0.5 per cent of sales on ads, one-quarter of what Kmart and Sears each spend. By running leaner, Wal-Mart can charge less—and make more.

In the process of understanding the Wal-Mart phenomenon, Stone began advising local merchant groups on how to parry the retailing giant's thrusts. In that capacity, he has gone to every state in which Wal-Mart has a store.

Wal-Mart in Maine

In 1991, Wal-Mart announced it was entering Maine—by building about 12 stores there. Sites shifted, as did opening dates. What emerged for sure was that Wal-Mart would build on the outskirts of Brunswick, 6 miles west of Bath; in Rockland, 45 miles north; and in Auburn, 30 miles northwest. Bath would not come under siege from the east because it was bordered by the ocean.

Bath, Maine, is a mostly blue-collar town dominated by shipbuilding. It has 10,000 residents. Bath Iron Works (BIW) has been building ships for the navy since World War I and, before that, Bath's shipyards built many clipper ships of the 19th century. With defense cutbacks, BIW, which once employed 10,000 people and drew workers from up to 100 miles away, has been in decline. Into that void, there have stepped—to some degree—specialty retailers. The specter of decline recedes in downtown Bath, with its occupied stores, brick sidewalks, and street lamps harking back to gaslit days.

The prospect of a Wal-Mart opening 6 miles away, on Brunswick's outskirts, divided Bath's business community. On one side, a comfortable old guard looked at the high occupancy rates in Bath's downtown and wondered what the fuss was about. "There was a fear on the part of some people that if you talked about something negative, it would make everything negative," says Jayne Palmer. "We, on the other hand, saw Wal-Mart's coming as the catalyst that would mobilize and organize the downtown merchants."

Palmer and Bill King, owner of RVI, which sells motorcycle and snowmobile accessories, led the group that split from the chamber of commerce to form the Bath Business Association (BBA), which claims 75 members. "Wal-Mart is a threat to every small business in Bath," says King. "That's not to say it's going to put everyone out of business, but there are things you have to do." He bought some Wal-Mart stock and "started copying its profit-and-loss statements and bringing them to our meetings just to scare people."

Bob Reny spent four days trooping through Wal-Marts in Florida and then spoke before the BBA about the company and its tactics. The BBA also organized two four-hour sessions in advance of Wal-Mart's arrival, amounting to a plumbing of the civic soul. "Each of us had to make a commitment of what we were willing to do to make the community move forward," says Halcyon Blake.

In spring 1992, Ken Stone came to Maine to address merchant groups from towns in the path of the Wal-Mart advance. His advice was simple: don't compete directly; specialize and carry harder-to-get and better-quality items; emphasize customer service; extend your hours; advertise more—not just your products but your business—and, perhaps most pertinent of all to this group of Yankee individualists, work together.

After hearing Stone's pep talk, Jayne Palmer increased her ad budget by 30 per cent. She computerized her inventory and tied her system in with General Electric Credit, enabling her to order GE products direct from the company and save money by getting better terms. She extended her hours and eased customer credit. She created a room in her store where people could watch TV while children played on the floor. She cut back on the low end of her inventory.

John Hichborn, who runs the True Value Hardware store in Bath, felt well positioned—although Ken Stone's Iowa data showed hardware stores took a big market-share hit when Wal-Mart came to the state: "Our customers know our inventory. Each department is run distinctly with two employees responsible for all decisions in it, including buying and merchandising."

Craig Burgess extended the hours of his family market and stepped up promotions: "It's important to keep emphasizing the low prices we have." He says Wal-Mart creates the illusion that it always undersells the market, based on a handful of heavily promoted items at rock-bottom prices, but that the rest of Wal-Mart's inventory is not as price competitive. He says if customers perceive that Wal-Mart consistently undersells specialty retailers, those retailers are as good as dead.

Many Bath retailers came together for the Christmas 1992 shopping season, with 39 of them kicking in $220 each to fund a campaign promoting downtown as a shopping destination, the first time that ever happened. They lit every tree in town. Sales were brisk. Bill King recalls how customers coming to his store told him how relieved they were to get out of the malls and go shopping in the relative peace of downtown Bath.

The merchants' efforts included informal intelligence gathering. Some of them hired the same contractors that had worked on Wal-Mart's construction. They tapped into them to guess at a completion date for the building, so they could mount a pre-emptive ad campaign. They comparison shopped at Wal-Mart stores in New Hampshire, in the process getting thrown out for taking notes. They then started using concealed tape recorders activated by voice.

Wal-Mart sent its vice-president of corporate affairs to Maine for two weeks to soothe local merchants. Jayne Palmer recalls few if any substantive answers to questions at the meeting she attended.

In early 1993, the Holiday Inn in Bath received a call from Wal-Mart asking for a quote on 30 rooms for six weeks—a tip-off of the grand opening. Which six weeks, the motel asked? We can't tell you that, replied Wal-Mart, just give us a price.

Matt Eddy, Bath's town planner, says, "Wal-Mart is exceptionally well organized. Before most people knew it was even coming to Maine, it had four or five building sites it had strong options on and was going through the simultaneous review-and-approval process."

Wal-Mart likes to move as quickly and as quietly as possible, given that wherever it goes, it sends ripples through local economies. Developers and bankers are avid followers of Wal-Mart because they know that when the company puts up a building, it immediately creates value for miles around. One Maine developer who has worked with Wal-Mart, notes that the firm tends to own land until it has a building up—it then sells the land and becomes a tenant: "That gives it control when the project is under construction, and flexibility once it's done." Wal-Mart recoups its investment and is on the hook only for its lease. As Ken Stone explains, "If Kmart comes into the market with a bigger store, you can bet that Wal-Mart will soon find a place for a bigger store." Wal-Mart only owns 16 per cent of the land on which there are Wal-Mart stores.

This is not atypical for large retailers. But Wal-Mart's tendencies implied a lack of commitment that worried people in Bath. Another troubling element involved the disjunction between how many jobs Wal-Mart claimed it would create and how many of them were really part-time—up to 60 per cent by some estimates. "That creates a hidden cost to the community," says Jayne Palmer; if Wal-Mart ends up "paying less than people can live on" and doesn't offer adequate benefits, local taxpayers end up subsidizing its work force.

Again, a high percentage of part-time jobs is not unusual in retailing, and Wal-Mart maintains that its work force is at least 60 per cent full-time. But Wal-Mart hardly defines full-time in a conventional way: A person working at least 28 hours a week is eligible for benefits and considered full-time.

Competing Against Wal-Mart's Muscle

Bob Reny has a thing about stores being open on Sunday. To him, Sunday is for church, rest, and family—and ice fishing and berry picking. For years, he fought the repeal of state blue laws that denied major stores Sunday hours: "I believed that if you rescinded those blue laws, you would irrevocably change the face of Maine." Reny lost the battle when opponents, backed by $600,000 from large retailing interests, won a referendum by only two percentage points, having outspent Reny's side 12 to 1.

Earlier, on the New Hampshire side of the border, Wal-Mart had built a distribution center and was ready to open in Maine—only if the blue laws were rescinded. Bob Reny says 100,000 Mainers work in retailing, "and a lot of those people have families. Now, some of them will have to work on Sundays." He notes that this puts the squeeze not only on people working for large retailers who can afford to pay their employees time-and-a-half to work on Sundays but also on small retailers who are forced to keep pace.

Another example of the muscle Wal-Mart could bring to bear occurred in Augusta, Maine's capital, when the legislature voted to allow the newly built Augusta Mall—to be anchored by a Wal-Mart—to use $7 million of the sales-tax receipts that it generated for improvements around the mall. Reny considers such a tax break outrageous, since it uses public dollars to give an advantage to the mall against downtown merchants, who are already reeling from the flight of business to the mall.

During November 1992, Wal-Mart opened its Rockland, Maine store, 45 miles north of Bath. In one week, it received 2,800 work applications and hired 200 people. Some left their jobs to work for Wal-Mart, believing it would offer steadier employment. In December, the Rockland Wal-Mart's first full month of operation, Rockland had a 55 per cent gain in retail sales. The surrounding towns showed declines ranging from 6 to 17 per cent. After the Christmas rush, the Rockland Wal-Mart laid off some newly hired workers.

Some of Rockland's gain could be chalked up to curiosity about the new Wal-Mart, but it also pointed out the two-edged sword that the store embodied with its pulling power. Before Wal-Mart arrived, Rockland's leakage was 50 per cent: The city lost half its retail business to nearby towns—for every $1 Rockland consumers spent in Rockland, they also spent $1 elsewhere. That spoke directly to the quandary Wal-Mart created for small towns wherever it went.

If your town doesn't attract a Wal-Mart, then a neighboring town might, leading to higher trade and tax revenues for the neighbor—and less for you. The neighbor's pulling power creates your leakage. That was the problem faced by Amy Naylor, Brunswick's town planner, when Wal-Mart bought land in Cook's Corner, two miles east of Brunswick and four miles west of Bath: "We had just finished a townwide plan that really brought home citizens' desire to create neighborhoods, keep the town livable, and have a human scale. That came over clearly." Wal-Mart entered on the heels of that debate. "People were knocking on my door for two weeks, asking, 'How can Wal-Mart come in after we've just been through this process? This is not what we want,'" Naylor says.

Naylor "tried to call Wal-Mart and see if its people would come up and talk to us about it. They wouldn't set foot in the state until they had all the approvals." She also worried that Wal-Mart would accelerate the drift of business from Brunswick to Cook's Corner, where a new courthouse, a hospital, and a mall were going in: "Wal-Mart is not going to generate new sales. It's going to earn money from existing stores. It's not providing great jobs with a future. Wal-Mart will not do its banking in Brunswick or in Maine. It will use our consumers and our labor as its raw material, and everything except the low wages and the tax revenues it provides will be pumped out of state."

Yet, no matter what Naylor thought, she had little choice: "If I had gone to my town manager and said, 'We have to stop Wal-Mart because these are low-income jobs, Wal-Mart does all its banking out of state, and it will put a real strain on services,' I'd be told, 'It's 200 jobs, we'll get tax revenues, and if we don't take Wal-Mart, Bath will.' I couldn't go to the town council and say, 'I lost Wal-Mart.' If I did, I'd be out of a job."

As Wal-Mart readied to open its Brunswick store, concern prevailed in Bath. "I think that man's business is going to be devastated," stated Halcyon Blake, referring to Don Povich, a specialty clothier on Front Street. Povich said he wasn't worried. He endured the first wave of flight to the malls, 20 years ago. Another merchant worried that Jayne Palmer at Gediman's would get hurt, while Palmer pointed out that Wal-Mart seemed to be stalking Bob Reny by locating near his stores. Reny foresaw his sales initially falling 10 per cent, and then rebounding because Wal-Mart can't match him on value: "With Wal-Mart, there's a lot of hype and no reality."

By mid-1993, 7 Wal-Marts had opened in Maine. But, the firm would not confirm how many stores it will eventually have there: "Wal-Mart believes that the type of discount retailing we do will be fully appreciated in Maine. Regardless of where we locate, acceptance is going to be very good."

Wal-Mart Falls Short of Perfection

Despite Wal-Mart's confidence, some Bath locals displayed skepticism, feeling that Maine was different and that Wal-Mart's highly centralized operation—the Rockland store had its lights and thermostat controlled by a company computer in Oklahoma—would be a negative in a traditional state like Maine. On top of that, Wal-Mart had brought in a Florida manager to run its Rockland store.

Wal-Mart, these locals suspected, had done scant market research. A number of sources claim to have heard as much directly from Wal-Mart officials. One source, Amy Naylor, the planner in Brunswick, recalls a meeting where "they told us they just had a feeling it was going to be right."

A Wal-Mart spokesperson replies that it may move fast, but it moves with care: "You can rest assured that some of the finest marketing and real-estate minds in the country work for this company." That may be so, but to what extent were those minds, calling the shots from headquarters in Arkansas, oblivious to nuances in regional markets? When the firm built its Bangor store, it installed electric heat, which is three times more expensive than oil heat in Maine. In its first month, the store had an electricity bill of $80,000—it then ripped out its electric system and replaced it with oil.

The Bangor blunder, Wal-Mart's opponents contend, revealed the vanity of a large national corporation that was sure it could use its formula anywhere. But, would the formula work in Maine? A study commissioned by a large local business projects that retail sales in Maine will grow only 1 to 2 per cent in each of the next 15 years. The state's retail environment has already been honed by years of rigorous discounting in the form of numerous factory-outlet stores coupled with an enduring recession. Says Dave Morse, the publisher of a number of weekly Maine newspapers: "If you've survived in Maine to this point, you know what you're doing. You're not just a shopkeeper, you're a merchant."

Maine is not a wealthy state, and its population is older than the U.S. average. Older people tend to shop on Main Street. Living in the land of L.L. Bean, Mainers know the meaning of value and quality. "People will walk into a store, buy the one thing on sale, and walk out. They shop for value, and they shop hard. Many have found Wal-Mart lacking. Everybody I've talked to has said its inventory is phenomenal and the layout is nice, but its prices are not always the cheapest, and its quality is not always the best," says Morse.

What's more, Wal-Mart paid too much for the Rockland site, asserts John Morris, a local architect who six years ago built a nearby shopping center that now competes with Wal-Mart. Morris notes that Wal-Mart paid $2.3 million for an 8-acre site and added $1 million in improvements: "I know a development group that had an option on the site two years earlier for $800,000 and didn't exercise it." He doubts Wal-Mart will generate enough revenues in Rockland to turn an acceptable profit and believes Wal-Mart may have overpaid because it had an inflated view of what the Rockland store could produce.

Another possible misstep involved advertising. Wal-Mart prides itself on its low advertising costs, due in part to the economies of scale realized by generating print ads from Arkansas in the form of pre-printed inserts sent to local newspapers or distributed via direct mail 13 times a year. But local merchants can outflank a monthly insert by setting ads on their desktop PCs and getting them in the local paper weekly, to niche around Wal-Mart's less timely ads and more centralized marketing strategy.

Wal-Mart's slow start in Rockland led to strange financial dealings. The store strung out local suppliers for up to 10 weeks. The manager then abruptly resigned. Wal-Mart refused to specify if the manager resigned or was fired: "That's a personnel matter. Like any good business, we believe in paying our bills with a sense of urgency. Does that happen in each and every one of our stores? No, but when it doesn't, we react and respond as we did in Rockland."

Meanwhile, management in Rockland, in an effort to limit its labor costs to no more than 10 per cent of sales each week, would abruptly tell employees to go home, curtailing their hours, wages, and enthusiasm for their employer. When the local paper ran a story suggesting there was employee discontent at Wal-Mart, store managers turned the newspaper box outside the store face down on the sidewalk and called the paper to come retrieve it.

The Battle Lines Are Drawn

In Bath, various merchants sound confident. True Value's John Hichborn says "people have to drive six miles past my door to get to Wal-Mart. I'd be surprised if I had this place up for sale in two years."

Craig Burgess sees "no massive door closings." He believes that in today's economy, people "crave service," which Wal-Mart offers "only on a superficial level." Burgess envisions a swing away from price and back toward service.

Mary Danzer, an editor at Bath's weekly *Coastal Journal*, says people she knows who have visited the Rockland Wal-Mart were underwhelmed: "Everyone came back and said, 'What's the big deal? It's just Kmart with the stuff stacked a little higher.'" She adds: "When you think about the 1980s, Wal-Mart matches the excess of that decade. People are now talking new values, and it takes a while before that translates into action, but the trend is to decentralization. Megagovernment, megainvestment, and megaretailing are going the way of IBM and Sears. And Wal-Mart will be the next white elephant."

When measured against Wal-Mart's phenomenal success, that kind of talk could be considered wishful thinking. Walter Loeb, a noted retail analyst, says, "Wal-Mart is an amazing company, powered by the dedication and drive of its management people. I believe it will continue to grow."

To Bath merchants like Halcyon Blake, growth is not the issue: "We have to focus on being good citizens and giving back to the community. There's no argument that you can get a light bulb for 10 cents cheaper at Wal-Mart than you can at John Hichborn's hardware store. But do people know that John Hichborn is a major contributor to Elmhurst [a local trade school for the handicapped]? He works at finding jobs for people from Elmhurst. If Hichborn goes out of business because people want a cheaper light bulb, then you lose more than just the tax revenues that business generated."

In one way, Bob Reny likes Wal-Mart. It reminds him how he has already seen a lot of retailers—Sears, Penney's, Grant's, Woolworth's—come and go, while he has prospered. Reny has been in business 43 years and withstood them all. But now, he is confronted by a new force, perhaps more formidable than the others: "Wal-Mart thinks it's invincible. The problem is, it does not want just its share. It wants it all. A lot of small towns need to survive. Wal-Mart comes and goes, but after Wal-Mart goes, there's nothing left."

Questions

1. What are the general strengths and weaknesses of small retailers in competing with Wal-Mart?
2. What are the particular strengths and weaknesses of small retailers in Bath, Maine, in competing with Wal-Mart?
3. Besides the actions noted in the case, what else would you recommend that the Bath Business Association do to help its member firms?
4. React to this statement: "If customers perceive that Wal-Mart consistently undersells specialty retailers, those retailers are as good as dead."
5. What, if any, responsibilities does Wal-Mart have to the residents, workers, and businesses in the small towns in which it locates? Why?
6. What mistakes did Wal-Mart make when it opened a store in Rockland, Maine? How should it address them?
7. Comment on these remarks: "When you think about the 1980s, Wal-Mart matches the excesses of that decade. Megaretailing is going the way of IBM and Sears. And Wal-Mart will be the next white elephant."

Targeting Customers and Gathering Information

- In Part 3, various techniques for identifying and understanding consumers, and selecting a target market, are first presented. Information-gathering methods—which can be used in selecting a target market, as well as in developing and implementing an overall strategy—are then described.

- Chapter 6 discusses why it is necessary for a retailer to determine and respond properly to its target market, the customer group that the firm tries to satisfy. Consumer demographics, lifestyles, and decision making are all examined and related to retailing. Throughout the chapter, relevant research findings are noted.

- Chapter 7 deals with information gathering and processing in retailing. First, the difficulties that may arise from basing a retail strategy on nonsystematic research are considered. The retail information system, its components, and recent advances in information systems are then reviewed in depth. The chapter concludes by outlining and describing the marketing research process, with particular emphasis on the characteristics and alternative kinds of secondary data and primary data.

Identifying and Understanding Consumers

❖ Chapter Objectives

1. To discuss why it is important for a retailer to properly select, identify, and understand its target market
2. To enumerate and describe a number of consumer demographic and life-style factors, and explain how these concepts can be applied to retailing
3. To examine the consumer decision process and its stages: stimulus, problem awareness, information search, evaluation of alternatives, purchase, and post-purchase behavior
4. To differentiate among different types of consumer decision making
5. To present the findings of several studies on consumer characteristics and behavior

Retailers are paying greater attention to ethnic markets. As the president of one African-American advertising agency that works with retailers notes, "There is an increasing awareness that, despite the fact that America likes to think of itself as this great melting pot, and that the same message works for everybody, that is not the case."

Industry analysts cite three major reasons behind the growing emphasis on minority target markets: the high growth of ethnic subgroups, the improved use of scanning equipment by retailers, and the availability of targeted media. Although people of African, Asian, and Hispanic descent now comprise 25 per cent of the U.S. population, as of 2000, they will total one-third of the population. Improved store-based scanning lets retailers determine sales by store and region of specific items. Targeted media can efficiently reach ethnic markets.

Some retailers have always adapted their merchandise to meet the special needs of ethnic customers, but the current efforts of retailers are more focused. Many firms now order goods that are only bought by ethnic consumers, have set up ethnic specialty shops, and/or engage in joint promotions aimed at ethnic markets. Among the retailers that have targeted minority buyers are J.C. Penney, Luckys Stores, and Mary Kay.

J.C. Penney now places ethnically targeted goods in 170 suburban and urban stores. According to its special segments manager, a year-long study of eight markets resulted in the firm's more clearly focusing on ethnic markets. In some cases, appealing to a market is as simple as carrying fewer pastel colors; in others, it means different size distributions.

Luckys Stores, a supermarket chain, developed a year-long program with 156 all-night music events aimed at the Hispanic market in conjunction with Keebler, the cookie and cracker manufacturer. Attendees got $5 off the $15 admission price by presenting both a Luckys' receipt and a proof-of-purchase of a Keebler's product. One in five attendees took advantage of the discount.

To appeal to ethnic markets, Mary Kay has developed a line of cosmetics, Shades of Perfection, that complements the skin tones of African-Americans and Hispanics. The line includes face powder, eye shadow, lipstick, and nail polish. Mary Kay also aggressively recruits minority sales consultants to sell its products. About 7 per cent of its sales consultants are African-American and 3 per cent are Hispanic.[1]

[1] Cliff Edwards, "Retailers, Grocers Marketing to Segmented Ethnic Society," *Marketing News* (January 17, 1994), p. 8; "Ethnic Promotions," *Promo* (January 1994), pp. 24, 73–75; Bob Ortega, "J.C. Penney Adopts Sales Targeting of Minority Buyers," *Wall Street Journal* (September 9, 1993), p. B12; and "Direct Selling Cosmetics: Avon and Mary Kay Ahead," *Drug and Cosmetics Industry* (June 1992), pp. 46, 49.

Reprinted by permission of Mary Kay.

Overview

A retailer's ability to develop and apply a sound strategy depends on how well that retailer selects, identifies, and understands its customers. This entails selecting the type of target market to reach (mass market, market segment, or multiple segments), identifying the characteristics and needs of the firm's specific target market, and understanding how consumers make decisions:

> Retailers have long depended on their ability to size up people when they walk in the door. Customers give themselves away by their clothing, speech, and mannerisms. While gut instinct still works for some retailers, the era of successful scrutiny has passed. You can no longer pigeonhole at a glance since increasing consumer diversity has made stereotyping futile. Today, you need a more systematic way to understand your customers.[2]
>
> In 1800, a typical American had access to fewer than 300 products on sale in his or her hometown, one retail establishment (a country store), and about 500 feet of retail space. In contrast, a typical American in a city of a million people now has access to over a million consumer products, thousands of merchants, and 15 million square feet of selling space.[3]

A ***target market***, as defined in Chapter 2, is a customer group that a retailer seeks to satisfy. With a mass-market approach, a company like a supermarket or a drugstore sells goods and services to a broad spectrum of consumers; it does not really focus efforts on any one kind of customer. With a market-segment approach, a retailer tailors its strategy to the needs of one distinct consumer group, such as young working women; it does not attempt to satisfy people outside that segment. With a multiple-segment approach, a retailer aims at two or more distinct consumer groups, such as men and boys, with a different strategy mix for each segment; a firm can do this by operating more than one kind of outlet (such as separate men's and boys' clothing stores) or by having distinct departments grouped by market segment within a single store (as a department store might do). When deciding on the type of target market to reach, a firm would consider its goods/service category, its goals, what competitors are doing, the size of various consumer segments, the relative efficiency of each target-market alternative for the particular company, the resources required, and other factors.

After the retailer chooses a target-market method, it identifies the characteristics and needs of those customers to whom it wants to appeal and tries to understand how they make purchase decisions. Consumer characteristics include demographic and life-style factors. Consumer needs relate to a firm's store location, goods/service assortment, prices, and so on. Purchase decisions may be made impulsively or may encompass a detailed thought process.

In this chapter, we examine consumer characteristics and needs and the way purchase decisions are made.

Identifying Consumer Characteristics and Needs

Consumer characteristics and needs can be identified by studying various demographic and life-style factors. Then, the retailer can develop a profile of its target market by combining two or more of the factors.

As introduced in Chapter 3, ***demographics*** are objective and quantifiable population data that are easily identifiable and measurable; and ***life-styles*** are the ways in which individual consumers and families (households) live and spend time and money.

[2] Marvin Nesbit and Arthur Weinstein, "How to Size Up Your Customers," *American Demographics* (July 1986), p. 34.

[3] James H. Snider, "Consumers in the Information Age," *Futurist* (January–February 1993), p. 15.

CONSUMER DEMOGRAPHICS

Consumers can be identified in terms of such demographic variables as these: population size, household size, marital and family status, income, retail sales, age, birth rates, mobility, place of residence, gender, employment status, occupation, education level, and ethnic/racial background.

First, a retailer should have some basic knowledge of the overall demographics of the U.S. population. Next, it would determine the demographic attributes of its own target market.

A Demographic Snapshot of the United States[4]

Table 6–1 shows selected U.S. demographic data by region. These data are a useful starting point for retailers, since most firms are local and regional.

Here is a demographic overview of the United States:

As of 1995, there are 263 million people living in 100 million households. The four most-populated regions are the South Atlantic, East North Central, Pacific, and Middle Atlantic. The greatest proportion of single-person households reside in the Middle Atlantic, West North Central, New England, and East North Central regions.

About 56 per cent of the adult population is married, and one of every two marriages ends in divorce. The average age at first marriage is twenty-six for men and twenty-four for women. Just over 70 per cent of all households (a ***household*** is defined as one or more persons occupying a housing unit, whether related or not) consist of families (a ***family*** is defined as two or more related persons living together).

The typical American family has a total annual after-tax income of about $35,000. The top one-fifth of families have yearly incomes of $65,000 or more; but the lowest one-fifth earn under $18,000 per year. When earnings are high, consumers are more apt to have ***discretionary income***—money left over after paying taxes and buying necessities.[5] People in the New England, Middle Atlantic, and Pacific regions have the highest median incomes.

The average annual U.S. retail expenditures per household are about $22,000. Together, the South Atlantic, East North Central, Pacific, and Middle Atlantic regions account for two-thirds of all U.S. retail sales.

The median age of the U.S. population is 33.4. The average is lowest in the West South Central, Mountain, and Pacific regions. The national annual birth rate is 16.2 per thousand people. It is highest in the Pacific, West South Central, and Mountain regions.

About 15 to 20 per cent of the U.S. population changes residences each year; 60 per cent of all moves are in the same county. People in the Middle Atlantic, New England, East North Central, and East South Central regions are the most likely to have lived in the same residence for at least five years.

Almost 80 per cent of all people reside in urban or suburban areas. Urbanization is highest in the Pacific and Middle Atlantic regions. The fastest-growing cities and states are in the Mountain, Pacific, West South Central, South Atlantic, and Southwest regions. See Figure 6–1.

Nationwide, there are 6 million more females than males, and nearly three-fifths of females aged 16 and older are in the labor force (most full time). Female participation in the labor force is greatest in the West North Central and New England regions.

Most U.S. employment—male and female—is in the service sector. Also, there are now more professionals and white-collar workers than previously and far fewer blue-collar and agricultural workers.

[4] The data presented in this section are from various issues of *Current Population Reports* (Washington, D.C.: U.S. Bureau of the Census).

[5] See Cheryl Russell and Thomas G. Exter, "Mad Money," *American Demographics* (July 1993), pp. 26–32.

TABLE 6–1 Selected U.S. Demographics by Region (as of 1993)

Region	Per Cent of U.S. Population	Per Cent of Households That Are Single Person	Per Cent of U.S. Household Income	Per Cent of U.S. Retail Sales	Median Age of Population in Years
New England	5.2	25.1	6.1	5.7	34.3
Middle Atlantic	14.8	26.2	16.9	14.6	34.9
East North Central	16.7	25.0	16.6	16.8	33.5
West North Central	7.0	26.1	6.7	7.2	33.6
South Atlantic	17.7	24.4	17.0	18.2	34.3
East South Central	6.1	24.0	5.0	5.4	33.5
West South Central	10.8	24.4	9.6	10.4	31.7
Mountain	5.6	24.8	5.1	5.6	32.1
Pacific	16.1	24.1	17.0	16.1	32.3

Region	Annual Births Per 1,000 People	Per Cent of People in Same Residence for 5+ Years	Per Cent of People Living in Urban/Suburban Area	Per Cent of Adult Females in the Labor Force	Per Cent of Adults with 4-Year College Degree
New England	14.3	56.9	84.2	61.8	25.9
Middle Atlantic	15.2	62.1	91.3	54.3	22.1
East North Central	15.5	56.6	79.5	58.7	18.4
West North Central	14.5	55.1	58.3	62.8	19.5
South Atlantic	15.5	50.3	78.6	58.4	20.2
East South Central	14.9	56.4	55.6	53.9	15.4
West South Central	17.7	51.6	75.6	57.4	13.6
Mountain	17.5	46.3	70.3	59.1	21.7
Pacific	18.8	44.8	91.7	57.1	23.4

New England = Connecticut, Maine, Massachusetts, New Hampshire, Rhode Island, Vermont
Middle Atlantic = New Jersey, New York, Pennsylvania
East North Central = Illinois, Indiana, Michigan, Ohio, Wisconsin
West North Central = Iowa, Kansas, Minnesota, Missouri, Nebraska, North Dakota, South Dakota
South Atlantic = Delaware, District of Columbia, Florida, Georgia, Maryland, North Carolina, South Carolina, Virginia, West Virginia
East South Central = Alabama, Kentucky, Mississippi, Tennessee
West South Central = Arkansas, Louisiana, Oklahoma, Texas
Mountain = Arizona, Colorado, Idaho, Montana, Nevada, New Mexico, Utah, Wyoming
Pacific = Alaska, California, Hawaii, Oregon, Washington

Sources: Computed by the authors from U.S. Bureau of the Census data; except for the household income and retail sales data, which are from "1993 Survey of Buying Power," *Sales & Marketing Management* (August 30, 1993), pp. B-3–B-4.

More adults have attended some level of college than ever before. Over one-fifth of all adults aged twenty-five and older have graduated from college. The highest percentages of adults with college degrees are in the New England and Pacific regions. Young males and females are now graduating from college in roughly equal numbers.

The population comprises a number of different ethnic and racial groups. For example, in the United States, there are 33 million African-Americans and 26 million Hispanics; these groups represent large potential target markets.

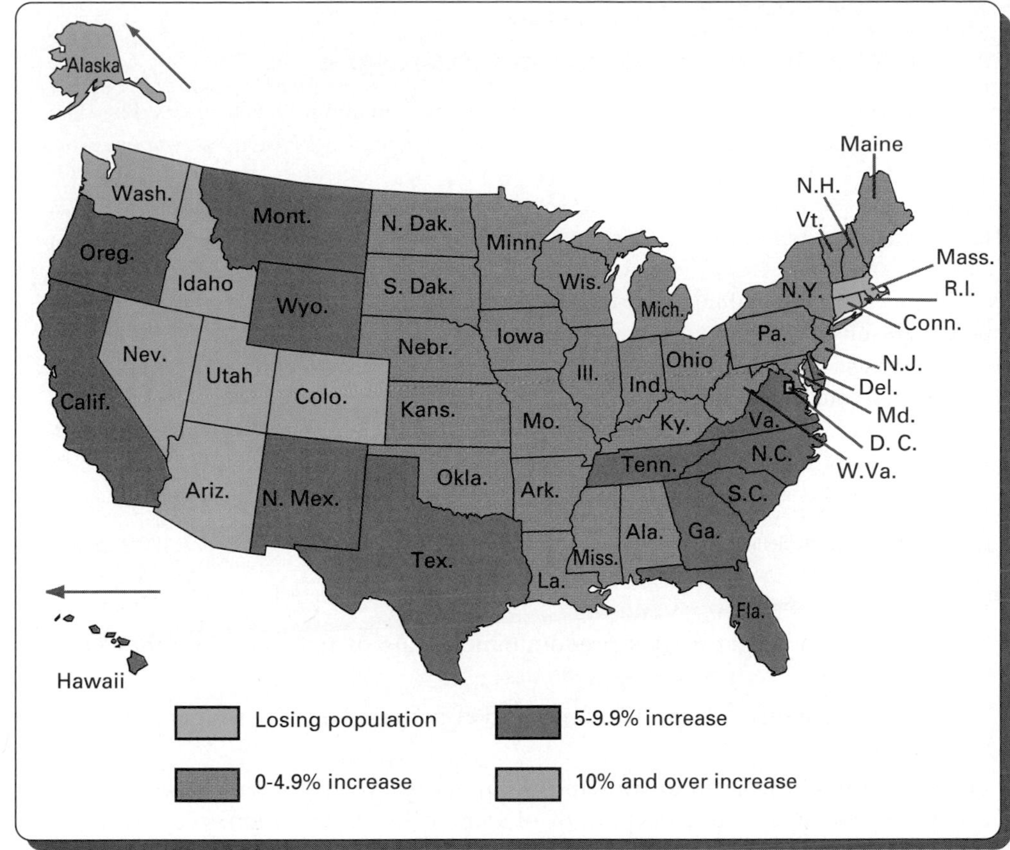

FIGURE 6–1
Population Growth in the United States, 1993 to 1998
Source: Sales & Marketing Management.

Relating Demographics to the Target Market

Although the preceding gives a good picture of the United States as a whole and by region, consumer demographics vary within geographic areas. Even within the same state or city, some locales have larger populations and more affluent, older, and better-educated residents than others. Because most retailers are local or operate in only parts of particular regions, they must compile information about the people living in their particular trading areas and/or those most likely to patronize them. A firm would use this information to develop a demographic profile of its specific target market.

A retailer could identify its target market in terms of some combination of the following demographic factors:

- Market size—How many consumers are in the target market?
- Household size—What size household is appropriate?
- Marital and family status—Are consumers single or married? Do families have children?
- Income—Is the target market lower income, middle income, or upper income? Is discretionary income available for luxury purchases?
- Retail sales—What is the retail sales potential for the retailer's goods/services category?
- Age—What are the prime age groups to which the firm appeals?
- Birth rates—How important are birth rates for the retailer's goods/services category?
- Mobility—What percentage of the target market moves each year (into and out of the trading area)?
- Where people live—How large is the trading area from which customers can realistically be drawn?

RETAILING IN ACTION

How Do You Sell High Fashion in Pittsburgh?

K. Barchetti Shops, consisting of a 3,500-square-foot men's apparel store and a newly opened 1,500-square-foot women's apparel store in Pittsburgh, had total sales of about $2.5 million in 1993. The two stores' sales per square foot are about 60 per cent greater than a major Pittsburgh competitor.

Although K. Barchetti specializes in expensive clothing and accessories, such as $1,400 Italian suits, the clothing sells quickly. A key competitive advantage is the store's knowledge of the buying preferences of its most important customers. The owner, Katherine Barchetti, knows about 500 of her customers on a first-name basis (she fishes, golfs, and plays squash with many of them); and she also has a comprehensive data base of about 28,000 clients. This data base contains each customer's size, style, and brand preferences.

Much of K. Barchetti's clothing is purchased to appeal to specific customers. And, shortly after merchandise that fits a particular customer's preferences arrives in one of the stores, that person is called by a salesperson who says something like, "I've got a great suit that looks like you. Interested?"

To stay abreast of the latest fashion developments and to be the first in Pittsburgh to stock trendy fashions, Katherine Barchetti made 27 buying trips to New York in one recent year.

Source: Based on material in Wendy Bounds, "Tenacity Sells High Fashion to Pittsburgh," *Wall Street Journal* (December 23, 1993), p. B1.

- Gender—Is the target market predominantly male or female, or are they equal in proportion?
- Employment status—Does the target market contain working women, retirees, and so on?
- Occupation—In what industries and occupations are customers working? Are they professionals, office workers, or of some other designation?
- Education—Are customers college-educated?
- Ethnic/racial background—Does the target market consist of a distinctive racial or ethnic subgroup?

CONSUMER LIFE-STYLES

Consumer life-styles are based on both social and psychological factors. They are greatly affected by people's demographic backgrounds.

As with demographics, a retailer should first have some basic knowledge of various consumer life-style concepts. Then, the retailer would determine the life-style attributes of its own target market.

Social Factors

These social factors are key elements in identifying consumer life-styles: culture, social class, reference groups, social performance, family life cycle, and time utilization.

A ***culture*** is a distinctive heritage shared by a group of people. It influences the importance of family, work, education, and other concepts by passing on a series of beliefs, norms, and customs. In the United States, there is an overall culture, which stresses individuality, success, education, and material comfort, as well as different subcultures for various demographic groups (such as Hispanic and Asian) because of the many countries from which residents have come.

A ***social class*** system is an informal ranking of people in a culture based on their income, occupation, education, dwelling, and other factors. There are people with similar values and life-styles in each social class category. See Table 6–2.

Reference groups influence people's thoughts and/or behavior. They may be categorized as aspirational, membership, and dissociative. An aspirational group is one to which a person does not belong but wishes to join, such as a higher social class, a professional club, or a fraternity. A membership group is one to which the person does belong, such as the current social class, his or her family, or a union. A dissociative group is one to which the person does not want to belong, such as a lower social class

TABLE 6–2 Social Classes in the United States

Class	Size	Characteristics
Upper Americans		
Upper-upper	0.3%	Social elite. Inherited wealth. Exclusive neighborhood. Summer home. Children attend best schools. Money not important in purchases. Secure in status.
Lower-upper	1.2%	Great earned wealth. Newly rich. Often business leaders and professionals. College educated. Seek the best for children. Active socially. Insecure. Conspicuous in consumption. Money not important in purchases.
Upper-middle	12.5%	Career-oriented. Successful business executives and professionals. Earnings over $60,000 per year. Status tied to occupation and earnings. Most educated in society, not from prestige schools. Demanding of children. Quality products purchased. Attractive home. Socially involved. "Gracious living."
Middle Americans		
Middle class	32%	"Typical Americans." Average-earning white-collar workers and the top group of blue-collar workers. Many college educated. Respectable. Conscientious. Try to do the right thing. Home ownership sought. Do-it-yourselfers. Family focus.
Working class	38%	The remaining white-collar workers and the bulk of blue-collar workers. "Working class" life-style. Some job monotony. Seek job security more than advancement. Usually high-school educated. Close-knit families. Brand loyal and interested in name brands. Not status-oriented.
Lower Americans		
Upper-lower	9%	Employed, mostly in unskilled or semiskilled jobs. Poorly educated. Low incomes. Hard to move up the social class ladder. Protective against lower-lower class. Standard of living at or slightly above poverty. Reside in affordable housing.
Lower-lower	7%	Unemployed or menial jobs. Poorest income, education, and housing. The "bottom layer." Present-oriented. Impulsive as shoppers. Overpay. Use credit.

Sources: This table is derived by the authors from Richard P. Coleman, "The Continuing Significance of Social Class in Marketing," *Journal of Consumer Research*, Vol. 10 (December 1983), pp. 265–280; James F. Engel, Roger D. Blackwell, and Paul W. Miniard, *Consumer Behavior*, Seventh Edition (Hinsdale, Ill.: Dryden, 1993), pp. 117–119; and William L. Wilkie, *Consumer Behavior*, Third Edition (New York: Wiley, 1993), pp. 347–351.

or an unpopular club. Those reference groups that are face-to-face, such as families, have the greatest impact on people. In addition, within reference groups, there are opinion leaders whose views are respected and sought.

Social performance refers to how well a person does his or her roles as worker, citizen, parent, consumer, and so on. A person's performance determines acceptance by peers and influences the types of goods and services bought. For example, a poor performer can emulate peers in an attempt to win approval, withdraw and become a loner, or buy expensive goods to "show off."

The ***family life cycle*** describes how a traditional family evolves from bachelorhood to children to solitary retirement. It is shown in Table 6–3. At each life cycle stage, a family's needs, purchases, and income change. In addition to planning for the traditional family life cycle, retailers need to be responsive to the increasing number of adults who never marry, divorced adults, single-parent families, childless couples, and so on. That is why more attention is being paid to the ***household life cycle***, which incorporates the life stages of both family and nonfamily households.[6]

Time utilization refers to the types of activities in which a person is involved and the amount of time allocated to them. Some of the broad categories of time utilization are work, transportation, eating, recreation, entertainment, parenting, sleeping, and (retailers hope) shopping. Today, many consumers allocate much less time to shopping activities than in the past.

[6] See, for example, Charles M. Schaninger and William D. Danko, "A Conceptual and Empirical Comparison of Alternative Household Life Cycle Models," *Journal of Consumer Research*, Vol. 19 (March 1993), pp. 580–594.

TABLE 6–3 Applying the Traditional Family Life Cycle to Retailing

Stage in Cycle	Characteristics	Relevance for Retailing
Bachelor (male or female)	Independent. Young. Early stage of career. Entry-level earnings.	Clothing. Car. Stereo. Travel. Restaurants. Entertainment. Appeal to status.
Newly Married	Two incomes. Relative independence. Present- and future-oriented.	Furnishing apartment. Travel. Clothing. Durables. Appeal to enjoyment and togetherness.
Full Nest I	Youngest child under 6. One to one-and-a-half incomes. Limited independence. Future-oriented.	Goods and services geared to child. Family-use items. Practicality of items. Durability. Safety. Drugs. Appeal to economy.
Full Nest II	Youngest child over 6, but dependent. One-and-a-half to two incomes. At least one spouse established in career. Future-oriented.	Savings. Home. Education. Family vacations. Child-oriented products. Some interest in luxuries. Appeal to comfort and long-range enjoyment.
Full Nest III	Youngest child living at home, but independent. Highest income level. Independent. Thoughts of retirement.	Education. Expensive durables for children. Replacement and improvement of parents' durables. Appeal to comfort and luxury.
Empty Nest I	No children at home. Independent. Good income. Thoughts of self and retirement.	Retirement home. Travel. Clothing. Entertainment. Luxuries. Appeal to self-gratification.
Empty Nest II	Retirement. Limited income and expenses. Present-oriented.	Travel. Recreation. Living in new home. Health-related items. Little interest in luxuries. Appeal to comfort at a fair price.
Sole Survivor I	Only one spouse alive. Actively employed. Present-oriented. Good income.	Immersion in jobs and friends. Interest in travel, clothing, health, and recreation areas. Appeal to productive citizen.
Sole Survivor II	Only one spouse alive. Retired. Some feeling of futility. Lower income.	Travel. Recreation. Health-related items. Security. Appeal to economy and social activity.

Psychological Factors

These psychological factors are key components in identifying consumer life-styles: personality, class consciousness, attitudes, perceived risk, and the importance of the purchase.

A ***personality*** is the sum total of an individual's traits, which make that individual unique. Personality traits include a person's levels of self-confidence, innovativeness, autonomy, sociability, emotional stability, assertiveness, and so on. Together, these attributes have a great impact on a consumer's life-style.

Class consciousness is the extent to which a person desires and pursues social status. It helps determine a consumer's use of reference groups and the importance of prestige purchases. A class-conscious person values the social status associated with particular goods, services, and retailers. A person who is not class conscious is more interested in pleasing himself or herself; actual goods/service/retailer quality, not status, is essential.

Attitudes (opinions) are the positive, neutral, or negative feelings a person has about the economy, politics, goods, services, institutions, and so on. They are also the feelings consumers have toward an individual retailer, its location, its personnel, the goods and services offered, the prices charged, and the displays and ads used. Of special concern to a retailer is whether the consumer believes its strategy is desirable, unique, and fairly priced.

Perceived risk is the level of risk a consumer believes exists regarding the purchase of a specific good or service from a specific retailer, whether or not that belief is factually correct. There are six types of perceived risk: functional (Will a good or service perform as expected?); physical (Can a good or service hurt me?); financial (Can I

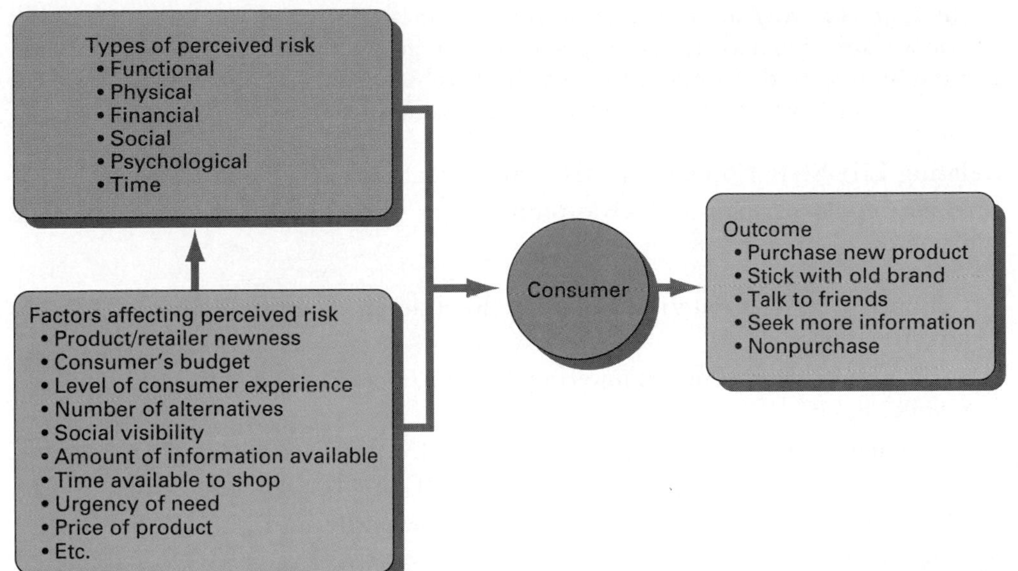

FIGURE 6–2
The Impact of Perceived Risk on Consumers

really afford the purchase?); social (What will peers think of my shopping with this retailer?); psychological (Am I doing the right thing?); and time (How much effort must I exert to make a purchase?).[7] Perceived risk will be highest if the retailer and/or the brands it carries are new, a person has a tight budget, a person has little experience, there are many alternatives from which to choose, a purchase is socially visible or complex, and so on. See Figures 6–2 and 6–3. Retailers must work to reduce perceived risk by providing ample information.

FIGURE 6–3
How Highland Stores Reduces Perceived Risk
Because Highland Stores sells major appliances and consumer electronics, its shoppers may have high perceived risk. To allay their concerns, Highland employs knowledgeable salespeople, offers good customer service, and stands behind the products its sells.
Photo by Derek Pierson. Reprinted by permission.

[7] Leon G. Schiffman and Leslie Lazar Kanuk, *Consumer Behavior,* Fifth Edition (Englewood Cliffs, N.J.: Prentice-Hall, 1994), pp. 562–563.

The ***importance of the purchase*** to the consumer affects the amount of time that person will spend in making a decision and the range of alternatives considered. When a purchase is viewed as important, perceived risk tends to be higher than when it is viewed as unimportant; and the retailer must act accordingly.

Relating Life-Style Concepts to the Target Market

A retailer could develop a life-style profile of its target market by analyzing these concepts:

- Culture—What cultural values, norms, and customs are most important to the target market?
- Social class—Are consumers lower, middle, or upper class? Are they socially mobile?
- Reference groups—To whom do people look for purchasing advice? Does this differ by good or service category? How can a firm target opinion leaders?
- Social performance—Are customers high or low performers? How is their shopping affected by this?
- Family (or household) life cycle—In what stage(s) of the cycle are the bulk of customers?
- Time utilization—How do people spend their time? How do they view the time spent shopping?
- Personality—Do customers have identifiable personality traits?
- Class consciousness—Are consumers status conscious? What does this signify for purchases?
- Attitudes—How does the target market feel about the retailer and its offerings in terms of specific strategy components?
- Perceived risk—Do customers feel risk in connection with the retailer? Which goods and services have the greatest perceived risk?
- Importance of the purchase—How important are the goods/services offered by the retailer to the target market?

SELECTED RETAIL RESEARCH FINDINGS

Retail research has examined consumer characteristics in various settings. Following are some examples of the findings. Please note: the results of the studies described in this and later sections may be limited to the specific product categories/retailer types investigated. By no means do the cited examples cover the full domain of retailing.

Shopper Profiles

Considerable research has been aimed at describing overall consumer shopping profiles, as well as more specific shopper profiles with regard to mall patronage, discount stores, supermarkets, and individual retailers (such as T.J. Maxx).

One very comprehensive research project of consumers, sponsored by the *Wall Street Journal*, surveyed people throughout the United States. It was able to identify seven major overall shopper profiles (market segments): agreeable shoppers, practical shoppers, trendy shoppers, value shoppers, top-of-the-line shoppers, safe shoppers, and status shoppers. Ninety-six per cent of all U.S. consumers could be placed in these categories.[8] The profiles are highlighted in Figure 6–4.

A study on mall-prone and mall-avoiding consumers found that shoppers who enjoy patronizing malls are mostly female, under age 45, and middle income. Three-quarters

[8] "Peter Hart's Showcase of Shoppers," *Wall Street Journal* (September 19, 1989), p. B4.

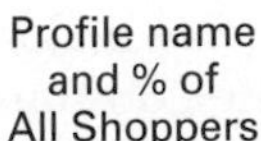

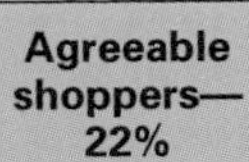

Profile name and % of All Shoppers	Description
Agreeable shoppers—22%	Get-along, go-along consumers, especially susceptible to advertising and most likely to shop at discount stores. Tend to be lower-middle income. Highest proportions of Hispanics and African-Americans. More likely than average to enjoy watching TV, shopping for groceries, and doing household work. High brand loyalty for everything from TV sets to tuna fish.
Practical shoppers—21%	Practical shoppers who research purchases and look for the best deal. Would shop at a store selling off-price, name-brand clothing. Highest proportion of women. Tend to be middle-income, younger, and better educated than average. More inclined than others to consider items such as remote control devices, CD players, and video cameras as modern frills. Pay more attention than most to food labels. Tend to be the least brand-loyal of any group.
Trendy shoppers—16%	Impulse buyers who love to shop and stay up with the latest fads. Like to go to fashion boutiques. Tend to be young, unmarried, and politically liberal. Have little brand loyalty. Do not carefully watch the kinds of foods eaten. Least likely group to say they have most everything they need in life. Less than one in three believes American-made products satisfy consumer tastes.
Value shoppers—13%	Cost-conscious but traditional shoppers who tend to believe the best products are those that have stood the test of time. Often do not have the money to buy the very best. Shop at mid-priced department stores. Middle-income persons who are apt to be homemakers and retirees. More likely than others to be very satisfied with the quality of their lives. More likely to view shopping as a chore. Care more about saving money than time, and rarely buy on impulse.
Top-of-the-line shoppers—10%	People who put a premium on a product's reputation for quality and believe they've earned the right to buy the best. Apt to shop at upscale department stores. Highest median income and the oldest group. Tend to believe foreign goods are better than American ones. Half say they have most everything they need in life. Less likely than most to enjoy browsing or window shopping. Less inclined to want the latest gadgets.
Safe shoppers—9%	Look for familiar products that make them feel comfortable, rather than research a purchase. Inclined to shop at well-known mass merchandisers. Most likely to be White and male. Most likely to feel they have the same values as their parents. Find shopping a chore. Less confident than any other group that they are savvy grocery shoppers and pay little attention to nutritional labels on foods.
Status shoppers—5%	Sometimes impractical in buying habits; "a day without a new gadget is a day without joy." Love to buy designer labels. Youngest group with highest percentage who have never married. Most politically conservative group. Second-highest median income group. Most apt to own cordless phones, CD players, and answering machines. Would like to own computers, car phones, and fax machines. Most likely to spend an extra hour browsing or shopping, and most likely to buy on impulse.

FIGURE 6–4 Seven Overall Shopper Profiles

Source: "Peter Hart's Showcase of Shoppers," *Wall Street Journal* (September 19, 1989), p. 84.

live in a house; and two-thirds have lived in the area for over five years. The majority are married, but often do not have children. Over one-half of mall-prone consumers are apt to visit a mall for less than an hour on each trip there. Another study discovered that only two-fifths of primary shoppers now go to a regional shopping mall at least once per month, down from more than one-half of primary shoppers in the late 1980s. A third study found that, on average, African-American and Hispanic shoppers visit malls more often, spend more per visit, and spend more annually than white shoppers.[9]

Research on the demographic attributes of discount-store customers found that

- Average monthly discount-store expenditures are $85 to $100.
- Two-thirds of shoppers are women.
- The average age of shoppers is 45.
- The average household income of shoppers is $36,000 per year.
- These shoppers patronize discount stores an average of 3 times per month.
- Three-fifths of shoppers use circulars for at least some discount-store buying.[10]

An analysis of supermarket customers determined that they could be classified into six market segments: Avid shoppers are active cooks/shoppers/bargain seekers who have been the traditional core market for supermarkets. Hurried shoppers are busy people interested in shortcuts for buying and cooking. Unfettered shoppers are mostly older, empty-nest people with good incomes and less need to shop carefully. Kitchen strangers are sophisticated, childless consumers who are more apt to rely on restaurants than supermarkets. Kitchen birds are older people who eat lightly and spend modestly. Constrained shoppers are unsophisticated, undereducated people with low incomes.[11]

T.J. Maxx is one of the largest U.S. off-price family apparel chains. It sells brand-name family apparel and accessories, women's shoes, domestics, jewelry, and giftware. According to the firm's own extensive studies of customers, its typical shoppers are women between the ages of 25 and 50, who are from families with middle and upper-middle incomes. These customers generally fit the profile of department-store shoppers.[12] See Figure 6–5.

In-Home Shopping

Over the years, studies of in-home shopping have uncovered some insightful results.[13] The in-home shopper is not always a captive audience. Shopping is often discretionary, not necessary. Convenience in ordering one item, without traveling for it, is important. In-home shoppers are often also active store shoppers, and they are affluent and well-educated. Many in-home shoppers are self-confident, younger, and venturesome.

[9] "Who Shops in Shopping Malls?" *Stores* (November 1989), p. 43; Laura Richardson, "Consumers in the 1990s: No Time or Money to Burn," *Chain Store Age Executive* (August 1993), p. 16A; and Greg Krikorian, "The Minority Community's Shopping-Mall Hard Sell," *New York Times* (May 20, 1990), Section 3, p. 5.

[10] Jeffrey Arlen, "Defining the Discount Shopper: Who Is She?" *Discount Store News* (August 2, 1993), pp. A12–A13; and "Circular Usage Ranks High in Consumer Poll," *Discount Store News* (April 19, 1993), pp. 3, 46.

[11] *Supermarket Merchandising for the 1990's: A Framework for Competing* (Atlanta: Coca-Cola Retailing Research Council, May 1989).

[12] *TJX Companies 10K, 1993,* p. 5.

[13] See Harvey D. Braun, "The Catalog Shopper of the '90s," *Direct Marketing* (March 1993), pp. 15–18; Patrick M. Reilly, "TV Shopping Hooks High-Toned Viewers," *Wall Street Journal* (November 16, 1993), pp. B1, B10; Jean C. Darian, "In-Home Shopping: Are There Consumer Segments?" *Journal of Retailing,* Vol. 63 (Summer 1987), pp. 163–186; and Robert A. Peterson, Nancy M. Ridgway, and Gerald Albaum, "Consumers Who Buy from Direct Sales Companies," *Journal of Retailing,* Vol. 65 (Summer 1989), pp. 273–286.

UNDERSTANDING
OUR CUSTOMER
In order to successfully meet our customers' needs, T.J. Maxx has long recognized the importance of market research which provides us with valuable insights about our customers. We know, for instance, that our customers are fashion conscious and looking for excellent value — defined by T.J. Maxx as brand names, fashion, quality and price. We are always seeking ways to enhance the appeal of our stores through the addition of new and exciting merchandise categories. Recently our market research supported the need to expand our giftware departments. T.J. Maxx responded by opening 29 new "Home Collections" departments in certain key locations which have proven very successful.
One of the most important reasons for our success is that we have never confused our customers! While we have updated and changed T.J. Maxx stores over the years, we have not had the need to make radical alterations. With their "no-frills" format, our stores provide a pleasant shopping experience that suggests a sense of current fashion as well as a value oriented atmosphere. Our customers know where to come for value and when they enter T.J. Maxx, there is no doubt — they know they've come to the right place!

FIGURE 6–5 T.J. Maxx: Knowing Your Customers
Reprinted by permission of TJX Companies, Inc.

They like in-store shopping but have low opinions of local shopping conditions. For some catalog shoppers, time is not an important shopping variable. In households with young children, in-home shopping is more likely if the female is employed part time or not at all than if she works full time.

When appealing to in-home shoppers, the retailer should recognize the differences between in-home and store purchases. In particular, in-home shoppers usually have a limited ability to comparison shop; may be unable to touch, feel, handle, or examine products firsthand; are concerned about customer service (such as the return policy); and may not have a salesperson from whom information can be acquired.

Outshopping

Outshopping (out-of-hometown shopping) is important for both local and surrounding retailers. The former want to minimize this behavior, whereas the latter want to maximize it. Accordingly, research on outshopping has been conducted for two decades.[14]

Outshoppers are often male, young, members of a large family, and new to the community. Income and education vary by situation. Outshoppers differ in their life-styles from those who patronize neighborhood or hometown stores. They enjoy fine foods, like to travel out-of-town, are active, like to change stores, and read out-of-town newspapers more than hometown shoppers. They also downplay hometown stores and compliment out-of-town stores. This is important information for suburban shopping centers.

Outshoppers have the same basic reasons for patronizing out-of-town shopping areas whether they reside in small or large communities. Among these reasons are easy access, liberal credit terms, store diversity, product assortments, prices, the presence of large chain outlets, entertainment facilities, customer services, and product quality.

ADDRESSING CONSUMER NEEDS

While developing an in-depth profile of its target market, the retailer should also identify the most important consumer needs. These are just a few of the questions that could be considered:

- How far will customers travel to get to the retailer?
- How important is convenience?
- What store hours are desired? Are evening and weekend hours required?
- What level of customer services is preferred?
- How extensive a goods/service assortment is desired?
- What level of goods/service quality is preferred?
- How important is price?
- What retailer actions are necessary to reduce perceived risk?
- Do different market segments have special needs? If so, what are they?

[14] See Fred D. Reynolds and William R. Darden, "Intermarket Patronage: A Psychographic Study of Consumer Outshoppers," *Journal of Marketing,* Vol. 36 (October 1972), pp. 50–54; N. G. Papadopoulos, "Consumer Outshopping Research: Review and Extension," *Journal of Retailing,* Vol. 56 (Winter 1980), pp. 41–58; A. Coskun Samli, Glen Riecken, and Ugur Yavas, "Intermarket Shopping Behavior and the Small Community: Problems and Prospects of a Widespread Phenomenon," *Journal of the Academy of Marketing Science,* Vol. 11 (Winter 1983), pp. 1–14; R. Eric Reidenbach, M. Bixby Cooper, and Mary Carolyn Harrison, "A Factor Analytic Comparison of Outshopping Behavior in Larger Retail Trade Areas," *Journal of the Academy of Marketing Science,* Vol. 12 (Spring 1984), pp. 145–158; James R. Lumpkin, Jon M. Hawes, and William R. Darden, "Shopping Patterns of the Rural Consumer: Exploring the Relationship Between Shopping Orientations and Outshopping," *Journal of Business Research,* Vol. 14 (1986), pp. 63–81; and Vicki L. Blakney and William S. Sekely, "A Product-Specific Examination of Shopping Mode Choice," *Journal of Marketing Management,* Vol. 3 (Spring–Summer 1993), pp. 23–38.

RETAILING AROUND THE WORLD

Will McDonald's Do Well with Beefless Burgers in India?

During 1995, McDonald's is beginning operations in India with 20 restaurants. However, McDonald's will offer no beef products in its Indian restaurants—because Hindus make up 80 per cent of the Indian population and they regard the cow as sacred.

Although McDonald's has been unsure as to what it will use in place of beef, many experts have been guessing that lamb will be the substitute. Lamb is popular in India; and, it is used by Nirula's, a fast-food competitor with outlets in India.

Aside from the decision not to offer beef products, McDonald's faces other obstacles in India. The overall population of India, with an annual per-capita income of less than $400, is so poor that a McDonald's meal would be a luxury to many. McDonald's conventional foods are also bland in comparison to typical Indian fare.

McDonald's is undaunted. The Indian market, with about 850 million people, is virtually untapped. And, even though the Indian middle class may be small on a relative basis, it is larger than the population of the entire United States. Furthermore, McDonald's believes the lessons it has learned by adapting menus in Moscow, Japan, China, and Saudi Arabia—among other nations—will help it to succeed in India.

Sources: Based on material in Rahul Jacob, "Where's the Beef?" *Fortune* (January 24, 1994), p. 16; and Valerie Reitman, "India Anticipates the Arrival of the Beefless Big Mac," *Wall Street Journal* (October 20, 1993), pp. B1, B3.

When the retailer gears its strategy toward satisfying consumer needs, it is appealing to their ***motives***, the reasons for their behavior. The better the firm addresses the most desired needs of its target market, the more motivated (likely to purchase) the customers will be.

For example, it is important for retailers to know that only about one-half of U.S. consumers enjoy shopping for clothes or for food and that the average time spent in a mall is roughly one hour (down from 90 minutes a decade ago); however, more people like to shop if they feel they have the time. Almost twice as many women as men feel shopping is a great way to relax. Two-thirds of U.S. consumers like "watching for sale advertisements from their favorite stores and shopping for bargains." Yet, "value alone, while still important to today's consumer, is not enough. Rather, the '90s shopper is seeking out the right combination of quality, selection, price, and service. This shift is hitting many retailers hard and rewarding others."[15]

Here are three illustrations of how specific retailers are addressing the needs of various target markets:

- Middle class and blue collar—At Consolidated Stores' Odd Lots and Big Lots closeout stores, the "core shoppers consist of two groups. The first is a large group of savvy shoppers who can afford to shop anywhere they choose, yet regularly shop Big Lots and Odd Lots looking for the incredible closeout deals that have become our hallmark. They are attracted by the "treasure hunt" opportunities at our stores. The second group consists of blue-collar working people, folks who have watched their purchasing power erode over the last decade. They shop Big and Odd Lots often, finding our stores the opportunity to buy brand-name products that would otherwise be out of their price range. These are our most loyal shoppers, and we find that when their finances improve, they retain their loyalty to our stores."[16]
- Children—To attract more young customers (a market segment dominated by McDonald's), Burger King has established a "Kids Club" for children ages 2 to

[15] Richardson, "Consumers in the 1990s: No Time or Money to Burn," pp. 15A–17A; Barry Berman, "The Changing U.S. Consumer: Implications for Retailing Strategies," *Retail Strategist*, Vol. 1 (Number 1, 1991), pp. 17–18; "Shopping Still a 'Favorite' Pastime," *Promo* (February 1993), p. 52; and *Standard & Poor's Industry Surveys: Retailing* (May 13, 1993), p. R76.

[16] *Consolidated Stores 1992 Annual Report*, pp. 10–11.

FIGURE 6–6 Burger King's Kids Club
Reprinted by permission.

13. Members get a bimonthly newsletter containing games, short articles on items such as bicycle care, and Burger King stories. They also receive special gifts and prizes. See Figure 6–6.

- Hispanics—In the Los Angeles area, where there are more than two million Hispanics, Vons operates a number of Tianguis supermarkets to appeal to Hispanic consumers. During 1993, the nine Tianguis stores had total annual sales of $160 million. In a typical Tianguis supermarket, there are a tortilleria (where fresh tortillas are made), hundreds of different items in the produce section (including large assortments of chili peppers, beans, salsa, and cheese), a relatively small frozen-food section, a salchichoneria (where fresh sausages are made), and a cut fruit and juice bar.[17]

Understanding How Consumers Make Decisions

In addition to identifying the characteristics of its target market, a retailer should have an understanding of how its customers make decisions. This requires some knowledge of ***consumer behavior***, which involves the process by which people determine whether, what, when, where, how, from whom, and how often to purchase goods and services.[18] Such behavior is influenced by a person's background and traits.

THE CONSUMER DECISION PROCESS

The ***consumer decision process*** consists of two parts: the process itself and the factors affecting the process. The decision process has six basic steps: stimulus, problem awareness, information search, evaluation of alternatives, purchase, and post-purchase behavior. Factors that affect the process are a consumer's demographics and life-style. The complete consumer decision process is shown in Figure 6–7.

Each time a person buys a good or service, he or she goes through a decision process. In some cases, all six steps in the process are utilized; in others, only a few

[17] *Vons Companies, Inc. 1993 Annual Review*; and authors' estimates.
[18] Adapted by the authors from Schiffman and Kanuk, *Consumer Behavior*, p. 7.

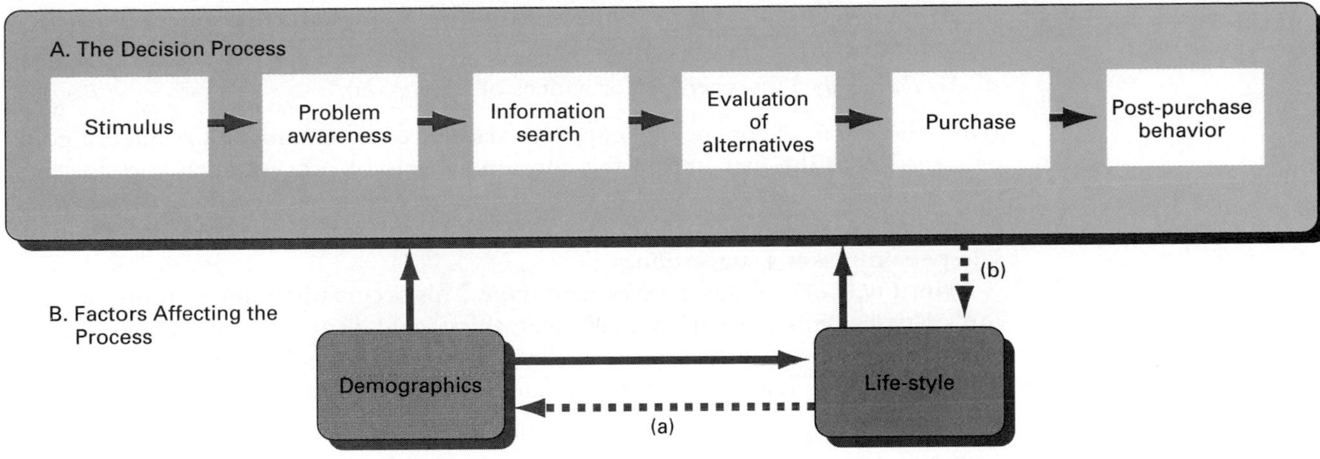

Note: Solid arrows connect all the elements in the decision process and show the impact of demographics and life-style upon the process. Dashed arrows show feedback. (a) shows the impact of life-style on certain demographics, such as family size, location, and marital status. (b) shows the impact of a purchase on elements of life-style, such as social class, reference groups, and social performance.

FIGURE 6–7 The Consumer Decision Process

of the steps are employed. For example, a consumer who has previously and satisfactorily bought luggage at a local store may not use the same extensive decision process as a person who has never bought luggage.

The decision process outlined in Figure 6–7 assumes the end result is the purchase of a good or service by the consumer. It is important to realize that at any point in the process, a potential customer may decide not to buy; the process then stops. The good or service may be unnecessary, unsatisfactory, or too expensive.

Before we consider the different ways in which the consumer uses the decision process, the entire process depicted in Figure 6–7 is explained.

Stimulus

A ***stimulus*** is a cue (social or commercial) or a drive (physical) meant to motivate or arouse a person to act. When one talks with friends, fellow employees, professors, and so on, a ***social cue*** is received. These cues may activate behavior. Some examples of social cues are:

"Gee Ed, I hear that the Tivoli Theater has a good movie. Let's go."

"We haven't been to a football game in a long time, and the Super Bowl is next month. Let's get tickets tomorrow."

"It's Thursday. Please meet me at the supermarket."

"Alice, I found an excellent new hair salon. You really should try it."

Each of these cues is a hint at arousing some action, which the person on the receiving end may ignore, treat as unimportant, or follow through on. The special attribute of a social cue is that it comes from an interpersonal, noncommercial source.

A second type of stimulus is a ***commercial cue***. This is a message sponsored by a retailer, a manufacturer, a wholesaler, or some other seller. The objective of a commercial cue is to interest a consumer in a particular retailer, good, or service. Ads, sales pitches, and point-of-purchase displays are commercial stimuli. Here are some examples of commercial cues:

"Our store is going out of business. If you are thinking about a winter coat, *now* is the time for a bargain."

"When was the last time you treated yourself to a night on the town? At the Palace, we will wine and dine you with service fit for royalty."

"Happiness Health Spas. A younger, healthier, more attractive you. You'll love the new you. *They'll* love the new you."

"*My Fair Lady.* Last seven performances of this revival."

While the intent of commercial cues is to create excitement about a retailer, a good, or a service as the first step in the consumer decision process, such cues may not be regarded as highly as social ones by consumers because the messages are seller-controlled. A consumer may receive a cue differently when a friend rather than a salesperson makes a suggestion.

A third type of stimulus is a ***physical drive.*** This occurs when one or more of a person's physical senses are affected. Hunger, thirst, cold, heat, pain, or fear could cause a physical drive. A strong drive normally impels some type of action. However, if the stimulus is weak, it may be ignored. Examples of physical drives follow:

"It's five after one. My stomach is awfully noisy. Another homework problem and I'll break for lunch."

"We've been driving for five hours, and I am really thirsty. We better stop for a soda before my mouth gets too dry."

"When I went out yesterday, it was 80 degrees. Today, it's 45. I'm freezing. And I don't even have a winter coat."

"This summer has been a real scorcher. Last night, I tossed and turned. I couldn't sleep at all."

"My eyes really hurt when I woke up last Thursday morning. I knew that I had to think about making an appointment with an optometrist."

"My car broke down. I was afraid that I would be late for my job interview."

In each of these scenarios, the person's physical senses are affected, and there is some desire to act to rectify the situation. However, the remaining steps in the decision process help determine whether a person will really act or just think about doing so.

A potential consumer may be exposed to any or all three stimuli for any good or service. If a person is aroused (motivated), he or she will go to the next step in the decision process. If a person is not sufficiently aroused, he or she will ignore the stimulus—thus terminating the decision process for the given good or service.

Problem Awareness

At the ***problem awareness*** stage in the decision process, the consumer not only has been aroused by social, commercial, and/or physical stimuli, but also recognizes that the good or service under consideration may solve a problem of shortage or unfulfilled desire.

It is sometimes difficult to determine why a consumer is motivated enough to move from the stimulus stage to the problem awareness stage. This is especially so because many consumers shop at the same store or buy the same good or service for different reasons (convenience, price, image, quality, service, durability, and so on); consumers may not know their own motivation (it may be subconscious); and consumers may not tell a retailer their real reasons for shopping there or buying a certain good or service.

Recognition of shortage occurs when a consumer discovers that a good or service may need to be repurchased. A good could wear down beyond repair (automobile, refrigerator, watch, clothing), or the consumer might run out of an item (milk, bread, tissues, hair spray). Service may be required when a good can be repaired (automobile, refrigerator, watch) or a service wears out (hair cutting, lawn mowing, car washing). In each case, the consumer would see a possible need to replenish a good or service. These are examples of stimuli interacting with problem awareness (recognition of shortage):

"The sun is strong today. I'll need eye protection *(stimulus)*, but my old sunglasses are broken *(recognition of shortage)*."

"Why did I have to get a flat tire *(stimulus)*? I don't even have a spare *(recognition of shortage)*."

"Debbie said she didn't like the way my hair looked *(stimulus)*. Maybe it is too long *(recognition of shortage)*."

"I really want a cough drop *(stimulus)*. But I gave my last one to Herb *(recognition of shortage)*."

Recognition of unfulfilled desire occurs when a consumer becomes aware of a good or service that has not been purchased before—or a retailer that has not been patronized before. A good or service may improve the person's life-style, self-image, status, looks, and so on in a new, untried way (contact lenses, Carribean vacation, diet center), or it may offer new, unheard-of performance characteristics (self-cleaning oven, pot-cleaning dishwasher, pen-operated computer). In this case, the person is aroused by an urge to improve him- or herself and considers the necessity of fulfilling these desires. These are examples of stimuli interacting with problem awareness (recognition of unfulfilled desires):

"I don't like the way I look. I've worn glasses since I was 14 and always hated them *(stimulus)*. Why don't I find a good optician and try on contact lenses? I may even look at the ones that give you a different eye color. Then, I'll be the life of the party *(recognition of unfulfilled desire)*."

Henry: "We've been married 31 years and have never been on a real vacation *(stimulus)*."
Barbara: "Why can't we go on a trip where it's sunny and the sand is beautiful *(recognition of unfulfilled desire)*?"

"One of the reasons why I hate to cook is that I dislike washing pots *(stimulus)*. But, I just read that GE has a line of dishwashers that do a great job of cleaning pots, as well as dishes *(recognition of unfulfilled desire)*."

"Our friends eat at good restaurants and have fine meals at least once a week, but we eat at fast-food places *(stimulus)*. Once in a while, I'd like to go into a restaurant, have a maitre d' show us to a table, drink a bottle of fine wine, and enjoy a delicious meal *(recognition of unfulfilled desire)*."

Most consumers are more hesitant to react to unfulfilled desires than to shortages. There are greater risks and benefits may be harder to determine. This is especially true when the consumer has had substantial satisfactory experience with the good or service to be replaced.

Whether the consumer becomes aware of a shortage or an unfulfilled desire, he or she will act only if it is perceived as a problem worth solving. Otherwise, the decision process will terminate. A strong stimulus does not necessarily mean the presence of a worthy problem. For instance:

"The sun is strong today. I'll need eye protection. My old sunglasses are broken, but I can tape the frame together."

"Debbie said she didn't like the way my hair looked, but she would criticize Mel Gibson."

Henry: "We've been married 31 years and have never been on a real vacation. But, with two children in college, we can't afford to take any kind of trip this year."

Information Search

After a person decides a shortage or unfulfilled desire is worth further consideration, information is sought. The ***information search*** has two parts: (1) determining the alternative goods or services that will solve the problem at hand and (2) ascertaining the characteristics of each alternative.

First, the consumer compiles a list of various goods or services that address the problem encountered in the previous step of the decision process. This list does not have to be very formal nor even in written form. It may simply be a group of alternatives the consumer thinks about. The key is that the consumer enumerates potential solutions to his or her problem. This aspect of information search may be internal or external.

A consumer with a lot of purchasing experience (in the specific area) will normally utilize an internal search of his or her memory to determine the goods or services that would be satisfactory for the solution of the current problem. A typical thought process of this type is:

> "It's raining *(stimulus)*. My old raincoat is torn; I really need a new one *(problem awareness)*. The question is: Will I buy a London Fog, a Botany, or a Harbor Master raincoat *(internal search for listing alternatives)*?"

A consumer with little purchasing experience will often use an external search to develop a list of goods or services that would solve the current problem. Thus, the consumer seeks information outside his or her memory. An external search can involve commercial sources (mass media, salespeople), noncommercial sources (*Consumer Reports*, government publications), and social sources (family, friends, colleagues). Here are examples of how each type of information source may be used in listing alternatives:

> "Our roof is leaking *(stimulus)*. This house is getting on my nerves. Let's look for a new one *(problem awareness)*. Sunday's edition of the *Gazette* will have a listing of all the new houses in our area. We should use it to develop a list of possibilities *(commercial source for listing alternatives)*."
>
> "It just cost me $400 for a new transmission. I am worried the car will cause me more problems *(stimulus)*. Now is the time to look for a new car before this one breaks down again *(problem awareness)*. *Consumer Reports* lists the new-model cars in its next issue. Let's get that issue and see what's available this year *(noncommercial source for listing alternatives)*."
>
> Alice: "We haven't eaten out in a long time. I'm in the mood to have a good meal tonight *(stimulus)*."
> Dean: "You're right, I didn't realize how long it has been since we have gone out *(problem awareness)*. Where should we go?"
> Alice: "We can go to the Mandarin Inn, the Elm Tree Restaurant, or the Homestead Cafe *(social source for listing alternatives)*."

Second, the consumer gathers information relating to the characteristics of each alternative. Once the list of possible alternatives is known, the consumer must determine their attributes. This kind of information may be obtained internally (memory) or externally, in much the same manner as the list of alternatives is generated.

An experienced consumer will search his or her memory for the attributes (pros and cons) of each good or service alternative:

> "It's raining *(stimulus)*. I need a new raincoat because my old one is torn *(problem awareness)*. I want to choose from among London Fog, Botany, and Harbor Master *(list of alternatives)*. London Fog makes a fine product, but it's rather expensive. Botany makes a fine product, but I can't get it in my area. Harbor Master makes an equally fine product, but I have trouble with the fit *(internal search for characteristics of alternatives)*."

A consumer with little experience or a lot of uncertainty will search externally for information about each alternative under consideration. Commercial, noncommercial, and social sources are available for the collection of information about good or service attributes:

"My wife and I want to go to Europe for a vacation *(stimulus* and *problem recognition)*. Your ad mentioned six different packages *(list of alternatives)*. Please explain the details and costs of each one *(commercial source for characteristics of alternatives)*."

"I am interested in a new refrigerator *(stimulus* and *problem recognition)*, so I want to read *Consumer Reports*. Not only are all major models listed, but each is described in depth *(noncommercial source for list* and *characteristics of alternatives)*."

"I agree we should go to the Mandarin Inn, the Elm Tree Restaurant, or the Homestead Cafe *(stimulus, problem awareness,* and *list of alternatives)*. But let's consider the quality of food, service, and prices before we make a decision *(social source for characteristics of alternatives)*."

The extent to which a consumer searches for information depends, in part, on that person's perception of the risk attached to the purchase of a specific good or service. Risk varies among individuals and by situation. For some, it is inconsequential; for others, it is quite important.

The retailer's role in a consumer's search process is to provide enough information for him or her to feel comfortable in making decisions, thereby reducing the consumer's perceived risk. Point-of-purchase advertising, product displays, and knowledgeable sales personnel help provide consumers with the information they need to make decisions.

Once the consumer's search for information is completed, he or she must decide whether the current shortage or unfulfilled desire can be met by any of the alternatives. If one or more are satisfactory, the consumer moves to the next step in the decision process. However, the consumer will discontinue the process should no satisfactory goods or services be found. For example, when all big-screen televisions are perceived as too expensive or all diet centers are unappealing, the consumer will not continue the purchase process.

Evaluation of Alternatives

At this point, the consumer has enough information to select one good or service alternative from the list of choices. Sometimes, this is quite easy—if one alternative is clearly superior to the others across all attributes. An alternative that is of excellent quality and has a low price will be the easy choice over more expensive, average-quality ones.

A choice is often not that simple, and the consumer must carefully engage in an ***evaluation of alternatives*** before making most decisions. When two or more alternatives seem attractive, the consumer will determine which criteria (attributes) to evaluate and the relative importance of the criteria (attributes). Then the alternatives will be ranked, and a choice will be made.

The criteria for a decision are those good or service attributes that the consumer considers to be relevant. These criteria may include price, quality, fit, color, durability, warranty, and so on. The consumer sets standards for these characteristics and evaluates each alternative according to its ability to meet the standards. The importance of each criterion is also determined by the consumer. And the attributes of a good or service are usually of different importance to each consumer. As an example, for some people, the initial price may be more important than the operating costs (as measured by electrical consumption) of a new air conditioner. In selecting an air-conditioner brand, this type of consumer will choose a less expensive product that consumes a lot of energy over a more expensive, more efficient product.

Next, the consumer ranks the alternatives under consideration (from most favorite to least favorite) and selects one from among the list. This illustration shows the entire process of evaluating alternatives:

Judy and Larry talked about visiting California for quite a while. This year they finally decided they would leave Vermont for the first time and go to California.

They talked with friends, read magazines and newspapers, and consulted a travel agent. They zeroed in on three alternatives: a 14-day bus trip, a 17-day car trip, and a 10-day plane trip. Judy and Larry agreed their choice of a trip would depend on cost, time available for sightseeing, and the quality of sightseeing. Cost was important, but the time available for sightseeing and the sightseeing itself were more important. The bus trip was the cheapest; the plane trip was the most expensive. The car trip left the least time for sightseeing; the plane trip provided the most. The car trip offered the best-quality sightseeing because it was so flexible; the bus trip provided the worst because it included a fixed itinerary. Judy and Larry decided that, on the basis of their criteria and the order of these criteria, the plane trip was the best available alternative. The bus trip was the worst.

For some goods or services, it is especially difficult for consumers to evaluate the characteristics of the available alternatives because the items are technical, intangible, new, or poorly labeled. When this occurs, consumers often use price, brand name, or store name as an indicator of quality, and choose an alternative based on this criterion.

Once a consumer examines the attributes of alternatives and ranks them, he or she chooses the good or service that is most satisfactory. In situations where no alternative proves adequate, a decision not to purchase is made.

Purchase

Following the choice of the best alternative, the consumer is ready for the ***purchase act***—an exchange of money or a promise to pay for the ownership or use of a good or service. Important decisions are still made during this step in the process. From a retailing perspective, the purchase act may be the most crucial aspect of the decision process because the consumer is mainly concerned with three factors: place of purchase, terms, and availability. See Figure 6–8.

The consumer must determine where to buy the good or service. The place of purchase may be a store or a nonstore location. Many more items are bought at store locations (such as department, drug, and furniture stores) than at nonstore locations (such as home, work, and school). The place of purchase is evaluated in the same manner as the good or the service itself: alternative places of purchase are listed; their characteristics are defined; and they are ranked. The most desirable place of purchase is then chosen.

Criteria for selecting a store-based retailer include such factors as store location, store layout, customer service, sales help, store image, and level of prices. Criteria for selecting a nonstore retailer include such factors as image, customer service, level of

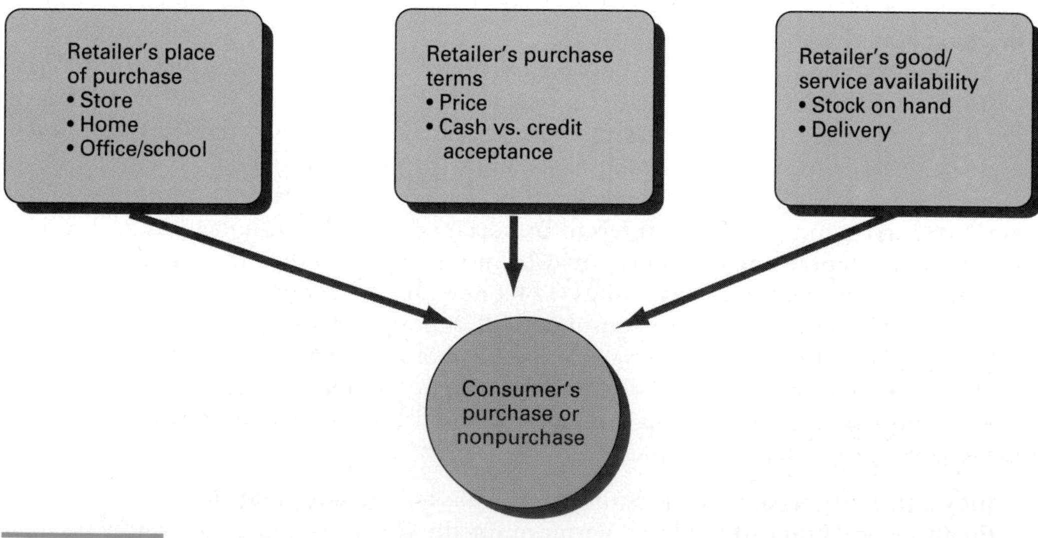

FIGURE 6–8 Key Factors in the Purchase Act

ETHICS IN RETAILING

What Rights Do Consumers Have?

Although specific consumer rights vary from state to state, here is a basic primer on consumers' general rights:

- Every new product has an implied warranty that offers consumers protection against a product that does not perform adequately.
- Purchases made by mail, fax machine, telephone, and computer are covered by the U.S. Federal Trade Commission's 30-day rule. Under this rule, consumers can cancel an order if receipt is delayed beyond the promised time limit or beyond 30 days (if no time limit is stated).
- Under the FTC's cooling-off rule, consumers have three business days to cancel a purchase costing $25 or more that is made at their home or another place (but not the seller's permanent place of business). Sellers are required to provide customers with a cancellation form for purchases made in the home.
- Many credit sales (made in the consumer's home state or within 100 miles of his/her billing address for $50 or less) are protected by the Federal Credit Billing Act. The act allows a customer to withhold payment for goods or services that are unsatisfactory.

In addition, local Better Business Bureau offices, the Direct Marketing Association, local consumer protection offices, and other organizations will help consumers resolve disputes with retailers.

Source: Based on material in "Your Shopping Rights," *Consumer Reports* (December 1993), pp. 802–803.

prices, hours, and convenience. A consumer will shop with the store or nonstore retailer that offers the best combination of criteria, as defined by that consumer.

The consumer is also interested in purchase terms and the availability of the good or service. Purchase terms include the price and method of payment. Price is the dollar amount a person must pay to achieve ownership or use of a good or service. Method of payment is the way the price may be paid (cash, short-term credit, long-term credit). Availability relates to stock-on-hand and delivery. Stock-on-hand is the amount of an item that a place of purchase has in inventory. Delivery is the time span between the order and the receipt of an item and the ease with which an item is transported to its place of use.

If the consumer is pleased with these three components of the purchase act, the good or service will be bought. If there is dissatisfaction with the place of purchase, the terms of purchase, and/or availability, the consumer may not buy the good or service, although there is contentment with the item itself. Here are examples of each situation:

> Jenny wanted to buy a sofa to complete her living-room set. She already had two chairs and a coffee table, but until now, Jenny could not afford a new sofa. She knew exactly what she wanted, a SuperSofa convertible (Model 155). The questions were where to buy the sofa, how to pay for it, how soon it could be delivered, and how it would be delivered. Jenny selected the Living Room Store from among four possible stores and bought the sofa. She never considered buying by telephone or mail because she didn't trust nonpersonal shopping. The Living Room Store provided Jenny with what she wanted. She received good service at a convenient location and a special discount was given for paying cash. Because the sofa was in stock, it was delivered within one week. Delivery was included in the sofa's price.
>
> Ken wanted to buy a stereo system. He knew which system to get and had saved $100 for a down payment. But, after a month of trying to buy the stereo, Ken gave up in disgust. He explained why: "The system I wanted was sold in only three stores in my area and through a mail-order house. Two of the stores overpriced the stereo by about $75. The third store had a really good price, $599, but the owner insisted that I pay in cash. In addition, I would have had to drive to their warehouse, twenty miles away, and pick up the system myself. The mail-order company had a really good deal—low price, credit, and delivery. But they ran out of the model I was interested in and told me the wait would be four months. After I heard that, I just gave up. My portable CD player will have to suffice."

Post-Purchase Behavior

After the purchase of a good or service, the consumer is often involved in ***post-purchase behavior***. Such behavior falls into either of two categories: further purchases or re-evaluation. In many situations, buying one good or service leads to further purchases. For instance, the purchase of an automobile leads to buying insurance. The purchase of a new suit may be accompanied by the purchase of a new shirt and tie. Buying a stereo system will require tapes or CDs to play on it. Therefore, it can be stated that some purchases provide the impetus for others, and consumer decisions continue until the last purchase is made. Just as in the decision process for the original item, the characteristics of the supplementary items are noted and the alternatives ranked. A retailer that utilizes scrambled merchandising by stocking nonrelated items may also stimulate a shopper to further purchases, once the primary good or service is bought.

A warning: Retailers should carefully evaluate their expansion of product lines (related or nonrelated). The skills necessary to obtain a supplemental customer purchase may not be similar to those required for the major good or service category. For example, real-estate transactions and property insurance sales involve different skills; television sales and service contracts require different retailer activities; and muffler repairs and transmission overhauls are quite dissimilar.

The consumer may also re-evaluate the purchase of a good or service. Does it perform as promised? Do its actual attributes match the expectations the consumer had of these attributes? Has the retailer functioned as expected? Satisfaction may lead to customer contentment, a repurchase when the good or service wears out, and favorable conversations with friends interested in the same item. Dissatisfaction may lead to unhappiness, brand or store switching when the good or service wears out, and unfavorable conversations with friends interested in the same item.

The latter situation (dissatisfaction) may result from ***cognitive dissonance***, that is, doubt that the correct decision has been made. The consumer may regret that the purchase was made at all or may wish that another alternative from the list had been chosen. To overcome cognitive dissonance and dissatisfaction, the retailer must realize that the consumer decision process does not end with a purchase. Customer after-care (via a phone call, a service visit, or an ad) may be as important as anything the retailer can do to complete the sale. When items are expensive and/or important to a consumer, after-care takes on added significance because the person really wants to be right. In addition, when there are more alternatives from which to choose, doubt is greater after a decision is made, and after-care is more important.

Many retailers know that consumers often have doubts and second thoughts about recent purchases. Decades ago, Wanamaker and others pioneered the concept of a money-back guarantee, so customers could return merchandise if doubts or second thoughts became too great.

Realistic sales presentations and advertising campaigns can also minimize dissatisfaction because consumers' expectations do not then exceed reality. If overly high expectations are created, a consumer is more apt to become unhappy because a good or service does not perform at the level promised. The coupling of an honest sales presentation with good after-care of the consumer should reduce or eliminate cognitive dissonance and dissatisfaction.

TYPES OF CONSUMER DECISION MAKING

As noted earlier, every time a consumer purchases a good or service, he or she uses a form of the decision process described in the preceding subsections. Often, the process is used subconsciously, and a person is not even aware of its use. Also, as indicated in Figure 6–7, the decision process is affected by the characteristics of the consumer.

For example, older consumers may not spend as much time as younger ones in making purchase decisions because of their experience. Well-educated consumers may search out many information sources before making a decision. Upper-income consumers may spend little time making a decision because they can afford to buy again if a purchase is unsatisfactory. In a family with children, each member may have an input into a decision, thereby lengthening the process. Class-conscious consumers may be more interested in social sources than in commercial or noncommercial ones. Consumers with low self-esteem and/or high perceived risk may use all of the steps in the decision process in detail. And people who are under time pressure may skip steps in the process to save time.

The decision process is used differently in dissimilar situations. One situation (such as the purchase of a new home) may require the thorough use of each step in the process; perceived risk will probably be high regardless of the consumer's background. Another situation (such as the purchase of a magazine) may enable the consumer to skip certain steps in the process; perceived risk will probably be low regardless of the person's background.

There are three types of decision processes: extended decision making, limited decision making, and routine decision making. They are explained next.

Extended Decision Making

Extended decision making occurs when a consumer makes full use of the decision process shown in Figure 6–7. A considerable amount of time is spent gathering information and evaluating alternatives before a purchase is made. After a purchase is completed, the potential for cognitive dissonance is great. In this category are expensive, complex goods and services with which the consumer has had little or no experience. Perceived risk of all kinds is high. Examples of goods and services requiring extended decision making are a house, a first car, and a life insurance policy.

At any point in the purchase process, a consumer can stop, and for expensive, complex items, this occurs quite often. Consumer characteristics (such as age, education, income, marital status, time utilization, and class consciousness) have their greatest impact with extended decision making.

Because their customers tend to use extended decision making, retailers like real-estate brokers and auto dealers should emphasize personal selling, printed materials, and other methods of communication to provide as much information as possible. A low-key approach should be enacted, so shoppers feel comfortable and not threatened. In this way, the consumer's perceived risk can be minimized.

Limited Decision Making

Limited decision making occurs when a consumer uses each of the steps in the purchase process but does not need to spend a great deal of time on each of them. This type of decision making requires less time than extended decision making because the consumer typically has some experience. In this category are items the person has purchased before, but not regularly. Risk is moderate, and the consumer will spend some time shopping. The thoroughness with which the decision process is used depends mostly on the person's prior experience. Priority would probably be placed on evaluating known alternatives according to the person's desires and standards, although information search is also important for some. Examples of goods and services requiring limited decision making are a second car, clothing, a vacation, and gifts.

Consumer characteristics have an impact on decision making, but the effect lessens as perceived risk falls and experience rises. Income, the importance of the purchase, and motives play very strong roles in the uses of limited decision making.

This form of consumer decision making is most relevant to retailers like department and specialty stores that cater to in-store shopping behavior and carry goods and services that customers have bought before. The interior environment and assortment of the store are very important. Sales personnel should be available for questions and to differentiate among brands or models.

Routine Decision Making

Routine decision making takes place when the consumer buys out of habit and skips steps in the purchase process. The person wants to spend little or no time shopping, and the same brands are usually repurchased. In this category are items that are purchased regularly. These goods and services have little risk for the consumer because of experience. The key step for this type of decision making is problem awareness. When the consumer realizes that a good or service is needed, a repurchase is often automatic. Information search, evaluation of alternatives, and post-purchase behavior are less likely than in limited or extended decision making. These steps are not undertaken as long as a person is satisfied. Examples of goods and services often requiring routine decision making are weekly groceries, newspapers, and haircuts.

Consumer characteristics have little impact on purchases in routine decision making. Problem awareness almost inevitably leads to a purchase.

This type of consumer decision making is most relevant to retailers like supermarkets, dry cleaners, and fast-food outlets. For them, these strategic elements are crucial: a good location, long hours of operation, clear in-store displays, and, most important, product availability. Advertising should be reminder-oriented. The major task for store personnel would be completing the transaction quickly and precisely.

SELECTED RETAIL RESEARCH FINDINGS

Both the individual components of the consumer decision process and the level of decision making have been investigated in many different retail settings. Here are examples of the findings.

Problem Awareness

A survey of consumers who patronize shopping centers found that one-third go to the centers for a specific purchase and one-sixth go to visit a specific retailer. However, 40 per cent go for general shopping or to browse. According to another study, men are significantly more likely than women to know exactly what they're going to buy when they go on a shopping trip.[19]

Research on apparel shoppers was able to classify them on the basis of two problem-awareness styles. One segment includes people whose awareness is usually activated when a product wears out or breaks down (recognition of shortage); the other consists of people interested in change or novelty (recognition of unfulfilled desire). The latter would agree, "It's not unusual for me to buy new clothes simply because I want something new." They are more apt to view themselves as innovators, to like shopping, to be confident, to shop often, and to consult many information sources.[20]

Information Search

Research in this area has involved such topics as the impact of social class, perceived risk, and product category on the kind and amount of information sought.

One survey examined the effect of two factors (social class and perceived risk) on the information search behavior of working women. It found that lower-class women are more apt to seek information from friends and relatives on products such as clothing, sheets, and towels than are upper-class women. For major items such as cars, upper-class women more frequently consult with consumer guides than lower-class women. With regard to perceived risk, working women are often apt to avoid any level of information search for low-risk products such as food. As perceived risk increases,

[19] "Who Shops in Shopping Malls?" p. 43; and "Shopping Still a 'Favorite' Pastime," p. 52.

[20] Gordon C. Bruner II, "Problem Recognition Styles and Search Patterns: An Empirical Investigation," *Journal of Retailing*, Vol. 62 (Fall 1986), pp. 281–297.

they not only gather more information but also place greater emphasis on consumer guides, friends, sales personnel, and relatives; newspaper ads become less important.[21]

A study of media usage discovered that the information search depends on the product category. For example, the consumer's use of newspapers during information gathering is highest for goods and services like electronics products, major appliances, furniture, lawn and garden supplies, and floor coverings. It is lowest for goods and services like attorneys, insurance, tires, florists, and home contracting. Another study, on automobiles, found that the showroom is the leading first source of information, followed by articles, word-of-mouth from other people, and then advertisements.[22]

Evaluation of Alternatives

An important aspect in the consumer's evaluation of alternatives are the criteria set by that person. A study on supermarket characteristics determined that consumers rate these store attributes as most important in comparing outlets: cleanliness, low prices, all prices clearly labeled, accurate and pleasant clerks, and freshness dates marked on products. Older shoppers are more interested in a good meat department and helpful managers. Younger shoppers are more attracted by one-stop shopping, a good deli, hot takeout foods, and long hours. Overall, consumers rate the supermarkets at which they shop as 7.5 on a 10-point scale (with 10 being sensational).[23]

A survey of parents and their children found that the children have great impact in choosing the clothing, breakfast cereal, toys, ice cream and soft drinks, and videos to be purchased. They have little impact on the choice of a PC or a car.[24]

Purchase Behavior

Consumer purchase behavior has been researched from various perspectives. Surveys show that consumer interest in and enthusiasm for shopping have fallen in recent years. One-third of people say they spend less time shopping today than in 1990. And they visit fewer stores on each shopping trip.[25]

Surveys of supermarket shoppers show that Friday and Saturday are the most popular days of the week for the major store visit. On average, during a typical week, 37 per cent visit stores between 8 A.M. and noon, 35 per cent between noon and 5 P.M., 26 per cent between 5 P.M. and 9 P.M., and 2 per cent between 9 P.M. and 8 A.M. Early-morning visits are greatest on Wednesday and Thursday. Evening visits are greatest on Thursday and Friday. Only 5 per cent have a major weekly shopping trip on Saturday night.[26]

A study of coffee shoppers found that the number of brands carried by a store and its use of special displays have a significant effect on purchase behavior. For example, when a store has a large number of brands from which to choose and runs special displays, the consumer is apt to be susceptible to promotional offers and be less brand loyal.[27]

[21] Paul Hugstadt, James W. Taylor, and Grady D. Bruce, "The Effects of Social Class and Perceived Risk on Consumer Information Search," *Journal of Consumer Marketing,* Vol. 4 (Spring 1987), pp. 41–45.

[22] *Yellow Pages and the Media Mix* (Chesterfield, Mo.: American Association of Yellow Pages Publishers, n.d.); and John R. Hauser, Glen L. Urban, and Bruce D. Weinberg, "How Consumers Allocate Their Time When Searching for Information," *Journal of Marketing Research,* Vol. 30 (November 1993), pp. 452–466.

[23] "Consumers Show Cautious Optimism," *Progressive Grocer* (April 1993), pp. 88–90; and "Cleanliness Counts to Consumers," *Progressive Grocer* (Mid-April 1990), p. 57.

[24] Patricia Sellers, "The ABC's of Marketing to Kids," *Fortune* (May 8, 1989), p. 115. See also James U. McNeal and Chyon-Hwa Yeh, "Born to Shop," *American Demographics* (June 1993), pp. 34–39.

[25] *Standard & Poor's Industry Surveys: Retailing,* p. R76.

[26] "Consumers Show Cautious Optimism," p. 92.

[27] Kapil Bawa, Aradhna Krishna, and Jane T. Landwehr, "Consumer Response to Retailers' Marketing Environments: An Analysis of Coffee Purchase Data," *Journal of Retailing,* Vol. 65 (Winter 1989), pp. 471–495.

In-store purchase behavior is also affected by merchandise stockouts. One investigation determined that stockouts cause consumers to have a lower store image, less satisfaction with shopping, and lower purchase intentions for particular product categories. Sale shoppers are less sensitive to stockouts than nonsale shoppers. Stockout behavior does vary by product category.[28]

Figure 6–9 shows how retailers can affect shoppers' in-store behavior.

Consumer Satisfaction/Dissatisfaction

Retailers are quite interested in the causes of consumer satisfaction and dissatisfaction because they want to optimize their strategies. A study of mall shoppers discovered that people are most satisfied with the variety of merchandise, friendly employees, good sales prices, and quality merchandise. They are least satisfied with the convenience of the location, ease of parking, and the excitement of the shopping experience.[29]

According to a study of automobile purchases, consumers are most likely to say positive things to others, recommend the car they have purchased, and compliment the dealership where the car has been purchased if they are both satisfied with their purchases and believe they have been treated fairly by the dealer and the salesperson.[30]

A study of consumer dissatisfaction (involving grocery shopping, auto repair, medical care, and banking services) was able to segment people into four major groups. Passives are unlikely to state complaints to retailers or to take any other actions if unhappy. Voicers are most apt to complain to the retailer if dissatisfied; they do not usually complain to friends or outside parties, nor do they switch patronage. Irates are quite likely to complain to friends and switch patronage; they are not apt to contact parties such as the Better Business Bureau. Activists are quite likely to complain to friends, switch patronage, and contact parties such as the Better Business Bureau, the local newspaper, and others.[31]

Level of Consumer Decision Making

Three of the concepts that have been investigated with regard to the level of consumer decision making are shopping and travel time, impulse purchases, and store loyalty.

When a consumer utilizes extended or limited decision making, he or she is more willing to spend time shopping and traveling to a retailer than if routine decision making is involved. The type of decision making used depends on the consumer segment, as these research findings indicate: One-third of all women always feel rushed. This figure is higher for women who are ages 44 and younger, work full time, and have children.[32]

In San Antonio, one-fifth of shoppers go to a supermarket more than once a week; most drive to a store and have high sales per transaction. In New York City, over one-quarter of shoppers go to a supermarket more than once per week; many are in close proximity (often, walking distance) to a store and spend less per trip. New Yorkers trade lower travel time for multiple store visits.[33]

[28] Paul H. Zinzer and Jack A. Lesser, "An Empirical Evaluation of the Role of Stockout on Shopper Patronage Processes," in Richard P. Bagozzi et al. (Editors), *Marketing in the 80's* (Chicago: American Marketing Association, 1980), pp. 221–224.

[29] Stanley D. Sibley and Soo Young Moon, "Testing Satisfaction Models with the Mall Shopper," in Paul C. Thistlethwaite, Rolf Hackmann, and Charles Pettijohn (Editors) *Midwest Marketing Association 1993 Proceedings* (Macomb, Ill.: Western Illinois University, 1993), pp. 157–163.

[30] John E. Swan and Richard L. Oliver, "Post-Purchase Communications by Consumers," *Journal of Retailing*, Vol. 65 (Winter 1989), pp. 516–533.

[31] Jagdip Singh, "A Typology of Consumer Dissatisfaction Response Styles," *Journal of Retailing*, Vol. 66 (Spring 1990), pp. 57–99.

[32] Survey Research Center, University of Maryland, "Pressed for Time," *American Demographics* (February 1990), p. 33.

[33] Impact Resources, "Hispanic Shoppers: Fewer Trips to the Grocery," *Chain Store Age Executive* (July 1989), p. 90.

FIGURE 6–9 Influencing Purchase Behavior
Retailers can have a great impact on peoples' purchase behavior, their mood while in the store, the length of the shopping trip, the extent of impulse purchases, and other factors. Well-planned store interiors can facilitate shopping and generate a sense of excitement. Shown here are the customer-friendly layouts of a food store (upper left), a full-line discount store (upper right), and an off-price store (lower left).
Reprinted by permission of Nash Finch, Ames Department Stores, and Ross Stores.

In general, retailers need to emphasize a unique and broad product selection, good sales personnel, competitive prices, a pleasant shopping atmosphere, and goods/service guarantees to encourage consumers to spend more time in a store and to travel a greater distance to shop.[34] Consumers are apt to patronize nearby stores unless there are compelling reasons to do otherwise. ***Mapping*** is a good technique for a retailer to use in evaluating the trading area of a store. With it, a firm determines the distances people are likely to travel to get to a store, the population density of the geographic area surrounding the store, and the travel patterns and times from various locations. A map is then drawn showing these factors.

Impulse purchases occur when consumers purchase products and/or brands they had not planned on buying before entering a store, reading a mail-order catalog, seeing a TV shopping show, and so on. With impulse purchases, at least part of consumer decision making is influenced by the retailer. There are three kinds of impulse shopping:

- Completely unplanned—A consumer has no intention of making a purchase in a goods or service category before he or she comes into contact with a retailer.
- Partially unplanned—A consumer intends to make a purchase in a goods or service category but has not chosen a brand before he or she comes into contact with a retailer.
- Unplanned substitution—A consumer intends to buy a specific brand of a good or service but changes his or her mind about the brand after coming into contact with a retailer.

With partially unplanned and substitution kinds of impulse purchases, some decision making takes place before a person interacts with a retailer. In these cases, the consumer may be involved with any type of process (extended, limited, or routine). Completely unplanned shopping is usually related to routine decision making or limited decision making; there is little or no time spent shopping, and the key step is problem awareness. Impulse purchases are more susceptible to in-store displays than pre-planned purchases.

According to a major supermarket study, on a given shopping trip, about 52 per cent of purchases are completely unplanned, 11 per cent are partially unplanned, and 3 per cent are unplanned substitutions. Over 80 per cent of the purchases of these products involve some level of impulse behavior: candy, gum, snacks, pasta, cookies, crackers, and condiments.[35]

When ***store loyalty*** exists, a consumer regularly patronizes a particular retailer that he or she knows, likes, and trusts. Such loyalty lets a person reduce decision making because he or she does not have to invest time in learning about and choosing the retailer from which to make purchases.

Over the years, research has addressed various aspects of store loyalty. For example, store-loyal consumers tend to be time-conscious, use the entertainment media, enjoy shopping locally, be fashion leaders, not rely on credit, and not be engaged in outshopping. In a service setting, such as an auto repair shop, customer satisfaction with service quality often leads to store loyalty; price has little bearing on decisions. One-quarter of supermarket shoppers patronize only one store in a typical week; and over 70 per cent of grocery spending is done in a consumer's main supermarket.[36]

[34] Richardson, "Consumers in the 1990s: No Time or Money to Burn," pp. 15A–17A.

[35] Point-of-Purchase Advertising Institute, "Impulse Buying," *New York Times* (August 18, 1991), Section 3, p. 4.

[36] Fred D. Reynolds, William R. Darden, and Warren S. Martin, "Developing an Image of the Store-Loyal Customer," *Journal of Retailing*, Vol. 50 (Winter 1974–75), pp. 73–84; L. W. Turley and Ronald P. LeBlanc, "An Exploratory Investigation of Consumer Decision Making in the Service Sector," *Journal of Services Marketing*, Vol. 7 (Number 4, 1993), pp. 11–18; and "Store Loyalty Lives," *Progressive Grocer* (April 1993), p. 94.

SUMMARY

1. *To discuss why it is important for a retailer to properly select, identify, and understand its target market* To properly develop and apply a strategy, a retailer must determine which type of target market to reach, identify the characteristics and needs of the specific chosen target market, and understand how consumers make decisions.

2. *To enumerate and describe a number of consumer demographic and life-style factors, and explain how these concepts can be applied to retailing* Consumer characteristics and needs can be identified by studying demographic and life-style factors. Demographics are easily identifiable and measurable population statistics; life-styles are the ways in which consumers live and spend time and money.

   People can be described in terms of these demographic factors: population size, household size, marital and family status, income, retail sales, age, birth rates, mobility, place of residence, gender, employment status, occupation, education level, and ethnic/racial background. Based on these factors, this chapter presents a demographic overview of the United States and relates demographics to a retailer's identification of a target market.

   Consumer life-styles are comprised of social and psychological elements and are greatly affected by demographics. Social factors include culture, social class, reference groups, social performance, the family life cycle, and time utilization. Psychological factors include personality, class consciousness, attitudes, perceived risk, and the importance of a purchase. As with demographics, a retailer can generate a life-style profile of its target market by analyzing these concepts.

   When a retailer gears its strategy toward satisfying consumer needs, that firm is appealing to their motives—the reasons for behavior. The better a company addresses the needs of its customers, the more likely they are to make purchases.

3. *To examine the consumer decision process and its stages* Retailers require a knowledge of consumer behavior—the process whereby individuals decide whether, what, when, where, how, from whom, and how often to purchase goods and services. The consumer decision process has six basic steps: stimulus, problem awareness, information search, evaluation of alternatives, purchase, and post-purchase behavior. The process is influenced by a person's background and traits.

   A stimulus may be a social or commercial cue or a physical drive meant to motivate a person to act. At problem awareness, the consumer not only has been aroused by a stimulus, but further recognizes that the good or service under consideration may solve a problem of shortage or unfulfilled desire. Next, an information search determines the available alternatives and the characteristics of each. The alternatives are then evaluated and ranked. In the purchase act, a consumer considers the place of purchase, terms, and availability. After a purchase is made, there may be post-purchase behavior in the form of additional purchases or re-evaluation. The consumer may have cognitive dissonance if there is doubt that a correct choice has been made.

4. *To differentiate among different types of consumer decision making* Every time a consumer makes a purchase, he or she uses a form of the decision process. However, the process may be used subconsciously, and it is affected by consumer characteristics. Extended decision making occurs when a person makes full use of the six steps in the decision process. In limited decision making, each of the steps in the process is used, but not in great depth. Routine decision making takes place when a person buys out of habit and skips steps in the purchase process.

5. *To present the findings of several studies on consumer characteristics and behavior* Retail research findings provide insights into various aspects of consumer demographics, life-styles, and decision making, such as shopper profiles, in-home shopping, outshopping, information search, impulse purchases, and store loyalty.

KEY TERMS

target market (p. 188)
demographics (p. 188)
life-styles (p. 188)
household (p. 189)
family (p. 189)
discretionary income (p. 189)
culture (p. 192)
social class (p. 192)
reference groups (p. 192)
social performance (p. 193)
family life cycle (p. 193)
household life cycle (p. 193)
time utilization (p. 193)
personality (p. 194)
class consciousness (p. 194)
attitudes (opinions) (p. 194)
perceived risk (p. 194)
importance of the purchase (p. 196)
outshopping (p. 200)
motives (p. 201)
consumer behavior (p. 202)
consumer decision process (p. 202)
stimulus (p. 203)
social cue (p. 203)
commercial cue (p. 203)
physical drive (p. 204)
problem awareness (p. 204)

recognition of shortage (p. 204)
recognition of unfulfilled desire (p. 205)
information search (p. 205)
evaluation of alternatives (p. 207)
purchase act (p. 208)
post-purchase behavior (p. 210)
cognitive dissonance (p. 210)
extended decision making (p. 211)
limited decision making (p. 211)
routine decision making (p. 212)
mapping (p. 216)
impulse purchases (p. 216)
store loyalty (p. 216)

Questions for Discussion

1. Comment on this statement: "Retailers have long depended on their ability to size up people when they walk in the door. Today, you need a more systematic way to understand your customers."
2. Contrast the mass-market approach used by a supermarket with the market-segment approach used by a bakery featuring expensive pastries and breads. Could a retailer combine these two approaches? If so, how?
3. Describe how a national fast-food chain could use the demographic information presented in the chapter.
4. Develop demographic profiles for two different market segments to which a stationery store could appeal.
5. Contrast the family life-cycle concept with the household life-cycle concept. What is the value of each?
6. Explain how a retailer selling do-it-yourself furniture (with pre-cut wood) could reduce the six types of perceived risk.
7. Distinguish between in-home shopping and out-shopping. In each case, what should be the strategic emphasis of retailers?
8. What could a retailer learn from studying the consumer decision process?
9. Describe how the consumer decision process would operate for the following goods and services:
   a. Word-processing software.
   b. A fitness center.
   c. A new car.
   d. A portable CD player.
10. For each item cited in Question 9, which elements of the decision process are most important to retailers? Develop appropriate strategies.
11. What criteria could a consumer use in deciding which drugstore to patronize? How would these criteria differ by market segment?
12. Why should a real-estate broker care whether its clients have cognitive dissonance? The seller moves after the transaction and the buyer will not be in the market for another house again until a great many years have elapsed.
13. Differentiate among the three types of impulse purchases. Give an example of each.
14. How does store loyalty benefit both the retailer and the consumer?

CASE 1
Personal Cleansing: Cleaning Up on a Changing Category*

Although supermarkets sell approximately 65 per cent of bar soap in the United States, they have been losing market share for 25 years. Since 1970 (when virtually all bar-soap sales were made in supermarkets), mass merchants, drug chains, and membership clubs have steadily increased their market share at the expense of supermarkets. Analysts predict that supermarkets' market share will drop still further—to 60 per cent. According to *Progressive Grocer's* "Sales Manual/Data-Bank," supermarket sales of bar soap declined by 1.9 per cent between 1991 and 1992; and the total volume for bar soap sold through supermarkets was $758 million in 1992. Many retail experts attribute the supermarkets' loss of market share of bar soap to their failure to understand and react to important changes by people buying soap.

There are five basic segments to the soap market: super cleaning (40 per cent of the total market), basic cleaning (26 per cent), cosmetic and skin improvement (21 per cent), liquid soap (10 per cent), and all others (3 per cent). Supermarket category managers need to be cognizant of each of these five segments and their respective market size in ordering soap, allocating shelf space to each segment, and placing soap in the store. For example, many final consumers are likely to view cosmetic and skin improvement-style soap as more of a cosmetic than a soap and detergent product. Thus, a more appropriate display area for this soap product would be in the health-and-beauty section, near facial creams, rather than in the traditional hand soap area.

Even though the overall sales of basic bar soaps (the basic cleaning segment) account for 2.5 times the sales of liquid soap, the supermarket sales pattern for these two product categories differs. According to *Progressive Grocer* data, bar soap outsells liquid soap in supermarkets by a ratio of 5.4 to 1. Retail analysts can interpret this data two ways. The first suggests that supermarket customers are more apt to purchase bar soap than shoppers in other retail stores. The second implies that supermarkets have not effectively marketed liquid soap products.

Some retail experts have been critical of the ways in which supermarkets marketed soap in the past. According to these experts, the "buy three, get one free" promotion has been particularly overused. With this promotion, supermarkets receive special pricing allowances from soap manufacturers when the supermarkets purchase deal packs with four bars of soap attached in a common outer package. By passing on the cost savings to final consumers, supermarkets are able to offer the equivalent of a free soap bar for each three bars purchased.

These promotions were very successful originally, when used for only one brand at a time. They encouraged shoppers to engage in long-term usage of a brand, which often led to brand loyalty. The promotions also had the effect of "mother loading"—the large household inventory of soap (several weeks' supply) made members less susceptible to promotions from competing brands. Yet, the effectiveness of the promotions fell as additional soap manufacturers began to use them (the strategy lost its uniqueness) and as manufacturers overused the tactic (which caused consumers to refuse to purchase brands at nonsale prices as they expected the brands to always be on sale).

To effectively sell soap in its full-line discount stores, Target now carries soap in club-size packs. It stocks soap at the beginning of the health-and-beauty-aids section, where it has the most exposure to consumers. To ensure an adequate selection of leading brands, sizes, and market segments, Target handles 90 different varieties of soap (including liquid and bar soaps) in its stores. Target makes it easy to find particular brands and sizes of soap by using multiple shelf facings (placing two or more identical sizes of a particular soap next to each other) for popular sizes and brands.

* The material in this case is drawn from Glenn Snyder, "HBA Beefs Up for Battle," *Progressive Grocer* (June 1992), pp. 21–25; and "Sales Manual Databank: Soaps and Detergents," *Progressive Grocer* (July 1993), p. 114.

As a result, one-half of Target stores have 24 linear feet of shelf space devoted to soap. To increase consumer interest in soap, Target is constantly looking for new soap products (like liquid soap refills packaged in plastic pouches) and good promotions from soap manufacturers.

These are among the suggestions that have been made to increase the sales of soap in supermarkets:

- Treat soap as a core category.
- Devote sufficient shelf space to growing segments of the soap market.
- Aggressively merchandise new soap items.
- Review the distribution of "price-based" brands.
- Place soaps of the same brand name in adjacent positions.
- Use year-round soap displays.

QUESTIONS

1. How would supermarkets benefit by better understanding the five basic segments of the soap market?
2. Explain how the consumer decision process can be applied to the purchase of a cosmetic and skin improvement soap in a supermarket.
3. What types of soap products can be most effectively sold in a supermarket? Explain your answer using the extended, limited, and routine decision making processes.
4. How could a supermarket increase its impulse sales of liquid soap? Develop specific strategies using the concepts of completely unplanned, partially unplanned, and unplanned substitution.

VIDEO QUESTIONS ON PERSONAL CLEANSING

1. Discuss the new developments in packaging that have increased sales of soap at supermarkets.
2. Some consumers position soap as a health-and-beauty-care item. How can a conventional supermarket best merchandise soap to these people?

CASE 2

Profiling Catalog Shoppers[†]

Many studies have looked into the relationship between people's shopping orientations and shopper decision-making styles; but, few have examined nonstore shopping behavior. This case reports on a major study on mail-order catalog shopping, involving nearly 1,500 U.S. female heads of households. The survey participants were similar to the U.S. population in terms of age, marital status, employment, income, and education.

Respondents were asked to report on several apparel-catalog attribute ratings and their purchase histories, catalog and store shopping patterns, life-styles, and demographic data. Catalog transaction information from the prior twelve months was used to compile respondents' purchase histories and to classify them as either repeaters or switchers. Respondents were defined as repeaters if they bought more than one-half of their items from the same catalog, regardless of sequence. In contrast, switchers purchased more than one-half of their items from different catalogs, regardless of sequence.

The study also grouped people by decision-making styles. An inventory of styles was devised using eight attributes of decision making: high quality consciousness, brand consciousness, novelty fashion consciousness, hedonistic shopping consciousness, price and value shopping consciousness, impulsiveness, confusion from overchoice, and brand-loyalty orientations.

Here are the major findings of the study:

- Within the prior year, 30.7 per cent of the respondents did not buy an item from an apparel catalog, 28.4 per cent made one or two purchases, and 40.9 per cent made three or more purchases.
- On average, the women who ordered apparel had significantly higher household incomes than nonbuyers.
- Catalog shoppers were more likely to be young to middle-aged, employed, and married.
- No relationship was present between a consumer's education and her frequency of ordering apparel.
- Repeaters represented 36.5 per cent of those who purchased three or more items in the prior year; switchers accounted for 63.5 per cent. In general, repeaters purchased less frequently than switchers, were older, and were more likely to be married. There was no significant difference between repeaters and switchers on household income and education.
- Six shopper profiles were developed for the segment that purchased three or more apparel items from the catalogs in the prior year: loyalist shoppers, value shoppers, fashionable shoppers, diverse shoppers, recreational shoppers, and emotional shoppers. The characteristics of each of these groups and their relative size are described in Table 1. Overall, switchers were more represented in the fashionable, value, and diverse segments. Repeaters were more apt to be in the loyalist shopper segment. See Table 2.
- The best predictors of repeat buying behavior among the seven variables reviewed (age, income, education, employment, marital status, purchasing frequency, and decision-making style segment) were decision-making style segment, marital status, age, and purchasing frequency. Fashionable and value shoppers were greater switchers than loyalist shoppers. Being married was associated with repeat behavior. Older women were more likely to be repeaters. Less frequent purchases was predictive of repeat behavior.

[†] The material in this case is drawn from William J. McDonald, "The Roles of Demographics, Purchase Histories, and Shopper Decision-Making Styles in Predicting Consumer Catalog Loyalty," *Journal of Direct Marketing*, Vol. 7 (Summer 1993), pp. 55–65.

Table 1 Decision-Making Styles for Heavy Catalog Shoppers of Apparel (611 Respondents)

Decision-Making Style	Description/Size
Loyalist shoppers	Have the greatest scores on loyalty due to their interest in repeatedly buying from the same catalog. This group also outscores most other segments on the quality and image styles. (14.7 per cent of heavy catalog shoppers)
Value shoppers	Have the highest score on value because they are most interested in getting the best combination of price and quality. This group is the least image-oriented segment. (31.1 per cent of heavy catalog shoppers)
Fashionable shoppers	Have the highest score on fashion due to their interest in the latest clothing and the variety of apparel. This group is image-oriented, emotional, and confused, but less concerned with quality and value. (18.2 per cent of heavy catalog shoppers)
Diverse shoppers	The most difficult segment to categorize because it does not have any outstanding or dominant style. There are low scores on quality and high scores on recreation. (16 per cent of heavy catalog shoppers)
Recreational shoppers	Have the greatest interest in the fun and enjoyable activity aspects of apparel catalog shopping. Less quality- and value-oriented than some other segments. (15.5 per cent of heavy catalog shoppers)
Emotional shoppers	Have the highest scores on the emotional and confused styles. This segment is less systematic and more impulsive in its approach to shopping; it is more disoriented and uncertain about available choices. It is more image- and fashion-oriented than many other segments. (4.3 per cent of heavy catalog shoppers)

Note: The percentages do not equal 100.0 due to small rounding errors.

Table 2 The Relationship Between Decision-Making Style and Repeaters/Switchers for Heavy Catalog Shoppers of Apparel

Decision-Making Style	Per Cent of All Heavy Shoppers (n = 1,494)	Per Cent Repeaters (n = 223)	Per Cent Switchers (n = 388)
Loyalist shoppers	14.3	37.7	1.5
Value shoppers	26.2	23.8	35.6
Fashionable shoppers	17.6	7.2	24.5
Diverse shoppers	18.1	12.1	18.3
Recreational shoppers	17.1	14.3	16.2
Emotional shoppers	6.6	4.9	3.9
Total shoppers	99.9[a]	100.0	100.0

[a] Rounding error.

A mathematical model based upon these findings correctly classified 78.9 per cent of total regular catalog shoppers (in terms of their repeater/ switcher behavior). The model correctly classified 58.3 per cent of the repeaters and 90.7 per cent of the switchers.

QUESTIONS

1. How can a catalog-based retailer use the findings of this study that relate to shoppers' decision-making styles?
2. How can a catalog-based retailer use the findings of this study that relate to repeat buying behavior?
3. What other factors could be used to explain repeat catalog shoppers' buying behavior? Explain your answer.
4. Could the findings on repeat buying behavior be applied to store-based retailers? Explain your answer.

Information Gathering and Processing in Retailing

❖ Chapter Objectives

1. To show why retailers should systematically collect and analyze information when developing and modifying their strategies
2. To examine the role of the retail information system, its components, and the recent advances in such systems
3. To describe the marketing research process: problem definition, secondary data search, generating primary data (if needed), data analysis, recommendations, and implementing findings
4. To discuss the characteristics and types of secondary data and primary data

In the past, retailers used their customer data bases as a means of contacting individual people or groups of people with standardized promotions. With newer data-base systems, retailers can now divide consumers into specific groups on the basis of differences in their purchase behavior, tailor specific promotions to customer buying habits, and pinpoint the success of particular promotions.

Marks & Spencer, Great Britain's largest retailer, has used its data-base system to learn that 30 per cent of its charge-card customers are wine drinkers and to gain valuable information on the wine vintages and price levels that specific segments of this group favor. Bloomingdale's data base has both demographics and past sales histories for its customers. This data base has been used for targeted promotions, such as special sales on men's shirts and accessories for customers who have recently purchased suits.

Although the newer data-base systems can be highly effective, they require a rather sophisticated retail information system—one that can add new customers, merge customer records from multiple sources, and organize customer purchase histories. Many modern information systems work with data from transactions involving the retailers' own credit cards; some also capture data based on general purpose credit-card and check transactions.

Unlike Marks & Spencer's and Bloomingdale's customer data bases, which are largely drawn from customer sales histories, Kay-Bee Toy Stores (a 1,200-store division of Melville Corporation) has used its retail information system to generate a data base of households that live within a 10-minute drive of a Kay-Bee store and have children aged four to 14. These households receive Kay-Bee's *GoodTimes* magazine, which has separate stories for adults and children—as well as coupon offers from manufacturers. According to a study by an outside marketing research firm, 59 per cent of the readers of *GoodTimes* have bought an advertised product and 63 per cent recall seeing an ad from the publication. Kay-Bee is currently looking for other data-base marketing programs. One project under development is a Spanish version of *GoodTimes* magazine for Hispanic areas, such as those around its Southern California stores.[1]

[1] Kevin Higgins, "Retailers Join Race to Data-Base Marketing, But Few Have Success," *Marketing News* (May 24, 1993), pp. 1, 6; and Junu Bryan Kim, "Data Bases Open Doors for Retailers," *Advertising Age* (February 15, 1993), p. 38.

Reprinted by permission of Melville Corporation.

Overview

Whether a retailer is developing a new strategy or modifying an existing one, information gathering and processing can be valuable. Such aspects of a retail strategy as the attributes and purchase behavior of current and potential customers, alternative store locations, store management and operations, goods and service offerings, pricing, and store image and promotion can be studied—so as to make the best possible strategic decisions. Illustrations of research in these and other areas are provided throughout this chapter.

Acting on the basis of good information reduces a retailer's chances of making wrong decisions. Without proper information, a firm's risk of weak performance is higher because it may act on the basis of too little knowledge or on knowledge gained nonsystematically. The extent of research activity should, to a large degree, be determined by the level of risk involved in a decision. For instance, there is considerable risk for a department store considering a new branch-store location. There is much less risk if a retailer is deciding whether a store should carry a new line of sweaters. In the branch-store location situation, several thousand dollars for research and many months of study may be necessary. In the case of ordering new sweaters, limited research may be sufficient.

Information gathering and processing should be conducted in an ongoing manner, yielding enough data for planning and control. Unless information is obtained on a regular basis, it may focus on short-run problems (crises), as opposed to the long-range strategy-planning needs of the retailer.

In this chapter, the shortcomings of nonsystematic research are noted. Then, the retail information system and the marketing research process (with an emphasis on secondary data and primary data) are discussed in detail.

Retail Strategies Based on Nonsystematic Research

Retailers are often tempted to rely on nonsystematic and/or incomplete ways of obtaining information in the development and evaluation of their strategies due to time constraints, cost constraints, and/or the lack of research skills. Here are examples of nonsystematic ways of information gathering and processing:

- The use of intuition (e.g., "My gut reaction is to order 100 dozen quartz watches and sell them for $50 each as Christmas gifts.")
- A continuation of what was done before (e.g., "I have never sold jewelry on credit. Why should I do so now?")
- The copying of a successful competitor's strategy (e.g., "Bloomingdale's has had great success with the sale of gourmet foods. We should stock and promote those products.")
- The development of a strategy after speaking to a few individuals about their perceptions (e.g., "My friends Bill and Mary feel that our prices are too high. We ought to lower them to improve sales and profits.")
- The assumption that past trends will continue into the future (e.g., "The wholesale prices of compact disc players have fallen 25 per cent in the last year. So, we can wait another six months to make a purchase and get a really low price. We can then underprice our competitors, who are buying now.")

Now, let us look at several decisions made by retailers that have not obtained information in a systematic way and analyze their strategic errors.

A movie theater charges $6 for tickets throughout the entire week. The manager cannot understand why attendance is poor during weekday afternoons. That manager feels because all patrons are seeing the same movie, prices should be the same for a Monday matinee as a Saturday evening show. Yet, by looking at data stored in the theater's retail information system, the manager would learn that attendance is much lower on Mondays than on Saturdays. This would indicate that because people prefer Saturday evening performances, they are willing to pay $6 to see a movie at that time. On the other hand, weekday customers have to be attracted, and a lower price is one means of doing so.

A toy store orders conservatively for the holiday season because the previous year's sales were poor. The store sells out two weeks before the peak of the season, and additional merchandise cannot be delivered to the store in time for holiday sale. The toy store uses a technique employed by many firms: incremental budgeting. Under that policy, a percentage is added to or subtracted from the prior year's budget to arrive at the present year's budget. In this case, the store owner assumed the previous year's poor sales would occur again. However, a survey of consumers would have revealed a new degree of optimism and an increased desire to give gifts. A research-based retailer would have planned its inventory accordingly.

A chain bookstore decides to open a new branch unit seventy miles from its closest current store. The decision is based on the growing population in the area and the present absence of an outlet there by the chain. After a year, the new store is doing only 40 per cent of its expected business. A subsequent study by the chain reveals that the store name (and image) was relatively unknown in the area and the choice of advertising media was incorrect. In planning the new branch, these two important factors were not researched.

A mail-order retailer is doing well with small appliances, portable TVs, and moderately priced cameras. The firm has developed a good reputation in its traditional product lines and attracted loyal customers. It wants to add other product lines to capitalize on its name and customer goodwill. However, recent expansion into furniture and stereo systems has yielded poor results because the firm did not first conduct research on the consumer behavior of mail-order customers: People will readily buy standard, branded merchandise through the mail; but they are reluctant to buy most furniture and stereos that way. The latter items must be experienced or tried out before a purchase.

A florist cuts the price of two-day-old flowers from $4 to $1 because they have a shorter life expectancy when purchased by customers; but they don't sell. The florist assumes bargain-hunting consumers will buy them as gifts or for floral arrangements. What the florist does not know (due to no research) is that people perceive the older flowers to be of very poor quality, color, and smell. The reduced price is actually too low and turns off customers!

The conclusion to be drawn from these examples is that nonsystematic and/or incomplete means of collecting and/or analyzing information can cause a retailer to enact an inappropriate strategy.

The Retail Information System

Data gathering and analysis should not be approached as a one-shot resolution of a single problem or issue. Thus, the gathering of useful information should be viewed as an ongoing, well-integrated process or system. A ***retail information system*** anticipates the information needs of retail managers; collects, organizes, and stores relevant data on a continuous basis; and directs the flow of information to the proper retail decision makers.

In the following subsections, these topics are covered: developing and using a retail information system, data-base management, and gathering information through the UPC and EDI.

DEVELOPING AND USING A RETAIL INFORMATION SYSTEM

Figure 7–1 presents a general retail information system. With such a system, a retailer begins by clearly stating its business philosophy and objectives. The philosophy and objectives are influenced by environmental factors (such as competitors, the economy, and government).

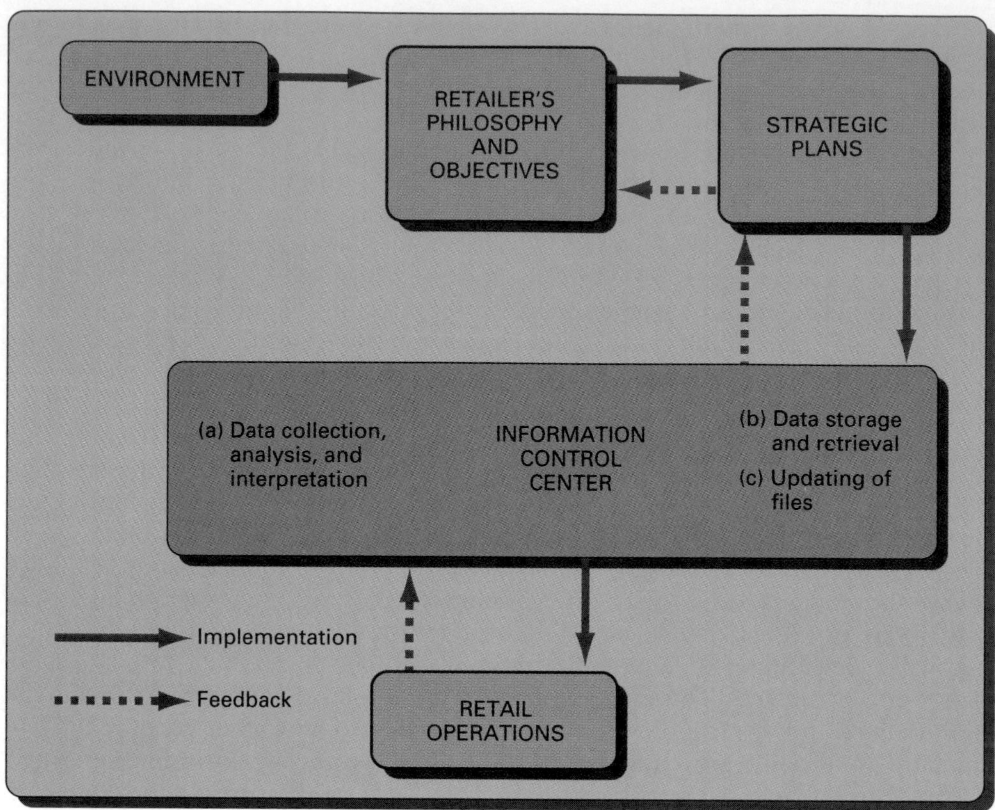

Figure 7–1
A Retail Information System

The retailer's philosophy and objectives provide very broad guidelines, which direct strategic planning. Some aspects of strategic plans are routine and, in the long run, may require little re-evaluation. Other aspects are nonroutine and will require careful evaluation each time they arise.

Once the retail strategy is outlined, the data needed to implement it are collected, analyzed, and interpreted. If the data are already available, they are retrieved from storage in the company's files. Each time new data are acquired, the files are updated. All of this takes place in the firm's information control center. Then, based on the data in the control center, decisions are made and put into operation.

After decisions are operationalized, performance results are fed back into the information control center and compared with pre-set standards. Data are retrieved from files, or further data are collected. Routine adjustments are implemented immediately. Regular reports and, when needed, exception reports (explanations of deviations from expected performance) are fed back to the appropriate managers. If needed, a retailer may have to react to performance results in a way that affects its overall philosophy or goals (like revising the firm's image if it is perceived as old-fashioned or sacrificing short-run profits to introduce a new, computerized checkout counter).

All types of information should be stored in the control center for future and ongoing use; and the control center should be integrated with the short- and long-run planning and operations of the company. Information should not be gathered sporadically and haphazardly, but systematically—consistent with management objectives, plans, and operations.

Having a retail information system offers several advantages. First, information collection is organized and broad (companywide) in perspective. Second, data are continuously collected and stored. Therefore, opportunities can be foreseen and crises avoided. Third, the elements of retail strategy can be coordinated. Fourth, new strategies can be developed more quickly. Fifth, quantitative results are obtainable, and cost-benefit analysis can be done. However, devising a retail information system may not be easy. It may require high initial time and labor investments. Complex decision making may be necessary to set up and follow through on such a system.

Recent studies of department stores, mass merchants, specialty stores, and supermarkets have found that retail information systems have these attributes:

- Retailers typically spend just less than one per cent of sales on their information systems efforts.
- Many firms have set up information systems departments.
- Formal, written annual plans are often produced for information systems departments.
- Microcomputers are used by most companies using information systems analysis.
- Substantial growth in the use of retail information systems is expected.
- There are many differences among retailers, on the basis of sales and type of stores operated.[2]

As computer technology has become more sophisticated and less expensive, greater numbers of retailers (of all types) have developed comprehensive information systems. For example, in 1978, only 200 supermarkets used computerized scanning systems; now, 25,000 supermarkets (90 per cent of all chains and 70 per cent of all independents) have installed such systems.[3] In the mid-1970s, most computerized systems were used only to reduce clerical cashier errors and improve inventory control. Today, computers often form the foundation for a retail information system and are involved in consumer surveys, ordering, transfers of merchandise between stores, and other diverse activities. Figure 7–2 shows just some of the capabilities of a computerized retail information system.

These are illustrations of how retailers are placing greater emphasis on computerizing their information systems. At Deb Shops, a 370-store apparel chain, "We pride ourselves on specific knowledge of the marketplace. Our point-of-sale merchandise data system provides detailed daily sales results from each store. This information is essential to merchandise managers, who are able to react immediately to consumer buying trends. Accurate decisions for purchasing and markdowns are vital to maintaining a competitive position in today's retail environment. Our data processing system also helps our merchandising personnel properly distribute goods and restock stores. We are continually investigating innovative new ways to complement and improve upon our current computer systems." Each Deb store has NCR 7052 DOS-based cash registers, which are polled nightly by Xcellenet's RemoteWare software via 9,600-baud UDS Motorola Fastalk modems. In-store data banks are regularly updated.[4] See Figure 7–3.

Over the past several years, Kmart has spent a total of $1+ billion on its information system. Half the outlays involve capital investments in new point-of-sale equipment and a satellite communications linkup among stores, and half involve labor costs, in-house software, and computer-processing support. With its system, Kmart can improve customer service, better detect trends and buying behavior, and make better decisions on prices, inventory levels, assortments, and advertising.[5]

At Dylex, Canada's biggest specialty retailer (with several leading men's and women's apparel chains), the information-systems department has a key role. This sums up the department's ongoing orientation:

> [We want] solid, reliable information from the day-to-day operations. That's the backbone that has to be there. Number two, turning the data into information

[2] "Ernst & Young's Survey of Retail Information Technology Expenses and Trends," *Chain Store Age Executive* (October 1993), Section 2; and "Retail Technology Investment: Toward a Brighter Future," *RIS News* (October 1993), special supplement.

[3] "60th Annual Report of the Grocery Industry," *Progressive Grocer* (April 1993), pp. 49, 80.

[4] *Deb Shops, Inc. 1992 Annual Report*, pp. 4–5; and "Not the Same Old Polling," *Chain Store Age Executive* (November 1992), pp. 86, 90.

[5] "The Technology That Drives Kmart," *Chain Store Age Executive* (June 1993), Section Two.

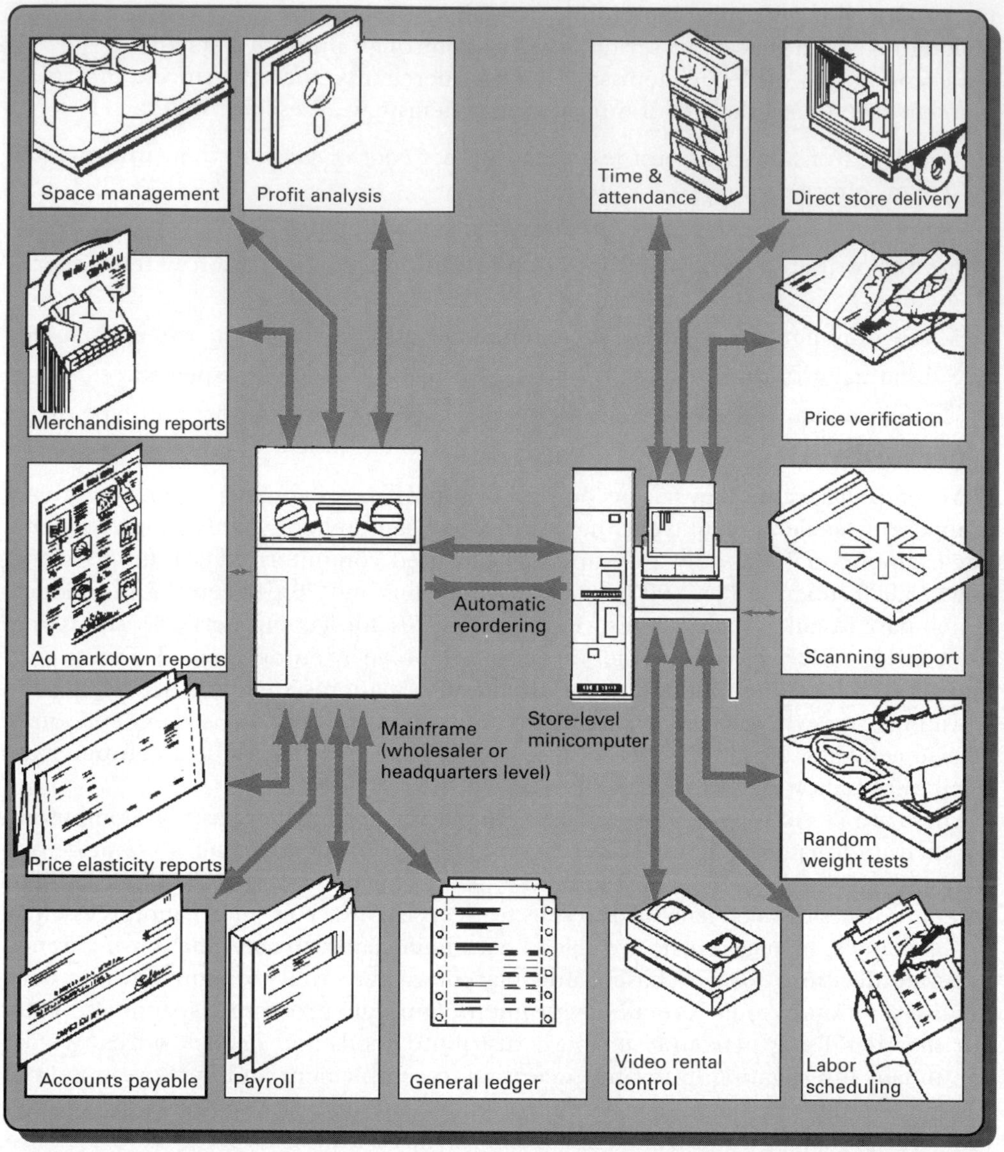

Space management
Profit analysis
Time &
attendance
Direct store delivery
Merchandising reports
Price verification
Ad markdown reports
Automatic
reordering
Scanning support
Mainframe
(wholesaler or
headquarters level)
Store-level
minicomputer
Price elasticity reports
Random
weight tests
Accounts payable
Payroll
General ledger
Video rental
control
Labor
scheduling

FIGURE 7–2
Selected Capabilities of a Computerized Retail Information System
Source: "The Capability of Computerization," *Progressive Grocer* (January 1987), p. 41. *Reprinted by permission.*

370 STORES
41 STATES
NCR 7052 POS
REGISTERS WITH
80-COLUMN PRINTERS
XCELLENET
CENTRAL SITE
SERVER
9,600 BAUD
UDS MODEMS
7 LINES
80486
RUNNING
OS/2
DECNET
3 CENTRAL SITE
DEC VAXs

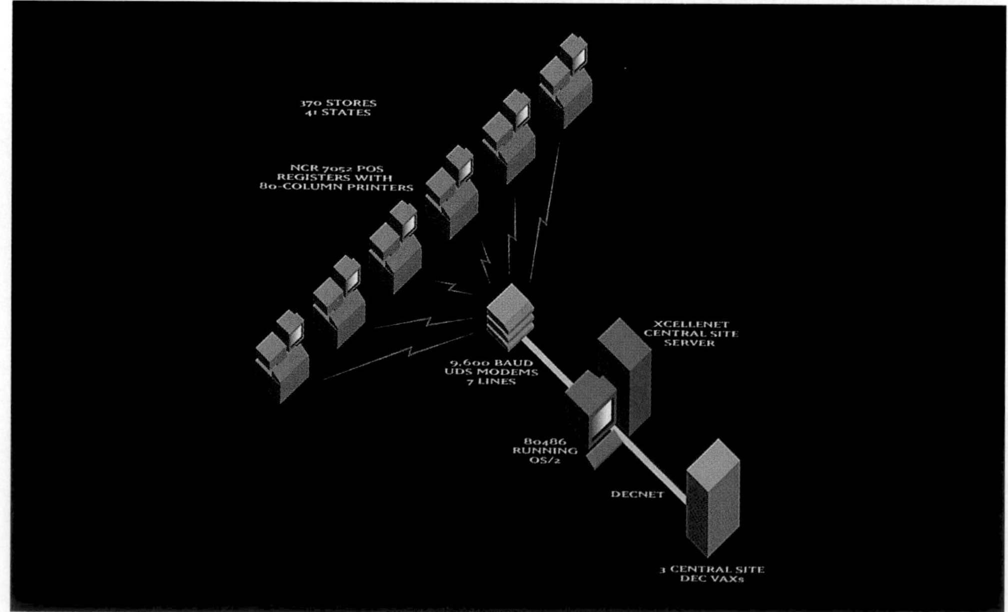

FIGURE 7–3
How Deb Stores Uses Xcellenet's RemoteWare for Its Retail Information System
Reprinted by permission of Xcellenet, Inc.

RETAILING AROUND THE WORLD

Are Information Systems the Key for Wal-Mart in Mexico?

Wal-Mart has established a joint venture with Cifra, a Mexican firm, to open a chain of membership clubs in Mexico. Due to Wal-Mart's long-term prowess, a major competitive advantage of the joint venture is the use of the Wal-Mart information system. The system, developed at an overall cost of more than $700 million, enables Wal-Mart to analyze sales performance and to control audio and digital programs for each store.

The sales performance of Wal-Mart's Mexican venture can be reviewed quarterly on a store-by-store basis by using information collected and kept over a 65-week period (five quarters). These data are utilized in inventory planning. For example, although the general merchandise carried in the Wal-Mart store near the Mexico City airport is similar to that in many U.S. locations, a large number of the products are Mexican-made (including both Mexican and American brand names). The sales analysis system lets Wal-Mart emphasize the appropriate product mix and minimize stockouts.

Wal-Mart's information system also controls the audio programming (such as music and in-store advertising) in each store by adapting the programming to reflect customer characteristics. And digital controls enable Wal-Mart to centrally control each store's temperature by regulating the heating and air conditioning.

Source: Based on material in Mary Ellen Kelly, "Wal-Mart's Kahn Advises Mexicans on Retailing Basics," *Discount Store News* (October 18, 1993), p. 12.

and providing easy access. Number three, which is really coupled with number two, the use of PCs. People should not be wasting time keying in data and regurgitating reports if it could be done in a better manner. Number four is development. We must be able to develop systems speedily. Number five: How do I keep the cost of the operation down?"[6]

Rite Aid drugstores did not have a comprehensive information system until 1982: "The chain had no POS network and clerks were checking out customers on electronic cash registers; the only data being collected were sales and department totals. Store personnel would manually record sales information on scanning documents that were mailed to the Harrisburg headquarters, where they were read by an optical scanner and fed into the mainframe. It was a paperwork jungle." Today, Rite Aid has a sophisticated store-based point-of-sale system providing detailed data on all phases of company operations.[7]

DATA-BASE MANAGEMENT

Data-base management is the procedure used to gather, integrate, apply, and store information related to specific subject areas. It is a key element in a retail information system and may be employed with customer data bases, vendor data bases, product-category data bases, and so on. For instance, a retailer may compile and store data on the characteristics and purchase behavior of customers, compute and save sales figures by vendor, and maintain historical records by product category. Each of these would represent a separate data base.

Federated Department Stores is one of the many retailers now placing more emphasis on data-base management, especially for its customer data base:

> Our primary function at the Financial and Credit Services group [which oversees Federated's total credit-card data base of 30 million customers] is to gather data, make sure it is the right data, and make sure that it is accurate. We have been capturing the data for many years, so we have a lot of data that up until the last couple of years was not used very effectively. It is now used much more

[6] Gary Robins, "Dylex's Norman Shaw: MIS Is Not Just an Expense," *Stores* (January 1991), pp. 112–114.

[7] "Hands Off, System On," *Chain Store Age Executive* (January 1986), pp. 94, 98; and *Rite Aid 1993 Annual Report.*

> effectively because we now know who buys, what their store of preference [within the Federated system] is, how often they buy, what their buying cycle is, and what it is they buy.
>
> When you know people's buying cycle, you can fairly accurately predict when they are about to buy the same merchandise again. You also know how they buy: some people just buy in the stores, some respond to the mail, others use the phone system. It is important to know where the customer buys. Then, we begin to segment the file to create buyer-behavior patterns and buyer preferences, and once you get it segmented—and we can segment it 75 to 100 different ways—the store marketing departments take over. Thus, if they want to send out a cosmetics catalog, they may request a list of the customers who buy cosmetics in our stores and then segment down to those who have bought in the last 12 months.[8]

Data-base information can come from internal and external sources. A retailer can develop its data bases internally by keeping detailed records and arranging them properly. To illustrate, a firm could generate data bases containing such information as this:

- By customer—frequency of purchases, goods and services bought, average purchase amount, demographic background, and typical method of payment.
- By vendor—total purchases by the retailer per time period, total sales to customers per time period, the most popular items, the retailer's profit margins, average delivery time, and quality of service.
- By product category—total category's sales per time period, each model's sales per time period, the retailer's profit margins, and the percentage of items sold at a discount.

There are also a number of companies that compile data bases and make them available (for a fee) to retailers. One such company is Donnelley Marketing, which has a data base called DQI²: "It consists of two comprehensive files. Information on more than 60 million households is gathered from 4,500+ phone directories. This information is merged with motor-vehicle registration data from over 35 states. The result is a data base with extensive information on length of residence, car ownership, etc.—89 million households and 150 million shoppers in all."[9]

With either internally- or externally-generated data bases, a retailer can identify opportunities and problems, and undertake the best actions (which may be customized due to the information provided by the data bases) to address them. The retailer must be sure its data bases are kept current, the privacy of customers and vendors is not violated, and the effectiveness of actions aimed at various data bases is regularly reviewed. As Williams-Sonoma, the home-products retailer, notes, "Our sophisticated systems—many of them unique to our firm—eliminate unprofitable names, cross-market all of our catalogs to promising customers, and target mail to specific geographic areas. At the same time, we are sensitive to our customers' privacy concerns and use manual, as well as computer-matching, methods to verify names and addresses and minimize duplicate mailings."[10]

GATHERING INFORMATION THROUGH THE UPC AND EDI

To gather and process data more efficiently for use in their information systems, a growing number of retailers now rely on the Universal Product Code (UPC) and electronic data interchange (EDI).

[8] James J. Amann, "FACS Boosts Marketing Power," *Stores* (December 1993), p. 42.

[9] *Donnelley Marketing Inc. Consumer Data Base DQI²* (Stamford, CT: Donnelley Marketing, 1993).

[10] *Williams-Sonoma 1992 Annual Report*, p. 9.

With the ***Universal Product Code (UPC)***, products (or tags attached to them) are marked with a series of thick and thin vertical lines, representing each item's identification code. UPC-A labeling—the preferred format—also includes numbers, as well as the lines. The vertical lines are "read" by optical scanning equipment at checkout counters. Cashiers do not have to enter transactions manually—although they can, if needed. Because the UPC is not readable by humans, the retailer or vendor must attach a ticket or sticker to every product specifying its size, color, and other information (if these data are not on the package or the product itself). Because the UPC does not include price information, this too must be added by a ticket or sticker.

By using UPC-based technology, retailers are able to record information instantaneously on a product's model number, size, color, and other factors when an item is sold, and to transmit the information to a computer that monitors unit sales, inventory levels, and other factors. Retailers' goals are to generate better merchandising data, improve inventory management and control, speed up transaction time, increase productivity, reduce clerical errors in processing transactions, and coordinate the flow of information. Over the years, UPC technology has substantially improved. Today, it is the accepted industry standard for both food retailers and general merchandise retailers (including specialty stores). Figure 7–4 illustrates how far UPC technology has come with regard to information gathering and processing.

Initially, the UPC was widely accepted by food retailers (due to their volume of routine transactions and the impact of this on inventory management) and not popular among general merchandise retailers. But according to one survey, of all mass merchandisers (such as Kmart and Wal-Mart), 87 per cent of traditional department stores, and 88 per cent of specialty stores indicated they were or shortly would be using UPC technology in their retail information systems. Among smaller general merchandise retailers, 63 per cent said they were committed to utilizing bar-coding technology.[11] The UPC is discussed further in Chapter 14 ("Financial Merchandise Management").

Through ***electronic data interchange (EDI)***, retailers and their suppliers regularly exchange information via their computers with regard to inventory levels, delivery times, unit sales, and so on, of particular items. As a result, both parties can enhance their decision-making capabilities, better control inventory levels, and be more responsive to consumer-demand trends. As the director of information systems at Pennsylvania's Boscov's Department Stores says:

> EDI is the only way to accomplish speedy communications on both the retailer and vendor ends and to avoid potential failure. Smart trading partners recognize this; they are putting aside their fear of automation or the notion that technology does not yield fast-enough payback and are abandoning paper-based ways of doing business.[12]

The use of the UPC greatly facilitates EDI. Accordingly, most retailers that are involved with UPC-based technology have also embraced some form of EDI with their suppliers. EDI is covered further in Chapter 12 ("Operations Management: Operational Dimensions").

The Marketing Research Process

Marketing research in retailing entails the collection and analysis of information relating to specific issues or problems facing a retailer. At farsighted firms, marketing research is just one element in a thorough retail information system. At other firms, marketing research may be the only type of information gathering and processing that is done.

The ***marketing research process*** embodies a series of activities: defining the issue or problem to be studied, examining secondary data, generating primary data (if

[11] "Retailer Commitment to EDI on the Upswing," *Chain Store Age Executive* (May 1990), p. 216.

[12] "Retail Technology Investment: Toward a Brighter Future," special supplement, p. 11.

FIGURE 7–4 State-of-the-Art Uses of UPC Technology

As this photo montage shows, Symbol Technologies has devised a host of scanning products (some of which are wireless) that make UPC data capture and processing quite simple. For example, Symbol products can be used at the point of sale to enter transaction data and transmit them to a central office, at product displays to verify shelf prices, at storage areas to aid in taking physical inventories, at receiving stations to log in the receipt of new merchandise, and at delivery points to track the movement of customer orders.
Reprinted by permission of Symbol Technologies.

needed), analyzing data, making recommendations, and implementing findings. It is not a single act. The use of this process will enable a retailer to conduct research systematically—rather than haphazardly—and to make better decisions.

Figure 7–5 outlines the research process. Note that each activity is conducted sequentially. For instance, secondary data cannot be examined until after the issue or problem is defined. The dashed line around the primary data stage means that these data need to be generated only when the secondary data search does not yield enough information to make a decision. The components of the research process are described next.

Issue (problem) definition involves a clear statement of the topic to be studied. What information does the retailer want to obtain in order to make a decision? With-

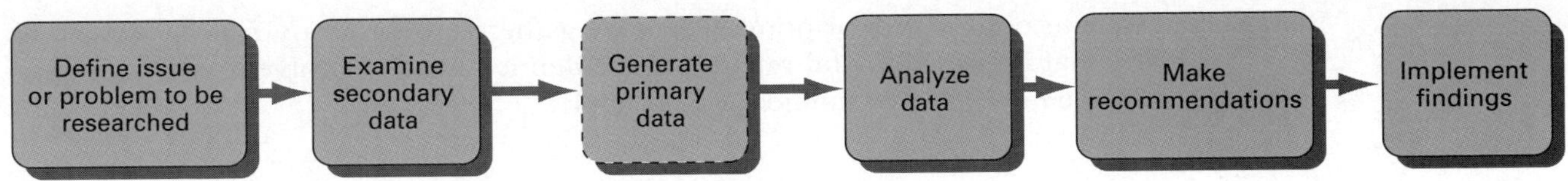

FIGURE 7–5 The Marketing Research Process in Retailing

out a clear understanding of the topic to be researched, potentially irrelevant and confusing data could be collected. Here are examples of issue (problem) definitions for a downtown shoe store:

1. "Of three potential new store locations, which should we choose?"
2. "What store hours should we keep?"
3. "How can we improve the sales of our men's shoes?"
4. "Why is our competitor doing well? How can we draw customers away from that store?"

It should be discerned from these examples that research issues (problems) may differ in nature. Whereas the first one relates to a comparison of three locations and is fairly structured, the third one is much more open-ended.

After the research issue (problem) has been defined, secondary data sources are examined. ***Secondary data*** are those that have been gathered for purposes other than addressing the issue or problem currently under study. Secondary data may be internal (such as company records) or external (such as government reports and trade publications). Secondary data are described in more depth in the next section.

Primary data are those collected to address the specific issue or problem under study. This type of data may be generated via surveys, observations, experiments, and simulation. Primary data are discussed more fully later in this chapter.

In some instances, secondary data are relied upon; in others, primary data are crucial. Other times, both are important. Three points are noteworthy. First, the diversity of possible data collection (types and costs) is great. Second, only data relevant to the problem or issue under investigation should be amassed. Third, as indicated earlier, primary data are usually acquired only if the secondary data search yields insufficient information (hence, the dashed box in Figure 7–5).

By gathering secondary and/or primary data, these kinds of information can be compiled for the shoe-store issues (problems) that were just stated:

Issue (Problem) Definition	Information Needed to Solve Issue (Problem)
1. Which store location?	1. Data on access to transportation, traffic, consumer profiles, rent, store size, and types of competition are gathered from government reports, trade publications, and observation by the owner for each of the three potential store locations.
2. What store hours?	2. Local ordinances for store hours are reviewed, as are the hours of neighboring and competing stores. Consumer attitudes are determined.
3. How to improve sales of shoes?	3. Store sales records for the past five years by product category are gathered. A consumer survey in a nearby mall is conducted.
4. How to draw consumers away from a competitor's store?	4. Extensive information about the competitor's strategy is gathered through observation. Consumers exiting the competitor's store are questioned outside.

After secondary and/or primary data are gathered, ***data analysis*** is performed to assess that information and relate it to the defined issue or problem. Alternative solutions are also clearly outlined. For example:

Issue (Problem) Definition	Alternative Solutions
1. Which store location?	1. Each location is ranked for all of the criteria (access to transportation, traffic, consumer profiles, rent, store size, and types of competition).
2. What store hours?	2. The advantages and disadvantages of different store hours are compared (in terms of increased sales and increased costs).
3. How to improve sales of shoes?	3. Alternative strategies to boost shoe sales are analyzed and ranked.
4. How to draw consumers away from a competitor's store?	4. The reasons for the competitor's success are studied, and possible reactions are listed.

Then, the advantages and disadvantages of each alternative are enumerated. See Table 7–1.

At this point, ***recommendations*** are made as to the strategy the retailer should enact to best address its issue or problem. Of the available options, which is best? Table 7–1 shows the recommendations for the shoe-store issues (problems) discussed throughout this section.

Last, but not least in importance, is the ***implementation*** of the recommended strategy. If research is to replace intuition in developing and enacting a retail strategy, a decision maker must follow the recommendations from research studies, even if they seem to contradict his or her own ideas.

Secondary Data

ADVANTAGES AND DISADVANTAGES

In the marketing research process, secondary data (information collected for other purposes) have several advantages over primary data. The assembly of data is inexpensive. Company records, trade journals, and government publications are all rather inexpensive to use. No data-collection forms, interviewers, and tabulations are needed.

Secondary data can be gathered quickly. Company or library records can be analyzed immediately, whereas the generation of primary data can take up to several months. And when a firm keeps past reports and other materials in its retail information system, secondary data are often stored in an easy-to-find and organized manner.

For many retailing issues (problems), several sources of secondary data are available. These allow a company to receive many perspectives and large quantities of data. With a primary study, limited data and only one perspective are obtained.

A secondary source may possess information the retailer would otherwise be unable to get. For example, government publications often have statistics no private company could acquire on its own. Furthermore, the data contained in government literature may be more honest and accurate than those a private company could collect.

When secondary data are assembled by a source such as *Progressive Grocer,* A.C. Nielsen, *Business Week,* or the federal government, the results are believable. Each of these sources has a high level of credibility and a reputation for thoroughness.

TABLE 7–1 Research-Based Recommendations

Issue (Problem)	Alternatives	Pros and Cons of Alternatives	Recommendation
1. Which store location?	Site A.	Best transportation, traffic, and consumer profiles. Highest rent. Smallest store space. Extensive competition.	Site A: the many advantages far outweigh the disadvantages.
	Site B.	Poorest transportation, traffic, and consumer profiles. Lowest rent. Largest store space. No competition.	
	Site C.	Intermediate on all criteria.	
2. What store hours?	9 A.M.–8 P.M.	Hours maintained by neighboring stores. Not early enough for customers. No legal violations.	7 A.M.–6 P.M.: satisfy customers and show results of informal survey to other merchants.
	7 A.M.–6 P.M.	Hours desired by customers Violation of voluntary retail dealers' agreement. No legal violations.	
3. How to improve sales of shoes?	Increased assortment.	Will attract and satisfy many more customers. High costs. High level of inventory. Reduces turnover for many items.	Lower prices and increase ads: additional customers offset higher costs and lower margins; combination best expands business.
	Drop some lines and specialize.	Will attract and satisfy a specific consumer market. Excludes many segments. Costs and inventory reduced.	
	Slightly reduce prices.	Unit sales increase. Markup and profit per item decline.	
	Advertise.	Will increase traffic and new customers. High costs.	
4. How to draw consumers away from a competitor's store?	Sharply reduce prices, increase inventories, add salespeople.	Similar to successful strategy of competitor. Will increase costs and appeal to a different consumer market (old customers may be lost). Imitation.	Modernize facilities and improve image: competitive advantages are kept and improved; poor strategy to imitate competitor and lose present customers.
	Modernize facilities and advertise high-quality image.	Retains old customers and attracts new ones with a distinctive image. Expensive and time-consuming.	

A retailer may often have only a rough idea of the topics it wants to investigate. In this instance, a search of secondary data may help that firm to define issues (problems) more specifically. In addition, background information about a given issue or problem can be gathered from secondary sources before a primary study is undertaken.

Although secondary data have many advantages, there are several potential disadvantages. Available data may not suit the purposes of the current study because they have been collected for other reasons. As an illustration, the units of measurement may be different. A retailer normally needs local demographic and other types of information. Yet, neighborhood statistics are rarely found in secondary sources (which typically contain federal, state, and city statistics). Data may also be categorized in an unusable fashion. For example, a service-station owner would be interested in the number of local citizens having cars. He or she would want this information broken down by year, model, and mileage driven, so as to stock parts. A motor-vehicle bureau could provide statistics on the models but not the mileage driven.

Secondary data may be dated. Because the information was assembled for another purpose, it may also have outlived its usefulness. Conclusions reached five or even two years ago may not be valid today. As an example, the *Census of Retail Trade* is conducted every five years. The last fully-published retail census is based on data gathered in 1987, and many statistics contained in that census are outdated. Furthermore, there is often a long time delay between the completion of a census and the release of that information to the public. Some of the data from the 1992 retail census are not scheduled for distribution until 1996.

The accuracy of secondary data must be evaluated. The retailer needs to decide whether data have been compiled in an unbiased, objective manner. Thus, the purpose of the original research, the data-collection techniques used, and the method of analysis should each be examined for bias—if they are available for review. This is especially important when the research was undertaken by a company that has a stake in the study's findings. The supporting evidence (raw data) should be read, as well as summary reports.

The source of secondary data can be a disadvantage, as well as an advantage. A partisan, profit-making company usually does not provide competitors with information that will hurt it. Generalities and omissions should be noted by the retailer. Also, some sources are known for their poor data-collection techniques, and they should be avoided. When conflicting data are found, it is important to distinguish among sources and select the one with the best reputation for accuracy. Conflicting results presented by equally accurate sources may lead a retailer into primary research (the collection of its own data).

Lastly, the reliability—the ability to replicate a study and get the same outcome—of secondary data is not always known. In retailing, many research projects are not retested; the user of secondary data may have to hope that the results from one narrow study are applicable to his or her firm.

Thus, a retailer desiring information to resolve an issue (problem) has many criteria to consider when contemplating the use of secondary data. In particular, low costs, speed, and access to materials must be weighed against improper fit, out-of-date statistics, and data accuracy.

Whether secondary data resolve the retailer's issue (problem) or not, their low cost and immediate availability require that primary data not be collected until after a thorough search of secondary data. Only if secondary data prove unsatisfactory or incomplete should primary data be collected.

A variety of secondary data sources for retailers are now detailed.

Sources

There are various sources and types of secondary data. The major distinctions are between internal and external sources. ***Internal secondary data*** are available within the company, sometimes from the data bank of a retail information system. ***External secondary data*** are available from sources outside the firm.

Internal Secondary Data

Before spending time and money searching for external secondary data or primary data, the retailer should look at the information that is available inside the company. Among the major sources of internal secondary data are budgets, sales reports, profit-and-loss statements, customer billing reports, inventory records, prior company research reports, and written reports on company performance.

At the beginning of the year, most retailers develop budgets for the next 12 months of that year. These budgets, based on sales forecasts, outline planned expenditures during the coming year. A firm's budget and its performance in attaining budgetary goals (adhering to the outlined plan of expenditures) are good sources for secondary data.

Retailers often use sales reports as indicators of performance. For many, this information is accurately and rapidly available via point-of-sale cash registers. By examining the sales of each store, department, item, and salesperson and comparing them with prior periods, a firm can get a sense of growth or contraction. But this feeling, and overdependence on sales data, may be misleading. Higher sales do not always mean higher profits. To be valuable, sales data should be used in conjunction with profit-and-loss statistics.

A retailer's profit-and-loss statements may provide a lot of information. If profit goals have been set, actual achievements can be measured against these goals. Trends in company success can be determined over time. Profits can be analyzed by store, department, item, and salesperson. A detailed breakdown of profits and losses can show strengths and weaknesses in operations and/or management and can lead to improvements.

Customer billing reports provide a host of information. A retailer could learn about inventory movement, sales made by different personnel, peak selling times, and sales volume. For credit customers, the retailer could examine sales by geographic area, outstanding debts, length of repayment time, and types of purchases made. Company invoices could show the retailer its own past purchase history and allow the firm to evaluate that performance against budgetary or other goals.

Inventory records show the levels of merchandise carried by a retailer throughout the year and the movement of this merchandise. Knowledge of the lead time needed to place and receive orders from suppliers and of the amounts of safety stock (excess merchandise kept on hand to prevent running out) held at different times during the year can aid in inventory planning. These are valuable sources of secondary data.

If a retailer conducts primary research, the resultant report should be retained for future use (hopefully in the information control center of a retail information system). When a research report is used initially, it involves primary data. However, later reference to that report is secondary in nature (because the report is no longer being used for its "primary" purpose). A detailed report should have some validity in the future unless conditions change drastically, although the datedness of the report must be noted.

Written reports on company performance are another source of internal secondary data. The reports may be composed by senior executives, buyers, sales personnel, or stockroom workers. For example, sales personnel turnover and customer responses to in-store displays are the kinds of information available through written reports. With proper direction, all phases of retail management can be improved via formal report procedures.

External Secondary Data

After checking internal sources, a retailer should consult external secondary data sources—if the internal information is not sufficient for a decision to be made regarding the defined issue (problem). External secondary data sources are comprised of government and nongovernment categories.

To use either source of external secondary data properly, one should be familiar with the appropriate reference guides. Such guides contain listings of written (sometimes computer-based) materials for a specified time. These listings are usually by subject or topic heading. Here are several reference guides (including computerized data bases), chosen because of their retailing importance. They are available in any business library or other large library:

- *ABI/INFORM* (data base). Covers hundreds of journals in business/management. Articles are indexed, classified by subject and abstracted.
- *Business Index*. Monthly. Completely indexes hundreds of periodicals, including newspapers. Selectively indexes another 1,100 periodicals.

- *Business Periodicals Index.* Monthly, except for July. Cumulations quarterly, semiannually, and annually. Subject index of hundreds of English language periodicals.
- *Census Catalog and Guide* (Washington, D.C.: U.S. Bureau of the Census). Cites the programs and services of the Census Bureau. Lists reports, diskettes, microfiche, and maps.
- *Dialog Information Retrieval Service* (data base). Contains hundreds of data bases covering a wide variety of disciplines. Information on public companies, economic data, financial news, and business news.
- *Predicasts F&S Index: Europe.* Monthly, with quarterly and annual cumulations. Covers industries and companies.
- *Predicasts F&S Index: International.* Monthly, with quarterly and annual cumulations. Covers industries and companies.
- *Predicasts F&S Index: United States.* Weekly, with monthly, quarterly, and annual cumulations. Covers industries and companies.
- *Wall Street Journal Index.* Monthly, with quarterly and annual cumulations.

The government distributes a wide range of statistics and written materials. Here are several publications, chosen because of their retailing importance. They are available in any business library or other large library:

- *Census of Retail Trade.* Every five years ending in 2 and 7. Detailed statistics by store classification and metropolitan region. Data include multiple ownership, employment, goods/service categories, and sales.
- *Census of Service Industries.* Every five years ending in 2 and 7. Similar to *Census of Retail Trade* but covers service industries organized by SIC code.
- *Combined Annual and Revised Monthly Retail Trade.* Compiled annually. Ten-year statistics on retail sales and retail inventories by kind of business for specified areas and cities.
- *Monthly Retail Trade.* Monthly. Survey of retail sales, inventories, and other data by kind of retail store.
- *Statistical Abstract* (Washington, D.C.: U.S. Superintendent of Documents, Government Printing Office). Annual. Detailed summary of U.S. statistics.
- *Survey of Current Business.* Monthly, with weekly supplements. On all aspects of business, as reported by the U.S. Department of Commerce.
- *Other.* Registration data (births, deaths, automobile registrations, etc.). Available through a variety of federal, state, and local agencies.

Government agencies, such as the Federal Trade Commission, also provide a variety of pamphlets and booklets on topics like franchising, unit pricing, deceptive advertising, and credit policies. The Small Business Administration helps smaller retailers, providing literature and managerial advice. Pamphlets and booklets are either distributed free of charge or sold for a nominal fee.

Nongovernment secondary data come from various sources, many of which are listed in reference guides. Four of the major sources of nongovernment data are regular periodicals; books, monographs, and other nonregular publications; other channel members; and commercial research houses. Table 7–2 contains a selected listing of these sources.

Regular periodicals are available in most libraries or via personal subscriptions. Some periodicals are quite broad in scope (like *Business Week* and *Fortune*) and discuss a great many business topics. Others have specialized coverage (like *Chain Store Age Executive* and *Stores*) and deal mostly with topics of concern to retailers. Solutions to retail problems can be found in both the broad and the narrow publications. It is

TABLE 7–2 Selected Sources of External Secondary Data: Nongovernment

Regular Periodicals

Advertising Age. Weekly, with applications to retailing.

American Demographics. Monthly, with articles on important population trends affecting retailers.

Business Week. Weekly, with articles on all phases of business.

Chain Store Age Executive. Monthly, focuses on chain store and shopping center information.

Dealerscope Merchandising. Monthly, with articles on appliance and electronics retailing.

Direct Marketing. Monthly, with articles on all aspects of the field.

Discount Store News. Biweekly, with articles on industry developments.

Drug Store News. Biweekly, with articles on current trends, health and beauty aids, and productivity statistics.

Fortune. Semimonthly, with articles on all phases of business.

Journal of the Academy of Marketing Science. Quarterly, with articles in all areas of marketing.

Journal of Advertising Research. Bimonthly, includes articles on advertising in retailing.

Journal of Consumer Marketing. Quarterly, with applied articles on all aspects of marketing.

Journal of Direct Marketing. Quarterly, with articles on all aspects of direct marketing.

Journal of Marketing. Quarterly, with articles in all areas of marketing.

Journal of Marketing Research. Quarterly, with articles on research developments in all areas of marketing.

Journal of Retailing. Quarterly, with articles on theories and developments in all aspects of retailing.

Journal of Services Marketing. Quarterly, with articles on all aspects of service marketing.

Marketing News. Biweekly, covers all aspects of marketing.

Progressive Grocer. Monthly, with emphasis on food retailing trends.

Restaurant Business. Eighteen times per year, covers developments in the restaurant field.

Retail Control. Bimonthly, with focus on credit, store security, and inventory management.

Sales & Marketing Management. Monthly, of interest to retailers: annual survey of buying power by county (based on income, retail sales, and population in each county).

Standard & Poor's Industry Surveys. Retailing Basic Analysis. Yearly (and periodic updates), with information on all aspects of retailing.

Stores. Monthly, with emphasis on department stores, specialty stores, and off-price retailing.

Supermarket Business. Monthly, with articles on supermarket retailing.

Supermarket News. Weekly, includes articles on market share, changes in markets, and financial data on the industry.

Wall Street Journal. Five times weekly, with articles on all aspects of business.

Women's Wear Daily. Five times weekly, with emphasis on fashion information.

Books, Monographs, and Other Nonregular Publications[a]

The following publish a variety of information pertaining to retailing:

Academy of Marketing Science.
American Collegiate Retailing Association.
American Management Association.
American Marketing Association.
Better Business Bureau.
Chamber of Commerce.
Conference Board.
Direct Marketing Association.
Food Marketing Institute.
International Association of Chain Stores.
International Council of Shopping Centers.
International Franchise Association.
International Mass Retail Association.
Marketing Science Institute.
National Retail Federation.
National Retail Furniture Association.
National Retail Hardware Association.
Point-of-Purchase Advertising Institute.
Radio Advertising Bureau.
Super Market Institute.

Other Channel Members

Advertising agencies.
Franchise operators.
Manufacturers.
Wholesalers.

Commercial Data[b]

More specialized information can be obtained from these research companies:

Audits & Surveys. Conducts physical audits of merchandise in stores.

Information Resources Inc. Gathers information via in-store scanning equipment and consumer household panels.

A.C. Nielsen. Conducts a Retail Index service. Continuous data on food, drug, cosmetic, tobacco, toiletry, and other products sold in food stores and drugstores.

R.L. Polk. Provides mailing lists and automobile registrations.

Standard Rate & Data Service. Collects information on advertising rates for various media. Consumer data include income, retail sales, etc.

[a] Many other sources can be found in any business library.

[b] This is a sampling of commercial researchers. Others may be found in the classified section of local telephone directories.

critical for readers of periodicals to know the differences in orientation and quality among various publications. These examples are intended to provide an overview of the diversity of information available in the periodic literature:

- Store location—Articles have appeared on computer-based models for site selection, location theories, small-town sites, the status of shopping centers, specialty shopping areas, and factory outlet centers.
- Operations—Articles have appeared on different management styles, customer-conscious employees, drug testing of employees, cost control, store remodeling, and shoplifting.
- Merchandising—Articles have appeared on the retail product mix, fads versus trends, the buyer's role, vendor selection, and inventory management.
- Pricing—Articles have appeared on consumers' use of information, price regulations, everyday low prices, discounts, one-price stores, pricing by direct marketers, and coping in a price-sensitive environment.
- Store image and promotion—Articles have appeared on how store image is developed, store atmosphere, the promotion mix, merchandise promotions, and customer service.
- Evaluating the strategy—Articles have appeared on company mergers, strategy execution, attaining goals, and competitive distinctiveness.

A number of organizations publish books, monographs, and other nonregular literature on retailing. Some are traditional publishers (like Prentice-Hall) that produce textbooks and practitioner-oriented books. Others, like the firms listed in Table 7–2, have distinct goals in publishing their materials.

One type of organization (such as the American Management Association and the American Marketing Association) distributes information in the hope of increasing the awareness and level of knowledge of its readers with regard to various topics. A second type (such as the Better Business Bureau and the Chamber of Commerce) is interested in improving the public's image of business and in expanding the role of industry self-regulation. These associations provide literature to familiarize firms with efficient and legal practices. A third type (such as the National Retail Federation and the Direct Marketing Association) describes current industry practices and emerging trends, and it also acts as a spokesperson and lobbyist in advocating the best interests of member firms. All of these organizations publish and distribute materials for moderate fees or free of charge (to members). Besides the associations cited in Table 7–2, others can be uncovered by consulting Gale's *Encyclopedia of Associations* in the library.

RETAILING IN ACTION

How Could Retailers Plan for the Weather?

Few retailers subscribe to independent weather services. For instance, Commercial Weather Services of Flint, Michigan, reports that its only retailer customer is Frank's Nursery & Crafts. That chain uses Commercial Weather Services' forecasts so that its weekend ads will reflect actual weather conditions. Weather Services Corporation of Bedford, Massachusetts, has only two retail clients: Macy's and TJX. Both firms use the weather reports to explain major differences between planned and actual sales.

There are a number of other potential uses for weather forecasts by retailers. A hardware chain could authorize the purchase of additional pumps for areas that anticipate flooding. An appliance chain could decide to sell its current inventory of air conditioners at reduced prices early in the season based upon reports of a cool summer. And many retailers could "de-weatherize" their historic sales patterns by incorporating actual weather conditions.

A new weather-forecasting company that might attract more retailer attention is Strategic Weather Services in Wayne, Pennsylvania. It claims to predict weather conditions 12 to 15 months in advance; and says its forecasts are 70 per cent accurate (defined as being within two degrees of actual temperatures in 15 major cities throughout North America).

Source: Based on material in Gary Robins, "Tracking Sales Climate," *Stores* (November 1993), pp. 52–54.

Retailers can often obtain information from channel members: advertising agencies, franchise operators, manufacturers, and wholesalers. Whenever any of these firms undertake research for their own purposes (such as determining the kind of advertising message that is most effective, what type of consumer is most likely to buy a particular product, or the sort of retailer the consumer will patronize in making a purchase) and then presents some or all of the findings to their retailers, external secondary data are involved. Channel members will pass along findings in order to enhance their sales and relations with retailers. They usually do not charge retailers for the information.

The last external secondary data source is the commercial research house that conducts ongoing studies and makes the results of those studies available to many clients for a fee. The fee can be quite low, or it can range into the thousands of dollars, depending on the complexity of the issue or problem examined. This type of research is secondary when the retailer acts as a subscriber and does not request specific studies pertaining only to itself.

Several large commercial houses specializing in secondary data for retailers are shown in Table 7–2. The firms provide a host of subscription services at much lower costs (and probably with greater expertise) than the retailer would incur if the data were collected only for its primary use.

Primary Data

ADVANTAGES AND DISADVANTAGES

After a firm has exhausted the available secondary data, its defined issue or problem may still not be resolved. In this instance, primary data (those collected to resolve the specific topic at hand) are necessary. In cases where secondary data research is sufficient, primary data are not collected.

There are several advantages associated with primary data. They are collected to fit the specific purposes of the retailer. The data are current. The units of measure and the data categories are designed to address the issue or problem under investigation. In addition, the retailer either collects the data itself or hires an outside party to do so. Thus, the source is known and controlled, and the methodology is constructed for the specific study. There are no conflicting data from different sources, and the reliability of the research can be determined, if desired. When secondary data do not resolve an issue or problem, primary data are the only alternative.

There are also several possible disadvantages often associated with primary data. They are normally more expensive to obtain than secondary data. The collection tends to be more time consuming. Some types of information cannot be acquired by an individual firm. If only primary data are collected, the perspective may be limited. Irrelevant information may be collected if the issue or problem is not stated specifically enough.

A retailer desiring information to resolve an issue or problem has many criteria to consider when evaluating the use of primary data. In particular, specificity, currentness, and reliability must be weighed against high costs, time, and limited access to materials. The benefits of primary research must be weighed against the limitations.

A variety of primary data sources for retailers are discussed next.

SOURCES

The first decision to be made in collecting primary data is who will undertake it. A retailer can gather the data itself (internal) or hire a research firm (external). Internal data collection is usually quicker and cheaper. External data collection is usually more objective and formalized.

Second, a sampling methodology would be specified. Instead of gathering data from all stores, all products, all customers, and so on, a retailer can obtain accurate information by studying a sample of stores, products, or customers. Sampling saves time and money.

FIGURE 7–6
Survey Research at Food Lion
At Food Lion, a leading supermarket chain, surveys are regularly used to obtain shopper feedback on customer service, product displays, and other topics. As shown here, company employees are often involved as interviewers.
Reprinted by permission.

There are two broad sampling approaches: probability (random) and nonprobability (nonrandom). In a ***probability (random) sample***, every store, product, or customer has an equal or known chance of being chosen for study. In a ***nonprobability sample***, stores, products, or customers are chosen by the researcher—based on judgment or convenience. A probability sample is more accurate but is also more costly and difficult to undertake. A further discussion of sampling is beyond the scope of this book.

Third, the retailer must choose among four basic types of primary data collection: survey, observation, experiment, and simulation. All of these methods are capable of generating data for each element of a retail strategy.

Survey

The ***survey*** is a research technique whereby information is systematically gathered from respondents by communicating with them. Surveys may be used in a variety of retail settings. For instance, Circuit City surveys 25,000+ customers each month to determine their satisfaction with each aspect of the selling process. Spiegel combines an in-house computer-assisted telephone interviewing system (CATI) with mail questionnaires, small-group personal surveys, and on-site shopper surveys (at its Eddie Bauer stores) to regularly determine customer tastes and needs. And Food Lion uses in-store surveys to find out how satisfied its customers are and what their attitudes are on various subjects.[13] See Figure 7–6.

A survey may be conducted in person, over the phone, or via the mail. In almost all cases, a questionnaire is used. A personal survey is face-to-face, flexible, and able to elicit lengthy responses; and any question ambiguity can be explained. It may be costly, and interviewer bias is possible (such as interviewers inadvertently suggesting ideas to respondents). A telephone survey is fast and relatively inexpensive. Yet, responses are usually short, and nonresponse may be a problem. It must be verified that the desired respondent is contacted. A mail survey can reach a wide range of respondents, has no interviewer bias, and is relatively inexpensive. Slowness of return, high nonresponse rates, and participation by incorrect respondents are the major potential problems. The technique chosen depends upon the objectives and the requirements of the research project.

It must also be decided whether a survey is nondisguised or disguised. In a ***nondisguised survey***, the respondent is told the real purpose of the study. Figure 7–7 shows how a nondisguised survey could be used to learn about shopper attitudes toward a particular specialty-store chain. With this survey, respondents (those answering ques-

[13] *Circuit City Stores Inc. 1993 Annual Report*; "Spiegel Keeps in Touch," *Stores* (October 1993), pp. 78–79; and *Food Lion 1993 Annual Report.*

Please indicate how you feel about each of the following statements describing Foot Locker shoe stores. For each statement, indicate your level of agreement or disagreement by checking the appropriate space. We are interested in your honest opinions about Foot Locker.

	Strongly agree	Agree	Neither agree nor disagree	Disagree	Strongly disagree
1. Foot Locker has a wide assortment of items.	___	___	___	___	___
2. The products carried are of high quality.	___	___	___	___	___
3. Foot Locker is very dependable.	___	___	___	___	___
4. The employees are quite helpful.	___	___	___	___	___
5. Prices are high.	___	___	___	___	___
6. Foot Locker is old-fashioned.	___	___	___	___	___
7. Returns are handled promptly and reliably.	___	___	___	___	___
8. The displays in the store are confusing.	___	___	___	___	___
9. Foot Locker is a friendly store.	___	___	___	___	___
10. When Foot Locker runs a sale, real bargains can be found.	___	___	___	___	___

FIGURE 7–7
An Attitudinal Survey for a Specialty-Store Chain

tions) are told the true purpose of the study, and a questionnaire is used to enter answers. In a ***disguised survey***, the respondent is not told the study's real purpose. Otherwise, the person may answer what he or she thinks a firm wants to hear. Disguised surveys may use word associations, sentence completions, cartoon analysis, and/or projective questions (such as "Do your friends like shopping at this store? Do they find the styles to be in fashion?").

The ***semantic differential***—a listing of bipolar adjective scales—is a survey technique that may be disguised or nondisguised, depending on whether the respondent is told the study's true purpose. The respondent is asked to rate one or more retailers on several criteria; each criterion is evaluated along a bipolar adjective scale, such as unfriendly-friendly or untidy-neat. By computing the average rating of all respondents for each criterion, an overall store profile can be developed. A semantic differential comparing two furniture retailers appears in Figure 7–8. Store A is a pres-

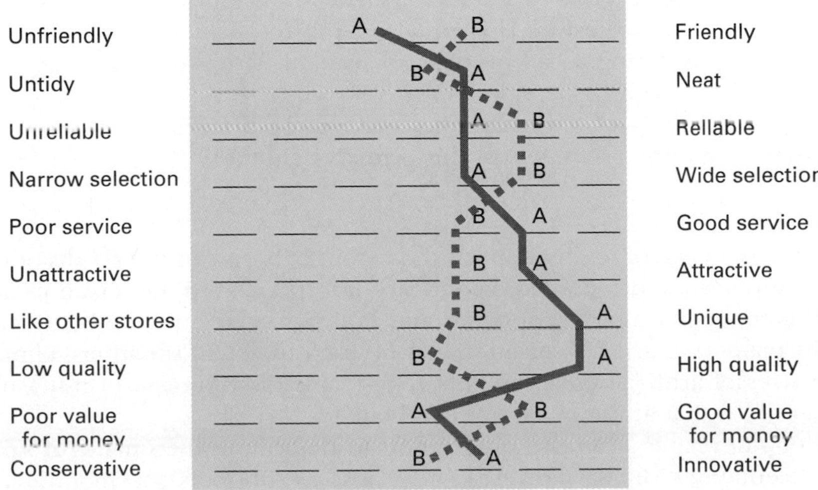

FIGURE 7–8
A Semantic Differential for Two Furniture Stores

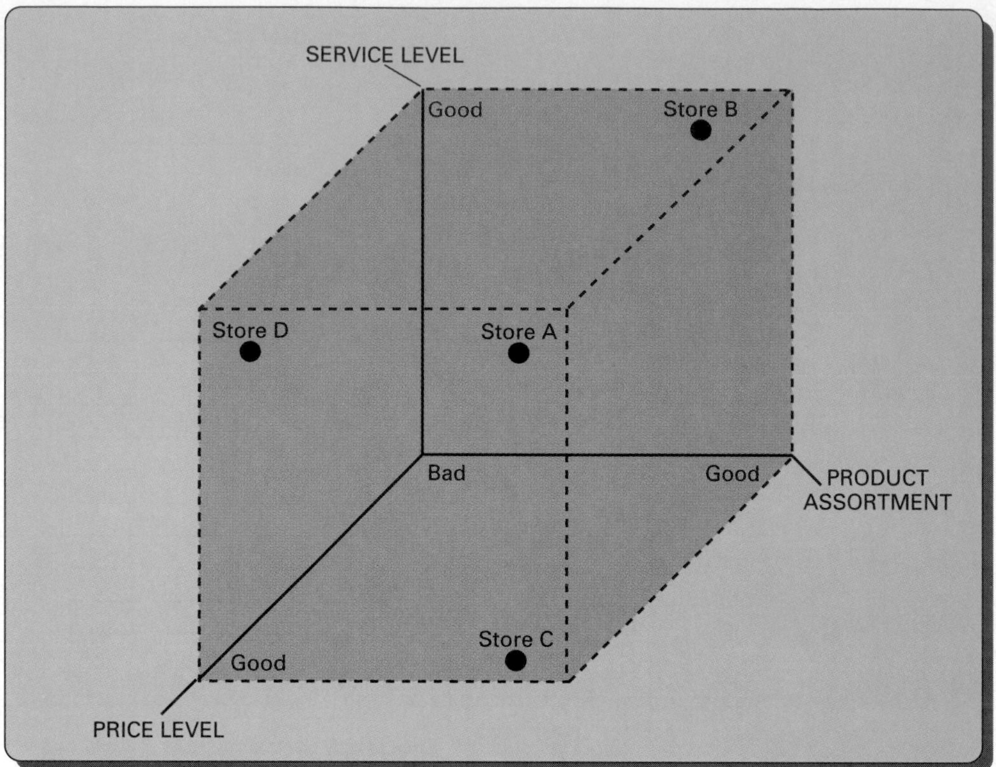

FIGURE 7–9
Multidimensional Scaling Applied to Drugstores

tige, high-quality store and Store B is a medium-quality, family-run store. The semantic differential reveals the overall images of the stores and graphically portrays them.

A survey-related tool gaining popularity is ***multidimensional scaling***, a technique by which attitudinal data are collected for several attributes in a manner that allows data analysis to produce a single overall rating of a retailer (rather than a profile of individual characteristics). A further description of the technique is beyond the scope of this text, but Figure 7–9 shows how multidimensional scaling can be used to construct single overall ratings. In this example, service level, product assortment, and price level are the criteria used to create profiles for four competing drugstores. These ratings reveal consumer perceptions by store, show the stores' strengths and weaknesses, and aid in strategy development and modification.

From Figure 7–9, these conclusions can be reached: Drugstore A is rated as good on all three criteria; it is the best-liked store. Drugstore B is equal to A in terms of service level and product assortment; it is viewed as having high (bad) prices. Drugstore C is equal to A in terms of product assortment and price level; it is viewed as providing bad service. Drugstore D is equal to A in terms of service level and price level; it is viewed as having a bad product assortment. Drugstores B, C, and D need to improve their strategies to compete with A.

Other types of survey-related techniques also can be utilized, but those described should demonstrate the usefulness of this primary-data tool.

Observation

Observation is a form of research in which present behavior or the results of past behavior are observed and recorded. People are not questioned. Observation may not require the cooperation of respondents, and interviewer or question biases are minimized. In many instances, observation can be used in actual situations, eliminating the influences of artificial environments. The major disadvantage of using observation (by itself) is that attitudes cannot be obtained.

For example, retailers can use observation to determine the quality of sales personnel presentations (by having researchers pose as shoppers), to monitor related-item buying by consumers, to determine store activity by time of day and day of week, to make pedestrian and vehicular traffic counts (to measure the potential of new locations), and to determine the proportion of shopping-center patrons using public transportation.[14]

When observation is utilized, decisions are necessary as to whether it should be natural or contrived, disguised or nondisguised, structured or unstructured, direct or indirect, and human or mechanical.

Natural observation occurs if a real, ongoing situation is involved—such as actual customers being viewed entering, shopping in, and/or leaving a store. Contrived observation takes place under more artificial conditions, such as observers posing as customers to determine a salesperson's "pitch" or "dummy" displays being set up to see shoppers' reactions.

In disguised observation, the shopper or company employee is not aware that he or she is being watched. A two-way mirror or hidden camera provides disguised observation. In nondisguised observation, the participant knows he or she is being observed—such as a department manager's observing the behavior of a cashier.

Structured observation calls for the observer to watch for and note specific behavior. Unstructured observation requires the observer to watch and note all actions performed by the person being studied, such as a researcher's watching the total in-store behavior of customers to determine the actions they take and the items they buy.

With direct observation, the observer watches the present behavior of people. With indirect observation, the observer examines evidence of past behavior. Food products in consumer pantries are examples of items that could be analyzed via indirect observation.

Human observation is carried out by people and is flexible. It may be disguised; but the observer may enter biased notations or interpretations and may miss behavior. Mechanical observation eliminates viewer bias and does not miss any behavior. A movie camera that films in-store consumer activity is an example of mechanical observation.

Experiment

An ***experiment*** is a type of research in which one or more elements of a retail strategy mix are manipulated under controlled conditions. An element may be, for example, an item's price, the layout of a department in a store, a shelf display, or store hours. In an experiment, just the element under investigation is manipulated; all others remain constant. For instance, if a retailer is interested in finding out the effects of a price change on a brand's unit sales, only the price of that brand is varied (such as making this week's price $0.99 and next week's $1.19, and then comparing unit sales for each week). The other elements of the retail strategy remain the same. This way, only the effect of the price change is measured.

An experiment may utilize survey or observation techniques to record data. In a survey, questions are asked about the experiment: Did you buy Brand Z because of its new shelf display? Are you buying extra ice cream because it's on sale? In observation, behavior is watched during the experiment: The revenues of Brand Z increase by 20 per cent when a new display is used. Ice cream sales go up by 25 per cent during a special sale.

Surveys and observations are experimental in nature if they take place under closely-controlled situations. But when surveys ask broad attitudinal questions or observations of unstructured behavior occur, experimental procedures are not involved. In a retail setting, an experiment can be hard to undertake since many factors beyond the command of the retailer (such as weather, competition, and the economy) may influence results. On the other hand, a well-controlled experiment can provide a lot of good, specific data.

[14] See Paco Underhill, "Store Snooping," *Marketing Management*, Vol. 2 (Number 1, 1993), pp. 6–7; and Michael J. McCarthy, "James Bond Hits the Supermarket: Stores Snoop on Shoppers' Habits to Boost Sales," *Wall Street Journal* (August 25, 1993), pp. B1, B5.

ETHICS IN RETAILING

How Can Mailing Lists Be Developed While Still Maintaining Consumer Privacy?

Everyone has opened his or her mailbox and taken out unsolicited catalogs, special promotions, and other unsolicited mail. The mailing lists for these items are usually developed from sources such as voter registration records, magazine subscriptions, and past purchases. Although some people like getting unsolicited mail, others view this as an invasion of their privacy. An area of particular concern involves the disclosure of consumers' purchase histories.

To protect people against unwanted solicitations, the Direct Marketing Association (DMA) began a Mail Preference Service (MPS) in 1971 and a Telephone Preference Service (TPS) in 1985. Under these programs, people who do not want to be solicited can request that their names be removed from firms' mail and telephone lists. People can also ask that organizations not rent or sell their names to other retailers. The DMA maintains and distributes the names of people who do not want unsolicited mail or phone calls to member firms. The DMA also recommends that direct marketers clearly state these options on their order forms and bill stuffers, as well as in their catalogs.

Because only large firms tend to participate in the MPS and TPS, people are unable to limit unsolicited mail and phone calls from local merchants, political candidates, charitable organizations, and others.

Sources: Based on material in *Privacy: The Key Issue of the 90's* (Washington, D.C.: Direct Marketing Association, 1993); and *How Did They Get My Name?* (New York, N.Y.: Direct Marketing Association, 1991).

The major advantage of an experiment lies in its ability to show cause and effect (for instance, a lower price equals higher sales). It is also systematically structured and implemented. The major potential disadvantages are high costs, contrived settings, and uncontrollable factors.

Simulation

A ***simulation*** is a type of experiment whereby a computer-based program is used to manipulate the elements of a retail strategy mix rather than test them in a real setting. Two types of simulations are now being employed in retail settings: those based on a mathematical model and those involved with "virtual reality."

For the first type of simulation, a mathematical model of the expected controllable and uncontrollable factors (and their interactions) facing the retailer is first constructed. These factors are then manipulated via a computer so their effects on the overall retail strategy and specific elements of it are learned. No consumer cooperation is needed, and many different factors and combinations of factors can be manipulated in a controlled, rapid, inexpensive, and relatively risk-free manner. This kind of simulation is becoming more popular for retailers because their level of mathematical and computer sophistication is rising and appropriate software is becoming available. However, it is still somewhat difficult to use.

For the second type of simulation, the retailer must devise or purchase interactive software that enables participants to simulate actual behavior in a format that is as realistic as possible. Here is an example (depicted in Figure 7–10) of the exciting possibilities via virtual-reality simulations:

> From virtual reality to virtually real shopping—but no less real marketing research on consumer behavior. That's what MarketWare Corp. believes it has captured in its new software, Visionary Shopper, for studying consumer behavior in retail stores. The system, which runs on PCs, allows consumers to stroll through store aisles on a computer screen, allowing examination of packages as though the shelf was really in front of them. Consumers are recruited through store and mall intercepts and given about five minutes' training on the software. MarketWare personnel then leave them alone to do their shopping so that they'll rely on themselves to "walk through" the virtual store aisles. The anonymity also helps boost real consumer responses to the variables being tested.

FIGURE 7–10
A Virtual-Reality Simulation
MarketWare Corporation's Visionary Shopper simulation, developed by Professor Raymond Burke of the Harvard Business School, enables participants to simulate an in-store shopping experience. Retailers can learn a great deal from the results of people's "shopping."
Reprinted by permission.

> The impact of a multitude of factors can be measured through the process, which for most brands and categories runs about 30 minutes per consumer. Using a track ball and touch-screen technology, participants can move around displays, "pick up" products, rotate them, zoom in and out, and place products in simulated shopping carts. They can react to shelf-layout changes or promotional and pricing considerations—all without setting foot in a store. Visionary Shopper keeps an electronic record of each consumer's movements, and compiles information on which products were looked at, which were purchased, and which were returned to shelves.[15]

It should be noted that, at present, there is limited software for virtual-reality simulations and people must be trained in how to use the software.

THE DATA COLLECTION ROLE OF RETAILERS IN A DISTRIBUTION CHANNEL

Retailers can have a key role in collecting primary data due to their position at the last stage in a distribution channel. Of all the firms in a channel, often only retailers have direct contact with and easy access to shoppers.

These are some of the ways in which retailers can assist other channel members in collecting primary data. They can

- Provide informal feedback on supplier prices, ads, and so on, based on their past experience.
- Allow data to be gathered on their premises. Many marketing-research firms seek to conduct interviews at shopping centers because a large and broad base of people is available.

[15] *Visionary Shopper Fact Sheet* (Norcross, GA: MarketWare, 1994); and Howard Schlossberg, "Shoppers Virtually Stroll Through Store Aisles to Examine Packages," *Marketing News* (June 7, 1993), p. 2.

- Gather specific information requested by suppliers, such as how shoppers are reacting to prescribed in-store displays.
- Pass along information on the characteristics of consumers purchasing particular brands, models, and so on. Because, for many retailers, credit transactions account for a significant portion of sales, these retailers can link purchases with consumer age, income, occupation, and other factors.
- Participate in single-source data collection by allowing their stores to have specially equipped computerized checkouts. In ***single-source data collection***, a research firm (like Information Resources Inc.) develops a sample of consumer households, determines the demographic and life-style backgrounds of those households via surveys, observes television viewing behavior via in-home cable hookups to the firm's computers, and monitors shopping behavior by having people make purchases in designated stores. At these stores, consumers present an identification card similar to a credit card; all items bought are then recorded by computerized scanning equipment. This system is more accurate than multisource data collection (whereby the people surveyed are often different from those whose behavior is observed). It is a relatively new and somewhat expensive way of amassing data, and it has thus far been mostly limited to purchases in supermarkets.

SUMMARY

1. *To show why retailers should systematically collect and analyze information when developing and modifying their strategies* Whether developing a new retail strategy or modifying an existing one, good information is necessary. Acting on the basis of proper information reduces a retailer's chances of making incorrect decisions. Retailers that rely on nonsystematic and/or incomplete methods of research, such as intuition, increase their probabilities of failure.

2. *To examine the role of the retail information system, its components, and the recent advances in such systems* Obtaining useful information should be viewed as an ongoing, well-integrated process. Thus, a retail information system anticipates the information needs of retail managers; continuously collects, organizes, and stores relevant data; and directs the flow of information to the proper retail decision makers. Such a system has several components: environment, retailer's philosophy, strategic plans, information control center, and retail operations. The most important component is the information control center. It directs data collection, stores and retrieves data, and updates files.

   Data-base management is the procedure used to collect, integrate, apply, and store information related to specific topics (such as customers, vendors, and product categories). Data-base information can come from internal—company generated—and external—purchased from outside firms—sources.

   In recent years, retailers have greatly increased their use of computerized retail information systems, and the Universal Product Code (UPC) has become the dominant technology for recording and processing product-related information. Through electronic data interchange (EDI), the computers of retailers and their suppliers regularly exchange information.

3. *To describe the marketing research process* Marketing research in retailing involves a process consisting of a series of activities: defining the issue or problem to be researched, examining secondary data, gathering primary data (if needed), analyzing the data, making recommendations, and implementing findings. It is systematic in nature and not a single act. The steps should be undertaken sequentially.

4. *To discuss the characteristics and types of secondary data and primary data* Secondary data (information gathered for other purposes) offer several advantages: they are inexpensive, can be collected quickly, may have several sources, and may provide otherwise unattainable information. Some sources are quite credible. And when the problem is ill defined, a secondary data search can clarify it. There are also a number of potential disadvantages to secondary data: they may not suit the purposes of the study; the units of measurement and the categories of data may not be specific enough; information may be dated and/or inaccurate; a source may be disreputable, and different sources may present conflicting results; and the data may not be reliable.

   Secondary data should always be consulted before primary data are obtained. Internal secondary data are available within the firm. External secondary data are available from government and nongovernment sources outside the company. Reference guides, regular periodicals, nonregular publications, channel members, and commercial research houses all provide external secondary data.

Primary data (those gathered for the resolution of the specific topic at hand) are collected when secondary data do not adequately address the issue or problem at hand. Primary data have several advantages: they are precise and current; the data are collected and categorized with the measures desired; the methodology is known; there are no conflicting results; and the level of reliability can be determined. When secondary data do not exist, primary data are the only alternative. The potential disadvantages of primary data are the costs, time, limited access, narrow perspective, and amassing of irrelevant information.

Primary research may be done internally or externally. Four types of primary data collection are available: survey (personal, telephone, or mail), observation (natural-contrived, human-mechanical), experiment, and simulation. Each technique has its own advantages and disadvantages.

Retailers often have a major role in collecting primary data because of their position at the final stage in a distribution channel. Retailers can provide informal feedback to suppliers, allow data to be gathered on their premises, assist in monitoring consumer behavior, pass along information on consumer characteristics, and participate in single-source data collection.

KEY TERMS

retail information system (p. 227)
data-base management (p. 231)
Universal Product Code (UPC) (p. 233)
electronic data interchange (EDI) (p. 233)
marketing research in retailing (p. 233)
marketing research process (p. 233)
issue (problem) definition (p. 234)
secondary data (p. 235)
primary data (p. 235)
data analysis (p. 236)
recommendations (p. 236)
implementation (p. 236)
internal secondary data (p. 238)
external secondary data (p. 238)
probability (random) sample (p. 244)
nonprobability sample (p. 244)
survey (p. 244)
nondisguised survey (p. 244)
disguised survey (p. 245)
semantic differential (p. 245)
multidimensional scaling (p. 246)
observation (p. 246)
experiment (p. 247)
simulation (p. 248)
single-source data collection (p. 250)

QUESTIONS FOR DISCUSSION

1. At the beginning of this chapter, several unsuccessful strategies were described. What types of information gathering and processing would you recommend for each of the retailers?
   a. Movie theater.
   b. Toy store.
   c. Chain bookstore.
   d. Mail-order retailer.
   e. Florist.
2. How could a small retailer devise a retail information system?
3. How could a small retailer develop and maintain a customer data base?
4. What are the value of the Universal Product Code (UPC) and electronic data interchange (EDI) with regard to the retail information systems of general merchandise retailers?
5. How do the terms *retail information system* and *marketing research in retailing* differ?
6. What are the steps in the marketing research process? May any of these steps be skipped? Why or why not?
7. Cite the major advantages and disadvantages of secondary data.
8. As an apparel-store owner, what kinds of secondary data would you want to obtain from Levi Strauss or Wrangler?
9. Under which circumstances should a retailer collect primary data?
10. Describe the major disadvantage of each method of gathering primary data: survey, observation, experiment, and simulation.
11. What are the benefits and risks of using disguised consumer surveys?
12. Develop a ten-item semantic differential for a local delicatessen to judge its image. Who should be surveyed? Why?
13. Under which circumstances should the following kinds of observation be used?
    a. Contrived.
    b. Nondisguised.
    c. Structured.
    d. Direct.
14. Discuss some of the potential problems a retailer could face in conducting an in-store display experiment.

CASE 1
Information Power at 7-Eleven Japan*

Although many analysts credit Wal-Mart with having the best information system in retailing, according to one expert, "no other retailer in the world has defined its business so tightly around information" as 7-Eleven Japan. Through its parent company, Ito-Yokado, 7-Eleven Japan owns 64 per cent of Southland Corporation, the worldwide franchisor and operator of convenience stores. In Japan, 97 per cent of the 5,100 7-Eleven stores are operated by franchisees, with the rest owned by 7-Eleven Japan.

The average 7-Eleven store in Japan is just 1,080 square feet in size, less than one-half of the size of a typical U.S. 7-Eleven store. Each Japanese 7-Eleven store has its point-of-sales register directly linked to a NEC personal computer that is custom-made for 7-Eleven Japan. Besides entering sales data, clerks are trained to key in such information as the customer's gender and approximate age. This allows every store to track specific purchases by target market group and time of day.

A good retail information system is especially critical in Japan. The small store size means that each outlet must receive multiple deliveries per day or face stockouts. And because Japanese consumers are quite concerned with freshness, all 7-Eleven Japan stores electronically send orders to their vendors less than five hours prior to actual delivery times. The retail information system also lets 7-Eleven shift the storage function to suppliers. This not only eliminates the need for costly distribution centers, but reduces the number of daily deliveries per store.

Because most of 7-Eleven Japan's franchisees are former mom-and-pop store owners, the retail information system is easy-to-use. Many of the analyses can be conducted by pressing a single key; and brightly-colored graphics are used to indicate performance trends.

Here is how the 7-Eleven Japan information works at one company-owned store in western Tokyo: The store manager uses his decentralized computer system to monitor the sales of the 3,000 items in his store. Sales information that is entered into the computer can be displayed in a graphical format by pressing a simplified keyboard. The store's PC system then shows what items sell best by time of day and by specific weather condition. For example, this store's retail information system has revealed that 72 per cent of shoppers are male, that several types of rice dishes are popular with male customers between 7 P.M. and 9 P.M., and that potato chips are an especially popular snack for children returning home from school. By pressing a certain button on the computer, the store manager can find out which of the 3,000 items are the most important contributors to sales and to profits.

In addition to analyzing sales data, the information system monitors the Tokyo store's inventory levels, evaluates sales trends based upon systemwide data, and monitors the store's refrigeration and air-conditioning systems. For example, the store manager can determine when to discard overordered items, such as cold noodle dishes. He can also find out which brands are doing well throughout 7-Eleven

* The material in this case is drawn from Gale Eisenstodt, "Information Power," *Forbes* (June 21, 1993), pp. 44–45.

Japan's stores. A message may even flash on his computer monitor like a news bulletin to tell the manager that a new drink is very popular at other locations. According to an executive at a large consulting firm, "As the process is repeated, ordering precision increases." The computer even regulates the store's refrigeration and air-conditioning equipment and automatically calls the maintenance firm if a given temperature or humidity level cannot be reached within a given time period.

Data—involving the daily purchases of five million customers—are fed into the companywide information system from each store and centrally analyzed at 7-Eleven Japan's main office. There, the firm's 650 field counselors review the aggregate data to further direct each store's buying and operations. The firm uses these data to centralize purchases, reduce ordering costs, outline specifications for exclusive products, and obtain special services.

Companywide data are also shared with key vendors so they can minimize their inventory levels, maintain sufficient quantities of fast-selling goods, reduce product spoilage, forecast demand, and develop new-product concepts. For example, Delica Ace, a producer of sandwiches and prepared dishes, uses the sales data to forecast demand. This is critical since it takes 10 hours to prepare its perishable foods, yet most stores order only 5 hours in advance of their needs. If Delica Ace prepares too much food, spoilage occurs; if it prepares too little food, there are lost sales opportunities. Aggregate data from 7-Eleven has been used by another supplier to develop Dekavita C, a highly profitable vitamin-enriched drink.

7-Eleven Japan's retail information system is an important contributor to the firm's overall success. For instance, average daily sales are more than 30 per cent higher than at Family Mart, its leading competitor. In its latest fiscal year, 7-Eleven Japan's net earnings increased by almost 11 per cent despite the softness in the Japanese economy. And 7-Eleven Japan's operating margin is also 43 per cent; double the level of Family Mart. These factors explain why royalty fees for a Japanese 7-Eleven are higher than for competing convenience-store franchises.

At this point in time, the use of this powerful retail information system is limited to 7-Eleven's Japanese stores. The chairman of 7-Eleven Japan hopes to develop and implement a similar computer system for the firm's 6,200 U.S. stores in the near future. The chairman wants its U.S. franchisees to first understand the importance of such information before investing in software, hardware, and training.

QUESTIONS

1. List the benefits of a retail information system for 7-Eleven Japan franchisees. Are there any limitations? Explain your answer.
2. How can these benefits be quantified to arrive at a dollar value?
3. Describe the pros and cons of a specially-developed keyboard as an input into 7-Eleven's retail information system.
4. What series of steps must 7-Eleven Japan implement before a retail information system is used in U.S. stores? Be specific in your answer.

CASE 2

The Marsh Super Study†

Marsh Supermarkets, an Indianapolis-based chain, recently conducted a major two-part consumer behavior study. In the first phase of the study, Marsh recorded all customer transactions in five of its stores (located in upscale metropolitan, blue-collar metropolitan, and county-seat rural areas) using point-of-sale equipment that was equipped with scanners. These data were employed to analyze sales, profit, and productivity relationships. For example, by varying advertising during the study, Marsh was able to determine the impact of different promotions on sales.

The second phase of the study tracked 1,600 shoppers in two Marsh test stores over a three-week period. One outlet was a combination store with a large general merchandise department and a pharmacy. Many shoppers there were from younger, larger families who lived in new residential areas. The second store was a conventional supermarket with general merchandise integrated into the grocery area. During the second phase, Marsh learned how many shoppers use lists, where shoppers go in the store, how many shoppers talk with employees, and how long typical shoppers spend in a supermarket. To avoid influencing shopper behavior, trackers used walkie-talkies to communicate with each other as they observed customers from catwalks located above the store. Shopper behavior was then linked to purchases for each person. Behavior was recorded from 7 A.M. to 7 P.M. on Wednesdays, Fridays, and Saturdays.

The results of the two-part study have yielded what some industry experts call "the most detailed shopper profile analysis ever compiled," with consumers divided into three groups based on their behavior: fill-in shoppers, routine shoppers, and stock-up shoppers. Fill-in shoppers, who comprised 43 per cent of the test stores' total customers, buy 10 or fewer items on a given shopping trip. The average fill-in shopper spends $12.51 weekly at the supermarket, completes a shopping trip in 11 minutes, and buys 5 items per trip. Routine shoppers, who accounted for 41 per cent of the test stores' total customers, buy 11 to 35 items per shopping trip. The average routine shopper spends $39.40 per trip, completes a shopping trip in 23 minutes, and buys 20 items per trip. Stock-up shoppers, who accounted for only 16 per cent of the test stores' total shoppers, buy 36 or more items per shopping trip. On average, stock-up shoppers spend $85.30 weekly, stay in the store for 39 minutes, and buy 48 items.

Here are several other findings from the Marsh study that are important to the supermarket industry:

- Once considered the slowest day of the week, the study indicates that Sunday sales now comprise 15 per cent of the weekly total. This calls into question the traditional practice whereby few supermarkets are restocked with fresh perishables on Saturday night.
- Shopping patterns differ by type of area. Consumers in the blue-collar metropolitan area make the smallest average purchases, are the most price sensitive, and are most likely to purchase store specials. Shoppers in the county-seat rural area are least apt to shop between 8 P.M. and 8 A.M. and on Sundays. In comparison to

† The material in this case is drawn from Robert E. O'Neill, "Customer Behavior: Seeing is Believing," *Progressive Grocer* (January 1993), pp. 57–62; Robert E. O'Neill, "How Consumers Shop," *Progressive Grocer* (December 1992), pp. 62–64; and Glenn Snyder, "Shedding Light on Bulb Sales," *Progressive Grocer* (June 1993), p. 117.

the upscale metropolitan group that favors Saturday and Sunday shopping, the blue-collar group favors Thursday and Friday shopping.

- Average department penetration (the percentage of shoppers who pass through a given department) is highest for the first department encountered in a store's traffic-flow pattern. The penetration rate declines for each department that is a further distance from the first department. Meat, produce, and dairy are penetrated by 74 per cent, 56 per cent, and 47 per cent of shoppers, respectively.
- The success ratio (the percentage of shoppers who buy a good in a given department) varies by department. Only 10 per cent of the departments studied have success rates higher than 50 per cent. One-third have success rates between 26 per cent and 50 per cent; and 56 per cent have success rates of 25 per cent or less.

The Marsh Super Study also reported specific findings for a number of different product categories. As an example, for light bulbs, consumer demographics, the selling season, and a store's marketing program all have a great impact on sales. The upscale metropolitan store has light-bulb sales of $1.59 per $1,000 of total sales, versus $1.06 and $1.41 per $1,000 in the blue-collar metro and county-seat rural stores, respectively. Light-bulb sales are highest during the third and fourth quarters, when days are shortest. Temporary price reductions, newspaper advertising, and displays are effective in generating light-bulb sales. Although a temporary price reduction alone generated a 9.6 per cent increase in sales; the combined effect of price, advertising, and displays resulted in a 430.1 per cent increase in sales.

While supermarket owners and managers can question the applicability of these findings for their individual store(s), the Marsh study has presented a useful methodology, as well as posed a number of important questions, for owners and managers to consider. These include whether stock-up shoppers require additional services, the advisability of staffing key departments (such as produce and meats) on Sundays, whether different stores should receive different merchandise mixes and promotion strategies based on the demographic characteristics of their shoppers, how stores can best plan their layouts, and what factors affect the sales of specific product categories.

QUESTIONS

1. To a retailer using the Marsh Super Study as secondary data, what are the strengths and weaknesses of the methodology employed in the study?
2. What could a nonsupermarket retailer learn from the Marsh study?
3. What other kinds of primary and secondary data could a supermarket use in researching the behavior of shoppers? Explain your answer.
4. Describe how Marsh could integrate its shopper study into its retail information system.

VIDEO QUESTIONS ON MARSH SUPER STUDY

1. Discuss the Marsh Super Study findings for light bulbs.
2. How should a supermarket owner or manager use these findings to increase sales and profitability?

Part 3 Comprehensive Case

What About the Consumer?*

Introduction

The key to more targeted merchandising is a sharper analysis of the customer base. Here's how to group stores according to a consumer map you can use to jump-start profits.

Exploiting the Differences in Neighborhoods

Knowing how to exploit the differences in neighborhoods plays a greater role in store success or failure than knowing the subtle differences of competing products. Increasingly, a brand's selling point is its appeal to a precise segment of consumers.

What's needed in management is not a keen eye for buying one brand or another on deal. What's really needed is a retailer's vision for developing a profitable product category and, ultimately, a more profitable store.

Long-term profitability springs from a very different definition of effectiveness. In this era of efficient consumer response, the key to higher sales at full price is matching the product mix and promotion schedule for each product category with the wants and needs of real live shoppers. At the store level, the key is tailoring merchandising and promotion for each store cluster according to the neighborhoods they serve.

Being More Consumer Oriented

This means that everyone in retail management has to think in a more consumer-oriented manner. It also means that information about the consumer has to be used in a more focused and intelligent way.

The flood of data measuring each aspect of how consumers live needs to be ordered in a useful format that lets a retail manager spot the opportunities for virtually every product in his or her store and understand the impact on other products.

You can start by weighing sales and profits for every category against the performance of the store as a whole. Isolate the heavy sellers versus the laggards. Determine what products you absolutely have to carry. Then, compare how each product moves in stores relative to other stores of like size and similar shopper composition.

The assistance of committed manufacturers can improve this process. First, though, the retailers' and manufacturers' roles in the marketing process have to be redefined. To work well together, both manufacturers and retailers have to be realistic about what the other party can bring to the planning table.

Manufacturers can hone in on their categories and provide portraits of the consumers who buy individual products. Using the proper integrated information approach, a manufacturer can analyze a category according to customer life-styles; map out sales by brand; identify which brands outperform or underperform what we call the product opportunity index; and recommend merchandising and promotion that will most effectively increase a product's appeal to the stores' consumer base. By bringing an integrated informational approach to category analysis, a manufacturer can lead the way to defining store clusters that make sense.

The retailer must first analyze product category and store sales and profits in a number of ways. Total store sales should be measured against shopper traffic. Sales and profits are measured against stores with similar customer bases and merchandising philosophies. Only the retailer can focus on competing stores to any great extent.

Secondly, the retailer must apply micromarketing tools to cluster stores according to precise profiles of the consumers who shop them. That permits the retailer to develop appropriate merchandising mixes and promotional strategies for each cluster. It is then up to the retailer to explore additional ways to use micromarketing tools to improve category and storewide performance.

Of course, everyone must understand the true meaning of micromarketing. Contrary to many definitions buzzing around the industry, micromarketing is really the planning version of integrated marketing. It is the process of using every available informational tool to portray every aspect of a consumer's life. Put simply, that means finding out: where the consumer lives, where she [he] works, what she [he] needs, what media she's [he's] exposed to, when she [he] shops, what products she [he] buys in which stores, and more. That provides opportunity targets that marketing-minded retailers can really exploit. The opportunity is evident in the interrelationship between different life-style activities.

This more sophisticated capability is what is revolutionizing the concept of product category management. Progressive retailers are discovering that the tools exist to define which products will appeal—and for what reasons—to smaller and smaller subsegments of consumers. These retailers are taking the initial bold steps

* The material in this case was prepared and written by Tom Dailey and Monika Torrence, president and vice-president, respectively, of Spectra Marketing Systems. It originally appeared in "What About the Consumer?" *Progressive Grocer* (September 1993), pp. 27–32. Copyright *Progressive Grocer*. Reprinted by permission.

toward a lasting competitive advantage by grouping their stores into clusters based on the dynamics of shopper composition. They then can establish separate shelf strategies, display strategies, and overall promotional strategies accordingly.

Five Steps Toward Customer Clustering

How does clustering and opportunity targeting really work? Let's analyze Marsh Supermarkets, an 80-store chain based in Indianapolis.

Step 1: Develop a Shopper Profile for the Entire Chain.

This step is essential as a benchmark and requires a relatively simple analysis. Build a store's trading area by starting at the block group level and accumulating appropriate block groups. Then pull together data on grocery expenditures, population, age, housing, children, income, and education levels by each block group.

Overall, Marsh draws its business from combined store trading areas consisting of 2.86 million consumers, with 1.08 million households and five-year-growth rates of 4.5 per cent for population and 6.9 per cent for households.

Median annual household income (HHI) for Marsh shoppers is $33,689, with 53.9 per cent of households having incomes under $35,000. Fifty-five per cent of Marsh shoppers are in white-collar jobs and 30 per cent are blue-collar. The population is evenly spread out in age and there is very little ethnic diversity—6.4 per cent are black and less than one per cent are Hispanic or Asian. Relatively few households, 36.6 per cent, have children.

Step 2: Cluster Each Store According to More Accurate Shopper Profiles.

Most retailers are unable to do this. They may have consumer demographic or life-style data, but they don't have a system for combining the information and accounting for the presence of children—perhaps the most important factor in determining purchasing levels [in supermarkets]. For Marsh, we are able to create five distinct clusters:

1. Upscale Suburbs This cluster is exemplified by the Marsh store in Carmel, Indiana. Home ownership is significantly higher for shoppers of this store (70.8 per cent) than it is for shoppers throughout the chain (55.3 per cent). Annual income is also significantly higher: Sixty per cent of the households have incomes of more than $50,000 versus 26.4 per cent for the chain. Some 48 per cent of these shoppers are between the ages of 25 and 54. There are more children: 42.3 per cent of the households have children compared with 36.6 per cent for the chain overall. In addition, 48.6 per cent of these shoppers have completed at least four or more years of college versus only 18 per cent for all Marsh shoppers.

2. Upper-Midscale/Urban/Urban Fringe This cluster is represented by the Marsh store on West 86th Street in Indianapolis. It shows relatively high degrees of rental housing (53.6 per cent) and white-collar occupations (81.2 per cent). The age range is lower (36.3 per cent are 25 to 44), and only 29.6 per cent of households have children. In addition, the overall ethnic population is high here: 12.4 per cent are black, 1.1 per cent Hispanic, and 1.9 per cent Asian.

3. Upper-Midscale Suburbs This cluster is illustrated by the store in Greenwood, Indiana. The store caters to young families (40.4 per cent have children, and 34.2 per cent are between the ages of 25 and 44). The shoppers here are more affluent than the chain's average—38 per cent have an annual HHI of more than $50,000. White-collar occupations run relatively high (64.5 per cent) and the neighborhood is almost exclusively white.

4. Downscale/Rural This cluster is epitomized by the store in Marion, Indiana. Shoppers at the store are below the chain average in income (41 percent with an annual HHI under $25,000). A greater percentage, 38.9, have blue-collar jobs, and the average age is slightly older (37.7 per cent over 45). The presence of children (34.8 per cent) is lower than average, while ethnic concentration (5.5 per cent are black, 2.2 per cent Hispanic) runs higher.

5. Mid-to-Downscale/Urban This cluster is exemplified by the store on Madison Avenue in Indianapolis. It serves a mixed occupation base (51.5 per cent are white collar and 33.0 per cent are blue collar), with lower annual incomes (47.6 per cent are under $25,000 and 67.7 per cent are under $35,000), lower home values (54.4 per cent are under $50,000), and a lower presence of children (31 per cent). The trading area skews toward both younger people (30.9 per cent 25 to 54) and older people (14.9 per cent over 65).

Step 3: Determine Brand and Category Opportunity.

The key to sizing up opportunity is to index product purchasing by consumer life-stage (age and presence of children) within each life-style cluster.

Start with an index of consumption across the entire United States. Significantly heavier consumption will be evident immediately. Then, analyze each cluster and store according to the presence of high-indexing shoppers. Table 1 shows opportunity indexes for several different products in each of Marsh's five consumer life-style clusters. An index of 100 equals the norm. The further an index is above 100, the heavier the consumption level.

Table 1 Product Opportunities

Product Category	Index by Store Type[a]				
	Upscale Suburbs	Upper-Midscale/ Urban/Urban Fringe	Upper-Midscale Suburbs	Downscale/ Rural	Mid-to-Downscale/ Urban
Artificial sweeteners	104	102	100	101	92
Diet cola	108	105	102	98	88
Nondiet soda	82	87	100	108	111
Greeting cards	102	99	101	102	91
Friendship greeting cards	104	104	104	98	86
Sweetened instant iced tea	104	97	100	100	101
Plain paper disposable plates	98	91	103	106	89
Coated paper disposable plates	106	99	103	102	84
	104	97	102	103	89
Light bulbs					
Energy-saving light bulbs	99	95	102	105	89

[a] Product opportunity index: 100 equals the average for all Marsh stores. Above 100 means the opportunity is greater than average.
Source: Spectra Marketing.

Let's examine some sample products to see how it works. For instance, as Table 2 indicates, nondiet soda is bought by younger, midscale to downscale households with and without children. The reason for this is that children like sugar and the downscale population is not as highly educated on health matters.

In contrast, for diet cola, the opportunity lies with young upper/midscale to upscale families with and without children. For artificial sweeteners, the opportunity index climbs with age. The highest sales come from households with people above the age of 55, probably because of health concerns. Sweetened instant iced tea is strongest in upscale suburban, midscale urban, and downscale urban households with children.

Step 4: Apply Opportunity Index to Clusters.

Examine the indexing versus the store clusters. Using the sample products in Table 1 as an as an example, we find the following for each store type:

1. Upscale suburban store shoppers present the greatest opportunity for diet cola and coated paper plates, and relatively strong opportunities for artificial sweeteners, friendship greeting cards, sweetened instant iced tea, and light bulbs.
2. Upper-midscale/urban/urban fringe stores show the strongest opportunity for diet cola and friendship greeting cards. Nearly every other product in this sample shows a below-average opportunity.
3. Upper-midscale suburban stores show the strongest opportunity in friendship greeting cards. All other products fall into the average to above-average range.
4. Downscale/rural shoppers show very strong opportunities for nondiet soda, plain paper plates, and energy-saving light bulbs. Other categories are about average.
5. Mid-to-downscale/urban stores offer particularly strong opportunities for nondiet soda, but the opportunities in nearly every other category are well below average.

Step 5: Change Shelf Sets and Adjust Promotion According to Category Opportunity.

Smart merchandising starts with a sound analysis of product versus product. Take the light bulb category. Within Marsh stores, the upscale suburbs cluster presents the best sales opportunity for light bulbs, especially for decorative and outdoor lines. The sales opportunity is rather good in the upper-midscale suburbs and downscale/rural clusters. The opportunity is weakest for all light bulbs in mid-to-downscale urban stores.

Table 2 A Tale of One Product/Two Markets, Product: Nondiet Soda

Consumer Households	Index by Store Type[a] Upscale Suburbs	Downscale/Rural
Head of household, ages 18–34		
With children	85	138
Without children	83	159
Head of household, ages 35–54		
With children	80	147
Without children	66	82
Head of household, 55 and older		
Ages 55 to 64	66	81
65 and older	90	87

[a] Product opportunity index: 100 equals the average for all Marsh stores. Above 100 means the opportunity is greater than average.

Source: Spectra Marketing.

Based on that analysis, the simplest way for Marsh to increase light bulb sales would be to give light bulbs the most shelf-space in upscale suburbs, upper-midscale suburbs, and downscale/rural stores. In the upscale suburban stores, Marsh should set the shelf by brands, giving prominence to outdoor and decorative bulbs.

Manufacturers can be catalysts for this kind of profitable category management. A partnership between Coors and a major Midwestern chain provides a strong example. The chain wanted to sample Coors Killian's Red Irish beer before committing to the product, However, Coors couldn't afford to sample more than 100 stores and the retailer couldn't justify giving the product a strong presence in all stores.

Using demographic information, Coors identified 30 stores that fit the Killian's consumer profile and the chain approved a limited three-month sampling test. The test was a success and now Killian's is prominently displayed in those 30 stores, while it gets less prominent space in the chain's other stores.

Questions

1. Discuss this statement: "Knowing how to exploit the differences in neighborhoods plays a greater role in store success or failure than knowing the subtle differences of competing products."
2. Describe the five steps toward customer clustering.
3. What recommendations would you make on the basis of the data in Tables 1 and 2?
4. Besides the data reported in this case, what other target-market information should Marsh study? Why?
5. How could Marsh use the information presented in this case to set up a customer data base? What steps must Marsh take to best manage such a data base?
6. What kinds of information about Killian's Red Irish beer should Marsh gather and examine before agreeing to introduce it in more stores? State several performance criteria that Marsh could use.
7. As noted in this case, what are the proper roles of manufacturers and retailers in collecting and applying consumer-oriented information? Comment on these roles.

Choosing a Store Location

- After a retailer conducts a situation analysis, sets objectives, and identifies consumer characteristics and needs, it is ready to develop and implement an overall strategy. In Parts 4 through 7, the major elements of such a strategy are examined: choosing a store location, managing a business, merchandise management and pricing, and communicating with the customer. Part 4 concentrates on store location.

- Chapter 8 discusses the crucial nature of store location for retailers and outlines a four-step approach to location planning. Step 1, trading-area analysis, is covered in this chapter. Among the topics studied are the use of geographic information systems, the size and shape of trading areas, how to determine the trading areas of existing and new stores, and the major factors to consider in assessing trading areas. Several data sources are described.

- Chapter 9 deals with the last three steps in location planning: deciding on the most desirable type of location, selecting a general location, and choosing a particular store site within that location. Isolated store, unplanned business district, and planned shopping center locations are contrasted. And criteria for evaluating each location are outlined and detailed.

Trading-Area Analysis

❖ Chapter Objectives

1. To demonstrate the importance of store location for a retailer and outline the process for choosing a store location
2. To discuss the concept of a trading area and its related components
3. To show how trading areas may be delineated for existing and new stores
4. To examine three major factors in trading-area analysis: population characteristics, economic base characteristics, and competition and the level of saturation

When the rest of the United States was going through a building boom in shopping-center development during the 1980s, the Midwest (comprising the East North Central and West North Central regions) was rather quiet. Now, while much of the United States is witnessing little building growth, many retailers and real-estate developers are sensing new opportunities in the Midwest.

According to retailing experts, the Midwest's growth opportunities are due to three key factors. One, major retail chains such as Best Buy, Sports Authority, Oshman's, Wal-Mart, Dillard's, Builders Square, and Marshalls have recently begun to expand into the area. Two, various Midwest regional malls have been upgraded to effectively compete against Minnesota's new Mall of America, the largest shopping center in the United States. Three, retailers have shown increased interest in such cities as Chicago. For example, 17 major tenants were either new to Chicago or increased facilities there during 1993.

Fueling the retail growth in this area is the financial and household stability of Midwesterners. According to survey research on Midwesterners by Stillerman Jones & Co., 80 per cent of them live in houses (compared to 73 per cent nationwide) versus apartment-type units. Sixty per cent of Midwestern adults are married (compared to 55 per cent elsewhere). The annual household income in the Midwest is a little less than the national average; however, this does not take into account the lower cost of living in the Midwest.

One reason for the relative health of the Midwest economy is its diverse economic base. As an executive with a leading real-estate developer says, "most of our Ohio cities are really strong because they're not one-horse towns tied to a single industry." A diverse economic base softens the impact of poor performance in one industry sector and enables workers to shift from one industry to another, based upon employment opportunities. As a result of the strong economic base in the Midwest and its strong demographics, one developer decided to build a one-million-square-foot regional shopping center in Dayton, Ohio. This was one of the few centers that big to be built in the United States during 1993.[1]

[1] Paul Doocey, "Powering Up the Midwest," *Stores* (March 1993), pp. 33–34; and Edward McKinley, "Power Play in the Heartland," *Stores* (September 1993), pp. 68–71.

Marshalls photo. Reprinted by permission of Melville Corporation.

Overview

The selection of a store location is one of the most consequential strategic decisions a retailer makes. This chapter and Chapter 9 explain why the choice of the proper store location is so crucial; and they describe the steps a retailer should take when choosing a location for a store and deciding whether to build, lease, or purchase facilities.

The Importance of Location to a Retailer

The importance of store location to a retailer should not be underestimated. Decision making can be complex, costs can be quite high, there is typically little flexibility once a location has been chosen, and the attributes of a location have a strong impact on the retailer's overall strategy. In general, a good location may enable a retailer to succeed even if its strategy mix is relatively mediocre. For example, a hospital gift shop may do very well, although its merchandise assortment is limited, prices are above average, and it does not advertise. On the other hand, a poor location can be such a liability that even the most able retailer may be unable to overcome it. For example, a small mom-and-pop grocery store may not do well if it is situated across the street from a food-based superstore; while the small firm features personal service and long hours, it cannot match the product selection and prices of the superstore. Yet, at a different site, it might do quite well.

The selection of a store location generally requires extensive decision making by the retailer because of the number of criteria to be considered. These include the size and characteristics of the surrounding population, the level of competition, access to transportation, the availability of parking, the attributes of nearby stores, property costs, the length of the agreement, population trends, legal restrictions, and other factors.

A store location usually requires a sizable financial investment and a long-term commitment by the retailer. Even a retailer seeking to minimize its investment by leasing (rather than owning a building and land) can have a substantial investment. Besides lease payments that are locked in for the term of an agreement, the retailer must spend money on lighting, fixtures, the storefront, and so on.

Although leases of less than five years are common in less desirable retailing locations, leases in good shopping centers or shopping-district locations are often five to ten years or more. It is not uncommon for a supermarket site to be leased for 15, 20, or 30 years. Department stores and large specialty stores, which locate on major downtown thoroughfares, have been known occasionally to sign leases longer than thirty years.

Because of its fixed nature, the amount of the investment, and the length of lease agreements, store location is the least flexible element of a retailer's strategy mix. A retailer such as a department store cannot easily move to another site or be converted into another type of retail operation. In contrast, advertising, prices, customer services, and the goods/service assortment can be modified rather quickly if the environment (consumers, competition, economy, and so on) changes. Furthermore, if a retailer breaks a lease, it may be responsible for any financial damages incurred by the property owner. In some instances, a retailer may be prohibited from subleasing its location to another party during the term of an agreement.

A retailer owning the building and land on which it is situated may also find it difficult to change locations. It would have to find an acceptable buyer, which might take several months or longer; and it may have to assist the buyer in financing the property. It may incur a financial loss, should it sell during an economic downturn.

Any retailer moving from one location to another faces three potential problems. First, some loyal customers and employees may be lost; the greater the distance between the old and the new locations, the greater the loss. Second, a new location may not possess the same characteristics as the original one. Third, the store fixtures and renovations at an old location often cannot be transferred to a new one; their remaining value is lost if they have not been fully depreciated.

Store location has a strong impact on a retailer's long-run and short-run planning. In the long run, the choice of a location affects the firm's overall strategy. The retailer needs to be at a store site that will be consistent with its organizational mission, goals, and target market over an extended period of time. The company also needs to regularly study and monitor the status of its location with regard to population trends, the distances people travel to the store, and the entry and exit of competitors—and to adapt long-run plans accordingly.

In the short run, store location influences the specific elements of a retail strategy mix (product assortment, prices, promotion, and so on). For example, a retailer located in a downtown area populated by office buildings may have little pedestrian traffic on weekends. Therefore, it would probably be inappropriate to sell items such as major appliances at this location (because these items are generally purchased jointly by husbands and wives). The firm would have to either close on weekends and not stock certain types of merchandise or remain open on weekends and try to attract customers to the area by using extensive promotion and/or aggressive pricing. If the retailer closes on weekends, it is adapting its strategy mix to the attributes of the location. If it stays open, it must invest additional resources in advertising to attempt to alter consumer buying habits. A retailer trying to overcome its location, by and large, faces greater risks than one adapting to its site.

In choosing a store location, retailers should follow these four steps:

1. Evaluate alternate geographic (trading) areas in terms of the characteristics of residents and existing retailers.
2. Determine whether to locate as an isolated store, in an unplanned business district, or in a planned shopping center within the geographic area.
3. Select the general isolated store, unplanned business district, or planned shopping-center location.
4. Analyze alternate sites contained in the specified retail location type.

This chapter concentrates on Step 1. Chapter 9 details Steps 2, 3, and 4. The selection of a store location must be viewed as a process involving each of these four steps.

Trading-Area Analysis

A ***trading area*** is "a geographical area containing the customers of a particular firm or group of firms for specific goods or services."[2] It is also defined as

> A district the size of which is usually determined by the boundaries within which it is economical in terms of volume and cost for a marketing unit or group to sell and/or deliver a good or service.[3]

The first step in the choice of a retail store location consists of describing and evaluating alternate trading areas and then deciding on the most desirable one. After a trading area is picked, it should be scrutinized regularly.

A thorough analysis of trading areas provides the retailer with several benefits:

- The demographic and socioeconomic characteristics of consumers can be detailed. Government and other published data can be utilized to obtain this information. For a new store, the study of proposed trading areas reveals market opportunities and the retail strategy necessary for success. For an existing store, it can be determined if the current retail strategy still matches the needs of consumers.

[2] Peter D. Bennett (Editor), *Dictionary of Marketing Terms* (Chicago: American Marketing Association, 1988), p. 202.

[3] Ibid., p. 203.

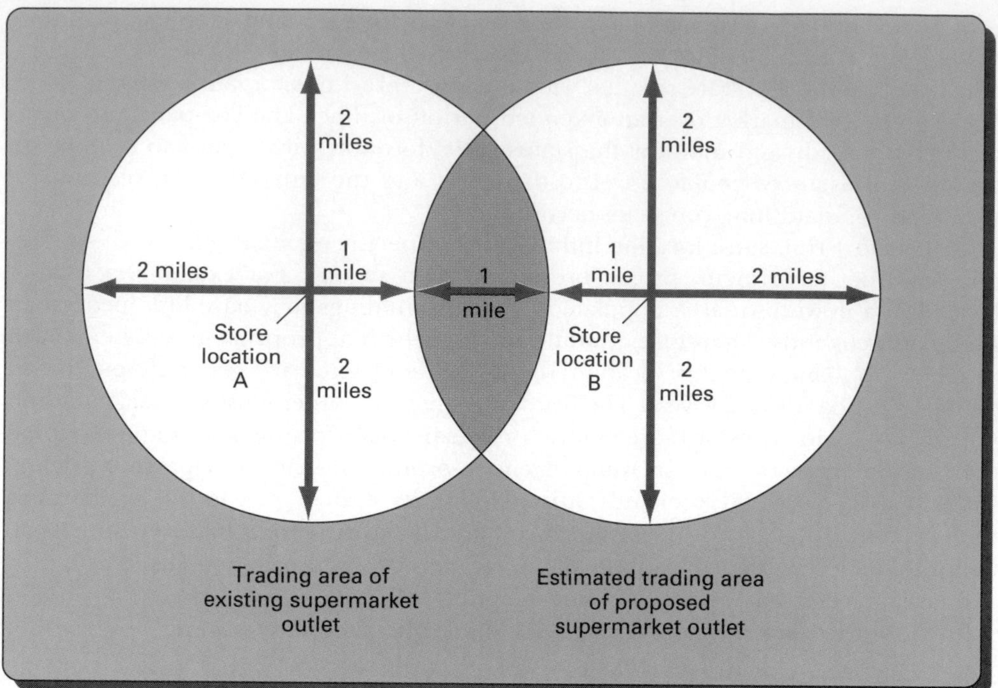

FIGURE 8–1
The Trading Areas of Current and Proposed Supermarket Outlets

- The focus of promotional activities can be ascertained. For example, a retailer finding that 95 per cent of consumers live within a three-mile radius of a store location would have a considerable amount of waste if it advertises in a newspaper with a citywide audience. To avoid wasted circulation, the retailer could assess the media coverage patterns of proposed or existing locations.
- It can be determined whether the location of a proposed branch store will service new customers or take away business from existing stores in a chain or franchise. For example, suppose a supermarket chain currently has an outlet in Jackson, Mississippi. This outlet has a trading area of two miles. The chain is considering adding a store, three miles from the Jackson one. Figure 8–1 shows the distinct trading areas and expected overlap of the two outlets. The shaded portion represents the ***trading-area overlap*** between the stores, in which the same customers are served by both branches.

  The chain needs to find out the overall net increase in sales if it adds the proposed location shown in Figure 8–1 (total revised sales of existing store + total sales of new store − total previous sales of existing store).
- Chain management can anticipate whether competitors want to open stores at nearby locations if the firm does not expand there itself. That is why BJ's Wholesale Club is often willing to open a BJ's club at a new site even though this would initially reduce sales at an existing BJ's store. The firm feels this strategy limits competitive entries into its market areas.[4]
- The proper number of outlets operated by a chain retailer in a geographic region can be calculated. How many outlets should a bank, a travel agency, and so on situate in a region to provide adequate service for customers (without raising investment costs too much or having too much overlap)? For instance, a leading upscale clothing chain now has a new store in Wausau, Wisconsin, after determining that its existing stores were not close enough to properly service the residents there. And a major competitive advantage for Canadian Tire Corporation

[4] *Waban Inc. Annual Report 1993*, p. 4.

RETAILING AROUND THE WORLD
How Far Will People Travel to Shop?

Until recently, foreign shoppers represented a significant target market only for those U.S. retailers located in exclusive shopping areas such as Madison Avenue in New York City, the Magnificent Mile in Chicago, and Rodeo Drive in Beverly Hills. Now, shopping areas such as the Mall of America in Bloomington (outside Minneapolis-St. Paul), Sawgrass Mills in Ft. Lauderdale, and factory outlet stores in Fall River, Massachusetts, report that a growing proportion of their sales comes from tourists who live in Australia, Japan, and Western Europe.

For example, Sawgrass Mills, a factory outlet mall, finds that almost one-half of its 18 million annual visitors are foreign. The mall estimates that a foreign visitor spends an average of $500 to $1,000 on a shopping trip, compared to $200 for a typical local customer.

The increased patronage of foreign shoppers can be explained by four factors. One, some foreign travel agencies now organize shopping trips and promote these visits as part of organized U.S. tours. Two, some malls have begun to advertise overseas. Third, the prices of many items are considerably cheaper in the United States, due to both the competitive environment in this country and the low relative value of the U.S. dollar. Fourth, many U.S. retailers feature goods and services that are unavailable in foreign markets.

Source: Based on material in Barnaby J. Feder, "U.S. Malls Luring Foreign Shoppers," *New York Times* (December 13, 1993), pp. D1, D3.

is that 77 per cent of the Canadian population lives within a 15-minute drive of a Canadian Tire Associate Store.[5]

- Geographic weaknesses can be highlighted. Suppose a suburban shopping center conducts a trading-area analysis and discovers that a significant number of people residing south of town do not shop there. Then, suppose a more comprehensive study reveals that residents are afraid to drive past a dangerous railroad crossing on the southern outskirts of town. As a result of its research, the shopping center could exert political pressure to make the crossing safer. This would lead to a lot of shoppers from south of town.
- Other factors can be described and evaluated. Competition, availability of financial institutions, transportation, availability of labor, location of suppliers, legal restrictions, projected growth, and so on can each be determined for the trading area(s) being examined.

THE USE OF GEOGRAPHIC INFORMATION SYSTEMS IN TRADING-AREA DELINEATION AND ANALYSIS

Increasingly, retailers are using geographic information systems software in their trading-area delineation and analysis. ***Geographic information systems (GIS)*** combine digitized mapping with key locational data to graphically depict such trading-area characteristics as the demographic attributes of the population, data on customer purchases, and listings of current, proposed, and competitor locations. Thus, GIS software enables retailers to rather easily research the attractiveness of alternative locations and to present the findings on computer-screen maps.[6] Prior to GIS software, retailers often placed different color pins on paper-based maps to represent their current and proposed locales—as well as competitor sites—and typically had to do their own data collection and analysis.

[5] Rick Tetzeli, "Mapping for Dollars," *Fortune* (October 18, 1993), p. 92; and *Canadian Tire Corporation, Limited 1992 Annual Report*, p. 11.

[6] See Michael F. Goodchild, "Geographic Information Systems," *Journal of Retailing*, Vol. 67 (Spring 1991), pp. 3–15.

Among the firms producing GIS software are Strategic Mapping, Thompson Associates, Urban Decision Systems, Environmental Systems Research Institute, Intergraph, EDS/GDS, Tactics International, and Mapinfo.[7] A montage of GIS software uses appears in Figure 8–2.

Although GIS software programs differ by vendor (many of which offer trading-area consulting services, in addition to selling software), they generally can be purchased for as little as $500 to $2,500 each, are designed to work with PCs, and allow for some manipulation of trading-area data. For the most part, GIS software programs are based on the 1990 *Census of Population* and the U.S. Census Bureau's national digital map, which is known as TIGER (topologically integrated geographic encoding and referencing). TIGER incorporates all streets and highways in the United States. *The GIS Sourcebook*, published annually by GIS World Inc. of Fort Collins, Colorado, lists many GIS software products.

GIS software can be applied in a variety of ways. For instance, a chain retailer could use GIS software to learn which of its stores have trading areas containing households with a median annual income of more than $50,000. That retailer could derive the sales potential of proposed new-store locations and those stores' potential effect on sales at existing branches. The firm could utilize GIS software to learn the demographic attributes of customers at its best locations, and then dervive a model to enable it to scan locations throughout the country to find the ones with the most-desirable trading-area characteristics. The retailer could even use GIS software to find out the chain's market penetration by zip code and to pinpoint its geographic areas of strength and weakness.

Many firms are now employing GIS software in their retail trading-area delineation and analysis. Here are some examples:

- PepsiCo uses GIS technology to help pinpoint the best locations for new Pizza Hut and Taco Bell outlets.[8]
- A&P Canada uses GIS software to determine how many customers come from within one, two, and three miles of each store. The software even draws a border to show where 70 per cent of each store's customers reside. A&P Canada also looks to see whether its advertising media coverage matches each store's trading area; and it can learn each store's relative attractiveness for specific market segments via GIS computer mapping.[9]
- Dayton Hudson's Target stores division uses GIS software to determine the trading area's household income and population growth for each of its stores. This analysis lets Target see which trading areas have sufficient income and population to support additional stores. GIS computer mapping also better enables Target to match its stores' merchandise mixes with the demographic characteristics of the population.[10]
- Western Auto (a division of Sears, Roebuck) uses GIS software to establish the appropriate demographics for proposed locations, to help prepare direct-marketing campaigns, and to better adjust the merchandising mix to the characteristics of each trading area. According to Sears' corporate planning manager, the use of GIS software has enabled Western Auto to reduce the time needed for new stores to break even. It now takes six months to break even on operating expenses, down from 18 months before.[11]

[7] An extensive listing of firms can be found in *National Clearinghouse for Census Data Services* (Washington, D.C.: U.S. Bureau of the Census, June 1993).

[8] Eric Schine and Geoffrey Smith, "Computer Maps Pop Up All Over the Map," *Business Week* (July 26, 1993), pp. 75–76.

[9] Gary Robins, "Retail GIS Use Growing," *Stores* (January 1993), p. 46.

[10] Ibid., p. 47.

[11] Rick Tetzeli, "Mapping for Dollars," *Fortune* (October 18, 1993), p. 92.

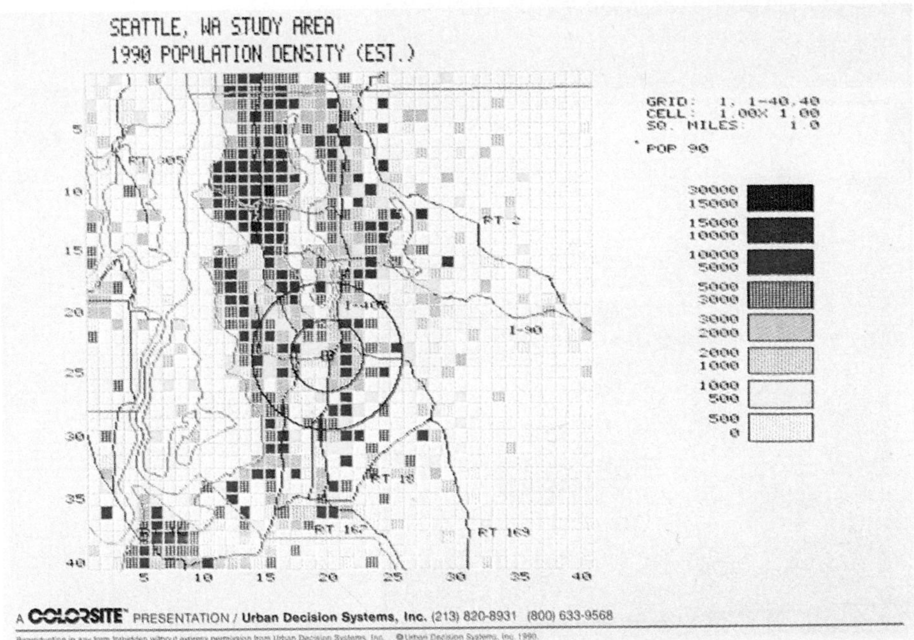

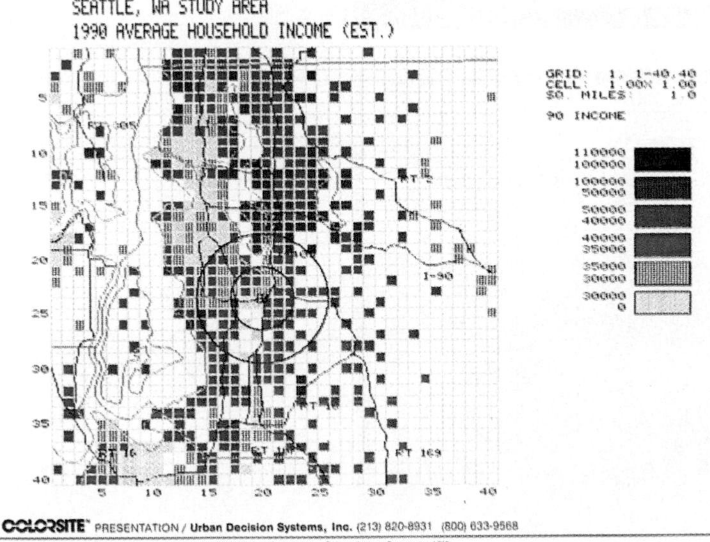

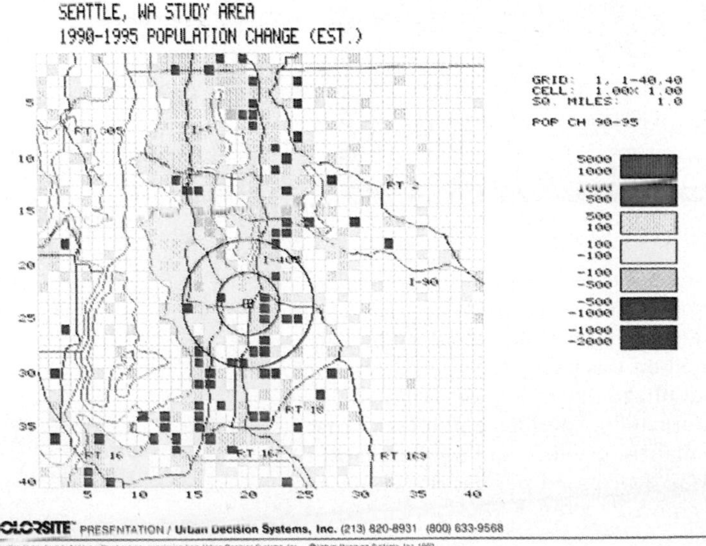

FIGURE 8–2

GIS Software in Action

When delineating and analyzing trading areas, their characteristics need to be studied and compared. Through geographic information systems (GIS) software, such as that represented here, retailers can learn about such trading-area characteristics as population density, average household income, and future population changes for each trading area being considered, and then decide on the most appropriate area in which to situate.

Reprinted by permission of Urban Decision Systems.

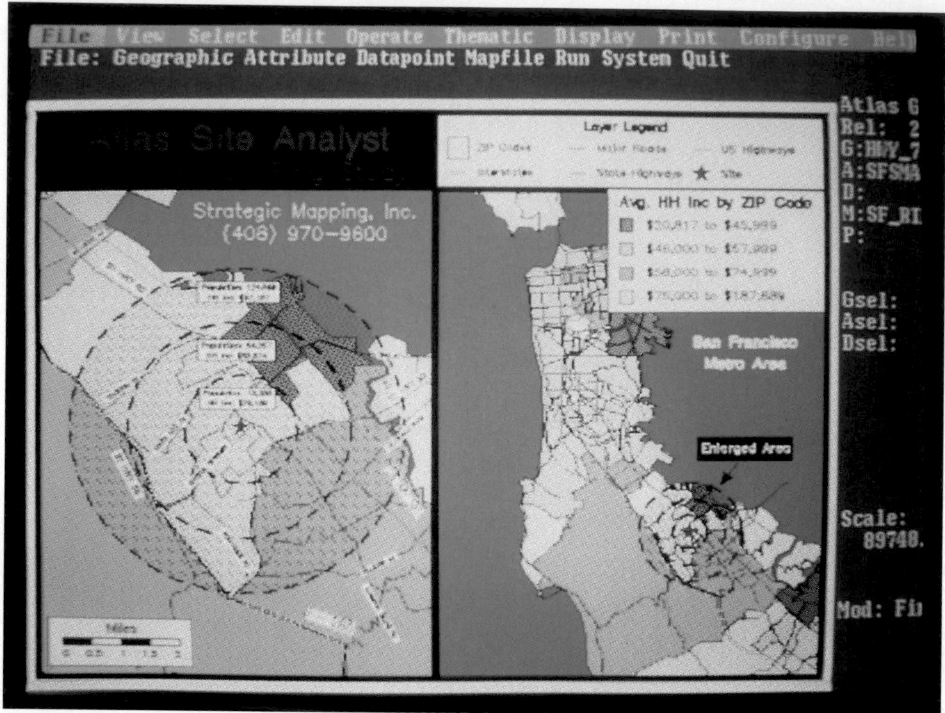

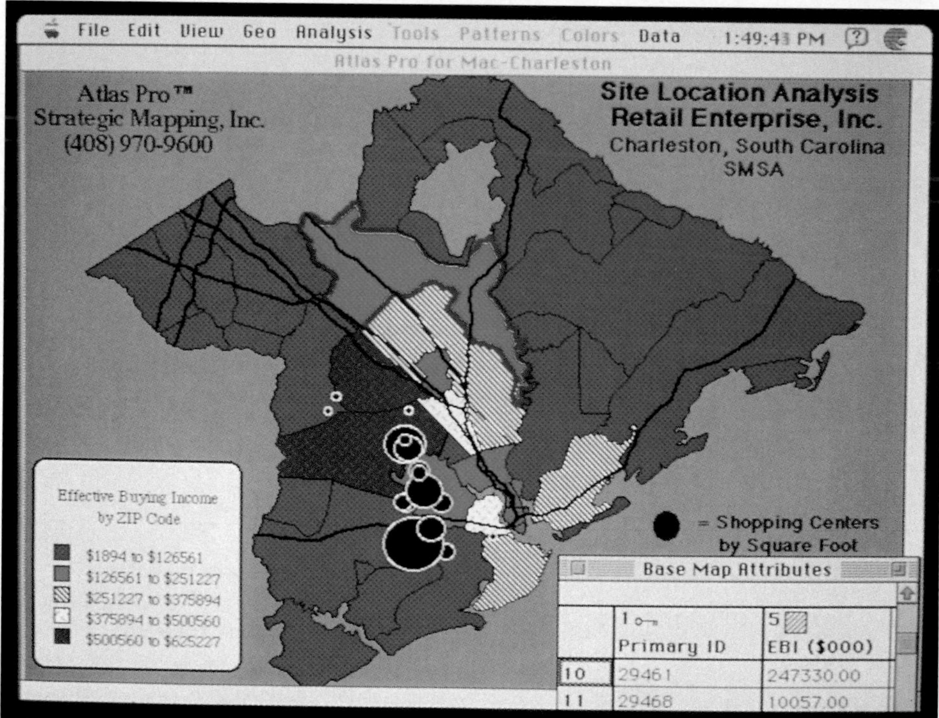

Figure 8–2 (Continued)

Strategic Mapping is well known for its GIS software. Among its retailing clients are Arby's, Circuit City, Citibank, Marriott, and May. The firm's most popular software is its Atlas series—which consists of Atlas GIS, Atlas Site Analyst (an add-on module for Atlas GIS), and Atlas Pro. Atlas Site Analyst and Atlas Pro are highlighted on this page. As Strategic Mapping states, "GIS offers the retailer numerous competitive advantages including the ability to: base decisions on both quantitative facts and geographic information; consider multiple alternatives through easy, interactive 'what if' and 'show me' analysis; produce and update maps and reports quickly and easily; and present conclusions in a clear and persuasive fashion with boardroom-quality maps and corresponding data-base reports."

Reprinted by permission of Strategic Mapping, Inc.

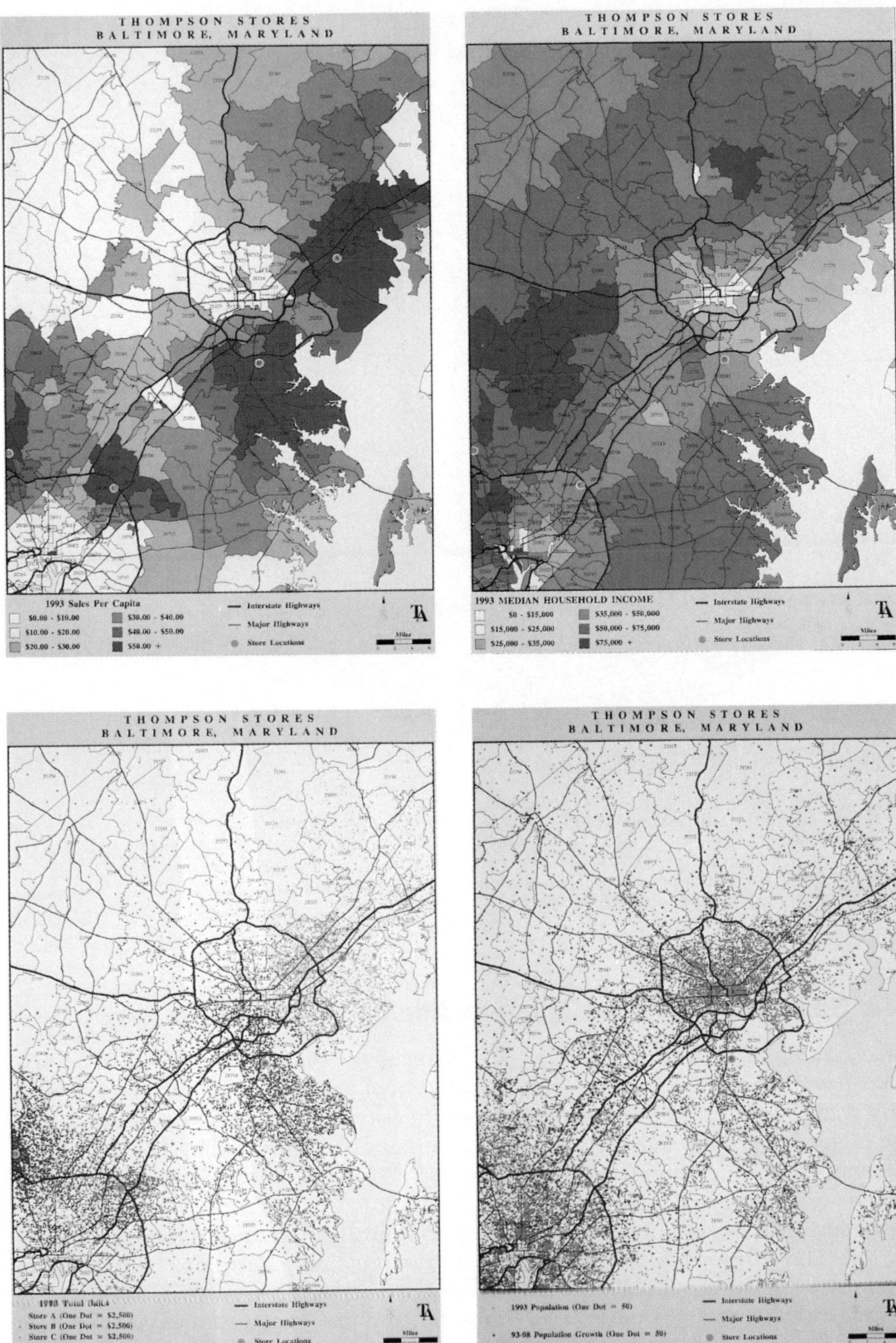

FIGURE 8–2 (Continued)

Thompson Associates combines sophisticated research methodologies with hands-on experience in virtually every retail category and tailors its services to individual clients. It has both cartographers and research experts. Every market and location study employs at least two different measures to ensure the greatest reliability of Thompson's recommendations. The firm uses "Forecast Convergence," a proprietary process to compare the results of each measure. Statistical forecasts are tied directly to actual store performance, and comprehensive recommendations are made to clients. Among Thompson's 1,000 retailing clients are Burger King, Home Depot, Kroger, Spencer Gifts, and Sports Authority.

Reprinted by permission of Thompson Associates.

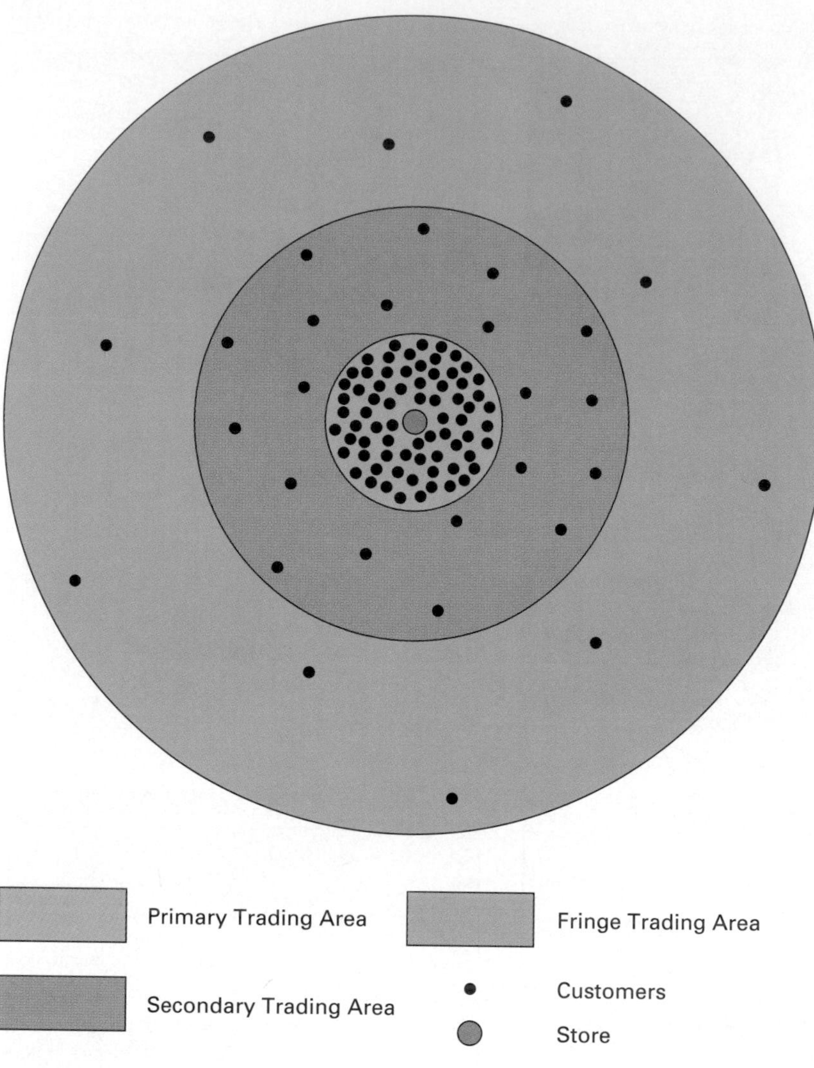

FIGURE 8–3
The Segments of a Trading Area

THE SIZE AND SHAPE OF TRADING AREAS

Each trading area consists of three parts: primary, secondary, and fringe. The ***primary trading area*** encompasses 50 to 80 per cent of a store's customers. It is the area closest to the store and possesses the highest density of customers to population and the highest per-capita sales. There is little overlap with other trading areas (both intracompany and intercompany).

The ***secondary trading area*** contains an additional 15 to 25 per cent of a store's customers. It is located outside the primary area, and customers are more widely dispersed. The ***fringe trading area*** includes all the remaining customers, and they are the most widely dispersed. For example, a store could have a primary trading area of four miles, a secondary trading area of five miles, and a fringe trading area of eight miles. The fringe trading area typically includes some outshoppers, who are willing to travel greater distances to patronize particular stores.

Figures 8–3 and 8–4 contain illustrations of trading areas and their segments. In reality, trading areas do not usually follow such concentric or circular patterns. They adjust to the environment. The size and shape of a trading area are influenced by a large variety of factors, among them: store type, store size, the location of competitors, residential housing patterns, travel time and traffic barriers (such as toll bridges or poor roads), and availability of media. These factors are discussed next.

Two types of stores can have different-sized trading areas although they are both located in the same shopping district or shopping center. One store could offer a

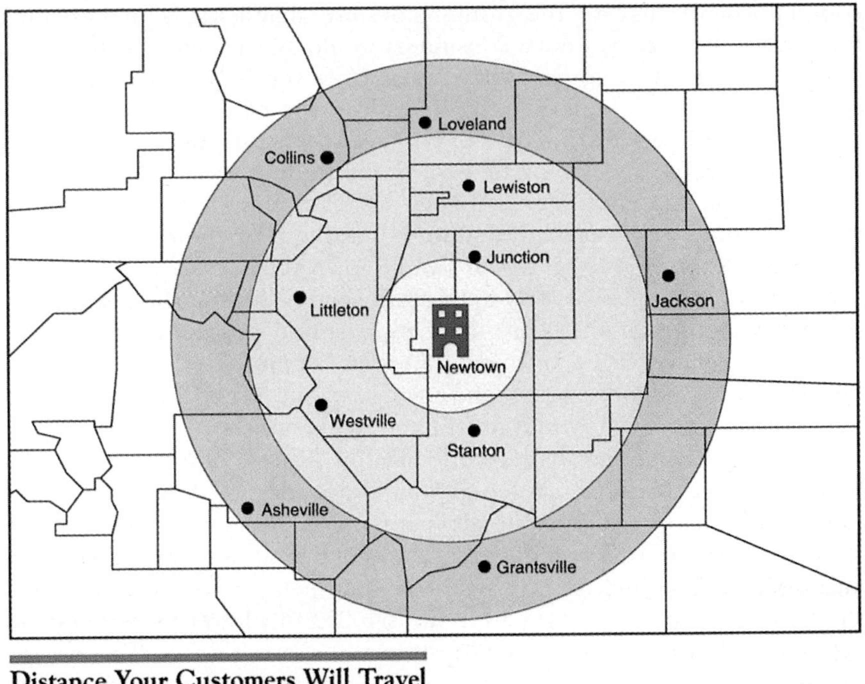

FIGURE 8–4
Delineating Trading-Area Segments by Customer Willingness to Travel
Through its DQI[2] data base (which was discussed in Chapter 7), Donnelly Marketing can help retailers identify customers and where they live in relation to where they shop. Patterns of cross-shopping between adjacent stores can also be identified. Thus, as indicated here, retailers can accurately determine their primary, secondary, and fringe trading areas.
Reprinted by permission of Donnelley Marketing Inc.

better merchandise assortment in its product category(ies), promote more extensively, and create a stronger image. Thus, this store—known as a ***destination store***—would have a trading area much larger than that of a competitor with a less unique appeal to consumers. As an illustration, situated in the same shopping center could be an outlet of a leading apparel specialty chain with a distinctive image and shoppers willing to travel up to thirty miles and a shoe store perceived as "average" and shoppers willing to travel up to ten miles. That is why, in comparing itself to other retailers, Dunkin' Donuts has used the slogan, "It's worth the trip."

Another type of outlet, called a ***parasite store***, does not create its own traffic and has no real trading area of its own. The store depends on customers who are drawn into the location for other reasons. A magazine stand in a hotel lobby and a snack bar in a shopping center are both parasites. Customers are not drawn to a location because of them but patronize these stores while they are there.

The size of a store's trading area is affected by its own size. As a store gets larger, its trading area usually increases. This relationship exists because the size of a store generally reflects the assortment of goods and services provided for customers. Yet, trading-area size does not rise proportionately with increasing store size. As a rule, trading areas for supermarkets are much greater than those for convenience stores; because of their size, supermarkets have a better product selection and convenience stores appeal to consumers' needs for fill-in merchandise. In a regional shopping center, department stores typically have the largest trading areas, followed by apparel stores. Gift stores in such a center have comparatively small trading areas.

The locations of a retailer's competitors determine their impact on the size of its trading area. Whenever potential customers are situated between two stores, the size of the trading area is often reduced for each; and the size of each store's trading area normally increases as the distance between them grows (then the target markets do not overlap as much). On the other hand, when stores are situated very near each other, the size of each's trading area would not necessarily be reduced because of competition. In this case, the grouping of stores may actually increase the trading area for each store because more consumers would be attracted to the general location due to the variety of goods and services. However, it is important to recognize that each store's market penetration (the percentage of total retail sales in the trading area) may be low with this type of competition. Also, the entry of a new store may change the shape and/or create gaps in the trading areas of existing stores.

Residential housing patterns affect a store's trading area. In many urban communities, people are clustered in multiunit housing near the center of commerce. With such population density, it is worthwhile for a retailer to locate quite close to consumers; and trading areas tend to be small because several shopping districts (in close proximity to one another) are likely to exist and prosper, particularly in the most densely populated cities. In many suburban communities, people live in single-unit housing—which is more geographically spread out. Accordingly, to generate sufficient sales volume, a retailer would need to attract shoppers from a greater distance.

Travel or driving time has an influence on the size of a trading area that may not be clear from a study of the geographic distribution of the population. Physical barriers (such as toll bridges, tunnels, poor roads, rivers, railroad tracks, and one-way streets) usually reduce trading areas and contribute to their odd shapes. Economic barriers (such as differences in sales taxes between two towns) also affect the size and shape of trading areas. If one town has significantly lower taxes than another, it may entice consumers to travel longer in return for saving on purchases.

The size of a trading area is often affected by a retailer's promotion efforts. Therefore, in a community where a newspaper and/or other forms of local advertising media are available, a retailer could easily afford to use these media and enlarge its trading area. However, if local media are not available in a community, the retailer would have to weigh the costs and probable waste of advertising in citywide or countywide media against the possibilities of increasing the trading area.

DELINEATING THE TRADING AREA OF AN EXISTING STORE

The size, shape, and characteristics of the trading area for an existing store (or shopping district or shopping center) can usually be delineated quite accurately. Store records (secondary data) and/or a special study (primary data) can be used to measure the trading area. In addition, as noted earlier in the chapter, many firms offer computer-generated data and maps based on census and other statistics. This information can be tailored to individual retailers' needs.

Store records can reveal the addresses of both credit and cash customers. Addresses of credit customers can be obtained via a retailer's billing department; addresses of cash customers can be acquired by analyzing delivery tickets, cash sales slips, store contests (sweepstakes), and check-cashing operations. In both instances, the analysis of addresses is relatively inexpensive and quick because the data were originally collected for other purposes and are readily available.

Since many big retailers have their own computerized credit-card systems, they can delineate trading areas by studying the addresses of these customers. Primary, secondary, and fringe trading areas can be described in terms of

- The frequency with which people from various geographic localities shop at a particular store.
- The average dollar purchases at a store by people from given geographic localities.
- The concentration of a store's credit-card holders from given geographic localities.

Though it may be easy to get data on credit-card customers, conclusions drawn from these data might not be valid if cash customers are excluded from analysis. Credit use may vary among customers from different localities, especially if consumer characteristics in the localities are dissimilar. Thus, an evaluation of only credit customers may overstate or understate the total number of shoppers from a particular locality. This problem is minimized if data are collected for both cash and credit customers.

A retailer can also collect primary data to determine the size of a trading area. It can record the license plate numbers of cars parked near a store, find the general addresses of the owners of those vehicles by contacting the state motor vehicle office or the local treasurer's office, and then note them on a map. For a few thousand dollars or less, a retailer could have R.L. Polk (a marketing research company) record the license plate numbers and determine the general owner addresses and demographics of parked vehicles. In either case, only general addresses (zip code and street of residence, but not the exact house number) are given out, to protect people's privacy. When using license plate analysis, nondrivers and passengers must not be omitted. Customers who walk to a store, use public transportation, or are driven by others should be included in the research. To collect data on these customers, questions must usually be asked (survey).

If a retailer desires still more detailed demographic information about consumers in particular localities, it can purchase those data from such firms as Claritas Corporation. Claritas has developed a computerized system (which extrapolates census data) for identifying communities by demographic cluster. Sixty-two different types of neighborhoods have been identified and described using names like "Rural Industria," "Urban Gold Coast," and "Kids & Cul-de-Sacs." This system, known as PRIZM, initially was based on zip codes; it now is also based on census tracts, block groups and enumeration districts, telephone exchanges, and postal routes. Standard PRIZM reports can be bought for as little as $99 each; costs are higher if the reports are tailored to the individual retailer.[12]

No matter the manner by which a trading area is delineated, the retailer should realize that a time bias may exist. For example, a downtown business district is patronized by different customers during the week (people who work there) than on weekends (people who travel there to shop). And special events may attract customers from great distances for only brief periods of time; after the events are over, the size of the trading area may drop. Therefore, an accurate estimate of the size of a store's trading area can be obtained only through complete and continuous investigation.

After any trading area is delineated, a retailer should map out the locations and densities of customers. This may be done in either of two ways: manually or with a geographic information system. In the manual method, a paper map of the area surrounding a store is used. Different colors of dots or pins could be placed on this map to represent population locations and densities, incomes, and other factors. Customer locations and densities are then indicated; and the primary, secondary, and fringe trading areas are noted by zip code. Customers can be reached by promotions aimed at particular zip codes. With a geographic information system, key customer data (such as the frequency of purchases and the amounts purchased) are combined with other information sources (such as census data) to yield computer-generated digitized maps that depict primary, secondary, and fringe trading areas.

DELINEATING THE TRADING AREA OF A NEW STORE

A new store opening in an established trading area can use the techniques detailed in the prior section. This section refers more to a trading area with less well-defined shopping and traffic patterns.

Prospective trading areas for a new store must frequently be evaluated by assessing market opportunities rather than current customer patronage and traffic (pedestrian and vehicular) patterns. Since the techniques used in delineating the trading area of an established store are often insufficient, additional tools must be utilized.

[12] Christina Del Valle and Jon Berry, "They Know Where You Live—And How You Buy," *Business Week* (February 7, 1994), p. 89.

Trend analysis and/or surveys can be employed. Trend analysis—estimating the future based on the past—involves examining government and other data concerning predictions about population location, automobile registrations, new housing starts, mass transportation, highways, zoning, and so on. Consumer surveys can be used to gather information about the time and distance people would be willing to travel to various possible retail locations, the features attracting people to a new store, the addresses of the people most likely to visit a new store, and other topics. Either or both of these techniques may provide a basis for delineating alternate new-store trading areas.

On a more advanced level, there are three basic types of computerized trading-area analysis models that could be used to assess new store locations: analog, regression, and gravity. An ***analog model*** is the simplest and most popular trading-area analysis model. Potential sales for a new store are estimated on the basis of existing store revenues in similar areas, the competition at a prospective location, the new store's expected market share at that location, and the size and density of the location's primary trading area. A ***regression model*** develops a series of mathematical equations showing the association between potential store sales and various independent variables at each location under consideration. The impact of such independent variables as population size, average income, the number of households, nearby competitors, transportation barriers, and traffic patterns are studied. A ***gravity model*** is based on the premise that people are drawn to stores that are closer and more attractive than competitors'. Such factors as the distance between consumers and competitors, the distance between consumers and the site, and store image are included in this model.

Computerized trading-area analysis models offer several benefits to retailers: They operate in an objective and systematic manner. They can offer insights as to how each locational attribute should be weighted. They are useful in screening a large number of locations. They can be used to assess management performance by comparing forecasts with results.

Several more-specific methods for delineating new trading areas are described next.

Reilly's Law

The traditional means of trading-area delineation, devised by William J. Reilly in 1929, is called ***Reilly's law of retail gravitation.***[13] The law's purpose is to establish a point of indifference between two cities or communities, so the trading area of each can be determined. The ***point of indifference*** is the geographic breaking point between two cities (communities)—at which consumers would be indifferent to shopping at either. According to Reilly's law, more consumers will be attracted to the larger city or community because a greater amount of store facilities (assortment) will exist, making the increased travel time worthwhile.

The law may be expressed algebraically as[14]

$$D_{ab} = \frac{d}{1 + \sqrt{\frac{P_b}{P_a}}}$$

where

D_{ab} = limit of city (community) A's trading area, measured in miles along the road to city (community) B

d = distance in miles along a major roadway between cities (communities) A and B

P_a = population of city (community) A

P_b = population of city (community) B

[13] William J. Reilly, *Method for the Study of Retail Relationships*, Research Monograph No. 4 (Austin: University of Texas Press, 1929), University of Texas Bulletin No. 2944.

[14] Richard L. Nelson, *The Selection of Retail Locations* (New York: F.W. Dodge, 1959), p. 149.

Based on this formula, a city with a population of 90,000 (A) would draw people from three times the distance as a city with 10,000 (B). If the cities are 20 miles apart, the point of indifference for the larger city is 15 miles, and for the smaller city, it is 5 miles:

$$D_{ab} = \frac{20}{1 + \sqrt{\frac{10,000}{90,000}}} = \frac{20}{1 + \sqrt{\frac{1}{9}}} = \frac{20}{1 + \frac{1}{3}} = \frac{20}{\frac{4}{3}} = 15 \text{ miles}$$

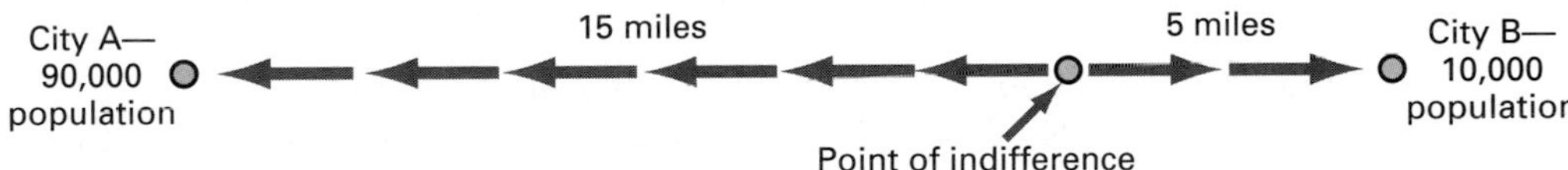

Reilly's law rests on these major assumptions: (1) two competing areas will be equally accessible from the major road; and (2) retailers in the two areas will be equally effective. Other factors (such as the dispersion of the population) are held constant or ignored.

The law of retail gravitation is an important contribution to trading-area analysis because of its ease of calculation and the research that has been conducted on it. Reilly's law is most useful when other data are not available or when the costs of compiling other data are too great. By combining this technique with others, a retailer could generally determine if the most appropriate trading area is being considered.

Despite its usefulness, Reilly's law has at least two key limitations. First, distance measurement is confined to major thoroughfares and does not involve cross streets; yet, many people will travel shorter distances along these slower cross streets. Second, actual distance to a store may not correspond with consumer perceptions of distance. A store offering few customer services and crowded aisles is likely to be a greater perceived distance from the customer than a similarly located store with a more pleasant shopping environment.

Huff's Law

In the 1960s, David L. Huff isolated several variables (rather than just one, as Reilly had done) and related them to trading-area size. ***Huff's law of shopper attraction*** delineates trading areas on the basis of the product assortment (of the items desired by the consumer) carried at various shopping locations, travel times from the consumer's home to alternative shopping locations, and the sensitivity of the kind of shopping to travel time. The assortment variable is measured by the total square feet of selling space a retailer expects all firms at a shopping location to allocate to a product category. Sensitivity to the kind of shopping entails the purpose of a trip (restocking versus shopping) and the type of good/service sought (such as furniture versus clothing versus groceries).[15]

Huff's law is expressed as

$$P_{ij} = \frac{\frac{S_j}{(T_{ij})^{\lambda}}}{\sum_{j=1}^{n} \frac{S_j}{(T_{ij})^{\lambda}}}$$

[15] David L. Huff, "Defining and Estimating a Trading Area," *Journal of Marketing*, Vol. 28 (July 1964), pp. 34–38; and David L. Huff and Larry Blue, *A Programmed Solution for Estimating Retail Sales Potential* (Lawrence: University of Kansas, 1966). For an empirical evaluation of the Huff model, see Christophe Benavent, Marc Thomas, and Anne Bergue, "Application of Gravity Models for the Analysis of Retail Potential," *Journal of Targeting, Measurement, and Analysis for Marketing*, Vol. 1 (Winter 1992–1993), pp. 305–315.

where

P_{ij} = probability of a consumer's traveling from home i to shopping location j

S_j = square footage of selling space in shopping location j expected to be devoted to a particular product category

T_{ij} = travel time from consumer's home i to shopping location j

λ = a parameter used to estimate the effect of travel time on different kinds of shopping trips

n = number of different shopping locations

λ must be determined through research or via a computer program.

This formula may be applied as follows: Assume a leased-department operator is studying three possible shopping locations with 200, 300, and 500 total square feet of store space expected to be allocated to men's cologne (by all retailers in the areas). A group of potential customers lives 7 minutes from the first location, 10 minutes from the second, and 15 minutes from the third. From previous research, the operator estimates the effect of travel time to be 2. Therefore, the probability of consumers' shopping for men's cologne is 43.9 per cent at Location 1; 32.2 per cent at Location 2; and 23.9 per cent at Location 3:

$$P_i1 = \frac{(200)/(7)^2}{(200)/(7)^2 + (300)/(10)^2 + (500)/(15)^2} = 43.9\%$$

$$P_i2 = \frac{(300)/(10)^2}{(200)/(7)^2 + (300)/(10)^2 + (500)/(15)^2} = 32.2\%$$

$$P_i3 = \frac{(500)/(15)^2}{(200)/(7)^2 + (300)/(10)^2 + (500)/(15)^2} = 23.9\%$$

As a result, if 200 males live 7 minutes from Location 1, about 88 of them will shop there.

These points should be considered in using Huff's law:

- To determine the overall trading area for Location 1, the same type of computations would have to be made for consumers living 5, 10, 15, 20 minutes, and so on away. The number of consumers at each distance who would shop there are then summed. In this way, the stores in Location 1 would be able to estimate their total market, the size of the trading area, and the primary, secondary, and fringe areas for a particular product category.
- When new retail facilities (square footage of selling space) in a product category are added to a location, the percentage of consumers living at every travel time from that location who will shop there goes up.
- The probability of consumers' shopping at a particular location is highly dependent on the effect of travel time for the product category. In the previous example, if the product is changed to a more important item, such as men's dress watches, consumers would be less sensitive to travel time. A λ value of 1 would result in these probabilities: Location 1, 31.1 per cent; Location 2, 32.6 per cent; and Location 3, 36.3 per cent. Location 3 becomes much more attractive for this product category because of its assortment.
- All of the variables are somewhat difficult to calculate; and for mapping purposes, travel time needs to be converted to distance in miles. In addition, travel time depends on the form of transportation used.
- On different shopping trips, consumers buy different items. That means the trading area would vary from trip to trip.

Other Trading-Area Research

Over the years, a number of other researchers have examined trading-area size in a variety of settings. They have introduced additional factors and sophisticated statistical techniques to explain the consumer's choice of shopping location.[16] For example, in his model, David A. Gautschi added to Huff's analysis by including shopping-center descriptors (such as center design and hours of operation) and transportation conditions (such as cost, performance, and safety).[17] Glen E. Weisbrod, Robert J. Parcells, and Clifford Kern studied the attractiveness of shopping centers on the basis of expected population changes, expected store characteristics, and the evolving transportation network.[18] Avijit Ghosh developed a consumer behavior model that takes into consideration multipurpose shopping trips.[19] Mark R. Young and Roger J. Calantone developed a model to assess customer perceptions of destination attractiveness, the distance to locations, retailer-to-retailer accessibility, customer interchange, and access to competing locales.[20] Paul LeBlang demonstrated that consumer life-styles could be used to predict sales at new department-store locations.[21]

Characteristics of Trading Areas

After the size and shape of various alternative trading areas (existing and/or proposed) have been determined, the retailer should study the characteristics of those areas. Of special interest are the attributes of residents and how well they match with the retailer's definition of its target market. Thus an auto-repair franchisee may compare the opportunities available in several areas by examining the number of car registrations; a hearing-aid retailer may evaluate the percentage of the population 65 years of age or older; and a bookstore retailer may be concerned with the educational level of residents.

Among the trading-area characteristics that should be studied by most retailers are the population size and features, availability of labor, closeness to supply, promotion facilities, economic base, competition, availability of locations, and regulations. The ***economic base*** refers to an area's industrial and commercial structure—the companies and industries that residents depend on to earn a living. The dominant industry (company) in an area is very important because its drastic decline may have adverse effects on a large proportion of the area's residents. An area with a diverse economic base, where residents work for a variety of nonrelated industries, is more secure than an area dependent on one major industry. Table 8–1 summarizes a number of the major factors to consider in evaluating retail trading areas.

Much of the information necessary to describe an area can be obtained from the U.S. Bureau of the Census, the *Survey of Buying Power, Editor* & *Publisher Market Guide, Rand McNally Commercial Atlas* & *Market Guide, American Demographics, Standard Rate* & *Data Service,* regional planning boards, public utilities, chambers of commerce, local

[16] A good summary of the research up to the early 1980s is C. Samuel Craig, Avijit Ghosh, and Sara McLafferty, "Models of the Retail Location Process: A Review," *Journal of Retailing,* Vol. 60 (Spring 1984), pp. 5–36.

[17] David A. Gautschi, "Specification of Patronage Models for Retail Center Choice," *Journal of Marketing Research,* Vol. 18 (May 1981), pp. 162–174.

[18] Glen E. Weisbrod, Robert J. Parcells, and Clifford Kern, "A Disaggregate Model for Predicting Shopping Area Market Attraction," *Journal of Retailing,* Vol. 60 (Spring 1984), pp. 65–83.

[19] Avijit Ghosh, "The Value of a Mall and Other Insights from a Revised Central Place Model," *Journal of Retailing,* Vol. 62 (Spring 1986), pp. 79–97.

[20] Mark R. Young and Roger J. Calantone, "Advances in Spatial Interaction Modeling of Consumer-Retailer Interaction" in William Bearden, Rohit Despande, and Thomas J. Madden, et al. (Editors), *1990 AMA Educators' Proceedings* (Chicago: American Marketing Association, 1990), pp. 264–267.

[21] Paul LeBlang, "A Theoretical Approach for Predicting Sales at a New Department-Store Location Via Life-Styles," *Direct Marketing,* Vol. 7 (Autumn 1993), pp. 70–74.

TABLE 8–1 Major Factors to Consider in Evaluating Retail Trading Areas

Population Size and Characteristics
- Total size and density
- Age distribution
- Average educational level
- Per cent of residents owning homes
- Total disposable income
- Per-capita disposable income
- Occupation distribution
- Trends

Availability of Labor
- Management
- Management trainees
- Clerical

Analysis of:
a. High school and college graduates
b. Outmigration of graduates
c. Average wages in the area vs. average wages in the United States

Closeness to Sources of Supply
- Delivery costs
- Timeliness
- Number of manufacturers and wholesalers
- Availability and reliability of product lines

Promotion
- Availability and frequency of media
- Costs
- Waste

Economic Base
- Dominant industry
- Extent of diversification
- Growth projections
- Freedom from economic and seasonal fluctuations
- Availability of credit and financial facilities

Competitive Situation
- Number and size of existing competitors
- Evaluation of strengths and weaknesses for all competitors
- Short-run and long-run outlook
- Level of saturation

Availability of Store Locations
- Number and type of locations
- Access to transportation
- Owning versus leasing opportunities
- Zoning restrictions
- Costs

Regulations
- Taxes
- Licensing
- Operations
- Minimum wages
- Zoning

government offices, shopping-center owners, and renting agents. In addition, GIS software programs provide data on the potential buying power in an area, the location of competitors, and highway access. Both consumer demographic and life-style information are also included in these programs.

Although the yardsticks noted in Table 8–1 are not equally important in all retail location decisions, each should be considered (to prevent an oversight). The most

RETAILING IN ACTION

To Be Great(land) in Columbus, Ohio?

Target Greatland is Dayton Hudson's new full-line discount store prototype, with three stores opened in Columbus, Ohio, in October 1991. *Discount Store News* commissioned an independent marketing research firm to conduct a 1993 phone survey of the chief shoppers from 200 households in Columbus to determine their shopping patterns at Target Greatland. The survey was completed about 16 months after the store openings.

These are among the relevant findings:

- Three-fifths of the households knew that there was a Target Greatland within easy driving distance.
- 58 per cent of the households shopped at Target Greatland in 1992; they averaged 9 trips and spent a total of $235 for the year. In contrast, 89 per cent shopped at Kmart in 1992; they averaged 24 trips and spent a total of $355 for the year. And 90 per cent shopped at Meijer in 1992; they averaged 36 trips and spent a total of $675 for the year.
- The demographics of Target Greatland shoppers closely mirrored those of the Columbus population. The average household size for Greatland shoppers was 3.0 persons; 31 per cent of Greatland shoppers were college graduates; and the average age of Greatland shoppers was 41 years. Similarly, the ethnic backgrounds of Greatland shoppers closely matched Columbus'.

Source: Based on material in "Greatland Lags Behind Columbus Discounters," *Discount Store News* (April 5, 1993), pp. 26–28.

important yardsticks should be viewed as "knockout" factors: if a location does not meet minimum standards on key measures, it should be immediately dropped from further consideration.

These are examples of desirable trading-area attributes, as developed by a diverse group of retailers:

- Casey's General Stores, a convenience-store chain that specializes in small towns, seeks locations where the population in the immediate area is between 500 and 20,000 persons, there are no competing convenience stores in the market area, and highway locations are available.[22]
- Dairy Mart Convenience Stores seeks areas with favorable demographics, population densities, population trends, traffic and commuting patterns, and zoning and other restrictions. Its stores are usually in densely-populated, high-traffic areas—close to single-family homes and apartments.[23]
- The Delchamps supermarket chain looks for locations in suburban shopping areas with middle- and upper-middle-class populations.[24]
- The Helig-Meyers supermarket chain focuses on locales that have fewer than 50,000 people and that are at least 25 miles from a metropolitan area and within 200 miles from an existing or a planned distribution center. Since a distribution center needs 30 to 40 stores to be efficient, the chain tries to expand within each distribution center's zone of market coverage.[25]
- Gottschalks, a department store chain, prefers to concentrate locations in secondary cities, where there is strong demand for nationally-advertised merchandise but less competition. In selecting locations, Gottschalks studies the demographic characteristics of the surrounding population, the economic conditions within trading areas, and the extent of competition. It is aware that the current economic climate has had a greater effect on its California stores than on other geographic areas.[26]

[22] *Casey's General Stores, Inc. 1993 10K*, pp. 1, 7.

[23] *Dairy Mart Convenience Stores, Inc. 1993 10K*, pp. 6, 8.

[24] *Delchamps, Inc. 1993 10K*, p. 5.

[25] *Helig-Meyers Company 1993 Annual Report*, p. 13.

[26] *Gottschalks, Inc. 1993 10K*, p. 9.

- The Syms off-price apparel chain seeks locations near major highways or thoroughfares in suburban areas that are populated by a least one million persons and that are readily accessible to customers by car. In certain areas, where there is a population of over two million people, Syms has opened more than one store.[27]
- The S&K off-price apparel chain has predominantly looked for locations in mid-sized markets—opening 3,000- to 4,000-square-foot stores in the 30th to the 150th biggest communities in the United States. It is now testing its Menswear Mega Center, which is designed for larger markets.[28]
- Tuesday Morning—which operates in about 30 states with closeout stores that feature gift merchandise, dinnerware, silver serving pieces, gourmet housewares, and household accessories—carefully reviews demographic data for each new market area and generally wants potential store locations to be in upscale communities.[29]
- The Revco drugstore chain wants to open additional stores within its existing market areas where it has poor market coverage. It is also searching for locations in inner cities.[30]

Several stages of the process involved in gathering information to analyze retail trading areas are shown by the flowchart in Figure 8–5. This chart incorporates not only the characteristics of residents, but also those of the competition. By studying both of these factors, a retailer can determine how saturated an area is for its type of business.

In the next sections, three factors in trading-area selection are discussed: population characteristics, economic base characteristics, and the nature of competition and the level of saturation.

CHARACTERISTICS OF THE POPULATION

A lot of knowledge about a trading area's population characteristics can be gained from secondary data sources. These sources can provide information about an area's population size, number of households, income distribution, education level, age distribution, and more. Because the *Census of Population* and the *Survey of Buying Power* are such valuable sources, each will be briefly described.

Census of Population

The ***Census of Population*** supplies a wide range of demographic data for all U.S. cities and surrounding vicinities. Such data are organized on a geographic basis, starting with blocks and continuing to census tracts, cities, counties, states, and regions. As a rule, fewer data are available for blocks and census tracts than for larger units because of concerns about individuals' privacy. The major advantage of census data is that they provide valuable demographic information on small geographic units.

After a retailer has outlined the boundaries of a trading area, it can use census data to gather information for each of the geographic units contained in the area and then study aggregate demographics. A major breakthrough for retailers occurred with the 1970 census, when the U.S. Bureau of the Census created a computer file for the storage and retrieval of population data by geographic area. The 1980 census added useful data categories for retailers interested in segmenting the market—including racial and ethnic data, small-area income data, and commuting patterns. An on-line computer system was also introduced to make census data more accessible.

[27] *Syms Corporation 1993 10K*, p. 4.

[28] Paul Doocey, "S&K Debuts Mega Center," *Stores* (March 1993), pp. 42–44.

[29] *Tuesday Morning 1992 10K*, p. 4.

[30] *Revco 1993 Annual Report*, p. 9.

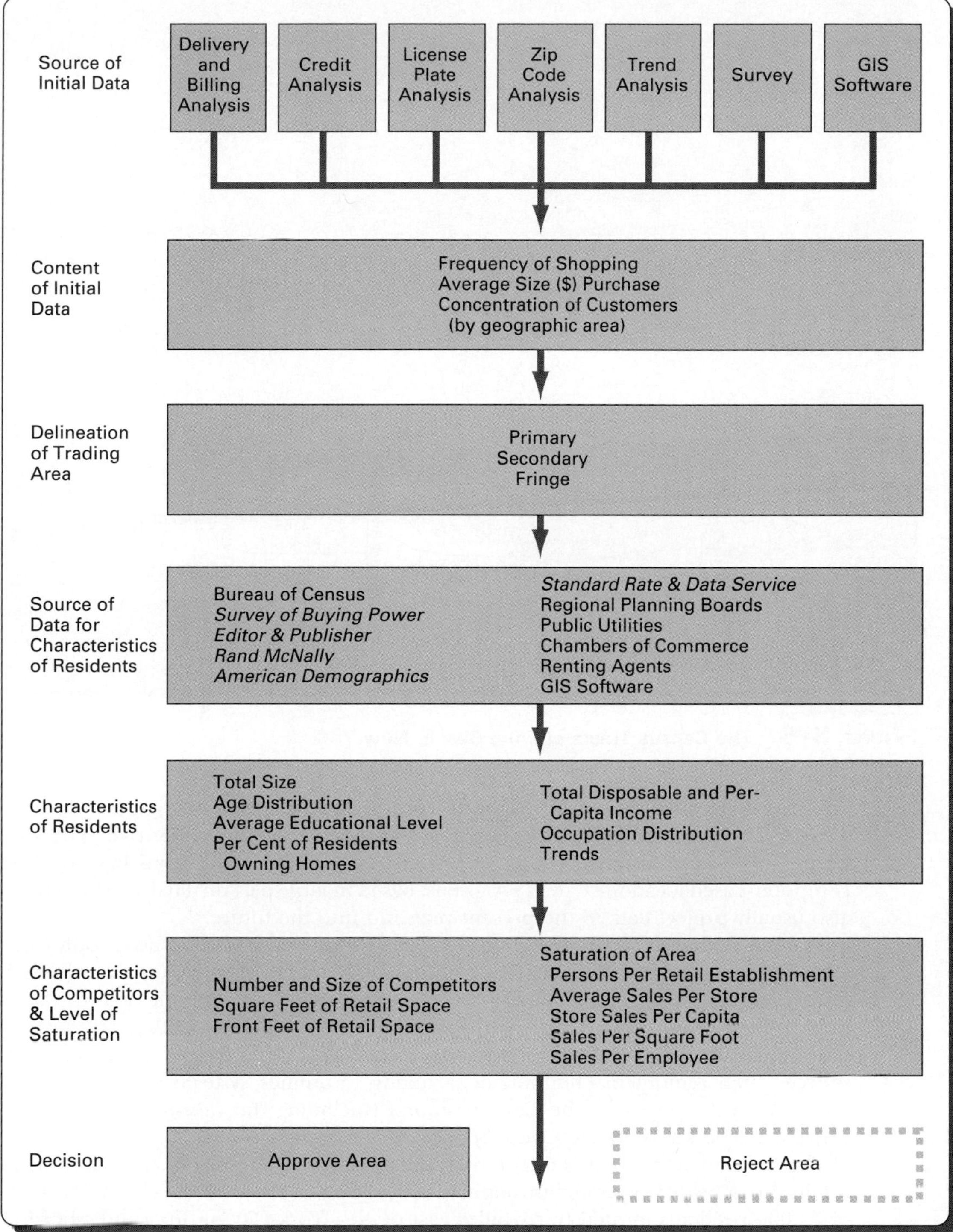

FIGURE 8–5 Analyzing Retail Trading Areas

The 1990 census further expanded the availability of detailed information via computer formats—such as computer tapes, floppy disks, CD-ROM (compact disk-read only memory), and on-line services. But the biggest advance with the 1990 census involved the introduction of TIGER (topologically integrated geographic encoding and referencing) computer tapes, which contain the most detailed physical breakdowns of U.S. areas ever produced. ***TIGER computer tapes*** comprise a computer-readable data base that contains digital descriptions of geographic areas (such as area bound-

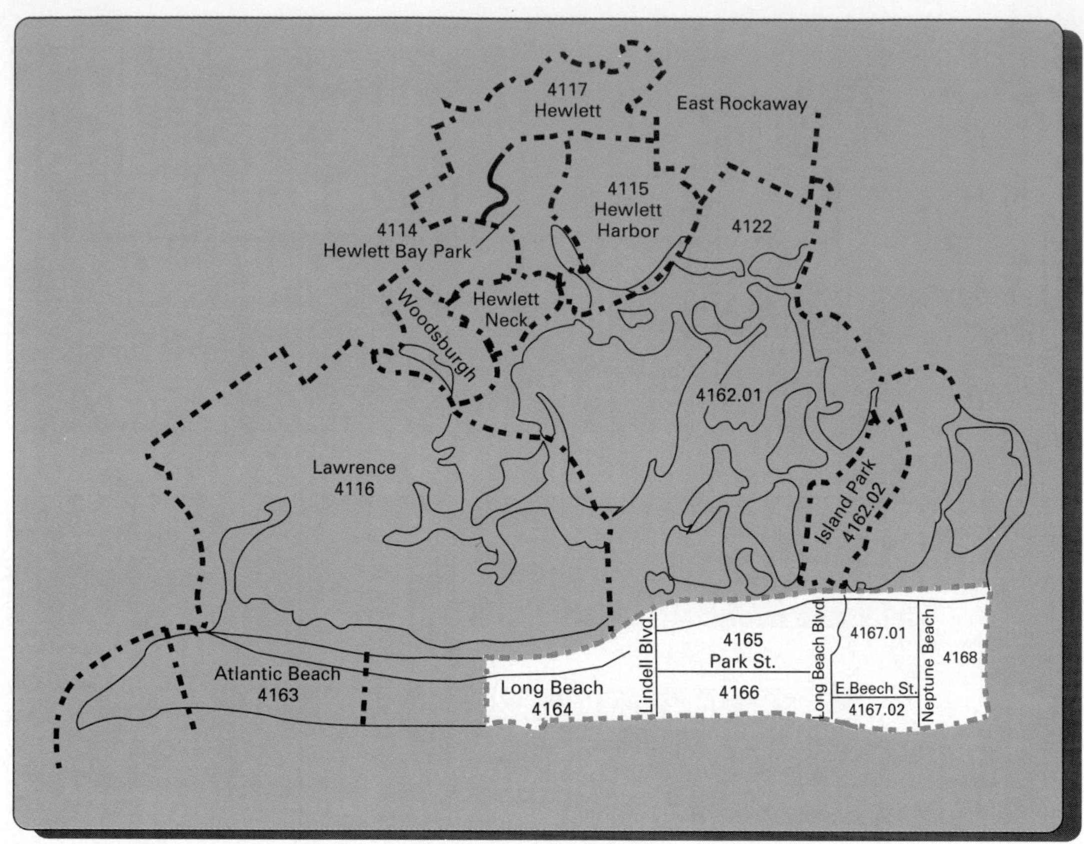

FIGURE 8–6 The Census Tracts of Long Beach, New York

aries and codes, latitude and longitude coordinates, and address ranges). Because TIGER tapes must be used in conjunction with population and other data, GIS software is necessary. As noted earlier in this chapter, many private firms have devised computer-based location-analysis programs, based in large part on TIGER. These firms also usually project data to the present year and into the future.[31]

The major drawbacks of the *Census of Population* are that it is undertaken only once every ten years and that all data are not immediately available when they are collected. For example, information from the 1990 *Census of Population* was released in phases from 1991 through 1993. Thus, census material can become out of date and inaccurate—particularly several years after its collection. Accordingly, supplementary sources, such as municipal building departments or utilities, state government offices, and other U.S. Bureau of the Census reports (including the *Current Population Survey*) must be used to update *Census of Population* data.[32]

The value of actual census tract data (available only via the *Census of Population*) to retailers can be demonstrated through an illustration of Long Beach, New York, a city of 34,000 residents located thirty miles east of New York City on the south shore of Long Island. Long Beach encompasses six census tracts, numbers 4164, 4165, 4166, 4167.01, 4167.02, and 4168. See Figure 8–6. Although census tract 4163 is contiguous with Long Beach, it represents Atlantic Beach, another community.

Table 8–2 contains a variety of population statistics for each of the census tracts in Long Beach. The characteristics of the residents in each tract differ markedly; thus, a retailer might choose to locate in one or more tracts but not in others.

[31] See *TIGER: The Coast-to-Coast Digital Map Data Base* (Washington, D.C.: U.S. Bureau of the Census, November 1990); and *TIGER Resource List* (Washington, D.C.: U.S. Bureau of the Census, October 1993).

[32] See Dowell Myers, "How to Use Local Census Data," *American Demographics* (June 1993), pp. 52–54.

TABLE 8–2 Selected Characteristics of Long Beach, New York, Residents by Census Tract, 1980 and 1990

	Tract Number					
	4164	4165	4166	4167.01	4167.02	4168
Total population:						
1980	6,921	5,480	6,059	4,299	5,008	6,308
1990	7,082	5,694	5,613	4,162	4,479	6,480
1990 population 25 and older	5,315	3,331	4,306	3,003	3,620	5,074
Number of households:						
1980	2,582	1,791	2,183	1,559	2,526	2,976
1990	2,735	1,812	2,219	1,465	2,295	3,066
Education:						
College graduates (% of population 25 and older, 1990)	15.2	13.1	17.8	17.1	20.4	19.5
Income:						
Median household income, 1980	$16,651	$14,089	$11,883	$21,955	$12,606	$21,341
Median household income, 1990	$26,250	$25,211	$30,826	$25,972	$30,135	$26,615
Selected occupations:						
Managerial and professional specialty occupations (% of employed persons 16 and older, 1990)	17.3	12.2	17.3	14.6	17.8	19.6

Sources: *Census of Population and Housing* (Washington, D.C.: U.S. Bureau of the Census, 1980 and 1990), Census Tracts Nassau-Suffolk New York Standard Metropolitan Statistical Area; and authors' computations.

For example, suppose a growing bookstore chain is evaluating two potential trading areas. Area A corresponds roughly with census tracts 4165 and 4166. Area B is similar to census tracts 4167.01, 4167.02, and 4168. The population data for these two areas have been extracted from Table 8–2 and are presented in Table 8–3. Some interesting comparisons can be made.

Area A is substantially different from Area B, despite their geographic proximity and similar physical size:

- The population in Area B is about one third larger than the population in Area A.
- Although both areas declined in population from 1980 to 1990, the rate of population decline was greater in Area B.
- The number of Area B residents aged 25 and older with college degrees is almost two times greater than that of Area A.
- The annual median income in Area A is slightly higher than that of Area B.
- The percentage of workers who are managers or are in professional specialty occupations is greater in Area B than in Area A.

The management of the bookstore chain would probably select Area B since its residents have the attributes desired for the target market. Area A would probably be rejected since it does not rate as high on those attributes.

TABLE 8–3 Selected Population Statistics for Long Beach Trading Areas A and B

	Area A (Tracts 4165 and 4166)	Area B (Tracts 4167.01, 4167.02, and 4168)
Total population, 1990	11,307	15,121
Population change, 1980–1990	−2.0%	−3.2%
Number of college graduates, 25 and older, 1990	1,203	2,245
Median household income, 1990	$28,302	$27,661
Managerial and professional specialty occupations (% of employed persons 16 and older), 1990	14.5%	17.8%

Survey of Buying Power

The ***Survey of Buying Power***, published yearly by *Sales & Marketing Management* magazine, reports current demographic data on metropolitan areas, cities, and states. It also provides some information not available from the *Census of Population*, such as total annual retail sales by area, annual retail sales for specific product categories, annual effective buying income, and 5-year population and retail sales projections.

The most important disadvantage of the *Survey* is its use of broad geographic territories. These territories may not correspond with a store's trading area (they are often much larger than a trading area) and cannot be broken down easily.

The value of the *Survey of Buying Power* can be seen by showing how a prospective new-car dealer could apply it during trading-area analysis for a store location. This dealer is investigating three counties near Chicago: Du Page, Kane, and Lake. Table 8–4 lists selected relevant 1992 population and retail sales data (as well as 1997 projections) for each county under consideration. The *Survey* updates these data each year.

To fully understand the information in Table 8–4, two key terms used in the *Survey of Buying Power* must be defined.[33] ***Effective buying income (EBI)*** is personal income (wages, salaries, interest, dividends, profits, rental income, and pension income) minus federal, state, and local taxes and nontax payments (such as personal contributions for social security insurance). EBI is commonly known as disposable personal income.

The ***buying power index (BPI)*** is a single weighted measure combining effective buying income, retail sales, and population size into an overall indicator of an area's sales potential, expressed as a percentage of total U.S. sales:

Buying power index = 0.5 (the area's percentage of U.S. effective buying income)
+ 0.3 (the area's percentage of U.S. retail sales)
+ 0.2 (the area's percentage of U.S. population)

Each of the three criteria in the index is assigned a weight, based on its relative importance.

The buying power indexes for Du Page, Kane, and Lake Counties are computed in Table 8–5. The BPI of Du Page is over three times greater than that of Kane and 60 per cent greater than that of Lake. As the data in Table 8–4 indicate, Du Page has a larger population and more people 18 and older than either Kane or Lake. These

[33] "Definitions of Terms in the Survey of Buying Power," *Sales & Marketing Management: 1993 Survey of Buying Power* (August 30, 1993), pp. A-16–A-19.

TABLE 8–4 Selected Data from *Survey of Buying Power* Relating to the Automobile Market in Three Illinois Counties, 1992

	County		
	Du Page	Kane	Lake
December 31, 1992			
Total population	827,500	339,300	550,500
Number of people 18 and over	606,600	236,800	396,900
Percentage of population 18 and over	73.3	69.8	72.1
Number of households	296,100	113,900	185,300
Total effective buying income (EBI)	$18,958,202,000	$5,892,344,000	$13,352,026,000
Median household EBI	$55,351	$45,641	$54,745
Per-capita EBI	$22,910	$17,366	$24,254
Percentage of households with $35,000–$49,999 EBI	17.8	20.6	17.8
Percentage of households with $50,000+ EBI	55.4	44.1	55.2
Total retail sales	$11,325,584,000	$2,656,928,000	$5,644,141,000
Buying power index (%)	0.4795	0.1423	0.2996
Percentage of U.S. EBI	0.4840	0.1504	0.3409
Percentage of U.S. retail sales	0.5767	0.1353	0.2874
Percentage of U.S. population	0.3223	0.1322	0.2144
Automobile retail sales, 1992	$1,964,649,000	$507,822,000	$1,523,648,000
Projections for December 31, 1997			
Total population	897,900	374,200	606,600
Percentage of change in population, 1992–1997	8.5	10.3	10.2
Total EBI	$26,978,753,000	$8,428,885,000	$19,239,772,000
Percentage change in total EBI, 1992–1997	42.3	43.0	44.1
Total retail sales	$18,034,912,000	$3,447,694,000	$8,078,565,000
Percentage change in total retail sales, 1992–1997	59.2	29.8	43.1
Buying power index (%)	0.5139	0.1432	0.3110

Source: Adapted from *Sales & Marketing Management: 1993 Survey of Buying Power* (August 30, 1993), pp. B-2, B-3, C-51, C-54; and *Sales & Marketing Management: 1993 Survey of Media Markets* (October 25, 1993), p. 59. Reprinted by permission of Sales & Marketing Management Inc. (c) 1993, S&MM Survey of Buying Power.

are vital statistics for an auto dealer. In addition, 73.2 per cent of Du Page's residents have effective buying incomes of $35,000 or better, compared to 64.7 per cent of Kane's residents and 73.0 per cent of Lake's. In 1992, automobile sales were $1.97 billion in Du Page, compared to $508 million in Kane and $1.52 billion in Lake.

A Cadillac dealer using *Survey of Buying Power* data might select Du Page and a Chevrolet dealer might select Kane. But, because *Survey* statistics are broad in nature,

TABLE 8–5 Computations of Buying Power Indexes: Du Page, Kane, and Lake Counties, 1992[a]

Du Page County
Buying power index = 0.5 (0.4840%) + 0.3 (0.5767%) + 0.2 (0.3223%)
= 0.4795%

Kane County
Buying power index = 0.5 (0.1504%) + 0.3 (0.1353%) + 0.2 (0.1322%)
= 0.1423%

Lake County
Buying power index = 0.5 (0.3409%) + 0.3 (0.2874%) + 0.2 (0.2144%)
= 0.2996%

[a] BPI = 0.5 (area's % of U.S. effective buying income) + 0.3 (area's % of U.S. retail sales) + 0.2 (area's % of U.S. population)

several subsections of Kane may be superior choices to subsections in Du Page (based on census data) for the Cadillac dealer. And the level of competition in each area also must be noted.

Different retailers require different kinds of information about an area's population. The location decision for a bookstore or an automobile dealer usually requires more data than are needed for a fast-food franchise. For a fast-food franchisor, the prime criterion in trading-area analysis is often population density.[34] Thus, many fast-food franchisors seek communities having a large number of people living or working within a three- or four-mile radius of their stores. On the other hand, bookstore owners and automobile dealers cannot locate merely on the basis of population density. They must consider a more complex combination of population attributes in evaluating areas and should look at the sources of data described in this chapter.

ECONOMIC BASE CHARACTERISTICS

It is essential to study the characteristics of each area's economic base. This base reflects the commercial and industrial infrastructure of a community and the sources of income for its residents. A retailer seeking stability will normally prefer an area with a diversified economic base (one with a large number of nonrelated industries and financial institutions) to one with an economic base keyed to one major industry. The latter area is more affected by a strike, declining demand for one product line, and cyclical fluctuations.

In evaluating a trading area, a retailer should investigate such economic base factors as the percentage of the labor force in each industry or trade grouping, the transportation network, banking facilities, the potential impact of economic fluctuations on the area and particular industries, and the future of individual industries (firms). These data can be obtained from *Editor & Publisher Market Guide,* regional planning commission studies, regional industrial development organizations, chambers of commerce, and other sources.

Editor & Publisher Market Guide provides a lot of economic base data for cities on a yearly basis, including principal sources of employment, transportation networks, bank deposits, auto registrations, the number of gas and electric meters, newspaper circulations, and major shopping centers. It also contains statistics on population size and total households by city. Like the *Survey of Buying Power, Editor & Publisher Market Guide* has one serious drawback for retailers. The data cover broad geographic areas and are difficult to disaggregate.

[34] See Robert A. Simons, "Site Attributes in Retail Leasing: An Analysis of a Fast-Food Restaurant Market," *Appraisal Journal* (October 1992), pp. 521–531.

The value of *Editor & Publisher* can be shown by examining some important economic base data from the 1993 description of Sacramento, California. Sacramento is the capital of California. Among its principal industries (each employing at least 24,000 people) are retail and wholesale trade, manufacturing, government, construction, transportation and public utilities, insurance and real estate, and other services. More specifically, Sacramento is involved with U.S. aircraft repair and modification, aerospace, and mobile home manufacturing; and even has an Army depot and training center. It has a large transportation system involving several railroads, motor freight carriers, intercity bus routes, and airlines. The population of several hundred thousand has access to 67 commercial banks, 46 savings and loan associations, and 1 newspaper; and residents own 592,875 passenger autos. There are a number of major shopping centers and retail outlets.[35]

The bookstore chain noted earlier would find *Editor & Publisher* information on shopping centers and retailers to be quite helpful in analyzing cities. The auto dealer would find *Editor & Publisher* information on the transportation network, the availability of financial institutions, and the number of passenger cars to be very useful. In trading-area analysis, *Editor & Publisher Market Guide* is best used to supplement census and *Sales & Marketing Management* statistics.

THE NATURE OF COMPETITION AND THE LEVEL OF SATURATION

A retailing opportunity in an area cannot be accurately assessed unless the competitive structure is studied. Although a trading area may have residents who match the retailer's desired market and may have a strong economic base, it may be a poor location for a new store if competition is too extensive. Similarly, an area with a small population and a narrow economic base may be a good location if competition is minimal.

When examining competition in an area, such factors as these should be analyzed: the number of existing stores, the size distribution of existing stores, the rate of new-store openings, the strengths and weaknesses of all stores, short-run and long-run trends, and the level of saturation. These factors should be evaluated in relation to an area's population size and growth, not just in absolute terms.

For example, over the past decade, many retailers have expanded into states in the Southeast and Southwest due to their growing populations. Thus, Tiffany, Saks Fifth Avenue, Gumps, Target, Marshall Field, Lord & Taylor, and Macy's are among the retailers that have entered the New Orleans, Dallas, Orlando, and/or Phoenix markets to be in areas with expanding populations. However, there is some concern that localities such as these may become oversaturated because of the influx of new stores. Furthermore, while the population in the Northeast has been declining relative to the Southeast and the Southwest, one of its major strengths—population density—should not be disregarded by retailers. According to the U.S. Bureau of the Census, the population density (as expressed by the number of persons residing per square mile) in the Northeast is much higher than in the Southeast and Southwest. In Massachusetts, there are 760 people per square mile. In Louisiana, there are 100; in Texas, 70; in Florida, 250; and in Arizona, 35.

The level of retail saturation in a trading area can be defined as understored, overstored, or saturated. An ***understored trading area*** has too few stores selling a specific good or service to satisfy the needs of its population. An ***overstored trading area*** has so many stores selling a specific good or service that some retailers will be unable to earn an adequate profit. A ***saturated trading area*** has the proper amount of retail facilities to satisfy the needs of its population for a specific good or service, as well as to enable retailers to prosper.

For example, according to research by Vons, the largest supermarket chain in Southern California, the South Central area of Los Angeles is understored. Vons re-

35 "Sacramento," *Editor & Publisher Market Guide 1993*, p. II-44.

ETHICS IN RETAILING

Is Taco Bell Overstepping Its Bounds?

Taco Bell's vigorous store expansion plan, which resulted in 37 per cent more units being opened during one recent five-year period, has significantly boosted the firm's sales and profits. And besides its traditional stores, Taco Bell has also added Taco Bell Express units (a limited-menu prototype with no seating) and street carts.

Many Taco Bell franchisees have complained that the additional stores have led to oversaturated markets. According to these franchisees, Taco Bell does not care how its store-expansion plans affect individual franchised locations. Its contracts with franchisees grant Taco Bell the right to open further outlets within existing franchisees' trading areas.

Some franchisees are fighting back. One franchisee who owns nine Taco Bell units has filed a law suit against the firm. The suit alleges that Taco Bell's plan to build a company-owned restaurant next to his most profitable restaurant is motivated by the franchisor's desire to buy back his location at a low price. A recent law in Iowa, designed to protect franchisees, bans franchisors from opening new stores within three miles of existing franchised stores of the same franchise system.

Source: Based on material in Amy Barrett, "Indigestion at Taco Bell," *Business Week* (December 14, 1992), pp. 66–67.

search shows that as many as 1.2 million people in this inner-city area of Los Angeles do not have access to a supermarket. Thus, Vons plans to spend more than $100 million to build 12 stores there. As one retailing analyst says, "the inner-city strategy makes sense because Vons is going into underserved markets. It will work because people in poor areas like nice stores just like everyone else."[36]

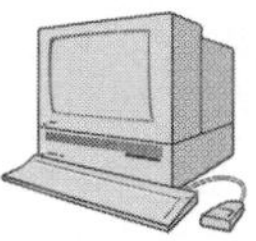

Measuring Trading-Area Saturation

When measuring the level of retail saturation in a trading area, this premise should be kept in mind: any trading area can support only a given number of stores or square feet of selling space per goods/service category. The ratios mentioned in this subsection attempt to quantify retail store saturation. These ratios are meaningful only if norms are established; the level of saturation in a trading area can then be measured against a standard set by the retailer, or it can be compared with that of other trading areas.

For example, the owner of a chain of auto-accessory stores recently found that his current trading area was saturated by computing the ratio of accessory sales to household income. On the basis of this calculation, the owner decided to expand into a nearby metropolitan area with a lower ratio rather than adding another store in the more-established trading area.[37]

Among the ratios that retailers most often use to determine a trading area's level of retail saturation are the

- Number of persons per retail establishment;
- Average sales per retail store;
- Average sales per retail store category;
- Average store sales per capita or household;
- Average sales per square foot of selling area; and
- Average sales per employee.

The statistics necessary to compute these and other ratios can be obtained from a company's records on its own performance, city and state license and tax records, telephone directories, personal visits to locales, consumer surveys, economic census data, *Dun & Bradstreet* reference books, *Editor & Publisher Market Guide, County Business Patterns,* trade association publications, and other sources. Retail sales by product cat-

[36] Calvin Sims, "Vons Opens New Store in a City Torn by Riots," *New York Times* (January 14, 1994), p. D4.

[37] *How People Use Economic Census Data* (Washington, D.C.: U.S. Bureau of the Census, 1992).

egory, the population size, and the number of households per market area can be found in the *Survey of Buying Power.*

While investigating an area's level of saturation for a specific good or service, saturation ratios must be interpreted carefully. Variations among areas sometimes may not be reliable indicators of differences in saturation. For example, car sales per capita are usually different for a suburban area than for an urban area because suburban residents have a much greater need for their cars. Thus, each area's level of saturation should be evaluated against different standards—based on optimum per-capita sales figures in that area.

In calculating the saturation level in an area based upon sales per square foot of selling space, the retailer must remember to take its proposed store into account. If that proposed store is not part of the calculations for the level of saturation, the relative value of each trading area may be distorted; sales per square foot of selling area decline the most when new outlets are added in small communities. Furthermore, the retailer should consider whether a new store will expand the total consumer market for a specific good or service category in a trading area or just increase the firm's market share in that area without expanding the total market.

Table 8–6 shows 1993 background data and selected measures of trading-area saturation for the supermarket industry (including conventional supermarkets, food-

TABLE 8–6 Background Data and Selected Measures of Trading-Area Saturation for Supermarkets (of All Types) in Three Major Texas Markets, 1993

	Dallas	Houston	San Antonio
Background Data:			
Total supermarket sales (mil.)	$8,457	$5,749	$4,489
Total population (in 000s)	6,840	4,802	4,512
Total number of households (in 000s)	2,589	1,751	1,544
Total number of supermarkets	853	524	431
Total square footage for all supermarkets (in 000s)	24,721	15,835	11,348
Total number of employees for all supermarkets	47,811	35,030	26,268
Average square footage per supermarket	28,981	30,219	26,329
Average employees per supermarket	56	67	61
Measures of Trading-Area Saturation:			
Number of persons/supermarket	8,019	9,164	10,469
Average sales per supermarket (in 000s)	$9,914	$10,971	$10,415
Average supermarket sales per capita	$1,236	$1,197	$995
Average supermarket sales per household	$3,267	$3,283	$2,907
Average supermarket sales per square foot	$342	$363	$396
Average supermarket sales per employee (in 000s)	$177	$164	$171

Source: *Marketing Guidebook*, 1994 Edition (Trade Dimensions, Inc.: Stamford, CT: 1993), various pages; and authors' computations.

based superstores, and so on) in three major Texas market areas: Dallas, Houston, and San Antonio. As compiled by Trade Dimensions, Inc., the market areas depicted in the table are quite broad because they include the cities noted, as well as the cities, suburbs, and communities surrounding them.

Dallas is the least saturated on the basis of two of the six ratios: average sales per capita and average sales per employee. It also has the largest population. Houston is the least saturated in terms of average sales per supermarket and average sales per household. Its high average sales per supermarket are due to the larger-than-average supermarkets. San Antonio is the least saturated in terms of the number of persons per supermarket and average sales per square foot. There are far fewer supermarkets in San Antonio than in the other areas, which accounts for the greater number of people per supermarket. Thus, all three areas offer some positive and negative attributes for prospective supermarkets; and the choice of an area must be linked to the saturation factors deemed most critical by the particular retailer.

SUMMARY

1. *To demonstrate the importance of store location for a retailer and outline the process for choosing a store location* The choice of a store location is significant because of the complex decision making involved, the high costs, the lack of flexibility once a site is chosen, and the impact of a site on a retailer's strategy. A good location may let a retailer succeed even if its strategy mix is relatively mediocre.

   The selection of a store location consists of four steps: (1) evaluating alternative trading areas; (2) determining the most desirable type of location; (3) picking a general site; and (4) settling on a specific site. This chapter concentrates on Step 1. Chapter 9 details Steps 2, 3, and 4.

2. *To discuss the concept of a trading area and its related components* A trading area is the geographical area from which a retailer draws its customers. When two or more shopping locales are near to one another, they may have trading-area overlap.

   Today, more and more retailers are utilizing geographic information systems (GIS) software to delineate and analyze their trading areas. This software combines digitized mapping with key locational data to graphically depict trading-area characteristics, thereby allowing retailers to research alternative locations and display the findings on computer-screen maps. Several vendors market GIS software.

   Every trading area has primary, secondary, and fringe components; the farther consumers live from a shopping area, the less likely they are to travel there. The size and shape of a trading area depend on store type, store size, the location of competitors, residential housing patterns, travel time and traffic barriers, and media availability. Due to their distinctiveness, destination stores have much larger trading areas than parasite stores.

3. *To show how trading areas may be delineated for existing and new stores* The size, shape, and characteristics of the trading area for an existing store or group of stores can be identified quite accurately. A retailer can gather data by examining store records, sponsoring contests, recording license plate numbers and linking them to customer addresses, surveying consumers, purchasing specialized computer-generated data, and so on. Time biases must be considered when amassing data. Results should be mapped and customer densities noted.

   Alternate trading areas for a new store must often be described in terms of opportunities rather than current patronage and traffic patterns. Trend analysis and consumer surveys may be used. There are three computerized trading-area models that could be used for planning a new store location: analog, regression, and gravity. These models offer several benefits.

   Two techniques for delineating new trading areas are Reilly's law of retail gravitation, which relates the population size of different cities to the size of their trading areas; and Huff's law of shopper attraction, which is based on each area's shopping assortment, the distance of people from various retail locales, and the sensitivity of people to travel time.

4. *To examine three major factors in trading-area analysis: population characteristics, economic base characteristics, and competition and the level of saturation* Once the size and shape of each possible trading area have been determined, these key factors should be studied in depth. The best secondary sources for population data are the *Census of Population* and the *Survey of Buying Power*. These sources have complementary strengths and weaknesses for retailers. Census data are the most detailed and specific for retailers; they can become dated. The buying power index is available through the *Survey of Buying Power*; but it reports on broader geographic areas.

A trading area's economic base reflects the commercial and industrial infrastructure of the community and the income sources for its residents. A retailer should look at such economic base factors as the percentage of the labor force in each industry grouping, the transportation network, banking facilities, the potential impact of economic fluctuations on the area, and the future of individual industries. *Editor & Publisher Market Guide* is a good source of data on economic base characteristics.

A trading area cannot be properly analyzed without studying the nature of competition and the level of saturation. An area may be understored (too few retailers), overstored (too many retailers), or saturated (the proper number of retailers). Store saturation may be measured in several ways, such as the number of persons per retail establishment, the average sales per retail store, the average store sales per capita or household, average sales per square foot of selling space, and average sales per employee.

KEY TERMS

trading area (p. 265)
trading-area overlap (p. 266)
geographic information systems (GIS) (p. 267)
primary trading area (p. 272)
secondary trading area (p. 272)
fringe trading area (p. 272)
destination store (p. 273)
parasite store (p. 273)
analog model (p. 276)
regression model (p. 276)
gravity model (p. 276)
Reilly's law of retail gravitation (p. 276)
point of indifference (p. 276)
Huff's law of shopper attraction (p. 277)
economic base (p. 279)
***Census of Population* (p. 282)**
TIGER computer tapes (p. 283)
***Survey of Buying Power* (p. 286)**
effective buying income (EBI) (p. 286)
buying power index (BPI) (p. 286)
***Editor & Publisher Market Guide* (p. 288)**
understored trading area (p. 289)
overstored trading area (p. 289)
saturated trading area (p. 289)

QUESTIONS FOR DISCUSSION

1. If a retailer has a new twenty-year store lease, does this mean the next time it studies the characteristics of its trading area should be fifteen years from now? Explain your answer.
2. What is trading-area overlap? Are there any advantages to a chain retailer's having some overlap among its various stores? Why or why not?
3. Describe three ways in which an optical chain could use geographic information systems (GIS) software in its trading-area analysis.
4. How could an off-campus video store situated near a college campus determine its primary, secondary, and fringe trading areas? Why should the video store obtain this information?
5. Why do few trading areas look like concentric circles?
6. How could a parasite store increase the size of its trading area?
7. Explain Reilly's law. What are its advantages and disadvantages?
8. Use Huff's law to compute the probability of consumers' traveling from their homes to each of three shopping areas: square footage of selling space—Location 1, 3,000; Location 2, 5,000; Location 3, 8,000; travel time—to Location 1, 8 minutes; to Location 2, 15 minutes; to Location 3, 30 minutes; effect of travel time on shopping trip—2. Explain your answer.
9. What are the major advantages and disadvantages of *Census of Population* data in delineating trading areas?
10. Describe the kinds of retail information contained in the *Survey of Buying Power.* What is its most critical disadvantage?
11. Look at the most recent buying power index in the *Survey of Buying Power* for the area in which your college is located. What retailing-related conclusions do you draw?
12. Look at the most recent issue of *Editor & Publisher Market Guide* and study the economic base characteristics for the area in which your college is located. What retailing-related conclusions do you draw?
13. If a retail area is acknowledged to be "saturated," what does this signify for existing retailers? For prospective retailers considering this area?
14. Calculate several supermarket saturation ratios for cities A and B, based upon the following data:

	City A	City B
Supermarket sales (millions)	$ 7,000	$ 6,000
Population (thousands)	8,000	5,000
Households (thousands)	3,000	2,200
Supermarkets	800	600
Supermarket employees	40,000	35,000

Which city is better to locate a new store? Explain your answer.

CASE 1

Arby's: The Use of Strategic Mapping Software*

Since 1983, Strategic Mapping, Inc. has been the world's leading producer of geographic information systems (GIS) software for personal computers. Its traditional software, Atlas GIS, sells for about $3,000 and runs on IBM compatibles (in DOS, Windows, and UNIX operating systems). Its newest product, Atlas Pro, is available in versions for both IBM compatibles and Macintoshes, and sells for less than $1,000.

Atlas GIS enables the user to generate reports on a retail site's trading area characteristics, after the user first "points and clicks" with a computer's mouse to identify the borders of a site's trading area. Natural boundaries such as rivers, highways, and major cross streets are often used as trading area borders; and the locations of major competitors can also be placed on maps. Atlas GIS reports can detail a trading area's population size, the number of households, the total male and female population, the median age, the value of owner-occupied housing, and per-capita income. These data can also be analyzed in a variety of ways. For example, a retailer user may wish to determine the total population within 3, 5, and 8 miles of a site. A trading area's current population can also be contrasted with its population in 1980 or with a 1997 forecast population.

Retailers utilizing Atlas GIS can evaluate trading-area data through four commands:

- View—Lets users see relationships, determine concentrations of customers, and identify locational opportunities. For instance, a firm could use the view function to see how sales decline as the consumer's distance from a given retail site increases. This analysis is often used to divide a trading area into primary, secondary, and fringe trading-area components.
- Ask—Presents data upon the users' request. For example, a firm could ask for a listing of all retail sites where the median household income exceeds $50,000 per year.
- Analyze—Lets users combine different types of data. For instance, a firm may want to identify areas for expansion based upon multiple site-selection constraints. Thus, the user could apply the analyze function to generate a list of areas that are between 10 and 15 miles from an existing store, and within a mile from a major department store location.
- Present—Lets users depict relationships using different shadings, dot densities, symbol sizes, and colors. The present command enables firms to develop reports and slides.

One user of Atlas GIS is Arby's, a fast-food franchisor that specializes in selling fresh, hot roast beef. Prior to using the Atlas software, Arby's denoted its current locations by first placing a dot on a road map and then drawing a circle around it. Market surveys of competition were done in a similar fashion.

Conducting trading-area analysis with Atlas GIS software has several advantages for Arby's. First, it avoids the tedious process of producing hand-made maps. Sec-

* The material in this case is drawn from John C. Freed, "Mapping Software for Everybusiness," *New York Times* (February 16, 1992), Section 3, p. 9; John Freehling, "Use Drive Times to Build Trading Areas and Market Segments," *Marketing News* (May 10, 1993), p. 2; and *Geographic Analysis: A Key to Retailing Success* (Santa Clara, CA: Strategic Mapping, Inc., n.d.).

ond, maps can easily be related to a data base, such as the number of residents within a given distance of each site. Third, a larger number of potential sites can be identified based upon desirable trading-area characteristics. And fourth, "what if" scenarios—such as the impact of a new franchise location on an existing unit's sales—can more easily be determined. According to an Arby's executive, "You can imagine what they'd have to go through to make a change [in the manual method]."

In employing Strategic Mapping, Inc.'s Atlas GIS software for its trading-area analysis, Arby's works with two urban geographers. And it can easily determine the trading areas for existing, as well as new, locations, evaluate the trading-area characteristics of potential sites, and examine the level of saturation in each area. Through this software, Arby's has found that 75 per cent of its customers usually travel 11 minutes or less from their home or workplace to a location. The firm has also learned each store's primary, secondary, and fringe trading areas on the basis of travel time (less than 5 minutes, 5 to 10 minutes, and 10 to 15 minutes). The analysis is based upon a detailed data base of road characteristics (which outline each road's normal traffic speed and the distance of a location to an entrance or exit ramp of an interstate highway). These drive times have been placed into a GIS computer program to develop maps based on driving times from every Arby's location.

Arby's is using these findings to segment the market for its food services by travel time to each outlet. Customers located less than 5 minutes from an existing Arby's represent a good target market for the firm's quick-service message or for programs that increase a customer's frequency of purchase. On the other hand, for customers who live or work more than 15 minutes from an existing store, Arby's would use a marketing program that stresses the fresh preparation and sliced-to-order benefits of its roast beef.

QUESTIONS

1. Compare the pros and cons of Atlas GIS versus manual systems for describing the characteristics of trading areas to Arby's.
2 Develop specific criteria that Arby's can use to evaluate Strategic Mapping, Inc. as a GIS software vendor.
3. In deciding whether to open a second outlet in a particular trading area, what criteria should Arby's use? How could Arby's use Atlas GIS to improve its decision making in this situation?
4. Would you recommend the use of Atlas GIS or similar software for a retailer with one store? Explain your answer.

VIDEO QUESTIONS ON STRATEGIC MAPPING

1. The video lists five functions for Atlas GIS: present data geographically, query the map, retrieve information, query the data base, and show results geographically. Explain each of these functions.
2. Offer three trading-area-based applications for Arby's that are not mentioned in the video.

CASE 2
Abernathy's: Assessing Saturation Data

Abernathy's is a Pennsylvania-based supermarket chain that is exploring growth opportunities in Connecticut, New Jersey, and New York. The firm acknowledges that it has saturated the Pennsylvania market and believes these neighboring states offer excellent growth opportunities:

- A high percentage of people who live in areas that border on Pennsylvania are already aware of Abernathy's. Many have visited its Pennsylvania stores. Some local television advertising has also spilled over into these states.
- In the short-run, Abernathy's can serve new stores in these states from its current distribution center. According to Abernathy's management, the firm's distribution center is currently operating at 85 per cent of capacity.
- Abernathy's store format offers several competitive advantages over a lot of the older stores located in these states. For example, Abernathy's stores feature a bakery, a florist, a prepared-foods section (including a fresh pasta, a salad bar, and a

Table 1 Supermarket Saturation Data

	State		
	Connecticut	New Jersey	New York
Number of supermarkets, 1992	329	696	1,717
Total supermarket sales, 1992 (millions)	$3,994	$9,505	$16,941
Total food sales, 1992 (millions)	$6,106	$13,658	$25,546
Total retail sales, 1992 (millions)	$29,412	$67,702	$126,079
Total population, 12/31/92 (thousands)	3,277	7,827	18,188
Total effective buying income, 12/31/92 (millions)	$68,604	$162,125	$312,648
Area's percentage of U.S. retail sales, 12/31/92	1.498	3.447	6.419
Area's percentage of U.S. population, 12/31/92	1.276	3.048	7.083
Area's percentage of U.S. effective buying income, 12/31/92	1.751	4.139	7.982
Projections for December 31, 1997			
Total annual retail sales (millions)	$38,166	$88,611	$153,991
Total population (thousands)	3,217	7,972	18,439
Total annual effective buying income (millions)	$91,988	$219,802	$407,604

Sources: Adapted by the authors from "For the Record," *Progressive Grocer*, (April 1993), p. 107; *Sales & Marketing Management: 1993 Survey of Media Markets* (October 25, 1993), pp. 55, 67, and 69; and *Sales & Marketing Management: Survey of Buying Power* (August 30, 1993), pp. B-2, B-3, B-4, C-28, C-107, C-114. Reprinted by permission of Sales & Marketing Management Inc. © 1993, S&MM Survey of Buying Power.

Table 2 Ratios Used to Estimate Store Saturation

	State		
	Connecticut	New Jersey	New York
Supermarket sales as a per cent of total food sales	65.4	69.6	66.3
Supermarket sales as a per cent of total retail sales	13.6	14.0	13.4
Annual supermarket sales per capita	$1,219	$1,214	$932
Supermarket sales as a per cent of effective buying income	5.8	5.9	5.4
Average annual sales per supermarket	$12,139,817	$13,656,609	$9,866,628

Chinese wok-style kitchen), an expresso/coffee bar, and a catering section. Abernathy's also has a full-service butcher and a separate seafood department. Its produce department stocks quality items. Besides traditional seasonal fruits and vegetables, Abernathy's strives to stock most produce on a year-round basis by importing these foods.

Abernathy's has hired Location Consultants Inc., a site location specialist, to study the degree of market saturation by supermarkets in Connecticut, New Jersey, and New York. For now, Abernathy's is interested in learning which of the states offers the best overall expansion opportunities. At a later point, Location Consultants Inc. will be asked to assemble and compute store-saturation data on a county-by-county basis to help Abernathy's focus on specific trading areas.

Among the sources of data being analyzed by Location Consultants Inc. are "For the Record" from *Progressive Grocer* and *Sales & Marketing Management's Survey of Buying Power* and *Survey of Media Markets* issues. Although Location Consultants has sought to obtain other relevant secondary data, such as the mix of traditional supermarkets, superstores, and combination stores in each state, these data are unavailable. The firm's preliminary figures are shown in Tables 1 and 2.

QUESTIONS

1. Compute the buying power index for each state. Explain your answer.
2 Interpret Tables 1 and 2. Which state is the most saturated? The least saturated? Explain your answer.
3. What factors are *not* taken into account In Tables 1 and 2.
4. What sources of county-based data exist? Comment on their accuracy.

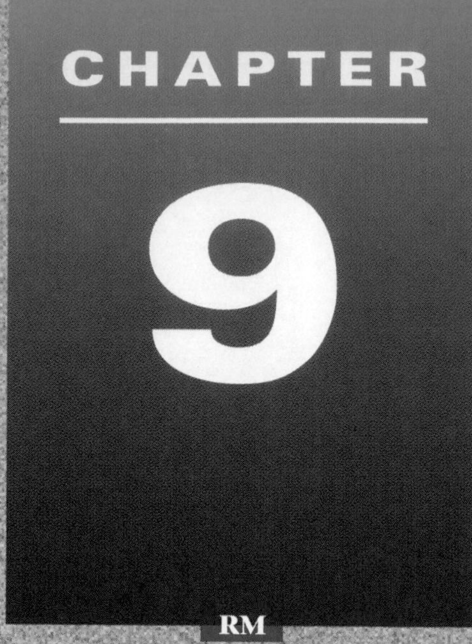

Site Selection

❖ Chapter Objectives

1. To thoroughly examine the types of locations available to a retailer: isolated store, unplanned business district, and planned shopping center
2. To note the decisions necessary in choosing a general retail location
3. To describe the concept of the one-hundred per cent location
4. To discuss several criteria for evaluating general retail locations and the specific sites within them
5. To contrast alternative terms of occupancy

Shopping centers range in size from small strip centers that serve the convenience needs of neighborhoods to giant megamalls (such as West Edmonton Mall and Mall of America) that have millions of square feet of retail space and serve as major tourist destinations.

Unlike larger malls, many smaller strip centers are dominated by small independent retailers and have not instituted cooperative advertising programs that are co-sponsored by the retail tenants and the centers' management. Yet, Baita International is an example of a strip-center owner that is using a marketing director to devise a detailed marketing plan for 12 of the centers it owns in Florida. Baita also has an in-house advertising agency, which enables its tenants to receive a 15 per cent discount on their advertising. While the owners of larger centers often invest in promotional programs as a way to increase rent payments (because many big chains pay rent as a percentage of sales), smaller center owners typically invest in marketing programs as a means of keeping existing tenants in business.

At the extreme upper end of the shopping-center size spectrum are the West Edmonton Mall (located in West Edmonton, Alberta, Canada) and the Mall of America (located in Bloomington, Minnesota). They are the two largest enclosed combination retail and family entertainment complexes in the world. Because these megamalls combine huge retail facilities and family entertainment in one complex, they are able to serve as leading tourist destinations for their respective geographic areas. The West Edmonton Mall boasts well over 800 retail stores, eleven of which are department stores. For entertainment and lodging, the West Edmonton Mall has theme streets, over 150 restaurants, half a dozen amusement centers (such as a water park and a National Hockey League-sized ice rink), and a 360-room Fantasyland hotel.

West Edmonton Mall attracts about 20 million visitors per year. The Edmonton Convention and Tourist Authority estimates that over 60 per cent of all inquiries at its Visitor Information Centers are related to that mall. Similarly, one-half of all out-of-town visitors to the Minneapolis-St. Paul, Minnesota, area say the Mall of America is their main reason for visiting that area.[1]

[1] Gary Belsky, "Watch Out, Disneyland!" *Money* (October 1992), pp. 213–220; West Edmonton Mall 1994 press kit; "Mall of America: A Merchant," *TIAA/CREF: The Participant* (November 1993), p. 6; and "Who Says You Can't Market a Strip Center?" *Chain Store Age Executive* (October 1993), p. 52.

Reprinted by permission of Triple Five Corporation Ltd. Photo by the Postcard Factory.

Overview

After a retailer investigates alternative trading areas (Step 1), it then determines what type of location is desirable (Step 2), selects the general location (Step 3), and evaluates alternative specific store sites (Step 4). Steps 2, 3, and 4 are discussed in this chapter.

Types of Locations

There are three basic location types a retailer should distinguish among: the isolated store, the unplanned business district, and the planned shopping center. Each type of location has its own characteristics relating to the composition of competing stores, parking facilities, nearness to nonretail institutions (such as office buildings), and other factors.

Step 2 in the location process is a determination of which type of location to use.

The Isolated Store

An ***isolated store*** is a freestanding retail outlet located on either a highway or a street. There are no adjacent retailers with which this type of store shares traffic.

The advantages of this type of retail location are many:

- There is no competition.
- Rental costs are relatively low.
- There is flexibility.
  1. No group rules must be abided by in operation.
  2. Larger space may be attained.
  3. Location is by choice.
- Isolation is good for stores involved in one-stop or convenience shopping.
- Better road and traffic visibility is possible.
- Facilities can be adapted to individual specifications.
- Easy parking can be arranged.
- Cost reductions are possible, leading to lower prices.

There are also various disadvantages to this retail location type:

- Initial customers may be difficult to attract.
- On an ongoing basis, many people will not travel very far to get to one store.
- Most people like variety in shopping.
- Advertising costs may be high.
- Operating costs cannot be shared, such as outside lighting, security, maintenance of grounds, and trash collection.
- The prior existence of other retailers and community zoning laws may restrict access to desirable locations.
- Often, a store must be built rather than rented.
- Generally, unplanned business districts and planned shopping centers are much more popular among consumers; they generate the bulk of retail sales.

The difficulty of attracting and holding a target market is the major reason large retailers (such as Wal-Mart) or convenience-oriented retailers (such as 7-Eleven) are usually those best suited to isolated locations. For example, a smaller specialty store would probably be unable to develop a customer following at this type of location because people would be unwilling to travel to or shop at a store not having a very large assortment of products (width and/or depth) and a strong image for merchandise and/or prices.

Years ago, when discount operations were frowned on by traditional retailers, numerous shopping centers forbade the entry of discounters. This forced various discounters to become isolated stores or to build their own centers, and they have been successful.

Today, diverse retailers operate in isolated locations, as well as at business-district and shopping-center sites. Examples of retailers using a mixed-location strategy are Kmart, Kinney Shoes, McDonald's, Carvel, Sears, Toys "R" Us, Wal-Mart, and 7-Eleven. Some retailers, such as many gasoline stations and convenience stores, continue to emphasize isolated locations.

The Unplanned Business District

An ***unplanned business district*** is a type of retail location where two or more stores are situated together or (in close proximity) in such a manner that the total arrangement or mix of stores in the district is not the result of prior long-range planning. Stores situate on the basis of what is best for them, not for the district. Accordingly, four shoe stores may exist in an area that has no pharmacy.

There are four kinds of unplanned business districts: the central business district, the secondary business district, the neighborhood business district, and the string. A brief description of each of these follows.

Central Business District

A ***central business district (CBD)*** is the hub of retailing in a city. It is the largest shopping area in that city and is synonymous with the term "downtown." The CBD exists in the part of a town or city with the greatest concentration of office buildings and retail stores. Vehicular and pedestrian traffic are highly concentrated. The core of the CBD usually does not exceed a square mile. Cultural and entertainment facilities surround it. Consumers are drawn from the whole urban area and include all ethnic groups and all classes of people.

The CBD has at least one major department store and a broad grouping of specialty and convenience stores. The arrangement of these stores follows no format; it depends on history (first come, first located), retail trends, and luck.

Here are some of the strengths that enable CBDs to attract a large number of shoppers and potential shoppers:

- Excellent goods/service assortment.
- Access to public transportation.
- Variety of store types and images within one area.
- Wide range of prices offered.
- Variety of customer services.
- High level of pedestrian traffic.
- Nearness to commercial and social facilities.

In addition, chain headquarters stores are often situated in CBDs.

These are some of the inherent weaknesses of the CBD:

- Inadequate parking.
- Traffic and delivery congestion.
- Travel time for those living in the suburbs.
- Age of many of the retail facilities.

- Declining condition of some central cities relative to their suburbs.
- Relatively poor image of central cities to some potential consumers.
- High rents and taxes for the most popular sites.
- Movement of some popular downtown stores to suburban shopping centers.
- Discontinuity of offerings (such as four shoe stores and no pharmacy).

Although the CBD remains a major force in retailing, over the past four decades, its share of overall store sales has fallen substantially, compared to the planned shopping center. Besides having the weaknesses just cited, much of the CBD's decline has been due to the continuing suburbanization of the population. In the first half of the twentieth century, most urban workers lived right near their jobs, and central cities had a large well-balanced mix of income, racial, and cultural groups. But gradually, many people (especially middle-class and upper-income ones) have moved to the suburbs—where they are served by planned shopping centers.

Nonetheless, a number of CBDs are doing quite well and others are striving to return to their former stature. Many are using such tactics as modernizing storefronts and equipment, forming strong cooperative merchants' associations, planting trees to create "atmosphere," building vertical malls (with several floors of stores), improving transportation networks, closing streets to vehicular traffic, and integrating a commercial and residential environment—known as mixed-use facilities. There are signs of turnarounds and continuing strong retail developments in numerous cities.[2]

One of the best examples of a CBD turnaround involves Cleveland, where the business community has worked hard to strengthen the central city to make it more competitive with suburban shopping centers and to stimulate office construction. As a vice-president of May Department Stores noted: "Cleveland is one of the great turnaround cities in the U.S. The community is a lot healthier than it has been for a long long time."[3]

A cornerstone of Cleveland's downtown renaissance is the new upscale $400-million Tower City Center, a mixed-use pre-planned enclosed project with 6.5-million square feet of space for commercial, retail, hotel, and entertainment facilities—located on 34 acres above a renovated commuter railroad station on Public Square. It has a three-level Skylight Concourse and is situated in an area with 250,000 workers nearby. Tower City Center will eventually have 120 specialty stores, major office complexes, a multiscreen cinema, restaurants, and up to four anchor stores. There is a Ritz-Carlton Hotel in the Tower City Center; and the first retailer to commit to having an anchor store was Neiman-Marcus. According to observers, "Getting Neiman's in particular is going to make Tower City a very important place."[4]

Faneuil Hall in Boston is a different type of successful CBD renovation. When developer James Rouse took over the 6.5-acre site containing three 150-year-old, block-long former food warehouses, it had been abandoned for almost ten years. Rouse creatively used landscaping, fountains, banners, open-air courts, informal entertainment (street performers), and colorful graphics to enable Faneuil Hall to capture a festive spirit. Faneuil Hall has combined shopping, eating, and watching activities and made them fun. Today, Faneuil Hall attracts millions of shoppers and visitors yearly.

Other major CBD projects include The Gallery at Harborplace (Baltimore), Union Station (St. Louis), Circle Centre (Indianapolis), St. Louis Centre, Metropolis Times Square (New York City), Horton Plaza (San Diego), New Orleans Centre, and Underground Atlanta. See Figure 9–1.

[2] See "Things Are Much Better Downtown," *Chain Store Age Executive* (October 1993), pp. 60–64; and Susan Diesenhouse, "As Suburbs Slow, Supermarkets Return to Cities," *New York Times* (June 27, 1993), Section 3, p. 5.

[3] Jon Connole, "Retailing in Cleveland Heads Downtown for New Wave of Growth," *Advertising Age* (March 12, 1990), p. M-4.

[4] Ibid.; and "Discounters Find Cleveland," *Chain Store Age Executive* (January 1994), pp. 71–72.

ETHICS IN RETAILING

Should Stores Head Downtown?

After being neglected by major retail chains, downtown shopping areas have recently been rediscovered. Filene's Basement, Kmart, Toys "R" Us, and Target are among the leading chains that have recently been placing more stores in downtown sites. Various reasons have been given for the resurgence in downtown retailing: the high population densities, the relatively low rents, the strong customer base, the large lunch-time crowds, and the oversaturation of many suburban locations.

The growth in downtown retailing has lead to a number of important ethical issues. Here are some of them:

- Should retailers situate in inner-city locations, as well as mainstream downtown locations?
- Should the merchandise mix be tailored to reflect the characteristics of local shoppers?
- Should prices be higher to reflect insurance, security, pilferage, and store renovation costs? Or lower to reflect the below-average incomes in certain communities?
- What special obligations do retailers have to residential tenants who live above or adjacent to stores (in terms of garbage pickup, noise control, and delivery times)?
- What added security measures are required to protect the store's shoppers and employees?
- Should special efforts be made to hire employees and managers who are inner-city residents?
- Should retailers work with community groups to revitalize blighted areas?

Source: Based on material in Gregory A. Patterson, "All Decked Out, Stores Head Downtown," *Wall Street Journal* (February 15, 1994), pp. B1–B2.

Secondary Business District

A ***secondary business district (SBD)*** is an unplanned shopping area in a city or town that is usually bounded by the intersection of two major streets. Cities—particularly larger ones—often have multiple SBDs, each having at least a junior department store (which may be a branch of a traditional department store or a full-line discount store), a variety store, and/or some larger specialty stores—in addition to many smaller stores. This type of location has grown in importance as cities have increased in population and "sprawled" over larger geographic areas.

The kinds of goods and services sold in an SBD mirror those in the CBD. However, an SBD has smaller stores, less width and depth of assortment, and a smaller trading area (consumers will not travel as far) and sells a higher proportion of convenience-oriented items.

The major strengths of the SBD include good product assortments, access to thoroughfares and/or public transportation, less crowding and more personal service than the CBD, and placement nearer to residential areas than the CBD. The major weaknesses of the SBD include the discontinuity of offerings, the sometimes high rent and taxes (but not as high as in the CBD), traffic and delivery congestion, aging facilities, parking difficulties, and the existence of fewer chain-store outlets than in the CBD. In general, these weaknesses have not affected the SBD to the extent they have affected the CBD—and parking problems, travel time, and congestion are less for the SBD.

Neighborhood Business District

A ***neighborhood business district (NBD)*** is an unplanned shopping area that appeals to the convenience-shopping and service needs of a single residential area. An NBD contains several small stores, such as a dry cleaner, a stationery store, a barber shop and/or a beauty salon, a liquor store, and a restaurant; the leading retailer is typically a supermarket, a large drugstore, or a variety store. This type of business district is situated on the major street(s) of its residential area.

An NBD offers consumers a good location, long store hours, good parking, and a less hectic atmosphere than the CBD or the SBD. On the other hand, there is a limited selection of goods and services, and prices (on the average) tend to be higher because competition is less than in the CBD or the SBD.

FIGURE 9–1
Revitalized Central Business Districts
Large business districts rely on the customer traffic drawn by office buildings, as well as cultural and entertainment facilities. Three popular, revitalized business districts are Faneuil Hall, Boston (1); The Gallery at Harborplace, Baltimore (2 and 3); and Union Station, St. Louis (4).
Photos courtesy of Rouse Company.

String

A ***string*** is an unplanned shopping area comprising a group of retail stores, often with similar or compatible product lines, located along a street or highway. There is little extension of the shopping area onto streets perpendicular to the string street. A string may start as an isolated store, success then breeding competitors. Car dealers, antique stores, and clothing stores are examples of stores commonly situating in strings.

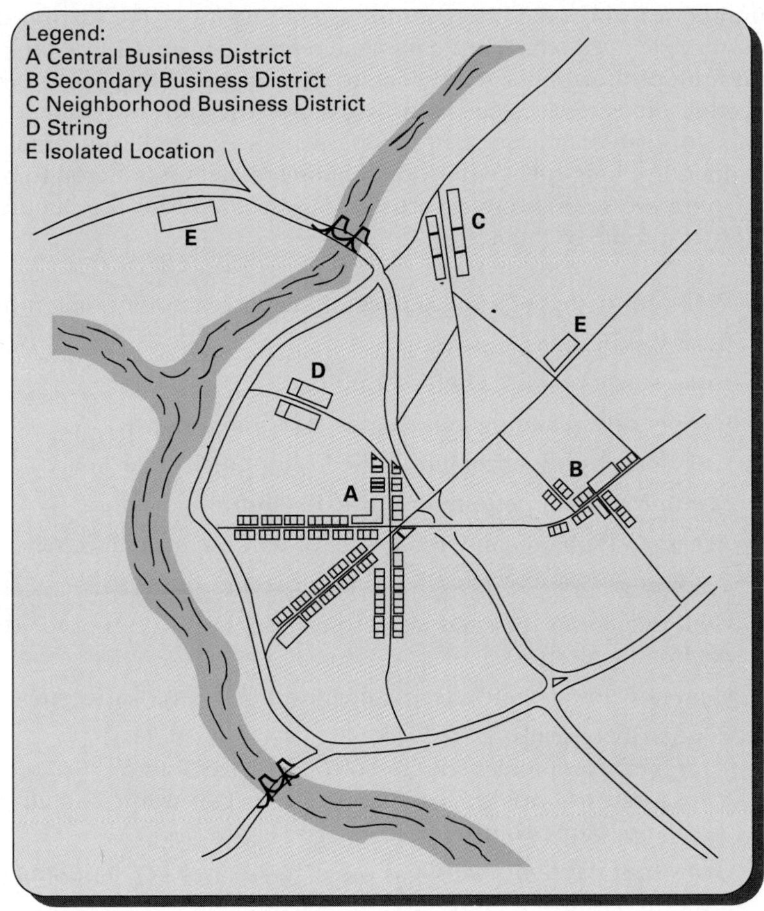

FIGURE 9–2
Unplanned Business Districts and Isolated Locations
Courtesy Kenneth Cooperman.

A string location possesses many of the advantages associated with an isolated store site (such as lower rent, more flexibility, better road visibility and parking, lower operating costs), along with some of its disadvantages (such as the limited variety of products, the increased travel time for many consumers, higher advertising costs, zoning restrictions, and the need to build premises). Unlike an isolated store, a string store has competition at its location. This attracts more customer traffic to the string area and allows for some sharing of common costs among firms. It also leads to less control over prices and lower store loyalty for each outlet there. But an individual store's increased traffic flow, due to locating in a string rather than an isolated site, may be greater than the customers lost to competitors. This may explain why four gas stations will locate on opposing corners.

Figure 9–2 shows a map depicting the various forms of unplanned business districts and isolated locations.

THE PLANNED SHOPPING CENTER

A ***planned shopping center*** consists of a group of architecturally unified commercial establishments built on a site that is centrally owned or managed, designed and operated as a unit, based on balanced tenancy, and surrounded by parking facilities. Its location, size, and mix of stores are related to the trading area being served.[5] A typical shopping center has one or more anchor, or generator, stores and a diversity of smaller stores.

Through ***balanced tenancy***, the stores in a planned shopping center complement each other in the quality and variety of their product offerings, and the kind and

[5] *Statistical Abstract of the United States 1993* (Washington, D.C.: U.S. Bureau of the Census, 1993), p. 781.

number of stores are linked to the overall needs of the surrounding population. To ensure balanced tenancy, the management of a planned shopping center usually specifies the proportion of total space to be occupied by each kind of retailer, limits the product lines that can be sold by each of the various retailers, and stipulates what kinds of firms can acquire unexpired leases. At a well-run center, a coordinated and cooperative long-run, centerwide retailing strategy is adhered to by all member stores.

There are several positive attributes associated with the planned shopping center. Here are some of them:

- Well-rounded goods and service offerings because of long-range planning.
- Strong suburban population.
- Interest in one-stop, family shopping.
- Cooperative planning and sharing of common costs.
- Creation of distinctive, but unified, shopping-center images.
- Maximization of pedestrian traffic for individual stores.
- Access to highways and availability of parking for consumers.
- Declining appeal of city shopping for some consumers.
- Generally lower rent and taxes than CBD stores (except for the more-costly, enclosed-mall sites).
- Generally lower theft rates than central business district stores.
- Popularity of malls.
    1. Open (shopping area closed to vehicular traffic).
    2. Closed (shopping area closed to vehicular traffic and all stores under one temperature-controlled roof). See Figure 9–3.
- Growth of discount malls and other newer types of shopping centers.

Despite this overwhelming list of positive qualities for the planned shopping center, there are also some limitations with this arrangement:

- Regulations that reduce each retailer's operating flexibility, such as required store hours.
- Generally higher rent than for an isolated-store location (with some regional shopping centers being quite expensive).
- Restrictions as to the goods/services that can be sold by each store.
- Competitive environment within the center.
- Required payments for items that may be of little or no value to an individual retailer, such as membership in a merchants' association.
- Overexpansion and overstoring in a number of areas (some observers call this "the malling of America").
- Rising consumer boredom with and disinterest in shopping as an activity.
- Aging facilities of some older centers.
- Domination by large anchor stores.

The importance of planned shopping centers is evident from the following. First, 35 years ago, there were fewer than 1,000 U.S. shopping centers; now, there are 39,000+, ten per cent of which are closed shopping malls. Shopping center revenues exceed $750 billion annually and account for almost 40 per cent of total U.S. retail-store sales (including automobiles and gasoline). Over nine million people work in shopping centers. Second, many shopping center customers are active. And nine out of ten Americans over age 18 visit some type of center at least once each year. Third, individual retail chains have large stakes in shopping centers. For example, The Lim-

FIGURE 9–3
A Closed Shopping Mall
Shown here is the popular White Flint Mall in Chevy Chase, Maryland.
Reprinted by permission of Browning-Ferris Industries.

ited, B. Dalton Bookseller, and J.C. Penney are among the vast number of chains deriving substantial sales and profits from shopping center outlets.

Fourth, some big retailers have been involved in shopping-center development. Typically, these firms buy a site of their choosing, years in advance, and contact another major retailer (depending on the center's size). They then bring in a developer, who builds, owns, and leases the center and connects it to the anchor stores. For instance, Sears has participated in the construction of dozens of shopping centers, and Publix Super Markets operates centers with hundreds of small-store tenants. Fifth, each year, numerous new centers of all kinds and sizes are built and tens of millions of square feet of retail space are added to existing centers.[6]

To sustain their long-term growth, shopping centers are engaging in such practices as these:

- Several older centers have been or are being renovated, expanded, or repositioned. Belle Promenade in New Orleans; County East Mall in Antioch (a San Francisco suburb); Newmarket North Center in Hampton, Virginia; Speedway Center in Indianapolis; and the Promenade in Fort Lauderdale are among the 10- to 30-year-old centers that have recently been revitalized.

[6] See Robert E. O'Neill and Sandra M. Sutton, "A History of the Shopping Center Industry," *Monitor* (August 1990), pp. 11–59; and Avijit Ghosh and Sara McLafferty, "The Shopping Center: A Restructuring of Post-War Retailing," *Journal of Retailing*, Vol. 67 (Fall 1991), pp. 253–267.

- Certain derivative types of centers are being used to foster consumer interest and excitement. Two of these, megamalls and power centers, are discussed later in this chapter.
- The retailer mix is broadening at many centers to attract people interested in one-stop shopping. In particular, more centers than before are apt to include such service-oriented businesses as banks, stock brokers, dentists, beauty salons, television repair outlets, and/or car-leasing offices.
- There is increased interest by shopping center management in providing convenience and customer service for patrons. As an example, "When people first go onto a shopping center, they want information. In any kind of center, that is what they are looking for. Our job is to make the shopping experience easier."[7]

There are three major types of planned shopping centers: regional, community, and neighborhood. The characteristics of these centers are displayed in Table 9–1, and they are described next.

Regional Shopping Center

A ***regional shopping center*** is a large, planned shopping facility appealing to a geographically dispersed market. It has at least one or two full-sized department stores (each with a minimum of 100,000 square feet) and 50 to 150 or more smaller retailers, as illustrated in Figure 9–4. A regional center features a very broad and deep assortment of shopping-oriented goods, as well as a number of services intended to enhance the consumer's experience at the center. The market for a typical regional center is 100,000+ people, who live or work up to 30 minutes' driving time from the center. On average, people travel fewer than 20 minutes.

The regional center is the result of a planned effort to re-create the shopping variety of a central city in suburbia. Some experts even credit the regional shopping center with becoming the social, cultural, and vocational focal point of an entire suburban area. Frequently, a regional center is used as a town plaza, a meeting place, a concert hall, and a place for a brisk indoor walk. And despite people's declining overall interest in shopping (which does pose a significant problem for retailers), according to *Chain Store Age Executive*, on a typical visit to one of the 1,850 or so regional centers in the United States, almost 40 per cent of all customers spend one to two or more hours there.

The first regional center—shown in Figure 9–5—opened in 1950 in Seattle, Washington, anchored by a branch of Bon Marche, a leading downtown department store. Southdale Center (outside Minneapolis), built in 1956 for the Dayton Hudson Corporation, was the first fully enclosed, climate-controlled mall.

One current derivative form of regional center, known as the megamall, is particularly interesting. A ***megamall*** is an enormous planned shopping center with one-million+ square feet of retail space, multiple anchor stores, up to several hundred specialty stores, food courts, and entertainment facilities. Its goal is to heighten consumer interest in shopping and greatly expand the trading area. There are about 375 U.S. megamalls, including the giant Mall of America in Bloomington, Minnesota. The Mall of America has four anchor stores (Bloomingdale's, Macy's, Nordstrom, and Sears), hundreds of specialty stores, more than one dozen theaters, a health club, numerous restaurants and nightclubs, the world's largest indoor amusement park (Knott's Camp Snoopy, created and managed by Knott's Berry Farm of California), and 12,000 parking spaces—all on 4.2-million square feet of space. Why build this megamall? Mall of America's marketing experts "believe it will draw customers not just from Minnesota but from seven other states, plus Japan."[8]

[7] "Lower Prices, But Not Low Class," *Chain Store Age Executive* (March 1994), pp. 186, 188.

[8] Jeffrey A. Trachtenberg, "Largest of All Malls in the U.S. Is a Gamble in Bloomington, Minn.," *Wall Street Journal* (October 30, 1990), pp. A1, A14; "Mall of America Fallout," *Stores* (May 1993), pp. 44–47; and William M. Stern, "Bumpbacks in Minneapolis," *Forbes* (April 11, 1994), pp. 48–49.

TABLE 9–1 Characteristics of Typical Neighborhood, Community, and Regional Types of U.S. Planned Shopping Centers

Features of a Typical Center	Type of Center		
	Regional	Community	Neighborhood
Total site area (acres)	30–100+	10–30	3–10
Total sq. ft. leased to retailers	400,000–2,000,000+	100,000–400,000	30,000–100,000
Principal tenant	One, two, or more full-sized department stores	Branch department store (traditional or discount), variety store, and/or category killer store	Supermarket or drugstore
Number of stores	50–150 or more	15–25	5–15
Goods and services offered	Largest assortment for customers, focusing on goods that encourage careful shopping and services that enhance the shopping experience (such as a food court)	Moderate assortment for customers, focusing on a mix of shopping- and convenience-oriented goods and services	Lowest assortment for customers, emphasizing convenience-oriented goods and services
Minimum number of people living/working in the trading area needed to support center	100,000+	20,000–100,000	3,000–50,000
Trading area in driving time	Up to 30 minutes	Up to 20 minutes	Fewer than 15 minutes
Location	Outside central city, on arterial highway or expressway	Close to one or more populated residential area(s)	Along a major thoroughfare in a single residential area
Layout	Mall, often enclosed with anchor stores at major entrances/exits	Strip or L-shaped	Strip
Per cent of all centers	5	32	63
Per cent of all centers' selling space	30	45	25
Per cent of all centers' retail sales	30	41	29

Source: Percentage data are from *Shopping Center World* (March 1993).

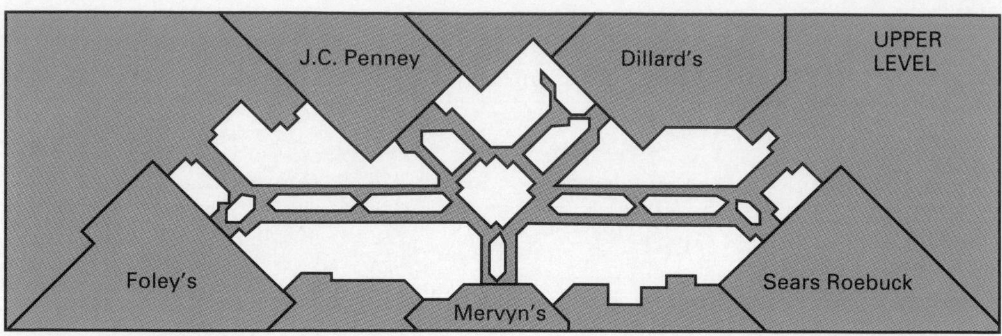

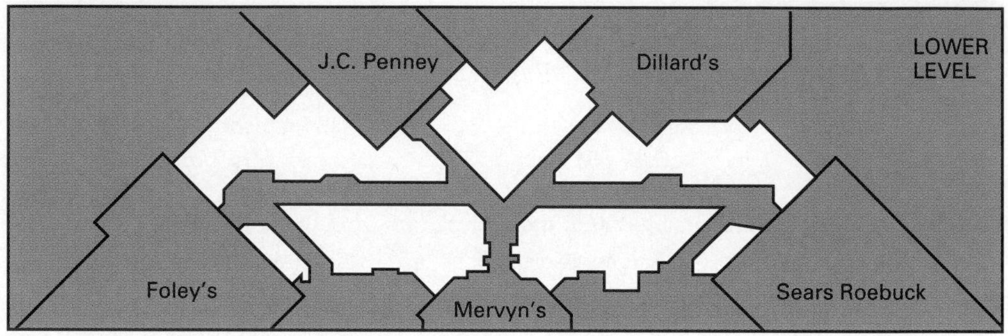

FIGURE 9–4
The Collin Creek Mall, Dallas, Texas
The Collin Creek Mall is anchored by the five department stores shown here. The mall also contains more than 160 other shops and restaurants (which are situated in the white spaces adjacent to the anchor stores). Over 250,000 people live within 10 miles of Collin Creek.
Courtesy Collin Creek Mall.

Community Shopping Center

A ***community shopping center*** is a moderate-sized, planned shopping facility with a branch department store (traditional or discount), a variety store, and/or a category killer store, in addition to several smaller stores (which usually are similar to those in a neighborhood center). It offers a moderate assortment of both shopping- and convenience-oriented goods and services to consumers from one or more nearby, well-populated, residential areas. From 20,000 to 100,000 people, who live or work within 10 to 20 minutes of the center, are serviced by this type of retail location.

Greater and superior long-range planning is used for a community shopping center than for a neighborhood shopping center. For example, balanced tenancy is usually better enforced and cooperative promotion expenditures are more likely. Thus, store composition and the center's image are kept pretty consistent with pre-set goals.

A rapidly emerging type of community center is the ***power center***, a shopping site with (a) a half-dozen or so category killer stores and a mix of smaller stores or (b) several complementary stores specializing in one product category. A power center usually occupies 200,000 to 400,000 square feet and is situated on a major highway or road intersection. Its goals are to be quite distinctive—thus providing consumers with a strong motivation to go there—and to better compete with regional shopping centers. There are about 2,000 U.S. power centers. For instance, the 360,000+-square-foot 280 Metro Center in Colma, California, is a category killer power center. It has such anchor stores as Nordstrom Rack, Marshalls, Home Depot, and Kids "R" Us—plus about 30 smaller stores and a movie theater. The 200,000-square-foot Towne Center Village in Marietta, Georgia, is a specialized home furnishings power center. It features furniture, custom sofa, and Oriental rug stores.[9]

Neighborhood Shopping Center

A ***neighborhood shopping center*** is a planned shopping facility with the largest store being a supermarket and/or a drugstore. Other retailers in the center often include a bakery, a laundry-dry cleaner, a stationery store, a barbershop and/or a beauty

[9] Barbara Solomon, "Power Centers: The New Face of Retailing," *Management Review* (April 1993), pp. 50–53; "Centering on the Home," *Chain Store Age Executive* (March 1990), Section Two, pp. S4, S6; and "The Food Factor: Will Supermarkets Enter Power Centers?" *Chain Store Age Executive* (September 1993), pp. 40, 42.

Figure 9–5
The Grand Opening of the First U.S. Regional Shopping Center
When this Seattle, Washington, shopping center—anchored by a Bon Marche department store—opened in 1950, it ushered in an exciting new era of retailing.
Reprinted by permission of Bon Marche.

parlor, a hardware store, a restaurant, a liquor store, and a gas station. This center focuses on convenience-oriented goods and services for people living or working in the immediate vicinity. It serves 3,000 to 50,000 people who are within 15 minutes' driving time (usually fewer than 10 minutes).

A neighborhood shopping center is usually arranged in a strip. When first developed, it is carefully planned, and tenants are balanced. Over time, the planned aspects of this center may diminish and newcomers may face fewer restrictions. For example, a liquor store may be allowed to replace a barber shop. In this case, there would be no barbershop. A center's ability to maintain balance depends on its continuing attractiveness to potential tenants (as expressed by the extent of the store vacancy rate).

In number, but not in selling space or sales, neighborhood centers account for nearly two-thirds of all U.S. shopping centers.

The Choice of a General Location

The last part of Step 2 in location planning requires the retailer to select one of the three basic types of locations: isolated, unplanned district, or planned center. The decision would depend on the firm's strategy and a careful evaluation of the advantages and disadvantages of each type of location.

Once the type of location is picked, the retailer must choose a broadly defined site for its store(s), Step 3. Two decisions are needed here. First, the specific kind of isolated store, unplanned business district, or planned shopping center location must be picked. If a retailer wants an isolated store, it must decide whether to locate on a highway or side street. Should the retailer desire an unplanned business area, it must decide whether to locate in a CBD, an SBD, an NBD, or a string. A retailer seeking a planned area must decide whether to locate in a regional, community, or neighborhood shopping center; and it needs to choose whether to situate in a derivative form of shopping center such as a megamall or power center.

RETAILING AROUND THE WORLD

What's a Shopping Mall Like in South Africa?

Masakhane Mall is a shopping center with twenty-four stores—including a supermarket, a dry cleaner, a liquor store, a photo studio, and a hair salon. One of the things that makes this mall unique is that it is built from converted 8-foot by 20-foot cargo ship containers.

Located on the edge of a black settlement in Lawaikamp, South Africa, Masakhane Mall stands as an example of the hope of the neighboring black community. Planners of the mall expect that it will attract shoppers who would otherwise have to walk two miles for convenience goods and services. They also want the mall to serve as an impetus for black entrepreneurship. Until recently, most of the businesses in the area were owned and operated by white businesspeople.

The Masakhane Mall was developed and built by a non-profit development agency with the assistance of a few white businesspeople. The agency persuaded a shipping line to sell it the used containers that were employed in the mall's construction. It also secured a loan guarantee from a major supermarket chain for a local black resident who intended to open an independent supermarket. Revenues were even generated from a life insurance company that advertised on the mall's wall.

Source: Based on material in Bill Kelley, "A South African Mall That Black Know-How Built," *New York Times* (September 12, 1993), Section 1, p. 3.

Here are the preferences of a variety of retailers:

- Lechters, a chain of houseware stores, "considers its ability to obtain attractive, high-traffic store locations to be critical. Accordingly, the majority of the company's stores are situated in regional enclosed shopping malls having at least two major department stores as anchors and at least 200,000 square feet containing specialty retailers."[10]
- 7-Eleven stores "are located in neighborhood areas, on main thoroughfares, in shopping centers, or at other sites that are easily accessible and have ample parking for in-and-out shopping."[11]
- At Dollar General, "75 per cent of stores are situated in communities with populations of 25,000 or less. About 55 per cent of the firm's stores are located in strip shopping centers, with the balance in freestanding or downtown store buildings."[12]
- Cato, a chain of women's apparel stores, locates "primarily in strip shopping centers anchored by major discount stores, with approximately 50 per cent in centers anchored by Wal-Mart stores."[13]

Second, a retailer must determine the general placement of its store(s). For an isolated store, this means selecting a specific highway or side street. For an unplanned district or planned center, this means designating a specific district (e.g., downtown Los Angeles or Pittsburgh) or center (e.g., Seminary South in Fort Worth, Texas, or Chesterfield Mall in Richmond, Virginia).

In Step 3, the retailer narrows down the decisions made in the first two steps and then chooses a general location. Step 4 requires the retailer to evaluate alternative specific sites, including their position on a block (or in a center), the side of the street, and the terms of tenancy. The factors to be considered in assessing and choosing a general location and a specific site within that location are described together in the next section because many strategic decisions are similar for these two steps.

[10] *Lechters, Inc. 1993 10K*, p. 4.

[11] *Southland Corporation 1992 10K*, p. 4.

[12] *Dollar General Corporation 1993 10K*, p. 4.

[13] *Cato Corporation 1993 10K*, p. 2.

Location and Site Evaluation

The evaluation of each general location and the specific sites contained within them both require extensive analysis. Site selection is as crucial as the choice of a retail area, especially for stores relying on customer traffic patterns to generate business.

The optimum site for a particular store is called the ***one-hundred per cent location.*** Because different retailers need different locations, a location classified as 100 per cent for one retailer may be less than optimal for another retailer.

For instance, an upscale ladies' apparel shop would seek a location with different strengths from those desired by a convenience store. The specialty shop would benefit from heavy pedestrian traffic, closeness to major department stores, and proximity to other specialty stores. The convenience store would rather locate in an area with ample parking and heavy vehicular traffic. It does not need to be close to other stores.

Figure 9–6 contains a checklist for location and site evaluation. In choosing a location, a retailer would rate every alternative location (and specific site) on all of the criteria and develop an overall rating for each alternative. Two firms may rate the same location quite differently, depending on their stores' requirements. This figure should be used in conjunction with the trading-area data noted in Chapter 8, not instead of them.

PEDESTRIAN TRAFFIC

Probably the most important measures of a location's and site's value are the number and type of people passing by. The site with the highest pedestrian traffic is often best.

Because everyone passing a location or site is not necessarily a good prospect for all types of stores, many retailers employ selective counting procedures, such as counting only males and females carrying shopping bags. Otherwise, pedestrian traffic totals may include too many nonshoppers. As an example, it would be improper for an appliance retailer to count as prospective shoppers all the people who pass a downtown site on the way to work. In fact, much of the pedestrian traffic in a downtown location may be from people who are in the area for nonretailing activities.

A proper pedestrian traffic count should encompass these four elements:

- A separation of the count by age and gender (children under a certain age should not be counted).
- A division of the count by time (this allows the study of peaks, low points, and changes in the gender of the people passing by the hour).
- Pedestrian interviews (these enable researchers to find out the proportion of potential shoppers).
- Spot analysis of shopping trips (these allow observers to verify the stores visited).

VEHICULAR TRAFFIC

The quantity and characteristics of vehicular traffic must be examined, especially by retailers appealing to customers who drive there. Convenience stores, outlets in regional shopping centers, and car washes are examples of retailers that rely on heavy vehicular traffic. Automotive traffic studies are quite important in suburban areas, where pedestrian traffic is often limited.

Some adjustments to the raw count of vehicular traffic should be made. For instance, some retailers count only homeward-bound traffic. Some exclude vehicles passing on the other side of a divided highway. And many retailers omit out-of-state license plates in their counts. Data on traffic patterns are usually available from the state highway department, the county engineer, or the regional planning commission.

In addition to traffic counts, the retailer should study the extent and timing of congestion (caused by heavy traffic, detours, narrow and poor roads, and so on). Vehicular customers will normally avoid heavily congested areas, and shop in areas where driving time and driving difficulties are minimized.

Rate each of the following criteria on a scale of 1 to 10, with 1 being excellent and 10 being poor		
Pedestrian Traffic	Number of people	______
	Type of people	______
Vehicular Traffic	Number of vehicles	______
	Type of vehicles	______
	Traffic congestion	______
Parking Facilities	Number and quality of parking spots	______
	Distance to store	______
	Availability of employee parking	______
Transportation	Availability of mass transit	______
	Access from major highways	______
	Ease of deliveries	______
Store Composition	Number and size of stores	______
	Affinity	______
	Retail balance	______
Specific Site	Visibility	______
	Placement in the location	______
	Size and shape of the lot	______
	Size and shape of the building	______
	Condition and age of the lot and building	______
Terms of Occupancy	Ownership or leasing terms	______
	Operations and maintenance costs	______
	Taxes	______
	Zoning restrictions	______
	Voluntary regulations	______
Overall Rating	General location	______
	Specific site	______

Figure 9–6
A Location/Site Evaluation Checklist

Parking Facilities

The importance of good parking facilities must not be overlooked in assessing a location and specific sites in it. The vast majority of retail stores built in the United States since the end of World War II include some provision for nearby off-street parking. In many business districts, parking facilities are provided by individual stores, cooperative arrangements among stores, and municipal governments. In planned shopping centers, parking facilities are shared by all the stores in those centers. The number and quality of parking spots, their distances from store sites, and the availability of employee parking should all be evaluated.

It is hard to generalize about a retailer's needs for parking facilities because they depend on such factors as the trading area of the store, the type of store, the portion of shoppers using an automobile, the existence of other parking facilities, the turnover of spaces (which depend on the length of the shopping trip), the flow of shoppers throughout the day and the week, and parking by nonshoppers. Nonetheless, a shopping center normally requires about 4 or 5 parking spaces per 1,000 square feet of gross floor area; and whereas a supermarket usually requires 10 to 15 parking spaces per 1,000 square feet of gross floor area, a furniture store would need only 3 or 4.

Sometimes, free parking in shopping locations that are in or close to commercial areas creates problems. Commuters and employees of nearby businesses may park in these facilities, reducing the number of spaces available for shoppers. This problem can be lessened by the validation of shoppers' parking stubs and requiring payment from nonshoppers.

Another problem may occur if total selling space in a location goes up due to the addition of new stores or the expansion of current ones. Parking facilities may then be inadequate because space formerly allocated to parking might be given to the new stores or the extensions, and because parking needs rise to accommodate new employees, new shoppers, and longer shopping trips.

Double-deck parking or parking tiers are possible solutions to this problem. In addition to saving land, these types of parking shorten the distance from a parked car to a store. This is important when one recognizes that many customers of a regional shopping center may be unwilling to walk more than a few hundred feet from their cars to the center.

Having too large a parking facility may also cause difficulties. If the facility is not full, the location's image may suffer because an illusion of emptiness is created—and customers would wonder why. A parking lot may contain 150 cars, but if the capacity of the lot is 500 cars, it might appear that the lot is empty and the stores unpopular.

Transportation

The availability of mass transportation, access from major highways, and ease of deliveries must be examined in assessing a location and specific sites.

In a downtown area, closeness to mass transportation is important, particularly for people who do not own cars, who commute to work there, or who would not otherwise shop in an area with heavy traffic congestion and limited parking. The availability of buses, taxis, subways, trains, or other kinds of public transit must be investigated for any area not readily serving vehicular traffic. Because most downtown shopping areas are at the hub of a mass transportation network, they allow people from all over a city to shop there.

Locations dependent on vehicular traffic should be rated on the basis of their access to major thoroughfares. As mentioned in the previous chapter, driving time is an important consideration for many customers. In addition, drivers heading eastbound on a highway often do not like to make a U-turn to get to a store on the westbound side of that highway.

The transportation network should also be studied for its ability to convey delivery trucks to and from the store. Many thoroughfares are excellent for customer traffic but ban large trucks or cannot bear their weight.

Store Composition

The store composition in the area should be studied. How many stores are there? How large are they? The number and size of stores should be consistent with the kind of location selected. For example, a retailer interested in an isolated site would want no stores nearby; a retailer interested in a neighborhood business district would want to locate in an area with ten or fifteen small stores; and a retailer interested in a regional shopping center would desire a location with more than fifty stores, including at least one or two large department-store anchors (to generate lots of customer traffic).

A retailer should weigh its store's compatibility with adjacent or nearby retailers in evaluating locations and sites. When the various stores at a given location (be it an unplanned district or a planned center) complement, blend, and cooperate with one another, and each benefits from the others' presence, then ***affinity*** exists. With a strong level of affinity, the sales of each store would be greater, due to the high level of customer traffic, than if the stores are situated apart from each other.

The practice of similar or complementary stores locating near each other is based on two major premises: (1) customers like to compare the offerings of similar stores as to price, style, selection, and service, and (2) customers like one-stop shopping (A variety of products is often bought from different stores on the same shopping trip). Thus, affinities can exist among competing stores, as well as among complementary stores. Because many more people will travel to shopping areas with large selections than to convenience-oriented areas, the sales of all stores would be enhanced.

One measure of compatibility is the degree to which stores exchange customers. The stores in these categories are very compatible with each other and have a high level of customer interchange:

- Supermarket, drugstore, bakery, fruit-and-vegetable store, meat store.
- Department store, apparel store, hosiery store, lingerie shop, shoe store, jewelry store.

For example, Publix supermarkets are often in neighborhood shopping centers that have Eckerd drugstores. Publix does not locate in regional centers due to the different nature of the shopping and the low turnover of parking spaces.

As one expert says about affinity: "The department stores of Boulevard Haussmann in Paris, the outfitters of London's Oxford Street, the electrical retailers of Akihabara in Tokyo, and the theaters and cinemas of Broadway are among the better-known examples of this phenomenon. But the clustering of similar outlets is a truly universal trait, ranging from the hamburger alleys and automobile rows of most American cities to the pronounced clusters of goldsmiths and banana sellers in the marketplaces of the third world."[14]

A location's retail balance should also be considered. ***Retail balance*** refers to the mix of stores within a district or shopping center. Proper balance occurs when the number of store facilities for each merchandise or service classification is equal to the location's market potential; when a wide range of goods and service classifications is provided to ensure one-stop shopping; when there is an adequate assortment within any good or service category; and when there is a proper mix of store types (balanced tenancy).

Specific Site

Besides the factors already detailed, the specific site should be evaluated on the basis of visibility, placement in the location, size and shape of the lot, size and shape of the building, and condition and age of the lot and building.

Visibility refers to a site's ability to be seen by pedestrian and/or vehicular traffic. A site on a side street or at the end of a shopping center would not achieve the same visibility as a site on a major road or at the entrance of a shopping center. High visibility makes passersby aware that a store exists and is open. Furthermore, some shoppers are hesitant to go down a side street or to the end of a center.

[14] Stephen Brown, "Retail Location Theory: The Legacy of Harold Hotelling," *Journal of Retailing,* Vol. 65 (Winter 1989), p. 451.

Placement in the location refers to a site's relative position in the district or center. A corner location is often desirable since it is situated at the intersection of two streets and has "corner influence." A corner site is usually more expensive to own or lease because it offers these advantages: greater pedestrian and vehicular passersby due to converging traffic flows from two streets, increased show-window display area, and less traffic congestion via the use of two or more entrances. Corner influence is greatest in high-volume retail locations. That is why numerous Pier 1 stores and Kay jewelry stores occupy corner lots in shopping districts or corner spots in shopping malls. See Figure 9–7.

Some advantages of a corner location are reduced in a shopping center. For instance, traffic on the streets perpendicular to many neighborhood and community centers is usually sparse. Accordingly, fewer additional customers would be attracted to a corner store. Also, because many stores in larger shopping centers have two entrances (one in the mall and one in the parking area), shoppers can go from parking spots to the main mall without using the designated walkways, stores have more window display space without the need for corner locations, and traffic flows to and through the center are eased.

Placement decisions should be keyed to retailer needs. As an example, a convenience-oriented retailer, such as a stationery store, would be more concerned about the side of the street, the location relative to other convenience-oriented stores, the nearness to parking, the access to a bus stop, and the distance from homes. A shopping-oriented retailer, such as a furniture store would be more interested in the use of a corner site to increase window display space, the proximity to wallpaper and other related retailers, the accessibility of its pickup platform to consumers, and the ease of deliveries to the store.

The size and shape of the lot should be evaluated. For instance, a department store would require significantly larger space than a boutique; and a department store may desire a square site, whereas the boutique may seek a rectangular one. Any site should be assessed in terms of the total space needed: parking, walkways, selling, nonselling, and so on.

When a retailer buys or rents an existing building, its size and shape should be examined. In addition, the condition and age of the lot and the building should be investigated. These site characteristics would then be measured against the needs of the firm.

FIGURE 9–7
Corner Influence and Pier 1
When it has the opportunity, Pier 1 likes to situate stores at corner sites to gain additional visibility, greater window-display space, and vehicular and pedestrian traffic from two streets. Shown here is a corner store in Northern California.
Reprinted by permission.

RETAILING IN ACTION

A 140,000-Square-Foot Store at an Outlet Mall?

Burlington Coat Factory, a leading off-price clothing chain, recently opened its largest store in Franklin Mills, a huge discount mall in Pennsylvania. That was the first outlet-mall site for Burlington.

Part of this Burlington store had been a Macy's Close Out outlet and the rest was an entertainment complex that never opened. Thus, the site required substantial renovations. For instance, the men's wear department is now where a bowling alley was located; the coat department is where a skating rink was situated. Interestingly, some of the improvements at the site were actually paid for by former tenants (so the space could be leased). For example, the store has hardwood floors, a mezzanine level, and a decorative house-like building in the middle of the first floor. As Burlington's chairman says, "I would never pay for this, but it's nice to have."

The Franklin Mills location marks the beginning of a different phase in Burlington's site selection. Although most of its new stores will continue to be in freestanding or strip mall locations, outlet mall locations will also be considered. Of the twenty-four new stores scheduled for 1994, several were to be in outlet malls. Burlington has also announced a new store in Juarez, Mexico—its first international venture.

Source: Based on material in Jill Lettich, "Burlington Coat's Newest Unit Shows Shrewd Real-Estate Dealing," *Discount Store News* (November 1, 1993), p. 4.

TERMS OF OCCUPANCY

Terms of occupancy—including ownership versus leasing, the type of lease, operations and maintenance costs, taxes, zoning restrictions, and voluntary regulations—must be evaluated for each prospective site.

Ownership Versus Leasing

A retailer with adequate financial resources can either own or lease premises. Ownership is more common in small stores, in small communities, and/or at inexpensive locations. It has several advantages over leasing. There is no risk that an outside property owner will not renew a lease or will double or triple the rent when a lease expires. With ownership, monthly mortgage payments are stable. Operations are flexible; the retailer can engage in scrambled merchandising, break down walls, and so on. It is also likely that property value will appreciate over time, giving the retailer a tangible asset if it decides to sell the business. The disadvantages of ownership are the high initial costs, the long-term commitment that is necessary, and the inflexibility in changing sites.

If a retailer chooses to own the store premises, it must decide whether to construct a new facility or purchase an existing building. In weighing these alternatives, a retailer should consider the purchase price and maintenance costs, zoning restrictions, the age and condition of existing facilities, the adaptability of existing facilities to its needs, and the time necessary to erect a new building. To encourage building rehabilitation in small towns (5,000 to 50,000 people), Congress enacted the Main Street program of the National Trust for Historic Preservation in 1981. Retailers have benefited via participation in this program by getting tax credits and low-interest loans.

Despite the advantages of ownership, most retailers lease store sites. For example, Caldor (a full-line discount store chain) "has long-term leases with a typical initial term of 20 years and renewal options of 10 to 30 years." And T.J. Maxx apparel-store leases "are generally for 10 years with options to extend for one or more 5-year periods. The company has the right to terminate certain leases before the expiration date under given circumstances and for a specified payment."[15]

Leasing enables retailers to minimize their initial investment, reduce their risk, acquire leases at prime locations that could not accommodate additional stores, gain immediate occupancy and customer traffic, and reduce their long-term commitment

[15] *Caldor Corporation 1993 10K*, p. 5; and *TJX Companies, Inc. 1993 10K*, p. 8.

(if they so desire). Many retailers also feel they can open more outlets or spend more on other elements of their strategy mixes by leasing. Firms that lease also accept the disadvantages of this approach: the limits on operating flexibility, the restrictions on subletting and selling the business, possible nonrenewal problems, future rent increases, and no benefit from the rising value of real estate.

Some large retailers build new stores and then sell them to real-estate investors who lease the property back to the retailers on a long-term basis. This is called a ***sale-leaseback.*** Retailers using sale-leasebacks can construct stores to their specifications and have bargaining power in leasing terms—while they reduce their capital expenditures.

Tax-exempt industrial revenue bonds have also been used to finance retail facilities. In this arrangement, a state or municipality uses bond proceeds to build stores or warehouses and gives retailers long leases (with payments used to pay bond principal and interest). The practice reduces investment costs for retailers, but requires them to commit to a site for an extended period.

Types of Leases

Because most retailers lease (rent) store facilities, it is important to be familiar with several of the major types of leases being used by property owners, including the straight lease, percentage lease, graduated lease, maintenance-increase-recoupment lease, and net lease. Property owners no longer rely solely on constant rent leases, partly because of their concern about the rate of inflation and the related rise in many of their operating costs; thus, terms can become quite complicated. Although a typical lease runs from five to twenty years, some are shorter and others are longer.

The simplest, most direct arrangement is the ***straight lease,*** whereby a retailer pays a fixed dollar amount per month over the life of the lease. Rent usually ranges from $1 to $50 annually per square foot, depending on factors like the location's desirability, and store traffic. At some sites, rents can be much higher (up to hundreds of dollars per square foot).

A ***percentage lease*** stipulates that rent is related to the retailer's sales or profits. This differs significantly from a straight lease, which provides for constant payments each month, regardless of revenues or earnings. For example, a drugstore may be required to pay 4 per cent of sales, a toy store 6 per cent, and a camera store 12 per cent (with these figures being keyed to the space occupied and sales per square foot). A percentage lease enables a property owner to be protected against the effects of inflation, as well as to benefit when a store is successful; it also allows a tenant to view the lease as a variable cost—which means rent is lower when its performance is weak and higher when performance is good. The percentage rate varies by type of shopping district or center and by type of store.

Percentage leases have variations. In one, a minimum or maximum rent is noted:

- Percentage lease with specified minimum—This recognizes that low sales are partly the retailer's responsibility and that the property owner should receive some minimum payments (as in a straight lease) that at least partially cover the mortgage, taxes, and property maintenance.
- Percentage lease with specified maximum—This recognizes that a very successful retailer should not pay more than a maximum rental charge. Superior merchandising, promotion, and pricing should reward the retailer.

A second variation is the sliding scale. In this form of percentage lease, the ratio of rent to sales changes as sales increase. A sliding-down scale has the retailer pay a lower percentage of sales as sales go up; 5 per cent of the first $100,000 in sales and 3 per cent of all sales over $100,000 is an example. A sliding-down scale gives an incentive to the effective retailer, while it generates added rent for the property owner.

A ***graduated lease*** calls for precise rent increases over a specified period of time. Thus, rent may be $4,000 per month for the first five years, $4,800 per month for the next five years, and $5,600 per month for the last five years of a lease. Rental payments are known in advance by both the retailer and the property owner and are based on anticipated increases in sales and costs. There is no problem in auditing sale or profit figures, as there is for percentage leases. The graduated lease is often used with small retailers, whose financial statements and controls are weak.

A ***maintenance-increase-recoupment lease*** has a provision that allows for increases in rent if a property owner's taxes, heating bills, insurance, or other expenses rise beyond a certain point. This provision most often supplements a straight rental-lease agreement.

A ***net lease*** calls for all maintenance expenses, such as heating, electricity, insurance, and interior repair, to be paid by the retailer—which is responsible for the satisfactory quality of these items. A net lease allows a property owner to be freed from management of the facility and enables a retailer to have control over the maintenance of the store. It would be used to supplement a straight lease or a percentage lease.

Table 9–2 shows 1993 rent payments by location type for several cities.

Other Considerations

After assessing ownership and leasing opportunities, a retailer must look at the costs of operations and maintenance. Mortgage or rental payments are only one part of a site's costs. The age and condition of a facility may cause a retailer to have high total monthly costs, even though the mortgage or rent is low. Furthermore, the costs of extensive renovations should be calculated.

Taxes must be evaluated, especially in an ownership situation. Long-run projections, as well as current taxes, must be examined. Differences in sales taxes (those that customers pay) and business taxes (those that the retailer pays) among alternative sites must be weighed. Business taxes should be broken down into real-estate and income categories.

Zoning restrictions should be analyzed. There may be legal limitations pertaining to the kind of stores allowed, store size, building height, the type of merchandise carried, and other factors that have to be overcome (or another site chosen). For example, it took 12 years for the Redmond Town Center in the state of Washington

TABLE 9–2 Effective Annual Rent Per Square Foot, 1993 (Selected Metropolitan Areas)

Metropolitan Area	Central Business District	Regional Mall	Community/ Neighborhood Shopping Center
Bergen, New Jersey	$14.00	$50.00	$20.00
Charleston, South Carolina	15.00	14.00	9.00
Charlotte, North Carolina	14.00	25.00	12.00
Cleveland, Ohio	24.00	25.00	10.00
Dallas, Texas	14.00	35.00	11.50
Memphis, Tennessee	9.00	15.00	10.00
Miami, Florida	40.00	45.00	10.00
Orlando, Florida	20.00	25.00	12.00

Note: Effective annual rent includes common-area charges.

Source: Various issues of *Chain Store Age Executive*.

to receive all the necessary approvals for construction to begin on this mixed-use shopping facility. As one observer stated, "getting the land was the easiest part."[16]

Voluntary restrictions, those not mandated by the government, should also be examined. These are most prevalent in planned shopping centers and may include required membership in merchant groups, uniform store hours, and cooperative security forces. For instance, leases for many stores in regional shopping centers have included clauses protecting anchor tenants (large department stores) from too much competition—especially from discounters. These clauses may involve limits on product lines, bans against discounting, fees for common services, and specifications as to acceptable store practices. Anchors have been given such protective clauses by developers since the latter need their long-term commitments to finance the building of their centers.

Some shopping-center practices have been limited by the Federal Trade Commission (FTC). As an illustration, the FTC discourages "exclusives"—whereby only a particular retailer in a shopping center can carry specified merchandise, and "radius clauses"—whereby a tenant agrees not to operate another store within a certain distance of the center.[17]

Because of the overbuilding of retail facilities in many areas and the recent economic downturn in the U.S. economy, some retailers are now in a better position to bargain over the terms of occupancy. For example, "There are more centers looking for retail tenants than retailers looking for space. While conditions are different from center to center, retailers are calling more shots right now."[18]

OVERALL RATING

The last task in selecting a general location, and the specific site within it, is to compute overall ratings. First, each location under consideration is given an overall rating based on its performance on all the criteria displayed in Figure 9–6. The overall ratings of alternative locations are then compared, and the best location is chosen. The same procedure is used to evaluate the alternative sites within the location.

It is often difficult to compile and compare composite evaluations because some attributes may be positive while others are negative. For example, the general location may be a good shopping center, but the site in the center may be poor; or an area may have excellent potential but it will take two years to build a store. Therefore, the attributes in Figure 9–6 need to be weighted according to their importance to the retailer. An overall rating should also include certain knockout factors, those that would preclude consideration of a site. Possible knockout factors are a short-duration lease (fewer than three years), no evening or weekend pedestrian traffic, and poor tenant relations with the landlord.

SUMMARY

1. *To thoroughly examine the types of locations available to a retailer: isolated store, unplanned business district, and planned shopping center* After a retailer assesses alternative trading areas, it determines which type of location is desirable, selects the general location, and chooses a particular store site. There are three basic types of locations a retailer should distinguish among.

   An isolated store is a freestanding retail establishment, not adjacent to other stores. This type of location has several advantages, including no competition, low rent, flexibility, road visibility, easy parking, and lower property costs. There are also distinct disadvantages: difficulty in attracting traffic, no variety for shoppers, no shared costs, and zoning restrictions.

   An unplanned business district is a shopping area where two or more stores are located together or in close proximity. Store composition is not based on long-range planning. Unplanned business dis-

[16] "Worth Its Wait," *Chain Store Age Executive* (June 1990), p. 32.

[17] Eric C. Peterson, "New Lease Language," *Stores* (January 1990), pp. 111–112.

[18] Mike Reynolds, "Leasing Shoe on Other Foot," *Stores* (January 1991), p. 146.

tricts can be broken down into four categories: the central business district, the secondary business district, the neighborhood business district, and the string.

An unplanned business district generally has such points as these in its favor: variety of goods, services, and prices; access to public transit; nearness to commercial and social facilities; and pedestrian traffic. However, the shortcomings of this type of location have led to the growth of the planned shopping center: inadequate parking, older facilities, high rents and taxes in popular CBDs, discontinuity of offerings, traffic and delivery congestion, high theft rates, and some declining central cities.

A planned shopping center is a centrally owned or managed, well-balanced shopping area. It usually has one or more large (anchor) stores and many smaller stores. During the past several decades, the growth of the planned shopping center has been great. This is due to the extensive goods and service offerings, expanding suburbs, shared strategy planning and costs, attractive locations, parking facilities, lower rent and taxes (except for most regional shopping centers), lower theft rates, popularity of malls, and lesser appeal of inner-city shopping. The negative aspects of the planned center include the inflexibility of operations, restrictions on the merchandise lines carried, and domination by anchor stores. There are three forms of planned shopping centers: regional, community, and neighborhood.

2. *To note the decisions necessary in choosing a general retail location* First, the specific form of isolated store, unplanned business district, or planned shopping-center location must be determined, such as whether to locate on a highway or side street; in a CBD, an SBD, an NBD, or a string; or in a regional, community, or neighborhood shopping center. Then, the general location for a store must be specified, such as singling out a particular highway, business district, or shopping center.
3. *To describe the concept of the one-hundred per cent location* Extensive analysis is required when evaluating each general location and the specific sites contained within it. Most importantly, the optimum site for a given store must be determined. Such a site is called the one-hundred per cent location; and it differs by store.
4. *To discuss several criteria for evaluating general retail locations and the specific sites within them* These factors should be studied: pedestrian traffic, vehicular traffic, parking facilities, transportation, store composition, the attributes of each specific site, and terms of occupancy. Then, an overall rating would be computed for each location and site, and the best one would be selected.

   Affinity occurs when the stores at the same location complement, blend, and cooperate with one another; each benefits from the others' presence.
5. *To contrast alternative terms of occupancy* Terms of occupancy are critical in choosing a site. A retailer must decide whether to own or lease. If it leases, an agreement must be negotiated via a straight lease, percentage lease, graduated lease, maintenance-increase-recoupment lease, and/or net lease. Operating and maintenance costs, taxes, zoning restrictions, and voluntary restrictions also need to be weighed.

KEY TERMS

isolated store (p. 300)
unplanned business district (p. 301)
central business district (CBD) (p. 301)
secondary business district (SBD) (p. 303)
neighborhood business district (NBD) (p. 303)
string (p. 304)
planned shopping center (p. 305)
balanced tenancy (p. 305)
regional shopping center (p. 308)
megamall (p. 308)
community shopping center (p. 310)
power center (p. 310)
neighborhood shopping center (p. 310)
one-hundred per cent location (p. 313)
affinity (p. 316)
retail balance (p. 316)
terms of occupancy (p. 318)
sale-leaseback (p. 319)
straight lease (p. 319)
percentage lease (p. 319)
graduated lease (p. 319)
maintenance-increase-recoupment lease (p. 320)
net lease (p. 320)

QUESTIONS FOR DISCUSSION

1. A hardware-store chain has decided to open outlets in a combination of isolated locations, unplanned business districts, and planned shopping centers. Comment on this strategy.
2. Why do supermarkets often locate in shopping centers or business districts, whereas convenience stores, such as 7-Eleven, often operate at isolated sites?

3. From the retailer's perspective, compare the advantages of locating in unplanned business districts versus planned shopping centers.
4. Differentiate among the central business district, the secondary business district, the neighborhood business district, and the string.
5. Develop a brief plan to revitalize a neighborhood business district nearest your campus.
6. What is a megamall? What is a power center? How should other retailers react to a megamall or power center locating near them?
7. Evaluate the community shopping center nearest your campus.
8. What are some of the problems that planned shopping centers will probably have to address in the future? How should they respond?
9. Explain why a one-hundred per cent location for The Gap chain may not be a one-hundred per cent location for a local clothing store.
10. What criteria should a small retailer use in selecting a general store location and a specific site within it? A large retailer?
11. What difficulties are there in using a rating scale such as that shown in Figure 9–6? What are the benefits?
12. How do the parking needs for a membership club, a dry cleaner, and a movie theater differ?
13. Under what circumstances would it be more desirable for a retailer to build a new store rather than to buy or lease an existing facility?
14. What are the pros and cons of a straight lease versus a percentage lease for a prospective retail tenant?

CASE 1

Whistle & Flute: Evaluating a New Location for a Men's Apparel Store*

Whistle & Flute is a small, but prosperous, independent men's apparel store situated in a rapidly growing area. When founded, the store was located in a neighborhood shopping district that also contained a supermarket, a drugstore, and a local bakery; soon thereafter, a much larger group of stores opened in the immediate area—transforming it into a secondary shopping district. The larger concentration of stores improved customer traffic and provided some affinities for many of the retailers. Over a period of four years, Larry Simmons, the owner of Whistle & Flute, has seen his store's annual sales grow from $150,000 to $500,000. Part of this increase is due to the increased strength of the location. The rest is due to the store's well-balanced stock, high level of customer service, and excellent reputation.

Whistle & Flute offers a broad selection of men's apparel. Although the store does a satisfactory sales volume with men's suits, sports coats, and slacks, Simmons has also developed a significant business for such men's accessories as sport shirts, neckties, and robes. Many of these items are purchased by women, who visit the store to buy items for their husbands and friends. Accessories account for 40 per cent of the store's overall sales.

Larry Simmons recently became aware that a new regional shopping center is planning to open within three miles of his Whistle & Flute store within the next 18 months. Even though the total store composition of the center is unknown at this time, Arlin's, a large regional department-store chain, has signed a long-term lease and will be one of the anchor stores. The center's developer is actively pursuing other tenants for the 100-store mall, including at least one other department store as an anchor. The developer has an excellent reputation among the retailer tenants in its other regional malls with regard to enforcing balanced tenancy agreements, fairness in lease renewal negotiations, and maintenance of common areas. The center's estimated primary trading area will consist of a 30-minute driving radius, about 15 miles in all directions from the center. The developer will provide ample free parking for shoppers.

For several reasons, Simmons is quite concerned about the new center's possible impact on Whistle & Flute. One, the center's primary trading area will directly overlap with his store's, and traffic will be deflected away from his current shopping-district location. Two, the modern shopping center will be very attractive to the women who make up a large proportion of his accessories' customers. Three, Arlin's carries medium-priced merchandise—similar to the goods now carried by Whistle & Flute. Four, the shopping-center developer has been known to engage actively in joint promotions with tenants during such major shopping periods as Thanksgiving, Christmas, Easter, and July 4th. This will no doubt hurt Whistle & Flute's business.

Accordingly, Larry Simmons has begun to evaluate his options:

1. He could continue in his present location with his current strategy. To undertake this option, Simmons needs to be convinced that his present customers have a

* This case was prepared and written by John L. Roman, Director of Stores, Rochester Institute of Technology, Rochester, New York.

high level of store loyalty. While this is a status-quo strategy, he recognizes that it entails considerable risk.

2. He could give up his current store and seek a new shopping-center location as of the end of the year. His current lease (which expires at year's end) provides for a five-year renewal option, but he does not have to renew the lease. At the new location, Simmons would seek to attract new customers, as well as maintain the existing ones. With this option, some store fixtures could be moved to the new location; others would have to be sold.
3. He could convert the current site to an off-price outlet and also open a new store at the regional shopping center. This is a multiple-segmentation strategy and it would allow him to compete at the present site by reducing labor costs (due to a self-service, no-alterations strategy), purchasing opportunistically, and using all of the store's existing fixtures. The option would require a new store image, as well as access to new sources for merchandise. It could also require him to change the existing store's name to avoid confusion with the new outlet in the shopping center (which would continue the traditional Whistle & Flute strategy).

While considering the potential impact of the new shopping center on his business, Simmons received a phone call from the leasing agent for the center. The agent suggested that he lease a location directly adjacent to Arlin's. The leasing agent offered him a 20-year percentage lease (four 5-year leases, each with a renewal option).

Larry Simmons views the percentage lease and the renewal options as signs of confidence in his ability as a merchant and in the viability of the shopping center to develop and sustain a high level of customer traffic. He also recognizes certain other advantages with the new site. He knows that Arlin's, coupled with a large number of specialty stores, will bring ample customer traffic to the mall. In contrast to his current locale (which does not have a strong anchor store or true balanced tenancy), the new site will have balanced tenancy of apparel, shoe, and accessory stores—which will help Whistle & Flute. The new site will also have high pedestrian traffic each day of the week.

At the same time, Simmons fears that he cannot compete with Arlin's selection, buying clout, or mass promotion emphasis. Furthermore, he is hesitant to become a "small fish in a big pond," to give up the flexibility of setting his own store hours, and to give up the right to expand into other merchandise categories (such as women's accessories).

QUESTIONS

1. Discuss the pros and cons of unplanned business districts and planned shopping centers from the perspective of Larry Simmons.
2. What criteria should Larry Simmons use to evaluate the four options?
3. React to this statement: "Larry Simmons views the percentage lease and the renewal options as signs of confidence in his ability as a merchant and in the viability of the shopping center to develop and sustain a high level of customer traffic."
4. Rank the four options Larry has identified. Explain your answer, emphasizing the strengths and weaknesses of each option.

CASE 2

Donut Village: Developing Site-Selection Criteria for Nontraditional Locations

Donut Village is a successful franchisor of donut shops throughout the United States. One of the most significant services that the firm provides to its franchisees is site-selection research. Donut Village recognizes that even the most successful operator would be hindered by a poor location and that a marginal operator would greatly benefit from a superior site. Because the company typically negotiates for twenty-year leases, it also knows the long-term consequences of site selection for both Donut Village and its franchisees. For example, Donut Village derives much of its revenues from the royalty fees paid by franchisees on a continuing basis. Thus, a poor location would greatly impair its earnings potential. Likewise, because franchisees are bound to locations for the duration of their franchise agreements, poor sites could cause weak earnings or even bankruptcy.

Donut Village applies these site-selection criteria to its traditional main-road suburban stores:

- The correct side of the street is extremely critical. The firm is aware that many of its potential customers do not like to cross double-lined roads or highways or to make U-turns, even if these are legal. Therefore, when it conducts vehicular traffic counts for prospective sites, vehicles traveling on the opposite side of the road are heavily discounted.
- The busiest time for donut shops is typically before work (6:30 A.M. to 8:45 A.M.) on weekdays. Traffic counts at other hours, and on weekends or holidays, are generally much less important.
- Site visibility from the road is a major consideration. A site with poor visibility means that potential consumers might pass the shop before they actually see it. This would drastically reduce sales potential. Corner locations generally have much better visibility than locations in the middle of a block.
- Donut stores need to be close to a large population base to prosper. The most successful stores are often located near major office buildings, factories, and colleges and universities.
- The firm's required ratio of parking spots to store square footage is less stringent than McDonald's or Burger King's, since the average customer time in a donut shop is much less than in a hamburger-based outlet (due to the donut shop's high take-out business and limited menu).
- Factors such as retail balance and the characteristics of the residents in a community (in terms of income, age, or education) are rather unimportant for Donut Village.

At present, Donut Village is contemplating the use of nontraditional sites for new outlets. Because good traditional sites are increasingly difficult to obtain, it must seek new kinds of locations if it is to maintain its present growth rate. By studying the operations of McDonald's and Burger King, Donut Village executives discovered that they each have been creative in their use of nontraditional locations. For example, McDonald's and Burger King have outlets in U.S. naval installations, high schools, zoos, hospitals, office buildings, and parks and on turnpikes. Many of these outlets serve "captive populations." Burger King also has mobile units that can be moved to different sites, such as a college football-field parking lot.

Despite the popularity of McDonald's and Burger King's new locales, Donut Village executives understand that the nature of their business is quite different from hamburger-based franchising: the donut business is more snack-oriented, a high proportion of donuts are consumed at breakfast, donuts have a higher percentage of take-out business, and donuts are frequently purchased in multiple units for group consumption.

This is how Donut Village executives view a number of nontraditional sites that are under consideration:

- Office buildings—Franchisees can sell products from coffee wagons in office buildings that provide high concentrations of people. The office environment fits well with the breakfast, coffee-break, and snack orientation of Donut Village. Special arrangements would have to be worked out with each property owner for the rental of a small basement-area facility for the storage of carts, the receipt of fresh donuts, and the preparation of coffee.
- Mobile units—These units can be dispatched to specific sites with high but temporary concentrations of people, such as sporting events, parades, and dog shows. This is a flexible location approach. Separate arrangements would have to be made with each event manager for the right to sell Donut Village products. The mobile units could be operated by existing nearby franchisees as an additional source of revenues or by individuals seeking part-time work.
- Highway locations—Donut Village quick-stop units can be developed. These sites would provide an ideal place for car drivers and their passengers, bus passengers, and truck drivers to take a coffee break. Donuts and coffee could also be consumed in customers' cars. This operation could be open twenty-four hours a day. Units could also be operated in conjunction with independent frozen-yogurt shops or pizza parlors that typically have different hourly sales trends. These stores, however, would have to comply with specific Donut Village requirements for fixtures, signs, and so on.
- College/university cafeterias—Self-contained operations located alongside schools' conventional cafeterias could be developed in a standardized prototype format. Such operations would provide quick service, portability (students and faculty can take a donut and coffee to class), large concentrations of people, and would not require added parking facilities. Although there would be some evening and weekend business in selling to dorm students and in catering special events and small parties, this business would be relatively small. Special arrangements would have to be made with each school since the cafeteria operator often has the exclusive right to sell food on campus.

Questions

1. What are the pros and cons of each of these options for donut shops: isolated store locations, unplanned business district sites, and planned shopping-center sites?
2. Evaluate the criteria used by Donut Village in planning for its traditional sites.
3. Develop a site-location checklist for use by Donut Village in assessing nontraditional sites. How would you weight each criterion?
4. Evaluate the four nontraditional sites proposed by Donut Village. What kind of site is best? Explain your answer.

Part 4 Comprehensive Case

De-Enclosing Malls: Will This Be a Long-Term Trend?*

Introduction

By the time Ross Schaub of the First City Company took charge of Valley Green Mall in 1990, the then three-year-old center was already in a state of decline. Although strongly anchored by a Jamesway discount department store, Thrift Drugs outlet, and a Superfresh supermarket, the 380,000-square-foot enclosed mall was only 60 per cent leased, had anemic rent rates of $2.50 to $5 per square foot, and had lost roughly $10 million in value, according to officials at Mass Mutual, the Springfield, Massachusetts-based owner of the mall's property. Some thought the Newberry Township, Pennsylvania, mall was beyond salvaging.

But, the reports of Valley Green Mall's demise were greatly exaggerated. Today, the shopping center, renamed Newberry Commons, boasts a lease occupancy rate of 74 per cent and climbing, with rents ranging from $8 to $12 per square foot. The center has since regained $6 million in lost value, based on recent appraisals of the property.

It took more than a name change to turn this property around. A $2.5 million renovation featured a new twist: The enclosed mall was opened up and converted into a strip center.

"What was originally built was a cross between a mall and a strip shopping center that was neither one nor the other," says Schaub, who is a marketing representative for First City, a Pittsburgh-based development and management firm responsible for more than 4-million square feet of retail space. "The space in the enclosed portion of the mall was almost worthless. There was no market for it. We felt something had to be done . . . [so we] took the space that was enclosed, opened it up, and created a strip center."

De-Malling the Mall

Newberry Commons is not the only shopping center property to undergo such a drastic transformation. A handful of malls in Canada and the United States have been "de-malled" and converted into either strip or community centers. On paper, de-malling offers owners of obsolete or uncompetitive properties a chance for profitable renewal by converting retail space for big box use.

"We had a regional property that had a new 1-million-square-foot mall built right next to it," says R. Jeffrey Gwin, director of shopping centers for Sarakreek USA, a Dutch firm that recently converted South Hills Mall, a 750,000-square-foot property in Poughkeepsie, New York. "Instead of competing with them in a market that couldn't support two full-blown fashion malls, we decided to convert our property into a value or power center format."

But de-enclosing malls is not a universal cure for ailing shopping center projects. The process is expensive, intricate, time-consuming, and very site specific.

"There is no set way of doing it," says John Felix, project architect for Arrowstreet, the Somerville, Massachusetts-based design firm that helped convert South Hills Mall. "You can't decide you have an enclosed center and you are going to create a power center with all exterior entries. You have to design with tenants in mind and what positions they are willing to accept. It's an interesting mix of thought processes to put it all together."

But, as older regional shopping centers continue to decline in the face of competition from newer centers and the demise of traditional mall retailers, many owners see de-malling as a future trend in shopping center development.

"Let's face it, it is a hard bullet to bite," says Tom Schriber, a principal of Donahue Schriber, a Newport Beach, California-based company that is currently de-enclosing Anaheim Plaza in Anaheim, California. "Properties have to get really distressed before somebody is willing to take that bullet. But, it is going to happen, and it will happen nationwide."

Some projects that have already been or are being demalled include:

- Newberry Commons: The former Valley Green Mall is now a 230,000-square-foot community center still anchored by Jamesway, Thrift Drug, and Superfresh. Fashion Bug has also become a tenant on the property.
- South Hills Mall: This property started life as a 700,000-square-foot fashion mall anchored by Hess's, Sears, and Kmart. After undergoing a $20 million renovation in which common area and store space were rehabbed for big box use, the mall is now a 92 per cent-leased power center anchored by Kmart, Bob's, Price Chopper, Farmhouse, Service Merchandise, Burlington Coat, T.J. Maxx, and Dick's Sporting Goods.

* The material in this case was prepared and written by Paul Doocey, a White Plains, N.Y.-based analyst who reports on the shopping center industry. It originally appeared in "De-Enclosing Malls: Will This Be a Long-Term Trend?" *Stores* (May 1993), pp. 31–35. Reprinted by permission.

- Anaheim Plaza: At one time, this 600,000-square-foot mall was anchored by Robinson's, The Broadway, and Mervyn's. However, for the past few years, the mall has limped along with one anchor—Mervyn's. In summer 1993, demolition work began to convert the property into a 500,000-square-foot power center. Mervyn's, Wal-Mart, Comp USA, Ross, Fashion Bug, and SuperCrown Books have already signed on to anchor the project.
- Shopper's World: This Framingham, Massachusetts, property is one of the few remaining open-air regional centers in the eastern United States. Currently 750,000 square feet and anchored by Toys "R" Us, Bradlees, and General Cinema, the shopping center will be converted into a power strip with Toys "R" Us, Kids "R" Us, Bradlees, Sears Home Life, Jordan Marsh Furniture, and General Cinema as tenants. The project is being developed by Homart Community Centers, Chicago.
- Cassinelli Square: This Cincinnati-based power center was once an enclosed mall until a newer, larger regional opened nearby. It was then converted into a 315,000-square-foot power center anchored by Service Merchandise, Toys "R" Us, Marshalls, and Hechinger Home Quarters. It is owned by Joseph J. Freed & Associates, Wheeling, Illinois.
- Mayfield Common: Formerly known as The Centennial Village Mall, this shopping center had the misfortune of being the closest regional to West Edmonton Mall [the world's largest planned shopping center] when it first opened in 1981. After dropping to a 55 per cent lease rate and having the ignominy of being anchored by a car dealership, the mall was de-enclosed in 1991. Mayfield Common is now a 370,000-square-foot power center owned by Lehndorff Commercial Developments and anchored by Woolco, Save-On Foods & Drugs, H.Q. Office Supplies, House of Tools, and Independent Jewelers. The center was over 97 per cent leased as of 1992.
- Trans Canada Mall: A 165,000-square-foot enclosed mall in Calgary, Alberta, it is undergoing a conversion into a 185,000-square-foot community center featuring a Kmart and a Safeway supermarket. The mall is owned by Morguard Investments, a Toronto-based pension fund investor.

The Logic Behind De-Enclosing Malls

In most cases, a de-malling was pursued because the enclosed regional centers became obsolete, either in physical form, tenant mix, or location.

"For years, we were the only mall in the area that had all the fashion tenants," says Gwin, describing South Hills Mall before its transformation to an enclosed power center. "Then, a new 1.2 million-square-foot brass and glass and waterfalls and marble mall with all the big fashion anchors opened nearby. So, it was either sit here and be second class and fight it out with them as a fashion mall or differentiate ourselves and see if between the two properties we could actually expand the trade area."

Whatever the reasons, de-malling has essentially been the conversion of enclosed mall space into retail areas that can be utilized by expanding promotional tenants.

"The key to the whole thing is having the right product and appealing to the right parties," says Sam Kubiak, director of real-estate investment for the Washington, D.C., office of Mass Mutual, owner of Newberry Commons.

Making a failed or obsolete regional shopping center attractive to big box users usually entails some sort of physical reconstruction of the property. Common area space is often sacrificed in order to get the square foot sizes needed to house larger tenants. Many promotional tenants insist on their own entrances and exits from the mall and storefronts that can be seen from the street level.

Types of De-Malling

Sometimes, roofs and walls need to be torn away in order to get the required sight lines and stand-alone configurations. Parking is important, so vital that potential retail space is often sacrificed for it.

The most common type of de-malling is the partial demolition of an existing property, where store space in advantageous locations is left untouched, and new retail space for promotional tenants is created by opening up common areas or large retail spaces.

For example, at Newberry Commons, anchor space remained as it was and new space was taken out of the center by tearing down walls and reconfiguring common areas. "Original plans called for eliminating the whole plaza area," Kubiak says. "But, instead, we tore down the front side of the building and knocked away the majority of the plaza. The old building was built like a bunker. It really had no appeal to anybody."

But, by no means are all de-mallings the same. The developers in charge of Shopper's World and Anaheim Plaza found it necessary to more or less tear down the existing center and start from scratch. Most developers and owners, however, like to avoid total demolition, largely because of what it does to the value of the property. "Needless to say, when you tear it down you lose a considerable amount of value," Schriber says, "because you are going to have to write down the property almost to the value of the land."

To avoid this and other problems associated with total or partial demolition, some developers are attempting to de-mall within the existing footprint of a property. For example, although de-malled, South Hills Mall still has an enclosed common area and other features associated with more traditional shopping centers. "We didn't rip the roof off the building, there is still what you would call a mall there," says Gwin. "It is essentially an enclosed mall with all strip center tenants."

But, it is hard to avoid some sort of demolition or construction cost in a de-malling. Even at a largely untouched center such as South Hills, a food court in the front of the mall had to be torn out, the common area space narrowed, the store spaces faced forward, and the entrances made more accessible to the parking lot.

"The idea is to find blocks of space in the mall that are between 10,000 square feet and 75,000 square feet and put mini-anchors in those spaces," says Felix of Arrowstreet. "At South Hills, we had to move out the storefront, which actually gained a lot of value for the owners because they were able to gain a strip of lease space that wasn't being used before."

The Advantages of De-Malling

Increased leasing space is not the only advantage that can be gained by a de-malling. Developers of successfully converted malls point out that shifting retail reliance away from small tenants and troubled department stores to healthy and growing big-box retailers can, in the long run, improve the value of the property.

"It takes a lot of effort because you are putting more money into what has already lost a lot of money," Kubiak says. "But, the results can be dramatic. [At Newberry Commons], we increased $6 million in value in less than a year. The money that has been spent on the project to date we have recovered four-fold in value. That is not a bad return."

Although developers are working with less than successful projects, many have found it somewhat easier to get financing for the rehabilitations as opposed to ground-up developments. "Go out there today and try to find financing to buy a piece of land and build a shopping center. It is very difficult to do," says Schriber. "But if you already have a mall, especially one that is older with no or very little debt and a lot of equity, you can usually find money to convert."

Not only is financing easier to get, but some developers also report that it is easier to obtain community and tenant approval to alter the existing site, especially if it is in a state of decline. "They [retailers and the local community] were delighted we were putting money into Valley Green Mall," Kubiak says. "This center required major surgery and everybody knew it. It required something drastic, and when we did that drastic thing, it sent a signal to the community and brought back a lot of people who had left because they thought it was a dying center."

"If the site is already a shopping center, we feel the fight with the town is shorter—especially if the mall is not doing well," adds Gwin.

De-Malling Is Not for Every Enclosed Shopping Center

Despite these positive results, developers are quick to point out that de-malling is not the answer for all failed enclosed shopping centers. Certain criteria must be met for a site to be successfully de-malled. Primary among them is that the property must have the location and demographics to entice big box retailers.

In addition, it helps to have a deep-pocket owner involved that is staying with the project long-term and understands that sometimes money has to be spent in order to make money, say developers. An understanding owner is essential because de-malling can be a taxing process. People involved with a de-enclosing are quick to point out that the process can be expensive and time-consuming. For example, the turnaround time at South Hills Mall took more than three years. Officials at Newberry Commons allocated five years to complete the de-malling and fully lease the project. Often, delays can stem from having to get approval from reluctant tenants and/or uninformed local communities.

"It was a long and laborious process," Gwin says. "We had to convince the town this was the right thing to do. They did not like the idea that we were putting outside entrances on the mall or that we wanted to put signs up. We had to make them understand what the power center format was.

"For the tenants," Gwin adds, "there were rent releases and concessions made during the reconstruction. We had a 75 per cent turnover. There was a lot of relocation. Some tenants changed their formats. Altogether, it was a three-year process."

Despite these problems, some developers that have already undertaken a de-malling are seemingly willing to do more as the need arises. "We are going to try to develop this as our market niche," Gwin says. "In the Northeast, where it is hard to find 40 acres of flat land on which to build, difficult to get the equity requirements necessary to build and where retail is moving toward category killers [huge specialty-type stores], I think it is going to be more feasible to look at an existing project and reconfigure as opposed to waiting to see if you can build a new center."

Questions

1. How could a shopping center determine the size, shape, and characteristics of its trading area?
2. a. In a regional shopping center, which stores are most likely to be destination stores? Which are most likely to be parasite stores? Why?
   b. In a neighborhood shopping center, which stores are most likely to be destination stores? Which are most likely to be parasite stores? Why?

3. As the operator of the Newberry Commons shopping center, state what could you learn by studying data from these sources:
   a. *Census of Population.*
   b. *Survey of Buying Power.*
   c. *Editor & Publisher Market Guide.*
4. Do you think "de-malling" is a good idea? Why or why not?
5. What kinds of retailers should *not* situate in shopping centers that have been de-malled? Explain your answer.
6. How should an enclosed shopping center react to a nearby rival's converting to a de-enclosed mall? Why?
7. What criteria would you use to determine whether a shopping center is performing well or poorly?

PART

5

Managing a Retail Business

❖ In Part 5, the elements in managing a retail enterprise are discussed. First, the steps in setting up a retail organization and the special human resource management environment of retailing are presented. Then, operations management is examined—from financial and operational perspectives.

❖ Chapter 10 details how a retailer can use an organization structure to assign tasks, policies, resources, authority, responsibilities, and rewards to satisfy the needs of the target market, employees, and management. It also shows how human resource management can be used to have that structure work properly. Human resource management consists of recruiting, selecting, training, compensating, and supervising personnel.

❖ Chapter 11 focuses on the financial dimensions of operations management in implementing a retail strategy. These topics are discussed: profit planning, asset management—including the strategic profit model and other key business ratios, budgeting, and resource allocation.

❖ Chapter 12 deals with the operational aspects of operations management. These specific operations-management concepts are analyzed: store format and size, space allocation, personnel utilization, store maintenance, energy management, inventory management, store security, insurance, credit management, computerization, and crisis management.

RM

CHAPTER

10

Retail Organization and Human Resource Management

RM

❖ Chapter Objectives

1. To study the procedures involved in setting up a retail organization
2. To examine the various organizational arrangements utilized in retailing
3. To consider the special human resource environment of retailing
4. To describe the principles and practices involved with the human resource management process in retailing

Albertson's operates approximately 660 supermarkets in 19 states, mostly in the western and southern regions of the United States. Ten per cent of its stores are conventional supermarkets, 38 per cent are superstores, 46 per cent are combination stores, and 6 per cent are warehouse stores. Since starting with one store in 1939, Albertson's has grown to become one of the largest retail chains in the country. In recent years, the firm's return on equity and sales growth have been about double the supermarket industry's average.

Albertson's is known in the industry for excellence in human resource management, especially its focus on training, employee motivation, and affirmative action. All employees receive a basic training program when they are hired. Continuing education is provided through on-the-job training, special videos, and classroom-type lectures. Training is also supplied via the *Albertson's Today Video News Magazine*, which has contemporary information on merchandising, customer service, and training topics in a video format. Albertson's has recently introduced a new graduate-level management training program for its district sales managers. This program is designed to keep the managers current on new theories and strategies, as well as to further develop their management skills.

Employees are motivated to provide superior customer service through the firm's Service First award program. The awards were developed to recognize exceptional employees who consistently provide customers with more than they expect. Regular employee evaluations and advancement opportunities offer further motivation.

Albertson's is involved with providing equal opportunities for all of its 71,000 employees. The firm understands the diversity of employees in terms of gender, race, national origin, age, experience, skills, and abilities. In 1992, Albertson's created the position of Equal Employment Opportunity Specialist. This manager is responsible for implementing equal opportunity programs, including those designed to identify, encourage, and train women and minority candidates. As part of its equal opportunity efforts, Albertson's posts all job openings, conducts career interest surveys, and has initiated a new mentoring program. The mentoring program, called the Management Advisory Program, is designed to put women and minority employees in direct contact with specially-trained store directors who are not the employee's supervisors. The directors are trained to answer questions and provide advice concerning career advancement.[1]

[1] *Albertson's 1992 Annual Report*; and Toddi Gutner, "Food Distributors," *Forbes* (January 3, 1994), p. 148.

Reprinted by permission of Albertson's.

Overview

There are three basic steps to managing a retail business properly: setting up an organization structure, hiring and managing personnel, and managing operations—both financially and nonfinancially. In this chapter, the first two steps are covered. Chapters 11 and 12 deal with operations management.

Setting Up a Retail Organization

Through a ***retail organization***, a firm structures and assigns tasks (functions), policies, resources, authority, responsibilities, and rewards in order to efficiently and effectively satisfy the needs of its target market, employees, and management. Figure 10–1 shows a variety of needs that a retailer should take into account when planning and assessing an organization.

As a rule, a retailer cannot survive unless its organization structure satisfies the needs of the target market, regardless of how well employee and/or management needs are met. Thus, an organization structure that reduces costs via centralized buying but results in the retailer's insensitivity to geographic differences in customer preferences would probably be improper.

Even though many retail firms carry out similar tasks or functions (e.g., buying, pricing, displaying, and wrapping merchandise), there are many ways of organizing to perform these functions and focus on the needs of customers, employees, and man-

TARGET MARKET NEEDS

Are there a sufficient number of personnel (salespeople, deliverypersons, cashiers, etc.) available to provide customer service at the appropriate levels?
Are personnel knowledgeable and courteous?
Are store facilities well maintained?
Are the specific needs of branch store customers met?
Are changing needs promptly addressed?

EMPLOYEE NEEDS

Are positions challenging enough?
Is there an orderly promotion program?
Is the employee able to participate in the decision making?
Are the channels of communication clear and open?
Are jobs satisfying?
Is the authority-responsibility relationship clear?
Does the firm promote from within?
Does each employee get treated fairly?
Is good performance rewarded?

MANAGEMENT NEEDS

Is it relatively easy to obtain and retain competent personnel?
Are personnel procedures clearly defined?
Does each worker report to only one supervisor?
Can each manager properly supervise and control the number of workers reporting to him (her)?
Do operating departments have adequate staff support (i.e., computerized reports, market research, and advertising)?
Are the levels of organization properly developed?
Are the organization's plans well integrated?
Are employees motivated?
Is absenteeism low?
Does the organization provide continuity so that personnel can be replaced in an orderly manner?
Is the organization flexible enough to adapt to changes in customer preference and/or regional growth patterns?

FIGURE 10–1
Selected Factors That Must Be Considered in Planning and Assessing a Retail Organization

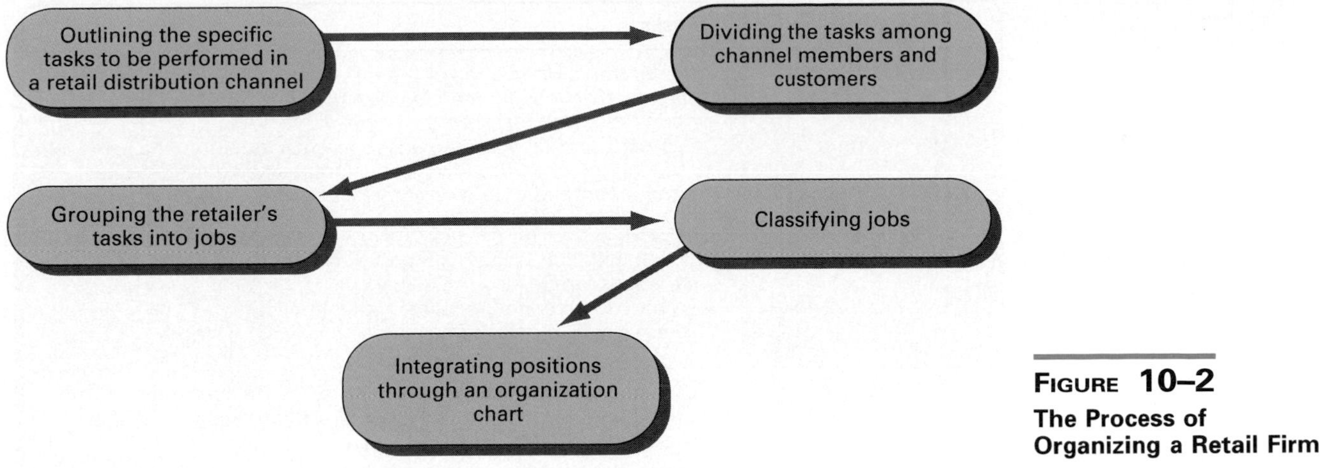

FIGURE 10–2
The Process of Organizing a Retail Firm

agement. The process of setting up a retail organization is outlined in Figure 10–2 and described in the following subsections.

SPECIFYING TASKS TO BE PERFORMED

The general tasks to be performed in a retail channel of distribution must be enumerated. Among the typical tasks are

- Buying merchandise.
- Shipping merchandise.
- Receiving merchandise.
- Checking incoming shipments.
- Setting prices.
- Marking merchandise.
- Inventory storage and control.
- Preparation of merchandise and window displays.
- Facilities maintenance (e.g., keeping the store clean).
- Customer research.
- Customer contact (e.g., advertising, personal selling).
- Facilitating shopping (e.g., convenient site, short checkout lines).
- Customer follow-up and complaint handling.
- Personnel management.
- Repairs and alteration of merchandise.
- Billing customers.
- Handling receipts and financial records.
- Credit operations.
- Gift wrapping.
- Delivery.
- Return of unsold or damaged merchandise to vendors.
- Sales forecasting and budgeting.
- Coordination.

The proper performance of these activities, keyed to the strategy mix chosen, is necessary for effective retailing to occur.

Performer	Tasks
Retailer	Can perform all or some of the tasks listed in the preceding section, from buying merchandise to coordination.
Manufacturer or Wholesaler	Can perform few or many functions, such as: shipping, marking merchandise, inventory storage and control, display preparation, research, sales forecasting, etc.
Specialist(s)	Can include the following types: buying office, delivery firm, warehouse, marketing research firm, advertising agency, accountant, credit bureau, computer service firm. Each specializes in the performance of a particular task.
Consumer	Can assume responsibility for delivery, credit (cash-only sales), sales effort (self-service or direct marketing), product alterations (do-it-yourselfers), etc.

FIGURE 10–3
The Division of Retail Tasks

DIVIDING TASKS AMONG CHANNEL MEMBERS AND CUSTOMERS

Although the tasks just cited are often performed in a retail channel of distribution, they do not necessarily have to be performed by a retailer. Some can be undertaken by a manufacturer, a wholesaler, a specialist, or the consumer. Figure 10–3 shows the types of activities that could be carried out by each party. The following illustration indicates some of the criteria to be considered in allocating the tasks related to consumer credit.

A task should be carried out only if desired by the target market. Unless a retailer, such as a convenience store chain, finds that a number of its customers disapprove of cash-only transactions, it should not accept credit-card sales. For some retailers, liberal credit policies may provide significant advantages over competitors. For others, a cash-only policy may reduce their overhead and lead to lower prices.

A task should be performed by the party with special competence and/or equipment. Credit collection may require a legal staff and a computer-based record-keeping system. These are usually affordable only by medium-sized or large retailers. Smaller retailers would rely on bank credit cards to overcome the lack of necessary resources.

The retailer should consider the loss of control over an activity when it is delegated to another party. A credit collection firm, pressing hard to receive payment on a past-due account, may antagonize a customer to the point of losing future sales for the retailer.

The institutional framework of the retailer can have an impact on the allocation of tasks. Franchisees are readily able to get together to set up their own credit bureau. Independents cannot do this as easily.

Task allocation should take into consideration the savings achieved by sharing or shifting tasks. The credit function can be better performed by an outside credit bureau if its personnel are specialized, it has ongoing access to financial information, it uses tailored computer software, and/or it pays lower rent (due to an out-of-the-way location), and so on. Many retailers cannot gain these savings themselves.

GROUPING TASKS INTO JOBS

After the retailer decides which functions to perform, tasks are grouped into jobs. These jobs must be clearly defined and structured. Some examples of grouping tasks into jobs are

Tasks	Jobs
Displaying merchandise, customer contact, gift wrapping, customer follow-up	Sales personnel
Entering transaction data, handling cash receipts, processing credit purchases, gift wrapping, inventory control	Cashier(s)
Receiving merchandise, checking incoming shipments, marking merchandise, inventory storage and control, returning merchandise to vendors	Inventory personnel
Window dressing, interior display set-ups, use of mobiles	Display personnel
Billing customers, credit operations, customer research	Credit personnel
Repairs and alterations of merchandise, resolution of customer complaints, customer research	Customer service personnel
Cleaning store, replacing old fixtures	Janitorial personnel
Personnel management, sales forecasting, budgeting, pricing, coordination of tasks	Management personnel

When grouping tasks into jobs, the retailer must consider the use of specialization. Under specialization, each employee is responsible for limited functions (as opposed to each employee's performing many diverse functions). Specialization has the advantages of clearly defined tasks, greater expertise, reduced training costs and time, and hiring personnel with narrow education and experience. Problems can result through extreme specialization: poor morale (boredom), personnel not being aware of the importance of their jobs, and the need for an increased number of employees.

The proper use of specialization involves assigning specific duties and responsibilities to individuals so that a job position encompasses a relatively homogeneous cluster of work tasks. These tasks should have an essential and enduring purpose within the retail organization.

After work tasks are grouped, job descriptions are constructed. These outline the job titles, objectives, duties, and responsibilities for every position. They are used as a hiring, supervision, and evaluation tool. Figure 10–4 contains a job description for a store manager.

Classifying Jobs

Jobs can then be broadly categorized via a functional, product, geographic, or combination classification system. In a ***functional classification***, jobs are divided among functional areas such as sales promotion, buying, and store operations. Expert knowledge is utilized.

Product classification divides jobs on a goods or service basis. For example, a department store can hire personnel for clothing, furniture, giftware, appliances, and so on. Product classification recognizes that differences exist in the personnel requirements for different products. Tighter control and responsibility are also possible.

Geographic classification is useful for multiunit stores operating in different areas. Personnel are adapted to local conditions. Job descriptions and qualifications are under the control of individual branch managers.

For larger retailers, combinations of these three classifications are often used. As an example, a branch unit of a department store may hire and supervise its own selling staff, while buying personnel for each product line are centrally hired and controlled by the headquarters' store. Thus, the functional, product, and geographic forms of organization are combined.

JOB TITLE: Store Manager for 34th Street Branch of Pombo's Department Stores

POSITION REPORTS TO: Senior Vice-President

POSITIONS REPORTING TO STORE MANAGER: All personnel working in the 34th Street store

OBJECTIVES: To properly staff and operate the 34th Street store

DUTIES AND RESPONSIBILITIES:

1. Personnel recruitment, selection, training, motivation, and evaluation
2. Merchandise display
3. Inventory storage and control
4. Approving orders for merchandise
5. Transferring merchandise among stores
6. Sales forecasting
7. Budgeting
8. Handling store receipts
9. Preparing bank transactions
10. Locking and unlocking store
11. Reviewing customer complaints
12. Reviewing computer data forms
13. Semiannual review of overall operations
14. Forwarding reports to top management

COMMITTEES AND MEETINGS:

1. Store Managers' Review Committee
2. Attendance at monthly meetings with Senior Vice-President
3. Supervision of weekly meetings with department managers

FIGURE 10–4
A Job Description for a Store Manager

DEVELOPING AN ORGANIZATION CHART

When planning its organization structure, a retailer should not look at jobs as individual units but as parts of the whole. Thus, the format of a retail organization must be planned in an integrated, coordinated way. Jobs must be defined and distinct; yet, interrelationships among positions must be clear.

RETAILING AROUND THE WORLD

What Organizational Factors Influence Internationalization?

A recent research study examined British-based retailers that operate at least one store within and one store outside Great Britain to determine the organizational characteristics that affect the level of internationalization for these retailers.

Four organizational and decision-maker traits were found to be associated with internationalization:

- British orientation—This trait is appropriate for firms with minimal commitment to international retailing, such as firms that have just started foreign operations.
- Pace-setting/market leadership orientation—This trait is proper for firms with considerable experience in international retailing. They prefer to lead, not follow, competitors.
- Cautious orientation—This trait symbolizes a "go-slow" approach to international retailing due to the higher risks, the greater uncertainty, and a lack of knowledge of foreign markets.
- Innovative business orientation—This trait depicts organizations with creative retail business concepts and senior managers who are willing to accept change. These firms hope to earn profits by being the first into foreign markets with unique concepts, rather than setting up extensive domestic activities.

Although some retailers with a British orientation may be forced to internationalize to sustain their growth (despite their domestic inclination), others with similar traits may be unable to internationalize due to limited resources.

Source: Based on material in David E. Williams, "Retailer Internationalization: An Empirical Inquiry," *European Journal of Marketing*, Vol. 26 (Number 8/9, 1992), pp. 8–24.

The ***hierarchy of authority*** outlines the job relationships within a company by describing the reporting relationships among employees (from the lowest level to the store manager or board of directors). Coordination and control are provided through this hierarchy.

The levels in a retail organization are reflected by the number of positions separating the top official from the lowest employee. A firm with a large number of subordinates reporting to one supervisor has a ***flat organization.*** Some benefits of a flat organization are good communication, quicker handling of problems, and better employee identification with a job. The major problem tends to be too many employees reporting to one manager.

A ***tall organization*** has several levels of managers. This arrangement leads to close supervision and fewer employees reporting to each manager. The problems include a long channel of communication, an impersonal impression given to employees, and inflexible rules.

With these factors in mind, a retailer can develop an ***organization chart,*** which graphically displays the hierarchal relationships within the firm. Table 10–1 lists the principles to be considered in establishing an organization chart. Figure 10–5 contains examples of functional, product, geographic, and combination organization charts.

Organizational Patterns in Retailing

Retail organization structures differ by institutional type. For example, an independent retailer has a much simpler organization than a chain retailer. An independent does not have to manage units that may be distant from the main store, the owner-manager usually personally supervises all employees, and workers have ready access

TABLE 10–1 Principles for Organizing a Retail Firm

- An organization should be concerned about its employees. Job rotation, promotion from within, participatory management, recognition, job enrichment, etc. improve worker morale.
- Employee turnover, lateness, and absenteeism should be monitored, as they may indicate personnel problems.
- The line of authority should be traceable from the highest to the lowest positions. In this way, employees know whom to report to and who reports to them (chain of command).
- A subordinate should only report to one supervisor. This avoids the problem of workers' receiving conflicting orders (unity of command).
- Responsibility should be associated with adequate authority. A person responsible for a given objective needs the power to achieve it.
- Although a supervisor can delegate authority, he/she retains responsibility for the acts of subordinates. The delegation of authority cannot be an excuse for a manager's failing to achieve a goal. This concept requires that a manager actively evaluate the performance of subordinates while they are working to reach a goal.
- There is a limit to the number of employees a manager can directly supervise (span of control).
- The firm should strive to limit the number of organization levels. The greater the number of levels, the longer the time for communication to travel and the greater the coordination problems.
- An organization has an informal structure aside from the formal organization chart. Informal relationships exercise power in the organization and may bypass formal relationships and procedures.

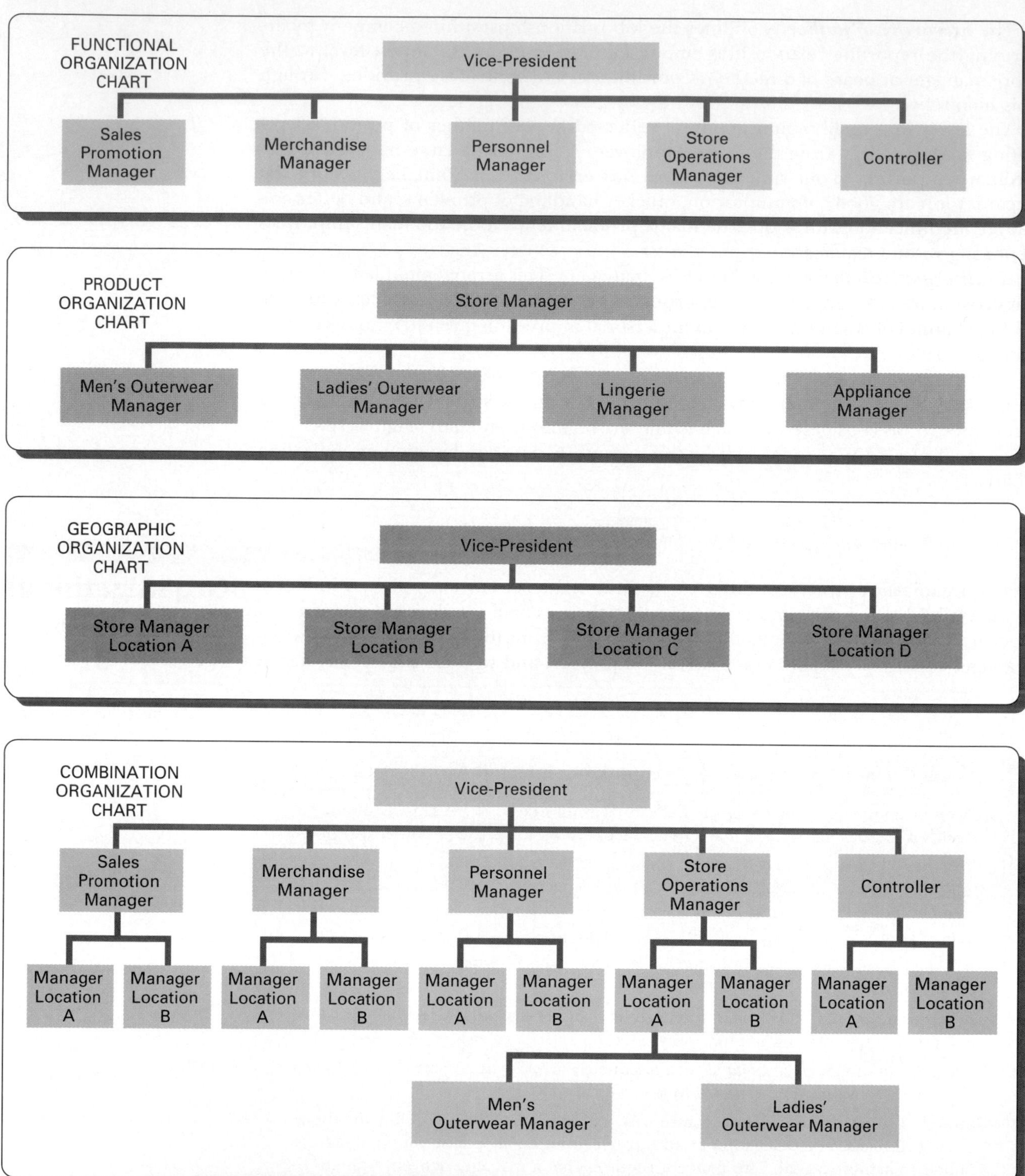

FIGURE 10–5 Different Forms of Retail Organization

to the owner-manager in the event of any personal or work-related problems. In contrast, a chain must specify how tasks are to be delegated, coordinate multiple-store operations, and establish common policies for all employees.

A discussion of organizational arrangements used by independent retailers, department stores, chain retailers, and diversified retailers follows.

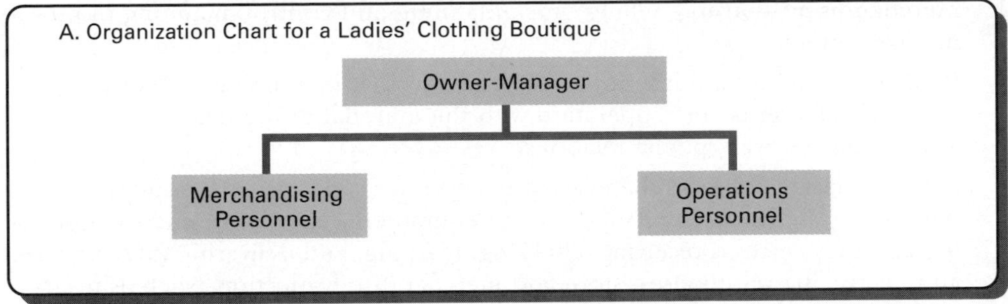

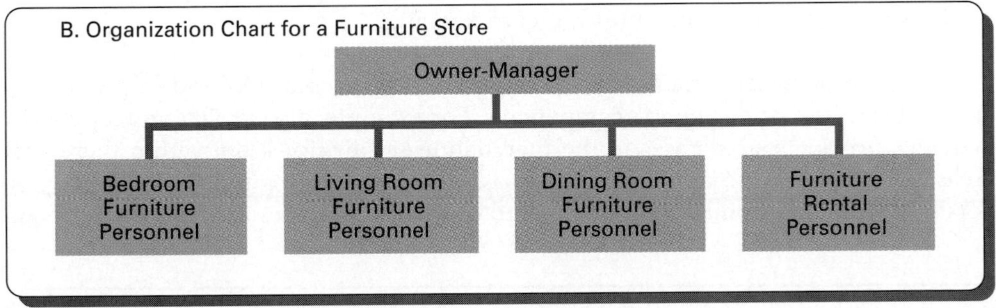

FIGURE 10–6
Organization Structures Used by Small Independents

ORGANIZATIONAL ARRANGEMENTS USED BY SMALL INDEPENDENT RETAILERS

Small independent retailers generally use simple organizational arrangements because they contain only two or three levels of personnel (the owner-manager and employees), and the owner-manager personally runs the business and supervises employees. There are few workers and little departmentalization (specialization). There are no branch units. Yet, this does not mean fewer activities must be performed.

The small retailer has little specialization of functions since there are many tasks to be performed relative to the number of workers available to do them. Thus, each worker must allot part of his or her time to several duties.

Figure 10–6 shows the organization structures of two small independents. In A, a boutique is organized on a functional basis: merchandising versus operations. Merchandising personnel are responsible for buying and selling goods and services, assortments, displays, and ads. Operations personnel are responsible for store maintenance and operations (e.g., inventory management and financial reports). In B, a furniture store is organized on a product-oriented basis, with the personnel in each category responsible for selected activities. All of the product categories get appropriate attention, and some expertise is developed. This expertise is particularly important because different skills are necessary to buy and sell each type of furniture.

ORGANIZATIONAL ARRANGEMENTS USED BY DEPARTMENT STORES

Many medium-sized and large department stores use organizational arrangements that are a modification of the Mazur plan, which was first introduced in 1927. The basic ***Mazur plan*** divides all retail activities into four functional areas: merchandising, publicity, store management, and accounting and control.[2] These functional areas include the following activities:

[2] Paul M. Mazur, *Principles of Organization Applied to Modern Retailing* (New York: Harper & Brothers, 1927).

1. Merchandising—buying, selling, stock planning and control, planning of promotional events.
2. Publicity—window and interior display, advertising, planning and executing promotional events (in cooperation with the merchandising department), advertising research, public relations.
3. Store management—merchandise care, customer services (such as adjustment bureaus), purchasing store supplies and equipment, store maintenance, operating activities (such as receiving, checking, marking, and delivering merchandise; and overseeing warehouse), store and merchandise protection (such as insurance and security), training and compensating personnel, workroom operations.
4. Accounting and control—credit and collection, expense budgeting and control, inventory planning and control, record keeping.

These four areas are organized in terms of line (direct authority and responsibility) and staff (advisory and support) components. For example, a controller and a publicity manager provide staff services to the merchandising divisions, but within these staff areas, personnel are organized on a line basis. This principle can be more clearly understood from an examination of Figure 10–7, which illustrates the basic Mazur plan.

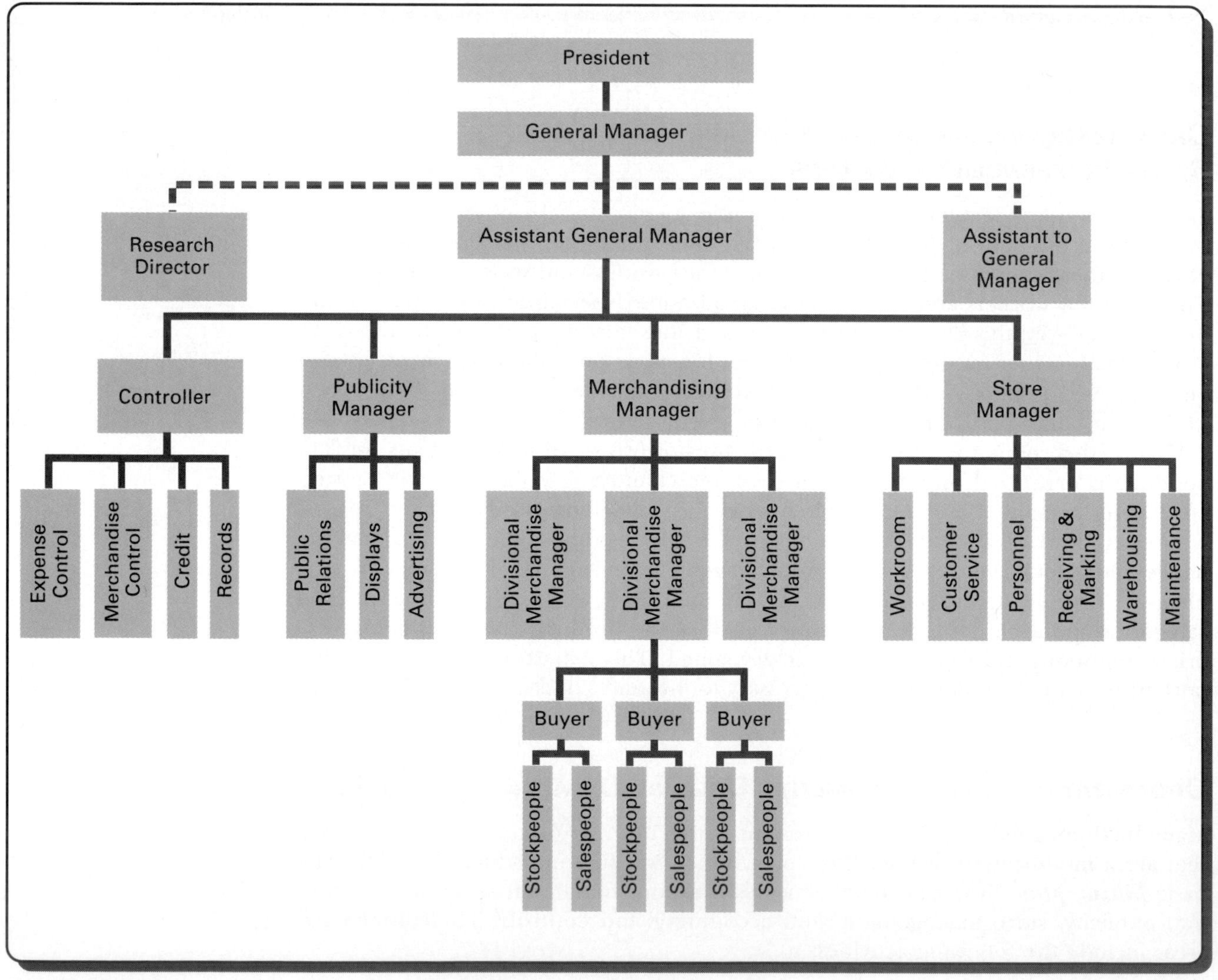

FIGURE 10–7 The Basic Mazur Organization Plan for Department Stores

Source: Adapted from Paul Mazur, *Principles of Organization Applied to Modern Retailing* (New York: Harper & Brothers, 1927), frontispiece. Reprinted by permission.

As shown in Figure 10–7, the merchandising division is responsible for buying and selling activities and is headed by a merchandising manager. This executive is often regarded as the most important area executive in the store and is responsible for supervising buyers, developing a financial control system for each department, coordinating department merchandise plans and policies (so a store has a consistent image among departments), and interpreting economic data and their effect on the store. In some stores, divisional merchandise managers are utilized, so the number of buyers reporting to a single manager does not become unwieldy.

The buyer, under the basic Mazur plan, has complete responsibility for controlling expenses and reaching profit goals within his or her department. The buyer's duties include preparing preliminary budgets, studying fashion trends, bargaining with vendors over price, planning the number of salespeople needed, and informing sales personnel about merchandise purchased and fashion trends. The grouping of buying and selling activities into one job (buyer) may present a major problem. Since buyers are not constantly on the selling floor, control of personnel (training, scheduling, and supervision) may suffer.

The growth of branch stores has led to three derivative forms of the Mazur plan: the ***mother hen with branch store chickens organization***, whereby headquarters executives oversee and operate the branches; the ***separate store organization***, whereby each branch has its own buying responsibilities; and the ***equal store organization***, whereby buying is centralized and branches become sales units with equal operational status.

In the "mother hen" organization, most authority remains with managers at the main company store. Merchandise planning and buying, advertising, financial controls, store hours, and many other areas are centrally managed. To a great extent, this organization standardizes the performance of all outlets. Branch store managers hire and supervise the employees in their stores and are responsible for making sure day-to-day operations conform to company policies. This organization works well when there are few branches and the buying preferences of branch customers are similar to those of the main store's customers. However, as the branch stores increase in number, the buyers, the advertising director, the controller, and others may become overworked and give too little attention to the branches. In addition, because the main store's personnel are physically removed from the branches, differences in customer preferences may easily be overlooked.

The "separate store" organization places merchandise managers directly in branch stores. Each branch outlet has autonomy for merchandising and operations decisions. Customer needs are quickly identified, but duplication by managers in the main store and the branches is possible. Coordination can also be a problem (e.g., maintaining a consistent image from outlet to outlet). Transferring stock between branches becomes more complex and more costly. This organization is best when individual stores are large, branches are geographically separated, and/or local customer tastes vary widely.

With the "equal store" organization, department stores try to achieve the benefits of both centralization and decentralization. It is probably the most popular arrangement today for multiunit department stores. Buying functions—such as forecasting, planning, buying, pricing, merchandise distribution to branches, and promotion—are centrally managed. Selling functions—such as presenting merchandise, selling, customer services, and store operations—are managed in each outlet. All outlets, including the main store, are treated equally; and buyers are freed from supervising main-store personnel. Data gathering is critical because buyers have less customer and store contact, and responsibility is more widely dispersed (and harder to pin down—buyers versus sales manager).

ORGANIZATIONAL ARRANGEMENTS USED BY CHAIN RETAILERS

Chain retailers of various types often use a version of the equal-store organizational format explained in the preceding section and shown in Figure 10–8. Although chain-store organization structures may differ, they generally have these characteristics:

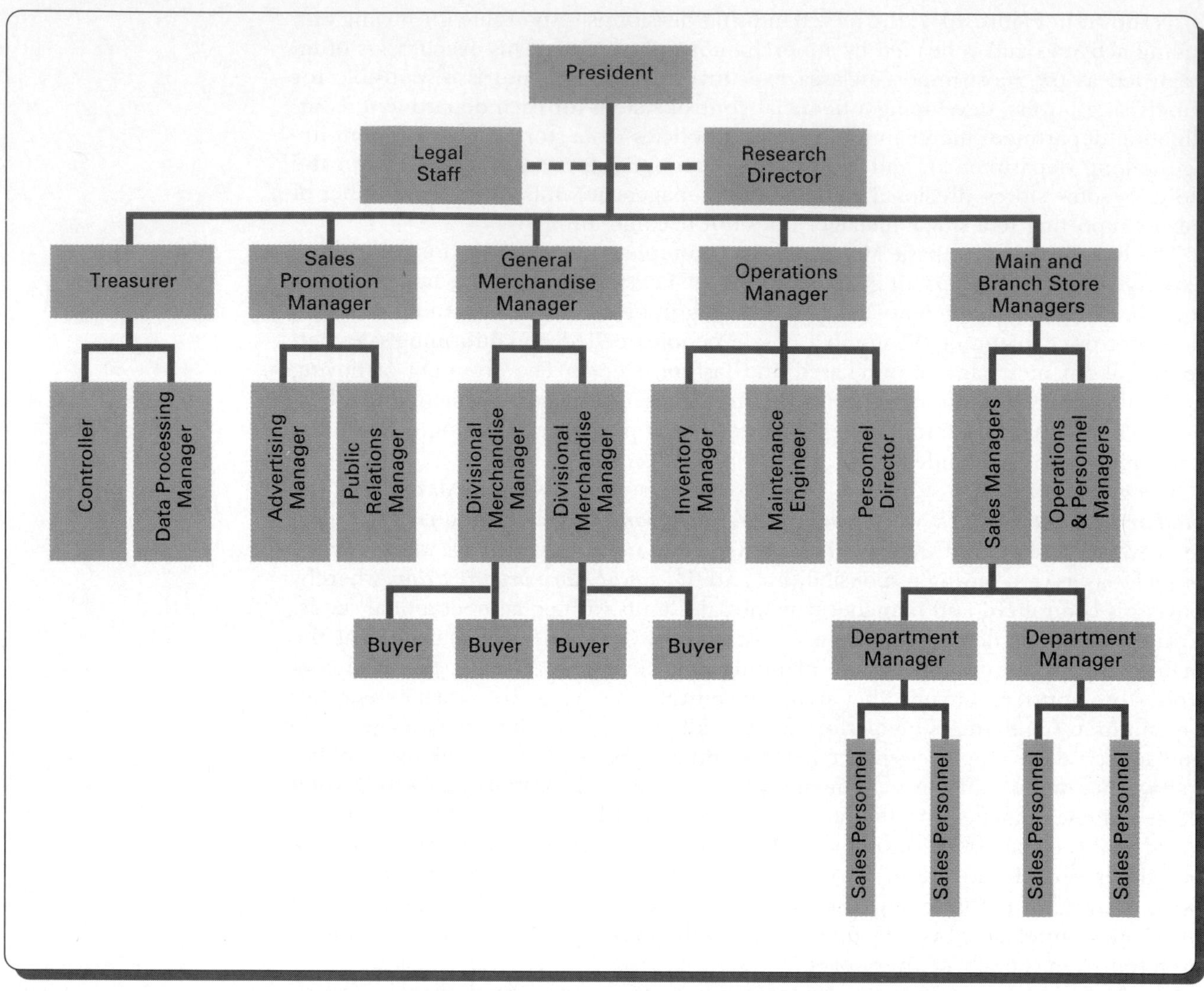

FIGURE 10–8 The Equal-Store Organizational Format Used by Many Chain Stores

- There are a large number of functional divisions, such as sales promotion, merchandise management, distribution, store operations, real estate, personnel, and information systems.
- Overall authority and responsibility are centralized, with individual store managers responsible for sales.
- Many operations are standardized (fixtures, store layout, building design, merchandise lines, credit policy, and store service).
- An elaborate control system keeps management informed.
- A limited amount of decentralization enables branch stores to adapt better to local conditions and increases the store manager's responsibilities. For example, while some large chains standardize 80 to 90 per cent of the merchandise carried by their outlets, store managers are free to fine-tune 10 to 20 per cent of the mix to appeal to local markets—be they rural or urban, African-American or Hispanic, high or low income.

Figure 10–9 shows the organizational structure for the United States' Toys "R" Us store division of Toys "R" Us, Inc. It is an equal-store format organized by function and geographic area.

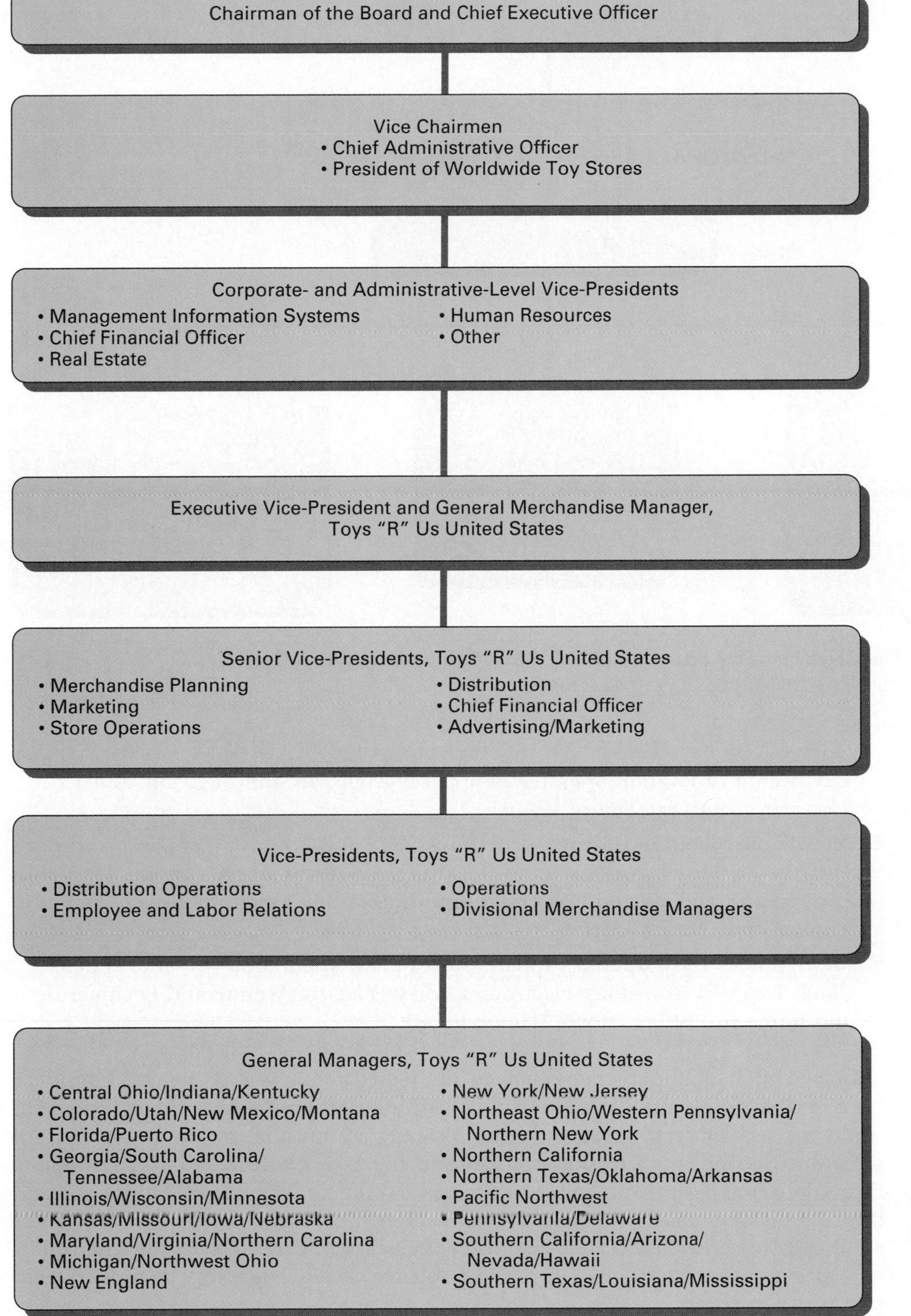

FIGURE 10–9
The Organizational Structure of Toys "R" Us (United States Only)
Source: Adapted by the authors from the *Toys "R" Us 1993 Annual Report.*

ORGANIZATIONAL ARRANGEMENTS USED BY DIVERSIFIED RETAILERS

A ***diversified retailer***, also known as a retail conglomerate or conglomerchant, is a multiline merchandising firm under central ownership. Like a chain, a diversified retailer has more than one outlet; however, unlike a typical chain, these outlets cover different types of retail operations. These are some examples of diversified retailers:

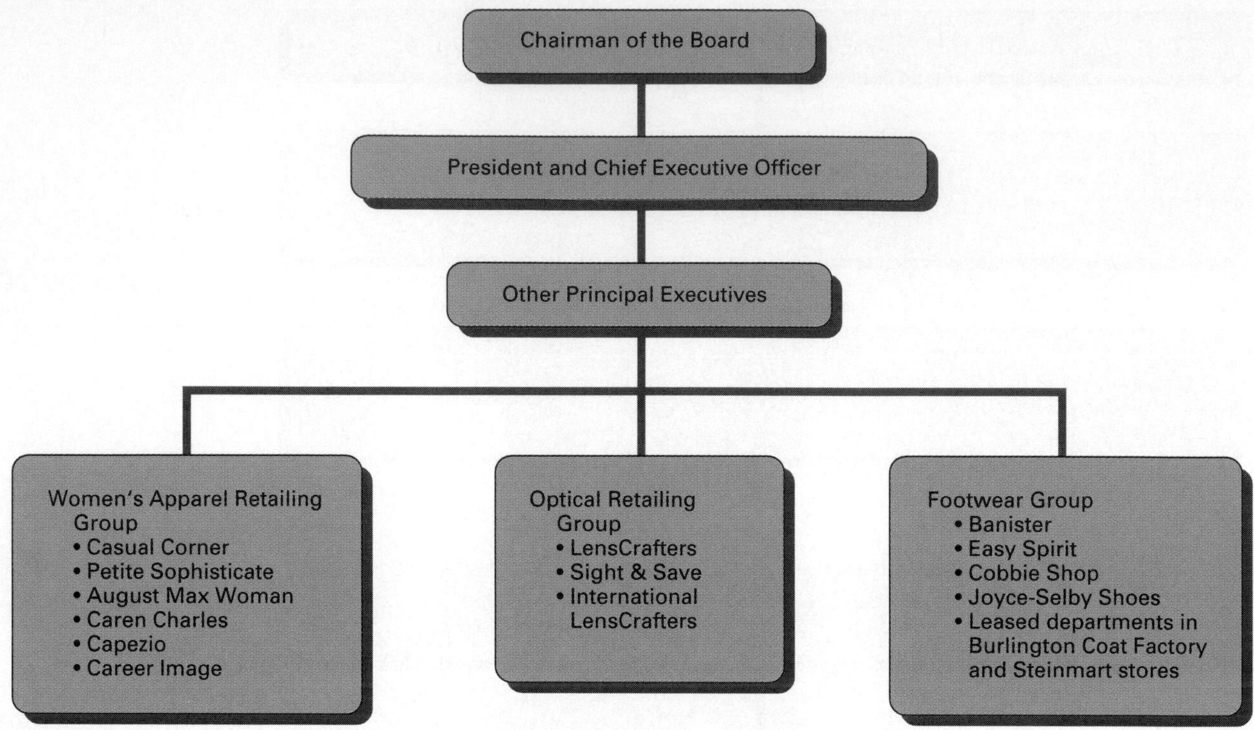

FIGURE 10–10 The Organizational Structure of U.S. Shoe Corporation (Retail Only)
Source: Adapted by the authors from the *U.S. Shoe 1992 Annual Report*.

- U.S. Shoe Corporation operates an apparel group, an optical group, and a footwear group. See Figure 10–10.
- Melville Corporation operates drugstores (CVS and Freddy's), apparel stores (such as Marshalls, Wilsons, and Chess King), footwear stores (Thom McAn and FootAction), and toy and household furnishings stores (such as Kay-Bee, Linens 'n Things, and This End Up).
- Montgomery Ward operates apparel stores (The Apparel Store), auto centers (Auto Express), consumer electronics stores (Electric Avenue and Lechmere), and home furnishings stores (Home Ideas).

Due to their multiple strategy mixes, diversified retailers face atypical considerations in developing and maintaining an organization structure. First, interdivision control is needed. Operating procedures and clear goals must be communicated among divisions. Second, interdivision competition must be coordinated (e.g., Should a firm's department stores and discount stores carry the same brands?). Third, resources must be divided among different divisions. Fourth, potential image and advertising conflicts must be avoided. Fifth, management skills must be adapted to rather different operations. Accordingly, a diversified retailer usually has a very complex organization structure.

Human Resource Management in Retailing

Human resource management involves the recruitment, selection, training, compensation, and supervision of personnel in a manner consistent with the retailer's organization structure and strategy mix. It is required of all retailers, with policies dependent on their line of business, the number of employees, the location of outlets, and other factors.

Because good personnel are needed to develop and carry out retail strategies, and labor costs can amount to 50 per cent or more of some retailers' operating expenses, the importance of effective human resource management is clear. This is further illustrated through the following:

- U.S. retailing now employs twenty million people and this will rise to 23 million by the year 2000; thus, there is a constant need to attract new employees. However, from 1980 to the present, the number of available U.S. workers aged 16 to 24 has dropped by several million people. This has made the recruitment and retention of full- and part-time employees harder. For example, over two million fast-food workers are aged 16 to 20, and they must be regularly replaced since they stay in their jobs for only short times.[3]
- After determining that many teenagers quit their jobs once they reach specific goals (such as earning enough money to buy new clothes), some McDonald's franchise operators decided to try to make the jobs more fun. They now allow employees to select the music they listen to in work areas, wear their own clothing rather than uniforms one day a week, and so on. Thus far, the approach has been promising.[4]
- Dollar General has a progressive human resource mission, keyed to such principles as these: "We believe in the dignity of the person and the work. Our productivity is, therefore, attained by emphasizing strengths, not by dwelling on weaknesses. We believe that any success is short-lived if it does not involve mutual gain."[5]
- The highest entry-level position at Home Depot is usually assistant store manager; store managers are typically not hired from outside the company. Although Home Depot is a large and growing chain, the firm's co-founders and other senior executives have been personally involved in the training of virtually every manager. They want to be sure that the basic operating philosophy is clearly communicated to and carried out by all employees.[6]
- At Nordstrom, "unlike most large chains, the company has buyers in each store to respond directly to reports from sales clerks and comments from customers. Salespeople decide on such things as special orders, when the goods are delivered, obtaining extra garments if needed, and handling problems. But, mainly, they are urged to be attentive."[7]
- At West Point Market, an Akron, Ohio, supermarket, new employees are given performance reviews every 30, 60, and 90 days—"both to give positive reinforcement and to pinpoint specific problems."[8]

THE SPECIAL HUMAN RESOURCE ENVIRONMENT OF RETAILING

Retailers face a special human resource environment, which is characterized by a large number of inexperienced workers, long hours, highly visible employees, many part-time workers, and variations in customer demand. These factors often make the hiring, staffing, and supervision of employees a difficult process.

[3] Jules Abend, "Personnel Strategies," *Stores* (September 1990), pp. 42–44; Laura Liebeck, "Working Moms Can Ease Chains' Labor Problems," *Discount Store News* (May 7, 1990), p. 125; and *Standard & Poor's Industry Analysis: Retailing Basic Analysis* (April 19, 1990), p. R90.

[4] Joel Dreyfuss, "Get Ready for the New Work Force," *Fortune* (April 23, 1990), p. 181.

[5] *Dollar General Corporation 1993 Annual Report*, p. 8.

[6] *Home Depot 1992 Annual Report*, pp. 2–5.

[7] Isadore Barmash, "Nordstrom Opens Store in New Jersey, Despite Odds," *New York Times* (September 7, 1990), p. D8.

[8] Mary Ann Linsen, "Searching for Solutions," *Progressive Grocer* (May 1993), pp. 183–188.

The greatest personnel difficulty for many retailers is probably the relative inexperience of a lot of their workers. As previously noted, there is a need for a large labor force in retailing, and persons with little or no prior experience are frequently hired. For numerous new workers, a position in retailing represents their first "real" job. People are attracted to retailing because they find jobs near to their homes; and retail positions may require limited education, training, and skill (e.g., checkout clerks, wrappers, stock clerks, and some types of sales personnel). Also, the low wages paid for some positions call for the hiring of inexperienced people. Thus, there are high employee turnover and cases of poor performance, lateness, and absenteeism.

The long working hours generally encountered in retailing, including Saturdays and Sundays in various locales, turn off some prospective employees; and there is a strong trend toward longer store hours, because family shoppers and working-women shoppers look for stores with evening and weekend hours. As a result, some retailers must have at least two shifts of full-time employees.

In retailing, employees are highly visible to the customer. Therefore, when a retailer selects and trains personnel, special care must be taken with regard to their manners and appearance. Unfortunately, some small retailers may not recognize the importance of employee appearance (e.g., being neatly groomed and appropriately attired).

Due to the long hours of retail stores, firms often have to hire part-time personnel. In many supermarkets, over half the workers are part-time; and problems can arise accordingly. Part-time employees may be more apt to be lackadaisical, late, absent, or quit their jobs than full-time employees (who are more career-oriented). This means they must be closely monitored.

Last, variations in customer demand by day, time period, or season may cause personnel planning problems. For example, the majority of consumers make their major supermarket shopping trips on Thursday, Friday, or Saturday. So, how many employees should a supermarket have on the premises Sunday (or Monday) through Wednesday, and how many should be used Thursday through Saturday? Demand differences during the day (e.g., morning, afternoon, evening) and by season (e.g., fall, Christmas) also affect personnel planning.

In general, retailers should consider points such as these:

- Employee recruitment and selection procedures must be able to generate a sufficient number of applicants efficiently.
- Some training programs must be intensive and short in duration because many workers are inexperienced and temporary.

RETAILING IN ACTION

Why Is Sears Making a Comeback?

Upon joining Sears in 1992 as chief executive officer of the merchandising group, Arthur Martinez was astonished to learn that its top executives did not have access to information on profits by store, that the corporate culture valued seniority as more important than performance, and that store managers had little voice in how their stores were run.

In his first year at Sears, Martinez reduced costs by firing 50,000 workers (15 per cent of Sears' work force), offered buyouts to 4,000 of Sears's 15,000 managers, closed 113 stores, and disbanded Sears' catalog operation (which lost $160 million during its last year of operation).

His greatest challenge, however, was to persuade working women to buy clothes for work at Sears. Although apparel accounts for only 26 per cent of Sears' sales, it makes up 64 per cent of profits. A successful advertising campaign, "The Softer Side of Sears," was developed to play off the Sears' reputation for hard goods (such as consumer electronics and appliances) and more stylish clothing was added. Sears also upscaled its target market to include families in the $25,000 to $60,000 income range.

In comparison to 1992, when Sears' merchandise group lost $8 million, the unit earned a profit of several hundred million dollars for 1993.

Source: Based on material in John McCormick, "The Savior at Sears," *Newsweek* (November 1, 1993), pp. 43–46.

- Opportunities for advancement must be available to employees who look at retailing as a career.
- Employee appearance and work habits must be explained and reviewed.
- Morale problems may result from the high rate of employee turnover and the large number of part-time workers.
- Full- and part-time employees may have conflicts, especially when part-time personnel are used to minimize overtime for full-time workers.

THE HUMAN RESOURCE MANAGEMENT PROCESS IN RETAILING

The ***human resource management process*** in retailing consists of these interrelated personnel activities: recruitment, selection, training, compensation, and supervision. The goals of this process are to obtain, develop, and retain employees. In the next subsections, each activity in the process is discussed for retail sales and middle-management positions.

Recruitment of Retail Personnel

Recruitment is the activity whereby a retailer generates a list of job applicants. Sources of potential employees include educational institutions, other channel members, competitors, advertisements, employment agencies, unsolicited applicants, and current and former employees who are looking for new positions or who recommend friends. Table 10–2 indicates the characteristics of these sources.

TABLE 10–2 Recruitment Sources and Their Characteristics

Sources	Characteristics
1. Outside the Company	
Educational institutions	a. High schools, business schools, community colleges, universities, graduate schools b. Good for training positions; ensure minimum educational requirements are fulfilled; especially useful when long-term contacts with instructors are developed
Other channel members, competitors	a. Employees of wholesalers, manufacturers, ad agencies, competitors; leads from each of these b. Reduce extent of training; can evaluate performance with prior firm(s); must instruct in company policy; some negative morale if current employees feel bypassed for promotions
Advertisements	a. Newspapers, trade publications, professional journals b. Large quantity of applicants; average applicant quality may not be high; cost/applicant is low; additional responsibility placed on screening; can reduce number of unacceptable applicants by noting job qualifications in ads
Employment agencies	a. Private organizations, professional organizations, government, executive search firms b. Must be carefully selected; must be determined who pays fee; good for applicant screening; specialists in personnel
Unsolicited applicants	a. Walk-ins, write-ins b. Wide variance in quality; must be carefully screened; file should be kept for future positions
2. Within the Company	
Current and former employees	a. Promotion or transfer of existing full-time employees, part-time employees; rehiring of laid-off employees b. Knowledge of company policies and personnel; good for morale; honest appraisal from in-house supervisor
Employee recommendations	a. Friends, acquaintances, relatives b. Value of recommendations depends on honesty and judgment of current employees

For entry-level sales personnel, retailers are apt to rely on educational institutions, ads, walk-ins (or write-ins), and employee recommendations. For middle-management positions, retailers are likely to use employment agencies, competitors, ads, and current employees.

Often during recruitment, the retailer's major goal is to generate a large list of potential employees, which will be sharply reduced during selection. However, retailers that accept applicants for further consideration only if they meet minimum background standards (e.g., education, experience) can save a lot of time and money during selection.

Selection of Retail Personnel

Next, the retailer selects its new employees from among those it has recruited. The major objective in a selection procedure is to match the traits of potential employees with the requirements of the jobs to be filled. Such a procedure should include job analysis and description, the application blank, interviewing, testing (optional), references, and a physical examination. These steps should be followed in an integrated manner.

Job analysis consists of gathering information about each job's functions and requirements: duties, responsibilities, aptitude, interest, education, experience, and physical condition. It is used for selecting personnel, setting job performance standards, and salary administration. For example, a study of department managers at a variety of general merchandise stores found that they typically supervise other sales associates, serve as the main sales associates for their departments, have some administrative and analytical responsibilities, report directly to the store manager, are eligible to receive bonuses, and are paid from $15,000 to $35,000+ annually. The majority have been with their companies for two or more years.[9]

Job analysis should lead to written job descriptions. A ***traditional job description*** contains each position's title, supervisory relationships (superior and subordinate), committee assignments, and the specific roles and tasks to be performed on an ongoing basis. Figure 10–4 showed a traditional job description for a store manager.

However, the use of the traditional job description alone has been criticized. This approach may limit the scope of a job, as well as its authority, responsibility, and decision-making power; be static and not allow a person to grow; limit activities to those listed; and not describe how positions are coordinated. Thus, as a supplement to a traditional job description, many personnel experts now advocate using a ***goal-oriented job description***, which enumerates basic functions, the relationship of each job to overall goals, the interdependence of positions, and information flows. Figure 10–11 is an illustration of a goal-oriented job description.

An ***application blank*** is usually the first tool used in screening applicants; it provides data on education, experience, health, reasons for leaving previous jobs, organizational memberships, hobbies, and references. It is relatively short, requires little interpretation, and can be used as the basis for probing during an interview.

One refinement of the basic application form is the ***weighted application blank***. Retailers using such a form typically have analyzed the performance of current and past employees and determined which criteria (education, experience, and so on) are best correlated with job success (as measured by longer tenure, higher sales volume, less absenteeism, and so on). Factors having a high relationship with success are given more weight than others, and a certain number of points are assigned to each rated factor. After weighted scores are given to all job applicants (based on information they provide), a minimum total score can be used as a cutoff point for hiring. An effective weighted application blank would aid a retailer in reducing job turnover and identifying high achievers.

An application blank should be used in conjunction with a job description. Those who meet the minimum requirements of a job are processed further (interview). Those who do not are immediately rejected. In this way, the application blank provides a quick and inexpensive method of screening.

[9] Ernst & Young, "Study: Store Management," *Stores* (September 1990), pp. 48–49.

Attributes Required	Ability	Desire	In the Retailing Environment
ANALYTICAL SKILLS: ability to solve problems; strong numerical ability for analysis of facts and data for planning, managing, and controlling.			Retail executives are problem solvers. Knowledge and understanding of past performance and present circumstances form the basis for action and planning.
CREATIVITY: ability to generate and recognize imaginative ideas and solutions; ability to recognize the need for and be responsive to change.			Retail executives are idea people. Successful buying results from sensitive, aware decisions, while merchandising requires imaginative, innovative techniques.
DECISIVENESS: ability to make quick decisions and render judgments, take action, and commit oneself to completion.			Retail executives are action people. Whether it's new fashion trends or customer desires, decisions must be made quickly and confidently in this ever-changing environment.
FLEXIBILITY: ability to adjust to the ever-changing needs of the situation; ability to adapt to different people, places, and things; willingness to do whatever is necessary to get the task done.			Retail executives are flexible. Surprises in retailing never cease. Plans must be altered quickly to accommodate changes in trends, styles, and attitudes, while numerous ongoing activities cannot be ignored.
INITIATIVE: ability to originate action rather than wait to be told what to do and ability to act based on conviction.			Retail executives are doers. Sales volumes, trends, and buying opportunities mean continual action. Opportunities for action must be seized.
LEADERSHIP: ability to inspire others to trust and respect your judgment; ability to delegate and to guide and persuade others.			Retail executives are managers. Running a business means depending on others to get the work done. One person cannot do it all.
ORGANIZATION: ability to establish priorities and courses of action for self and/or others; skill in planning and following up to achieve results.			Retail executives are jugglers. A variety of issues, functions, and projects are constantly in motion. To reach your goals, priorities must be set, work must be delegated to others.
RISK-TAKING: willingness to take calculated risks based on thorough analysis and sound judgment and to accept responsibility for the results.			Retail executives are courageous. Success in retailing often comes from taking calculated risks and having the confidence to try something new before someone else does.
STRESS TOLERANCE: ability to perform consistently under pressure, to thrive on constant change and challenge.			Retail executives are resilient. As the above description should suggest, retailing is fast-paced and demanding.

FIGURE 10–11
A Goal-Oriented Job Description for a Management Trainee
Source: *Rate Yourself as a Retail Executive* (New York: Abraham & Straus), p. 1. Reprinted with permission.

The interview seeks to obtain information that can be amassed only through personal questioning and observation. It enables the prospective employer to determine the oral ability of the candidate, note his or her appearance, ask questions based on the application blank, and probe into career objectives.

Several decisions about the interviewing process must be made: the level of formality, the number of interviews and the length of each, the physical location of interviews, the person(s) to do interviewing, the use of a relaxed or tense atmosphere, and the degree to which interviewing is structured. These decisions often depend on the interviewer's ability and a job's requirements.

Many, particularly smaller, retailers hire an applicant if he or she performs well during the interview. Other, usually larger, retailers use an additional selection device: testing. In this case, a candidate who does well during the interview is asked to complete psychological tests (which measure personality, intelligence, interest, leadership skills) and/or achievement tests (which measure learned knowledge).

Such tests need to be administered and interpreted by qualified people. It is important that standardized examinations not be used unless they are proven as effective predictors of job performance. Because achievement tests deal with specific skills or information, such as industry knowledge, the ability to make a sales presentation, and insights into the principles of retailing, they are much easier to interpret than psychological tests; and direct relationships between knowledge and ability can be determined. When giving tests to job applicants, retailers must be careful not to violate any federal, state, or local law. For example, the federal Employee Polygraph Protection Act of 1988 prohibits firms from using lie detector tests in most retail employee hiring situations (drugstores are exempt from this law).

In conjunction with interviewing and testing, retailers usually gather references from job applicants. These references can be checked either before or after the interview stage. The purposes of contacting references are to see how enthusiastically others recommend an applicant, to check the honesty of the applicant, to ask a prior employer why the applicant left an earlier job, and to review the types of people who will vouch for the applicant. Mail and telephone reference checks are inexpensive, fast, and easy to do.

When a candidate successfully completes the interview, testing, and reference check steps, many retailers require a physical examination before giving a job. This is especially important because of the physical activity, long hours, and tensions involved in many retailing positions. A clean bill of health would mean the candidate is offered a job. Again, federal, state, and local laws must be followed.

Each step in the selection process complements the others; together they give the retailer a total information package upon which to base personnel decisions. As a rule, retailers should use job descriptions, application blanks, interviews, and reference checks. The use of follow-up interviews, psychological and achievement tests, and physical examinations depends on the nature of the retailer and the open positions.

Inexpensive tools (such as application blanks) should be used in the early screening stages, whereas more expensive, in-depth tools (such as personal interviews) should be used after the number of applicants has been reduced substantially. Federal and state regulations require that only questions directly linked to job performance be asked in the selection process. Equal opportunity, nondiscriminatory practices must be followed.

Training Retail Personnel

When a new employee first joins the company, he or she should be exposed to a pre-training session. ***Pre-training*** is an indoctrination on the history and policies of the retailer and a job orientation on the hours, compensation, chain of command, and job duties. In addition, the new employee would be introduced to his or her co-workers.

Training programs are used to teach new (and existing) personnel how best to perform their jobs or how to improve themselves. Training can range from one- or two-day sessions on writing up sales forms, operating a cash register, personal selling techniques, or compliance with affirmative action programs to two-year programs for executive trainees on all aspects of the retailer and its operations.[10] For example, at Sterling (one of the largest jewelry-store chains in the United States):

> The Management Training Program is quite comprehensive in nature. It has five phases and takes up to two years to complete. A Manager Trainee
> - Learns the management, operations, credit, and loss-prevention skills required of managerial candidates.
> - Is responsible for high personal sales and helps achieve store goals.
> - Maintains the appearance of sales and display areas, enforces all policies regarding security, and implements the merchandising and advertising programs generated from the Home Office.

[10] See *A Survey of Employer Interests and Attitudes Regarding Education and Training in the Retail Industry* (Washington, D.C.: National Retail Institute, 1993).

TABLE 10–3 Selected Training Decisions

1. When does training occur? (At the time of hiring and/or after being at the workplace?)
2. How long should training be?
3. What training programs are for new employees? For existing employees?
4. Who should conduct each training program? (Supervisor, co-worker, training department, or outside specialist?)
5. Where should training take place? (At the workplace or in a training room?)
6. What material (content) should be learned? How should it be taught?
7. Should audiovisuals be used?
8. How can the effectiveness of training be measured?

- Follows a systematic, structured store management training program.
- Completes a Diamontology course.
- Benefits from on-the-job training and coaching by the firm's management team.
- Has performance reviewed on a regular basis to provide continuous feedback.
- Strives to reach the realistic goals set for advancement to management. The appropriate District Manager will encourage and share ideas, impressions, and suggestions throughout the program.[11]

Effective retailers realize training is an ongoing activity. New equipment, changes in laws, and new product lines, as well as motivating current personnel, employee promotions, and employee turnover, necessitate not only training but retraining as well. Thus, Sharper Image has "ongoing programs conducted at each store that are designed to keep each salesperson up to date on each new product offered." And Lechters has existing managers "attend periodic meetings to review store procedures and merchandising."[12]

Several training decisions need to be made, as shown in Table 10–3. Those decisions can be divided into three categories: identifying needs, devising appropriate training methods, and evaluation.

Immediate training needs for both new and existing employees can be identified by the retailer's measuring the gap between the skills those employees already possess and the job skills desired by the firm (for each position). Training should also prepare employees for possible job rotation, promotions, and emerging changes in company operations. A five-year plan for personnel development would enable a firm to identify future needs and train workers accordingly. Both short- and long-run training needs can be unearthed via communications with top management, formal evaluation programs, informal observations, group discussions, employee requests, and employee performance.

After needs are identified, the best training method(s) for addressing them must be uncovered from among lectures, demonstrations, films, programmed instruction, conferences, sensitivity training, case studies, role playing, behavior modeling, and competency-based instruction. The characteristics of these methods are noted in Table 10–4. Retailers often use two or more techniques during training to reduce boredom and cover the material better.

For training to be successful, an environment conducive to learning must be created. These are essential principles for enacting such an environment:

- All people can learn if taught properly.
- A person learns better when motivated; intelligence alone is not sufficient.

[11] Joel R. Evans and Barry Berman, *Careers in Retailing* (Hempstead, NY: Hofstra University, 1993), p. 123.

[12] *Sharper Image Corporation 1993 10K*, p. 9; and *Lechters, Inc. 1993 10K*, p. 6.

TABLE 10–4 The Characteristics of Retail Training Methods

Method	Characteristics
Lecture	Factual, uninterrupted presentation of material; can use professional educator and/or expert in the field; no active participation by trainees
Demonstration	Good for showing equipment or sales presentation; exhibits relevance of training; active participation by trainees
Video	Animated; good for demonstration; can be used many times; no active participation by trainees
Programmed Instruction	Presents information in a structured manner; requires response from trainees; provides performance feedback; adjustable to trainees' pace; high initial investment
Conference	Useful for supervisory training; conference leader must encourage participation; reinforces training
Sensitivity Training	Extensive interaction; good for supervisors as a tool for understanding employees
Case Study	Actual or hypothetical problem presented, including circumstances, pertinent information, and questions; learning by doing; exposure to a wide variety of problems
Role Playing	Trainees placed into real-life situations and act out roles
Behavior Modeling	Trainees taught to imitate models shown on videotape or in role-playing sessions
Competency-Based Instruction	Trainees given a list of tasks or exercises that are presented in a self-paced format

- Learning should be goal-oriented.
- A trainee learns more when he or she participates and is not a passive listener.
- The teacher must provide guidance.
- Learning should be viewed as a process of steps rather than a one-time occurrence.
- Learning should be spread out over a reasonable period of time rather than be compressed.
- The learner should be encouraged to do homework or otherwise practice.
- Different methods of learning should be combined.
- Performance standards should be set and good performance recognized.
- The learner should feel a sense of achievement.
- The teacher should adapt to the learner and to the situation.

A training program must be systematically evaluated for effectiveness. Comparisons may be made between the performances of those who have received training and those who have not. Comparisons may also be made among employees receiving different types of training for the same job. When a retailer measures the success of a training program, evaluations should always be made in relation to stated training goals. In addition, the effects of training should be measured over several time intervals (e.g., immediately, thirty days later, six months later), and appropriate records maintained.

Compensation of Retail Personnel

Compensation includes both direct monetary payments (such as salaries, commissions, and bonuses) and indirect payments (such as paid vacations, health and life insurance benefits, and retirement plans). To motivate employees better, some retailers

ETHICS IN RETAILING

Has Lucky Learned an Expensive Human Resources Lesson?

In late 1993, Lucky Stores Inc. agreed to pay almost $75 million in damages to female employees who were denied opportunities for promotion. The firm was also ordered to invest $20 million in affirmative action programs for female workers.

This class-action settlement was one of the largest ever negotiated in a sex discrimination case. About 14,000 women who were employed at Lucky Stores between 1983 and 1992 were covered by the agreement; and they were expected to receive amounts from $100 to $50,000 each, depending upon seniority. The settlement also required Lucky to revise its personnel practices and to pay additional fines if specific hiring and promotion targets are not met.

The suit alleged that a group of female employees in the firm's 188 North California stores were systematically denied desirable assignments, access to management training, and the ability to transfer from part- to full-time positions. The plaintiffs also alleged that they were given jobs that were "dead-end." According to the Federal District court judge who presided over the case, "sex discrimination was standard operating procedure at Lucky." The judge found that the Lucky's defense that women were not promoted to better jobs because they were not interested in them was "unpersuasive."

Source: Based on material in Jane Gross, "Big Grocery Chain Reaches Landmark Sex-Bias Accord," *New York Times* (December 17, 1993), pp. A1, B10.

also have profit-sharing plans. Smaller retailers often pay salaries, commissions, and/or bonuses, with little emphasis on fringe benefits. Bigger firms generally pay salaries, commissions, and/or bonuses plus fringe benefits. Total compensation should be fair to both the retailer and its employees to be effective.

For many larger retailers, compensation levels for certain positions are set through collective-bargaining contracts. As an example, 44 per cent of supermarket chains employ unionized clerks; in contrast, only 12 per cent of independent supermarkets have unionized clerks.[13] Union contracts also frequently affect nonunion personnel, who ask for similar compensation.

In a straight-salary plan, a worker is paid a fixed amount per hour, week, month, or year. Earnings are not directly tied to productivity. Advantages of a straight-salary plan are retailer control, security for employees, and known expenses. Disadvantages are retailer inflexibility, limited worker incentive to increase productivity, and fixed costs. Lower-level retail personnel (e.g., clerks, cashiers) are usually paid salaries.

With a straight-commission plan, employee earnings are directly tied to productivity (e.g., sales volume). A fixed amount is not paid. Advantages of this plan are retailer flexibility, the tie to worker productivity, no fixed costs, and employee incentive. Disadvantages are the retailer's potential lack of control over the tasks employees perform, the risk of low earnings to employees, the instability of retail costs, and the lack of limits placed on worker earnings. Sales personnel for automobiles, real estate, insurance, furniture, jewelry, and other expensive items are often paid on straight commission—as are direct-selling personnel.

To combine the attributes of both salary and commission plans, some retailers pay their employees a salary plus commission. Shoe salespeople, major appliance salespeople, and some management personnel are among the employees paid in this manner. At times, bonuses are awarded as supplements to salary and/or commission. These are normally given for outstanding company or individual performance. At Dairy Mart Convenience Stores, "Area supervisors and store managers participate in various cash incentive programs, which are generally based on store results as compared to budgeted projections."[14]

Sometimes, top retail management is paid via a "compensation cafeteria," whereby those executives can choose their own combination of salary, bonus, deferred bonus, fringe benefits, life insurance, stock options, and deferred retirement benefits.

[13] "60th Annual Report of the Grocery Industry," *Progressive Grocer* (April 1993), p. 86.

[14] *Dairy Mart Convenience Stores, Inc. 1993 10K*, p. 6.

Supervision of Retail Personnel

Supervision is the manner of providing a job environment that encourages employee accomplishment. The objectives of supervision are to oversee personnel, achieve good performance, maintain employee morale and motivation, control expenses, minimize redundancies, communicate company policies, and resolve problems. Supervision is provided through personal contact, meetings, and written reports between managers and subordinates.

A key element of supervision is the continued motivation of employees. ***Job motivation*** is the drive within people to attain work-related goals. The role of supervision is to motivate employees to achieve company objectives and thereby harness human energy to the retailer's needs. As one astute grocery-store owner noted, "We need to keep the staff happy because they're the first line of defense when customers come into the store."[15]

Several theories of motivation have been developed. Three of them are McGregor's Theory X and Theory Y, Herzberg's theory of satisfiers and dissatisfiers, and Theory Z (popularized by the Japanese and now in growing use in the United States).

Theory X is the traditional view of motivation and has been applied to lower-level retail positions:

- Management is responsible for organizing money, materials, equipment, and people resources.
- Personnel should be directed, motivated, controlled, and modified in accordance with the needs of the organization.
- Management must actively intervene with personnel; otherwise, people are passive and resistant to organizational needs.
- The average worker lacks ambition, dislikes responsibility, and prefers to be led.
- The average worker is self-centered and resistant to change.[16]

Theory Y is a more modern view of motivation and applies to all levels of retail personnel:

- Management is responsible for organizing money, materials, equipment, and people resources.
- People are not by nature passive or resistant to organizational needs.
- Motivation, potential for development, capacity for assuming responsibility, and readiness to achieve company goals are all present in people. Management must make it possible for people to recognize and develop their abilities.
- The essential management task is to arrange the organizational environment so employees can achieve their own goals by directing their efforts toward company objectives.[17]

Theory X assumes employees must be closely supervised and controlled; economic inducements provide motivation. Theory Y assumes employees can use self-management and be delegated authority, motivation is social and psychological, and management is decentralized and participatory.

[15] Phaedra Hise, "The Motivational Employee-Satisfaction Questionnaire," *Inc.* (February 1994), p. 73.

[16] Douglas McGregor, "The Human Side of Enterprise" in Warren G. Bennis and Edgar Schein (Editors), *Leadership and Motivation: Essays of Douglas McGregor* (Cambridge, Mass.: MIT Press, 1966).

[17] Ibid.

Herzberg's theory offers another perspective on motivation. According to this theory, the factors involved in producing job satisfaction and motivation (satisfiers) differ from those leading to job dissatisfaction (dissatisfiers). Factors that can cause job satisfaction are achievement, recognition for achievement, the job itself, responsibility, and growth or advancement. Factors that can result in job dissatisfaction are a worker's unhappiness with company policies and their administration, the method of supervision, interpersonal relationships, work conditions, salary, and job security.[18]

Theory Z adapts elements from Theory Y and Herzberg's theory, but advocates more employee involvement in defining their jobs and sharing decision making with management. There is mutual loyalty between the firm and its workers, and both parties enthusiastically cooperate for the long-term benefit of the firm (and employees).[19] Though Theory Z has been most widely used by manufacturing firms in the United States, applications by retailers are growing. Here is an example:

> Carol DeJardin and Gary Smith, owners of two Thriftway supermarkets (one in West Linn, Oregon, and the other in Williamette, Oregon), encourage their managers and employees to exercise initiative when it comes to operations and customer service. Together with DeJardin and Smith, managers set their own gross margins, sales volumes, and labor percentages. They also buy, hire, perform employee evaluations, and participate in decisions about whom to promote. Employees are urged to search for ways to improve the shopping experience, whether it means solving a problem, making good on an exchange of a product, or simply serving them cheerfully. DeJardin and Smith even have a name for this: "Positively Outrageous Service."
>
> At the same time, DeJardin and Smith try to treat their employees royally. They provide union-scale wages, benefits, and profit sharing. Work schedules are posted two weeks ahead of time, so that employees can request changes. Employees can purchase deli meals at cost, and they are given grocery charge accounts with a two per cent rebate. Each year, the owners throw a summer picnic for employees of the two stores.[20]

It is critical that supervision motivate employees in a manner yielding job satisfaction, low turnover, low absenteeism, and high productivity.

[18] Frederick Herzberg, "One More Time: How Do You Motivate Employees?" *Harvard Business Review,* Vol. 46 (January-February 1968), pp. 53–62.

[19] William Ouchi, *Theory Z* (Reading, Mass.: Addison-Wesley, 1981).

[20] Stephen Bennett, "People Who Serve People," *Progressive Grocer* (March 1993), p. 58.

SUMMARY

1. *To study the procedures involved in setting up a retail organization* A retail organization is used to structure and assign tasks, policies, resources, authority, responsibilities, and rewards in order to efficiently and effectively satisfy the needs of a firm's target market, employees, and management. Five steps are involved in setting up an organization: outlining the specific tasks to be performed in the distribution channel, dividing tasks among channel members and customers, grouping tasks into jobs, classifying jobs, and integrating positions through an organization chart.

   Specific tasks include buying, shipping, receiving, checking, pricing, and marking merchandise; inventory control; display preparation; facilities maintenance; research; customer contact and follow-up; personnel management; merchandise repairs; finances and credit; gift wrapping; delivery; returns; forecasting; and coordination. These tasks may be divided among retailers, manufacturers, wholesalers, specialists, and customers.

   Next, tasks are grouped into jobs, such as sales personnel, cashiers, inventory personnel, display personnel, credit personnel, customer service personnel, janitorial personnel, and management. Then jobs are categorized via functional, product, geographic, or combination classifications. Finally, an organization chart graphically displays the hierarchy of authority and the relationship among jobs, and coordinates personnel.

2. *To examine the various organizational arrangements utilized in retailing* Retail organization structures differ by institutional type. Small, independent retailers generally use simple organizations, with little specialization. Many department stores use a version of the Mazur plan, whereby they separate functions into four categories: merchandising, publicity, store management, and accounting and control. The equal store organization, a version of the Mazur plan, is used by a number of chain retailers. Diversified retailers have particularly complex organizations.

3. *To consider the special human resource environment of retailing* Retailers have a unique human resource environment because of the large number of inexperienced workers, long hours, highly visible employees, many part-time workers, and variations in customer demand.

4. *To describe the principles and practices involved with the human resource management process in retailing* This process is composed of several interrelated activities: recruitment, selection, training, compensation, and supervision.

   Recruitment is the activity of generating job applicants. Sources include educational institutions, channel members, competitors, ads, employment agencies, unsolicited applicants, and current and former employees.

   The selection of retail personnel requires thorough job analysis, creating job descriptions, using application blanks, interviews, testing (optional), reference checking, and physical examinations. After personnel are selected, employees go through pre-training (job orientation) and job training. An effective training program revolves around identifying needs, devising appropriate training methods, and evaluating the results. Training is usually necessary for continuing, as well as new personnel.

   Employees are compensated via direct monetary payments and/or indirect payments. The alternative direct compensation plans are straight salary, straight commission, and salary plus commission and/or bonus. Indirect payments involve such items as paid vacations, health benefits, and retirement plans.

   Supervision and motivation are necessary to obtain good employee performance. Supervision can be provided via personal contact, meetings, and written reports. Motivation theories include McGregor's Theory X-Theory Y, Herzberg's satisfiers-dissatisfiers, and Theory Z.

KEY TERMS

retail organization (p. 336)
functional classification (p. 339)
product classification (p. 339)
geographic classification (p. 339)
hierarchy of authority (p. 341)
flat organization (p. 341)
tall organization (p. 341)
organization chart (p. 341)
Mazur plan (p. 343)
mother hen with branch store chickens organization (p. 345)
separate store organization (p. 345)
equal store organization (p. 345)
diversified retailer (p. 347)
human resource management (p. 348)
human resource management process (p. 351)
recruitment (p. 351)
job analysis (p. 352)
traditional job description (p. 352)
goal-oriented job description (p. 352)
application blank (p. 352)
weighted application blank (p. 352)
pre-training (p. 354)
training programs (p. 354)
compensation (p. 356)
supervision (p. 358)
job motivation (p. 358)
Theory X (p. 358)
Theory Y (p. 358)
Herzberg's theory (p. 359)
Theory Z (p. 359)

QUESTIONS FOR DISCUSSION

1. Cite at least five objectives retailers should take into consideration when setting up their organization structures.
2. Why are employee needs important in developing a retail organization?
3. Are the steps involved in setting up a retail organization the same for small and large retailers? Explain your answer.
4. Present a five-item checklist that could be used in assigning tasks to members in a retail channel of distribution.
5. How would the hierarchy of authority in a flat organization differ from that in a tall organization? What are the potential ramifications?
6. What are the pros and cons of analyzing a retailer on the basis of its organization chart?
7. Describe the greatest similarities and differences in the organization structures of small independents, department stores, chain retailers, and diversified retailers.
8. How would small and large retailers act differently for each of the following?
   a. Recruitment.
   b. Selection.
   c. Training.
   d. Compensation.
   e. Supervision.
9. Why are the job description and the application blank so important in employee selection?
10. What problems can occur while interviewing and testing prospective employees?
11. Present a plan for the ongoing training of both existing lower-level and middle-management-level employees without making it seem punitive.
12. Describe the goals of a compensation plan in a retail setting.
13. Under what circumstances should Theory X be used? Theory Y?
14. Comment on Herzberg's theory of satisfiers and dissatisfiers, and contrast it with Theory Z.

CASE 1

Fieldhouse Department Stores: Improving Employee Motivation and Job Performance*

Fieldhouse Department Stores is a large, regional, family-owned department store chain. It has approximately 300 stores in 14 Southeastern states and employs over 30,000 people—3,000 of whom are in management positions. The founder of the organization intended for Fieldhouse to be a "general store" located in the heart of small Southern towns. Although Fieldhouse was, at one time, viewed as the dominant department-store chain in each of its trading areas, the mergers and acquisitions involving other regional department-store chains have generated several strong competitors in its key markets.

Fieldhouse has always been very interested in customer service, customer loyalty, and consumer satisfaction. Besides selling a broad selection of national brands at fair prices, the firm has always viewed a customer's satisfaction with his or her shopping experience as a major determinant of store choice. To Fieldhouse, the shopping experience includes such factors as store ambiance, the ease of parking, salespeople's product knowledge, and promptness of delivery.

To increase its competitive advantages, Fieldhouse has recently embarked on a five-year plan that addresses store atmosphere, merchandising, and human resources. Each store's interior and exterior atmosphere are to be evaluated; and stores will be renovated and refixtured as required. In some stores, this may merely consist of new carpeting or updated fixtures in several key departments. Other stores will be completely refurbished. Merchandise lines will also be reviewed to determine that goods reflect life-style trends and consumer demand for attractive merchandise at major price points.

A key portion of the five-year plan relates to the improvement of employee motivation and job performance. Fieldhouse's top management realizes the importance of motivation and job performance for all of its employees—from the part-time sales clerks to company vice-presidents. One of the firm's senior vice-presidents recently read a book on employee motivation. A central premise of the book was that the success of employees at the bottom of the corporate ladder is dependent on the job satisfaction of middle managers. Thus, the senior vice-president convinced Fieldhouse's top management to retain a consultant to study employee motivation and job satisfaction at the chain. Marky Consulting, a small, but well-regarded, human-resources firm, was selected to analyze employee motivation and job satisfaction. Marky was given a retainer of $20,000 and committed itself to completing and presenting a full report to Fieldhouse's top management within four months.

Marky randomly selected 30 of the 300 stores in the chain to use for its sample. Then, with the cooperation of Fieldhouse's corporate office, Marky mailed questionnaires to the 295 people having management positions in the 30 selected stores. A cover letter by the Human Resources Office endorsing the project was included. To encourage a high response rate, each of the 30 stores was assigned a representative to distribute the questionnaires, collect the completed responses, and return the questionnaires to corporate headquarters. While responses were coded by store, each person's responses were completely anonymous. Marky and Fieldhouse's top

* This case was prepared and written by Professor Nancy A. Oliver and Professor Ginger A. Woodard, East Carolina University.

management believe the answers were a true reflection of respondent perceptions and not "what management wanted to hear."

Of the 295 managers given questionnaires, 237 filled them out. Respondents were geographically distributed: 39 per cent were from rural stores, 47 per cent were from suburban stores, and 11 per cent were from urban stores. Their stores were mostly located in major malls, with 77 per cent in enclosed malls and 16 per cent in shopping centers. Forty-two per cent of the managers had been with Fieldhouse for over ten years, 29 per cent for between five and ten years, and 38 per cent for between one month and four years. Twelve per cent of the respondents were store managers, 33 per cent were department managers, and 29 per cent were either store or department buyers.

Marky used a well-known and respected questionnaire to measure motivation. One part of the survey analyzed employee preferences for specific job features that the employees would like to receive, such as pay raises. Scores were computed on a scale of 1 to 100. A low score indicated that there was little relation between an employee's hard work and effort and the desired outcome from that hard work, such as a pay raise. However, if the score was high, this indicated that the employee felt there was a strong relationship between hard work and achieving personal goals.

The results of the questionnaire and individual scores were computed for each employee. One-third of the respondents scored from 0 to 35, one-third from 36 to 49, and one-third from 50 to 85. This meant that two-thirds of the respondents scored less than one-half of the highest possible score. These results indicate that two-thirds of Fieldhouse's middle managers were poorly motivated and did not believe that effort and good job performance would lead to what they valued in a job.

Another part of the questionnaire dealt with which aspects of a job were most important to the managers. The findings reveal that Fieldhouse's middle managers desired the following job features (in order of mention): feelings of accomplishment, keeping their jobs, personal growth and satisfaction, and giving help to others.

Top management was perplexed with the results of the survey, believing that Fieldhouse had a comprehensive performance-evaluation system that rewarded middle managers with pay raises, bonuses, and other monetary benefits. Yet, these were not the rewards most desired by respondents.

As part of the report Marky prepared for Fieldhouse, a list of questions was included that upper management might address in its assessment of employee satisfaction and motivation. Here are two of the questions: What can top management do to improve overall motivation for middle managers? How can top management improve job satisfaction among middle managers?

Questions

1. What can Fieldhouse's top management do to improve the motivation of middle managers?
2 What can Fieldhouse's top management do to improve the job satisfaction of middle managers?
3. Relate the study's findings to Theory X, Theory Y, and Theory Z.
4. What types of training programs do you recommend for Fieldhouse, based upon the consultant's findings?

CASE 2

Supervalu: Performance Appraisal†

Supervalu is the largest U.S. food distributor. It serves about 4,350 stores, most of which are independently owned. The firm also owns and operates 250 conventional supermarkets, warehouse stores, and food-based superstores.

Supervalu uses a management-by-objectives (MBO) process in evaluating its buyers and other key personnel. This process is based on (1) the establishment of clear priorities, (2) a results orientation, (3) an appreciation of the critical skills needed to succeed, and (4) joint discussions between employees and their managers. To reduce ambiguity, goals are quantified, if possible.

According to advocates of MBO programs, when objectives are properly quantified, employees have a good understanding of performance expectations; and they are able to judge their own level of success during the year. As active participants in the creation of their personal objectives, employees are also more likely to accept challenging goals.

This case describes Supervalu's performance-appraisal process by focusing on Bill Edwards, a Supervalu buyer, and Teresa Harrison, his supervisor. The discussion covers one year—from their meeting to discuss suitable objectives for the upcoming year to the recent meeting in which Edwards was evaluated.

One year ago, as part of the performance-appraisal process, Bill Edwards and Teresa Harrison mutually agreed to hold Edwards accountable for fulfilling these specific objectives for the forthcoming year: improving gross profits, increasing inventory turnover, reducing the number of vendor complaints, and building and sustaining good vendor relations in his department. Each goal was quantified; for example, Edwards agreed to "negotiate mutually beneficial joint promotions with one-half of his vendors" as part of Supervalu's increased emphasis on its partnering program.

Two incidents are noteworthy in portraying Edwards' performance during the year. In one incident, he initiated a meeting with Vasco, one of Supervalu's major suppliers, to complain about late deliveries and back orders. Although he ultimately resolved the problem through a creative solution, some ill will was created when Edwards initially suggested that Supervalu temporarily switch vendors until Vasco's new computer system functioned as planned. In another situation, Edwards initially refused to immediately inspect damaged freight at a loading dock. Instead, he tried to get the loading dock supervisor to accept the freight "as is," arguing that ultimately it would be accepted in its damaged condition by his customers. Only after he was reminded that this was against company policy, did Edwards work out another solution to the problem.

About eleven months after their initial meeting (when Edwards and Harrison agreed on Edwards' goals for the year), Harrison began to prepare for his performance-evaluation meeting. She gathered information from a variety of sources, including financial data from Edwards' department, letters from vendors, specific behavior that Harrison had observed, and information from Edwards' co-workers.

One letter she received indicated that Edwards had done "an outstanding job in getting products needed quickly" and that Edwards' "ideas are original and fresh." Another letter, however, was critical. It noted that "he has discounted the firm's needs, and has side-stepped Supervalu's management policies. Edwards has a success at any price mentality."

Harrison decided to call Sara Karnsby, one of Edwards' co-workers, to inquire about his performance. Harrison assured her that this discussion was confidential.

† The material in this case is drawn from data supplied by Supervalu.

Karnsby's evaluation of Edwards was somewhat mixed. These are some of the comments she made:

> Bill's been a lot better lately, in that he has great ideas and is more organized. But he is still hard to deal with sometimes.
>
> Bill's most successful promotion won a prize for the most effective store display. This promotion was especially liked by our store managers. Bill wrote the promotion piece and was responsible for getting the merchandise to the stores quickly.
>
> While Bill is light on detail work, he gets things done. His customers really like him.

In commenting about a particularly difficult problem associated with Bill Edwards, Sara Karnsby told Teresa Harrison about a major holiday promotion when Edwards did not get an order to a supplier on time. Edwards told Karnsby that he had misplaced the paper work, but he tried to cover up the problem by purchasing another firm's products. Even though the alternate product did not meet the client store's high quality standards, Edwards got his customers to accept the product substitution by convincing them it was more profitable to the stores than the product he originally ordered.

At the annual performance evaluation, Harrison reminded Edwards that the meeting was a two-way dialogue and that Edwards was free to ask questions and to comment about her evaluations. At first, Edwards was very upset that he was only judged as "average" on overall performance. He said that he had "made his numbers," worked hard, established relations with vendors, and demonstrated his creativity. While Harrison agreed with him that he had made his numbers, she was critical of his human-relations skills. She was especially concerned about his relations with his co-workers and his vendors—and his domineering personality. Several co-workers had fought with Edwards; some others had been intimidated by him. This resulted in poor relationships and a poor team effort.

As part of the MBO process for the next year, Edwards and Harrison have agreed that his key area for development will involve building human-relations skills. Edwards has agreed to work on a joint promotion with a colleague; Harrison has agreed with Edwards' suggestion that he attend a special training seminar on negotiating skills. They plan to meet in two months to discuss what he has learned from the seminar and how he will apply the material to his job.

Questions

1. Describe the pros and cons of an MBO system of employee assessment.
2. Describe the relationship between an MBO evaluation system and a goal-oriented job description.
3. How can this appraisal system be tied into the development and evaluation of management training programs?
4. Was Edwards fairly evaluated? Explain your answer.

Video Questions on Supervalu

1. Evaluate Supervalu's performance-appraisal system.
2. What other suggestions could Harrison have given Edwards?

CHAPTER

11

Operations Management: Financial Dimensions

RM

❖ Chapter Objectives

1. To define operations management
2. To discuss profit planning
3. To describe asset management, including the strategic profit model and other key business ratios
4. To look at retail budgeting
5. To examine resource allocation

Merry-Go-Round Enterprises (MGR) grew from one store catering to hippies in the 1960s to a 1,450-store chain—featuring young men's and women's clothing and accessories—in 44 states under the names of Merry-Go-Round, Cignal, DeJaiz, and Chess King in the 1990s. Until recently, MGR was a shining star. For the period 1988–1992, its average return on equity and sales growth were both well above the average for other apparel retailers.

However, to finance its expansion, MGR became highly leveraged (meaning that its debt-to-equity ratio was high) and this led to tough times. In 1993, only 5 of the 26 apparel retailers studied by *Forbes* were more highly leveraged; and MGR's debt left it little room for error. Its performance was especially hampered due to poor sales at its Chess King stores, which were bought from Melville Corporation in May 1993.

On December 2, 1993, MGR reported a loss of $38.5 million for the quarter ended October 30th, as well as a 15 per cent drop in sales for stores open at least one year. Most of the loss was due to a $35.1 million write-down for slow-moving merchandise. Together, the quarterly loss, the cumulative loss for the first nine months of the year, and poor sales in December placed MGR in "technical violation" of credit agreements with major institutional lenders. These agreements specified that MGR had to comply with minimum working capital allowances and that its current assets-to-current debt ratio be a minimum figure. On December 10th, the firm missed payments to factors (firms that advanced money to MGR's suppliers and guaranteed that they would be paid for all products shipped to the firm), vendors, and suppliers. MGR attempted to conserve its cash by delaying these payments.

MGR's strategy backfired. Factors refused credit approval for spring 1994 orders; and vendors not using factors began to notify MGR that they would refuse to ship spring merchandise. Institutional lenders were also unwilling to waive the existing financial requirements that were part of its financing agreement or to restructure its debts.

On January 11, 1994, Merry-Go-Round Enterprises filed for Chapter 11 bankruptcy protection. Under Chapter 11, MGR was able to continue in business without paying its existing creditors. It could also get out of leases on unprofitable store locations. And payments for new merchandise would be guaranteed under a $125 million debtor-in-possession financing package.[1]

[1] "No Brass Ring For Merry-Go-Round," *Business Week* (January 24, 1994), p. 44; Patrick M. Reilly, "Merry-Go-Round Fails in Effort to Win Concessions, Makes Bankruptcy Filing," *Wall Street Journal* (January 12, 1994), pp. A1, A4; and Liz Comte Reisman, "Merry-Go-Round's Spin Cycle," *Smart Money* (March 1994), p. 100.

Reprinted by permission.

Overview

After a retailer develops an organization structure and establishes a human resource management plan, it concentrates on ***operations management***—the efficient and effective implementation of the policies and tasks necessary to satisfy the firm's customers, employees, and management (and stockholders, if a publicly owned company).

Retailers should recognize that the way they operate their businesses has a major impact on sales and profitability. For example, large inventory levels, long store hours, expensive fixtures, extensive customer services, and heavy advertising may encourage consumers to shop and lead to higher sales volume. But at what cost? If a supermarket must pay night-shift salaries that are 25 per cent higher than day-shift salaries, is staying open 24 hours per day worthwhile (i.e., Do the increased sales justify the increased costs and add to overall profit?)?

This chapter covers the financial aspects of operations management, with an emphasis on profit planning, asset management, budgeting, and resource allocation. The operational dimensions of operations management are explored in detail in Chapter 12.

Profit Planning

The ***profit-and-loss (income) statement*** represents a summary of a retailer's revenues and expenses over a particular period of time, usually on a monthly, quarterly, and/or yearly basis. It enables the retailer to review its overall and specific revenues and costs during similar periods (for example, January 1, 1994 to December 31, 1994, versus January 1, 1993 to December 31, 1993), as well as to analyze profitability. By having frequent profit-and-loss statements, a retailer can monitor its progress toward goals, update performance estimates, and revise strategies and tactics.

In comparing profit-and-loss performance over time, it is crucial that the same time periods be used (such as the fourth quarter of 1994 with the fourth quarter of 1993) due to seasonality considerations. The retailer should also note that some yearly periods may have an unequal number of weeks (such as 53 weeks in one fiscal year versus 52 weeks in another). In addition, retailers that have increased the number of stores or the square footage of existing stores between accounting periods should take into account the larger facilities in their analysis. Thus, yearly sales growth should reflect both the total revenue growth and the rise in same-store sales.

The profit-and-loss statement consists of these major components:

- ***Net sales***—The revenues received by a retailer during a given time period after deducting customer returns, markdowns, and employee discounts.
- ***Cost of goods sold***—The amount a retailer has paid to acquire the merchandise that is sold during a given time period. It is based on purchase prices and freight charges, less all discounts (such as quantity, cash, and promotion).
- ***Gross profit (margin)***—The difference between net sales and the cost of goods sold; consists of operating expenses plus net profit.
- ***Operating expenses***—The cost of running a retail business.
- ***Net profit before taxes***—The profit earned after all costs have been deducted.

Table 11–1 shows an annual profit-and-loss statement for Donna's Gift Shop, an independent retailer. These observations can be made from the table:

- Donna's net sales were $220,000; this was computed by deducting returns, markdowns on the items sold, and employee discounts from total sales.
- Donna's cost of goods sold was computed by taking the total purchase amount for the merchandise that was sold, adding freight charges, and subtracting quantity, cash, and promotion discounts. The cost of goods sold was $120,000.

TABLE 11–1 Donna's Gift Shop, 1994 Profit-and-Loss Statement

Net sales	$220,000	
Cost of goods sold	$120,000	
Gross profit		$100,000
Operating expenses:		
Salaries	$50,000	
Advertising	3,300	
Supplies	1,100	
Shipping	1,000	
Insurance	3,000	
Maintenance	3,400	
Other	1,700	
Total	$63,500	
Other costs	$17,500	
Total costs		$ 81,000
Net profit before taxes		$ 19,000

- Donna's gross profit was $100,000, calculated by subtracting the cost of goods sold from net sales. This sum was used for operating and other expenses, with the remainder accounting for net profit and the payment of local, state, and federal taxes.
- Donna's operating expenses included salaries, advertising, supplies, shipping, insurance, maintenance, and other operating costs—for a total of $63,500.
- Donna's unassigned costs were $17,500.
- Donna's net profit before taxes was $19,000, computed by deducting total costs of $81,000 from gross profit. This amount would be used to cover federal, state, and local taxes, as well as company profits.

Overall, 1994 was a good year for Donna; her personal salary was $35,000 and the store's before-tax profit was $19,000. A further analysis of Donna's Gift Shop's profit-and-loss statement will be conducted in the budgeting section of this chapter.

Asset Management

Each retailer has various assets to manage and liabilities to control. This section presents the basic components of a retailer's balance sheet, and describes the strategic profit model and other key business ratios.

A ***balance sheet*** itemizes a retailer's assets, liabilities, and net worth at a specific point in time; it is based on the principle that assets = liabilities + net worth. Table 11–2 has a balance sheet for Donna's Gift Shop.

Assets are any items a retailer owns that have a monetary value. Current assets consist of cash on hand (or in the bank) and items readily converted to cash in the short run, such as inventory on hand (or in transit to the retailer) and accounts receivable (amounts owed to the retailer by its customers). Fixed assets consist of the property, buildings (a retail store, a warehouse, and so on), store fixtures, and equipment such as cash registers and trucks; these are used in operations over a long period of time. The most significant asset for most retailers is real estate.[2]

[2] See Lois A. Huff, "Restructuring Corrects Problems with Fixed Assets," *Chain Store Age Executive* (August 1993), pp. 19A–23A.

TABLE 11–2 A Retail Balance Sheet for Donna's Gift Shop (as of December 31, 1994)

Assets			*Liabilities*			
Current:			Current:			
Cash on hand	$ 13,300		Payroll expenses payable	$ 4,000		
Inventory	24,100		Taxes payable	9,000		
Accounts receivable	1,100		Accounts payable	21,400		
Total		$ 38,500	Short-term loan	700		
			Total		$ 35,100	
Fixed (present value):						
Property	$125,000		Fixed:			
Building	42,000		Mortgage	$65,000		
Store fixtures	9,700		Long-term loan	4,500		
Equipment	1,700		Total		$ 69,500	
Total		$178,400				
			Total liabilities			$104,600
Total assets		$216,900				
			Net Worth			$112,300
			Liabilities + net worth			$216,900

Unlike current assets, which are recorded on a balance sheet on the basis of cost, fixed assets are recorded on the basis of cost less accumulated depreciation. This may create some difficulties in asset management, as records may not accurately reflect the true value of a firm's assets. For instance, many retailing analysts use the term ***hidden assets*** to describe depreciated assets, such as office buildings and shopping centers, that are reflected on a retailer's balance sheet at low values relative to their actual worth. In some instances, investors have been attracted to acquire retailers because of the high value of these hidden assets.

Liabilities are any financial obligations a retailer incurs in operating a business. Current liabilities comprise payroll expenses payable, taxes payable, accounts payable (amounts owed to suppliers), and short-term loans; these obligations must be paid in the coming year. Fixed liabilities comprise mortgages and long-term loans; these obligations are generally repaid over several years.

A retailer's ***net worth*** is computed as its assets minus its liabilities. Net worth is also known as owner's equity and represents the value of a retail business after deducting all financial obligations.

In operations management, the retailer's goal is to use its assets in the manner providing the best results possible. There are three basic, and commonly accepted, ways of measuring those results: net profit margin, asset turnover, and financial leverage. Each of these components is discussed next.

Net profit margin is a performance measure based on a retailer's net profit and net sales:

$$\text{Net profit margin} = \frac{\text{Net profit}}{\text{Net sales}}$$

In the case of Donna's Gift Shop, the net profit margin was a little over 8.6 per cent; for a gift shop, this is a very good percentage. To enhance its profit margin, a retailer could seek to either increase its gross profit as a percentage of sales or reduce its operating expenses as a percentage of sales. The firm could seek to raise its gross profits through opportunistic buying, selling exclusive product lines, avoiding price competition by having excellent customer service, minimizing markdowns because of more focused buying, and selling a mix of goods with high profit margins. A retailer could reduce operating expenses by emphasizing self-service, lowering personnel costs

RETAILING AROUND THE WORLD

Why Isn't Harrods of London Performing Better Financially?

Harrods is viewed by many retail analysts as one of London's top attractions for residents and tourists. Its 11 million shoppers per year are drawn by its collection of historical items (such as a pharaoh's head borrowed from the British museum), the live music from a harpist and a troop of marching bagpipers, and unique products (such as a rhinoceros doll that sells for over $3,700).

Unfortunately, according to one retail analyst, "providing an exceptional shopping experience does have a cost. It's a balance that management must strike between attracting people to the store and running a business." Even after renovating Harrods with new carpeting, display tables, and brass fixtures at a cost of almost $300 million, its sales dropped by 5 per cent. And although operating profits recently increased by 10 per cent from the prior year, Harrods' profits are still below those of some previous years.

Some experts believe that Harrods' low profits are in part due to its policy of charging premium prices on items available elsewhere. For example, a Pictionary game at Harrods sells for 20 per cent more than at a Toys "R" Us store. Harrods also runs only two sales a year. And many of the people who visit Harrods just browse and do not buy anything at all.

Source: Based on material in Kevin Helliker, "Harrods: Grandeur Comes at Grand Cost," *Wall Street Journal* (December 1, 1993), pp. B1, B5.

(via better scheduling and automation), refinancing a mortgage to take advantage of lower interest rates, cutting energy costs, and so on. However, a firm would have to be careful not to lessen customer service to the extent that sales and profit would decline.

Asset turnover is a performance measure based on a retailer's net sales and total assets:

$$\text{Asset turnover} = \frac{\text{Net sales}}{\text{Total assets}}$$

For Donna's Gift Shop, asset turnover was a very low 1.0143; this means the shop averaged just over $1.01 in sales per dollar of total assets. To improve its asset turnover ratio, a firm would have to generate increased sales via the same level of assets or maintain the same sales with a reduced asset base. A firm might increase sales by staying open longer hours, accepting mail-order sales, training employees to cross-sell additional products and services to consumers, or stocking well-known national brands instead of local brands. None of these tactics requires the asset base to be expanded. Or, a company might maintain sales on a lower asset base by moving to a smaller store (less wasted space), simplifying store fixtures (or having suppliers install and own the fixtures), keeping a more basic inventory on hand, and negotiating with property owners for them to pay part of the costs of store renovation.

By looking at the relationship between a retailer's net profit margin and its asset turnover, ***return on assets (ROA)*** can be computed:

$$\text{Return on assets} = \text{Net profit margin} \times \text{Asset turnover}$$

$$\text{Return on assets} = \frac{\text{Net profit}}{\text{Net sales}} \times \frac{\text{Net sales}}{\text{Total assets}}$$

$$= \frac{\text{Net profit}}{\text{Total assets}}$$

Thus, Donna's Gift Shop had an ROA of 8.8 per cent, computed as:

$$= .0864 \times 1.0143 = 0.0876 = 8.8\%$$

This return on assets is below average for gift stores because the firm's good net profit margin does not adequately offset its low asset turnover.

Financial leverage is a performance measure based on the relationship between a retailer's total assets and net worth:

$$\text{Financial leverage} = \frac{\text{Total assets}}{\text{Net worth}}$$

Donna's Gift Shop had a financial leverage ratio of 1.9314. This means assets were just under double Donna's net worth, and total liabilities and net worth were almost equal. As a result, Donna's financial leverage was a little above the average leverage for U.S. gift stores (which are rather conservative as a group). However, the store is in no danger.

A firm with a high financial leverage ratio has a sizable degree of debt, while a financial leverage ratio of 1 means the retailer has no debt—assets equal net worth. If financial leverage is too high, there may be too much emphasis on cost cutting and short-run revenues due to the need to make large interest payments on a periodic basis; net profit margins may suffer because of interest charges; and, sometimes, a retailer even may be forced into bankruptcy if its debts cannot be paid in an orderly way.

Over the last decade or so, the use of the ***leveraged buyout (LBO)***, whereby a retail ownership change is mostly financed by loans from banks, investors, and others, has had a major effect on retail budgeting and cash flow. One study found that over half of the revenues of publicly-owned food-based retailers came from firms with high levels of leverage.[3]

At times, because debts incurred in LBOs can be excessive, some large retailers have had to concentrate more on covering the interest payments on their debts than in investing in their businesses; have had to run sales just to generate enough cash to cover operating costs and the purchase of new merchandise; and have had to sell off store units to pay off debt. Among the retailers whose operations have been affected by LBOs are Macy's, Ralphs, Stop & Shop, Piggly Wiggly Southern, Pathmark, Carter Hawley Hale, and Revco.[4] Safeway, which was involved in an LBO, seems to have done well by reducing costs, reducing prices, and improving customer service. For example, its 1992 cash flow was 2.6 times its debt service.[5]

On the other hand, if financial leverage is too low, a firm may be too conservative. The firm may be limiting its ability to renovate and expand existing stores, as well as to expand into new markets. In general, financial leverage would be too low if the owner's equity is relatively high; and that equity could be partially replaced by increasing the amount of short- and long-term loans and/or accounts payable. Thus, some equity funds could be taken out of a business by the owner (stockholders, if a public firm).

THE STRATEGIC PROFIT MODEL

The mathematical relationship among net profit margin, asset turnover, and financial leverage is expressed via the ***strategic profit model***, which results in a performance measure known as ***return on net worth (RONW)***. See Figure 11–1. The strategic profit model can be used in planning or controlling a retailer's asset management. For example, a firm could determine that the major cause of its poor return on net worth is less-than-satisfactory asset turnover or too-low financial leverage. According to the strategic profit model, a retailer can increase its return on net worth by raising its net profit margin, asset turnover, or financial leverage. And because these measures are multiplied to determine a firm's return on net worth, a doubling of any of them—for example—would result in the doubling of a firm's return on net worth.

3 Steve Weinstein, "The Legacy of Leverage," *Progressive Grocer* (June 1993), pp. 70–76.

4 See Susan Caminiti, "R.H. Macy: A High-Priced Game of Catch-Up," *Fortune* (September 6, 1993), pp. 73–74.

5 See Russell Mitchell, "Safeway's Low-Fat Diet," *Business Week* (October 18, 1993), pp. 60–61.

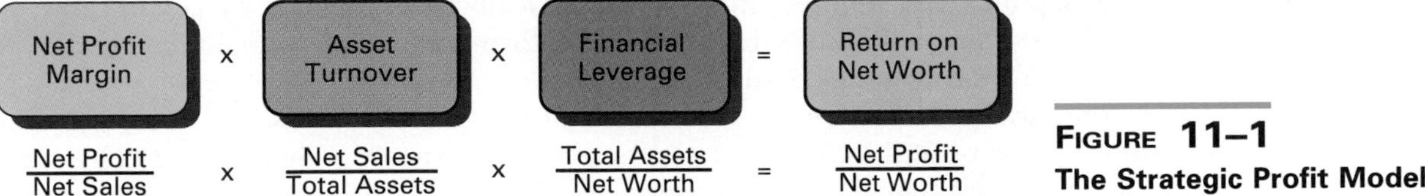

FIGURE 11–1
The Strategic Profit Model

This is how the strategic profit model can be applied to Donna's Gift Shop:

$$\text{Return on net worth} = \frac{\text{Net profit}}{\text{Net sales}} \times \frac{\text{Net sales}}{\text{Total assets}} \times \frac{\text{Total assets}}{\text{Net worth}}$$

$$= \frac{\$19{,}000}{\$220{,}000} \times \frac{\$220{,}000}{\$216{,}900} \times \frac{\$216{,}900}{\$112{,}300}$$

$$= .0864 \times 1.0143 \times 1.9314$$

$$= .1692 = 16.9\%$$

Overall, Donna's return on net worth was about average for all gift stores.

Table 11–3 applies the strategic profit model to various retailers. In evaluating the data in this table, it is best to make comparisons among the firms within given retail institutional categories. For example, the net profit margins of clothing retailers such

TABLE 11–3 Application of Strategic Profit Model to Selected Retailers, 1992 Data

Retailer	Net Profit Margin	×	Asset Turnover	×	Financial Leverage	=	Return on Net Worth
General Merchandise							
Discount-Oriented							
Service Merchandise	2.28%		2.17		8.80		43.54%
Wal-Mart	3.60		2.70		2.35		22.84
Toys "R" Us	6.10		1.35		1.84		15.15
Kmart	2.49		1.99		2.51		12.44
Department Stores							
J.C. Penney	4.07		1.41		2.88		16.53
Nordstrom	3.89		1.71		1.95		12.97
Dillard's	4.84		1.19		2.24		12.90
Federated	1.60		1.01		3.38		5.46
Specialty Clothing							
The Gap	7.12		2.15		1.55		23.73
The Limited, Inc.	6.60		1.79		1.70		20.08
Home Improvement							
Home Depot	5.08		1.82		1.71		15.81
Lowe's	2.20		2.39		2.19		11.51
Food-Based							
Winn-Dixie	1.90		5.23		2.08		20.67
Albertson's	2.65		3.45		2.12		19.38
Food Lion	2.47		2.85		2.64		18.58
Safeway	0.28		2.90		21.50		17.46
Publix	2.47		3.76		1.53		14.21
Giant Food	2.50		2.79		2.01		14.02
Vons	0.96		2.71		4.19		10.90
Great Atlantic & Pacific Tea	0.61		3.61		2.56		5.64

Source: Computed by the authors from data in "The 50 Largest Retailing Companies," *Fortune* (May 31, 1993), p. 220.

as The Gap and The Limited, Inc., have historically been much higher than those of supermarket chains. Because the financial performance of individual retailers differs from year to year, caution is advised in studying these data.

A comparison of Service Merchandise, Wal-Mart, Toys "R" Us, and Kmart (based on the data reported in Table 11–3) shows that Service Merchandise's 1992 return on net worth was 3.5 times that of Kmart, 2.9 times that of Toys "R" Us, and 1.9 times that of Wal-Mart. An analysis of the components of the strategic profit model indicate that Service Merchandise's performance was largely due to its very high financial leverage. If Service Merchandise's financial leverage was 2.23 (the average of the other three firms) and its net profit margin and asset turnover were as indicated in Table 11–3, its return on net worth would only have been 11.03 (2.28 × 2.17 × 2.23). This would have been the lowest of all the firms in the discount category.

The data on the department stores listed in Table 11–3 indicate that even though Nordstrom and Dillard each had a 1992 return on net worth of 12.9 to 13.0 per cent, the two chains each had different factors leading to their results. Dillard's net profit margin and financial leverage were both greater than Nordstrom's; but Nordstrom's asset turnover was greater than Dillard's. Thus, for instance, Dillard's could seek better asset turnover. Yet, in attempting to improve this turnover, Dillard's needs to be careful not to affect its relatively high net profit margin. By reducing inventory levels, Dillard might lift its asset turnover at the expense of profits, as well as sales. This could adversely affect the net profit margin.

OTHER KEY BUSINESS RATIOS

Key business ratios may be used to measure a retailer's success or failure in reaching particular performance standards. Such ratios have a strong impact on a retailer's short- and long-run performance. Accordingly, here are the definitions of several other key business ratios, besides those covered in the preceding discussion:

- Quick ratio—cash plus accounts receivable divided by total current liabilities, those due within one year. This ratio shows a retailer's liquidity. A ratio greater than 1 to 1 means the firm is liquid and therefore easily able to cover short-term liabilities.
- Current ratio—total current assets (including cash, accounts and notes receivable, merchandise inventories, and marketable securities) divided by total current liabilities. A ratio of 2 to 1 or more is considered good.
- Collection period—accounts receivable divided by net sales and then multiplied by 365. This ratio measures the quality of accounts receivable (the amounts due, but not yet paid by customers). In general, when most sales are on credit, any collection period one-third or more over normal selling terms (such as 40.0 for 30-day credit arrangements) indicates slow-turning accounts receivable.
- Accounts payable to net sales—accounts payable divided by annual net sales. This compares how a retailer pays suppliers relative to volume transacted. A figure larger than the industry average may indicate that the firm relies on suppliers to finance operations.
- Overall gross profit—net sales minus the cost of goods sold and then divided by net sales. This net firmwide average takes markdowns, discounts, and shortages into account. It is used by retailers to cover both operating costs and net profit.[6]

Table 11–4 presents several median key business ratios—including net profit margin, asset turnover, and return on net worth—for a number of retailer categories. From this table, a hardware store manager or owner would learn that the industry av-

[6] *Industry Norms and Key Business Ratios: Desk-Top Edition 1992–93* (New York: Dun & Bradstreet, 1993), pp. v–vi.

TABLE 11–4 Median Key Business Ratios for Selected Retailer Categories, 1992

Line of Business	Quick Ratio (times)	Current Ratio (times)	Collection Period (days)	Accounts Payable to Net Sales (%)	Overall Gross Profit (%)[a]	Net Profit Margin (%)	Asset Turnover (times)	Return on Net Worth (%)
Auto & home supply stores	0.9	2.6	22.6	6.2	33.6	2.3	2.6	8.3
Car dealers	0.2	1.3	6.2	0.9	13.2	0.8	3.8	9.3
Department stores	1.2	3.5	20.6	4.9	33.9	1.2	2.0	4.6
Direct-selling companies	1.2	2.4	22.6	3.2	42.1	3.7	3.3	19.2
Drug & proprietary stores	1.0	2.9	15.7	4.5	27.1	2.7	3.9	15.6
Eating places	0.7	1.2	4.4	2.7	52.5	3.3	3.5	20.3
Family clothing stores	1.1	4.8	12.4	4.3	35.0	4.1	1.9	9.2
Florists	1.1	2.2	24.1	4.0	48.7	3.4	3.3	15.9
Furniture stores	1.0	3.1	24.7	4.7	36.7	2.8	2.1	8.4
Gasoline service stations	0.8	1.8	6.9	2.4	18.3	1.1	5.3	9.2
Gift, novelty, & souvenir shops	0.8	3.6	8.2	4.5	41.0	4.8	2.2	16.8
Grocery stores	0.6	2.1	2.6	2.5	21.1	1.4	5.5	13.8
Hardware stores	0.8	3.6	17.5	4.5	33.4	2.5	2.1	8.0
Hobby, toy, & game shops	0.6	3.3	4.0	4.6	38.6	3.0	2.4	15.3
Jewelry stores	0.7	3.3	22.6	8.3	44.3	4.1	1.5	10.0
Lumber & other materials dealers	1.1	2.8	33.6	4.7	26.5	1.7	2.6	7.9
Mail-order firms	0.9	2.5	14.6	5.1	39.2	3.0	3.2	19.7
Men's & boys' clothing stores	0.7	3.4	12.8	5.4	39.0	3.8	2.1	11.0
Newsstands & dealers	0.6	2.3	18.5	6.6	26.6	1.3	2.8	13.2
Radio, TV, & electronics stores	0.6	2.0	12.8	5.2	34.8	3.0	2.9	14.0
Sewing & needlework stores	0.5	3.9	5.3	5.2	39.5	4.8	2.3	15.1
Shoe stores	0.5	3.4	5.8	6.2	37.2	4.2	2.3	12.1
Sporting-goods & bicycle stores	0.5	2.7	6.6	6.8	32.9	4.1	2.5	15.1
Variety stores	0.6	3.5	6.6	4.1	33.8	2.8	2.5	10.8
Vending-machine operators	0.4	1.3	3.7	3.1	42.7	1.6	3.4	8.7
Women's clothing stores	1.0	4.0	12.8	4.4	35.9	4.3	2.4	11.5

[a] Gross margins are reported as means rather than medians and represent net figures, which take into account all deductions (such as markdowns, discounts, and shortages).

Source: *Industry Norms and Key Business Ratios: Desk-Top Edition 1992–93* (New York: Dun & Bradstreet, 1993), pp. 142–167. Reprinted by permission.

erage is an extremely poor quick ratio of 0.8; liquid assets are less than current liabilities. The current ratio of 3.6 is quite good, mostly because of the value of inventory on hand. The collection period of 17.5 days is moderate, considering that many small purchases are paid for by cash. Accounts payable of 4.5 per cent of sales is good. The overall gross profit of 33.4 per cent would be used to cover both operating costs and profit. The net profit margin of 2.5 per cent is a relatively low figure for nonfood retailing. The asset turnover ratio is conservative, 2.1, another indicator of the value of inventory. The return on net worth percentage of 8.0 is quite low. In sum, on average, hardware stores require high inventory and other investments and yield low-to-medium returns.

Budgeting

Budgeting outlines a retailer's planned expenditures for a given time period based on its expected performance. In this way, a retailer's costs can be linked to satisfying target market, employee, and management goals. For example, what should planned personnel costs be if the retailer wants to provide a certain level of customer service, such as no shopper waiting in a supermarket checkout line for more than ten minutes? What compensation level should be planned to motivate sales personnel? What amount of total planned expenses will enable management to generate satisfactory sales revenue and reach profit goals?

There are several reasons why a retailer should systematically develop a detailed budget. By budgeting,

- Expenditures are clearly related to expected performance, and costs can be adjusted as goals are revised. This enhances productivity.
- Resources can be allocated to the appropriate departments, product categories, and so on.
- Expenditures for various departments, product categories, and so on can be coordinated.
- Because management is able to plan in a structured and integrated manner, the goal of efficiency can be given more prominence.
- Cost standards can be set, such as advertising equals 5 per cent of sales.
- The retailer can prepare for the future rather than react to it.
- Expenditures can be monitored during a budget cycle. For example, if a firm has allocated $50,000 to purchase new merchandise over a budget cycle, and it has spent $33,000 on such merchandise halfway through that cycle, it has planned expenditures of $17,000 remaining.
- The retailer can analyze and explain the differences between its expected and actual costs and performance.
- A company's expected and actual costs and performance can be contrasted with industry averages. For instance, how do a specialty-store chain's total net operating expenses as a percentage of sales compare to the industry average?

In establishing a budget, the retailer should be aware of the effort and time involved in the process, recognize that expectations may not be fully accurate (because of unexpected consumer demand, competitors' tactics, and so on), and be willing to modify plans as necessary. It should not allow itself to become overly conservative (or inflexible) or simply add a percentage to each current expense category to arrive at the next year's budget, such as increasing expenditures by 3 per cent across the board based on an anticipated sales growth of 3 per cent.

The budgeting process is shown in Figure 11–2 and described next.

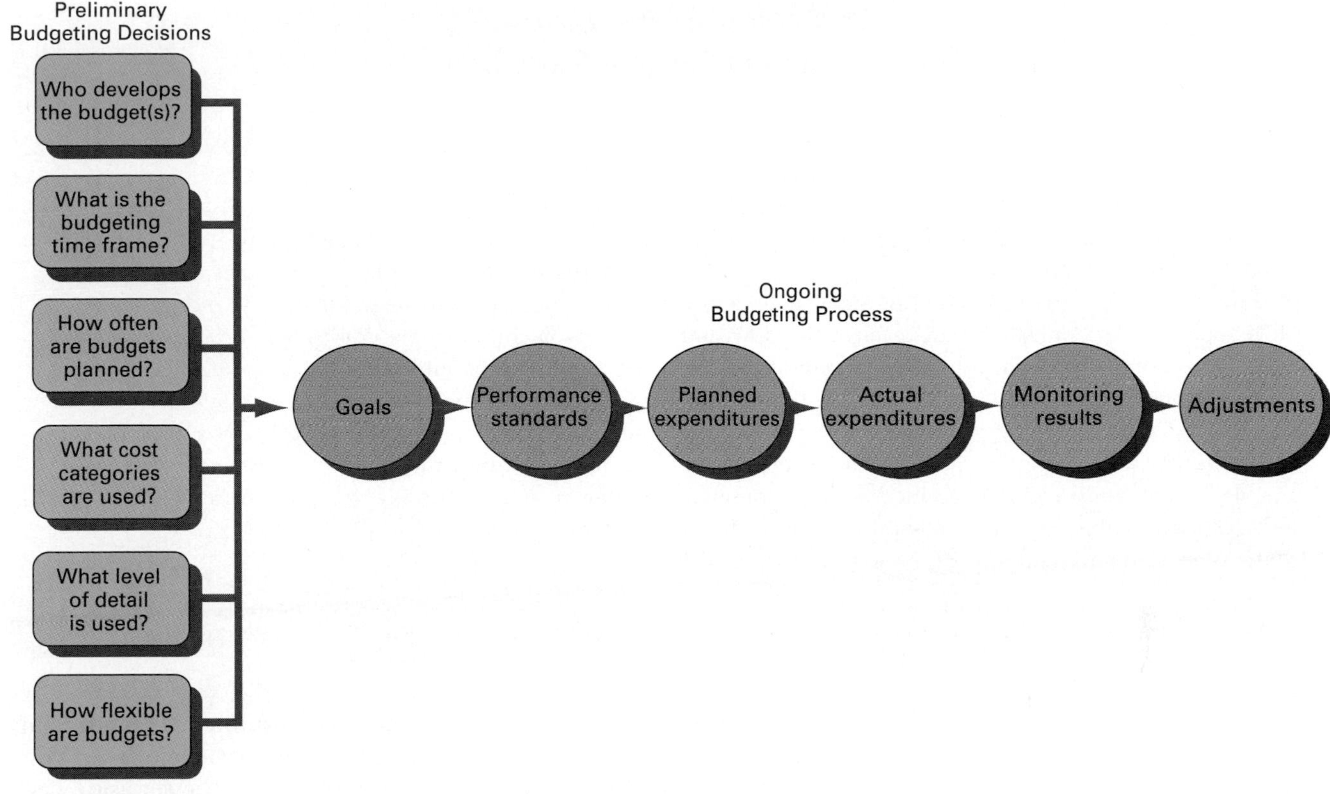

FIGURE 11–2 The Retail Budgeting Process

PRELIMINARY BUDGETING DECISIONS

A retailer must make six preliminary budgeting decisions.

First, the person(s) responsible for budgeting decisions is specified. ***Top-down budgeting*** places financial decisions with upper management; these decisions are then communicated down the line to succeeding levels of managers. For example, the Chairman's Group at Woolworth establishes overall strategic priorities and financial objectives for the firm and allots capital to projects.[7] ***Bottom-up budgeting*** requires lower-level executives to develop budget requests for their departments; these requests are then assembled, and an overall companywide budget is designed. With top-down budgeting, senior management centrally directs and controls budgets. With bottom-up budgeting, varied perspectives are included, managers are held accountable for their own decisions, and employee morale is enhanced. For these reasons, many firms combine aspects of the two approaches.

Second, the budgeting time frame is defined. Most retailers set budgets with yearly, quarterly, and monthly components. In this way, annual spending can be planned; and expected versus actual costs and performance can be reviewed on a regular basis. As a result, a firm can control overall costs, while responding to seasonal or other fluctuations. Sometimes, the time frame can be longer than a year or shorter than a month. For example, when a firm such as Dayton Hudson decides to open a number of new stores over a five-year period, it would specify capital expenditures (property, construction, and other investment costs) for the entire five years. When a supermarket chain such as Safeway orders milk, baked goods, and other perishable goods, it would have daily or weekly budgets for each item.

7 *Woolworth Corporation 1993 Fact Book*, p. 5.

ETHICS IN RETAILING

Will Consumers Forgive Stew Leonard?

Stew Leonard, founder of two Connecticut supermarkets bearing his name, was cited in the 1985 edition of Tom Peters' *A Passion for Excellence* as an extremely effective retailer. In 1986, he was presented with the Presidential Award for Entrepreneurial Achievement by President Ronald Reagan.

But, in July 1993, the reputation of Stew Leonard as a "legendary retailer" quickly began to tarnish—as he and three other company executives were charged with not reporting more than $17 million of sales from the Norwalk store. One month later, the Connecticut Department of Consumer Protection also charged that the Norwalk store was significantly misweighing products so that customers were actually getting less than they thought. In October 1993, Stew Leonard and the other executives pleaded guilty to the tax evasion charges. Stew Leonard was sentenced to more than four years in prison and ordered to pay $16+ million in taxes, penalties, and interest costs.

Immediately after the settlement of the tax case, the *Danbury News-Times* interviewed shoppers to determine their reaction to the guilty plea and the short-weighting charges. According to the newspaper, a typical reaction was "The problem is people don't know how to deal with it when they get too much money." However, 87 per cent of the 5,232 callers to a call-in poll stated that they would continue to shop at Stew Leonard's. According to Stew Leonard, Jr., the firm's current president, "what attracts customers to a store is the store, not the image of the person who founded it."

Sources: Based on material in Bruce Fox, "The Customer Is Always Forgiving," *Chain Store Age Executive* (November 1993), pp. 26, 28; and Jacques Steinberg, "Connecticut Store Owner Sentenced in Tax Fraud," *New York Times* (October 21, 1993), pp. B1, B6.

Third, the frequency with which budgets are planned is determined. Though many retailers review their budgets on a regular, ongoing basis, the great majority of companies plan them once a year. In some firms, several months may be set aside each year for the budgeting process to be undertaken; this lets all participants have ample time to gather information and allows retailers to take their budgets through several drafts before giving final approval.

Fourth, cost categories are established:

- Capital expenditures involve major long-term investments in land, buildings, fixtures, and equipment. Operating expenditures include the short-term selling and administrative expenses of running a retail business.
- Fixed costs are those that remain relatively constant for the period of a budget, such as store-security expenses and real-estate taxes, regardless of the retailer's performance. Variable costs are those related to the firm's performance during the budget period, such as sales commissions. If performance standards are high, these expenses often rise.
- Direct costs are incurred by specific departments, product categories, and so on, such as the earnings of department-based salespeople and cashiers. Indirect costs such as exterior store displays and centralized cashiers are shared by two or more departments, product categories, and so on.
- Natural account expenses are reported by the names of the costs, such as salaries, and not assigned by their purpose. Functional account expenses are classified on the basis of the purpose or activity for which expenditures are made, such as cashier salaries.

Tables 11–5 and 11–6 show the natural and functional account expense categories enumerated by the National Retail Federation (formerly the National Retail Merchants Association). Please note: Individual firms may use different categories from those shown in these tables, and for some retailers, certain categories may not be appropriate (such as executive office and central wrapping and packing expenses for a small retailer).

Fifth, the level of budgeting detail is ascertained. For example, should planned expenditures be allocated by department (e.g., produce), product category (e.g., fresh

TABLE 11–5 Natural Account Expense Categories

01	Payroll
02	Allocated fringe benefits
03	Media costs
04	Taxes
06	Supplies
07	Services purchased
08	Unclassified
09	Travel
10	Communications
11	Pensions
12	Insurance
13	Depreciation
14	Professional services
16	Bad debts
17	Equipment rentals
18	Outside maintenance and equipment service contracts
20	Real property rentals
90	Expense transfers in
91	Expense transfers out
92	Credits and outside revenues

Source: *Retail Accounting Manual*, Revised (New York: National Retail Merchants Association, Financial Executive Division, 1984).

fruit), product subcategory (e.g., apples), or product item (e.g., McIntosh apples)? If a retailer has a very detailed budget, it must be sure every expense subcategory is adequately covered.

Sixth, the amount of flexibility in the budget is set. On the one hand, the budget should be rigid enough to serve its purpose in guiding planned expenditures and linking costs to goals. On the other hand, a budget that is too inflexible would not allow a retailer to adapt to changing market conditions, to capitalize on unexpected opportunities, and/or to minimize the costs associated with a strategy that is poorly received by the target market. Thus, many retailers express budget flexibility in quantitative terms. For example, a buyer could be allowed to increase his or her quarterly budget by a certain maximum percentage if customer demand is higher than anticipated.

ONGOING BUDGETING PROCESS

After preliminary budgeting decisions are made, the retailer would engage in the ongoing budgeting process shown in Figure 11–2:

- Goals are set. These goals are based upon customer, employee, and management needs (as discussed in Chapter 10).
- Performance standards to achieve these goals are specified. Such standards include customer service levels, the compensation amounts needed to motivate employees and minimize personnel turnover, and the sales and profit levels needed to satisfy management. Frequently, the budget is related to a sales forecast, which is a projection of expected revenues for the next budget period. Forecasts are usually broken down by department or product category.

TABLE 11–6 Functional Account Expense Categories[a]

010 Property and equipment
- 020 Real estate, buildings, and building equipment
- 030 Furniture, fixtures, and nonbuilding equipment

100 Company management
- 110 Executive office
- 130 Branch management
- 140 Internal audit
- 150 Legal and consumer activities

200 Accounting and management information
- 210 Control management, general accounting, and statistical
- 220 Sales audit
- 230 Accounts payable
- 240 Payroll and time-keeping department
- 280 Data processing

300 Credit and accounts receivable
- 310 Credit management
- 330 Collection
- 340 Accounts receivable and bill adjustment
- 350 Cash office
- 360 Branch-store/selling-location offices

400 Sales promotion
- 410 Sales promotion management
- 420 Advertising
- 430 Shows, special events, and exhibits
- 440 Display

500 Service and operations
- 510 Service and operations management
- 530 Security
- 550 Telephones and communications
- 560 Utilities
- 570 Housekeeping
- 580 Maintenance and repairs

600 Personnel
- 610 Personnel management
- 620 Employment
- 640 Training
- 660 Medical and other employee services
- 670 Supplementary benefits

700 Merchandise receiving, storage, and distribution
- 710 Management of merchandise receiving, storage, and distribution
- 720 Receiving and marking
- 730 Reserve stock shortage
- 750 Shuttle services

800 Selling and supporting services
- 810 Selling supervision
- 820 Direct selling
- 830 Customer services
- 840 Selling support services
- 860 Central wrapping and packing
- 880 Delivery

900 Merchandising
- 910 Merchandising management
- 920 Buying
- 930 Merchandise control

[a] These are also known as expense centers.

Source: *Retail Accounting Manual*, Revised (New York: National Retail Merchants Association, Financial Executive Division, 1984).

- Expenditures are planned to allow the firm to attain performance goals. With ***zero-based budgeting***, a firm starts each new budget from scratch and outlines the expenditures needed to reach the goals during that period. All costs must be justified each time a budget is done. In ***incremental budgeting***, a firm uses current and past budgets as guides and adds or subtracts from these budgets to arrive at the coming period's expenditures. Despite its conservative nature, most retailers apply incremental budgeting because it is easier to use, less time-consuming, and less risky.
- Actual expenditures are made. The retailer pays rent and employee salaries, buys merchandise, places advertisements, and so on.
- Results are monitored. This involves two types of analysis. One, actual expenditures are compared with planned expenditures for each expense category previously specified by the retailer, and reasons for any deviations are considered. Two, the firm determines whether or not goals and performance standards have been met and tries to explain any deviations.
- The budget is adjusted. Major or minor revisions in the original budget would be made, depending on how closely a retailer has come to achieving its goals. The funds allocated to some expense categories may be reduced, while greater funds may be provided to other categories.

Table 11–7 compares budgeted (planned) and actual revenues, expenses, and profits for Donna's Gift Shop in 1994. The actual data come from Table 11–1, which was discussed earlier in the chapter. The variance figures in Table 11–7 compare the expected and actual results for each profit-and-loss item. The variances are positive numbers when actual performance was better than expected and negative numbers when performance was worse than planned. As the table indicates, net profit before taxes was $10,500 higher than anticipated. Actual sales turned out to be $20,000 higher than expected; thus, the cost of goods sold was $10,000 more than anticipated. However, because of solid cost controls, actual operating expenses were $500 lower than expected.

TABLE 11–7 Donna's Gift Shop, 1994 Budgeted Versus Actual Profit-and-Loss Statement (in Dollars)

	Budgeted		Actual		Variance[a]	
Net sales	$200,000		$220,000		+$20,000	
Cost of goods sold	$110,000		$120,000		−$10,000	
Gross profit		$90,000		$100,000		+$10,000
Operating expenses:						
Salaries	$50,000		$50,000		—	
Advertising	3,500		3,300		+$ 200	
Supplies	1,200		1,100		+$ 100	
Shipping	900		1,000		−$ 100	
Insurance	3,000		3,000		—	
Maintenance	3,400		3,400		—	
Other	2,000		1,700		+$ 300	
Total	$64,000		$63,500		+$ 500	
Other costs	$17,500		$17,500		—	
Total costs		$81,500		$ 81,000		+$ 500
Net profit before taxes		$ 8,500		$ 19,000		+$10,500

[a] Variance was a positive number when actual sales or profits were higher than expected or actual expenses were lower than expected. The variance was a negative number when actual sales or profits were lower than expected or when expenses were higher than expected.

TABLE 11–8 Donna's Gift Shop, 1994 Budgeted Versus Actual Profit-and-Loss Statement (Expressed as a Per Cent of Sales)

	Budgeted		Actual	
Net sales	100.00		100.00	
Cost of goods sold	55.00		54.55	
Gross profit		45.00		45.45
Operating expenses:				
Salaries	25.00		22.73	
Advertising	1.75		1.50	
Supplies	0.60		0.50	
Shipping	0.45		0.45	
Insurance	1.50		1.36	
Maintenance	1.70		1.55	
Other	1.00		0.77	
Total	32.00		28.86	
Other costs	8.75		7.95	
Total costs		40.75		36.81
Net profit before taxes		4.25		8.64

Table 11–8 recomputes the actual performance data in Table 11–7 to yield a percentage profit-and-loss statement for Donna's Gift Shop. A ***percentage profit-and-loss (income) statement*** summarizes a retailer's revenues and expenses for a specific period of time, with data expressed as per cents of net sales. This statement lets a firm set goals and performance standards—and evaluate budgeted versus actual performance—on a per-cent-of-sales basis.

As can be seen from Table 11–8, actual net profit before taxes was 8.64 per cent of sales; this compares very favorably to the planned level of 4.25 per cent. Most of the increased net profit before taxes was due to actual operating expenses being 40.75 per cent of sales versus planned operating expenses of 36.81 per cent of sales.

While planning and implementing a budget, a retailer must carefully consider ***cash flow***, which relates the amount and timing of revenues received to the amount and timing of expenditures made during a specific time period. In cash flow management, the retailer's intention is usually to make sure revenues are received prior to expenditures' being made.[8] Otherwise, short-term loans may have to be taken out or profits tied up in the business to pay off inventory expenses and so on. For seasonal businesses, this may be unavoidable. Table 11–9 provides two examples of cash flow.

According to the Small Business Administration, underestimating costs and overestimating revenues, both of which affect cash flow, are the leading reasons why one-quarter of all new businesses fail within two years and three-fifths fail within six years.[9]

Resource Allocation

In allotting financial resources, a retailer should examine two basic factors: the magnitude of various costs and productivity. Each has significance for asset management and budgeting.

[8] See Robert A. Mamis, "Money In, Money Out," *Inc.* (March 1993), pp. 96–103.

[9] Brent Bowers, "This Store Is a Hit but Somehow Cash Flow Is Missing," *Wall Street Journal* (April 13, 1993), p. B2.

TABLE 11–9 The Effects of Cash Flow

A.
A retailer has relatively consistent sales throughout the year. Therefore, the cash flow during any given month is positive. This means no short-term loans are needed, and the owner can withdraw funds from the firm if she so desires:

Linda's Luncheonette, Cash Flow for January

Cash inflow:		
Net sales		$11,000
Cash outflow:		
Cost of goods sold	$2,500	
Operating expenses	3,500	
Other costs	2,000	
Total		$ 8,000
Positive cash flow		$ 3,000

B.
A retailer has highly seasonal sales that peak in December. Yet, to have a good assortment of merchandise on hand during December, it must order merchandise in September and October and pay for it in November. As a result, it has a negative cash flow in November that must be financed by a short-term loan. All debts are paid off in January, after the peak selling season is completed:

Dave's Party Favors, Cash Flow for November

Cash inflow:		
Net sales		$14,000
Cash outflow:		
Cost of goods sold	$12,500	
Operating expenses	3,000	
Other costs	2,100	
Total		$17,600
Net cash flow		–$ 3,600
Short-term loan (to be paid off in January)		$ 3,600

THE MAGNITUDE OF VARIOUS COSTS

As noted earlier in the chapter, retail expenditures can be divided into capital and operating categories. ***Capital expenditures*** are the long-term investments in fixed assets. ***Operating expenditures*** are the short-term selling and administrative costs of running a business. Before making decisions, it is imperative for retailers to have a sense of the magnitude of various capital and operating costs. The following examples illustrate this point.

In 1993, these were the average capital expenditures for erecting a single store for a range of retailers. The amounts include the basic building shell; heating, ventilation, and air-conditioning; lighting; flooring; fixtures; ceilings; interior signage; and roofing:

- Supermarket—$2.8 million.
- Department store—$6.7 million.
- Full-line discount store—$2.8 million.
- Apparel specialty store—$640,000.
- Drugstore—$940,000.
- Home center—$1.2 million.[10]

[10] Estimated by the authors from "Budget-Minded Retailers Maximize Dollars," *Chain Store Age Executive* (July 1993), pp. 56–61.

RETAILING IN ACTION

F.A.O. Schwarz: How Can Results Be Pumped Up?

F.A.O. Schwarz is considered by many to be the world's premier upscale toy chain. Yet, although sales at the chain's 25 stores have more than tripled over the past ten years, it has had difficulty turning a profit. High rents and salaries are major problem areas; but the firm's biggest resource drain has been its smaller mall-based stores.

Schwarz' 30,000- to 40,000-square-foot flagship stores in New York, Boston, Chicago, and San Francisco are all successful. It is the mall-based locations that have not been profitable. The firm's chief executive officer feels that his biggest challenge is to find a new format to replace the smaller stores, some of which occupy as little as 3,000 square feet. For example, 11,000-square-foot stores could duplicate the flagship stores in the classes of merchandise carried and the mechanized displays used. These stores should yield a 15 per cent return on investment with the same sales per square foot that would be needed to break even in smaller mall-based stores.

Koninlijke Bijenkorf Beheer (KBB), the Dutch firm that is Schwarz' current parent company, also wants to broaden the chain's marketing appeal without damaging its strong image. Besides replacing Schwarz' smaller stores, it plans to revise the merchandise mix to include more exclusive and less expensive merchandise, and to reduce the retailer's dependence on the Christmas selling season.

Source: Based on material in Stephanie Strom, "Palace of Toys Finds Profits Elusive," *New York Times* (December 23, 1993), pp. D1, D4.

Thus, a typical home-center chain must be prepared to invest $1.2 million to build each new outlet it opens. This does not include land and merchandise costs, and the total could be higher if a larger-than-average store is built.

Besides new-building construction costs, remodeling costs can also be expensive. A study by the International Mass Retail Association found that, among the store types examined, drugstore chains remodeled most frequently—averaging once every 6.6 years. The remodeling cycle for other retailers was 7.9 years for off-price retail chains, 8.5 years for full-line discount stores, and 9.2 years for department stores. Remodeling has been prompted by competitive pressures, the requirement of complying with Title II of the Americans with Disabilities Act, and environmental concerns.[11]

To reduce their investments, some retailers have insisted that real-estate developers help pay for building, renovating, and fixturing costs. These increased demands by retail tenants reflect the oversaturation of some retail areas, the increased retail space that is available due to the bankruptcy of some retailers (as well as mergers), and the increased interest by developers in gaining retailers that generate consumer traffic (such as category killers). For example, Oshman's Sporting Goods requires that developers contribute capital to its new-store locations. 50-Off Stores, Inc., a general-merchandise discounter, and Cache, Inc., a ladies clothing chain, also require construction allowances from landlords to help defray the costs of improvements to leased space.[12]

Regarding operating expenses, these costs are usually expressed as a percentage of sales and range from an average of 20 per cent in supermarkets to over 40 per cent in some specialty stores. To succeed in the marketplace, a retailer's operating costs must be in line with those of its competitors. Thus, Wal-Mart's five-per-cent advantage on operating costs over Kmart is significant when viewed in the context of Kmart's overall lower net profit margin and its inability to regularly meet the everyday low prices offered by Wal-Mart.[13]

Resource allocation must also take opportunity costs into account. ***Opportunity costs*** involve forgoing possible benefits that may occur if a retailer could make expenditures in another opportunity rather than the one chosen. For example, if a supermarket chain decides to renovate ten existing stores at a total cost of $2.8 million,

[11] "IMRA Poll: Retailers Prefer to Remodel Stores," *Discount Store News* (March 1, 1993), p. 3.

[12] *Oshman's Sporting Goods, Inc. 1992 Annual Report*, p. 4; *50-Off Stores, Inc. 1993 Annual Report*, p. 8; and *Cache, Inc. 1993 Annual Report*, p. 3.

[13] Bill Saporito, "The High Cost of Second Best," *Fortune* (July 26, 1993), pp. 99–102.

it would be unable to open a new outlet requiring a $2.8-million investment (excluding land and merchandise costs). Because financial resources are finite, firms often face either/or decisions. In this case, because the supermarket chain expects to earn greater profits by renovating than by building a new store, the latter becomes a lost opportunity—at least for now.

PRODUCTIVITY

Due to erratic sales, mixed economic growth, rising labor costs, increasing competition, and other factors over the last several years, many retailers are now placing priority on improving ***productivity***, the efficiency with which a retail strategy is carried out. The key question is: How can sales and profit goals be reached while keeping control over costs?

Productivity can be described in terms of costs as a percentage of sales, the time it takes a cashier to complete a transaction, the percentage of customers a salesperson sees during an average day who actually make purchases, profit margins, sales per square foot, inventory turnover, sales growth, and so on. For each of these measures, productivity goals require a firm to implement its strategy as efficiently as possible.

Because different retail strategy mixes have distinct resource needs in terms of store location, fixtures, the level of personnel, and other elements, productivity measures must be related to norms for each type of strategy mix (like department stores versus full-line discount stores). Sales growth should also be measured on the basis of comparable seasons, using the same stores as in previous periods. Otherwise, the data will be affected by seasonality and/or the increased square footage of stores. For instance, the productivity of Kmart can be evaluated by comparing its sales per square foot with its key competitors. Thus, although Kmart's Builders Square stores have averaged about $15 million in sales for each 109,000 square-foot outlet, Home Depot's average store has sales of $40 million in the same size facility.[14] This suggests that Kmart's asset management is weak relative to Home Depot.

Another example contrasts Circuit City and Best Buy, the two largest consumer-electronics chains. Best Buy's overhead expenses as a per cent of sales have averaged 15.3 per cent, versus 22.8 per cent for Circuit City. This gives a major pricing advantage to Best Buy.[15]

In general, productivity can be enhanced in two ways. A firm can improve employee performance, sales per foot of shelf space, and other factors by enhancing training programs, increasing advertising, and so on. And/or, it can reduce costs by automating, requiring suppliers to perform certain tasks, taking advantage of quantity discounts, seeking out cheaper suppliers, and being flexible in operations, and so on. One example of flexibility is Woolworth's converting almost all of its Susie's and Sportelle women's apparel stores into better-performing concepts such as Foot Locker, Lady Foot Locker, Champs Sports, Northern Reflections, and Afterthoughts.[16] Another example would be a retailer that employs a small core of full-time workers during its nonpeak times and supplements them with many part-time workers during its peak times.

Retailers need to keep in mind that productivity must not be measured strictly from the perspective of cost-cutting. Excessive cost-cutting can undermine customer loyalty. This happened to Rally's, a Louisville, Kentucky, fast-food franchisor, when it sought to reduce operating costs by developing a new burger that was 20 per cent smaller than its predecessor and consisted of frozen—rather than fresh—meat. Although the new burger recipe and Rally's reduction in advertising (from 8 per cent of sales to 4.9 per cent) helped the firm reduce its costs as a per cent of sales, sales

[14] Ibid.

[15] Marcia Berss, "High Noon," *Forbes* (December 20, 1993), pp. 44–45.

[16] Huff, "Restructuring Corrects Problems with Fixed Assets," pp. 19A–23A.

slipped by 4 per cent. At the same time, a competitor increased its market share by 5 per cent. In addition, some franchisees decided to refuse to sell the smaller-size burger.[17]

These are two strategies that retailers have used to raise productivity:

- Department stores such as Sears have paid attention to space productivity. Sears has cleared 700,000 square feet of space in its stores—by moving some furniture departments into freestanding stores and converting space that was previously used by its affiliated home-improvement contractors to retail use.[18]
- Tuesday Morning Corporation, a seller of quality closeout merchandise, opens its stores for only four sales events each year. The stores are not in use when there are no sales events, other than to house inventory and to restock for the next sales event.[19] Operating costs are low because the stores save on labor expenses (part-time workers are used extensively), utilities, insurance, and so on. The firm further reduces its costs by locating in low-rent sites. The firm realizes it operates destination stores that are sought out by loyal customers.

SUMMARY

1. *To define operations management* Operations management involves efficiently and effectively implementing the tasks and policies necessary to satisfy the retailer's customers, employees, and management. This chapter covered the financial aspects of operations management. Operational dimensions are studied in Chapter 12.
2. *To discuss profit planning* The profit-and-loss (income) statement summarizes a retailer's revenues and expenses over a specific period of time, typically on a monthly, quarterly, and/or yearly basis. It consists of these major components: net sales, cost of goods sold, gross profit (margin), operating expenses, and net profit before taxes.
3. *To describe asset management, including the strategic profit model and other key business ratios* Each retailer has various assets and liabilities that it must manage. A balance sheet itemizes a retailer's assets, liabilities, and net worth at a specific point in time. Assets are any items owned by a retailer that have a monetary value; some retail assets actually appreciate and may have a hidden value. Liabilities are any financial obligations that are incurred in running a business. The retailer's net worth, also known as owner's equity, is computed as assets minus liabilities.

   The results of asset management may be measured by reviewing a firm's net profit margin, asset turnover, and financial leverage. Net profit margin equals net profit divided by net sales. Asset turnover equals net sales divided by total assets. By multiplying the net profit margin by asset turnover, a retailer can determine its return on assets—which is based on net sales, net profit, and total assets. Financial leverage equals total assets divided by net worth. With leveraged buyouts (LBOs), firms may take on too much debt.

   The strategic profit model incorporates asset turnover, profit margin, and financial leverage to yield a measure known as return on net worth. As an overall measure, with three specific components, it allows a retailer to better plan or control its asset management.

   These are among the other key business ratios with which retailers should be familiar: quick ratio, current ratio, collection period, accounts payable to net sales, and overall gross margin.
4. *To look at retail budgeting* Budgeting outlines a retailer's planned expenditures for a given time period based on its expected performance; costs are linked to satisfying goals.

   There are six preliminary decisions. First, responsibility is defined via top-down and/or bottom-up arrangements. Second, the time frame is specified. Third, the frequency of budget planning is set. Fourth, cost categories are established. Fifth, the level of detail is ascertained. Sixth, the amount of flexibility is determined.

   The ongoing budgeting process then proceeds: goals, performance standards, planned expendi-

[17] Claire Poole, "Easy on the Beef," *Forbes* (March 15, 1993), p. 74.

[18] Gregory A. Patterson, "Department Stores, Seemingly Outmoded, Are Perking Up Again," *Wall Street Journal* (January 4, 1994), pp. A1, A6.

[19] *Tuesday Morning Corporation 1992 Annual Report*, p. 9; and *Tuesday Morning Corporation 1992 10K*, p. 1.

tures, actual expenditures, monitoring results, and adjustments. With zero-based budgeting, each new budget is started from scratch; with incremental budgeting, current and past budgets serve as guides. The budgeted versus actual profit-and-loss (income) statement and the percentage profit-and-loss (income) statement are vital budgeting tools. In all budgeting decisions, the impact of cash flow, which relates the amount and timing of revenues received with the amount and timing of expenditures made, must be considered.

5. *To examine resource allocation* In resource allocation, both the magnitude of costs and productivity need to be examined. Costs can be divided into capital and operating categories; the amount of both must be regularly reviewed. Opportunity costs involve forgoing possible benefits that may occur if a retailer could invest in an opportunity other than the one chosen. Productivity is the efficiency with which a retail strategy is carried out; the goal is to maximize sales and profits while keeping costs in check.

KEY TERMS

operations management (p. 368)
profit-and-loss (income) statement (p. 368)
net sales (p. 368)
cost of goods sold (p. 368)
gross profit (margin) (p. 368)
operating expenses (p. 368)
net profit before taxes (p. 368)
balance sheet (p. 369)
assets (p. 369)
hidden assets (p. 370)
liabilities (p. 370)
net worth (p. 370)
net profit margin (p. 370)
asset turnover (p. 371)
return on assets (ROA) (p. 371)
financial leverage (p. 372)
leveraged buyout (LBO) (p. 372)
strategic profit model (p. 372)
return on net worth (RONW) (p. 372)
key business ratios (p. 374)
budgeting (p. 376)
top-down budgeting (p. 377)
bottom-up budgeting (p. 377)
zero-based budgeting (p. 381)
incremental budgeting (p. 381)
percentage profit-and-loss (income) statement (p. 382)
cash flow (p. 382)
capital expenditures (p. 383)
operating expenditures (p. 383)
opportunity costs (p. 384)
productivity (p. 385)

QUESTIONS FOR DISCUSSION

1. Describe the relationship of assets, liabilities, and net worth for a retailer. How is a balance sheet useful in examining these items?
2. A retailer has net sales of $600,000, net profit of $40,000, total assets of $500,000, and a net worth of $200,000.
   a. Calculate net profit margin, asset turnover, and return on assets.
   b. Compute financial leverage and return on net worth.
   c. Evaluate the financial performance of this retailer.
3. How can a supermarket increase its asset turnover?
4. Is too low a financial leverage necessarily bad? Why or why not?
5. Under what circumstances would you recommend bottom-up budgeting rather than top-down budgeting?
6. How can a retailer combine top-down and bottom-up budgeting?
7. What is zero-based budgeting? Why do most retailers utilize incremental budgeting, despite its limitations?
8. What are the disadvantages of a slow-turning accounts receivable?
9. How could a seasonal retailer improve its cash-flow situation during periods when it must buy goods for future selling periods?
10. Distinguish between capital and operating expenditures. Why is this distinction important to retailers?
11. Describe three retailers that use risk-minimization retailing.
12. What factors should retailers consider when assessing opportunity costs?
13. What are several ways for these retailers to improve productivity?
    a. Gasoline station
    b. Restaurant
    c. Dry cleaner
    d. Off-price chain
14. Comment on Tuesday Morning Corporation's strategy for maximizing its productivity.

CASE 1
Cost-Driven Retail Strategies*

While traditional retailers have sought to maximize their profit margins, cost-driven retailers (CDRs) such as Wal-Mart have focused on expanding their customer bases by decreasing both their costs and profit margins. CDRs seek to develop and sustain a long-term competitive advantage by containing the overall costs associated with store fixtures, merchandise presentation, store location, physical distribution, and information systems; and they strive to take advantage of the lower operating costs due to larger volumes. As new opportunities occur for CDRs to further reduce costs due to quantity discounts, negotiating ability, or economies of scale, they will try to drive their profit margins even lower.

CDRs generally pay more attention to operating efficiency (via centralized buying, computerization, and mechanization) than to either buying or selling activities. Many of them sell the same or similar items (such as nationally advertised brands) as their competitors, but differentiate their offerings through a low price appeal. An important part of the value message that CDRs present is that they sell major brands at lower prices than competitors. A major attribute of CDRs is their appeal to price-sensitive customers by being on the "low" end of the locational, service, and facility continuum.

Home Depot, Food Lion, and Price/Costco are also examples of CDRs—besides Wal-Mart. Although their individual cost-containment strategies differ, these retailers seek to carefully control costs through low-cost locations, the use of pallets or cut cases as fixtures, self-service merchandising, centralized buying, low advertising costs, and tight controls on inventory levels. The overall expense structure of these firms is typically below that of their direct competitors. Thus, the low-expense structure enables them to make profits at prices that would involve losses for non-CDR competitors.

Two academic researchers isolated three critical success factors for CDRs. These are effective operations, distribution, and information systems. Successful CDRs also manage customer satisfaction from a production (efficiency) perspective. And they keep track of competitors' strategies, particularly their current prices on key items.

Those researchers interviewed executives (at least one from buying/merchandising and at least one from logistics/operations) at 24 different large-scale retailers (such as supermarkets, drugstores, and mass merchants). Respondents were questioned about decision making in three areas: assortment planning, supplier evaluation and selection, and supplier relationships. Each interview lasted about two hours. Of the firms studied, 8 were CDRs. Because the study was interview-based and the sample size was small, the research findings should be treated as exploratory in nature. Nevertheless, the results suggest important differences in orientation between traditional retailers and CDRs.

A key distinction between CDRs and other retailers relates to assortment planning. Although not all CDRs try to maintain limited assortments, many are reluctant to increase their assortments because of the increased costs. Traditional retailers may want to add to their assortments to appeal to new market segments, but CDRs fear that deeper assortments could increase their costs of doing business and result in their losing lowest-cost-provider status. According to a statement by a merchandise manager at one CDR:

> If you think of all the costs associated with buying, handling, controlling, and merchandising, we're simply better off with one brand and one size. If the customer isn't satisfied with the selection, (s)he can go elsewhere. But (s)he can't buy as cheaply anywhere else. And we couldn't possibly sell it at that low price if we increased the assortment and selection.

* This case was prepared and written by Professor Roger Dickinson, University of Texas at Arlington, and Professor Bixby Cooper, Michigan State University. The case is based upon their article, "The Emergence of Cost-Based Strategies in Retailing," *Journal of Marketing Channels*, Vol. 2 (Number 1, 1992), pp. 29–45.

CDRs also appear to be more prone to adopt a supply-chain perspective. Through this perspective, the concern of CDRs extends beyond themselves to their suppliers. CDRs are also more apt to have a total-cost viewpoint in doing business with suppliers. They are more aware of the importance of on-time delivery, full-order fulfillment, and damage- and error-free delivery. CDRs are more likely to favor suppliers that have strong operations support, and will not typically consider national-brand suppliers that cannot provide this support. They favor third or fourth market-share brands with superior support to best-selling brands with poor or inconsistent support. CDRs are also more willing to have longer relationships with suppliers and to use quick response, electronic data interchange, and new technologies than non-CDRs.

CDRs tend to avoid forward buying (purchasing larger than needed amounts to receive greater discounts) despite the appeal of higher profits due to lower costs. CDRs typically feel that forward buying requires additional costs in terms of more warehousing space, multiple merchandise handling, greater chances of damage, and greater obsolescence. They favor everyday low pricing, primarily due to the cost reductions that can be passed on to consumers—not because of its promotional possibilities.

CDRs are also more likely to manage in-bound transportation by preferring suppliers that offer high pick-up allowances. For example, in some cases, CDRs will use their own truck fleet or hire contact carriers to pick up goods. The pick-up allowances are viewed as sources of revenue if the CDRs can transport the goods for less than the pick-up allowance credits.

CDRs also look at the retailing environment differently than traditional retailers:

- Even though some retailing analysts feel many locales are overstored, CDRs believe it is relatively easy to take business away from noncost-driven retailers.
- CDRs are more concerned about the number of people located near a given location than the traffic counts. They assume that people will travel to a CDR, even if is located in a somewhat inconvenient spot.
- Price is a more important element in their retail strategies.

QUESTIONS

1. Discuss profit planning for a CDR from the perspective of gross margin and operating expense management.
2. How could a CDR retailer use the strategic profit model? Look at each component separately.
3. Describe resource allocation decision making for a CDR.
4. Is risk minimization a form of cost-driven retailing? Explain your answer.

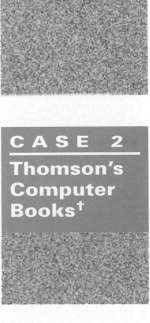

CASE 2
Thomson's Computer Books†

Thomson's Computer Books has established a reputation for stocking an extensive selection of computer books and manuals, including hard-to-find books and technical material. Its customers generally consist of computer "whizzes" who seek specialized texts that are not available elsewhere and consumers seeking a broad selection of computer manuals for current or older versions of major software packages. Many of the latter consumers desire manuals that go beyond the documentation provided by software producers.

† This case was prepared and written by Professor Raymond A. Marquardt and Lynn Samsel, University of Nebraska-Lincoln.

Thomson's operates two stores approximately three miles apart in Plainview, a Midwestern city of 200,000 residents. Owners Mae and Bill Thomson work at both stores as needed.

Thomson's North location, consisting of 2,300 square feet, opened October 1, 1991. It is situated at the center of town in a high-traffic strip center, between a very large discount store and a very large grocery store. Four employees work at the North store, three full-time and one part-time. The store has a toll-free number for out-of-town customers; and it receives 36 per cent of sales from customers who live out-of-town (even out-of-state). By appealing to customers in a four-state trading area, Mae and Bill Thomson have been able to increase the sales of this store. Thomson's North store enjoys a good reputation among purchasing agents in the Plainview business community as 'the' source for hard-to-find items. Although 35 per cent of the store's sales are to institutions, Thomson's North is steadily building its retail traffic as people learn of it and discover its low prices.

Thomson's South store has 1,000 square feet and opened November 1, 1993. It is across the street from a community college with a small bookstore of its own. The neighborhood surrounding the community college is old and stable—a lower-middle-class residential area. One full-time employee works at the South store. Unlike Thomson's other shop, the South store has no real institutional business. This store was the only computer bookstore in the southern part of town until a recent curriculum change brought computer classes to the community college and computing books to the campus bookstore. The South store is located in a small strip center with four small stores and eight parking spots. While the South store did some fairly effective advertising on the radio when it opened, its recent advertising via flyers sent to previous customers and new radio spots has had little effect in terms of increasing store traffic or sales. Table 1 contains selected financial information for the two stores for 1992 through May 1994. Table 2 contains a profit-and-loss statement for each store for 1993.

Bytes 'N Books (BNB) is Thomson's main competitor. BNB is located in a strip shopping center in the central part of the city and has gross sales exceeding $1 million. In comparison to Thomson's, BNB charges slightly higher prices and occupies

Table 1 Selected Financial Information for Thomson's Computer Books—North and South Stores (1/1/92 to 5/31/94)

North Store:	1992	1993	Five Months Ending 5/31/94
Net Sales	$281,705	$338,058	$125,085
Cost of Goods Sold	183,644	214,329	79,429
Gross Profit	98,061	123,729	45,656
Operating Expenses	113,323	115,752	49,820
Net Profit (Net Loss)	(15,262)	7,977	(4,164)
South Store:	**1992**	**1993**	**Five Months Ending 5/31/94**
Net Sales	–	$ 3,480	$ 8,180
Cost of Goods Sold	–	2,395	5,301
Gross Profit	–	1,085	2,879
Operating Expenses	–	6,881	8,409
Net Profit (Net Loss)	–	(5,796)	(5,530)

Note: The North location opened on October 1, 1991; the South store opened on November 1, 1993.

TABLE 2 Profit-and-Loss Statements for Thomson's Computer Books—North and South Stores (Fiscal Year 1993)

	North Store	South Store
Sales		
Software manuals/learning aids	$143,564	$ 478
Programming books	48,278	473
General computer books	45,649	1,114
Technical manuals	40,881	849
Wiring diagrams	17,680	240
Computer disks	11,690	198
Computer accessories	5,387	58
Miscellaneous	24,929	70
Total	$338,058	$ 3,480
Total Cost of Goods Sold	214,329	2,395
Total Gross Profit	$123,729	$ 1,085
Operating Expenses		
Wages	$ 35,736	$ 1,777
Rent	28,909	$ 950
Advertising and promotion	9,053	233
Freight and postage	5,763	41
Interest expense	4,765	–
Insurance	3,417	–
Taxes and permits	3,219	10
Telephone	3,144	169
Legal and accounting	2,891	302
Utilities	2,726	105
Operating supplies	1,600	150
Office expense	–	2,834
Miscellaneous	14,529	310
Total	$115,752	$ 6,881
Total Profit (Loss)	$ 7,977	($5,796)

5,000 square feet. Like Thomson's North location, BNB has a toll-free phone number for out-of-town customers. BNB has a separate section for parents to leave their young children to entertain themselves with educational software and video games while their parents shop elsewhere in the store. BNB's sales are 20 per cent institutional and 80 per cent retail. Unlike both of Thomson's stores, BNB carries a full line of greeting cards, some stationery items, and some magazines.

Because about 30 per cent of the population of Plainview and the surrounding area own computers or use them on the job, Mae Thomson believes the sales potential for Thomson's Computer Books has not been fully reached. Table 2 provides sales data by line of merchandise for both stores, as well as operating cost data.

QUESTIONS

1. Analyze the financial data in Tables 1 and 2.
2. What are the difficulties in evaluating the data in Tables 1 and 2?
3. What should Mae and Bill Thomson do next with the North and South stores? Give separate recommendations for the two stores.
4. Present several short-run and long-run financial goals for each of the two Thomson's stores. Explain your answer.

Operations Management: Operational Dimensions

❖ Chapter Objectives

1. To describe the operational scope of operations management
2. To study several specific operational aspects of operations management: store format and size, space allocation, personnel utilization, store maintenance, energy management, inventory management, store security, insurance, credit management, computerization, and crisis management

Fred Meyer, based in Portland, Oregon, has more than 100 combination stores—ranging from 150,000 to 200,000 square feet in size—in seven Western states. Each store has about 20 departments, with the food-based departments accounting for about one-third of total sales. In addition to its combination stores, Fred Meyer operates chains of nutrition stores and jewelry stores.

The diversity of locations, store formats, and types of goods and services sold places high demands on the firm's overall computer system. At Fred Meyer, the computer system is used to plan, implement, and control many operations—including labor scheduling, store remodeling, and inventory management.

Until 1989, employee hours worked, attendance, and scheduling were based on manual inputs and analysis. Now, the firm uses a computerized time-and-attendance program to save a lot of the employee and manager time that used to be devoted to completing time sheets and editing, correcting, and processing them manually. Fred Meyer's conversion to a computerized labor-scheduling program was especially hard because it has 22,000 employees who are covered by more than 250 union and 100 nonunion contracts. In addition, some stores have as many as nine managers. The computerized labor-scheduling system now helps Fred Meyer better match the supply and demand for labor, while meeting the provisions of labor contracts.

Fred Meyer uses computers in its drafting and store design departments. These enable the firm to quickly redesign and remodel stores. By using computer-assisted design (CAD) software, Fred Meyer can see the impact of alternate designs on a department's appearance, the total amount of shelf space available, and fixturing requirements and costs.

A third important application of computer technology at Fred Meyer is in the communication of merchandise orders and sales history information with 350 key suppliers. Fred Meyer's system enables it to use a quick response (QR) inventory system, in which fast-moving merchandise is ordered quickly, but in relatively small quantities. By doing so, the firm can minimize its inventory investment without facing stockouts on its best-selling goods.[1]

[1] "Fred Meyer: Meeting the Demands of a Diverse Business," *Chain Store Age Executive* (November 1993), p. 66; and "For Fred Meyer, Less Is Better," *Chain Store Age Executive* (October 1993), pp. 115–117.

Reprinted by permission of Fred Meyer.

Overview

As defined in Chapter 11, operations management is the efficient and effective implementation of the policies and tasks necessary to satisfy a retailer's customers, employees, and management (and stockholders, if a publicly owned company). In contrast to Chapter 11, which examined the financial dimensions of operations management, this chapter covers the operational aspects of operations management.

For retailers to ensure their long-run success, operational areas need to be managed as well as possible. Thus, for example, a decision to change the store format or to introduce new anti-theft equipment should be carefully considered because these acts could greatly affect a retailer's performance.

The Operational Dimensions of Operations Management

In running their businesses, retail executives need to make a wide range of operating decisions, such as these:

- What is the optimal format and size of a store?
- What is the relationship among shelf space, shelf location, and sales for each item in the store? How would total store sales change by varying space allocations and shelf locations?
- How can personnel best be matched to customer traffic flows? Would increased staffing improve or reduce productivity?
- What impact would the use of self-service versus sales personnel have on the sales of each product category?
- What effects do the uses of various building materials have on store maintenance?
- How can energy costs be better controlled?
- How can inventory be managed appropriately?
- How can inventory losses due to theft be reduced without disturbing most customers or employees?
- What levels of insurance are required?
- How can credit transactions be managed most effectively?
- How can computer systems improve operating efficiency?
- What kinds of crisis management plans should be in place?

In this chapter, these aspects of operations management are analyzed: store format and size, space allocation, personnel utilization, store maintenance, energy management, inventory management, store security, insurance, credit management, computerization, and crisis management.

Store Format and Size

With regard to store format, a retailer should consider whether productivity would be increased by such tactics as locating in a planned shopping center rather than in an unplanned business district, using prefabricated materials rather than customized ones in construction, and/or implementing certain kinds of store design and display layouts (which are discussed in Chapter 16). As always, decisions must be related to the retail strategy mix. A crucial store format decision for chain retailers is whether to use ***prototype stores***, whereby each outlet conforms to relatively uniform construction, layout, and operations standards.

Prototype stores offer several benefits. They make construction and centralized management control easier, reduce construction costs, enable operating methods to be standardized, facilitate the interchange of employees among outlets, allow fixtures and other materials to be purchased in quantity, and enforce a consistent chain image. However, a strict reliance on prototypes may lead to inflexibility, a failure to adapt to and/or capitalize on local customer needs, and a lack of creativity. Kmart, Pep Boys (an auto-accessory and repair-center chain), Radio Shack, Toys "R" Us, fast-food outlets, and various supermarket chains are among those with prototype stores.

Together with prototype stores, some chains are using ***rationalized retailing*** programs that involve a high degree of centralized management control combined with rigorous operating procedures for every phase of business. The aspects of a chain's operations would be performed in a virtually identical manner in a number of its outlets. Rigid control and standardization make this technique an easy one to implement and manage. In addition, a firm can add a significant number of units in a relatively short time period. Radio Shack and Toys "R" Us are examples of firms applying rationalized retailing. Each operates many stores that are similar in size, the number of items carried, store layout, merchandising, and sales approaches to others in that chain.

In their quest to be distinctive, and because of high rents and store saturation in many major metropolitan U.S. markets, many firms are engaging in one or both of two contrasting store-size approaches. On the one hand, various retailers—including Home Depot, Barnes & Noble, and Tandy (through its Incredible Universe outlets)—are opening category killer-sized stores so they can try to dominate smaller-sized stores by having extensive assortments. To do this, food-based warehouse stores and large discount-oriented stores are sometimes opening in secondary sites, where rents are much lower. These stores are confident they can draw customers from large trading areas. Cub Foods (a food-based warehouse chain), Wal-Mart, and others are applying this approach.

On the other hand, a number of retailers which believe that large stores are not efficient in serving saturated (or small) markets or that are now situated in high-rent areas have been downsizing their stores. For instance,

- According to a vice-president of the firm, Rose's new strategy is "to fit a 100,000-square-foot [full-line discount] store into a 50,000-square-foot box" by reducing the number of product variations stocked, as well as the store's average inventory on hand. Among the tactics used to accomplish this objective are vendor deliveries of slower-moving items directly to customers, requiring trucks to arrive at stores on a scheduled basis, and letting stores order smaller amounts—like less-than-full cartons."[2]
- Tandy plans to open several dozen smaller versions of its Radio Shack stores and Computer City stores in downtown areas. The units, called Radio Shack Express, will be about half as large as traditional Radio Shack outlets, but will offer about 75 per cent of the selection of the bigger stores. The units will be located in downtown areas such as Manhattan and Philadelphia, where rents are high and large retail sites are difficult to obtain. In addition to the smaller downtown locations, Radio Shack plans to establish Energy Express kiosks, which will be located in malls that currently have full-sized Radio Shack stores.[3]

SPACE ALLOCATION

Retailers need to place considerable emphasis on allocating store space. They must use facilities as productively as possible and determine the amount of space and its placement for each product category. Sometimes, retailers may decide to drop merchandise lines altogether because they occupy too much store space in relation to their sales and profit. That is why J.C. Penney dropped its home electronics, large sporting goods, and photographic equipment lines from its department stores.

[2] "Rose's Team Streamlines Operations to Run a Tight, Profitable Ship," *Discount Store News* (August 16, 1993), p. 79.

[3] Robert Johnson, "Tandy Bucks Retail Trend, Thinks Small," *Wall Street Journal* (May 5, 1993), pp. B1, B8.

With the ***top-down approach to space management***, a retailer starts with its total available store space (by store and for the overall firm, if a chain), divides the space into categories, and then works on in-store product layouts. This is in contrast to a ***bottom-up approach to space management***, where planning starts at the individual product level and then proceeds to the category, total store, and overall company levels.

Micro-merchandising is a strategy that enables a retailer to adjust shelf-space allocations to respond to customer and other differences among local markets. Thus, Dominick's Finer Foods, a supermarket chain, now allots shelf space to children's and adult's cereals on the basis of the demand patterns at its different stores; sales and inventory turnover have gone up accordingly. And Wal-Mart makes adjustments in the space it allocates to various product lines to reflect the demographics, weather, and popularity of different sporting events at its various stores.[4]

An emerging technique that some retailers, particularly supermarkets, are beginning to utilize to improve their shelf-space productivity is known as ***category management***—which is "a philosophy of managing a retailer's business which recognizes that category groupings of products are strategic business units for meeting consumer needs and achieving sales and profit goals." Category management orients retail managers toward the buying and selling decisions that are necessary to maximize the return on the assets assigned to them (including shelf space).[5] A fundamental notion in category management is that a retailer must empower someone to be responsible for the financial performance of each product category. As with micro-merchandising, category management also means customizing a retailer's merchandising strategy in each store or region to better satisfy customers. Thus,

> The advent of category management is shaking up the way many retailers approach merchandising. Items are no longer managed on their own. Now, many are managed in concert with the items around them to help a store make an improved pricing, promotion, or variety statement. Vons, for example, has dismantled its greeting-card department in some stores and replaced it with a party shop encompassing 5,500 items. And Cub Foods uses shelf management to rank an item's performance—in terms of movement and profitability—against the rest of its subcategory or category.[6]

In deciding upon the proper space allocation per product category, these are several of the crucial measures of performance to retailers:

- ***Sales per linear foot of shelf space***—equals annual sales divided by the total linear footage devoted to the product category.
- ***Gross profit per linear foot of shelf space***—equals annual gross profit divided by the total linear footage devoted to the product category.
- ***Return on inventory investment***—equals annual gross profit divided by average inventory at cost.
- ***Inventory turnover***—equals the number of times during a given period, usually one year, that the average inventory on hand is sold.
- ***Days supply***—equals the number of days of supply of an item that is on the shelf; it is a similar measure to inventory turnover.
- ***Direct product profitability (DPP)***—equals an item's gross profit less its direct retailing costs (such as warehouse and store support, occupancy, inventory, and direct labor costs, but not general overhead).

[4] "Dominick's Micro Approach: Chain Goes Beyond Space Management," *Chain Store Age Executive* (September 1993), pp. 31–32; and "Wal-Mart Fishing for a Niche in New Jersey," *Discount Store News* (September 6, 1993), p. 47.

[5] Brian F. Harris, "Category Management: What Is It?" *Promo/Progressive Grocer Special Report* (December 1993), p. 9.

[6] Michael Garry and Glenn Snyder, "Turning Partnering into Reality," *Progressive Grocer* (September 1993), pp. 44–46.

RETAILING IN ACTION

What Is a WinCMS?

After reorganizing its merchandising department by creating category management teams, Hannaford Bros., a Maine-based supermarket chain, was able to get a clearer view of each vendor. However, the category managers needed a better information system to implement "what, if" type analyses. Thus, during fall 1992, the firm began to install WinCMS (Windows-based Category Management System) software. The information used in this system is generated from products' UPC codes.

Through WinCMS, Hannaford can

- Analyze promotion results by item and category.
- Analyze profitability at the item, category, and store level.
- Study the effect of price changes.
- Identify poorly-performing products.
- List products (by item, category, department, store, and group of stores) that are either fast-selling or slow-selling.
- Allocate shelf space to increase profitability.
- Compare sales on a week-to-week, holiday-to-holiday, vendor-to-vendor, item-to-item, department-to-department, and store-to-store basis.

A major advantage of the system is its ability to perform vendor reviews. Rather than rely on data supplied by vendors, Hannaford can now analyze its own data—for individual stores and specific geographic areas.

Source: Based on material in Quita Ryder, "Making Technology Pay," *Progressive Grocer* (September 1993), pp. 35–38.

Comparisons can be made by studying company data from period to period and by looking at categorical statistics that are published in trade magazines.

Currently, the companywide use of category management in retailing is in its relative infancy. Although a lot of firms are employing the concept in selected product categories, according to one expert, only a handful of major U.S. retailers have fully-integrated category management programs and another 10 to 15 firms are 70 per cent to 80 per cent of the way there.[7]

Category management data can be analyzed with software from such firms as Information Resources Inc., MarketMax (SpaceMax), Strategic Merchandising Applications (Spacemaster), and Nielsen Retail Information Group (Spaceman III). A few large retailers have even developed their own category-management software. All of the software programs base the allocation of in-store space on sales, inventory turnover, and profits at the individual store level. Because data are store specific, space allocations can reflect actual customer purchases at individual stores.[8]

Figure 12–1 indicates how a firm could use category management to better merchandise liquid detergent. One axis of the figure deals with direct product profitability (DPP). For the supermarket depicted in this example, $0.69 per item is the average DPP for all liquid detergents. Those with higher amounts would be placed in the top half of the grid; those with lower amounts would be placed in the lower half. The other axis classifies liquid detergents in terms of their unit sales (an indicator of inventory turnover), with 12.3 items per week being the dividing line between slow- and fast-moving detergents. On the basis of this two by two grid, all detergents could be placed into one of four categories: high potential ("sleepers")—products with high profitability but low unit sales; winners—products with high profitability and high weekly sales; underachievers ("dogs")—products with low profitability and low weekly sales; and traffic builders—products with low profitability and high weekly sales. Specific strategies are recommended in this figure.

Here are just some of the other tactics being used to increase the productivity of store space: Many retailers have vertical displays, which occupy less room than horizontal displays; they may hang displays on store walls or from ceilings. Formerly free space is now devoted to vending machines and small point-of-sale displays; product

[7] Christopher W. Hoyt, "Category Management Is Inevitable, So See Where You Stand," *Brandweek* (January 11, 1993), p. 19.

[8] See Ray Pearson, "Space Management: From Product to Store," *Progressive Grocer* (December 1993), pp. 31–32.

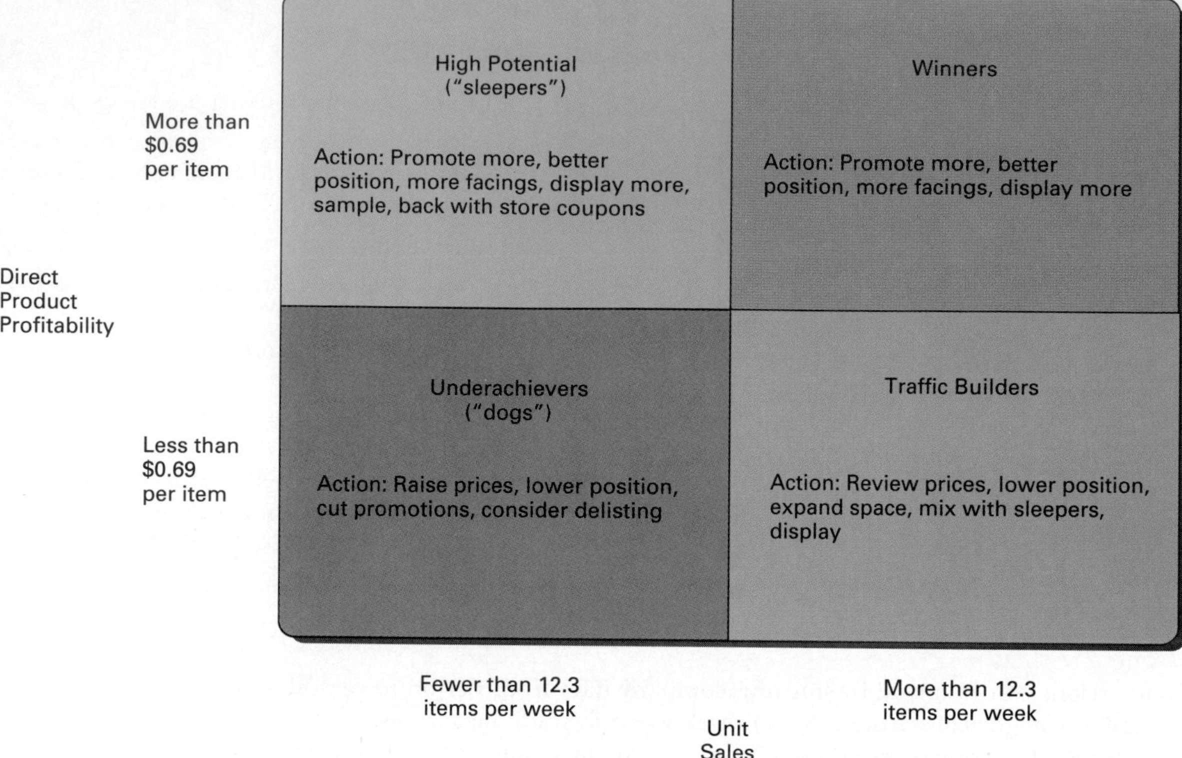

Note: The criteria are based on the average profit and movement of the items in the product category of heavy-duty liquid detergent. The averages change for each product category.

FIGURE 12–1 Applying Category Management to Heavy-Duty Liquid Detergent
Source: Walter H. Heller, "Profitability: Where It's Really At," *Progressive Grocer* (December 1992), p. 27. Copyright *Progressive Grocer*. Reprinted by permission.

displays are also being located in front of stores. Open doorways, mirrored walls, and vaulted ceilings give small, cramped stores the appearance of being larger. Some retailers allocate up to 75 to 80 per cent or more of their total floor space to selling; the rest is used for storage, rest rooms, and so on. Scrambled merchandising (involving high-profit, high-turnover items) is occupying more square feet in a wider range of stores and more space in mail-order catalogs than ever before. By staying open longer hours, retailers are also using space better.

UTILIZATION OF PERSONNEL

From an operations perspective, the efficient utilization of retail personnel is important for several reasons. First, labor costs are high. As an example, in independent supermarkets, wages and benefits account for 57 per cent of total operating costs; and in supermarket chains, the average starting part-time clerk is paid about $5 an hour, the average full-time clerk about $6 an hour, and the average meat cutter about $10 an hour; the latter two also receive fringe benefits.[9]

Second, high employee turnover leads to increased recruitment, training, and supervision costs. Third, poor personnel may not have good selling skills, mistreat customers, misring sales transactions, and make other costly errors. Fourth, productivity gains in technology have taken place much more rapidly than those in labor; yet, many retailers remain quite labor-intensive.

[9] Computed by the authors from "60th Annual Report of the Grocery Industry," *Progressive Grocer* (April 1993), pp. 82, 86.

Fifth, labor deployment decisions are often subject to unanticipated fluctuations in customer demand. For instance, even though retailers know they should increase sales personnel in peak sales periods and reduce them in slow periods, they may still be over- or understaffed if the weather changes, competitors run special sales, or suppliers increase promotion support.

Finally, unionization places restrictions on retailers that have unionized employees. In these cases, working conditions, compensation, job tasks, overtime rates, performance measurement, termination procedures, seniority rights, promotion criteria, and other factors are generally specified in written contracts. Not only must retailers abide by the terms of these contracts, but their flexibility in deploying workers may be affected.

Among the tactics retailers may use to maximize personnel productivity are these:

- Hiring process—By carefully screening potential employees before they are offered jobs, turnover can be reduced and better performance secured.
- Workload forecasts—For each season, week, day, and time period, the needed number and type of personnel can be pre-determined. Thus, a drugstore may have one pharmacist, one cashier, and one stockperson in the store from 2 P.M. to 5 P.M. on Wednesdays and add a pharmacist and a cashier from 5 P.M. to 7:30 P.M. (to accommodate people shopping after work). In doing workload forecasts, personnel costs must be balanced against the possibilities of lost sales if customer waiting time is excessive. It is important to be both efficient (cost-oriented) and effective (service-oriented). Today, a number of retailers are using computer software to aid them in the scheduling of personnel.[10]
- Job standardization and cross-training—With ***job standardization***, the tasks of personnel with similar positions in different departments, such as cashiers and stockpersons in clothing and candy departments, are kept rather uniform. With ***cross-training***, personnel learn tasks associated with more than one job, such as cashier, stockperson, gift wrapper, and customer complaints handler. A firm can increase personnel flexibility and minimize the total number of employees needed at any given time via job standardization and cross-training. As an example, if one department is slow, a cashier could be assigned to another that is busy; and a salesperson could also process transactions, help set up displays, and handle customer complaints. Cross-training can even reduce employee boredom.
- Employee performance standards—Each employee must have clear performance standards and be accountable for meeting them. Cashiers can be judged on the basis of transaction speed and misrings; buyers can be judged on the basis of departmental revenues and the need for markdowns; and senior executives can be judged on the basis of the firm's reaching sales and profit goals. Personnel are usually more productive when they work toward specific goals.
- Compensation—Financial compensation, promotions, and recognition can reward good performance. They serve to motivate employees better. Thus, a cashier will be motivated to reduce misrings if he or she knows there is a bonus for keeping mistakes under a certain percentage of all transactions processed.
- Self-service—Personnel costs as a percentage of sales can be reduced significantly if self-service facilities are used, thus lessening the need for personnel. However, two points should be taken into account. First, self-service requires better in-store displays, well-known brands, ample assortments on the selling floor, and goods/services with simple features. Second, by reducing or eliminating sales personnel, some customers may feel they are receiving inadequate service; and there is no cross-selling (whereby customers are encouraged to buy complementary goods they may not have been thinking about).

[10] See Terry Hennessy, "Scheduling That Works," *Progressive Grocer* (December 1993), pp. 35–36; and "New Use for ShopperTrak," *Chain Store Age Executive* (March 1994), pp. 166, 168.

TABLE 12–1 Selected Store Maintenance Decisions

- What should be the responsibility of the retailer for maintaining outside facilities? For example, does a lease agreement make the retailer or the property owner responsible for snow removal in the parking lot?
- Should store maintenance activities be performed by the retailer's own personnel or by outside specialists? Will that decision differ by type of facility (e.g., air-conditioning versus flooring) and by type of service (e.g., maintenance versus repairs)?
- What repairs should be classified as emergencies? How promptly should nonemergency repairs be made?
- How frequently is store maintenance required for each type of facility (e.g., daily vacuuming of floors versus weekly or monthly washing of exterior windows)? How often should special maintenance activities be undertaken (e.g., waxing floors and restriping the spaces in a parking lot)?
- How should store maintenance vary by season and by time of day (e.g., when a store is open versus when it is closed)?
- How long should existing facilities be maintained before acquiring new ones? What schedule should be followed?
- What performance standards should be set for each element of store maintenance? Do these standards balance costs against a desired level of maintenance?

- Length of employment—Long-term employment can be encouraged. As a rule, full-time workers who have been with a company for a long time are more productive than those who are part-time and/or who have worked for the firm for a short time. The former are often more knowledgeable, are more anxious to see their company succeed, require less supervision, are popular with their customers, can be promoted to higher-level positions, and are more likely to accept and adapt to the special environment of retailing. In many cases, the high productivity associated with full-time, long-term employees far outweighs their relatively high compensation.

STORE MAINTENANCE

Store maintenance encompasses all of the activities involved in managing the retailer's physical facilities. These are just some facilities that must be managed as productively as possible: exterior—parking lot, points of entry/exit, outside signs and display windows, and common areas adjacent to a store (e.g., sidewalks); interior—windows, walls, flooring, climate control and energy use, lighting, displays and signs, fixtures, and ceilings. Selected store maintenance decisions are shown in Table 12–1.

The quality of store maintenance affects consumer perceptions of the retailer, the life span of facilities, and operating expenses. Consumers do not like to patronize stores that are unsanitary, decaying, or otherwise poorly maintained. This means the regular cleaning of light fixtures, the replacement of burned-out lamps, and the periodic cleaning or repainting of room surfaces to optimize light reflection. Some chains even go so far as to replace all lamps at the same time to assure constant color and light levels throughout the chain.[11]

Ongoing and thorough maintenance can enable a retailer to use its current facilities for an extended period before having to invest in new ones. At home centers, for instance, the heating, ventilation, and air-conditioning equipment lasts an average of

[11] "Maintenance: Group Relamping Maximizes Efficiency," *Chain Store Age Executive* (December 1993), pp. 44–45; and "Partnerships for Progress: Creating Effective Lighting in the 1990s," *Chain Store Age Executive* (January 1994), Section Three.

15 years; flooring an average of 15 years; and interior signs an average of 6 years. But store maintenance can be costly. During a typical year, a 38,000-square-foot home center spends about $9,500 on floor maintenance alone.[12]

ENERGY MANAGEMENT

Today, due to the rise in costs over the last two decades (although prices have stabilized in recent years), energy management is a major consideration in store operations for many retailers. At companies with special needs, such as food stores and florists, energy management is especially critical. A typical outlet of a supermarket chain has annual energy costs amounting to 1.1 to 1.4 per cent of sales.[13]

To better manage their energy resources, more firms are now:

- Using better-quality insulation materials when constructing and renovating stores to obtain long-run monthly savings in energy bills.
- Carefully adjusting interior temperature levels during nonselling hours. In summer, air-conditioning is reduced for off-hours; in winter, heating is lowered for off-hours.
- Using computerized systems, which can be programmed by store department and to fractions of a degree, to closely monitor temperature levels.
- Using centralized computer-controlled systems, whereby operators can monitor and manipulate temperature, lighting, heat, and air-conditioning in multiple store units from a single office. Such systems can even enable the operators to learn whether managers have left lights on within closed stores and to turn those lights off from their consoles. Vast cost savings are possible.
- Substituting high-efficiency bulbs and fluorescent ballasts for traditional lighting, thus reducing energy costs significantly.
- Installing specialized "targeted desiccant" air-conditioning systems to better control the humidity levels in specific areas of the store, such as refrigerated and freezer locations, and thereby minimizing moisture condensation.[14]

Here are two examples of how seriously retailers are taking energy management: First, the compact fluorescent bulb system (now used by such retailers as Venture Stores) requires about one-third of the electricity as alternative lighting sources. Compact bulbs also deliver as much light as standard 4-foot fluorescent bulbs; and they have a rated life of 20,000 hours, compared with 2,000 hours for the average incandescent bulb. In addition, the higher lumen output of the fluorescents helps to reduce the number of fixtures required per store. After refitting 54 existing stores and a general office with energy-efficient fluorescent lamps on electronic ballasts, Venture's energy manager said, "the lighting system at these stores and office is saving Venture $1.23 million annually."[15]

Second, Lord & Taylor worked closely with Boston Edison to design and engineer a lighting retrofit, a new air-conditioning system, and an energy-management system for its downtown Boston store. The retrofit has resulted in reduced annual operating costs of $87,000; and the investment in the retrofit was reduced by rebates from the local utility (Boston Edison) that totalled $129,000. Lord & Taylor replaced its central air-conditioning system with a new system that requires 150 tons less capacity. And the firm installed an energy-management system to oversee all aspects of the Boston store's energy output. That system lets Lord & Taylor monitor and control tempera-

12 "Budget-Minded Retailers Maximize Dollars," *Chain Store Age Executive* (July 1993), pp. 56–61.

13 Warren Thayer, "Five Ways to Cut Your Energy Bill," *Progressive Grocer* (January 1991), p. 21.

14 Marianne Wilson, "Genuardi's New System," *Chain Store Age Executive* (March 1994), p. 62.

15 "Venture Uses Compact Fluorescents," *Chain Store Age Executive* (February 1993), p. 84.

RETAILING AROUND THE WORLD

What Do Germans Have Against Longer Store Hours?

The German labor union that represents 420,000 of Germany's 2.8 million retail workers has vowed to aggressively fight a recent proposal for longer store hours that was made by the governing Christian Democratic Party. Currently, nearly all retail stores must close promptly at 6:30 P.M. on most weekdays, at 2 P.M. on most Saturdays, and all day on Sunday.

Many economists and businesspeople feel that longer store hours could help Germany out of its worst economic situation in 40 years. Those favoring longer store hours cite as evidence the large crowds that run to stores on Saturday morning before closing times. They also point to the German court ruling that now allows gasoline stations to sell newspapers, candy, cigarettes, and other sundries. Many of these sales are at the expense of traditional retailers.

Labor unions have argued against longer hours because they believe the longer hours will further reduce competition. According to the union, there were 160,000 grocery stores in Germany in 1960, but only 69,000 in 1993. The unions fear that longer hours would perpetuate the decline of smaller grocery and other stores. The majority of the firms in the German retailers federation are also not in favor of longer hours. Many fear they would have to match the hours of the larger chains.

Source: Based on material in Craig R. Whitney, "Longer Store Hours? Germans Are Aghast," *New York Times* (October 31, 1993), p. 6.

ture levels in every department from any remote location via a modem. It also manages different lighting levels for each department by time of day. This means the system can increase the lighting at an employee entrance in the morning and reduce it in the afternoon.[16]

INVENTORY MANAGEMENT

Through ***inventory management***, a retailer seeks to acquire and maintain a proper merchandise assortment while ordering, shipping, handling, and other related costs are kept in check. From an operations vantage point, inventory management has three interrelated phases: retailer to supplier, supplier to retailer, and retailer to consumer. See Figure 12–2.

First, the retailer places an order with a supplier based on a sales forecast and/or actual customer behavior. Both the number of items and their variety (such as assorted colors, sizes, and materials) are requested in ordering. Order size and frequency depend on quantity discounts and various inventory costs. Second, the supplier fills the retailer's order and sends merchandise to a warehouse or directly to the store(s). Third, the retailer receives merchandise, makes items available for sale (e.g., by removing items from shipping cartons, marking prices on them, and placing them on the selling floor), and completes transactions with consumers. Sometimes, transactions are not complete until merchandise is delivered to the customer. The cycle starts anew when the retailer places another order.

These are some factors retailers should consider in inventory management, from an operations perspective:

- How can the handling of merchandise received from different suppliers be coordinated?
- How much inventory should be on the selling floor versus in a warehouse or storage area?
- How often should inventory be moved from nonselling to selling areas of the store?
- What inventory functions can be performed during nonstore hours rather than while the store is open?

[16] "Lord & Taylor's Energy Efficient Overhaul," *Chain Store Age Executive* (October 1993), pp. 144–146.

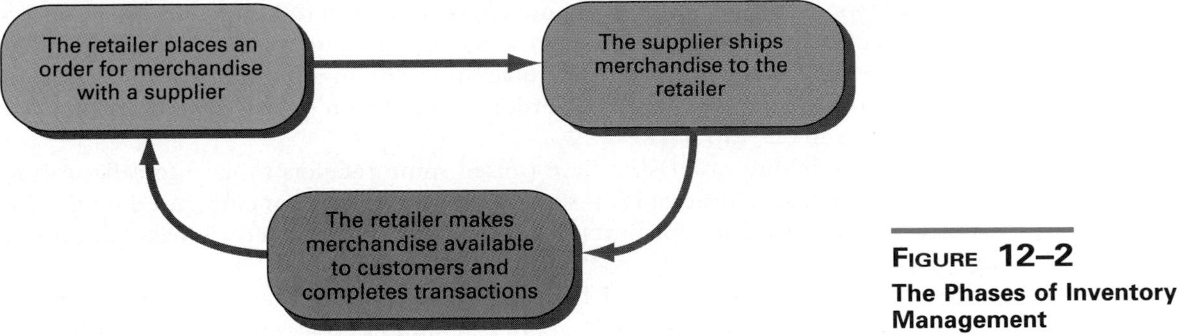

FIGURE 12–2
The Phases of Inventory Management

- What are the trade-offs between faster delivery times from suppliers and higher shipping costs?
- What support is expected from suppliers in storing merchandise and/or setting up displays?
- What level of in-store merchandise breakage is acceptable?
- Which items require delivery to customers? How should this be accomplished (e.g., timing and responsibility)?

To improve their inventory management performance, a number of retailers are now involved with quick response inventory planning—which, until a few years ago, was mostly used by manufacturers. With ***quick response (QR) inventory planning***, a retailer reduces the amount of inventory it keeps on hand by ordering more frequently and in lower quantity. A QR system requires a retailer to have good relationships with suppliers, coordinate shipments, monitor inventory levels closely to avoid running out of stock, and regularly communicate with suppliers via electronic data interchange and other means.

For the retailer, a QR system allows inventory costs to be reduced, minimizes the space required for product storage, and enables the firm to better match its orders with market conditions—by replenishing stock more quickly. For the manufacturer, a QR system can also improve inventory turnover and better match supply and demand by giving the vendor the ability to track actual sales. These data were less available to the manufacturer in the past. In addition, a QR system that operates effectively makes it more difficult for a retailer to switch suppliers.

According to one study of retail operations executives, 42 per cent of retailers are now using a QR system to make purchases from vendors. Generally, the most active users of QR are full-line discount stores, department stores, home centers, supermarkets, and drugstores.[17] Among the individual firms using QR systems with at least some products are Dillard's, Carter Hawley Hale, Belk, Shaw's Supermarkets, Home Depot, The Limited, Dayton Hudson, Mercantile, Kmart, Ross, Sears, J.C. Penney, and Wal-Mart.

A QR system is most effective when used in conjunction with floor-ready merchandise, lower minimum order sizes, newly formatted store fixtures, and electronic data interchange: ***Floor-ready merchandise*** refers to items that are received at the store in condition to be put directly on display without any preparation by retail workers. For example, with this approach, apparel manufacturers are responsible for preticketing merchandise (with information specified by the retailer) and placing it on hangers. Similarly, Safeway supermarkets require that vendors put Safeway tags on apples and grapefruit, freeing produce clerks for other tasks.[18]

[17] "The Impact of Information Technologies," *Chain Store Age Executive* (May 1993), Section Two, p. 16A.

[18] Russell Mitchell, "Safeway's Low-Fat Diet," *Business Week* (October 18, 1993), p. 61.

Quick response also means that manufacturers need to rethink their minimum order sizes. For instance, while a minimum order size of 12 for a given size or color used to be required by sheet and towel manufacturers, the minimum order size is now as low as two units. Likewise, minimum order sizes for men's shirts have been reduced from six to as low as two units.[19]

The new minimum order sizes have caused some retailers to have to refixture instore departments. Prior to quick response, fixtures were often configured on the basis of a retailer's stocking full inventories. Today, retailers need to make an impact with smaller inventories.

Electronic data interchange, EDI (defined in Chapter 7), lets retailers use QR inventory planning efficiently—via a paperless, computer-to-computer relationship between retailers and their vendors. As an example, the results of one study suggest that the prices of dry grocery items could be reduced an average of 10.8 per cent with the industrywide usage of QR and EDI.[20] These illustrations show the use of EDI and QR at specific retailers:

- "On Saturday afternoon, a customer buys a package of Hanes underwear at a Dayton's department store. That evening, Dayton Hudson's headquarters in Minneapolis polls the store and records the sale. On Sunday morning, the central computer transmits data to the chain's automatic reorder system. A few hours later, that system sends an order to an electronic mailbox, where Hanes picks it up Monday morning. The vendor packs the order Tuesday, and ships it to Dayton Hudson's warehouse Wednesday. By Thursday night, the shipment is in the store, ready for purchase by another customer."[21] See Figure 12–3.
- Mercantile Stores shares sales data with suppliers on a daily basis through EDI technology. The firm has implemented a Basic Automatic Replenishment system, which reorders and restocks fast-selling merchandise throughout the selling season.[22]
- Tesco (a supermarket chain with 400 stores throughout Great Britain) has been using EDI since 1984. Tesco now has electronic links with over 1,200 suppliers. According to its retail systems controller, before EDI, "we held three to four weeks worth of stock in every store and our warehouses held several weeks worth of stock. Today, at the store level, we hold half a week's stock at most. We haven't got this great overhead of capital tied up in stock that's just sitting there."[23]
- VF Corporation—the apparel manufacturer—has devised a QR system, called Market Response System, for its retailers. The Market Response System enables VF to manage the inventories of its customers and provide them with sophisticated analytical tools. The system reviews sales/stockout data on a daily basis and replenishes retailers' inventories as frequently as required. VF is moving toward 24-hour replenishment.[24]

Some retailers are going further than QR planning and becoming more actively involved with ***logistics***—which is the total process of moving goods from a manufacturer to a customer in the most timely and cost-efficient manner possible. Unlike other methods of inventory management, logistics regards transportation, storage, order processing, packaging, purchasing, and customer service as interdependent. It also oversees inventory management decisions as items travel through the retail supply chain (from manufacturers to warehouses to distribution centers to stores or, in some

[19] Gary Robins, "Quick Response," *Stores* (March 1993), pp. 21–22.

[20] "Jenkins Leads EDI Effort," *Chain Store Age Executive* (March 1993), pp. 147–148.

[21] "Quick Response: The Right Thing," *Chain Store Age Executive* (March 1990), p. 49.

[22] *Mercantile Stores 1992 Annual Report.*

[23] Bruce Fox, "To Tesco, EDI Is Nothing New," *Chain Store Age Executive* (July 1993), pp. 40, 45.

[24] Robins, "Quick Response," pp. 21–22.

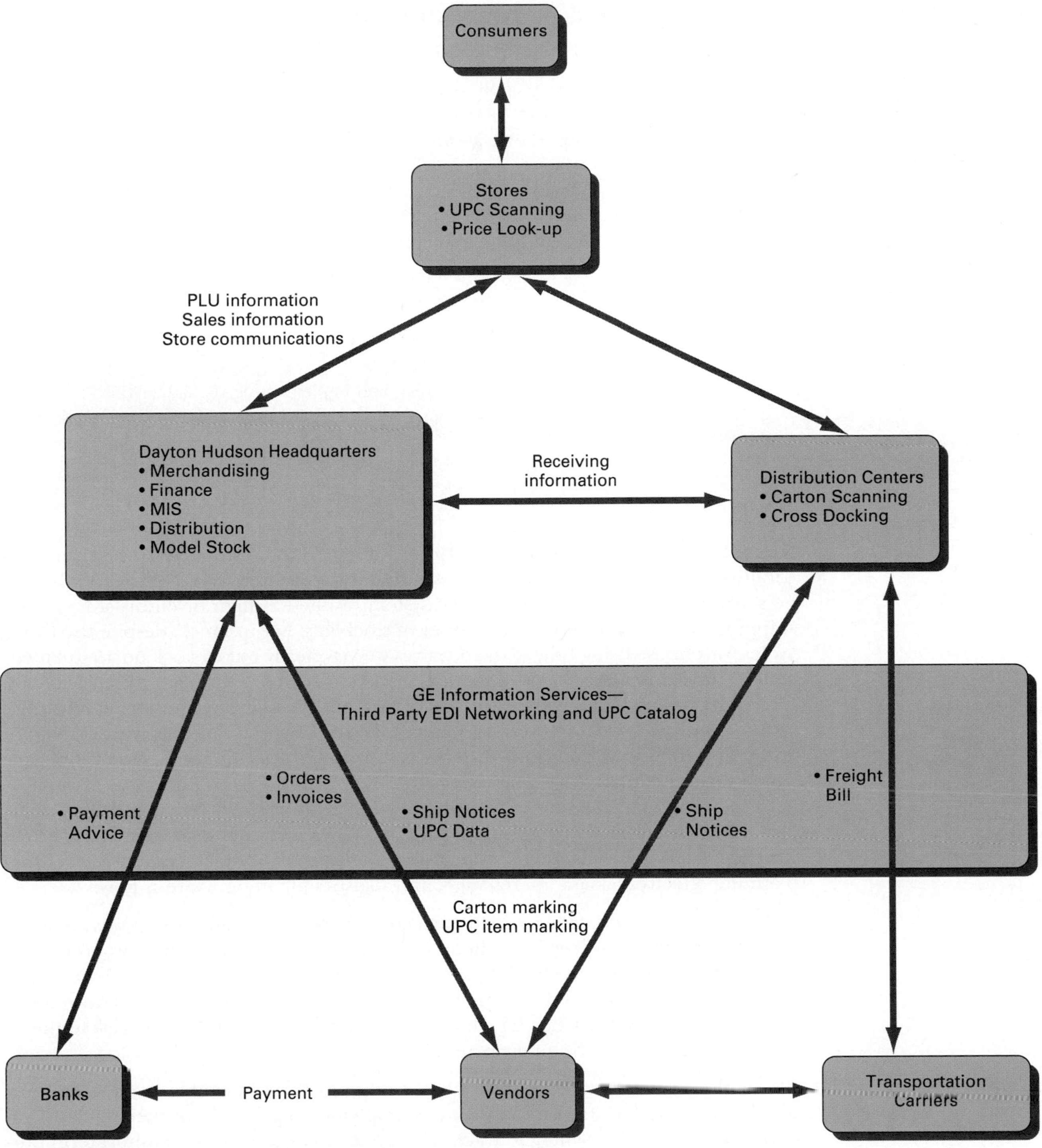

FIGURE 12–3 Quick Response at Dayton Hudson

Source: GE Information Services, "Quick Response at Dayton Hudson," *Chain Store Age Executive* (March 1990), p. 49. Reprinted by permission. Copyright Lebhar-Friedman, Inc., 425 Park Avenue, New York, NY 10022.

cases, even to homes of consumers). If the logistics system works well, retailers can reduce stockouts, hold down inventories, and improve customer service—all at the same time.

Laura Ashley, a well-known designer of wallpaper and dresses, has relied upon a logistics approach to untangle its "knotted" supply chain: The firm acquires goods from fifteen countries and deals with 500+ stores worldwide. Originally, all of Laura Ash-

ETHICS IN RETAILING

How Can Food Retailers Better Deal with Safety Issues?

Many retailing analysts believe that shopper sensitivity to food handling and safety has dramatically increased since *Prime Time Live* showed alleged abuses in food handling at Food Lion supermarkets. According to a Food Marketing Institute annual *Trends* survey, consumers now say that spoilage is the greatest threat to food safety. Consumers are especially interested in product freshness, shelf life and expiration dates, germs, and improper packaging.

Food safety experts say that the most important factor in food protection is the time and temperature principle: All potentially hazardous food must be kept at an internal temperature of below 40 degrees fahrenheit or above 140 degrees fahrenheit during transport, storage, handling, preparation, display, and service. Bacteria can rapidly multiply outside this temperature range.

Among the actions that food retailers are taking to better ensure food safety are:

- Investing in blast-chilling equipment that cools food rapidly. This equipment enables food to quickly pass outside the danger temperature zone.
- Enforcing requirements for food-handling personnel to wear gloves and hats.
- Cleaning of cutting surfaces with hot water and cleansing solutions.
- Developing and implementing regular self-inspection programs.

Source: Based on material in Mary Ann Linsen, "Safety First," *Progressive Grocer* (December 1993), pp. 83–89.

ley's blouses that were produced in Hong Kong had to be shipped to the firm's distribution center in Wales. Then, blouses that were ordered by a Tokyo store had to be rerouted back to the Far East. That system resulted in high inventory-storage and shipping costs, as well as a large amount of stockouts. For instance, despite the firm's Wales warehouse being fully stocked, stores were typically out of stock on 15 to 20 per cent of Laura Ashley's items; and too many goods were in-transit. Today, Federal Express' Business Logistics Services Division manages Laura Ashley's new inventory system, having signed a ten-year agreement. Federal Express consults with each store and determines what goods need to be received as of specific times. Goods are now shipped from manufacturers directly to stores.[25]

In the supermarket sector of retailing, a number of firms are striving to apply their own form of logistics management, known as ***efficient consumer response (ECR)***. Through ECR, supermarkets are incorporating aspects of quick response inventory planning, electronic data interchange, and logistics planning. Here is how:

> Phase one concentrates on initiating electronic data interchange programs aimed at efficient inventory replenishment. Even at this stage, results can be impressive with reductions of paperwork by more than half their previous levels. Phase two addresses continuous replenishment, which can help dramatically to reduce inventory levels even further. The last stage links retail sales all the way back to the manufacturer's ordering raw materials.[26]

Although U.S. supermarket retailers believe that ECR could enable them to cut tens of billions of dollars in distribution costs, implementing it will not be easy. Most supermarkets are still unwilling to trade their ability to negotiate special short-term purchase terms with vendors in return for routine order fulfillment without special deals. And as one expert says, "Supermarkets and their suppliers are still living with outdated systems. From a technology standpoint, they are not ready for the requirements of ECR."[27]

Merchandising decisions are discussed thoroughly in Chapters 13 and 14.

[25] Stephanie Strom, "Logistics Steps onto the Retail Battlefield," *New York Times* (November 3, 1993), pp. D1–D2; and "Logistics Mean Service," *Chain Store Age Executive* (October 1993), p. 139.

[26] R. Craig MacClaren, "Manufacturers Are Setting a Fast Pace for ECR," *Promo* (March 1994), p. 42.

[27] "ECR: Harder Than It Looks," *Chain Store Age Executive* (December 1993), pp. 104, 106.

STORE SECURITY

Nearly $35 billion in U.S. retail sales are lost annually because of ***inventory shrinkage*** caused by employee theft, customer shoplifting, and vendor theft (mostly short shipping). According to one study, employees account for 46 per cent of the amount, customers 46 per cent, and vendors 8 per cent.[28] Thus, some store security program is needed by all retailers.

To reduce losses due to theft, three key points should be incorporated into retailers' operating plans. First, loss prevention should be considered as stores are designed and built. For example, the placement of store entrances, dressing rooms, and delivery areas should be planned from a security standpoint. Second, a combination of security measures should be enacted, like employee background checks, in-store guards, electronic security equipment, and merchandise tags. Third, retailers need to communicate the importance of loss prevention to employees, customers, and vendors, as well as the actions they will take to reduce losses (such as firing workers).

Here are some activities being used to reduce losses due to theft:[29]

- Product tags, security guards, in-store cameras, point-of-sale computers, employee surveillance, and burglar alarms are each being used by a growing number of retailers. Storefront protection is also quite popular.
- Many general merchandise retailers and some supermarkets are using ***electronic article surveillance***, by which specially designed tags or labels are attached to products. These tags can be sensed by electronic devices that are placed at store exits. If the tags are not removed by store personnel or desensitized by electronic scanning equipment, an alarm goes off. Retailers also have greater access to non-electronic tags. These are tightly attached to products and must be removed by special detachers; otherwise, the products would be unusable. See Figure 12–4.
- A lot of firms are performing detailed background checks for every employee. According to one study, close to 17 per cent of the applicants for retail positions would be classified as high risk.
- Various retailers have employee training programs on the impact of losses and offer incentives for reducing them. Others distribute clear, written policies on ethical behavior that are signed by all personnel, including owners and senior management. For example, Target Stores enrolls store managers in problem outlets in a Stock Shortage Institute. Neiman-Marcus shows employees a film containing interviews with convicted shoplifters in prison to demonstrate the seriousness of the problem.
- More retailers are now likely to fire employees and prosecute shoplifters involved with theft. Courts are imposing stiffer penalties; and in some areas, store detectives are empowered by local police to make arrests. In 43 states, there are civil restitution laws, whereby shoplifters must pay for stolen merchandise or face arrests and criminal trials. In most states, fines are higher if goods are not returned or they are damaged. Shoplifters must also contribute to court costs. By imposing its own fines, Jack Eckerd (the drugstore chain) saves time and imme-

[28] "Ernst & Young's Fourteenth Annual Survey of Retail Loss Prevention Expenses and Trends," *Chain Store Age Executive* (January 1993), p. 4; Terry Considine Williams, "Supermarkets Wage Hi-Tech War on Theft," *New York Times* (December 26, 1993), Section 13, pp. 1, 4–5; and Diane Filipowski, "For Millions of Employees, Crime Does Pay," *Personnel Journal* (April 1993), p. 49.

[29] See "The National Shopping Center Security Report," *Chain Store Age Executive* (May 1993), pp. 84–113; Gary Robins, "EAS: What to Look For," *Stores* (March 1993), pp. 29–30; Junda Woo, "Most States Now Have Laws Permitting Stores to Impose Civil Fines on Shoplifters," *Wall Street Journal* (September 9, 1992), pp. B1, B8; Jack Hayes, "The Question Still Remains: Is Employee Theft Declining?" *Discount Store News* (April 5, 1993), p. 19; and Scott Dawson, "Consumer Responses to Electronic Article Surveillance Alarms," *Journal of Retailing*, Vol. 69 (Fall 1993), pp. 353–362.

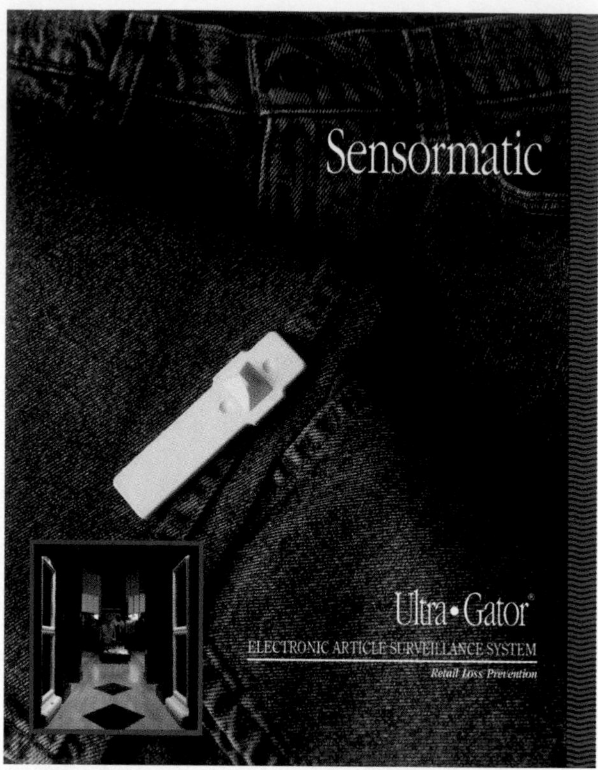

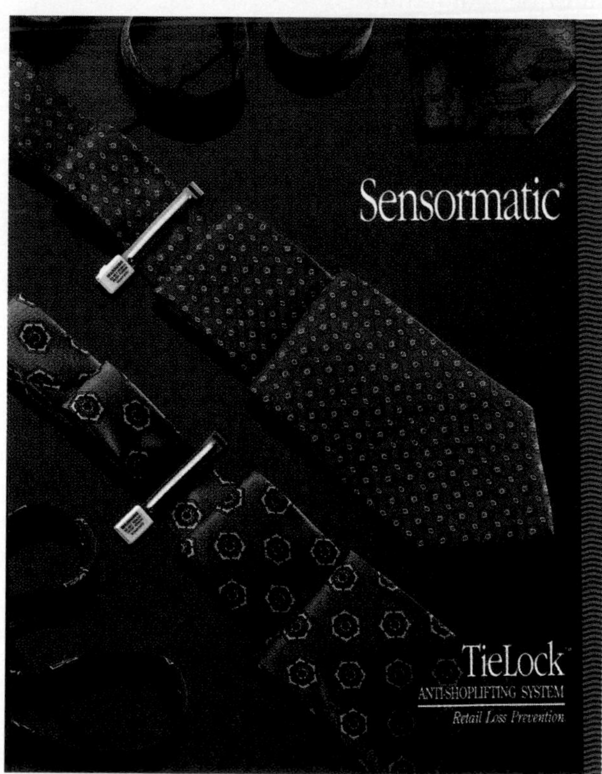

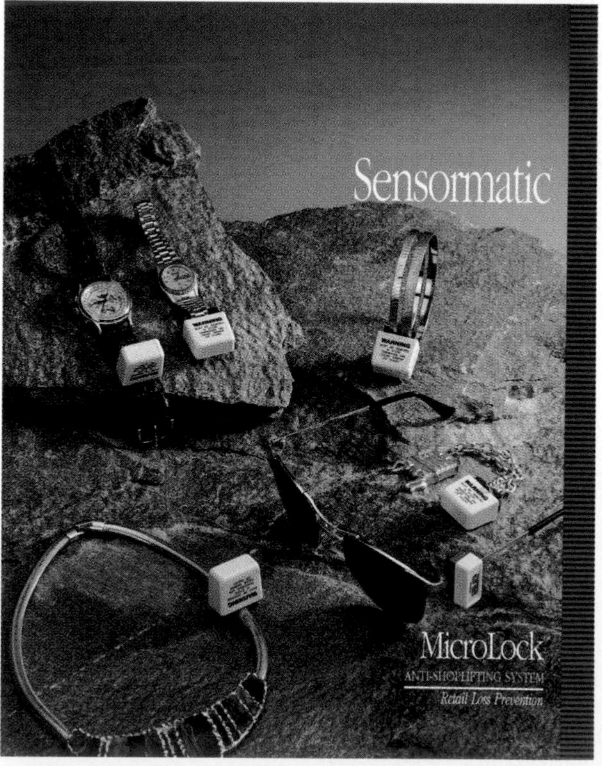

FIGURE 12–4 Using Electronic and Nonelectronic Product Tags to Reduce Losses Due to Theft
The top two photos show electronic product tags. If these tags are not removed at the checkout counter, an alarm would be set off when a person goes through a specially equipped store exit. The bottom two photos show nonelectronic product tags. If these tags are not removed at the checkout counter, the products would be almost unusable because the tags could not be detached without special tools.
Reprinted by permission of Sensormatic Electronics Corporation.

diately gets its merchandise back, rather than handing goods to police for evidence. In a recent three-year period, Eckerd took in $700,000 to $1 million per year with its fines.

Figure 12–5 presents a detailed list of the tactics that retailers can use to combat employee and shopper theft, by far the leading causes of losses.

A. Employee Theft

- Using pencil-and-paper honesty tests, voice stress analysis, and psychological tests as employee screening devices.
- Developing a system of locking up trash to prevent merchandise from being thrown out and then retrieved.
- Verifying through use of undercover personnel whether all sales are rung up.
- Utilizing cameras and mirrors to monitor activities.
- Implementing central control of all exterior doors to monitor opening and closing.
- Properly identifying deliverypeople.
- Verifying receipts and goods taken out.
- Sealing all trucks after they are loaded with goods.
- Inspecting worker packages, tool boxes, lunch boxes.
- Dividing responsibilities (e.g., having one employee record sales; another making deposits).
- Giving rewards for spotting thefts.
- Having training programs.
- Vigorously investigating all known losses.
- Firing offenders immediately.

B. Shopper Theft While Store Is Open

- Using in-store detectives or uniformed guards.
- Prosecuting all individuals charged with theft.
- Using electronic article surveillance wafers, electromagnets, or stick-ons for high-value and theft-prone goods.
- Developing comprehensive employee training programs.
- Providing employee bonuses based upon overall reduction in shortages or based on value of recovered merchandise.
- Inspecting all packages brought into store.
- Utilizing self-closing/self-locking showcases for high-value items such as jewelry.
- Chaining down expensive samples, such as high-fidelity equipment, to fixtures.
- Placing goods with high value/small size in locked showcases.
- Attaching expensive clothing together.
- Alternating the direction of hangers on clothing near doors.
- Limiting the dollar value and quantity of merchandise displayed near exits.
- Limiting the number of entrances and exits to the store.
- Utilizing cameras and mirrors to increase visibility, especially in low-traffic areas.
- Using two-way mirrors where appropriate.

C. Employee/Shopper Theft While Store Is Closed

- Conducting thorough check of the building at night to make sure no one is left in store.
- Locking all exits, even fire exits, at night.
- Utilizing ultrasonic/infrared detectors, burglar alarm traps, or guards with dogs when store is closed.
- Placing valuables in safe.
- Using shatterproof glass and/or iron gates on display windows to prevent break-ins.
- Making sure exterior lighting is adequate when store is closed.
- Periodically testing burglar alarms.

FIGURE 12–5
Ways Retailers Can Deter Employee and Shopper Theft

When developing and implementing a store security plan, a retailer must assess the impact of such a plan on employee morale, shopper comfort, and vendor relations. For example, J.C. Penney has been reluctant to offer rewards for employees to report co-workers involved in theft: "We want employees to pay attention to selling—not have them watching each other or wondering if someone's looking over their shoulder."[30] Likewise, by setting overly strict rules for fitting rooms (like severely limiting the number of garments to be brought in at one time) and/or placing chains on expensive furs and suede coats, a retailer may cause some people to try on and buy less clothing.

INSURANCE

In retail operations, the purchase of insurance that covers the firm in case of losses due to fire, customer lawsuits regarding on-premises accidents, and other causes must be carefully planned. Among the types of such insurance bought by retailers are workers' compensation, public liability, product liability, property, and directors' and officers' liability. In addition, many retailers offer some type of health insurance option to their full-time employees; sometimes, the retailers pay the entire premiums, other times, employees pay part or all of the premiums.

Insurance decisions are important for several reasons. First, over the past decade, premiums have risen dramatically—in some cases, doubling. Second, insurers have been reducing the scope of their coverage. Many now require higher deductibles before paying claims and/or will not provide coverage on all aspects of operations (such as the professional liability of pharmacists). Third, there are fewer insurance carriers servicing retailers today than a decade ago; this limits the choices of retailers.

As a result, a number of retailers have embarked on costly programs aimed at lessening their vulnerability to employee and customer claims due to dangerous or unsafe conditions and at holding down insurance premiums:

> They entail installing no-slip floors, carpeting, and rubber mats at entrances; frequent mopping and inspection of wet floors; training fixture designers to design risk-free fixtures; conducting frequent elevator and escalator maintenance checks; conducting fire drills; designing and constructing fire resistant stores, warehouses, and distribution centers; building separate structures to warehouse aerosols; implementing employee training programs; and documenting that proper maintenance has been done, in the event of legal action. The list is as long as a retailer—or its insurance company—wants to make it.[31]

CREDIT MANAGEMENT

Credit management involves the policies and practices retailers follow in receiving payments from their customers. These are some major operational decisions that must be made:

- What form of payment is acceptable? A retailer may accept cash only; cash and personal checks; cash and credit card(s); or all of these.
- Who administers the credit plan? The firm can have its own credit system and/or accept major credit cards (such as Visa, MasterCard, American Express, and Discover).
- What are customer eligibility requirements to make a check or credit purchase? For a check purchase, identification such as a driver's license might be sufficient. For a credit purchase, a new customer would have to satisfy requirements

[30] David J. Solomon, "Hotlines and Hefty Rewards: Retailers Step Up Efforts to Curb Employee Theft," *Wall Street Journal* (September 17, 1987), p. 37.

[31] Holly Klokis, "A Bad Break for Retailers," *Chain Store Age Executive* (June 1986), p. 16; and "Slip/Fall Liability for Upscale Retailer," *Chain Store Age Executive* (November 1992), p. 112.

regarding age, employment, annual income, and so on; and an existing customer would be evaluated in terms of his or her outstanding balance and credit limit. A minimum purchase amount may also be specified before a credit transaction is allowed.

- What are the tradeoffs between the cost of credit and the increased profits generated by credit sales?
- What credit terms will be used? A retailer using its own plan needs to determine when interest charges will begin, what the rate of interest would be, and minimum monthly payments.
- How will late payments or nonpayments be handled? Some retailers that have their own credit plans rely on outside collection agencies to follow up on past-due accounts.

In credit management, a retailer generally needs to balance the ability of credit to generate additional revenues against the cost of processing credit payments. The latter can include screening, transaction, and collection costs, as well as bad debts. If a firm completes all credit functions itself, it will incur these costs; if outside credit arrangements (e.g., Visa) are used, that firm covers the costs via its payments to the credit organization.

According to one recent study, the average sales transaction involving payment by check is 80 per cent higher than one involving payment by cash; and the average sales transaction involving payment by credit card is more than double the amount involving payment by cash. Forty-five per cent of all retail transactions and 29 per cent of all revenues entail cash payments, 26 per cent of transactions and 30 per cent of revenues entail check payments, and 29 per cent of transactions and 41 per cent of revenues entail credit-card payments. Among the retailers that accept credit-card payments, about one-third have their own company card, 95 per cent accept MasterCard and/or Visa, 80 per cent accept Discover, and 65 per cent accept American Express. Most handle two or more cards.[32]

Credit-card fees paid by retailers generally range from 1.5 per cent to 3.5 per cent of sales for Visa, MasterCard, and Discover—depending mostly on the retailer's credit volume. American Express charges 2.5 to 3.5 per cent of sales. MasterCard, Visa, and Discover also have transaction fees of 5 to 25 cents per charge and monthly statement fees of $5 to $25. American Express' rates include these fees. In contrast, the costs of retailers' own credit operations as a per cent of credit sales are 2.0 per cent.[33]

Many supermarkets, gas stations, and drugstores—among others—have begun to place greater emphasis on some form of ***debit transfer system***, whereby the purchase price of a good or service is automatically and immediately deducted from a consumer's bank account and entered into a retailer's account by using an appropriate computer terminal. The retailer's risk of nonpayment is eliminated and its costs are reduced with debit rather than credit transactions. For traditional credit cards, end-of-month billing is employed (with no interest charges if payments are made promptly); with debit cards, monetary account transfers are made at the time of the purchase—delayed billing carries interest charges from the day an item is bought.

There has been, and will continue to be, some resistance to debit transactions by consumers who like the delayed-payment benefit of conventional credit cards. Some people may also dislike debit cards because of privacy or security issues (such as: Can a retailer look at a customer's bank balance? Can a retail clerk gain access to a cus-

[32] Arthur Andersen, "The Fourth Annual Survey of Retail Credit Trends," *Chain Store Age Executive* (January 1994), Section Two.

[33] Ibid.; and Timothy L. O'Brien, "Merchants' Ire Flares Over Fees on Credit Cards," *Wall Street Journal* (October 11, 1993), pp. B1–B2.

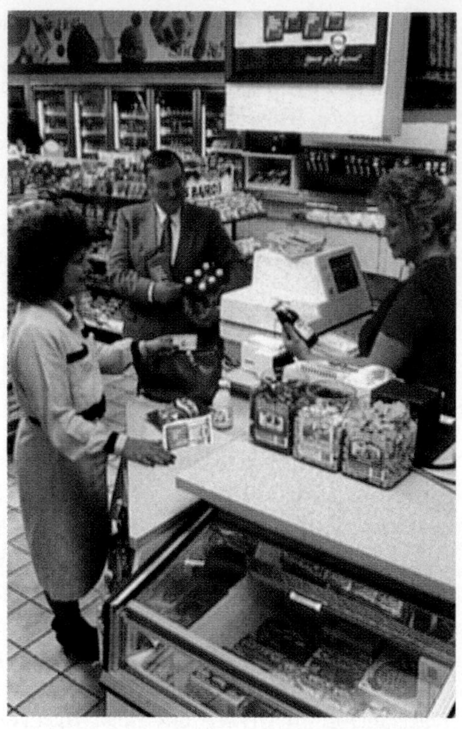

FIGURE 12–6
The Value of Computerized Checkouts
Because of continuing technological advances (and the associated cuts in the prices of equipment), even the smallest stores are now able to computerize their operations, thus making them more efficient and responsive to consumers. Shown here is a Fina convenience store, which has a relatively inexpensive (but fully functional) computer terminal and the ability to electronically process credit-card transactions.
Reprinted by permission of American Petrofina.

tomer's checking account by learning the person's access code?). According to the *Nilson Report*, a major news and advisory service for credit/debit card executives, at present, only 0.6 per cent of retail store sales involve debit-card transactions. However, the number is expected to exceed 2 per cent by 2000.[34]

Regardless of the payment plan adopted, it is imperative for a retailer to communicate all policies clearly to both employees and customers. Credit is discussed further in Chapter 16 in the section on customer services.

COMPUTERIZATION

Many retailers are improving operations productivity via computerization. And with the declining prices of computer systems and related software, even more firms will do so in the near future. In this section, computerized checkouts and electronic point-of-sale systems, other operations applications, and several specific examples of computerized operations are presented.

The ***computerized checkout*** is used by many types of retailers (large and small), so these firms are able to efficiently process transactions and maintain strict control over inventory. As noted in Chapter 7, retailers will increasingly rely on UPC-based systems, whereby cashiers manually ring up sales or pass items over or past optical scanners. Computerized registers instantly record and display sales, customers are given detailed receipts, and all inventory data are stored in the computer's memory bank. See Figure 12–6.

This type of checkout lowers costs by reducing transaction time, employee training, misrings, and the need for price markings on items. In addition, retailers can increase their productivity because of better inventory control, reduced spoilage, and improved ordering. Firms are also able to get in-depth data on an item-by-item basis—which aids in determining store layout and merchandise plans, establishing the amount of shelf-space per item, and automatically replenishing inventory.

There are two potential problems facing retailers using computerized checkouts. First, UPC-based systems will not reach peak efficiency until all manufacturers attach

[34] Gary Levin, "Debit Cards Receive Bigger Push," *Advertising Age* (June 28, 1993), p. 18.

UPC labels to their merchandise; otherwise, retailers must incur labeling costs. Second, because UPC symbols are unreadable by humans, some states have enacted laws making price labeling on individual packages mandatory; some others are considering such legislation. This lessens the labor savings of retailers that would like to post only shelf prices, rather than enter prices on all individual items.

There have been a number of recent technological developments related to computerized checkouts. These include wireless scanners that let workers scan heavy items without having to pick them up, radio frequency identification tags (RFID) which emit a unique radio frequency code when placed near an appropriate transmitter receiver (this is faster than UPC codes and more appropriate for harsh climates), and speech recognition (that can tally up an order for one hamburger and a diet Coke, for example, on the basis of a clerk's verbal order).[35]

Many retailers are and will be expanding beyond the computerized checkout to an ***electronic point-of-sale system***, which performs all the tasks of a computerized checkout and also verifies check and charge transactions, provides instantaneous sales reports, monitors and changes prices, sends intra- and interstore messages, evaluates personnel and profitability, and stores information. In most cases, a point-of-sale system would be used in conjunction with a firm's retail information system. The terminals in the electronic point-of-sale system can either stand alone (the "intelligent" type) or be integrated with an in-store minicomputer or a headquarters mainframe. In any case, keyboards, printers, scanners, wands, and screens can be used as needed by the retailer.

Among the other basic ways in which retailers are using computers in their operations are these:

- To train, schedule, and compensate personnel.
- To coordinate inventory orders and handling.
- To reduce checkout time and cashier misrings.
- To communicate with suppliers.
- To obtain current information.
- To preserve and retrieve credit records.
- To generate and maintain mailing lists.
- To allocate shelf space and advertising expenditures.
- To analyze performance.

Here are several examples of how particular retailers are computerizing so as to improve operations:

- Elliott's Ace Hardware, a chain in Milwaukee, Wisconsin, has automated payroll processing for its 275 workers. Previously, the firm used mechanical time clocks and punch cards. Besides being labor intensive, the old system was error prone; and because each bookkeeper interpreted the firm's policies differently, workers in the same job category could be paid differently. The new Atlas time-management system is PC-based. It can track up to 12 wage rates and 18 job categories. In addition, the system is able to generate the reports required by the Wisconsin Labor Department. And workers who used to be involved in payroll have been shifted to the sales floor. As the firm's vice-president says, "It just makes sense to have employees spend more time helping customers and less time on tedious duties.[36]

[35] See Gary Robins, "Auto ID Technologies: An Update," *Stores* (May 1993), pp. 54–57; and Gary Robins, "Wireless POS Systems," *Stores* (February 1994), pp. 47–48.

[36] "Mom and Pop Goes Modern," *Chain Store Age Executive* (February 1993), pp. 60, 62.

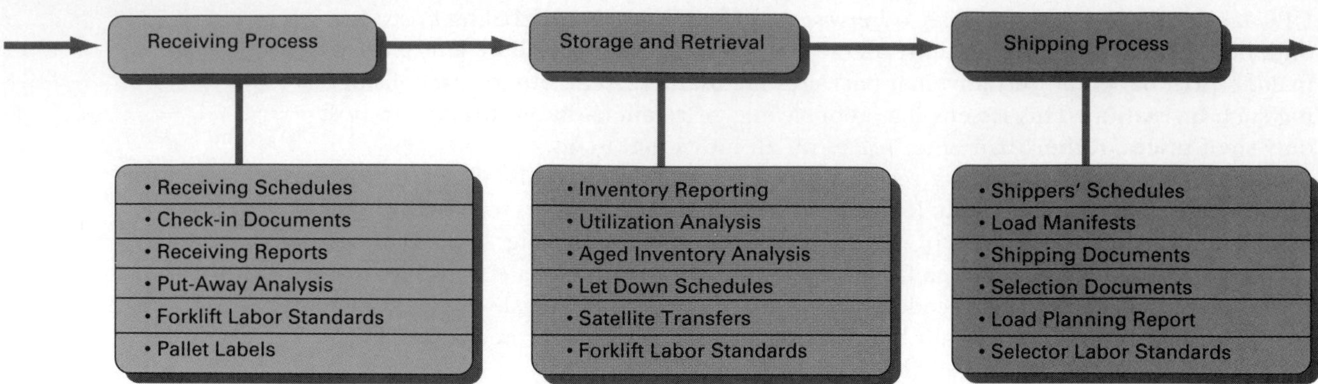

FIGURE 12–7 Hannaford's Distribution Center Management and Control System
Source: "DCMCS—Distribution Center Management and Control System," *Chain Store Age Executive* (April 1990), p. 56. Reprinted by permission. Copyright Lebhar-Friedman, Inc., 425 Park Avenue, New York, NY 10022.

- Sears Apparel System (SAMS) is utilized to forecast sales for single stores and for groups of stores and to develop performance reports at the item, color, size, price, and vendor levels. SAMS can make adjustments to account for the impact of planned markdowns; it can also adjust forecasts based upon an item's current inventory status. According to Sears' national director of logistics for soft lines, SAMS has been instrumental in the firm's efforts to stock the right apparel at the right price and to ensure that each store has the proper product mix.[37]
- The Hannaford supermarket chain uses sophisticated computer software to manage its distribution centers. One software package is the Distribution Center Management and Control System (DCMCS) developed by Dallas Systems. DCMCS is a warehouse inventory control package used on an IBM 9370 computer: "Because everything is tracked so carefully, the system can go beyond telling us that we have 400 cases of Campbell's tomato soup in a warehouse. It can tell us that we have 50 cases in one location, 50 in another, and 300 in a satellite location across town. It tracks sales, predicts future sales, and recommends what product should be transferred from satellite warehouses to the main distribution center to be more accessible."[38] Figure 12–7 highlights the DCMCS used by Hannaford.
- Montgomery Ward has shifted its architectural operations completely over to Computer Aided Design (CAD), including even rough sketches. CAD projects include both new-store planning and the remodeling of some of Ward's existing stores. Due to the productivity of CAD, Montgomery Ward can now perform three to four times the number of design projects with the same staff as it did with manual operations. CAD lets Montgomery Ward communicate with local architects via modems (over telephone lines), instead of through the mail. It also enables the retailer to more easily make changes and to see how the revised drawings look. Lastly, the firm benefits from using an existing drawing as a template and then adapting each store to unique zoning or space requirements.[39]
- P.C. Richard and Son, a New York electronics and appliance chain, has installed an Electronic Signature Capture (ESC) terminal throughout the chain. So, in-

[37] "At Sears, SAMS Aids Planning," *Chain Store Age Executive* (October 1993), p. 139.
[38] "Distribution Software Eases Growth Pains," *Chain Store Age Executive* (April 1990), pp. 55–56.
[39] "CAD Dominates at Ward," *Chain Store Age Executive* (July 1993), p. 48.

stead of signing credit-card slips, customers sign their names with a penlike stylus directly on terminal screens; itemized receipts are printed at the terminals for customers and P.C. Richard's copies of the transactions are stored directly on optical disks. The data are digitized and are capable of being retrieved by the firm in a few seconds.[40]

- Federated Department Stores' Sabre Group (not to be confused with American Airlines' Sabre reservation system) services other retailers—for a fee—via the same computerized inventory-management and record-keeping system that is used with Federated's stores. It tracks inventory from the time a purchase order is placed through the delivery and distribution process until a sale is made. R.H. Macy has been a Sabre user since 1990; and in 1993 alone, Macy's paid Federated about $70 million for the service.[41]

Crisis Management

Sometimes, despite their best intentions, retailers may be faced with crisis situations that need to be managed as smoothly as possible. Crises may be brought on by such occurrences as an in-store fire or broken water pipe, bad weather breaking the store's front window, access to a store being partially blocked due to a road widening, a car accident in the parking lot, a burglary, a sudden illness by the owner or a key employee, storms that knock out a retailer's power, unexpectedly high or low consumer demand for a good or service, a sudden increase in a supplier's prices, a natural disaster like a flood or an earthquake, or other factors.[42]

Although crises cannot always be anticipated, and some adverse effects may take place regardless of a retailer's efforts, several general principles should be followed in developing operations management plans. First, contingency plans should be established for as many different types of crisis situations as possible; that is why retailers buy insurance, install backup lighting in anticipation of power failures, and prepare management succession plans in the event of sudden illnesses of key officers. For example, a retailer could have a checklist of steps to follow if there is an in-store fire or a parking-lot accident. Second, essential information should be communicated to all affected parties, like the fire or police department, employees, customers, and the media, when a crisis occurs. Third, there should be cooperation and not conflict among the involved parties. Fourth, responses should be as quick as feasible; indecisiveness may worsen the situation. Fifth, the chain of command for decisions should be clear and the decision maker given adequate authority to act.

As one expert once noted, "Unless we have a means of dealing with crises when they hit, all the dollars and energies spent on operating a retail business can either be quickly wiped out or reduced. We've got to be prepared for whatever comes down the road."[43]

[40] Bruce Fox, "A First for Electronic Signature Capture," *Chain Store Age Executive* (May 1993), p. 151.

[41] Stephanie Strom, "Computerized Record-Keeping for Retailers," *New York Times* (May 20, 1992), p. D6; and Laura Zinn and Philip L. Zweig, "Happy New Year, Macy's—You're Under Attack," *Business Week* (January 17, 1994), p. 32.

[42] See Paul Doocey, "Gone with the Wind," *Stores* (February 1993), pp. 63–66; Michael Garry, "Grace Under Pressure," *Progressive Grocer* (March 1993), pp. 62–63; and Stephen Bennett, "Crisis Management: Making the Best of It," *Progressive Grocer* (March 1992), pp. 50, 53.

[43] "Warning to Mall Managers: Plan Ahead," *Chain Store Age Executive* (May 1987), pp. 64–70.

SUMMARY

1. *To describe the operational scope of operations management* As defined in Chapter 11, operations management involves efficiently and effectively enacting the policies needed to satisfy a retailer's customers, employees, and management. In contrast to Chapter 11, which dealt with the financial aspects of operations management, this chapter covered the operational facets. While running their businesses, retail executives need to make a wide range of operating decisions.
2. *To study several specific aspects of operations management* Store format and size considerations include the use of prototype stores and the size of stores. Firms that operate prototype stores often do so under the aegis of rationalized retailing. Some retailers are emphasizing large, category-killer size stores; others are opening smaller, targeted stores.

   Many firms use a top-down approach to space planning; a number use a bottom-up approach. In micro-merchandising, allocations are responsive to local needs. With category management, product groupings are set up as strategic business units that satisfy consumer needs, while maximizing profits. Among the performance measures for space allocation are sales per linear foot, gross profit per linear foot, return on inventory investment, inventory turnover, days supply, and direct product profitability.

   Personnel utilization activities that could improve productivity range from workload forecasts to job standardization and cross-training. In job standardization, the tasks of people with similar positions in different departments are kept rather uniform. In cross-training, people learn tasks associated with more than one job. A firm can elevate its personnel flexibility and minimize the total number of workers needed at any given time via job standardization and cross-training.

   Store maintenance includes all of the activities involved in managing the retailer's physical facilities. The quality of store maintenance influences people's perceptions of the retailer, the life span of facilities, and operating expenses.

   Energy management is a major operational concern for many retailers. For firms with special needs, energy management is crucial. To better control energy resources, retailers are doing everything from using better-quality insulation materials when building and renovating stores to substituting high-efficiency bulbs and fluorescent ballasts for traditional lighting.

   With inventory management, retailers strive to acquire and maintain proper merchandise assortments while ordering, shipping, handling, and other related costs are kept in check. To improve performance, many retailers are now involved with quick response inventory planning—whereby they reduce the amount of inventory they keep on hand by ordering more often and in lower quantity. A QR system works best if used in conjunction with floor-ready merchandise, lower minimum order sizes, newly formatted store fixtures, and electronic data interchange. Some retailers are more actively involved with logistics—the total process of moving goods from a manufacturer to a customer in the most timely and cost-efficient manner possible. A number of supermarkets are trying to apply their own form of logistics management, known as efficient consumer response (ECR).

   Store security techniques are needed to prevent the inventory shrinkage caused by employee theft, customer shoplifting, and vendor theft. To reduce theft, loss prevention should be considered as stores are designed and built; a combination of security measures should be enacted, like employee background checks and electronic security systems; and firms must communicate the importance of loss prevention to employees, customers, and vendors, as well as the actions they will take to reduce losses.

   Insurance covers the retailer against losses arising from fire, customer lawsuits, and other causes. Among the types of insurance that retailers buy are workers' compensation, public liability, product liability, property, and directors' and officers' liability. In addition, many firms offer some type of health insurance option.

   Credit management pertains to the policies and practices that retailers follow in receiving payments from customers. In general, credit and check payments mean larger transactions than cash payments. Forty-five per cent of retail transactions entail cash, 26 per cent checks, and 29 per cent credit cards. Some retailers are placing greater emphasis on debit transfers, whereby purchase prices are automatically and immediately deducted from consumer bank accounts and entered into retailer accounts by using appropriate computer terminals.

   With the declining prices of computer systems and related software, more and more retailers are computerizing elements of operations. Computerized checkouts and electronic point-of-sale systems are especially helpful. Electronic point-of-sale systems perform all the tasks of computerized checkouts—and also verify check and charge transactions, provide instant sales reports, monitor and change prices, send intra- and interstore messages, evaluate personnel and profitability, and store data.

   Crisis management is needed to handle unexpected situations as smoothly as possible. There should be contingency plans; key information should be communicated to all affected parties; there should be cooperation among the involved parties; responses should be as quick as feasible; and the chain of command for decisions should be clear.

KEY TERMS

prototype stores (p. 394)
rationalized retailing (p. 395)
top-down approach to space management (p. 396)
bottom-up approach to space management (p. 396)
micro-merchandising (p. 396)
category management (p. 396)
sales per linear foot of shelf space (p. 396)
gross profit per linear foot of shelf space (p. 396)
return on inventory investment (p. 396)
inventory turnover (p. 396)
days supply (p. 396)
direct product profitability (DPP) (p. 396)
job standardization (p. 399)
cross-training (p. 399)
store maintenance (p. 400)
inventory management (p. 402)
quick response (QR) inventory planning (p. 403)
floor-ready merchandise (p. 403)
logistics (p. 404)
efficient consumer response (ECR) (p. 406)
inventory shrinkage (p. 407)
electronic article surveillance (p. 407)
credit management (p. 410)
debit transfer system (p. 411)
computerized checkout (p. 412)
electronic point-of-sale system (p. 413)

QUESTIONS FOR DISCUSSION

1. What are the pros and cons of prototype stores? For which kinds of retailers are they most desirable?
2. Differentiate between micro-merchandising and category management. Give an example of each concept.
3. Discuss Figure 12–1.
4. Why would a retailer be interested in job standardization for its employees? In cross-training?
5. Comment on this statement: "The quality of store maintenance efforts affects consumer perceptions of the retailer, the life span of facilities, and operating expenses."
6. Talk to two local retailers and ask them what they have done to maximize their energy efficiency. Present your findings.
7. Could a small retailer use a quick response inventory system? Why or why not?
8. Describe why floor-ready merchandise, reduced order sizes, and electronic data interchange are important to a quick response inventory system.
9. Differentiate between logistics and inventory management.
10. Would you offer a reward to retail employees who report theft on the part of co-workers? Explain your answer.
11. A mom-and-pop store does not accept checks because of the risks involved. However, it does accept Visa and MasterCard. Evaluate this strategy.
12. As the owner of a local supermarket, how would you persuade customers that they should use debit cards (since you are interested in expanding business, but do not want to accept credit cards)?
13. What potential problems may result if a retailer relies on its computer to implement too many actions (such as employee scheduling or inventory reordering) automatically?
14. Outline contingency plans a retailer could have in the event each of these occurs:
    a. An in-store fire.
    b. A hurricane.
    c. A manufacturer's product recall.
    d. The bankruptcy of a key supplier.

CASE 1

Category Management: Soft Drink Sales and Profitability*

Marsh Supermarkets, the Indianapolis-based supermarket chain, recently conducted a major consumer behavior study. (This study was also the subject of Case 1 in Chapter 7.) In the first phase of the study, Marsh recorded all transactions in five of its supermarkets using point-of-sale equipment that was equipped with scanners. These data were utilized to analyze sales, profit, and productivity relationships. In the second phase of the study, the in-store behavior of 1,600 shoppers was carefully tracked in two test stores over a three-week period. The second phase was used to learn how many shoppers use lists, where shoppers go in the store, how many shoppers talk with employees, and how long typical shoppers spend in a supermarket.

This case describes the aspects of the Marsh study that pertain to soft drink sales and profitability. Besides tracking transactions, Marsh executives reviewed the profitability of soft drinks by employing such measures as gross margins, gross margin return per dollar of inventory investment, and direct product profitability (gross margin minus handling costs).

For soft drinks, Marsh keeps an average of 4.5 days of inventory on shelves. Thus, with an annual turnover rate of 80.6 times, soft drinks are the fastest-selling items in the grocery department. The second-fastest-selling item—bread—has a turnover rate of 66.7 times; and the third-fastest-selling item—cereal—has a turnover rate of 35.5 times.

At the two Marsh supermarkets in the study, only produce, meat, deli, and paper products are purchased more frequently than soft drinks. And research by the International Coffee Organization indicates that soft drinks have had the highest usage rate of any beverage since 1985. Prior to 1985, coffee had a higher consumption rate. Products with high purchase frequencies are often heavily promoted by supermarkets as a means of generating customer traffic and building store loyalty.

Table 1 reveals the relationship between gross margin and direct product profitability (DPP) for soft drinks, using 1992 data supplied by Marsh. As the table shows, the Marsh stores had weekly soft drink sales of $10,003.92, which represented 3.3 per cent of total store sales. This jibes with the national average reported in *Progressive Grocer's Supermarket Sales Manual.*

The table shows that raw-data calculations can be very misleading in that they do not reflect key adjustments. In this case, the raw data indicate that soft drinks lost money, when, in fact, they were quite profitable. Thus, to be more accurate in their analysis, Marsh executives adjusted the raw data to reflect the special incentives provided by soft drink vendors. These included cooperative advertising allowances, special pricing allowances, slotting fees (payments for shelf space for new products), and other special offers. The combined effect of these adjustments was to increase the raw gross margin from 3.11 per cent to an adjusted gross margin of 13.48 per cent.

Cost data were analyzed by Marsh's operations research department for such functions as warehousing, store transportation, labor, occupancy, inventory, and other store costs. These expenses were then subtracted from the gross margin on soft drinks to yield their direct product profitability. Therefore, in 1992, the raw direct product profitability for soft drinks was −2.94 per cent and the adjusted direct product profitability was 7.43 per cent. This represented −$0.04 and $0.11 DPP per unit, respectively (with an average selling price per unit of $1.48).

The expenses for handling soft drinks were low (6.05 per cent of sales) because 90 per cent of all soft drinks were delivered directly to the store by the bottler. In comparison, items that are first delivered to a supermarket's distribution center have

* The material in this case is drawn from Stephen Bennett, "Putting Soft Drinks to Work," *Progressive Grocer* (February 1993), pp. 89, 92; and Walter H. Heller, "Profitability: Where It's Really At," *Progressive Grocer* (December 1992), pp. 26–31.

Table 1 Marsh's 1992 Profitability Data on Soft Drinks

	Raw Data	Adjusted Data
Weekly dollar sales	$10,003.92	$10,003.92
Weekly gross margin dollars	$ 311.03	$ 1,349.75
Per cent gross margin[a]	3.11	13.48
Gross margin dollars per unit[b]	$ 0.05	$ 0.20
Per cent DPP[c]	−2.94	7.43
Weekly DPP dollars[d]	$ −294.48	$ 744.24
DPP dollars per unit[e]	$ −0.04	$ 0.11

[a] Gross margin = (Sales − Cost of goods sold)/Sales. Adjusted gross margin reflects special incentives such as advertising and pricing allowances.
[b] Assumes an average unit selling price of $1.48.
[c] Per cent DPP = Per cent gross margin − handling costs. For both raw data and adjusted data, handling costs were 6.05 per cent of sales.
[d] Weekly DPP dollars = Per cent DPP × Weekly dollar sales.
[e] DPP dollars per unit = Per cent DPP × $1.48.
Source: Data from "The Profit Iceberg," *Progressive Grocer* (December 1992), p. 28.

higher handling costs to reflect that supermarket's warehousing costs, transportation expenses from the distribution center to the store, and labor costs for stocking shelves.

The per-dollar return on inventory investment for soft drinks is the second-highest among all grocery items. This is due to the high turnover of soft drinks—so high that soft drinks can be sold as many as three to five times before the retailer has to pay for the drinks. Thus, soft drinks add materially to retailers' cash flow.

Retailers can further increase soft-drink profitability via promotions. According to data from Marsh, sales of soft drinks rose an average of 41.7 per cent when there were special consumer promotions. The biggest increase was 397 per cent—the result of a combination of a price discount, advertising, and displays. Therefore, Marsh is more frequently featuring 24-packs due to their increased visibility of the display and the higher purchase amount.

QUESTIONS

1. Why should retailers be careful when examining raw data?
2. How could Marsh improve its soft-drink performance? Be sure to comment on Table 1 in your answer.
3. What other measures of sales and profit performance could Marsh use?
4. If you owned a supermarket chain, would you allocate the same amount of space for soft drinks in each store? Would you locate the soft-drink department in the same place in each store? Explain your answer.

VIDEO QUESTIONS ON SI FORUM: SOFT DRINK PROFITABILITY

1. What factors must be considered in comparing the profitability of branded and private-label soft drinks?
2. What are the major opportunities for retailers to increase soft-drink sales?

CASE 2

Sensormatic: Pilferage Control†

Sensormatic Electronics, with annual sales exceeding $500 million, has a 70 per cent U.S. market share for anti-pilferage equipment. Its major competitors are Knogo (with a 12 per cent market share) and Checkpoint Systems (with a 9 per cent market share). Sensormatic has an annual research and development budget of $15 million; as a result, three-quarters of its revenues come from products introduced over the past six years. In 1992, Sensormatic acquired ALP, Europe's largest distributor of anti-shoplifting equipment.

Although Sensormatic makes a variety of electronic article surveillance (EAS) products (such as an ink tag that marks the thief and damages stolen goods, sophisticated cameras that monitor stores and warehouses, and unobtrusive labels that can be hidden under a product's regular label), its most popular product is the Ultra-Max system.

The Ultra-Max system uses raised plastic tags that resemble chicklet gum in both size and shape. Unlike other products, Ultra-Max tags can be reactivated if customers return products to the store. Because Ultra-Max tags are clearly visible to the shopper, they are an active deterrent to theft. The Ultra-Max system is based upon acousto-magnetic technology. When an Ultra-Max tag that has not been deactivated enters a magnetic field located near a store's exit, the material inside the tag vibrates. This vibration sets off an alarm. Each Ultra-Max tag costs about six cents.

In contrast, the anti-shoplifting devices made by Checkpoint Systems and other major manufacturers are based on radio frequency technology. Unless these tags are deactivated at the checkout counter, an alarm is set off when the tags pass through an electrical field generated by two panels that are placed near store exits. Checkpoint tags cost 3 to 4 cents each. Unlike Ultra-Max tags, Checkpoint tags can be easily hidden under a product's price tag or inside a carton. These tags cannot be reused if packages are returned.

One of the most important emerging developments in pilferage control is source tagging, whereby manufacturers place anti-theft devices on products before shipment to retailers. At present, most EAS tags are attached to goods by retailers. However, source tagging relieves retailers of the labor expense of placing sensors on each product and increases sales of manufacturers' products. Without source tagging, many retailers would lock up small valuable products in glass cases that need to be opened by sales clerks. Although this practice results in lower pilferage costs, it also reduces revenues for both manufacturers and retailers.

The effectiveness of source tagging was recently proven in a four-month field experiment during which Target (the discount-department store chain) studied the impact of tagging on both sales and pilferage of calculators. One Target store displayed the calculators with a noticeable anti-theft tag in a self-service environment. A second Target store had a similar display, but with no noticeable anti-theft tag. At a third Target store, tagged calculators were placed in a glass case that required a sales clerk equipped with a key to open the display. According to Target's vice-president

† The material in this case is drawn from "Anti-Theft Tag Is Rejected," *New York Times* (November 12, 1993), p. D5; Pan Demetrakakes, "Packaging Can Offer Safety From Theft, Too," *Packaging* (October 1993), p. 25; Peter Nulty, "Sensormatic: Why Not to Kill Your Competitor," *Fortune* (May 3, 1993), pp. 71–72; and *Sensormatic 1993 Annual Report*.

for loss prevention, "in the store where the calculators were tagged and accessible, the sales rate was much greater and shortage was virtually nonexistent. It certainly proved our point to the manufacturer that source tagging will increase both sales and reduce shoplifting."

There are several obstacles to source tagging. One, because different retailers use incompatible anti-pilferage systems, manufacturers would have to ship their products with different pilferage control devices based upon each retailer's installed system. Even if a trade association recommends one system as standard for one type of retailer (such as a drugstore), many products such as batteries, calculators, and film are sold by a wide variety of retailers. Two, while source tagging is particularly effective against customer theft, it is not as effective against employee-based theft. Many employees know how to deactivate the tags and have access to deactivation devices. Three, some retail analysts believe that manufacturers have little motivation to protect their retailers' inventories since high pilferage rates may increase the manufacturers' short-term sales.

Drugstores, home centers, and supermarkets are thinking about adopting a common anti-theft tagging standard, but none currently exists. The National Association of Recording Merchandisers (NARM), which represents music retailers, originally endorsed Sensormatic's Ultra-Max tags for use with cassette tapes, videotapes, and compact discs. But, after further testing by six music distributors, NARM withdrew support: Sensormatic's deactivation process reduced the sound quality of tapes to "an unacceptable degree." Because the liquor industry has moved to adopt a common standard, many manufacturers have begun to insert anti-theft devices under their labels.

Despite the difficulties with source tagging, several products are already being tagged by manufacturers. And industry observers feel that the greatest use for source tagging is with small, high-value items. For example, Johnnie Walker scotch that is sold to Lucky Stores in the Los Angeles area has Checkpoint tags installed under their labels. Film manufactured by 3M for sales in Snyder's drugstores is source tagged with 3M's Quadra tag.

Questions

1. Compare the pros and cons of a retailer's using Ultra-Max tags versus tags produced by Checkpoint Systems.
2. What are the advantages and disadvantages of source tagging versus tagging by retailers?
3. How can the obstacles to source tagging be overcome?
4. How can a specialty store determine the value of source tagging for compact cameras?

Video Questions on Ultra-Max Training Tape

1. Describe the guidelines for installing Sensormatic labels.
2. Develop a procedure for a sales clerk to approach a customer who has set off a store alarm.

PART 5 COMPREHENSIVE CASE

Growth Through Portfolio Retailing*

Introduction

Some retailers are growing robustly, drawing market share from all competitors in their path. Single-business firms—such as Home Depot, a fast-growing chain of home-improvement warehouse stores, and The Container Store, a small chain selling household storage and organization products—are among the winners. Other retailers are growing rapidly with multibusiness strategies. Examples include Toys "R" Us, which developed the Kids "R" Us apparel chain, and The Limited, Inc., which operates jewels such as Express and Victoria's Secret.

The idea of building a portfolio of retail businesses is not new. Indeed, diversification seems to be losing cachet, with the proportion of highly diversified U.S. corporations declining markedly in the 1980s. Yet, portfolio retailing is not just assembling a collection of firms: it blends the strategy of diversification with the strategy of focus. It is not diversification that is passé, but unfocused diversification. Focused diversification is an approach that many respected U.S. retailers are using to grow. Portfolio retailing, when executed properly and under the right conditions, lets a retail firm prosper in both troubled and good times.

Focusing on Competencies

Portfolio retailers leverage a common set of core competencies across multiple retail concepts targeted to fit the shopping preferences and buying patterns of specific market segments. They are best understood not by their formats—department store, specialty store, catalog, and so on—but by their core competencies, which are their integral capabilities. Core competencies are not resources like capital, facilities, or information systems, but rather the shared intellect that shapes their development.

The leveraging of core competencies provides the focus characteristic of successful portfolio retailers. Various businesses in a portfolio may appear unrelated when, in fact, they require a common set of core capabilities. Circuit City, America's largest home electronics chain, surprised many with its announcement that it planned to enter used-car retailing on a test basis. Yet, its customer-service skills, operating controls, and expertise in selling high-ticket durable goods on credit provide synergies with auto retailing.

There are three tests for identifying core competencies in a firm: They must provide access to various markets, contribute significantly to perceived customer benefits, and be hard for competitors to imitate. Core competencies are hard to imitate because they are intellectual or service activities. The more dispersed the critical knowledge and skills are in a firm, the harder it is for competitors to imitate them. Competitors may duplicate Wal-Mart's use of "people greeters," but few can match the efficiencies of its cutting-edge inventory management and distribution system. The former is one idea; the latter is the product of many ideas from many people.

Toys "R" Us, in operating its Kids "R" Us stores, passes the three tests. The large, clean, colorful stores—specializing in children's apparel and linked to the famous toy store—offer visible price and assortment benefits. Toys "R" Us' expertise in running supermarket-like stores gives it access to a children's clothing market via similarly-run stores. Toys "R" Us' knowledge of large-store operations, its vendor credibility and purchasing power, and its prowess in inventory management make competitive imitation difficult.

Portfolio retailers use their core competencies to meet customer demand innovatively. They are oriented toward satisfying customer preferences rather than to sustaining a particular retail concept. They test new retail concepts aggressively, push strong concepts hard, and reinvent or jettison faltering concepts. Internal response to external change is a constant.

In portfolio retailing, timing is critical—knowing when to push a new concept and when to redesign or let go of an existing one. Thus, America's best portfolio retailers are masters of using information technology to listen to the market. Executives know immediately what is selling and what is not, who is buying and who is not, and which concepts are working and which aren't.

Portfolio Retailing: Not for Everyone

Many retailers have no core competencies, no specific knowledge or skills that offer market access. These firms must first develop competencies to support their established business before diverting resources into new ones. Spreading mediocrity from one retail concept to multiple ones rarely makes sense.

Multiple concepts may also not make sense for a firm with a strong retail concept, limited geographic coverage, and modest growth resources. A Pea in the Pod, which sells fashionable maternity clothes for the profes-

* The material in this case was adapted by the authors from Leonard L. Berry and Kathleen Seiders, both of Texas A&M University, "Growing Through Portfolio Retailing," *Marketing Management*, Vol. 2 (Number 3, 1993), pp. 9–20. Reprinted by permission of the American Marketing Association.

sional woman, has about 40 stores in 19 cities. It has a small management staff, strong quality control, and many more geographic markets to enter. Multiple retail concepts would be an unneeded diversion of management attention and resources.

Dominant regional firms that excel with a specific type of business may choose to grow via geographic expansion rather than by adding other concepts. Dillard's, with state-of-the-art operating systems and controls, has achieved strong growth by acquiring mediocre local chains and turning them into solid performers. Dillard's may eventually diversify, but for now, it seems unnecessary and—from a resources standpoint—unwise.

Walgreen, the leading U.S. drugstore chain, is a classic example of a firm that is far stronger as a single-business retailer than as a diversifier. In the 1960s, it acquired department stores, supermarkets, and fast-food chains, among other businesses, only to divest them during the 1980s to concentrate on its original drugstore business. Between 1970 and 1980, with its potpourri of businesses, Walgreen opened only 100 new drugstores. In a five-year period spanning the late 1980s and early 1990s, Walgreen opened or remodeled 1,230 drugstores. It also has invested heavily in pharmacy computerization.

Walgreen's diversification efforts stretched management and financial resources. The various businesses made money but were not integrated. Walgreen could not transfer its competencies in drugstore operations to the other businesses; at the same time, the firm's drugstore growth was stunted. As Walgreen President Daniel Jorndt once remarked, "How much can you have on your plate at one time and still manage it well? During the 1980s, nearly 90 per cent of our stores were either opened or remodeled. That money would not have been there if we hadn't 'cut bait' on some of our other operations."

Portfolio retailing makes the most sense for those with a mature and possibly vulnerable base business, ample management and financial resources to add new businesses, and competencies that can be transferred synergistically to related businesses. Firms that need new growth opportunities, and have the wherewithal to seize them, are the best candidates for portfolio retailing.

With these criteria in mind, Circuit City's test entry into used-car retailing seems less extreme. Circuit City is a mature chain in a fiercely price-competitive business. It has management and financial resources. It is known for customer service and operating controls. Electronic durables and autos have some parallels. And the used-car business is fragmented among thousands of retailers, many small and lacking Circuit City's capabilities.

Notable Examples

Two firms demonstrating portfolio retailing's potential are Spiegel and Woolworth. We interviewed senior officials at these companies and studied management presentations and writings, publicly available financial reports, and literature to develop profiles of their diversification strategies.

More Than a Catalog Company

"One big idea is no longer enough," according to John Shea, chairman of Spiegel Inc. "We need continuing ideas. Spiegel's one big idea was to mail a big catalog, an idea that sustained us for 70 years. I try not to use the expression 'mail order' anymore. We are in the merchandise distribution business and have to be open to all ways of doing it."

Founded in 1865, Spiegel is America's largest direct marketer. Besides its 500-page semiannual "Big Book" offering a "department store in private," the company distributes dozens of specialty catalogs.

During the 1980s, increasingly difficult conditions in the catalog sector stimulated Spiegel to diversify. More than 4,000 new catalog firms entered the business, yet catalog share of total retail sales did not increase during the late 1980s and early 1990s. Moreover, catalog operating costs climbed sharply, primarily from increased postal and shipping rates. Spiegel sought to offset those market conditions via a portfolio strategy. Spiegel operates today in both specialty-store retailing and mail order with varied concepts.

In 1988, it bought Eddie Bauer, a Seattle-based sportswear and casual apparel retailer. Spiegel accelerated expansion of both the store and catalog divisions of Eddie Bauer, increasing retail locations from 80 in 1988 to 266 in 1992—and raising Bauer's total sales from $200 million to $800+ million.

Eddie Bauer, in turn, introduced two new store concepts in 1991: Home Collection, with Northwest-style home furnishings, and All Week Long, with women's sportswear and special occasion attire. Both store concepts convey an image of craftsmanship and product quality consistent with the Eddie Bauer tradition. Store interiors feature hardwoods to convey a naturalistic ambience to upscale customers. By year-end 1992, Eddie Bauer had 11 Home Collection stores and 6 All Week Long stores.

Spiegel gets catalog ideas from its stores and store ideas from its catalogs. With one-half of its customer base having children at home, the firm opened children's apparel test stores, Crayola Kids, in 1991. Crayola Kids products were then featured in several catalogs. Another concept, For You from Spiegel—size 14-and-up women's apparel—had a catalog-to-store evolution.

Knowledge of Customers Spiegel's knowledge of its customers—who they are, where they are, what they buy—facilitated by its vast data-base capability, is a core competency. By analyzing sales data, Spiegel segments customers into precise demographic and life-style units.

It uses data to chart the Eddie Bauer expansion and make site-selection decisions. New locations are chosen on the basis of the buying behavior of Eddie Bauer catalog customers living in a given geographic area. In advance of store openings, Eddie Bauer promotional literature and catalogs are sent to Spiegel customers in the area fitting the Bauer shopper profile.

Data-base intelligence supports Spiegel's specialty catalogs, such as the E Style catalog clothing line for the African-American market—a joint venture with Johnson Publications, *Ebony* magazine's publisher. E Style is sent to selected *Ebony* subscribers, as well as to Spiegel customers.

The Spiegel SHOPS catalog offers a collection of 13 specialty concepts in a 300-page format. While Spiegel's Big Book is based on the traditional department store concept, SHOPS is modeled after a specialty shopping mall. Individual "stores" feature merchandise ranging from special-event fashions to workout equipment to bedroom furnishings to electronic games and video.

Powerful Order-Entry System The order-entry system shared by all Spiegel businesses encompasses 69,000 products for 7.6 million active customers. Operators at order centers enter purchasing information directly into the data base. A common system provides flexibility in managing the flow of customer calls, such as diverting calls from Spiegel to Eddie Bauer phone centers during peak shopping periods. Integrating this system with the retail point-of-sale network quickens the pace of merchandising decisions because there is on-line access to inventory transactions. The technological strength extends to Spiegel's distribution: Automated warehouses can process up to 100,000 orders per eight-hour shift.

Spiegel's portfolio is both catalog- and store-based. It has extended the resources and expertise required to operate a first-rate catalog business to the operation of specialty stores. The stores, in turn, promote the catalogs. Management does not view Spiegel as a "catalog company"; instead, the aim is to use market intelligence to reach diverse customers in different ways.

Thousands of Stores

Woolworth operates thousands of stores in 21 countries on four continents. Its variety stores date from 1879, and Woolworth still has a presence in urban America with these outlets. In the mid-1970s, the firm sought renewal via an aggressive portfolio-building strategy in specialty retailing, adding more than 3,600 stores in 40 specialty-store divisions between 1982 and 1991.

Woolworth has developed its specialty businesses in three company-defined categories: footwear/athletic apparel and equipment (e.g., Kinney Shoes, Foot Locker, Champs Sports); apparel (e.g., Kid's Mart, Northern Reflections, Lady Plus); and other specialty (e.g., Afterthoughts, The Rx Place, The Best of Times). Woolworth's portfolio includes both internally developed stores, such as Foot Locker, and acquisitions, such as Kid's Mart.

It is one of America's oldest multinational retailers, having entered Canada in 1897, Great Britain in 1909, and Germany in 1927. Woolworth's 3,000 foreign stores accounted for 43 per cent of its 1992 revenues.

The long-term payoff of this portfolio strategy is evident in the fact that Woolworth doubled its revenue in about 10 years, from $5.1 billion in 1981 to almost $10 billion in 1992. In the United States, about one-half of sales and three-quarters of profits come from the specialty-store businesses. It would be a dying firm today had it remained strictly a variety-store chain.

Short-term, Woolworth's earnings are being affected by weak variety-store sales, poor business conditions in Canada (which produces nearly a quarter of the firm's sales), and a marketwide slowdown in athletic apparel sales.

Woolworth allocates assets according to demand patterns. Its resources are now channeled into specialty retailing because its specialty stores average $360 in sales per square foot and its variety stores average $150. Even within its specialty-retailing business, Woolworth invests dollars where they will do the most good. In 1991, the firm announced the closing or redeployment (into other formats) of 900 underperforming specialty and general merchandise units.

Between 1993 and 2000, Woolworth plans to open 800 specialty stores and close 300 annually, for a net gain of 4,000 stores. These additions will bring the total store count to 13,000 and could raise sales to about $20 billion.

Detecting Consumer Trends Woolworth's ability to identify emerging consumer trends has propelled its specialty businesses. The Foot Locker chain, marketing athletic footwear and apparel in more than 1,700 stores worldwide, has been the growth leader with division sales of approximately $2 billion. When research showed that female customers disliked "intruding" in stores they perceived as male-oriented, Woolworth created Lady Foot Locker in 1982. Kids Foot Locker stores were introduced in 1987. By 1992, the firm had opened 745 Lady Foot Locker stores worldwide and 94 Kids Foot Locker stores in the United States. Because of cooling U.S. sales, Woolworth has shifted recent expansion efforts to Europe, where 1,000 Foot Locker units are projected by the decade's end.

Woolworth opened its first World Foot Locker stores—10,000-square-foot stores for athletic apparel and footwear—in 1992. (A conventional Foot Locker store has 1,300 square feet.) World Foot Locker stores reflect Woolworth's fashion sense: Not only must products be fashion-forward, but the stores must be fashionable too The firm hopes to build 300+ of these superstores by 2000.

Champs Sports is another strong concept benefitting from the popularity of athletic accessories. It sells sporting goods, as well as athletic footwear and apparel—targeting merchandise to young, sports-conscious males. Acquired in 1987 as an 89-store business, 400 Champs stores operated in 41 states at year-end 1992, and Woolworth projects expansion to 700 stores by 1997.

Developing Retail Concepts Woolworth's skill in detecting consumer trends provides ample opportunity to practice another core competency: creating and expanding highly specialized retail concepts. Although the firm's roots are in general merchandise, its experience in developing Foot Locker and other concepts has helped Woolworth branch out into the specialty-store arena.

It constantly develops, tests, and modifies new specialty-retailing concepts. Shopping malls are considered R&D labs, and division management regularly presents ideas for new businesses or acquisitions. When Woolworth adopts a new concept, it opens 2 stores the first year, 10 the second year, and then "explodes it" if early results are promising. Woolworth's real-estate expertise and position of strength with mall developers permit rapid rollout.

In the span of six years (1987–1992), Woolworth took four concepts—Champs Sports, Lady Foot Locker, Afterthoughts (costume jewelry, handbags, and accessories), and Northern Reflections (women's casual sportswear)—from combined revenue of $118 million to more than $1 billion.

Merchandise Management Woolworth's merchandise management is another core competency. Specialty divisions use interactive on-line systems to track sales by product category. Worldwide EDI connects headquarters, regional offices, distribution centers, and stores to major suppliers. Joint forecasting and sales analysis with suppliers such as Reebok and Nike help Woolworth maintain in-stock positions.

Woolworth has changed itself from a variety-store chain to a multiconcept mall retailer. It operates as many as 13 different stores in a given mall. It aggressively seeks new businesses, investing in what works and curtailing what doesn't. It continues to capitalize on athletic footwear while searching for the next "Foot Locker" through market research, trial, error, refinement, and rollout. The firm's portfolio of retail concepts is a protective buffer from slowdown in particular markets, its cash flow spigot for trying new concepts and exploding strong concepts, and its source of redeployment flexibility.

Essentials of Portfolio Retailing

Instead of operating one business well, portfolio retailers must run multiple businesses and know their markets well. They must continue to invest big in the short term to reap long-term gains. They must stay focused on their core competencies, nurturing them, developing them, staying ahead of competitors. They must stay hungry, aggressive, and bold, despite the new-concept failures that will occur, and despite the success, growth, and praise that may occur.

The two firms featured in this case offer insight into the essentials. Spiegel and Woolworth both have exceptional knowledge of the customer; unusual merchandise distribution capability; a culture celebrating innovation; internally generated investment capital; and strong real-estate expertise.

Four of these five essentials are core competencies; the fifth, capital, is a resource. Executives considering portfolio retailing need to carefully consider its benefits and drawbacks in light of these essentials. Does the company possess them? If not, is it prepared to develop them?

Portfolio retailing means aligning investment in retail concepts with customer demand, as well as changing as consumers change. It means becoming a "listening company" through market intelligence activities and information systems that reveal who is buying what and where. Few, if any, retailers have been better at this than Spiegel. Its data bases help managers make decisions such as which section of the big catalog to spin-off into a new specialty catalog, which households should receive the new catalog, where to locate test stores that might be developed from the catalog, and which households will receive direct mail announcing the opening of the test stores.

Although knowing what merchandise to sell and where to sell it is a core competency, it is not enough. The merchandise still must be moved in a timely, cost-effective manner from manufacturer to distribution center to store to customer. Both Spiegel and Woolworth have made, and continue to make, massive investments in infrastructure to move merchandise quickly and inexpensively to selling locations. This "invest now to benefit later" mentality is a must.

Portfolio retailing offers an incentive to invest in distribution because fixed costs can be spread over multiple retail concepts. All of Woolworth's specialty store chains share the same distribution and inventory management infrastructure. Thus, Woolworth typically faces low incremental investment to handle and distribute goods when adding a new retail concept to its portfolio.

A corporate culture that demands innovation and entrepreneurship is a third key in portfolio retailing. Executives who are unwilling to experiment and innovate do not succeed in this culture.

Companies need ample capital to develop, test, and expand retail concepts. Spiegel and Woolworth use internally generated cash flow to fund new concepts. Woolworth's variety stores are past their prime, but they generate cash flow for new concepts. Strong cash flows and balance sheets nurture the long-term perspective needed in building true core competencies. Readily available funds also allow a portfolio retailer to accelerate the growth of a strong concept, as illustrated by Woolworth's expansion of Champs Sports. Woolworth was not even in the sporting-goods business prior to acquiring Champs in 1988. By 1992, Champs was the largest mall-based U.S. sporting-goods chain.

Real-estate expertise is needed to determine where to locate new stores and to acquire retail space. Vigorous rollouts of strong concepts need well conceived real-estate strategies, intimate knowledge of potential store sites, and the expertise and relationships to negotiate attractive deals quickly. For example, Woolworth knows malls. Its executives know where they want to place the stores within the mall. They know the developers with whom they will negotiate. They know how to use the firm's considerable presence as a mall tenant to make a far better deal than almost any other mall tenant.

Implementing Portfolio Retailing

The experiences of Spiegel and Woolworth suggest six guidelines that other retailers can use to develop portfolio retailing strategies.

Build the Base Business First

Portfolio retailers need a healthy base around which to build additional, related businesses. For Spiegel, the base is its catalog. For Woolworth, it is the Foot Locker chains. A solid base provides three crucial "Cs" in portfolio retailing: cash flow to fund newer ventures, credibility with vendors and other suppliers, and confidence within the firm to pursue the ventures.

The base points out the pathways for developing a portfolio by defining the boundaries within which new ventures should fit, by shaping management's overall conceptualization of the firm, and by representing the firm's most advanced exercise of its core competencies. The relative maturity of the base business, combined with newer ventures demanding attention and capital, creates the risk of insufficient support. Ensuring that the base gets the attention and resources it needs is imperative in portfolio retailing.

Focus on Core Competencies

No guideline for portfolio retailing is more important than this. Successful portfolio retailers can attribute much of their success to knowing what they are good at, honing these capabilities over time, and using the competencies as criteria to decide which businesses to add and which to avoid.

This seems simple but is not. Many retailers don't have any competencies, but think they do, rendering focus inconsequential. Others may misjudge their competencies and stress the wrong ones. Some portfolio retailers may have and know their competencies, but be too ambitious and overdiversify.

Portfolio retailers must learn to ask, debate, and answer these questions regularly at the highest management levels:

- What are the specific core competencies we possess?
- How do we know these are true core competencies? What is the proof?
- How can we develop core skills and knowledge further and make it harder for competitors to match them?
- What criteria do our core competencies reveal that can be used to judge all business opportunities?

With approximately 40 specialty-store chains in its portfolio, Woolworth does not appear on the surface to be an example of corporate focus. In fact, Woolworth is so focused that its senior vice-president of corporate planning disdains the term "diversification." He says, "I don't think of it as diversification. I think of it as growth in related businesses."

Woolworth has identified the operation of highly specialized stores as one of its core competencies. Management seeks to develop or acquire concepts that focus on a specific category of merchandise with a high gross margin and can be sold without in-depth product knowledge. Its San Francisco Music Box Company, which sells only music boxes—priced from $10–$3,000—is an example, as is Best of Times, which sells only watches and clocks.

Stress Quality over Quantity

The portfolio's quality, not the quantity of concepts, is what counts.

Mediocre concepts divert attention and resources away from strong ones, so firms must set stringent criteria for new concepts to meet. Financial tests such as ROI projections are important but insufficient; retailers also must establish market-based criteria. Does the concept fill an unmet need in the market? Does it have a reason for being? These criteria are in addition to those for assessing concepts relative to a firm's resources and competencies. One question firms always should ask is, "Do we bring something important to the table?" If the answer is "no," the venture probably isn't worth pursuing.

Among other capabilities, Spiegel brought credit purchases to Eddie Bauer. The fact that Spiegel, via the consumer bank it owns, could offer credit to Eddie Bauer customers was one reason for the acquisition. Eddie Bauer boosted catalog sales 50 per cent the first year after issuing a private credit card.

Build for the Future

Another key in portfolio retailing is having the capacity to explode strong concepts as Woolworth is doing with its "rising stars": Champs Sports, Lady Foot Locker, Afterthoughts, and Northern Reflections. Afterthoughts, which Woolworth started in 1985, had more than 700 stores at year-end 1992, and the company projects more than 1,300 units by 1997.

Explosive growth that doesn't unravel into mediocrity (or worse) requires investing in capacity before it is needed, flexibility in using assets so they can be reallocated to the best uses, and partnerships with suppliers who can accommodate growth. Companies wanting to run hard with hot concepts need to establish the necessary supply lines for products, manpower, and money.

It's easy to outrun supply lines, as Spiegel did with Eddie Bauer in the early 1990s: "Eddie Bauer stands for one thing: casual outdoor wear of the highest quality. This evolved to a wide assortment of price-oriented goods outside the concept. We were hiring store managers from other firms who weren't trained in the Bauer style and culture. We are back on track now, but we almost lost our focus. We went too fast."

A fine line exists between strong growth and too much growth, which leads to poor execution. Building for the future means preparing today for a big crowd on another day. It does not mean sacrificing execution of the concept if the crowd is even bigger than planned.

Create Multiple Listening Posts

Quick reaction to changing consumer preferences and attitudes is a hallmark of successful portfolio retailers. Knowing which merchandise and retail concepts to support and which to curtail—and implementing these changes in a timely manner—is a function of listening to the market better than competitors do. Managers must listen to the market in multiple ways.

Nurture Innovation

Portfolio retailing means continually testing ideas. Accommodating change is not enough; the best portfolio retailers embrace change, seek it out, and nurture it.

Woolworth's top management encourages the divisions to try new concepts by earmarking special innovation funds and using capital to reward successful new ventures. Division executives know that failing to try new ideas is a greater risk than trying new ideas that fail. The person who started Woolworth's very successful Afterthoughts chain previously developed several failed startups.

Spiegel has a Concept Committee whose mandate is to bring new ideas to management. The E Style catalog came from the committee, which is a champion for change within the organization. Promising ideas go to task groups for further development.

Woolworth and Spiegel have brought innovative strategies to the market, in part because one of their strategies is to be innovative. Senior managers use structural and financial tools—and encourage constant discussion about innovation—to stimulate entrepreneurial thinking in their organizations. They are not leaving innovation to chance.

Questions

1. Comment on this statement: "Portfolio retailers leverage a common set of core competencies across retail concepts targeted to fit the shopping preferences and buying patterns of specific market segments."
2. Under what circumstances should a firm pursue portfolio retailing? Avoid it?
3. In setting up an organizational arrangement, what special considerations do portfolio retailers face? How would you overcome them?
4. From an asset management perspective, how is Woolworth using portfolio retailing to improve its overall performance?
5. In this case, it is stated that portfolio retailing offers an incentive to invest in distribution. Why? How can portfolio retailing also be an inefficient method of distribution?
6. From an operational perspective, present three reasons why portfolio retailing has worked out so well for Spiegel.
7. What are the benefits and limitations of job standardization and cross-training for portfolio retailers?

PART

6

Merchandise Management and Pricing

- In Part 6, the merchandise management and pricing aspects of the retail strategy mix are presented. Merchandise management consists of the buying, handling, and financial aspects of merchandising. Pricing decisions are crucial because of their impact on the financial aspects of merchandise management and their interaction with other retailing elements.

- Chapter 13 deals with buying and handling merchandise. Each stage in the buying and handling process is described: organization, merchandise plans, information about customer demand, merchandise sources, evaluation methods, negotiations, concluding the purchase, merchandise handling, reordering, and re-evaluation.

- Chapter 14 concentrates on financial merchandise management. First, the cost and retail methods of accounting are introduced. Next, the merchandise forecasting and budgeting process is presented. Then, unit control systems are discussed. The last part of the chapter integrates dollar and unit financial inventory controls.

- Chapter 15 covers pricing. The outside factors affecting decisions are discussed: consumers, government, suppliers, and competitors. A framework for developing a price strategy is described: objectives, broad policy, basic strategy, implementation, and adjustments.

RM

Buying and Handling Merchandise

❖ Chapter Objectives

1. To examine nonfinancial merchandise planning and management
2. To outline the merchandise buying and handling process: organization, merchandise plans, information about customer demand, merchandise sources, evaluation methods, negotiations, concluding the purchase, merchandise handling, reordering, and re-evaluation
3. To discuss each element in the merchandise buying and handling process in detail
4. To place special emphasis on what merchandise a retailer should carry, how much to stock, when to stock items, and where to store items

Gottschalks is a 24-unit department-store chain with outlets mainly in small and mid-sized cities in California. A key aspect of the firm's overall strategy is that an estimated 90 per cent of its sales are from manufacturer brands. At many of its locations, Gottschalks is the only outlet that sells such brands as Liz Claiborne, Calvin Klein fragrances, Levi Strauss, Mikasa, Samsonite, and Sony.

According to Gottschalks' chief financial officer, it is particularly strong in national brands of cosmetics, "the kind that women would kill to get. We know a lot of customers drive an hour or hour and a half to buy cosmetics and presumably stick around to buy other things." The cosmetics brands sold by Gottschalks include Estée Lauder and Clinique.

There are several advantages to Gottschalks' branding strategy: One, large, current selections of well-known brands contribute to and reinforce its fashion leadership image. Two, Gottschalks receives cooperative advertising allowances and promotional assistance from manufacturers. This assistance gives the chain its "biggest bang per dollar" of promotional expenditures. Three, because many consumers seek out well-known brands, Gottschalks' trading area is increased. Four, unlike with private brands, Gottschalks can generally return unsold items to the manufacturer; much of this merchandise is then sold by the manufacturer to off-price chains or through their own factory outlets.

In contrast to Gottschalks' approach, other stores use a mixed-brand strategy that places an emphasis on both private brands and manufacturer brands. For instance, Studio B is a Bloomingdale's private brand and Real Clothes is a Saks private brand. Typically, the private brands offered by retailers are priced lower than manufacturer brands; at the same time, they offer higher profit margins to the retailer. Sometimes, private brands carry gross margins of 60 to 70 per cent versus 50 per cent for manufacturer brands.

A private-brand strategy is most successful when a retailer has a strong positive image that can be leveraged. That is why firms such as Bloomingdale's, Saks, Bergdorf Goodman, Marshall Field, Neiman-Marcus, and Nordstrom have the necessary cachet to implement a successful private-brand strategy.[1]

[1] *Gottschalks Annual Report 1992*; and Gretchen Morgenson, "Back to Basics," *Forbes* (May 10, 1993), pp. 56–58.

Reprinted by permission of Gottschalks.

Overview

Developing and implementing a merchandise plan is a key phase in a retail strategy. To be successful, a firm must have the proper assortments of goods and services when they are in demand and sell them in a manner consistent with the overall strategy. Thus, ***merchandising*** consists of the activities involved in acquiring particular goods and/or services and making them available at the places, times, and prices and in the quantity that will enable a retailer to reach its goals.

Even for the best retailers, merchandising decisions can dramatically affect performance. This is illustrated by The Gap's recent sluggish results:

> Famous for its jeans and T-shirts and not much else, Gap Inc. is now out to convince consumers that the "Gap look" also encompasses stretch pants and leather vests. The once-invincible company doesn't have much choice. Competitors have copied its basic look and are selling the knockoffs cheaper. Consumers, particularly women, grew tired of The Gap's boxy, unisex look and started going elsewhere for more feminine styles. To shore up slipping profit margins, the San Francisco-based specialty retailer is aggressively piling more fashionable, higher-priced goods into stores. "We can't afford not to change," says President Millard "Mickey" Drexler.[2]

In this chapter, the buying and handling aspects of merchandise planning and management are discussed. Merchandising's financial side is described in Chapter 14. Retail pricing is covered in Chapter 15. Planning for a service retailer is examined in Chapter 18.

The Merchandise Buying and Handling Process

Figure 13–1 shows the ***merchandise buying and handling process***, which consists of an integrated and systematic sequence of steps from establishing a buying organization through regular re-evaluation. It is essential for each step to be used in merchandising.

ESTABLISHING A FORMAL OR INFORMAL BUYING ORGANIZATION

The first stage is establishing a buying organization. Merchandising cannot be conducted in a thorough, systematic manner unless the buying organization is well defined—specifying who is responsible for merchandise decisions, the tasks of these people, the authority to make decisions, and the relationship of merchandising to overall retail operations. Figure 13–2 highlights the range of buying-organization attributes from which retailers may choose.

A ***formal buying organization*** exists if merchandising is viewed as a distinct retail task and a separate department is set up. Then, all or most functions involved in acquiring merchandise and making it available for sale (Figure 13–1, Steps 2 through 10) are under this department's control. A formal organization most often occurs with larger firms and involves distinct buying personnel. In an ***informal buying organization***, merchandising is not viewed as a distinct task. Then, the same personnel handle both merchandising and other retail functions; responsibility and authority are not always clear-cut. Informal organizations generally occur in smaller retailers.

The major advantages of a formal buying organization are the well-defined responsibilities and authority and the use of full-time, specialized merchandisers. The major disadvantage is the cost of having a separate department. The important advantages of an informal buying organization are the low costs and flexibility. The

[2] Christina Duff, "Gap's New Line Goes Beyond the Basics," *Wall Street Journal* (August 12, 1993), p. B1. See also Russell Mitchell, "The Gap Dolls Itself Up," *Business Week* (March 21, 1994), p. 46.

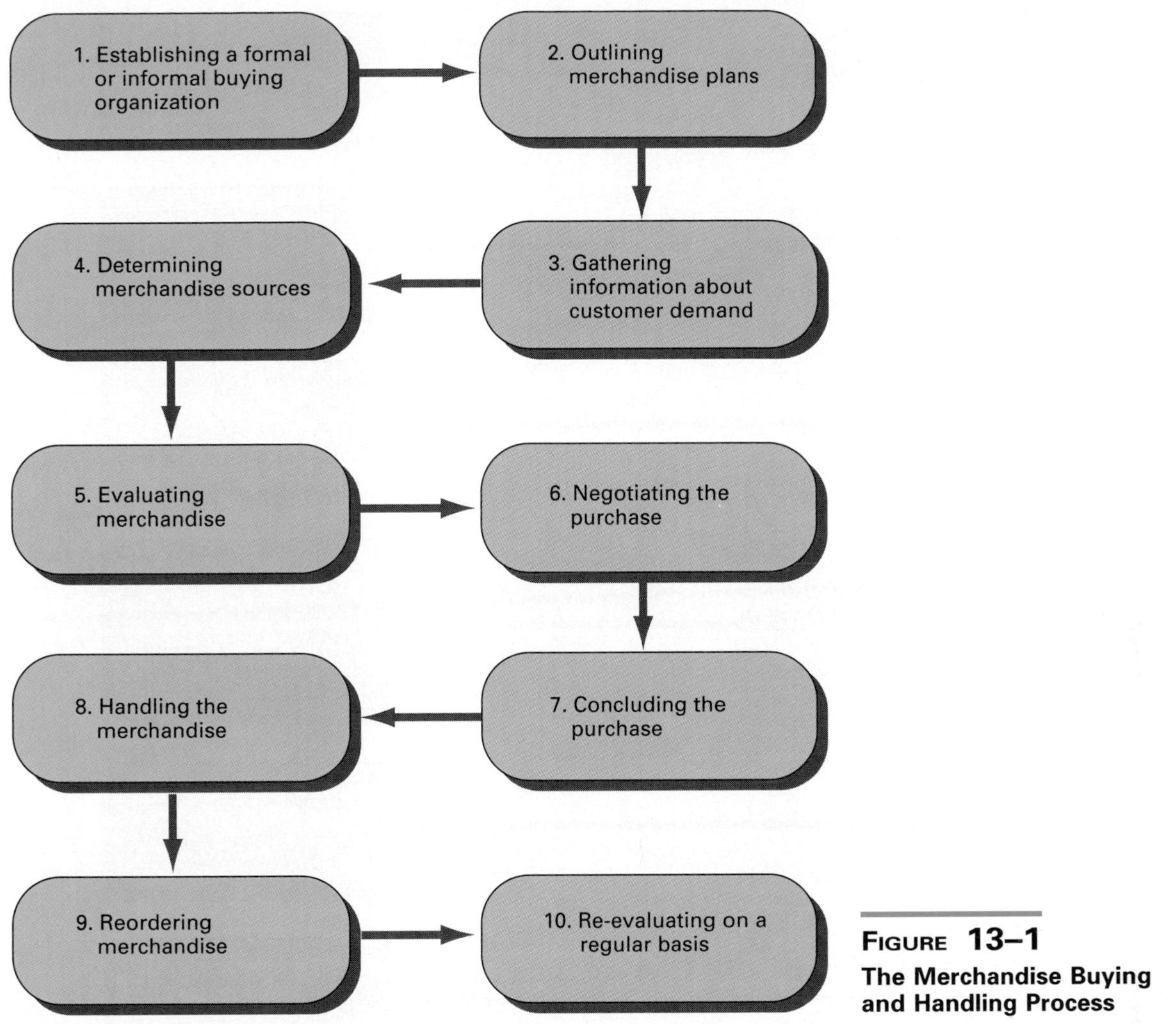

FIGURE 13–1
The Merchandise Buying and Handling Process

important disadvantages are less-defined responsibilities and authority, and the de-emphasis on merchandise planning.

Both structures exist in great numbers. It is not crucial that a retailer use a formal organization. But, it is crucial that the firm realize the role of merchandising and ensure that responsibility, activities, authority, and the interrelationship with store operations are properly defined and enacted.

Multiunit retailers must also determine whether to create a centralized buying organization or a decentralized one. In a ***centralized buying organization***, all purchase decisions emanate from one office. For instance, a chain may have eight stores, with all merchandise decisions made at the headquarters store. In a ***decentralized buying organization***, purchase decisions are made locally or regionally. As an example, a 12-store chain may allow each outlet to select its own merchandise or divide the branches into geographic territories (such as four branches per region) with regional decisions made by the headquarters store in each territory.

Among the advantages of a centralized buying organization are the integration of effort, strict controls, consistent image, proximity to top management, staff support, and discounts through volume purchases. Among the possible disadvantages are the inflexibility, time delays, poor morale at local stores, and excessive uniformity.

Decentralized buying offers these advantages: adaptability to local market conditions, quick order processing, and improved morale because branches have autonomy. The potential disadvantages are the disjointed planning, an inconsistent image, limited management controls, little staff support, and loss of volume discounts.

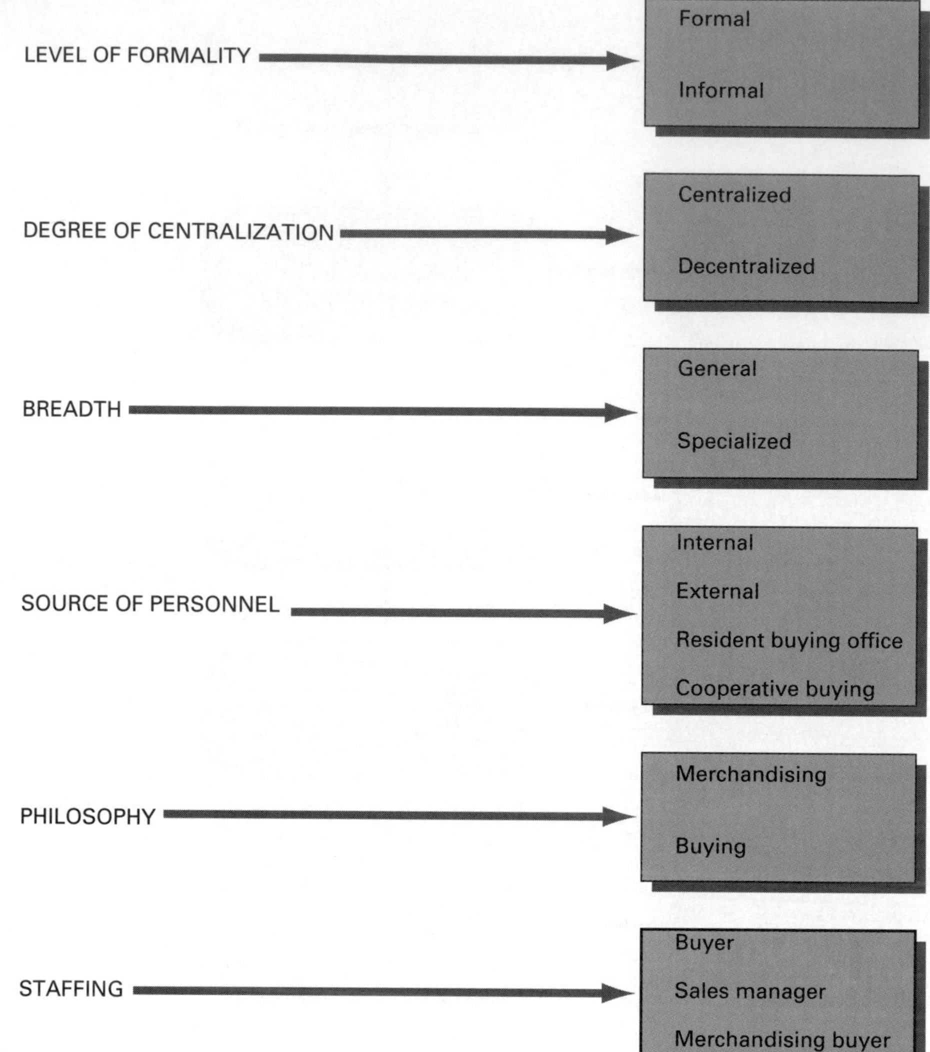

FIGURE 13–2
The Attributes of Buying Organizations

Many chains have combined the benefits of both systems by using a centralized buying organization while also giving regional or local store managers the power to revise orders or place their own orders. At Federated Department Stores, which operates a number of department-store chains:

> We have made significant strides over the past several years to improve and differentiate our merchandise offering—while controlling costs and enhancing value for our customers. Federated's buying process has been reformulated into a unique team approach that brings a specialty-store focus to our department-store business. We harness and fuse the thinking of the company's top merchants in every category to direct and coordinate common assortments. The percentage of merchandise in our stores that now is team-directed ranges between 50 and 85 per cent, depending on product category. The team process then allows divisional merchants to tailor the remainder of their assortments to local demographics, regional climate, and their customers' distinct fashion preferences.[3]

A choice must be made between a general buying organization and a specialized one. In a general organization, one or several people buy all of a firm's merchandise.

[3] *Federated Department Stores, Inc. 1992 Annual Report*, p. 3.

RETAILING IN ACTION

How Does Teamwork Pay Off in Merchandise Planning?

Team-based buying has been in place at Federated Department Stores since 1990 for all of Federated's divisions except Bloomingdale's. According to the principal team sponsor for accessories and shoes, the biggest challenge of team buying is to create a single merchandising strategy that works well in each of Federated's store divisions. A Federated team-buying committee typically consists of two buyers from different divisions and a merchandise manager. This group is further supported by a group merchandise manager and a Federated vice-president.

The conversion to team buying required that Federated develop a common merchandise department/classification system throughout all of its stores. Such a system allows every Federated store to monitor its performance relative to the others. Team buying also called for the development of a corporatewide merchandising strategy.

In comparison to the old independent-buying system, these are among the strengths of team buying: the better possibility of partnership opportunities with key vendors, the greater bargaining power for the overall company, the better opportunities to share information among store divisions, the greater ability to transfer merchandise among store divisions, and the ability to function with fewer buyers. The weaknesses of team buying relate to the inability to reflect regional and divisional differences, and the fear that a committee will settle on a compromise mentality.

Source: Based on material in "Russell Stravitz Answers Strategic Challenge with Teamwork: Group Dynamics," *Stores* (December 1993), p. 49.

For example, the owner of a small hardware store may buy all merchandise for his or her store. With a specialized organization, each buyer is responsible for a product category. As an example, a department store usually would have separate buyers for girls', juniors', and women's clothes.

The general approach is better when the retailer is small or there are few different goods/services involved. The specialized approach is better when the retailer is large or many goods/services are handled. Through specialization, knowledge is improved and responsibility well defined; however, costs are higher and extra personnel are usually required.

A retailer can choose an inside buying organization and/or an outside one. An ***inside buying organization*** is staffed by a retailer's own personnel and merchandise decisions are made by permanent employees of the firm. See Figure 13–3. With an ***outside buying organization***, a company or personnel external to the retailer are hired, usually on a fee basis. Although most retailers use either an inside or an outside buying organization, some employ a combination of the two.

An outside organization is most frequently used by small or medium-sized retailers or those far from their sources of supply. In these cases, it is more efficient for the

FIGURE 13–3
Michaels Stores' Inside Buying Organization
Michaels Stores is a growing chain of arts, crafts, and decorative products shops. Each of its outlets carries about 30,000 items that are selected by the firm's full-time buyers. Michaels has a corporate merchandising group to choose products from and negotiate purchase terms with about 1,000 vendors. Merchandising personnel often travel to meet with vendors. Shown here is a recent buying trip to the Orient.
Reprinted by permission.

retailers to hire outside buyers than to use company personnel. An outside organization has clout in dealing with suppliers (because of purchase volume), usually services noncompeting retailers, offers marketing research expertise, and sometimes sponsors private-label goods. Outside buying organizations may be paid by retailers that subscribe to their services, or by manufacturers, which give commissions. Sometimes, an individual retailer decides to set up its own internal organization if it believes its outside group is dealing with direct competitors or the firm finds it can buy merchandise more efficiently on its own.

A ***resident buying office***, which can be an inside or outside organization, is used when a retailer wants to keep in close touch with key market trends and cannot do so through just its headquarters buying staff. Such offices are usually situated in important merchandise centers (sources of supply) and provide valuable information and contacts. There are a few hundred outside resident buying offices in the United States, the majority in New York City, serving several thousand retailers. For example, five years ago, Carter Hawley Hale (which had relied on its own inside buying organization) decided to join Associated Merchandising Corporation's worldwide network of buying offices to get more marketing research data, better identify emerging fashion trends, and obtain recommended sources of supply.[4]

Smaller, independent retailers are now using cooperative buying to a greater degree than ever before (to compete with bigger chains). Under ***cooperative buying***, a group of independent retailers gets together to make large purchases from a supplier. Volume discounts are then achieved. It is most popular among food and hardware retailers. In some cases, retailers initiate the cooperative; in others, the wholesaler or manufacturer may form the cooperative as an attempt to cut operating costs.

Another decision involves a retailer's determination of whether the buying organization is to be concerned with merchandising or buying. As noted at the beginning of the chapter, merchandising includes the broad range of activities involved in buying and selling goods and services, such as purchases, pricing, storage, and display. Buying includes only product purchases and not their sale. Many firms consider merchandising the key to their success, and buyers (or merchandise managers) are involved with both buying and selling tasks. However, some retailers consider their buyers to be highly skilled specialists who should not be active in the selling function, which is undertaken by other skilled specialists. Thus, a recent study of store managers at full-line discount stores found that most of these managers have great influence as to the way items are displayed; but they have rather little influence with regard to decisions as to whether to stock particular brands or to promote them.[5]

The advantages of a merchandising philosophy are that a smooth chain of command is enacted by an integrated effort; the buyer's expertise is used in selling; responsibility and authority are clear (a buyer does not blame sales personnel for poor sales efforts and vice versa); the buyer ensures that items are properly displayed; costs are reduced (fewer staff specialists); and the buyer is close to consumers via his or her involvement with selling.

The advantages of separate buying and selling functions are that similar skills are not needed for each function; the morale of in-store personnel goes up as they get more authority; selling is not viewed as a secondary function; salespeople are closer to customers than buyers; specialists can develop in each area; and buyers may not be good supervisors due to their time away from the store and the differences in managing buying and selling personnel.

Both approaches are used, and the advantages of a merchandising versus a buying philosophy are still open to debate. An individual retailer must evaluate which procedure is better for carrying out its overall strategy.

[4] *Carter Hawley Hale 1989 Annual Report*, p. 12.

[5] "Areas Where Managers Feel They Have the Most Influence," *Discount Store News* (October 4, 1993), p. 29.

The last decision in this stage of buying and handling merchandise centers on staffing the buying organization. What positions must be filled, and what qualifications should a retailer require? Firms with a merchandising vantage point are most concerned with hiring good buyers. Firms that take a buying and selling perspective are concerned with hiring both buyers and sales managers.

Many large retailers hire college graduates whom they place in extensive training programs and promote internally to positions as buyers and sales managers. A buyer must be attuned to the marketplace, must be assertive in bargaining with suppliers, must make extensive use of buying plans (detailed shopping lists that completely outline purchases), and may have to travel to major marketplaces. A sales manager must be a good organizer, supervisor, and motivator. A merchandising buyer must possess the attributes of each.

Today, more retailers than ever feel that the most important qualification for good buying personnel is the ability to relate to their customers and systematically anticipate future needs. In addition, to some extent, buyers are involved with each of the remaining activities described in the balance of this chapter and many of those detailed in Chapter 14.

Outlining Merchandise Plans

Merchandise planning centers on four basic decisions: what merchandise to stock, how much merchandise to stock, when to stock merchandise, and where to store merchandise.

What Merchandise Is Stocked

First, a retailer must determine what quality of merchandise to carry. Should it carry top-line, expensive items and sell to upper-class customers? Or should it sell middle-of-the-line, moderately priced items and cater to middle-class customers? Or should it sell bottom-line, inexpensive items and attract lower-class customers? Or should it try to draw more than one market segment by offering a variety in quality, such as middle- and top-line merchandise for middle- and upper-class shoppers? The firm must also decide whether to carry promotional merchandise (low-priced closeout items or special buys used to generate store traffic).

In deciding on merchandise quality, the retailer should take several factors into consideration: the desired target market(s), competition, store image, store location, stock turnover, profitability, manufacturer versus private brands, customer services, personnel, the perceived goods/service benefits, and constrained decision making. See Table 13–1.

For example, Dollar General (the variety-store chain) has an overall merchandising strategy that is very consistent with its approach to merchandise quality:

> Dollar General Corporation operates more than 1,500 neighborhood stores in 23 states. We market the basics in soft goods, including apparel for the whole family, shoes, and domestics (such as table cloths). We also offer hard goods, including health and beauty aids, cleaning supplies, stationery, and seasonal goods. We present these basics in low price points which make sense to our customers: $1, two for $5, $10, etc. When negotiating with vendors, our buyers look for value at price points such as these. As a result, we offer more than 1,800 items which sell for $1 or less, as well as $5 flannel shirts, $9 Rustler jeans, and $10 irons. Our stores have always invited cost-conscious customers to "Count on Us" every day for value in quality, basic merchandise.[6]

[6] *Dollar General Corporation 1992 Annual Report,* various pages.

TABLE 13–1 The Factors to Be Considered in Planning Merchandise Quality

Factor	Relevance for Planning
Target market(s)	Merchandise quality must be matched to the wishes of the desired target market(s).
Competition	A retailer can sell similar quality (follow the competition) or different quality (to appeal to a different target market).
Store image	Merchandise quality must be directly related to the perception that customers have of the retailer.
Store location	The location affects store image and the number of competitors, which, in turn, relate to quality.
Stock turnover	High quality and high prices usually yield a lower turnover than low quality and low prices.
Profitability	High-quality merchandise generally brings greater profit per unit than low-quality merchandise; however, turnover may cause total profits to be greater for low-quality merchandise.
Manufacturer versus private brands	For many consumers, manufacturer (national) brands connote higher quality than private (dealer) brands.
Customer services to be offered	High-quality merchandise requires personal selling, alterations, delivery, and so on. Low-quality merchandise may not.
Personnel	Skilled, knowledgeable personnel are necessary for quality merchandise. Limited personnel are needed for low-quality merchandise.
Perceived goods/service benefits	Low-quality merchandise attracts customers who desire functional product benefits (e.g., warmth, comfort). High-quality merchandise attracts customers who desire extended product benefits (e.g., status, services, style).
Constrained decision making	a. Franchise or chain operators have limited or no control over product quality. They either buy directly from the franchisor (chain) or must abide by quality standards. b. Independent retailers who buy from a few large wholesalers will be limited to the range of quality offered by those wholesalers.

Dollar General is so successful that its annual sales exceed $800 million. See Figure 13–4.

The second major decision a retailer makes on what merchandise to handle involves determining how innovative to be. Several factors should be examined: target market(s), goods/service growth potential, fashion trends and theories (if applicable), store image, competition, customer segments, responsiveness to consumers, investment costs, profitability, risk, constrained decision making, and dropping declining goods/services. See Table 13–2.

An innovative retailer, one carrying new goods and services and planning for upcoming trends, faces a great opportunity (being first in the market) and a great risk (possibly misreading customer interests and being stuck with large inventories). By evaluating each factor in Table 13–2 and developing a thorough plan for handling new goods and services, a retailer should be able to capitalize on its opportunities and reduce its risks.

Here are two illustrations of innovative merchandising strategies:

- "Books "R" Us is one of several special departments Toys "R" Us is testing to expand the reach and enhance the ambiance of its standard warehouse-store format. The company, which also operates Kids "R" Us children's clothing stores, is even testing Parties "R" Us, a department stocking candles, paper plates, favors, and other party gear, and Movies "R" Us. Two stores have Lego boutiques, and the company is testing a new in-store shop for stuffed toys, which have never lent themselves to the warehouse environment."[7]

[7] Stephanie Strom, "Bookshelf Space at Toys "R" Us," *New York Times* (August 25, 1993), pp. D1–D2.

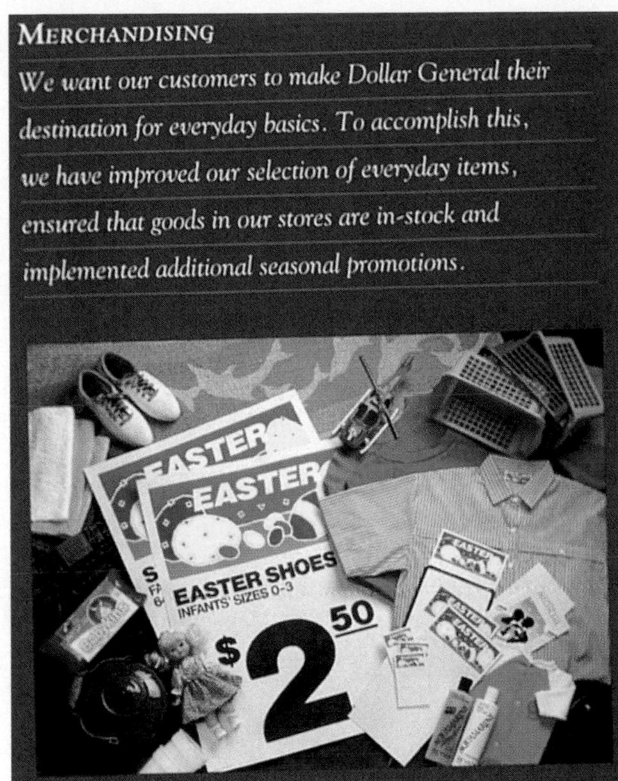

FIGURE 13–4
Dollar General's Merchandising Philosophy
Reprinted by permission.

- Sharper Image has "returned to a product mix which emphasizes unique products available either exclusively at the company or which are not available in broad distribution. Such products enable the firm to sustain a higher gross margin by reducing the ability of a customer to comparison shop. The company also emphasizes recreation, fitness, and stress reduction products, and selected apparel and footwear which serve a purpose of improving the quality of customers' lives. Brand-name consumer electronics have been scaled back; however, the firm continues to introduce the newest in electronics and technology, a market niche in which it has succeeded. The current strategy is to offer an assortment of 500 to 600 products which includes carefully pre-selected products that are best for the customer on the basis of newness and value, or the most innovative solution to people's needs and wants, and that offer high margins."[8]

The retailer should evaluate the growth potential for each new good or service it carries. Three elements of growth are of special interest: the rapidity of initial sales, maximum sales potential per time period, and the length of selling life. How fast will a new good or service generate sales? What are the most sales (dollars and units) that can be achieved in a season or a year? Over what time period will a good or service continue to sell?

A useful tool for assessing growth potential is the ***product life cycle***, which shows the expected behavior of a good or service over its life. The traditional product life cycle has four stages: introduction, growth, maturity, and decline—as depicted and described in Figure 13–5. A knowledge of this tool is quite helpful to a retailer in strategy planning.

During the introductory stage, the retailer should anticipate a limited target market, consisting of higher-income and more innovative consumers. The good or service will probably be supplied in one basic version, not a choice of alternatives. The manufacturer (supplier) may limit distribution to "finer" stores. However, new convenience

[8] *Sharper Image Corporation 1993 10K*, pp. 6–7.

TABLE 13–2 The Factors to Be Considered in Planning Merchandise Innovativeness

Factor	Relevance for Planning
Target market(s)	Evaluate whether the target market is conservative or progressive.
Goods/service growth potential	Consider each new offering on the basis of rapidity of initial sales, maximum sales potential per time period, and length of sales life.
Fashion trends and theories	Understand the "trickle-down" and "trickle-across" theories, if selling fashion merchandise.
Store image	The kinds of goods/services a retailer carries are influenced by its image. The level of innovativeness should be consistent with this image.
Competition	Lead or follow competition in the selection of new goods/services.
Customer segmentation	Customers can be segmented by dividing merchandise into established-product displays and new-product displays.
Responsiveness to consumers	New offerings should be handled when they are requested by the target market.
Amount of investment	These types of investment are possible for each new good/service: product costs, new fixtures, and additional personnel (or further training for existing personnel).
Profitability	Each new offering should be assessed for potential profits (for the particular item, as well as the overall profits of the retailer).
Risk	The major risks involve the possible tarnishing of store image, investment costs, and opportunity costs.
Constrained decision making	Franchise and chain operators may be restricted in the new goods/services they can purchase.
Dropping declining goods/services	Old goods/services should be deleted when sales and/or profits are too low.

items such as food and houseware products are normally mass distributed. Items that are initially distributed selectively generally have a high (skimming) price strategy. Merchandise that is mass distributed typically involves low (penetration) pricing to encourage faster acceptance by consumers. In either case, introductory promotion must be explanatory, geared to informing consumers. At this stage, there is only one or very few possible suppliers.

As innovative consumers buy a new good or service and recommend it to their friends, sales increase rapidly and the product life cycle enters the growth stage. The target market expands to include middle-income consumers who are somewhat more innovative than the average. Variations of the basic offering appear; width and depth of assortment expand. The number of retailers carrying the product increases. Price discounting is not widely employed, but a wide variety of retailers offer a large range of prices, customer services, and quality. Retail promotion is more persuasive and is aimed at acquainting consumers with product availability and extended services. There is an increasing number of suppliers.

In maturity, good or service sales reach their maximum level. The largest portion of the target market is reached during this period. Lower-, middle-, and upper-class consumers select from a very wide variety of offerings and options. All types of retailers (discount to upscale) carry the good or service in some form. Prestige retailers continue to emphasize brand names and customer services, but other retailers enter into active price competition. Price is more prominently mentioned in promotional activities. For retailers and their suppliers, the maturity stage is the most competitive.

With the traditional product life cycle, a good or service would then enter decline, often brought on by two factors: the target market shrinks (due to product obsolescence, the availability of newer substitutes, and consumer boredom) and price cutting lessens profit margins. During decline, the target market may become the lowest-

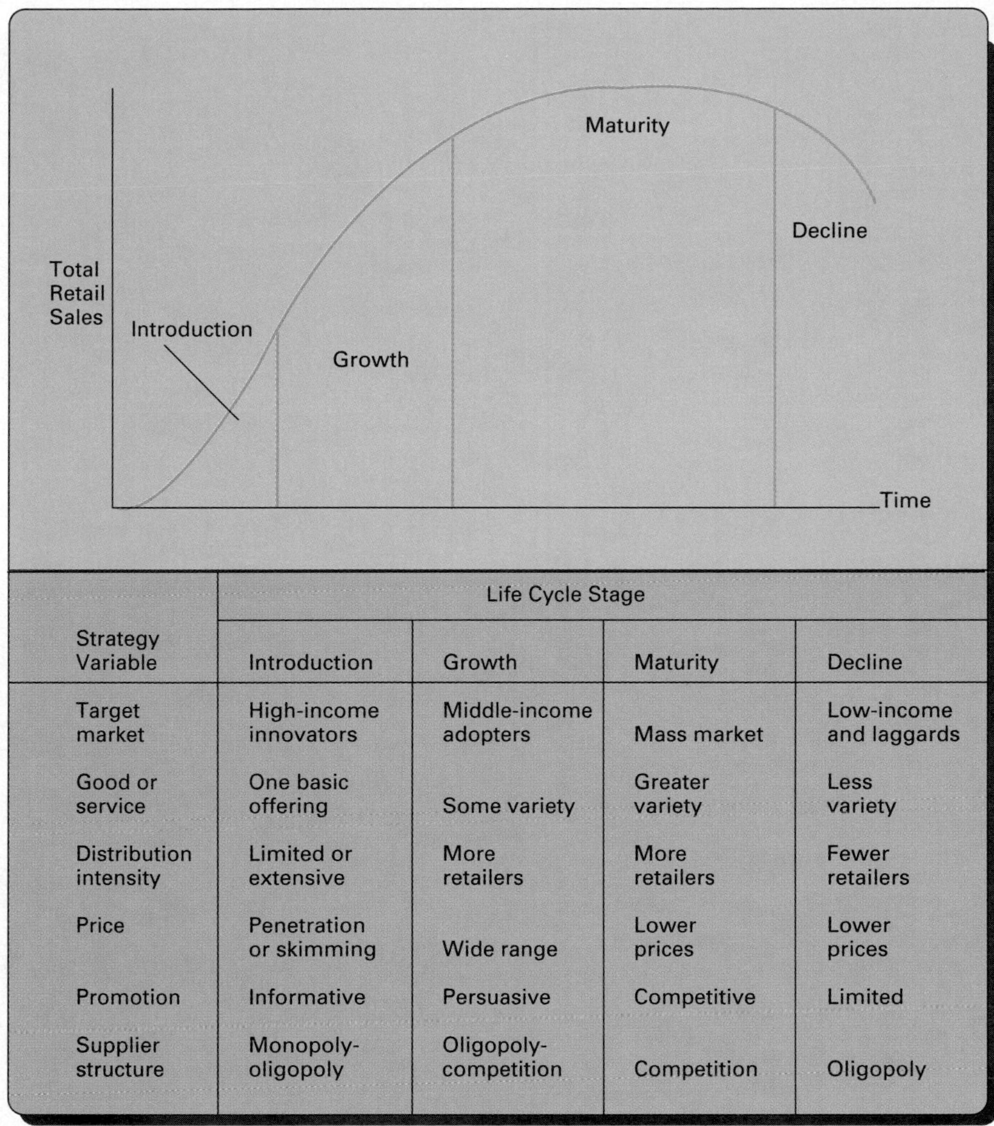

Strategy Variable	Life Cycle Stage			
	Introduction	Growth	Maturity	Decline
Target market	High-income innovators	Middle-income adopters	Mass market	Low-income and laggards
Good or service	One basic offering	Some variety	Greater variety	Less variety
Distribution intensity	Limited or extensive	More retailers	More retailers	Fewer retailers
Price	Penetration or skimming	Wide range	Lower prices	Lower prices
Promotion	Informative	Persuasive	Competitive	Limited
Supplier structure	Monopoly-oligopoly	Oligopoly-competition	Competition	Oligopoly

FIGURE 13–5
The Traditional Product Life Cycle

income consumer and laggards. Some retailers cut back on their variety (to reduce the space allotted to these items); others drop the good or service for profit and image reasons. At the retailers still carrying the items, low prices are offered, and promotion is reduced and geared to price. There are fewer suppliers, as many turn to other items.

It should be noted that not all goods and services conform to the traditional product life cycle just detailed. Some derivatives are shown in Figure 13–6. In a boom sales pattern, sales rise quickly and maintain a high level for a long period of time. Many cosmetics, pharmaceutical products, and rental services can be placed in this category.

A fad curve occurs when a good or service generates a lot of sales, but only for a short time. The retailer must be careful not to overorder because of enthusiasm over high early sales. Often, toys and games are short-lived fads, such as products tied in with the 1993 *Jurassic Park* movie. An extended fad is like a fad, except that residual sales continue for a longer period at a fraction of earlier sales. Clothing with designer insignias is an example of a product that can be classified as an extended fad.

A seasonal or fashion curve results when a good or service sells well during nonconsecutive time periods. Seasonal items, such as ski equipment and air-conditioner servicing, have excellent sales during one season per year. Because the strongest sales

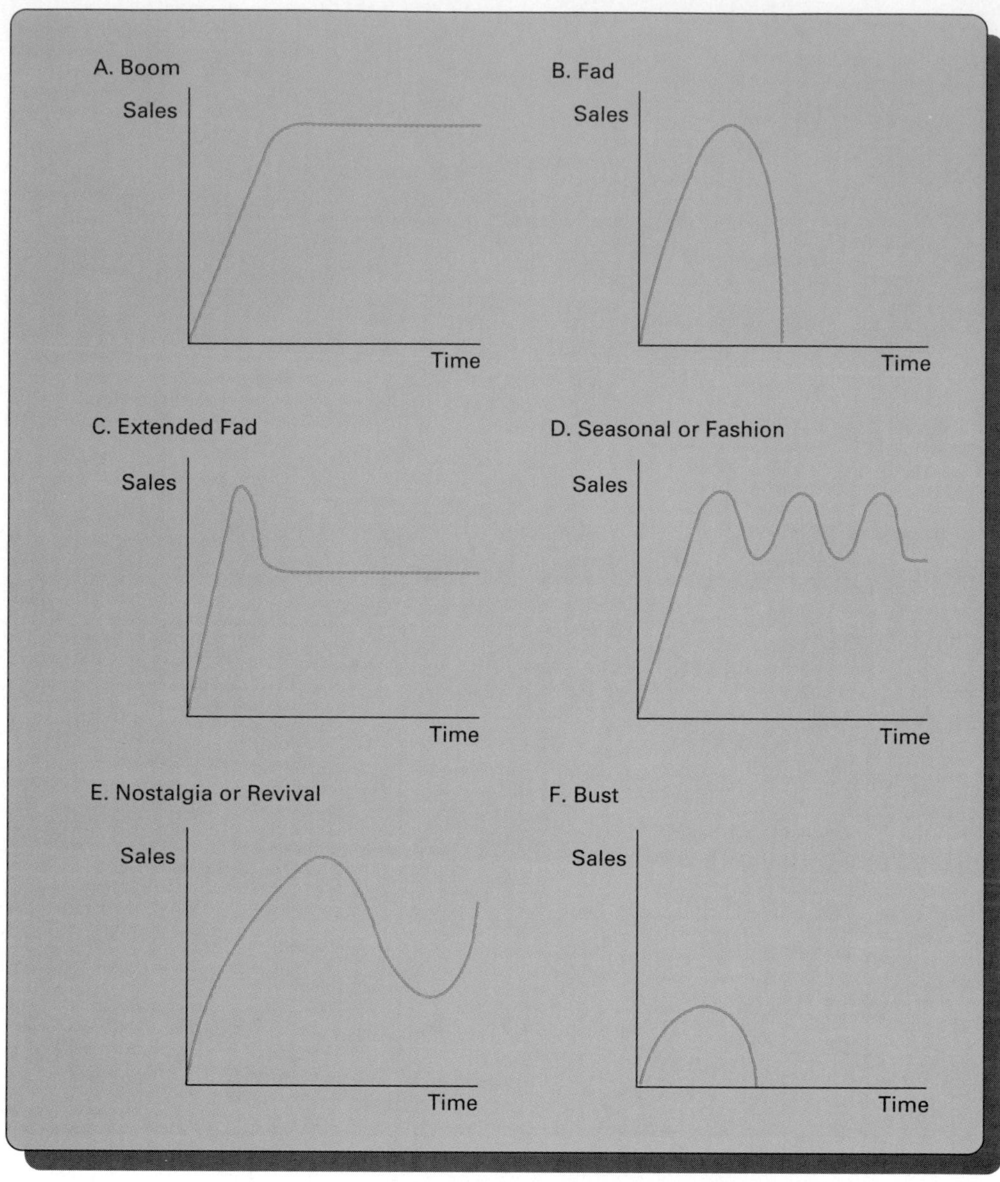

FIGURE 13–6
Selected Product Life Cycles

of seasonal goods and services usually occur at the same time each year, retail planning is rather simple. Fashion products are much less predictable. Sales of items like bow ties or miniskirts are often sizable for a number of years, become unpopular for a number of years, and then become popular again. For these items, retail planning is harder.

With a nostalgia or revival curve, a seemingly obsolete good or service is revived. An innovative retailer will recognize potential in this area and merchandise accordingly. For example, direct marketers often use television commercials to sell records, cassettes, and compact discs emphasizing music or artists who were previously successful. They also heavily promote "greatest hits" recordings featuring combinations of artists.

A bust product cycle is one in which a good or service is not successful at all (unlike a fad), and the retailer loses money and, sometimes, status. This occurred with Pizza Hut's original attempt to sell a "light" pizza; despite extensive testing, the product did not do well and never made it into full distribution. Sometimes, retailers have to slash prices to sell a huge amount of excess inventory for an unpopular item. This takes place with books that are expected to be best-sellers but fail to attract enough readers.

A retailer carrying apparel must be familiar with fashion trends and related theories. Such trends may be divided into vertical and horizontal categories; fashions may go through one or a combination of the two. A vertical trend occurs when a fashion is first accepted by an upscale market segment and undergoes changes in its basic form before it is sold to the general public. According to the ***trickle-down theory***, a fashion passes from the upper to the lower social classes through three vertical stages: distinctive (original designs, designer dress shops, custom-made, worn by high society); emulation (modification of original designs, finer stores, alterations, worn by the middle class); and economic emulation (simple copies of originals, discount and bargain stores, mass produced, mass marketed). With this theory, Paris has often been considered the fashion capital of the world.

In recent years, the importance of horizontal fashion trends has also been recognized. A horizontal trend occurs when a new fashion is accepted by a broad spectrum of people when it is introduced, while retaining its basic form. According to the ***trickle-across theory***, within any social class, there are innovative customers who act as opinion leaders. New fashions must be accepted by these leaders, who then convince other members of the same social class (who are more conservative) to buy the items. Merchandise is sold across the class and not from one class down to another.

By understanding both theories and determining which is more appropriate for a specific item, a retailer is better able to predict fashion successes and the types of customers who will buy in each stage of the product life cycle. Figure 13–7 contains a checklist for predicting fashion adoption.

In planning innovativeness, a retailer's emphasis is too often on new-product additions. Equally important are the decisions involved in dropping existing goods or services. Because of limited resources and shelf space, some items have to be dropped when others are added. Instead of intuitively removing existing offerings, the retailer should use structured guidelines:

1. Select items for possible elimination on the basis of declining sales, prices, and profits; the appearance of substitutes; the loss of usefulness; and excessive demands on executives' time.
2. Gather and analyze information about these items, including profits, financial considerations, employee relations, and promotion factors.

		Yes	No
1.	Does the fashion satisfy a consumer need?	___	___
2.	Is the fashion compatible with emerging consumer life-styles?	___	___
3.	Is the fashion oriented toward the mass market? Toward a market segment?	___ ___	___ ___
4.	Is the fashion radically new?	___	___
5.	Are the reputations of the designer(s) and the retailers carrying the fashion good?	___	___
6.	Are several designers marketing some version of the fashion?	___	___
7.	Is the price range for the fashion appropriate for the target market?	___	___
8.	Will extensive advertising be used?	___	___
9.	Will the fashion change over time?	___	___
10.	Will consumers view the fashion as a long-term trend?	___	___

FIGURE 13–7
A Checklist for Predicting Fashion Adoption

RETAILING AROUND THE WORLD

How Exotic Is the Merchandise Mix at Italy's 10 Corso Como?

A new European retailing phenomenon involves boutiques that cross the boundaries of traditional retail product categories. For example, some of these boutiques sell clothing, books, furniture, decorative objects, and food in a single unit. According to one retail analyst, these stores rely "more on serendipity than strategy for their impact." One such store is 10 Corso Como.

10 Corso Como is part store, part design studio, and part exhibition gallery. The owner, former magazine editor Carla Sozzani, appeals to young Italians who are looking for "things that express their personalities rather than labels." The store features clothing from Sozzani's NN (No Name) design studio, other designers, and collections of clothing from the 1950s and 1960s.

The store's selection of other goods is eclectic. For example, on a recent buying trip to Morocco, Sozzani bought carpets, pillows, and bowls of spices for sale at her store. In addition, lingerie, cosmetics, and men's shoes are stocked. The NN design studio plans to add furniture, ceramics, towels, and perfumes to its line. And, at 10 Corso Como, Galleria Carla Sozzani also holds art and photography exhibitions.

Like other such retailers, 10 Corso Como does not advertise and depends largely on word-of-mouth promotion.

Source: Based on material in Mary Krienke, "Boutiques Exotiques," *Stores* (September 1993), pp. 65–67.

3. Consider nondeletion strategies such as cutting costs, revising promotion efforts, adjusting prices, and cooperating with other retailers.
4. After a deletion decision is made, consider timing, parts and servicing, inventory, and holdover demand.[9]

As an illustration, several years ago, Montgomery Ward stopped selling hunting equipment, skates, hardware, cabinets, and flooring and lessened its emphasis on paint, lawn mowers, tillers, grills, lawn furniture, garbage disposals, and ceiling fans. At that time, only six per cent of total company sales were in these products. In their place, Montgomery Ward now carries more of its better-selling merchandise, such as automotive goods, appliances, apparel, and home furnishings.[10]

How Much Merchandise Is Stocked

After a retailer decides what merchandise to carry, it must determine how much of that merchandise to stock. Thus, the width and depth of assortment should be planned. ***Width of assortment*** refers to the number of distinct goods/service categories with which a retailer is involved. ***Depth of assortment*** refers to the variety in any one goods/service category with which a retailer is involved. As noted in Chapter 5, product assortment can range from wide and deep (a department store) to narrow and shallow (a box store). Selected advantages and disadvantages of each type of assortment strategy are shown in Table 13–3.

Assortment strategies vary widely. For example, KFC's thousands of worldwide outlets emphasize chicken and related quick-service products. They do not sell hamburgers, pizza, or other popular fast-food items; these do not fit with KFC's merchandising approach. On the other hand, Wal-Mart's huge Supercenters feature a full range of both general merchandise and food. This is Egghead's approach:

> All of Egghead's stores carry a "core" list of computer software and computer accessories, with optional software and peripherals to meet the individual store's clientele and market. Downtown stores offer more business-oriented titles than suburban stores, which carry more software games. Trends shift, and so does the product mix in our stores.[11]

[9] Adapted from the classic article by Ralph S. Alexander, "The Death and Burial of 'Sick' Products," *Journal of Marketing*, Vol. 28 (April 1964), pp. 1–7.

[10] *Montgomery Ward: Leadership in Retailing* (Chicago: Montgomery Ward, 1989); and *Montgomery Ward 1993 Annual Report*.

[11] *Egghead, Inc. 1992 Annual Report*, p. 15.

TABLE 13–3 Retail Assortment Strategies

Advantages	Disadvantages
Wide and Deep (many goods/service categories and a large assortment in each category)	
Broad market	High inventory investment
Full stocking of items	General image
High level of customer traffic	Many items with low turnover
Customer loyalty	Some obsolete merchandise
One-stop shopping	
No disappointed customers	
Wide and Shallow (many goods/service categories and a limited assortment in each category)	
Broad market	Low variety within product lines
High level of customer traffic	Some disappointed customers
Emphasis on convenience customers	Weak image
Less costly than wide and deep	Many items with low turnover
One-stop shopping	Reduced customer loyalty
Narrow and Deep (few goods/service categories and a large assortment in each category)	
Specialist image	Too much emphasis on one category
Good customer choice in category(ies)	No one-stop shopping
Specialized personnel	More susceptible to trends/cycles
Customer loyalty	Greater effort needed to enlarge the size of the trading area
No disappointed customers	
Less costly than wide and deep	Little (no) scrambled merchandising
Narrow and Shallow (few goods/service categories and a limited assortment in each category)	
Aimed at convenience customers	Little width and depth
Least costly	No one-stop shopping
High turnover of items	Some disappointed customers
	Weak image
	Limited customer loyalty
	Small trading area
	Little (no) scrambled merchandising

Several factors should be considered in planning the width and depth of assortment to carry. Sales and profit should be evaluated. If goods/service variety is increased, will overall sales go up? Will overall profits? Carrying ten varieties of cat food will not necessarily yield greater sales or profits than stocking four varieties. The retailer should be sure to look at the investment costs that occur with a large variety.

Space requirements should be examined. How much space is required for each good or service category? How much space is available? Because selling space is limited, it should be allocated to those goods and services generating the greatest customer traffic and sales. The turnover rate should also be considered in assigning shelf space.

A distinction should be made among scrambled merchandising, complementary goods and services, and substitute goods and services. With scrambled merchandising, the retailer adds unrelated items to generate greater customer traffic and lift profit margins (e.g., a florist adding umbrellas). Handling complementary goods/services lets the retailer sell basic items and related offerings (e.g., stereo and CDs, lawn service and tree spraying). Scrambled merchandising and complementary goods/services are both intended to increase the retailer's overall sales. Yet, carrying many substitute goods/services (e.g., competing brands of toothpaste) may simply shift sales from one brand to another and have little impact on a retailer's overall sales.

For some firms, especially supermarkets, the proliferation of substitute products has created a difficult problem: how to offer consumers an adequate choice without tying up too much investment and floor space in one product category. For example, the shelves at the Apples supermarket in Canton, Ohio, are stocked with 25 types of apples, 20 varieties of low-sodium and salt-free meats and cheeses, 40 kinds of store-made salads, and 26 varieties of bread and rolls. Yet, as one expert says, "If variety is healthy for a supermarket, too much duplication can harden its arteries."[12]

Sometimes, a retailer may have no choice about stocking a full assortment within a product line. A powerful supplier may insist that the retailer carry its entire line or else it will not distribute via the retailer at all. But large retailers—and smaller ones that belong to cooperative buying groups—are now standing up to suppliers; and many retailers stock their own brands next to manufacturers'. As retail chains (and buying groups) have grown bigger, this phenomenon has increased. When retailers and manufacturers compete for the shelf space allocated to various brands and for control over the location of displays, this is known as the ***battle of the brands***.

A retailer needs to consider the appropriate mix of manufacturer, private, and generic brands to carry. ***Manufacturer (national) brands*** are produced and controlled by manufacturers. They are usually well known, are supported by manufacturer advertising, are somewhat pre-sold to consumers, require limited retailer investment, and often represent maximum product quality to consumers. Manufacturer brands dominate sales in most product categories. Among the most popular manufacturer brands are Kraft, Coke, Pepsi, Levi's, Kodak, Rubbermaid, Sony, Maybelline, and Fisher-Price.

Private (dealer) brands contain names designated by wholesalers or retailers, are more profitable to retailers, are better controlled by retailers, are not sold by competing retailers, are less expensive for consumers, and lead to customer loyalty to retailers (rather than to manufacturers). Yet, with most private-label products, retailers must line up suppliers, arrange for physical distribution and warehousing, sponsor ads, create in-store displays, and absorb losses from unsold items. Retailers' interest in the sales of their own brands can be shown through these examples:

- Private-brand apparel accounts for over one-fifth of all U.S. apparel sales. Private brands provide 27 per cent of men's wear sales, 18 per cent of boys' wear and women's wear sales, and 15 per cent of girls' wear sales.[13]
- Industrywide, private brands account for 15 per cent of U.S. supermarket revenues and 20 per cent of U.S. supermarket unit sales. Loblaw, a Canada-based chain, carries 1,300 items under its President's Choice brand and exports the brand to 1,500 U.S. supermarkets. As a result, "Loblaw has the highest operating margin in Canadian food retailing."[14]
- J.C. Penney has a Merchandise Development Organization "to build the firm's private brands into coordinated collections to compete with dominant manufacturer brands. Its strategic direction is "to court long-term customer loyalty by continuing to improve the components of the merchandise value equation—the right fashion, the right quality, the right price." There is special emphasis on Penney's Worthington, Stafford, Original Arizona Jean Company, Hunt Club, By Design, and Classic Tradition brands.[15]

[12] Richard M. Petreycik, "Variety Adds Spice to Apples," *Progressive Grocer* (February 1990), pp. 72–78; and Steve Weinstein, "How to Avoid Product Duplication," *Progressive Grocer* (July 1993), p. 103.

[13] "PL: Winners and Sinners," *Stores* (May 1990), p. 80.

[14] Kathleen Deveny, "Private-Label Unit Sales Drop, But Can Big Marketers Relax Yet?" *Wall Street Journal* (February 10, 1994), p. B10; and Kathleen Morris, "No-Name Power," *FW* (March 16, 1993), pp. 28–33.

[15] *J.C. Penney Company, Inc. 1992 Annual Report*, p. 4.

- The top 11 private brands at Kmart generate a total of more than $750 million per year in revenues.[16]
- More firms are marketing private brands aggressively: "Private-label products are getting wake-up calls in the form of slick packaging, catchy names, broadcast ad campaigns, promotional programs—even in-store sampling. In other words, retailers are enthusiastically mimicking the sales tactics that manufacturers of packaged goods have used for decades."[17]

As one expert has noted:

> Private label is here to stay in a very strong way. And it is likely to grow, but probably at a somewhat more modest pace than in the past few years. We are seeing large chains going heavily into private label and exploiting it, such as The Limited, which carries only its own labels. Then there are some, such as Dillard's, that believe it is their basic business and their principal approach to specialize in designer or name-brand merchandise, and they do little or no private label.[18]

Nonetheless, care must be taken by retailers in deciding how much emphasis to place on their private brands. There are many consumers who are loyal to manufacturer brands and would shop elsewhere if those brands are not stocked. For instance, when A&P introduced its own Master Choice brand of premium ice cream, "we thought we had a great product—and we did; people loved it in taste tests. But there was a strong brand loyalty to Ben & Jerry's and other premium ice-cream brands, and we weren't able to crack that. We've taken the products off the market and are reassessing them."[19]

Generic brands have generic names for brands (such as canned peas or instant coffee); they are no-frills goods stocked by some retailers. These items usually receive secondary shelf locations, have little or no promotion support, are sometimes of less overall quality than other brands, are stocked in limited assortments, and have plain packages. Generics are controlled by retailers and are priced well below other brands. In U.S. supermarkets carrying them, generics have stabilized at less than one per cent of sales. However, in the prescription drug industry, where the product quality of manufacturer brands and generics is similar, generics account for one-third of unit sales.

There are other considerations that take on added importance if a retailer moves toward a wider and deeper merchandising strategy, including these:

- Risks, merchandise investments, damages, and obsolescence may increase.
- Personnel may be spread too thinly, sometimes over dissimilar goods and services.
- Both the positive and negative ramifications of scrambled merchandising may occur.
- Inventory control procedures may become much more difficult. Merchandise turnover probably will slow down.

Assortment planning should be conducted with the use of a basic stock list (for staples), a model stock plan (for items such as fashion merchandise), and a never-out list (for best-sellers). Staple merchandise consists of regular items carried by a retailer. To a supermarket, staples are such items as milk, bread, canned soup, and facial tissues. To a department store, staples include such items as luggage, cameras, glassware, and housewares. Because these items have relatively stable sales (sometimes seasonal) and their nature does not change much over time, a retailer can clearly outline the requirements for each item. A ***basic stock list*** specifies the inventory level, color, brand,

[16] Bruce Fox, "Brand Erosion Potential," *Chain Store Age Executive* (February 1994), p. 37.

[17] Stuart Elliott, "Advertising," *New York Times* (March 22, 1994), p. D23.

[18] Penny Gill, "Private Label: More or Less," *Stores* (May 1990), p. 71.

[19] Elliott, "Advertising," p. D23.

style category, size, package, and so on for every staple item carried by the retailer. At Wal-Mart, "merchandisers and distribution associates have identified more than 250 key items that have been made a part of the basic stock in our distribution centers. These fast-moving basic stock items also facilitate our [quick response] inventory management system."[20]

Planning assortments for fashion merchandise, furniture, and other nonstandardized items is harder than for staples due to variations in demand, changes in styles, and the number of sizes and colors that must be carried. For these items, decisions involve two stages. First, product lines, styles, designs, and colors are selected. Second, a ***model stock plan*** is used to order specific items, such as the number of green, red, and blue pullover sweaters of a certain design by size. With a model stock plan, many items of popular sizes and colors are ordered; and small amounts of less-popular sizes and colors are ordered to fill out the assortment. Thus, a specialty store may stock one Size 18 dress and six Size 10 dresses for each style carried.

A ***never-out list*** is used when a retailer plans stock levels for best-sellers. Items accounting for high sales volume are stocked in a manner that ensures they are always available. Products are added to and deleted from this list as their popularity and importance to the retailer change. For example, when a new Stephen King novel is released, bookstores order large quantities to be sure they can meet anticipated demand. After it disappears from newspaper best-seller lists, smaller quantities are kept.

For virtually all types of retailers, it is usually a good strategy to use a combination of a basic stock list, a model stock plan, and a never-out list. In some cases, these lists may overlap.

When Merchandise Is Stocked

Next, a retailer should ascertain when each type of merchandise would be stocked. For new goods and services, the retailer must decide when they would first be displayed and sold. For established goods and services, the retailer must plan the regular merchandise flow during the year.

To order merchandise properly, the retailer should forecast sales during the year and take into account various other factors: peak seasons, order and delivery time, routine versus special orders, stock turnover, discounts, and the efficiency of inventory procedures.

As noted earlier in the chapter, some goods and services have peak seasons during the year. For these items (e.g., winter coats and boat rentals), a retailer should plan large inventories during peak periods and less for the off-season. Because some customers like to shop during the off-season, the retailer should not eliminate the items.

A retailer should plan merchandise purchases based on order and delivery time. How long does it take the retailer to process an order? After the order is sent to the supplier, how long does it take to receive delivery of the merchandise? By adding these two time periods together, the retailer can get a good idea of the lead time necessary to restock its shelves. For example, if it takes a retailer seven days to process an order and the supplier an additional fourteen days to deliver merchandise, the retailer should begin to order new merchandise at least 21 days before the old inventory runs out.

Planning differs for routine versus special orders. Routine orders involve the restocking of staples and other regularly sold items. Deliveries are received weekly, monthly, and so on. Accordingly, planning and problems are minimized. Special orders involve the purchase of merchandise that is not sold regularly. These orders involve a lot of planning and close cooperation between retailer and supplier. Specific delivery dates are usually arranged. Custom furniture is an example of a product requiring special orders.

Stock turnover (how quickly merchandise sells) greatly influences how often items must be ordered. Convenience items like milk and bread (which are also highly perishable) have a high turnover rate and must be restocked quite often. Shopping items like refrigerators and color TV sets have a lower turnover rate and are restocked less often.

20 *Wal-Mart 1989 Annual Report*, p. 2.

In deciding when and how often to purchase merchandise, a retailer should consider quantity discounts. Large purchases may result in lower per-unit costs. Also, the use of efficient inventory procedures, such as electronic data interchange and quick response planning procedures, would decrease costs and order times while increasing merchandise productivity.

Where Merchandise Is Stored

The last basic merchandise planning decision involves where products are handled. A single-unit retailer usually must determine how much merchandise to place on the selling floor, how much to place in the stockroom, and whether to use a warehouse. A chain must also allocate merchandise among its stores.

Some firms focus almost entirely on warehouses as central—or regional—distribution centers. Products are shipped from suppliers to these warehouses, and then allotted and shipped to individual outlets. For instance, Burlington Coat Factory's 420,000-square-foot New Jersey warehouse processes up to 125,000 pieces of merchandise a day and services stores nationwide; and Toys "R" Us' regional distribution center in Rialto, California, houses over 80,000 pallets (storage bins) of merchandise—stacked fifty feet high.[21]

Other retailers, such as many supermarket chains, do not rely as much on central warehouses. Instead, they have at least some goods shipped directly from suppliers to individual stores. As an example, Vons has high-volume products shipped directly to its supermarkets rather than to a Vons warehouse for further distribution.[22]

The advantages of central warehousing include the efficiency in transportation and storage, the mechanized processing of goods, improved security, the efficient marking of merchandise, the ease of returns, and the smooth and coordinated flow of merchandise. Central warehousing's major disadvantages are the excessive centralized control, the extra handling of perishables, the high operating costs for small retailers, and potential order-processing delays. In addition, centralized warehousing may reduce the capability of quick response systems by adding another stage in distribution.

In allocating merchandise among its outlets, a retailer should consider the target market(s). Products should be carried by branch stores only if they address the tastes and needs of the customers served by those stores. The more geographically dispersed a retailer is, the more essential it is to pinpoint the differences in store product assortments.

Store size should also be studied in allotting products among branch stores. When the outlets' target markets are similar, the allotment should be based on sales. If Store A has sales of $1 million and Store B has sales of $2 million, Store B should receive twice as many items as A. However, refinements must be made when the target markets differ. Woolworth learned this several years ago, after placing the wrong items in some of its variety stores:

> Oh, let's say a lady's skirt was selling well in the larger stores where we carried eight different varieties. The theory was: take the two best-selling skirts and put them in the smaller stores. Well, it doesn't work that way. There are different customer profiles. Different traffic patterns.[23]

GATHERING INFORMATION ABOUT CONSUMER DEMAND

After overall merchandising plans are established, information about the target market is needed. A retailer should gather data about consumer demand before purchasing or repurchasing any merchandise. The marketing research process, as related to retailing, was detailed in Chapter 7.

[21] "Burlington Warehouse Gets Trigger-Happy," *Chain Store Age Executive* (June 1989), p. 31; and Susan Caminiti, "The New Champs of Retailing," *Fortune* (September 24, 1990), p. 94.

[22] *Vons Companies, Inc. 1992 Annual Report*, p. 12.

[23] Geoffrey Smith, "We're Moving! We're Alive!" *Forbes* (November 21, 1983), pp. 66 ff.

ETHICS IN RETAILING

When Should a Retailer Decide to Pull a Questionable Product Off Its Shelves?

A week after Congress held hearings on the amount of sex and violence in the video-game industry (and after getting complaints from parents), Toys "R" Us announced that it would stop selling Sega Entertainment's *Night Trap* video game. And Toys "R" Us, by far the nation's largest toy chain, decided to send back all of the remaining *Night Trap* stock that it had in inventory to Sega.

The goal of the *Night Trap* game is for the players to protect scantily-clad sorority sisters against attacking zombies. If the zombies win, they suck the sorority sisters' blood with a giant syringe. As a Toys "R" Us spokesperson remarked, "*Night Trap* was a good seller for us, but corporate executives decided to remove the game from the shelf."

Despite Toys "R" Us' actions, a spokesperson for Sega said, "There continues to be a misperception about our industry that it is a kiddie-based industry. But in reality we have many adults playing our games as well." Sega has no plans to limit "its ability to produce a variety of software." However, the firm does intend to continue with its current age-rating mix for video games: About 4 per cent of its games are rated by the company as being suitable for people 17 and older; the balance are for general audiences or for those 13 and older.

Source: Based on material in Joseph Pereira, "Toys "R" Us Says It Decided to Pull Sega's *Night Trap* From Store Shelves," *Wall Street Journal* (December 17, 1993), p. B5F.

Superior merchandise management depends on a retailer's ability to generate a relatively accurate sales forecast. After all, the most important merchandising functions performed by a retailer are the anticipation and satisfaction of customer demand. See Figure 13–8.

In gathering data for merchandising decisions, the retailer has several possible sources of information. The most valuable source is the consumer. By researching the target market's demographics, life-styles, and potential shopping plans, a retailer is able to study consumer demand directly.

Other sources of information can be used when direct consumer data are unavailable or insufficient. Suppliers (manufacturers and/or wholesalers) usually do their own sales forecasts and marketing research (e.g., test marketing). They also know how much outside promotional support a retailer will get, and this affects sales. When closing a deal with the retailer, a supplier may present charts and graphs, showing forecasts and promotional support. However, the retailer should remember one significant point: it is the retailer that has direct access to the target market and its needs.

Retail personnel can provide input about consumer demand. Sales and display personnel have direct contact with customers and can pass their observations along to management. A retailer can use a ***want book*** or a ***want slip*** system. These are tools for recording consumer requests on unstocked or out-of-stock merchandise. The want book is used in smaller stores; want slips are requests for specific items that are used in larger stores. These tools are very helpful to a retailer's buyers. Personnel should be encouraged to offer feedback and not be shut off from making comments based on interaction with consumers. Outside of customers, salespeople may provide the most useful information for merchandising decisions.

Buying personnel can learn a lot about consumer demand by visiting suppliers, talking with sales personnel, and observing customer behavior. Usually, buyers are responsible for complete sales forecasts and merchandise plans in their product categories; top management combines the forecasts and plans of individual buyers to obtain overall company projections.

Competitors are another source of information. A conservative retailer may not stock an item until the competition does so. Therefore, comparison shoppers (who look at the offerings and prices of competitors) may be employed. In addition, trade publications report on trends in each area of retailing and provide a legal way of gathering information from competitors. See Figure 13–9 for an example of a competition shopping report.

Other sources may offer useful pieces of information: government sources can show unemployment, inflation, and product safety data; independent news sources conduct

"Because I order all the sports merchandise for my store, I talk to my customers to learn what they want. That's a major difference between Fred Meyer and other stores. Here, we let our buyers know what products our customers are looking for and work hard to keep those products in stock."
NICK HILL, SPORTS ORDER CLERK
Coleman
Crowded
Ruffles
COLEMAN

FIGURE 13–8 How Fred Meyer, Inc. Anticipates and Satisfies Customer Demand
Reprinted by permission.

COMPETITION SHOPPING REPORT

Store #_____ Date_____

Dept. #_____ Qualified Competition Shopped:

1._____
2._____

Our Style No.	Mfr. Model or Style	Description	Our Price	1st Compet. Price	2nd Compet. Price	Store's Recom. Price	Buyer's Recom. Price

Item Seen at Our Competitor's Store Which We Should Carry:					
Manufacturer	Mfr. Model or Style	Description	Reg. or List Price	Sale Price	Buyer's Comments

Signature of Shopper *Store Manager*

FIGURE 13–9
A Competition Shopping Report

their own consumer polls and do investigative reporting; and commercial data can be purchased.

Information should be gathered from several of these sources; one type of data may be insufficient. Whatever the amount of information acquired, a retailer should feel comfortable that it will be able to make decisions as accurately as possible. For routine merchandising decisions (e.g., staple products), limited information may be sufficient. On the other hand, new-car sales can fluctuate widely and require extensive data for sales forecasts.

DETERMINING MERCHANDISE SOURCES

The next step in merchandise buying and handling is to determine the sources of merchandise. Three major sources exist: company-owned; outside, regularly used; and outside, new.

With the company-owned supplier, a large retailer owns a manufacturing and/or wholesaling facility. The company-owned supplier handles all or part of the merchandise that the retailer requests.

An outside, regularly used supplier is one not owned by the retailer but used regularly by it. The retailer knows the quality of the goods and services and the reliability of the supplier through its own experience.

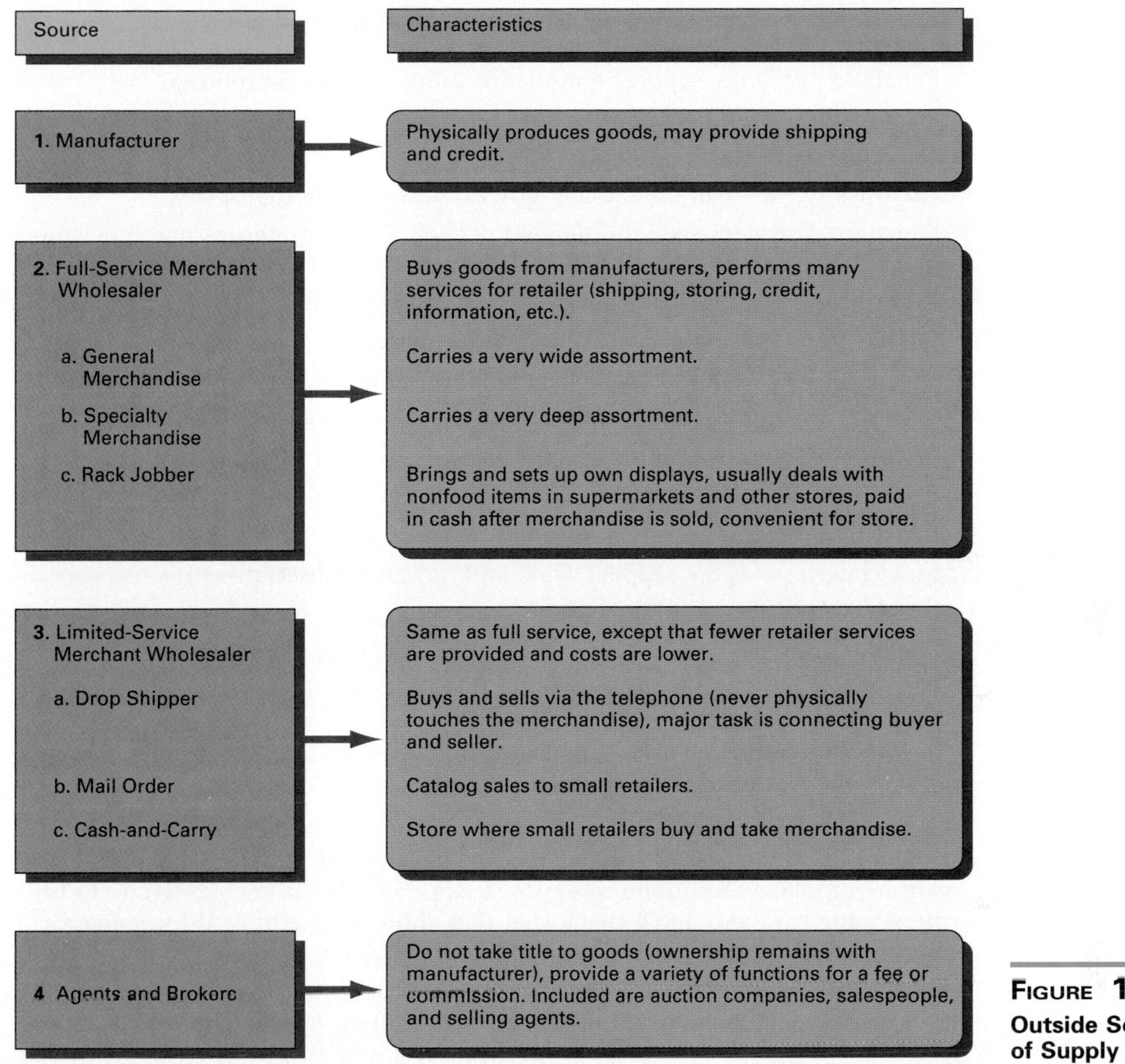

Source
Characteristics
1. Manufacturer
Physically produces goods, may provide shipping and credit.
2. Full-Service Merchant Wholesaler
Buys goods from manufacturers, performs many services for retailer (shipping, storing, credit, information, etc.).
a. General Merchandise
Carries a very wide assortment.
b. Specialty Merchandise
Carries a very deep assortment.
c. Rack Jobber
Brings and sets up own displays, usually deals with nonfood items in supermarkets and other stores, paid in cash after merchandise is sold, convenient for store.
3. Limited-Service Merchant Wholesaler
Same as full service, except that fewer retailer services are provided and costs are lower.
a. Drop Shipper
Buys and sells via the telephone (never physically touches the merchandise), major task is connecting buyer and seller.
b. Mail Order
Catalog sales to small retailers.
c. Cash-and-Carry
Store where small retailers buy and take merchandise.
4. Agents and Brokers
Do not take title to goods (ownership remains with manufacturer), provide a variety of functions for a fee or commission. Included are auction companies, salespeople, and selling agents.

Figure 13–10
Outside Sources of Supply

An outside, new supplier is one that is not owned by the retailer and has not been dealt with before by it. Thus, the retailer may be unfamiliar with the quality of the merchandise and the reliability of this supplier. The basic types of outside suppliers (regularly used and new) are shown in Figure 13–10.

These two examples show the complexity involved with choosing suppliers. Sears purchases products from 5,000 primary suppliers in the United States alone; this means constantly assessing potential vendors and the performance of existing ones. To improve its efficiency in dealing with suppliers, Sears has been working on an EDI linkup with all of its primary suppliers. And it has developed a computer software program, which it is making available to suppliers at no charge.[24]

The annual International Home Furnishings Market in High Point and Thomasville, North Carolina, is the world's largest wholesale furniture fair. The fair lasts more than a week, takes place in over 150 separate buildings, involves 1,600 domestic and international home furnishings exhibitors, and draws in excess of 50,000 people (over half of whom are retail buyers), and results in transactions worth several hundred million dollars.[25]

[24] Eve Tahmincioglu, "Sears to Implement Standard EDI Link with 5,000 Suppliers," *Women's Wear Daily* (July 12, 1990), p. 15.

[25] International Home Furnishings Market correspondence.

In choosing vendors, such criteria as these should be considered:

- Reliability—Will the supplier consistently fulfill all written promises?
- Price-quality—Who provides the best merchandise at the lowest price?
- Order-processing time—How fast will deliveries be made?
- Exclusive rights—Will the supplier give exclusive selling rights?
- Functions provided—Will the supplier provide shipping, storing, and other functions, if needed?
- Information—Will the supplier pass along any important goods/service data?
- Ethics—Will the supplier fulfill all verbal promises?
- Guarantee—Does the supplier stand behind its offerings?
- Credit—Can credit purchases be made from the supplier? On what terms?
- Long-run relations—Will the supplier be available over an extended period?
- Reorders—Can the supplier promptly fill reorders?
- Markup—Will markup (price margins) be adequate?
- Innovativeness—Is the supplier's line innovative or conservative?
- Local advertising—Does the supplier advertise in local media?
- Investment—How large are total investment costs with a supplier?
- Risk—How much risk is involved in dealing with the supplier?

Sometimes, retailers and their suppliers work well together. Other times, there are problems. Here is an illustration of each situation:

> Creating a power merchandising approach to apparel in the new Kmart prototype was facilitated by the strong working partnerships that the retailer had forged with its suppliers. According to senior vice-president Don Keeble, "We went to the vendor base and asked them what they think we ought to do to enhance their products. Because it is a partnership, we want their opinions on how to sell more at the mass-merchandising level."[26]
>
> Best Buy's retailing approach depends, in part, upon its ability to offer a wide selection of name-brand products to customers and is, therefore, dependent upon satisfactory supplier relationships. Best Buy's 25 largest suppliers account for around 73 per cent of the merchandise purchased by the retailer. In spring 1992, General Electric advised Best Buy that it would stop selling major appliances to the retailer because Best Buy's discount-store format was inconsistent with GE's marketing strategy.[27]

EVALUATING MERCHANDISE

Whatever source is chosen, the retailer needs a procedure for evaluating the merchandise under consideration for purchase. Should each individual unit be examined, or can an item be bought by description?

Three types of evaluation are possible: inspection, sampling, and description. The choice of technique depends on the cost of the item, its attributes, and its regularity of purchase. Inspection occurs when each individual unit is examined before purchase and after delivery. Jewelry and art are two examples of expensive, relatively unique purchases where the retailer would carefully inspect every item.

Sampling takes place when a large quantity of breakable, perishable, or expensive items is regularly purchased. It becomes inefficient to inspect each piece of mer-

[26] "Supplier Partnership Spurs Power Apparel," *Discount Store News* (February 1, 1993), p. 34.

[27] *Best Buy, Inc. 1993 10K*, pp. 7–8.

chandise in this situation. Therefore, items are sampled for quality and condition. For example, a retailer ready to purchase several hundred light fixtures, bananas, or watches would not inspect each fixture, banana, or watch. Instead, a number of units (a sample) would be examined. The entire selection would be purchased if the sample is satisfactory. An unsatisfactory sample might cause a whole shipment to be rejected (or a discount negotiated). Sampling would also occur on receipt of merchandise.

Description buying takes place when a retailer purchases standardized, nonbreakable, and nonperishable merchandise. The items are not inspected or sampled; they are ordered in quantity from a verbal, written, or pictorial description. For example, a stationery store can order paper clips, pads, typing paper, and so on from a catalog or order form. When it receives an order, only a count of those items is conducted.

NEGOTIATING THE PURCHASE

After a merchandise source has been chosen and pre-purchase evaluation has been conducted, a retailer has to negotiate the purchase and its terms. A new or special order usually results in a ***negotiated contract.*** In this case, a retailer and a supplier carefully negotiate all aspects of the purchase. On the other hand, a regular order or reorder usually results in a ***uniform contract.*** In this instance, terms are standard or have already been agreed on, and the order is handled in a routine manner.

Many purchase terms must be specified, whether a negotiated or a uniform contract is involved, including

- Delivery date.
- Quantity purchased.
- Price and payment arrangements.
- Discounts.
- Form of delivery.
- Point of transfer of title.

The delivery date and the quantity purchased must be clearly stated. A retailer should be able to cancel an order if either provision is not carried out satisfactorily. The retailer's purchase price, payment arrangements, and permissible discounts are also important. What is the retailer's cost per item (including handling charges)? What forms of payment are permitted (e.g., cash versus credit)? What discounts are permitted? Often, retailers' purchase prices are discounted for early payments (e.g., "2/10/net 30" means a 2 per cent discount is given if the full bill is paid in ten days; the full bill is due in thirty days), trade activities (such as setting up displays), and quantity purchases. Stipulations are necessary for the form of delivery (water, air, truck, rail, and so on) and the party responsible for shipping charges (e.g., FOB factory—free on board—means a supplier places merchandise with the shipper, but the retailer pays the freight). Last, the point of transfer of title—when ownership changes from supplier to buyer—should be noted in a contract.

CONCLUDING THE PURCHASE

For many medium-sized and large firms, purchases are concluded automatically; computers are used to complete and process orders, and each purchase is fed into the computer's data bank. Smaller retailers usually conclude their purchases manually; orders are written up and processed manually, and purchases are added to the store's book inventory in the same manner.

Multiunit retailers must determine whether to use central, regional, or local approval to conclude purchases: Should central or regional management have the final okay in a purchase, or should the local manager have the final say? This issue was discussed in the buying organization part of the chapter. Advantages and disadvantages accrue to each approval technique.

As mentioned in the previous section, ***transfer of title*** should be carefully specified with the supplier. Several alternatives are possible:

1. The retailer takes title immediately upon purchase.
2. The retailer assumes ownership after merchandise is loaded onto the mode of transportation.
3. The retailer takes title when a shipment is received.
4. The retailer does not take title until the end of a billing cycle, when the supplier receives payment.
5. The retailer accepts merchandise on consignment and does not own the items. The supplier is paid after merchandise is sold.

It is important for a retailer to understand the differences among these alternatives, because its responsibilities and rights differ in each case.

A consignment or memorandum deal can be made when a vendor is in a rather weak position and wants to persuade the retailer to carry its items. In a ***consignment purchase***, the retailer runs no risk because title is not taken; the supplier owns the goods until they are sold. In a ***memorandum purchase***, risk is still low, but the retailer takes title on delivery and is responsible for damages. With both options, the retailer does not pay for items until they are sold and has the right to return merchandise.

HANDLING THE MERCHANDISE

During this phase, a retailer physically handles merchandise, which involves such varied tasks as receiving and storing goods, price and inventory marking, setting up displays, figuring on-floor quantities and assortments, completing customer transactions, arranging for customer delivery or pickup, processing returns and damaged goods, monitoring pilferage, and controlling merchandise.

First, items are usually shipped from a supplier to warehouses, for storage and disbursement, or directly to a retailer's store(s). For example, Rose's, a chain with 235 full-line discount stores, has a fully automated warehouse that stocks thousands of products and speeds their delivery throughout the Southeast. See Figure 13–11. On the other hand, rather than rely on deliveries from suppliers, The Limited orders apparel via satellite, picks it up from manufacturers in the United States and Asia (with a chartered Boeing jet making several flights a week to Hong Kong and back); ships items to its own central warehouse in Columbus, Ohio; and then delivers them to its stores. J.C. Penney has three large distribution centers for its stores, six catalog distribution centers, and ten "deliverable lines" centers. The latter's function is to supplement the storage space the firm has in selected markets. Few goods are stored at the deliverable lines centers: "Almost 80 per cent of the work here involves receiving freight from domestic suppliers and shipping it out to stores."[28]

Next, prices and inventory information are marked on merchandise. Supermarkets estimate that price marking on individual items costs them an amount equal to their annual profits, and they look forward to the time when shelf prices will be sufficient.

Price and inventory marking can be conducted in various ways. Small retailers often hand-post prices and manually keep inventory records. Many larger retailers use their own computer-generated price tags and rely on pre-printed UPC data on packages for maintaining inventory records. Others purchase tags, with computer- and human-readable price and inventory data, from outside suppliers. Still other retailers expect their vendors to provide source tagging.

[28] *Rose's Stores Inc. 1992 Annual Report*; Jeremy Main, "The Winning Organization," *Fortune* (September 26, 1988), p. 56; Walecia Konrad, Russell Mitchell, and Laura Zinn, "Why Leslie Wexner Shops Overseas," *Business Week* (February 3, 1992), p. 30; and "Retrofit Speeds Throughput at Penney DC," *Chain Store Age Executive* (November 1990), pp. 160–164.

FIGURE 13–11
Rose's State-of-the-Art Distribution Center
Rose's is a Henderson, North Carolina-based full-line discount store chain. It operates over 235 stores in several states. Its high-tech distribution center greatly facilitates its merchandise handling and shipping functions.
Reprinted by permission.

The more information that labels or tags possess, the more efficient the inventory control system. For example, Kimball Systems makes various product tags that include a wide range of data. Dennison Manufacturing makes a system for receiving, marking, and routing merchandise to sales floors. With the portable printers developed by Monarch Marking Systems, a retailer can use hand-held devices to print UPC-based labels; and the devices can also be connected to a store's computer system.

Store displays and on-floor quantities and assortments depend on the type of store and merchandise involved. Supermarkets typically use bin and rack displays and place most inventory on the sales floor. Traditional department stores have all kinds of interior displays (such as ensemble displays) and place a lot of inventory in the back room, off the sales floor. Displays and on-floor merchandising are discussed more fully in Chapter 16.

Merchandise handling is not completed until the customer purchases and receives it from the retailer. This involves order taking, credit or cash transactions, packaging, and delivery or pickup. Automation has improved retailer performance in each of these areas.

A procedure for processing returns and damaged goods is also needed. In particular, a retailer needs to determine which party is responsible for customer returns (the supplier or the retailer) and the provisions under which damaged goods would be accepted for refund or exchange (such as the length of time a warranty is honored).

As discussed in Chapter 12, monitoring and reducing inventory losses due to theft is an aspect of merchandise handling that has rapidly grown in importance. More retailers are taking aggressive actions in dealing with this problem than before because of the high costs of merchandise theft.

Merchandise control involves evaluating sales, profits, turnover, inventory shortages, seasonality, and costs for each goods/service category and item carried by a retailer. Control is generally achieved by developing and maintaining book (perpetual) inventory data, and then periodically conducting a physical inventory count to check the accuracy of the book figures. The latter usually must be adjusted to reflect damaged goods, pilferage, customer returns, and other factors. An in-depth discussion of this topic appears in the next chapter.

REORDERING MERCHANDISE

A plan for reordering merchandise must be developed and implemented for those items purchased more than once. Four factors are most important in devising such a plan: order and delivery time, inventory turnover, financial outlays, and inventory versus ordering costs.

Order and delivery time need to be determined. How long would it take for a retailer to process an order and a supplier to fulfill and deliver that order? It is possible that delivery time could be so lengthy that a retailer must reorder while a full inventory still exists. On the other hand, overnight delivery may be available for some items.

The turnover rate for each type of merchandise needs to be calculated. How long would it take for a retailer to sell out its inventory? A fast-selling product allows a retailer to have two choices: order a surplus of items and spread out reorder periods, or keep a low inventory and order frequently (short order periods). A slow-selling item may enable a retailer to reduce its initial inventory level and spread out the reorder period.

The financial outlays to be made under various purchase options need to be considered. A large order, which would provide a discount, may involve a large cash outlay. A small order, although more expensive per item, would result in lower total costs at any one time (because less inventory is maintained).

Finally, inventory holding versus ordering costs must be weighed. The advantages of maintaining a large inventory are customer satisfaction, quantity discounts in purchases, low per-item transportation charges, and ease of control and handling. Potential disadvantages are high investment costs; the greater possibility of obsolescence, deterioration, and damages; storage costs; insurance costs; and opportunity costs. The advantages of placing many orders and keeping a small inventory are low investment costs, low opportunity costs, low storage costs, and low damages and obsolescence. The potential disadvantages are disappointing customers by being out of stock, higher per-unit costs, the impact of order-fulfillment delays, the need for partial shipments, extra service charges, and more complex control and handling. Retailers normally try to trade off these two costs by maintaining a large enough inventory to satisfy customers while not keeping a high surplus inventory. Quick response inventory planning reduces both inventory and ordering costs via closer retailer-supplier relationships.

RE-EVALUATING ON A REGULAR BASIS

Once a well-integrated merchandise buying and handling plan is in place, the retailer should not ignore this process. Re-evaluation should take place on a regular basis. Management should review the buying organization (Step 1 in Figure 13–1), and that organization should review the buying and handling process (Steps 2 through 9). The overall procedure, as well as the handling of individual goods and services, should be monitored.

SUMMARY

1. *To examine nonfinancial merchandise planning and management* A key element in a successful retail strategy is developing and implementing a merchandise plan. Merchandising consists of the activities involved in a retailer's buying goods and services and making them available for sale.

2. *To outline the merchandise buying and handling process* A merchandise buying and handling plan is an integrated, systematic process for acquiring and processing merchandise. Ten steps are involved: (1) setting up a buying organization; (2) outlining merchandise plans; (3) gathering information about

consumer demand; (4) determining merchandise sources; (5) evaluating merchandise; (6) negotiating the purchase; (7) concluding the purchase; (8) handling the merchandise; (9) reordering merchandise; and (10) re-evaluating on a regular basis.

3. *To discuss each element in the merchandise buying and handling process in detail* Buying-organization decisions include the level of formality, degree of centralization, amount of specialization, inside versus outside personnel, cooperative efforts, merchandising versus buying, and staffing. A buying philosophy includes only the purchase of goods and services and not the sale of them; a merchandising philosophy entails both activities. Some retailers separate the buying and selling functions.

Merchandise plans involve the four basic decisions noted under this chapter's objective 4.

Data from customers, sources of supply, personnel, competitors, and others must be collected to help the retailer forecast and adapt to demand.

A retailer must choose among company-owned; outside, regularly used; and/or outside, new sources of supply. Inspection, sampling, and/or description techniques of merchandise evaluation must be planned.

Purchase terms may have to be negotiated in their entirety or uniform contracts may be used. The purchase must also be concluded (automatic-manual, management approval, and transfer of title).

Merchandise handling must be outlined, including receiving and storing, price and inventory marking, displays, on-floor assortments, customer transactions, delivery or pickup, returns and damaged goods, monitoring pilferage, and control.

Reorder procedures are necessary and depend on order and delivery time, inventory turnover, financial outlays, and inventory versus ordering costs.

Both the overall merchandising procedure and specific goods and services need to be regularly reviewed.

4. *To place special emphasis on what merchandise a retailer should carry, how much to stock, when to stock items, and where to store items* First, in determining what items to handle, a retailer must decide on the quality of merchandise (below average, above average, or medium) to stock and how innovative (progressive or conservative) to be. The product life cycle is a useful tool for projecting the sales of a product over its life and the types of customers who purchase during different time periods.

Second, how much merchandise to stock is a decision involving width and depth of assortment. A product assortment can range from wide and deep to narrow and shallow. When planning an assortment, many factors should be examined: sales, profit, investment costs, space requirements, turnover, complementary and substitute products, manufacturer insistence, and the brand mix (manufacturer, private, and/or generic).

A third required decision involves when merchandise is to be stocked. An accurate sales forecast is necessary for efficient planning. Among the points to be considered are peak seasons, order and delivery time, routine versus special orders, stock turnover, discounts, and the efficiency of inventory procedures.

A fourth decision concerns where merchandise is stored. The retailer must determine whether to use warehouses or to have items shipped directly to its store(s). Merchandise also has to be allocated among store branches.

KEY TERMS

merchandising (p. 432)
merchandise buying and handling process (p. 432)
formal buying organization (p. 432)
informal buying organization (p. 432)
centralized buying organization (p. 433)
decentralized buying organization (p. 433)
inside buying organization (p. 435)
outside buying organization (p. 435)
resident buying office (p. 436)
cooperative buying (p. 436)
product life cycle (p. 439)
trickle-down theory (p. 443)
trickle-across theory (p. 443)
width of assortment (p. 444)
depth of assortment (p. 444)
battle of the brands (p. 446)
manufacturer (national) brands (p. 446)
private (dealer) brands (p. 446)
generic brands (p. 447)
basic stock list (p. 447)
model stock plan (p. 448)
never-out list (p. 448)
want book (want slip) (p. 450)
negotiated contract (p. 455)
uniform contract (p. 455)
transfer of title (p. 456)
consignment purchase (p. 456)
memorandum purchase (p. 456)

QUESTIONS FOR DISCUSSION

1. Why is proper merchandising so critical to a retailer's success or failure?
2. What are the advantages and disadvantages of a decentralized buying organization?
3. Under what circumstances could a retailer carry a wide range of merchandise quality without hurting its image? When should the quality of merchandise carried be quite narrow?
4. How innovative should each of these retailers be in planning its merchandise? Explain your answers.
   a. Convenience store.
   b. Women's shoe store.

 c. Small fruit-and-vegetable store.
 d. Mail-order luggage firm.

5. How should a toy store use the product life-cycle concept?
6. If you were a franchise operator, how would you feel about enforcing constrained decision making with regard to merchandise planning? Why?
7. Why are some retailers hesitant to drop fading goods and services?
8. Give examples of retailers fitting into each of these merchandise assortment plans.
 a. Narrow-shallow.
 b. Narrow-deep.
 c. Wide-deep.
9. How could a college store use a basic stock list, a model stock plan, and never-out lists?
10. What problems may occur if a retailer mistimes purchases?
11. What types of information should a specialty store gather before adding a new brand of computer?
12. Cite the advantages and disadvantages associated with these merchandise sources for a small art gallery. How would your answers differ for a large art gallery chain?
 a. Company-owned.
 b. Outside, regularly used.
 c. Outside, new.
13. Develop a checklist a retailer could use in negotiating purchase terms with its suppliers.
14. Which is more difficult, merchandise planning for a restaurant or a children's clothing store? Explain your answer.

CASE 1
Supervalu: Produce Power*

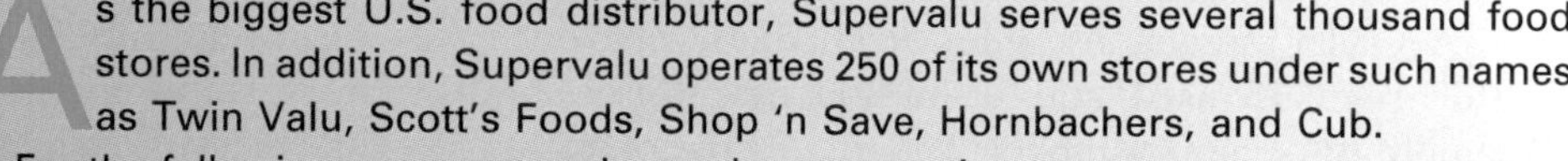

As the biggest U.S. food distributor, Supervalu serves several thousand food stores. In addition, Supervalu operates 250 of its own stores under such names as Twin Valu, Scott's Foods, Shop 'n Save, Hornbachers, and Cub.

For the following reasons, produce sales are very important to supermarkets. One, many firms see the produce department as a way of differentiating themselves from competitors. Some executives believe an excellent produce department is the leading reason why people visit a particular supermarket. Two, the produce department is a key contributor to supermarket sales and profits. According to *Progressive Grocer*, the produce department currently accounts for 9.9 per cent of total supermarket sales; retail analysts predict that produce may account for nearly 12 per cent of supermarket sales by the year 2000. And industrywide, produce yields higher gross profits than dry groceries. Three, supermarkets still dominate the marketplace with regard to the sale of fresh fruits and vegetables. One study found that 90 per cent of respondents say the supermarket is the place where fresh fruits and vegetables are purchased.

Yet, despite the value of produce to supermarkets, research has shown that these retailers have not increased the size of the produce buying department in recent years. The average supermarket chain has two produce buyers at headquarters, the same as in prior years. Some firms are even operating with fewer buyers than before due to the increased use of computers.

Although many supermarket chains use produce brokers, Supervalu has its own field buyers. The advantages of using produce brokers include their having specialized knowledge on the availability of produce (especially when a crop's yield is low due to poor climate conditions), and the access to their research reports. Some of the better brokers prepare weekly reports which contain data on wholesale and retail prices, suggest the products to advertise in upcoming weeks, and forecast product availability. The reports are often tailored to store climates and consumer profiles.

Field buyers are used by the largest retailers, including Supervalu. Since 1968, Supervalu's produce buyers have been actively involved in all of the stages of produce preparation and selection—from the seedling to the store. These steps include packaging, cooling, loading, shipping, storage, and distribution. Supervalu's total commitment to buying ensures that consumers can rely on Supervalu for consistent quality at competitive prices.

* The material in this case is drawn from Stephen Bennett, "A Healthy Prognosis for Produce," *Progressive Grocer* (January 1994), pp. 81–86; and Mary Ann Linsen, "Clubs: How Big a Threat?" *Progressive Grocer* (September 1993), pp. 107–115.

Table 1 The Rating of Product Attributes by Produce Buyers

Attribute	Rating
Best quality available	4.9
Strong demand	4.5
Appropriate current season	4.3
High gross margin	4.1
Price competitive	4.0
High net margin/Direct product profitability	3.8
Innovative packaging	3.7
Year-round availability	3.6
Competitors added item	3.4
Produce branded	2.8

Note: A rating of 1 means that the attribute is not important; a rating of 5 means that the attribute is very important.
Source: "Fresh Fruit and Vegetable Procurement Dynamics/The Rise of the Supermarket Buyer," Cornell University's Food Industry Management Program.

An example of Supervalu's commitment to securing quality produce is its employment of permanent inspectors in prime growing regions of California, Florida, and Washington throughout the year. Supervalu also hires temporary inspectors in seasonal growing areas. The firm does not use third-party inspectors. Its inspectors are responsible for checking the appearance, shape, color, and maturity level of all produce. In addition, buyers are responsible for evaluating packaging, cooling facilities, and trucking facilities.

Unlike other buyers who have no or little loyalty to important vendors, Supervalu buyers typically build long-term relationships with growers and shippers. These relationships may prove to be most helpful when there are shortages of a given crop due to heat, cold, drought, or hail.

Table 1 shows data on the rating of 10 product attributes by produce buyers. Each attribute is rated on a 1 to 5 scale, with 1 being not important and 5 being very important. As can be seen from the table, the three most important attributes are best quality available, strong demand, and appropriate current season. The three least important attributes are year-round availability, competitors added item, and produce branded.

Table 2 lists various measures of produce buyers' performance. Of the seven measures cited, overall sales and shrinkage/loss are the most-often used to evaluate buyers, and sales per square foot and direct product profitability are the least-often used.

Table 2 The Use of Various Measures to Assess Produce Buyers' Performance

Performance Measure	Frequency of Use
Overall sales	2.8
Shrinkage/loss	2.7
Sales per labor hour	2.7
Gross margin/return on investment	2.6
Sales per customer	2.5
Sales per square foot	1.8
Direct product profitability	1.5

Note: A rating of 1 means that the performance measure is never used; a rating of 3 means that the performance measure is always used.
Source: "Fresh Fruit and Vegetable Procurement Dynamics/The Rise of the Supermarket Buyer," Cornell University's Food Industry Management Program.

QUESTIONS

1. Evaluate the pros and cons of centralized buying for Supervalu.
2. Evaluate the data in Tables 1 and 2, and describe how the information in these tables can be used by Supervalu produce buyers.
3. Under what conditions should Supervalu use produce brokers? Explain your answer.
4. What can supermarkets do to improve the effectiveness of their produce departments?

VIDEO QUESTIONS ON SUPERVALU

1. Evaluate Supervalu's seedling-to-store produce buying strategy.
2. Describe the pros and cons of Supervalu's long-term relationships with its growers, shippers, and retailers.

CASE 2 Lillian Vernon: Order Processing†

The Lillian Vernon company was founded in 1951 by a young woman who placed a $495 ad in *Seventeen Magazine*. The ad, which offered inexpensive purses and belts (personalized with the customer's initials), generated $32,000 in orders and launched a promising mail-order business. The firm went public in 1987.

Today, Lillian Vernon is a direct marketer that sells gift, household, gardening, decorative, and children's products through four types of catalogs: the Lillian Vernon core catalog, Lilly's Kids, Christmas Memories, and sale catalogs. During 1993, the firm mailed 20 editions of its catalogs and had a total circulation of 141 million. The average catalog was 108 pages in length and displayed over 700 products. Total revenues exceeded $172 million in 1993.

Lillian Vernon's customer data base includes nearly 15 million names, five million of which have bought products from the firm within the past two years. Over 90 per cent of the company's customers are women; they average 43 years of age and have an average annual household income of $53,000. The firm continually refines its data base to better target mailings, reduce costs, and increase sales per catalog. Lillian Vernon sorts its data base by demographic factors so that each mailing is aimed at the most likely customer group.

The company accepts phone and fax orders 24 hours a day, 7 days a week. In 1993, it received over 1.8 million orders by phone, and it filled more than 4.4 million orders in all. Over the six weeks of the 1993 Christmas season, Lillian Vernon processed 50,000+ orders daily. The average customer order was $40 and involved two to three items.

Order processing at Lillian Vernon is rather complex because the firm personalizes many of its brass, wood, lucite, and textile products by inscribing names or initials free of charge. A full order often requires that multiple items be picked, personalized, packed, and then shipped. Lillian Vernon has one of the largest personalization departments in the country.

When mail orders are received, they are opened, reviewed, batched, and entered into the firm's computer system. That system checks for inventory availability and prints lists, places work orders, and bar codes packing materials and shipping labels.

† The material in this case is drawn from *Lillian Vernon 1993 Annual Report*; *Lillian Vernon Corporate Overview: Fact Sheets*; Stephanie Strom, "A Downside of Mail-Order Mania," *New York Times* (December 10, 1993), pp. D1, D3; and "On Target: Lillian Vernon Focuses on Customers," *Management Review* (May 1993), pp. 22–24.

It even automatically selects the optimal shipping carton; this saves packaging and postage costs. Inventory movements are tracked with scanners and terminals that are located on forklift trucks. As a result of its procedures, Lillian Vernon can process an order within days. In contrast, some competitors require 4 to 6 weeks.

Inventory management is somewhat simplified for the firm because most items at Lillian Vernon are not sized. This also reduces the company's return rate. Lillian Vernon offers a 100 per cent satisfaction guarantee. It will accept returns years after purchases, and even if the items are personalized.

Before orders are shipped out, they are reviewed by checkers to insure completeness. And to better assure correctness, all orders get two accuracy and quality control checks.

After orders are sealed, they are passed through a laser scanner. The scanner reads and directs the packages to the proper trucks for shipment. The scanner also deducts the items from Lillian Vernon's stock records, updates the computer order file, weighs the packages, and calculates postage.

The computerization and mechanization have enabled the firm to reduce its fulfillment and delivery costs despite a 14 per cent increase in United Parcel Service rates that went into effective in February 1992. The cost reduction was accomplished by using alternate methods of shipment and other cost-control measures.

The Lillian Vernon distribution center is located in Virginia Beach. The center encompasses the company's entire fulfillment efforts; all orders are shipped from this facility. It also contains its telemarketing department, computer center, and customer-service center. This enables the firm to more easily verify that ordered goods are in stock, fulfill orders, and handle returns. The distribution center, located on a 57-acre site, is the size of 10 football fields and holds 23,000 pallets of merchandise.

Lillian Vernon introduces 1,100+ new products annually; each year, over one-half of the products in its catalogs are new. It buys products from around the world. All items are purchased directly from manufacturers; the firm does not deal with intermediaries (wholesalers). Its 20 buyers regularly travel to such major markets as Paris, London, Milan, and Hong Kong. In addition, Lillian Vernon has buying and quality-control offices in Florence and Hong Kong. Buyers choose new products on the basis of focus groups and consumer surveys, and make store visits to view new products. Many of its products are designed by Lillian Vernon's own artists and are protected by copyright.

As a result of these combined strategies, the firm's annual profit has been growing strongly.

QUESTIONS

1. Describe why order processing is complex at Lillian Vernon. How would you simplify it?
2. Under what circumstances should the firm ship a partial order? Explain your answer.
3. What additional opportunities for mechanization of Lillian Vernon's order processing exist?
4. Comment on Lillian Vernon's buying practices.

VIDEO QUESTIONS ON LILLIAN VERNON

1. Develop a flowchart describing all of the steps in order processing at Lillian Vernon. Explain the sequencing of these steps.
2. Evaluate Lillian Vernon's order-processing system.

Financial Merchandise Management

❖ Chapter Objectives

1. To describe the major aspects of financial merchandise planning and management
2. To explain the cost and retail methods of accounting
3. To study the merchandise forecasting and budgeting process
4. To examine alternative methods of inventory unit control
5. To integrate dollar and unit merchandising control concepts

A Coopers & Lybrand survey of physical-inventory performance among supermarkets found that 74 per cent of respondents feel their current inventory-counting systems are failing to meet their needs. In general, the respondents say there must be more accurate and precise data on inventory levels. As of 1996, 36 per cent of these respondents expect to be recording inventory data by stock-keeping unit (SKU) or UPC; and 33 per cent plan to be counting inventories by scanning bar codes.

This study also learned that, besides the actual counting of merchandise, retail prices are the most commonly recorded data during physical inventories (collected by 87 per cent of respondents), followed by the items' department or merchandise codes (collected by 54 per cent of respondents) and the items' cost (collected by 15 per cent of respondents). Gross profit margin is the most important financial measure of inventory performance, closely followed by gross margin dollars; respondents rank inventory turnover, sales per square foot, and gross margin return on investment as being less important.

Many convenience-store retailers are emphasizing better merchandise management and inventory planning as a means of improving their profitability. 7-Eleven has implemented a new inventory management system called Accelerated Inventory Management (AIM) that provides each store manager with the ability to create a merchandise assortment based upon his or her store's local market.

Dairy Mart, a regional convenience-store chain with annual revenues of $600 million, is another firm that uses a sophisticated computer-based inventory management system. Its new retail stores are mostly "super pumper" units; they stress gasoline sales and have an expanded food-service area. The average new "super pumper" location has almost two times the sales volume of nongasoline-related merchandise as the firm's traditional convenience stores and almost three times the gas volume. Dairy Mart has recently established a point-of-sale (POS) automation team with the responsibility for developing and implementing an appropriate inventory management system for all of its stores. Dairy Mart hopes its POS system will increase inventory turnover, reduce stockouts, better enable each store to stock merchandise that reflects local buying patterns, and reduce the spoilage of perishable goods.[1]

[1] Coopers & Lybrand, "Utilizing Inventory Information for Enhanced Supply Chain Management," *Chain Store Age Executive* (1993); *Dairy Mart 1992 Annual Report*; and Doug Zaper, "Convenience Store Industry Embraces Change," *Chain Store Age Executive* (August 1993), pp. 27A–28A.

Reprinted by permission of Dairy Mart.

Overview

Through ***financial merchandise management***, a retailer specifies exactly which products (goods and services) are purchased, when products are purchased, and how many products are purchased; both dollar and unit controls are employed. ***Dollar control*** involves planning and monitoring a retailer's financial investment in merchandise over a stated time period. ***Unit control*** relates to the quantities of merchandise a retailer handles during a stated time period. Dollar controls usually precede unit controls, as a retailer must plan its dollar investment before making assortment decisions.

Well-structured financial merchandise plans offer such benefits as these:

- The value and amount of inventory in each department and/or store unit during a given period of time can be delineated. Stock is thus balanced, and fewer markdowns may be necessary.
- The amount of merchandise (in terms of investment) that a buyer can purchase during a given period can be stipulated. This gives a buyer direction.
- A buyer can study the inventory investment in relation to planned and actual revenues. This improves the return on investment.
- The retailer's space requirements can be partly determined by estimating beginning-of-month and end-of-month inventory levels.
- A buyer's performance can be evaluated. Various measures may be used as performance standards.
- A buyer can determine the level of stock shortages, giving an estimate of bookkeeping errors and pilferage.
- Slow-moving items can be classified, thus allowing increased sales efforts or markdowns to be made.
- A proper balance between inventory levels and out-of-stock conditions can be maintained.

This chapter divides financial merchandise management into four areas: methods of accounting, merchandise forecasting and budgeting, unit control systems, and financial inventory control. The hypothetical Handy Hardware Store is used throughout the chapter to illustrate the concepts covered.

Inventory Valuation: The Cost and Retail Methods of Accounting

Retail inventory accounting systems can be complex because they entail a great deal of data (due to the number of items sold). A typical retailer's dollar control system must provide such information as the sales and purchases made by that retailer during a budget period, the value of beginning and ending inventory, the extent of markups and markdowns, and merchandise shortages.

Table 14–1 shows a profit-and-loss statement for Handy Hardware Store for the period from January 1, 1994, through June 30, 1994. The sales amount represents the store's total receipts during this period. Beginning inventory is computed by counting the merchandise in stock on January 1, 1994—recorded at cost. Purchases (at cost) and transportation charges (costs incurred in shipping items from the supplier to the retailer) are derived by adding the invoice slips for all merchandise bought by the store during this period.

Together, beginning inventory, purchases, and transportation charges equal the cost of ***merchandise available for sale***. Since Handy does a physical inventory twice yearly, ending inventory is figured by counting the merchandise in stock on June 30, 1994—recorded at cost (Handy codes items so costs can be derived for each item in stock). The ***cost of goods sold*** equals the cost of merchandise available for sale minus the cost value of ending inventory. Sales less cost of goods sold yields ***gross profit***, while ***net profit*** is gross profit minus retail operating expenses.

TABLE 14–1 Handy Hardware Store Profit-and-Loss Statement, January 1, 1994–June 30, 1994

Sales		$208,730
Less cost of goods sold:		
Beginning inventory (at cost)	$ 22,310	
Purchases (at cost)	144,700	
Transportation charges	1,300	
Merchandise available for sale	$168,310	
Ending inventory (at cost)	45,250	
Cost of goods sold		123,060
Gross profit		$ 85,670
Less operating expenses:		
Salaries	$ 35,000	
Advertising	12,500	
Rental	8,000	
Other	13,000	
Total operating expenses		68,500
Net profit before taxes		$ 17,170

Retailers typically have different information needs than manufacturers. Retail assortments are larger; costs cannot be printed on cartons unless coded (due to customer inspection). Stock shortages are higher; sales are conducted more often; and retailers require monthly, not quarterly, profit data.

Two inventory accounting systems are available to a retailer: the cost and retail methods of accounting. The cost accounting system values merchandise at cost plus in-bound transportation charges. The retail accounting system values merchandise at current retail prices.

Next, the cost and retail inventory methods are examined on the basis of such factors as the frequency with which data are obtained, the difficulties in doing a physical inventory, the difficulties in keeping records, the ease of settling insurance claims (in case of inventory damage), the extent to which stock shortages can be calculated, and the complexities of the systems.

THE COST METHOD

In the ***cost method of accounting***, the cost to the retailer of each item is recorded on an accounting sheet and/or is coded on a price tag or merchandise container. When a physical inventory is conducted, every item's cost must be ascertained, the quantity of every item in stock counted, and the total inventory value at cost calculated.

One method of coding merchandise cost is to use a ten-letter equivalency system, such as M = 0, N = 1, O = 2, P = 3, Q = 4, R = 5, S = 6, T = 7, U = 8, and V = 9. An item coded with the letters STOP would have a cost value of $67.23. The technique is useful as an accounting tool and for retailers that allow price bargaining by customers (profit per item is easy to calculate).

The cost method can be used while a retailer computes physical or book inventories. A physical inventory involves an actual count of merchandise, whereas a book inventory depends on record-keeping entries.

A Physical Inventory System Using the Cost Method

With a ***physical inventory system***, ending inventory is measured by an actual count of the merchandise still in stock at the close of a sales period; ending inventory is then recorded at cost. The retailer cannot calculate gross profit until after ending inventory is valued. Thus, a firm using the cost method and relying on a physical inventory system can derive its gross profit only as often as it does a complete physical

TABLE 14–2 Handy Hardware Store Perpetual Inventory System, July 1, 1994–December 31, 1994[a]

Date	Beginning-of-Month Inventory (at Cost)	+	Net Monthly Purchases (at Cost)	−	Monthly Sales (at Cost)	=	End-of-Month Inventory (at Cost)
7/1/94	$45,250		$ 20,000		$ 31,200		$ 34,050
8/1/94	34,050		14,000		19,200		28,850
9/1/94	28,850		13,800		14,400		28,250
10/1/94	28,250		22,000		14,400		35,850
11/1/94	35,850		25,200		20,400		40,650
12/1/94	40,650		7,950		30,600		18,000
		Total	$102,950		$130,200		(as of 12/31/94)

[a] Transportation charges are not included in computing inventory value in this table.

inventory. Because most retailers take physical inventories just once or twice a year, reliance on a physical inventory system would impose severe limitations on merchandise planning.[2]

By using only a physical inventory system, a firm could also be unable to compute inventory shortages (due to pilferage, unrecorded breakage, and so on) because ending inventory value is set by simply adding the costs of all items in stock. What the ending inventory level *should be* is not computed.

A Book Inventory System Using the Cost Method

A ***book inventory system*** (also known as a ***perpetual inventory system***) avoids the problem of infrequent financial analysis by keeping a running total of the value of all inventory on hand at cost at a given time. Therefore, end-of-month inventory values can be computed without a physical inventory, and frequent financial statements can be developed. In addition, a book inventory lets a retailer uncover stock shortages by comparing projected inventory values with actual inventory values via a physical inventory.

A retailer maintains a perpetual system by regularly recording purchases and adding them to existing inventory value; sales transactions are then subtracted to arrive at the new current inventory value (all at cost). Table 14–2 shows a book (perpetual) inventory system for Handy Hardware for the period from July 1, 1994, to December 31, 1994. Note that the ending inventory in Table 14–1 becomes the beginning inventory in Table 14–2.

Table 14–2 assumes merchandise costs are relatively constant and monthly sales at cost are easily computed. However, suppose merchandise costs rise. How, then, would inventory be valued? Two ways to value inventory are the FIFO (first-in-first-out) and LIFO (last-in-first-out) methods.

The ***FIFO method*** logically assumes old merchandise is sold first, while newer items remain in inventory. The ***LIFO method*** assumes new merchandise is sold first, while older stock remains in inventory. FIFO matches inventory value with the current cost structure—the goods remaining in inventory are the ones bought most recently, while LIFO matches current sales with the current cost structure—the goods sold first are the ones bought most recently. During periods of rising inventory values, LIFO offers retailers a tax advantage because lower profits are shown.

[2] See Coopers & Lybrand, "Inventory Management for Improved Profitability," *Chain Store Age Executive* (December 1992), Section Two.

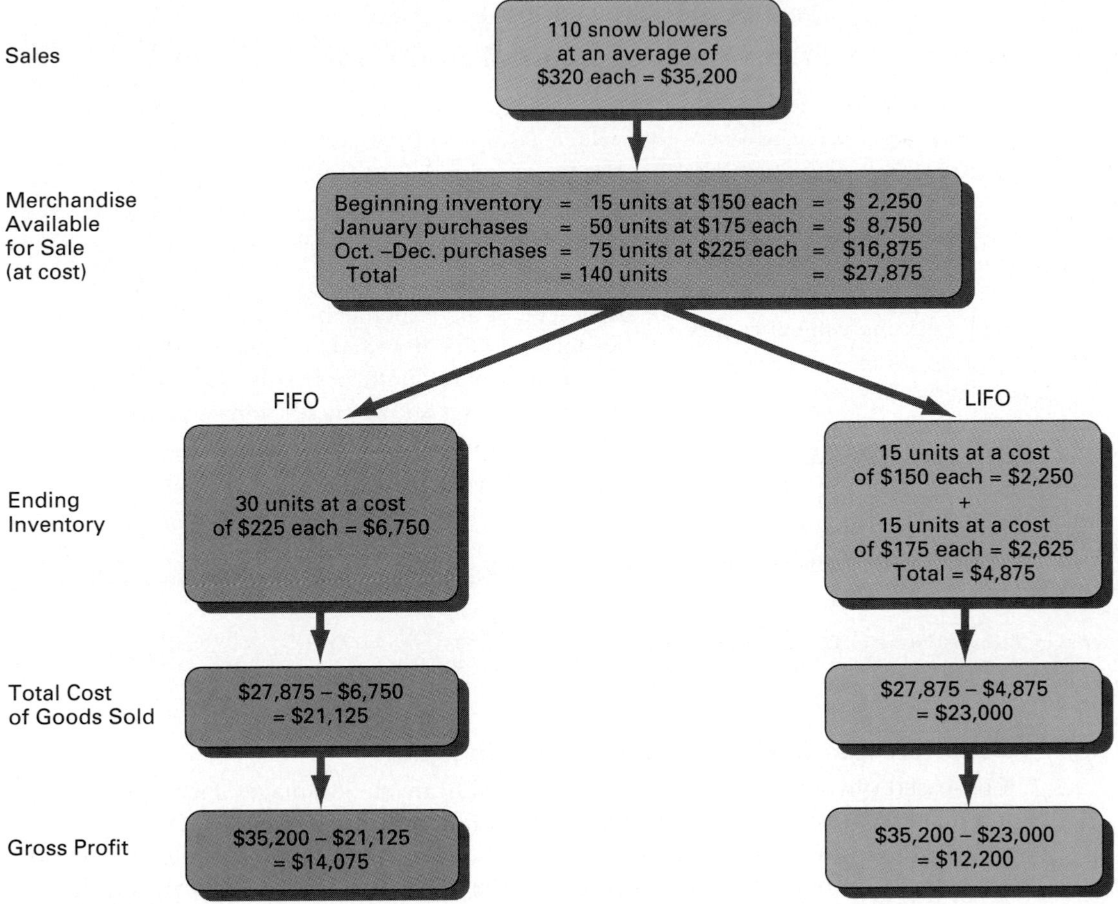

FIGURE 14–1 Applying FIFO and LIFO Inventory Methods to Handy Hardware, January 1, 1994–December 31, 1994

In Figure 14–1, the FIFO and LIFO methods of inventory valuation are illustrated for Handy Hardware's snow blowers for the period January 1, 1994, to December 31, 1994; the store carries only one model of snow blower. Handy has found that it sold 110 snow blowers in 1994 at an average retail price of $320. Handy knows it started 1994 with a beginning inventory of 15 snow blowers, which it had bought for $150 each. During January 1994, it bought 50 snow blowers at $175 each; from October to December 1994, Handy bought another 75 snow blowers for $225 apiece. Because Handy sold 110 snow blowers in 1994, as of the close of business on December 31, it had 30 units left in inventory.

Using the FIFO method, Handy would assume that its beginning inventory and initial purchases were sold first. The 30 snow blowers remaining in inventory would have a cost value of $225 each, resulting in a total cost of goods sold of $21,125 and a gross profit of $14,075. Using the LIFO method, Handy would assume that the most recently purchased items were sold first and that the remaining inventory would consist of beginning goods and early purchases. Of the snow blowers remaining in inventory, 15 would have a cost value of $150 each and 15 a cost value of $175 apiece, resulting in a total cost of goods sold of $23,000 and a gross profit of $12,200. Thus, the FIFO method presents a more accurate picture of the cost of goods sold and the true cost value of ending inventory. The LIFO method indicates a lower profit, leading to the payment of lower taxes, but an understated cost ending-inventory value.

The retail method of inventory, which combines FIFO and LIFO concepts, is explained later in this chapter. A fuller discussion of FIFO and LIFO may be found in a basic accounting text.

ETHICS IN RETAILING

What's the Ethics Role for Internal Auditors?

Recently, 129 chief internal auditors of firms whose securities are traded on the New York Stock Exchange were subjects of a major ethical issues survey. The topics covered by the study included conflicts of interest, supplier relations, gifts and gratuities, political contributions, health and safety, and compliance with the Foreign Corrupt Practice Act. The survey was conducted by a Wayne State University faculty member and the general auditor of Kmart.

Here is a summary of the survey's key results:

- Most respondents say their companies have charters that outline the duties of the internal auditor.
- 77 per cent of respondents say their firms have printed booklets outlining ethical standards of business conduct.
- 55 per cent of respondents say their companies have written examples of policies of appropriate conduct relating to "ethical dilemmas."
- 53 per cent of respondents say their firms mention their ethical policies or internal audit operations in their annual reports.
- Almost all of the respondents believe their companies are following the procedures recommended by the Treadway Commission Report with regard to internal financial controls and financial auditing practices.
- 53 per cent of respondents say their department serves as an ombudsman to determine that financial and other policies are properly followed.

Source: Based on material in Michael Hartnett, "Business Ethics Trends," *Stores* (June 1993), pp. 34–35.

Disadvantages of Cost-Based Inventory Systems

Cost-based physical and book systems have significant disadvantages. First, both require a retailer to assign costs to each item in stock (and to each item sold). Therefore, during periods when merchandise costs are changing, cost-based inventory valuation systems are most useful only for retailers that have low inventory turnover, limited variety and assortments, and high average prices. Examples of retailers with these characteristics are car dealers, furriers, furniture stores, and major-appliance dealers.

Second, neither cost-based method provides for adjusting inventory values to reflect style changes, end-of-season markdowns, or sudden surges of demand (which may increase prices). Thus, the ending value of inventory, based on the cost of the merchandise, may not reflect its actual worth. This discrepancy could be quite troublesome if the ending inventory value is used in computing required insurance coverage or in filing insurance claims for losses.

Despite these disadvantages, retailers that make the products they sell—such as bakeries, restaurants, and furniture showrooms—often keep records on a cost basis. A department store with these operations (or others involving manufacturing) could use the cost method for them and the retail method for other departments.

THE RETAIL METHOD

With the ***retail method of accounting***, closing inventory value is determined by calculating the average relationship between the cost and retail values of merchandise available for sale during the period. Though the retail method overcomes the disadvantages of the cost method, it requires a detailed record-keeping system. The retail method is more complex because ending inventory is first valued in retail dollars and then converted to cost for a retailer to compute gross margin (gross profit).

There are three basic steps in computing an ending inventory value via the retail method:

1. Calculating the cost complement.
2. Calculating deductions from retail value.
3. Converting retail inventory value to cost.

TABLE 14–3 Handy Hardware Store, Calculating Merchandise Available for Sale at Cost and at Retail, July 1, 1994–December 31, 1994

	At Cost	At Retail
Beginning inventory	$ 45,250	$ 69,600
Net purchases	102,950	170,263
Additional markups	—	8,200
Transportation charges	1,746	—
Total merchandise available for sale	$149,946	$248,063

Calculating the Cost Complement

In the retail method, the value of beginning inventory, net purchases, additional markups, and transportation charges are all included. The value of beginning inventory and the net purchase amounts (purchases less returns) are recorded at both cost and retail levels. Additional markups represent the extra revenues received by a retailer when it increases its selling prices during the period covered, due to inflation or unexpectedly high demand. Transportation charges are the retailer's costs for shipping the merchandise it buys from suppliers to the retailer. Table 14–3 shows the total merchandise available for sale at cost and at retail for Handy Hardware for the period from July 1, 1994 to December 31, 1994, using cost data from Table 14–2.

By using Table 14–3 data, the average relationship of cost to retail value for all merchandise available for sale by Handy Hardware during the six-month period can be computed. This concept is called the ***cost complement***:

$$\text{Cost complement} = \frac{\text{Total cost valuation}}{\text{Total retail valuation}}$$

$$= \frac{\$149{,}946}{\$248{,}063}$$

$$= 0.6045$$

Since the cost complement is 0.6045 (60.45 per cent), on average, 60.45 cents of every retail sales dollar is made up of Handy Hardware's merchandise cost.

Calculating Deductions from Retail Value

The ending retail value of inventory must reflect all deductions from the total merchandise available for sale at retail. Besides customer sales, deductions would include markdowns (such as special sales and reduced prices on discontinued, end-of-season, and shopworn goods), employee discounts, and stock shortages (due to pilferage, unrecorded breakage, and so on). Although sales, markdowns, and employee discounts can be recorded throughout an accounting period, a physical inventory is needed to compute stock shortages.

From Table 14–3, it is known that Handy Hardware had a retail value of merchandise available for sale of $248,063 during the period from July 1, 1994, to December 31, 1994. This amount was reduced by sales of $211,270 and recorded markdowns and employee discounts of $7,017. The ending book value of inventory at retail as of December 31, 1994, was $29,776. See Table 14–4.

Once a physical inventory is taken, stock shortages are simple to compute under the retail method. A firm would just compare the retail book value of ending inventory with the actual physical ending inventory value at retail. If a book inventory figure exceeds a physical ending inventory amount, a ***stock shortage*** exists. Table 14–5 shows the results of a physical inventory by Handy Hardware. There are shortages of

TABLE 14–4 Handy Hardware Store, Computing Ending Retail Book Value, as of December 31, 1994

Merchandise available for sale (at retail)		$248,063
Less deductions:		
Sales	$211,270	
Markdowns	5,817	
Employee discounts	1,200	
Total deductions		218,287
Ending retail book value of inventory		$ 29,776

$1,541 (at retail), and the book value is adjusted accordingly. Although Handy recognizes that the shortages are due to pilferage (by customers and/or employees), bookkeeping errors (not recording markdowns, employee discounts, and breakage), and overshipments not billed to customers, it cannot determine the proportion of the shortages caused by each of these factors.

Occasionally, a physical inventory may reveal a ***stock overage***, which represents the excess of physical ending inventory value over book value. An overage may be due to errors in conducting a physical inventory or in maintaining a book inventory. If overages occur, the ending retail book value of inventory must be adjusted upward.

Because a retailer must do a physical inventory to compute stock shortages (overages), and a physical inventory is taken only once or twice a year, shortages (overages) are often estimated for monthly merchandise budgets.

Converting Retail Inventory Value to Cost

Next, the retailer must convert the adjusted ending retail book value of inventory to cost in order to compute dollar gross profit (gross margin). The ending inventory at cost equals the adjusted ending retail book value multiplied by the cost complement. For Handy Hardware, this would be:

$$\text{Ending inventory (at cost)} = \text{Adjusted ending retail book value} \times \text{Cost complement}$$
$$= \$28{,}235 \times .6045$$
$$= \$17{,}068$$

The equation does not yield the exact ending inventory value at cost for Handy but approximates the value based on the average relationship between cost and the retail selling price for all merchandise available for sale.

The adjusted ending inventory at cost can then be used to find gross profit. See Table 14–6. For Handy Hardware, the July 1, 1994, to December 31, 1994, cost of goods sold was $132,878, resulting in gross profit of $78,392. By deducting operating expenses of $69,500, Handy sees that net profit before taxes for this six-month period was $8,892.

TABLE 14–5 Handy Hardware Store, Computing Stock Shortages and Adjusting Retail Book Value, as of December 31, 1994

Ending retail book value of inventory	$29,776
Physical inventory (at retail)	28,235
Stock shortages (at retail)	1,541
Adjusted ending retail book value of inventory	$28,235

TABLE 14–6 Handy Hardware Store Profit-and-Loss Statement, July 1, 1994–December 31, 1994

Sales		$211,270
Less cost of goods sold:		
Total merchandise available for sale (at cost)	$149,946	
Adjusted ending inventory (at cost)[a]	17,068	
Cost of goods sold		132,878[b]
Gross profit		$ 78,392
Less operating expenses:		
Salaries	$ 35,000	
Advertising	12,500	
Rental	8,000	
Other	14,000	
Total operating expenses		69,500
Net profit before taxes		$ 8,892

[a] Adjusted ending inventory (at cost) = Adjusted retail book value × Cost complement = $28,235 × .6045 = $17,068

[b] Cost of goods sold = Monthly sales (at cost) + Transportation charges + Stock shortages (at cost) = $130,200 + $1,746 + $932 = $132,878

Advantages of the Retail Method

In comparing the cost and retail accounting methods, several strengths of the retail method are evident:

1. The retail method is easier to use when taking a physical inventory. The chances of making errors in valuing merchandise are thus reduced because the physical inventory is recorded at retail value and costs do not have to be decoded.
2. Because undertaking a physical inventory is simpler, it can be completed more frequently. This enables a retailer to be more aware of slow-moving items and stock shortages and to take appropriate corrective actions.
3. The physical inventory method at cost requires a physical inventory for the preparation of a profit-and-loss statement. In contrast, the retail method lets a firm prepare a profit-and-loss statement by using book inventory figures. The figures can be adjusted to account for estimated stock shortages between physical inventory periods. Since frequent statements are needed if a firm is to examine profit trends by department, a book inventory system is superior to a physical system at cost.
4. A complete record of ending book values is extremely important in determining the appropriate level of insurance coverage and in settling insurance claims The retail book method gives a firm an estimate of inventory value throughout the year. Because physical inventories are usually taken when merchandise levels are low, the book value at retail allows companies to plan insurance coverage during peak periods and shows the values of the goods on hand (in case of a claim adjustment). The retail method is accepted in insurance claims.

Limitations of the Retail Method

The greatest limitation of the retail method is the bookkeeping burden of recording a lot of cost- and price-related data. Ending book inventory figures can be correctly computed only if the following are accurately noted: the value of beginning inventory (at cost and at retail), purchases (at cost and at retail), transportation charges, markups, markdowns, employee discounts, transfers from other departments or stores, returns, and sales. Although store personnel are freed from the burden of taking many physical inventories, the ending book value at retail may be inaccurate unless all the required data are precisely recorded. With computerization, this potential problem is reduced.

A second limitation of the retail method is that the cost complement is an average figure based upon the total cost of merchandise available for sale and its total retail value. It is therefore possible that the resultant ending cost value of inventory only approximates the true cost of the items on hand. This is especially true if fast-selling merchandise has different markups from slow-selling merchandise and/or if there are wide variations among the markups of goods within a single department.

Familiarity with the retail and cost methods of inventory is essential for understanding the financial merchandise-management material described in the balance of this chapter.

Merchandise Forecasting and Budgeting: Dollar Control

As noted at the beginning of the chapter, dollar control involves planning and monitoring a retailer's inventory investment during a specified time period. Figure 14–2 illustrates the dollar control process for merchandise forecasting and budgeting, which is broken down into six successive stages: designating control units, forecasting sales, inventory-level planning, retail-reduction planning, planning purchases, and profit-margin planning.

It is important that the sequential nature of this process be followed since a change in any one stage affects all the stages after it. For instance, if a retailer's sales forecast is too low, it may run out of items because it does not plan to have enough inventory on hand during a selling season and its planned purchases will also be too low.

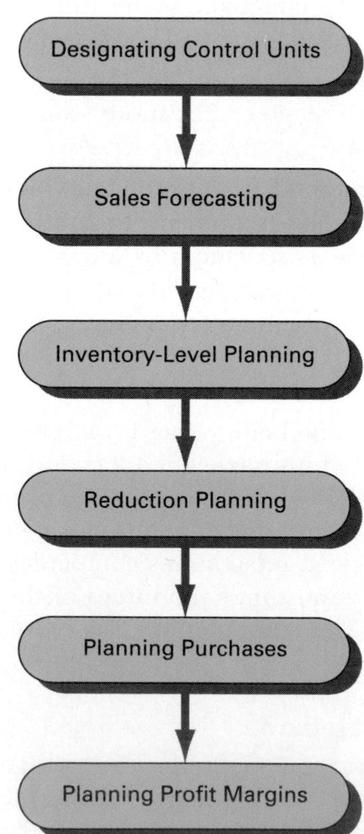

FIGURE 14–2
The Merchandise Forecasting and Budgeting Process: Dollar Control

DESIGNATING CONTROL UNITS

Merchandise forecasting and budgeting require the selection of ***control units***, the merchandise categories for which data are gathered. It is important for control unit classifications to be narrow enough to isolate opportunities and problems with specific lines of merchandise. A retailer wishing to control merchandise within departments must record data relating to dollar allotments separately for each category.

As an example, knowing that total markdowns in a department are 20 per cent above last year's level is less valuable than knowing the specific merchandise lines in which large markdowns are taken. A retailer can broaden its control system by summarizing the categories that comprise a department. However, a broad category cannot be broken down into components. Therefore, it is better to err on the side of too much information than too little.

It is also helpful to select control units consistent with other internal company data and with trade association data, wherever possible. Intracompany comparisons are meaningful only when classification categories are stable over time. A classification system that shifts over time does not allow comparisons between periods. And valid external comparisons can be made only if control categories are similar for a given retailer and its trade association(s).

Control units may be set up on the basis of departments, classifications within departments, price line classifications, and standard merchandise classifications. A discussion of each follows.

At the very least, most retailers should keep financial records in terms of specified departmental categories. Thus, even a small firm like Handy Hardware needs to acquire data on a departmental basis (such as tools and equipment, supplies, housewares, and so on) for buying, inventory control, and markdown decisions. The broadest practical division is the department, which allows a retailer to assess the performance of each general merchandise grouping or buyer.

To obtain more financial information than available through departmental categories, ***classification merchandising*** can be used, whereby each specified department is subdivided into further categories for related types of merchandise. Thus, in planning merchandise for its tools and equipment department, Handy Hardware can keep financial records not only on the overall performance of that department but also on the individual performance of such categories as lawn mowers/snow blowers, power tools, hand tools, and ladders.

One special form of classification merchandising involves ***price line classifications***, whereby retail sales, inventories, and purchases are analyzed by retail price category. This analysis is quite valuable if a firm offers the same type of product at vastly different prices to different target markets (such as Handy Hardware carrying $20 power tools for do-it-yourselfers and $135 power tools for contractors). Retailers with deep assortments are most frequently involved with price line control. As a case in point, a men's clothing store may want to differentiate between sports jackets selling in the $79–$99 price range and those selling in the $149–$189 price range. Such diverse categories of sports jackets are usually sold to different customers or to the same customers for different purposes.

To best compare company financial data with industry averages, a firm's merchandise categories should conform to those cited in respected trade publications. As an example, many years ago, the National Retail Federation (then the National Retail Merchants Association) developed a ***standard merchandise classification*** to list the most common merchandise-reporting categories—useful for a wide range of retailers and products. The Federation annually publishes *Merchandising and Operating Results of Department and Specialty Stores*, using its classifications. Industry-specific standard merchandise classifications are also popular for different retailer types. For instance, published yearly is *Progressive Grocer*'s "Supermarket Sales Manual," which relies on standard classifications applicable to that industry.

RETAILING AROUND THE WORLD

How Does Ikea Sharpen Its Financial Merchandising Plans in Eastern Europe?

Ikea's new furniture store in Warsaw, Poland, is the largest of its seven Eastern European outlets. The store also presents an important financial merchandising challenge to Ikea.

Ikea's Eastern European stores carry significantly fewer products than its Western European stores. For example, except for the Polish store, Ikea's largest Eastern European outlet stocks 3,000 products, only one-quarter the items offered in the typical Western European store. Ikea is stocking 6,000 products in the Polish store. Yet, even with less selection, Ikea's Budapest, Hungary, store has more than 40,000 visitors per week—about double the number for a typical Western European unit.

Ikea's merchandise selection must reflect the relatively lower disposable incomes of its Eastern European customers. In Western European markets, it takes the average customer slightly more than one week to earn the $400 needed to pay for Ikea's Klippan sofa model. In contrast, it takes a Polish consumer about two months of work to pay for the same sofa. To accommodate the lower incomes, Ikea sells Polish customers one spoon or a single teacup at a time and keeps products in stock for long periods. It also works with Polish suppliers to bring Ikea's prices within reach of the Polish mass market.

Source: Based on material in Stephen D. Moore, "Sweden's Ikea Forges Into Eastern Europe," *Wall Street Journal* (June 28, 1993), p. A9A.

After each appropriate dollar control unit is set, all transactions—such as sales, purchases, transfers, markdowns, and employee discounts—must be recorded under the proper classification number. For instance, if house paint is denoted as Department 25 and brushes as 25-1, all transactions must carry these category designations.

SALES FORECASTING

Through ***sales forecasting***, a retailer estimates expected future revenues for a given time period. Sales forecasts may be companywide, on a departmental basis, and/or for individual merchandise classifications. Perhaps the most important step in any financial merchandise-planning process is accurate sales forecasting. Because of its effect on subsequent steps, an incorrect estimate of future sales throws off the entire process.

Companywide and departmentwide sales of larger retailers are often forecast by the use of statistical techniques such as trend analysis, time series analysis, and multiple-regression analysis. A discussion of these techniques is beyond the scope of this text. It should be noted that few small retailers use those methods; they rely more on "guesstimates," projections based on past experience.

Sales forecasting for merchandise classifications within departments (or price lines) generally relies on more qualitative techniques, even for larger firms. One way of forecasting sales for these narrower categories is first to project sales on a companywide basis and by department, and then to break down these figures judgmentally into merchandise classifications.

Sales forecasts must carefully anticipate and take into account external factors, internal company factors, and seasonal trends. Among the external factors that could affect a retailer's future sales are consumer demographic and life-style trends, competitors' actions, the state of the economy, changes in the tastes of the target market, and new offerings from suppliers. For example, *Stores* has a Consumer General Merchandise Index to regularly measure consumers' willingness to purchase clothing, household furnishings, and other products.[3] Among the internal company factors that could impact on a retailer's future sales are additions and deletions of merchandise lines, changes in promotion and credit policies, changes in the hours of business, the opening of new outlets, and the remodeling of existing stores. With a number of

[3] See "Buying Plans," *Stores* (April 1993), p. 70.

TABLE 14–7 Handy Hardware Store, A Simple Sales Forecast Using Product Control Units

Product Control Units	Actual Sales 1994	Projected Growth/ Decline (%)	Sales Forecast 1995
Lawn mowers/ snow blowers	$100,000	+10.0	$110,000
Paint and supplies	64,000	+3.0	65,920
Hardware supplies	54,000	+8.0	58,320
Plumbing supplies	44,000	−4.0	42,240
Power tools	44,000	+6.0	46,640
Garden supplies/ chemicals	34,000	+4.0	35,360
Housewares	24,000	−6.0	22,560
Electrical supplies	20,000	+4.0	20,800
Ladders	18,000	+6.0	19,080
Hand tools	18,000	+9.0	19,620
Total year	$420,000	+ 4.9	$440,540

retailers, seasonal variations must be considered in developing monthly or quarterly sales forecasts. As an example, Handy Hardware's yearly snow-blower sales should not be estimated from December sales alone.

A retailer can develop a sales forecast by examining past trends and projecting future growth (based on external and internal factors). Table 14–7 shows such a forecast for Handy Hardware. However, this forecast should be regarded as an estimate, subject to revisions. For this reason, a financial merchandise plan needs some flexibility.

The firm should be aware that some factors may be particularly hard to incorporate when devising a sales forecast, such as merchandise shortages, consumer reactions to new products, strikes by suppliers' personnel, the rate of inflation, and new government legislation.

After a yearly forecast is derived, it should be broken into quarterly or monthly planning periods. In retailing, monthly sales forecasts are usually required. Thus, for example, jewelry stores know that December typically accounts for a very strong 22 per cent of annual sales, while drugstores know that December typically accounts for 9 per cent of annual sales (only slightly above the monthly average).[4]

To acquire more specific estimates, a retailer could use a ***monthly sales index***, which is calculated by dividing each month's actual sales by average monthly sales and multiplying the results by 100. Table 14–8 shows actual monthly sales and monthly sales indexes for Handy Hardware in 1994. The data reveal the store is quite seasonal, with peaks during late spring and early summer (for lawn mowers, garden supplies, house paint and supplies, and so on), as well as December (for lighting fixtures, snow blowers, and gifts).

According to Table 14–8, average monthly sales for the year are $35,000 ($420,000/12). The monthly sales index for January is 67 [($23,400/$35,000) × 100]; other monthly indexes are calculated similarly. Each monthly index shows the percentage deviation of that month's sales from the average month's. Thus, the May index of 160 means sales in May are 60 per cent higher than average monthly sales. The October index of 67 means sales in October are 33 per cent below the average.

[4] Melissa Campanelli (Editor), " 'Tis the Season for Shopping," *Sales & Marketing Management* (December 1993), p. 44.

TABLE 14–8 Handy Hardware Store, 1994 Sales by Month

Month	Actual Sales	Monthly Sales Index[a]
January	$ 23,400	67
February	20,432	58
March	24,000	69
April	32,800	94
May	56,098	160
June	51,900	148
July	52,280	149
August	31,400	90
September	23,452	67
October	23,400	67
November	33,442	96
December	47,396	135
Total yearly sales	$420,000	
Average monthly sales	$ 35,000	
Average monthly index		100

[a] Monthly sales index = (Monthly sales/Average monthly sales) × 100

Once monthly sales indexes are determined, a retailer can forecast monthly sales, based on a yearly sales estimate. Table 14–9 shows how Handy Hardware's monthly sales can be forecast if the next year's (1995's) average monthly sales are expected to be $36,712. May sales are projected to be $58,739 ($36,712 × 1.60). October sales would be $24,597 ($36,712 × 0.67).

INVENTORY-LEVEL PLANNING

After a retailer forecasts sales for a specified time period, it must plan the inventory levels for that period. Inventory must be sufficient to meet sales expectations, allowing a margin for error. Among the techniques used to plan inventory levels are the basic stock, percentage variation, weeks' supply, and stock-to-sales methods.

With the ***basic stock method***, a retailer carries more items than it expects to sell over a specified period. Beginning-of-month planned inventory equals planned sales plus a basic stock amount:

Basic stock (at retail) = Average monthly stock at retail − Average monthly sales

Beginning-of-month planned inventory level (at retail) = Planned monthly sales + Basic stock

This method gives a firm a cushion if sales are higher than anticipated, shipments are delayed, or customers want to select from a variety of items. It is best when inventory turnover is low or sales are erratic during the year.

If Handy Hardware, with an average monthly 1995 sales forecast of $36,712, wants to have extra stock on hand equal to 10 per cent of its average monthly sales forecast (or $3,671) and expects January 1995 sales to be $24,597:

TABLE 14–9 Handy Hardware Store, 1995 Sales Forecast by Month

Month	Actual Sales 1994	Monthly Sales Index	Monthly Sales Forecast for 1995[a]	
January	$ 23,400	67	$36,712 × .67 =	$ 24,597
February	20,432	58	36,712 × .58 =	21,293
March	24,000	69	36,712 × .69 =	25,331
April	32,800	94	36,712 × .94 =	34,509
May	56,098	160	36,712 × 1.60 =	58,739
June	51,900	148	36,712 × 1.48 =	54,334
July	52,280	149	36,712 × 1.49 =	54,701
August	31,400	90	36,712 × .90 =	33,041
September	23,452	67	36,712 × .67 =	24,597
October	23,400	67	36,712 × .67 =	24,597
November	33,442	96	36,712 × .96 =	35,244
December	47,396	135	36,712 × 1.35 =	49,561
Total sales	$420,000		Total sales forecast	$440,540[b]
Average monthly sales	$ 35,000		Average monthly forecast	$ 36,712

[a] Monthly sales forecast = Average monthly forecast × (Monthly index/100). In this equation, the monthly index is computed as a fraction of 1.00 rather than 100.

[b] There is a small rounding error.

Basic stock = ($36,712 × 1.10) − $36,712
= $40,383 − $36,712 = $3,671

Beginning-of-January planned inventory level (at retail) = $24,597 + $3,671 = $28,268

With the ***percentage variation method***, the beginning-of-month planned inventory level during any month differs from the planned average monthly stock by only half of that month's variation from estimated average monthly sales. This method is recommended when stock turnover is more than six times a year or relatively stable, since it results in planned monthly inventories that are closer to the monthly average than other techniques:

Beginning-of-month planned inventory level (at retail) = Planned average monthly stock at retail × 1/2 [1 + (Estimated monthly sales/Estimated average monthly sales)]

If Handy Hardware plans average monthly stock of $40,383 and November 1995 sales are expected to be 4 per cent less than average monthly sales of $36,712, the store's planned inventory level at the beginning of November 1995 would be:

Beginning-of-November planned inventory level (at retail) = $40,383 × 1/2 [1 + ($35,244/$36,712)]

= $40,383 × 1/2 (1.96) = $39,575

However, for Handy Hardware, the percentage variation method is not a good one to use because of the firm's variable sales. With that method, Handy would plan a beginning-of-December 1995 inventory level of $47,450 (based on planned average monthly stock of $40,383), less than it expects to sell.

The ***weeks' supply method*** involves forecasting average sales on a weekly basis, so beginning inventory is equal to several weeks' expected sales. This method assumes the inventory carried is in direct proportion to sales. Thus, too much merchandise may be stocked in peak selling periods and too little during slow selling periods:

Beginning-of-month planned inventory level (at retail) = Average estimated weekly sales × Number of weeks to be stocked

If Handy Hardware forecasts average weekly sales of $5,478.54 during the period from January 1, 1995, through March 31, 1995, and it wants to stock 13 weeks of merchandise (based on expected turnover in the first part of 1995), beginning inventory would be $71,221:

Beginning-of-January planned inventory level (at retail) = $5,478.54 × 13 = $71,221

With the ***stock-to-sales method***, a retailer wants to maintain a specified ratio of goods-on-hand to sales. A stock-to-sales ratio of 1.3 means that if Handy Hardware plans sales of $34,509 in April 1995, it should have $44,862 worth of merchandise (at retail) available during the month. Like the weeks' supply method, the stock-to-sales ratio tends to adjust inventory levels more drastically than changes in sales require.

Industrywide stock-to-sales ratios are available from such sources as *Merchandising and Operating Results of Department and Specialty Stores* (New York: National Retail Federation, annual), *Industry Norms and Key Business Ratios* (New York: Dun & Bradstreet, annual), and *Annual Statement Studies* (Philadelphia: Robert Morris Associates). A retailer can thus compare its ratios with other firms'.

REDUCTION PLANNING

Besides forecasting sales, a firm should estimate the extent of its expected ***retail reductions***, which represent the difference between beginning inventory plus purchases during the period and sales plus ending inventory. These planned reductions should encompass anticipated markdowns (price reductions to stimulate merchandise sales), employee and other discounts (price reductions given to employees, senior citizens, clergy, and others), and stock shortages (caused by pilferage, breakage, and bookkeeping errors) over the budget period. It is essential for a retailer to estimate and plan reductions, not just wait for them to occur:

Planned reductions = (Beginning inventory + Planned purchases) − (Planned sales + Ending inventory)

A retailer's reduction planning involves two major factors: estimating the expected total reductions for the budget period and distributing the estimates by month. A firm should study the following in planning total reductions for the budget period:

- Past experience with reductions.
- Markdown data for similar retailers.
- Changes in company policies.

RETAILING IN ACTION

Will Pay Less' New Purchasing System Pay Off?

The inventory turnover at Pay Less Drug Stores' distribution center in Wilsonville, Oregon, has increased from 8.2 times to 11.0 times since 1990. In addition, since 1991, the chain's in-stock service level has gone from 86 per cent to 93 per cent. These improvements in inventory management are mostly due to Pay Less' implementing a new purchasing system and organizational changes.

Pay Less' new purchasing system is based upon inputs from the company's accounting, data processing, distribution center, transportation, and merchandising departments. Working with Pay Less' director of merchandise information systems, these departments re-evaluated the company's buying practices, order frequency, deal buying, and lead time requirements. Then, Pay Less was able to re-engineer its purchasing system to better control costs and inventory levels.

As part of the new system,

- Buyers negotiate all deals, vendor terms, and price-increase notifications.
- Basic replenishment and promotional orders are grouped together, wherever possible, to reduce ordering and handling costs.
- Items with excess inventories are noted, and orders for this merchandise are reduced.
- Buying practices are adjusted through a seasonality index. Pay Less is particularly concerned with having low inventory levels at the end of a selling season.

Source: Based on material in "New Efficiencies at Pay Less," *Chain Store Age Executive* (December 1993), pp. 100–102.

- Merchandise carryover from one budget period to another.
- Price trends.
- Stock-shortage trends.

Past experience is a good starting point in reduction planning. This information can then be compared with that of similar firms—by reviewing the available data presented on markdowns, discounts, and stock shortages in trade publications. For instance, a retailer having more (higher) markdowns than competitors should investigate and correct this situation by adjusting its buying practices and price levels or training sales personnel better.

In evaluating past reductions, a firm must consider its own procedures. Changes in policy during a budget period often affect the quantity and timing of markdowns. For instance, a retailer's expanding its assortment of seasonal and fashion merchandise would probably lead to an increase in markdowns.

Merchandise carryover, price trends, and stock-shortage trends also affect planning. If such items as gloves and antifreeze are held in stock during off-seasons, markdowns are usually not needed to clean out inventory. However, the carryover of fad merchandise merely postpones reductions. Price trends of product categories influence retail reductions. For example, many microwave ovens are now available for under $200, down considerably from earlier prices. This means higher-priced microwave ovens have to be marked down accordingly.

A firm can use its recent stock-shortage trends (determined by comparing book and physical inventory values over prior budget periods) to project future reductions due to employee, customer, and vendor theft; breakage; and bookkeeping mistakes. Generally, about one-quarter of all stock shortages in retailing are the result of clerical and handling errors. If a firm has total stock shortages amounting to less than 2 to 4 per cent of its annual sales, it is usually deemed to be doing well. Figure 14–3 shows a checklist retailers could use to reduce shortages from clerical and handling errors. Suggestions for reducing shortages arising from theft were discussed in Chapter 12.

Answer yes or no to each of the following questions. A no answer to any question means corrective measures must be taken.

Buying

1. Is the exact quantity of merchandise purchased always specified in the contract?
2. Are purchase quantities recorded by size, color, model, etc.?
3. Are special purchase terms clearly noted?
4. Are returns to the vendor recorded properly?

Marking

5. Are retail prices clearly marked on merchandise?
6. Are the prices marked on merchandise checked for correctness?
7. Are markdowns and additional markups recorded by item number and quantity?
8. Does a cashier check with a manager if a price is not marked on an item?
9. Are the prices shown on display shelves checked for consistency with those marked on the items themselves?
10. Are old price tags removed when an item's price is changed?

Handling

11. After receipt, are purchase quantities checked against contract specifications?
12. Is merchandise handled in a systematic manner?
13. Are goods separated by merchandise classification?
14. Are all handling operations monitored properly (e.g., receiving, storing, distribution)?
15. Is enough merchandise kept on the selling floor (to reduce excessive handling)?
16. Are items sold in bulk (such as produce, sugar, candy) measured accurately?
17. Are damaged, soiled, returned, or other special goods handled separately?

Selling

18. Do sales personnel know correct prices or have easy access to them?
19. Are markdowns, additional markups, etc., communicated to sales personnel?
20. Are misrings by cashiers made on a very small percentage of sales?
21. Are special terms noted on sales receipts?
22. Do sales personnel confirm that all items are rung up by cashiers?
23. Are employee discounts noted?
24. Is the addition on sales receipts done mechanically or double checked if computed by hand?
25. Are sales receipts numbered and later checked for missing invoices?

Inventory Planning

26. Is a physical inventory conducted at least annually?
27. Is a book inventory maintained throughout the year?
28. Are the differences between physical inventory counts and book inventory always accounted for?
29. Are sales and inventory records reviewed regularly?

Accounting

30. Are permanent records on all transactions kept?
31. Are both retail and cost data maintained?
32. Are all types of records monitored for accuracy?
33. Are inventory shortages compared with industry averages to determine acceptability of performance?

FIGURE 14–3 A Checklist to Reduce Inventory Shortages Due to Clerical and Handling Errors

After total reductions are determined, they must be planned by month because reductions as a percentage of sales would not be the same during each month. For example, stock shortages may be much higher during busy periods, when stores are more crowded and transactions happen more quickly.

PLANNING PURCHASES

The formula for calculating planned purchases for a period is

Planned purchases (at retail) = Planned sales for the month + Planned reductions for the month + Planned end-of-month stock − Beginning-of-month stock

If Handy Hardware projects June 1995 sales to be $54,334 and total planned reductions to be 5 per cent of sales, plans end-of-month inventory at retail to be $36,000, and has a beginning-of-month inventory at retail of $40,000, planned purchases for June would be

Planned purchases (at retail) = $54,334 + $2,717 + $36,000 − $40,000 = $53,051

Because Handy Hardware expects merchandise costs to be about 60 per cent of retail selling price, it is planning to purchase $31,831 of goods at cost in June 1995:

Planned purchases (at cost) = Planned purchases at retail × Merchandise costs as a percentage of selling price

= $53,051 × 0.60 = $31,831

Open-to-buy is the difference between planned purchases and the purchase commitments already made by a buyer for a given time period, often a month. It represents the amount the buyer has left to spend for that month and is reduced each time a purchase is made. At the beginning of a month, a firm's planned purchases and open-to-buy would be equal if no purchases have been committed prior to the start of that month. Open-to-buy is recorded at cost.

At Handy Hardware, the buyer has made purchase commitments for June 1995 valued in the amount of $27,500 at retail. Accordingly, Handy's open-to-buy at retail for June is $25,551:

Open-to-buy (at retail) = Planned purchases for the month − Purchase commitments for that month

= $53,051 − $27,500 = $25,551

To calculate the June 1995 open-to-buy at cost, $25,551 is multiplied by Handy Hardware's merchandise costs as a percentage of selling price:

Open-to-buy (at cost) = Open-to-buy at retail × Merchandise costs as a percentage of selling price

= $25,551 × 0.60 = $15,331

The open-to-buy concept has two significant strengths. First, it assures the retailer that a specified relationship between stock on hand and planned sales is maintained, which avoids overbuying and underbuying. Second, it enables a firm to adjust merchandise purchases to reflect changes in sales, markdowns, and so on. For instance, if Handy Hardware revises its June 1995 sales estimate to $60,000, it would automatically increase planned purchases and open-to-buy by $5,666 at retail and $3,400 at cost.

From a strategic perspective, it is usually advisable for a retailer to keep at least a small open-to-buy figure for as long as possible. This lets the firm take advantage of special deals, purchase new models as they are introduced, and fill in merchandise that sells out. Sometimes, an open-to-buy limit must be exceeded due to underestimates of demand (low sales forecasts).

PLANNING PROFIT MARGINS

When developing a merchandise budget, a retailer is quite interested in profitability (as expressed by dollar and percentage profit margins) and must consider its anticipated net sales level, retail operating expenses, profit, and retail reductions in pricing merchandise:

$$\text{Required initial markup percentage} = \frac{\text{Planned retail expenses} + \text{Planned profit} + \text{Planned reductions}}{\text{Planned net sales} + \text{Planned reductions}}$$

The required markup figure is an overall company average; individual items may be priced according to demand and other factors, as long as the company average is maintained. A more complete discussion of markup is contained in the next chapter. The concept of initial markup is introduced at this point for continuity in the description of merchandise budgeting.

Handy Hardware has an overall 1995 sales forecast of $440,540 and expects annual operating expenses to be $145,000. Reductions are anticipated to be $22,000. The total net dollar profit margin goal is $30,000, representing 6.8 per cent of sales. Therefore, its required initial markup is 42.6 per cent:

$$\text{Required initial markup percentage} = \frac{\$145{,}000 + \$30{,}000 + \$22{,}000}{\$440{,}540 + \$22{,}000} = 42.6\%$$

$$\text{Required initial markup percentage (all factors expressed as a percentage of net sales)} = \frac{32.9\% + 6.8\% + 5.0\%}{100.0\% + 5.0\%} = 42.6\%$$

Figure 14–4 summarizes the merchandise forecasting and budgeting process. It expands on Figure 14–2 by including the bases for each decision stage.

Unit Control Systems

Unit control systems deal with quantities of merchandise in units rather than in dollars. Information typically contained in unit control systems includes

- The identification of items that are selling well and those that are selling poorly.
- A focus on opportunities and problem areas for buyers in terms of price, color, style, size, and so on.
- The computation (where a perpetual inventory system is used) of the quantity of goods on hand. This minimizes overstocking and understocking.
- An indication of the age of the inventory, highlighting those items that are candidates for markdowns or special promotions.

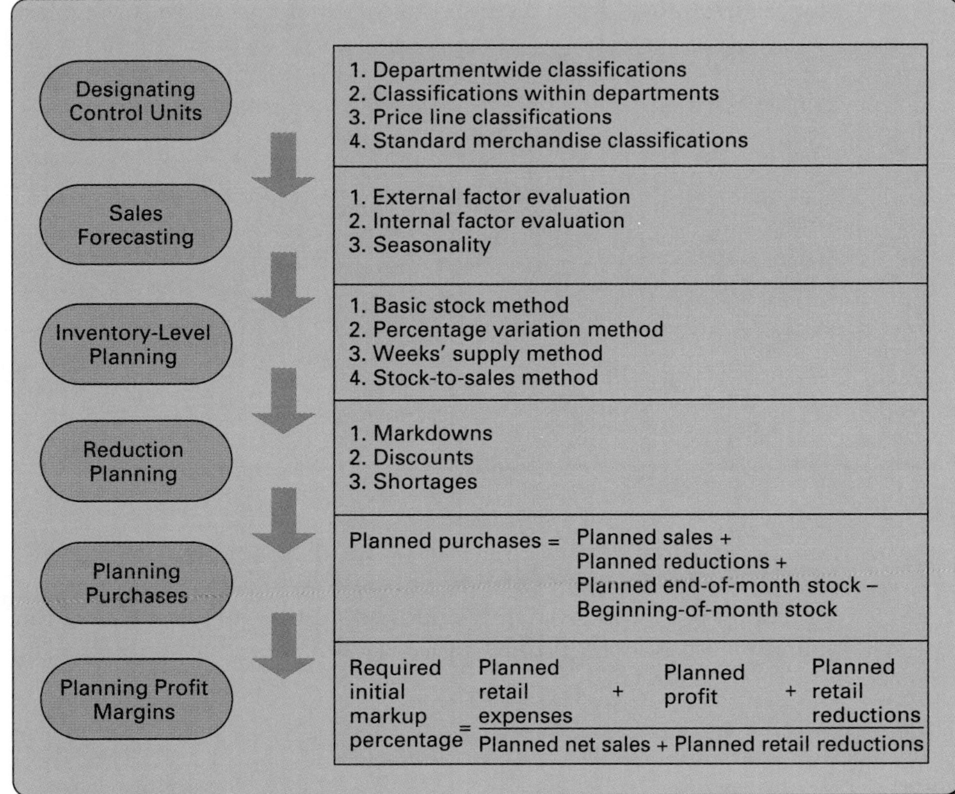

FIGURE 14–4
The Merchandise Forecasting and Budgeting Process: Dollar Control

- A determination of the optimal time to reorder merchandise.
- An examination of experiences with alternative sources (vendors) when problems arise.
- The level of inventory and sales for each item in each store branch. This improves the flow of goods transfer between branches and alerts sales personnel as to which branches have desired products. Also, less stock can be maintained in each store, reducing costs.

PHYSICAL INVENTORY SYSTEMS

A physical-inventory unit-control system is relatively similar to a physical-inventory dollar-control system. But whereas a dollar control system is concerned with the financial value of inventory, a unit control system examines the number of units by item classification. In a unit control system, someone within a retail firm is given the task of monitoring inventory levels of merchandise, either by visual inspection or by actual count.

With a typical ***visual inspection system***, merchandise is placed on pegboard (or similar) displays, with each item numbered on the back of its package on a stock card. Minimum inventory quantities are clearly noted on the merchandise, and sales personnel are responsible for reordering when the number of items on hand reaches a minimum level. In this system, accuracy occurs only if merchandise is placed in numerical order on the displays (and sold accordingly). The system is used in the houseware and hardware displays of various discount, department, variety, and hardware stores.

Although a visual inspection system is easy to maintain and inexpensive, it has two shortcomings. First, it does not provide information on the rate of sales of individual items. Second, minimum stock quantities may be arbitrarily defined and not drawn from in-depth analysis.

The other physical inventory system, actual counting, requires a firm to regularly compile the number of units on hand. A ***stock-counting system*** records—in units—inventory on hand, purchases, sales volume, and shortages during specified periods. For example, Handy Hardware could use the system for its insulation tape:

	Number of Rolls of Tape for the Period 12/1/94–12/31/94
Beginning inventory, December 1, 1994	50
Total purchases for period	35
Total units available for sale	85
Closing inventory, December 31, 1994	30
Sales and shortages for period	55

A stock-counting system requires more clerical work than a visual system, but it lets a firm obtain sales data for given periods and stock-to-sales relationships as of the time of each count. A physical system is not as sophisticated as a perpetual inventory system, and its use is more justified with low-value items having predictable sales rates.

PERPETUAL INVENTORY SYSTEMS

A ***perpetual-inventory unit-control system*** keeps a running total of the number of units handled by a retailer via ongoing record-keeping entries that adjust for sales, returns, transfers to other departments or stores, receipt of merchandise shipments, and other transactions. All additions to and subtractions from beginning inventory are recorded.

Perpetual (book) inventory systems can be maintained manually, use merchandise tags that are processed by computers, or rely on point-of-sale devices such as optical scanning equipment. Technological advances have greatly improved retailers' abilities to develop strong perpetual inventory systems and to utilize computers.

A manual system requires employees to gather information by examining sales checks, merchandise receipts, transfer requests, and other merchandise documents. This information is then coded and tabulated.

A merchandise-tagging system relies on pre-printed tags attached to each item in stock. These tags include data on department, classification, vendor, style number, date of receipt, color, and material. When an item is sold, one copy of the merchandise tag is removed and sent to a tabulating facility, where the coded information is analyzed by computer. Because pre-printed merchandise tags are processed in batches, they can be used by small and medium-sized retailers (which subscribe to independent service bureaus) and by branches of chains (with data being processed at a central location).

Point-of-sale systems, developed and sold by firms such as IBM, Digital Equipment Corporation, and NCR, feed data from merchandise tags or product labels directly to in-store computer terminals for immediate data processing. Computer-based systems are quicker, more accurate, and of higher quality than manual systems. And because of the access to PCs, computerized checkout equipment, and service bureaus, costs are reasonable for smaller retailers.

Newer point-of-sale systems can be easily networked, have battery backup capabilities (in case of power interruptions), and use industry-standard components (which enables retailers to better choose printers, keyboards, and monitors). Many point-of-

When the checker passes an item with the UPC symbol over a scanning device, the symbol is read by a low-energy laser.

The UPC symbol is found on many supermarket products and looks like this.

Each product has its own unique identification number. For example, the first five digits, 11146, represent the manufacturer, Giant in this case. The second five digits represent the specific items; 01345 identifies 24 ounce iced tea mix.

Note that the price is not in the symbol. The symbol identifies the product, not the price.

11146 01345

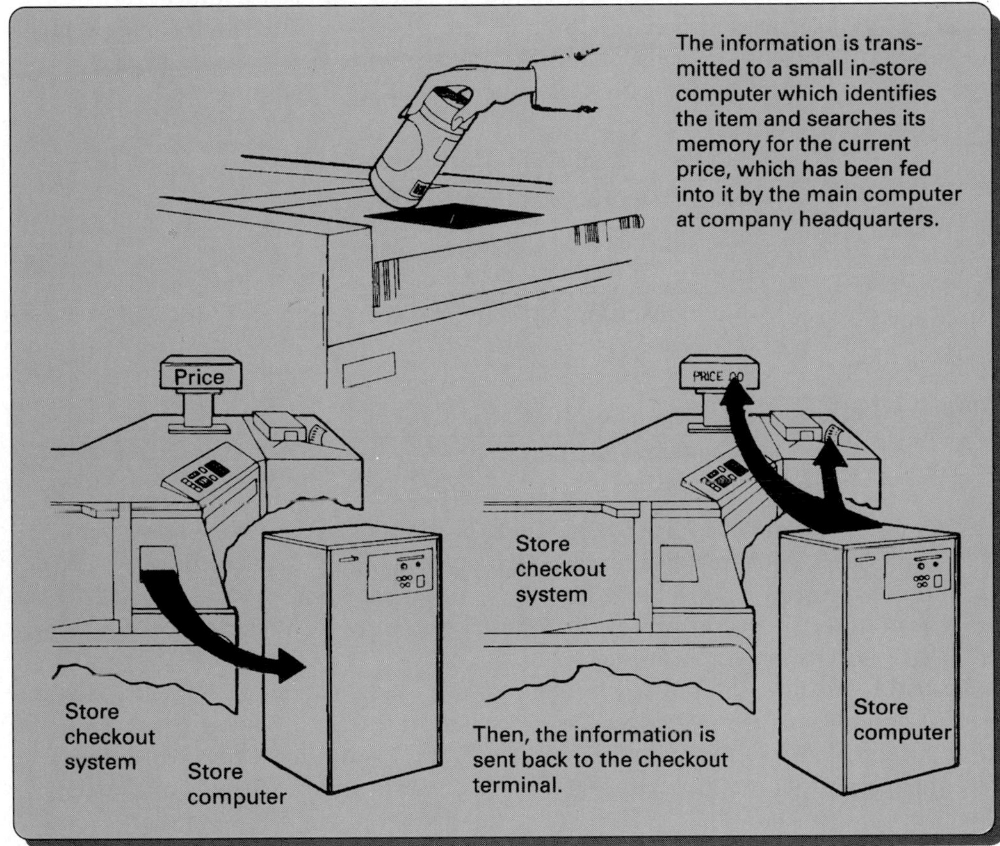

The information is transmitted to a small in-store computer which identifies the item and searches its memory for the current price, which has been fed into it by the main computer at company headquarters.
Price
Store checkout system
Store computer
Store checkout system
Then, the information is sent back to the checkout terminal.
Store computer

Figure 14–5
How Does a UPC-Based Scanner System Work?
Courtesy Giant Food Inc.

sale systems use optical scanners that transfer data from merchandise to computers via wands or stationary devices that interact with sensitized strips on the merchandise. Figure 14–5 shows how a UPC-based scanner system works. As discussed earlier in the text, the Universal Product Code (UPC) has become the dominant format for coding data onto merchandise.

A retailer does not have to use a perpetual system for all of its inventory. Many firms combine perpetual and physical systems. Key items, accounting for a large proportion of sales, could be controlled through a perpetual system, and other items could be controlled through a physical inventory system. In this way, attention could be properly placed on the retailer's most important products.

Financial Inventory Control: Integrating Dollar and Unit Concepts

Up to this point, dollar and unit control concepts have been discussed as separate entities. However, in practice, dollar and unit controls are directly linked. For example, the decision on how many units to buy at a given time affects and is affected by dollar investment, inventory turnover, quantity discounts, warehousing and insurance costs, and so on.

Three aspects of financial inventory control are described in this section: stock turnover and gross margin return on investment, when to reorder, and how much to reorder.

Stock Turnover and Gross Margin Return on Investment

Stock turnover represents the number of times during a specific period, usually one year, that the average inventory on hand is sold. Stock turnover can be measured by store, by product line, by department, and by vendor. A high level of stock turnover has several virtues. Inventory investments are productive on a per dollar basis. Merchandise on the shelves is fresh. Losses due to changes in styles and fashion are reduced. Costs associated with maintaining inventory (such as interest, insurance, breakage, and warehousing) are lessened.

Stock turnover can be computed in units or dollars (at retail or cost):

$$\text{Annual rate of stock turnover (in units)} = \frac{\text{Number of units sold during year}}{\text{Average inventory on hand (in units)}}$$

$$\text{Annual rate of stock turnover (in retail dollars)} = \frac{\text{Net yearly sales}}{\text{Average inventory on hand (at retail)}}$$

$$\text{Annual rate of stock turnover (at cost)} = \frac{\text{Cost of goods sold during the year}}{\text{Average inventory on hand (at cost)}}$$

The choice of a turnover formula depends on the retailer's accounting system.

In computing stock turnover, the average inventory level for the entire period covered in the analysis needs to be reflected. Turnover rates will be invalid if the true average is not used, as occurs when a firm mistakenly views the inventory level of a peak or slow month as the yearly average.

Table 14–10 shows overall stock turnover rates for a variety of retailers. Gasoline service stations and grocery stores have very high rates. They rely on sales volume for their success. Jewelry, shoe, clothing, and hardware stores have very low rates. They rely on larger profit margins for each item sold and maintain a sizable assortment for their customers.

A retailer can increase its stock turnover via a number of different strategies, such as reducing the assortment, eliminating slow-selling items, maintaining minimal inventory for slow-sellers, buying in an efficient and timely manner, applying quick response inventory planning, and utilizing reliable distributors.

Despite the advantages of high stock turnover, there are instances in which it can have adverse effects. First, purchasing items in small amounts could increase merchandise costs because quantity discounts may be lost and transportation charges may rise. Second, since a high turnover rate could be due to low width and/or depth of assortment, some customer sales may be lost. Third, high stock turnover could result in low profits if prices must be reduced in order to move inventory quickly. A retailer's return on investment depends on both turnover and profit per unit.

Gross margin return on investment (GMROI) shows the relationship between the gross margin in dollars (also known as total dollar operating profits) and the average inventory investment (at cost) by combining profitability and sales-to-stock measures:

TABLE 14–10 Annual Median Stock Turnover Rates for Selected Types of Retailers

Type of Retailer	Annual Median Stock Turnover Rate (Times)
Auto and home supply stores	6.5
Department stores	4.6
Family clothing stores	3.7
Furniture stores	4.7
Gasoline service stations	34.6
Grocery stores	18.2
Hardware stores	4.0
Household appliance stores	6.0
Jewelry stores	2.5
Lumber and other building materials dealers	6.8
Men's and boys' clothing stores	3.6
New and used-car dealers	5.8
Shoe stores	3.4
Women's accessory and specialty stores	4.3

Source: *Industry Norms & Key Business Ratios: Desk-Top Edition 1992–93* (New York: Dun & Bradstreet, 1993).

$$\text{Gross margin return on investment (GMROI)} = \frac{\text{Gross margin in dollars}}{\text{Net sales}} \times \frac{\text{Net sales}}{\text{Average inventory at cost}}$$

$$= \frac{\text{Gross margin in dollars}}{\text{Average inventory at cost}}$$

In this formula, the gross margin in dollars is defined as net sales minus the cost of goods sold. The gross margin percentage (a profitability measure) is derived by dividing the dollar gross margin by net sales. A sales-to-stock ratio is provided by dividing net sales by average inventory at cost. [Note: A sales-to-stock ratio may be converted to stock turnover by multiplying that ratio by (100 − Gross margin percentage)/100]. According to a recent study of department stores, GMROI was ranked as the most important profitability measurement linked directly to inventory management.[5]

GMROI is a useful concept for several reasons:

- It shows how different kinds of retailers can prosper despite different gross margins and sales-to-stock ratios. For example, a conventional supermarket may have a gross margin percentage of 20 and a sales-to-stock ratio of 22, resulting in a GMROI of 440 per cent (20% × 22). A department store may have a gross margin percentage of 44 and a sales-to-stock ratio of 10, resulting in a GMROI of 440 per cent (44% × 10). The GMROIs of the two stores are the same because of the trade-off between profitability per item and turnover.
- It is a good indicator of a manager's performance because it focuses on factors controlled by that person. Interdepartmental comparisons can also be made.

[5] Coopers & Lybrand, "Utilizing Inventory Information for Enhanced Supply Chain Management," p. 4.

- It is simple to plan and understand, and data collection is easy.
- A retailer can determine if GMROI performance is consistent with other company goals, such as its image and cash flow.

When using the GMROI formula, it is important for the gross margin percentage and the sales-to-stock ratio to be examined individually. If only the overall GMROI is studied, performance may be assessed improperly. Some retailing experts have also suggested that the basic GMROI formula shown in this section be expanded to include accounts receivable, accounts payable, and inventory carrying costs.

WHEN TO REORDER

One way to control inventory investment is to establish stock levels at which new orders must be placed. Such a stock level is called a ***reorder point***. The determination of a reorder point depends on three factors: order lead time, usage rate, and safety stock. ***Order lead time*** is the time span from the date an order is placed by a retailer to the date merchandise is ready for sale (received, price-marked, and put on the selling floor). The ***usage rate*** refers to average sales per day, in units, of merchandise. ***Safety stock*** is the extra inventory kept on hand to protect against out-of-stock conditions due to unexpected demand and delays in delivery. Safety stock is planned in accordance with a retailer's policy toward running out of merchandise (service level). For example, Lands' End increased its inventory by $20 million during one recent Christmas selling season based upon its goal of being in stock 90 per cent of the time.[6]

This is the formula if a retailer does not plan to carry safety stock, believing that demand is stable and orders are promptly filled by suppliers:

Reorder point = Usage rate × Lead time

If Handy Hardware sells 10 paint brushes a day and needs eight days to order, receive, and display merchandise, it would have a reorder point of 80 brushes. Thus, it would reorder brushes once inventory on hand reaches 80. By the time brushes from that order are placed on shelves (eight days later), stock on hand will be zero, and the new stock will replenish the inventory.

This strategy would be correct only if Handy Hardware has a perfectly steady customer demand of 10 paint brushes per day and it takes exactly eight days for all stages in the ordering process to be completed. However, this does not normally occur. For example, should consumers buy 15 brushes per day during a given month, Handy would run out of merchandise in 5-1/3 days and be without brushes for 2-2/3 days. Similarly, should an order take ten days to process, Handy would have no brushes for two full days, despite correctly estimating demand. Figure 14–6 graphically demonstrates how these stockouts may occur if safety stock is not planned.

When a retailer incorporates safety stock, the reorder formula becomes:

Reorder point = (Usage rate × Lead time) + Safety stock

As a rule, retailers should include safety stock in merchandise planning because demand is rarely constant from day to day or week to week and deliveries from suppliers can be delayed.

Suppose Handy Hardware decides to plan a safety stock of 30 per cent for paint brushes; then its reorder point is

Reorder point = (10 × 8) + (.30 × 80) = 80 + 24 = 104

[6] Tim W. Ferguson, "Shrink Inventory? Lands' End Likes It Loose," *Wall Street Journal* (January 18, 1994), p. A17.

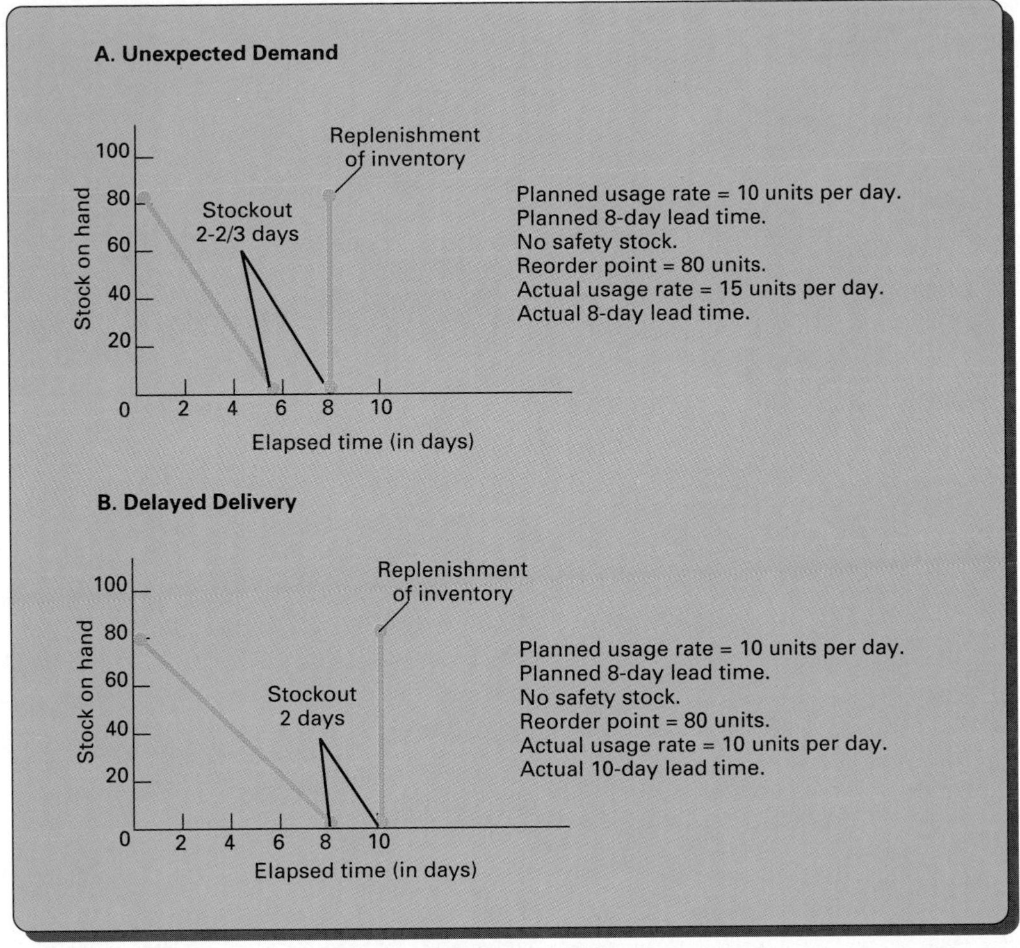

FIGURE 14–6 **How Stockouts May Occur**

In this case, Handy still expects to sell an average of 10 brushes per day and receive orders in an average of eight days. A safety stock of 24 extra brushes is kept on hand to protect against unexpected demand or a late shipment.

For retailers dealing with staples (products with small sales variations during the year or their primary selling season), a procedure is available for estimating safety stock. It is based on the Poisson probability distribution and is shown in Table 14–11. According to this method, if Handy Hardware estimates its paint-brush basic reorder point to be 80 for the spring and summer, it would plan a safety stock of 9 to have an 80 per cent probability of not running out of stock; 14 to have a 95 per cent probability of not running out of stock; and 21 to have a 99 per cent probability of not running out of stock. Therefore, Handy Hardware would take a 20 per cent chance of being out of stock by planning a reorder point of 89 (including safety stock).

As Table 14–11 shows, the safety stock required is proportionately greater for low-turnover items than for high-turnover items. For instance, at the 99 per cent level, safety stock for a retailer having an estimated basic reorder point of 40 is 37.5 per cent (15/40) of that reorder point. At the same level, safety stock for a retailer having an estimated basic reorder point of 400 is 11.5 per cent (46/400) of that reorder point.

By combining a perpetual inventory system and reorder point calculations, a merchandise ordering process can be programmed into a computer and reorders can take place automatically when stock-on-hand reaches the reorder point. This is referred to as an ***automatic reordering system***. However, intervention by a store manager

TABLE 14–11 Safety Stock Levels Required to Obtain Various Probabilities of Not Running Out of Staples

Estimated Basic Reorder Point	Retail Stock Policy Chance of Not Running Out of Stock (%)	Safety Stock Needed to Achieve Stock Policy	Required Reorder Point[a]
25	99	$2.3\sqrt{\text{Estimated reorder point}} = 2.3\sqrt{25} = 12$	37
40	99	$2.3\sqrt{40} = 15$	55
80	99	$2.3\sqrt{80} = 21$	101
100	99	$2.3\sqrt{100} = 23$	123
200	99	$2.3\sqrt{200} = 33$	233
400	99	$2.3\sqrt{400} = 46$	446
25	95	$1.6\sqrt{\text{Estimated reorder point}} = 1.6\sqrt{25} = 8$	33
40	95	$1.6\sqrt{40} = 10$	50
80	95	$1.6\sqrt{80} = 14$	94
100	95	$1.6\sqrt{100} = 16$	116
200	95	$1.6\sqrt{200} = 23$	223
400	95	$1.6\sqrt{400} = 32$	432
25	80	$\sqrt{\text{Estimated reorder point}} = \sqrt{25} = 5$	30
40	80	$\sqrt{40} = 6$	46
80	80	$\sqrt{80} = 9$	89
100	80	$\sqrt{100} = 10$	110
200	80	$\sqrt{200} = 14$	214
400	80	$\sqrt{400} = 20$	420

[a] Required reorder point = Estimated basic reorder point + Safety stock

or buyer must be possible, especially when monthly sales fluctuate greatly. As of 1994, approximately 26 per cent of Federated Department Stores' merchandise was being replenished through an automatic reordering system; the firm's goal is to be at 33 per cent.[7]

HOW MUCH TO REORDER

The decision about how much to order affects how often a retailer must order merchandise. A firm placing large orders generally reduces ordering costs but increases inventory-holding costs. A firm placing small orders often minimizes inventory-holding costs while ordering costs may rise significantly (unless electronic data interchange and a quick response inventory system are used).

The ***economic order quantity (EOQ)*** is the quantity per order (in units) that minimizes the total costs of processing orders and holding inventory. Order-processing costs include computer time, order forms, labor, and handling new merchandise.

[7] "Stock Answers: Tom Cole Tackles Challenge of Boosting Turnover Statistics," *Stores* (December 1993), pp. 37–39.

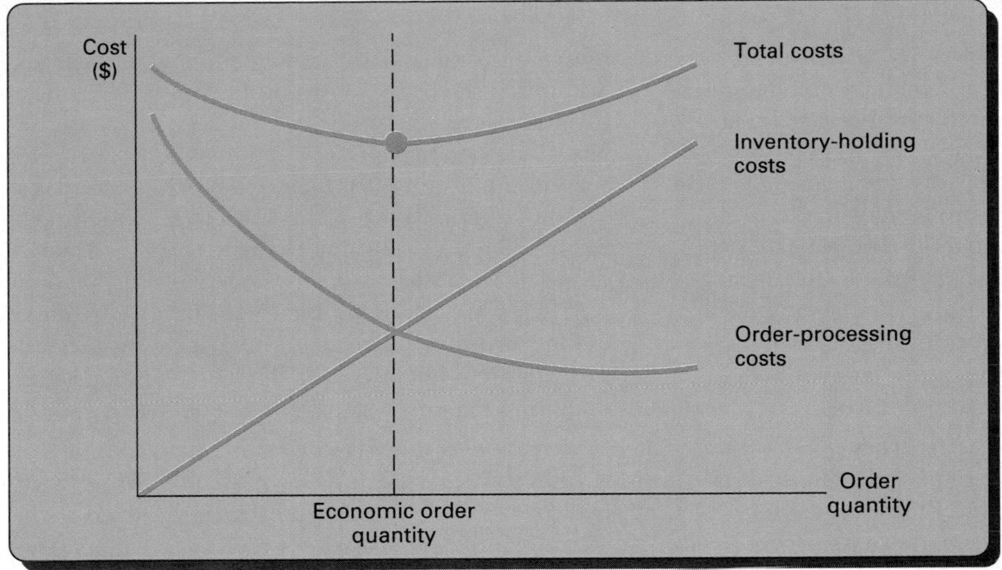

FIGURE 14–7
Economic Order Quantity

Holding costs include warehousing, inventory investment, insurance, taxes, depreciation, deterioration, and pilferage. EOQ can be utilized by both large and small firms.

As shown in Figure 14–7, order-processing costs drop as the quantity per order (in units) goes up because fewer orders are needed to purchase the same total annual quantity, and inventory-holding costs increase as the quantity per order goes up because more units must be maintained in inventory and they are kept for longer periods. The two costs are summed into a total cost curve.

Mathematically, the economic order quantity is

$$EOQ = \sqrt{\frac{2DS}{IC}}$$

where

EOQ = quantity per order (in units)
D = annual demand (in units)
S = costs to place an order (in dollars)
I = percentage of annual carrying cost to unit cost
C = unit cost of an item (in dollars)

Handy Hardware estimates it can sell 150 power-tool sets per year. They cost Handy \$90 each. Breakage, insurance, tied-up capital, and pilferage equal 10 per cent of the costs of the sets (or \$9 each). Order costs are \$25 per order. The economic order quantity is

$$EOQ = \sqrt{\frac{2(150)(\$25)}{(0.10)(\$90)}} = \sqrt{\frac{\$7{,}500}{\$9}} = 29$$

The EOQ formula must often be modified to take into account changes in demand, quantity discounts, and variable ordering and holding costs.

SUMMARY

1. *To describe the major aspects of financial merchandise planning and management* Financial merchandise management stipulates which products are bought, when products are bought, and how many products are bought. Dollar control involves planning and monitoring the inventory investment made during a given period, while unit control relates to the quantities of merchandise handled during that period. Financial merchandise management encompasses methods of accounting, merchandise forecasting and budgeting, unit control systems, and integrated dollar and unit controls.

2. *To explain the cost and retail methods of accounting* The two accounting techniques available to retailers are the cost and retail methods of inventory valuation. Physical and book (perpetual) procedures are possible with each. Physical inventory valuation requires the actual counting of merchandise at prescribed intervals. Book inventory valuation relies on accurate bookkeeping and a smooth flow of data.

   The cost method obligates a retailer to maintain careful records for each item purchased or code its cost on the package. This is necessary to determine the exact value of ending inventory at cost. Many retailers use the LIFO method of accounting to approximate that value, which enables them to reduce taxes by placing a low value on ending inventory. With the retail method, closing inventory value is determined by calculating the average relationship between the cost and retail value of merchandise available for sale during the period. Though the retail method more accurately reflects market conditions, it is also more complex.

3. *To study the merchandise forecasting and budgeting process* Merchandise forecasting and budgeting is a form of dollar control that consists of six stages: designating control units, sales forecasting, inventory-level planning, retail-reduction planning, planning purchases, and profit-margin planning. Adjustments at any stage of the process would require all later stages to be modified accordingly.

   Control units are the merchandise categories for which data are gathered. They must be narrow enough to isolate problems and opportunities with specific lines of merchandise. Sales forecasting—whereby expected future sales are estimated for a given time period—may be the key stage in the merchandising and budgeting process because its accuracy affects so many other stages. Through inventory-level planning, a firm sets merchandise levels for specified periods. Popular ways of inventory-level planning are the basic stock, percentage variation, weeks' supply, and stock-to-sales methods. Retail-reduction planning estimates expected markdowns, discounts, and stock shortages. Planned purchases are based on planned sales, reductions, ending inventory, and beginning inventory. Profit margins are related to a retailer's planned net sales, operating expenses, profit, and reductions.

4. *To examine alternative methods of inventory unit control* A unit control system deals with physical units of merchandise. Key unit control data include the identification of best-sellers and poor sellers, the quantity of goods on hand, inventory age, reorder time, and so on. A physical-inventory unit-control system may use visual inspection or a stock-counting procedure. A perpetual-inventory unit-control system keeps a running total of the number of units a retailer handles via ongoing record-keeping entries that adjust for sales, returns, transfers, new items received, and so on. A perpetual system can be applied manually, by merchandise tags processed by computers, or by point-of-sale devices.

5. *To integrate dollar and unit merchandising control concepts* The aspects of financial inventory control that integrate dollar and unit control concepts are stock turnover and gross margin return on investment, when to reorder, and how much to reorder. Stock turnover represents the number of times during a specified period that the average inventory on hand is sold. Gross margin return on investment shows the relationship between the gross margin in dollars (total dollar operating profits) and average inventory investment (at cost). A reorder point calculation—when to reorder—would include the retailer's usage rate, order lead time, and safety stock. The economic order quantity—how much to reorder—aids a retailer in choosing how large an order to place, based on both ordering and inventory costs.

Throughout the chapter, a number of important mathematical merchandising equations are introduced and illustrated.

KEY TERMS

financial merchandise management (p. 466)
dollar control (p. 466)
unit control (p. 466)
merchandise available for sale (p. 466)
cost of goods sold (p. 466)
gross profit (p. 466)
net profit (p. 466)
cost method of accounting (p. 467)
physical inventory system (p. 467)
book inventory system (perpetual inventory system) (p. 468)

FIFO method (p. 468)
LIFO method (p. 468)
retail method of accounting (p. 470)
cost complement (p. 471)
stock shortage (p. 471)
stock overage (p. 472)
control units (p. 475)
classification merchandising (p. 475)
price line classifications (p. 475)
standard merchandise classification (p. 475)
sales forecasting (p. 476)
monthly sales index (p. 477)
basic stock method (p. 478)
percentage variation method (p. 479)
weeks' supply method (p. 480)
stock-to-sales method (p. 480)
retail reductions (p. 480)
open-to-buy (p. 483)
visual inspection system (p. 485)
stock-counting system (p. 486)
perpetual-inventory unit-control system (p. 486)
stock turnover (p. 488)
gross margin return on investment (GMROI) (p. 488)
reorder point (p. 490)
order lead time (p. 490)
usage rate (p. 490)
safety stock (p. 490)
automatic reordering system (p. 491)
economic order quantity (EOQ) (p. 492)

QUESTIONS FOR DISCUSSION

1. What kinds of retailers can best use a perpetual inventory system involving the cost method?
2. Since the FIFO method of costing inventory seems more logical than the LIFO method, because it assumes the first merchandise purchased is the first merchandise sold, why do many more retailers use LIFO?
3. Explain the cost complement concept in the retail method.
4. Distinguish between the basic stock method and the weeks' supply method of merchandise planning.
5. Present two situations in which it would be advisable for a retailer to take a markdown, instead of carrying over merchandise from one budget period to another.
6. What are the pros and cons of a low stock turnover?
7. How does an automatic reordering system work? What are its advantages and disadvantages?
8. Why is the formula for the economic order quantity shown in this chapter an oversimplification?
9. A retailer has yearly sales of $950,000. Inventory on January 1 is $400,000 (at cost). During the year, $800,000 of merchandise (at cost) is purchased. The ending inventory is $425,000 (at cost). Operating costs are $125,000. Calculate the cost of goods sold and net profit, and set up a profit-and-loss statement. There are no retail reductions in this problem.
10. A retailer has a beginning monthly inventory valued at $20,000 at retail and $14,000 at cost. Net purchases during the month are $60,000 at retail and $35,000 at cost. Transportation charges are $2,000. Sales are $60,000. Markdowns and discounts equal $14,000. A physical inventory at the end of the month shows merchandise valued at $5,000 (at retail) on hand. Compute the following:
    a. Total merchandise available for sale—at cost and at retail.
    b. Cost complement.
    c. Ending retail book value of inventory.
    d. Stock shortages.
    e. Adjusted ending retail book value.
    f. Gross profit.
11. The monthly sales of a full-line discount store are listed here. Calculate the monthly sales indexes. What do they mean?

January	$ 40,000	July	$ 40,000
February	45,000	August	60,000
March	45,000	September	70,000
April	60,000	October	50,000
May	60,000	November	80,000
June	50,000	December	120,000

12. If the planned average monthly stock for the discount store in Question 11 is $80,000, how much inventory should be planned for July if the retailer uses the percentage variation method? Comment on this retailer's choice of the percentage variation method.
13. The discount store in Questions 11 and 12 knows that its cost complement for all merchandise purchased last year was 0.64; it projects this figure to remain constant. For the current year, it expects to begin and end December with an inventory valued at $30,000 at retail and estimates reductions for December to be $4,000. The company has already made purchase commitments for December worth $60,000 (at retail). What is the open-to-buy at cost for December?
14. A retailer sells an average of 12 standard touch-tone telephones per day and desires a safety stock of 24 phones. If it takes seven days for an order to be placed and received by the retailer, what is its reorder point? Explain your answer.

CASE 1
Appliances Plus: Financial Merchandise Planning

Appliances Plus is a 5,000-square-foot retail store situated in downtown Portland, Oregon. The store, which opened in January 1993, sells a full complement of major appliances, including refrigerators, freezers, stoves, microwave and traditional ovens, dishwashers, clothes washers and dryers, and trash compactors. Among the brands carried by Appliances Plus are White-Westinghouse, General Electric, Whirlpool, Frigidaire, and Roper.

Within each of its product categories, Appliances Plus stocks a wide variety of merchandise. For example, the store carries regular refrigerators, refrigerators with freezers, refrigerators with freezers and extra features (such as ice makers and ice-water dispensers), and custom-made models (which can be modified to fit with a kitchen's decor and cabinetry). Portable and full-size models are sold.

Unlike some competitors that order items from a buying cooperative's warehouse at the same time they are sold, Appliances Plus maintains its own warehouse. Although this increases the inventory-carrying costs, it gives the retailer greater control over delivery times and the types of products that are stocked. Thus, Appliances Plus is generally able to deliver the most popular models and colors of a refrigerator or a freezer within four hours of receiving an order.

Appliances Plus' delivery policy has increased the sales of refrigerators and freezers, but has had little impact on the sales of washing machines, dryers, and trash compactors. Even though it has been hard to quantify the advantages of its fast-delivery strategy, Appliances Plus' owner feels that it allows the firm to charge a 5 to 10 per cent price premium on refrigerators and freezers. There is no associated price premium keyed to the early delivery of any other appliances.

Recently, Appliances Plus completed its first annual physical and book inventories for the period January 1, 1994, through December 31, 1994. The results are shown in Tables 1 to 4. The data was prepared by the store's bookkeeper and verified by its certified public accountant (CPA).

QUESTIONS

1. Compute the following for Appliances Plus during 1994:
   a. Stock shortages (at retail).
   b. Adjusted ending retail book value of inventory.
   c. Cost complement.
   d. Closing inventory (at cost).
   e. Gross profit.
   f. Monthly sales index.
2. What was the annual rate of stock turnover in retail dollars for Appliances Plus during 1994 if the average inventory on hand (in retail dollars) was $175,000? Is this good or bad?
3. Which inventory-level planning methods should Appliances Plus employ? Why?
4. Evaluate Appliances Plus' inventory-management system for refrigerators.

Table 1 Appliances Plus—Physical Inventory, as of December 31, 1994

Product Categories	Value of Inventory (at Retail)
Refrigerators/freezers	$ 71,500
Stoves/ovens/microwaves	61,600
Dishwashers	40,700
Clothes washers/dryers	55,000
Trash compactors	22,000
Accessories	11,000
	$261,800

Table 2 Appliances Plus—Perpetual Inventory System, for the Period January 1–December 31, 1994

Date	Beginning-of-Month Inventory (at Cost)	Monthly Purchases (at Cost)	Monthly Sales (at Cost)	End-of-Month Inventory (at Cost)
1/1/94	$148,500	$ 66,000	$ 66,000	$148,500
2/1/94	148,500	66,000	66,000	148,500
3/1/94	148,500	44,000	55,000	137,500
4/1/94	137,500	33,000	44,000	126,500
5/1/94	126,500	44,000	44,000	126,500
6/1/94	126,500	44,000	44,000	126,500
7/1/94	126,500	44,000	44,000	126,500
8/1/94	126,500	44,000	44,000	126,500
9/1/94	126,500	66,000	55,000	137,500
10/1/94	137,500	77,000	66,000	148,500
11/1/94	148,500	121,000	93,500	176,000
12/1/94	176,000	115,500	104,500	187,000
		$764,500	$726,000	(as of 12/31/94)

Table 3 Appliances Plus—Merchandise Available for Sale, for the Period January 1–December 31, 1994

	Cost Method	Retail Method
Beginning inventory	$148,500	$ 214,500
Net purchases	764,500	1,056,000
Additional markups	—	—
Freight-in	16,500	—
	$929,500	$1,270,500

Table 4 Appliances Plus—Ending Retail Book Value, as of December 31, 1994

Merchandise available for sale		$1,270,500
Less deductions:		
Sales	$968,000	
Markdowns	27,500	
Total deductions		995,500
Ending retail book value of inventory		275,000

CASE 2

Magnum Stores: Reversing a Downward Sales Trend in Junior Sportswear*

Liz Collins has just been appointed as Department Manager/Buyer of Junior Sportswear for Magnum Stores. The firm is headquartered in Oklahoma City and specializes in moderate- to better-quality junior sportswear and accessories. Collins had previously worked in a large regional department-store chain for three years as an assistant buyer for junior sweaters. She graduated from the University of Oklahoma with a specialization in marketing, and accepted the job at the department-store chain shortly after graduation.

When she accepted the position with Magnum Stores, Collins learned that the previous manager of this department had been fired, shortly after his annual performance review. Although Collins could not confirm the reason for his being fired, persistent rumors in the office suggested that it was due to the department's poor performance and the person's being "too nice."

In Liz's initial meeting with her immediate supervisor, John Bennett, the Divisional Merchandise Manager, commented:

> Your appointment to this position is a significant opportunity and promotion. Junior Sportswear is one of the most important departments to our company in terms of sales, profits, and customer traffic generated. Although the previous manager was viewed as hard-working and enthusiastic, sales and profit performance had declined. I want you to spend the next two weeks in the headquarter's store's Junior Sportswear department observing sales patterns, speaking to sales personnel and customers, and reviewing the department's financial data. Let's meet again in about three weeks to discuss your analysis of the department's problem areas and your preliminary comments about financial planning in the department.

For the following two weeks, Collins spoke with salespeople and customers, carefully reviewed the department's merchandise forecasting and budgeting process, and visited the Junior sportswear departments of two competing retailers that had excellent reputations among Magnum's target market.

At this point, Liz Collins concluded that:

- The sales staff appeared to be professional, well motivated, and to work well together. A few of the better salespeople commented to Liz: "It seems that we sell out of the 'hot new fashions' too quickly, and that regular customers increasingly leave without making a purchase."
- Discussions with several customers confirmed the salespeople's comments. Several of the customers said the department has "lost its luster." Others said they used to stop at Magnum first when looking for moderate-priced sweaters, but that they now visit the store only when dissatisfied with the offerings of other retailers.
- In comparing sales data for the past twelve months with those of the prior year for corresponding months, Collins found out that the department had failed to meet the previous year's monthly sales level objectives for each of the last eight months. She was well aware that the previous department manager/buyer was responsible for buying decisions in this eight-month period and that revenues in other departments of the store were on target during the same time period.
- Markdowns were comparatively low. Markdowns in the department have averaged 14 per cent of sales this year; two years ago, they were 20 per cent of sales. Trade association data for women's apparel indicates that about 24 per cent is an industry average figure for Magnum's geographic area.
- Stock turnover has increased significantly over the past year:

* This case was prepared and written by John L. Roman, Director of Stores, Rochester Institute of Technology.

Season	Stock Turnover Last Year	This Year
Spring	2.3	3.0
Fall	2.5	4.0

Collins found that the stock turnover rates for the department this year are much higher than average and that last year's rate was about average.

- Collins also evaluated retail sales, inventories, and purchases by retail price category over the past two years. She found that the number of price lines per subclassification of merchandise (such as long-sleeved solid-color cotton sweaters) had been reduced from three to four as of two years ago to one or two lines now. In addition, the dollar range between the lowest and highest prices in these subclassifications had narrowed significantly during this period. See Table 1 for pricing data on classic-styled sweaters sold in the spring.
- There had been no significant difference in the quantity of advertising, in the scheduled sales promotion activities, or in the competitive environment over the past two years.

Table 1 Magnum Stores' Spring Pricing Data for Classic-Styled Sweaters

Sweater Description	Prices Two Years Ago	Prices Now
Cotton, solid color, crew neck, long sleeves. Available in red, navy, and ivory.	$55, 47, 38, 30	$60, 52
Cotton, stripes with reverse stitching, crew neck, long sleeves. Available in navy/white, yellow/white, and jade/white.	$47, 35, 22	$50, 43
Ramie/cotton, padded shoulders, short turned-back sleeves. Available in red, navy, and white.	$62, 48, 35	$70, 62
Updated wool, buttons on shoulder, oversized, ribbed crew neck, long sleeves. Available in red, navy, and white.	$72, 57, 45	$77, 64
Wool jacquard pattern, shoulder pads, ribbed trim, long sleeves. Available in blue/yellow and green/pink.	$64, 58, 42	$70, 62

QUESTIONS

1. Comment on the salesperson's statement: "It seems that we sell out of the 'hot new fashions' too quickly, and that regular customers increasingly leave without making a purchase."
2. Examine the relationship among the decrease in markdowns, the increase in stock turnover, and the reduction in price lines stocked. Use numbers in your analysis.
3. If markdowns have been reduced and stock turnover has risen over the past year, do you think the gross margin return on investment has increased, decreased, or remained the same? Explain your answer.
4. What specific actions should Liz Collins recommend to reverse the decline in sales? Explain your answer.

CHAPTER 15

RM

Pricing in Retailing

❖ Chapter Objectives

1. To describe the role of pricing in a retail strategy and to show that pricing decisions must be made in an integrated and adaptive manner
2. To examine the impact of consumers; government; manufacturers, wholesalers, and other suppliers; and current and potential competitors on pricing decisions
3. To present a framework for developing a retail price strategy: objectives, broad policy, basic strategy, implementation, and adjustments

One basic pricing decision involves whether or not a retailer should use everyday low pricing (EDLP). With EDLP, retailers charge relatively low prices for all of their goods and services throughout the year. An opposite approach to EDLP is known as "high-low" pricing, in which retailers regularly offer specials on a few items, but charge higher prices on their other products.

Among the leading retailers with EDLP philosophies are Wal-Mart, Home Depot, Food Lion, and Winn-Dixie. These firms feel everyday low prices build brand and store loyalty, reduce their advertising costs, lessen staffing needs, and reduce inventory costs. To stabilize prices, EDLP retailers often pay the same amounts for specific items on a year-round basis. They also do not get promotional allowances from suppliers for putting items on sale.

In contrast, retailers that favor the high-low approach believe specials add excitement and provide a stimulus for consumers to shop during limited sale periods. High-low pricing is used by Target, Sears, Giant Foods, and Safeway. As an example, Target has a steady stream of in-store promotions and sales designed to keep customers coming back. The amounts paid by these chains for the same items varies. Many times, the firms stock up when they are offered special deals.

Research on the effectiveness of EDLP and high-low pricing has yielded mixed results. For instance, a University of Chicago study found that EDLP supermarkets have not matched the profits generated by high-low pricing supermarkets. Although the EDLP stores have slightly better revenues, their profits are much less than those earned by stores using high-low pricing—due largely to the higher profit margins obtained on items that are not on sale. On the other hand, an analysis of supermarket profitability by the Ryan Management Group found that the top five supermarket chains that use EDLP have higher net profits than the top five that use the high-low strategy.[1]

[1] Melissa Campanelli, "What's in Store for EDLP," *Sales & Marketing Management* (August 1993), pp. 56–57; Richard Gibson, "Broad Grocery Cuts May Not Pay," *Wall Street Journal* (May 7, 1993), pp. B1, B8; and Tibbett Speer, "Do Low Prices Bore Shoppers?" *American Demographics* (January 1994), pp. 11–13.

Reprinted by permission of Home Depot.

Overview

A retailer must price goods and services in a way that achieves profitability for the firm and satisfies customers, while adapting to various constraints.

Pricing is a crucial strategic variable for a retailer because of its direct relationship with a firm's goals and its interaction with other retailing-mix elements. A retailer's pricing strategy must be consistent with its overall sales, profit, and return-on-investment goals. For example, a retailer interested in an early recovery of its investment, due to expansion plans, might enact a mass-marketing strategy. That approach uses low prices.

The interaction of price with other retailing-mix elements can be shown through the following example. Tie Town is an off-price tie shop. Thus, its two partners have developed a broad strategy consisting of

- A target market of price-conscious men.
- Selling inexpensive ties (in the $9 to $12 range).
- A limited range of merchandise quality.
- Self-service.
- A downtown location.
- A deep assortment.
- Quantity purchases at discount from suppliers.
- An image of efficiency and variety.

This chapter divides retail pricing into two major sections: the external factors affecting a price strategy and developing a price strategy.

External Factors Affecting a Retail Price Strategy

Before detailing how a retail price strategy is developed, it is necessary to explore the external factors affecting price decision making. Consumers, government, manufacturers and wholesalers, and competitors each have an impact on the pricing strategy of a retailer, as shown in Figure 15–1. In some cases, these factors may have only a minor effect; in others, they may severely restrict a retailer's options in setting prices.

THE CONSUMER AND RETAIL PRICING

A retailer must understand the relationship between price and consumers' purchases and perceptions. Two economic principles help to explain this relationship: the law of demand and the price elasticity of demand.

The ***law of demand*** states that consumers usually purchase more units at low prices than at high prices. The ***price elasticity of demand*** relates to the sensitivity of buyers to price changes in terms of the quantities they will purchase. If relatively small percentage changes in price result in substantial percentage changes in the number of units purchased, then price elasticity is high. This occurs when the urgency for a pur-

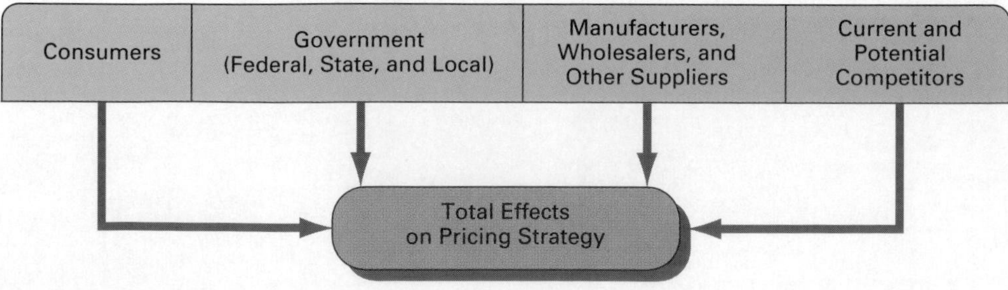

FIGURE 15–1
Factors Affecting Retail Price Strategy

chase is low or acceptable substitutes exist. However, when large percentage changes in price have small percentage changes in the number of units purchased, demand is considered inelastic. This occurs when purchase urgency is high or there are no acceptable substitutes (as takes place with store loyalty). Unitary elasticity occurs in cases where percentage changes in price are directly offset by percentage changes in quantity.

Price elasticity is computed by dividing the percentage change in the quantity demanded by the percentage change in the price charged:

$$\text{Elasticity} = \frac{\dfrac{\text{Quantity 1} - \text{Quantity 2}}{\text{Quantity 1} + \text{Quantity 2}}}{\dfrac{\text{Price 1} - \text{Price 2}}{\text{Price 1} + \text{Price 2}}}$$

Because, according to the law of demand, the quantities purchased decline as prices go up, elasticity is usually a negative number.

Table 15–1 shows the calculation of price elasticity for a 1,000-seat movie theater (with elasticities converted to positive numbers). The table demonstrates that the quantity demanded (tickets sold) declines at every price level from $4.00 to $7.00; fewer customers patronize the theater at $7.00 than at $4.00. Demand is inelastic from $4.00 to $5.50; total ticket receipts increase because the percentage change in price

TABLE 15–1 A Movie Theater's Elasticity of Demand

Price	Tickets Sold (Saturday Night)	Total Ticket Receipts	Elasticity of Demand[a]
$4.00	1,000	$4,000	
			$E = \dfrac{\dfrac{1{,}000 - 950}{1{,}000 + 950}}{\dfrac{\$4.00 - \$4.50}{\$4.00 + \$4.50}} = 0.44$
4.50	950	4,275	
			E = 0.57
5.00	895	4,475	
			E = 0.67
5.50	840	4,620	
			E = 1.00
6.00	770	4,620	
			E = 1.55
6.50	680	4,420	
			E = 2.38
7.00	570	3,990	

[a] Expressed as a positive number.

RETAILING AROUND THE WORLD

Has Discounting Really Come to Japan?

According to retail analysts, discounting has finally come to Japan, where shoppers have long been accustomed to paying full prices for their goods and services. In recent years, some discounters have reported Japanese sales increases of 10 to 18 per cent per year while department store sales have been sluggish. For instance, in 1992, department store sales fell 3.3 per cent—the first annual decline in 27 years. The relatively weak performance of Japanese department stores has been attributed to intense competition, the entry of new retailers such as Toys "R" Us, and the factory outlets that have been established on a nationwide basis.

The explosion of discounting has been especially strong for clothing, furniture, and electronic goods. The growth of electronics discounting stems largely from the current ability of retailers to buy merchandise from any manufacturer. In the past, they were limited to buying the goods of a single manufacturer.

Some regulatory impediments to the growth of discounting in Japan still exist. As an example, although the waiting period for approval to expand a store's size has decreased, delays of one year or more are still common. And government regulations require that many imported goods carry seals to identify the importers. These seals often restrict sales by discounters that have legally avoided paying duties on imported merchandise.

Sources: Based on material in Larry Holyoke, "What? Everyday Bargains? This Can't Be Japan," *Business Week* (September 6, 1993), p. 41; and Yumiko Ono, "Japanese Department Stores Fall From 1980s Heyday," *Wall Street Journal* (February 8, 1993), p. B4.

is greater than the percentage change in tickets sold. Demand is unitary from $5.50 to $6.00; total ticket receipts are constant because the percentage change in tickets sold exactly offsets the percentage change in price. Demand is elastic from $6.00 to $7.00; total ticket receipts decline because the percentage change in tickets sold is greater than the percentage change in price.

For this example, total ticket receipts are highest at $5.50 or at $6.00. But what about the total revenues for the theater? If patrons spend an average of $2.25 each at the concession stand, the best price would be $5.50 (total overall revenues of $6,510). The theater is most interested in total revenues generated because operating costs would be the same whether there are 840 or 770 patrons. But generally, retailers should evaluate the costs, as well as the revenues, from serving additional customers.

In retailing, computing price elasticity is often difficult for two reasons. First, as in the case of the movie theater, demand for individual events or items may be hard to predict. One week, the theater may attract 1,000 patrons to a movie, and the following week, it may attract 400 patrons to a different movie. Second, retailers such as supermarkets and department stores sell thousands of items and could not possibly compute elasticities for each one. Thus, many firms rely on average markup pricing, competition, tradition, and industrywide data as indicators of price elasticity.

Retailers need to recognize that consumer price sensitivity varies by market segment, based on shopping orientation.[2] Here are several segments:

- Economic consumers—They perceive competing retailers as similar to one another and shop around for the lowest possible prices. This segment has grown dramatically in recent years.
- Status-oriented consumers—They perceive competing retailers as quite different from one another. They are more interested in prestige brands and customer services than in price.

[2] See Kirk L. Wakefield and J. Jeffrey Inman, "Who Are the Price Vigilantes? An Investigation of Differing Characteristics Influencing Price Information Processing," *Journal of Retailing*, Vol. 69 (Summer 1993), pp. 216–233; Tridib Mazumdar and Kent B. Monroe, "Effects of Inter-Store Price Comparisons on Price Recall Accuracy and Confidence," *Journal of Retailing*, Vol. 68 (Spring 1992), pp. 66–89; Peter R. Dickson and Alan Sawyer, "The Price Knowledge and Search of Supermarket Shoppers," *Journal of Marketing*, Vol. 42 (July 1990), pp. 42–53; and William D. Diamond, "Just What Is a 'Dollar's Worth'? Consumer Reactions to Price Discounts Versus Extra Promotions," *Journal of Retailing*, Vol. 68 (Fall 1992), pp. 254–269.

- Assortment-oriented consumers—They seek retailers with strong assortments in the product categories under consideration. They look for fair prices.
- Personalizing consumers—They like to shop where they are known. There is a strong personal attachment with retail personnel and the firm itself. These consumers are willing to pay slightly above-average prices.
- Convenience-oriented consumers—They shop only because they must. They are looking for nearby locations and long store hours, and often shop via catalogs. These consumers are willing to pay above-average prices.

After identifying potential segments, retailers must determine which of the segment(s) forms their target market.

THE GOVERNMENT AND RETAIL PRICING

When examining the impact of government on planning a pricing strategy, it must be remembered that three levels of government exist: federal, state, and local. Although many key laws are federal, these laws apply only to interstate commerce. Therefore, a retailer operating exclusively within the boundaries of one state may not be restricted by federal legislation.

Government actions focus on seven major areas: horizontal price fixing, vertical price fixing, price discrimination, minimum price levels, unit pricing, item price removal, and price advertising.

Horizontal Price Fixing

Horizontal price fixing involves agreements among manufacturers, among wholesalers, or among retailers to set certain prices. Such agreements are illegal according to the Sherman Antitrust Act and the Federal Trade Commission Act, regardless of how "reasonable" resultant prices may be. It is also illegal for retailers to reach agreements with one another regarding the use of coupons, rebates, or other price-oriented tactics.

Although few large-scale legal actions have been taken in recent years, the penalties for horizontal price fixing can be severe. For example,

- The managers of three supermarkets (First National, Fisher Foods, and Stop 'N Shop) met weekly in parking lots late at night and jointly decided what "specials" each would offer and at what prices. These managers knew their actions were not legal and worked hard to keep them secret. As a result, the supermarkets were fined a total of $1.7 million, and four executives were fined $100,000 each. The executives also received suspended jail sentences and were placed on five years' probation.[3]
- Four supermarket chains (Waldbaum's, Pathmark, King Kullen, and LAMM) had a private agreement to limit their use of double and triple coupons. With such coupons, the chains would match or exceed the coupon values offered by manufacturers with their own store discounts. It was charged that the chains conspired to stop double- and triple-couponing during certain periods. They were ordered to pay fines totaling $830,000.[4]

Vertical Price Fixing

Vertical price fixing occurs when manufacturers or wholesalers are able to control the retail prices of their goods and services. Until 1976, this practice was allowed in

[3] Michael A. Duggan, "United States v. First National Supermarkets," *Journal of Marketing*, Vol. 47 (Fall 1983), pp. 127–128.

[4] "Four Supermarket Concerns Are Fined Total of $830,000," *Wall Street Journal* (November 27, 1984), p. 64.

the United States because of the belief that manufacturers and wholesalers had the right to protect the reputations of their brands and that these reputations could be diluted via indiscriminate price cutting by retailers. In addition, vertical price fixing was viewed as providing ***fair trade*** protection for smaller and full-service retailers in competition with discounters. Manufacturers enforced fair trade laws by setting uniform retail prices for their items and refusing to sell to those retailers utilizing price cutting or by seeking legal intervention.

However, fair trade laws were criticized by consumer groups and many manufacturers, wholesalers, and retailers as being anticompetitive, keeping prices artificially high, and allowing inefficient retailers to stay in business. As a result, the Consumer Goods Pricing Act, which terminated the interstate use of fair trade practices and resale price maintenance, was enacted. At present, retailers cannot be required to adhere to list prices developed by manufacturers and wholesalers.

Today, manufacturers and wholesalers can legally control retail prices only via one of these methods: they can carefully screen retailers; they can set realistic list prices; they can pre-print prices on products (which retailers do not have to use); they can set regular prices that are accepted by consumers (such as 50 cents for a newspaper); they can use consignment selling, whereby the supplier owns items until they are sold and assumes costs normally associated with the retailer; they can own retail facilities; and they can refuse to sell to retailers that advertise discount prices to enforce their written policies. Although a manufacturer has a right to announce a general policy regarding pricing by dealers and can refuse to sell to those that do not comply with it, the manufacturer cannot use coercion or conspire with other dealers to prohibit a retailer from advertising low prices.[5]

Many discount retailers nonetheless believe that, in the 1980s, the Federal Trade Commission and the Department of Justice did not adequately protect their right to compete on the basis of price. From 1981 through 1990, the FTC did not bring any actions to curb vertical price fixing, even though numerous discount retailers contended that they were denied access to product lines and that consumers had been forced to pay higher prices as a result.

Since early 1991, the FTC has become more involved in this area, settling complaints filed against Nintendo, Kreepy Krauly (a maker of swimming-pool cleaning devices), and others. In addition, for several years, a number of the nation's state attorneys general have actively policed manufacturers that engage in vertical price fixing, such as getting Stride Rite to agree to pay $7.2 million to New York consumers to avoid charges of price fixing on its popular Keds sneakers in 1993.[6] Similar settlements have been made with Nintendo (a $25 million fine) and Mitsubishi Electric (an $8 million fine). And the Clinton administration promised to more vigorously enforce vertical price fixing laws and "treat vertical price fixing as per se illegal."[7]

Price Discrimination

The ***Robinson-Patman Act*** prohibits manufacturers and wholesalers from discriminating in price or sales terms when dealing with individual retailers if these retailers are purchasing products of "like quality" and the effect of such discrimination would be to injure competition. The intent of the Robinson-Patman Act is to prevent large retailers from using their power to obtain discounts not justified by the cost savings achieved through sizable orders. It is feared that, without the Robinson-Patman Act, smaller retailers could be driven out of business because of noncompetitive final prices due to significantly higher merchandise costs.

[5] See Dorothy Cohen, "Commodore Business Machines vs. Montgomery Grant," *Journal of Marketing*, Vol. 57 (October 1993), p. 130; and Ken Rankin, "Sony Gives Clinton Chance to Act on Price Fixing," *Discount Store News* (December 6, 1993), p. 31.

[6] Joseph Pereira, "Stride Rite Agrees to Settle Charges It Tried to Force Pricing by Retailers," *Wall Street Journal* (September 28, 1993), p. A5.

[7] Joe Davidson, "Rules Allowing Manufacturers to Fix Prices with Distributors Are Rescinded," *Wall Street Journal* (August 11, 1993), p. A3.

There are exceptions to the Robinson-Patman Act, that allow justifiable price discrimination when

- Products are physically different.
- The retailers paying different prices are not competitors.
- Competition is not injured.
- Price differences are due to differences in the supplier's costs.
- Market conditions change.
  a. Manufacturing or other costs increase or decrease.
  b. Competing suppliers change their prices.

Discounts are not illegal, as long as a supplier follows the preceding rules, makes discounts available to competitive retailers on an equitable basis, and offers discounts sufficiently graduated so small (as well as large) retailers can qualify. Discounts for cumulative purchases (total orders during the year) and for multistore purchases by chains may be difficult to justify.

For example, in fall 1993, a group of 20 chain and independent drugstores initiated a law suit against seven major pharmaceutical makers, charging that those manufacturers had refused to give the drugstores the same discounts as mail-order retailers and managed-care organizations. The plaintiff group represents about 10 per cent of all U.S. drugstores; and its suit claims that the drug manufacturers have violated the Robinson-Patman Act.[8]

Although the Robinson-Patman Act seems to restrict sellers more than buyers, retailers do have specific liabilities under Section 2(F) of the Act:

> It shall be unlawful for any person engaged in commerce, in the course of such commerce, knowingly to induce or receive a discrimination in price which is prohibited in this section.

From a strategic perspective, a retail buyer must attempt to receive the lowest prices charged to any competitor in its class; yet, it must also be careful not to bargain so hard that the discounts received cannot be justified by one of the acceptable exceptions.

Minimum-Price Laws

Twenty-three states have ***minimum-price laws*** preventing retailers from selling certain merchandise for less than its cost plus a fixed percentage to cover overhead.[9] Merchandise costs are defined in various ways; typically, they are purchase or replacement costs, whichever are lower.

Minimum-price laws are intended to protect small retailers from predatory pricing by larger competitors. In ***predatory pricing***, big retailers attempt to destroy competition by selling goods and services at extremely low prices, which causes small retailers to go out of business.

With ***loss leaders***, retailers price selected items below cost to attract more customer traffic for those retailers. Firms such as supermarkets frequently use loss leaders to increase their overall sales and profits under the assumption that consumers will buy more than one item once drawn to a store. Although loss leaders are restricted by some minimum-price laws, because this approach is usually consumer-oriented, the laws are rarely applied (as long as predatory pricing is not involved).

Besides general laws, many states have acts setting minimum prices for specific products. For instance, in New Jersey and Connecticut, laws require the retail price of liquor to be not less than the wholesale cost (including taxes and delivery charges).

[8] Elyse Tanouye, "Drug Makers Sued by Stores Over Pricing," *Wall Street Journal* (October 15, 1993), pp. A2, A4; and Kenneth N. Gilpin, "For Drugstores, Pushing Pills Is Much Less Profitable," *New York Times* (January 2, 1994), Section 3, p. 5.

[9] Bob Ortega, "Wal-Mart Loses Predatory Pricing Case in Arkansas Court But Plans to Appeal," *Wall Street Journal* (October 13, 1993), pp. A3, A8.

In one recent, widely watched case, three independent pharmacies in Conway, Arkansas, filed a predatory pricing suit claiming that Wal-Mart had deliberately sold products below cost in an attempt to reduce competition. During fall 1993, Wal-Mart was found guilty in an Arkansas court, ordered to pay $289,407 in damages to the pharmacies, and ordered to stop selling health and beauty aids and over-the-counter drugs at prices below cost in its Conway store. This was the first time that Wal-Mart was unable to settle a predatory pricing case out of court. Wal-Mart agreed that it had priced products below cost to meet or beat rivals' prices, but not to harm small competitors. Wal-Mart announced that it would appeal the verdict to the Arkansas Supreme Court and further, if necessary.[10]

Unit Pricing

The proliferation of package sizes has led to ***unit-pricing*** laws in many states. The aim of such legislation is to enable consumers to compare the prices of products available in many sizes (e.g., small, medium, and large).

Food stores are most affected by unit-price regulations, and in many cases, these stores are required to express both the total price of an item and its price per unit of measure. For example, a 6.5-ounce can of tuna fish priced at 99 cents would also have a shelf label showing this represents $2.44 per pound. With unit pricing, a consumer could determine that a 12-ounce can of soda selling for 35 cents (2.9 cents per ounce) is more expensive than a 67.6-ounce—two-liter—bottle of soda selling for $1.49 (2.2 cents per ounce).

Unit-pricing laws are intended to give basic information to consumers who feel price is an important decision factor and to provide added data for those customers who consider brand-name or other factors as most important. Although early research studies questioned the effectiveness of unit pricing, later findings have indicated it is advantageous for both retailers and consumers.

Not all retailers must comply with unit-pricing laws. Generally, there are exemptions for retailers with low-volume sales or for those operating only one outlet. In addition, grocery items are much more heavily regulated than nongrocery items.

The costs of unit pricing to affected firms include calculating per-unit prices, printing product and shelf labels, and maintaining computer records. These costs are influenced by the way prices are attached to goods (manually versus machine), the number of items in a store subject to unit pricing, the frequency of price changes, sales volume, and the number of stores in a chain. A number of supermarket chains have reported that the costs of unit pricing are not excessive, whereas smaller food stores report that costs are high.

Unit pricing can be an advantageous strategy for retailers to follow, even when not required by law. For instance, Giant Food has found its unit-pricing system more than pays for itself in terms of decreased price-marking errors, better inventory control, and improved space management.

Item Price Removal

The expansion of computerized checkout systems has led many retailers, especially supermarkets, to advocate ***item price removal***—whereby prices are marked only on shelves or signs and not on individual items. Electronic scanning equipment reads the pre-marked codes on product labels and enters price information at the checkout counter. This practice is banned in several states and local communities.

Supermarkets assert that item price removal would significantly reduce labor costs and enable them to offer lower prices. Opponents argue that item price removal would lead to more checkout errors against consumers and make it virtually impossible for consumers to verify prices as they are rung up.

[10] Kate Fitzgerald, "Court Decision Stings Wal-Mart," *Advertising Age* (October 10, 1993), p. 8; Ken Rankin, "Winning Predatory Price Appeal Won't Be Easy for Wal-Mart," *Discount Store News* (November 15, 1993), p. 12; and "Wal-Mart Appeals Drug Price Suit," *Discount Store News* (November 1, 1993), pp. 1, 53.

ETHICS IN RETAILING

Can Consumers Trust Electronic Scanners?

According to *Information Week*, a trade publication for computer systems managers, scanner system overcharges (caused when prices are recorded at higher-than-correct levels) cost U.S. consumers an estimated $2.5 billion per year. Yet, the president of the Food Marketing Institute, a supermarket trade association, says the scanner error rate is only 2 per cent and that scanner errors are more often in favor of consumers than the stores.

An informal research study by *Consumer Reports* found that most of the supermarkets visited had no scanner errors. However, one shopper reported being overcharged $.70 on a $2.29 jar of cheese and another was not charged the sale price for a jar of peanut butter.

Consumer Reports believes that many of the scanner errors occur because store employees incorrectly input prices into the computer data bank or because stores do not update shelf tags often enough. In addition, shelf tags are sometimes located in the wrong place or are missing, making it impossible for many shoppers to compare scanner and store prices in states that do not have item-pricing laws.

To increase trust in scanner pricing, some stores now offer free products or other incentives to consumers if they are overcharged via scanner error.

Source: Based on material in "Checkup on the Checkout: Can You Trust the Scanner?" *Consumer Reports* (September 1993), p. 561.

Giant Food practices item price removal in its supermarkets, and there have been little consumer resistance and considerable cost savings. Giant carefully maintains accurate, highly visible shelf prices and gives items free to consumers if the prices processed by its electronic cash registers (equipped with scanners) are higher than those posted on shelves.

Price Advertising

The FTC has guidelines for price advertising. These guidelines deal with advertising price reductions, advertising prices in relation to competitors' prices, and bait-and-switch advertising.

In general, FTC guidelines state that a retailer cannot claim or imply that a price has been reduced from some former level (such as a manufacturer's list or suggested list price) unless the former price was an actual, bona fide one at which the retailer offered a good or service to the public on a regular basis during a reasonably substantial, recent period of time.

When a retailer claims its prices are lower than those of other firms, FTC guidelines state that it must make certain the price comparisons pertain to competitors selling large quantities in the same trading area. A particularly controversial, but basically legal, practice involves price matching: "When a store pledges to match a competitor's advertised prices, it isn't promising that all its prices are the lowest in town. What's more, such stores expect only a small percentage of shoppers to try to collect on price-matching promises. Critics question the fairness of a policy which allows merchants to cut special deals with only the most conscientious comparison shoppers."[11]

Bait advertising, or ***bait-and-switch advertising***, is an illegal practice whereby a retailer lures a customer by advertising goods and services at exceptionally low prices; then, once the customer contacts the retailer (by entering a store or calling a toll-free 800 number), he or she is told that the good/service of interest is out of stock or of inferior quality. A salesperson tries to convince the customer to purchase a better, more expensive substitute that is available. In bait advertising, the retailer has no intention of selling the advertised item.

In determining whether a promotion constitutes bait advertising, the FTC may consider how many sales were made at the advertised price, whether a sales commission was paid on sale items, and the total amount of sales relative to advertising costs.[12]

[11] Francine Schwadel, "Are Price-Matching Policies Largely PR?" *Wall Street Journal* (March 16, 1989), p. B1.

[12] Stephen P. Durchslag, "FTC Is on the Lookout For 'Bait and Switchers'," *Promo* (April 1993), p. 62.

MANUFACTURERS, WHOLESALERS, AND OTHER SUPPLIERS—AND RETAIL PRICING

Manufacturers, wholesalers, and other suppliers have an impact on a retail pricing strategy. In cases where suppliers are unknown or products are new, retailers may seek price guarantees to ensure that inventory values and profits will be maintained. ***Price guarantees*** protect retailers against possible price declines. For example, suppose a new manufacturer sells a retailer radios having a final list selling price of $20 and guarantees the price to a retailer. If that retailer is unable to sell the radios at this price, the manufacturer pays the difference. Should the retailer have to sell the radios at $15, the manufacturer would give a rebate of $5 per radio. Another type of price guarantee is one where a supplier guarantees to a retailer that no other retailer will be able to buy an item for a lower price. If anyone does, the retailer will get a rebate. The relative power of the retailer and its suppliers determines whether such guarantees are provided.

There are often conflicts between manufacturers (and other suppliers) and their retailers in setting final prices because each would like some level of input and control. Usually, manufacturers want to gain and retain a certain image and to let all retailers, even those that are rather inefficient, earn profits. In contrast, most retailers would rather set prices based upon their own image, objectives, and other factors.

A manufacturer can control prices by using an exclusive distribution system, refusing to sell to price-cutting retailers, and/or operating its own retail facilities. A retailer can gain control by being important to its manufacturers as a customer, threatening to stop carrying manufacturers' lines, selling private brands, or selling gray market goods.

In many instances, manufacturers set the selling prices to their retailers by estimating final retail prices and then subtracting the required retailer and wholesaler profit margins from these figures. For example, in the men's haberdashery industry, the common retail markup (gross profit) is 50 per cent of the final selling price. Thus, a man's shirt retailing at $24 can be sold to the retailer for no more than $12. If a wholesaler is involved, the manufacturer's price to the wholesaler must be far less than $12.

Retailers sometimes carry manufacturers' brands and place high prices on them. When they do this, rival brands (such as private-label merchandise) can be sold more easily. This is called ***selling against the brand*** and is disliked by manufacturers because sales of their brands are likely to decline. Some retailers also sell ***gray market goods***, generally brand-name products purchased in foreign markets or goods transshipped from other retailers. Manufacturers particularly dislike gray market goods because they are often sold at low prices by unauthorized dealers. Firms such as Givenchy have begun to limit the sales of gray market goods on the basis of copyright and trademark infringement.[13]

A retailer also has suppliers other than manufacturers and wholesalers. These include employees, fixtures manufacturers, landlords, and outside parties (such as advertising firms). Each of these suppliers has an impact on price because of their costs to the retailer.

The effect of manufacturers, wholesalers, and other suppliers on retail pricing strategies can be seen from these two examples:

- The presence of low-cost airlines in some markets has caused a problem for travel agents. These airlines provide lesser commission revenues (which are generally 10 per cent of the fare), while requiring more work—because many of the airlines do not participate in a computer-reservation system. Some travel agents

[13] See "Givenchy Wins Damages in Suit," *New York Times* (February 11, 1994), p. D3; and Stephanie Strom, "Givenchy Wins a Major Round in Discount Fight," *New York Times* (September 4, 1993), p. 37.

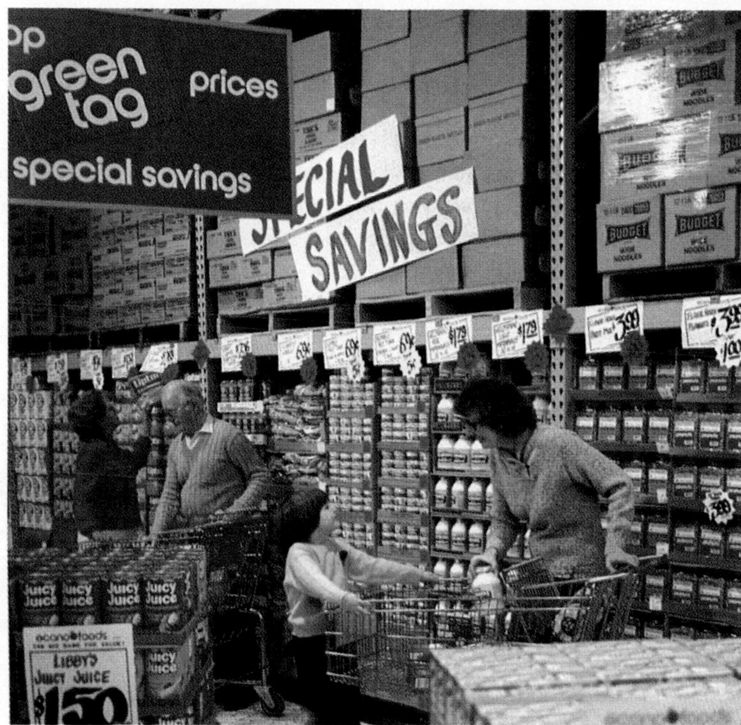

Figure 15–2
Market Pricing
Due to competitive pressures, many supermarkets engage in market pricing.
Reprinted by permission of Nash Finch.

have begun to add surcharges on tickets under $100. As one travel agent says: "If the airline can figure out a way to offer a $99 fare profitably, that is good news for the airline and good news for the traveler. But it's the agent who's the most vulnerable."[14]

- A small number of manufacturers, such as Step 2 (a toy maker), have recently revised their distribution policies and are refusing to sell to certain mass merchandisers in an effort to win the loyalty of independent retailers and to prevent their products from being used as price leaders. Although Step 2 will sell to Toys "R" Us, Kmart and Target, it has "an understanding" that its toys won't be offered below a certain price to increase store traffic. Other manufacturers, such as Scotts (a manufacturer of lawn care products), sell only certain product lines to mass merchants and reserve others for independent retailers. This reduces price competition among the different types of retailers.[15]

Competition and Retail Pricing

The degree of control an individual firm has over prices often depends on the competitive environment it faces. In a market-pricing situation, there is a lot of competition and people seek the lowest prices. Firms price similarly to each other and have low control over price. Supermarkets, fast-food firms, and gas stations are in very competitive industries and tend to sell similar goods and services; thus, firms in these categories use ***market pricing***. Demand for specific retailers is weak enough so that a number of customers would switch to a competitor if prices are raised much. See Figure 15–2.

With ***administered pricing***, a retailer seeks consumer patronage on the basis of a distinctive retailing mix. If strong differentiation from competitors can be reached, a

[14] James S. Hirsch, "Fare Cuts Test Travel Agents' Reliability," *Wall Street Journal* (January 19, 1994), pp. B1, B3.

[15] Valerie Reitman, "Manufacturers Start to Spurn Big Discounters," *Wall Street Journal* (November 30, 1993), pp. B1, B11.

firm can control the prices it charges. This occurs when shoppers consider image, assortment, personal service, and other factors to be more important than price and they will pay above-average prices for goods and services when shopping with desirable retailers (under the assumption that less desirable retailers do not offer as good an image, assortment, personal service, and so on). Traditional department stores, fashion apparel stores, and upscale restaurants are among those that work hard to create distinct offerings and have some control over their prices.

Because most price-oriented strategies can be easily copied in a short time, the reaction of competitors is predictable when the leading firm is successful. Therefore, a retailer should view price strategy from a long-run, as well as a short-run, perspective.

If the competitive environment becomes too intense, a ***price war*** may occur—whereby various retailers continually lower prices below regular amounts and sometimes below merchandise costs to attract consumers away from competitors. Price wars can lead to low profits, losses, or even bankruptcy for some competitors.

For example, a budding price war started when Circuit City announced a major price initiative primarily targeting Best Buy, its key competitor, at the winter 1994 Consumer Electronics Show. Best Buy has been expanding into markets once dominated by Circuit City. Many analysts believe Circuit City can undercut Best Buy due to the former's highly profitable service-contract business. In turn, Best Buy can compete through its full selection and simply not stock the specific items that Circuit City is promoting.[16]

Developing a Retail Price Strategy

As depicted in Figure 15–3, there are five steps (objectives, policy, strategy, implementation, and adjustments) in a retail price strategy. Like any other strategic activity, pricing begins with a clear statement of goals and ends with an adaptive or corrective mechanism. Pricing policies must be integrated with the total retail mix; this occurs in the second step of price planning. This process can be complex due to the often erratic nature of demand and the number of items carried by many retailers. And all aspects of the process are affected by the external factors already discussed.

RETAIL OBJECTIVES AND PRICING

A retailer's pricing strategy must be consistent with and reflect overall objectives. As noted in Chapter 2, financial goals can be stated in terms of sales and profits. Besides its broad objectives, a retailer needs to set more specific pricing goals to avoid such potential problems as confusing people by having too many prices, spending too much time bargaining with customers, having to use frequent sales to stimulate customer traffic, having inadequate profit margins, and placing excessive emphasis on price in the strategy mix.

Overall Objectives and Pricing

Sales goals are often stated in terms of dollar revenues and/or unit volume. An example of a sales goal and a resultant pricing strategy is a car dealer's desire to capture large dollar revenues by setting low prices and selling a high unit volume. This aggressive low-price strategy is known as ***market penetration.*** It is proper when customers are highly sensitive to price, low prices discourage actual and potential competition, and total retail costs do not increase as much as sales volume increases.

Profit-in-dollars objectives are sought when a retailer concentrates on total profit or profit per unit. With a ***market skimming*** strategy, a firm charges premium prices and attracts customers less concerned with price than service, assortment, and status. Though this approach typically does not maximize sales, it does achieve high profit

[16] Pete Hisey, "Price Wars Erupt at CES," *Discount Store News* (February 7, 1994), p. 3.

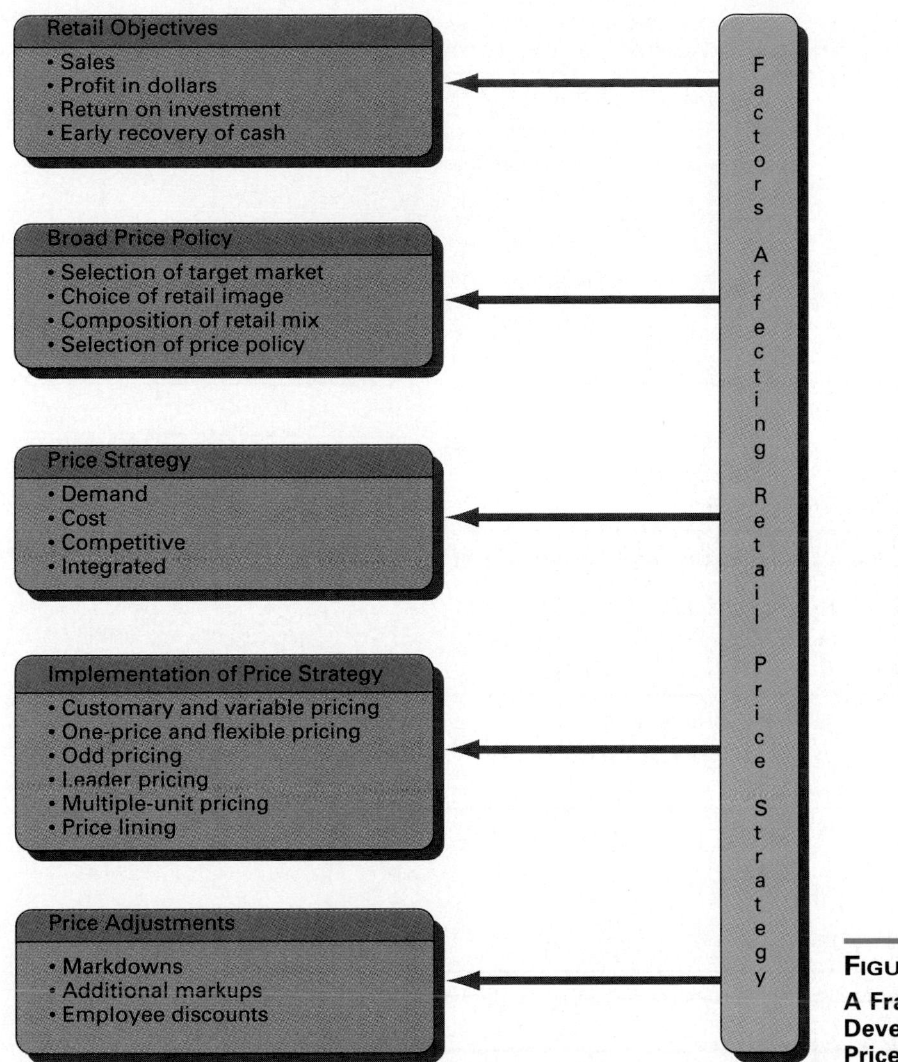

FIGURE 15–3
A Framework for Developing a Retail Price Strategy

per unit. It is appropriate if the market segment a retailer defines as its target market is insensitive to price, new competitors will not enter the market, and additional sales will greatly increase total retail costs.

Return on investment and early recovery of cash are two other profit-based objectives. A return-on-investment goal is sought if a retailer stipulates that profit must be a certain percentage of its investment, such as profit being 20 per cent of inventory investment. Early recovery of cash is a goal set by retailers that may be short on funds, wish to expand, or be uncertain about the future. A market skimming strategy is often used by retailers with return on investment or early recovery of cash as a goal.

Tie Town, the off-price tie shop cited at the beginning of the chapter, may be used to illustrate how a retailer could be interested in sales, profit, and return-on-investment goals. Tie Town sells inexpensive ties (avoiding competition with department and haberdashery stores), uses a single selling price for all ties (to be set for the next year from within the range of $9 to $12), minimizes operating costs, maximizes self-service, and carries a large variety to generate traffic.

Table 15–2 contains data gathered by Tie Town pertaining to demand, costs, profit, and return-on-inventory investment at various prices between $9 and $12. It must select the most appropriate price within that range. Table 15–3 shows the methods used to arrive at the figures in Table 15–2.

From Table 15–2, several conclusions concerning the best price for Tie Town can be drawn:

TABLE 15–2 Tie Town: Demand, Costs, Profit, and Return on Investment[a]

Selling Price (in $)	Quantity Demanded (in units)	Total Sales Revenue (in $)	Average Cost of Merchandise (in $)	Total Cost of Merchandise (in $)	Total Nonmerchandise Costs (in $)	Total Costs (in $)
9.00	57,000	513,000	7.60	433,200	52,000	485,200
10.00	52,000	520,000	7.85	408,200	47,000	455,200
11.00	40,000	440,000	8.25	330,000	44,000	374,000
12.00	30,000	360,000	8.75	262,500	40,000	302,500

Selling Price (in $)	Average Total Costs (in $)	Total Profit (in $)	Profit/Unit (in $)	Markup at Retail (in %)	Profit/Sales (in %)	Average Inventory on Hand (in units)
9.00	8.51	27,800	0.49	16	5.4	6,000
10.00	8.75	64,800	1.25	22	12.5	6,500
11.00	9.35	66,000	1.65	25	15.0	7,000
12.00	10.08	57,500	1.92	27	16.0	8,000

Selling Price (in $)	Inventory Turnover (in units)	Average Investment in Inventory at Cost (in $)	Inventory Turnover (in $)	Return on Investment (in %)
9.00	9.5	45,600	9.5	61
10.00	8.0	51,025	8.0	127
11.00	5.7	57,750	5.7	114
12.00	3.8	70,000	3.8	82

Note: Average cost of merchandise reflects quantity discounts. Total nonmerchandise costs include all retail operating expenses.

[a] Numbers have been rounded off.

- A sales objective would lead the company to a selling price of $10. At that price, total sales are highest ($520,000).
- A dollar profit objective would lead the firm to a selling price of $11. At that price, total profit is highest ($66,000).
- A return-on-investment objective would also lead the store to a selling price of $10, at which return-on-inventory investment is 127 per cent.
- Although a large quantity can be sold at $9, that selling price would lead to the lowest profit ($27,800).
- A selling price of $12 would yield the highest profit per unit and as a percentage of sales, but total dollar profit is not maximized at this price.
- High inventory turnover would not necessarily lead to high profits.

As a result, Tie Town's partners have decided that a price of $11 would enable them to earn the highest dollar profits, while also generating good profit per unit and profit as a percentage of sales.

Specific Pricing Objectives

Table 15–4 provides a list of specific pricing objectives other than sales and profits. Although a number of pricing objectives are enumerated in this table, each firm must determine the relative importance of the various goals in its particular situation and

TABLE 15–3 Derivation of Tie Town Data

Column in Table 15–2	Source of Information or Method of Computation
Selling price	Trade data, comparison shopping, experience
Quantity demanded (in units) at each price level	Consumer surveys, trade data, experience
Total sales revenue	Selling price × Quantity demanded
Average cost of merchandise	Contacts with suppliers, quantity discount structure, estimates of order sizes
Total cost of merchandise	Average cost of merchandise × Quantity demanded
Total nonmerchandise costs	Experience, trade data, estimation of individual retail operating expenses
Total costs	Total cost of merchandise + Total nonmerchandise costs
Average total costs	Total costs/Quantity demanded
Total profit	Total sales revenue − Total costs
Profit per unit	Total profit/Quantity demanded
Markup (at retail)	(Selling price − Average cost of merchandise)/ Selling price
Profit as a percentage of sales	Total profit/Total sales revenue
Average inventory on hand	Trade data, merchandise turnover data (in units), experience
Inventory turnover (in units)	Quantity demanded/Average inventory on hand (in units)
Average investment in inventory (at cost)	Average cost of merchandise × Average inventory on hand (in units)
Inventory turnover (in $)	Total cost of merchandise/Average investment in inventory (at cost)
Return-on-inventory investment	Total profit/Average investment in inventory (at cost)

plan accordingly. And some goals in the table may be incompatible with one another, such as "to not encourage customers to become overly price-conscious" and a "'we-will-not-be-undersold' philosophy."

BROAD PRICE POLICY

A broad price policy enables a retailer to generate a coordinated series of actions, a consistent image (especially important for chain and franchise units), and a strategy incorporating short- and long-run considerations (where the retailer balances immediate and long-term goals).

A useful way to plan a broad price policy is via the ***multistage approach***, which divides the major elements of pricing into six successive steps, with each placing limits on those that follow: selecting a target market, choosing a retail image, outlining the retail strategy mix, selecting a broad price policy, selecting a price strategy, and choosing specific prices.[17] The first four steps concentrate on the evolution of a broad policy; the last two steps center on specific price decisions and their implementation (which are discussed later in this chapter).

The starting point in developing any price policy is the selection of a target market. Once it is selected, an appropriate retail image is created to establish relevant as-

[17] Alfred R. Oxenfeldt, "Multi-Stage Approach to Pricing," *Harvard Business Review*, Vol. 38 (July–August 1960), pp. 125–133.

Table 15–4 Selected Specific Pricing Objectives

1. To maintain a proper image.
2. To not encourage customers to become overly price-conscious.
3. To be perceived as fair by all parties (including suppliers, employees, and customers).
4. To be consistent in setting prices.
5. To increase customer traffic during slow periods.
6. To clear out seasonal merchandise.
7. To match competitors' prices without starting a price war.
8. To promote a "we-will-not-be-undersold" philosophy.
9. To be regarded as the price leader in the market area by consumers.
10. To provide ample customer service.
11. To minimize the chance of government actions relating to price advertising and anti-trust matters.
12. To discourage potential competitors from entering the marketplace.
13. To create and maintain customer interest.
14. To encourage repeat business.

sociations in the minds of that market. Thus, the selection of a target market limits the retailer's choice of an image. In composing its retail strategy mix, the firm must assign a role to price, such as appealing to customers through extensive price cutting or generating store traffic through convenience, quality of service, and so on, rather than price.

Next, a retailer determines its broad price policy, which translates price decisions into an integrated framework. For example, a company must decide whether prices should be established for individual items, interrelated for a group of goods and services, or based on an extensive use of special sales.

These are some of the price policies from which a retailer could choose:

- No competitors will have lower prices; no competitors will have higher prices; or prices will be consistent with competitors'.
- All items will be priced independently, depending on the demand for each; or the prices for all items will be interrelated to maintain an image and ensure proper markups.
- Price leadership will be exerted; competitors will be price leaders and set prices first; or prices will be set independently of competitors.
- Prices will be constant throughout the year or season; or prices will change if merchandise costs change.

Price Strategy

A price strategy can be demand, cost, and/or competitive in orientation. In ***demand-oriented pricing***, a retailer sets prices based on consumer desires. It determines the range of prices acceptable to the target market. The top of this range is called the demand ceiling, the maximum consumers will pay for a good or service.

With ***cost-oriented pricing***, a retailer sets a price floor, the minimum price acceptable to the firm so it can reach a specified profit goal. A retailer usually computes merchandise and retail operating costs and adds a profit margin to these figures.

For ***competition-oriented pricing***, a retailer sets its prices in accordance with competitors'. The price levels of key competitors and how they affect the firm's sales are studied.

RETAILING IN ACTION

How Can a Small Retailer Compete on Price?

North Shore Farms is part of a three-store produce chain based in Long Island, New York. Low prices are the heart of each store's retail strategy. For example, North Shore Farms has sold cucumbers at 8 cents each, as compared to three for $1 at competitors.

The firm is able to undercut its larger competitors by applying these tactics:

- All produce racks have been built by the chain's owner and its employees. They are coated with an epoxy-based paint to protect them from moisture.
- To reduce energy costs, the produce racks are unrefrigerated. The produce is hosed throughout the day to reduce spoilage. At night, the wet produce is placed in coolers.
- To lower shipping costs, each store receives one trailer full of produce daily. Although much of the merchandise is ordered from food brokers, North Shore Farms also buys some produce directly from farmers. These farmers typically deliver their produce directly to the store.

To communicate its low-price strategy, the North Shore's store design resembles a farmer's market. And almost every week, the chain offers consumers a free produce item (such as a pineapple, a honeydew melon, or a package of mushrooms) with every purchase.

Source: Based on material in Stephen Bennett, "Produce Power Play," *Progressive Grocer* (November 1993), pp. 83–87.

As a rule, retailers should use an integrated combination of all three approaches when setting a price strategy. These approaches should not be viewed as operating independently of one another.

Demand-Oriented Pricing

Demand-oriented pricing is often used by retailers whose goals are listed in terms of sales or market share. It seeks to estimate the quantities customers would demand at various price levels and concentrates on the prices associated with stated sales goals. Whereas a cost-oriented pricing strategy examines costs, a demand-oriented approach looks at demand irrespective of costs.

When using demand-oriented pricing, it is necessary to understand the psychological implications. The term ***psychological pricing*** refers to consumer perceptions of retail prices. Two aspects of psychological pricing are the price-quality association and prestige pricing.

The ***price-quality association*** is a concept stating that many consumers believe high prices connote high quality and low prices connote low quality. This association is particularly important if competing retailers or products are difficult to judge on bases other than price, consumers have little experience or confidence in judging quality (as with a new retailer or product), buyers perceive large differences in quality among retailers or products, and brand names are an insignificant factor in product choice.

Though various studies have documented the price-quality relationship, research indicates that when other quality cues, such as retailer or product features and the stocking of well-known brands, are introduced, these factors may be more important than price in a person's judgment of overall retailer or product quality.

Prestige pricing is drawn from the price-quality association. With ***prestige pricing***, it is assumed that consumers will not buy goods and services at prices considered too low. Consumers may feel that too low a price would mean that quality and status are poor. In addition, some consumers look for prestige pricing when selecting retail stores and do not shop at stores having prices that are too low. For example, Saks Fifth Avenue and Neiman-Marcus do not generally carry the least expensive versions of items because their customers may perceive them to be inferior. See Figure 15–4.

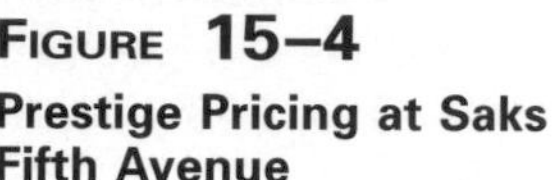

FIGURE 15–4
Prestige Pricing at Saks Fifth Avenue
Because it appeals to an upscale target market with a distinctive retail strategy mix, Saks is able to charge above-average prices for the items it carries.
Reprinted by permission.

Prestige pricing does not apply to all people. That is why the target market must be defined before a retailer reaches this stage. Some people may be economizers and always shop for bargains. Neither the price-quality association nor prestige pricing may be applicable for these consumers.

Cost-Oriented Pricing

One form of cost-oriented pricing, known as markup pricing, is the most widely practiced retail-pricing technique. In ***markup pricing***, a retailer sets prices by adding per-unit merchandise costs, retail operating expenses, and desired profit. The difference between merchandise costs and selling price is the retailer's ***markup***. For example, if a retailer buys a desk for $200 and wants to sell it for $300, the extra $100 is needed to cover retail operating expenses and profit. The markup is 33-1/3 per cent on the retail price, or 50 per cent on cost.

The markup percentage depends on such factors as a product's traditional markup, the manufacturer's suggested list price, inventory turnover, the competition, rent and other overhead costs, the extent to which a product must be altered or serviced, and the selling effort required.

Although markups can be computed on the basis of retail selling price or cost, they are typically calculated in terms of retail selling price. There are several reasons for this. First, retail expenses, markdowns, and profit are always stated as a percentage of sales. Thus, if markups are expressed as a percentage of sales, they are quite meaningful. Second, manufacturers quote their selling prices and trade discounts to retailers as percentage reductions from retail list prices. Third, retail selling-price data are more readily available than cost data. Fourth, profitability statistics appear to be smaller if expressed on the basis of retail price instead of cost; this can be useful when dealing with the government, employees, and consumers.

A ***markup percentage*** is calculated as

$$\text{Markup percentage (at retail)} = \frac{\text{Retail selling price} - \text{Merchandise cost}}{\text{Retail selling price}}$$

$$\text{Markup percentage (at cost)} = \frac{\text{Retail selling price} - \text{Merchandise cost}}{\text{Merchandise cost}}$$

TABLE 15–5 Markup Equivalents

Percentage at Retail	Percentage at Cost
5.0	5.3
10.0	11.1
15.0	17.6
20.0	25.0
25.0	33.3
30.0	42.9
35.0	53.8
40.0	66.7
45.0	81.8
50.0	100.0
60.0	150.0
75.0	300.0
80.0	400.0
90.0	900.0

As shown in these equations, the difference is in the denominator used. In both formulas, merchandise cost is the per-unit invoice and freight cost to the retailer, less per-unit trade or quantity discounts.

Table 15–5 shows a range of markup percentages at retail and at cost. As markups increase, the disparity between retail and cost percentages grows. For example, suppose a retailer buys a watch for $20 and considers whether to sell it for $25, $40, or $80. The $25 price yields a markup of 20 per cent (at retail) or 25 per cent (at cost), the $40 price yields a markup of 50 per cent (at retail) or 100 per cent (at cost), and the $80 price yields a markup of 75 per cent (at retail) or 300 per cent (at cost).

The markup concept has various applications in pricing and purchase planning. These illustrations detail its usefulness:

- A discount clothing store can purchase a shipment of men's jeans at $12 each and wants to obtain a 30 per cent markup at retail. What retail price should the store charge to achieve this markup?

$$\text{Markup percentage (at retail)} = \frac{\text{Retail selling price} - \text{Merchandise cost}}{\text{Retail selling price}}$$

$$0.30 = \frac{\text{Retail selling price} - \$12.00}{\text{Retail selling price}}$$

$$0.30(\text{Retail selling price}) = \text{Retail selling price} - \$12.00$$

$$0.70(\text{Retail selling price}) = \$12.00$$

$$\text{Retail selling price} = \$17.14$$

  The store should charge $17.14 to achieve a 30 per cent markup at retail.*

- A stationery store desires a minimum 40 per cent markup at retail for legal-sized envelopes. If the store feels the envelopes should retail at 79 cents per box, what is the maximum price the firm can pay for the envelopes?

* Selling price may also be computed by transposing the markup formula into

$$\text{Retail selling price} = \frac{\text{Merchandise cost}}{1 - \text{Markup}} = \frac{\$12.00}{1 - 0.3} = \frac{\$12.00}{0.7} = \$17.14$$

$$\text{Markup percentage (at retail)} = \frac{\text{Retail selling price} - \text{Merchandise cost}}{\text{Retail selling price}}$$

$$0.40 = \frac{\$0.79 - \text{Merchandise cost}}{\$0.79}$$

$$\$0.79 - \text{Merchandise cost} = (0.40)(\$0.79)$$

$$\$0.79 - \text{Merchandise cost} = \$0.316$$

$$\text{Merchandise cost} = \$0.79 - \$0.316$$

$$\text{Merchandise cost} = \$0.474$$

To achieve at least a 40 per cent markup, the retailer cannot pay more than 47.4 cents per box of legal-sized envelopes.†

- A sporting-goods store has been offered a closeout purchase on an imported line of bicycles. The per-unit cost of each bicycle is \$105, and the bikes should retail for \$160 each. What markup at retail will the store obtain?

$$\text{Markup percentage (at retail)} = \frac{\text{Retail selling price} - \text{Merchandise cost}}{\text{Retail selling price}}$$

$$\text{Markup percentage} = \frac{\$160.00 - \$105.00}{\$160.00}$$

$$\text{Markup percentage} = \frac{\$55.00}{\$160.00}$$

$$\text{Markup percentage} = 34.4$$

The store will receive a markup of 34.4 per cent on these bikes.

Markup may also be determined by examining planned retail operating expenses, profit, and net sales:

$$\text{Markup percentage (at retail)} = \frac{\text{Planned retail operating expenses} + \text{Planned profit}}{\text{Planned net sales}}$$

As an example, suppose a florist estimates retail operating expenses (rent, salaries, electricity, cleaning, bookkeeping, and so on) to be \$55,000 per year. The desired profit is \$50,000 per year, including the owner's salary. Net sales are forecast to be \$250,000. The planned markup is

$$\text{Markup percentage (at retail)} = \frac{\$55{,}000 + \$50{,}000}{\$250{,}000} = 42$$

Because flowers cost the florist an average of \$8.00 a dozen, the retailer's selling price per dozen is

$$\text{Retail selling price} = \frac{\text{Merchandise cost}}{1 - \text{Markup}}$$

$$\text{Retail selling price} = \frac{\$8.00}{1 - 0.42} = \$13.79$$

The florist will need to sell about 18,129 dozen flowers at \$13.79 per dozen to achieve its sales and profit goals. And to reach these goals, all flowers must be sold at the \$13.79 price.

† Merchandise cost may also be computed by transposing the markup formula into

$$\text{Merchandise cost} = (\text{Retail selling price})(1 - \text{Markup})$$

$$\text{Merchandise cost} = (\$0.79)(1 - 0.40) = (\$0.79)(0.60) = \$0.474$$

Because it is highly unusual for a retailer to sell all items in stock at their original prices, it is necessary to understand and compute initial markup, maintained markup, and gross margin. ***Initial markup*** is based on the original retail value assigned to merchandise less the costs of the merchandise. ***Maintained markup*** is based on the actual prices received for merchandise sold during a time period less merchandise cost. Since maintained markups are related to actual prices received, it can be hard to estimate them in advance. The difference between initial and maintained markups is that the latter reflect adjustments from original retail values caused by markdowns, added markups, shortages, and discounts.

The initial markup percentage depends on planned retail operating expenses, profit, reductions, and net sales:

$$\text{Initial markup percentage (at retail)} = \frac{\text{Planned retail operating expenses} + \text{Planned profit} + \text{Planned retail reductions}}{\text{Planned net sales} + \text{Planned retail reductions}}$$

If planned retail reductions are zero, the initial markup percentage is equal to planned retail operating expenses plus profit, both divided by planned net sales. This results in the markup formula just explained.

To return to the florist example, suppose the firm projects that its retail reductions will be 20 per cent of estimated sales, or $50,000. To reach its goals, the initial markup will have to be

$$\text{Initial markup percentage (at retail)} = \frac{\$55{,}000 + \$50{,}000 + \$50{,}000}{\$250{,}000 + \$50{,}000} = 51.7$$

and the original selling price will be

$$\text{Retail selling price} = \frac{\text{Merchandise cost}}{1 - \text{Markup}} = \frac{\$8.00}{1 - 0.517} = \$16.56$$

This means the original retail value of 18,129 dozen flowers will be about $300,000. Retail reductions of $50,000 will result in net sales of $250,000. Therefore, the retailer must begin selling flowers at $16.56 per dozen if its goal is to have an average selling price of $13.79 per dozen and a maintained markup of 42 per cent.

The maintained markup percentage can be viewed as

$$\text{Maintained markup percentage (at retail)} = \frac{\text{Actual retail operating expenses} + \text{Actual profit}}{\text{Actual net sales}}$$

or

$$\text{Maintained markup percentage (at retail)} = \frac{\text{Average selling price} - \text{Merchandise cost}}{\text{Average selling price}}$$

Gross margin is the difference between net sales and the total cost of goods sold. The total cost figure, as opposed to the gross cost figure, adjusts for cash discounts and additional expenses:

$$\text{Gross margin (in \$)} = \text{Net sales} - \text{Total cost of goods}$$

For the florist, gross margin (which is the dollar equivalent of maintained markup) is approximately $250,000 − $145,000 = $105,000. The total cost of goods is merchandise cost times the number of units purchased.

Although a retailer must set an overall companywide markup goal, markups for categories of merchandise or even individual products may differ. In fact, markups can vary significantly. For instance, in full-line discount stores, maintained markup as a percentage of sales ranged from 12.0 per cent for health and beauty aids to 48.3 per cent for videos in 1993.[18]

The use of a ***variable markup policy***, whereby a retailer designedly varies markups by merchandise category, achieves four major purposes. First, such markups recognize that the costs associated with separate goods/service categories may fluctuate widely. Some items require extensive alterations (such as clothing) or installation (such as carpeting). Even within a product line like women's clothing, expensive fashion items require higher end-of-year markdowns than inexpensive items. Therefore, the more expensive line would receive a higher initial markup.

Second, variable markups allow for differences in product investments. For instance, in a major-appliance department where the retailer orders regularly from a wholesaler, lower markups would be needed than in a fine jewelry department, where the retailer would have to maintain a complete stock of merchandise.

Third, a variable policy accounts for differences in selling efforts and merchandising skills. Selling a food processor may necessitate substantial sales effort, whereas selling a blender may involve significantly less effort and skill.

Fourth, a variable markup policy may enable a retailer to generate more store traffic by advertising certain products at especially attractive prices. This involves leader pricing and is further discussed later in this chapter.

One emerging technique for planning variable markups is ***direct product profitability (DPP)***, which was introduced in Chapter 12. It is growing in popularity among supermarkets, discount stores, and other types of retailers. With DPP, a retailer determines the profitability of each category or unit of merchandise by computing adjusted per-unit gross margin and assigning direct product costs for expense categories such as warehousing, transportation, handling, and selling. In this way, the appropriate markup for each category or item can be set. The major problem with DPP is the complexity and difficulty of allocating costs accurately.[19]

Figure 15–5 shows how DPP works. In this example, each of two items has a retail selling price of $20. With Item A, the retailer has a merchandise cost of $12. Its per-unit gross margin is $8. Because the firm gets a $1 per-unit allowance (rebate) for setting up a special display for Item A, its adjusted gross margin is $9. Total direct retail costs for Item A are estimated at $5. Thus, the direct product profit for Item A is $4, or 20 per cent of sales.

With Item B, the retailer has a merchandise cost of $10. Its per-unit gross margin is $10, and there are no special discounts or allowances. Since Item B requires a greater selling effort, its total direct retail costs are $6. And its direct profit is $4, or 20 per cent of sales. To attain the same direct profit per unit, Item A has a markup of 40 per cent (per-unit gross margin/selling price) and Item B has a markup of 50 per cent.

For many reasons, cost-oriented (markup) pricing is very popular among retailers. It is fairly simple, especially as a retailer can apply a standard markup for a category of products much more easily than it can estimate demand at various price levels; the firm also can adjust prices according to changes in demand, or it can segment a market. Markup pricing has an inherent sense of equity in that the retailer earns a fair profit. In addition, when retailers have similar markups, price competition is significantly reduced. Last, markup pricing is quite efficient if it takes into account competition, seasonal factors, and difficulties in selling specific merchandise categories.

[18] "Full-Line Discount Store Productivity," *Discount Store News* (August 2, 1993), p. 34.

[19] See James F. Wolter and Bennett L. Rudolph, "Direct Product Profit (DPP): Opening the Door for Relationship Marketing for Packaged Goods Marketers," in Paul C. Thistlethwaite, Rolf Hackmann, and Charles Pettijohn (Editors), *Midwest Marketing Association 1993 Proceedings* (Macomb, Ill.: Western Illinois University, 1993), pp. 170–174.

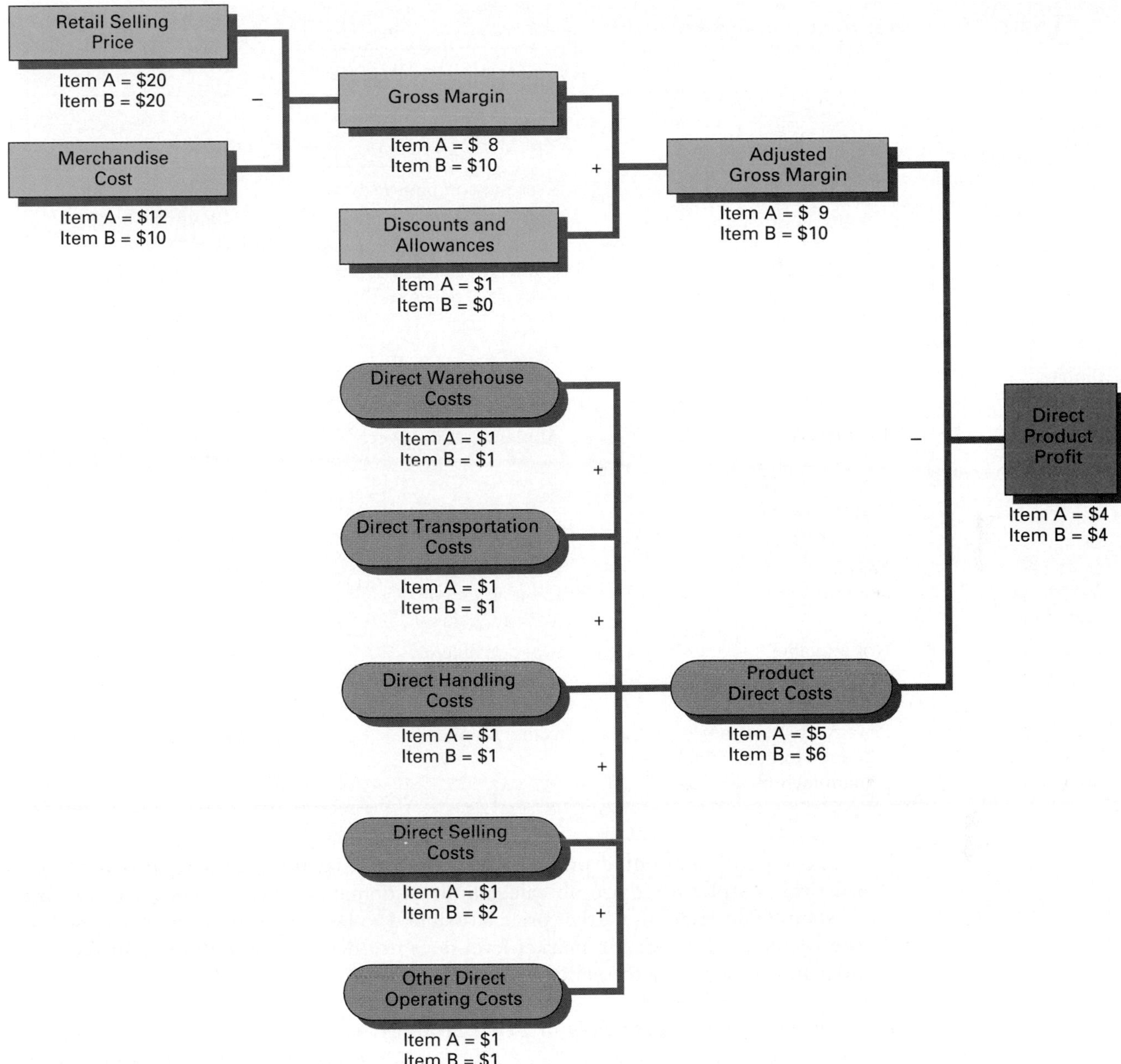

FIGURE 15–5 **How to Determine Direct Product Profit**

Competition-Oriented Pricing

In competition-oriented pricing, a retailer uses competitors' prices as a guide, rather than demand or cost considerations. A competition-oriented firm might not alter its prices to react to changes in demand or costs unless competitors alter theirs. Similarly, such a retailer might alter its prices when competitors do, even if demand or cost factors remain the same.

A competition-oriented retailer can price below the market, at the market, or above the market. Table 15–6 outlines the conditions influencing a firm's choice of one of these levels. It is clear from this table that a pricing strategy must be integrated with the overall retail strategy mix. For example, a firm with a strong site, superior customer service, good product assortment, favorable image, and exclusive brands could set its prices above competitors'. On the other hand, above-market pricing would not be suitable for a retailer that has an inconvenient location, relies on self-service, concentrates on best-sellers, is a fashion follower, and stresses private-label merchandise.

TABLE 15–6 Competition-Oriented Pricing Alternatives

Retail Mix Variable	Alternative Price Strategies: Pricing Below the Market	Pricing At the Market	Pricing Above the Market
Location	Poor, inconvenient site	Close to competitors, no locational advantage	Absence of strong competitors, convenient to consumers
Customer service	Self-service, little product knowledge on part of salespeople, no displays	Moderate assistance by sales personnel	High levels of personal selling, delivery, exchanges, etc.
Product assortment	Concentration on best-sellers	Medium assortment	Large assortment
Atmosphere	Inexpensive fixtures, little or no carpeting or paneling, racks for merchandise	Moderate atmosphere	Attractive, pleasant decor with many displays
Role of fashion in assortment	Fashion follower, conservative	Concentration on accepted best-sellers	Fashion leader
Special services	Not available	Not available or extra charge to customers	Included in price
Merchandise lines carried	Private labels, name-brand closeouts, small manufacturers	Name brands	Exclusive name brands

A competition-oriented pricing approach could be used for several reasons. It is relatively simple; there are no calculations of demand curves or concern with price elasticity. The ongoing market price is assumed to be fair for both the consumer and the retailer. Pricing at the market level does not disrupt competition and therefore does not usually lead to retaliation.

Integration of Approaches to Price Strategy

The three approaches for setting a retail price strategy should be integrated, so that demand, cost, and competition are all taken into account. To do this, a firm should answer questions such as these before enacting a price strategy:

- If prices are reduced, will revenues increase greatly? (Demand orientation)
- Should different prices be charged for a product, based on negotiations with customers, seasonality, and so on? (Demand orientation)
- Will a given price level allow a traditional markup to be attained? (Cost orientation)
- What price level is necessary for a product requiring special costs in purchasing, selling, or delivery? (Cost orientation)
- What price levels are competitors setting? (Competitive orientation)
- Can higher prices than competitors' be charged due to a firm's reputation and image? (Competitive orientation)

By no means is this list complete, but it should give some idea as to how a retailer can integrate demand, cost, and competitive orientations to pricing. Figure 15–6 illustrates an integrated pricing approach.

FIGURE 15–6

Integrated Pricing at Perry Drug Stores

Perry's price strategy is targeted at price-conscious customers, is tied to a low-cost operating structure, and takes competitors' prices into account ("Compare & Save"). In its "Perry Lowers Prices" campaign, the objective is to assure customers of the firm's price competitiveness while continuing to build on its strengths of convenient locations, a broad product mix, and responsive customer care. *Reprinted by permission.*

IMPLEMENTATION OF PRICE STRATEGY

The implementation of a price strategy involves a wide variety of separate but interrelated specific decisions in addition to those broad concepts already discussed. A checklist of selected decisions is shown in Table 15–7. In this section, many of the specifics of pricing strategy are detailed.

Customary and Variable Pricing

Customary pricing occurs when a retailer sets prices for goods and services and seeks to maintain them for an extended period. Prices are not altered during this time. Examples of goods and services with customary prices are newspapers, candy, mass transit, pay phones, arcade games, vending-machine items, and foods on restaurant menus. In each of these cases, a retailer seeks to establish customary prices and have consumers take them for granted.

A version of customary pricing is ***everyday low pricing (EDLP)***, whereby a retailer strives to sell all of its goods and services at consistently low prices throughout the selling season. Under EDLP, the retailer sets low prices initially; and there are no

TABLE 15–7 A Checklist of Selected Specific Pricing Decisions

1. How important is price stability? How long should prices be maintained?
2. Is everyday low pricing desirable?
3. Should prices change if costs and/or customer demand vary?
4. Should the same prices be charged of all customers buying under the same conditions?
5. Should customer bargaining be permitted?
6. Should odd pricing (e.g., $5.99) be used?
7. Should leader pricing be utilized to draw customer traffic? If yes, should leader prices be above, at, or below costs?
8. Should consumers be offered discounts for purchasing in quantity?
9. Should price lining be used to provide a price range and price points within that range?
10. Should pricing practices vary by department or product line?

advertised specials, except on discontinued merchandise or on end-of-season closeouts. The retailer reduces its advertising and product relabeling costs, and the manufacturer reduces its added production and shipping costs that are caused by uneven sales levels. EDLP also increases the credibility of the retailer's prices to the consumer. On the other hand, with EDLP, manufacturers usually eliminate the special trade allowances that are designed to encourage retailers to offer price promotions during the year. Although these allowances enable wholesalers and retailers to buy large amounts at a discount, some items have been resold by the wholesalers and retailers at regular prices.[20]

In many instances, a retailer cannot or should not use customary pricing. A firm *cannot* maintain constant prices if its costs are rising. A firm *should not* maintain constant prices if customer demand varies. Under ***variable pricing***, a retailer alters its prices to coincide with fluctuations in costs or consumer demand. Variable pricing may also provide excitement due to special sales opportunities for customers.

Cost fluctuations can be seasonal or trend-related. Seasonal fluctuations affect retailers selling items whose production peaks at certain times during the year. Thus, prices in supermarkets and floral shops vary over the year due to the seasonal nature of many agricultural and floral products. When items are scarce, their costs to the retailer go up. Trend-related fluctuations, common to retailers today, refer to the constant upward (or downward) spiral of costs to the retailer. As these costs rise, the retailer must raise prices permanently (unlike seasonal fluctuations, which cause temporary changes).

Demand fluctuations can be place- or time-based. Place-based fluctuations exist for retailers selling seat locations (such as concert theaters) or room locations (such as hotels). Different prices can be charged for different locations; for example, tickets close to the stage command higher prices. If variable pricing is not followed, location is based on a policy of first come, first served. Time-based fluctuations occur when consumer demand differs by hour, day, or season. For example, demand for a movie theater is greater on Saturday than on Wednesday; demand for an airline is greater during December than in February. Thus, prices should be lower during periods of low demand.

It is possible to combine customary and variable pricing. For instance, a theater can charge $3 every Wednesday night and $6 every Saturday. An airline can lower prices by 20 per cent during off-seasons.

One-Price Policy and Flexible Pricing

Under a ***one-price policy***, a retailer charges the same price to all customers seeking to purchase an item under similar conditions. A one-price policy may be used in conjunction with customary pricing or variable pricing. In the latter case, all customers interested in a particular section of seats or arriving at the same time would pay the same price.

The one-price policy was begun by John Wanamaker, who was the first major merchant to mark prices clearly on each item in stock. This marking system did away with price bargaining, found favor with consumers, and was quickly copied by others. Throughout the United States, one-price policies are the rule for most retailers, and bargaining over price is usually not permitted.

In contrast, ***flexible pricing*** allows consumers to bargain over selling prices, and those consumers who are good at bargaining obtain lower prices than those who are not. Many jewelry stores, auto dealers, house painters, flea markets, and consumer electronics stores use flexible pricing. Retailers employing flexible pricing do not clearly post their bottom-line prices; consumers must have prior knowledge in order to bargain successfully.

[20] See Jennifer Lawrence, "Will P&G's Pricing Policy Pull Retailers Over to Its Side?" *Advertising Age* (April 19, 1993), pp. 1, 42; "The Concept of EDLP Is Changing," *Advertising Age* (August 16, 1993), pp. 33–34; and Steve Weinstein, "EDLP: Fact and Fiction," *Progressive Grocer* (November 1992), pp. 50–58.

FIGURE 15–7
Odd Pricing and Floral Picks
Odd pricing is used by a wide range of retailers, including Michaels Stores (the chain of arts, crafts, and decorative products shops).
Reprinted by permission.

A one-price policy speeds up transactions, reduces labor costs, and permits self-service, catalog, and vending-machine sales. Flexible pricing requires high initial prices and qualified sales personnel. Today, some auto dealers are changing from a flexible pricing to a one-price policy (known as "no-haggle pricing") so as to enhance their image, raise consumer confidence, and shift the discussion to car attributes and away from price.[21]

Odd Pricing

With ***odd pricing***, retail prices are set at levels below even dollar values, such as $0.49, $4.98, and $199.00. The assumption is that people feel these prices represent bargains or that the amounts are beneath consumers' price ceilings. For example, realtors hope that consumers setting a price ceiling of less than $100,000 will be attracted to houses selling for $99,500. From this perspective, odd pricing is a form of psychological pricing (which was discussed earlier in this chapter). See Figure 15–7.

Originally, odd prices were used to force sales clerks to give change on each purchase, thus preventing the clerks from pocketing receipts without ringing up sales. Now, odd prices are accepted as part of the U.S. system of retailing and are used more for psychological reasons.

Odd prices that are 1 cent or 2 cents below the next highest even price (e.g., $0.29, $0.99, $2.98) are most common up to the $10.00 level. Beyond that point and up to $50.00, 5-cent reductions from the highest even price (e.g., $19.95, $49.95) are more usual. For higher-priced merchandise, odd endings are in dollars (e.g., $399; $4,995).

Despite the widespread use of odd pricing in retailing, there has been little research on its psychological effects.

[21] See James Bennett, "Buying Without Haggling as Cars Get Fixed Prices," *New York Times* (February 1, 1994), pp. A1, A12; and Arlena Sawyers, "No-Haggle Pricing Going Full Throttle," *Advertising Age* (March 22, 1993), pp. S-10, S-28.

Leader Pricing

In ***leader pricing***, a retailer advertises and sells key items in its goods/service assortment at less than the usual profit margins. The goal is to increase customer traffic for the retailer in the hope of selling regularly priced goods and services in addition to the specially priced items. Leader pricing is different from bait-and-switch, in which sale items are not sold.

Leader pricing often involves frequently purchased, nationally branded, high-turnover goods and services because it is easy for customers to detect low prices and they generate high customer patronage. For example, Goody's Family Clothing, a 127-store chain based in the Southeast, is widely known for its low prices on brand-name jeans, such as Levi's 550, Goody's most popular item. These jeans are used to attract customers who also buy higher-margin products on the same shopping trip.[22]

There are two kinds of leader pricing: loss leaders and sales at lower than regular prices (but higher than cost). As noted earlier in this chapter, loss leaders are regulated on a statewide basis under minimum-price laws.

Multiple-Unit Pricing

In ***multiple-unit pricing***, a retailer offers discounts to customers who buy in quantity. For example, by selling items at two for $0.75 or six for $2.19, a retailer would attempt to sell more products than at $0.39 each.

There are two reasons for using multiple-unit pricing. First, a retailer could seek to have customers increase total purchases of an item. However, if customers buy multiple units and stockpile them, instead of consuming more, the firm's sales would not increase. Second, multiple-unit pricing could enable a retailer to clear out slow-moving and end-of-season merchandise.

Price Lining

Instead of stocking merchandise at all different price levels, retailers often employ ***price lining*** and sell merchandise at a limited range of price points, with each point representing a distinct level of quality. In price lining, retailers first determine their price floors and ceilings in each product category. They then set a limited number of price points within the range. For example, department stores typically carry good, better, and best versions of merchandise consistent with their overall price policy and set individual prices accordingly.

Price lining benefits consumers and retailers. For consumers, price lining lessens shopping confusion. If the price range for a box of personalized stationery is $6 to $15 and the price points are $6, $9, and $15, consumers would know that distinct product qualities exist. However, should a retailer have prices of $6, $7, $8, $9, $10, $11, $12, $13, $14, and $15, the consumer could be confused about product qualities and differences.

For retailers, price lining greatly aids the merchandise buying and handling process. Retail buyers can seek out only those suppliers carrying products at appropriate prices; and the buyers can use final selling prices in negotiating with suppliers. Retailers would automatically disregard products not fitting within price lines and thereby reduce inventory investment. Also, stock turnover would be greatly increased by limiting the models carried.

Four difficulties do exist with price lining. First, depending on the price points selected, a price-lining strategy may have gaps between prices that are perceived as too large by consumers. Thus, a parent shopping for a graduation gift might find a $30 briefcase to be too inexpensive and a $120 briefcase to be too expensive. Second, inflation can make it difficult to maintain price points and price ranges. When costs rise, retailers can either eliminate lower-priced items or reduce markups. Third, mark-

[22] Amy Feldman, "Blue Jeans as Tuna Fish," *Forbes* (April 26, 1993), pp. 78–79.

PRICE CHANGE AUTHORIZATION 418651

MARK THE BLANK BOX TO THE LEFT OF EACH STORE AFFECTED WITH AN "X"

HQ | SC | WE | PA | VS | RF | BS | ST | CO | WH

ALL (SOUTH ONLY) | ME | CH | UD | NE | MO | KP | EC | LA | OX | GR

TYPE OF PRICE CHANGE: MARK "X" NEXT TO TYPE

MARKDOWN 1 | MARKDOWN CANCELLATION 2 | MARKUP 3 | MARKUP CANCELLATION 4 | ACTION DATE MM DD YY | DEPT

MARKING INSTRUCTIONS: NEW TICKET 1 PEN 2 CHANGE CHECKS 3 | PERMANENT | DIVISION
POS FROM BEFORE AND AFTER COUNTS 2 POS FROM SALESCHECKS 3 | TEMPORARY

REASON FOR PRICE CHANGE/ ORIGINAL AUTHORIZATION NO. | AD MERCHANDISE NO YES | DATES OF SALE FROM / TO / | STOCK STATUS DEPARTMENTS: CIRCLE ONE CODE ONLY FOR ALL STYLES 1 TO BE REPORTED IN REGULAR SELECTION OF STOCK STATUS 3 TO BE REPORTED IN MARKDOWN SECTION OF STOCK STATUS

SPECIAL INSTRUCTIONS

	% OFF	MERCHANDISE DESCRIPTION (CC 1-31)	CLASS	SKU NUMBER		UNIT RETAIL	UNIT RETAIL	CHANGE	EST COUNT (ALL STORES)	TOTAL DOLLARS
				VENDOR	STYLE	OLD	NEW	PER UNIT		
01			0							
02			0							
03			0							
04			0							
05			0							
06			0							
07			0							
08			0							
09			0							

REASON (CIRCLE)	LEAD TIME	REASON (CIRCLE)	LEAD TIME
1. COMPETITION	2 DAYS	5. NORMAL CLEARANCE	5 DAYS
2. STOREWIDE EVENTS DIV/DEPT SALE	5 DAYS	6. SLOW SELLING LIQUIDATION	5 DAYS
3. EQUALIZATION	5 DAYS	7. CURRENT RECEIPTS NOT SELLING	4 DAYS
4. MARKOUT/SALVAGE BREAKAGE	5 DAYS		

MEMO TOTAL

BUYER | DATE | BUYER EXT | DIV MDSE MGR | DATE | GEN MDSE MGR | DATE | PRICE CHANGE CONTROL | DATE

PRICE CHANGE CONTROL COPY

FIGURE 15–8
A Price Change Authorization Form

downs or special sales may disrupt the balance in a price line, unless all items in that line are reduced proportionally. Fourth, price lines must be coordinated for complementary product categories, such as blazers, skirts, and shoes.

PRICE ADJUSTMENTS

Price adjustments enable retailers to use price as an adaptive mechanism. Markdowns and additional markups may be necessary in adapting to such factors as competition, seasonality, demand patterns, merchandise costs, and pilferage. Figure 15–8 shows a price change authorization form.

A ***markdown*** from the original retail price of an item may be used to meet the lower price of another retailer, adapt to inventory overstocking, clear out shopworn merchandise, reduce assortments of odds and ends, and increase customer traffic. An ***additional markup*** is an increase in a retail price after—and in addition to—the original markup; it is used when demand is unexpectedly high or when costs are rising.

A third price adjustment, discounts to employees, is mentioned here since such discounts may affect the computation of markdowns and additional markups. Also, while employee discounts are not an adaptive mechanism, they influence morale. Some firms give employee discounts on all merchandise and also let workers buy sale items before they are made available to the general public.

Computing Markdowns and Additional Markups

Markdowns and additional markups can be calculated in dollars (total dollar markdown or markup) or percentages. Two ways of calculating a markdown are the markdown percentage and the off-retail percentage.

The ***markdown percentage*** is the total dollar markdown as a percentage of net sales (in dollars) and is computed as

$$\text{Markdown percentage} = \frac{\text{Total dollar markdown}}{\text{Net sales (in \$)}}$$

A difficulty with this formula is that additional markups and employee discounts must be reflected in net sales (along with dollar markdowns). Also, this formula does not enable a retailer to determine the percentage of items that are marked down as compared to those sold at the original price.

A complementary measure is the ***off-retail markdown percentage***, which looks at the markdown for each item or category of items as a percentage of original retail price:

$$\text{Off-retail markdown percentage} = \frac{\text{Original price} - \text{New price}}{\text{Original price}}$$

With this formula, the markdown percentage for each item can be computed, as well as the percentage of items marked down.

For example, suppose a gas barbecue grill sells for \$100 at the beginning of the summer and is reduced to \$70 at the end of the summer. The off-retail markdown is 30 per cent [(\$100 – \$70)/\$100]. If 100 grills are sold at the original price and 20 are sold at the sale price, the percentage of items marked down is 17 per cent, and the total dollar markdown is \$600.

The ***additional markup percentage*** looks at total dollar additional markups as a percentage of net sales, while the ***addition to retail percentage*** measures a price rise as a percentage of original price:

$$\text{Additional markup percentage} = \frac{\text{Total dollar additional markups}}{\text{Net sales (in \$)}}$$

$$\text{Addition to retail percentage} = \frac{\text{New price} - \text{Original price}}{\text{Original price}}$$

Retailers should be aware that price adjustments affect their markups per unit, and that significantly more customers would have to be attracted at reduced prices to attain a total gross profit equal to that at higher prices. The impact of a markdown or an additional markup on total gross profit may be ascertained through this formula:

$$\begin{array}{l}\text{Unit sales required to}\\ \text{earn the same total}\\ \text{gross profit with a}\\ \text{price adjustment}\end{array} = \frac{\text{Original markup (\%)}}{\begin{array}{c}\text{Original markup (\%)}\\ +/- \text{ Price change (\%)}\end{array}} \times \begin{array}{l}\text{Expected unit}\\ \text{sales at}\\ \text{original price}\end{array}$$

For example, at a specialty store, suppose a Sony Walkman with a cost of \$50 has an original retail price of \$100, a markup of 50 per cent. The firm expects to sell 500 units over the next year, leading to a total gross profit of \$25,000 (\$50 × 500). How many units would the retailer have to sell if it reduces the price to \$85 or raises it to \$110 and still earn a \$25,000 gross profit? This is how to compute the answer:

$$\begin{array}{l}\text{Unit sales required}\\ \text{(at \$85)}\end{array} = \frac{50\%}{50\% - 15\%} \times 500 = 1.43 \times 500 = 714$$

$$\begin{array}{l}\text{Unit sales required}\\ \text{(at \$110)}\end{array} = \frac{50\%}{50\% + 10\%} \times 500 = 0.83 \times 500 = 417$$

A retailer's judgment regarding price adjustments would be affected by its operating expenses at various sales volumes and customer price elasticities.

Markdown Control

Through ***markdown control***, a retailer evaluates the number of markdowns, their proportion of sales, and their causes. This control must be such that buying plans can be altered in later periods to reflect markdowns. A good technique for evaluating the causes of markdowns is to have retail buyers record the reasons for each markdown and to examine these reasons on a regular basis. Examples of possible buyer notations are "end of season," "to match the price of a competitor," "worn merchandise," and "obsolete style."

Markdown control enables a firm to monitor its policies, such as the way merchandise is stored and late acceptance of fashion shipments. In addition, careful planning may allow a retailer to avoid some markdowns by increasing advertising, training and compensating employees better, shipping goods more efficiently among branch units, and returning items to vendors. Table 15–8 cites ten ways to control markdowns.

The need for markdown control should not be interpreted as meaning that all markdowns can or should be minimized or eliminated. In fact, too low a markdown percentage may indicate that a retailer's buyers have not assumed enough risk in purchasing goods.

Timing Markdowns

Although there is some disagreement among retailers as to the best timing sequence for markdowns, much can be said about the benefits of implementing an early markdown policy. First, this policy offers merchandise at reduced prices when demand is still fairly active. Second, an early markdown policy requires lower markdowns to sell products than markdowns late in the selling season. Third, early markdowns free selling space for new merchandise. Fourth, a retailer's cash flow position can be improved.

The main advantage of a late markdown policy is that a retailer has every opportunity to sell merchandise at original prices. However, the advantages associated with an early markdown policy cannot be achieved under a late markdown policy.

TABLE 15–8 Ten Ways to Control Markdowns

1. Adhere to a buying plan in terms of the quantities to be ordered, and the timing of receipt of merchandise. Do not buy too much merchandise to secure an additional quantity discount or promotional allowance. Learn to say "no" to vendors' salespeople.
2. Be an important customer. Limit the number of vendors with which you deal. Bargain for the right to exchange slow-selling merchandise during the season, if necessary.
3. Evaluate the reasons for slow-selling merchandise. Can additional displays or sales incentives quicken the sales pace?
4. Carefully study the impact of special purchases on the sale of traditional merchandise.
5. Be careful in size selection. It may be wise to risk being out of stock, for example, in very small and very large sizes versus having to take drastic markdowns.
6. Maintain a perpetual inventory of large-ticket items to avoid large markdowns.
7. Limit spoilage by properly caring for and displaying perishable or breakable goods, and by using appropriate packaging and containers.
8. Monitor layaway payments. Beware of an item being held back for a long period of time and then not being wanted by a customer. Request partial pre-payments to hold a layaway item.
9. Make sure that salespeople are properly motivated and trained.
10. Staple merchandise can generally be carried over to next year. The carrying costs must be weighed against the size of the necessary markdown, potential increases in price next year, shelf space occupied, shipping costs, etc.

Source: Adapted by the authors from William Burston, *A Checklist of 38 Ways of Controlling Markdowns* (New York: National Retail Federation, n.d.).

Retailers can also use a staggered markdown policy, whereby prices are marked down throughout the selling season. One totally pre-planned staggered markdown policy for reducing prices through a selling season involves an ***automatic markdown plan.*** In such a plan, the amount and timing of markdowns are controlled by the length of time merchandise remains in stock. For example, Filene's Basement applies markdowns under this timetable:

Length of Time in Stock	Percentage Markdown (from Original Price)
12 selling days	25
18 selling days	50
24 selling days	75
30 selling days	Given to charity

Such a plan ensures fresh stock and early markdowns.

A storewide clearance, usually conducted once or twice a year, is another way of timing markdowns. Often a storewide clearance takes place after peak selling periods like Christmas and the Fourth of July. The goal is to clean out merchandise before taking a physical inventory and beginning the next season. The advantages of a storewide clearance over an automatic (staggered) markdown policy are that a longer period is provided for selling merchandise at original prices; frequent markdowns can destroy a consumer's confidence in a retailer's regular pricing policy: "Why buy now, when it will be on sale next week?" And an automatic policy may encourage a steady stream of bargain hunters who are not potential customers for the firm's regular merchandise, while clearance sales limit bargain hunting to once or twice a year.

Retailers should be concerned about too frequent a use of markdowns. In the past, many retailers would introduce merchandise at high prices and then mark down prices on many items by as much as 60 per cent to increase store traffic and improve inventory turnover. This caused customers to wait for price reductions and treat initial prices with skepticism. Today, a great number of retailers lower initial markup percentages, run fewer sales, and apply fewer markdowns than before.

SUMMARY

1. *To describe the role of pricing in a retail strategy and to show that pricing decisions must be made in an integrated and adaptive manner* Pricing is important to a retailer because of its interrelationship with overall objectives and the other components of the retail strategy mix. A price strategy must be well integrated and responsive.

2. *To examine the impact of consumers; government; manufacturers, wholesalers, and other suppliers; and current and potential competitors on pricing decisions* Before developing a price strategy, a retailer must study the factors affecting pricing. In some instances, these factors have only a minor effect on a retailer's pricing discretion; in others, they severely limit pricing options.

   With regard to consumers, retailers should be familiar with the law of demand and the price elasticity of demand. Government restrictions deal with horizontal and vertical price fixing, price discrimination, minimum prices, unit pricing, item price removal, and price advertising. Manufacturers, wholesalers, and other suppliers may be required to provide price guarantees (if they are in a position of weakness) and there may be conflicts about which party controls retail prices. The competitive environment may foster market pricing, which could lead to price wars, or administered pricing.

3. *To present a framework for developing a retail price strategy* Such a framework consists of five stages: objectives, broad price policy, price strategy, implementation of price strategy, and price adjustments.

   Retail pricing objectives can be chosen from among sales, dollar profits, return on investment, and/or early recovery of cash. After goals are chosen, broad policy is set and a coordinated series of actions is outlined, consistent with the firm's image and oriented to the short and long run. In setting policy, a retailer could use the multistage approach to pricing.

A price strategy integrates demand, cost, and competitive concepts. Each of these orientations must be understood separately and jointly. Psychological pricing, markup pricing, alternative ways of computing markups, gross margin, direct product profitability, and pricing below, at, or above the market are among the key aspects of strategy planning.

When implementing a price strategy, several specific tools can be used to supplement the broad base of strategy. Retailers should be familiar with and know when to use customary and variable pricing, one-price policies and flexible pricing, odd pricing, leader pricing, multiple-unit pricing, and price lining.

Price adjustments may be necessary for a retailer to adapt to various internal and external conditions. Adjustments include markdowns, additional markups, and employee discounts. It is important that adjustments be controlled by a budget, that the causes of markdowns be noted, that future company buying reflects earlier errors or adaptations, and that adjustments be properly timed.

KEY TERMS

law of demand (p. 502)
price elasticity of demand (p. 502)
horizontal price fixing (p. 505)
vertical price fixing (p. 505)
fair trade (p. 506)
Robinson-Patman Act (p. 506)
minimum-price laws (p. 507)
predatory pricing (p. 507)
loss leaders (p. 507)
unit pricing (p. 508)
item price removal (p. 508)
bait advertising (bait-and-switch advertising) (p. 509)
price guarantees (p. 510)
selling against the brand (p. 510)
gray market goods (p. 510)
market pricing (p. 511)
administered pricing (p. 511)
price war (p. 512)
market penetration (p. 512)
market skimming (p. 512)
multistage approach (p. 515)
demand-oriented pricing (p. 516)
cost-oriented pricing (p. 516)
competition-oriented pricing (p. 516)
psychological pricing (p. 517)
price-quality association (p. 517)
prestige pricing (p. 517)
markup pricing (p. 518)
markup (p. 518)
markup percentage (p. 518)
initial markup (p. 521)
maintained markup (p. 521)
gross margin (p. 521)
variable markup policy (p. 522)
direct product profitability (DPP) (p. 522)
customary pricing (p. 525)
everyday low pricing (EDLP) (p. 525)
variable pricing (p. 526)
one-price policy (p. 526)
flexible pricing (p. 526)
odd pricing (p. 527)
leader pricing (p. 528)
multiple-unit pricing (p. 528)
price lining (p. 528)
price adjustments (p. 529)
markdown (p. 529)
additional markup (p. 529)
markdown percentage (p. 529)
off-retail markdown percentage (p. 530)
additional markup percentage (p. 530)
addition to retail percentage (p. 530)
markdown control (p. 531)
automatic markdown plan (p. 532)

QUESTIONS FOR DISCUSSSION

1. Why is it important for retailers to understand the concept of price elasticity even if they cannot compute it?
2. Comment on each of the following from the perspective of a small retailer:
   a. Horizontal price fixing.
   b. Vertical price fixing.
   c. Price discrimination.
   d. Minimum-price law.
   e. Item price removal.
3. Why do some retailers sell gray market goods?
4. Give an example of a price strategy that integrates demand, cost, and competitive criteria.
5. Explain why markups are usually computed as a percentage of selling price rather than of cost.
6. A floor tile retailer wants to receive a 40 per cent markup (at retail) for all merchandise. If one style of tile retails for $9 per tile, what is the maximum that the retailer would be willing to pay for a tile?
7. A car dealer purchases multiple-disc CD players for $175 each and desires a 40 per cent markup (at retail). What retail price should be charged?
8. A photo store charges $11.00 to process a roll of slides; its cost is $6.50. What is the markup percentage (at cost and at retail)?
9. A retailer has planned operating expenses of $110,000, a profit goal of $52,000, and planned reductions of $28,000 and expects annual sales to be $600,000. Compute the initial markup percentage.
10. At the end of the year, the retailer in Question 9 determines that actual operating expenses are $120,000, actual profit is $42,000, and actual sales are $600,000. What is the maintained markup percentage? Explain the difference in your answers to Questions 9 and 10.

11. What are the advantages and disadvantages of the direct product profitability concept?
12. What are the pros and cons of everyday low pricing to a retailer? To a manufacturer?
13. What is the difference between markdown percentage and off-retail percentage?
14. A retailer buys merchandise for $25. At an original retail price of $50, it expects to sell 1,000 units.
    a. If the price is marked down to $35, how many units must the retailer sell to earn the same total gross profit it would attain with a $50 price?
    b. If the price is marked up to $60, how many units must the retailer sell to earn the same total gross profit it would attain with a $50 price?

CASE 1
Dahl's Fair Practices*

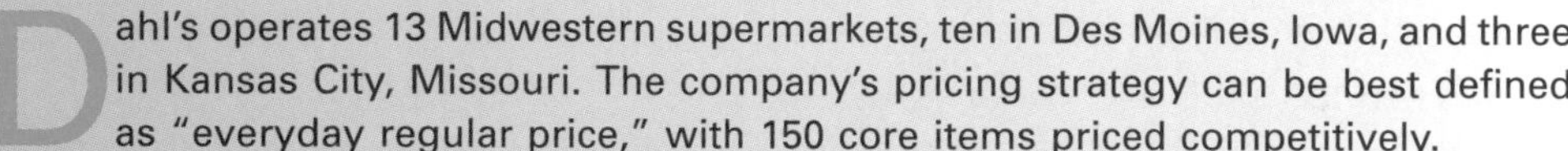

Dahl's operates 13 Midwestern supermarkets, ten in Des Moines, Iowa, and three in Kansas City, Missouri. The company's pricing strategy can be best defined as "everyday regular price," with 150 core items priced competitively.

Dahl's pricing practices are governed by a fair-practices statement that clarifies its relationships with suppliers and customers. Table 1 shows its expectations with regard to suppliers. Dahl's also endorses the *Fairness Statement* published by the Grocery Manufacturers of America and the *Ten Point Addendum* published by the National Grocers Association.

Table 1 Selected Pricing Strategies and Tactics Covered by Dahl's Fair-Practices Statement

- Dahl's wants to be viewed by all of its suppliers as a customer that handles business dealings professionally, equitably, and fairly.
- Dahl's will not request special prices, allowances, or services from manufacturers or their sales agents if they know that such prices, allowances, or services would force the manufacturer to unlawfully discriminate against other customers within the same market area.
- Dahl's expects all of its suppliers to deal fairly with the company.
- Dahl's expects manufacturers, their sales agents, and distributors to observe the spirit and the letter of the Robinson-Patman Act.
- Manufacturers should not make distinctions among competing distributor customers within the same market area based upon the "class of trade" or distributor format in the same market area. If the manufacturer develops prices, terms, promotions, deals, or packs designed to meet the marketing needs or desires of a particular class or distributor format, the manufacturer should inform ALL competing distributor customers within the same market area, regardless of their class of trade, of their availability and should grant these distributors an equal opportunity to qualify for these offerings.
- Dahl's plans to carefully review all policies and practices to be sure that they will be applied equitably to all of its suppliers. It does not want any of its suppliers to have an unfair advantage over its competitors.
- According to Dahl's, this statement "has been read and understood by all members of our organization. (All executives, all store managers, and all department managers). Individually and collectively, we are committed to its ongoing implementation."

* The material in this case is drawn from *Dahl's Food Fairness Statement* (Des Moines, Iowa: 1992); *Fairness Statement* (Washington, D.C.: Grocery Manufacturers of America, 1989); *Ten Point Addendum* (Reston, Virginia: National Grocers Association, 1992); and "What's in Store for EDLP?" *Sales & Marketing Management* (August 1993), pp. 56–59.

Dahl's fair-practices statement effectively meets these objectives:

- By eliminating the usual "give-and-take" of negotiations, Dahl's and its suppliers save time and money. Dahl's is assured that it is receiving the lowest legal price for its products in each market area.
- It is recognized that intertype competition among different types of food-based retailers (such as traditional supermarkets and membership stores) has increased within each market area. Dahl's statement gives its supermarkets access to the same offers as other classes of retailers. For example, compliance with fair practices means that manufacturers offer the same value-sized packages of goods to supermarkets as they have offered to membership chains.
- Adherence to the Robinson-Patman Act is specifically addressed.
- The retailer abuses of forward buying and diverting (that have been used by some firms to obtain profits at the expense of suppliers) are not allowed.

With forward buying, retailers receive special discounts, such as "$5 off the invoiced price per case," for buying a given quantity of merchandise. In return for the discounts, retailers agree to buy the manufacturers' products over a specified period, provide suitable shelf space, and pass on the savings to final consumers via sales prices. However, an abuse of the system takes place if supermarkets (or other retailers) buy three weeks of merchandise during the last week of a promotion and then charge their customers the full retail price for three additional weeks beyond the promotion.

In diverting, manufacturers provide special discounts to retailers to gain market share in specific market areas. Yet, an abuse occurs when retailers buy a large quantity and would then resell much of it to retailers located outside the market areas where the special promotions are offered. Retailers that divert can profit by pocketing the difference between their cost and the resale price to the other retailers. Through a single diversion deal, a supermarket could earn a net profit of $2,200 on a $19,600 investment; and a firm could do dozens of these transactions each week. For manufacturers, diverting results in their being unable to meet regional sales goals and in their loss of distribution control. Thus, a manufacturer's specially-priced goods aimed at the Milwaukee market could end up in a New York store that is not a recognized manufacturer's account.

Implementing Dahl's fair-practices agreement is rather complicated. For instance, even though the Robinson-Patman Act requires that suppliers offer promotional allowances on a proportionate basis to all buyers, Dahl's does not use run-of-press advertising, Sunday newspaper freestanding inserts, or radio or television advertising.

Questions

1. Comment on Table 1 from Dahl's perspective.
2. Comment on Table 1 from the perspective of Dahl's suppliers.
3. What is the impact of everyday low pricing on forward buying?
4. How can a manufacturer control diverting?

Video Questions on Dahl's

1. What portions of Dahl's fair-practices statement are governed by the Robinson-Patman Act?
2. Can a membership chain retailer legally secure a lower price than Dahl's? Explain your answer.

CASE 2

Thomas Teaberry's, Inc.: Evaluating the Pricing Abilities of Employees†

Tom Teaberry, Jr., executive vice-president of the $60 million (annual sales) department-store chain bearing his family's name, winced as he studied the results of a report prepared by the Retail Consulting Services Division of a major accounting firm. The report presented the results of an examination given to key merchandising personnel—divisional merchandise managers (DMMs), buyers, and assistant buyers—of a big East Coast department-store chain. The exam consisted of five sections: (1) knowledge of basic terms associated with pricing, merchandise planning, and inventory management and control, (2) understanding of basic merchandising arithmetic and profitability, (3) invoice mathematics and terms of sales, (4) pricing and repricing, and (5) dollar planning and control.

Teaberry was particularly disturbed with these highlights of the test results that the accounting firm's analysts seemed to feel were representative of the results that would emerge if the same test were given to other groups of retailing executives:

- On the average, the group tested (99 participants) answered only 19 per cent of the questions correctly—although they all dealt with basic merchandising procedures on a daily basis.
- The highest overall score of any participant was 52 per cent.
- DMMs answered an average of 30 per cent of the questions correctly; buyers averaged 25 per cent and assistant buyers averaged only 13 per cent. All of the assistant buyers had previously attended the firm's one-year training program.
- Merchandising arithmetic and profitability questions were correctly answered by 43 per cent of those tested; but only 8 per cent correctly answered dollar planning and control questions. And only 9 per cent defined "gross margin" correctly.
- Buyers and DMMs with 3 to 10 years' experience scored higher than those who worked fewer than 3 years or more than 10 years.
- As a whole, the group had very little understanding of overall store operations and their role in them. They also did not know how the store determined profitability.
- Despite the respected positions held by those who took the examinations, the results reveal a lack of understanding of such basic concepts as markups and markdowns.

Teaberry discussed the test findings with Angela Ott, the director of training, for his own company. Ms. Ott commented, "I shudder to think of how our own executives would perform if given a similar test." Teaberry responded, "There's no better time to find out than right now. But I have no intention of asking a bunch of elementary questions such as 'Compare the terms *initial markup* and *maintained markup*.' Frankly, if my sophisticated executives are unable to answer questions related to basic merchandising tools that are used every day of the week, they shouldn't be working for Teaberry's. I'm going to ask three or four thought-provoking questions and the answers will tell me whether my merchandising people are prepared to plan, analyze, and execute their responsibilities profitably."

Table 1 contains the test devised by Teaberry. Of his 27 merchandising executives, only one answered all of the questions correctly. This made Teaberry furious. He pro-

† This case was prepared and written by Professor Marvin A. Jolson, University of Maryland, College Park, Maryland.

Table 1 Teaberry's Mini-Exam (time allowed, 30 minutes)

1. The buyer for the home-entertainment department is determined to have an overall gross margin of 40.0 per cent on 9-inch color television sets after all markdowns have been taken. One hundred sets are purchased for $240 each, and an initial price of $425 is used for each. After selling 80 sets, the buyer decides to clear out the remaining units at a reduced price. What should the per-unit price of the 20 units be to reach the maintained markup objective?
(Answer: $300.00)

2. A suit is priced at $225 and subsequently reduced and sold for $150. What is the store's markdown percentage (using net sales as a base) on this item?
(Answer: 50 per cent)

3. In a channel of distribution for ladies' sweaters, wholesalers earn a 30 per cent markup and retailers earn 40 per cent (all markups are on selling price). If, for cashmere turtlenecks, the producer's selling price is $25.20, what should be the suggested retail price of the item?
(Answer: $60.00)

4. A new buyer has just taken over the appliance department at Teaberry's. One of the best-sellers has been a deluxe vacuum cleaner the store previously purchased for $130 and has retailed for $299.50. At the present time, 200 units are in stock. The buyer wishes to buy 1,000 additional units, but the vendor's price on the item is now $160. The profit target for the month on this item is $20,000, and operating expenses for the month (allocated to this product), including vigorous advertising, are planned at $62,000. The buyer feels that at the end of the month all units will be sold, but plans total reductions including markdowns at 10 per cent of net sales. How should the store price these items, initially assuming that merchandise on hand and new merchandise will be priced the same? What initial markup percentage will the department realize on this item?
(Answer: Price = $245.67
Markup = 36.9 per cent)

Note: Answers were not made available to Teaberry employees taking the exam.

posed to his father, the store's president, that all merchandising executives undergo an intensive 40-hour training program (on their own time) and then take a similar test again. Those still answering any questions incorrectly would be placed on probation until they could answer all of these types of questions.

QUESTIONS

1. How do you explain the dismal showing on both the accounting firm's and the Teaberry tests?
2. Take the Teaberry exam yourself, within the 30-minute time limit.
3. What parts of the exam are the most difficult? Why?
4. Do you agree that poor performance on this exam would be an indicator that a manager is ill prepared to plan, analyze, and execute responsibilities profitably? Explain your answer.

PART 6 COMPREHENSIVE CASE

Survival of the Fittest*

Introduction

Robert Nourse created a niche in furniture retailing that has effectively blocked all imitators. But, he keeps reinventing his company anyway.

Twenty years ago, when he was a pipe-smoking college professor, Robert Nourse never dreamed that one day he'd be a retailer. Yet, here he is at the controls of one of the hottest retail chains in North America. A peculiar turn of events, perhaps, but not really surprising. If anyone had the credentials to run a fast-track company, it was Nourse.

Equipped with a doctorate in marketing from Harvard Business School, he taught undergraduate and graduate courses at the University of Western Ontario for nine years. Along the way, he did a good deal of consulting. He then spent four years with a venture-capital firm, managing some of its holdings. His projects included chairing one of the world's largest aerial-mapping firms, running an Arctic airline, and overseeing the construction of water slides.

Those four years served as a kind of entrepreneurial boot camp. "I got the daylights kicked out of me the first two years. But, it was wonderful training in the art of growing businesses," he says. In 1979, at the age of 40, Nourse felt ready to run a business of his own. But what?

While at his last venture-capital job, managing a soft-drink firm, Nourse had dinner with an old friend during a bottlers' convention in Bermuda. "He was a wealthy guy who'd invested in this little mail-order startup in New Orleans," Nourse says. "He was really excited about it, said I should see it."

The company sold replicas of 18th- and 19th-century English furniture, small wooden pieces such as butler's tables, plant stands, and nightstands. They were advertised in magazines and shipped to customers in boxes, ready to be assembled. Usually, all the customer had to do was screw on the legs.

The founder was Brad Harper, and to him the mahogany-stained reproductions conjured up the glory days of the British Empire. The jewel of the empire was Bombay, so he called his business the Bombay Company. "Brad thought everyone would make the connection," Nourse says. "But nobody ever did."

Intrigued, Nourse met Harper for lunch when he was next in New Orleans. Bombay was losing money on sales of about $1.5 million, but Nourse saw that it had potential. First, he liked the value offered. Here were some nice styles of furniture sold at reasonable prices. Second, the items came flat-packed in boxes—or as "knockdowns," in furniture-business lingo. That kept storage space to a minimum. It was the sort of opportunity Nourse was looking for. So, at the end of an eight-hour lunch, he bought full Canadian rights to the Bombay Company for a dollar plus 4 per cent in royalties. He and Harper wrote up the deal on the back of a napkin.

In buying those rights, Nourse got one thing of special importance—access to the overseas supply channels Harper had developed, mainly in Taiwan.

Developing a Merchandising Strategy

Mapping his strategy back home in Toronto, Nourse came up with some innovative retailing ideas.

In his view, mail order was not the best way to market the Bombay line. Building a customer list would take too long and be too costly. Malls—that was the ticket. Malls had more foot traffic than most other retail locations. The rents were high, however, and furniture just didn't turn over fast enough to justify expensive real estate. But, Nourse thought he had a solution.

"You need an impulse component to your business to be in malls", he says. "When you pay those high rents, you are buying people going by your door. You've got to be able tap into those people. That means you've got to have fashion—the product has to be eye-catching and attractively designed. And then, you have to offer value."

Nourse believed he could deliver fashion and value, and something more—immediate gratification. He'd sell the same items Harper had, knocked-down small tables and plant stands and get them from the same factories in Taiwan and other Asian nations. But, his items could be carried right out to the car. Since it usually takes 6 to 12 weeks to get furniture delivered, consumers, he reasoned, would love the idea. Indeed, here was a way to develop an impulse business in home furnishings.

The ideal first location, Nourse concluded, was Toronto's Eaton Centre. "It is without question the preeminent mall in all of Canada," he says. "I didn't know then that the only retailers who get stores in places like that are major chains." But, luckily, Eaton's leasing agent had reserved space for someone with a new idea, and Bombay fit the bill.

Nourse threw his life savings—$125,000—into the business and borrowed an equal sum from a bank. He

* The material in this case was developed and written by Jay Finegan of *Inc.* It originally appeared in "Survival of the Fittest," *Inc.* (December 1993), pp. 78–88. Reprinted by permission. Copyright © 1993 Goldhirsh Group, Inc., 38 Commercial Wharf, Boston, MA 02110.

then hired a store designer to help him fulfill his vision. The Eaton Centre Bombay store was 2,000 square feet and modeled on England's Fountain Court at Hampton Court, Henry VIII's palace.

The store opened in April 1980, stocked with 35 styles of furniture. Sales were so strong that Nourse soon needed much more capital for inventory and expansion. From the start, he'd planned to build a chain. But, with interest rates at 20 per cent, he was stymied about how to proceed.

Meanwhile, Tandy Brands Inc., a holding company based in Fort Worth, had acquired Harper's mail-order outfit. In 1981, Tandy turned its sights on Canada. "I had mixed feelings about its buying me out," Nourse says. "If capital had been available at a reasonable cost, I never would have sold. But at the time, it was the only way to grow the company."

Under the terms of the deal, Nourse retained complete control of the Canadian operation. And backed by Tandy's financing, he had built 13 stores by 1983. They were all profitable.

In the United States, however, Tandy had a disaster on its hands. It had opened 36 Bombay stores and was losing its shirt. In late 1983, its CEO wanted to merge the Canadian and U.S. units, and make Nourse president of the whole Bombay division. Nourse couldn't refuse. "If I didn't do it, somebody else might have. That would have killed me," he says.

Once in Fort Worth, he lost no time in cleaning up Tandy's fiasco. By 1985, after a full fiscal year at the helm, he had turned a $3-million operating loss into a $500,000 profit. In 1986, profits hit $2 million.

Nourse credits much of the success to his wife, Aagje (pronounced "Akia"), Bombay's executive vice-president of marketing. Before she married Nourse, in 1980, she had marketed cosmetics for the largest cosmetics company in her native Holland. She also had an advertising background, and her initial job at Bombay was writing newspaper ads for the first store in Toronto.

"She's got a wonderful eye—a commercial eye—for developing products, for layouts, for color, for advertising, and for how to coordinate all those things," Nourse says. "You wouldn't want me as the driving force on that end of the business."

Together, with Aagje as the merchandising guru and Bob as the operations whiz, they created a very profitable store model. "Then, the trick was to roll it out at a rate you could manage financially, and to be able to grow the people and the organization to support it," Nourse says.

As Bombay grew from 75 stores in 1986 to 272 in 1990, the other divisions of Tandy, smaller and less profitable, were sold, spun off, or closed. The final parting came in December 1990, when the corporate name, Tandy Brands, was changed to the Bombay Company. In 1991, Nourse became president and CEO.

Bombay in Boom Times

Since then, Bombay has become one of the real success stories in retail. From 1990 through 1992, it opened 119 new stores. It planned to open 120 more by June 30, 1994. Sales reached $232 million in 1993, up from 1992's $176 million—making Bombay the 16th-largest home-furnishings retailer in North America, out of roughly 50,000 such retailers. Nourse aimed for sales of $300 million during the 1994 fiscal year, which would push Bombay into the top 10.

Bombay's average sales per square foot, at $340, clobber the $110 industry average. "You could almost say we cheat a little by staying away from the huge sofas and things that don't turn very quickly," Nourse says. "But that's part of tailoring our concept to the malls."

Equally impressive, in 1992, at a time when the industry was down overall, Bombay's same-store sales rose by 13 per cent. Then, in 1993, they jumped by 15 per cent. That might be enough success for some company builders, but instead of throttling back, Nourse is lighting the after-burners. "Our original ambition was to have 400 to 500 stores," he says. "We're now almost there. But, we never dreamed that we'd just be scratching the surface of a whole new generation of growth."

Indeed, Bombay has embarked on a massive expansion. Last year, the company started adding some larger pieces of furniture to its stock. "We know our customers are really keying in on functional items," says Aagje Nourse. "So, we made a chest of drawers that's somewhat bigger to fit with everyday life. We also went into headboards. And, with a lot of people working at home, it seemed reasonable to go into desks."

Everything still came flat-packed in boxes, but the stores were getting cramped displaying the larger new products. So, in the spring of 1992, as an experiment, Bombay opened a superstore in lower Manhattan. It then converted two more stores from the regular size of about 1,700 square feet to the large format—3,500 to 4,000 square feet.

The test went so well that the company decided in February 1993 to convert nearly all its stores to superstores. Between the conversions and new construction (all new stores will be superstores), Bombay now has about 100 superstores and plans to add about 50 more per year. "I believe a business, and certainly a retail business that changes so quickly, has to keep reinventing itself or it will wither and die," Nourse explains.

He says his favorite part of the job is change, and he's making plenty of it happen. While building superstores, he's also rolling out a second retail concept, called Alex & Ivy. It will copy Bombay's formula in everything except merchandise. The Alex & Ivy line will feature not Bombay's formal English styles but French and American country and casual furniture and accessories.

So far, the Bombay superstores have exceeded goals. And, if Alex & Ivy hits its targets, Nourse projects $1 billion in sales by the end of the decade. Marcia Aaron, a retail analyst with Montgomery Securities in San Francisco, finds that "Two years ago, I thought the company would reach a saturation point and top out at $500 million [in annual sales]," she says. "But with Alex & Ivy, the superstores, and the new product lines, I think this could be a $1 billion company. Bombay is outperforming all of retail, not just the furniture business. "To generate these results in a rather mature company, they have to be doing a lot of things right."

The Keys to Bombay's Success

Mind you, the explosive growth is occurring in a lackluster retail environment. What's driving it?

Bombay focuses on delivering furniture at reasonable prices. Exact comparisons are impossible because all of Bombay's furniture and most of its accessories are exclusives; but, according to analysts, the company's prices are 30 per cent to 60 per cent below competitors'. Nothing is more than $500, even though the line now includes some large pieces. Most items are less than $150, and the average sale is $80.

Keeping prices low while remaining highly profitable is no small feat. What makes it possible is the company's structure and its vigilance in keeping costs down. Bombay is a vertically-integrated soup-to-nuts business that controls the flow of its products from factory to shop floor. With some 2,900 employees, including a headquarters staff of 175, Bombay runs what amounts to a global enterprise. And it has its operations down to a science.

The key elements of its system are the following:

Sourcing

Most furniture retailers buy whatever comes out of the factories in and around the Carolinas. Bombay could not be more different. It runs what is undoubtedly the most sophisticated sourcing network in the industry, using 130 vendors from around the world.

At the core of the network are contract factories, mostly in Asia, which mass-produce furniture according to Bombay's technical specifications. The blueprints are trademarked, and the plants are barred from making the same furniture for anyone else.

Nourse has always worked closely with his vendors. "Relationships are very important," he says, "and they go back a long time in our case. We've used some of the same factories for 10 years. They are very loyal to us, and we are to them, and we both know what's expected."

Nourse and his staff consult with the vendors, especially about design: "It makes a big difference which way a curve goes on the apron of a side table. It affects the configuration of manufacturing equipment. So, we work together to hold down costs. We then work hard on ready-to-assemble technology so we can save on shipping and distribution. Flat-packing is very important—I can put 8,000 wine tables in a 40-foot container."

Another challenge is the wood finishing. Bombay gets items from dozens of factories in many different countries, but they're all sold in the same store and have to match.

Taiwan is the cornerstone. Of the 30 Asian factories making Bombay furniture, 24 are in Taiwan, 5 are in Malaysia, and one is in Korea. It has taken years of nurturing and hard work to build that sourcing network. It's so elaborate, no one has ever tried to copy it. "If we were going to get imitators, that would have happened when we had 50 or 75 stores," Nourse says. "It would be pretty hard to do now. That whole string of different factories with different capabilities is a complex thing to administer, and that's a deterrent. I wouldn't want to start trying to compete with us today."

Bombay's sourcing system is evolving under some new pressures. The expansion to superstores and the advent of Alex & Ivy mean the demand for products will grow dramatically. With Asian wages rising, the labor cost differential is shrinking, and Bombay is seeking to develop more domestic production. For technical reasons, however, U.S. furniture factories cannot easily accommodate contract manufacturing. As a result, Nourse says, "they have not been very aggressive in going after our business." But, with Bombay the fastest-growing furniture retailer in America for the past several years, some U.S. manufacturers are beginning to make the switch.

Shipping and Distribution

Bombay products are shipped from Asia in standard 40-foot containers. Cost control begins by making sure a container is full before it crosses the Pacific, which can entail a multicountry consolidation. For example, a container might start out in Thailand, work its way down to Malaysia, and end up in Taiwan.

For this fiscal year, Bombay negotiated a "bundled" transportation rate of approximately $2,500. For that amount, a container is brought into a U.S. port, moved across the country by rail, and trucked to loading docks at the distribution centers. All told, $2,500 is quite a value, considering that ordinarily it costs $1,800 just to truck a container from Los Angeles to Fort Worth. On the store-delivery side, the contract drivers also unload the boxes and, in some cases, even put the merchandise on the stockroom shelves. It's cheaper than hiring stockpeople.

The huge distribution centers are cost savers, as well. The one in Fort Worth, for example, is 150,000 square feet, and Bombay gets the most out of it. "With the furniture in flat boxes, we're able to achieve a high storage density," says Mark Winkelman, vice-president of distribution and logistics. "What we can fit into 100,000 feet would take up 700,000 feet at Pier 1 Imports. So, flat-packing is a very big cost advantage."

The object is to keep inventory in the warehouses rather than in the stores, which is much cheaper. Moreover, the store stockrooms are small—about 800 square feet in a superstore. They hold just enough inventory to satisfy demand—which is crucial when the aim is to have the customer carry the product out the door, yet keep most of the store's space as selling area. Consequently, Bombay replenishes its stores quickly. Based on data from the company's point-of-sale computer system, the three distribution centers can resupply 70 per cent of the stores in 24 hours and 90 per cent in 72 hours.

So, from factory to store, it's all Bombay's show. "We deal directly with the factories, we never buy from third parties, and there are no wholesalers," Nourse says. "We save broker margins. We do a lot of functions not usually done by retailers, and each little savings contributes to the bottom line."

Store Locations

Nourse has always been picky about the malls Bombay goes into. They must have upscale clientele and be heavily trafficked. Since 60 per cent of the business is walk-in, the busier the spot, the better. One near a food court is ideal.

Although the United States has a surplus of malls from the building binge of the 1980s, it has only about 400 topflight ones. Bombay is already in most of those, and Alex & Ivy will follow suit. Research shows "cannibalization" between the two stores to be around 5 per cent, an unexpectedly low crossover rate. To Nourse, that's proof that the concepts appeal to two kinds of people with the same purchasing power but different tastes.

Stephen King, president of Bombay's realty division, competes for prime sites with the other retailers in Bombay's league—like Williams-Sonoma, Crate & Barrel, and Ann Taylor. Nourse, however, also pays keen attention to Bombay's real-estate dealings. "I still sign every lease, because a lease is an enormous financial commitment in retail," he says. "It may involve $150,000 a year for 10 years. If you're doing that on 120 leases a year, and then you're also committing $200,000 worth of inventory to each store, you're talking some major commitments. I want to stay close to the pulse on that."

Merchandising

The merchandising cycle starts with product design, a department headed by Aagje Nourse and staffed by a large group of artists, draftspeople, and computer operators. While many of Bombay's styles are true reproductions of English antiques, others are modified versions, which are easier and cheaper to mass produce. And Aagje herself is a wellspring of ideas. "She devotes an enormous amount of effort to watching what's going on in the world of design and fashion," Nourse says. "She has a real talent for understanding fashion and anticipating it. In a commercial sense, she's got a great track record."

In the course of a year, Bombay replaces 25 per cent of its furniture styles, 50 per cent of its wall decor, and nearly all its accessories. Merchandise freshness is further assured by a major change in store layout every two months, an ambitious pace by retail standards. Detailed plans and schematics are developed in Fort Worth, and Bombay's "visual merchandisers" work with store managers under Aagje's direction to make sure all the stores look alike.

Those theme-based revampings require a constant flow of new products. Each theme is set three years in advance so the buyers can find fitting items. But, the extensive planning pays off in a high level of repeat business. "We treat this as a fashion business," Nourse says. "If what you put on your back is fashion, why wouldn't the things you surround yourself with be fashion, too?"

Bombay has a list of 1.2 million active customers, and each one gets its catalog seven times a year, including two for Christmas. Although the catalog costs more than $6 million annually to produce and generates 3 per cent of total sales, the firm doesn't go out of its way to support it. For instance, Bombay doesn't buy mailing lists, and sends the catalog only to its customers.

Customer Support

Bombay backs up its products with an unconditional guarantee. The best time to capture customers for life, Nourse says, is when they need a refund. "We'll take the thing back with no hassle, no questions, no guff about 'Where's the receipt?' The cost is peanuts compared to what you gain in customer loyalty."

Bombay's training crew works with store personnel to keep them abreast of new products and sales techniques. "The goal is to greet customers within 29 seconds, welcome them and hand them a catalog, and then drop back," says Alex & Ivy president Mel Baskin. If customers need help assembling a product or carrying it to the car, they get it. "Too many retailers have forgotten what service means," Nourse says. "When you treat customers like a million dollars, they'll come back."

Employee Compensation

Most companies with 401(k) retirement plans match employee contributions at 50 cents on the dollar. Not Bombay; it matches the first 5 per cent of earnings contributed at $1.50 on the dollar. Beyond that, employees can invest up to 10 per cent of their salary in the stock-purchase plan, and Bombay matches contributions at 50 per cent.

Executives are expected to accumulate substantial equity holdings in the company, and they have timetables to meet. "The best way to get managers to identify with shareholders is to make them shareholders," Nourse says. The arrangement has worked out nicely all around. Bombay's stock price has risen significantly in the past few years, making more than a few Bombay people millionaires.

Store managers get 6 per cent of store profits, and every other employee is eligible for bonuses. Executive salaries are well below market rates, but if the firm hits its targets for the year, the bonuses can be proportionally higher than they are elsewhere. In 1992, Nourse's salary was $265,000, but his bonus hit $810,000.

Planning

"In a small company, you run on informal systems," Nourse says. "Any formal system would bury or suffocate a small business. As you get bigger, you've got to move gradually. So, one of the perils you face is anticipating what changes you'll need for things like control and information systems, and how to organize and motivate your people. You really have to prepare for it because if you don't, it just murders you, and everything breaks down."

In laying the groundwork for Bombay's growth surge, for example, Nourse made sure he had high-caliber executives in place to help manage it. One of his first moves as CEO was to bring in Jim Herlihy, a chief financial officer with vast experience. Another was to lure retailing veteran Michael Glazer as president of the Bombay division and executive vice-president of the company.

Still, any company can stumble, so Bombay plans for contingencies. Consider its giant expansion now in full swing. "We're going to be taking some real operating risks," Nourse says, "risks that we can get enough product, that we can recruit enough quality people, that we can distribute effectively. I like risk—I think that's where you make money."

He wasn't willing to take operating and financial risks simultaneously, however. Bombay already had $10 million in cash, with no long-term debt, but earlier in 1993, management decided to issue more stock as a buffer. It expected the one-million-share offering to net $30 million, but since Bombay stock suddenly rose before the offering, it ended up netting $42.2 million.

"If we hit our targets, we won't have to touch that money," Nourse says. "But, what if we miss? Even then, we'll be in no financial difficulty whatsoever. We have eliminated the financial risk of a major aggressive expansion plan."

What Will the Future Bring?

Near the end of a long interview, Nourse settles his six-foot-five frame back in a chair to ponder the future. "If we had stopped with the original idea of building a few hundred Bombay stores, it would all be over," he says. "I'd be wearing woolen socks and sitting beside a fireplace."

Instead, he intends to lead Bombay into its third act, once Alex & Ivy gets in gear. "When building 120 stores a year becomes a habit, what are we going to do next?" he asks. "We'll need the next big growth vehicle." The opportunities are there. It might be another retail concept, or maybe a marketing move into Japan or Europe. He's not sure. "We'll know the answer long before we hit saturation," says Nourse. He is a living model of his own belief that to succeed, a business has to keep reinventing itself.

Questions

1. Describe and analyze Bombay's overall merchandising philosophy.
2. On the basis of the factors listed in Figure 13–2, recommend a buying organization structure for Bombay. Explain your choices.
3. Comment on this statement: "You could almost say we cheat a little by staying away from the huge sofas and things that don't turn very quickly," Nourse says. "But that's part of tailoring our concept to the malls."
4. What do you think are the benefits and risks of Bombay's merchandise sourcing system?
5. Why is *classification merchandising* an important concept for a firm such as Bombay to understand and apply?
6. Based on the information presented in the case, what is Bombay's policy with regard to safety stock? Evaluate this policy.
7. Is Bombay's price strategy consistent with the other elements of its merchandising plan? Why or why not?

Communicating with the Customer

- In Part 7, the elements involved in a retailer's communicating with its customers are discussed. First, the role of a retail image and how it is developed and maintained are covered. Various aspects of a promotional strategy are then detailed.
- Chapter 16 shows the importance of communications for a retailer. The significance of image in the communications effort and the components of a retailer's image are explained. The creation of an image depends heavily on a retailer's atmosphere—which is comprised of all of its physical characteristics, such as the store exterior, the general interior, layouts, and displays. The impact of customer services on a firm's image and the value of community relations are also studied.
- Chapter 17 focuses on promotional strategy, specifically how a retailer can inform, persuade, and remind its target market. The first part of the chapter deals with the four basic types of retail promotion: advertising, publicity, personal selling, and sales promotion. The second part describes the steps in a promotional strategy: objectives, budget, mix of forms, implementation of mix, and review and revision of the plan.

Establishing and Maintaining a Retail Image

❖ Chapter Objectives

1. To show the importance of communicating with customers
2. To examine the concept of retail image
3. To describe how a retailer's image is established through the use of atmosphere via its exterior, general interior, layout, and displays
4. To consider the impact of customer services and community relations on a retailer's image

Charming Shoppes, Inc., which operates Fashion Bug and Fashion Bug Plus apparel stores, plans to open 170 new stores each year through 1998. During the same period, the firm also intends to expand 90 of its existing stores annually. During 1993, Charming Shoppes had 1,300 stores and sales of $1.3 billion.

Fashion Bug and Fashion Bug Plus stores are targeted to working women from blue-collar households that have annual incomes of $30,000 to $35,000. The stores carry blazers, cardigan sweaters, coats, casual jewelry, shoes, girls' clothes, and men's sportswear. Many of the stores' customers want to dress well, but are on a limited budget and are pressed for time.

To appeal to its target market, Charming Shoppes strives to be a low-cost retailer. Its location and branding strategies reflect this orientation. When mall rents increased in the mid-1970s, the firm decided to place new stores in strip malls, where rents were up to 60 per cent less. Today, Fashion Bug and Fashion Bug Plus stores are typically located in strip malls that are anchored by a mass retailer such as Kmart or even a supermarket chain.

To hold down its selling prices, Charming Shoppes shifted its branding strategy from manufacturer brands to private brands in the mid-1980s. This enabled the company to design merchandise to its specifications, gain store loyalty through exclusive merchandise offerings, and pass on the savings from obtaining large quantities of given styles to customers.

Although Charming Shoppes wants to convey a "fashion on a budget" image, the firm is proud of the ambience of its stores. Fashion Bug and Fashion Bug Plus stores are carpeted and neat, have colorful and imaginative displays, and show coordinated apparel (such as sweaters and blouses) on the same rack. Customers are free to browse: "Our progressive visual-merchandising program and store design are created with our customer in mind. Outfits are easy to find and dressing rooms are consumer-friendly. Everything we do in our stores is done to maximize sales and satisfy every customer."[1]

[1] *Charming Shoppes, Inc. 1993 Annual Report*; and Howard Rudnitsky, "Full Speed Ahead, Damn the Recession," *Forbes* (October 25, 1993), pp. 94–96.

Reprinted by permission of Charming Shoppes.

Overview

A retailer needs a well-devised and well-executed communications strategy to properly position itself in customers' minds. Every firm has information about itself to present to customers, and this information must be interpreted by the target market as intended if sales are to be made. In addition, it is imperative for the retailer to create a proper shopping mood for customers. A variety of physical and symbolic cues can be used to do this. For instance,

> Several years ago, HMV Shops, a British retailer, entered the Canadian market and reinvented the music store. Like many of today's supermarkets, music stores then were sound asleep—dusty bins, tacky merchandising, and a painful dearth of customer service. Every store carried an almost identical product assortment, leaving it to retailers to fight it out on the basis of price. HMV then installed soft lights and lush carpeting. Giant video screens flashed music videos. A small studio was built for local garage bands to record demo tapes at bargain-basement rates. Visiting recording artists could promote their new material in live performances on the store's sound stage. Within eighteen months, HMV's Canada annual sales rose from $35 million to $84 million. The concept worked mainly because it gave shoppers a reason to go to the store.[2]

In this chapter, the establishment and maintenance of a retail image are described. The use of atmosphere, storefronts, store layouts, displays, customer services, and community relations are enumerated, as they relate to communicating with customers. Chapter 17 concentrates on the common promotional tools available to retailers in reaching their customers: advertising, publicity, personal selling, and sales promotion.

Please note that although the discussion in this chapter focuses more on store-based retailers, the overall principles also apply to nonstore-based firms. As an example, for mail-order retailers, storefronts are the covers of each catalog, and the layouts and displays are the interior pages devoted to product categories and the individual items and brands within them.

The Significance of Retail Image

As defined in Chapter 2, ***image*** refers to how a retailer is perceived by consumers and others. To be successful, a retailer must create and maintain a distinctive, clear, and consistent image. Once established, this image permeates all goods and service offerings; and in the consumer's mind, a retailer is placed in a niche relative to competitors. It is rather difficult to break out of a niche once it is firmly implanted in consumers' minds.

To further amplify, let us add these descriptions of retail image. It is

> the way in which a retailer is defined in a shopper's mind, partly by its functional qualities and partly by an aura of psychological attributes.[3]

> *not* simply someone's impersonal observations of a [retailer's] characteristics. Thus, I consider image a combination of factual and emotional material. The customer reacts to the retailer's characteristics, as he or she views them, in an emotional way.[4]

[2] Hunter Hastings, "At Retail Level, Brands Must Entertain, Involve, Inform," *Advertising Age* (March 7, 1994), p. 26.

[3] Pierre Martineau, "The Personality of the Retail Store," *Harvard Business Review*, Vol. 36 (January–February 1958), p. 47.

[4] Alfred R. Oxenfeldt, "Developing a Favorable Price-Quality Image," *Journal of Retailing*, Vol. 50 (Winter 1974–1975), p. 9.

> a subjective phenomenon that results from the acquisition of knowledge about the [retailer] as it is perceived relative to other retailers and in accordance with the consumer's unique cognitive framework.[5]

> unable to be all things to all people. Different groups of consumers might place different importance on various retail attributes. Retailers may thus emphasize different image attributes as part of their marketing strategy, and ideally, the image attributes stressed by the store should be those to which the target market attaches the most importance.[6]

> critical whenever a retailer enters a new market or analyzes its situation in a current market, and the firm considers how it is perceived relative to others in the trading area. Is the firm perceived as being the same (undifferentiated), generally the same but having some distinguishing feature (differentiated), or filling a unique market niche (subtyped)?[7]

Common to the definitions are these points: image is comprised of functional (physical) and psychological (emotional) elements which are organized into perceptual frameworks by shoppers, and the frameworks determine shoppers' expectations about a retailer's overall policies and practices.

COMPONENTS OF RETAIL IMAGE

Numerous factors contribute to a retailer's image, and it is the totality of these factors which determines an overall image. In different settings, it has been stated that retail image is composed of

- Quality, prices, and assortment.[8]
- Fashionability, salespersonship, outside attractiveness, and advertising.[9]
- Clientele mix, institutional maturity, merchandise offerings, locational convenience, shopping pleasure, transaction convenience, promotional emphasis, integrity, and image strength and clarity.[10]
- Locational convenience, prices, cleanliness of facilities, ease of credit, merchandise quality, shopping excitement, customer sophistication, the friendliness of salespeople, congestion, and other criteria.[11]
- Time, treatment, efficiency, price, physical, and technology factors.[12]

[5] Elizabeth C. Hirschman, "Retail Research and Theory," in Ben N. Enis and Kenneth J. Roering (Editors), *Review of Marketing* (Chicago: American Marketing Association, 1981), p. 119.

[6] Jan-Benedict E. M. Steenkamp and Michel Wedel, "Segmenting Retail Markets on Store Image Using a Consumer-Based Methodology," *Journal of Retailing*, Vol. 67 (Fall 1991), p. 301.

[7] Susan M. Keaveney and Kenneth A. Hunt, "Conceptualization and Operationalization of Retail Store Image: A Case of Rival Middle-Level Theories," *Journal of the Academy of Marketing Science*, Vol. 20 (Spring 1992), p. 172.

[8] Don L. James, Richard M. Durand, and Robert A. Dreves, "The Use of a Multi-Attribute Attitude Model in a Store Image Study," *Journal of Retailing*, Vol. 52 (Summer 1976), p. 30.

[9] Ronald B. Marks, "Operationalizing the Concept of Store Image," *Journal of Retailing*, Vol. 52 (Fall 1976), p. 44.

[10] Edgar A. Pessemier, "Store Image and Positioning," *Journal of Retailing*, Vol. 56 (Spring 1980), pp. 96–97.

[11] Linda L. Golden, Gerald Albaum, and Mary Zimmer, "The Numerical Comparative Scale: An Economical Format for Retail Image Measurement," *Journal of Retailing*, Vol. 63 (Winter 1987), p. 404.

[12] Joe Peritz, "Retailers Who Keep Score Know What Their Shoppers Value," *Marketing News* (May 24, 1993), p. 9.

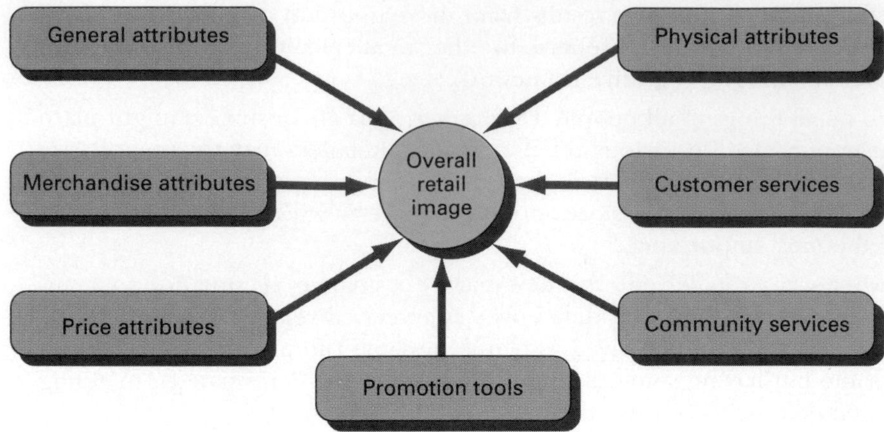

FIGURE 16–1
The Elements of a Retail Image

From these lists, the following is offered as a detailed summary of the components of a retailer's image:

1. Characteristics of the target market.
2. Retail positioning.
3. Store location (geographic coverage).
4. Merchandise assortment.
5. Price levels.
6. Attributes of physical facilities (atmosphere).
7. Customer services.
8. Community service.
9. Mass advertising and publicity.
10. Type and extent of personal selling.
11. Sales promotions.

Items 1 through 5 and their relation to image have been examined in earlier chapters in the text. Items 6 through 11 are the focal points for the discussion involving communications with the consumer in this and the next chapter. Figure 16–1 contains a breakdown of the elements of a retail image (incorporating Items 1 through 11).

THE DYNAMICS OF CREATING AND MAINTAINING A RETAIL IMAGE

Creating and maintaining a retail image is a multistep, ongoing process, as these three examples show. Tiffany & Co. is a 150-year-old upscale retailer of jewelry, tableware, time pieces, gift items, and "extraordinary objects for everyday life." It realizes that "the 1990s is no time for resting on one's laurels. Shoppers expect superior value and excellent customer service." The firm "can meet, and usually exceed, these expectations—so it has refined and intensified its efforts to clearly convey that message. Ads in major daily newspapers and in magazines more specifically communicate product value to consumers in over a dozen countries." In addition, Tiffany does marketing research and distributes various informative booklets: "Our intent is to heighten awareness, build confidence, attract more shoppers, and keep them coming back for more." And "as always, we will host consumer attractions and press briefings where our newest stores are opening and when new products are launched. Our stores have never been more outgoing and inviting."[13]

[13] *Tiffany & Co. 1992 Annual Report*, inside front cover and p. 8.

Caldor, a full-line discount-store chain, feels that a successful retailer must "provide an enjoyable shopping experience. If a store is fun to shop, people will come back. From the easily identifiable red shirts worn by our associates to our attractive new and remodeled stores, Caldor has implemented a range of programs designed to improve customer satisfaction and create a friendly environment. All of its stores "are based on a warm and inviting store prototype that features improved and defined merchandising areas, better fixtures, bright color schemes, better lighting, and wider aisles. Caldor has also "worked to establish and strengthen a customer-driven culture among managers and sales associates to enhance shopping experiences. Each store's 'friendliness' rating is compiled from monthly customer surveys."[14]

Through its multiple store formats, Designs, Inc. (which was founded in 1987) is the leading retailer that exclusively sells apparel and accessories made by Levi Strauss & Co. Each store format has a distinct retail image:

> Design Stores are located in enclosed regional malls and offer the broadest selection of Levi Strauss & Co. merchandise for the entire family. The layout and design of the Designs shops highlight the attractiveness and quality of the Levi's and Dockers brand products.
>
> Levi's Outlet Stores range in size from 8,000 to 17,000 square feet and are located in manufacturers' outlet parks and destination shopping areas. Designs, Inc. is the country's largest retailer of irregular and closeout Levi Strauss & Co. merchandise, and is the only operator of Levi's Outlet Stores in the Eastern United States.
>
> Original Levi's Stores and Dockers Shops are concept stores that allow Designs, Inc. to expand into new areas of retail development in which it concentrates on creating different environments—one focused on the jeans customers and another on the Dockers customer.[15]

Of particular concern to chain retailers and franchisors is maintaining a consistent image among all branches and units. However, despite the best planning, a number of factors may vary widely and have an effect on image. These factors include management and employee performance, consumer profiles, competitors, convenience in reaching the store, parking, safety, the ease of finding merchandise, and the qualities of the surrounding area.

Sometimes, retailers with good images receive negative publicity. This must be countered in order for them to maintain their desired standing with the public. Recently, Honda dealers had a potential image problem on their hands due to the media coverage regarding the past kickbacks that some of them had been required to make to U.S. Honda Motor Company executives in order for those dealers to be able to acquire scarce models (such as the Accord, which was then the best-selling car in America). To remedy matters, the way in which Honda dealers get scarce models has been changed and a number of U.S. Honda Motor Company executives have been forced from the company; these actions have also been reported by the media.[16]

Atmosphere

Creating and maintaining an image depend heavily on a firm's atmosphere. For a store-based retailer, ***atmosphere*** refers to the store's physical characteristics that are used to develop an image and to draw customers. For a nonstore-based retailer, the physical characteristics of such strategic-mix factors as catalogs and vending machines affect its image. This section looks at atmosphere from the perspective of store-based retailing.

[14] *Caldor Corporation 1992 Annual Report,* p. 8.

[15] *Designs, Inc. 1993 Annual Report,* pp. 5–6, 9.

[16] Martin Everett, "Honda Hits Emergency Brake After Sales Scandal," *Sales & Marketing Management* (May 1994), p. 13.

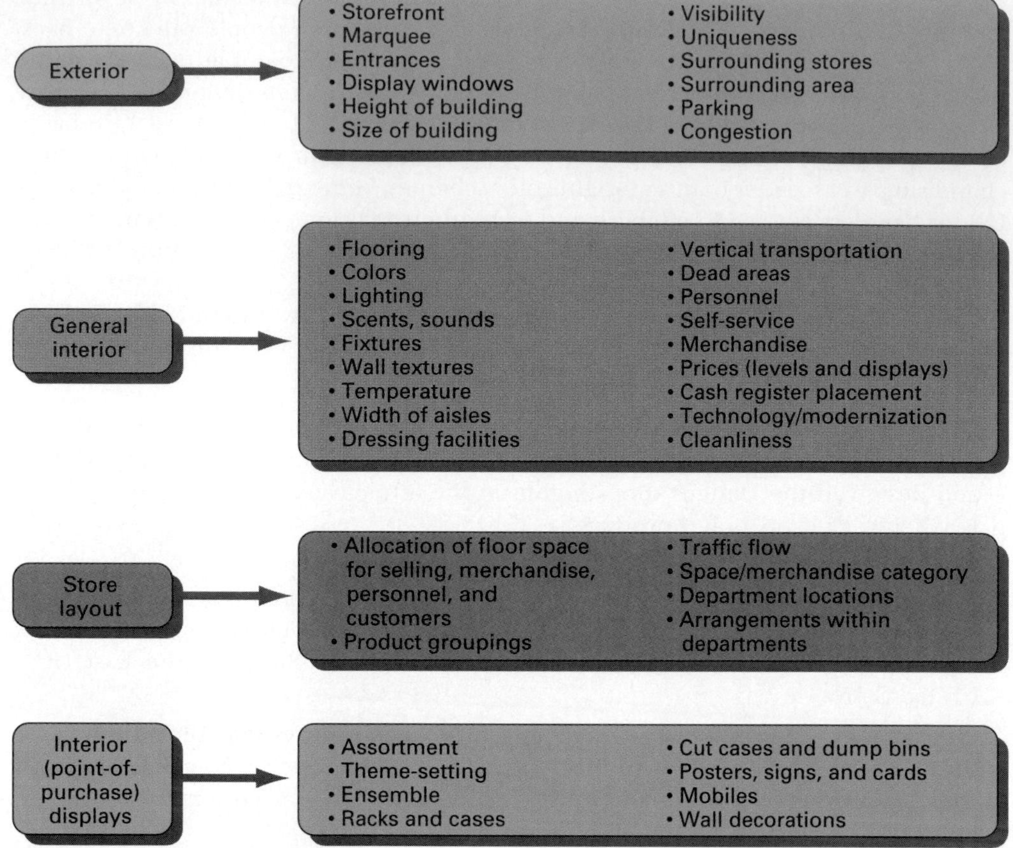

Exterior
• Storefront
• Marquee
• Entrances
• Display windows
• Height of building
• Size of building
• Visibility
• Uniqueness
• Surrounding stores
• Surrounding area
• Parking
• Congestion
General interior
• Flooring
• Colors
• Lighting
• Scents, sounds
• Fixtures
• Wall textures
• Temperature
• Width of aisles
• Dressing facilities
• Vertical transportation
• Dead areas
• Personnel
• Self-service
• Merchandise
• Prices (levels and displays)
• Cash register placement
• Technology/modernization
• Cleanliness
Store layout
• Allocation of floor space for selling, merchandise, personnel, and customers
• Product groupings
• Traffic flow
• Space/merchandise category
• Department locations
• Arrangements within departments
Interior (point-of-purchase) displays
• Assortment
• Theme-setting
• Ensemble
• Racks and cases
• Cut cases and dump bins
• Posters, signs, and cards
• Mobiles
• Wall decorations

FIGURE 16–2
The Elements of Atmosphere

The sights, sounds, smells, and so on of a store contribute greatly to the image that is projected to consumers. It is important that atmosphere be understood as the psychological feeling a customer gets when visiting a store or as the personality of the store.

Many people form impressions of a store before entering (due to location, storefront, and other factors) or just after entering (due to merchandise displays, the width of aisles, and other factors). These people could judge a store prior to closely examining merchandise and prices. Store atmosphere may thus influence people's enjoyment of shopping, their time spent browsing and examining a retailer's offerings, their willingness to converse with personnel and to use such facilities as dressing rooms, their tendency to spend more money than originally planned, and their likelihood of future patronage.

Atmosphere can be divided into these key elements: exterior, general interior, store layout, and displays. Figure 16–2 contains a detailed breakdown of these elements.

EXTERIOR

The exterior characteristics of a store have a powerful impact on its image and should be planned accordingly.

A ***storefront*** is the total physical exterior of the store itself. It includes the marquee, entrances, windows, lighting, and construction materials. Via its storefront, a retailer can present a conservative, progressive, lavish, discount, or other image to the consumer. A firm should not underestimate the importance of the storefront as a determinant of image, particularly for new customers. When passing through an unfamiliar business district or shopping center, consumers often judge a store by its exterior.

There are various alternatives a retailer could consider when planning its basic storefront. Here are a few of them:

RETAILING AROUND THE WORLD

What Image Can Kmart Carve Out in the Czech Republic and Slovakia?

Kmart's 1992 purchase of thirteen of the best stores in the then Czechoslovakia is viewed by many retailing experts as a tremendous opportunity for the firm. Kmart was allowed to choose the stores by the Czechoslovakian government because the country had no traditional U.S. discounters. When the country was split into the Czech Republic and Slovakia in January 1993, Kmart ended up with stores in both nations. Thus, the purchase provided Kmart with access to a huge population. And by the end of 1993, the firm had spent a total of $120 million to purchase and renovate the thirteen stores.

But the road to profitability for Kmart has been harder than anticipated. In contrast to its U.S. stores, none of the Czech and Slovakian stores had parking facilities or computer systems. Kmart also has had difficulties in getting employees to be receptive to customer-service training. For example, "Sales clerks, mostly women accustomed to leaning on countertops, were sent to the floor wearing tags announcing 'I'm here for you.' Problem was, many of them weren't. It didn't take long to realize the clerks were finding places to hide. They felt a little shy about getting out among the customers. Their hiding spots are gone now."

Kmart's Prague store was the first one to be renovated. The store's layout is now more open, and new lighting and store lighting fixtures have been installed. Due to shortages of Czech-made goods, Kmart plans to sell some German foods, some private-label foods (such as Nature's Classics cookies and crackers) that have been successful in the U.S., and groceries and snacks.

Sources: Based on material in "Czech Stores Key to Kmart's European Push," *Discount Store News* (September 6, 1993), pp. 1, 57; "Kmart's Czech Invasion Lurches Along," *Wall Street Journal* (June 8, 1993), p. A12; and Susan Reda, "Aga's Maj Summer," *Stores* (November 1993), pp. 28–30.

- A modular structure—This is a one-piece rectangle or square that sometimes attaches several stores.
- A prefabricated (prefab) structure—This utilizes a store frame built in a factory and assembled at the store site.
- A prototype store—This is used by franchisors and chains. Because a consistent image is sought, uniform storefronts are constructed.
- A recessed storefront—In this case, the store is one of many at its locale. To lure people, the storefront is recessed from the level of other stores. Customers have to walk in a number of feet to examine the storefront.
- A unique building design—For example, round structures are distinctive.

In addition to the actual storefront, atmosphere can be enhanced by trees, fountains, and benches placed in front of the store. These intensify the consumer's feelings about shopping and about the store by establishing a relaxed environment.

A ***marquee*** is a sign used to display the store's name. The marquee can be painted or a neon light, printed or script, and alone or mixed with a slogan (trademark) and other information. To be effective, the marquee should stand out and attract attention. Image is influenced because a marquee can be gaudy and flashy or subdued and subtle. Probably the most widely known marquee in the world is the McDonald's golden arch, which some communities consider too overpowering.

The entrances to the store should be designed carefully, and three major decisions must be made. First, the number of entrances is determined. Many smaller stores have only one entrance. Larger department stores may have four to eight or more entrances. A store hoping to draw vehicular and pedestrian traffic should have at least two entrances (one in front to lure pedestrians, another in the rear—adjacent to the parking lot). Because front and back entrances serve different purposes, they should be designed separately. One factor limiting the number of entrances is potential pilferage. Some urban stores have closed off entrances to reduce the size of their security forces.

Second, the type of entrance(s) is chosen from among many options. The doorway is selected: revolving; electric, self-opening; regular, push-pull; or climate-controlled.

The latter is an open entrance with a curtain of warm or cold air, set at the same temperature as inside the store. This entry makes a store inviting, reduces pedestrian traffic congestion, and lets customers see inside the store. Entrance flooring is picked: cement, tile, or carpeting. Lighting is ascertained: traditional or fluorescent, white or colors, and/or flashing or constant.

Third, the walkways are considered. A wide, lavish walkway creates a very different image and mood from a narrow, constrained one. In the construction of the storefront, ample room must be provided for the walkways. Large window displays may be very attractive, but customers would not be pleased if there is insufficient space for a comfortable entry into the store.

Display windows serve two main purposes: to identify the store and its offerings, and to induce customers to enter. They give a wide variety of information about a store. By showing a representative merchandise offering, a store can create an overall image. By showing fashion or seasonal goods, a store can show that it is contemporary. By showing sale items, a store can lure price-conscious consumers. By showing eye-catching displays that have little to do with its merchandise offering, a store can attract pedestrians' attention. By showing public service messages (e.g., a window display for the Jerry Lewis Telethon), the store can indicate its concern for the community.

Considerable planning is needed to develop good display windows. Thus, many retailers hire specialists to set up their displays properly. Decisions include the number, size, shape, color, and themes of display windows—and the frequency of changes per year. Some retailers, especially ones in shopping malls, do not use display windows for the side of the building facing the parking lot; there are solid building exteriors. Those firms feel vehicular patrons are not lured by expensive outside display windows, but they do invest in display windows for the storefronts inside the malls.

The height and the size of the exterior building also contribute to a store's image. The height of a building can be disguised or nondisguised. Disguised building height occurs when part of a store—or shopping center—is beneath ground level. As a result, the building is not so intimidating to consumers who are turned off by a large, impersonal structure. Nondisguised building height occurs when an entire store—or center—can be seen by pedestrians (all floors are at ground level or higher). The overall size of a building cannot really be disguised; therefore, the target market should be researched to see how people feel about patronizing different-sized facilities. An intimate boutique image cannot be generated with a block-long building. Nor can a department store image be linked to a small site.

Few retailers are able to succeed without good exterior visibility for their stores and/or shopping centers. This means that pedestrian and/or vehicular traffic can clearly see the storefront or marquee. Accordingly, a store located behind a bus stop has poor visibility for vehicular traffic and pedestrians across the street. Many retailers operating near highways must use billboards for visibility because drivers quickly pass by.

Visibility is gained via a combination of exterior features. The goal is to have the store appear unique, make it stand out, and catch the consumer's eye. A distinctive store design, an elaborate marquee, recessed open-air entrances, decorative windows, and different building height and building size are one grouping of storefront features that could attract consumers through uniqueness. In the process, a retail image is fostered.

Uniqueness, although it provides excellent visibility, may not be without shortcomings. An example is Macy's in Elmhurst, Queens, New York, which is a multilevel "store-in-the-round." Because the store (which occupies a square city block) is round-shaped, parking is provided on each store level to make the walking distances of customers very short. However, a rectangular store would provide greater floor space on a lot of the same size; convenient on-floor parking may minimize customer shopping on other floors; added entrances increase chances for pilferage; many customers dislike inclined and circular driving; and architectural costs are higher for unique buildings.

Figure 16–3
Attractive Store Exteriors
As depicted here, retailers often place a lot of emphasis on their store exteriors to establish their overall atmosphere. Some exteriors may be seen from roads and streets, others are viewed from shopping mall walkways.
Reprinted by permission of Tandy, Dillard's, and Spencer Gifts.

When a retailer plans a store exterior, the surrounding stores and the surrounding area should both be examined. Each contributes to the store's image, regardless of the retailer's distinctive storefront and building. The surrounding stores present image cues to consumers that may be progressive or conservative, high price, personal service, and so on. An overall area image rubs off on the individual firm because people tend to have a general image of a shopping center or a business district. Thus, an individual storefront should be distinctive but not contradictory to the overall image of the site.

The surrounding area includes the demographics and life-styles of people living near a store. A store's image is affected by the type of neighborhood in which it is located. An unfavorable atmosphere would exist if vandalism and crime are high, the people living near the store are not part of the target market, and the area is rundown.

Parking facilities can add to or detract from a store's atmosphere. Plentiful, free, nearby parking (with large parking spaces) creates a more positive atmosphere than scarce, costly, distant parking (with tiny parking spaces). Countless potential shoppers may never enter the store if they drive around looking for on-street parking and, not finding it, go elsewhere or return home disgruntled. Other customers may run in and out of a store so they can complete their shopping before their parking meters expire. In assessing parking facilities, retailers should keep in mind that some people may have a limit on the distance they will walk from a parking space to the most distant stores in a shopping district or center, and many people dislike multilevel garages (because of discomfort in driving or a concern for safety).

Allied with the potential parking problem is that of congestion. A store's atmosphere would be diminished if its parking lot, sidewalks, and/or entrances are jammed. Consumers who feel crushed in the crowd generally spend less time shopping and are in poorer moods than those who feel comfortable.

Figure 16–3 shows some of the exciting things retailers are doing with their store exteriors, as does this example:

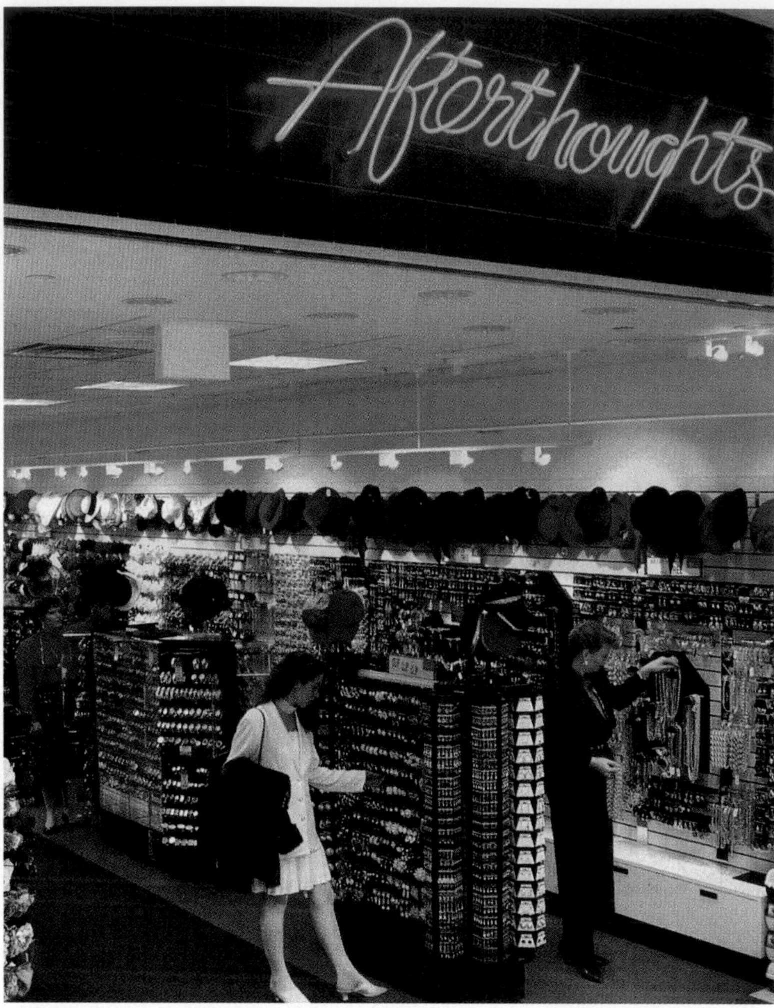

FIGURE 16–4
Capitalizing on the General Store Interior
At Afterthoughts specialty stores, the flooring, colors, lighting, fixtures, and other interior factors all contribute to a pleasant shopping experience.
Reprinted by permission of Woolworth Corporation.

It isn't often that the word dramatic is used to describe the exterior of a supermarket. But with a stunning all-glass facade that rises more than two stories at highest point, few supermarkets are as monumental in design scope or as visually stunning as Kroger's outlet in Alpharetta, Georgia. The all-inclusive nature and depth of the 80,000-square-foot store are introduced in its sweeping exterior, which is made of wirecut brick with light and dark brick accents (corvel stucco is used at the roof line). The glass is tinted green and grey reflective. A large gabled entrance (with a pre-finished standing seam metal roof) is positioned at either end of the sweeping facade. A flat metal canopy, supported by steel tube trusses, runs across the top front of the building.[17]

GENERAL INTERIOR

Once a customer is inside a store, there are numerous elements affecting his or her perception of it. The general interior elements of atmosphere are cited in Figure 16–2, illustrated in Figure 16–4, and described here.

Flooring can be made of cement, wood, linoleum, carpet, and so on. A plush, thick carpet creates one kind of image, and a cement floor causes another. Because people use cues to form store perceptions, flooring materials and designs are important. For instance, Genovese Drug Stores is installing carpeting, rather than tile, in its new

[17] "Kroger Lights the Night," *Chain Store Age Executive* (April 1994), p. 116.

and renovated stores to present a better appearance: "The sales area features a sculpted loop pattern done in black with flecks of gray and burgundy. The same carpeting accentuates the cosmetics department. The rose shading highlights the mauve fixturing."[18]

Colors and lighting affect a store's image. Bright, vibrant colors contribute to a different atmosphere than light pastels or plain white walls. Lighting can be direct or indirect, white or colors, constant or flashing. For instance, a teen-oriented apparel boutique could use bright colors and vibrant, flashing lights to foster one atmosphere, and a maternity dress shop could use pastel colors and indirect lighting to form a different atmosphere.

Scents and sounds can be used to influence the customer's mood and to contribute to a favorable atmosphere.[19] A restaurant uses kitchen scents to increase customers' appetites. A pet store wants the natural scents and sounds of its animals to woo customers. A beauty salon plays soft music or rock, depending on its target market. A cosmetics store uses an array of perfume scents to attract people. Slow-tempo music in supermarkets encourages consumers to move more slowly. A record/CD store plays its top-sellers.

Store fixtures can be planned not only on the basis of their utility but also because of their aesthetics. Pipes, plumbing, vents, beams, doors, storage rooms, and display racks and tables can be considered in the interior decorating. A store seeking a high-price, high-quality image disguises and decorates those fixtures. A store seeking a low-price, low-quality image might leave the fixtures exposed. Because the latter choice is inexpensive, it reinforces the desired image.

Wall textures can enhance or diminish a store's image. Prestigious stores often use fancy, raised wallpaper. Department stores are more likely to use flat wallpaper, while discount stores may have barren walls. Upscale stores might also have elaborate chandeliers, while discount stores would have simple lighting fixtures.

The customer's mood is affected by the temperature of the store and its way of achieving it. A person would be uncomfortable if there is insufficient heat in the winter and coolness in the summer. This can hasten his or her trip through the store. In another vein, the store's image is influenced by the use of central air-conditioning, unit air-conditioning, fans, or open windows.

The width of the aisles has an impact on retail image. Wide, uncrowded aisles create a better atmosphere than narrow, crowded ones. Customers shop longer and spend more when they are not pushed and shoved while walking or looking at merchandise. In Boston, the basement in Filene's department store has many items at bargain prices; yet, overcrowding keeps some customers away.

Dressing facilities can be elaborate, plain, or nonexistent. A prestigious store uses carpeted, private dressing rooms. An average-quality store uses linoleum-floored, semi-private rooms. A discount store uses small stalls or has no dressing facilities at all. For some apparel customers, dressing facilities (and their maintenance) are a major factor in store selection. To them, atmosphere and type of dressing facility are closely intertwined.

Multilevel stores must have some form of vertical transportation. The choices are elevator, escalator, and/or stairs. Larger stores may have a combination of all three. Traditionally, the operator-run elevator has appeared in finer stores and stairs have appeared in discount stores. Today, escalators are quite popular and are gaining stature. They provide consumers with a quiet ride and a panoramic view of the store. Finer stores decorate their escalators with fountains, shrubs, and trees. The placement and design of vertical transportation determine its contribution to atmosphere. Stairs remain important for discount and smaller stores.

18 "Genovese Rolls Out the Carpet," *Chain Store Age Executive* (March 1994), p. 59.

19 See Cyndee Miller, "Scent as a Marketing Tool: Retailers—and Even a Casino—Seek Sweet Smell of Success," *Marketing News* (January 18, 1993), pp. 1–2; and Richard Yalch and Eric Spangenberg, "Effects of Store Music on Shopping Behavior," *Journal of Consumer Marketing*, Vol. 7 (Spring 1990), pp. 55–63.

Light fixtures, wood or metal beams, doors, rest rooms, dressing rooms, and vertical transportation can cause dead areas for the retailer. ***Dead areas*** are awkward spaces where normal displays cannot be set up. In some cases, it is not possible for such areas to be deployed profitably or attractively. However, in general, retailers are learning to use dead areas better. For example, mirrors can be attached to exit doors. Vending machines can be located near rest rooms. Ads can be placed in dressing rooms.

The most creative use of a dead area involves the escalator. For a long time, retailers considered it an ugly fixture in the middle of the store. Now, it is viewed differently. The escalator enables the consumer to view the whole floor of the store, and sales of impulse items go up when placed at the entrance or exit of an escalator. In addition, most retailers plan escalators so customers must get off at each floor and pass by appealing displays.

The number, manner, and appearance of store personnel reflect a store's atmosphere. Polite, well-groomed, knowledgeable personnel generate a positive atmosphere. Ill-mannered, poorly groomed, unknowing personnel engender a negative one. Research findings generally show that customers like to deal with personnel having demographics similar to their own; thus, store personnel should resemble the target market as closely as possible. A store using self-service minimizes its personnel and creates a discount, impersonal image. A store cannot develop a prestigious image if it is set up for self-service.

The goods and services a retailer sells influences its image. Top-line items yield one kind of image, and bottom-line items yield another. The mood of the customer is affected accordingly.

Store prices contribute to image in two ways. First, price levels yield a perception of retail image in the consumer's mind. Second, the way prices are displayed is a vital part of atmosphere. Prestigious stores have few or no price displays and rely upon hidden price tags. Sales are de-emphasized. Discount stores accentuate price displays and show prices in large print. The placement of cash registers is associated with the type of price displays a store uses. Prestigious stores place cash registers in inconspicuous areas such as behind posts or in employee rooms. Discount stores locate their cash registers centrally and have big signs pointing them out.

The technology used by the store and the modernization of its building and fixtures also affect its image. A store with state-of-the-art technology, such as computerized cash registers and automated inventory procedures, impresses people by its efficiency and speed of operations. A store with slower, older technology can have long lines and impatient shoppers. A store with a modern building (new storefront and marquee) and new fixtures (lights, floors, and walls) fosters a more favorable atmosphere than one with older facilities.

These overall observations can be made about modernizing a store:

- Renovations are easier, faster, and less costly than building or opening new stores.
- Improving store appearance, updating facilities, expansion, and the need to reallocate space are the main reasons for remodeling.
- It results in strong sales and profit increases after completion.
- Almost all stores are kept open during a renovation.

Last, but certainly not least, a retailer must have a plan for keeping the store clean. No matter how impressive a store's exterior and interior may be, an unkempt store will be perceived negatively by customers. As one store manager remarked:

> I think cleanliness is the most important thing in a store. It sets the tone. Housekeeping is many things; keeping showcases clean; keeping bases clean where they are rapped by the vacuum cleaner. Everybody thinks of a store as the place where

the merchandise is. But are your toilet facilities taken care of properly? Are the trash baskets empty? It's not merely going through with a vacuum cleaner. It's the cleaning of the doors, of the countertops, of dust on top of seven-foot units.[20]

Store Layout

Next, the specifics of store layout are planned and set up.

Allocation of Floor Space

Each store has a total square footage of floor space available and must allot it among selling, merchandise, personnel, and customers. ***Selling space*** is the area set aside for displays of merchandise, interactions between sales personnel and customers, demonstrations, and so on. A retailer such as a supermarket or other self-service firm often allots a large amount of total store space to selling. At the upper extreme is Everything's a Dollar discount stores, which allocate 90 per cent of their space to selling.[21]

Merchandise space is the area where nondisplayed items are kept in stock or inventory. A traditional shoe store is a good example of a retailer whose merchandise space takes up a large percentage of total space.

Store personnel often require space for changing clothes, lunch and coffee breaks, and rest rooms. Firms may try to minimize ***personnel space*** by insisting on off-the-job clothes changing and other tactics. Because floor space is so valuable, that part allotted to personnel is usually controlled strictly. However, when planning personnel space, a retailer should consider employee morale and personal appearance.

Customers also require space, and it contributes greatly to a store's image. ***Customer space*** can include a lounge, benches and/or chairs, dressing rooms, rest rooms, a restaurant, vertical transportation, a nursery, parking, and wide aisles. Low-image retailers generally skimp on or omit most of these areas; those with consumer-oriented images provide their customers with adequate amounts of space for many or all of these factors.

A retailer cannot go further in its store-layout planning until floor space is properly allocated among selling, merchandise, personnel, and customers. Without that allocation, the firm would have no conception of the space available for displays, signs, rest rooms, and so on.

Today, a growing number of retailers (especially supermarkets) are using planograms to allocate their store space.[22] A ***planogram*** is a visual (graphical) representation of the space to be allotted to selling, merchandise, personnel, and customers—as well as to product categories. It also lays out their placement in a store. A planogram may be drawn by hand or generated by computer software (like the Pegman software noted in Chapter 3).

Classification of Store Offerings

Next, a store's offerings are classified into product groupings. Four types of groupings and combinations of them can be employed: functional, purchase motivation, market segment, and storability. With ***functional product groupings***, a store's merchandise is categorized and displayed by common end uses. For example, a men's clothing store might carry these functional groups: shirts, ties, cuff links, and tie pins; shoes, laces, and shoe polish; T-shirts, undershorts, and socks; suits; and sports jackets and slacks.

Purchase-motivation product groupings appeal to a consumer's urge to buy a product and the amount of time he or she is willing to spend in shopping. A committed

[20] Jules Abend, "Neat and Clean," *Stores* (November 1983), p. 15.

[21] *Value Merchants, Inc. 1993 10K*, p. 2.

[22] See Gary Robins, "Soft Lines, The New Frontier for Space Management Systems," *Stores* (April 1993), pp. 24–26.

customer with time to shop will visit the upper floors and extremities of a store; an uninterested customer with little time to spend will gravitate to displays on the first floor, near the exit. A retailer can capitalize on this fact by grouping its products by purchase motivation. Look at the first floor of a department store. The items located there tend to be impulse products and other relatively quick purchases. On the third floor of a department store are items encouraging and requiring more thoughtful shopping.

With ***market-segment product groupings***, various products that appeal to a given target market are placed together. Examples are a clothing store's dividing products into juniors', misses', and ladies' clothing categories; a music store's separating merchandise into rock, jazz, classical, rhythm and blues, country and western, gospel, and popular music sections; an art gallery's placing its paintings in different price groups; and a toy store's setting up distinct display areas for children and adult games.

For products requiring special handling, ***storability product groupings*** may be employed. A supermarket has freezer, refrigerator, and room-temperature sections. A florist keeps some flowers in a refrigerator and others at room temperature. The same is true for a bakery or a fruit store.

Many retailers often use a combination of product groupings and plan their store layouts accordingly. In addition to the considerations just covered, provisions must be made for minimizing shoplifting and pilferage. This means positioning product groups away from corners and doors.

Determination of a Traffic-Flow Pattern

The traffic-flow pattern of the store is then determined. There are two basic traffic-flow alternatives available to a retailer: straight and curving. With a ***straight (gridiron) traffic flow***, displays and aisles are constructed in a rectangular or gridiron pattern, as shown in Figure 16–5. With a ***curving (free-flowing) traffic flow***, displays and aisles are constructed in a free-flowing pattern, as shown in Figure 16–6.

A straight traffic pattern is most often used by food retailers, discount stores, hardware stores, and other convenience-oriented stores (such as stationery outlets). This layout has several advantages:

- An efficient atmosphere is created.
- People can shop quickly; regular customers especially desire clearly marked, distinct aisles and develop a routine way of walking through the store.
- All available floor space is utilized.
- Inventory control and security are simplified.
- Self-service is possible, thereby reducing labor costs.

The disadvantages of a gridiron pattern are an impersonal atmosphere, limited browsing by customers, and rushed shopping behavior.

A curving traffic pattern is most often used by boutiques, department stores, clothing stores, and other shopping-oriented stores. There are several benefits of this approach:

- A friendly atmosphere is present.
- Shoppers do not feel rushed and will browse around.
- People are encouraged to walk through the store in any direction or pattern they desire.
- Impulse or unplanned purchases are increased.

The disadvantages of a free-flow pattern are the potential customer confusion, wasted floor space, difficulties in inventory control and security, high labor-intensiveness, and possible encouragement of loitering. Also, free-flow displays are often more expensive than standardized gridiron displays.

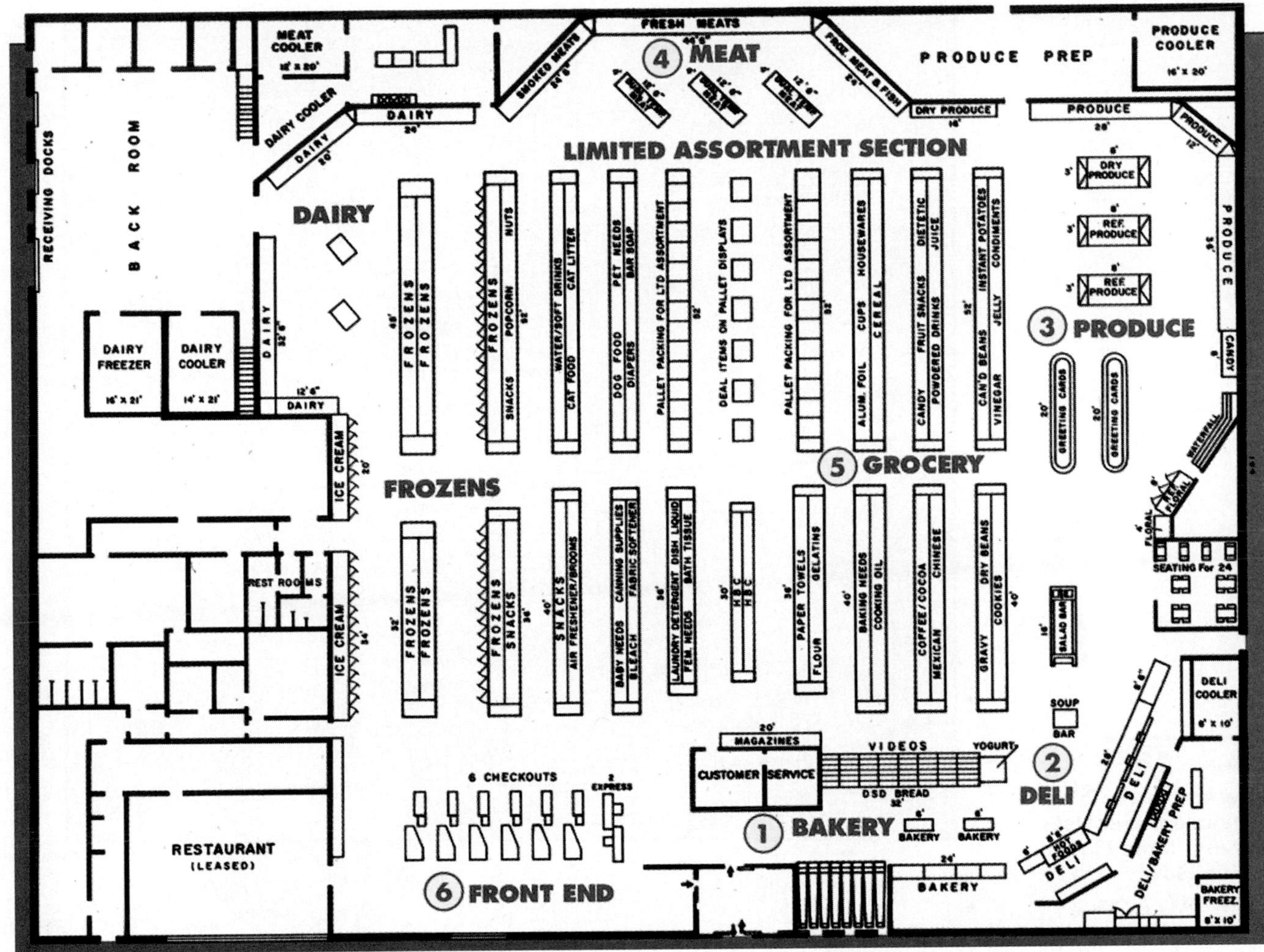

Figure 16–5 How Connersville IGA Plus in Connersville, Indiana, Uses a Staight (Gridiron) Traffic Flow

Copyright Progressive Grocer. Reprinted by permission.

Determination of Space Needs

At this point, the space for each product category is ascertained. Selling, as well as nonselling, space must be considered in any calculations.

Two approaches are possible for retailers: the model stock method and the space-productivity ratio. Under the ***model stock approach***, a retailer determines the amount of floor space necessary to carry and display a proper assortment of merchandise. Clothing stores and shoe stores are examples of retailers using the model stock method. With the ***sales-productivity ratio***, a retailer assigns floor space on the basis of sales or profit per foot. Highly profitable product categories receive large chunks of space; marginally profitable categories receive less space. Food stores and bookstores are examples of retailers using space-productivity ratios in planning floor space.

Mapping Out In-Store Locations

Department locations are mapped out now. For multilevel stores, this procedure includes assigning departments to floors and laying out the individual floors. What product categories should be placed on each floor? What should the layout of each floor be? The single-level store is concerned with only the second question. Generally speaking, here are some of the issues to be considered during this stage:

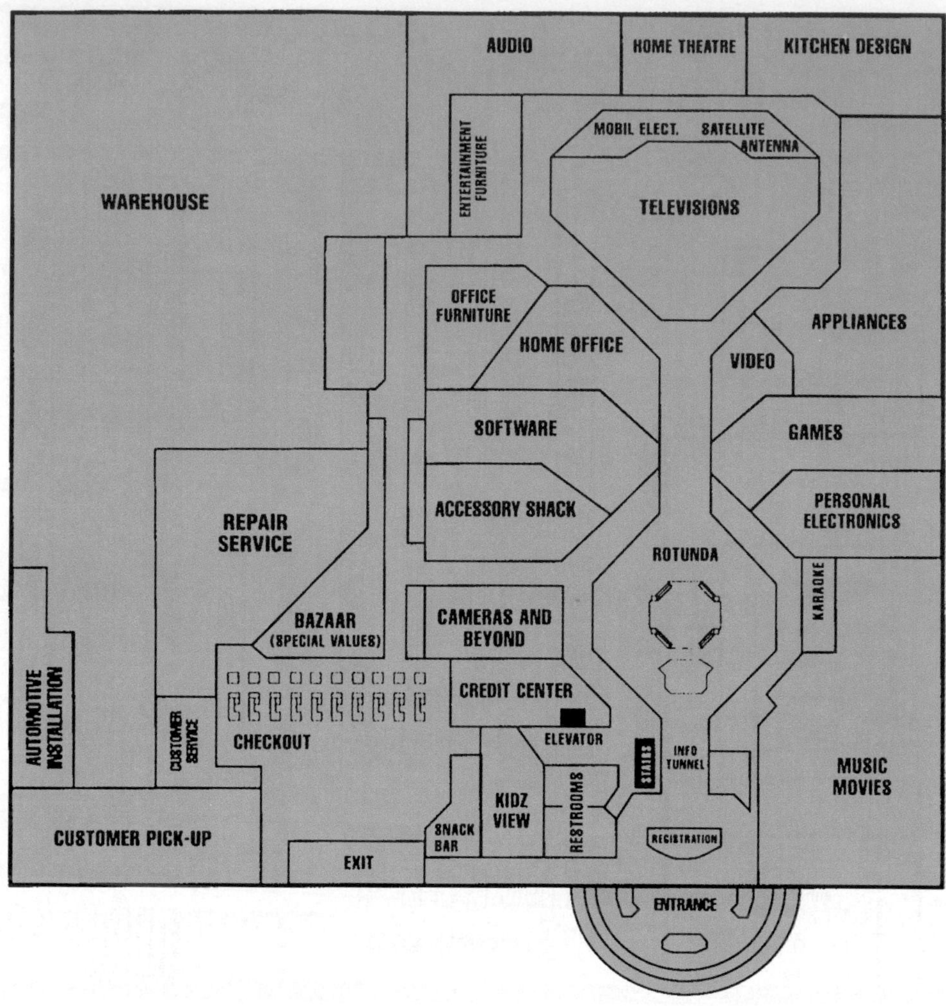

FIGURE 16–6
How the Incredible Universe Chain Uses a Curving (Free-Flowing) Traffic Flow
Reprinted by permission of Tandy.

- Which products should be placed in the basement, on the first floor, on the second floor, and so on?
- On a given floor, how should the groupings be placed in relation to doors, vertical transportation, and so on?
- Where should impulse or unplanned product categories be located in relation to categories that consumers pre-plan to buy?
- Where should convenience products be situated?
- How should associated product categories be aligned? See Figure 16–7.
- Where should seasonal and off-season products be placed?
- Where should space-consuming categories such as furniture be located?
- How close should product displays and stored inventory be to each other?
- What travel patterns do consumers follow once they enter the store?
- How can consumer lines be avoided near the cash register, and how can the overall appearance of store crowding be averted?

For example, research by American Greetings (the card maker) shows that just 40 per cent of the people who enter a stationery store walk through that store's greeting-card department. However, 90 per cent of those who do walk through the department typically purchase at least one greeting card. Thus, the placement of the greeting-card department within the store has a great impact on card sales.[23]

[23] *American Greetings 1992 Annual Report*, p. 12.

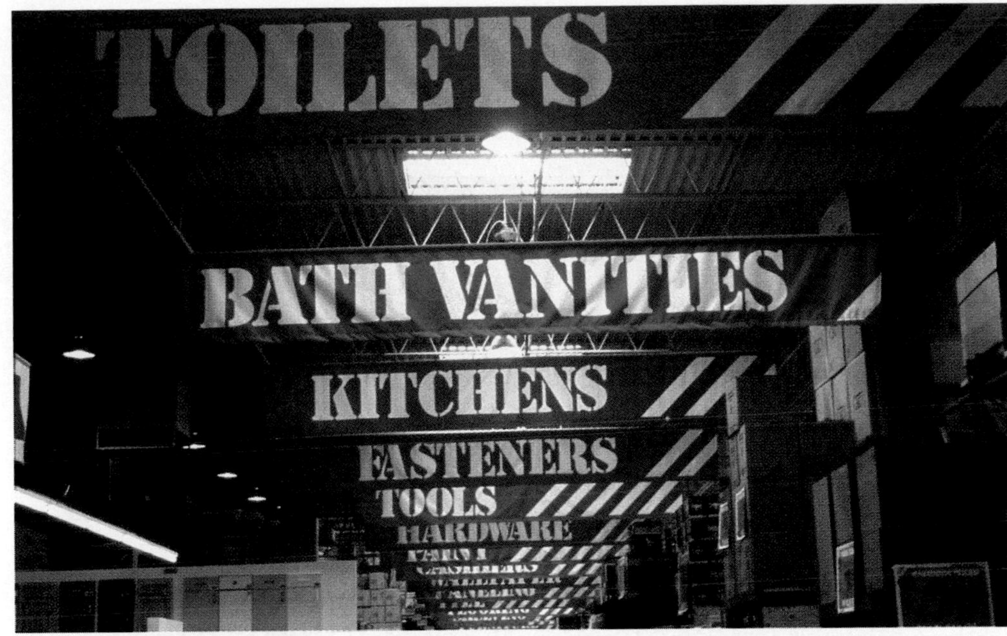

FIGURE 16–7
Home Depot's Department Location Displays
Reprinted by permission.

Arrangement of Individual Products

The last step in store layout planning is to arrange individual products within departments. Various criteria may be used in positioning them: The most profitable items and brands would receive favorable spots where consumer traffic is heavy. Products may also be arranged by package size, price, color, brand, level of personal service required, and/or customer interest.

End-aisle display positions, eye-level positions, and checkout-counter positions are the most apt to increase sales for individual items. Continuity of locations is also important; shifts in store layout may decrease sales. The least desirable display position is knee or ankle level, because consumers do not like to bend down.

Individual retailers should conduct their own research and experiments to measure the effects of different product positions on sales. In addition, it must be kept in mind that manufacturer and retailer goals may be dissimilar. A manufacturer often wants sales of its brand to be maximized and pushes for eye-level, full-shelf, end-aisle locations. On the other hand, a retailer is more involved in maximizing total store sales and profit, regardless of brand.

Self-service retailers have special considerations. The gridiron layout is normally used to minimize customer confusion. Similarly, aisles, displays, and merchandise must be clearly marked. A large selling space, with on-floor assortments, is necessary. Cash registers must be plentiful and accessible. It is difficult to sell complex and/or expensive items through self-service.

INTERIOR (POINT-OF-PURCHASE) DISPLAYS

After a store layout is fully detailed, a retailer devises interior displays. Each ***point-of-purchase (POP) display*** provides consumers with information, adds to store atmosphere, and serves a substantial promotional role. In this section, several types and forms of displays are described. Most retailers use combinations of some or all of these kinds of displays.[24]

An ***assortment display*** is one in which a retailer exhibits a wide range of merchandise for the customer. With an open assortment, the customer is encouraged to feel, look at, and/or try on a number of products. Greeting cards, pocketbooks, mag-

[24] For excellent examples, see "Stores of the Year," *Chain Store Age Executive* (March 1994), special section.

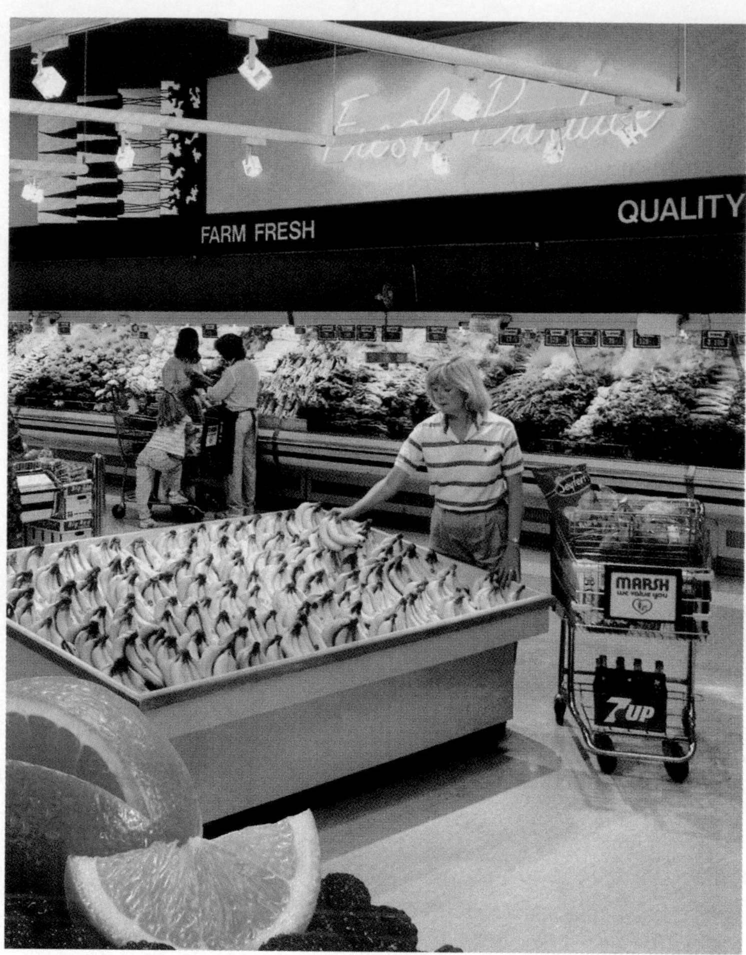

FIGURE 16–8
Open Assortment Displays at Marsh Supermarkets
Reprinted by permission.

azines, and gloves are the kinds of products for which firms use open assortments. In recent years, food stores have expanded the placement of items such as fruit, vegetables, and candy in open displays. See Figure 16–8. With a closed assortment, the customer is encouraged to look at a variety of merchandise but not touch it or try it on. Some shirts, games, and records are pre-packaged items a shopper is not allowed to open before buying.

A ***theme-setting display*** depicts a product offering in a thematic manner and lets a retailer portray a specific atmosphere or mood. Firms often change their displays to reflect seasons or special events; some even have employees dress to fit the occasion. All or part of a store may be adapted to a theme, such as Washington's Birthday, Columbus Day, Valentine's Day, Independence Day, or another concept. Each special theme is enacted to attract customer attention and make shopping more enjoyable (and not a chore).

An ***ensemble display*** has become very popular in recent years. Instead of grouping and displaying merchandise in separate categories (e.g., shoe department, sock department, pants department, shirt department, sports jacket department), complete ensembles are displayed. Accordingly, a mannequin could be dressed in a matching combination of shoes, socks, pants, shirt, and sports jacket, and these items would be readily available in one department or adjacent departments. Customers are pleased with the ease of a purchase and like being able to envision an entire outfit.

A ***rack display*** is often used by apparel retailers, houseware retailers, and others. The racks have a primarily functional use: to hang or present the products neatly. The major problems are possible cluttering and customers' returning items to the wrong place (thus disrupting the proper size sequence). Current technology allows retailers to use sliding, disconnecting, contracting/expanding, lightweight, attractive rack dis-

FIGURE 16–9 Rack Displays at Wilsons: The Leather Experts
Reprinted by permission of Melville Corporation. Photo by Derrick and Love.

plays. See Figure 16–9. A ***case display*** is employed to exhibit heavier, bulkier items than racks hold. Records, books, pre-packaged goods, and sweaters are typically contained in case displays.

A ***cut case*** is an inexpensive display, in which merchandise is left in the original carton. Supermarkets and discount stores frequently set up cut-case displays. These cases do not create a warm atmosphere. Neither does a ***dump bin***, which is a case that houses piles of sale clothing, marked-down books, or other products. Instead of neat, precise displays, dump bins contain open assortments of roughly handled items. The advantages of cut cases and dump bins are reduced display costs and a low-price image.

Posters, signs, and cards can be used to dress up all types of displays, including cut cases and dump bins. These tools provide information about in-store product locations and stimulate customers to shop. A mobile, a type of hanging display with parts that move, especially in response to air currents, serves the same purpose—but is more appealing to the eye and stands out. Wall decorations also enhance a store's atmosphere and add to displays; they are particularly useful with thematic and ensemble displays.

Customer Services

As defined in Chapter 1, ***customer services*** are the identifiable, but sometimes intangible, activities taken on by a retailer when selling its basic goods and services. The attributes of personnel who interact with customers (such as politeness and knowledge), as well as the number and variety of customer services offered by a firm, have a strong impact on and contribute to the image created. For instance, "Why do they call gas stations, 'service stations?' When was the last time you were approached by someone in a clean uniform with a smile who performed a series of services including washing your windows, checking your oil, and thanking you for coming?"[25]

[25] Murray Raphael, "Friendly Service?" *Direct Marketing* (June 1989), p. 20.

RETAILING IN ACTION

Are Personal Shoppers Good for Business?

To meet the special needs of time-pressured shoppers, personal shopping services have emerged. These services are being offered by department stores to assist shoppers at their stores, shopping centers, and independent firms.

With department store-based personal shoppers, the personal shoppers are employees of the particular store. By appointment, they accompany customers through the store and provide all kinds of assistance, from pre-selecting clothing wardrobes to processing payments. Many of the leading department stores have personal shoppers and offer their services at no charge.

Shopping center-based personal shoppers are free to assist customers with the purchase of goods and services at any store in a specific shopping center. They not only pick out gifts based upon suggestions of the customer, but they also arrange to have gifts wrapped and shipped to recipients. At the Downtown Plaza in Sacramento, California, mall shoppers were first employed to increase sales during a major construction project which disrupted traffic. The service became so popular that the mall continued it after the project was completed.

Independent personal shoppers make purchases from multiple retailers and are not restricted by location. Creative Resources Inc. is a 20-year-old independent shopping firm that specializes in atypical gifts such as antique toast racks and silver seltzer siphons. Although Creative Resources earns its profit based on a markup, other independent shoppers are often paid on an hourly basis—generally between $35 and $60 an hour.

Sources: Based on material in Christina Duff, "Personal Shoppers Hit the Malls So You Don't Have To," *Wall Street Journal* (December 15, 1993), pp. B1, B6; and Teri Agins, "You Think Your Christmas List Is Long? Try Shopping for 5,000," *Wall Street Journal* (December 15, 1993), pp. B1, B6.

On the other hand, "Suppose you go skiing several times during the winter, and as the ski season is ending, you notice the cuffs on the jacket are a little frayed and you don't think they should be. You call L.L. Bean and tell them about it, feeling somewhat nervous since you've had the jacket for so long. They immediately tell you to return it and that they'll give you your money back or provide a replacement. Needless to say, you're relieved, thrilled, and delighted. You also have no hesitation about ordering from L.L. Bean in the future because you know they'll take care of you."[26]

Planning the appropriate customer-services strategy can be complicated because retailers often face situations such as these:

> At the entrance to Bloomingdale's flagship Manhattan store, the security guard greets customers wearing a button that reads: "Ask me about coat and package check." Inside, shoppers can make free local calls at cash registers. Clerks even help shoppers hail cabs. With gestures like these, department stores are heralding a new era of service in which, they say, the customer is again king.
>
> But tell that to Christopher Nunes, a customer who recently searched in vain for a sales clerk at Bloomingdale's store in White Plains, New York. "They don't have the personnel," says Mr. Nunes, who adds that he felt swamped by an overabundance of merchandise and the busy Christmas decor. Did he use the free coat check? "I'll keep my coat on," he snaps. "I just want to find a clerk who will spend some time to help me."
>
> Service, it seems, is in the eye of the beholder. For department stores, it means a return to some of the customer-coddling amenities that used to be their trademark. Most shoppers, however, are less than dazzled by these feel-good flourishes, which they say can pale before frequent cash-register bottlenecks.[27]

[26] Barry Farber and Joyce Wycoff, "Customer Service: Evolution and Revolution," *Sales & Marketing Management* (May 1991), p. 46.

[27] Teri Agins, "Stores Try to Boost Service—But Cheaply," *Wall Street Journal* (December 16, 1992), p. B1.

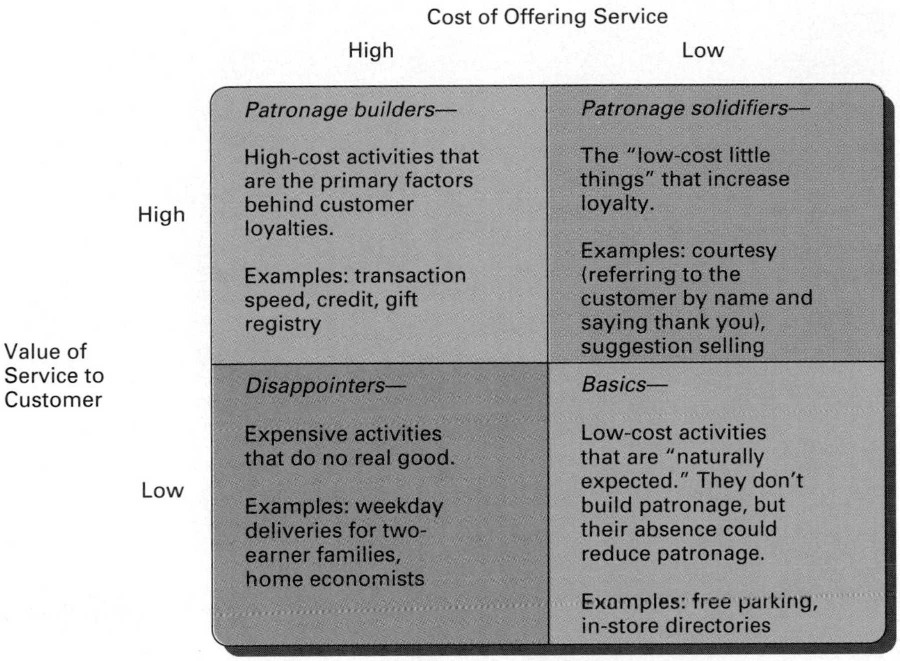

	Cost of Offering Service: High	Cost of Offering Service: Low
Value of Service to Customer: High	*Patronage builders—* High-cost activities that are the primary factors behind customer loyalties. Examples: transaction speed, credit, gift registry	*Patronage solidifiers—* The "low-cost little things" that increase loyalty. Examples: courtesy (referring to the customer by name and saying thank you), suggestion selling
Value of Service to Customer: Low	*Disappointers—* Expensive activities that do no real good. Examples: weekday deliveries for two-earner families, home economists	*Basics—* Low-cost activities that are "naturally expected." They don't build patronage, but their absence could reduce patronage. Examples: free parking, in-store directories

FIGURE 16–10
Classifying Customer Services
Source: Adapted by the authors from Albert D. Bates, "Rethinking the Service Offer," *Retail Isues Letter* (December 1986), p. 3. Reprinted by permission.

To use customer services properly, a firm must first outline an overall service strategy and then plan individual services.[28] Figure 16–10 shows one way a retailer may view customer services.

DEVELOPING A CUSTOMER SERVICES STRATEGY

In developing a customer services strategy, a retailer has to make decisions involving the range, level, choice, price, measurement, and retention of its services.

What services are primary and ancillary for a particular retailer? ***Primary customer services*** are those considered basic ingredients in the retail strategy mix; they must be provided. Examples are credit for a furniture retailer, new-car preparation for an auto dealer, and a liberal return policy for a gift shop. These services form an essential part of those retailers' strategy mixes, and they could not stay in business without them.

Ancillary customer services are extra elements that enhance a retail strategy mix. A retailer could cater to its target market adequately without these services, but using them enhances its competitive standing. Examples are home delivery for a supermarket, an extra warranty for an auto dealer, gift wrapping for a toy store, and credit for a flea market vendor.

It is vital that each retailer determine which customer services are primary and which are ancillary for its own situation. Primary services for one retailer, such as delivery, may be ancillary for another. Remember: Primary services have to be provided; ancillary services are not required but improve a firm's image. See Figure 16–11.

What level of customer services is proper to complement a firm's image? An upscale retailer would define more services as primary than a discounter because consumers expect that retailer to supply a wide range of services as part of its basic strategy mix. This is not true of a discounter. In addition, the performance of services would be different. As an example, customers of an upscale retailer may expect elaborate gift-wrapping facilities, valet parking, a restaurant, and a ladies' room attendant, whereas

[28] See, for example, Patricia Sellers, "Companies That Serve You Best," *Fortune* (May 31, 1993), pp. 74–88; and Marianne Wilson, "Big Hopes for Lil' Things," *Chain Store Age Executive* (January 1994), pp. 55–59.

FIGURE 16–11
Using Customer Services to Enhance a Retailer's Competitive Advantage
Luria's is a Florida-based discount chain that features jewelry, gift items, housewares, home furnishings, and consumer electronics. Yet, despite its discount orientation, the firm offers a number of customer services—including the computerized bridal registry that is highlighted here—to nurture its customers' loyalty.
Reprinted by permission of Luria's.

customers of a discounter may expect cardboard gift boxes, self-service parking, a lunch counter, and an unattended ladies' room. In these instances, the customer service categories are the same; however, the level of the services is not.

Should there be a choice of customer services? Some firms let customers select from among various levels of service; others provide only one level. For instance, a retailer may honor several credit cards or only its own. Trade-ins may be allowed on some items or all. Warranties may have optional extensions or fixed lengths. A retailer may offer one-month, three-month, and six-month payment plans or may insist on a one-month payment period.

Should customer services be free? Two factors are causing a number of retailers to charge for some services: rapidly increasing costs and consumer behavior. Delivery, gift wrapping, and other services are labor intensive, and their costs are steadily rising. Also, it has been found that people are more likely to remain at home for a delivery or a service call if a fee is imposed. Without a fee, retailers may have to attempt a delivery two or three times to find someone at home. In settling on a free or fee-based customer-service strategy, a firm must determine which services are primary (these are often free) and which are ancillary (these could be provided for a fee); competitors and profit margins should be watched closely, and the target market should be studied. In setting fees, a retailer must also decide whether its goal is to break even or to make a profit on the services.

How can a retailer measure the benefits of providing customer services against their costs? The purpose of customer services is to attract and retain consumers, thus maximizing sales and profits. This means that ancillary services should not be offered unless they raise a firm's overall sales and profits. Unfortunately, little research on the benefit-cost ratios of various services has been undertaken. Thus, a retailer should plan ancillary services on the basis of its experience, competitors' actions, and customer comments; and when the costs of providing these services increase, higher prices should be passed on to the consumer.

How can customer services be terminated? Once a retailer establishes an image, consumers are likely to react negatively to any reduction of services. Nonetheless, inefficient and costly ancillary services might have to be discontinued. When dropping customer services, a retailer's best strategy is to be forthright, and to explain why the services are being terminated and how the customer will benefit through lower prices

TABLE 16–1 Typical Customer Services

Credit
Delivery
Alterations and installations
Packaging (gift wrapping)
Complaints and returns handling
Gift certificates
Trade-ins
Trial purchases
Special sales for regular customers
Extended store hours
Mail and telephone orders
Miscellaneous

• Bridal registry	• Rest rooms
• Interior designers	• Restaurant
• Personal shoppers	• Baby-sitting
• Ticket outlets	• Fitting rooms
• Parking	• Beauty salon
• Water fountains	• Fur storage
• Pay telephones	• Shopping bags
• Baby strollers	• Information

and so on. Many times, a retailer may choose a middle ground, charging for previously free services and allowing the customers who want the services to continue to receive them.

As the president of Minnesota's Snyder's Drug Stores recently noted, "Service doesn't bring in the customers, but it keeps them coming back."[29]

PLANNING INDIVIDUAL SERVICES

After a broad customer-service strategy is outlined, individual services are planned. For example, a large department store might offer all of these customer services: gift wrapping, layaway plans, pay telephones, a bridal registry, parking, a restaurant, a women's beauty salon, credit, carpet installation, dressing rooms, clothing alterations, customer rest rooms and sitting areas, the use of baby strollers, home delivery, and fur storage. The range of typical customer services is shown in Table 16–1 and described next.

Today, most retailers allow their customers to make credit purchases. Even supermarkets and fast-food chains—two of the last major holdouts—are now experimenting with credit-card transactions. And almost all retailers accept personal checks with proper identification. Whereas smaller and medium-sized retailers rely on bank cards and companies such as American Express to process purchases made on credit, larger retailers often have their own credit systems and credit cards. In greater numbers, larger retailers have also begun to accept outside credit cards in addition to their own.

Credit's role in retail purchases can be seen through the following:

- Visa, MasterCard, American Express, Carte Blanche, Diners Club, and Discover are just some of the national credit cards accepted by various retailers.

29 Marianne Wilson, "Snyder's Drug: A Twin Cities' Staple," *Chain Store Age Executive* (January 1993), p. 77.

- 40 to 60 per cent of department and specialty store purchases are on credit.
- Consumers' use of credit rises greatly as the amount of a purchase goes up.
- Annually, tens of millions of people use a Sears credit card when shopping at one of the chain's stores.
- Computerization has eased the credit process and made it more efficient, thus encouraging more retailers to accept some form of credit system.

Retailer-generated credit cards have four advantages. One, the retailer saves the sales fee it would have to pay for outside card sales. Two, people are encouraged to shop with a given firm because its card would usually not be accepted elsewhere. Three, contact can be maintained with customers and information learned about them. Four, attractive card design contributes to overall company image. There are also disadvantages to retailer credit cards: startup costs are high, the retailer must worry about unpaid bills and slow cash flow, credit checks and follow-up tasks must be performed, and customers without that retailer's card may be discouraged from making purchases.

Bank and other commercial credit cards enable small and medium-sized retailers to offer credit, generate more business for all types of retailers, appeal to tourists and mobile consumers, provide advertising support from the sponsor, reduce bad debts, eliminate startup costs for the retailer, and provide information. Yet, these cards do charge a service fee per transaction (based on the purchase amount) and do not engender retailer loyalty.

As noted, both types of credit cards enhance the retailer's information capabilities. They provide data on credit sales (such as the size of the average transaction and the merchandise bought), customer demographics (such as place of residence and income), and branch store performance (such as credit versus cash sales by product category).

All bank cards and most retailer cards involve revolving accounts. With a ***revolving credit account***, a customer charges items and is billed monthly on the basis of the outstanding cumulative balance. An ***option credit account*** is a form of revolving account; no interest is assessed if a person pays a bill in full when it is due. See Table 16–2, Example 1. However, should a person make a partial payment, he or she will be assessed interest monthly on the unpaid amount. See Table 16–2, Examples 2 and 3.

The customer receives a credit limit with a revolving account, and his or her total balance cannot exceed this limit. Several states allow retailer and bank credit cards to charge up to 2 or more per cent interest per month (an annual rate of 24 per cent or more) on unpaid balances.

Some credit-card firms (such as American Express) and some retailers may rely more on open credit accounts. With an ***open credit account***, a consumer must pay his or her bill in full when it is due. Partial, revolving payments are not permitted. A person with an open account is also given a credit limit.

Under a ***monthly payment credit account***, the consumer pays for a purchase in equal monthly installments. Interest is usually charged. As an illustration, suppose a person buys a $300 camera and pays for it over 12 months. Equal monthly payments of $27.50 ($25 principal and $2.50 interest) yield a total cost of $330 for the camera. The true interest rate is 18.46 per cent on the average monthly balance.*

Deferred billing lets regular charge customers make purchases and not pay for them for several months, with no interest charge. Deferred billing may be used as a Christmas or other seasonal promotion tool. Customers couid be encouraged to buy in November and December and not pay until March.

A ***layaway plan*** allows any customer to give a retailer a deposit to hold a product. When the customer completes payment, he or she takes the item. In the meantime, the consumer does not have to worry about the store's running out of stock.

* The computation for this is ($30 interest)/[(1/2) ($300 initial principal + $25 last month's principal)] = ($30)/[(1/2)($325)] = ($30)/($162.50) = 18.46 per cent.

TABLE 16–2 How a Revolving Credit Account Works

Example 1: Revolving Account (no interest paid)		
Purchases in June	$100.00	
End-of-month bill		$100.00
Payment		$100.00
Balance due		$ 0.00
Example 2: Revolving Account (interest paid)		
Purchases in June	$100.00	
End-of-month bill		$100.00
Payment		$ 50.00
Balance due		$ 50.00
Purchases in July	$ 0.00	
Balance from June	$ 50.00	
One month's interest (at 1½% per month)	$ 0.75	
Total end-of-month bill		$ 50.75
Payment		$ 50.75
Balance due		$ 0.00
Example 3: Revolving Account (interest paid)		
Purchases in June	$400.00	
End-of-month bill		$400.00
Payment		$100.00
Balance due		$300.00
Purchases in July	$400.00	
Balance from June	$300.00	
Interest on balance	$ 4.50	
Total end-of-month bill		$704.50
Payment		$200.00
Balance due		$504.50
Purchases in August	$ 0.00	
Balance from July	$504.50	
Interest on balance	$ 7.57	
Total end-of-month bill		$512.07
Payment		$512.07
Balance due		$ 0.00

COD (collect on delivery) lets a customer have a product delivered to him or her before paying for it. Payment in full must be made when the merchandise is received. Direct marketers sometimes use COD.

As the preceding indicates, retailers have wide flexibility in choosing a credit strategy. The one that best fits a firm's image, customers, and needs should be selected. Although the trend to credit-card usage continues, some firms (such as a number of gas stations) have moved in the opposite direction and ended credit-card transactions to reduce costs and prices. In the proper setting (such as off-price chains), discounts for cash also seem feasible.

At a firm whose products and/or customers require that items be delivered, there are three considerations in setting up delivery service: the method of transportation, ownership versus rental of equipment, and timing. The shipping method can be car, van, truck, train, boat, mail, and/or plane. The costs and appropriateness of the methods depend on the merchandise involved.

Large retailers often find it economical to own delivery vehicles. This also enables them to advertise their company names, have control over delivery schedules, and have company employees handle deliveries. Small retailers serving limited trading areas may use their own personal vehicles. However, many small, moderate-sized, and even large retailers use a delivery firm such as United Parcel Service or utilize commercial truckers when consumers reside away from a delivery area, transportation is used sporadically, and shipments are not otherwise efficient (because less than full truckloads would be sent).

Last, the timing of deliveries must be planned. A retailer must decide how quickly orders are to be processed and how often deliveries are to be made to different geographic areas. For example, will customers residing in a Baton Rouge, Louisiana, suburb receive deliveries daily, once a week, or monthly?

For certain firms, alterations and installations are primary services and are treated accordingly—though more retailers now charge fees. However, many discounters have stopped offering alterations of clothing and installations of heavy appliances on both a free and a fee basis. They feel that the services are too ancillary to their business and not worth the effort. Other retailers offer only basic alterations: shortening pants, taking in the waist, and lengthening jacket sleeves. They do not adjust jacket shoulders or width. Some appliance retailers may hook up washing machines but not do plumbing work. Various clothing chains have centralized alteration systems to reduce costs.

Within a store, packaging (gift wrapping)—as well as complaints and returns handling—can be centrally located or decentralized. Centralized packaging counters and complaints and returns departments have several advantages: they may be situated in otherwise dead spaces; the main selling areas are not cluttered; specialized personnel can be used; and a common store policy is implemented. The advantages of decentralized facilities are that consumers are not inconvenienced; people are kept in the selling area, where a salesperson may resolve any problems or offer different merchandise; and extra personnel are not required. In either case, a clearly established store policy as to the handling of complaints and returns must be stated. The axiom "The customer is always right" should be followed when possible. Unfortunately, customers are often not convinced this policy is used.

Gift certificates encourage new and existing customers to shop with a given retailer. Many firms require that gift certificates be spent and not redeemed for cash. Customers thus come into contact with the store while shopping. Trade-ins induce new and regular customers to patronize a retailer. People get the feeling of a bargain and an accommodation. Trial purchases let shoppers test products before purchases become final, thus reducing risks. If customers like the products, they are kept and paid for; if customers dislike them, they can be returned. Mail-order retailers often allow trial purchases.

Retailers are increasingly offering special services to regular customers. Special sales, not open to the general public, are run to increase customer loyalty. Extended hours, such as evenings and weekends, are provided. This lengthens in-store shopping time and decreases rushing. Mail and telephone orders placed by regular customers are handled for convenience. All of these tactics give a firm an atmosphere of warmth for its most important customers.

Other useful customer services, some of them discussed previously, include a bridal registry, interior designers, personal shoppers, ticket outlets, free (or low-cost) and plentiful parking, in-store water fountains, pay telephones, baby strollers, rest rooms, a restaurant, baby-sitting, fitting rooms, a beauty salon, fur storage, shopping bags, and in-store information counters. The latter should not be underestimated; confused

ETHICS IN RETAILING

How Can a Small Retailer Carve Out a Societally-Oriented Niche?

The Village Market in Wilton, Connecticut, is an independent supermarket that is owned by Peter Keating. Although many other independents have succumbed to the competition of large supermarket chains, warehouse stores, and membership clubs, The Village Market has been quite successful due to its societally-oriented niche.

The Village Market donates $20,000 per year to local groups, ranging from the Little League to the local Y. It also matches funds that civic groups receive in their fund-raising efforts for items like a Wilton grade school piano and cheerleaders' uniforms. Peter Keating has even coached the local Brownie Troop on how to sell cookies.

The Village Market does not limit its community involvement to just child-oriented programs. For example, it actively promotes the local food bank. During one recent nine-month period, the store collected three tons of food from its customers and employees for the needy. The Village Market also regularly offers free water and free use of its freezers to community residents when local power fails.

As a highly ethical firm, the Village Market expects fair treatment from all of its suppliers. Thus, when a snack-food company regularly cut back on its deliveries, Peter Keating vigorously protested to the firm's president. The delivery problems were resolved shortly thereafter.

Source: Based on material in Andrew H. Malcolm, "Grocer Thrives with Personal Touches," *New York Times* (January 29, 1993), p. B5.

customers are less likely to be satisfied and/or to complete their shopping trips. A retailer's willingness to offer some or all of these services indicates to its customers its concern for them and is a strong contributor to image.

In particular, retailers need to be attentive to consumer needs and consider the impact of excessive self-service. Here are the observations of an executive at one supermarket chain:

> We're doing more self-service. But, by the same token, we do so with caution. It must be done carefully and by neighborhood—not just to make things simple for the home office. You have to have a good balance between service and self-service, depending on the neighborhood.[30]

And at Nordstrom, the award-winning Seattle-based chain:

> Legendary service has been the key to gaining customers in new markets. Salespeople commonly write thank-you notes or make home deliveries to customers. Each store employs a concierge stationed near the entrance to help customers with special requests. Such amenities have won Nordstrom loyalty and affection.[31]

Community Relations

The manner in which retailers interact with the communities around them also has an impact on image—and performance. Firms can enhance their images by actions such as:

- Making sure that stores are barrier-free for disabled shoppers.
- Showing a concern for ecology, such as recycling and clean streets.
- Supporting charities.
- Participating in anti-drug programs.
- Employing area residents.
- Running special sales for senior citizens and other groups.
- Sponsoring Little League and other youth activities.

[30] Mary Ann Linsen, "Service Vs. Self-Service: A Balancing Act," *Progressive Grocer* (November 1993), p. 92.

[31] Dori Jones Yang and Laura Zinn, "Will 'The Nordstrom Way' Travel Well?" *Business Week* (September 3, 1990), p. 83.

- Cooperating with neighborhood planning groups.
- Donating money and/or equipment to schools.

For example, McDonald's sponsors Ronald McDonald Houses worldwide. These are "homes-away-from-home," where families of seriously ill children stay while the children are being treated at nearby hospitals. Hills Department Stores, Kmart, and Wal-Mart are among the numerous retailers participating in some type of "Just Say No" anti-drug program. And Safeway and Giant Food are just two of the many supermarket chains that give money and/or equipment to schools in their neighborhoods.

Since 1990, at Safeway Stores alone, millions of dollars of Apple computer equipment have been donated to more than 2,000 California schools: "We were looking for a community relations project which would have an impact and be very tangible." Even though Safeway has not done research to determine how many customers have been drawn by its program (whereby schools collect Safeway sales receipts from parents and redeem them for free computers, printers, and software), "we believe the program is very worthwhile."[32]

SUMMARY

1. *To show the importance of communicating with customers* Customer communications are necessary for a retailer (store- or nonstore-based) to position itself in customers' minds. Various physical and symbolic cues can be used when communicating.

2. *To examine the concept of retail image* Creating and maintaining the proper image, the way a retailer is perceived by its customers, is an essential aspect of the retail strategy mix. The components of a firm's image are its target-market characteristics, retail positioning, store location, merchandise assortment, price levels, physical facilities, customer services, community service, mass advertising and publicity, personal selling, and sales promotions. Accordingly, a retail image requires a multistep, ongoing process. For chains, it is essential that there be a consistent image among branches.

3. *To describe how a retailer's image is established through the use of atmosphere via its exterior, general interior, layout, and displays* A retailer's image depends heavily on the atmosphere projected. For a store-based retailer, atmosphere is defined as the physical attributes of the store utilized to develop an image and is composed of the exterior, general interior, store layout, and displays. For a nonstore-based firm, the physical attributes of such strategic mix factors as catalogs and vending machines affect its image.

   The store exterior is comprised of its storefront, marquee, entrances, display windows, building height and size, visibility, uniqueness, surrounding stores and area, parking, and congestion. The exterior sets a mood or tone before a prospective customer even enters a store.

   The general interior of a store incorporates its flooring, colors, lighting, scents and sounds, fixtures, wall textures, temperature, width of aisles, dressing facilities, vertical transportation, dead areas, personnel, self-service, merchandise, price displays, cash register placement, technology/modernization, and cleanliness. The interior of an upscale firm would be far different from that of a discounter, portraying the retail image desired, as well as the costs of doing business.

   In laying out a store's interior, six steps are followed. One, floor space is allocated among selling, merchandise, personnel, and customers; and adequate space must be provided for each, based on the firm's overall strategy. More retailers are now using planograms to allocate their store space. Two, product groupings are determined; they could be based on function, purchase motivation, market segment, and/or storability. Three, traffic flows are planned, using a straight or curving pattern. Four, space per product category is computed via a model stock approach or sales-productivity ratio. Five, departments are located. Six, individual products are arranged within departments.

   Interior (point-of-purchase) displays provide information for consumers, add to store atmosphere, and have a promotional role. Interior display possibilities include assortment displays, theme displays, ensemble displays, rack and case displays, cut case and dump bin displays, posters, mobiles, and wall decorations.

[32] Alice Z. Cuneo, "Helping Schools Helps Grocers," *Advertising Age* (September 13, 1993), p. 39.

4. *To consider the impact of customer services and community relations on a retailer's image* Customer services are the identifiable, but mostly intangible, activities offered by a retailer when selling its basic goods and services. When a firm outlines its customer services strategy, several decisions must be made: What services are primary and ancillary? What level is needed to complement the company's image? Should a variety be presented? Should fees be charged? How can service effectiveness be measured? How can unprofitable services be terminated? Customer services include credit, delivery, alterations and installations, packaging, complaints and returns handling, gift certificates, trade-ins, and so on.

When determining a credit strategy, a retailer must decide whether to employ its own credit plan and/or accept outside credit cards. It must also choose which of these tactics to utilize: revolving accounts, option accounts, open accounts, monthly payment accounts, deferred billing, layaway plans, and COD.

Customers are apt to react favorably to retailers that show community interest and involvement in such activities as establishing stores which are barrier-free for disabled persons, supporting charities, and running special sales for senior citizens.

KEY TERMS

image (p. 546)
atmosphere (p. 549)
storefront (p. 550)
marquee (p. 551)
dead areas (p. 556)
selling space (p. 557)
merchandise space (p. 557)
personnel space (p. 557)
customer space (p. 557)
planogram (p. 557)
functional product groupings (p. 557)
purchase-motivation product groupings (p. 557)
market-segment product groupings (p. 558)
storability product groupings (p. 558)
straight (gridiron) traffic flow (p. 558)
curving (free-flowing) traffic flow (p. 558)
model stock approach (p. 559)
sales-productivity ratio (p. 559)
point-of-purchase (POP) display (p. 561)
assortment display (p. 561)
theme-setting display (p. 562)
ensemble display (p. 562)
rack display (p. 562)
case display (p. 563)
cut case (p. 563)
dump bin (p. 563)
customer services (p. 563)
primary customer services (p. 565)
ancillary customer services (p. 565)
revolving credit account (p. 568)
option credit account (p. 568)
open credit account (p. 568)
monthly payment credit account (p. 568)
deferred billing (p. 568)
layaway plan (p. 568)
(COD) collect on delivery (p. 569)

QUESTIONS FOR DISCUSSION

1. Why is it sometimes difficult for a retailer to convey its image to consumers? Give a local example of a retailer with a fuzzy image.
2. How could a restaurant project an upscale retail image? How could a furniture retailer project such an image?
3. Define the concept of *atmosphere*. How does this differ from that of *image*?
4. Which aspects of a store's exterior are controllable by the retailer? Which are uncontrollable?
5. What are the advantages and disadvantages of self-service?
6. How would the following differ for a luxury hotel and a discount motel?
   a. Flooring.
   b. Lighting.
   c. Fixtures.
   d. Personnel.
   e. Level of self-service.
   f. Placement of cash registers.
7. What are meant by selling, merchandise, personnel, and customer space?
8. Present a planogram for your college bookstore.
9. Develop a purchase-motivation product grouping for a gift store.
10. Which stores should not use a free-flowing layout? Explain your answer.
11. Why would a retailer use the sales-productivity ratio instead of the model stock approach when determining space needs? What are the limitations of the sales-productivity ratio?
12. For each of these services, give an example of a retailer that would consider it primary and a retailer that would consider it ancillary.
    a. Delivery.
    b. Credit.
    c. Alterations.
    d. Gift certificates.
    e. Extended store hours.
    f. Personal shoppers.
    g. Parking.
13. Distinguish among revolving, open, and monthly credit accounts. What are the pros and cons of each?
14. Why should a retailer contribute to a charity or pay to sponsor a Little League team?

CASE 1
Harris Teeter Goes for the Gold*

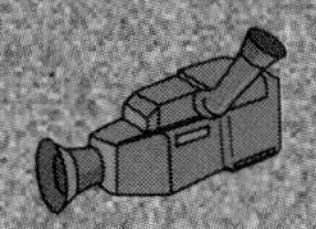

Harris Teeter is a regional chain with over 130 supermarkets. According to one retail analyst, the firm's new $5-million, 60,800-square-foot supermarket (with 43,561 square feet of selling space) in Charlotte, North Carolina, is the chain's biggest and best unit. The store is located in an affluent section of town, a block from a new mall in Morrocroft. The average household income within a two-mile radius of the store is $64,538. Although the store's 1993 weekly sales were $425,000 (its estimated break-even volume), Harris Teeter's management expects the store to have weekly sales of $725,000 when the nearby shopping center is fully rented.

The image projected by the Charlotte store is highly unusual for a supermarket. The store has a brick storefront designed to resemble a Jeffersonian architectural theme. The building's exterior looks more like a library or an office. No sign identifying the store as a Harris Teeter supermarket is visible from the street; and the storefront has no large picture windows. Only a small sign appears in the back of the store, on the side of the parking lot.

The store interior is also unique. Signs and murals help customers better locate each department and give each department a separate identity. For example, the perishables department features large murals with agricultural pictures. The murals are attached to the overhead signs with green lattice. The floral department is located around a fountain, set behind white columns. Signs in the produce department feature buying and preparation tips, as well as each item's price. The sign for cauliflower, for instance, suggests that customers "look for firm white to creamy-white heads."

The "star of the show" is the Charlotte store's deli/bakery department, which has been referred to as "almost like a supermarket Disneyland." A staff of 88 people (including seven full-time chefs, their assistants, and part-time workers) continuously create fresh prepared foods for this department. Of a total menu of 72 prepared foods, 40 are available at a given time. This lets shoppers buy their favorite take-out cuisine, while being able to sample newer dishes. Many of the store's chefs have been hired from local culinary schools. Among the most-popular items are Cajun chicken and lemon garlic chicken (both at $7.99 per pound), stuffed grape leaves (at $5.99 per pound), and seafood lasagna (at $5.49 per pound). Also featured are roasted and fried chicken, sandwiches, store-made pizza, a large selection of crusty breads (such as baguettes), and birthday cakes. All cake assembling and decorating is done on the premises. The deli/bakery even has a large catering business.

Sales in the deli/bakery department are high due to the large number of customers who would rather buy high-quality prepared foods and eat them at home than dine in a restaurant. The many offices and small businesses near the store also contribute to high deli/bakery sales. In total, the deli/bakery department accounts for 14.7 per cent of the store's total sales—versus 4.6 per cent in the average U.S. supermarket.

The labor intensity of the deli/bakery department and its size contribute to the high overall labor expense for the Charlotte store. Its labor expense is 13.5 per cent of sales, double that of other Harris Teeter stores and significantly higher than the 9.2 per cent labor rate among all independents.

Even though customer service and quality products are important to Harris Teeter, so is price. The chain uses a modified form of everyday low pricing (EDLP) in which its standard pricing policy is supplemented with weekly specials on 20 to 30 different items. Bold signs over end-of-aisle displays are used to convey a strong price image. The wording on these signs can easily be changed, based upon whether goods are priced at EDLP or on-sale levels.

Among the other features that contribute to the retail image of Harris Teeter's Charlotte store are these:

- The wine department has an extensive selection, ranging from inexpensive wines to a fine champagne that retails at $249.99 a bottle. This department is staffed by

* The material in this case is drawn from Stephen Bennett, "Best in the East," *Progressive Grocer* (March 1993), pp. 36–43.

a wine expert who is qualified to offer advice on the types of wine and preferred years. It also services shoppers in search of special vintages. The store has a special liquor license that allows shoppers to sample wines on the premises.

- The floral department will make deliveries and accepts phone orders. It has a staff of four full-time floral designers.
- The produce department stores fresh fruit on ice. None of its items are pre-bagged. Fresh-squeezed orange and carrot juice are made in the store to ensure freshness. All fresh-cut fruit is prepared in an open area, in full view of shoppers. This assures consumers that the cut fruit is fresh, ripe, and readied in a sanitary manner.
- The meat and seafood department is exemplary. "Heat and eat" meats, such as honey mustard chicken breasts and chicken kabobs, are regularly featured. A large amount of seafood is air-freighted to assure its freshness; some of the air-freighted seafood comes from China.

See Figure 1 for a visualization of the store's traffic-flow pattern.

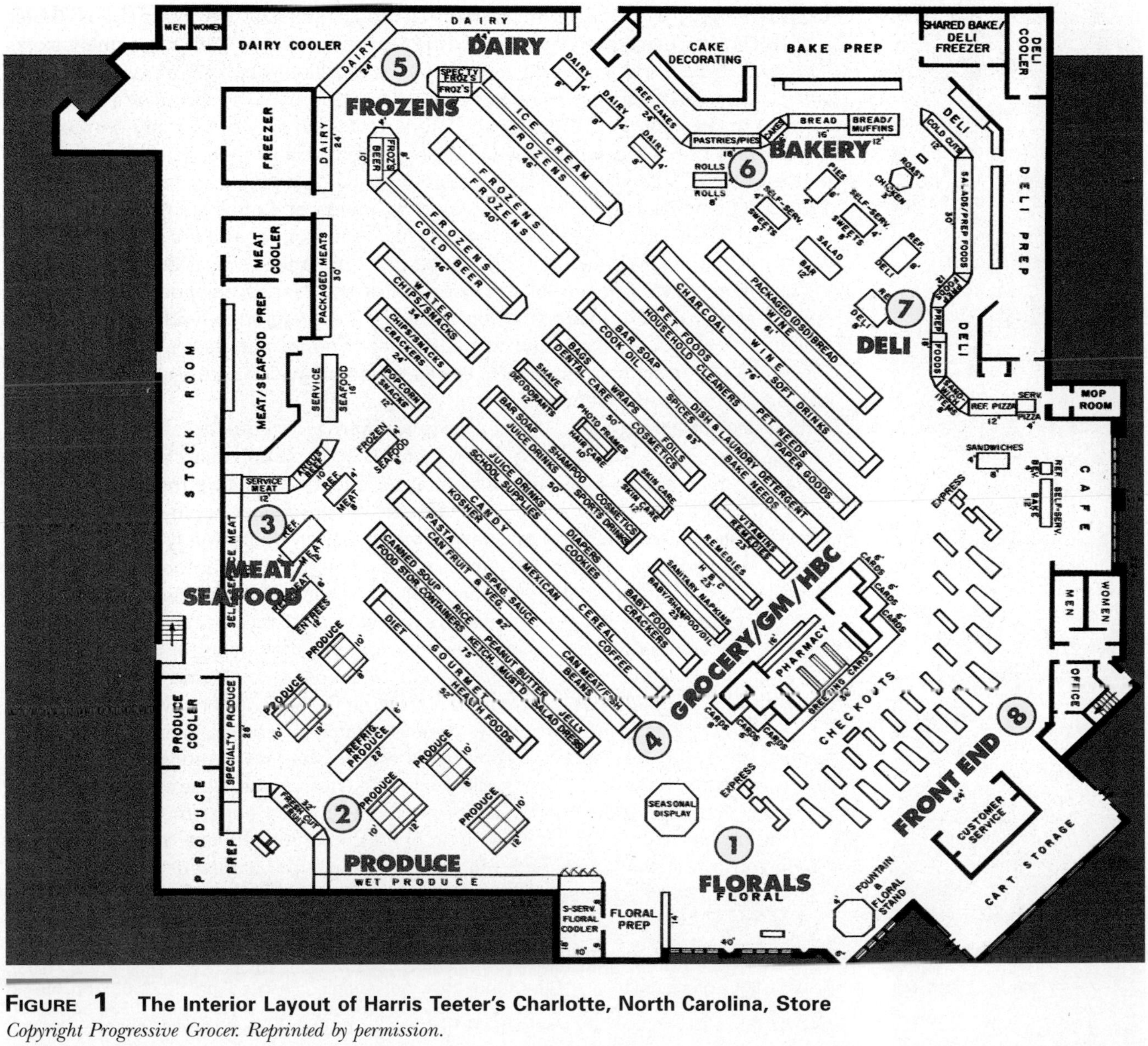

Figure 1 The Interior Layout of Harris Teeter's Charlotte, North Carolina, Store

Copyright Progressive Grocer. Reprinted by permission.

QUESTIONS

1. What are the pros and cons of the Harris Teeter's Charlotte supermarket having such a unique exterior?
2. Describe how the Charlotte store uses functional, purchase motivation, market segment, and storability product groupings.
3. Evaluate the store's traffic-flow pattern.
4. As the owner of a nearby supermarket, how would you compete with Harris Teeter's Charlotte store?

VIDEO QUESTIONS ON HARRIS TEETER

1. How can Harris Teeter develop a price image while selling labor-intensive gourmet foods?
2. What factors enable the Charlotte store to be more profitable than other Harris Teeter units?

CASE 2
J.C. Penney: Customer Service†

J.C. Penney is the fourth-largest general-merchandise retailer in the United States (after Wal-Mart, Kmart, and Sears). The firm operates over 1,300 department stores and 500+ Thrift Drug and Treasury Drug Stores throughout the United States and Puerto Rico. Catalog sales make up about 17 per cent of the company's total sales.

Until the mid-1970s, J.C. Penney offered goods and services largely on the basis of function, price, and reliability—rather than fashion and style. The firm closed its major appliance, lawn and garden, automotive, hardware, and paint departments in 1983 and its home electronics, major sporting-goods, and photography departments in 1988 so that it could emphasize women's and men's apparel lines. The lines that were dropped had represented over 30 per cent of Penney's overall sales.

To effectively implement its soft-goods strategy, Penney has spent $1 billion on store renovations. For example, interiors have been upgraded, with drab floors replaced with quarry tiles, wooden parquet, and carpeting; and glass-partioned display cases have been set up. In addition, stores now have wider aisles, a more open layout, and escalator wells topped with skylights.

Penney has also stepped up its efforts to improve the quality of its moderately-priced merchandise, recognizing that two-thirds of its current sales are derived from private brands. It has increased the number of quality inspectors from 20 in 1990 to 200 today. These inspectors audit the factories that produce Penney's merchandise, rank suppliers for quality, and evaluate competitors' products. Many of Penney's private brands, such as its Stafford men's suit line and its Worthington brand of women's suits, have national recognition, as well as a positive image. These brands have among the largest market shares of men's and women's suits. At the same time, Penney has placed greater focus on such highly-regarded manufacturer brands as Dockers, Bali, and Health-Tex. A recent marketing research study found that close to 50 per cent of consumers believe that J.C. Penney has changed for the better.

J.C. Penney is working hard to improve customer service by having special training programs for its sales associates. There are several reasons for the firm's added focus on customer service. One, high levels of customer service are needed to reinforce J.C. Penney's transition to a more fashion-oriented department store. Unlike discounters that rely on self-service merchandising, Penney wants to stress the advice given by its sales staff. Two, high levels of customer service lead to cross selling, by which sales associates recommend related purchases. Effective cross selling

† The material in this case is drawn from Gary Hoover, Alta Campbell, and Patrick J. Spain (Editors), *Hoover's Handbook of American Business 1994* (Austin, Texas: Reference Press, 1993), pp. 864–865; Zina Moukhiber, "Our Competitive Advantage," *Forbes* (April 12, 1993), pp. 59–62; Marianne Wilson, "J.C. Penney's New Look," *Chain Store Age Executive* (June 1993), pp. 70–71; and Wendy Zellner, "Penney's Rediscovers Its Calling," *Business Week* (April 5, 1993) pp. 51–52.

Table 1 J.C. Penney's Customer-Service Suggestions for Sales Associates

1. Greet the customer to make him or her feel welcome. This sets the tone for the customer's visit to your department.
2. Listen to customers to determine their needs.
3. Know your merchandise. For example, describe the quality features of Penney's private-brand merchandise.
4. Know merchandise in related departments, as well. This can increase sales, as well as lessen a customer's shopping time.
5. Learn to juggle several shoppers at once.
6. Pack the customer's merchandise carefully. Ask if the customer would want the merchandise on a hanger to prevent creasing.
7. Constantly work at keeping the department looking its best.
8. Refer to the customer by his or her name; this can be gotten from the customer's credit card.
9. J.C. Penney stresses a "hassle-free" return policy.

increases the average sales transaction. Three, improved customer service can result in sales associates "saving the sale," by suggesting that a customer who is returning a given item try a different color, style, or quality level. Four, improved customer service can lead to greater customer loyalty to Penney. See Table 1 for a listing of customer-service suggestions that Penney has made to salespeople.

Penney is also seeking to improve customer service via a more thoughtful department design. For example, the new prototype design for its bed and window covering department features a made-to-measure area and a sit-down area where customers can comfortably browse through sample books. A redesigned service counter offers semiprivate sit-down areas for catalog ordering and for discussions with Penney credit counselors.

Despite its new fashion focus, the renovated interiors, and the greater attention to customer service, some problems persist at Penney. One, in 1992, its sales per square foot were estimated at $118; this was significantly less than for Nordstrom ($372), May ($189), Mercantile ($172), and Dillard's ($142). Two, Penney still lacks many important national brands that are needed to attract and keep the more affluent shopper that Penney desires. For instance, although the firm carries some upscale cosmetics lines (such as Ultima II and Charles of the Ritz), Elizabeth Arden and Esteé Lauder will not sell to it. Liz Claiborne and Leslie Fay, makers of women's wear, will also not sell to Penney. Three, Sears—a once-dormant competitor—has begun to emerge more along the lines of Penney's strategy.

QUESTIONS

1. Has J.C. Penney's repositioning made its customer-service strategy more or less difficult to implement? Explain your answer.
2. Differentiate between primary and ancillary customer services for J.C. Penney.
3. Develop a list of the customer services offered by J.C. Penney based upon a visit to a nearby store. Comment on your experience.
4. Classify customer services offered by J.C. Penney using the patronage builder, patronage solidifier, disappointer, and basics grid described in Figure 16–10.

VIDEO QUESTIONS ON J.C. PENNEY

1. Evaluate the nine suggestions for improved customer service in Table 1.
2. How can J.C. Penney's sales associates be effectively trained in implementing these suggestions?

CHAPTER 17

Promotional Strategy

RM

❖ Chapter Objectives

1. To explore the scope of retail promotion
2. To study the elements of retail promotion: advertising, publicity, personal selling, and sales promotion
3. To discuss the strategic aspects of retail promotion: objectives, budgeting, the mix of forms, implementing the mix, and reviewing and revising the plan

In a heavily-quoted 1992 telecast, ABC's *Prime Time Live* charged that the Food Lion supermarket chain knowingly sold bad meat that was altered to appear fresh, and that it relabeled outdated meats. Within weeks of the telecast, Food Lion's same-store sales dropped by 9.5 per cent. The decline in sales and profits also forced the firm to reduce its expansion plans for 1993.

According to Food Lion, ABC was "unfair and inaccurate." First, the telecast did not mention that sanitation ratings had placed Food Lion among the top three supermarkets in every state that it operated. Second, the firm had a video clip that was not aired on *Prime Time Live*, which showed an employee discarding chicken soaked in a marinade. Third, Food Lion believed the charges were initiated by the United Food and Commercial Workers Union (UFCW), which had unsuccessfully tried to organize the firm's workers—as well as by disgruntled current and former employees.

Because of the *Prime Time Live* report, Food Lion spent "thousands of dollars and hours" reviewing its operating policies and inspecting its stores. It also spent many days reviewing the unedited videotape taken by ABC. This tape was obtained via a lawsuit against ABC.

In an effort to improve its image, Food Lion enacted a number of measures:

- It hired an outside advertising agency, the first in its history, in 1993. The agency devised a campaign that highlighted the firm's product quality.
- It began an "open tour" program—by which shoppers, media representatives, and members of Congress could view the food-preparation and handling areas to judge first-hand the cleanliness and quality of meats and fish.
- In new stores, it has windows to let shoppers see the meat-cutting area. Glass doors have been installed in renovated stores.
- It will no longer sell wholesome meat at a reduced price that is even one day past its expiration date.
- It filed a lawsuit against *Prime Time Live* and others involved in the production and distribution of the program.[1]

[1] *Food Lion 1992 Annual Report*; Michael Garry, "The Lion Talks," *Progressive Grocer* (June 1993), p. 19; and Gary Hoover, Alta Campbell, and Patrick J. Spain (Editors), *Hoover's Handbook of American Business 1994* (Austin, Texas: Reference Press, 1993), pp. 518–519.

Reprinted by permission of Food Lion.

Overview

Retail promotion is broadly defined as any communication by a retailer that informs, persuades, and/or reminds the target market about any aspect of that retailer. This chapter deals with developing a promotional strategy. In the first part of the chapter, promotion elements (advertising, publicity, personal selling, and sales promotion) are detailed. The second part centers on the strategic aspects of promotion: objectives, budget, mix of forms, implementation of mix, and review and revision of the plan.

Elements of the Retail Promotional Mix

Advertising, publicity, personal selling, and sales promotion are the four elements of promotion. Each is discussed here in terms of goals, advantages and disadvantages, and basic forms. Although these elements are described individually, a good promotional plan normally integrates them—based on the overall strategy of the retailer. A movie theater would concentrate more on advertising and sales promotion (point-of-purchase displays to prompt food and beverage sales) and would have less emphasis on personal selling and publicity. An upscale independent specialty store would stress personal selling, with less emphasis on advertising, publicity, and sales promotion.

Retailers spend significant sums on their promotion efforts. For example, in a typical department store, about 2.5 per cent of sales is spent on advertising and 8 to 10 per cent on personal selling.[2] In addition, most department-store chains invest heavily in sales promotions (such as special events) and employ internal or external public relations offices to generate favorable publicity and respond to media requests for information.

ADVERTISING

Advertising is any paid, nonpersonal communication transmitted through out-of-store mass media by an identified sponsor. Four aspects of this definition merit further clarification:

1. Paid form—This distinguishes advertising from publicity, for which no payment is made by the retailer for the time or space used to convey a message.
2. Nonpersonal presentation—In advertising, a standard message is delivered to the entire audience, and it cannot be adapted to individual customers.
3. Out-of-store mass media—These media include newspaper, radio, television, and other mass communication channels, rather than personal contacts. In-store communications (such as displays and radio announcements) are considered sales promotion.
4. Identified sponsor—Advertising clearly divulges the name of the sponsor, unlike publicity.

Sears annually has the highest dollar advertising expenditures among U.S. retailers—over $1 billion. About 2.3 per cent of its U.S. sales is spent on ads. In contrast, many other firms have higher advertising-to-sales ratios, despite lower dollar spending; these include McDonald's (5.6 per cent of systemwide sales) and Tandy Corporation, the parent of Radio Shack (5.0 per cent). Tandy even has its own in-house ad agency. On the other hand, Wal-Mart spends just 0.3 per cent of its sales on advertising. It relies more on word of mouth and its everyday low pricing strategy.[3] Table 17–1 shows 1992 advertising-to-sales ratios for a number of retailing categories.

[2] Schonfeld & Associates, "Advertising-to-Sales Ratios, 1993," *Advertising Age* (July 26, 1993), p. 27; and David P. Schulz, "MOR: Kidswear Gets 'A'," *Stores* (October 1990), p. 19.

[3] "100 Leading National Advertisers," *Advertising Age* (September 29, 1993), various pages.

TABLE 17–1 Selected U.S. Advertising-to-Sales Ratios by Type of Retailer

Type of Retailer	Advertising Dollars as Percentage of Sales Dollars[a]	Advertising Dollars as Percentage of Margin[b]
Apparel and accessories stores	2.4	6.1
Auto and home supply stores	1.4	4.7
Department stores	2.5	11.1
Drug and proprietary stores	1.5	5.4
Eating places	3.4	17.0
Family clothing stores	2.4	7.3
Furniture stores	6.5	13.5
Grocery stores	1.2	5.0
Hobby, game, and toy shops	1.3	4.1
Hotels/motels	3.5	12.5
Lumber and building materials	1.2	4.7
Mail-order firms	6.5	17.6
Movie theaters	5.7	9.0
Photofinishing labs	4.0	11.4
Radio, television, and consumer electronics stores	4.1	18.3
Record and tape stores	13.8	29.2
Shoe stores	3.7	9.6
Variety stores	1.6	6.9

[a] Advertising dollars as percentage of sales = Advertising expenditures/Net company sales

[b] Advertising dollars as percentage of margin = Advertising expenditures/(Net company sales − Cost of goods sold)

Source: Schonfeld & Associates, "Advertising-to-Sales Ratios, 1993," *Advertising Age* (July 26, 1993), p. 27. Reprinted by permission. Copyright Crain Communications Inc.

Differences Between Retailer and Manufacturer Advertising Strategies

Although the definition given applies to all advertising, it is important to examine some of the key differences between retailer and manufacturer advertising strategies. First, retailers usually have more geographically concentrated target markets than manufacturers. This means a retailer can adapt better to local needs, habits, and preferences than can a manufacturer. However, a retailer typically is not able to utilize national media as readily as a manufacturer. For example, only the largest retail chains and franchises can advertise on national TV programs. An exception is direct marketing because trading areas for even small firms can be geographically dispersed.

Second, retail advertising emphasizes immediacy. Individual items are placed for sale and advertised during specific, short time periods. Timely purchases are sought. In contrast, manufacturers are more often concerned with developing a favorable attitude toward a product or the company and not with short-run sales increases.

Third, many retailers stress prices in ads, whereas manufacturers usually emphasize several attributes of a product. In addition, many retailers display a number of different products in one advertisement, whereas manufacturers tend to minimize the number of products mentioned in a single ad.

Fourth, media rates are often lower for retailers than for manufacturers. Because of this factor and the desire of many manufacturers and wholesalers for wide distribution, the costs of retail advertising are sometimes shared by a manufacturer or wholesaler and a retailer. Two or more retailers may also share costs. This is known as ***cooperative advertising.***

Objectives

Retail advertising may be based on a wide variety of specific goals, including

- Short-term sales increases.
- Increases in customer traffic.
- Developing and/or reinforcing a retail image. See Figure 17–1.
- Informing customers about goods and services and/or company attributes.
- Easing the job for sales personnel.
- Developing demand for private brands.

A retailer would select one or more of these goals and base advertising efforts on it (them).

Advantages and Disadvantages

The major advantages of advertising are that

1. A large audience is attracted. Also, for print media, circulation is supplemented by the passing of a copy from one reader to another.
2. The costs per viewer, reader, or listener are low.
3. A large number of alternative media are available. Therefore, a retailer can match a medium to the target market.
4. The retailer has control over message content, graphics, timing, and size (or length), so a standardized message in a chosen format can be delivered to the entire audience.
5. In print media, a message can be studied and restudied by the target market.
6. Editorial content (a TV show, a news story, and so on) often surrounds an ad. This may increase its credibility or the probability it will be viewed or heard.
7. Since a customer can become aware of a retailer and its goods and services before shopping, self-service or reduced-service operations are possible.

FIGURE 17–1
Using Advertising to Project an Image
This ad is sponsored by Merry-Go-Round Enterprises.
Reprinted by permission.

RETAILING IN ACTION

1-800-Mattres?

Dial-A-Mattress uses a direct-marketing approach to sell mattresses via radio and television commercials. It also has several retail stores. The firm generates annual sales of about $40 million with its combined strategy.

Although Dial-A-Mattress' prices are often up to 60 per cent less than those at department stores, most retailing analysts view the firm's two-hour delivery time (from the time an order is placed) to be its most important competitive advantage. Although the firm's telemarketing operation is in New York, it has retail stores in Boston, Philadelphia, Chicago, San Francisco, San Jose, and Washington, D.C. Each location has a sufficient inventory and trucks to offer two-hour deliveries—day or evening, weekends, and holidays.

Consumers who call the firm's toll-free number (1-800-MATTRES) reach one of its 50 telemarketers. These employees are specially trained to provide brand and model suggestions, based upon consumer preferences, and to arrange for delivery.

A key Dial-A-Mattress sales promotion involves the eight $20 coupons that are included with each delivered mattress. The coupons provide $20 off any new mattress bought by a referred prospect, as well as a $20 payment to the referring customer. One-third of all new mattress sales result from this sales promotion.

Source: Based on material in "Barragan Family Sleeps Well At Night," *Direct Marketing* (October 1993), pp. 52–57.

The major disadvantages of advertising are that

1. Because a message is standardized, it is inflexible. The retailer is unable to focus on the needs of individual customers.
2. Some types of advertising require large investments. This may eliminate the access of small retailers to certain media (such as television).
3. Many media appeal to large geographic areas, and for retailers, waste may occur. For instance, a small supermarket chain may find that only 40 per cent of a newspaper's readers reside within its trading area.
4. Some media require an extremely long lead time for placing ads. This reduces a retailer's ability to advertise fad items or to react to some current-events themes.
5. Some media have a high throwaway rate. For instance, circulars and mail ads are often discarded without being read.
6. Ads must be brief. For example, a 30-second TV commercial or quarter-page newspaper advertisement cannot contain much information.

These are broad generalities about the entire field of advertising. The pros and cons of specific media are described in the following section.

Media

A retailer can choose from among newspapers, telephone directories, direct mail, radio, television, transit, outdoor, magazines, and flyers/circulars. A summary of the attributes of these media appears in Table 17–2.

Retailers annually spend billions of dollars on media advertising. For instance, each year, they spend about $20 billion on newspaper ads. According to one survey of traditional and discount department stores, specialty stores, home furnishings stores, and home/housewares stores, those firms spend an average of 55 per cent of their ad budgets on newspapers, 15 per cent on direct mail, 11 per cent on TV, 9 per cent on radio, 5 per cent on magazines, and 5 per cent on other media. *Progressive Grocer* has reported that 83 per cent of independent supermarkets advertise in newspapers, 53 per cent use radio, 22 per cent use TV, and 17 per cent use outdoor.[4]

[4] Estimated by the authors from Newspaper Advertising Bureau, "Retail Advertising in Newspapers," *New York Times* (January 15, 1990), p. D6; Retail Advertising Conference, "Where the Dollars Will Go," *Advertising Age* (February 6, 1989), p. 57; and "Circulars' Strength Grows Slowly," *Progressive Grocer* (April 1991), p. 29.

TABLE 17–2 Advertising Media Comparison Chart

Medium	Market Coverage	Particular Suitability	Major Advantages	Major Disadvantages
Daily newspaper	Single community or entire metro area; local editions may be available.	All larger retailers.	Wide circulation, short lead time.	Nonselective audience, heavy ad competition.
Weekly newspaper	Single community usually; maybe a metro area.	Retailers with a strictly local market.	Targeted readers, local identification.	Limited audience, little ad creativity.
Shopper papers	Most households in one community; chain shoppers can cover a metro area.	Neighborhood retailers and service businesses.	Targeted readers, low costs.	Small audience, a giveaway and not always read.
Telephone directories	Geographic area or occupational field served by the directory.	All types of goods- and service-oriented retailers.	Attract consumers who are ready to shop or purchase, permanent message.	Limited to active shoppers, long lead time needed.
Direct mail	Controlled by the retailer.	New and expanding firms, those using coupons or special offers, mail order.	Targeted readers, personalized and aimed at good prospects, can be tied to data base.	High throwaway rate, low image to many consumers.
Radio	Definable market area surrounding the station's location.	Retailers focusing on identifiable segments.	Relatively low costs, good market coverage.	No visual effect, must be used regularly to be of value.
Television	Definable market area surrounding the station's location.	Retailers of goods and services with wide appeal.	Dramatic impact, wide market coverage.	High cost of time and production, audience waste.
Transit	Urban or metro community served by transit system.	Retailers near transit routes, especially those appealing to commuters.	Targeted audience, repetition and length of exposure.	Clutter of ads, distracted or uninterested audience.
Outdoor	Entire metro area or single neighborhood.	Amusement and tourist-oriented retailers, well-known firms.	Dominant size, frequency of exposure.	Clutter of ads, distracted or uninterested audience.
Local magazine	Entire metro area or region; zoned editions sometimes available.	Restaurants, entertainment-oriented firms, specialty shops, mail-order firms.	Special-interest audience, creative options.	Long lead time, less sense of immediacy.
Flyers/circulars	Single neighborhood.	Restaurants, dry cleaners, service stations, and other neighborhood firms.	Very targeted audience, low costs.	High throwaway rate, poor image.

Newspapers can be classified as dailies, weeklies, and shoppers. As just noted, among retailers, the newspaper is the most preferred medium, having the advantages of market coverage, short lead time, reasonable costs, flexibility, longevity, graphics, and editorial association (ads next to columns or articles). Disadvantages include the possible waste (circulation to a wider geographic area than that containing the target market), the competition among retailers, the black-and-white format, and an appeal to fewer senses than television. To maintain their dominant position, many papers have redesigned their graphics, and some have begun running a limited number of color ads. Free-distribution shopper papers (also known as "penny savers")—delivered to all consumer households in a geographic area—are growing in use, sometimes at the expense of other types of newspapers.

Telephone directories (the White and Yellow Pages) are key advertising media. In the White Pages, a retailer receives a free alphabetical listing along with all other telephone subscribers, commercial and noncommercial. The major advantage of the White over the Yellow Pages is that a customer who is familiar with the retailer's name is not distracted by seeing competitors' names. The major disadvantage, in contrast with the Yellow Pages, is the alphabetical rather than type-of-business listing. For example, a customer unfamiliar with repair services in his or her area will usually look in the Yellow Pages under "Repair" and choose a firm that is listed.

In the Yellow Pages, a retailer pays for an alphabetical listing (and a larger display ad, if desired) in its business category. The overwhelming majority of retailers advertise in the Yellow Pages. The advantages include the widespread usage by people who are ready to shop or purchase and the long life (one year or more). The disadvantages are that retailer awareness is not stimulated and there is a long lead time for new ads. As a result of the breakup of AT&T, retailers now have multiple Yellow Pages firms vying for their business—sometimes at lower rates.

Direct mail is the medium whereby a retailer sends customers catalogs or advertisements via the U.S. mail. Some of its advantages are a targeted audience, a tailor-made format, controlled costs, quick feedback, and potential tie-ins (for example, a retailer with its own credit card can mail advertisements with the monthly billing statements). Computerized data bases have greatly improved the efficiency of direct-mail advertising. Among the disadvantages of direct mail are a high throwaway rate ("junk mail"), a poor image to some consumers, a low response rate, and outdated mailing lists (addressees may have moved).

Radio is used by a variety of retailers. Key advantages are its relatively low costs, its importance as a medium for car drivers and riders, its ability to use segmentation, its rather short lead time, and its wide reach. Key disadvantages include no visual impact, the need for repetition, the need for brevity, and waste. The use of radio by retailers has gone up in recent years.

Television, although increasing in importance because of the rise of national and regional firms, is far behind newspapers in retail advertising expenditures. Among the advantages of television are the dramatic effects of video messages, the large market, the creativity, and the program affiliation (for regular sponsors). Disadvantages of television include the high minimum costs, the audience waste, the need for brevity, the need for repetition, and the limited availability of time slots for nonregular sponsors.

Transit advertising is used by retailers in areas with mass-transit systems. Ads are displayed on buses and in subway cars and taxis. These ads have the advantages of a captive audience, a mass market, a high level of repetitiveness, and a geographically defined market. Disadvantages include the clutter of ads, a distracted or uninterested audience, a lack of availability in smaller areas, restricted travel paths, and graffiti. Besides the transit ads already mentioned, retailers often advertise on their delivery trucks.

Outdoor or billboard advertising is sometimes used by retailers. Posters and signs may be displayed in public places, on buildings, and alongside highways. Advantages are the large size of the ads, the frequency of exposure, the relatively low costs, and the assistance in directing new customers. Disadvantages include the clutter of ads, a distracted or uninterested audience, the limited information, and some legislation banning outdoor ads.

Magazines are growing more important for retailers due to three factors: the rise in national and regional retailers, the creation of regional and local editions, and the use by mail-order firms. Advantages of magazines are their tailoring to specific markets, creative options, editorial associations, the longevity of messages, and the use of color. Among the disadvantages are the long lead time, less sense of consumer urgency, and waste.

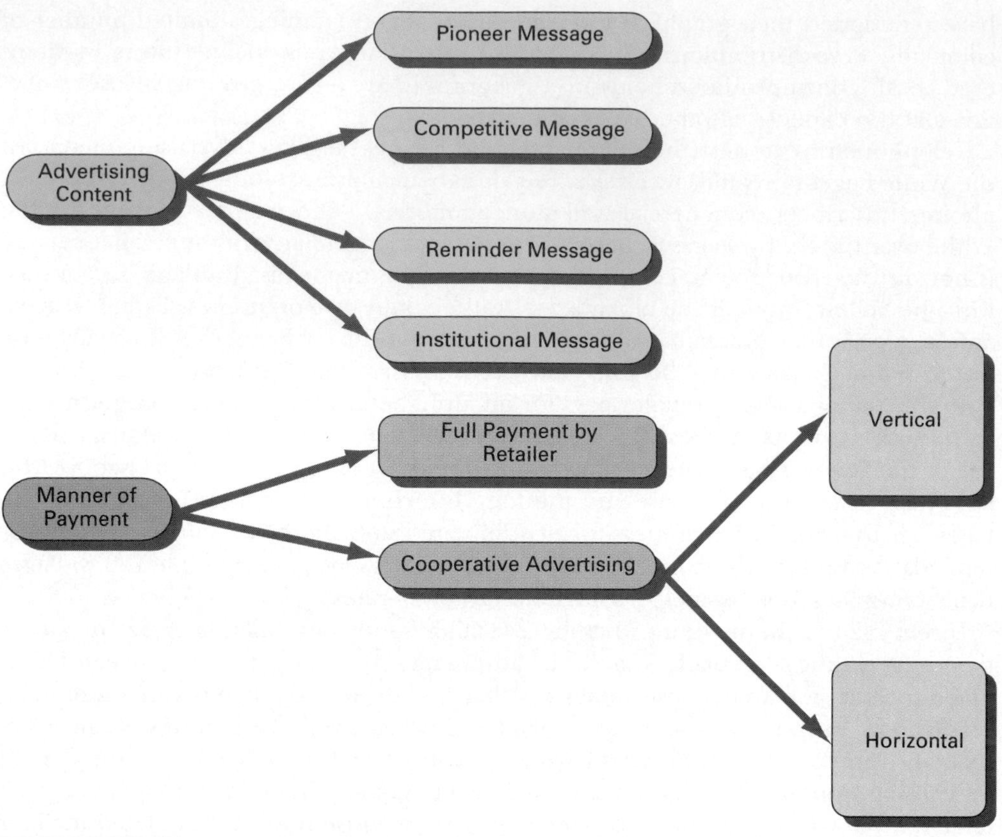

FIGURE 17–2 Types of Advertising

Flyers/circulars are also a significant advertising medium. Single-page (flyers) or multiple-page (circulars) ads can be distributed in parking lots or right to consumer homes. Advantages include a very targeted audience, low costs, flexibility, and speed. Among the disadvantages are the high level of throwaways, the poor image to some consumers, and clutter. Flyers are good for smaller retailers, while circulars are used by larger ones.

Types

Advertisements can be classed by content and payment method. See Figure 17–2.

An ad may be pioneering, competitive, reminder, or institutional. A ***pioneer advertisement*** has awareness as a goal and offers information (usually on a new firm or location). A ***competitive advertisement*** has persuasion as a goal. A ***reminder advertisement*** is geared to loyal customers and emphasizes the attributes that have made a retailer successful. An ***institutional advertisement*** strives to keep the retailer's name before the public without emphasizing the sale of goods or services. Public service messages (such as sponsorship of a telethon or a Little League team) are institutional in nature.

When placing ads, a retailer may pay its own way and/or seek cooperative ventures. For the retailer that pays its own way, the major advantages are control and flexibility. The major disadvantages are the costs and efforts required. A cooperative venture is one where two or more parties share the costs and the decision making. It is estimated that more than $10 billion is spent annually on U.S. cooperative advertising, most via vertical agreements. Newspapers are much preferred over other media for cooperative ads.[5]

[5] Julie S. Newhall, "The Care and Feeding of a Cash Cow," *Sales & Marketing Management* (May 1992), pp. 40–47. See also Mark Vogel and Walter J. Fiorentini, "Redefining Co-Op," *Sales & Marketing Management* (May 1993), pp. 63–65; and Sydney Roslow, Henry A. Laskey, and J. A. F. Nicholls, "The Enigma of Cooperative Advertising," *Journal of Business & Industrial Marketing*, Vol. 8 (Number 2, 1993), pp. 70–79.

In a ***vertical cooperative-advertising agreement***, a manufacturer and a retailer or a wholesaler and a retailer share an ad. Each party's duties and responsibilities are usually specified contractually. Retailers are typically not reimbursed until after ads are run and invoices are provided to the manufacturer or the wholesaler. Vertical cooperative advertising is subject to the Robinson-Patman Act; manufacturers and other suppliers must offer similar arrangements to all retailers on a proportional basis. The advantages of a vertical agreement to a retailer are its reduced ad costs, the assistance in preparing advertisements, greater coverage of the market, and less expenditure of the retailer's time. Disadvantages to a retailer include less control, flexibility, and distinctiveness. Some retailers have been concerned about the requirements they must satisfy to be eligible for support and the emphasis on the supplier's name in ads. Manufacturers and other suppliers are responding by being more flexible and understanding of their retailers' concerns. For instance, in the American Express cooperative program, restaurants can choose from among dozens of border designs and copy blocks (which can be tailored to a wide variety of cuisines). Restaurants can also insert their own logos and add other copy.

With a ***horizontal cooperative-advertising agreement***, two or more retailers—usually small, situated together in a shopping center, or franchisees of the same franchising company—share an ad. The advantages and disadvantages are similar to those in a vertical agreement. A further benefit is the increased bargaining power of retailers in dealing with the media.

While planning a cooperative advertising strategy, a retailer should consider such questions as these:

- What ads qualify, in terms of merchandise and special requirements?
- What percentage of advertising is paid by each party?
- When can advertisements be run?
- What media can be used?
- Are there special provisions regarding message content?
- What documentation is required for reimbursement?
- How does each party benefit?
- Do cooperative advertisements obscure the image of the individual retailer?

PUBLICITY

Publicity is any nonpersonal communication transmitted through mass media where the time or space provided by the media is not paid for and where there is no identified commercial sponsor.

The basic distinction between advertising and publicity is the nonpaid nature of the latter. Because of this difference, publicity messages are not as readily controllable by a retailer. For example, a story about a new store opening may not appear at all, appear after the fact, or not appear in the form desired. Yet, to consumers, publicity is often deemed more credible and important than ads. Thus, advertising and publicity should be complements, not substitutes, for each other. Many times, publicity could precede advertising.

Objectives

Retail publicity seeks to accomplish one or more of these goals:

- To increase awareness of the retailer and its goods and services.
- To maintain or improve a company's image.
- To show the retailer as a contributor to the public's quality of life.

- To demonstrate innovativeness.
- To present a favorable message in a highly believable manner.
- To minimize total promotion costs.

Advantages and Disadvantages

The major advantages of publicity are that

1. An image can be presented or enhanced.
2. An objective source presents the message for the retailer, providing credibility (e.g., a good review of a restaurant).
3. There are no costs for the message's time or space.
4. A mass audience is addressed.
5. Carryover effects are possible (for example, if a store is perceived as community-oriented, the products it carries would be viewed as good).
6. People pay more attention to news stories than to clearly identified ads.

The major disadvantages of publicity are that

1. There is little retailer control over the message, its timing, its placement, and its coverage by a given medium.
2. It is difficult to plan in advance and is more suitable in short-run, rather than long-run, planning.
3. Although there are no media costs, there are often costs for a public relations staff, planning activities, and the activities themselves (such as parades and store openings).

Types

The publicity that a retailer receives can be categorized as expected or unexpected, and favorable or unfavorable.

Expected publicity occurs when a retailer plans activities in advance and strives to have the media report on them, or anticipates that certain events will result in media coverage. Community services, such as donations and special sales; parades on holidays (such as the Macy's Thanksgiving Day Parade); the sales of new goods and services; and the opening of a new store are all activities that a retailer hopes will receive media coverage. The release of quarterly sales figures and publication of the annual report are events that a retailer can anticipate will be covered by the media.

Unexpected publicity takes place when the media report on the retailer's performance without the firm's having advance notice of the coverage. TV and newspaper reporters may visit restaurants and other retailers anonymously, and rate their performance and quality. A fire, robbery, or other newsworthy event may be cited. Investigative stories about company practices may appear.

There is positive publicity when the media report on the firm in a favorable manner, with regard to the excellent nature of its retailing practices, its efforts on behalf of its community, and so on. However, the media may also provide negative publicity about a firm. For instance, with a store opening, the media could describe the location in less than glowing terms, criticize the store's effects on the environment, and otherwise be critical. The retailer has no control over the message; and the media may not cover this or any other publicity event. Accordingly, publicity must be viewed as a component of the promotion mix, not as the whole mix.

PERSONAL SELLING

Personal selling involves oral communication with one or more prospective consumers for the purpose of making sales.

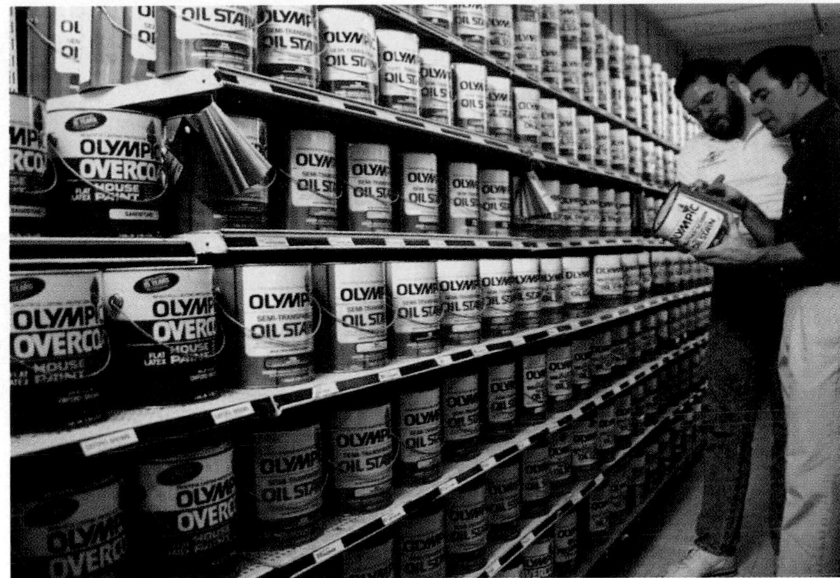

FIGURE 17–3
Personal Selling and Customer Service
Like many retailers, the P.M. home center in Aliquippa, Pennsylvania, which is highlighted here, realizes that personal selling is a key component of customer service.
Reprinted by permission of PPG Industries.

Objectives

Among the goals of personal selling are to

- Persuade customers to make purchases because they often enter a store after acquiring some information through advertising.
- Stimulate sales of impulse items or products related to consumers' basic purchases.
- Complete transactions with consumers.
- Create awareness of items marketed via in-home selling and telemarketing.
- Feed back information to company personnel.
- Provide adequate levels of customer service. See Figure 17–3.
- Improve and maintain customer satisfaction.

Advantages and Disadvantages

The major advantages of selling are related to the nature of personal contact:

1. A salesperson can adapt a message to the needs of the individual customer.
2. A salesperson can be flexible in offering ways to address customer needs.
3. The attention span of the customer is high.
4. For store-based retailers, there is little or no waste; most people who walk into a store are potential customers.
5. Customers respond more often to personal selling than to ads.
6. Immediate feedback is provided.

The major disadvantages of personal selling are that

1. Only a limited number of consumers can be reached at a given time.
2. The costs of interacting with each consumer can be high.
3. Consumers are not initially lured into a store through personal selling.
4. Self-service may be discouraged.
5. Consumers may not perceive salespeople as helpful and knowledgeable, but rather as pushy.

Types

Most types of retail sales positions can be categorized as either order taking or order getting. An ***order-taking salesperson*** is involved in routine clerical and sales functions, such as setting up displays, placing inventory on the shelves, answering simple questions, filling orders, and ringing up sales. This type of selling most often occurs in stores that have a strong mix of self-service with some personnel on the floor.

An ***order-getting salesperson*** is actively involved with informing and persuading customers, and with closing sales. This is the true "sales" employee. Order getters usually sell higher-priced or complex items, such as real estate, autos, apparel, appliances, and consumer electronics. On average, they are much more skilled and better paid than order takers.

In some instances, a manufacturer may help finance the personal selling function by providing ***PMs*** (defined as promotional money, push money, or prize money) for retail salespeople selling that manufacturer's brand. PMs are in addition to the compensation received from the retailer. Many retailers are concerned about this practice because it encourages their sales personnel to be loyal to the manufacturer, and salespersons may be less responsive to actual customer desires (if customers desire brands not yielding PMs).

Retail salespeople may operate in a store, visit consumers' homes or places where consumers work, and/or engage in telemarketing.

Functions

Store-based sales personnel may be responsible for all or many of these tasks: greeting customers, determining customer wants, showing merchandise, giving a sales presentation, demonstrating goods and/or services, answering objections, and closing the sale. See Figure 17–4. Nonstore-based sales personnel may also have to generate customer leads (by knocking on doors in residential areas or calling people who are listed in a local telephone directory).

Upon entering a store or a department in it (or being contacted at home), a customer would be greeted by a salesperson. Typical in-store greetings are

"Hello, may I help you?"

"Good morning [afternoon]. If you need any help, please call upon me."

"Hi, is there anything in particular you are looking for?"

With any greeting, the salesperson seeks to put the customer at ease and build rapport.

Next, the salesperson would determine what the customer wants:

- Is the person just looking, or is there a specific good or service in mind?
- For what purpose is the item to be used (such as gift or personal)?

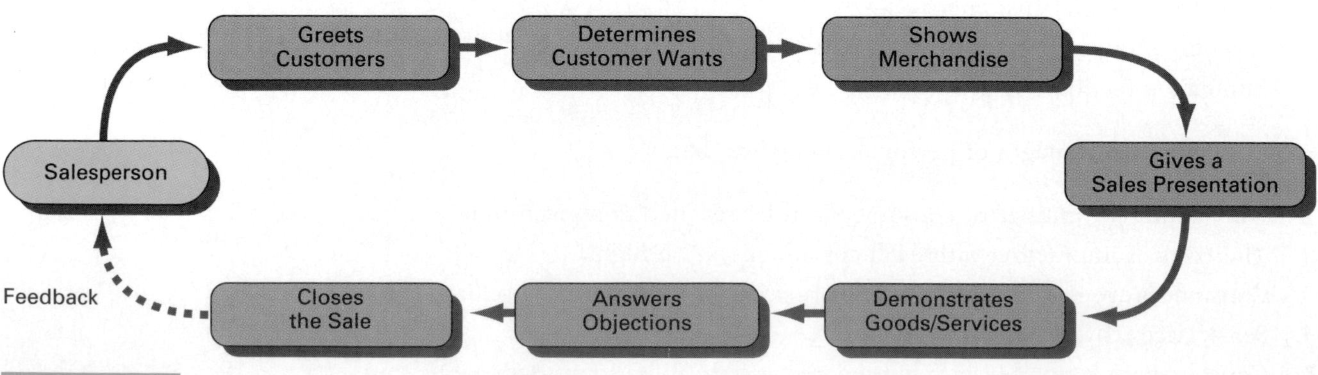

FIGURE 17–4 Typical Personal Selling Functions

Ethics in Retailing

What's Acceptable Behavior for Auto Salespeople?

Two researchers recently studied ten potentially unethical situations that exist in the auto industry by surveying the sales forces at ten car dealers in a medium-sized, Middle-Atlantic city. These were the situations examined:

- Informing a customer that someone else is interested in a car, whether or not this is true.
- Using high-pressure tactics to close a sale.
- Charging full price for a car, without the customer's knowledge.
- Accepting a trade-in auto that the dealer does not want.
- Making a promise the dealer will not honor.
- Not telling the customer the full truth about the specifications of an auto.
- Giving preferential treatment to certain customers.
- Selling a more costly auto than the customer needs.
- Taking customers away from other sales associates.
- Bowing to peer pressure not to report unethical behavior.

The researchers found that the 89 salespeople in the study did report using significant levels of preferential treatment, misinformation about people being interested in a car, and high pressure to close a sale. Of the situations studied, the salespeople were least likely to make promises that they knew the dealer would not keep, to be less than truthful about a car's specifications, and to take customers away from other sales associates.

Source: Based on material in Earl D. Honeycutt, Jr., "Ethical Dilemmas in the Automotive Industry" in David W. Cravens and Peter R. Dickson (Editors), *1993 AMA Educators' Proceedings* (Chicago: American Marketing Association, 1993), pp. 352–358.

- Does the person have a price range in mind?
- What other information can the person provide to help the salesperson?

From the perspective of the retailing concept, a salesperson could not be successful without first ascertaining the customer's wants.

At this point, a salesperson may show or present merchandise. Based on a determination of customer wants, he or she would select the good or service most apt to be satisfactory for that customer. The salesperson may decide to trade up (discuss a more expensive version) or present a substitute (especially if the retailer does not carry or is out of the requested item).

The salesperson would now make a sales presentation to influence the customer to make a purchase. The two most common ones are the canned sales presentation and the need-satisfaction approach. The ***canned sales presentation*** is a memorized, repetitive speech given to all customers interested in a particular item. The ***need-satisfaction approach*** is based upon the principle that each customer has a different set of wants and that the sales presentation should be geared to the demands of the individual customer. This approach is being utilized more and more in retailing.

In a sales presentation, a demonstration may be useful. This would show the actual utility of an item and allow customer participation. Demonstrations are often used to sell stereos, autos, TV sets, health club memberships, dishwashers, video games, and watches.

A customer may raise questions during the personal selling process, and the salesperson must address them satisfactorily. Then, after all questions are answered, the salesperson closes the sale. This involves getting the customer to conclude his or her purchase. Typical closing lines are

"Will you take it with you or have it delivered?

"Cash or charge?"

"Would you like this gift-wrapped?"

"Have you decided on the color, red or blue?"

For the personal selling process to be completed effectively, salespeople must be enthusiastic, knowledgeable about their firm and its offerings, interested in consumers, and able to communicate effectively. For example, when Toyota set up a new

TABLE 17–3 Selected Reasons Why Retail Sales Are Lost

- *Poor qualification of the customer:* Information should be obtained from the customer so that a salesperson can gear his or her presentation to the prospective buyer.
- *Salesperson does not demonstrate the good or service:* A good sales presentation should be built around the item shown in use; then, benefits can be easily visualized.
- *Failure to put feeling into the presentation:* The salesperson should be sincere and consumer-oriented in his or her presentation.
- *Poor knowledge:* The salesperson should know the major advantages and disadvantages of his or her goods and services, as well as competitors', and be able to answer questions.
- *Arguing with a customer:* A good salesperson should avoid arguments in handling customer objections, even if the customer is completely wrong.
- *No suggestion selling:* A salesperson should attempt to sell related items (such as service contracts, product supplies, and installation) along with the basic product.
- *Giving up too early:* If an attempt to close a sale is unsuccessful, it should be tried again.
- *Inflexibility:* A salesperson should be creative in analyzing alternative solutions to a customer's needs, as well as in adapting his or her message to the requirements of the individual consumer.
- *Poor follow-up:* A salesperson should be sure the order is correctly written, merchandise arrives at the agreed-on time, and the customer is satisfied.

dealer network for its luxury Lexus division, it sent hundreds of sales and service personnel to special training sessions in Chicago. The goal? "Know your product—and the competing models—thoroughly, as salespeople do at BMW. Shower customers with respect and courtesy, a la Mercedes. Avoid the cool, unemotional presentation common at Acura, Honda's upscale division. And shun the backslapping approach of Cadillac."[6]

Table 17–3 contains a selected list of how retail sales can be lost through poor personal selling, and how to correct these problems.

SALES PROMOTION

Sales promotion consists of the paid marketing communication activities—other than advertising, publicity, and personal selling—that stimulate consumer purchases and dealer effectiveness. Included are displays, contests, sweepstakes, coupons, frequent-shopper programs, prizes, samples, demonstrations, referral gifts, and other limited-time selling efforts outside of the ordinary promotion routine.

Objectives

Sales promotion goals include

- Increasing short-run sales.
- Maintaining customer loyalty.
- Emphasizing novelty.
- Supplementing other promotion tools.

Advantages and Disadvantages

The major advantages of sales promotion are that

1. It often has eye-catching appeal.
2. The themes and tools can be distinctive.

[6] Wendy Zellner, "Two Days in Boot Camp—Learning to Love Lexus," *Business Week* (September 4, 1989), p. 87.

3. The consumer may receive something of value, such as coupons, prizes, or calendars.
4. It helps draw customer traffic and maintain loyalty to the retailer.
5. Impulse purchases are increased.
6. Customers can have fun, particularly with contests and demonstrations.

The major disadvantages of sales promotion are that

1. It may be difficult to terminate special promotions without adverse customer reactions.
2. The retailer's image may be hurt if trite promotions are used.
3. Sometimes, frivolous selling points are emphasized rather than the retailer's product assortment, prices, customer services, and other factors.
4. Many sales promotions have only short-run effects.
5. It should be used only as a supplement to other promotional forms.

Types

Figure 17–5 lists many of the major types of sales promotions. Each is described here.

Point-of-purchase promotion consists of in-store displays designed to increase sales. The effect of these displays on retail image was discussed in Chapter 16. From a promotional perspective, the displays may remind customers, stimulate impulse behavior, allow self-service to be used, and reduce a retailer's promotion costs because many manufacturers provide displays. The long-run impact of point-of-purchase promotions must be carefully studied. For instance, in some product categories, total sales may not rise if special displays are used; instead, customers could stockpile items and purchase less when the special displays are removed.

Here are examples showing the use and value of point-of-purchase displays:

- The Point-of-Purchase Advertising Institute (POPAI) estimates that manufacturers and retailers annually spend $16 billion on in-store displays.
- Display ads appear on shopping carts in the majority of U.S. supermarkets. And thousands of supermarkets have in-store electronic signs above their aisles that promote such well-known brands as Clorox and Kraft.
- Retailers use about 65 per cent of all displays provided by manufacturers.
- Coca-Cola distributors have been giving out $2,000 display units to their retailers. These displays not only stock Coca-Cola products, they also hold gum, candy, and magazines.[7]

Contests and sweepstakes are similar in nature; they seek to attract and retain customers via participation in events that can lead to substantial prizes. A contest requires a customer to demonstrate some skill in return for a reward. A sweepstakes requires only participation, with the lucky winner chosen at random. The disadvantages of contests and sweepstakes are their costs, customer reliance on these tools as the reason for continued retailer patronage, the effort required of consumers, and entries by nonshoppers. Together, manufacturers and retailers spend over $200 million each year on contests and sweepstakes.

Coupons are used to present discounts from the regular selling prices of manufacturer and retailer brands. Each year, over 300 billion coupons are distributed in

[7] Glenn Heitsmith, "Selling an In-Store Strategy," *Promo* (January 1994), pp. 28–31; Alison Fahey, "Advertising Media Crowd into Aisles," *Advertising Age* (June 18, 1990), p. 18; and Patricia Winters, "Pepsi, Coke Battle at Express Checkout Lanes," *Advertising Age* (October 19, 1992), p. 20.

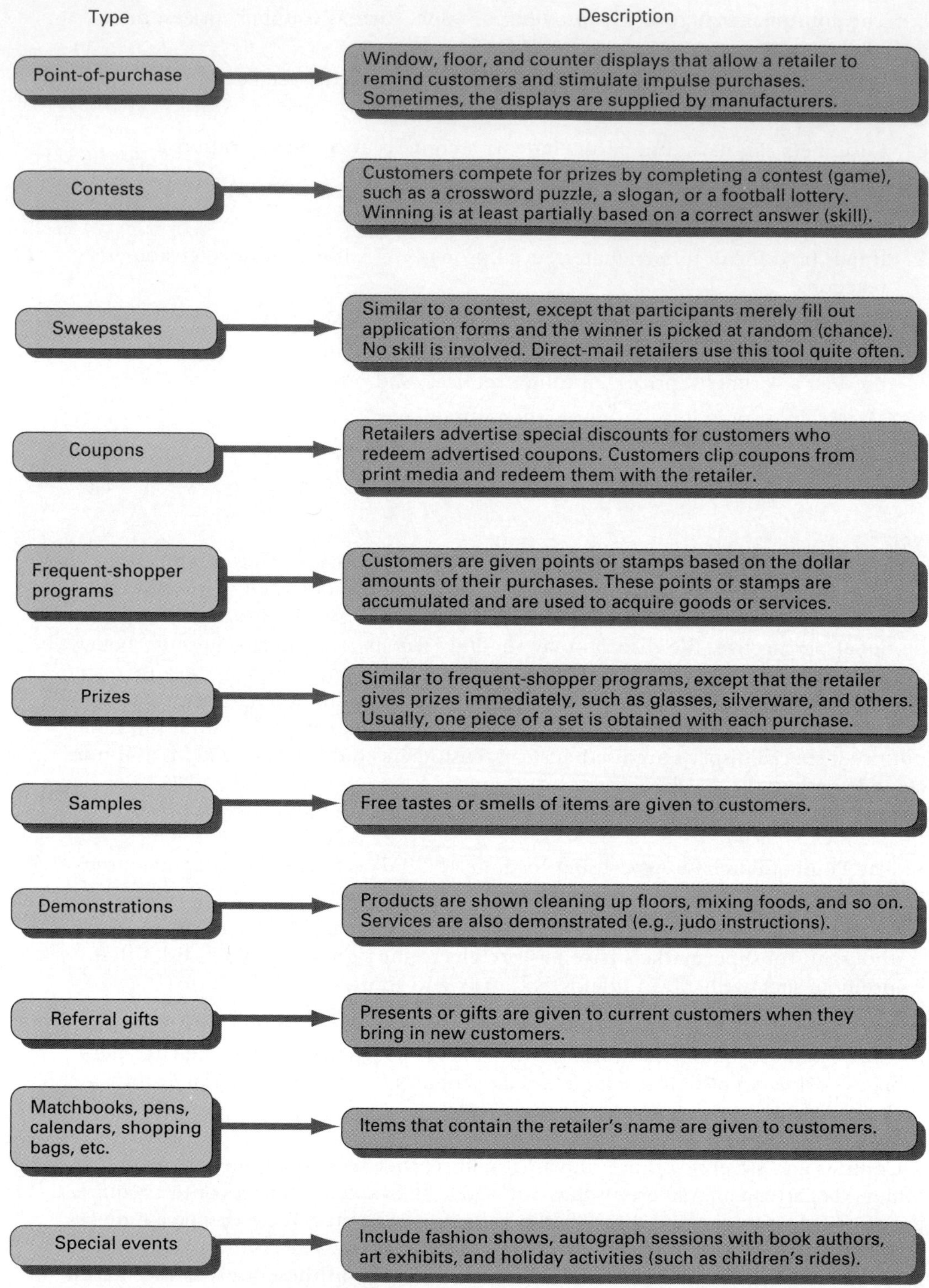

Type
Description
Point-of-purchase
Window, floor, and counter displays that allow a retailer to remind customers and stimulate impulse purchases. Sometimes, the displays are supplied by manufacturers.
Contests
Customers compete for prizes by completing a contest (game), such as a crossword puzzle, a slogan, or a football lottery. Winning is at least partially based on a correct answer (skill).
Sweepstakes
Similar to a contest, except that participants merely fill out application forms and the winner is picked at random (chance). No skill is involved. Direct-mail retailers use this tool quite often.
Coupons
Retailers advertise special discounts for customers who redeem advertised coupons. Customers clip coupons from print media and redeem them with the retailer.
Frequent-shopper programs
Customers are given points or stamps based on the dollar amounts of their purchases. These points or stamps are accumulated and are used to acquire goods or services.
Prizes
Similar to frequent-shopper programs, except that the retailer gives prizes immediately, such as glasses, silverware, and others. Usually, one piece of a set is obtained with each purchase.
Samples
Free tastes or smells of items are given to customers.
Demonstrations
Products are shown cleaning up floors, mixing foods, and so on. Services are also demonstrated (e.g., judo instructions).
Referral gifts
Presents or gifts are given to current customers when they bring in new customers.
Matchbooks, pens, calendars, shopping bags, etc.
Items that contain the retailer's name are given to customers.
Special events
Include fashion shows, autograph sessions with book authors, art exhibits, and holiday activities (such as children's rides).

FIGURE 17–5 Types of Sales Promotion

the United States, with grocery products accounting for nearly four-fifths of that amount. U.S. consumers actually redeem 7 billion coupons, resulting in their saving $4 billion; retailers receive $600 million to $700 million for handling redeemed coupons.[8] Coupons are offered to consumers via freestanding inserts in Sunday news-

[8] Glenn Heitsmith, "Sea Change or Tidal Shift?" *Promo* (April 1994), pp. 42–46, 80; and *Promo: The Sourcebook 1994*, pp. 128–129.

papers and placements in daily newspapers, direct mail, regular magazines, and Sunday newspaper magazines. They are also placed in or on packages and dispensed from electronic in-store machines.

There are four important advantages of coupons. First, in many cases, manufacturers pay for the advertising and redemption of coupons. Second, coupons are very helpful to an ongoing advertising campaign and increase store traffic. According to one survey of shoppers, 93 per cent of respondents said they scan newspapers for coupons.[9] Third, the use of coupons increases the consumer's perception that a retailer offers good value. Fourth, the effectiveness of advertisements can be measured by counting redeemed coupons.

The disadvantages of coupons include their possible negative effect on the retailer's image, consumers shopping only when coupons are available, the low redemption rates, the clutter of coupons (largely due to the expanding number of coupons distributed), retailer and consumer fraud, and handling costs. For example, just over 2 per cent of all coupons are redeemed by consumers because of the large number of them that are received by each American household.

Frequent-shopper programs award special discounts or prizes to customers for their continued patronage. In most such programs, customers must accumulate a certain number of points (or their equivalent) and the points are redeemed for cash or prizes. Here are examples of frequent-shopper programs:

- Twenty-three million people belong to American Airlines' AAdvantage program. By traveling on American Airlines or patronizing participating firms (such as Marriott and Hertz), people can earn free flights.
- Dunkin' Donuts' "Coffee Cash-In" program gives points to customers for purchases of medium and large coffee. The points (along with a nominal fee) may be redeemed for T-shirts, hats, tote bags, umbrellas, and other items.
- Egghead software stores have a Cue program, whereby its 1.6 million members save 5 per cent on all purchases.
- Frank's Nursery & Crafts has a Preferred Customer Card program with 800,000+ members. A $5 coupon is awarded every time a customer spends $100.[10]

Among the advantages of frequent-shopper programs are the loyalty bred (customers can accumulate points only through patronage of one or a few firms), the "free" nature of awards to many consumers, and the competitive edge for a retailer that is similar to others. On the other hand, a number of consumers feel frequent-shopper programs are not really free and therefore would rather shop at lower-priced stores without these programs; it may take customers a while to gather enough points to get meaningful gifts; and profit margins may be small if retailers with frequent-shopper programs try to price competitively with firms that do not have these programs.

Prizes are similar in concept to frequent-shopper programs, but instead of points, a prize is given immediately with each purchase. Prize giveaways are most effective when sets of glasses, silverware, dishes, place mats, and so on are distributed one at a time to shoppers. These encourage store loyalty. The problems are the cost of the prizes, the difficulty of termination, and the possible impact on image.

As a supplement to personal selling, free samples (such as a taste of a cake or a smell of a perfume) and/or demonstrations (such as cooking lessons) may be used. More than $125 million is spent annually on sampling in U.S. supermarkets—in addition to the samples given out in membership clubs, specialty stores, department stores, and elsewhere.[11] Sampling is effective because the customers become involved and impulse purchases increase. Loitering and costs may be problems.

[9] Scott Hume, "Coupons: Are They Too Popular?" *Advertising Age* (February 15, 1993), p. 32.

[10] Bruce Chemel, "Frequent Marketer," *Sales & Marketing Management* (April 1994), p. 13; "Dunkin' Donuts Offers Wake-Up Call," *Promo* (December 1993), p. 78; *Egghead, Inc. 1993 Annual Report*, p. 3; and *General Host Corporation 1992 Annual Report*, p. 11.

[11] Gabriella Stern, "With Sampling, There Is Too a Free Lunch," *Wall Street Journal* (March 11, 1994), pp. B1, B6.

Referral gifts are used to encourage existing customers to bring in new customers. Direct marketers, such as book and record clubs, often use this tool. It is a technique that has no important shortcomings and recognizes the value of friends in influencing purchasing decisions.

Items such as matchbooks, pens, calendars, and shopping bags are sometimes given to customers. They differ from prizes in that they promote a retailer's name and are usually not part of a set. These items should be used as supplements. Their advantage is longevity. There is no real disadvantage.

Retailers may use special events to foster consumer enthusiasm. The special events can range from elaborate grand openings to fashion shows to art exhibits. For example, when Toys "R" Us opens a store, it has giveways and activities for children, and there is always a guest appearance by the firm's Geoffrey the giraffe (a human in a costume). See Figure 17–6. In general, when a special event is planned, the potential increase in consumer awareness and store traffic needs to be weighed against that event's costs.

FIGURE 17–6

The Grand Opening of Toys "R" Us in Spain

Around the world, Toys "R" Us uses its popular Geoffrey the giraffe to launch new stores in spectacular fashion.
Reprinted by permission.

FIGURE 17–7
Planning a Retail Promotional Strategy

Planning a Retail Promotional Strategy

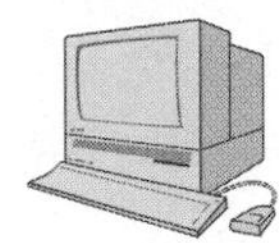

To communicate successfully with its customers, a retailer should plan its overall promotional strategy carefully. A systematic five-step approach to promotional planning is depicted in Figure 17–7 and explained next.

DETERMINING PROMOTIONAL OBJECTIVES

Broad promotional objectives include increasing sales, stimulating impulse and reminder buying, raising customer traffic, getting leads for sales personnel, developing and reinforcing a retailer's image, informing customers about the attributes of goods and services, popularizing a new store site, capitalizing on manufacturer support, offering customer service and improving customer relations, and maintaining customer loyalty.

In developing a promotional strategy, a retailer must determine which of these goals are most important. It is necessary for the firm to state its goals clearly in order to give direction to the selection of promotional types, media, and messages.

Goals must be stated as precisely as possible. As an example, increasing company sales is not a specific enough goal. However, increasing sales by 20 per cent is directional, quantitative, and measurable. With such an objective, a firm could devise a thorough promotional plan and evaluate its success.

ESTABLISHING AN OVERALL PROMOTIONAL BUDGET

Several procedures are available for setting the size of a promotion budget. Five techniques are discussed in this section.

With the ***all-you-can afford method***, a retailer first allocates funds for every element of the retail strategy mix except promotion. Then, whatever funds are left over are placed in a promotional budget. This is probably the weakest of the budgeting techniques. Its shortcomings are that little importance is placed on promotion as a crucial retail strategy-mix variable; expenditures are not linked to objectives; and if little or no funds are left over, the promotion budget is too small or nonexistent. The method is used predominantly by small, conservative retailers.

The ***incremental method*** of promotion budgeting relies on previous budgets in the allocation of funds. A percentage is either added to or subtracted from this year's budget to determine next year's budget. For instance, if this year's promotion budget is $10,000, next year's budget would be calculated by adding or subtracting a percentage to or from that amount. A 10 per cent increase means that next year's budget would be $11,000. This technique is useful for a small retailer. A reference point is used. The budget is adjusted based on the retailer's feelings about past successes and future trends. It is an easy method to use. However, important disadvantages do exist. The budget size is rarely tied to specific goals. Intuition or "gut feelings" are used. Evaluation of promotional effectiveness is also difficult.

For the ***competitive parity method***, a retailer's budget is raised or lowered according to the actions of competitors. Thus, if the leading retailer in an area raises its promotion budget by 8 per cent, competitors in the area could follow suit. This method has utility for small and large firms. The advantages are that it uses a point of comparison and is market-oriented and conservative. The disadvantages are that it is a following, not a leading, philosophy; it may be difficult to obtain data about competitors; and there is an assumption that competing firms are similar (in terms of the number of years in business, size, target market, location, merchandise, prices, and so on). The last point is particularly critical: competitors may actually need quite different promotional budgets.

In the ***percentage-of-sales method***, a retailer ties its promotion budget to sales revenue. First, the firm would develop a promotion-to-sales ratio. Then, during each succeeding year, the ratio of promotion dollars to sales dollars would remain constant, although the dollar amount would vary. For instance, a firm could set promotion costs at 10 per cent of sales. If this year's sales are expected to be $100,000, a $10,000 promotion budget is planned. If next year's sales are projected to be $140,000, a $14,000 budget would be planned. The benefits of this procedure are the use of sales as a base, its adaptability, and the correlation of promotion with sales. The shortcomings are that there is no relation to objectives (as an example, for an established retailer, an increase in sales may not require an increase in promotion); promotion is not used as a leader of sales, but as a follower; and promotion decreases during poor sales periods when increases might be beneficial. This technique provides too many promotional funds in periods of high sales and too few funds in periods of low sales.

Under the ***objective-and-task method***, a retailer clearly defines its promotional objectives and then determines the size of the budget needed to satisfy these objectives. For example, a retailer may decide that its goal is to have 70 per cent of the people in its trading area know the firm's name by the end of a one-month promotion campaign, up from 50 per cent currently. It then calculates what tasks and costs are required to achieve that goal:

Objective	Task	Cost
1. Gain awareness of homemakers.	Use eight quarter-page ads (in four successive Sunday editions of two area newspapers).	$ 8,000
2. Gain awareness of motorists.	Use forty 30-second radio commercials during prime time on local radio stations, at $125 each.	5,000
3. Gain awareness of pedestrians.	Give away shopping bags—5,000 bags at $0.75 each.	3,750
	Total budget	$16,750

The objective-and-task method is probably the best budgeting technique. Among its advantages are that objectives are clearly stated; expenditures are related to the completion of goal-oriented tasks; it is adaptable; and success (or failure) can be assessed. The major shortcoming is the complexity in setting goals and specific tasks, especially for small retailers.

FIGURE 17–8

Computerized Promotional Budgeting

Promotion Guardian is PC-based software from MarketWare that enables retailers to optimize the use and management of their promotional funds. It can manage cooperative advertising dollars, special salesperson incentives, grand opening investments, and all other promotion expenditures. Promotion Guardian software costs $19,800.

Reprinted by permission.

When deciding how to plan their promotion budgets, retailers should weigh the strengths and weaknesses of each technique in relation to their individual requirements and constraints. To assist firms in their budgeting efforts, there is now computer software available, as highlighted in Figure 17–8.

SELECTING THE PROMOTIONAL MIX

After a budget is set, a retailer must determine its promotional mix: the combination of advertising, publicity, personal selling, and sales promotion. A firm with a relatively small budget may rely on in-store displays, flyers, targeted direct mail, and publicity to generate customer traffic, whereas a firm with a large promotion budget may rely heavily on newspaper and TV ads.

The choice of promotional mix is often affected by the type of retailer involved. Figure 17–9 shows the use of sales promotion tools by independent and chain supermarkets. Product sampling, continuity programs (such as coupons and point-of-sale promotions), theme sales, bonus coupons, half-price sales, and register-tape plans are

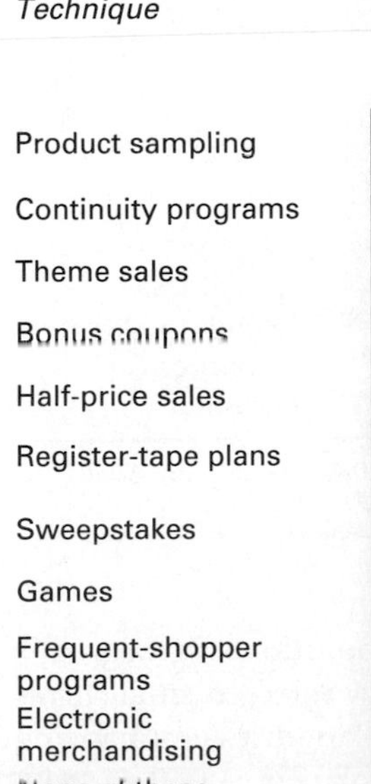

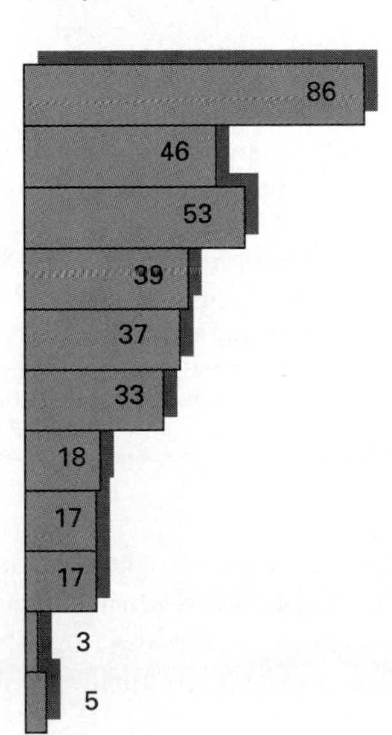

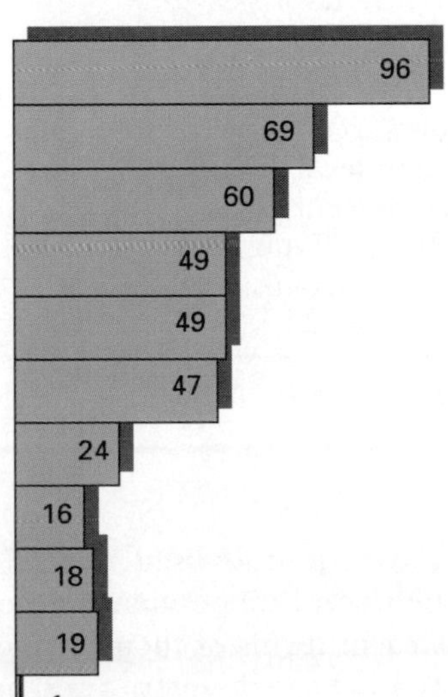

FIGURE 17–9

The Use of Sales Promotion Tools by Independent and Chain Supermarkets

Source: "60th Annual Report of the Grocery Industry," *Progressive Grocer* (April 1993), p. 70. Copyright *Progressive Grocer*. *Reprinted by permission.*

TABLE 17–4 The Promotion Mixes of Selected Small Retailers

Type of Retailer	Favorite Media	Emphasis on Personal Selling	Special Considerations	Promotional Opportunities
Apparel store	Weekly or suburban newspapers; direct mail; radio; Yellow Pages; exterior signs.	High.	Cooperative advertising available from manufacturers.	Fashion shows for community organizations or charities.
Auto supply store	Local newspapers; Yellow Pages; POP displays; exterior signs.	Moderate.	Cooperative advertising available from manufacturers.	For specialty stores, direct mail is a popular medium.
Bar and/or cocktail lounge	Yellow Pages; local newspapers (entertainment section); tourist publications; radio; specialties; exterior signs.	Moderate.	All product advertising from manufacturers.	Unusual drinks at "happy hour" rates; hosting post-event parties.
Bookstore	Newspapers; shoppers; Yellow Pages; local magazines; radio; exterior signs.	Moderate.	Cooperative advertising available from publishers.	Autograph parties.
Coin-operated laundry	Yellow Pages; flyers in area; local direct mail; exterior signs.	None.	None.	Coupons in newspaper ads for "free trial."
Gift store	Weekly newspapers; Yellow Pages; radio; direct mail; local magazines; exterior signs.	Moderate.	None.	Open houses; demonstrations of products such as cookware.
Hair-grooming/ beauty salon	Yellow Pages; newspapers; name credits for styles in feature articles; exterior signs.	Moderate.	Word-of-mouth communication very important to a salon's success.	Styling for area fashion shows; free beauty clinics and demonstrations.
Health food store	Local newspapers; shoppers; college newspapers; direct mail; POP displays; exterior signs.	Moderate.	None.	Educational displays and services.
Restaurant	Newspapers; radio; Yellow Pages; transit; outdoor; local entertainment guides or tourist publications; theater programs; exterior signs.	Moderate.	Word-of-mouth communication relied upon heavily by independently owned restaurants.	Publicity in critics' columns; specialties; birthday cakes or parties for customers.

Source: Adapted by the authors from "Advertising Small Business" (Bank of America NT & SA, 1982), p. 16. Reprinted with permission. *Small Business Reporter* 1982.

the techniques used most. However, the use of different sales promotions varies greatly between independent and chain outlets. Table 17–4 shows how selected small firms vary in terms of their promotion mixes—such as coin-operated laundries emphasizing Yellow Page directories and health food stores relying on local newspapers, as well as point-of-purchase displays.

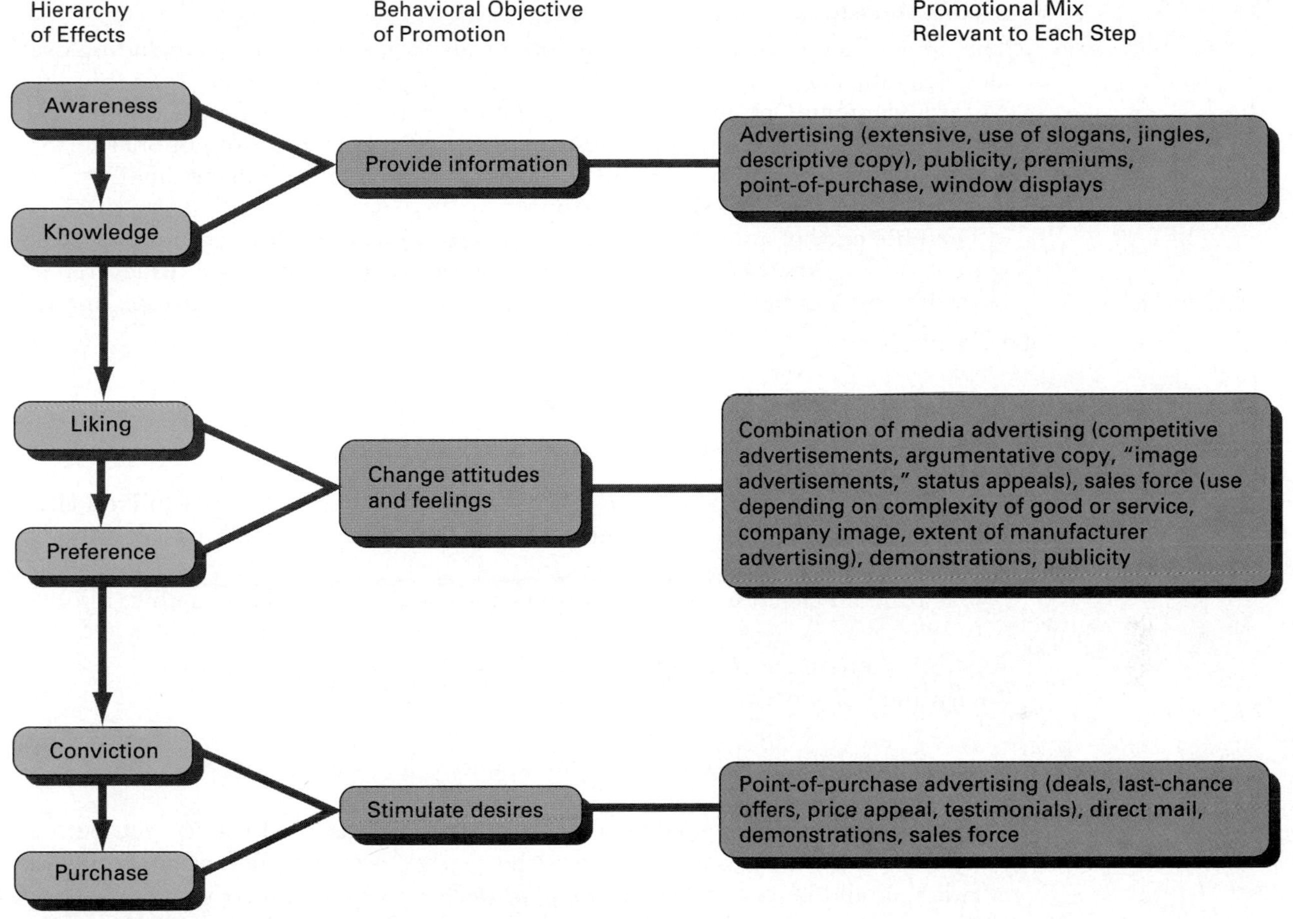

FIGURE 17–10 Promotion and the Hierarchy of Effects

Source: Adapted by the authors from Robert Lavidge and Gary A. Steiner, "A Model for Predictive Measurements of Advertising Effectiveness," *Journal of Marketing*, Vol. 25 (October 1961), p. 61. *Reprinted with permission of the American Marketing Association.*

Often, retailers use an assortment of promotional forms to reinforce each other. Thus, a melding of media advertising and point-of-purchase displays may be more effective in getting across a message than one form alone.

In reacting to a retailer's communication efforts, a consumer often goes through a sequence of steps called the ***hierarchy-of-effects model***, which leads him or her from awareness to knowledge to liking to preference to conviction to a purchase.[12] Different promotional mixes are required in each step, as noted in Figure 17–10. As a rule, advertising and publicity are most effective in developing awareness, and personal selling and sales promotion are most effective in changing attitudes and stimulating desires. This is especially true for expensive and complex goods or services.

IMPLEMENTING THE PROMOTIONAL MIX

The implementation of a promotional mix involves choosing which specific media to use (such as, Newspaper A and Newspaper B), the timing of promotion, the content of messages, the makeup of the sales force, specific sales-promotion tools, and the responsibility for coordination.

[12] Robert Lavidge and Gary A. Steiner, "A Model for Predictive Measurements of Advertising Effectiveness," *Journal of Marketing*, Vol. 25 (October 1961), pp. 59–62.

Media Decisions

The choice of specific media is based on a wide variety of elements, including overall costs, efficiency (the cost to reach a member of the target market), lead time, and editorial content. Overall costs are important because the extensive use of an expensive medium may preclude the implementation of a balanced promotional mix. In addition, a retailer may not be able to repeat a message in a costly medium, and ads are rarely effective when shown only once.

The efficiency of a medium relates to the cost of reaching a given number of target customers. Newspaper efficiency is measured by the milline rate, which reflects both the cost per ***agate line*** (there are 14 agate lines to an inch of space, one column wide) and the newspaper's circulation:

$$\text{Milline rate (newspaper efficiency)} = \frac{\text{Cost per agate line} \times 1{,}000{,}000}{\text{Circulation}}$$

The ***milline rate*** represents the cost to a retailer of one agate line per million circulation. A newspaper with a circulation of 400,000 and an agate-line rate of $160 has a milline rate of $400.

Magazine efficiency is based on cost per thousand (rather than a milline rate):

$$\text{Cost per thousand (magazine efficiency)} = \frac{\text{Cost per page} \times 1{,}000}{\text{Circulation}}$$

A magazine with a circulation of 2 million and a per-page rate of $80,000 has a cost per thousand of $40.

In both computations, total circulation is used to measure efficiency. Yet, because a retailer usually appeals to a limited target market, only the relevant portion of circulation should be considered. Thus, if 70 per cent of a magazine's readers are target customers for a particular firm (and the other 30 per cent live outside its trading area), the real cost per thousand is

$$\begin{aligned}\text{Cost per thousand (target market)} &= \frac{\text{Cost per page} \times 1{,}000}{\text{Circulation} \times \dfrac{\text{Target market}}{\text{Circulation}}}\\ &= \frac{\$80{,}000 \times 1{,}000}{2{,}000{,}000 \times 0.70}\\ &= \frac{\$80{,}000{,}000}{1{,}400{,}000} = \$57.14\end{aligned}$$

Different media require different lead times. For instance, a newspaper ad can be placed shortly before publication, whereas a magazine ad sometimes must be placed months in advance. In addition, the retailer must decide what kind of editorial content it wants near its ads (such as a sports story, the comics, a personal-care column, or a feature story).

Timing of the Promotional Mix

Advertising decisions involve a consideration of reach and frequency. ***Reach*** refers to the number of distinct people who are exposed to a retailer's ads during a specified time period. ***Frequency*** measures the average number of times each person who is reached is exposed to company ads during a given time period.

A retailer can advertise extensively or intensively. ***Extensive media coverage*** means ads reach many people but with relatively low frequency. ***Intensive media coverage*** means ads are placed in selected media and repeated frequently. Repetition is important, particularly for a retailer seeking to develop an image or selling new goods or services.

RETAILING AROUND THE WORLD

Why and How Do Dutch Retailers Control the Promotion Mix?

According to the marketing director of Coca-Cola Netherlands, five retail chains in the Netherlands control the distribution of more than 70 per cent of that country's consumer packaged goods. This concentration of sales has led to those five chains having tremendous "authority" over manufacturers. And other retailing analysts say that great retailer power is common throughout Europe.

As a result of their power, many Dutch retailers have refused to honor manufacturers' cents-off coupons; instead, they prefer price reductions. Some of them have also refused to stock packages that include premiums because they either lack shelf space or would rather sell the premiums separately.

Manufacturers that seek the cooperation of Dutch retailers need to develop targeted promotions that offer clear benefits to both the retailers and final consumers. One such type of promotion is based on brand-switching appeals. An example of such an appeal is Pepsi's offering Coke drinkers two free bottles of Pepsi-Cola in exchange for two empty Coca-Cola bottles. Joint promotions, such as Dutch manufacturers offering contest winners trips to EuroDisney, have also been effective.

Retailing experts expect that Dutch manufacturers will soon devise more "cross-the-border" promotions to capitalize on the new openness of the European Union.

Source: Based on material in Amie Smith, "Dutch Trade Seizes Power," *Promo* (April 1993), pp. 81–82.

In enacting its promotional mix, a retailer must consider peak seasons and whether to mass or distribute efforts. When peak seasons occur, all elements of the mix are usually utilized; in slow periods, promotional efforts are typically reduced. A ***massed advertising effort*** is used by retailers, such as Avon, that promote mostly in one or two seasons. A ***distributed advertising effort*** is employed by retailers, such as McDonald's, that promote constantly throughout the year.

Even though they are not really affected by seasonality as much as many other retailers, peak advertising is practiced by supermarkets, the majority of which use Wednesday as the day when major weekly newspaper ads are placed. This placement takes advantage of the fact that a heavy proportion of consumers conduct their major shopping trip on Thursday, Friday, or Saturday.

Sales-force size can vary by time (morning versus evening), day (weekdays versus weekends), and month (December versus January). Sales promotions also vary in their timing. Store openings and holidays are especially good times for sales promotions. See Figure 17–11.

Content of Messages

Whether written or spoken, personally or impersonally delivered, message content is important. In advertising, themes, wording, headlines, the use of color, size, layout, and placement must be decided on. Publicity releases need to be written. In personal selling, the greeting, the sales presentation, the demonstration, and the closing need to be applied. In sales promotion, the firm's message must be composed and placed on the promotional device.

FIGURE 17–11
Timing the Promotional Effort
Retailers such as Michaels Stores plan their promotions on a monthly basis and emphasize special events at selected times.
Reprinted by permission.

To a large extent, the characteristics of the promotional form influence the message. A shopping bag often contains no more than a retailer's name; a billboard (seen while driving at 55 miles per hour) is good for visual effect, but can hold only limited written material; and a salesperson may be able to maintain a customer's attention for a while, thus expanding the content of the message that is conveyed. Some shopping centers now use a glossy magazine format to communicate a community-oriented image, introduce new stores to consumers, and promote the goods and services carried at stores in the center.

In advertising, distinctiveness can be an aid to a retailer because of the proliferation of messages. For example, cluttered ads displaying many products may suggest a discounter's orientation, while fine pencil drawings and selective product displays may suggest a specialty store focus.

Recently, more retailers have become involved in ***comparative advertising***, whereby messages compare their offerings with those of competitors. Comparative ads are used to help position a retailer in relation to competitors, increase awareness of the firm, maximize the efficiency of a limited budget, and provide credibility. Yet, these ads provide visibility for competitors, may confuse people, and may lead to legal action by competitors. Some fast-food and off-price retailers are among those using comparative ads.

Makeup of Sales Force

Qualifications for sales personnel must be detailed, and such personnel must be recruited, selected, trained, compensated, supervised, and monitored. Personnel should also be classified (such as order takers versus order getters) and assigned to the appropriate departments. An in-depth discussion regarding human resource management was provided in Chapter 10.

Sales Promotion Tools

The specific sales promotion tools must be chosen from among those cited in Figure 17–5. The combination of tools depends on short-run (and changing) objectives and the other components of the promotion mix. Wherever possible, cooperative ventures with manufacturers or other suppliers should be sought, and tools inconsistent with the retailer's image would not be used.

Responsibility for Coordination

Regardless of a firm's size or organizational form, someone within the company must have authority over and responsibility for the promotion function. Larger retailers often assign this job to a vice-president of promotion, who oversees display personnel, works with the firm's advertising agency, supervises the retailer's own advertising department (if there is one), and supplies branch outlets with the necessary in-store materials. Personal selling is usually under the jurisdiction of the store manager in a large retail setting.

For a promotional strategy to be successful, its components have to be coordinated with other elements of the retail mix. Thus, sales personnel must be informed of special sales and must know product features; featured items must be received, marked, and displayed; and bookkeeping entries must be made.

Often, a shopping center or a shopping district runs a theme promotion, such as "back to school." In those instances, someone must have responsibility for coordinating the activities of all stores participating in the event.

REVIEWING AND REVISING THE PROMOTIONAL PLAN

An analysis of the success of a promotion plan depends on the objectives sought, and that analysis is simplified if promotional goals are clearly stated in advance (as suggested in this chapter). Revisions would be made for promotional tools not achieving their pre-set goals.

TABLE 17–5 Measuring Promotional Effectiveness

Behaviorally Oriented Promotion Objectives	Examples of Retail Promotion Objectives	Research Approaches for Evaluating Promotion Effectiveness
Cognitive: the realm of thoughts; promotion designed to provide information and facts.	Inform current customers about new credit plans; acquaint potential customers with new offerings.	Study company and product awareness before and after promotion; evaluate extent of promotion audience.
Affective: the realm of emotions; promotion designed to change attitudes and feelings.	Develop and reinforce a high-fashion image; maintain customer loyalty.	Study image via semantic differential, projective techniques, rank-order preference for retailers, and rating scales before and after promotion.
Conative: the realm of motives; promotion designed to stimulate or direct desires.	Increase customer traffic; produce leads for salespeople; increase sales over last year's; reduce customer returns from last year's.	Evaluate sales performance and number of inquiries; study customer intentions to buy before and after promotion; study customer trading areas and average purchases; study coupon redemption.

Source: Adapted by the authors from Robert Lavidge and Gary A. Steiner, "A Model for Predictive Measurement of Advertising Effectiveness," *Journal of Marketing*, Vol. 25 (October 1961), p. 61. Reprinted by permission of the American Marketing Association.

Table 17–5 lists a number of research approaches for testing the effectiveness of a promotional effort. Although difficulties may sometimes exist in assessing promotion efforts (for instance, increased sales may be due to a variety of factors, not just promotion), it is still necessary for a retailer to systematically study and adjust the promotional mix.

SUMMARY

1. *To explore the scope of retail promotion* Retail promotion involves any communication by a retailer that informs, persuades, and/or reminds the target market about any aspect of the retailer via advertising, publicity, personal selling, and sales promotion.

2. *To study the elements of retail promotion: advertising, publicity, personal selling, and sales promotion* Advertising involves any paid, nonpersonal communication and has the advantages of a large audience, low costs per person, many alternative media, and other factors. The disadvantages of advertising include an inflexible message, high absolute costs, and a wasted portion of the audience. Major advertising media are newspapers, telephone directories, direct mail, radio, television, transit, outdoor, magazines, and flyers/circulars. Of special importance are cooperative ads, by which a retailer shares the costs and message with manufacturers, wholesalers, or other retailers.

   Publicity is nonpersonal, nonpaid communication. Advantages include the enhanced image presented, the objectivity of the source to the consumer, and no costs for messages. Disadvantages include the lack of control over messages, the short-run nature, and the nonmedia costs. Publicity can be expected or unexpected, and positive or negative.

   Personal selling involves oral communication with one or more potential customers and is important for persuasion and in closing sales. Some advantages are the adaptability, flexibility, and immediate feedback. Some disadvantages are the small audience, high costs per customer, and the inability to help lure customers into the store. Order-taking (routine) and/or order-getting (creative) selling personnel can be employed. Sales functions include greeting the customer, determining wants, showing merchandise, making a sales presentation, demonstrating goods and/or services, answering objections, and closing the sale.

Sales promotion consists of paid supplements to advertising and personal selling. Among the advantages are that it is eye-catching, unique, and valuable to the customer. Among the disadvantages are that it may be hard to end, have a negative effect on image, and rely on frivolous selling points. Types of sales promotion include point-of-purchase displays, contests, sweepstakes, coupons, frequent-shopper programs, prizes, samples, demonstrations, referral gifts, matchbooks, pens, calendars, shopping bags, and special events.

3. *To discuss the strategic aspects of retail promotion: objectives, budgeting, the mix of forms, implementing the mix, and reviewing and revising the plan* First, objectives are stated in specific and measurable terms. An overall promotion budget is then determined on the basis of one of these techniques: the all-you-can-afford, incremental, competitive parity, percentage-of-sales, and objective-and-task methods.

Third, the promotional mix is outlined, based on the size of the retailer's budget, the type of retailing involved, the coverage of the media, and the stage in the hierarchy-of-effects model. Fourth, the promotional mix is implemented. Included are decisions involving specific media, promotional timing, message content, sales-force composition, particular sales promotion tools, and the responsibility for coordination. Last, the retailer systematically reviews and revises the promotional plan, consistent with its pre-set objectives.

KEY TERMS

retail promotion (p. 580)
advertising (p. 580)
cooperative advertising (p. 582)
pioneer advertisement (p. 586)
competitive advertisement (p. 586)
reminder advertisement (p. 586)
institutional advertisement (p. 586)
vertical cooperative-advertising agreement (p. 587)
horizontal cooperative-advertising agreement (p. 587)
publicity (p. 587)
personal selling (p. 588)
order-taking salesperson (p. 590)
order-getting salesperson (p. 590)
PMs (p. 590)
canned sales presentation (p. 591)
need-satisfaction approach (p. 591)
sales promotion (p. 592)
all-you-can-afford method (p. 597)
incremental method (p. 597)
competitive parity method (p. 598)
percentage-of-sales method (p. 598)
objective-and-task method (p. 598)
hierarchy-of-effects model (p. 601)
agate line (p. 602)
milline rate (p. 602)
reach (p. 602)
frequency (p. 602)
extensive media coverage (p. 602)
intensive media coverage (p. 602)
massed advertising effort (p. 603)
distributed advertising effort (p. 603)
comparative advertising (p. 604)

QUESTIONS FOR DISCUSSION

1. Are there any retailers that should not use advertising? Explain your answer.
2. How would an advertising plan for a small retailer differ from that of a large retail chain?
3. How do manufacturers' and retailers' cooperative advertising goals overlap? How do they differ?
4. How should a retailer try to generate positive publicity?
5. Give three examples each of order-taking salespeople and order-getting salespeople. Under which circumstances should each type be used?
6. How can advertising, personal selling, and sales promotion complement each other for a retailer?
7. Are there any retailers that should not use sales promotion? Explain your answer.
8. What are the pros and cons of frequent-shopper programs?
9. Develop sales promotions for each of the following:
   a. A new shopping center in a major metropolitan area.
   b. An existing restaurant now open on Sunday for the first time.
   c. An existing major appliance retailer.
   d. A new supermarket in a moderate-sized suburb.
10. Which method of promotional budgeting should a small retailer use? Why? A large retailer? Why?
11. Explain the hierarchy-of-effects model from a retail perspective. Apply your answer to a new travel agency.
12. Describe the difference between frequency and reach in retail advertising. Which is more important? Why?
13. Develop a checklist for a full-line discount store to coordinate its promotional plan.
14. For each of these promotional objectives, explain how to evaluate promotional effectiveness:
    a. Increase customer traffic by 10 per cent.
    b. Develop an innovative image.
    c. Maintain customer loyalty.

CASE 1
Selling at Bon Marche*

Bon Marche is a 39-store division of Federated Department Stores. The West Coast-based Bon Marche generates about $800 million in revenues annually.

Bon Marche's philosophy is to guarantee shopper satisfaction with regard to both merchandise and customer service. This is accomplished at four different levels: anticipation of customer needs, merchandise presentation, handling of returns and problems, and exceptional opportunities.

At Bon Marche, anticipating customer needs often means focusing on the little extras that shoppers might not even anticipate occurring at another chain. Such extras might include offering to take a product to the gift wrap area to save the customer time or suggesting to a busy shopper that a product could be delivered to the person's home as an added convenience. Some sales associates even offer to take packages to shoppers' cars if they appear to be too heavy for the shoppers to carry.

In presenting merchandise, sales associates are taught to know the features of every item sold, as well as their comparative benefits. Sources of product information include the department's buyer, vendor sales and catalog materials, product seminars, specialized magazine literature, and discussions with more experienced associates. The sales associates' product knowledge makes shoppers feel more secure, increases the chances that shoppers pick the proper items, reduces returns, and lessens customers' total time commitment.

Although many consumers feel uncomfortable entering a department to return an item, Bon Marche specifically trains sales associates to put them at ease. The sales associates are taught to accept for repair or replace those products that are not properly functioning, as well as to exchange wrong colors, sizes, or styles for the appropriate ones. In some cases, the consumer has erred by purchasing a low-priced item that will not properly perform the required task. The exchange situation should be seen as a way to make things right, not as a problem area.

Lastly, salespeople often have exceptional opportunities to capitalize on Bon Marche's "I guarantee it" philosophy. Examples include a sales associate's arranging for the installation of a headset on a television set to better enable a hard-of-hearing consumer to listen to the sound, making a special delivery to a consumer in an emergency situation, or installing equipment in a consumer's home.

John Hart, the sales manager for men's clothing at a branch of Bon Marche, has developed procedures for effective selling based upon the "I guarantee it" philosophy. These procedures are shown in Table 1. Hart intends to submit this material to a Bon Marche vice-president for review and possible chainwide adoption.

QUESTIONS

1. Evaluate the selling procedures outlined in Table 1. How would you improve these procedures?
2. How would you change these procedures to accommodate a semiannual sale that attracts shoppers who wait for this event?
3. How should a department manager respond to a sales associate who has the highest volume in the department yet refuses to abide by the procedures in Table 1? Explain your answer.
4. As a newly-hired sales associate in Bon Marche's camera department, you are concerned about developing an appropriate sales presentation, as well as providing superior customer satisfaction. Describe four different types of customer needs that are common for the $59 to $500 camera equipment that you are responsible for selling. Develop an appropriate presentation for each type of need.

* Based on material in Gary Hoover, Alta Campbell, and Patrick J. Spain (Editors), *Hoover's Handbook of American Business 1994* (Austin, Texas: Reference Press, 1993), pp. 492–493; and Bon Marche correspondence.

Table 1 Suggested Procedures for Effective Apparel Selling

- When meeting a new customer, the salesperson should explain the long-term relationship sought by Bon Marche. The customer's height and weight, as well as color, style, and texture preferences, should be ascertained and noted in the sales associate's log book. The person's desired price range for various items should also be recorded. Company policies, such as alteration costs, should be described.
- A sales associate should try to schedule appointments with loyal customers. In this way, undivided attention can be given to individual customers, the sales associate can assemble selections in advance of appointments, and customers can allocate adequate time for an in-store visit.
- All sales associates should be honest in appraising the style, color, and fit of garments. Bon Marche wants its customers to be satisfied.
- A sales associate should be aware of the opportunities available through cross-selling. For example, a sports jacket purchase could lead to the purchase of slacks and a tie. Suit buyers should be encouraged to look at ties and shirts. In general, customers should be reminded that the best time to purchase accessories is when the garments are in the store, so he/she can see how the combination of colors and textures actually look.
- A sales associate should stay with the customer throughout the in-store experience. It is important to verify the need for alterations and to remind the customer of the date when his/her garments will be ready. Nonetheless, the person should be allowed to browse throughout the store, if he or she so desires. The salesperson should be available at the person's request.
- A sales associate's job is not complete when the sale is made. The associate is expected to be present when the customer returns to pick up the altered garments to verify the fit. This is another opportunity to ensure client satisfaction and to suggest other items (in a subtle way).
- Customers should be encouraged to trade up to better-quality garments as they go through their career cycles.
- Regular customers should be contacted in advance of special sales to alert them to the opportunity to purchase at 10 to 50 per cent off usual Bon Marche prices. This gives the sales associate another reason to contact customers.

VIDEO QUESTIONS ON BON MARCHE

1. Should Bon Marche sales personnel use the canned sales presentation or the need-satisfaction approach in dealing with customers? Why? Would your answer be the same for a discount clothing store? Why?
2. Cite five exceptional opportunities for a sales associate in the china department of Bon Marche.

CASE 2A

Competitech 1: Telemarketing In Action†

Brenda Johnson, Vice-President of Marketing, has a major problem. Her firm, Competitech, a retailer of computer supplies, has recently started to feature a toll-free 800 number in all of its ads, direct-mail pieces, and catalogs. The public has been responding well to this easy-to-use, economical method of ordering. Response rate reports indicate that sales should be up by 12 to 15 per cent. Yet, actual revenues are the same as before Competitech started using telemarketing. In studying the reports, Johnson has found that her telemarketing representatives have received about 4,000 calls over the past 20 days. She is pleased to note that about 50 per cent of the callers had never previously bought anything from Competitech. The fact that the "phone has been ringing but the cash register has not" is cause for deep concern.

To review the matter further, Johnson has called a meeting of the managers of telemarketing, shipping and inventory management, mail order, and customer service. The goal of the meeting is to see where and how business is being lost, and to review the steps of order processing as depicted in Figure 1.

When telemarketing personnel get a call for a computer part or a software package, they record the customer's name, address, product-identification data, and credit-card information; they then ask the caller where he/she had seen a Competitech advertisement or other promotional information. Brenda Johnson considers this last bit of information vital to learn which media are stimulating the most responses. At the end of the workday, the telemarketers send all their orders to the mail-order department where that day's orders are combined. The orders are next passed to the shipping and inventory-management department to verify creditworthiness (if the orders need it), and order pickers fill each request and prepare the products for shipment.

If the requested merchandise is out of stock, a written notice of the shortage and the customer's name and address is given to the customer-service group. Customer service sends a letter apologizing for the temporary delay in completing the order and indicates when Competitech expects to ship the back-ordered product.

The telemarketing group is beginning to receive calls from customers stating that they do not want to wait for back orders and therefore wish to cancel their requests. In some situations, customers angrily say they would never have done business with Competitech if they had known about the delays.

Johnson realizes that Competitech is not only losing an opportunity to capitalize on new business but, even worse, is alienating some customers.

† This case was prepared and written by Professor John I. Coppett and Professor William A. Staples, University of Houston-Clear Lake, Houston, Texas.

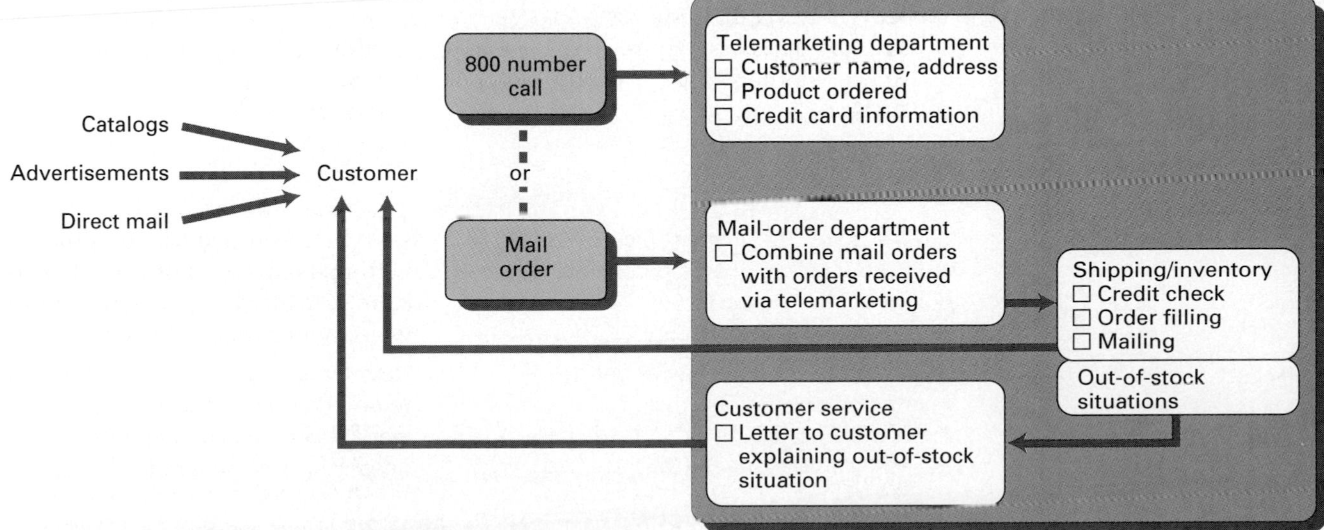

FIGURE 1 Order-Processing Operations

QUESTIONS

1. Evaluate the order-processing system shown in Figure 1.
2. How could Competitech use telemarketing to more efficiently support the customer-service function?
3. What should be the role of advertising at Competitech? The role of personal selling?
4. What kinds of sales promotions should Competitech utilize? Why?

CASE 2B
Competitech 2: Telemarketing in Action‡

The background material for this case is provided in the Competitech 1 case. You should read that case before analyzing Competitech 2.

The discussion that follows is taking place one year after the issues described in Competitech 1 were resolved. Brenda Johnson, Vice-President of Marketing, is meeting with Frank Thomas, the Telemarketing Center Manager.

JOHNSON: Frank, since we solved the problem of how to coordinate our telemarketing order-processing activity with the inventory control people, our sales and profits have really increased. Our sales are up thirty per cent over last year and customer complaints are much lower. Top management is greatly pleased with your department.

THOMAS: Thanks, Brenda. I'll pass that on to the people on the phones. You know I've been in the telemarketing business for almost ten years and this is the best group of people I have ever worked with. They're really customer-oriented.

JOHNSON: I know. Last week, I was at an AT&T seminar. One of the things they mentioned got me thinking about our center and how we could do an even better job with telemarketing.

THOMAS: What do you have in mind?

JOHNSON: Well, right now, all of our business is generated by incoming calls. Customers call us after they see one of our ads or get one of our catalogs. The customer, however, is taking the initiative in these situations. What the AT&T people were recommending was an "outcall" sales program. Rather than just wait for incoming calls to be placed, they recommended that we also make calls from our center to prospective customers. In that way, we can use our center more efficiently and increase our sales even more. We would still be selling the same products. What do you think?

THOMAS: There is a big difference between being an order taker and an order getter. Let me get back with you next week with a plan that will test the feasibility of this.

JOHNSON: Good!

QUESTIONS

1. What are the major factors that Frank Thomas needs to consider as he designs a plan?
2. Describe some of the major "people problems" that will need to be anticipated by Thomas if the expansion occurs.
3. Assuming that it is technically feasible for Competitech to proceed with this expanded use of telemarketing, with what target market would you suggest it start?
4. How would you suggest that the telemarketing operators obtain new leads from which additional business might be secured?

‡ This case was prepared and written by Professor John I. Coppett and Professor William A. Staples, University of Houston-Clear Lake, Houston, Texas.

PART 7 COMPREHENSIVE CASE

Position and Promos Boost Card Sales*

Introduction

Despite competing discounters, Ukrop's draws big profits from medium-sized greeting-card departments. How does it do it? It uses favored locations and cents-off promos via electronic shopper cards.

The Role of Greeting Cards at Ukrop's

"Where people and food come first." With a slogan like that, it's no surprise that nonfoods takes a secondary role at Ukrop's. The 21-store, Richmond, Virgina-based supermarket chain projects a powerful food presence, including expensive sit-down dining areas in several of its bigger stores and a central kitchen for its large service bakeries and delis.

But some nonfoods' action has taken place. Health and beauty care has been upgraded with larger sections and more promotion. General merchandise, on the other hand, is fully represented but held on a fairly tight leash.

Greeting cards is a modest exception. In rather tight quarters (as little as 20 square feet in Ukrop's smallest store, up to a maximum of 76 square feet), the category still manages to command nearly 0.6 per cent of overall chain sales. That's big business—about $2.4 million a year in a company with estimated annual sales of around $400 million and stores mostly in the 35,000- to 45,000-square-foot range.

The Power of Greeting Cards

Thanks to several factors, including more frequent promotion, the chain's greeting-card sales have tripled since 1986 (with only one store added during this time).

"Cards is sort of a pet department for us," says Harvey Sutton, Ukrop's general merchandise director. "You look at those 50 per cent margins and practically zero operating costs—full vendor service and no warehousing and delivery charges—and you can't help but be favorably disposed, even if your orientation is focused on food."

He also notes that because cards are driven by seasonal events and occasions, they relate particularly well with service bakery, deli, and floral operations, as well as grocery sections such as baking needs and candy. And Sutton points out that cards has become a demand department, that "customers expect to find greeting cards in their supermarket, especially younger women who are working and pressed for time. They're attracted by the colorful variety and attractive fixtures and shopping convenience."

Pumping Up Sales

The card department has long held a relatively favored position at Ukrop's. But, it was generally located in an alcove area, away from the primary customer traffic flow.

Then, in 1989, Ukrop's opened the first of its four in-store pharmacies. It was at that point, says Sutton, that "we began to loosen the reins a little bit." Cards gained some floor space, but perhaps even more importantly, the department began to move into the main sales area. Sutton explains that "greeting cards, along with health and beauty care, are part of the customer's mindset when she [he] sees a pharmacy."

That realization began to extend beyond the pharmacy stores, setting the stage for cards' move into the grocery grid. See Figure 1.

The Importance of In-Store Locations

Thomas Kearns, a key accounts manager for the greeting-card vendor, is among the supplier people fostering the upgrading of greeting cards at Ukrop's. He says greeting cards' success depends heavily on the same factor that underpins any store—location, location, location.

"Placement is critical for cards today for supermarkets," says Kearns. "Competition from other types of outlets is growing. Supermarkets have the best frequency of store visits, but to capitalize on this advantage supers must be sure customers know that the department is there. A prime location is the best insurance."

Kearns says alcove positions or other locations away from the main traffic flow are "tricky" and can be weak. With a location in the main grocery traffic area or facing the perimeter, sales opportunities are enhanced—if the section itself provides strong magnets. The grocery locations he says are preferable are near cookies and commercial bread. He gives an OK to breakfast cereals, but finds beer and soda less suitable. Sutton notes that the store achieving the chain's highest sales per foot for cards has a 60-foot section in the paper aisle. Kearns and Sutton regularly work together in planning the greeting-card department. See Figure 2.

Kearns cites several examples from Ukrop's where an improved location reaped sales benefits. In one store,

* The material in this case was prepared and written by Glenn Snyder of *Progressive Grocer*. It originally appeared in "Position and Promos Boost Card Sales," *Progressive Grocer* (May 1993), pp. 47–51. Copyright *Progressive Grocer*. Reprinted by permission.

FIGURE 1

Placing Greater Emphasis on Greeting Cards

For the last several years, Ukrop's has put greater in-store attention on greeting cards, recognizing the strong potential of this department.

the card section was switched with bread. Cards were pulled out of a front alcove and installed in-line 40 feet away (across from cookies), display footage was cut by 8 feet. "The bread people almost killed me until I pointed out they were getting more shelf space and two endcaps [end-of-aisle displays]," says Kearns. The swap boosted card sales by 24 per cent, netting the store an extra $200 a week even though the new 64-foot section was smaller.

What about the bread section? Kearns says he thinks it more than held its own. "People have no trouble remembering where the bread and rolls are," he says. "It's greeting cards that has the big need for impulse sales and memory reinforcement."

Store Fixtures and Displays

From a fixture standpoint, higher-density racks with up to 16 tiers of merchandise help broaden the assortment. But, they do not compensate for insufficient floor space.

They can also impede turnover if sales are not increased sufficiently, according to Kearns. He adds that strong, point-of-sale materials and seasonal decorations are important allies. "One way or another, we must make sure cards are never overlooked," Kearns says.

Investing in Promotion

Ukrop's nod to cards in terms of promotion began in 1988. At that time, freestanding half-page newspaper ads began appearing during peak seasons once or twice a year. Available with promotional monies, the ads included offers such as one card free with three and free stamps with a purchase. They were successful, but expensive.

Enter a whole new technique: Ukrop's Valued Customer Program. The program features a smart card that enables participating customers to receive, among other things, the stores' cents-off product offers deducted automatically at the checkout with a purchase. The program is based on a monthly mailing to more than 200,000 registered customers and includes a sheet listing about 75 items with coupons in 20 categories.

FIGURE 2

Cooperative Planning

Ukrop's general merchandise manager, Harvey Sutton (at left), and greeting-card salesperson, Thomas Kearns (at right) meet frequently to discuss the layout of the items in the card department.

Greeting cards were included in 1990, a few years after Ukrop's introduced the valued customer program in 1987. It was one of the first supermarket chains to do so.

At present, greeting cards receive six, month-long cents-off jolts a year—Valentine's Day, Easter, Mother's Day, Father's Day, graduation, and Christmas. In the past, most offers were for 25 cents off. But, Valentine's Day 1993 brought the first 50-cent coupon; and chainwide sales of Valentine's cards reached 59,862, about 2,800 per store and 14 per cent above 1992 when a 25-cent coupon was offered.

Aggressive greeting-card promotions, such as the 50-cent Valentine coupon, are necessary since competition from the discounters is tougher than ever. The discounters have increased the size of their card departments and their promotional push. For example, a Phar-Mor drugstore in the same shopping center as a Ukrop's has doubled the size of its department to about 250 linear base feet; card discounts are "up to" 50 per cent.

At first glance, the monthly coupon list in the valued customer mailing looks rather prosaic. Do customers really take notice of the items? Avidly, reports a company spokesperson, judging from sales results. The initial hit from cards offered with coupons and those being promoted for the first time is "astronomical," according to Thomas Kearns, the key accounts manager for the greeting-card vendor—a gain in the 40 per cent to 50 per cent range depending on the seasonal event.

The shopper card is reportedly used in more than 90 per cent of Ukrop's overall transactions. Point-of-sale signs remind customers of the coupon specials. See Figure 3.

Kearns says the savings from not purchasing newspaper ad space enables Ukrop's to run more frequent cents off offers throughout the year. Before the smart-card program, greeting cards received no more than two ad-supported coupon offers a year. Now, there are six regular promotions.

Not Giving Away the Store

Frequent couponing through the smart-card program also presents a forceful price image against greeting-card discounters without "giving away the store" with an everyday discount program.

It's generally held that everyday discounts on cards at a figure that makes a price impression seldom advance unit movement sufficiently to compensate for the decline in dollar profit. Kearns says cents-off offers during peak seasonal periods maintain the dollar profits, along with a price image. What's more, the promotional activity builds shopper recognition and, hence, sales throughout the year.

"Greeting cards are not particularly price sensitive during the year, but tend to become so during the major seasonal times," says Kearns. "So, by gearing offers to top seasonal times, we are achieving a good compromise." Also, he adds, cents-off coupons are a more effective way to use cooperative advertising funds than institutional [company image] ads. "In short," he says, "customer cards give us more bang for the buck."

Another advantage is that the offers can involve multiple purchases or can be attached to some other item to build the retail sale. With the single-purchase coupon, the customer intent on buying a single greeting card can take advantage of the offer, while multiple-card purchasers can enjoy multiple savings.

The electronic coupons do not always ride alone. Besides increasing the coupon value in its Valentine program mailing in 1993, Ukrop's added radio commercials. A few days before the deadline, radio listeners in rush-hour traffic were reminded that "The Day" was about to arrive; last call for greeting cards, flowers, and boxed candy at Ukrop's.

Harvey Sutton, Ukrop's general merchandise director, reports that the use of the smart cards salvaged a seg-

FIGURE 3
Promoting Smart-Card Usage
Point-of-sale signs showing smart-card coupon savings boost redemption. The greeting-card department also gets a line in the Valued Customer Program's monthly mailing about six times a year. Copyright *Progressive Grocer.* Reprinted by permission.

ment of the greeting-card business that had been virtually conceded to the discounters: boxed Christmas cards. "We decided to give it a shot in 1991 with a $2-off coupon," he says. "We sold 900 boxes in two days; this cleaned us out. We reordered and ended up selling about 8,000 boxes in two months."

Sutton has also observed an uplifting phenomenon. With cents-off electronic coupons (in greeting cards at least), shoppers tend to trade up. "They seem to be buying more of the higher-priced cards and boxes of cards rather than the cheaper ones, more $3 cards than $1.50 cards. Now that's good."

Questions

1. Based on the information presented in this case, describe and evaluate the image of Ukrop's greeting-card department. Is it consistent with the overall positioning of a supermarket? Explain your answer.
2. Describe the criteria that Ukrop's should use to determine how much space to devote to its greeting-card department and where to situate the department in the store.
3. Should Ukrop's advertise its greeting-card department? Why or why not?
4. What kind of cooperative promotions should Ukrop's expect from its greeting-card vendor? Why?
5. Comment on Ukrop's decision to offer six coupon promotions per year for greeting cards rather than use an everyday low pricing strategy.
6. Show how Ukrop's could use the objective-and-task method to devise a yearly promotion budget for its greeting-card department.
7. How should Ukrop's promotion strategy for greeting cards change during the year? Present a monthly plan.

Planning for the Future

- In Part 8, two aspects of retailing that are crucial in anticipating, planning for, and responding to the future are detailed.
- Chapter 18 focuses on how firms offering rented-goods, owned-goods, and nongoods services can develop and enact proper strategies, as well as prepare for the future. These retailers must address the intangibility of service offerings, the inseparability of services from their providers, the perishability of services, and the variability of service performance.
- Chapter 19 ties together the elements of a retail strategy that have been described throughout the text. The chapter examines planning and opportunity analysis, performance measures, productivity, and uses of new technology. The value of industry-wide data comparisons is assessed. Strategic control via the retail audit is covered.

Planning by a Service Retailer

❖ Chapter Objectives

1. To examine the scope of service retailing
2. To show how service retailing differs from goods-oriented retailing
3. To apply strategy concepts to service retailing: situation analysis, objectives, target marketing, overall strategy, implementation, and re-evaluation
4. To evaluate uncontrollable factors as they pertain to service retailers

The car-rental business is a tough one. It is highly seasonal, consumers often have specifications in mind (such as a sedan, convertible, or van), and vacationers and business travelers may require different rental locations. A car-rental firm also needs a host of facilitating services, such as providing data about terms, having a reservation system, handling a car's checkout and return, processing bills, and handling complaints.

For instance, to position itself more clearly, InterRent-Europcar of Sweden decided to design its basic service package around these facilitating services and to offer three service guarantees:

- A "get to the destination" guarantee—Customers are guaranteed to be on their way within 45 minutes of calling InterRent to report a breakdown. If the firm cannot meet this standard, it will send a taxi and pay all fees.
- A "lowest price" guarantee—Its computer system automatically determines the lowest price based on comparing all possible rates (such as daily or weekly rates and various mileage options).
- A "trouble-free service" guarantee—There will be no charge, if a rental car is delivered more than five minutes late.

According to InterRent, these guarantees have reversed an earlier sales decline without significantly increasing the firm's operating expenses.

The car-rental firm that is both an innovator and a leader in service quality is Hertz, which often scores first on Zagat's surveys of customers. Hertz' successful strategy is partly based on its #1 Club Gold program. As part of this program, members pay a $50 yearly fee and call ahead to reserve a car. Instead of waiting to see an attendant, waiting again to have credit checked, and waiting a third time to be driven to the rental car, Hertz' club members are driven directly to their reserved car after boarding the Hertz airport courtesy bus. The bus driver calls a Hertz attendant to advise him or her that a member has boarded the bus so the rental car can be started and the air-conditioning or heat turned on. All a club member has to do is to show the gate attendant a driver's license as he or she drives off. Says one club member, "This is the best thing that ever happened to rental cars."[1]

[1] Christian Grönroos and Hans Ake Sand, "A Winning Service Offer in Car Rental," *Management Decision*, Vol. 31 (Number 1, 1993), pp. 45–51; and Patricia Sellers, "Companies That Serve You Best," *Fortune* (May 31, 1993), pp. 74–80.

Reprinted by permission of Hertz.

Overview

Service retailing in the United States and elsewhere in the world is growing steadily and represents a very large portion of overall retail trade. Although the total revenues from service retailing are hard to estimate because key government data do not separate retail services from business services, the dimensions of service retailing can be seen from these examples. In the United States,

- Consumers spend three-fifths of their after-tax income on such services as travel, recreation, personal care, education, medical care, and housing.[2]
- Over 70 per cent of the labor force is employed in the service sector.[3]
- Consumers spend billions of dollars each year to rent such products as power tools and party goods (coffee urns, silverware, wine glasses, etc.).[4]
- People annually spend $120 billion to maintain and repair their cars.[5]
- The top five amusement parks (Walt Disney World, Disneyland, Universal Studios Florida, Universal Studios Hollywood, and Sea World of Florida) attract about 60 million visitors per year.[6]
- There are 76,000 beauty salons and barber shops, 50,000 laundry-service outlets, 39,000 hotels and motels, 17,000 video-rental stores, and 13,000 sports and recreation clubs.[7]
- At shopping centers, from the world's largest regional shopping center—the West Edmonton Mall—to the smallest neighborhood shopping center, service retailers such as restaurants, beauty salons and barber shops, and others play a key role in drawing customer traffic and providing a positive shopping atmosphere. See Figure 18–1.
- During the past 20 years, the prices of services have risen more than the prices of goods (excluding food and energy). Due to technological advances, automation has substantially reduced labor costs in manufacturing; but many services remain rather labor-intensive because of their personal nature.[8]

As noted in Chapter 5, ***service retailing*** encompasses rented goods, owned goods, and nongoods. With rented-goods services, consumers lease physical products for a specified period of time. With owned-goods services, consumers own the physical products that are repaired, maintained, or altered. With nongoods services, consumers receive personal expertise from a service provider; physical goods are not involved or have a small role in a business.

Service retailing's growth and the differences in strategic planning for a service retailer and a goods retailer make this a part of retailing to be thoroughly studied. In the future, the service sector will continue to expand. Opportunities will be plentiful for those who know how to react to them.

[2] *Statistical Abstract of the United States 1993* (Washington, D.C.: U.S. Department of Commerce, 1993), p. 443.

[3] Daniel Benjamin, "Some Germans Pin Hopes on Service Jobs," *Wall Street Journal* (November 10, 1993), p. A16.

[4] Clifford J. Levy, "Persuading People to Rent More Than Just Videos," *New York Times* (April 19, 1992), Section 3, p. 8.

[5] Julie Edelson Halpert, "Who Will Fix Tomorrow's Cars?" *New York Times* (November 7, 1993), Section 3, p. 4.

[6] Richard Turner, "New Theme Parks Will Take Owners on a Risky Ride," *Wall Street Journal* (December 2, 1993), pp. B1, B6.

[7] *Statistical Abstract of the United States 1993*, p. 788.

[8] See Myron Magnet, "Good News for the Service Economy," *Fortune* (May 3, 1993), pp. 46–52.

FIGURE 18–1 The Diversity of Service Retailing at the West Edmonton Mall
Reprinted by permission of Triple Five Corporation. Photos by The Postcard Factory.

Strategy Concepts Applied to Service Retailing

The unique aspects of services, which influence a retail strategy, are that (1) the intangible nature of many services makes a consumer's choice of competitive offerings more difficult than with goods; (2) the service provider and his or her services are sometimes inseparable (thus localizing marketing efforts and giving consumers a limited choice of alternatives); (3) the perishability of many services prevents storage and increases risks; and (4) the human nature of many services makes them more variable.

The intangible (and possibly abstract) nature of services make it tougher for a firm to develop a clear consumer-oriented strategy, particularly as many retailers (such as opticians, repairpersons, and landscapers) start service businesses on the basis of their product expertise. The inseparability of the service provider and his or her services means the owner-operator is often indispensable and good customer relations are necessary. Perishability presents a risk that in many instances cannot be overcome. For example, the revenues from an unrented hotel room are forever lost. Variability means service quality may differ for each shopping experience, store, or service provider. See Figure 18–2.

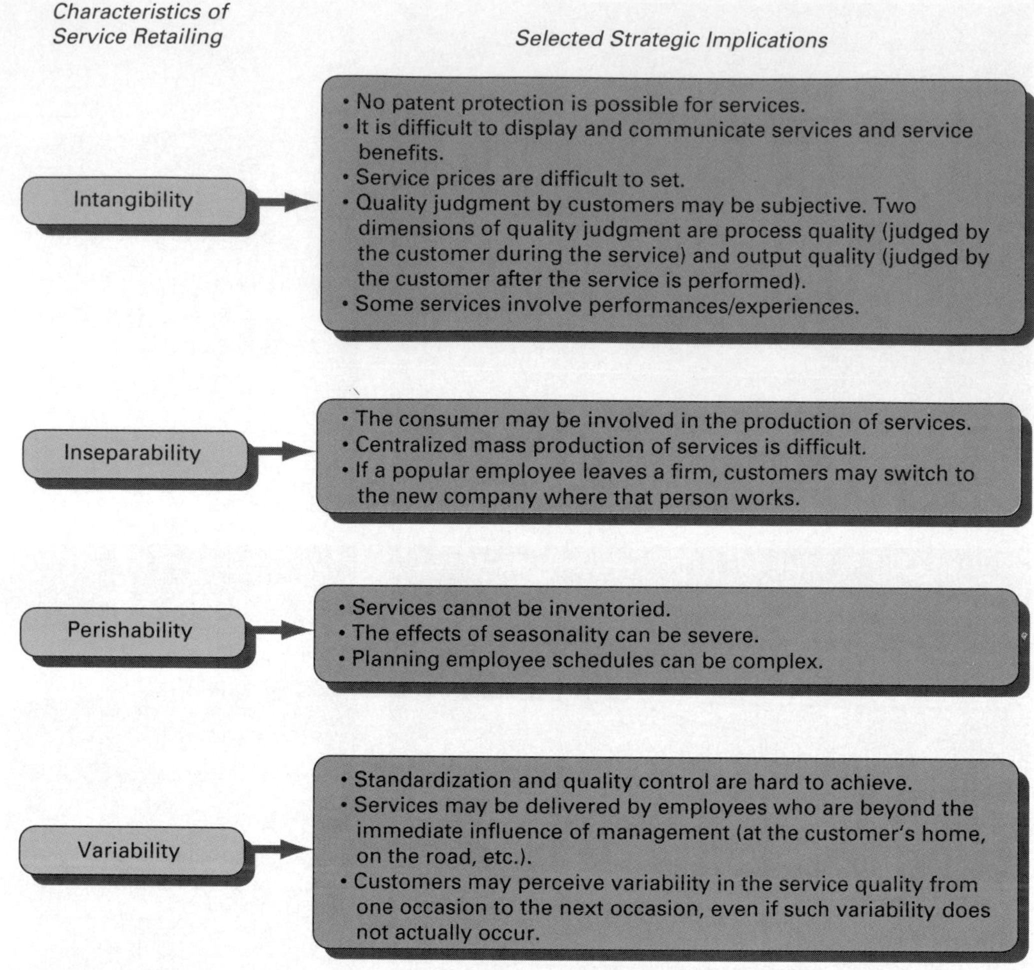

Characteristics of Service Retailing
Selected Strategic Implications
Intangibility
• No patent protection is possible for services.
• It is difficult to display and communicate services and service benefits.
• Service prices are difficult to set.
• Quality judgment by customers may be subjective. Two dimensions of quality judgment are process quality (judged by the customer during the service) and output quality (judged by the customer after the service is performed).
• Some services involve performances/experiences.
Inseparability
• The consumer may be involved in the production of services.
• Centralized mass production of services is difficult.
• If a popular employee leaves a firm, customers may switch to the new company where that person works.
Perishability
• Services cannot be inventoried.
• The effects of seasonality can be severe.
• Planning employee schedules can be complex.
Variability
• Standardization and quality control are hard to achieve.
• Services may be delivered by employees who are beyond the immediate influence of management (at the customer's home, on the road, etc.).
• Customers may perceive variability in the service quality from one occasion to the next occasion, even if such variability does not actually occur.

FIGURE 18–2 Characteristics of Service Retailing That Differentiate It from Goods Retailing and Their Strategic Implications

Source: Adapted by the authors from Valarie A. Zeithaml, A. Parasuraman, and Leonard L. Berry, "Problems and Strategies in Service Marketing," *Journal of Marketing*, Vol. 49 (Spring 1985), p. 35. Reprinted by permission of the American Marketing Association.

Figure 18–3 shows a system for classifying service retailers; an individual firm should precisely identify the combination of attributes in this figure that it possesses (or wants to possess) and act accordingly. Typically, a service retailer can be described in terms of each category depicted in Figure 18–3. For example, a car-rental firm may be classified as rented goods (degree of tangibility), nonprofessional (skill of service provider), equipment-based (degree of labor intensiveness), low contact (degree of customer contact), profit-oriented (goal), and relatively nonregulated (degree of regulation). However, this classification system is not ironclad. If a problem occurs (such as a rental car's not functioning properly or a promised car's being unavailable), a low-contact car-rental firm would become a high-contact firm.[9]

Although service-oriented retailing differs from goods-oriented retailing, strategy planning should be conducted by using the same overall procedure:

1. The situation is analyzed, including a definition of the service category.
2. The objectives of the firm are enumerated and ranked.

[9] For a further discussion on classifying services, see John Bowen, "Development of Taxonomy of Services to Gain Strategic Marketing Insights," *Journal of the Academy of Marketing Science*, Vol. 18 (Winter 1990), pp. 43–49.

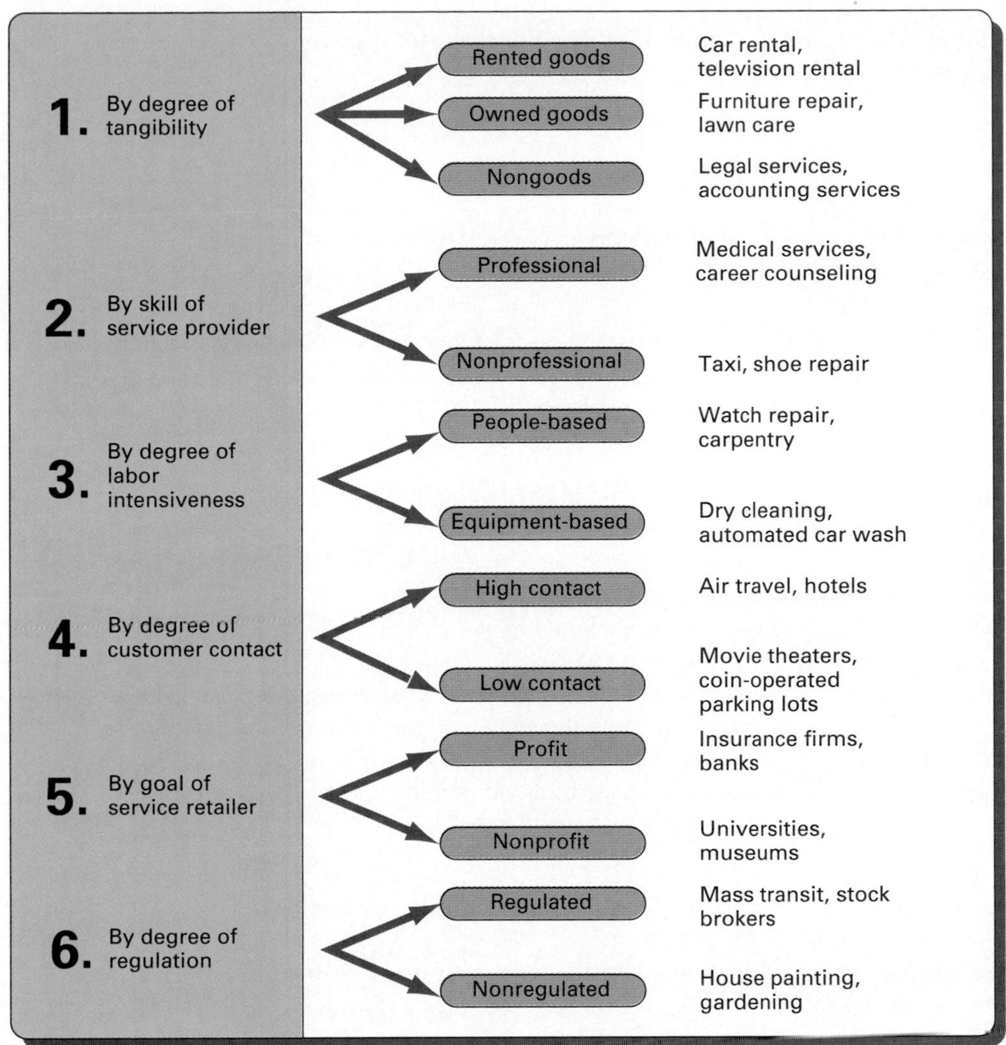

FIGURE 18–3
A Classification System for Service Retailers

3. Consumer characteristics and needs are identified.
4. The overall strategy is outlined.
5. The strategy is implemented.
6. The strategy is regularly re-evaluated and adjusted.

In particular, a service retailer must understand its organizational mission, efficiently select opportunities, set clear objectives, cater to consumer needs, be cost-effective, present a distinctive offering, determine how to set prices, communicate with customers, and plan for competition.

Table 18–1 points out how firms can plan for the differences between service and goods retailing.

SITUATION ANALYSIS

While developing a service strategy, a retailer must determine whether rented-goods, owned-goods, or nongoods services are involved because planning is different for each type of service. The service category must then be more narrowly defined, as these illustrations show:

TABLE 18–1 Special Managerial Considerations for Service Retailers in Seven Key Strategic Areas

Service Retailing as Compared with Goods Retailing	Managerial Adjustments Needed by Service Retailers
a. Store organization	
More specialized supervision is needed.	Separate management for service areas will be required.
More specific search for service employees is needed.	Nontraditional sources for identification of employees must be used.
Lower employee turnover is needed.	Frequent salary and performance reviews must be carried out.
Higher pay for skilled craftspeople than for merchandising personnel is needed.	Pay levels will need to be adjusted upward over periods of longevity for service employees.
b. Service production	
More involvement in producing the service is necessary.	Production skills will need to be obtained by supervisors.
More emphasis on quality control is needed.	Supervisors must be able to assess the quality of a service performed for a customer.
There is more need to monitor consumer satisfaction.	Prior customers should be researched to measure their satisfaction with the service.
There is more need to refine scheduling of employees.	Maximizing the service employees' time requires matching consumer purchasing with the employees' ability to produce the service.
Quality must be consistent among all outlets.	Standards for consistency of the service must be established and continually evaluated; central training may be required for workers in multiple-branch operations.
c. Pricing	
Services vary in cost; therefore, pricing is harder.	Prices may be quoted within a range instead of an exact figure before the purchase.
There is more difficulty in price competition or promotion based on price.	Services should be promoted on the basis of criteria other than price.
d. Promotion	
Value is more difficult for consumers to determine.	Consumers need to be convinced of value through personal selling.
It is difficult to display services within a store.	In-store signing or a service center is required to notify customers of services' availability.
Visual presentation is more important.	Before-and-after photographs may be possible with some services. Testimonials may be possible with other services.
Cross-selling with goods is important.	A quota or bonus for goods-oriented salespersons who suggest services will lead to increased service selling.
It is more difficult to advertise in catalogs.	Conditions for the sale and for away-from-the-store performance must be specified.
e. Complaints	
It is more difficult to return a service.	Policies must be established for adjusting the service purchased by a dissatisfied customer.
A customer is more sensitive about services involving a person (rather than a good).	Specific guarantees and policies about adjustments must be established; new types of insurance must be added to cover liabilities.
f. Controls	
There is a greater opportunity to steal customers.	Employees' assurances of loyalty must be established. Protection of store loyalty must be sought.

TABLE 18–1 (Continued)

Service Retailing as Compared with Goods Retailing	Managerial Adjustments Needed by Service Retailers
g. Measuring performance	
Capital expenditures vary widely for different services.	Return on net worth may not be the most important measurement of the value of a service to the retailer.
Small or no inventories are required to offer services.	Turnover, markdown controls, and other goods-related controls are not as appropriate.
Higher labor costs exist for services.	Profit after labor costs replaces the gross margin used with goods retailing.
Some services support the sale of goods.	Sales-supporting services should be evaluated differently from revenue-producing ones.
Cost accounting is more important.	Job-specific records will be required to assess the profitability of each sale.

Source: Adapted by the authors from J. Patrick Kelly and William R. George, "Strategic Management Issues for the Retailing of Services," *Journal of Retailing*, Vol. 58 (Summer 1982), pp. 40–42. Reprinted by permission.

- Is a retailer interested in opening a barber shop and giving haircuts? Or should a men's personal-care salon be opened, with such services as hair cutting, manicures, facial massages, hair coloring, and facial-care advice?
- Is a retailer going to operate an upscale resort hotel? Or should a discount motel chain be started?
- A potential dry cleaner is undecided: Should its focus be on clothing or household products? Or both?

These examples indicate the range of options available to a potential service retailer and demonstrate the necessity of defining the service category.

A retailer should decide on the service category before making any other strategic decisions. Too narrow a definition of the service category runs the risk of attracting a small target market and ignoring related services that may be vital to customer satisfaction. For example, a retailer that repairs televisions may also receive a lot of requests from customers to repair their VCRs. If the firm defines its offering too narrowly (and decides not to repair VCRs), it misses out on an opportunity to expand sales and it takes a chance of losing the television-repair business from these customers. On the other hand, too broad a definition of the service category (such as equipment repair) could result in a nonspecialist image and may require a larger operation and greater investment than desired.

When determining the service category, personal abilities, financial resources, and time resources should be matched to the requirements of the business. The personal abilities required of a service-oriented retailer are usually quite different from those of a goods-oriented retailer:

- In service retailing, the major value provided to the customer is some type of service, not the ownership of a physical product.
- Many specific skills may be required, and the skills may not be transferable from one type of service to another. For example, television repairpeople, beauticians, and accountants cannot easily change businesses or transfer skills. However, the owners of appliance stores, cosmetics stores, and toy stores (all goods-oriented firms) would have a much easier time changing and transferring their skills to another area.

RETAILING AROUND THE WORLD

Will KFC Make It in Venezuela on This Attempt?

In the late 1960s and 1970s, KFC's first attempt to enter the Venezuelan market failed due to a lack of commitment by its then-parent firm, Heublein. During the mid-1970s, under R.J. Reynolds (its next parent company), KFC made another try. However, over the next decade, the businessperson who was given countrywide franchising rights refused to expand beyond four restaurants. As a result, in the late 1980s, KFC again exited Venezuela.

Today, with PepsiCo as the parent company, KFC is making its third stab at succeeding in Venezuela. Plans are underway to open about 75 restaurants by the end of 1998. KFC's general manager for Venezuela is very optimistic about growth prospects, based on research that found growth patterns to be similar to those in Mexico, which is now KFC's largest market south of the Rio Grande, with more than 100 outlets.

To better appeal to Venezuelans, KFC is augmenting its "Americanized" menu with Venezuelan rice and bean dishes. It also hopes to sell beer, a popular beverage in Venezuela. KFC is also aware of the cultural differences between the U.S. and Venezuelan markets. For instance, many Venezuelans eat at KFC to celebrate important occasions, such as birthdays and holidays. Some McDonald's units in Venezuela even feature hostesses that seat customers, take their orders, and deliver meals to them.

Source: Based on material in Peter Wilson, "KFC Won't Chicken Out in Third Venezuelan Try," *Advertising Age* (December 13, 1993), pp. I-3, I-15.

- Many service operators must possess licenses or certification to run their businesses. Barbers, real-estate brokers, dentists, attorneys, plumbers, and others must pass examinations in their chosen fields.
- Owners of service businesses must enjoy their professions and have the aptitude for them. Because of the close personal contact with customers, these elements are essential and difficult to feign.

The financial resources necessary for a service-oriented retailer often differ significantly from those of a goods-oriented retailer. The major ongoing cost for many service retailers is labor. Whereas the opening of a service station demands a high capital investment, the compensation for mechanics is the largest ongoing cost of doing business. For goods retailers, the major ongoing investment is inventory.

Many service retailers can thus operate on lower overall investments and require less yearly revenue than goods retailers. A new service station can function with one gas attendant and one skilled mechanic. A tax-preparation firm can succeed with one accountant. A watch repair business needs only one repairperson. In each case, the owner may be the only skilled laborer. Costs can be held down accordingly. On the other hand, a goods retailer must have an adequate assortment and supply of inventory, which may impose financial obligations, require storage facilities, and be costly.

At times, this distinction between service and goods retailing is not as great as expected because suppliers may allow their goods-oriented retailers to receive inventory on consignment or may offer low-interest credit terms. Furthermore, some service retailing requires not only an initial capital investment but also other substantial ongoing nonlabor costs. For instance, an amusement park, a car wash, and a laundromat all have high electrical and maintenance costs.

In selecting a service category, it is crucial that all costs be computed. The owner's labor should not be viewed as cost-free since he or she could earn wages as someone else's employee (and because the owner needs a steady income to maintain a given life-style).

The time resources of a prospective retailer should be weighed in terms of the requirements of alternative business opportunities. Some businesses, like a self-service laundromat or a movie theater, require low time investments. Other businesses, like house painting or a travel agency, require large time investments because personal service is the key to profitability. More service retailers fall into the high rather than the low time-investment category.

Setting Objectives

Besides the sales, profit, and image goals sought by goods-oriented retailers, service-oriented retailers should set other objectives because of their unique characteristics. These include increasing service tangibility, matching demand and supply, standardizing services, and making services more efficient.

Service tangibility can be increased by stressing service-provider reliability, promoting a continuous slogan (for instance, at Delta Air Lines, "We love to fly and it shows"), describing specific service accomplishments (such as a car tune-up's improving gasoline consumption by 1 mile per gallon), and offering warranties. H&R Block promotes a program guaranteeing the tax refunds computed by its preparers.[10]

Demand and supply can be better matched by offering similar services to market segments with different demand patterns, new services with demand patterns that are countercyclical from existing services, new services that complement existing ones, special deals during nonpeak times, and new services not subject to existing capacity constraints (such as a restaurant's starting a home-delivery service).

Standardizing services reduces their variability, makes it easier to set prices, and improves efficiency. Services can be standardized by clearly defining each of the tasks involved, determining the minimum and maximum times needed to complete each task, selecting the best order for tasks to be done, and noting the optimum time and quality of the entire service. Standardization has been successfully applied to such firms as quick-auto-service providers (oil change, tune-up, and muffler repair firms), legal services (for wills, house closings, and similar proceedings), and emergency-medical-treatment centers. When services are standardized, there is often a trade-off: more consistent quality and convenience in exchange for less of a personal touch.

An important tool in standardizing labor-intensive services is a ***service blueprint***, which systematically lists all the functions to be performed and the average time required for each one to be completed. Figure 18–4 shows a service blueprint for a quick-oil-change firm's employees to follow. The blueprint identifies employee and customer activities (in order), as well as expected average performance times for each activity. Among the advantages of a service blueprint are that it helps standardize services (within a location and between locations), isolates points where the service may be weak or prone to failure (for example, do employees actually check transmission, brake, and power-steering fluid levels in one minute?), outlines a plan that can be evaluated for completeness (for example, should the customer be offered options for oil grades?), evaluates personnel needs (for example, should one employee change the oil and another wash the windshield?), and helps recommend productivity improvements (for example, should the customer or an employee drive the car into and out of the service bay?).

Besides standardizing services, retailers may be able to make services more efficient by automating them, thereby substituting machinery for labor. For instance, attorneys are increasingly using computerized word processing for common paragraphs in wills and house closings. This means better consistency in the way documents look, time savings, and neater—more error-free—documents. Among the service retailers that have been automating at least part of their operations are banks, car washes, bowling alleys, long-distance telephone services, real-estate brokers, and hotels.

Defining and Examining the Target Market

The target market must be defined and examined, and the consumer and the service offering carefully matched. Consumer demographics, life-styles, and decision making should all be studied. In this way, the retailer can develop a strategy in a logical and

[10] See Allan C. Reddy, Bruce D. Buskirk, and Ajit Kaicker, "Tangibilizing the Intangibles: Some Strategies for Services Marketing," *Journal of Services Marketing*, Vol. 7 (Number 3, 1993), pp. 13–17.

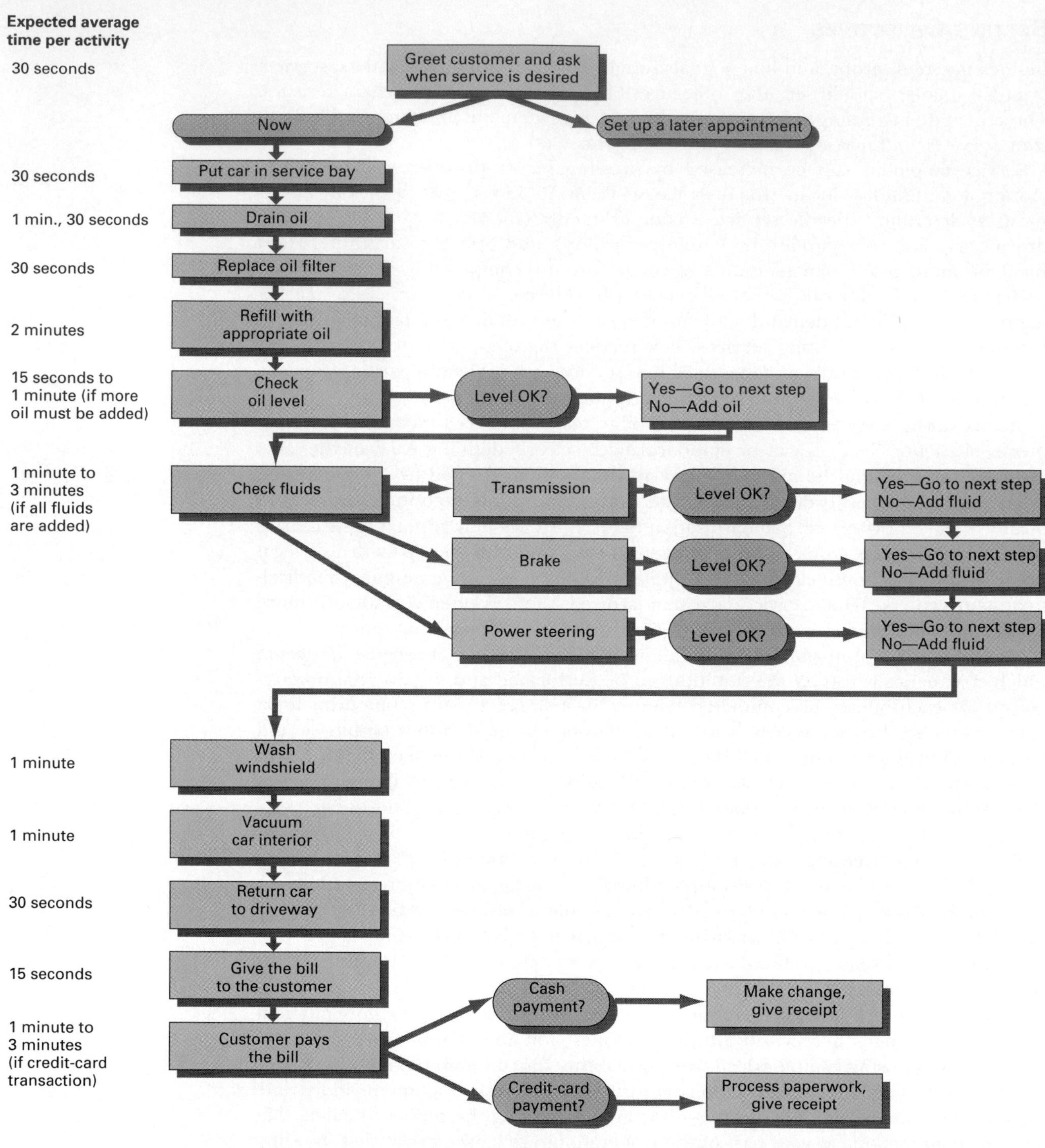

FIGURE 18–4 A Service Blueprint for a Quick-Oil-Change Firm's Employees

consistent manner. To illustrate with an earlier example, a barber shop would typically attract customers who are more conservative, less affluent, less mobile, and more convenience-oriented than those drawn to a personal-care salon.

Service retailers can use segmentation and/or mass marketing approaches. These examples show the variety of target market alternatives available:

- Different car-rental firms appeal to distinct market segments. Hertz and Avis have outlets at airport terminals; their convenient locations enable them to target full-service customers with above-average prices. Thrifty Rent-A-Car has outlets at sites near airports; it is more oriented to discount-oriented travelers. Snappy Rental specializes in replacement cars for people who need them because of insurance coverage after an accident.
- Sunrise Preschools, based in Phoenix, provides "high-end child care" services for the children of affluent professionals: "The type of parent we serve needs a lot of attention. They earn more, they're having fewer children per household than ever before, they're having children much later in life, and have more disposable income—so they're looking for a place that can take care of both the parents' and the child's needs." The per-child tuition at Sunrise averages well over $100 a week.[11]
- Boston-based BayBanks offers "value packages"—which include checking, savings, and credit services that are bundled together for a flat monthly fee. It has separate value packages for college students, young adults, and upper-income households.[12]
- There are 50+ hotel chains catering to the budget end of the U.S. market, with nightly accommodations averaging under $50. Days Inn and Motel 6 are the largest firms in this category, which overall accounts for one-fifth of all hotel rooms in the United States.[13]

OUTLINING OVERALL STRATEGY

In planning the overall strategy for operating a service business, the full range of controllable factors (store location and operations, service offering, pricing, and image and promotion) and uncontrollable factors (consumers, competition, technology, economic conditions, seasonality, and legal restrictions) must be examined. Figure 18–5 contains a list of the special considerations facing service retailers in each of these areas. They are detailed in the sections that follow.

Controllable Factors: Store Location and Operations

The store location and operations aspects of strategy must be outlined. The importance of store location to service retailers varies greatly. Sometimes, as with TV repairs, house painting, and lawn care, the service is "delivered" to the appropriate site. The firm's location becomes the client's home, and the actual office of the retailer is rather unimportant. Many clients might never even see a firm's office; they make contact by telephone or by personal visits, and customer convenience is optimized. In these instances, the firm incurs travel expenses, but it also has low (or no) rent and does not have to maintain store facilities, set up displays, and so on.

Other service retailers are visited on "specific-intent" shopping trips. Although a customer may be concerned about the convenience of a location, he or she usually does not select a skilled practitioner such as a doctor or a lawyer based on the location. It is common for doctors and attorneys to have offices in their homes or near hospitals or court buildings, respectively.

For some service retailers that are visited by customers, the location is critical. Car washes, travel agencies, movie theaters, hotels, and health spas are examples of re-

[11] Cathy Trost, "Marketing-Minded Child-Care Centers Become More Than 9-to-5 Baby Sitters," *Wall Street Journal* (June 18, 1990), p. B1.

[12] Eleena de Lisser, "Banks Court Disenchanted Customers," *Wall Street Journal* (August 30, 1993), p. B1.

[13] Updated by the authors from "Where to Stay?" *Consumer Reports* (September 1990), pp. 576–582.

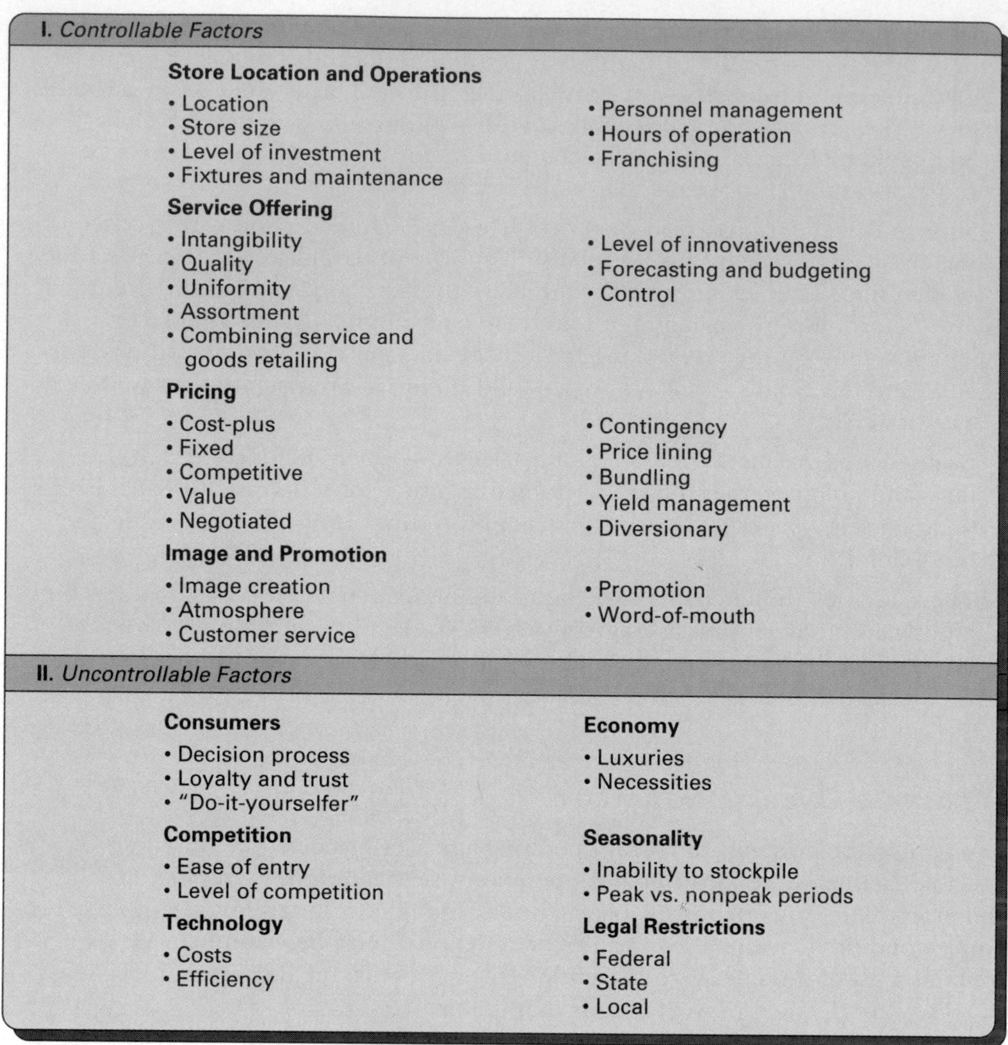

FIGURE 18–5 **Special Strategy Considerations for Service Retailers**

tailers that must be concerned about the convenience of their locations. That is why some car-rental agencies pay premium rents to be situated in airports rather than near them.

The store size and level of investment are considerably lower for many service-oriented retailers than they are for goods-oriented ones. A small store can often be utilized because little or no room is needed for displaying merchandise. As an example, a travel agency may have 12 salespeople and book several million dollars in trips; yet, it may fit into a store with less than 500 square feet. The investment factor relates to the absence of inventory, as discussed in the previous section. In addition, telephone business can further reduce the importance of store size and fixtures for service retailers.

Yet, sometimes, fixtures—as well as facilities maintenance—may be more crucial for service-oriented firms than goods-oriented ones. Because the sale of tangible, branded goods (which can be compared among different stores) is not the major focus of service retailing, a customer may base part of his or her opinion of a firm on the visible store fixtures and appearance. To use the travel agency example again, the desks, carpeting, light fixtures, computer terminals, and cleanliness level would be used by the customer to develop a perception of the firm—although these items are not part of a promotion mix.

Some aspects of personnel management can be difficult, and possibly frustrating, for a service retailer:

- When should the firm be staffed? Are there peak business hours?
- How can customer waiting time be minimized?
- What should permanent employees do during the time when no customers appear?
- How can employee performance be measured? How should the performance of technical personnel with high customer contact be evaluated?
- How can productivity be increased?
- How should employees be paid (salary, commission, or some combination)?
- If an employee quits or is fired, will customers follow him or her to another firm?

Because of the personal nature of many service businesses, these and other human resource issues must be considered before a strategy is implemented or revised. And the trade-offs involved with various service levels must be weighed. For example, "Seeking to improve their financial performance, most airlines are putting fewer attendants on board their aircraft. The result: Passengers wait longer for meals and beverages; meal carts clog aisles longer; dirty trays stack up; and obtaining the little extras of life aloft—a pillow, a magazine, a drink of water—is often a do-it-yourself experience."[14]

The decision on the hours of operation should be made in conjunction with personnel management decisions; and these hours must be planned on the basis of customer, not employee, convenience. Thus, a shoe repair store should be open during the morning, and a savings bank should have evening and/or Saturday hours. Although a shoe repair store can have one worker to open the store in the morning just to receive broken or worn shoes, as the work will be done later, a savings bank must plan to have enough employees during evening and/or weekend hours to handle all customer services while people wait.

Franchised services are expanding. Blockbuster, Fantastic Sam's, Jazzercise, and Century 21 Real Estate are some examples of franchises involved in service retailing. The greatest potential problem facing these chains involves a lack of uniformity in the services provided by different franchisees. Blockbuster must ensure that its franchisees offer similar video assortments at comparable prices. Fantastic Sam's must provide consistent hair-cutting services at all locales. Jazzercise must be sure that there are professional, knowledgeable fitness instructors at each studio. Century 21 must weed out unethical brokers and insist on certain performance standards.

As with goods-oriented franchising, if any unit in a service-oriented franchise performs poorly, the whole franchise would suffer. But because service-oriented franchising is more intangible, extra care needs to be given to generating and maintaining a clear and consistent company image. Employee training and supervision take on added importance.

Controllable Factors: Service Offering

A goods-oriented firm, carrying items such as perfume or cars or TV sets, has tangible products to offer. The merchandise can be seen, smelled, touched, heard, and, in some cases, tasted. A service firm that handles rentals and/or repair services deals with tangible items, but the service provided is still intangible. A nongoods service retailer, such as an accountant, has the most intangibility to overcome in marketing services to consumers because the services offered often cannot be seen, smelled, touched, heard, or tasted.

[14] James S. Hirsch, "With Fewer Attendants Aboard Jets, Mood of Passengers Turns Turbulent," *Wall Street Journal* (July 23, 1993), pp. B1, B5.

RETAILING IN ACTION

Should Banks Cut Back on Their Branch Outlets?

During 1992, U.S. banks closed 2,454 branches, while they opened only 1,120. Many closings were due to mergers and acquisitions. In other cases, the banks decided to close outlets that did not meet minimum deposit standards. The high number of closings means that many consumers will have to travel greater distances for their banking services and/or have less choice.

One banking consultant recommends that firms adopt a hub-and-spoke system, by which a bank's main branch would provide a full range of financial services and its branches would offer fewer services (tailored to each community). Thus, a branch in a community with young families could stress mutual fund investments as preparation for later college tuitions, while a branch in a business district could stress special services for retailers.

In contrast to banks that are closing branches, Fifth Third Bancorp is opening hundreds of branches. It is seeking sites in residential subdivisions, malls, and retail areas, and even opening minibranches in supermarkets. Although smaller branches offer only deposit- and withdrawal-related services, larger branches provide the full gamut of banking services.

Source: Based on material in Bridget O'Brian, "Bank Branches May Go the Way of Dime Stores and Dinosaurs," *Wall Street Journal* (December 16, 1993), pp. B1, B3.

Therefore, even though an airline rents plane seats to passengers, the quality of the service it offers depends on such intangibles as customer perceptions regarding flight attendant courtesy, the cleanliness of the aircraft, the smoothness of the flight, the firm's record for on-time flights, and the efficiency of baggage handling. As one airline president remarked, "We have thousands of 'moments of truth' out there every day."[15]

This is how one service retailer, a travel agency, might deal with the intangibility of its offering. The agency could emphasize the expertise of its agents and the types of travel arrangements it handles. Employees would be trained so they are aware of all available vacation packages—and their options—and they are able to design customized trips. The agency would have good relationships with popular airlines and hotels to provide one-stop shopping for customers. To present its service offering as tangibly as possible, the agency could use computer terminals in acquiring airline and other information and in processing orders (to demonstrate knowledge and efficiency), place certificates on office walls (to indicate the training received by employees, the awards recognizing the firm's past performance, and testimonials from satisfied clients), have a large assortment of colorful and well-written brochures (to show hotel accommodations, sightseeing excursions, and so on), and offer specific vacation packages (with the name of the hotel and airline, all package components, and pre-printed prices).

Like a goods-oriented firm, a service-oriented firm must consider the quality of its offering. Airlines always compete on the basis of "no frills" versus "extra service," trying to please various market segments. For example, many students want no-frills flights, whereas businesspeople are often more concerned about the time of departure, and tourists desire in-flight services.

Quality may also be difficult for a service retailer to plan because of the different customer perceptions of the same service. As an example, a tax-preparation service may be patronized because the consumer desires accurate mathematical computation, an opportunity for financial savings, advice, convenience, or freedom from responsibility. Different market segments could be lured by each of these perceived benefits. Figure 18–6 shows ten factors consumers may use in determining the quality of a service.

When a service retailer selects a level of service quality, its target market, competition, image, location, number of customer transactions, profitability, use of national versus private brands, services offered, personnel, perceived customer benefits, and constrained decision making should each be kept in mind. An additional factor (of greater importance than to a goods-oriented retailer), the uniformity of the service offering provided by the same firm, must be thoroughly planned.

[15] Kenneth Labich, "An Airline That Soars on Service," *Fortune* (December 31, 1990), p. 96.

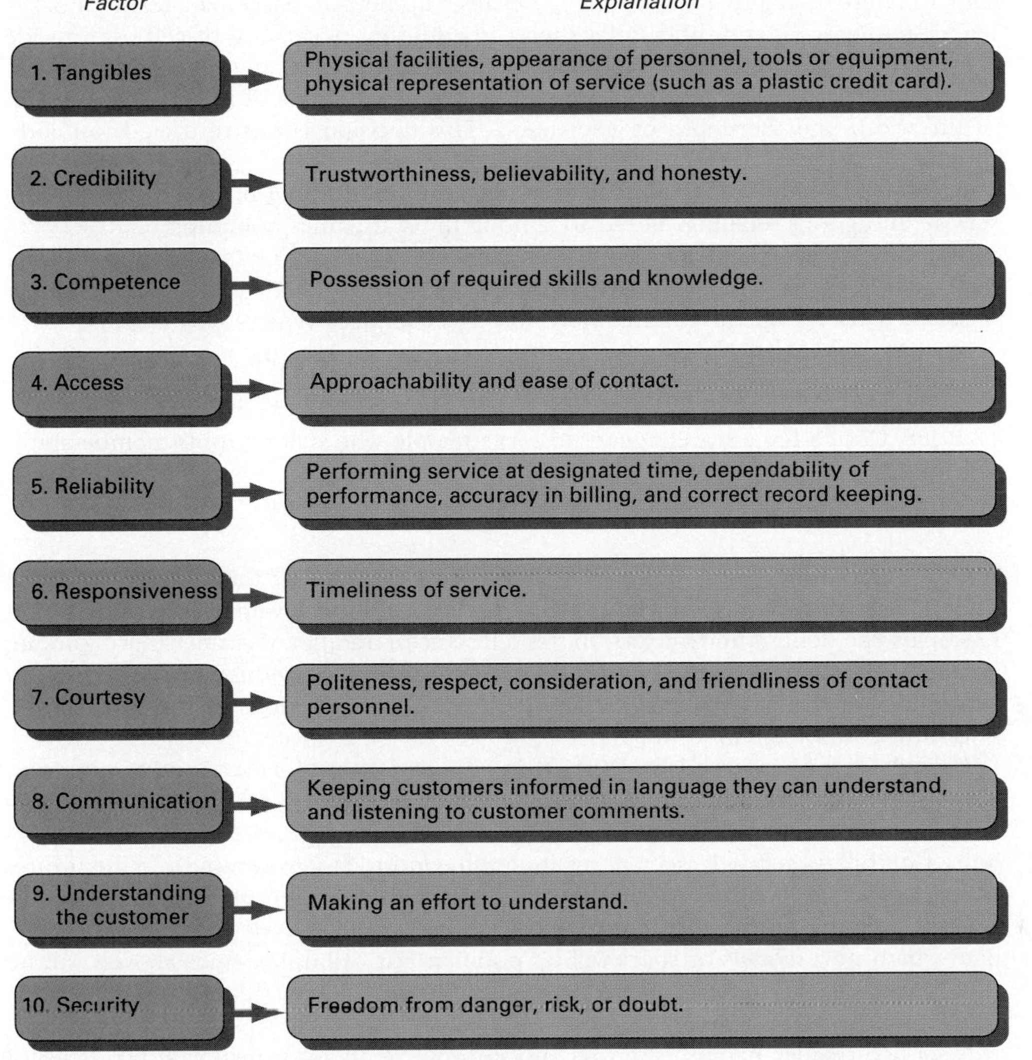

Factor
Explanation
1. Tangibles
Physical facilities, appearance of personnel, tools or equipment, physical representation of service (such as a plastic credit card).
2. Credibility
Trustworthiness, believability, and honesty.
3. Competence
Possession of required skills and knowledge.
4. Access
Approachability and ease of contact.
5. Reliability
Performing service at designated time, dependability of performance, accuracy in billing, and correct record keeping.
6. Responsiveness
Timeliness of service.
7. Courtesy
Politeness, respect, consideration, and friendliness of contact personnel.
8. Communication
Keeping customers informed in language they can understand, and listening to customer comments.
9. Understanding the customer
Making an effort to understand.
10. Security
Freedom from danger, risk, or doubt.

FIGURE 18–6
Ten Factors Consumers Use to Determine Service Quality
Source: Adapted by the authors from Valarie A. Zeithaml, A. Parasuraman, and Leonard L. Berry, *Delivering Quality Service* (New York: Free Press, 1990), pp. 21–22. Copyright Free Press. Reprinted by permission.

Customers are interested in receiving the same service level each time a particular retailer is patronized. For example, employees' appearance, skills, attitude, and performance must be consistent. Customer loyalty is predicated on this assumption. For instance, if a person eats at a restaurant where it usually takes an hour to complete dinner, this person would probably be very dissatisfied with a visit taking two hours to finish dinner (because of slow service). On the other hand, if a restaurant normally has two-hour service, its regular customers would not be unhappy with the length of the meal.

The width and depth of the service assortment, although different from those of a goods-oriented retailer, must be planned. Two illustrations can demonstrate this point. The width of assortment for a car-rental agency may consist of cars, trucks, vans, and/or camper-trailers. The depth of assortment would consist of the various models within any line (such as cars) and the range of services (such as daily, weekly, and monthly rentals; automatic and manual transmissions; and air-conditioned and non-air-conditioned). In Florida, some car-rental agencies concentrate on one product line (cars) and offer smaller economy cars only. This is a narrow-shallow service assortment that has proved very popular with the budget-oriented vacationer.

Sports arenas also make assortment decisions involving the events they will exhibit. Madison Square Garden in New York utilizes a wide-deep strategy. The assortment is wide because all types of sports and nonsports events are exhibited, including basketball and hockey games, tennis tournaments, boxing and wrestling matches, rodeos, circuses, dog shows, the Ice Capades, political conventions, rock concerts, and trade shows. There is depth of assortment because numerous basketball teams, hockey teams, tennis stars, and others play there. In addition, tickets are priced over a wide range and are available on a daily, seasonal (one sport), and all-events basis.

Every service retailer, small or large, must define the limits of its offering in terms of the width and the depth of assortment. This decision is not restricted to goods-oriented retailers.

Because of the growth of service retailing, many traditional firms are now joining service and goods retailing. These are among the companies operating retail services in the same stores where they sell merchandise:

- Some Stop N Go convenience stores offer fax services (Fax N Go).
- Various department stores own and operate restaurant facilities.
- Many supermarkets sell film processing and have automatic banking windows.
- Price/Costco has a travel agency to serve people who belong to its membership clubs.
- A number of stationery stores sell lottery tickets.

Other traditional goods-oriented retailers lease sections of their stores to service operators, such as banks, opticians, beauty parlors, and jewelry appraisers, and to professionals like dentists and lawyers. In some instances, traditional retailers have working arrangements with finance companies (most auto dealers do this) and repairpeople (a number of appliance stores do this) and receive commissions for performing the sales function for them.

A retailer combining goods and services in one setting must follow a consistent strategy. The goods and services should complement each other, be a logical extension for the retailer, and not adversely affect the firm's image. The coalitions just cited follow these guidelines. Combination goods/service retailing will continue to grow rapidly in the future.

Service-oriented retailers' innovation planning is quite different from that of goods-oriented retailers and sometimes unpredictable. A rented-goods retailer must anticipate which new models or styles will be popular. For example, which movies will be the most desirable videocassettes to be rented during the next 12 months? Which car models will customers prefer to rent?

A service retailer handling repairs and improvements must deal with two types of innovation planning. First, techniques for repairing or improving new merchandise must be learned. There is normally sufficient time to prepare for new items (such as large-screen rear-projection televisions) because these goods often have factory warranties for 90 days up to 1 year or longer. Second, new techniques must be developed and marketed for servicing existing items (such as a new way to tune up a car or treat the lawn). Customers must be sold on these techniques, which may require overcoming some resistance.

A nongoods-service firm has the toughest job in planning new services because it deals with the most intangibles. For example, an accountant has to determine which financial planning services to offer clients. A dance studio must decide which classes and programs to add and which to delete.

Forecasting and budgeting are central to any retailer's plans, but these tasks take on greater importance for a service firm due to the perishability of its services and the need to plan employee schedules carefully. Daily, weekly, monthly, and yearly sales must be forecast as accurately (and realistically) as possible. For established retailers, past sales data often provide good estimates for the future when combined with an analysis of competition, the target market, and the economy. Strong customer loyalty means repeat sales can be predicted. The new retailer must look at demographics and other factors but will rely essentially on estimates (usually keyed to the hours of work expected by the owner-operator) subject to large errors. The budget must be constructed on the basis of projected sales and the level of service quality to be offered, and it must allow for an acceptable profit.

A specified control mechanism is necessary in the evaluation and revision of the service retailer's strategy. Compared to a goods-oriented retailer, a service-oriented retailer has one area simplified and another magnified. Inventory control, including pilferage, is simple for nongoods retailers. For repair and rental retailers, the complexity of inventory is usually less than for goods-oriented retailers, although the rental retailer may be confronted with sloppy or malicious customers. On the other hand, service-oriented retailers may be hard pressed to measure productivity. After all, a fast worker may be a haphazard, incomplete, or messy worker. To overcome this difficulty, performance standards must be set, and, equally important, service employees must be compared with one another on their overall performances.

Controllable Factors: Pricing

In setting prices, a service firm has several options to consider: cost-plus, fixed, competitive, value, negotiated, contingency, price lining, bundling, yield management, and diversionary. Many of these methods may be combined.

Cost-plus pricing occurs when a retailer uses its costs of providing services as the basis for prices. The firm adds its costs to desired profit margins to arrive at selling prices. This is straightforward for some service retailers, such as coin-operated laundromats. For example, 55 to 60 per cent of revenues could cover a laundromat's lease; 17 to 20 per cent could go for repair, servicing, and collections expenses; 10 per cent could go for the purchase of new washing and drying machines; 8 per cent could cover operating expenses; and 5 to 10 per cent could be the expected net profit.

However, for many service retailers, service costs may be hard to determine. For instance, how does a self-employed repairperson determine labor costs? The simplest way is to find out the wages earned by a comparable repairperson working as an employee. But in addition to labor costs, materials, rent, taxes, and other factors must be included in calculations.

Cost-plus pricing has many disadvantages. It is not market-oriented; the price consumers are willing to pay for a given service is not ascertained. Idle time is seldom included in this technique. Total per-sale costs are difficult to compute. Cost cutting is rarely pursued actively.

Fixed pricing exists in situations where a branch of government has some degree of control and retailers must conform to the stated price structure. In some cities, parking-lot rates are fixed by law. Congress sets postage stamp rates. Taxi prices must often be government approved.

Fixed pricing produces mixed results. Advantages include the elimination of price wars, the protection of small firms, and consumer safeguards. Disadvantages include the lack of retailer control over an important marketing factor, inflexibility, and possible complacency.

Competitive pricing is a marketing-oriented strategy whereby a service retailer sets its prices on the basis of the prices charged by competitors. If a neighborhood theater charges $4 per ticket for a movie that has been in circulation for three months, a theater showing first-run movies might charge $6. Similarly, two hotels with comparable facilities and sites, catering to the same target market, would most likely have similar prices. Competitive pricing is the simplest, and probably the most effective, method for pricing services (because costs can usually be adjusted to accommodate prices). As always, pricing must be consistent with the overall strategy.

The use of competitive pricing is easy, responsive to the marketplace, and adaptive to the environment. It is conservative because a retailer goes along with its competitors. However, a firm might incorrectly assume its costs, image to consumers, and service offering are the same as those of competitors.

With ***value pricing***, prices are set on the basis of fair value for both the service provider and the consumer. For this approach to be effective, service firms must be in a strong competitive situation and have relative control over prices. Value pricing is common for such service professionals as doctors and lawyers. They set fees based upon the value of their time and the services performed.

Negotiated pricing occurs when a retailer works out pricing arrangements with individual customers because a unique or complex service is desired and a one-time price must be agreed upon. Unlike cost-plus, fixed, or competitive pricing (whereby each consumer pays the same price for a standard service), each consumer may be charged a different price under negotiated pricing (depending on the nature of the unique service). For example, a moving company charges different fees, depending on the distance of the move, who packs the breakable furniture, the use of stairs versus an elevator, access to highways, and the weight of such furniture as a piano.

Under negotiated pricing, a retailer can be very responsive to each consumer and develop tailor-made proposals. It is critical that negotiated prices be competitive with those of other service retailers and include a thorough cost analysis. This technique can also be quite time-consuming and expensive (because an estimate must usually be given to the consumer). Negotiated pricing is inefficient for standardized, recurrent services.

Contingency pricing is an arrangement whereby the retailer does not receive payment from the customer until after the service is performed and payment is contingent on the service's being satisfactory. A real-estate broker earns a fee only when a house purchaser (who is ready, willing, and able to purchase) is presented to the house seller. Several brokers may show a house to prospective buyers, but only the broker who actually sells the house earns a commission.

In some cases, such as real estate and lawn care, consumers prefer contingency payments; they want to be assured that the service is properly performed. This pricing technique presents some risks to the retailer because considerable time and effort may be spent without payment. A real-estate broker may show a house 25 times, may not sell it, and therefore is not paid.

Price lining is used by service retailers that provide a wide selection of services. A range of prices is matched to service levels. A travel agent handling European vacations can use price lining by creating several packages—with trips to Spain, France, and Italy priced from $1,500 to $5,000 per person. At each package price, a different combination of travel features is offered (from no frills to top of the line). A country club can use price lining by creating different types of membership: golf, tennis, and pool; golf and pool; golf only; tennis and pool; tennis only; and pool only. Each membership category is priced differently. Figure 18–7 shows how a restaurant can use price lining for different family members.

Price lining, as a supplement to one of the other pricing methods already mentioned, enables a retailer to expand its target market and to create a differentiated service offering. The latter point is very important because many consumers relate price to quality. Therefore, price lining helps a retailer to foster a diversified service image.

A service retailer may offer bundled and/or unbundled prices to its customers. With ***bundled pricing***, a retailer provides a number of services for one basic price. For example, a $60 air-conditioner tune-up could include in-home servicing, vacuuming the unit, replacing the air filter, unclogging all tubing, lubricating the unit, and checking air circulation. This approach helps standardize the service offering and makes bookkeeping simpler. However, it is not responsive to different customer needs.

As an alternative, many service retailers use ***unbundled pricing***, whereby they charge separate prices for each service provided. For example, a television-rental retailer could charge separate prices for the television rental, home delivery of the television set, and a monthly service contract. This approach enables the retailer to link its prices more closely with actual costs, present consumers with alternative service options, and perform only those services specifically requested. On the other hand, unbundled pricing may be harder to manage and may result in consumers buying fewer services than they would purchase under bundled pricing. When a retailer offers both bundled and unbundled pricing, it is engaged in a form of price lining.

In ***yield management pricing***, a service retailer determines the combination of prices that yield the highest level of revenues for a given time period. It is widely used

Figure 18–7
Price Lining at Morrison's
Morrison's family-style cafeterias use price lining to appeal to all members of the family—from children to big eaters.
Reprinted by permission.

in the airline and hotel industries. For instance, a crucial decision by an airline involves how many first-class, full-coach, intermediate-discount, and deep-discount tickets should be sold on each flight. Through yield management pricing, an airline would offer fewer discount tickets for flights during peak periods than for ones in nonpeak times. The airline has two goals: to try to fill as many seats as possible on every flight and to sell as many full-fare tickets as it can ("You don't want to sell a seat for $119 when a person will pay $500"). Yield management pricing is efficient and consumer-oriented, but it may be too complex for many small service retailers and it often requires sophisticated computer software.

Diversionary pricing is a practice used by deceptive service retailers. In this case, a low price is stated for one or a few services (which are emphasized in promotion) to give the illusion that all of the firm's prices are low. However, the prices of services that are not advertised are higher than the average. The intention is to attract consumers to the low-priced service and then entice them to purchase the high-priced ones, as well. A service station may promote an inexpensive tune-up to give the impression that all prices are low and then have high prices on repairs.

Because price and image are closely related for a service retailer, it is imperative that a cohesive pricing strategy be enacted. The methods described in this section provide good insights into the options available. The major difficulties lie in assessing market demand and measuring service costs.

Controllable Factors: Image and Promotion

Proper image creation is particularly crucial to a service retailer's success. People will patronize a retailer only if a unique and desirable image is created and reinforced. Every restaurant presents an image, whether it be clean and efficient, rustic, romantic, or a gourmet's delight. Each movie theater presents an image by virtue of its prices, selection of movies, cleanliness, parking, and waiting lines. Dry cleaners develop their images through the quality of cleaning, speed, and prices.

The most important element in a service retailer's image is the customer's perception of how well the basic service is performed. A clear image can be relatively easily created by a rental firm since tangible goods are involved; the consumer perceives a well-defined offering, which can be compared with that of other retailers. A repair or nongoods retailer may find it harder to carve out a distinct place in the market due to the intangibility of its offering (making it tougher for people to comparison shop). Thus, a repair or nongoods firm must generate an image based on a stated set of criteria (keyed to the factors cited in Figure 18–6), which are communicated to customers.

In creating an image, the proper atmosphere must be established. A clean and efficient restaurant image is aided by waxed floors, regularly washed windows, functional booths and tables, and counter service. A rustic image is fostered by early American furniture, lanterns, wooden fixtures, and pioneer attire for the waiters and waitresses. A romantic restaurant has secluded booths, candlelight, and soft background music. A gourmet's delight has the local newspaper critic's comments in the window, a lavish dessert display near the front door, and freshly cooked meals.

A movie theater's image is affected by its having extra cashiers on busy nights, separating smokers and nonsmokers (or not permitting smoking at all), cleaning popcorn and other debris from floors, and projecting a clear picture and sound. A dry cleaner's image can be influenced by using an easy-opening front door, having a clean countertop, displaying prices and cleaning data, and arranging clean clothes neatly on hangers.

A key part of atmosphere is store design. This includes the storefront, interior layout, and displays. The design must be constructed in a manner that is consistent with and adds to the service firm's image and atmosphere. Thus, in a dentist's office, cleanliness, good lighting, roominess, and reading materials in the reception area all contribute to patients' perceptions.

The level of customer service has a strong impact on image. Personal care, delivery, parking, credit, and telephone sales are some of the supplemental customer services for a service firm to consider. A self-service laundromat is perceived very differently from a laundry service that picks up, cleans, and returns clothes. A restaurant with metered, on-street parking is viewed as distinct from one with valet parking. A diet center allowing deferred billing has an image unlike one insisting on full payment before a class begins. A taxi service operating via the telephone is not the same as one requiring the patron to stand in the middle of a crowded street and wave. At We'll Clean Auto Spa, a Chicago car wash with two locations, "Car owners no longer have to choose between staring at the waiting room walls or watching scrubbers and water jets. It has installed rabbit-petting pens, an aquarium, a sun deck, cable TV, and a game table for kids. It also provides free popcorn."[16]

[16] Melissa Lee, "Service Providers Try to Make the Mundane Bearable," *Wall Street Journal* (July 13, 1993), p. B2.

At many banks, several customer services once provided free to all customers are now given free only to the most affluent ones. These banks may charge fees for "excessive" withdrawals from savings accounts, cashing social security checks, using live tellers, and balancing checkbooks. They believe the charges are needed to survive in today's highly competitive environment; in effect, they are now using unbundled pricing for customer services.[17]

Some service firms rarely use mass promotion. Seldom do barber shops, dry cleaners, repair retailers, house painters, laundromats, taxis, parking lots, or interior decorators advertise in media other than the Yellow Pages or neighborhood newspapers. They tend to be small and localized and to rely on loyal customers and/or convenient sites. Other service firms do rely heavily on promotion. These include hotels, motels, health spas, banks, and travel agents. They are usually larger and have a wider geographic market. In addition, multiple outlets are common.

Until the late 1970s, many professional associations did not let members advertise. Since then, the U.S. courts and the Federal Trade Commission have ruled that attorneys, physicians, pharmacists, optometrists, opticians, accountants, and others may advertise. Today, when advertising, professionals are expected to exhibit high standards of ethics, explain when services should be sought, and state what they can realistically provide to clients.

Virtually all types of service retailers stress personal selling in their promotion mixes. For instance, barbers, dry-cleaning attendants, repairpeople, painters, taxi drivers, and parking-lot attendants are each involved in a selling function, as well as in providing the primary service. So are hotel and motel personnel, health spa employees, bank tellers, and travel agents. Again, it must be mentioned that it is often personal attention which wins customers for service retailers.

Service retailers sometimes supplement their communication efforts with sales promotions. A health spa may offer a free month's membership for new enrollees. An airline may offer extra discounts for frequent passengers. A cruise ship may run coupon offers in newspapers. Premiums or prizes may be given by banks, movie theaters, and car-rental firms.

As a result of its good performance, a service retailer hopes to attain positive ***word-of-mouth communication***, which occurs when one consumer talks to others. If a satisfied customer tells his or her friends to use that retailer, this can build into a chain of customers. No service retailer can succeed if it receives extensive negative word-of-mouth communication (for example, "The hotel advertised that everything was included in the price. Yet it cost me thirty-five dollars to play golf"). Such comments would cause the retailer to lose substantial potential business.

A service-oriented retailer, more than its goods-oriented counterpart, must have positive word-of-mouth to attract new customers and retain existing ones. For example, many service firms credit word-of-mouth referrals with generating most new customers/clients/patients. As two experts have noted:

> Ads can only bring a person into an office once. If you are incompetent, don't treat people well, or overcharge, you're not going to get any repeat business. Word-of-mouth is still the key source of new customers.[18]

> Restaurants, unlike tennis players, get only one chance to serve. A customer dissatisfied with the service in a restaurant will probably never go back and is likely to tell dozens of other people about the experience.[19]

Uncontrollable Factors: Consumers

A service retailer must understand and respond to its consumers, who go through some form of decision process in selecting and purchasing services. The manner in

[17] See Kenneth H. Bacon, "Banks' Services Grow Costlier for Consumers," *Wall Street Journal* (November 18, 1993), pp. B1, B12.

[18] "Experience Belies Healthcare Professionals' Ad Fear," *Marketing News* (June 8, 1984), p. 1.

[19] Florence Fabricant, "New Focus on Service: Relearning a Lost Art," *New York Times* (July 25, 1990), p. C1.

ETHICS IN RETAILING

Will the Recycling Depot Appeal to Consumers?

Home Depot has opened a freestanding buy-back recycling center in the parking lot at its Duluth, Georgia, store as a joint venture with Mindis Recycling. The drive-through operation accepts common household waste (such as paper, plastic, and glass), as well as materials from home-improvement projects (such as electric wire, copper pipe, aluminum siding, and water heaters).

The two partners anticipate that this recycling venture will be self-supporting, based upon the monies obtained for the recycled materials. If the project is successful, they plan to expand it to other Home Depot stores.

For several reasons, both Home Depot and Mindis Recycling feel this project should appeal to customers. One, it targets ecologically-minded consumers and home-improvement professionals; all of the materials brought into the center will be recycled. Two, as an incentive to use this facility, customers can choose to accept either cash for their discarded goods or to have the proceeds donated to charity. Three, the concept should attract home-improvement professionals and home owners who can discard of unneeded items during a shopping trip to Home Depot. In the past, they would have had to make a special trip to a junk yard or dump.

Source: Based on material in "Home Depot Urges Recycling," *Chain Store Age Executive* (October 1992), pp. 33, 36.

which consumers use the process depends on the cost of the service, the newness of the service, the recurrence of the purchase, and other factors. Due to the intangible nature of many services, it is imperative that each element in the decision process be studied by the retailer: stimulus, problem awareness, information search, evaluation of alternatives, purchase, and post-purchase behavior. In addition, the relation of purchase behavior to consumer demographics and life-styles should be studied.

The thriving service retailer relies on the continued patronage and trust of customers, since many customers exhibit high levels of loyalty once they have selected a beautician, a dentist, a plumber, an accountant, a service station, or other service provider. This loyalty is usually much greater than for a goods-oriented firm because customers can easily switch among retailers selling the same merchandise. It is not as easy to switch among repair or nongoods retailers; satisfaction with these firms is due to a total offering that is hard to compare. In addition, loyal customers have a bond with their current service provider that may be impossible for a competitor to break.

Once a service firm becomes established, business should be good as long as a consumer orientation is maintained. In this situation, a new beautician, dentist, plumber, accountant, or service station would find it quite difficult to break into the market.

One customer type is often beyond the reach of some service retailers: the do-it-yourselfer. And the number of do-it-yourselfers in the United States is growing, as service costs increase. The do-it-yourselfer does car tune-ups, paints the house, mows the lawn, makes all plans for a vacation, and/or sets up a darkroom for developing film. Goods-oriented discount retailers do well by selling supplies to these people, but service retailers suffer because the major service (labor) is done by the customer. Market segmentation thus becomes desirable, and perhaps even necessary, to avoid the do-it-yourself segment or to serve it by offering low prices for basic services.[20]

Uncontrollable Factors: Competition

The ease of entry into service retailing differs for rental businesses versus repair and nongoods businesses. Because a rental retailer must often invest a large amount in the items to be rented (such as cars), the investment may limit entry into the market. On the other hand, a repair or nongoods retailer usually relies on labor (often his or her own) and tools, which minimizes investment costs. This makes entry into the marketplace easy. An exception occurs when extensive education and licensing provisions restrict entry.

[20] See Jane Larsen, "Getting Professional Help," *American Demographics* (July 1993), pp. 34–38.

Where easy entry exists, the level of competition will be high. In particular, small firms will arise, and they can be profitable if they appeal to specific target markets. Numerous small travel agencies, restaurants, and film processors flourish. Where entry is difficult, the level of competition is low. There are few bowling alleys, amusement parks, and country clubs operating in any geographic area.

When a prospective service retailer chooses a location, the amount of existing and potential competition should be measured. The site selected should have sufficient traffic and growth potential to accommodate that firm. For instance, a location with one profitable car wash may become a site with two unprofitable car washes if a second retailer opens and shares business with the first. And a car wash cannot easily be moved once it is constructed.

Uncontrollable Factors: Technology

A service retailer has a wide variety of technological options available in operating a business. A hotel could use an expensive computerized reservation system or older, less costly manual reservation procedures. A taxi service could feature old Yellow Cabs or new-model Chevrolets or Fords. A car wash could clean vehicles by hand or via large machines. A gardener could use a hand-operated cutting shears or elaborate automatic tools. An airline could fly 707s, 727s, 737s, 747s, 757s, 767s, 777s, and/or SSTs.

A business relying on older technology must provide superior personal service and rely on a loyal customer following. A firm depending on newer methods can eventually lower costs and do a more efficient and consistent job, which, in turn, results in an improved image and lower prices than those of competitors. A modern reservation system eliminates duplication, provides accurate information, and aids in strategy planning. A new, more compact taxi gets good gas mileage and is inexpensive to maintain. An automatic car wash has the capacity to clean and wax up to 100 or more cars per hour and leaves the cars sparkling. A gardener with automatic tools handles twice as many customers and does a more consistent job. A new jet allows an airline to schedule larger, more fuel-efficient flights, which cut down on expenses.

Uncontrollable Factors: The Economy

A service retailer should consider the effect of the economy on business. Because a number of services can be classified as luxuries, they are apt to be affected by economic conditions. If the economy is poor, air travel, overseas vacations, restaurants, lawn care firms, and others are adversely influenced. Laundromats, beauty salons, dry cleaners, and others are less affected because for many consumers they are necessities rather than luxuries.

In adapting to uncertain economic conditions, a service retailer can reduce sales fluctuations by offering a variety of services and de-emphasizing the luxury aspects of the services. It is important that business conditions be anticipated and included in strategy planning.

Uncontrollable Factors: Seasonality

Some service retailers are faced with seasonal demand for their services. Country clubs are most popular in the late spring, the summer, and the early fall. Many tourist hotels are busiest on weekends and holidays. Landscapers work most often in the fall and spring. Local buses and trains are most crowded during the morning and evening commuter rush hours.

The greatest problem for these service retailers is their inability to stockpile resources. If a country club has the capacity to accommodate 500 people, it cannot admit 750 people on Friday because there were only 250 on Thursday. A hotel cannot fill 1,000 rooms with 6,000 holiday visitors, even though, during midweek, half of the rooms were empty. A landscaper cannot handle two customers at the same time during the spring to make up for idle time in the winter. Buses and trains cannot sell 20,000 tickets for 5,000 seats during the rush hour to make up for a lack of passengers at other times.

Service businesses need to be oriented toward satisfying demand during peak periods. Employees must be deployed accordingly, and long-range planning must be based on realistic forecasting (including peak and nonpeak periods). Special services and offers can be used to attract customers during nonpeak times. Country clubs can introduce indoor activities. Hotels can offer low prices and additional services (such as the free use of a golf cart or free drinks at a show) for midweek patrons. Landscapers can offer snow removal and other winter services. Buses and trains can offer fare discounts and tie-ins with restaurants and theaters for off-hour riders.

Uncontrollable Factors: Legal Restrictions

All service retailers should be familiar with the federal, state, and local restrictions under which they must operate. On the federal level, various agencies, such as the Federal Aviation Administration and the Federal Deposit Insurance Corporation, oversee service retailers. In addition, many national self-governing bodies set guidelines for their members. These groups include the American Bar Association, the American Medical Association, and the American Institute of Certified Public Accountants.

In recent years, the federal government has actively pursued a policy of deregulating transportation, banking, communications, and other service industries. This has greatly increased the flexibility of firms in developing and carrying out their strategies. It has also led to a greater use of such marketing practices as consumer research.

On the state level, these are some of the restrictions facing service retailers: insurance companies and their rates are approved; licensing exams are administered and qualifications set for various professionals; utility rates are approved; trade schools are certified; and advertising messages may be limited. For instance, most state bar associations do not allow law firms to use movie stars, famous athletes, or former clients as spokespersons.

At the local level, the service retailer must be aware of zoning, operating, and other laws. Each municipality has different limitations (such as whether or not service professionals are allowed to operate home offices in residential areas), and this should be considered when selecting a location.

IMPLEMENTING A SERVICE STRATEGY

After a general strategy is outlined, the service retailer must put it into action. The tactics followed must conform to the overall strategy, and an integrated plan must be carried out. In addition, the strategy should be fine-tuned whenever necessary. Here are a variety of examples involving the implementation of service strategies.

Retail strategies used by service professionals vary greatly. On the one hand, there are many doctors, lawyers, dentists, and others who do not believe in retailing tactics or use them. They do not view themselves as involved with service retailing, think activities such as advertising are demeaning, deplore competitive tactics, and do not understand all the elements in strategic retail planning. These professionals believe their skills market themselves.

On the other hand, there are a growing number of service professionals who are quite involved in retail strategies in response to growing competition in their fields. For example, the number of U.S. dentists has grown dramatically since 1970. Yet, over this period, due to better prevention measures (such as fluoride toothpaste and fluoridated water), the number of cavities has dropped significantly. Many dentists have reacted to the situation by adopting such tactics as advertising in local papers, offering free initial examinations, and locating in neighborhood shopping districts or shopping centers.

Rented-goods retailing has grown as the costs of buying merchandise have risen sharply. Annually, U.S. consumers spend billions of dollars renting appliances, tools, household goods, computers, TV sets, pre-recorded videos, and other items. Car leasing is also popular, with 30 per of all new vehicles being leased; and that figure is expected to rise to 40 per cent by 1998:

> Consumers like leasing because it makes the vehicle more affordable, with 24- and 36-month lease monthly payments running about the same as a 60-month retail contract. Although they won't own a car at the end of the contract, they can lease another new car or arrange to buy or re-lease their current vehicle. Dealers like leasing because the newer, short-term leases ensure the consumer will be back for a new car within 36 months. That gives them the time to cultivate a relationship with these customers and lay the foundation for another lease contract—or a sale.[21]

The household-goods moving industry has undergone major changes because of deregulation. Before the Household Goods Transportation Act, interstate shippers could only haul used household goods at rates controlled by federal regulators. Today, carriers can ship a wide range of goods, offer various services, and control their prices. As one moving-company executive noted:

> We didn't pay a whole lot of attention to what the customer wanted before. Our services were pretty well governed by what the government would let us do. Now we're out battling for customers like everyone else in the competitive environment. There's more emphasis on sales and market training, guarantees, and other consumer attractions. We certainly have hiked our media advertising and our marketing research because of deregulation.[22]

Private storefront postal services rent mail boxes, receive and forward letters and packages, and pack boxes for consumers. At a time when the U.S. Postal Service has cut back on post office hours and some of the services provided, these private retailers are thriving. They offer customers longer hours of operation, quicker service, flexibility, and assistance with mailing problems. Some have telex and facsimile machines and offer word-processing, telephone-answering, and photocopying services. Because of the level of service offered, these firms have shipping prices far above those charged by the Postal Service and such nongovernmental carriers as United Parcel Service and Federal Express. The largest private postal service is Mail Boxes Etc., headquartered in San Diego; it has 2,100 franchised outlets throughout the United States and a number of other countries.

RE-EVALUATING THE SERVICE STRATEGY

Once a service strategy is in full operation, it should be monitored. For example, Figure 18–8 contains a simple form that deals with a service firm's marketing orientation. It could be used by virtually any service retailer.

Both the overall service strategy and its individual components should be re-evaluated regularly and adjustments made as needed. In this way, a service firm can quickly and accurately adapt to changes in the uncontrollable environment (consumers, competition, technology, economy, seasonality, and legal restrictions). The retail audit, described in Chapter 19, is as useful a tool for a service-oriented retailer as for a goods-oriented retailer.

Over the last several years, there has been heightened interest in devising ways to measure the quality of service retailing. The most well-known measurement tool is ***SERVQUAL***. It enables retailers to assess the quality of their service offerings by asking customers to react to a series of statements in five areas of performance (drawn from Figure 18–6): tangibles—the appearance of a firm's physical facilities, equipment, personnel, and communication materials; reliability—the firm's ability to perform the promised service in a dependable and accurate manner; responsiveness—the firm's willingness to help customers and provide prompt service; assurance—employees' knowledge and courtesy and their ability to convey trust; and empathy—the firm's

[21] Arlena Sawyers, "Short Leases: 'They'll Be Back,'" *Advertising Age* (March 28, 1994), p. S-20.

[22] Kevin Higgins, "Movers Grope for Marketing Orientation," *Marketing News* (May 11, 1984), p. 1.

Answer YES or NO to each of these statements:	YES	NO
1. There is a clearly defined mission for the firm.	_____	_____
2. There are stated long-term and short-term goals.	_____	_____
3. Key environmental trends are studied on a regular basis.	_____	_____
4. A target market has been identified and its characteristics are known.	_____	_____
5. The unique dimensions of service retailing are understood, with regard to		
a. Intangibility.	_____	_____
b. Inseparability.	_____	_____
c. Perishability.	_____	_____
d. Variability.	_____	_____
6. The strategic plan takes into account each of the factors noted in item 5.	_____	_____
7. Employees understand their special relationship with customers.	_____	_____
8. Customer service is stressed.	_____	_____
9. There are ongoing efforts to communicate the firm's image.	_____	_____
10. The pricing approach is keyed to the target market and the services and positioning of the firm.	_____	_____
11. A service blueprint is used to maximize productivity.	_____	_____
12. a. High-caliber personnel are hired and trained.	_____	_____
b. Employee turnover is low.	_____	_____
13. Service value is properly conveyed to customers.	_____	_____
14. Customer referrals are encouraged and rewarded.	_____	_____
15. Complaints are promptly resolved—to the customer's satisfaction.	_____	_____
16. The actions of competitors are monitored.	_____	_____
17. New services are added, so the firm's offering does not become stale.	_____	_____
18. A significant amount of time is spent in planning.	_____	_____

NOTE: ANSWERING NO TO ANY OF THE STATEMENTS MEANS THE SERVICE RETAILER HAS A DEFICIENCY THAT NEEDS TO BE CORRECTED.

FIGURE 18–8
Assessing a Service Retailer's Performance

level of caring, individualized customer attention.[23] Here are examples of SERVQUAL statements that can be used to assess the quality of a telephone repair service:

- XYZ company has modern-looking equipment. (tangibles)
- When XYZ promises to do something by a certain time, it does so. (reliability)
- Employees of XYZ are always willing to help you. (responsiveness)
- The behavior of employees of XYZ instills confidence in customers. (assurance)
- XYZ gives you individual attention. (empathy)[24]

[23] Valarie A. Zeithaml, A. Parasuraman, and Leonard L. Berry, *Delivering Quality Service* (New York: Free Press, 1990), pp. 23–33. See also Valarie A. Zeithaml, A. Parasuraman, and Leonard L. Berry, "Reassessment of Expectations as a Comparison Standard in Measuring Service Quality: Implications for Further Research," *Journal of Marketing,* Vol. 58 (January 1994), pp. 111–124.

[24] A. Parasuraman, Leonard L. Berry, and Valarie A. Zeithaml, "Refinement and Reassessment of the SERVQUAL Scale," *Journal of Retailing,* Vol. 67 (Winter 1991), pp. 420–450.

Regardless of the re-evaluation method used, this statement should be kept in mind by service retailers:

> Although the focus of many service firms is the continual improvement of service delivery, even the most customer-oriented culture and the strongest quality program will not entirely eliminate mistakes during service delivery. Unfortunately, one negative service encounter can undermine an extraordinary record of superior service, lowering evaluations of service quality and causing customers to search for other service providers. Yet, service organizations that are prepared to correct mistakes and handle customer concerns may be able to successfully differentiate themselves from competitors by implementing effective service recoveries. Service recovery refers to the actions a service provider takes in response to service failure.[25]

SUMMARY

1. *To examine the scope of service retailing* This form of retailing now represents a sizable share of overall retail sales and will continue to expand in the future. It encompasses a wide variety of businesses.

   Service retailing can be divided into three broad categories: rented goods, owned goods, and nongoods. In each category, the customer receives a service but does not obtain ownership of a physical product.

2. *To show how service retailing differs from goods-oriented retailing* Although the basic principles of planning and implementing a strategy are the cornerstones of any successful retail business, there are some major differences between service-oriented and goods-oriented firms. These distinctions exist largely due to the intangibility, inseparability, perishability, and variability associated with many services.

   Service retailers can be classified in terms of their tangibility, service provider skill, labor intensiveness, customer contact, goals, and the degree of regulation.

3. *To apply strategy concepts to service retailing* When conducting a situation analysis, the service category must be well defined. Personal abilities, financial resources, and time resources should be weighed in the category selection. Next, goals are set to reflect service tangibility, demand and supply, standardization (the use of a service blueprint can be quite helpful here), and the efficiency of services. The target market is then specified and described.

   The overall strategy is outlined, consistent with the service category and target market. In planning the general strategy, the retailer must consider various controllable factors. Store location and operations factors include location, store size, the level of investment, fixtures and maintenance, personnel management, hours, and type of ownership. Service-offering factors include intangibility, quality, uniformity, assortment, combinations of goods and services, innovativeness, forecasting and budgeting, and control. Pricing techniques include cost-plus, fixed, competitive, value, negotiated, contingency, price lining, bundling, yield management, and diversionary. Image and promotion factors include image creation, atmosphere, customer services, promotion, and word-of-mouth.

   After a service-retailing strategy is carefully outlined, it must be implemented as prescribed. The strategy is then regularly monitored and adjusted as necessary. SERVQUAL is one technique for measuring the quality of service retailing.

4. *To evaluate uncontrollable factors as they pertain to service retailers* While developing a strategy, the service retailer must also analyze relevant uncontrollable factors. Consumers, competition, technology, the economy, seasonality, and legal restrictions should each be investigated. The strategy should plan for and adapt to these variables.

KEY TERMS

service retailing (p. 618)
service blueprint (p. 625)
cost-plus pricing (p. 633)
fixed pricing (p. 633)
competitive pricing (p. 633)
value pricing (p. 633)
negotiated pricing (p. 634)
contingency pricing (p. 634)
price lining (p. 634)
bundled pricing (p. 634)
unbundled pricing (p. 634)
yield management pricing (p. 634)
diversionary pricing (p. 635)
word-of-mouth communication (p. 637)
SERVQUAL (p. 641)

[25] Scott W. Kelley and Mark A. Davis, "Antecedents to Customer Expectations for Service Recovery," *Journal of the Academy of Marketing Science*, Vol. 22 (Winter 1994), p. 52.

QUESTIONS FOR DISCUSSION

1. What are the unique aspects of service retailing? Give an example of each.
2. It is often stated that many service retailers are not consumer-oriented. Why do you think this comment is made? Is it accurate?
3. Should dental, accounting, and other services be considered a part of retailing? Why or why not?
4. In what kinds of service retailing are personal skills most important? In what kinds are they unimportant?
5. For each of the following, name several alternative final-consumer market segments to which they can appeal:
   a. Beauty salon.
   b. Bank.
   c. Movie theater.
   d. Plumber.
   e. Amusement park.
   f. Lawn service.
6. What reasons can you give for the growth of franchised services?
7. Apply the concepts cited in Figure 18–6 to a new fitness center opening near your college.
8. Why is personnel management especially difficult in service retailing?
9. Present an example of each type of pricing:
   a. Cost-plus.
   b. Fixed.
   c. Competitive.
   d. Value.
   e. Negotiated.
   f. Contingency.
   g. Bundled.
   h. Diversionary.
10. Explain the concept of atmosphere from a service-retailer perspective.
11. Discuss the importance of word-of-mouth to a service retailer.
12. Does the consumer use the decision process differently for services than for goods? Explain your answer.
13. What alternative strategies can service retailers use to deal with the do-it-yourselfer?
14. How could a real-estate broker use SERVQUAL to assess the quality of its sales force?

CASE 1

Domino's Pizza: Training by a Service Firm*

Domino's Pizza was started in 1960 when Thomas Monaghan and his brother, James, borrowed $900 to purchase DomiNick's, a bankrupt pizza parlor located in Ypsilanti, Michigan. In 1961, Thomas bought out his brother's half interest in the store. During the next several years, Monaghan developed a franchising strategy to sell only pizza, deliver it hot and fresh within 30 minutes, and locate new units near colleges and military bases. By 1978, Domino's Pizza operated 200 stores. The number of stores increased to 500 units by 1981 and to 1,000 by 1983. In 1989, sales reached $2.5 billion (with 5,185 stores); and a management team was appointed to oversee Domino's Pizza, as Thomas Monaghan stepped aside. However, Monaghan returned to an active role in 1991, as a result of stagnant sales between 1989 and 1991.

Today, Domino's Pizza has about 5,300 stores (nearly three-quarters of which are franchisee-operated) and yearly sales of $2.6 billion. It is the second-largest pizza chain, after Pizza Hut. Besides its traditional pizza, the firm now sells garlic sticks and salads at most stores. It has also been testing chicken wings, submarine sandwiches, and thin-crust pizza.

Domino's major competitors include Little Caesar's and Pizza Hut. In the past, Little Caesar's focused on the carry-out segment and Pizza Hut was positioned as a table-service restaurant. Each competitor has since changed its strategy. Little Caesar's has doubled the number of stores over the last few years and recently introduced spaghetti and salads. Pizza Hut currently accounts for a large per cent of the home-delivery market. To further blur the distinctions among competitors, Domino's new 300 square-inch "Dominator" pizza is only available on a carry-out basis.

According to one marketing research firm, the home-delivery segment represents about one-third of the $19.2 billion overall annual U.S. pizza market. Domino's has about a 45 per cent market share of the delivered-pizza market (down from 50 to 55 per cent in the mid- to late 1980s). Pizza Hut's share of the delivered market is 25 per cent.

* The material in this case is drawn from John Cortez, "New Direction for Domino's," *Advertising Age* (January 4, 1993), pp. 3, 34–35; "Domino's Settlement," *Wall Street Journal* (May 12, 1993), p. B5; and Leslie Albrecht Popiel, "New Fast-Food Rivalry Hits Big Pizza Chains," *Christian Science Monitor* (November 19, 1993), p. 10.

Domino's has changed its 30-minute delivery guarantee as the result of several deaths being attributed to franchisees' quest for speedy delivery. In one liability suit, the firm agreed to a $2.8 million settlement as damages for the death of a car driver who was involved in a collision with a Domino's pizza deliverer. In another case, a jury awarded $78 million to a woman who was hit and injured by a Domino's driver.

Training has become more difficult for Domino's. Although the firm still believes that fast delivery is an important competitive edge, many retailing experts question whether Domino's can accomplish consistent and quick delivery with a larger menu and the greater attention on safe delivery. In addition, Pizza Hut has been serious at making its delivery system work and is now a formidable competitor in every geographic market.

Domino's training program focuses on "the four-minute performance." This relates to the four minutes that the average customer is in contact with the employees at Domino's franchisee- and company-operated outlets. Domino's wants to "delight the customer" by "going out of the way" to satisfy him or her during this time period. According to the firm, its long-term success depends on how it performs during the four-minute performance, which is made up of one minute on the phone and three minutes at the door.

The person who answers the phone must be energetic, be friendly, and "let the customer see the smile on your face." This is an ideal opportunity to make a great first impression. Domino's telephone personnel should strive to pick up the phone on the first ring and not to put the customer on hold. In the event that a customer has to be placed on hold, the telephone order taker should respond, "Thank you for calling, will you hold on please?" The order taker should also offer the customer two free colas or a free topping as a way of saying "Thank you" for holding. The order taker should know the weekly specials, be confident, listen to the customer, confirm the order, and tell the customer the total price.

Because Domino's drivers are the only physical contact most customers have with the firm, they are an especially important part of the "four-minute performance." In delivering pizza, they should leave the delivery vehicle's lights on, turn the ignition off, and always close the door. Additional suggestions are that they should use their names; address the customer by name, or by sir, or madam; ask about the last pizza purchased from Domino's, and suggest that they call the store manager if they have any problems.

Domino's research suggests that its average customer purchases $600 in Domino's pizza per year and that happy customers convey their satisfaction to four friends. If a content customer discusses Domino's Pizza with just two friends, he or she influences $12,000 in sales over a ten-year period (plus $6,000 for his or her own purchases). The deliveryperson needs to see "$18,000 in purchases being influenced" by his or her performance at each delivery.

QUESTIONS

1. Comment on Domino's in terms of its service intangibility, inseparability, perishability, and variability.
2. Evaluate Domino's strategy on the basis of each of the seven special considerations cited in Table 18–1.
3. What special training considerations exist due to many Domino's outlets being owned by franchisees? Explain your answer.
4. How can Domino's Pizza differentiate itself from Pizza Hut and Little Caesar's?

VIDEO QUESTIONS ON DOMINO'S PIZZA

1. Evaluate Domino's suggestions to employees.
2. What additional suggestions should the firm consider?

CASE 2
Barbara Laine Insurance: Planning a Service Business

Barbara Laine is a former insurance saleswoman. While in college, she majored in marketing and became interested in personal selling. In her first job after college, Barbara worked as a management trainee at the Bank of America, but she was bored by the lack of personal contact with customers.

Laine left the Bank of America after six months and entered the sales program at the Prudential Insurance Company. Selling insurance really excited her, and she soon became the best saleswoman in her territory. Laine sold life, automobile, property, and other forms of insurance. She attended many insurance courses and received various insurance designations, such as CLU (Certified Life Underwriter). In addition, she completed an MBA with a specialization in finance.

Barbara Laine worked at Prudential for eight years and enjoyed all of them. However, she reached the point where opening an independent insurance company became important. Laine was particularly determined to be one of a handful of women who run their own insurance companies.

In 1990, Laine left Prudential to open her own independent insurance agency. Thus, instead of selling the services of just one firm (Prudential), she was now free to sell the services of many firms. This gave her the ability to better serve her clients by comparing the coverage and premiums of competitive insurance providers.

The first problem Barbara Laine had to wrestle with was whether to pull several large accounts of hers away from Prudential. Although Laine decided that she would not call any of her past accounts and ask them to come with her (that would be unethical), those accounts that asked to transfer their business would be gladly welcomed.

Because Laine decided not to solicit her old accounts, she began on a course of cold-canvassing commercial accounts. Many of the large commercial firms she contacted would not even seriously talk to her because of the following reasons:

- As a new company with a small advertising budget, Barbara Laine Insurance was unknown to them.
- They had doubts about Laine's long-term existence and were reluctant to buy insurance from a firm that might not be around when they had a claim.
- They were hesitant to deal with a small company.
- They were especially concerned about the agency's total reliance on the skills of Barbara Laine.
- Laine sometimes quoted rates higher than those advertised by other firms. She knew that promoted rates were often "come-ons" to attract consumers.
- They had strong relationships with their current insurance brokers and they wanted them to continue. Some used the same brokers for 20 years or longer.

At that point, Laine ascertained that homeowner's and auto insurance might yield greater returns. She again cold canvassed by selecting names from a telephone directory and then sought accounts. Although progress was slow, the endeavor proved profitable by 1992, especially with renewals and referrals.

During this time, Laine focused on advertising in the *Yellow Pages* and newspapers, appeared before civic and consumer groups, and met one-on-one with prospective clients in their homes. In general, Laine's presentations stressed these factors:

- Too few insurance brokers have encouraged their accounts to regularly review their insurance needs. For example, many policies significantly underinsure homes, since they do not have inflation riders that adjust policies' value to cover rising construction costs. Some homeowners who have not increased their coverage over a 10-year period may be underinsured by 50 per cent or more. Laine tries to get consumers to accept inflation riders. She also knows current construction costs for different types of homes.

- Some of the areas she serves are highly susceptible to flooding in the event of a hurricane. The federal government offers a comprehensive flood insurance policy, but less than 10 per cent of the residents have such coverage. Laine has sold many of these policies as a public service, despite low brokerage fees.
- Too few car owners have insurance clauses that cover losses up to $1 million in the event of a car-related accident. Laine feels this is critical in light of high medical care and hospitalization costs.
- She encourages clients to take out all of their insurance via her agency. Many insurance providers have discounts if households buy auto and homeowner insurance policies from one insurance agency. Most auto-insurance providers also have family discount plans.
- Laine realizes that many insurance policies involve joint decision making with both spouses present. Thus, she schedules evening meetings at clients' homes. In setting up appointments, she allocates sufficient time to explain the policies' features and premiums.

During late 1992, premiums reached the point where Laine was able to match her previous income with Prudential. In fact, she is now facing these very lucrative alternatives: (1) To open a large office and hire a full-time staff—This alternative is appealing to Laine based upon the self-satisfaction of building one's own business. However, it involves a significant investment. Barbara is also concerned that she will lose "the personal touch" with her current clients. (2) To merge with a slightly larger company—This would reduce some operating costs due to the ability to share administrative costs. This strategy involves less risk than the first alternative. (3) To bring her accounts with her and return to Prudential as a saleswoman—This option would free Laine to concentrate all of her efforts at selling. She could possibly earn the most money because of Prudential's lucrative compensation plan for very successful performers.

The first alternative is the most appealing to Laine, but she has never foreclosed any options without thoroughly evaluating them.

Questions

1. Has Barbara Laine done a good job of planning her service strategy? Explain your answer.
2. If she stays with her own business, should Laine try again to solicit commercial accounts? Explain your answer.
3. What are the pros and cons of each of the alternatives now confronting Barbara Laine?
4. If you were Prudential, would you want Laine back? Support your answer.

CHAPTER

19

RM

Integrating and Controlling the Retail Strategy

❖ Chapter Objectives

1. To demonstrate the importance of integrating a retail strategy
2. To examine four key factors in the development and enactment of an integrated retail strategy: planning procedures and opportunity analysis, performance measures, productivity, and the uses of new technology
3. To show how industrywide data can be used in strategy planning and analysis
4. To explain the principles of a retail audit, its utility in controlling a retail strategy, the difference between horizontal and vertical audits, and the possible difficulties with auditing
5. To provide examples of audit forms

The *Wall Street Journal* recently studied the largest retail outlet of twenty major retail chains to determine the factors responsible for each store's success. In some cases, success was strictly due to the location. For example, the leading Amoco oil station (which pumps five times the gas of a typical Amoco station) is in Indiana—right across the border from Illinois, where gasoline taxes are 13 cents per gallon higher. In other cases, sales performance is due to the unit's superior customer service. Thus, the top-selling U.S. Lexus dealer (in Margate, Florida) washed its customers' cars after Hurricane Andrew to remove acid rain that could pit a car's finish.

Let's also look at the best-selling U.S. outlets for Baskin-Robbins, H&R Block, FTD, Midas, and Radio Shack—and examine their characteristics.

Of Baskin-Robbins' 2,300 U.S. outlets, its top store is in the Royal Hawaiian Center, Honolulu. This store grosses about nearly $1 million per year. It has the advantage of weather that is summerlike all year-round, and it is the only food outlet (besides a coffee shop) in a major Waikiki mall.

H&R Block's downtown Stamford, Connecticut, store handles over 8,000 tax returns each year—almost two times the amount of the next busiest office. This facility has 19 tax-preparation stations and, unlike most of Block's outlets, it is open year-round.

McShan Florist Inc., in Dallas, Texas, fills more than 1,100 FTD floral orders per week, making it the leading flowers-by-wire retailer in the United States. Neiman-Marcus, the upscale department store, is a major customer. The store has partly achieved its reputation by landscaping many of the homes that surround it.

Wood's Car Care, in Vienna, Virginia, is the largest of 1,822 Midas dealers in terms of sales. The shop repairs over 40 cars per day. The strong sales volume is due to its location near office buildings, as well as its free customer pickup and delivery service.

Radio Shack's best-selling unit is located in Dadeland Mall, Miami. The store sells large amounts of "high-end" personal computers, video equipment, and other electronic goods for shipment to Puerto Rico and other tropical island locations. Despite being smaller than the average Radio Shack unit, the store's average purchase is 25 per cent or so higher than at other outlets.[1]

[1] Richard Gibson, "Location, Luck, Service Can Make a Store Top Star," *Wall Street Journal* (February 1, 1993), p. B1.

Reprinted by permission of Tandy.

Overview

Throughout the text, a number of individual factors pertaining to the development of retail strategies have been examined. This chapter focuses on integrating and controlling the retail strategy. Accordingly, the chapter ties together the material detailed previously, shows why it is necessary for retailers to plan and enact coordinated strategies, and describes how to assess success or failure.

Integrating the Retail Strategy

It is vital for a retailer to view strategy planning as an integrated and ongoing process, and not as a fragmented and one-time-only concept. As Figure 19–1 shows, Kay Jewelers understands that well.

One of this text's key goals has been to describe the interrelationships between the various stages in the enactment of a strategy and to demonstrate the need to operate in an integrated format. Figure 19–2, reproduced from Chapter 2, shows the overall development of a retail strategy and how steps are interconnected and integrated. Figure 19–3 highlights the integrated strategy of Bed Bath & Beyond, the New Jersey-based home-furnishings chain. In 1993, Bed Bath & Beyond was cited by *Chain Store Age Executive* as the leading "high performance retailer" among all publicly held U.S. retailers.[2]

In particular, four fundamental factors need to be considered in developing and enacting any integrated retail strategy: planning procedures and opportunity analysis, performance measures, productivity, and the uses of new technology. These factors are discussed next.

PLANNING PROCEDURES AND OPPORTUNITY ANALYSIS

Planning procedures can be optimized by undertaking several coordinated activities. Senior executives should first outline the retailer's overall direction and goals. This will provide written guidelines for middle- and lower-level managers, who should get input from all types of internal and external sources. Thus, middle- and lower-level managers are encouraged to generate new ideas at an early stage of planning. Then, top-down (generated by upper managers) and bottom-up or horizontal (generated by middle- and lower-level managers) plans can be combined. Last, specific plans should be enacted, including checkpoints and dates. By completing these tasks, planning is more systematic and data are acquired from all kinds of relevant sources.

For example, here is how Publix Super Markets' integrated planning works:

> At the store level, a store team consisting of the manager and department heads set both departmental and sales goals for the following year. They look at anticipated new competition, subdivision building going on or expected, and trends in tourism. After setting their goals, the store team discusses the wisdom and integrity of their objectives with their district manager. Store goals are combined with those of the district, and the result goes up the line to the divisional level and finally to corporate headquarters, where data are factored in such as where and when the chain will open stores in the following year. At least once a month, goal setters review their accomplishments and failings to date.[3]

Opportunities need to be systematically examined in terms of their impact on overall strategy, and not in an isolated manner. For example, the remaining Woolworth

[2] Marianne Wilson, "Home Furnishings Chain Takes Lead," *Chain Store Age Executive* (November 1993), pp. 21–24.

[3] Steve Weinstein, "How Retailers Set Goals—And Reach Them," *Progressive Grocer* (April 1990), p. 156.

At Kay Jewelers, the beauty of fine jewelry is combined with the business of merchandising. The "Kay Exclusive" jewelry design process profiled here shows the special Kay Jewelers approach to every aspect of merchandising, from initial design to final sale.

1. Merchandise Positioning.

Kay Jewelers buyers strive to anticipate consumers' desires. Our buyer notes that diamond and precious gem combinations are increasingly sought after, and suggests a necklace and ear-ring set.

2. Design Proposal.

A designer is given the parameters: a pear-shaped sapphire and round diamond combination in a necklace and earrings. More than a dozen preliminary sketches are assessed by the buyer and top management.

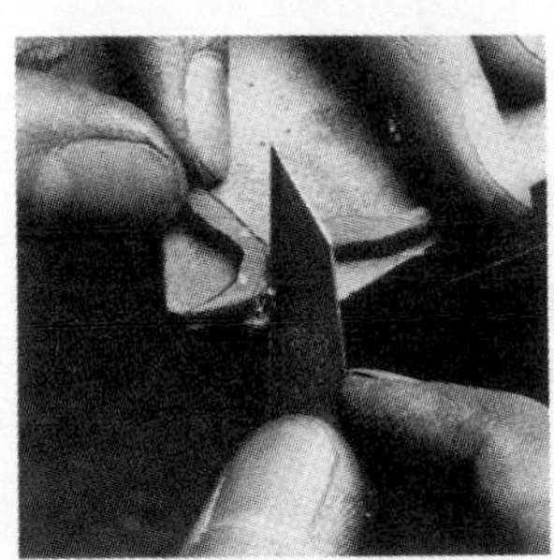

3. Preliminary Casting.

Designs selected for execution are carved in wax, a mold is made, and the jewelry is casted by artisans. With input from management, fine-tuning decisions are made about weight, polishing, angles, etc.

4. Test Marketing.

Kay Jewelers executives agree on a test market. Past experience shows that test marketing as few as 25 pieces over just six weeks can yield very accurate estimates, used to project chainwide distribution and sales figures.

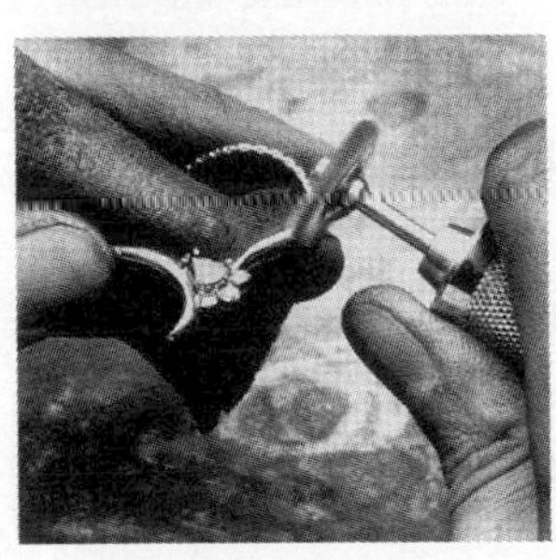

5. Manufacturing.

Kay's purchasing agents buy gems and precious metals strictly for projected need and do not maintain substantial inventories of raw materials vulnerable to wide fluctations in market value. Kay realizes cost efficiencies by subcontracting jewelry manufacture to outside goldsmiths.

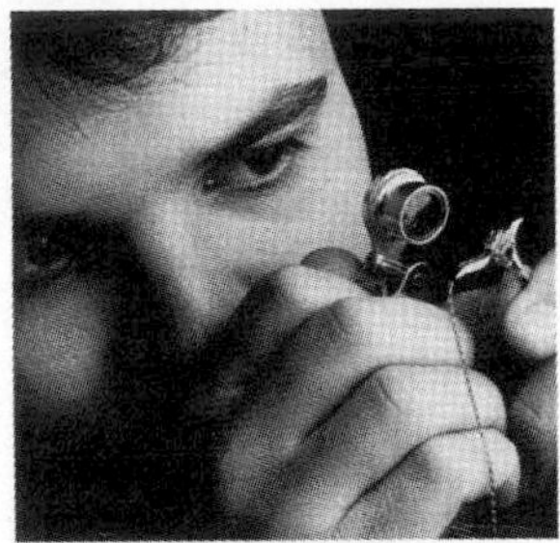

6. Quality Control.

Inspectors examine each item for gold content, quality of finish, gold and diamond weights, and proper setting. The items are scrutinized again in the store before they are put into inventory.

7. Retail Showcasing.

When the new merchandise arrives in the stores, the excitement among store personnel guarantees that it will be featured prominently in displays.

8. Advertising/Promotion

The public hears about the "Kay Exclusive Line" through advertising in print and on the radio. It is emphasized that these pieces are Company designs, meet high standards of quality, and are backed by Kay's warranties.

9. Warranty.

The new design carries our lifetime guarantee, the most extensive in the business, of a trade-in allowance at least 25% greater than the original purchase price after five years. Customers also are protected from the loss of a diamond from its setting.

10. Inventory Control.

Kay Jewelers salespeople tally all purchases on in-store point-of-sale terminals. Within 24 hours, a printout of sales results by specific item allows us to make accurate reordering and forecasting decisions.

This "Kay Exclusive" item, (pictured at right), a diamond and sapphire earring and necklace set, illustrates the step-by-step process through which fashion trends are transformed into new designs and increased sales.

FIGURE 19–1 Kay Jewelers' "Facets of a Sale"

Reprinted by permission.

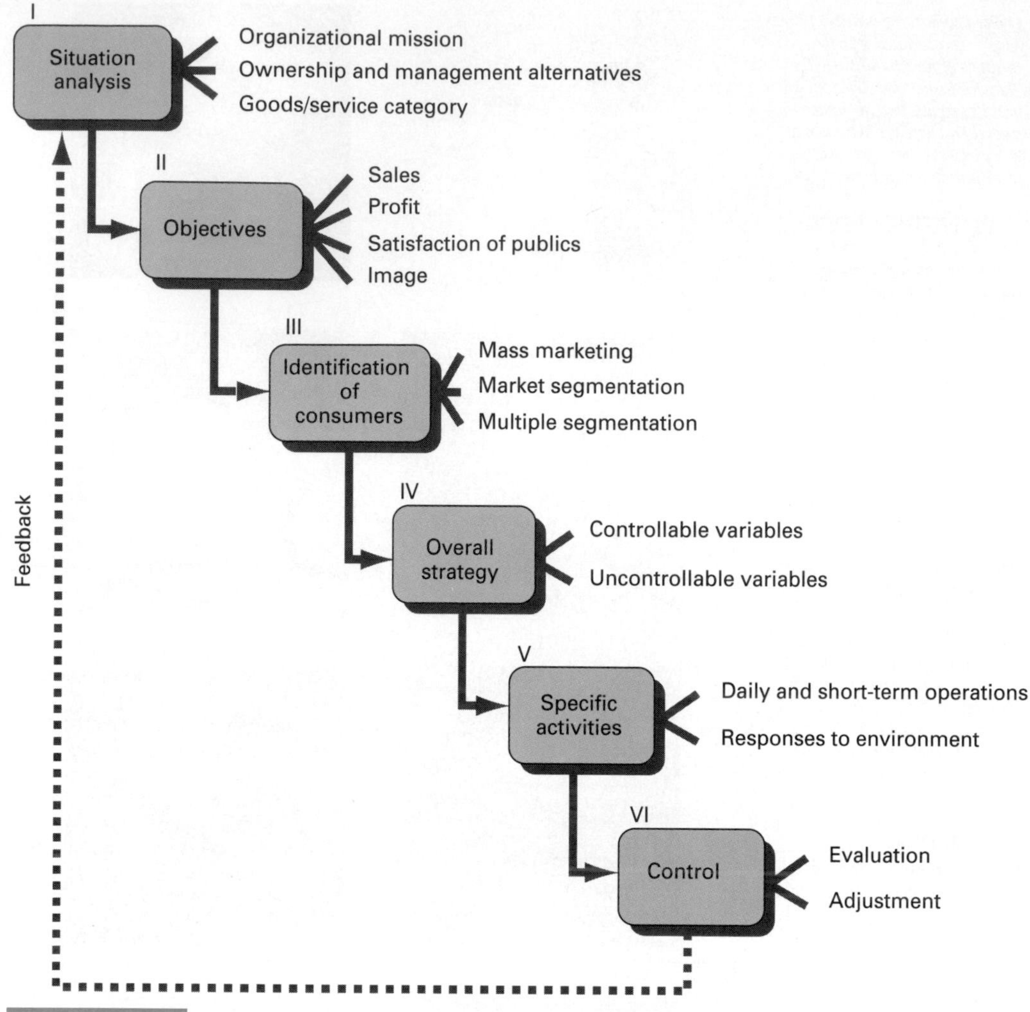

FIGURE 19–2 Elements of a Retail Strategy

variety stores now emphasize merchandise in which they can excel, such as health and beauty aids, candy, handbags, stationery, notions, children's wear, and hosiery. More ego-sensitive merchandise classifications (such as shoes and women's apparel) have been scaled down or eliminated.

When evaluating new opportunities, retailers should develop some form of ***sales opportunity grid***, which rates the promise of new goods, services, and/or store outlets across a variety of criteria. In this way, opportunities may be evaluated on the basis of the integrated strategies the retailers would follow if the opportunities are pursued.

Table 19–1 shows a sales opportunity grid for a large supermarket that wants to decide which of two brands of salad dressing to carry from among two alternatives. The supermarket's manager has specified the integrated strategy that would be followed for each brand; Brand A is established, whereas Brand B is new. Because of its newness, the manager believes initial sales of Brand B would be lower, but total first year sales would be similar. The brands would be priced the same and occupy identical floor space. Brand B would require more display costs but would offer the store a larger markup. Brand B would return a greater total gross profit ($781 to $613) and net profit ($271 to $193) than Brand A by the end of the first year. On the basis of the overall grid in Table 19–1, the store manager would choose Brand B. However, if the supermarket is more concerned about immediate profit, Brand A might be chosen because it is expected to take Brand B a while to gain consumer acceptance.

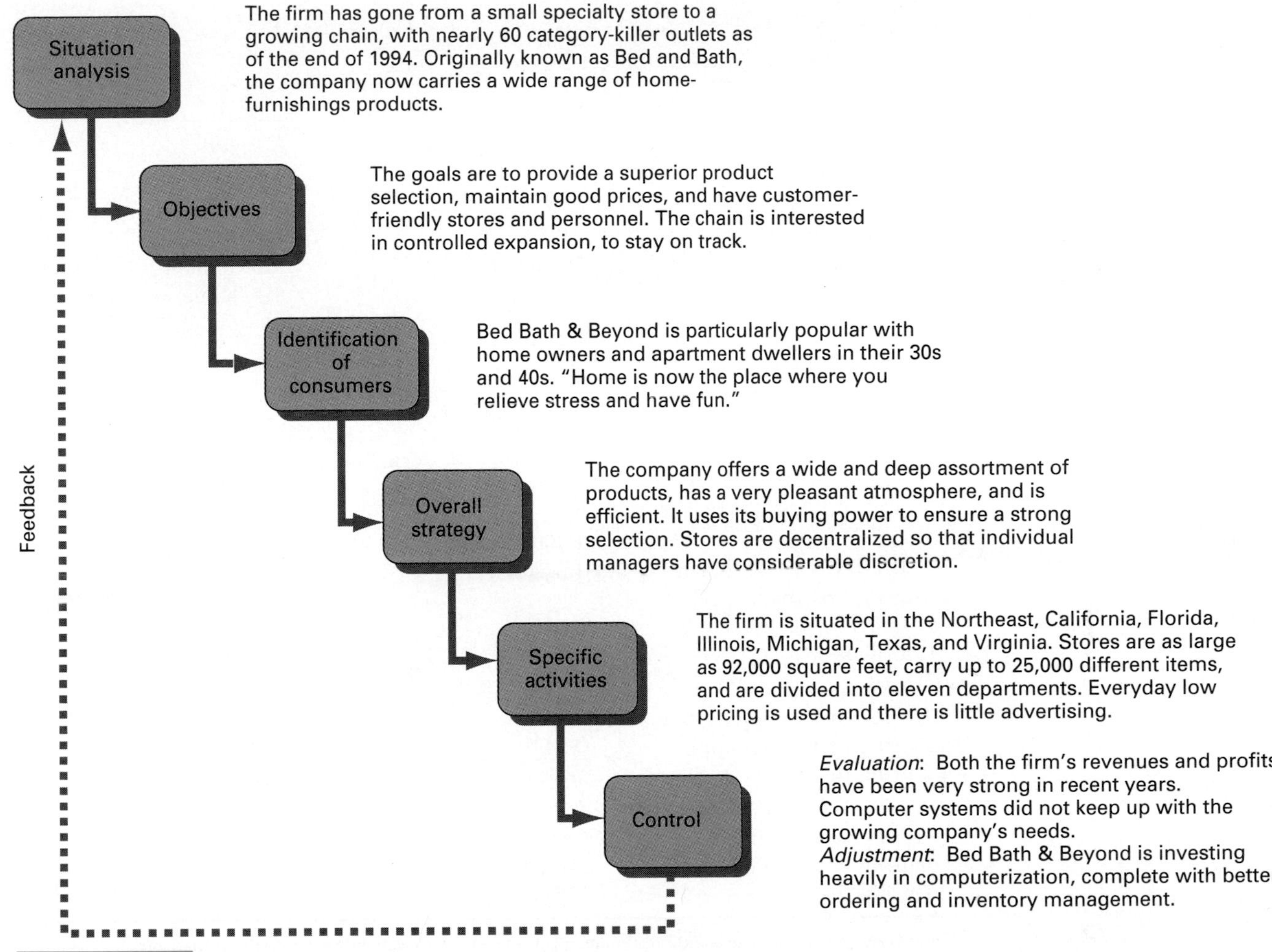

Situation analysis
The firm has gone from a small specialty store to a growing chain, with nearly 60 category-killer outlets as of the end of 1994. Originally known as Bed and Bath, the company now carries a wide range of home-furnishings products.
Objectives
The goals are to provide a superior product selection, maintain good prices, and have customer-friendly stores and personnel. The chain is interested in controlled expansion, to stay on track.
Identification of consumers
Bed Bath & Beyond is particularly popular with home owners and apartment dwellers in their 30s and 40s. "Home is now the place where you relieve stress and have fun."
Overall strategy
The company offers a wide and deep assortment of products, has a very pleasant atmosphere, and is efficient. It uses its buying power to ensure a strong selection. Stores are decentralized so that individual managers have considerable discretion.
Specific activities
The firm is situated in the Northeast, California, Florida, Illinois, Michigan, Texas, and Virginia. Stores are as large as 92,000 square feet, carry up to 25,000 different items, and are divided into eleven departments. Everyday low pricing is used and there is little advertising.
Control
Evaluation: Both the firm's revenues and profits have been very strong in recent years. Computer systems did not keep up with the growing company's needs.
Adjustment: Bed Bath & Beyond is investing heavily in computerization, complete with better ordering and inventory management.
Feedback

FIGURE 19–3 The Integrated Strategy of Bed Bath & Beyond

Source: Compiled by the authors from Marianne Wilson, "Home Furnishings Chain Takes Lead," *Chain Store Age Executive* (November 1993), pp. 21–24.

RETAILING AROUND THE WORLD

What's Ahead for European Retailers?

Many retailing experts anticipate major changes in European retailing as a result of significant internal and external changes in this region.

The major internal change involves the transformation of more than a dozen independent markets into a unified (common) market based upon European Union (EU) reforms. Some observers predict that by 2000 all of the countries in Europe, including Eastern European nations, will be EU members. As part of Europe's integration, various retailers have become more multinational, with greater operations in EU and non-EU nations. Great Britain, France, and Germany have been the home nations of the most active international retailers in Europe.

From an external perspective, a large number of U.S.-based retailers have recently opened stores in Europe. For the most part, these retailers are looking at Europe—with its large industrialized economies—as a means of adding to the sales in their mature, sometimes saturated, U.S. markets.

Most retailers (domestic and foreign) see Europe as being comprised of three different types of markets: Northern Europe, Southern Europe, and Eastern Europe. Northern Europe is the wealthiest of the three and has many chains. Southern Europe, still dominated by small independents, is a short-run prospect for growth by retailers. Eastern Europe has more long-run potential, as retail facilities and the economy advance in the future.

Sources: Based on material in "European Retailers Look Outward; Outsiders Eye Market," *Discount Store News* (August 2, 1993), p. 24; and "Multinationals Dominate International Retailing," *Discount Store News* (August 2, 1993), p. 23.

TABLE 19–1 A Supermarket's Sales Opportunity Grid for Two Brands of Salad Dressing

Criteria	Brand	
	A (established)	B (new)
Retail price	$1.29/8-ounce bottle	$1.29/8-ounce bottle
Floor space needed	8 square feet	8 square feet
Display costs	$10.00/month	$20.00/month for 6 mos., $10.00/month thereafter
Operating costs	$0.12/unit	$0.12/unit
Markup	19%	22%
Sales estimate		
During first month		
Units	250	50
Dollars	$323	$65
During first six months		
Units	1,400	500
Dollars	$1,806	$645
During first year		
Units	2,500	2,750
Dollars	$3,225	$3,548
Gross profit estimate		
During first month	$61	$14
During first six months	$343	$142
During first year	$613	$781
Net profit estimate		
During first month	$21	−$12
During first six months	$115	−$38
During first year	$193	$271

Note: Gross profit estimate = Sales estimate − [(1.00 − Markup percentage) × (Sales estimate)]

Example: Brand A gross profit estimate during first six months = $1,806 − [(1.00 − 0.19) × ($1,806)] = $1,806 − [(0.81) × ($1,806)] = $343

Net profit estimate = Gross profit estimate − (Display costs + Operating costs)

Example: Brand A net profit estimate during first six months = $343 − ($60 + $168) = $115

PERFORMANCE MEASURES

By determining the relevant ***performance measures***—the criteria used to assess effectiveness—and setting standards (goals) for each of them, a retailer can better develop and integrate its strategy. Among the performance measures frequently used by retailers are total sales, average sales per store, sales by goods/service category, sales per square foot, gross margins, gross margin return on investment, operating income, inventory turnover, markdown percentages, employee turnover, financial ratios, and profitability.

Retailers of varying sizes and in different goods or service lines can acquire a lot of industrywide data about firms like themselves from such secondary data sources as *Progressive Grocer, Stores, Discount Store News, Chain Store Age Executive,* Dun & Bradstreet, the National Retail Federation, and Robert Morris Associates. This information would enable the retailers to use industry norms to set company standards. Tables 19–2 through 19–6 contain a wide range of industry performance data for a number of retail categories and provide a large amount of information that could be used by individual retailers to set their own performance standards.

Tables 19–2 and 19–3 present industry performance data for supermarkets. Table 19–2 shows sales for each supermarket product category. For example, meat and seafood, produce, and dairy products account for the largest amount of overall store

TABLE 19–2 Supermarket Sales by Product Category, 1992[a]

Product Category	Performance Measure: Dollar Sales (Millions)	Per Cent of Overall Sales	Annual Sales Growth (Per Cent)[b]
Baby foods	2,458.19	0.86	8.77
Baking needs	5,378.81	1.88	2.24
Beer & wine	6,698.25	2.34	3.68
Breakfast foods	8,548.02	2.99	5.03
Candy & gum	2,868.84	1.00	2.95
Canned fish	1,667.42	0.58	−2.80
Canned fruit	1,300.85	0.45	0.85
Canned meat & specialty foods	2,138.46	0.75	2.83
Canned vegetables	3,001.13	1.05	0.98
Coffee & tea	3,704.59	1.29	−1.75
Cookies & crackers	5,952.92	2.08	3.30
Desserts & toppings	737.51	0.26	1.73
Juice (grocery)	3,686.23	1.29	4.25
Nuts & dried fruit	1,625.23	0.57	1.31
Pasta	2,177.18	0.76	3.56
Pickles & olives	1,216.60	0.42	2.22
Rice & dried vegetables	1,316.73	0.46	3.24
Sauces & dressings	5,787.09	2.02	4.56
Snacks	5,157.54	1.80	3.93
Soft drinks & mixes	11,374.29	3.97	3.48
Soup	2,556.63	0.89	4.44
Spices & extracts	1,200.94	0.42	3.06
Spreads & syrups	2,066.74	0.72	2.11
Total grocery edibles	***82,620.19***	***28.85***	***3.13***
Household supplies	8,683.40	3.03	1.40
Paper, plastic, film, & foil	9,622.04	3.36	1.18
Pet foods	5,209.39	1.82	0.76
Tobacco products	8,777.77	3.07	1.45
Total grocery nonfoods	***32,292.60***	***11.28***	***1.24***
Bakery foods, packaged	8,379.59	2.93	3.83
Dairy products	23,693.46	8.28	2.80
Deli	8,559.82	2.99	6.96
Florals	533.22	0.19	3.28
Frozen foods	15,401.75	5.38	1.91
Ice cream	4,351.51	1.52	2.21
In-store bakery	4,976.99	1.74	6.47
Meat & seafood	46,962.65	16.40	3.62
Produce	28,431.13	9.93	1.67
Total perishables	***141,290.12***	***49.36***	***3.73***
General merchandise	***11,685.18***	***4.08***	***2.45***
Health and beauty aids	***11,253.12***	***3.93***	***2.88***
Pharmacy	***4,100.00***	***1.43***	***NA***
Video rental	***1,206.61***	***0.41***	***NA***
Unclassified[c]	***1,852.14***	***0.66***	***NA***
Total supermarket	***286,299.96***	***100.00***	***3.56***

[a] There are small rounding errors in the table.

[b] 5-year compounded average annual growth rate.

[c] Because the items in this category change, the growth rate is not computed.

Source: "1993 Supermarket Sales Manual," *Progressive Grocer* (July 1993), p. 60. Copyright *Progressive Grocer*. Reprinted by permission.

TABLE 19–3 Selected Performance Data for Independent Supermarkets, 1992

Performance Measure	Annual Store Sales		
	$2–4 million	$6–8 million	$12+ million
Weekly sales/checkout	$14,439	$20,703	$32,962
Weekly sales/employee	$2,802	$3,248	$4,235
Sales/employee hour	$70.63	$81.72	$106.11
Store sales/hour	$599	$1,180	$2,901
Weekly sales/square foot of selling area	$5.52	$7.80	$11.07
Average selling area (square feet)	10,104	16,391	33,528
Average total store area (square feet)	13,605	22,215	42,543
Average number of items stocked	11,475	17,467	21,476
Average inventory value (thousands)	$234	$393	$863
Number of weekly transactions	5,317	9,467	16,651
Average customer transaction size	$10.62	$13.76	$22.99
Annual inventory turnover	10.0	14.7	18.3
Number of checkouts	4.0	6.3	11.6
Number of full-time employees	12.3	24.3	51.8
Number of part-time employees	14.7	30.7	81.5
Hours open per week (median)	93	102	135
Percentage open on Sunday	90	93	93
Percentage open 24 hours (seven days per week)	3	13	45

Source: "60th Annual Report of the Grocery Industry," *Progressive Grocer* (April 1993), pp. 102, 104.

revenues. The highest sales growth has been with baby foods, deli products, and the in-store bakery. And today, pharmacy products and video rental are important enough to be reported as separate categories; a few years ago, they were not.

Table 19–3 provides industrywide statistics for independent supermarkets, classified by store size. In this way, performance can be compared for small, medium, and large stores. From the table, it is clear that large supermarkets are much more efficient than smaller ones. Several facts support this, for example, sales per employee, sales per square foot of selling space, average customer transaction size, and inventory turnover. Smaller stores must keep this in mind when designing strategies and setting performance standards. The standards should realistically reflect the impact of store size on results.

Table 19–4 supplies performance data for nine department-store chains. Here are just a few of the conclusions reached by studying this table: Nordstrom, Dayton Hudson, and R.H. Macy have by far the highest annual sales per store and the highest annual sales per gross square foot. There appear to be three clusters with regard to average sales per store—$46 million to $49 million, $23 million to $33 million, and $12 million. As a percentage of sales, department-store operating results have been mixed, ranging from deficits at Carter Hawley Hale and R.H. Macy to strong results at Dayton Hudson and Dillard's. Yet, although Dayton Hudson is dominant in terms of

TABLE 19–4 1992 Performance Data on Selected Department Stores[a]

Company	Average Sales Per Store ($)	Operating Income as a % of Sales[b]	Sales Per Gross Square Foot ($)	Operating Income Per Gross Square Foot ($)	Operating Income Return on Assets (%)
Carter Hawley Hale	25,757,193	−0.5	141	−0.77	−0.6
Dayton Hudson	48,000,000	19.0	218	41.46	5.6
Dillard's	22,663,399	11.2	142	15.81	12.8
Federated Department Stores	32,626,456	6.1	171	10.40	6.1
R.H. Macy	46,394,856	−5.1	208	−10.65	−7.6
May Department Stores	27,913,183	8.3	175	14.60	8.4
Mercantile	30,022,429	6.0	173	10.32	8.1
Nordstrom	48,885,414	5.3	371	19.60	8.8
J.C. Penney	12,312,157	8.4	137	NA	11.2

[a] In a few instances, companywide data (rather than just department store data) are used in the table.

[b] Operating income = Sales − Cost of goods sold − Selling, general, and administrative expenses (including depreciation and amortization)

NA means data not available.

Source: Management Horizons, "J.C. Penney Leads the Department Store Industry's Comeback," *Chain Store Age Executive* (August 1993), p. 30A. Reprinted by permission. Copyright Lebhar-Friedman, Inc., 425 Park Avenue, New York NY 10022.

operating income per gross square foot, its operating income return on assets has been relatively weak; Dillard's and J.C. Penney have done far better with their return on assets. Overall, no firm is the leader in all of the categories depicted, which means that different strategies can succeed.

Table 19–5 displays performance statistics for several leading consumer electronics chains. An analysis of the table reveals that the approaches followed in this industry segment also vary widely: Circuit City is by far the leading firm in annual sales and earnings, yet Silo, with only 30 per cent of Circuit City's sales, has nearly 80 per cent as many outlets. The number of stores in the chains cited ranges from 2 to 260. Sales per store and store size differ dramatically; while BrandsMart USA's annual per-store sales are $88 million and its stores average 80,000 square feet, Rex/AV Affiliates has annual per-store sales of only $2.1 million and its stores average 7,000 square feet. Yearly sales per square foot range from $1,400 for Tops Appliances to $271 for Luskin's. For those publicly reporting their profits, pre-tax earnings as a percentage of sales tend to be low—reflecting the discount orientation of consumer electronics firms and the intense price cutting.

Since 1989, *Chain Store Age Executive* has published an annual listing of "high performance retailers." These are publicly-owned U.S. firms that perform well above average on a ***retail performance index***, which encompasses five-year trends in revenue growth and profit growth, and a six-year average return on assets. Due to its importance for publicly-held retailers, return on assets is weighted twice as much as either revenue growth or profit growth in the retail performance index. An overall performance index of 100 is considered average. Table 19–6 shows the leading high-performance retailers for 1992. A review of the table reveals there are various ways to be a high performance retailer. For example, Bed Bath & Beyond (the overall leader) trailed many other high-performance firms in revenue growth and profit growth, but its return on assets index was far ahead of any other firm. Furthermore, by deter-

TABLE 19–5 Selected 1992 Performance Data for the Leading Consumer Electronics Chains

Chain	1992 Sales (Millions)	Number of Stores (as of 1/93)	Estimated 1992 Sales/Store	Average Store Size (Square Ft.)	Estimated 1992 Sales/ Square Foot	1992 Pre-tax Earnings (Millions)[a]	Pre-tax Earnings as % of 1992 Company Sales
Circuit City	$3,270	260	$12,577,000	25,000	$ 503	$175.3	5.4
Best Buy	1,620	111	14,595,000	36,000	405	35.9	2.2
Silo	970	204	4,755,000	12,000	396	NA	NA
The Good Guys	504	41	12,293,000	10,000	1,229	6.3	1.3
Fretter/Fred Schmidt	362	86	4,209,000	15,000	281	8.7	2.4
Tops Appliances	350	5	70,000,000	50,000	1,400	NA	NA
The Wiz	315	40	7,875,000	15,000	525	NA	NA
American TV	310	8	38,750,000	100,000	388	NA	NA
BrandsMart USA	263	3	87,667,000	80,000	1,096	NA	NA
Rex/AV Affiliates	233	109	2,138,000	7,000	305	7.9	3.4
Trader Horn	160	18	8,889,000	10,000	889	NA	NA
J&R Music World	110	2	55,000,000	100,000	550	NA	NA
Luskin's	92	34	2,706,000	10,000	271	NA	NA

[a] Includes interest expenses, corporate expenses, and other unusual items.

NA means data not available.

Source: Computed by the authors from "Discount Industry Annual Report," *Discount Store News* (July 5, 1993), pp. 53, 55, 78. Reprinted by permission. Copyright Lebhar-Friedman, Inc., 425 Park Avenue, New York, NY 10022.

mining which are the key high-performance retailers in different industry categories, a prospective or existing company can study the strategies of those retailers and try to emulate their best practices.

By examining industrywide data, retailers can also determine whether their institutional category is declining. Thus, Best Products knows that it faces tough sledding in the future due to the flagging interest in retail catalog showrooms. In fact, it lost money in both 1991 and 1992. See Figure 19–4. To turn the situation around, Best is placing greater emphasis on its jewelry business.[4]

PRODUCTIVITY

As noted in Chapters 11 and 12, productivity refers to the efficiency with which a retail strategy is carried out; and it is in any retailer's interest to reach sales and profit goals while keeping control over costs. The most productive retail strategies are those that are well integrated in terms of the target market, the location(s), and operations, merchandising, pricing, and communications efforts.

A retailer must be careful when enacting its strategy. On the one hand, it does not want to incur unnecessarily high expenses. For example, a firm would not want to have eight salespeople working at the same time if four of them could satisfactorily handle all customers. Likewise, it would not want to pay a high rent for a location in a new regional shopping center if its customers would be willing to travel a few miles further to a less-expensive site. On the other hand, a retailer would not want to lose

[4] "Jewelry/Hard Lines Sales Lag Behind Discount Industry," *Discount Store News* (July 5, 1993), pp. 70, 93.

TABLE 19–6 High-Performance Retailers

Company	Compound Revenue Growth, 1987–1992	5-Year Revenue Growth Index	Compound Profit Growth, 1987–1992	5-Year Profit Growth Index	Average Return on Assets, 1987–1992	6-Year Return on Assets Index	Retail Performance Index[a]
Bed Bath & Beyond	27.18	276	22.62	292	25.69	637	460
50-Off Stores	41.89	426	67.15	866	9.26	229	438
Costco	36.43	370	86.02	1110	4.87	121	430
Quality Food Centers	19.40	197	49.30	636	15.01	372	394
Auto Zone	23.13	235	78.25	1010	6.20	154	388
Home Depot	37.51	381	46.33	598	10.06	249	369
Rag Shops	31.08	316	60.05	775	7.77	193	369
Babbage's	48.12	489	42.17	544	8.24	204	360
The Gap	22.76	231	24.80	320	17.04	422	349
One Price Clothing	34.89	354	20.20	261	13.97	346	327
Wet Seal	37.19	378	37.28	481	8.90	221	325
Designs	38.28	389	51.10	659	4.87	121	322
Men's Wearhouse	36.94	375	29.11	376	9.41	233	304
Merry-Go-Round Enterprises	28.02	285	30.38	392	10.84	269	304
Stein Mart	19.60	199	20.90	270	14.94	370	302
Wal-Mart	28.36	288	26.02	336	11.66	289	300
Cash America International	36.30	369	35.54	471	6.37	158	289
Frederick's of Hollywood	15.08	153	38.21	493	9.82	243	283
Bombay Company	32.96	335	19.11	247	10.78	267	279
Lands' End	16.92	172	7.99	103	16.34	405	271
Total Retailing Median	**9.84**	**100**	**7.75**	**100**	**4.03**	**100**	**100**

[a] Retail performance index = [Revenue growth index + Profit growth index + 2(Return on assets index)]/4

Source: Management Horizons, "High Performance Retailers 1987–1992," *Chain Store Age Executive* (January 1994), p. 3MH. Reprinted by permission. Copyright Lebhar-Friedman, Inc., 425 Park Avenue, New York NY 10022.

customers because there are insufficient sales personnel to handle the rush of shoppers during peak hours. And it would not want to be in a low-rent location if this could result in a significant decline in customer traffic.

This often means that neither the least expensive retail strategy nor the most expensive retail strategy would be the most productive retail strategy, since the former approach might not adequately service customers and the latter approach might be wasteful. The most productive approach would be one that implements a specific integrated retail strategy (such as a full-service jewelry store) as efficiently as possible. As a result, a productive strategy for an upscale retailer would be far different from that for a discounter.

For instance, an upscale retailer would not succeed with self-service operations, and it would be unnecessary (and inefficient) for a discounter to have a large sales staff. This was illustrated by the demise of Garfinckel's—the 85-year-old, Washington, D.C.-

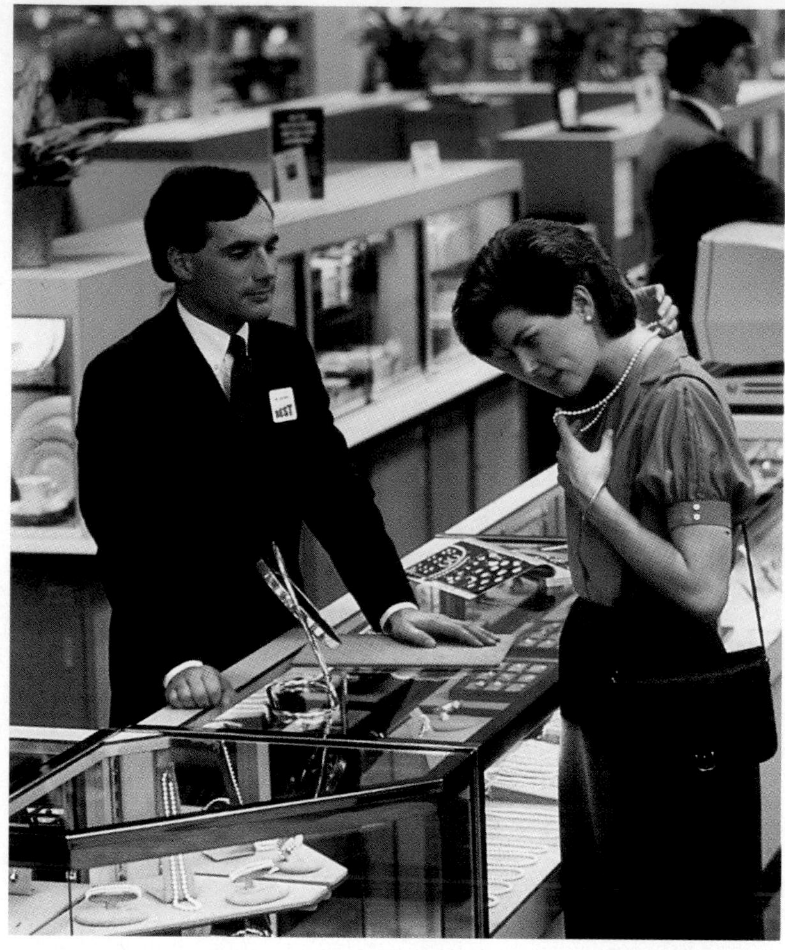

FIGURE 19–4
Dealing with a Troubled Retail Format
As the Best Products retail catalog-showroom chain has discovered, the performance of individual firms can be dramatically affected by the popularity of the institutional formats in which they operate. Thus, despite its superior customer service and other efforts, Best has been having a tough time in the retail catalog-showroom business.
Reprinted by permission.

based, upscale department-store chain, which lost appeal to its target market of affluent shoppers. As one former customer noted before Garfinckel's went out of business: "A store like Nordstrom offers wonderful service, so I'm willing to pay higher prices. Hecht's and Woodie's offer lots of variety at good prices, but you do more self-shopping. I didn't want to go to Garfinckel's, pay high prices, and still have self-shopping."[5]

Spiegel is one of the pre-eminent retailers in the United States. It is also an example of a firm with a well-integrated, productive strategy. Here are some reasons why:

> The mission is as clear as today's retail environment is complex. Through our catalogs and stores, we seek to provide the best specialty shopping experience around. *Bar none.* In pursuing this mission, Spiegel's management team and employees are committed to the following imperatives: (1) Know the customer. Our primary customer, the busy, working woman, is our most valued asset. We must understand her needs, desires, and demands. And we must adapt our product offerings and strategies to changes in her purchasing attitudes. (2) Apply state-of-the-art knowledge. We believe in the prudent application of the latest business information, systems, and technology to improve our understanding of customers and to gain a competitive advantage. (3) Offer real value. We recognize that today's working woman is a sophisticated shopper who demands real value. We strive to satisfy this need by offering an optimal combination of style, quality, service, and price in all product lines. (4) Build brand personality. Although the national and proprietary brands featured in our catalogs and stores address

[5] Edmund L. Andrews, "First Altman's, Now Garfinckel's," *New York Times* (June 28, 1990), pp. D1, D6.

RETAILING IN ACTION

Why Is the Cosmetic Center Chain Doing So Well?

The Cosmetics Center is a chain of category-killer stores that carries 25,000 different products. About 40 per cent of sales come from cosmetics, 40 per cent from fragrances, and 20 per cent from shampoo and jewelry.

By offering status brands (such as Lancome, Ultima II, and Elizabeth Arden) and mass-market items (such as Revlon, L'Oreal, and Max Factor), The Cosmetics Center boasts a broader selection than most department and specialty stores. It also discounts its products, selling them for 20 to 50 per cent below traditional retail prices. The firm has stores in strip malls in Washington, D.C., Chicago, Baltimore, Richmond, and Charlottesville, Virginia.

In contrast to department stores, where cosmeticians are often supplied by manufacturers, The Cosmetics Center employs all of its own cosmeticians. This enables the firm to shift employees from brand to brand (based upon demand), for one cosmetician to handle a customer's entire needs, and for the chain to emphasize the sale of higher-profit items.

The Cosmetic Center has a labeling system that is used to generate key sales data. And an automatic replenishment system enables the chain to maintain a 93 per cent in-stock rate.

Source: Based on material in Faye Brookman, "Cosmetic Center Set to Expand," *Stores* (September 1993), pp. 60–61.

different tastes and needs, we work to ensure that collectively, these brands make Spiegel synonymous in consumers' minds with the best specialty shopping experience. (5) Be a low-cost operator. We allocate human and financial resources in a disciplined manner across our businesses to control costs and to achieve real value for customers. These imperatives guide our management team as it formulates strategies to carry out the company's mission in today's increasingly competitive marketplace. They also provide a framework for employees as they implement these strategies through an ongoing process of research, response, and follow through. Most important, they keep Spiegel focused on the needs of our customers and shareholders as we strive to strengthen our position as a leader in specialty retailing.[6]

USES OF NEW TECHNOLOGY

Throughout the text, new retail technology, such as computerized retail information systems, has been described. In this section, examples of how retailers are using technology in integrating their strategies are presented.

Rite Aid has placed PCs in its 2,600 drugstores, enabling it to achieve several goals in planning, enacting, and monitoring its retail strategy mix:

- All outlets are electronically linked.
- Communications between individual stores and headquarters are enhanced.
- Individual store performance can be reviewed more quickly and accurately.
- Reporting is now easy, relatively paperless, and inexpensive.
- The computerization of the pharmacy end of the business means better records, more information maintained on patient profiles, enhanced drug interaction screening, improved processing of third-party prescription claims, and greater inventory control.[7]

Saks Fifth Avenue, unlike most other department-store chains, only began in-store computer scanning of merchandise a few years ago. Here's why: "The vendors who are doing massive UPC and EDI projects with retailers like Kmart and Sears are not the vendors we deal with at all. Our vendors are the small operators that are gener-

[6] *Spiegel, Inc. 1992 Annual Report*, p. 1.

[7] *Rite Aid Corporation 1993 Annual Report*, various pages.

FIGURE 19–5
Technology and Frank's Nursery & Crafts
Reprinted by permission. Frank's Nursery & Crafts, Inc., is a subsidiary of General Host Corporation.

ally not as sophisticated in their systems as the huge vendors like Levi and Haggar." Thus, Saks now prints its own bar codes on the price tags that are attached to merchandise: "Through scanning, we get more accurate information, and we get the customer's sale completed faster."[8]

Frank's Nursery & Crafts, a growing chain, has made a multimillion dollar commitment to technology (as highlighted in Figure 19–5):

> Frank's has the latest VSAT (very small aperture terminal) satellite communications system. A 15-foot diameter hub satellite dish is in place at Frank's Detroit headquarters, and all stores have received a six-foot satellite dish and other electronic equipment to support satellite communications. As a result, credit-card authorization response time is approaching seven seconds per transaction, down from the previous range of 45 to 60 seconds. This is particularly important because more than 25 per cent of sales involve credit cards. Frank's is also transmitting background music, special regionalized advertising, and messages through the system and will be sending training videos, new product presentations, and other information to the stores via satellite.
>
> Most recently, Frank's introduced a laser radio terminal that performs price verification and order entry in a single, integrated hand-held unit. Store personnel verify or change item pricing by scanning an item bar code and communicating with the in-store computer. Managers are able to track sales and inventory on a daily basis and respond to customer buying patterns by keeping desirable merchandise in stock and competitively priced. Managers also utilize the terminal for store ordering. Rather than wait for paper-based documentation, store employees can scan an item's bar code and check sales and pricing history; this cuts ordering time by more than one-fourth. Frank's is testing automatic inventory replenishment in a few locations with the intention of implementing this chainwide. The company also has initiated a pilot program with one of its vendors using an electronic data interchange system.
>
> Frank's business lends itself to computer technology because of its seasonality and large number of stock-keeping units—as many as 30,000 active items in any given period. Because technology enhances customer service, major investments in technology will continue.[9]

Some technological activities are more futuristic in approach than others, as companies prepare and gear up for the long run. For instance, Blockbuster Entertainment

[8] "Catching the Wave of the Future," *Chain Store Age Executive* (October 1990), Section Two, p. 29A.

[9] *General Host Corporation 1992 Annual Report,* pp. 14–16.

has been developing and testing a new high-tech inventory system called "Soundsational." At present, each of Blockbuster's 3,200 stores around the world carries about 7,000 video and audio titles. Yet, despite the high volume of inventory carried, the stores miss out on many sales opportunities because they cannot stock every title that customers might want—at least not in sufficient quantity. Furthermore, the music business is quite risky. Just one in 10 recordings makes money. Thus, at some point in the future, Blockbuster hopes Soundsational will remedy the situation. This is how:

> When a customer comes into a Blockbuster store, he or she will make use of a kiosk equipped with a touch screen to both identify and preview products of interest. After making a choice, the customer will tell a clerk behind the front desk, who will then use a PC to "order" the product from a central host computer. The host system will transmit the product to the store, where it will be manufactured—artwork and all—in minutes.
>
> Blockbuster will benefit from improved inventory management, better customer satisfaction, and increased sales and margins. Content providers will benefit from fewer returns, access to their entire catalogs, and new international opportunities—new content will be more available to new markets. Customers will benefit because they will be able to preview a product before buying or renting it; they will always get what they want—no more out of stock; and kiosks will make store visits more entertaining.
>
> Soundsational is currently in the testing phase and will not be fully implemented until several hurdles are cleared. These include licensing agreements with content providers and in-store equipment that can manufacture and assemble products rapidly and economically.[10]

Control: Using the Retail Audit

After a retail strategy has been developed and put into action, it must be continuously assessed, and necessary adjustments must be made. An important evaluation tool is the ***retail audit***, which may be defined as the systematic examination and evaluation of a firm's total retailing effort or some specific aspect of it. The purpose of a retail audit is to study what a retailer is presently doing, to appraise how well the retailer is performing, and to make recommendations for future actions.[11]

An overall company audit should include an investigation of a retailer's objectives, strategy, implementation, and organization. First, the firm's goals would be reviewed and evaluated for their clarity, consistency, and appropriateness. Second, the firm's strategy and its methods for deriving it would be analyzed. Third, how well the strategy has been implemented and actually received by customers would be reviewed. Fourth, the organizational structure would be analyzed; lines of command, types of organization charts, and other factors are the kinds of information studied in this phase.

Good retail auditing includes several key elements: Audits are conducted on a regular basis. In-depth analysis is involved. Data are amassed and analyzed in a systematic way. An open-minded, unbiased perspective is maintained during the audit process. There must be a company willingness to uncover weaknesses that must be corrected, as well as strengths that must be exploited. And once an audit is completed, the appropriate decision makers must be responsive to the recommendations made in the audit report.

[10] "Ernst & Young's Survey of Retail Information Technology Expenses and Trends," *Chain Store Age Executive* (October 1993), Section 2, pp. 10–11.

[11] See, for example, "Analyzing a Retailer," *Standard & Poor's Industry Surveys: Retailing Basic Analysis* (May 13, 1993), pp. R86–R88; and Scott W. Kelley, K. Douglas Hoffman, and Mark A. Davis, "A Typology of Retail Failures and Recoveries," *Journal of Retailing*, Vol. 69 (Winter 1993), pp. 429–452.

UNDERTAKING AN AUDIT

Several steps should be completed in undertaking a retail audit:

1. Determining who does the audit.
2. Determining when and how often the audit is conducted.
3. Determining areas to be audited.
4. Developing audit form(s).
5. Conducting the audit.
6. Reporting to management.

See Figure 19–6 for a description of the retail audit process.

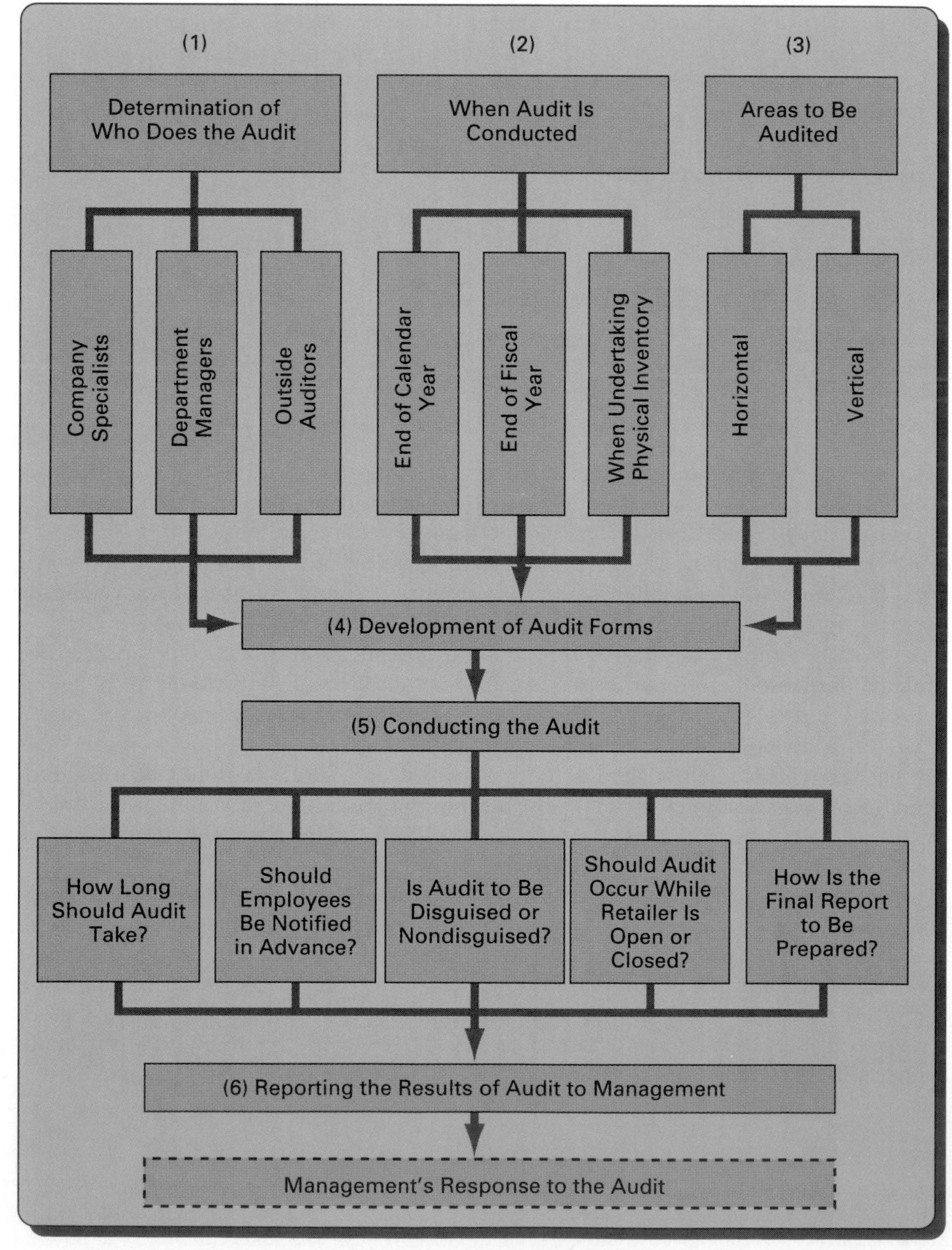

FIGURE 19–6
The Retail Audit Process

Determining Who Does the Audit

When a retail audit is conducted, one or a combination of three parties can be utilized: a company audit specialist, a company department manager, and an outside auditor. The advantages and disadvantages of each are noted here.

A ***company audit specialist*** is an internal employee whose prime responsibility is the retail audit. The advantages of this source include the auditing expertise, the thoroughness, the level of knowledge about the firm, and the ongoing nature (no time lags). Disadvantages include the costs (very expensive for small retailers, which do not need full-time auditors) and the limited independence of these auditors.

A ***company department manager*** is an internal employee whose prime responsibility is operations management, but he or she may also be asked to participate in the retail audit. The advantages of this source are that added personnel expenses are not needed and that such a manager is knowledgeable about the firm and has a complete understanding of day-to-day operations. Disadvantages include the manager's time away from the primary job, the potential lack of objectivity, the time pressure, and the complexity of conducting companywide audits.

An ***outside auditor*** is a person who is not a permanent employee of the retailer but who works as a consultant (usually for a fee). Advantages include the auditor's broad experience, objectivity, and thoroughness. Disadvantages include the high costs per day or hour (however, for small retailers, it may be cheaper to hire expensive, per diem consultants than to employ full-time auditors; the opposite is usually true for larger firms), the time lags while a consultant gains familiarity with the company, the failure of some retailers to use outside specialists on a continuous basis, and the reluctance of some employees to cooperate with outsiders.

Determining When and How Often the Audit is Conducted

Logical times for conducting an audit are at the end of the calendar year, at the end of the company's annual reporting year (fiscal year), or at the point of a complete physical inventory. Each of these is appropriate for evaluating a retailer's operations during the previous period.

An audit must be enacted at least annually, although some retailers desire more frequent analysis. It is important that the same period(s), such as January–December, be studied each year if meaningful comparisons, projections, and adjustments are to be made.

Determining Areas to be Audited

A retail audit typically includes more than financial analysis; it examines various aspects of a firm's strategy and operations. An audit can also be used during successful and unsuccessful periods to identify strengths and weaknesses. There are two basic types of audits—horizontal and vertical.

A ***horizontal retail audit*** involves an analysis of the overall performance of a retail firm, from its organizational mission to objectives to customer satisfaction to basic retail strategy mix and its implementation in an integrated, consistent manner. Because a horizontal audit studies the interrelation of many strategic elements and their relative importance, it may also be considered a "retail strategy audit."

A ***vertical retail audit*** involves an in-depth analysis of a retail firm's performance in one area of its strategy mix or operations, such as the credit function, customer service, merchandise assortment, or interior displays. A vertical audit is focused and specialized in nature.

The two audits should be used in conjunction with one another because a horizontal audit often reveals areas that merit further investigation via a vertical audit.

Developing Audit Forms

To be systematic and thorough, a retailer should use detailed audit forms. An ***audit form*** lists the area(s) to be examined and the exact information required in evaluating each area. Audit forms usually resemble questionnaires, and they are completed by the auditor.

ETHICS IN RETAILING

Why Is Ben & Jerry's Ahead of the Pack?

Unlike most firms, Ben & Jerry's publishes two types of audits in its annual report: financial and social. The social audit, conducted by an outside firm, evaluates Ben & Jerry's performance in such areas as employee benefits, plant safety, ecology, community involvement, and customer service. Ben & Jerry's supplies the social-audit analysts with all employee and corporate documents; it also agrees to publish the report in an unedited format.

Past social audits of Ben & Jerry's have been quite candid. For example, in its 1992 audit, the social auditor chided Ben & Jerry's plant-safety record and cited the increase in plant accidents from 52 in 1991 to 75 in 1992. Lost days due to accidents also increased from 902 to 1,702, an amount in excess of sales and production growth. The report also questioned Ben & Jerry's strategy of paying its highest-paid employee no more than seven times the salary of its lowest-paid worker in light of the number of vacant executive positions.

Public relations analysts believe that Ben & Jerry's social audit enhances its credibility among institutional investors, stockholders, and consumers. Few firms, however, have added a social audit to their annual report. Given Ben & Jerry's strong financial performance, maybe more should.

Source: Based on material in Betsy Wiesendanger, "Ben & Jerry Scoop Up Credibility," *Public Relations Journal* (August 1993), p. 20.

Without audit forms, the analysis becomes more haphazard and subjective, and it would not be standardized. Important questions may be omitted or poorly worded. The biases of the auditor may show through. And most significantly, questions may differ from one audit period to another, which could limit comparisons over time.

Examples of audit forms are presented later in the chapter.

Conducting the Audit

After the auditor is selected, the timing of the audit is determined, the areas to be analyzed are chosen, and audit forms are constructed, the audit itself is undertaken.

Management should specify in advance how long the audit will take and conform to this timetable. Prior notification of employees depends on management's perception of two factors: the need to compile some information in advance to increase efficiency and save time versus the desire to obtain a true picture and not a distorted one (which may occur if too much prior notification is given).

A ***disguised audit*** is one in which a retailer's employees are not aware an audit is taking place. It is useful if the auditor is investigating an area like personal selling and wishes to act out the role of a customer to elicit employee responses. A ***nondisguised audit*** is one in which a retailer's employees are aware an audit is being conducted. This is desirable if employees are asked specific operational questions and help in gathering data for the auditor.

The decision as to whether to perform an audit when the firm is open or closed depends on the type of information required. Some audits should be conducted while the retailer is open, such as analyses of the adequacy of the parking lot, in-store customer traffic patterns, the use of vertical transportation, and customer relations. Other audits should be completed while the retailer is closed, such as analyses of the condition of fixtures, inventory levels and turnover, financial statements, and employee records.

It must be determined what format the audit report will take. The report can be formal or informal, brief or long, oral or written, and a statement of findings or a statement of findings plus recommendations. A report has a better chance of acceptance if presented in the format desired by management.

Reporting Audit Findings and Recommendations to Management

The last step in the audit process is the presentation of findings and recommendations to management. It is the responsibility of management, not the auditor, to determine what adjustments (if any) to implement. It is essential that the proper company executives read the audit report thoroughly, consider each point made, and make the needed strategy changes.

Management should treat each audit report seriously and react accordingly. A serious mistake would be made if only lip service is paid to findings. A firm's long-term success is predicated on its evaluating the present and adapting to the future. No matter how well an audit is performed, it is a worthless exercise if not taken seriously by management.

RESPONDING TO AN AUDIT

After management has studied the findings of an audit, appropriate actions should be taken. Areas of strength should bc continued and areas of weakness revised. All actions must be consistent with the retail strategy and recorded and stored in the retail information system.

For example, TJX Companies, Inc., the parent company of several off-price apparel chains, places great reliance on its retail audits. Here is what it stated in one recent annual report:

> T.J. Maxx executed its business with the discipline that has led to its record of growth in sales and profits over the years. Merchandising, store operations, real estate, systems technology, marketing, and administration continued to perform their respective functions with precision, while seeking innovative ways in which to enhance their contributions to the bottom line. For instance, in merchandising, the misses sportswear department was revamped very successfully. While we've continued to concentrate on moderate sportswear, we separated career and casual sportswear in our store layout in order to give each a higher profile. Store operations continued to focus on efficiency and customer service. A major project was undertaken which analyzed and improved the back room operations of our stores, where merchandise is received and readied for the selling floor. The program was successful in improving efficiency, enhancing safety measures, lowering costs, and getting merchandise to the selling floor on a more timely basis. In addition, our mission to have the entire chain look fresh and current was continued with the refurbishing of stores to ensure that our customers have a pleasant shopping experience. Overall, T.J. Maxx had another year in which its consistency in management, mission, and execution led to record results.[12]

POSSIBLE DIFFICULTIES IN CONDUCTING A RETAIL AUDIT

There are several potential difficulties that may occur when conducting a retail audit; a retailer should be aware of them:

- An audit may be costly to undertake.
- An audit may be quite time-consuming.
- Performance measures may be inaccurate.
- Employees may feel threatened and not cooperate as much as desired.
- Incorrect data may be collected.
- Management may not be responsive to the findings.

At the present time, many retailers—particularly smaller ones—do not understand or perform systematic retail audits. But as these retailers move toward the year 2000, this must change if they are to analyze themselves properly and plan correctly for the future.

[12] *TJX Companies, Inc. 1992 Annual Report*, p. 2.

Answer YES or NO to Each Question

A Look at Yourself and Your Ability to Grow

____ 1. Do you keep abreast of changes in your field by subscribing to leading trade and general business publications?
____ 2. Do you plan for a profit (your net income) above a reasonable salary for yourself as manager?
____ 3. Are you an active member of a trade association?

Customer Relations

____ 4. Do you purposely cater to selected groups of customers rather than to all groups?
____ 5. Do you have a clear picture of the retail image you seek to implant in the minds of your customers?
____ 6. Do you evaluate your own performance by asking customers about their likes and dislikes and by shopping competitors to compare their assortments, prices, and promotion methods with your own?

Personnel Management and Supervision

____ 7. Do employees in your firm know to whom they each report?
____ 8. Do you delegate as much authority as you can to those immediately responsible to you, freeing yourself from unnecessary operating details?
____ 9. Do you seek your employees' opinions of stock assortments, choice of new merchandise, layout, displays, and special promotions?
____ 10. Do you apply the concept of "management by objectives," that is, do you set work goals for yourself and for each employee for the month or season ahead and at the end of each period check the actual performance against these goals?

Merchandise Inventory Control

____ 11. Do you keep sales, inventory, and purchase records by types of merchandise within your departments?
____ 12. Do you control your purchases in dollars by means of an open-to-buy system?
____ 13. For staple and reorder items, do you prepare a checklist (never-out list) that you frequently check against the actual assortment on hand?
____ 14. Do you make certain that best-sellers are reordered promptly and in sufficient volume and that slow-sellers are processed swiftly for clearance?
____ 15. Are you taking adequate safeguards to reduce shoplifting and pilferage in your store?

Budgetary Control and Productivity

____ 16. In controlling your operations, do you frequently compare actual results with the budget projections you have made; and do you then adjust your merchandising, promotion, and expense plans as indicated by deviation from these projections?
____ 17. Do you study industry data and compare the results of your operation with them?
____ 18. Do you think in terms of ratios and per cents, rather than exclusively in dollars-and-cents?
____ 19. Do you use a variety of measures of performance, such as:
  ____ a. Net profit as a per cent of your net worth?
  ____ b. Stockturn (ratio of your sales to the value of your average inventory)?
  ____ c. Gross profit margin per dollar of cost investment in merchandise (dollars of gross margin divided by your average inventory at cost)?
  ____ d. Sales per square foot of space (net sales divided by total number of square feet of space)?
  ____ e. Selling cost per cent for each salesperson (remuneration of the salesperson divided by that person's sales)?

Buying

____ 20. Are you continually searching the market for the most suitable merchandise, prices, and sources rather than relying too much on established sources?
____ 21. When reordering new items that have shown volume potential, do you make it a point to order a sufficient number?
____ 22. Do you keep up assortments through important selling seasons, such as Christmas and Easter, in spite of the probability of markdowns on the remainders?
____ 23. For goods having a short selling season (such as straw hats), do you pre-determine the following dates: (a) when first orders are to be placed, (b) when retail stocks are to be complete, (c) extent of peak selling period, (d) start of clearance, and (e) final cleanup?
____ 24. Do you take advantage of all available discounts—trade, quantity, seasonal, and cash—and do you include them on your written orders?

FIGURE 19–7 A Management Audit Form for Retailers

Source: This figure is adapted from John W. Wingate and Elmer O. Schaller, *Management Audit for Small Retailers* (Washington, D.C.: Small Business Administration, Small Business Management Series No. 31, Third Edition, 1977).

Illustrations of Retail Audit Forms

In this section, a management audit form for retailers and a retailing performance checklist are presented. These forms demonstrate how both small and large retailers can inexpensively, yet efficiently, conduct retail audits.

An internal or external auditor (or department manager) would complete one of the forms in a systematic, periodic way and then discuss the findings with management. The examples noted are both horizontal audits. A vertical audit would consist of an in-depth analysis of any one area in these forms.

Pricing

_____ 25. Do you figure markup as a percentage of retail selling price rather than as a percentage of costs?
_____ 26. Do you set price lines or price zones?
_____ 27. Do the prices you set provide adequate markups within the limits of competition?
_____ 28. In retail pricing of new items and in evaluating their cost quotations, are you guided by what you think the typical customer will consider good value?
_____ 29. Before you mark down goods for clearance, do you consider alternate supplementary ways of moving them—such as special displays, repackaging, or including them in a deal?

Advertising and Sales Promotion

_____ 30. Do you advertise consistently in at least one appropriate medium: newspapers, direct mail, flyers, local television, or radio?
_____ 31. Does each of your ads specifically "sell" your firm in addition to the merchandise advertised?
_____ 32. Do you regularly and systematically familiarize your salespeople with your plans for advertised merchandise and promotions?
_____ 33. Do you consult your suppliers about dealer aids helpful to the promotion of their merchandise in your store?
_____ 34. Do you use "co-op" ads with other merchants in your community?
_____ 35. Do you conduct a continuing effort to obtain free publicity in the local press or broadcast media?

Display

_____ 36. Are your window displays planned to attract attention, develop interest, create desire, and prompt a customer to enter your store for a closer inspection?
_____ 37. Do you give as much attention to your interior display as to your windows?

Equipment and Layout

_____ 38. Are goods that the customers may not be specifically looking for but are likely to buy on sight (impulse merchandise) displayed near your store entrances and at other points that have heavy traffic?
_____ 39. Are your cash registers well located?
_____ 40. Are nonselling and office activities kept out of valuable selling space?
_____ 41. Do you receive, check, and mark incoming goods at central points rather than on the selling floor?

Cash and Finance

_____ 42. Does someone other than the cashier or bookkeeper open all mail and prepare a record of receipts that will be checked against deposits?
_____ 43. Do you deposit all of each day's cash receipts in the bank without delay?
_____ 44. Do you calculate your cash flow regularly (monthly, for example) and take steps to provide enough cash for each period's needs?
_____ 45. Have you established, in advance, a line of credit at your bank, not only to meet seasonal requirements but also to permit borrowing at any time for emergency needs?

Credit

_____ 46. Do you have a credit policy?
_____ 47. Are your bad-debt losses comparable with those of other similar retailers?
_____ 48. Periodically, do you review your accounts to determine their status?

Insurance

_____ 49. Is your company's insurance handled by a conscientious and knowledgeable agent?
_____ 50. Have you updated your insurance needs to insure adequate protection for buildings, equipment, merchandise, and other assets, as well as for public liability?

Accounting Records

_____ 51. Do you have your books balanced and accounts summarized each month?
_____ 52. Do you use a modern point-of-sale register for sales transactions and modern equipment to record accounts receivable?
_____ 53. Do you keep data on sales, purchases, inventory, and direct expenses for different types of merchandise?

Taxes and Legal Obligations

_____ 54. To be sure you are not overpaying your taxes, do you retain a tax accountant to review your accounting records and prepare your more complicated tax returns?
_____ 55. Do you retain a good lawyer to confer with on day-to-day problems that have legal implications?

Planning for Growth

_____ 56. Over the past few years, have you done much long-range planning for growth?
_____ 57. When you find that change is called for, do you act decisively and creatively?
_____ 58. Do you make most of your changes after thoughtful analysis rather than as reactions to crises?
_____ 59. Are you grooming someone to succeed you as manager in the not too distant future?

FIGURE 19–7 (Continued)

A MANAGEMENT AUDIT FORM FOR RETAILERS

The Small Business Administration has published a *Management Audit for Small Retailers* (Small Business Management Series No. 31, Third Edition), by John W. Wingate and Elmer O. Schaller.* This booklet, although written for small retailers, provides a series of questions and discussions applicable to all retailers; it comprehensively details the components of a retail audit.

Figure 19–7 contains selected questions from each of the 16 areas covered in the *Management Audit for Small Retailers.* "Yes" is the desired answer to every question in

* In addition to the information presented here, *Management Audit for Small Retailers* discusses each point of the audit in great detail.

Rate your firm's performance for each of the following criteria on a scale of 1 to 5, with 1 being excellent and 5 being poor.

I. Development of strategy
1. Adherence to the philosophy of business ______
2. Clear objectives ______
3. Consistent objectives and image ______
4. Well-defined goods and/or service offerings ______
5. Well-defined and ongoing budget ______
6. Proper use of research ______
7. Thorough short-run planning ______
8. Thorough long-run planning ______
9. Reactions to external environment ______
10. Well-established evaluation criteria ______
11. Adjustments in strategy ______

II. The consumer
1. Well-defined target market ______
2. Consistency with image ______
3. Size of target market ______
4. Knowledge of consumer needs ______
5. Demographic trends for target market ______

III. Store location
1. Consistency with image ______
2. Size of trading area ______
3. Popularity of trading area ______
4. Access to vehicular traffic ______
5. Access to mass transportation ______
6. Parking facilities ______
7. Composition of existing stores ______
8. Affinity with existing stores ______
9. Turnover of stores ______
10. Visibility of store ______
11. Condition of building ______
12. Terms of occupancy ______
13. Store hours ______
14. Store facilities ______
15. Maintenance of facilities ______

IV. Retail organization and human resource management
1. Clarity of retail organization ______
2. Appropriateness of retail organization ______
3. Adaptability of retail organization ______
4. Employee recruitment ______
5. Employee selection ______
6. Employee training ______
7. Employee compensation ______
8. Employee supervision ______
9. Employee motivation ______
10. Opportunities for advancement ______

FIGURE 19–8
A Retailing Performance Checklist

the Figure. For those questions answered in the negative, a retailer would need to determine the causes for the responses and adjust strategy accordingly. Figure 19–7 should be viewed as a single, overall horizontal audit, not as fragmented pieces.

A RETAILING PERFORMANCE CHECKLIST

Figure 19–8 shows another type of audit form, a retailing performance checklist, which can be used to evaluate overall strategy performance. Included are each of the components of a retail strategy. The checklist can also be used by small and large retailers alike.

The checklist's purpose is to identify strengths and weaknesses, so a strategy can be adjusted. Unlike the yes-no answers in Figure 19–7, the checklist lets a retailer rate performance in each area, thus providing more in-depth information. A total score is not computed. Because all items are not equally important, a simple summation would not present a meaningful score.

V. Operations management
1. Return on assets ______
2. Return on net worth ______
3. Appropriateness of budgeting style ______
4. Cash flow ______
5. Store size ______
6. Space allocation ______
7. Employee turnover ______
8. Store maintenance ______
9. Inventory management ______
10. Store security ______
11. Use of insurance ______
12. Credit management ______
13. Level of computerization ______
14. Crisis management ______

VI. Merchandising
1. Buying organization ______
2. Appropriateness of merchandise quality ______
3. Level of innovativeness ______
4. Width of assortment ______
5. Depth of assortment ______
6. Availability of manufacturer brands ______
7. Availability of private brands ______
8. Knowledge of merchandise sources ______
9. Caliber of merchandise sources ______
10. Purchase terms ______
11. Reordering procedures ______
12. Use of dollar control systems ______
13. Use of unit control systems ______
14. Inventory valuation procedures ______
15. Accuracy of records ______
16. Merchandise forecasting and budgeting process ______
17. Stock turnover ______
18. Gross margin return on investment ______

VII. Pricing
1. Consistency with other retail strategy mix factors ______
2. Awareness of consumer sensitivity to price ______
3. Awareness of and compliance with government restrictions ______
4. Relations with suppliers ______
5. Competitive pricing environment ______
6. Use of multistage approach to pricing ______
7. Use of demand-, cost-, and competition-based pricing techniques ______
8. Adaptability ______
9. Use of price lining ______
10. Level of markdowns ______

VIII. Communications
1. Appropriateness of image ______
2. Customer perception of image ______
3. Storefront(s) ______
4. Cleanliness of facilities ______
5. Traffic flow ______
6. Width of aisles ______
7. Use of dead space ______
8. Displays ______
9. Customer service ______
10. Amount of promotion ______
11. Quality of promotion ______
12. Diversity of promotion ______
13. Amount of personal selling ______
14. Quality of sales force ______
15. Uses of publicity ______
16. Uses of sales promotion ______

FIGURE 19–8 (Continued)

SUMMARY

1. *To demonstrate the importance of integrating a retail strategy* This chapter shows why it is necessary for retailers to plan and implement coordinated strategies, and describes how to assess success or failure. The various parts of a retail strategy must be viewed as an ongoing, integrated system of interrelated steps—not as a fragmented, one-time-only concept.

2. *To examine four key factors in the development and enactment of an integrated retail strategy: planning procedures and opportunity analysis, performance measures, productivity, and the uses of new technology* Planning procedures can be optimized by following a series of specified actions, from situation analysis to control. Opportunities need to be examined in terms of their impact on overall strategy, and not in an isolated manner. The sales opportunity grid is a good tool for comparing various strategic options.

   By determining the relevant measures of performance and setting standards for them, a retailer can better develop and integrate strategy. Such measures include total sales, average sales per store, sales by goods/service category, sales per square foot, gross margins, gross margin return on investment, operating income, inventory turnover, markdown percentages, employee turnover, financial ratios, and profitability. The retail performance index devised for *Chain Store Age Executive* combines sales growth, profit growth, and return-on-assets measures.

   To maximize productivity, retailers need to make the implementation of their strategies as efficient as possible. However, efficiency does not necessarily mean having the lowest possible expenditures on operations (since this may lead to customer dissatisfaction), but rather keying spending to the performance standards required by a retailer's chosen strategy mix and niche in the market (such as upscale versus discount). By using new technology, retailers are often able to better integrate strategies and raise their performance.

3. *To show how industrywide data can be used in strategy planning and analysis* In this chapter, industrywide performance data have been presented for supermarkets, department stores, consumer electronics chains, and other retailer categories.

4. *To explain the principles of a retail audit, its utility in controlling a retail strategy, the difference between horizontal and vertical audits, and the possible difficulties with auditing* A retail strategy needs to be regularly monitored, evaluated, and fine-tuned or revised. The retail audit is one technique that can accomplish this control function; it is a systematic, thorough, and unbiased review and appraisal. With an audit, a firm's objectives, strategy, implementation, and organization could each be investigated.

   The retail audit process consists of six steps: determining who does the audit (company audit specialists, company department managers, and/or outside auditors); determining when and how often it is conducted; setting the areas to be audited; developing audit forms; conducting the audit; and reporting results and recommendations to management. After the appropriate executives read the audit report, necessary revisions in strategy should be made.

   With a horizontal audit, a retailer's overall strategy and performance are assessed. With a vertical audit, one element of a firm's strategy is evaluated in detail.

   Among the potential difficulties with auditing may be the costs, the time commitment, the inaccuracy of performance standards, the poor cooperation from some employees, the collection of incorrect data, and an unresponsive management. A number of retailers do not utilize audits; they may have problems evaluating their positions and planning for the future.

5. *To provide examples of audit forms* Two illustrations of audit forms have been presented in the chapter: a management audit for retailers and a retailing performance checklist.

KEY TERMS

sales opportunity grid (p. 652)
performance measures (p. 654)
retail performance index (p. 657)
retail audit (p. 663)
company audit specialist (p. 665)
company department manager (p. 665)
outside auditor (p. 665)
horizontal retail audit (p. 665)
vertical retail audit (p. 665)
audit form (p. 665)
disguised audit (p. 666)
nondisguised audit (p. 666)

QUESTIONS FOR DISCUSSION

1. Why is it so important for a retailer to view its strategy as an integrated and ongoing process?
2. Present an integrated strategy for Bed Bath & Beyond to increase sales by 12 per cent annually for each of the next three years. Refer to Figure 19–3 in your answer.
3. Develop a sales opportunity grid for a neighborhood beauty salon planning to add women's cosmetics to its product line.
4. Cite five performance measures commonly used by retailers, and explain what could be learned by studying each.
5. As a small independent supermarket ($2–4 million in annual sales), what could you learn by studying Table 19–3? Be specific in your answer.
6. What do you think are the pros and cons of the retail performance index described in this chapter and highlighted in Table 19–6?
7. Comment on this statement: "Often neither the least expensive retail strategy nor the most expensive retail strategy would be the most productive retail strategy." Does this mean that off-price chain stores should upgrade their strategies? Explain your answer.
8. How could the use of new technology be helpful in a retailer's efforts to better integrate its strategy?
9. Distinguish between horizontal and vertical retail audits. Develop a vertical audit form for a retailer selling exterior house siding.
10. What are attributes of good retail auditing?
11. Distinguish among the following auditors. Under what circumstances would each be preferred?
    a. Outside auditor.
    b. Company audit specialist.
    c. Company department manager.
12. Under what circumstances should a nondisguised audit be used?
13. How should management respond to the findings of an audit? What may happen if the findings are ignored?
14. Why do many retailers not conduct any form of retail audit? Are these reasons valid? Explain your answer.

CASE 1 Marks & Spencer: The Winning Team*

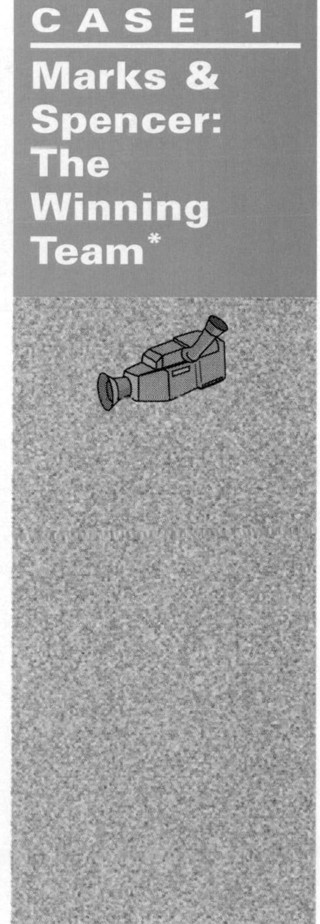

According to a survey by *The Economist,* Marks & Spencer is Great Britain's most admired company. Affectionately called "Marks & Sparks" by consumers throughout the country, its 300+ stores account for 17 per cent of Great Britain's total retail clothing sales and 25 per cent of its clothing exports. Marks & Spencer's 1993 revenues were 5.95 billion pounds (about $11 billion dollars), and its net income was 8.3 per cent of revenues.

The firm's strategy is based on its offering consumers a good value for clothing and food products, as well as on the growth of its retail operations. The firm applies its strategy by purchasing items directly from manufacturers, bargaining hard, and constantly being concerned about product quality—and via worldwide growth from both internal expansion and acquisitions.

Because Marks & Spencer accounts for such a big per cent of manufacturers' overall sales (as much as 90 per cent for some suppliers), the firm can be tough in bargaining and hold them accountable for high quality standards. Many of Marks & Spencer's products feature the firm's private brand, St. Michael, which originated in 1927.

In the past, Marks & Spencer was most successful with clothing. But it recently moved aggressively into the food business. Thus, its food business now accounts for about 40 per cent of the company's annual revenues and Marks & Spencer has a 5 per cent share of total food sales in Great Britain. Specialty foods are sold at its department stores and at its 20 British food-only stores. As with clothing, the firm uses a distribution approach for food that bypasses wholesalers and gets high-quality products from suppliers.

* The material in this case is drawn from Sunita Wadekar Bhargava, "What's Next, Grunge Bathrobes?" *Business Week* (June 21, 1993), pp. 64, 68; Alan Chai, Alta Campbell, and Patrick J. Spain (Editors), *Hoover's Handbook of World Business 1993* (Austin, Texas: Reference Press, 1993), pp. 318–319; Bernice Kanner, "Seams Like Old Times," *New York* (January 3, 1994), pp. 14–15; and Marks & Spencer: Store of Value," *The Economist* (June 26, 1993), p. 63.

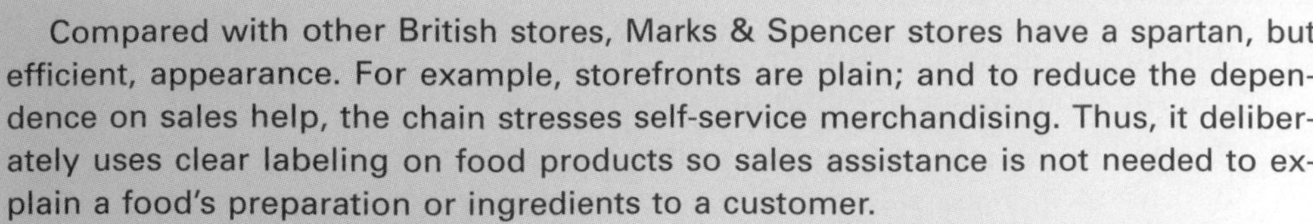

Compared with other British stores, Marks & Spencer stores have a spartan, but efficient, appearance. For example, storefronts are plain; and to reduce the dependence on sales help, the chain stresses self-service merchandising. Thus, it deliberately uses clear labeling on food products so sales assistance is not needed to explain a food's preparation or ingredients to a customer.

Revenues outside Great Britain account for 12.4 per cent of Marks & Spencer's companywide revenues. The firm has been in Canada since the early 1970s, through its purchase of People's (a general-merchandise chain), D'Allaird's (a women's clothing chain), and Walker's (a clothing shop whose stores were later renamed Marks & Spencer). Marks & Spencer purchased Brooks Brothers (an upscale U.S. men's and women's clothing retailer) and Kings Super Markets (a New Jersey-based regional chain) in 1988. During 1992, it opened a clothing store in Hungary in partnership with a Vienna-based trading company. Marks & Spencer also has 19 stores in France, Holland, Belgium, and Spain, as well as five stores in Hong Kong. It plans to use its Hong Kong stores as a platform to enter China, Thailand, Indonesia, Taiwan, and Japan (where it already has Brooks Brothers stores).

Brooks Brothers, a 175-year-old retailer known for its high-caliber, conservative clothing for men and women, was Marks & Spencer's most famous acquisition. Although Brooks Brothers currently accounts for only 3.4 per cent of Marks & Spencer's total revenues, many retailing analysts believe that its relative importance to Marks & Spencer will greatly increase as Brooks Brothers expands and repositions itself.

To replace its somewhat dowdy image, Brooks Brothers is trying to reach a younger target market, to expand into Great Britain and continental Europe (from its 54 locations in the United States and 44 in Japan), and to better focus on professional females (mostly with suits and blazers). Brooks Brothers hopes that women's wear will soon account for 20 per cent of its sales.

Under Marks & Spencer's ownership, Brooks Brothers has also sought to reduce costs by using computer systems for better control, reducing the number of salespeople, and closing many of its factories (except for three that produce shirts and ties). Brooks Brothers' future success will depend on its ability to keep its older, more conservative customers, while appealing to a younger clientele with more affordable merchandise.

Like Marks & Spencer, Brooks Brothers is fastidious about quality. For example, Brooks Brothers recently developed new standards and specifications for the 300 vendors that supply the store's 5,000 items. Accordingly, fabrics are now washed 30 times to determine their color fastness, shrinkage, and washability. The clothing industry judges 40 launderings as a garment's average life expectancy. Product-testing costs are borne by manufacturers.

While Marks & Spencer's overall performance can be characterized as very good, it has several areas of concern. These relate to new competition in Great Britain, its plans for Brooks Brothers, and its past problems with worldwide expansion.

Even though Marks & Spencer has increased its fashion emphasis in Europe, many analysts believe it still lacks a basic fashion orientation. New competitors in Great Britain—such as Next, Habitat, Mothercare, and Burton—have been successful at taking clothing sales away from Marks & Spencer.

Many analysts also feel Marks & Spencer greatly overpaid for Brooks Brothers (its purchase price of $750 million was two times Brooks Brothers' revenues). By comparison, InvestCorp's acquisition of Saks Fifth Avenue and Dayton Hudson's acquisition of the Marshall Field's chain were at one times revenues. The debate as to the appropriateness of the Brooks Brothers' acquisition will ultimately be settled after the results of its expansion and repositioning efforts are known.

Lastly, not all of Marks & Spencer's prior acquisitions were profitable. For example, the company ultimately sold its People's general-merchandise chain, after finding out that Canadians did not accept British tastes.

QUESTIONS

1. Evaluate Marks & Spencer's overall retailing strategy.
2. What are the pros and cons of Marks & Spencer's purchasing goods directly from manufacturers (and bypassing wholesalers)?
3. How did the purchase of Brooks Brothers fit into Marks & Spencer's overall retail strategy? What are the pros and cons of its repositioning strategy for Brooks Brothers? Explain your answer.
4. What criteria would you use to judge Marks & Spencer's performance? Explain your answer.

VIDEO QUESTIONS ON MARKS & SPENCER

1. Evaluate Marks & Spencer's strategy of expanding into foreign markets.
2. Develop a horizontal retail audit to judge the success of Marks & Spencer's five-year plan.

CASE 2

Home Depot: The Growth of a Home-Center Giant†

In 1980, Atlanta-based Home Depot had one store and sales of $22 million. During 1993, it was the largest home-center chain in the United States, with sales exceeding $9.2 billion (and net earnings of $457 million). Yet, although it is the leader in the industry, Home Depot still has less than a 7 per cent market share of home-improvement sales. The firm has been compared with such retailing stars as Toys "R" Us (in terms of its being a power retailer and saturating a market with stores), Nordstrom (in terms of its customer service), and Wal-Mart (in terms of its use of everyday low pricing and incentives for sales associates).

Besides the growth rate since its founding, market analysts have noted that the chain's average sales per foot are almost $400. And some Home Depot outlets in the Northeast have annual sales per square foot in excess of $600. This also indicates that Home Depot is fulfilling an unmet need and that existing competition is a poor match for the chain. Table 1 shows selected 1990–1992 financial data on Home Depot. Among the key elements in the firm's overall long-run strategy are national expansion, maintaining a large inventory, a high level of customer service, and everyday low pricing.

As of the end of 1992, Home Depot had 214 stores in 19 states; but three-quarters of them were located in only five states: Georgia, Florida, Texas, California, and Arizona. Thus, in recent years, Home Depot has expanded its market presence in the Northeast and in Nevada, North Carolina, South Carolina, and Oklahoma. By 1996, Home Depot plans to have 516 stores in 35 states, as well as some international units.

The firm believes the Northeast is an ideal expansion target; it opened 14 stores in this region in 1992 alone. Much of the suburban housing is over thirty years old, and various suburban garden apartment developments have been converted into co-operatives (making thousands of tenants into homeowners). The chain has been particularly effective on Long Island. For example, one Long Island store has been so successful that its 740-car parking lot generally fills up on weekends. Furthermore, Home Depot feels some home-center chains in the Northeast are especially weak. For example, even though Pergament (a Long Island-based chain) has a strong local identity, it has a heavy debt load due to a leveraged buyout. In contrast, Home Depot's long-term debt is only 21 per cent of its total assets.

† The material in this case is drawn from Karl Haller, "Warehouse Stores Lead Home Improvement Push," *Chain Store Age Executive* (August 1993), pp. 25A–27A; *Home Depot 1992 Annual Report*; "The Business Week 1000," *Business Week* (March 28, 1994), pp. 80–81; and Patricia Sellers, "Companies That Serve You Best," *Fortune* (May 31, 1993), pp. 71–83.

Table 1 Selected Financial Data for Home Depot, 1990–1992

	1990	1991	1992
Statement of Earnings Data			
Net sales (in 000s)	$3,815,356	$5,136,674	$7,148,436
Earnings before taxes (in 000s)	$259,828	$396,120	$575,973
Net earnings (in 000s)	$163,428	$249,150	$362,863
Gross margin (% of sales)	27.9	28.1	27.6
General and administrative expenses (% of sales)	2.4	2.3	2.1
Pre-opening expenses (% of sales)	0.4	0.3	0.4
Advertising expenses (% of sales)	0.9	0.7	0.5
Net earnings (% of sales)	4.3	4.8	5.1
Balance Sheet Data and Financial Ratios			
Total assets (in 000s)	$1,639,503	$2,510,292	$3,931,790
Working capital (in 000s)	$300,867	$623,937	$807,028
Merchandise inventories (in 000s)	$509,022	$662,257	$939,824
Current ratio (times)	1.73	2.17	2.07
Inventory turnover (times)	6.0	6.1	6.3
Return on average equity (%)	27.6	18.5	18.1
Customer and Store Data			
Number of states	12	15	19
Number of stores	145	174	214
Square footage at year-end (in 000s)	13,278	16,480	20,897
Number of customer transactions (in 000s)	112,464	146,221	189,493
Average sale per transaction	$33.92	$35.13	$37.72
Comparable-store sales increase (%)[a]	10	11	15
Weighted-average sales per square foot[a]	$322	$348	$387

[a] 1990 figures are adjusted to reflect the first 52 weeks of a 53-week fiscal year.
Source: *Home Depot 1992 Annual Report.*

Each Home Depot store stocks 30,000 home-improvement items (more than any major competitor)—such as tools, lumber, lighting equipment, and plumbing fixtures and supplies. The firm prides itself on having low stockouts; top management believes the three worst words that can be said to a customer are "It's on order." Yet, even with its high inventory levels, Home Depot has an inventory turnover of 6.3 times per year (the highest level in the industry). Store managers are given the latitude to vary product offerings to match consumer needs.

The chain prides itself on the quality of its customer service. To track its overall service quality, Home Depot has retained a marketing research firm that interviews more than 5,000 of its customers per year. As the research firm's president notes: "They keep closer track of customer satisfaction than any other company we work for. Unlike a lot of clients, they always react to what they hear."

Experts agree that no other firm in the home-center industry can match or even come close to Home Depot in attracting and retaining workers with good customer-service skills. The firm understands that qualified employees are essential in instructing do-it-yourselfers in home-improvement projects. It seeks to attract experienced workers by offering new employees comparatively high starting salaries. The firm is so attractive as an employer that it is able to hire only two people for every 100 that apply. Nearly every employee receives a four-week training program. To reduce turnover, a clear career path to assistant manager and store manager exists. All assistant managers are eligible for stock options. And scores of store managers have each accumulated $1 million or more in Home Depot stock. Because of store growth, new store openings, and a policy of promotion from within (employees are rarely hired from outside beyond the level of assistant manager), there are numerous opportunities for career openings.

Another important element of Home Depot's strategy is everyday low pricing, which the firm adopted in 1987. This policy enabled it to reduce advertising expenses from 3.2 per cent of sales in 1985 to 0.5 per cent of sales in 1992. Home Depot's television ads stress its service—not low prices.

In preparing for the future, Home Depot's management also needs to keep such factors as these in mind:

- The firm's recent emphasis on services like customized kitchens may make it more vulnerable to a regional recession.
- The firm's corporate culture may not stay intact as it expands. For example, Home Depot's chairman, president, and chief financial officer can no longer participate as actively in assistant manager and manager training programs. Instead, they have to broadcast training sessions over the firm's closed circuit television network.
- Some Home Depot store managers have "burned-out" after working from 5:30 A.M. to after 10 P.M., six days per week.
- Past growth was at the expense of independent hardware stores, lumber yard, and weaker chains. Now, Home Depot is increasingly facing competition from such large chains as Lowe's, Builder's Square, Hechinger, and HomeBase. These units are well-run and well-financed.
- Several markets have become saturated. For example, during 1993, Home Depot opened stores with millions of square feet of selling space.

QUESTIONS

1. Is Home Depot's retailing strategy well integrated? Explain your answer.
2. Comment on Home Depot's financial performance on the basis of the data shown in Table 1.
3. What performance data besides the information in Table 1 should Home Depot look at in assessing how well it is doing?
4. Design a vertical audit form to evaluate Home Depot's customer-service performance.

PART 8 COMPREHENSIVE CASE

Saint Louis Bread Company: Minding the Store*

Introduction

Before he opened his first bakery and became expert in the nuances of sourdough starters and espresso-brewing times, Ken Rosenthal knew he wanted a chain of stores. His friends thought he was making a big mistake and tried to warn him off. A few had grown up in bakery families, and to a person they cautioned him that there was a reason most bake shops had long since shut down: they're ridiculously exhausting to run. "I'll never forget one story," says Rosenthal, 50, a lanky, even-keeled man. "This guy was working around the clock. He'd come home, get in the shower, turn on the water, and sit on the floor to rest. When the hot water ran out and the shower ran cold, it was time to go back to work." Rosenthal shudders. "What a terrible story that is!"

It is terrible, but it reinforced his point: While a single shop wouldn't give him the life or the kind of business he wanted, a chain might. He and his wife, Linda, had spent 17 years running a women's clothing store, and the experience had left its mark. They had little control over what they sold, buying a line of clothing only to be undercut on price by the big chains.

The bakery idea came to Rosenthal when he was visiting his brother in San Francisco. After the two had spent some time hanging out in North Beach cafes, Rosenthal's brother suggested taking the idea back to St. Louis. Rosenthal liked hearty bread, and he liked the idea of creating his own product line. "Once I developed it and perfected it, it would be my line—good, bad, or indifferent." Since the cafe culture of the West Coast had yet to hit St. Louis, the market was wide open.

As it turns out, it was wide open and then some. No matter that when Rosenthal started, in 1987, all he knew about baking was that he didn't want to be the guy in the shower. By mid-1993, Saint Louis Bread Company employed 565 people at its corporate office, central baking plant, and 17 bakery/cafes throughout the city. The company has been profitable almost since year one, with 1992 revenues of more than $13 million and a five-year sales-growth rate of 5,325 per cent.

The Basic Strategy

Standout success in the brutally competitive restaurant industry has come partly on the strength of the concept: the 11 bread varieties, along with the more than 25 types of muffins, Danish, and croissants, are baked the day they're sold. The old-time bakery counter at the stores brings in customers, while the soup-and-sandwich counter alongside does the volume—two times that of the bakery. What's more, national food chains with similar concepts have so far let Saint Louis Bread Company establish a pre-eminent position.

But, the company also has gotten where it is—and set itself up for where it hopes to go, which is geographically out and financially up—through small and steady steps of back-room improvements. Ken Rosenthal and the team of managers he's added over the years have combined aggressive development with cautious calculation and a sense of what part of the operation must take priority each step of the way.

In its evolution, Saint Louis Bread has passed through distinctive stages: after pre-startup, that period of planning and self-education, came 15 months of operating one store. An initial expansion, over a year and a half, took the company to five stores. A more furious rollout, over two years, brought on another 12 stores. Then, in early 1993, the company decided to slow down its growth, quietly preparing itself for further expansion both within St. Louis and into new territories outside the city.

"Each time you decide to grow again, you realize you're starting at the bottom of another ladder," says Rosenthal. "When we went from one to two stores, we had to commit to getting a refrigerated truck. We could have stopped at two stores and made a nice living, but we decided to move into the central baking plant and take on a tremendous overhead. We wanted to bring on a chief executive officer, and MIS and accounting people, and each time you do that you make a commitment to grow the company a little more."

The decisions were consistent with what Rosenthal had always wanted, to run a chain. Through steady improvement in product mix, behind-the-scenes operations, public personality, and management—to name four critical areas—the company has blossomed. It is now, Rosenthal and his partners hope, poised for its next big surge. Here's how it all began:

The Idea Stage

For over a year, Ken and Linda Rosenthal worked to nail down their product concept: the deli and, especially, the

* The material in this case was developed and written by Leslie Brokaw of *Inc.* magazine. It originally appeared in "Minding the Store," *Inc.* (November 1993), pp. 66–75. Reprinted by permission.

bread. Rosenthal threw himself into a self-education process in 1986 and 1987, traveling to San Francisco six times to visit bakeries. At one of them, he got the concept of using a central baking facility for preparation and then doing final baking at the shops; at others, he took hundreds of photos, often getting tossed out for doing so. Still other bakers took him on for tutoring by day and baking by night. In all, Rosenthal logged thousands of hours and paid out $50,000 for training and sourdough recipes.

The Rosenthals picked a storefront in a strip mall in Kirkwood, Missouri, an upscale suburb that seemed primed to pay slightly more for better quality bread. The location also fed the "neighborhood bakery" image the Rosenthals wanted to develop. Startup capital totaled $350,000: the Rosenthals took $125,000 from their savings, got a Small Business Administration loan, and took out a second mortgage. The point of no return came when they bought equipment from a bankrupt bakery.

In October 1987, sailing on a $10,000 marketing campaign consisting of a 50,000-postcard mailing (the only explicit marketing the company would do until 1993), and with Ken, Linda, and 15 full- and part-timers at the helm, Saint Louis Bread Company opened its doors.

On-the-Job Learning

"We made lots of mistakes, but we were in a very forgiving neighborhood," says Rosenthal. The product took a while to perfect: If a loaf of bread turns out to be doorstop material, it's hard to pinpoint what in the process went awry—maybe the mixer put in the wrong ingredients or someone put the dough in the cooler too early. The Rosenthals invested in an expensive espresso maker, even though cappuccino quaffing wasn't even close to a rage. "We wanted to be sure that when coffee did hit, people would took at us as being at the forefront," Rosenthal says.

At the same time, the company's community image began to take shape. The Rosenthals decided not to sell day-old bread, in part so that customers would have no question about freshness. Instead, the company began a relationship that continues to this day with church groups and Operation Food Search, an organization that picks up and delivers goods to food pantries in St. Louis. From day one, the store gave away all its leftover bread each evening.

Within a few months, Saint Louis Bread had a regular clientele. The good part was that the Rosenthals were getting orders for bread. The bad part was that they were still figuring out how to fill them. Two months after the company's launch, they completely misjudged their Christmas sales. "We didn't know what we didn't know," says Rosenthal. "To make a long story short, we thought we had five hours more than we did, but everybody showed up for their bread orders at 7 A.M. We weren't ready for them. It got to the point where the counter people wouldn't go out front." That was the day Rosenthal started documenting things: what times of what days got busy; how much product was moving when.

In an attic crawl space above the baking area, the Rosenthals crafted an office. (An exposed pipe at forehead level was wrapped in towels to keep people from getting knocked out.) The fiscally conservative Rosenthal, loath to string along suppliers, paid his bills as they came in. He also resisted bringing in equity partners, determined to finance through cash flow and whatever bank debt he could muster up. It often was not easy. "I lived," he admits, "in constant fear that we weren't going to succeed." Sales the first nine months were $245,600, almost at break-even.

The First Expansion

By late 1988, the Rosenthals felt ready to expand. They picked a site in funky University City, just west of St. Louis. The spot was too small to have its own full-scale production, so the first store trucked over partially made bread. The bread would still be proofed—the pre-baking process of humidifying the dough to make it rise quickly—and baked on-site. That store opened in January 1989. Eleven months later, with bank debt covering about half the $300,000 startup cost, Saint Louis Bread opened a third store; stores four and five came in April and June of 1990, also half financed by loans.

The product mix was now stable. The company's public personality was being shaped by having stores that reflected the "personality" of their locations (college-area shops, for instance, have blond wood floors and more small tables, for a cafe feel) and by expansion of the company's charitable programs into fund-raising for local schools.

Attention to operations was the critical focus at this phase of growth. The Rosenthals got hooked up with Stern Fixture Co., an equipment-supply firm, which helped them think about more efficient ways to design deli operations. "Sandwiches were something they were doing as an adjunct to their bread business," says Mal Dardick, a designer and the chairman of Stern. "And we said, 'What are you going to do if everybody likes the product and they all come at once and you can't turn the food out quickly and cleanly?' We helped them think about better layouts for mass production."

In fall 1989, the company moved its mixing and shaping operations to a factory, another significant step. The first stage of baking could be done there, and then the goods could be trucked out. Taking on the space was a commitment to expansion: the plant was 12,000 square feet, and Saint Louis Bread needed only 3,000 of that. "I truly felt we would never use all the space—all you could see was space," says Rosenthal. "We'd gone to the next plateau, but we were at the bottom of it."

Saint Louis Bread also began filling out its executive ranks. After the fourth store opened, Linda Rosenthal left the day-to-day management to care for the couple's four children, though she has continued to be involved in store design and product development. Shortly before that, Doron Berger, a neighbor and confidant, had joined as a partner, working on regulatory compliance and purchasing. In 1990, Myron Klevens, another old friend with extensive experience both in real estate (he was a local developer) and in management (10 years at $7.7-billion Emerson Electric) came on, also as a partner. Both Berger and Klevens, now 45 and 50, put in nominal amounts of cash—along with commitments of sweat equity—for 17 per cent equity each. A former employee of Seattle-based Starbucks Coffee Co., the coffee retailer and cafe chain, joined Saint Louis Bread to beef up its coffee purchasing and brewing training.

Becoming a Presence

As the company continued to expand, the pace of everything picked up. While savvy neighborhood site selection was crucial, it became clear, too, that the company had to keep getting better at every level if it were to grow without spinning out of control.

The factory began focusing on getting new products introduced every 90 days; the trick was to keep customers invigorated. In August 1991, the company opened its only non-Saint Louis Bread store, the Rendezvous Cafe, which is positioned as a slightly more sophisticated version of Saint Louis Bread. The menu is very similar, and the restaurant serves as a test site for new menu items, from salads to soups to desserts.

Still relying on its extensive community involvement instead of advertising to attract and retain customers, Saint Louis Bread introduced Operation: Dough-Nation in 1992 to collect cash contributions from customers for local food pantries and to match those donations with fresh bread offerings. "Saint Louis Bread is just a remarkable organization," says Bill Nordmann, the executive director of Operation Food Search, which coordinated the distribution of almost $9 million worth of food from 900 stores and restaurants last year. "Its generosity, its community spirit. . . ." All told, Saint Louis Bread's contributions to Operation Food Search alone totaled $700,000 in bread in 1992, and the firm was involved in 60 other fund-raising and community events.

By mid-1992, the company was up to 10 stores and already had another 7 in development to open that fall and winter. The pace, Doron Berger says, had begun to feel frantic. "It was like running so hard that you can't breathe, but you have to keep running." Things weren't out of control yet, but it was getting harder for the three partners to visit all the stores as often as they wanted: their dally visits began to drop to every other day, or once a week.

In addition, margins were a little soggy: 1990 sales were $2.8 million, with net income of 1.4 per cent, and 1991 sales were $5.8 million, with net income at 1.7 per cent. (Au Bon Pain, a publicly-traded cafe chain, has net income of 5.5 per cent.) Turnover also was only at the industry average.

So, the partners decided to do something that's anathema to people who thrive on growth: they would stop growing. After the flurry of openings in fall 1992, they wouldn't open any stores for at least 9 months. "It was time to take a breath, sit back, and make sure everyone was thinking about the same thing and that we all had the same vision," says Rosenthal. After planning in 3- to 6-month spurts, they figured they'd plan for the next one to two years.

"The opportunistic approach this company had taken," says Richard Happel, who came on in late 1991 as CFO (chief financial officer), "wouldn't work anymore. Everyone here knows we have a window of opportunity, and we're anxious to capitalize on it. But the owners, above all else, understood that without the substructure, the superstructure would never hold. We reached the point where the controls and the information systems we had in place were woefully inadequate for a larger organization. And if we didn't stop soon, we were going to reach the point where we had total chaos."

The partners decided to go through extensive strategic planning. They brought in an outside team of facilitators, which took a group of 10 managers through a two-month, 50-hour program of evaluating every aspect of the business. They reached agreement on how many stores there should be, where those stores should be, and what volume they wanted to plan for, and then they wrote out detailed schedules for every step needed to get there. Two documents emerged: a business plan and a calendar of actions to meet strategic goal.

As a result, the firm began investing, for instance, in state-of-the-art point-of-purchase registers (at $30,000 a pop) that would allow it to better track everything from sales per hour and sales per stock-keeping unit (SKU) to sales by store and labor per dollar generated. At the bakery, new equipment began automating processes on the line so the company could make more product with the same number of people. Thirty suppliers were given a seven-page synopsis of the strategic summary, to keep them up-to-date on the company's plans. "Most food-service people are not organized at all," says Paul Landsbaum, president of Stern Fixture, which now supplies Saint Louis Bread with all its furniture, fixtures, and equipment. "What makes Saint Louis Bread different is that it approached the food-service business from the viewpoint of a retailer," Landsbaum notes. "The company excels at displaying its wares and attracting the sale. And, because it gives us projections, we can go out to our suppliers and strike volume deals on Saint Louis Bread's behalf."

In management, Rosenthal brought on David Hutkin, a real-estate developer who found Saint Louis Bread its third site. Hutkin had decided, back in 1989, that he wanted to buy the company. "Ken was very polite, very gracious, and told me to get lost," he says. But, like a persistent suitor, Hutkin kept in touch with letters and phone calls, and continued finding real estate as the company expanded. By early 1992, he had asked to be a franchisee. The partners agreed, but then decided that what the company needed more was a franchise manager. By May 1992, Hutkin was set to come aboard in September as president of a new entity, The Bread Co., which would coordinate franchising efforts.

However, at the end of the strategic planning process, Rosenthal decided The Bread Co. should be less of a separate business and opted to make Hutkin, then 40, CEO and president of everything. The planning had helped refocus the partners on their strengths. "If we were going to really make this thing grow in a professional, well-managed way, it was going to require a much narrower view of things we each had to do," Rosenthal says. "I had been on the point for five years, and I started thinking that it might be nice not to be there."

Linda Rosenthal says that turning over the titles to Hutkin didn't seem to be a traumatic decision for her husband: "Ken just told me that that's what he thought he should do, since there are so many things to do as president—everybody comes to you with everything—and he wanted to concentrate on production." The company separated ownership from management—the Rosenthals remained two-thirds owners, with Ken becoming chairman and Hutkin took the helm. As hard as the decision may have been initially on Klevens and Berger, the four seem to have crafted a closely interconnected management team.

The firm finally had cash to hire more management talent: in addition to Happel, who was brought on as CFO from Western Union, where he'd been manager of financial operations, it hired a director of store operations with 20 years' experience in the restaurant and franchise business, and an MIS chief.

Preparing For The Future

1993 was the year the company deliberately prepared for further expansion not only within the city but also to locations well outside St. Louis. In addition, with new-product development continuing (forays into tiramisu and jalapeño bread, for example), Saint Louis Bread set up its first marketing budget. It began joint promotions with companies including Blockbuster Video, with whom it's offering a kind of buy-one-get-one deal. ("We're thinking about using an early Clint Eastwood still," says Hutkin, "with him holding a video in one hand and a baguette in the other.") Klevens' visual mantra, which he pulls from his desk, is a November 1991 *Business Week* cover. "Value Marketing," screech the cartoonish bubble letters. "Top Quality! A Fair Price! And Great Service! It's the Way to Sell in the 90s!"

The company's focus has been to prepare for franchising, which the Rosenthals had thought about—and put on the back burner—almost since day one. "You give away a big percentage," says Hutkin, "and you don't make as much money, but it's a cheaper way to grow."

Trudging through the tedious task of drawing up a legal document, Hutkin has been mapping out three types of areas for testing franchising—Kansas City, Missouri, a medium-size metro market; Springfield, Missouri, a smaller and less urbane city of 150,000; and a yet-unnamed small town of 25,000 in Missouri or Illinois. "Franchising is a lot of things, but in large part it's another layer of distribution," says Hutkin, whose office is ringed with maps of St. Louis and the United States, dotted with color-coded push-pins. "We have to make sure there's not a hitch."

Getting products to the farther sites was a matter of figuring out everything from what kinds of boxes to use to how you package the product to how you ensure quality. "We tested this in a prototype store for months," says Rosenthal, "running it as though it were 200 miles away." The first two people who signed on as franchisees both have territories, in which they're expected to operate four to six stores each.

The firm's plans also called for a ramp-up in the number of company-owned units: another 4 by the end of 1993, and 10 in 1994, mostly outside the city. The focus was on areas where there's a void—places that didn't already have upscale bakery restaurants.

To add to the management voices, Hutkin has begun setting up an advisory board of outsiders. The firm has also launched an advisory board of insiders. Staff people from all areas discuss and make recommendations on such issues as holiday schedules, vacations, and tuition reimbursement. Training, too, has been revamped by the director of store operations, Jeffrey Rains. "A new hire used to come through in a couple of hours," says Hutkin. "'Here's the creed, here's the mission statement, there's the store.' Now, new hires spend 10 hours paid time with a manager, getting cross-trained in how to run the register, how to make sandwiches, how to make cappuccino." There are 56 training modules, covering focused areas such as "Espresso Standards" and "Product Packaging," with different jobs requiring different combinations of training. All new hires are now being trained under this system.

Rosenthal and his team believe that, having stopped and put in place those changes, they're now in a position to take on the next stage of growth with more steadiness. "We know the concept works well, we know the acceptance is excellent, and we know it can be a bigger company," Rosenthal says. The executives' roles are better defined. A bonus program for store managers and assistant managers is in place. The company's deli and bakery products are updated regularly, its role in the community is solid, and its operations and new computer systems are helping track inventory, sales, and margins better (although the four partners—addicted as they are to the beepers and cellular phones that keep them in touch throughout the day—are unapologetically computer illiterate).

The company carries $900,000 in bank debt, which the owners don't think is excessive for a company tracking at more than $17 million annually. They are assuming that one day Saint Louis Bread will go public. For now, they're content to focus on expanding some more.

"How big, I don't think we can say, and I don't think anyone has visions beyond maybe a couple years down the road," muses Rosenthal, sitting across from a framed quotation by Calvin Coolidge about persistence being the root of success. "We sort of know where we're going immediately, and we know what the challenge is. How well can we do it outside of the St. Louis market?"

The first franchise opened in June 1993. The owner, Jim Magers, has 17 years' experience in restaurants as both a franchisee (with the 130-unit Penguin frozen-yogurt chain, in California) and as a franchisor (as an operations manager with a company that owned 70 franchises), and says it was the concept that made him put in the call to Ken Rosenthal. "We knew, from watching Saint Louis Bread in St. Louis, that it was doing very well—even before talking to them, we could tell sales volumes were high." Saint Louis Bread's sales per square foot average $404; the industry median is $177.

By 11:30 A.M. on a weekday, Magers' Springfield store is packed, with a line out the door. Baking here, as at all the shops, started around midnight and continues until about 11 A.M. Like most units, the shop opened at 6:30 A.M. and would stay open until 8 or 10 P.M. "Foolishly," says Magers, "I invested in a security system. We're closed for only about an hour a night." It takes 45 employees to run the cafe: seven in the back, baking, the rest out front. Walking through the store, chatting with customers, Magers taps at breads to check the crusts. (He himself bakes two nights a week.) His commitment is to build six units in all. In his second month, he'd already begun looking at sites. By its third month, the Springfield outlet was the third-highest-volume store in the system.

Back in St. Louis, the firm has two three-inch-wide loose-leaf notebooks (A-L and M-Z) filled with 400 inquiries from potential franchisees. But, the owners want some time to watch the ones already in the loop before making more commitments. They say the bread can go 500 to 700 miles from the plant before freight becomes economically disproportionate. "There's a big Midwest," says Klevens. "We'd like to be kind of the itsy-bitsy spider—here's St. Louis, and here's someplace else, here's someplace else, and sort of link them all up."

Questions

1. As a bakery/cafe chain, the Saint Louis Bread Company functions as both a goods retailer (the bakery) and a service retailer (the cafe). What are the ramifications of this for the firm?
2. Develop a service blueprint for the cafe aspect of the Saint Louis Bread Company.
3. Devise a SERVQUAL-style questionnaire that could be used to ask customers their opinions about the Saint Louis Bread Company.
4. Evaluate the Saint Louis Bread Company's current strategy in terms of the concepts noted in Figure 19–2.
5. What measures would you use to assess the Saint Louis Bread Company's current performance? Why?
6. What do you think about the Saint Louis Bread Company's decision to open outlets outside of the Saint Louis area? Of its decision to become involved in franchising? Explain your answer.
7. Describe three different vertical audits that the Saint Louis Bead Company could regularly conduct.

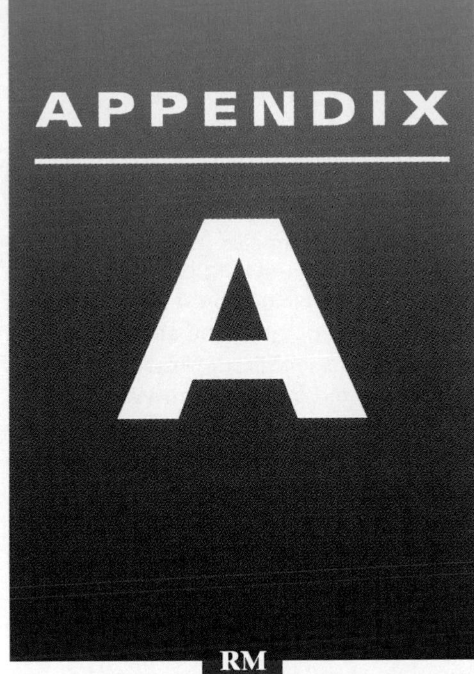

Careers in Retailing

A person looking for a career in retailing has two broad possibilities: owning a business or working for an employer. One alternative does not preclude the other. Many people open their own stores after getting experience as employees. A person can also choose franchising, which has elements of both entrepreneurship and managerial assistance. Franchising was discussed in Chapter 4.

Regardless of the specific retail career path chosen, it is important to note that recent college graduates often gain personnel and profit-and-loss responsibilities faster in retailing than in any other major industry. For instance, after an initial training program, an entry-level manager supervises personnel, works on in-store displays, interacts with customers, and reviews sales and other data on a regular basis. And an assistant buyer helps in planning merchandise assortments, interacting with suppliers, and outlining the promotion effort. Typically, new merchandise selections must be made at least once every four to six months.

Owning a Business

Owning a retail establishment is quite popular, and many opportunities exist. About four-fifths of all retail outlets are sole proprietorships. In addition, many of today's retail giants started out as independents. J.C. Penney, R.H. Macy, Kmart, Filene's, Toys "R" Us, McDonald's, and Sears illustrate this point. The founders of Lands' End, Petrie Stores, Body Shop, Wal-Mart, Weis Markets, and The Limited are profiled in Table 1.[1]

Too often, people overlook the possibility of owning a retail business. In a number of cases, initial investments can be quite modest (several thousand dollars). For example, many mail-order, vending-machine, direct-selling, and service retailers require relatively low initial investments—as do various franchising opportunities. In addition, financing may be available from banks, manufacturers, store-fixture firms, and equipment companies. Chapter 2 contained an in-depth discussion of starting and operating a retail business.

[1] For profiles of other successful retailing entrepreneurs, see James Barron, "The New Millionaires: Making It in Tough Times," *New York Times* (August 15, 1993), pp. 1, 10.

TABLE 1 Profiles of Leading Retail Entrepreneurs (as of 1993)

Gary Comer	He founded Lands' End, a mail-order retailer. Prior to that, Comer was an advertising copywriter for Young & Rubicam. Lands' End became a publicly held corporation in 1986; as of 1993, annual sales exceeded $800 million. Comer's personal wealth was estimated at $430 million.
Milton Petrie	He started in retailing as a $10-per-week department-store clerk in Indianapolis. As of 1993, his moderately priced clothing firm (consisting of Marianne's, Stuart's, and Petrie) had over 1,700 stores in 50 states and the Caribbean and annual sales $1.5 billion. Petrie had an estimated net worth of $1.1 billion.
Anita Roddick	In 1976, at the age of 33, she began to produce and sell natural cosmetics made from fruit and vegetable oils (instead of animal fats). Roddick used a $7,000 loan to supplement her startup capital. As of 1993, there were 700 Body Shop stores, most of them franchised, around the world. The personal wealth of Anita Roddick and her husband, Gordon, was estimated at $300 million.
Sam Walton	He opened his first retail store shortly after World War II; the first Wal-Mart discount department store was opened in 1962. While the chain grew, such other outlets as membership clubs and supercenters were also added. During 1993, Wal-Mart had over 2,000 stores and annual sales volume in excess of $67 billion. When Sam Walton died in 1992, he left 40 per cent of the firm's stock in his family's hands. In 1993, the Wal-Mart family had an estimated net worth of $23 billion.
Sigfried Weis and Robert Weis	The Weis cousins began by operating a cash-and-carry grocery store in 1912. As of 1993, there were 141 Weis Markets (supermarkets) in 6 states with annual sales of $1.4 billion. The personal wealth of Sigfried Weis was estimated to be about $410 million, while Robert Weis' personal wealth exceeded $355 million. In addition, other family members had stock worth over $260 million.
Leslie Wexner	He borrowed $5,000 from an aunt to start a ladies' apparel store in the early 1960s. As of 1993, his firm, The Limited, Inc., had over 4,400 stores (including The Limited, Express, Victoria's Secret, Lerner, Lane Bryant, Abercrombie & Fitch, and Henri Bendel) and annual sales of over $7 billion. Wexner's personal worth was estimated to be $1.6 billion in company stock alone.

Sources: Compiled by the authors from information in "The Forbes Four Hundred Richest People in America," *Forbes* (October 18, 1993), pp. 112–113 ff.; "The Business Week 1000," *Business Week* (March 28, 1994), pp. 72–73 ff.; "Corporate America's Most Powerful People: Paychecks of America's 800 Top Chief Executives," *Forbes* (May 23, 1994), pp. 144–147 ff.; and various other articles and company reports.

Opportunities as a Retail Employee

Retailing is a significant source of employment. As noted in Chapter 1, in the United States, about 20 million people work for traditional retailers. This does not include millions of others employed by service firms such as banks, insurance companies, and airlines. By any measure, more people work in retailing than in any other industry. For example, the 25 largest retailers in the United States employ 3.2 million people.[2]

Retail career opportunities are plentiful because of the number of new retail businesses opening each year and the labor-intensive nature of retailing. Nationally, thousands of new outlets open every year in the United States. Furthermore, certain segments of retailing are growing at particularly rapid rates. Thus, general merchandise retailers such as Wal-Mart and Kmart plan to open as many as 500 megastores (each being 200,000 square feet in size) by the year 2000.[3] See Table 2 for a listing of job prospects in selected retail careers.

The increases in employment due to new store openings and the sales growth of retail formats (such as power retailing) also mean there are significant opportunities for personal advancement for talented retail personnel. For instance, each time a chain opens a new outlet, there is a need for a store manager and other management-level people.

[2] "The 50 Largest Retailers," *Fortune* (May 30, 1994), pp. 214–215.

[3] "Supercenters—Growth Engine of the 90's," *Careers in Retailing 1994* (New York: Lebhar-Friedman), p. 5.

TABLE 2 Job Prospects in Selected Retail Career Positions[a]

Career	Employed persons in 1990	Projected Growth 1990–2005 (Per Cent)
Retail sales workers	4,754,000	25–34
Service sales representatives	588,000	35 or more
Insurance agents and brokers	439,000	14–24
Marketing, advertising, and public relations managers	427,000	35 or more
Real-estate agents, brokers, and appraisers	413,000	14–24
Wholesale and retail buyers	361,000	14–24
Counter and retail clerks	215,000	25–34
Securities and financial sales reps	191,000	35 or more

[a] Not all of these positions are exclusively retail.

Source: Wilton Woods, "The Jobs Americans Hold," *Fortune* (July 12, 1993), pp. 54–55; and the Bureau of Labor Statistics.

The following sections describe selected retailing positions, career paths, and compensation ranges for retail positions.

TYPES OF POSITIONS IN RETAILING

Employment in retailing is not confined to buying and merchandising. Career opportunities with retail firms encompass such areas as advertising, public relations, credit analysis, marketing research, warehouse management, data processing, personnel management, auditing, accounting, and real estate. See Table 3 for a listing and description of a variety of positions in retailing. From this table, one can see the range of employment opportunities available.

It should be noted that some highly specialized positions may be available only in large retail firms. As an illustration, Figure 1 shows the career possibilities that exist at Sears.

To a certain extent, the type of position a person seeks should be matched with the type of retailer likely to have such a position. For example, chain stores and franchises may have real-estate divisions. Department stores and chain stores may have large personnel departments. Mail-order firms and retail catalog showrooms may have large advertising production departments. If one is interested in travel, a buying position or a job with a retailer having geographically dispersed operations should be sought.

CAREER PATHS IN RETAILING

For new college graduates, the executive training programs of larger retailers offer good learning experiences and the potential for substantial advancement. These firms often offer careers in merchandising and nonmerchandising areas.

Here is how a new college graduate could progress through a career path at a typical department store or specialty store chain: He or she usually begins with a training program (which may last for a period ranging from three months to a year or more) on how to run a merchandise department. That program often involves both on-the-job and classroom experiences. On-the-job training usually includes working with merchandise records, reordering stock, planning displays, and supervising salespeople. Classroom activities normally include learning how to evaluate vendors, analyze computer reports, forecast fashion trends, and administer store policy.

TABLE 3 Selected Positions in Retailing

Job Title	Description
Accountant (internal)	Records and summarizes the retailer's transactions. Verifies reports. Provides financial information, budgets, forecasts, and comparison reports.
Advertising manager	Develops and implements a retailer's advertising program. Determines media, copy and message frequency. Recommends advertising budget and choice of advertising agency.
Assistant buyer	Works under the direction of a buyer, usually in a specific product category. Assists in sales analysis, order handling, buying, and setting up displays.
Assistant department manager	Works under the supervision of a department manager. Assists in managing personnel, controlling inventory, and other store operations.
Assistant store manager	Helps in implementing merchandising strategy and policies; interviews, hires, and trains sales personnel; takes inventory; and orders supplies.
Auditor (internal)	Analyzes data, interprets reports, verifies accuracy of data, and monitors adherence to the retailer's regular policies and practices.
Buyer	Develops and controls sales and profit projections for a product category (generally for all stores in a chain); plans proper merchandise assortment, styling, sizes, and quantities; negotiates with and evaluates vendors; and supervises in-store displays.
Catalog manager	Selects merchandise for inclusion in catalogs, works with vendors, orders catalogs, and monitors order fulfillment (particularly, timely shipments).
Commercial artist	Creates illustrations, layouts, and types of print to be used in the retailer's advertisements and catalogs, as well as on private-label packages.
Credit manager	Supervises the retailer's credit process, including credit eligibility, credit terms, late payment fees, and consumer credit complaints.
Data-processing manager	Oversees daily operations of a retailer's computer facility. Generates appropriate accounting, credit, financial, inventory, and sales reports. Recommends computer hardware and software for the retailer.
Department manager	Responsible for a department's merchandise displays, analyzing merchandise flow, and the training and direction of the sales staff. Assists buyers in selecting merchandise for branch stores.
District store manager	Responsible for management personnel, sales generation, merchandise presentation, expense control, and customer services in all stores in district.
Divisional merchandise manager	Plans, manages, and integrates buying for an entire merchandise division (composed of many departments).
Fashion coordinator	Directs buyers in evaluating fashion trends. Oversees fashion shows.
Fashion director	Responsible for developing and maintaining a retailer's overall fashion perspective.
Franchisee	Purchases a business from a franchisor. Benefits by common format, joint ads, and trouble shooting of franchisor. Decisions constrained by franchisor.
Franchisor	Develops a business format and image, then licenses the right to utilize this format and name to independent businesspeople. Oversees franchises, maintains operating standards, and receives royalty fees.
Group manager	Manages a number of department managers in different merchandise classifications. Trains, supervises, and evaluates these department managers.
Management trainee	First position for most college graduates entering retailing. Involves company orientation, classroom and on-the-job training, and close contact with buyers and group managers. Leads to department manager or assistant buyer.
Marketing research director	Acquires and analyzes relevant and timely information to assist executives in making important decisions. Heavily involved in methodology and data collection.
Merchandise administrator	Coordinates and evaluates the work of buyers in several related merchandise classifications (in a division).
Merchandise analyst	Plans and evaluates merchandise allocation to stores to ensure items are shipped at the right time, in proper amounts, and in the right assortment. Sets assortment strategy based on trends. Monitors reorder systems.

Table 3 Continued

Job Title	Description
Merchandise manager	Coordinates selling efforts among different departments (merchandise categories). Acts as liaison between store managers and buyers. Similar to group manager, but there are expanded merchandise responsibilities.
Operations manager	Responsible for receiving, checking, marking, and delivering merchandise; customer service; workroom operations; personnel; and maintaining the physical plant of the retailer.
Personnel manager	Devises a personnel policy. Analyzes long-run personnel needs. Recruits, selects, and trains employees. Works on compensation scales and supervision rules.
Public relations director	Keeps the public aware of the retailer's positive accomplishments. Measures public attitudes. Seeks to maintain a favorable image of the company.
Real-estate director	Evaluates retail sites. Negotiates lease or purchase terms. Works with builder on construction projects.
Sales promotion manager	Plans and enacts special sales, themes, and sales promotion tools (such as contests).
Salesperson	Assists customers in making proper choices. Handles minor complaints. Stocks some merchandise and sets up some displays. Notes understocked items. May also serve as a cashier.
Security supervisor	Responsible for minimizing pilferage among employees and customers. Recommends security systems and procedures. Manages a retailer's security personnel.
Senior vice-president for merchandising	Responsible for developing and evaluating all of the merchandise categories for performance. Has direct accountability for growth and profit.
Store manager	Oversees all store personnel and operations in a given outlet. Coordinates activities with other units in a chain. Responsible for customer service; implements merchandising and human resource policies.
Warehouser	Stores and moves goods within a retailer's warehouse. Maintains inventory records and rotates stock.

At the completion of the initial training program, the employee becomes an entry-level operations manager (often called a sales manager, assistant department manager, or department manager—depending on the firm) or an assistant buyer. An entry-level manager or assistant buyer works under the direction of a seasoned department (group) manager or buyer and analyzes sales, assists in purchasing goods, handles reorders, and assists in setting up displays. The entry-level manager supervises personnel and learns store operations; the assistant buyer is more involved in purchasing decisions than operations. Depending on the store's philosophy, either person may follow the same type of career path, or the entry-level operations manager may progress up the store management ladder and the assistant buyer up the buying ladder.

During this time, responsibilities and duties depend on the department (group) manager's or buyer's willingness to delegate and teach. They also depend on the autonomy given to that manager (buyer) to plan and implement a strategy. In a situation where a department (group) manager or buyer has the authority to make decisions, the entry-level manager or assistant buyer will usually be given greater responsibility. If a firm has a centralized management philosophy, a manager (buyer) is more limited in his or her responsibilities, as is the entry-level manager or assistant buyer. Further, an assistant buyer will gain more experience if he or she is in a store near a wholesale market center and can make trips to the market to buy merchandise.

The next step in a department store or specialty store chain's career path is a promotion to department (group) manager or buyer. This position can be viewed as entrepreneurial, the running of a business. The manager or buyer selects merchandise, develops a promotional campaign, decides which items to reorder, oversees depart-

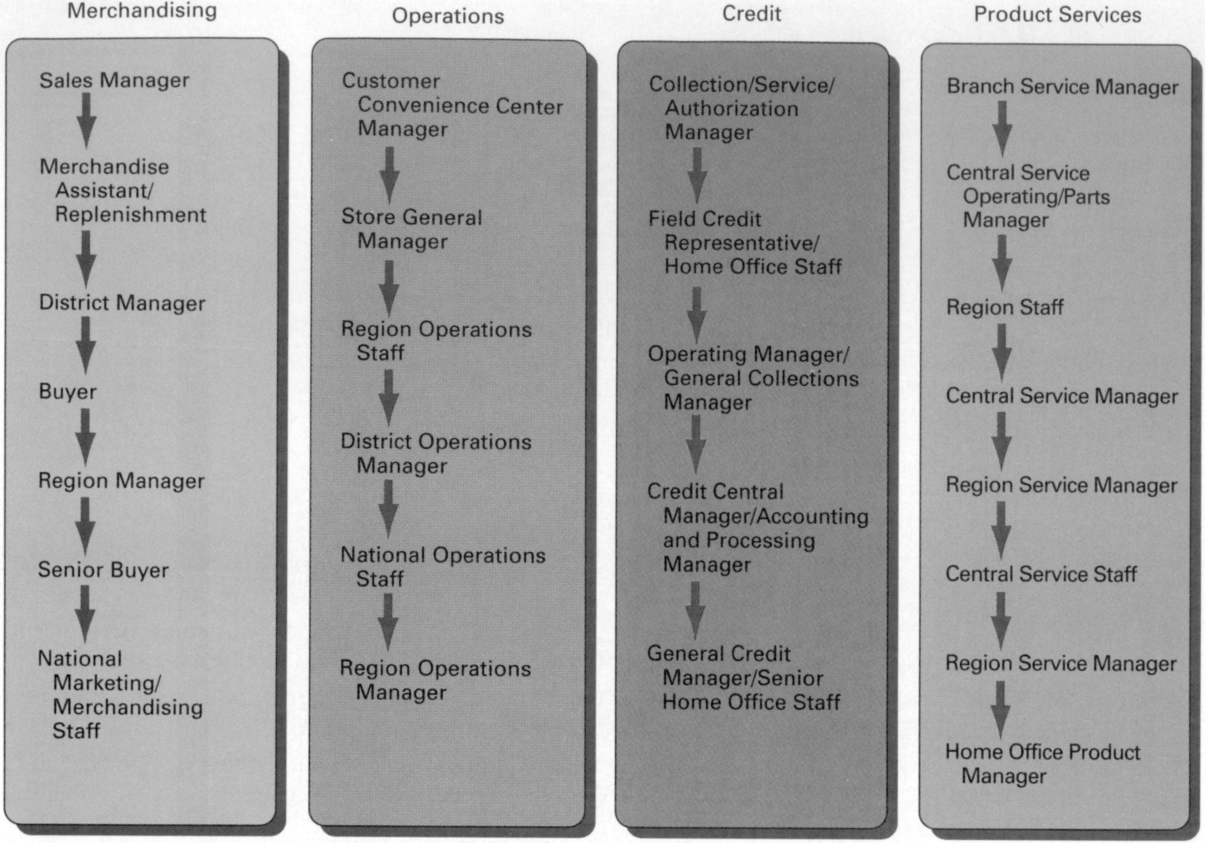

Career opportunities exist for significant advancement within each of the distinct categories above and, to a varying degree, between categories.

FIGURE 1 Sears' Career Opportunities After Management Training

Source: *Sears: Where New Beginnings Open New Career Opportunities.* Reprinted by permission.

mental personnel, and/or supervises record keeping. For some retailers, manager and buyer are synonymous terms. For others, the distinction is as just explained for entry-level positions. Generally, a person is considered for promotion to manager or buyer after two years.

Large department store and specialty store chains have additional levels of personnel to plan, supervise, and control merchandise departments. On the store management side, there can be group managers, store managers, branch vice-presidents, and others. On the buying side, there can be divisional managers, merchandising vice-presidents, and others.

At many firms, advancement is indicated by specific career paths. This enables employees to monitor their performance, know the next career step, and progress in a systematic, clear manner. Selected career paths at Pep Boys (an auto supply and service chain), Parisian (a fashion specialty-store chain), CVS (a drugstore chain), and Giant Food (a supermarket chain) are shown in Figures 2 through 5. At each succeeding step on these career ladders, a manager gains additional responsibility and authority.[4]

Over the last several years, retailing career opportunities for women have risen dramatically. According to a study by the *Wall Street Journal*, women now account for about

[4] For further information, see Joel R. Evans and Barry Berman, *Careers in Retailing* (Hempstead, NY: Hofstra University, 1993); and *Careers in Retailing*, a regular publication of Lebhar-Friedman, 425 Park Avenue, New York, NY 10022.

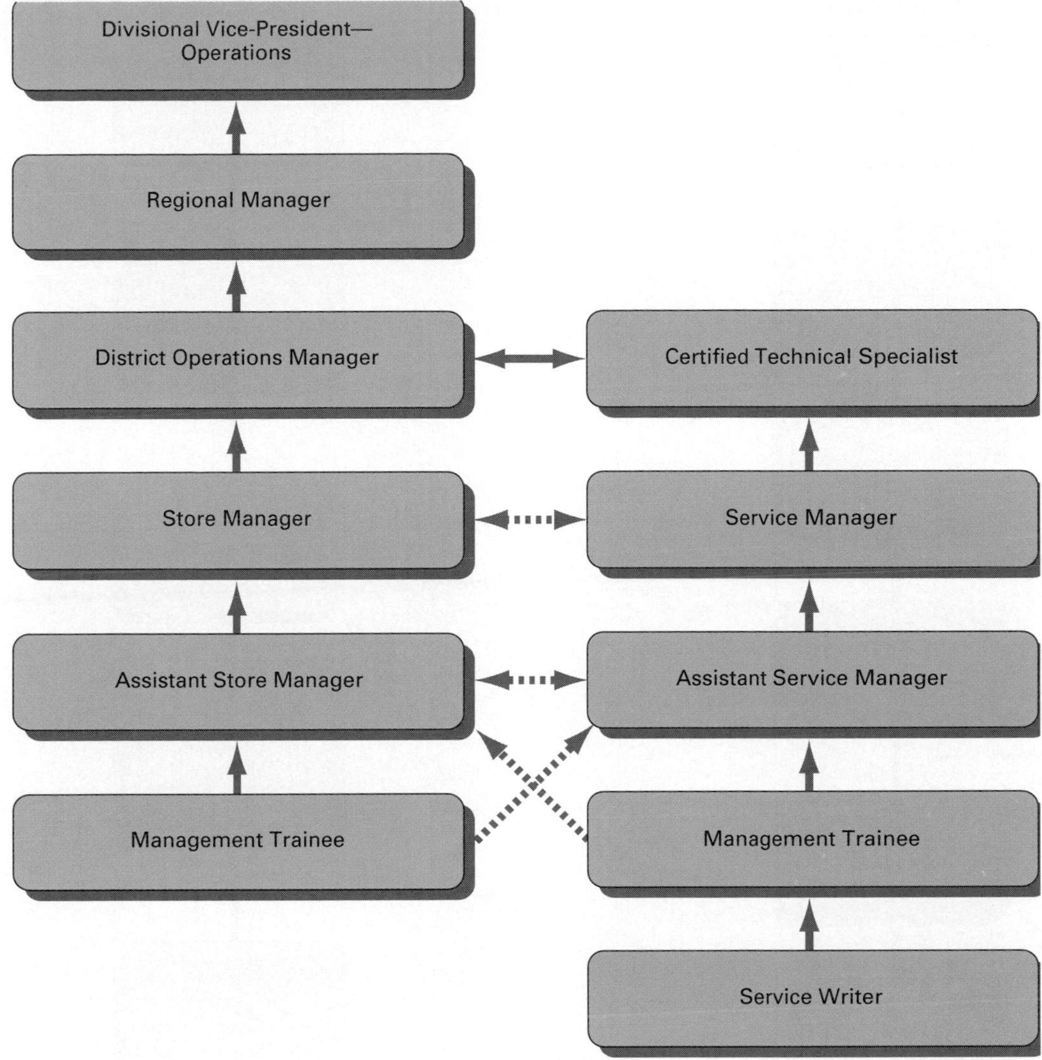

FIGURE 2 Pep Boys' Executive Career Ladder
Source: Pep Boys. Reprinted by permission.

two-fifths of all retailing executives; and among the nine major industry categories examined, retailing ranks third for the percentage of women executives (after finance, insurance, and real estate, and services). In the *Wall Street Journal* study, May Department Stores was rated as the retailer with the highest per cent of females as executives, 60 per cent.[5] And as reported elsewhere, at Dayton Hudson, almost 70 per cent of the management team for its department store division is female.[6]

Opportunities for women to own retail businesses have also increased in recent years. For example, between 1989 and 1994, the number of women owning McDonald's franchises tripled—to 450 of 2,500 franchisees.[7] Furthermore, the female-owned proprietorships in wholesaling and retailing have gone from 825,000 in 1980 to over 1.1 million today.[8]

[5] Rochelle Sharpe, "Women Make Strides, But Men Stay Firmly in Top Company Jobs," *Wall Street Journal* (March 29, 1994), pp. A1, A10.

[6] Teresa Andreoli, "These Women Mean Business," *Stores* (June 1993), pp. 24–26.

[7] Barbara Presley Noble, "The Women Behind McDonald's," *New York Times* (March 27, 1994), Section 3, p. 23.

[8] Wendy Zellner, Resa W. King, Veronica N. Byrd, et al., "Women Entrepreneurs," *Business Week* (April 18, 1994), p. 107.

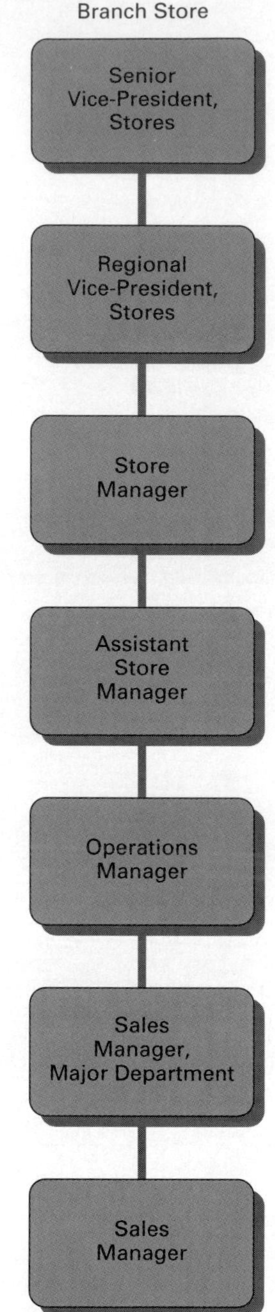

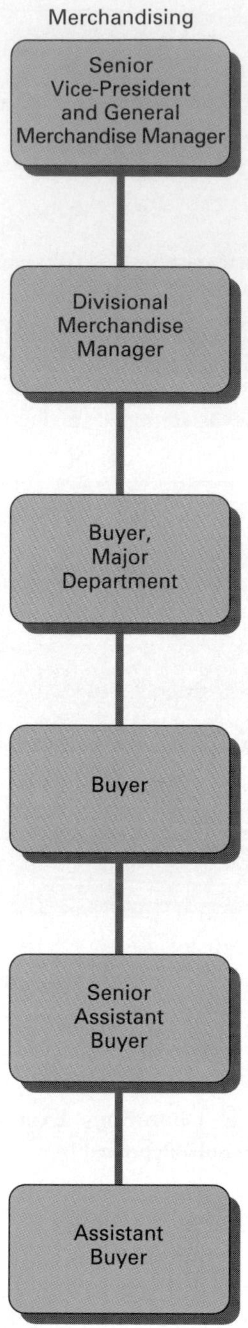

Figure 3
Parisian's Two Typical Executive Career Paths (Selected Positions)
Source: Parisian's. Reprinted by permission.

Compensation Ranges in Retailing

Table 4 lists compensation ranges for personnel in a number of retailing positions. Table 5 shows the total compensation for ten of the highest-paid chief executives in U.S. retailing during 1993.

Getting Your First Position as a Retail Professional

The search for career opportunities in retailing, interview preparation, and the evaluation of the retail career options available to you are important steps in getting your first professional position in retailing. It is essential that you devote sufficient time to these steps so your job hunt progresses as quickly and as smoothly as possible.

Next, there are some pointers to assist you in obtaining a rewarding first career-oriented position as a retail professional.

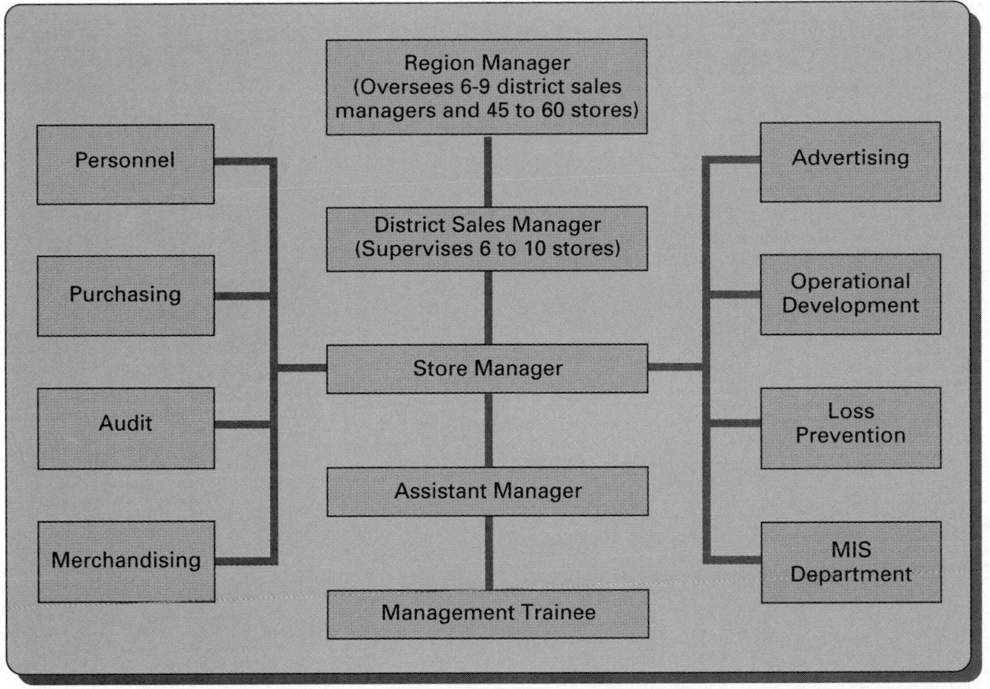

FIGURE 4
A Career Path at CVS Pharmacy
Source: *CVS: Together We Make a Great Team.* Reprinted by permission.

SEARCHING FOR CAREER OPPORTUNITIES IN RETAILING

Various sources should be consulted in the search for appropriate career opportunities. These sources should include your school's placement office, company directories (such as the one in Appendix B of this text), the placement services of your local American Marketing Association chapter, classified ads in your local newspapers, and networking (with professors, friends, neighbors, and family members).

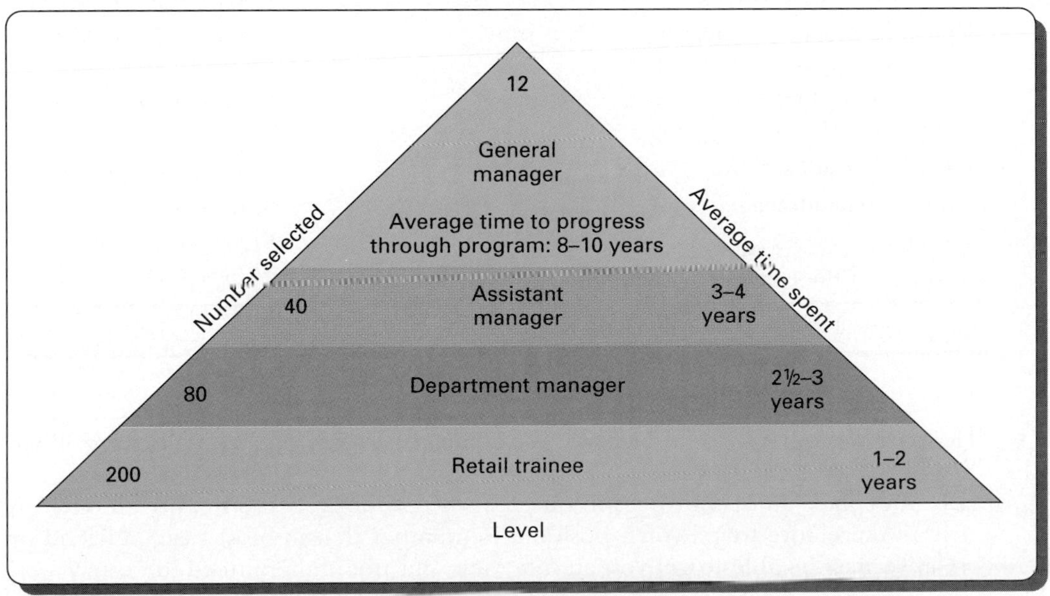

FIGURE 5 A Career Development Program at Giant Food
Source: *Giant Career Development Program: Steps to Future Success.* Reprinted by permission.

TABLE 4 Typical Compensation Ranges for Personnel in Selected Retailing Positions

Position	Compensation Range
Department manager—soft-line retailer	$ 15,000–$ 25,000+
Store management trainee	$ 17,000–$ 25,000+
Assistant buyer	$ 17,000–$ 35,000+
Department manager—department store	$ 17,000–$ 35,000+
Department manager—mass merchandiser	$ 17,000–$ 35,000+
Store manager—specialty store, home center, drugstore	$ 17,000–$ 55,000+
Market research junior analyst	$ 19,000–$ 30,000+
Department manager—hard-line retailer	$ 19,000–$ 35,000+
Store manager—soft-line retailer	$ 21,000–$ 45,000+
Buyer—specialty store, home center, drugstore, department store	$ 24,000–$ 50,000+
Warehouse director	$ 24,000–$ 90,000+
Market research analyst	$ 25,000–$ 40,000+
Buyer—discount store	$ 27,000–$ 50,000+
Market research senior analyst	$ 30,000–$ 50,000+
Market research assistant director	$ 30,000–$ 65,000+
Buyer—national chain	$ 32,000–$ 70,000+
Security director	$ 32,000–$ 70,000+
Store manager—department store	$ 33,000–$ 75,000+
Senior human resources executive	$ 33,000–$ 140,000+
Market research director	$ 35,000–$ 75,000+
Divisional merchandise manager	$ 42,000–$ 85,000+
Senior advertising executive	$ 42,000–$ 110,000+
Operations director	$ 47,000–$ 90,000+
General merchandise manager—drugstore, home center	$ 47,000–$ 90,000+
Senior real-estate executive	$ 47,000–$ 120,000+
General merchandise manager—specialty store, department store	$ 52,000–$ 100,000+
General merchandise manager—discount store, national chain	$ 63,000–$ 125,000+
Senior financial executive	$ 63,000–$ 200,000+
Senior merchandising executive	$ 75,000–$ 250,000+
President	$150,000–$ 800,000+
Chairman of the board	$150,000–$10,000,000+

Source: Estimated by the authors from various publications.

Here are some hints to consider when searching for career opportunities in retailing:

- Do not "place all of your eggs in one basket." Do not rely too heavily on one friend or relative to get you a position. Remember that in most cases, a friend or relative may be able to get you an interview, but not a guaranteed job offer.
- Treat your career search in a serious and systematic manner. Plan in advance and do not wait until the recruiting season at your school has started to generate a list of potential retail employers.

TABLE 5 The Compensation Levels of Ten of the Highest-Paid U.S. Retailing Chief Executives

Company of Chief Executive	Total 1993 Compensation of Chief Executive[a]
Auto Zone	$32,228,000
Blockbuster	15,557,000
Circuit City	13,565,000
Price/Costco	6,520,000
May Department Stores	4,706,000[b]
Sears Roebuck	4,173,000
Home Depot	2,844,000
Fred Meyer	2,534,000[b]
The Gap	2,490,000
J.C. Penney	2,346,000

[a] Includes salary, bonus, stock gains, and other payments (from long-term compensation plans, thrift-plan contributions, and so on).

[b] 1992 data.

Source: "Corporate America's Most Powerful People: Paychecks of America's 800 Top Chief Executives," *Forbes* (May 23, 1994), pp. 144–147 ff.

- Use directories with listings of retail firms. Such publications include *Fairchild's Manual of Retail Stores*; the College Placement Council's annual manual; the yearly *Peterson's Business & Management Jobs*; *Hoover's Handbook of American Business*, which profiles over 500 major U.S. companies of all kinds; *Dun's Million Dollar Directory*; *Standard & Poor's Register*; and the Yellow Pages in your area.
- Rely on the "law of large numbers." In sending out resumés, you may have to write to at least 10 to 20 retailers to get just two to four interviews.
- Make sure your resumé and accompanying cover letter highlight your most distinctive qualities. These may include school honors, officer status in a key organization, appropriate work experience, special computer expertise, and the proportion of college tuition you paid for yourself. Figure 6 shows a sample resumé that is geared to an entry-level position in retailing.
- Show your resumé to at least one of your professors for his or her reaction. Be receptive to the constructive comments made. Remember, your professor's goal is to help you get the best possible first job.

PREPARING FOR THE INTERVIEW

The initial and subsequent interviews for a retail position, which may last for 20 to 30 minutes or longer, play a large role in determining whether you are offered a job. For that reason, it is necessary that you prepare properly for all interviews.

These are some hints in preparing for a retail position interview:

- Adequately research the firm. Be aware of its goods/service category, current size, overall retail strategy, competitive developments, and so on.
- Anticipate such questions as these and plan general responses in advance: "Tell me about yourself." "Why are you interested in a retailing career?" "Why do you want a job with us?" "What are your major strengths?" "What are your major weaknesses?" "What do you want to be doing five years from now?" "Are you willing to relocate?" "Which college courses did you like most?" "Which courses did

Jennifer Marcus
17 Hart Drive
West Hartford, Connecticut 06117
(203) 555-7416

EMPLOYMENT OBJECTIVE:	Assistant Buyer Position, Formal Training Program Desired
EDUCATION:	Bachelor of Business Administration, December 1994 Hofstra University Hempstead, New York 11550-1090 Major: Marketing Minor: Psychology Class Rank: Top 10%
SCHOLARSHIPS AND AWARDS:	Hofstra University Distinguished Scholar Academic Award Dean's List for 6 semesters. Cum laude graduate.
EXTRACURRICULAR ACTIVITIES:	Vice-President, Retail Management Society, Spring 1993-Fall 1994. Responsible for recruitment of members, arranging for guest speakers, and budget preparation and control. Member, American Marketing Association; New York and National Chapters.
COMPUTER SKILLS:	Proficient in Word Perfect; working knowledge of Lotus and SPSS.
WORK EXPERIENCE:	
January 1992–present	Assistant to Store Manager, Fashion World. 200 Main Street, Hempstead, New York Responsible for setting up displays, providing product information to the sales staff, interacting with certain vendors, and handling returns.
January 1990–December 1991	Cashier, Thrifty Drug Stores. Green Fields Shopping Center, Valley Fields, New York Responsible for customer transactions, processing credit card sales, and restocking shelves. Paid half of tuition expenses by working 20 hours per week while attending college.
PERSONAL:	Willing to relocate. Hobbies include photography and personal computers.
REFERENCES:	Will be furnished upon request.

Figure 6 Sample Resumé

you like least?" "What would your previous employers say about you?" In your pre-interview preparation, role-play your answers to these questions with a parent, a friend, or a professor. Listen to their critical comments.

- Get ready for each interview as if it is the most important one you will be having. Otherwise, you may not be properly prepared when the position involved turns out to be more desirable than you had originally thought. Also, keep in mind that you represent both your college and yourself at every interview you go on.

- Be prepared to raise your own pertinent questions when asked to do so in the interview. Such questions should relate to career paths, training programs, and opportunities for advancement.
- Dress appropriately and be well groomed.
- Verify the date and place of the interview. Be prompt.
- Have a pen and pad available to record key information after the interview has been completed.
- Write a note to the interviewer within a week after the interview to thank him or her for spending time with you and to express a continuing interest in the company.

Evaluating Retail Career Opportunities

Graduating students often place too much emphasis on initial salary or the image of a retailer (in terms of fashion orientation or target market) when evaluating retail career opportunities. Yet, many other factors should be considered.

Here are several key questions to address while deciding what career opportunity to pursue. The questions should be linked to the attributes of each specific job offer you may receive:

- What activities do you like undertaking?
- What are your personal strengths and weaknesses?
- What are your current and long-term goals?
- Do you want to work for an independent, a chain, or a franchise operation?
- Does the opportunity offer an acceptable and clear career path?
- Does the opportunity include a formal training program?
- Will the opportunity enable you to be rewarded for good performance?
- Will you have to relocate?
- Will each promotion in the company result in greater authority and responsibility?
- Is the compensation level fair relative to other offers?
- Can a superior employee move up the career path significantly faster than an average one?
- If ownership of a retail firm is a long-term goal, which opportunity provides the best preparation?

Selected Firms Seeking College Graduates for Retail-Related Positions

Abraham & Straus
420 Fulton Street
Brooklyn, NY 11202
Department store chain
New York, New Jersey

Acme Markets, Inc.
75 Valley Stream Parkway
Malvern, PA 19355
Supermarket chain
East

Albertson's
250 Parkcenter Boulevard
Boise, ID 83726
Supermarket, superstore, and combination food/drug chains
West, South

American Stores Co.
P.O. Box 27447
Salt Lake City, UT 84127
Supermarket and drugstore chains
U.S.

Ames Department Stores
2418 Main Street
Rocky Hill, CT 06067
Discount department and variety store chains
Northeast, Mid-Atlantic

Associated Merchandising Corporation
1440 Broadway
New York, NY 10018
Affiliated with 30 department stores
Retail service organization
Northeast

J. Baker, Inc.
P.O. Box 231
Readville, MA 02136
Licensed shoe departments/shoe wholesaler and retailer
U.S.

Banana Republic
1 Harrison Street
San Francisco, CA 94107
Specialty clothing chain
U.S.

Banker's Note, Inc.
4900 Highlands Parkway
Smyrna, GA 30082
Specialty store chain
South

Barnes & Noble
120 Fifth Avenue, 5th Floor
New York, NY 10011
Bookstore chain
U.S.

W. Bell & Co., Inc.
12401 Twinbrook Parkway
Rockville, MD 20852
Showroom/warehouse/catalog chain
Washington, D.C.; Baltimore, Maryland; Chicago, Illinois

Best Products
1400 Best Plaza
Richmond, VA 23260
Catalog showroom and jewelry store chains
27 states

Big B, Inc.
P.O. Box 10168
Birmingham, AL 35202
Drugstore chain
South

Big V Supermarkets, Inc.
176 North Main Street
Florida, NY 10921
Supermarket chain
New York

Bloomingdale's
1000 Third Avenue
New York, NY 10022
Department store chain
8 states

Bon Marche
1601 Third Avenue
Seattle, WA 98101
Department store chain
Pacific Northwest, Rocky Mountain states

Boys Markets, Inc.
777 Harbor Boulevard
La Habra, CA 90631
Supermarket chain
California

Bradlees
1 Bradlees Circle
Braintree, MA 02184
Discount department store chain
Northeast

Brendle's Incorporated
1919 North Bridge Street
Elkin, NC 28621
Discount store chain
Georgia, North Carolina, South Carolina, Tennessee, Virginia

The Broadway—Southern California
3880 North Mission Road
Los Angeles, CA 90031
California

Brown Group, Inc.
P.O. Box 29
8400 Maryland Avenue
St. Louis, MO 63166
Shoe manufacturer and retailer/leased shoe departments/fabric store chain
U.S., Canada

Bruno's
P.O. Box 2486
Birmingham, AL 35201
Supermarket and convenience store chains
U.S.

Bullock's
800 South Hope Street
Los Angeles, CA 90014
Department store chain
California, Arizona, Nevada

Burdines
1333 East 163rd Street
North Miami, FL 33161
Department store chain
Florida

Burger King
P.O. Box 520783 GMF
Miami, FL 33152
Fast-food franchisor
U.S., International

Burlington Coat Factory Warehouse Corporation
1830 Route 130 N
Burlington, NJ 08016
Off-price apparel store chain
U.S.

Cache, Inc.
1460 Broadway, 16th Floor
New York, NY 10036
Women's specialty apparel chain
18 states and Washington, D.C.

Canadian Tire Corporation, Limited
2180 Yonge Street
P.O. Box 770, Station K
Toronto, Ontario, Canada
M4P 2V8
Gas stations/auto products store chain
Canada

Carson Pirie Scott & Co.
36 South Wabash Avenue
Chicago, IL 60603
Department and specialty store chains
Midwest

Carter Hawley Hale Stores
3880 North Mission Road
Los Angeles, CA 90031
Department store chains
Southwest and Western U.S.

Cato Corporation
P.O. Box 34216
Charlotte, NC 28234
Women's specialty store chain
South, Southwest

Circle K Corporation
4500 South 40th Street
Phoenix, AZ 85040
Convenience food store chain
South, West, Great Britian

Circuit City Stores, Inc.
9950 Mayland Drive
Richmond, VA 23233
Consumer electronics store chains
Southeast, California, Nevada

Ciro Inc.
6340 NW 5th Way
Ft. Lauderdale, FL 33309
Imitation jewelry store chains
U.S.

Clothestime, Inc.
5325 East Hunter Avenue
Anaheim, CA 92807
Women's apparel store chain
16 states

Consolidated Stores Corporation
300 Phillipi Road
P.O. Box 747
Columbus, OH 43216
Closeout store chain
Midwest, Southeast

County Seat Stores
17950 Preston Road, Suite 1000
Dallas, TX 75252
Retail apparel chain
Mideast, Midwest, California

Crown American Corporation
131 Market Street
Johnstown, PA 15907
Department store chain
10 states

Crown Books Corporation
3300 75th Avenue
Landover, MD 20785
Specialty book store chain
U.S.

CVS/Peoples Drugs
1 CVS Drive, Department MG
Woonsocket, RI 02895
Pharmacy chain
U.S.

Dairy Mart Convenience Stores, Inc.
240 South Road
Enfield, CT 06082
Owned and leased convenience store chain
Northeast, Midwest, Southeast

Dart Group Corporation
3300 75th Avenue
Landover, MD 20785
Discount auto parts, book, and grocery store chains
U.S.

Dayton's
700 On The Mall, Number 862
Minneapolis, MN 55402
Department store chain
Midwest

Deb Shops, Inc.
9401 Blue Grass Road
Philadelphia, PA 19114
Specialty apparel chain
32 states

Decor Corporation
2731 Espey Court Suite 7
Crofton, MD 21114
Graphic art and gift store chains
23 states and Washington, D.C.

Delchamps, Inc.
305 Delchamps Drive
P.O. Box 1668
Mobile, AL 36633
Supermarket chain
Alabama, Florida, Mississippi, Louisiana

Dillard Department Stores, Inc.
900 West Capital Avenue
Little Rock, AR 72201
Department store chain
18 states

Walt Disney Co.
500 South Buena Vista Street
Burbank, CA 91521
Leisure, recreation, entertainment
U.S.

Dollar General Corporation
104 Woodmont Boulevard, Suite 500
Nashville, TN 37205
Retail and wholesale general-merchandise chain
Southeast

Domino's Pizza
1190 Winterson Road, Suite 200
Linthacom, MD 21090
Fast-food franchisor
U.S., International

Dress Barn, Inc.
88 Hamilton Avenue
Stamford, CT 06902
Off-price women's apparel chain
27 states

Dylex Limited
637 Lake Shore Boulevard West
Toronto, Ontario, Canada
M5V 1A8
Apparel chains
Canada, U.S.

E&B Marine Inc.
201 Meadow Road
P.O. Box 747
Edison, NJ 08818
Marine supplies outlets
East

Eckerd Drug Company
8333 Bryan Dairy Road
Clearwater, FL 34618
Drugstore chain
East, Southeast

Edison Brothers Stores, Inc.
501 North Broadway, 3rd Floor
P.O. Box 14020
St. Louis, MO 63102
Women's shoe store chains/leased shoe departments
U.S.

Egghead, Inc.
22011 S.E. 51st Street
P.O. Box 7004
Issaquah, WA 98027
Personal computer software outlets
18 states; Washington, D.C.; British Columbia, Canada

Emporium Capwell
835 Market Street
San Francisco, CA 94103
Department store chain
California

Evans, Inc.
36 South State Street
Chicago, IL 60603
Specialty women's apparel store chains/leased fur salons
11 states and Washington, D.C.

Fabri-Centers of America, Inc.
5555 Darrow Road
Hudson, OH 44122
Fabric store chain
U.S.

Fabricland, Inc.
2035 N.E. 181st Avenue
Portland, OR 97230
Retail and wholesale fabric chain
West

Family Dollar Stores, Inc.
P.O. Box 1017
Charlotte, NC 28201
Discount variety store chain
East

Famous Footwear
203 East Olin Avenue
Madison, WI 53713
Shoe store chain
U.S.

Fay's Drug Company, Inc.
7245 Henry Clay Boulevard
Liverpool, NY 13088
Drugstore, discount auto parts, and discount office supply store chains
New York, Pennsylvania

Filene's
426 Washington Street
Boston, MA 02101
Department store chain
Northeast

Fisher Foods, Inc.
1365 Cherry Avenue
Canton, OH 44714
Supermarket chain
Ohio

Foley's
1110 Main Street
Houston, TX 77001
Department store chain
Texas, Oklahoma, New Mexico

Food Lion Stores, Inc.
P.O. Box 1330
Salisbury, NC 28145
Supermarket chain
U.S.

Foodarama Supermarkets, Inc.
303 West Main Street
P.O. Box 592
Freehold, NJ 07728
Supermarket chain
New York, New Jersey, Pennsylvania

Gantos, Inc.
P.O. Box 875
Grand Rapids, MI 49588
Women's apparel specialty store chain
U.S.

The Gap, Inc.
P.O. Box 60
900 Cherry Avenue
San Bruno, CA 94066
Specialty store chain
U.S., International

Gendis Inc.
General Distributors of Canada Ltd.
1370 Sony Place
Winnipeg, Manitoba, Canada
R3T 1N5
Junior department and family-clothing store chains
Canada

General Host Corporation
6399 East Nevada
Detroit, MI 48234
Nursery and craft store chain (Frank's)
U.S.

General Mills, Inc.
One General Mills Boulevard
P.O. Box 1113
Minneapolis, MN 55426
Restaurant chains
U.S.

General Nutrition Incorporated
921 Penn Avenue
Pittsburgh, PA 15222
Nutritional and health-related store chain
U.S.

Genesco Inc.
Genesco Park
Administration Building, Room 368
Nashville, TN 37217
Manufacturer, wholesaler, and retailer of shoes and specialty store operator
U.S.

Genovese Drug Stores, Inc.
80 Marcus Drive
Melville, NY 11747
Drugstore chain
Northeast

Giant Food Inc.
P.O. Box 1804
Washington, DC 20013
Supermarket and food/pharmacy chain
East

Gordon Jewelry Corporation
901 West Walnut Hill Lane
Irving, TX 75038
Jewelry store chain
U.S., Puerto Rico

Gottschalks Inc.
7 River Place East
P.O. Box 28920
Fresno, CA 93729
Department and clothing store chains
West

Grafton Group Limited
9 Sunlight Park Road
P.O. Box 108, Postal Station G
Toronto, Ontario, Canada
M4M 3G1
Apparel and footwear specialty retail chain
Canada, U.S.

Grand Auto, Inc.
7200 Edgewater Drive
Oakland, CA 94621
Automotive supply-store chain
California, Nevada, Washington, Alaska

Grand Union
201 Willowbrook Boulevard
Wayne, NJ 07470
Supermarket and community store chains
East, Puerto Rico, Virgin Islands

Great Atlantic & Pacific Tea Company, Inc. (A&P)
Box 418
2 Paragon Drive
Montvale, NJ 07645
Supermarket chains
U.S., Canada

Greenman Bros. Inc.
105 Price Parkway
Farmingdale, NY 11735
Toy store chains
31 states

Grossman's Inc.
200 Union Street
Braintree, MA 02184
Building materials and home-improvement store chains
17 states

Hancock Fabrics, Inc.
3406 West Main Street
P.O. Box 2400
Tupelo, MS 38801
Fabric store chain
29 states

Hannaford Bros. Co.
145 Pleasant Hill Road
Scarborough, ME 04074
Supermarket and drugstore chains
Maine, New Hampshire, Massachusetts, Vermont, upstate New York

Haverty Furniture Companies, Inc.
866 Peachtree Street NW
Atlanta, GA 30308
Home furnishings store chain
South

Heilig-Meyers Company
2235 Staples Mill Road
Richmond, VA 23230
Home furnishings store chain
South

Highland Superstores, Inc.
909 North Sheldon Road
Plymouth, MI 48170
Consumer electronics/home appliance stores
12 states

Hills Department Stores, Inc.
15 Dan Road
Canton, MA 02021
Discount department store chain
Middle Atlantic

Home Depot, Inc.
2727 Paces Ferry Road
Atlanta, GA 30339
Home-improvement store chain
U.S.

House of Fabrics, Inc.
13400 Riverside Drive
Sherman Oaks, CA 91423
Fabric, needlecrafts, and sewing supplies store chains
U.S.

Hudson's
700 On The Mall, Number 862
Minneapolis, MN 55402
Department store chain
Midwest

Hudson's Bay Company
401 Bay Street
Toronto, Ontario, Canada
M5H 2Y4
Department store chain
Canada

Ingles Markets, Incorporated
Highway 70
East of Asheville, NC 28816
Supermarket chain
North Carolina, South Carolina, Georgia, Tennessee, Virginia

Jay Jacobs, Inc.
1530 5th Avenue
Seattle, WA 98101
Apparel specialty store chain
West

Jacobson Stores Inc.
3333 Sargent Road
Jackson, MI 49201
Apparel and home furnishings store chain
Michigan, Ohio, Florida

Jamesway Corporation
40 Hartz Way
Secaucus, NJ 07096
Discount department store chain
New Jersey, New York, Pennsylvania, Virginia, Delaware, Maryland

Jewel Food Stores
1955 West North Avenue
Melrose Park, IL 60160
Supermarket, self-service drug, and department store chains
Midwest

Jewelcor Incorporated
100 North Wilkes Barre Boulevard
Wilkes-Barre, PA 18702
Jewelry and general merchandise catalog showroom chain
California, Florida, Illinois, New Jersey, Pennsylvania, Texas

Jordan Marsh
P.O. Box 9159
Boston, MA 02205
Department store chain
Northeast

Joslin's
934 16th Street
Denver, CO 80202
Apparel store chain
West

Judy's Inc.
7710 Haskell Avenue
Van Nuys, CA 91406
Apparel store chain
California, Nevada, Texas, Arizona, New Mexico

Jumping-Jacks Shoes, Inc.
100 Fifth Street
Monett, MO 65708
Shoe store chain
8 states, Puerto Rico

Kaufmann's
400 Fifth Avenue
Pittsburgh, PA 15219
Department store chain
U.S.

Kay-Bee Toy Stores
100 West Street
Pittsfield, MA 01201
Specialty toy chain
U.S.

Kenwin Shops, Inc.
4747 Granite Drive
Tucker, GA 30084
Ladies' and children's apparel store chain
South

Kinney Shoe Corporation
233 Broadway
New York, NY 10279
Shoe store chain
U.S.

Kmart Corporation
3100 West Big Beaver Road
Troy, MI 48084
Retail conglomerate
U.S., Puerto Rico, Canada

Kroger Co.
1014 Vine Street
Cincinnati, OH 45202
Supermarket and convenience store chains
Midwest, South, Southeast, Southwest

Lazarus Department Store
699 Race Street
Cincinnati, OH 45202
Department store chain
Ohio, Indiana, Kentucky, Michigan, West Virginia

Lechters Inc.
1 Cape May Street
Harrison, NJ 07029
Housewares chain
U.S.

Levitz Furniture Corporation
6111 Broken Sound Parkway NW
Boca Raton, FL 33487
Furniture and home-furnishings chain
U.S.

The Limited, Inc.
Three Limited Parkway
P.O. Box 16528
Columbus, OH 43230
Apparel store chains
U.S.

Liz Claiborne, Inc.
1441 Broadway
New York, NY 10018
Women's apparel manufacturer and retailer
U.S.

Loblaw Companies Limited
22 St. Clair Avenue East
Toronto, Ontario, Canada
M4T 2S8
Retail food chain
Canada, U.S.

Loehmann's
2500 Halsey Street
Bronx, NY 10461
Women's fashion apparel chain
East

Longs Drug Stores
P.O. Box 5222
Walnut Creek, CA 94596
Drugstore chain
California, Hawaii, Alaska, Nevada, Arizona, Colorado

Lord and Taylor
424 Fifth Avenue
New York, NY 10018
Specialty chain
East, Midwest, Southeast

Lowe's Companies, Inc.
Highway 268 East
North Wilkesboro, NC 28656
Home improvment centers
South

Lucky Stores, Inc.
6300 Clark Avenue
P.O. Box BB
Dublin, CA 94568
Food store chain
California, Nevada, Arizona, Florida

L. Luria & Son, Inc.
5770 Miami Lakes Drive
Miami Lakes, FL 33014
Catalog showroom chain
Florida

Luskin's, Inc.
7125 Columbia Gateway
Columbia, MD 21046
Specialty store chain
Maryland; Washington, D.C.; Virginia; Indiana; Ohio; Connecticut

Maas Brothers
P.O. Box 311
Tampa, FL 33602
Department store chain
Southeast

Macy's Atlanta, Inc.
180 Peachtree Street NW
Atlanta, GA 30303
Department store chain
South

Macy's New York, Inc.
151 West 34th Street
New York, NY 10001
Department store chain
Northeast

Macy's West, Inc.
170 O'Farrell Street
San Francisco, CA 94102
Department store chain
Midwest, Southwest, West

I. Magnin
135 Stockton Street
San Francisco, CA 94108
Department store chain
California, Arizona, Oregon, Washington, Illinois, Maryland

Marsh Supermarkets Inc.
P.O. Box 155
501 Depot Street
Yorktown, IN 47396
Supermarket, food-and-drug, and convenience store chains
Indiana, Ohio

Marshall Field's
700 On The Mall, Number 862
Minneapolis, MN 55402
Department store chain
U.S.

Marshalls
200 Brickstone Square
P.O. Box 9030
Andover, MA 01810
Off-price retail chain
U.S.

May Department Stores Company
611 Olive Street
St. Louis, MO 63101
Department store chains
U.S.

McDonald's Corporation
Kroc Drive
Oak Brook, IL 60521
Quick-service restaurant franchisor
U.S., International

Medicine Shoppe International, Inc.
1100 North Lindbergh
St. Louis, MO 63132
Franchise drugstore chain
U.S.

Meldisco
933 MacArthur Drive
Mahwah, NJ 07430
Leased shoe department chain
U.S., International

Melville Corporation
One Theall Road
Rye, NY 10580
Retail conglomerate
U.S., International

Mercantile Stores Company, Inc.
9450 Seward Road
Fairfield, OH 45014
Department store chains
U.S.

Merry-Go-Round Enterprises, Inc.
3300 Fashion Way
Joppa, MD 21085
Specialty apparel chains
U.S.

Fred Meyer, Inc.
P.O. Box 42121
Portland, OR 97242
Discount and specialty store chains
West

Michaels Stores, Inc.
P.O. Box 612566
Dallas, TX 75261
Specialty store chains
U.S.

Nash Finch Company
7600 France Avenue, South
P.O. Box 355
St. Louis Park, MN 55440
Retail and wholesale food distributor
Midwest, West

National Convenience Stores Incorporated
100 Waugh Drive
Houston, TX 77007
Convenience store chain
Texas, Florida, Georgia, Tennessee, California

Neiman-Marcus
1618 Main Street
Dallas, TX 75201
Specialty store chain
U.S.

S.E. Nichols Inc.
275 Seventh Avenue
New York, NY 10001
Discount department store chain
East, Ohio

Nordstrom, Inc.
1501 Fifth Avenue
Seattle, WA 98101
Specialty store chain/leased shoe departments
U.S.

Osco Drug
1818 Swift Avenue
Oak Brook, IL 60521
General merchandise, drug, and department store chains
Midwest, Northwest, New England

Oshawa Group Limited
302 The East Mall
Etobicoke, Ontario, Canada
M9B 6B8
Department store, supermarket, and drugstore chains
Canada

Oshman's Sporting Goods, Inc.
2302 Maxwell Lane
Houston, TX 77023
Sporting-goods specialty-store chain
California, Texas

Parisian Inc.
750 Lakeshore Parkway
Birmingham, AL 35211
Specialty department store chain
Southeast, Midwest

Pay 'N Pak Stores, Inc.
P.O. Box 97080
Kent, WA 98064
Home-improvement store chain
West, Midwest, Alaska, Hawaii

Payless Cashways, Inc.
2 Pershing Square, 2300 Main
P.O. Box 419466
Kansas City, MO 64141
Building materials store chains
Midwest, Southwest, New England, Pacific Coast

Payless Shoesource
3231 East Sixth
P.O. Box 1189
Topeka, KS 66607
Shoe store chain
U.S.

Penn Traffic Company
319 Washington Street
Johnstown PA 15901
Company-owned and franchised supermarket and department store chains
East

J.C. Penney Company, Inc.
P.O. Box 10001
Dallas, TX 75024
Department store, mail-order, and thrift drug chains
U.S., International

Pennington's Stores Limited
5101 Orbitor Drive
Mississauga, Ontario, Canada
L4W 4V1
Apparel store chains
Canada, U.S.

Peoples Jewellers Limited
1440 Don Mills Road
Don Mills, Ontario, Canada
M3B 3M1
Jewelry store chain
Canada

Pep Boys
3111 West Allegheny Avenue
Philadelphia, PA 19132
Auto supply, accessory, and service store chain
U.S.

Perry Drug Stores, Inc.
5400 Perry Drive
P.O. Box 1957
Pontiac, MI 48056
Drugstore and health care center chains
Michigan, Illinois, Wisconsin, Indiana

Petrie Stores Corporation
70 Enterprise Avenue
Secaucus, NJ 07094
Specialty apparel chains
U.S., Virgin Islands, Puerto Rico

Pic 'n' Save Corporation
2430 E. Del Amo Boulevard
Dominguez, CA 90220
Discount store chains
9 states

Pier 1 Imports, Inc.
P.O. Box 961020
Fort Worth, TX 76161
Gift store and home decorating store chains
U.S., International

Pizza Hut Inc.
200 Lanidex Center
Parsippany, NJ 07054
Quick-service restaurant franchisor
U.S., International

Price/Costco Company
10908 120th Avenue NE
Kirkland, WA 98033
Buying clubs
U.S., Europe

Publix Super Markets
1936 George Jenkins Boulevard
Lakeland, FL 33801
Supermarket chain
Southeast

Pueblo International, Inc.
1300 Northwest 22nd Avenue
Pompano Beach, FL 33069
Supermarket chains
Puerto Rico, Virgin Islands, Florida

Quality Food Centers, Inc.
10112 NE 10th Street
Bellevue, WA 98004
Supermarket chain
Washington

Reitman's (Canada) Limited
250 Sauve Street West
Montreal, Quebec, Canada
H3L 1Z2
Women's apparel store chain
Canada, U.S.

Revco Drug Stores
1925 Centerprice Parkway
Twinsburg, OH 44087
Drugstore chain
Midwest

Rhodes, Inc.
4370 Peachtree Road NE
Atlanta, GA 30319
Home-furnishings store chain
Southeast

Rich's Department Stores Inc.
35 Congress Street
Salem, MA 01970
Department store chain
Massachusetts, New Hampshire, Vermont, Maine

Rite Aid Corporation
P.O. Box 3165
Harrisburg, PA 17105
Drugstore chain
Middle Alantic

Rose's Stores
R.H. Rose Building
P.O. Drawer 947
Henderson, NC 27536
Variety store chain
East, Southeast

Ross Dress For Less
8333 Central Avenue
Newark, CA 94560
Off-price apparel and shoe store chains
South, Southwest, West

Safeway Stores
201 Fourth Street
Oakland, CA 94660
Supermarket chain
U.S.

Saks Fifth Avenue
12 East 49th Street, 4th Floor
New York, NY 10017
Fashion specialty-store chain
U.S.

Salant Corporation
1155 Avenue of the Americas
New York, NY 10036
Factory outlet store chain
Northeast, South

Sav-On, Inc.
1818 Swift Drive
Oak Brook, IL 60521
Drugstore chain
27 states

Schultz Sav-O Stores, Inc.
2215 Union Avenue
Sheboygan, Wisconsin 53081
Supermarket chain/food supplier
Wisconsin, Illinois

Scotty's, Inc.
P.O. Box 939
Winter Haven, FL 33882
Building supply store chain
Florida

Sears Canada Inc.
222 Jarvis Street
Toronto, Ontario, Canada
M5B 2B8
Department store and catalog chain
Canada

Sears, Roebuck & Co.
33-33 Beverly Road, E2-210A
Department 707-4
Hoffman Estates, IL 60179
Retail conglomerate
U.S., Puerto Rico

Seaway Food Town, Inc.
1020 Ford Street
Maumee, OH 43537
Food store and discount drugstore chains
Ohio, Michigan

Service Merchandise Company, Inc.
P.O. Box 24600
Nashville, TN 37202
Catalog showroom chain
U.S.

Sharper Image Corporation
650 Davis Street
San Francisco, CA 94111
Specialty store and mail-order chain
U.S.

Sherwin-Williams Company
101 Prospect Avenue NW
Cleveland, OH 44115
Manufacturer and retailer of paints and related products
U.S.

Southland Corporation
2828 North Haskill Avenue
Dallas, TX 75204
Convenience-food store chain and franchisor
U.S., International

Standard Brands Paint Company
4300 West 190th Street
Torrance, CA 90509
Paint/decorating centers and art materials chains
West

Staples—The Office Superstore
100 Pennsylvania Avenue
P.O. Box 9328
Framingham, MA 01701
Office supply retail chain
U.S.

Star Market Company
625 Mt. Auburn Street
Cambridge, MA 02138
Food store chain
Massachusetts, Rhode Island

Stern's
Route 4, Bergen Mall
Paramus, NJ 07652
Department store chain
New York, New Jersey

Stop & Shop Supermarket Company
P.O. Box 1942
Boston, MA 02105
Supermarket chain
Northeast

Strawbridge and Clothier
801 Market Street
Philadelphia, PA 19107
Department and discount variety store chains
Pennsylvania, New Jersey, Delaware

Stride Rite Corporation
5 Cambridge Center
Cambridge, MA 02142
Footwear manufacturer and retailer
U.S.

Sunshine-Jr. Stores, Inc.
June Avenue & 17th Street
P.O. Box 2190
Panama City, FL 32402
Supermarket and convenience store chains
Florida, Alabama, Georgia, Mississippi, Louisiana

Super Rite Foods, Inc.
3900 Industrial Road
P.O. Box 2261
Harrisburg, PA 17105
Supermarket chain
Maryland, Virginia

SuperValu Stores, Inc.
P.O. Box 990
Minneapolis, MN 55440
Food wholesaler/supermarket chain
U.S.

Syms Corporation
Syms Way
Secaucus, NJ 07094
Off-price apparel chain
U.S.

Taco Bell Corporation
17901 Von Karman
Irvine, CA 92714
Quick-service restaurant franchisor
U.S.

Tandy Corporation
500 One Tandy Center
Fort Worth, TX 76102
Company-owned and franchised consumer electronics store chains
U.S., International

Target
33 South 6th Street
P.O. Box 1393
Minneapolis, MN 55402
Discount department store chain
Midwest

Three D Departments, Inc.
P.O. Box 19773
Irvine, CA 92714
Leased departments and specialty store chain
Northeast, California

Tiffany & Co.
727 Fifth Avenue
New York, NY 10022
Fine jewelry and accessories chain
U.S., International

TJX Companies, Inc.
770 Cochituate Road
Framingham, MA 01701
Discount family and off-price ladies apparel chains
U.S.

Toys "R" Us/Kids "R" Us
461 From Road, MAC Center 6
Paramus, NJ 07652
Toy and clothing store chains
U.S., International

Tuesday Morning, Inc.
14621 Inwood Road
Dallas, TX 75244
Discount and household merchandise store chains
South

United States Shoe Corporation
One Eastwood Drive
Cincinnati, OH 45227
Retail conglomerate
U.S.

Venture Stores Inc.
2001 East Terra Lane, MS 224D
P.O. Box 110
O'Fallon, MO 63366
Upscale discount store chain
Midwest

Village Super Market, Inc.
733 Mountain Avenue
Springfield, NJ 07081
Supermarket chain
New Jersey, Pennsylvania

Volume Shoe Corporation
3231 East 6th Street
Topeka, KS 66607
Family shoe store chain
34 states

Vons Companies, Inc.
618 Michillinda Avenue
Arcadia, CA 91007
Supermarket and food-and-drug combination store chains
West

Wal-Mart Stores, Inc.
702 Southwest 8th Street
Bentonville, AR 72716
Retail conglomerate
U.S., International

Waldbaum's, Inc.
Hemlock Street and Boulevard Avenue
Central Islip, NY 11722
Supermarket chain
New York, Connecticut, Massachusetts

Walgreens
200 Wilmot Road
Deerfield, IL 60015
Drugstore chain
U.S., Puerto Rico

John Wanamaker
1300 Market Street
Philadelphia, PA 19101
Department store chain
New York, Pennsylvania

Wawa, Inc.
260 Baltimore Pike
Red Roof
Wawa, PA 19063
Convenience store chain
Northeast, Middle Atlantic

Weis Markets, Inc.
1000 South Second Street
Sunbury, PA 17801
Supermarket chain
Pennsylvania, New York, West Virginia, Maryland

Weisfield's, Inc.
375 Ghent Road
Akron, OH 44333
Jewelry store chain
9 states

Wendy's International
40 Shuman Boulevard, Suite 130
Naperville, IL 60563
Quick-service restaurant franchisor
U.S., International

Western Auto Supply Company
2107 Grand Avenue
Kansas City, MO 64108
Automotive products store chain
U.S.

Weyenberg Shoe Manufacturing Company
P.O. Box 1188
234 East Reservoir Avenue
Milwaukee, WI 53201
Men's footwear manufacturer, wholesaler, and retailer/leased shoe departments
U.S.

Wherehouse Entertainment, Inc.
19701 Hamilton Avenue
Torrance, CA 90502
Specialty home entertainment and information software chain
West

Wiener Enterprises, Inc.
5725 Powell Street
Harahan, LA 70123
Specialty apparel, shoe, and building materials store chains
South

Winn-Dixie Stores, Inc.
P.O. Box B
Jacksonville, FL 32203
Supermarket chain
13 states

Wisconsin Toy Company, Inc.
710 North Plankinton Avenue
Milwaukee, WI 53203
Closeout toy store chains
32 states

The Wiz
1300 Federal Boulevard
Carteret, NJ 07008
Consumer electronics store chain
New York, New Jersey, Connecticut

Wolohan Lumber Co.
1740 Midland Road
P.O. Box 3235
Saginaw, MI 48605
Building materials chain
Illinois, Indiana, Michigan, Ohio, Wisconsin, Kentucky

Woodward and Lothrop
2800 Eisenhower Avenue
Alexandria, VA 22314
Department store chain
Washington, DC; Maryland; Virginia

Woodward's Limited
101 West Hastings Street
Vancouver, British Columbia, Canada
V6B 4G1
Department and specialty apparel store chains
British Columbia and Alberta, Canada

Woolworth Corporation
233 Broadway
New York, NY 10279
Retail conglomerate
U.S., International

Zale Corporation
901 West Walnut Hill Lane
Irving, TX 75038
Jewelry store chain
U.S.

Zion's Co-operative Mercantile Institution
2200 South 900 West
Salt Lake City, UT 84137
Department store chain
Utah, Idaho

Retail Management Software

This appendix and an accompanying computer diskette let you engage in decision making under simulated conditions and apply many of the concepts studied during a course in retailing or retail management. The *Retail Management Software* diskette has three separate software packages: *Computer-Based Exercises in Retail Management*; *SUPERCO*, a retail simulation program; and *Appliance Data Base*, a customer and inventory data-base program for a small appliance-repair firm. Each of these packages is described in Appendix C.

The software is designed to run on a DOS-based PC and will work with a color or monochrome monitor. Although the overall quality of the graphics for these software packages is high, they do not require a graphics board.

General directions for copying the software onto a floppy disk or your hard drive are contained in the next section. Then, specific information on each package is presented.

Directions for Copying the Retail Management Software Diskette

To use the *Retail Management Software*, you need to purchase a blank computer diskette and make a personal copy of the master diskette that is available to your instructor.

These directions assume that your PC has two 3-1/2″ high-density drives or one 3-1/2″ high-density drive and a hard drive, and that you are using a version of DOS that is 5.0 or newer. If your computer system does not match this configuration, you will have to employ other procedures for copying your diskette. In that case, please refer to the DOS booklet that accompanies your computer system.

The following procedure creates three directories: EXERCISE, SUPERCO, and APPLDATA on your floppy disk or hard drive.

Using a Computer with Two Floppy Drives

If you are working with a two disk-drive computer with no hard drive, then follow these instructions. In this configuration, the floppy drives are known as drive "A" and drive "B."

To make your copy of the three software packages from the *Retail Management Software* master diskette, insert a disk operating system (DOS) diskette in drive A. Turn the computer on. Should the drive light come on for the drive with the diskette, fine. Otherwise, place DOS into the drive with the light on; for the computer you are using, this is drive A.

If your DOS diskette is configured with date and time options, it will be necessary to press the return key once when the date prompt appears and press the return key again when the time prompt appears. An "A>" automatically appears on the screen. When the screen displays "A>" (the A prompt), (1) type "XCOPY A:*.* B:/S" (without the quote marks), (2) remove the DOS diskette from drive A, (3) place the *Retail Management Software* master diskette in drive A, (4) place your blank formatted diskette in drive B, and (5) press return.

When copying is complete, remove both diskettes and turn off the computer. With a felt pen, mark your name on the copied diskette (the one from drive B). Return the master diskette to your instructor or the computer center operator.

Using a Computer with a Hard Drive

If you are working on a computer with a hard drive and one floppy drive (or two), then follow these instructions. In this configuration, the floppy drive is the "A" drive. NOTE: These instructions assume DOS is pre-loaded on your hard drive.

To make your copy of the three software packages from the *Retail Management Software* master diskette, turn on the computer. When the screen displays "C>" (the C prompt), (1) place the *Retail Management Software* master diskette in drive A and (2) type "XCOPY A:*.* C:/S" (without the quote marks). Make a backup by inserting a blank formatted diskette in drive A and then copying the individual software packages by (a) typing "XCOPY C:\EXERCISE A:\EXERCISE", pressing return, and typing "D" (all without the quote marks) when queried by the computer as to whether EXERCISE is a file or directory name; (b) typing "XCOPY C:\SUPERCO A:\SUPERCO", pressing return, and typing "D" (all without the quote marks) when queried by the computer as to whether SUPERCO is a file or directory name; and (c) "XCOPY C:\APPLDATA A:\APPLDATA", pressing return, and typing "D" (all without the quote marks) when queried by the computer as to whether APPLDATA is a file or directory name.

When copying is complete, remove the backup diskette and turn off the computer. With a felt pen, mark your name on the backup diskette. Return the master diskette to your instructor or the computer center operator.

Using a Network

Some colleges and universities have PC networks for student use. Because there are many differences in the way these networks are set up and operated, please consult with your professor or someone in the computer lab with regard to using *Retail Management Software.*

Computer-Based Exercises in Retail Management

The *Computer-Based Exercises in Retail Management* are designed to reinforce text material; to allow you to manipulate controllable retailing factors and to see their impact on costs, sales, and profits; to have you understand better the influence of uncontrollable factors; and to let you gain experience in using a PC to assess retailing opportunities and solve retailing problems. All 15 exercises are designed to be handed in for class assignments or for your own use. The exercises are balanced in terms of subject and level.

FEATURES

These are among the features of *Computer-Based Exercises in Retail Management*:

- The exercises are linked to important concepts discussed in *Retail Management: A Strategic Approach*, 6th Edition. Text page references are provided for each exercise on the computer diskette and in this appendix.
- Although each exercise parallels the text, it allows great flexibility in your data input. You are encouraged to manipulate data and compare the results attained under different assumptions. This provides you with "hands-on" experience.
- Each of the 15 exercises is "real-world" based. Significant retail management problems and opportunities are explored. There is at least one exercise corresponding to each of the eight parts in the text.
- The exercises are user-friendly. Directions are self-prompting. Numerous help screens may be called up. All exercises can be accessed from a main menu. You can easily refer to previous screens or skip screens. No knowledge of PCs, computer programming, or Lotus is required. In addition, no graphics board or spreadsheet software is needed. All screens can be printed.
- A "learn by doing" strategy is utilized. You can manipulate store image characteristics, questionnaire responses, markups, shopper travel time, operating expenses, square footage, purchase commitments, store service levels, ad budgets, and other factors—and see their effect on sales, profits, store positioning, trading area saturation, cash flow, and so on.
- The techniques used in the exercises vary widely to maximize student interest and diversify the learning environment. Among the techniques included are store positioning maps, trading-area saturation ratios, cash flow statements, retail accounting techniques, financial statements, open-to-buy reports, tabulation and cross-tabulation charts, spreadsheets, balance sheet statements, and various performance ratios.
- The exercises can be used to reinforce concepts in the text or to expand your knowledge further.
- After you have set up your copy of the exercise diskette, your name will appear at the top of each screen and on any pages you print from the screen.

HOW TO USE THE COMPUTER-BASED EXERCISE SOFTWARE

If you are using a two floppy-disk system, insert the DOS diskette in drive A and turn on the computer. At the "A>" (the A prompt), remove the DOS diskette, insert your *Retail Management Software* diskette, type "CD EXERCISE" (without the quote marks), and press the return key. When "A>\EXERCISE>" (the A exercise directory prompt) shows up on the screen, type "RETAIL" (without the quote marks) and press the return key. The computer will do the rest.

If you are using a computer with a hard drive, turn on the computer and at the "C>" (the C prompt), type "CD EXERCISE" (without the quote marks) and press the return key. When "C>\EXERCISE" (the C exercise directory prompt) next shows up on the screen, type "RETAIL" (without the quote marks) and press the return key. The computer will do the rest.

At this point, you are ready to insert your name, class, and section on the exercise program; once you enter this information, it will appear on every computer screen and printout. At the screen prompts, enter your name, class, and section. The information becomes a permanent part of your exercise software. If you desire, you may now continue on to the exercise menu and do an exercise. After you finish, turn off the computer.

Each subsequent time you want to use the exercise program, turn on the computer and repeat the preceding directions, depending on your computer's configuration. The software program will do the rest and guide you to the main menu.

While using the exercise diskette, you may print any screen for your own reference or for the submission of a class assignment. Turn on the printer (dot-matrix, letter-quality, or laser) connected to the PC you are using. Then, press the [Print Screen] key and the screen displayed on your monitor will automatically be printed—including your name, class, and section.

When using your diskette, all exercises can be accessed from the MAIN MENU screen. To run an exercise, move the up and down arrow keys to the appropriate text part and then press the return key. Entering "Q" (without the quote marks) will enable you to quit the program.

The menu is arranged in the same order as the topics appear in the text and shows pages references, so that you may review concepts before (or while) doing an exercise.

Computer-Based Exercises in Retail Management

	MAIN MENU	Text Page Reference
PART 1:	Store Positioning	42
PART 2:	Planning an Appropriate Retail Strategy Mix	110
PART 3:	Attitudinal Survey	244
PART 4:	Retail Location Analysis	276
PART 5:	Operations Management	372
PART 6:	Financial Merchandise Management	470
PART 7:	Promotional Planning	597
PART 8:	Sales Opportunity Grid	650

Please note: Several parts contain multiple exercises: Part 2—Franchising, The Wheel of Retailing, and Scrambled Merchandising; Part 4—Reilly's Law of Retail Gravitation, Buying Power Index, and Measuring Trading Area Saturation; Part 5—The Strategic Profit Model, Key Business Ratios, and Budgeting and Cash Flow Management; and Part 6—The Retail Method of Accounting and Open-to-Buy.

In the following subsections, each exercise is discussed. For every exercise, we present objectives, a list of the relevant key terms and concepts from the text, an explanation of the exercise, and questions/assignments to be answered or completed.

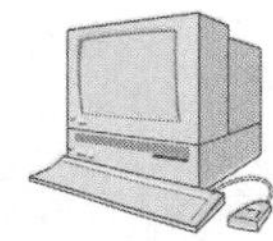

Part 1: Store Positioning (Exercise 1)

Objectives

1. To evaluate the components of a retailer's overall image
2. To show how a store's positioning map may change
3. To analyze the images of different types of retailers
4. To illustrate how consumers' judgments of fashion leadership and price level affect a retailer's image

Key Terms and Concepts

image	**mass market**
positioning	**market segment**
target market	**multiple segments**

Explanation of Exercise

As a retailing consultant to Bloomingdale's, a major department store chain, you have been asked to evaluate its store positioning relative to that of several key competitors.

The store positioning map changes to reflect the ratings assigned to fashion and price emphasis on 10 questions.

The computer screen highlights and places an asterisk next to the fashion or price question to be rated. Up and down arrow keys are used to choose the question to be rated. The default rating on each question is 0. The ratings can range from +2 (Strongly Agree) to −2 (Strongly Disagree). Pressing the right arrow key raises a rating on a specific question, and pressing the left arrow key lowers a rating on a specific question.

The positioning of Bloomingdale's changes its market share and the market share of its competitors. Refer to Table 1 in the exercise to see the impact of positioning changes on market share for Bloomingdale's and its competitors.

The exercise is keyed to pages 42–44 in the text.

Questions/Assignments

1. How does Bloomingdale's positioning relative to competitors change as it becomes more fashion conscious? More price conscious? What is the relevance of these changes for Bloomingdale's? How easy would they be to implement?
2. What is the ideal store positioning map for Bloomingdale's? Why?
3. Abraham & Straus is also a department store chain of Federated Department Stores. Which store positioning strategy for Bloomingdale's maximizes sales at both department store chains?
4. Evaluate the questionnaire used in this exercise. Make recommendations as to how it could be improved.

PART 2: PLANNING AN APPROPRIATE RETAIL STRATEGY MIX (EXERCISES 2–4)

Exercise A: Franchising

Objectives

1. To review the factors that a prospective franchisee considers when choosing which franchised outlet to operate
2. To weigh the relative merits of operating a franchise versus independent ownership of a retail business
3. To consider that different types of franchises have different profit margins and operating costs
4. To determine a franchise's profitability under different sales levels
5. To analyze how costs change with sales revenues

Key Terms and Concepts

independent
franchising
product/trademark franchising
business format franchising
constrained decision making

Explanation of Exercise

As a prospective franchisee, you are considering the purchase of one of several franchised outlets: a fast-food store (F), a shoe store (S), and an ice cream shop (I). After choosing the type of franchise by typing the appropriate letter (F, S, or I), this exercise allows you to vary sales levels and other factors, and determine their effect on performance. Each type of franchise has different default values for each factor.

The arrow keys are used to choose the factor to change. After the chosen factor is highlighted, the screen prompts for an acceptable value:

Factor	Range of Acceptable Values
Sales	$500,000–$3,000,000
Cost of Goods Sold	15%–75%
Salaries	$100,000–$500,000 (includes franchisee)
Royalty Expense	0%–8%
Utilities	$10,000–$300,000
Accounting and Legal Services	$10,000–$100,000
Ongoing Advertising Fee	0%–4%
Loan	$100,000–$1,500,000 (interest is at 9%)
Insurance	$10,000–$200,000
Investment	$50,000–$500,000
Yearly Hours Worked	1,000–3,000

Sales and expenses can be changed in $1,000 increments. The exercise automatically computes gross profit, total operating expenses, net profit before tax, return on investment, and profit per hour. Do not use decimals for per cents or $ and commas in entering dollar values. For example, enter a cost of goods sold of 40 per cent as '40'.

The exercise is keyed to pages 110–113 in the text.

Questions/Assignments

1. Compare the financial characteristics of each type of franchising (fast-food store, shoe store, and ice cream shop) using the default values in this exercise.
2. Compute the profitability of a franchised ice cream shop with the following factor inputs: sales = $700,000, cost of goods sold = 40%, salaries = $150,000, royalty expense = 8% of sales, utilities = $20,000, accounting and legal services = $25,000, ongoing advertising fee = 4% of sales, loan = $300,000, insurance = $20,000, investment = $100,000, and yearly hours worked = 2,000. How would relative profitability change if sales were increased to $850,000? Explain your answer.
3. An independent ice cream shop that has been established for twenty years can be purchased for $450,000 (with one-third down and two-thirds via a loan). This store is similar to the one in question 2 in every regard, except that there are no royalty fee and no advertising fee. Instead of a royalty fee, you would have to pay monthly rent of $4,000. Use the computer program and your own calculations to determine the profitability of buying the independent store. Contrast the results with the franchised outlet in question 2. Which store would you select? Why?
4. In deciding what retail business to purchase, what other factors would you consider besides those noted in the exercise? Explain your answer.

Exercise B: The Wheel of Retailing

Objectives

1. To determine an appropriate competitive strategy for each stage of the wheel of retailing: discounting, trading up, vulnerability, and maturity
2. To study the impact of markups, store facilities, store service levels, and other annual fixed operating expenses on sales and profit in each stage of the wheel of retailing
3. To evaluate appropriate differences in strategy in each stage of the wheel of retailing

Key Terms and Concepts

wheel of retailing	**medium strategy**
low-end strategy	**high-end strategy**

Explanation of Exercise

As a store manager, you know the optimal retail strategy mix varies in each wheel-of-retailing stage: discounting, trading up, vulnerability, and maturity. This exercise lets you vary gross profit margins (markups), facility costs, and service level costs and learn their effect on annual sales and net profit in each wheel-of-retailing stage. Other fixed costs cannot be changed.

The arrow keys are used to choose the factor to change. After the chosen factor is highlighted, the screen prompts for an acceptable value. Here is the range of acceptable values and the optimal values for each variable:

	Range of Acceptable Values		
Stage of the Wheel of Retailing	Markup (%)	Store Facility Costs ($000)	Store Service Costs ($000)
(1) Discounting	20–35	200–300	200–300
(2) Trading Up	30–40	350–500	350–600
(3) Vulnerability	35–45	400–700	500–700
(4) Maturity	40–60	500–1000	500–800

Markups can be changed in 1 per cent increments; store facility costs and store service costs can be changed in $1,000 increments. Other annual fixed operating expenses are $200,000 at each wheel-of-retailing stage. Do not use decimals for markups or $ and commas in entering dollar values. For example, enter a markup of 24 per cent as '24'. Because all data are in $000, enter $230,000 as '230'. In the exercise, Profit = Annual sales × Markup − (Store facility costs + Store service costs + Other annual fixed operating expenses).

The exercise is keyed to pages 135–136 in the text.

Questions/Assignments

1. At what markup, store facility costs, and store service cost does a firm maximize its profitability in each stage of the wheel of retailing? Why?
2. What factors explain the differences between an optimal strategy in the trading up and maturity stages of the wheel? Explain your answer.
3. Evaluate the wheel-of-retailing theory on a conceptual level.
4. Is this exercise realistic?

Exercise C: Scrambled Merchandising

Objectives

1. To determine an appropriate strategy for an independent pharmacy during these stages of scrambled merchandising: original business, supermarket scrambles, and pharmacy scrambles
2. To study the impact of changing marketing budget levels on the pharmacy's performance during each stage of scrambled merchandising
3. To evaluate the appropriate differences in strategy in each scrambled merchandising stage

Key Terms and Concepts

scrambled merchandising	**contagious nature of scrambled merchandising**

Explanation of Exercise

As manager of a pharmacy, you can vary the marketing budget levels of drug and nondrug products in your store in three different scrambled merchandising stages: original business, supermarket scrambles, and pharmacy scrambles. The optimal strategy to maximize profits differs in each stage.

The computer screen highlights the marketing budget to be adjusted. The arrow keys are used to select the marketing budget to be changed. The marketing budget for drugs can be between \$0 and \$100,000 (in \$1,000 increments); the marketing budget for nondrugs can vary between \$0 and \$100,000 (in \$1,000 increments). Do not use \$ and commas in entering dollar values. Because all data are in \$000, enter \$40,000 as '40'.

The markup for drugs is fixed at 35 per cent; the markup for nondrugs is fixed at 48 per cent. The drug department is charged with \$35,000 for general overhead; the nondrug department is charged with \$18,000 for general overhead:

Net profit for drugs = (Total drug sales × .35) − (\$35,000 + Marketing budget for drugs)

Net profit for nondrugs = (Total nondrug sales × .48) − (\$18,000 + Marketing budget for nondrugs)

The exercise is keyed to pages 136–137 in the text.

Questions/Assignments

1. Describe the contagious nature of scrambled merchandising using the Cureall Pharmacy example and data.
2. What is the proper role of marketing expenditures for Cureall Pharmacy at the original business, supermarket scrambles, and pharmacy scrambles stage of scrambled merchandising?
3. At what marketing expenditure levels does Cureall Pharmacy maximize its profits for drugs and nondrugs in each stage of scrambled merchandising? Explain your answer.
4. Are the optimal marketing expenditure values for each scrambled merchandising stage for nondrugs realistic? Why or why not?

PART 3: ATTITUDINAL SURVEY (EXERCISE 5)

Objectives

1. To illustrate the use of marketing research via a consumer attitude study on customer service of a department store near to your college
2. To encourage you to actually collect attitude data
3. To engage in tabulation and cross-tabulation of retailing survey data
4. To develop recommendations based on attitude survey data

Key Terms and Concepts

survey
nondisguised survey
disguised survey

Explanation of Exercise

As research director of a major department store chain, you have been asked to conduct a survey of consumer attitudes towards your firm. This exercise lets you enter data on customer service based on interviews; the computer program generates overall respondent percentage tabulations, an overall average rating by question, and cross-tabulations (by percentages and averages) for each demographic group.

A blank copy of the survey form can be printed by pressing "P" (without the quote marks) when asked. Because this exercise can store and analyze data on up to 40 respondents at a time, you can hand out surveys to respondents (by printing one copy and then photocopying additional ones) and enter the answers in the computer all at once, or you can have respondents answer directly on the computer screen. You can enter the data at different times or at one time. Use the arrow keys to select Yes for a new survey or No for continuation of an old survey. If you choose Yes, all data from past surveys will be erased.

The survey consists of 10 attitude and 4 demographic questions. Up and down arrow keys are used to choose the question to be rated, which is then highlighted. Ratings on attitude questions can range from +2 (Strongly Agree) to −2 (Strongly Disagree); the default rating is 0. Pressing the right arrow key raises a rating on a specific question; pressing the left arrow key lowers the rating. After entering a set of responses (ending with question 14), pressing "S" will save the responses. After saving data, you can go directly to question 1 by pressing "Y" to the screen query relating to shortcuts; otherwise, you will have to use the page up key to go back to question 1. As just noted, up to 40 surveys can be stored on the disk, which cannot be write-protected when implementing the save function for this exercise.

The exercise is keyed to pages 244–246 in the text.

Questions/Assignments

1. Collect data from respondents relating to their attitudes toward a nearby major department store. Evaluate the survey results using both tabulation and cross-tabulation data (by major demographic groups).
2. Combine your results with those of three other classmates and perform an overall analysis of the store's customer service strategy. How do the results compare with those you gathered individually? Why?
3. Evaluate the questionnaire form.
4. Develop a similar attitudinal questionnaire using a semantic differential. Contrast the questionnaire to the one in this exercise.

PART 4: RETAIL LOCATION ANALYSIS (EXERCISES 6–8)

Exercise A: Reilly's Law of Retail Gravitation

Objectives

1. To have you better understand the formula for Reilly's law
2. To demonstrate the impact of both the mileage between two cities (towns) and the population of each city on trading-area size
3. To discuss the limitations of Reilly's law

Key Terms and Concepts

Reilly's law of retail gravitation | **point of indifference**

Explanation of Exercise

As real-estate director for a specialty store chain, you wish to use Reilly's law to compute the point of indifference (based on the distance in miles between cities A and B, the population of city A, and the population of city B). The computer program automatically computes and graphs the point of indifference on the basis of the data supplied. The calculation is shown on the computer screen.

Up and down arrow keys are used to choose the value to change, and this value is highlighted. New amounts within the acceptable range can then be entered. You can change the distance in miles between cities A and B from 1 to 30 miles, the population of city A from 10,000 to 100,000, and the population of city B from 10,000 to 100,000 in increments of 1 mile and 1 unit of population. Do not use commas in entering population data. For example, a population of 10,001 for city A is entered as '10001'.

The exercise is keyed to pages 276–277 in the text.

Questions/Assignments

1. What are the major assumptions of Reilly's law? How realistic are these assumptions? Explain your answer.
2. What type of retail areas best fit the assumptions of Reilly's law? Why?
3. Compute the points of indifference for four different population sizes and four different distances between cities A and B. Discuss how the answers differ.
4. How could a small city overcome its size and increase its trading area? Is this possibility covered by Reilly's law? Explain your answer.

Exercise B: Buying Power Index

Objectives

1. To consider the relevance of the buying power index for retailers
2. To better understand the buying power index formula
3. To demonstrate the relative impact of an area's per cent of U.S. effective buying income, per cent of U.S. retail sales, and per cent of U.S. population on its overall buying power index

Key Terms and Concepts

Survey of Buying Power
effective buying income
buying power index (BPI)

Explanation of Exercise

As the prospective owner of a new-car dealership, you want to analyze an area's suitability for this business. This exercise allows you to vary an area's per cent of overall U.S. effective buying income, U.S. retail sales, and U.S. population. The computer program calculates the area's buying power index; this is then shown on the computer screen.

Up and down arrow keys are used to choose the value to change, which is highlighted on the screen. New amounts within acceptable ranges can then be entered. You can vary Area A's per cent of U.S. effective buying income from 0.01 to 0.40, Area A's per cent of U.S. retail sales from 0.01 to 0.40, and Area A's per cent of U.S. population from 0.01 to 0.40 in increments of 0.01.

All data in this exercise are recorded in per cent. Do not enter new amounts in decimal form; for example, enter 0.35 per cent as '35'.

The exercise is keyed to pages 286–288 in the text.

Questions/Assignments

1. What is the merit of the buying power index for retailers? What is the major advantage of using a weighted buying power index instead of examining a single factor in assessing the desirability of an area?
2. Compute the buying power index for Area A using four different sets of values for effective buying income, retail sales, and population size. Explain how the answers differ.
3. What is the most important factor in computing the buying power index? Why?
4. Relate the buying-power index concept to (a) the concept of economic base and (b) the concept of trading-area saturation.

Exercise C: Measuring Trading-Area Saturation

Objectives

1. To consider the relevance of retail saturation measures for retailers
2. To have you better understand the computation of a trading area's saturation
3. To look at the differences among understored, saturated, and overstored retail areas

Key Terms and Concepts

understored area **saturated area**
overstored area

Explanation of Exercise

As a retailing consultant, you have been asked to assess the degree of retail saturation in a specific geographic area on the basis of multiple measures of retail saturation. In this exercise, you can vary an area's population, total supermarket sales, and total number of supermarkets. The computer program then automatically computes three measures of retail saturation: average persons per supermarket, average sales per supermarket, and average sales per capita and the area's degree of saturation. Calculations assume that the average supermarket is 30,000 square feet and has 60 employees.

Up and down arrow keys are used to select the value to change, which is highlighted. New amounts within acceptable ranges can then be entered for the highlighted factors. You can vary the total population in an area from 50,000 to 200,000; total supermarket sales (in 000) from \$100,000 to \$400,000; and the total number of supermarkets from 10 to 40. The total population, total supermarket sales, and total number of supermarkets can each be changed in increments of 1 unit.

Do not use \$ and commas when entering values. For example, enter \$120,000 as '120000'.

The exercise is keyed to pages 289–292 in the text.

Questions/Assignments

1. Why is trading-area saturation a useful concept for supermarkets?
2. How could you use the three measures of trading-area saturation in this exercise to determine whether an area is understored, overstored, or saturated?
3. Compute the trading-area saturation measures for three different sets of data for total population, total supermarket sales, and total number of supermarkets. Explain how the answers differ.
4. Should a prospective supermarket use trading-area saturation data differently than an existing one? Explain your answer.

PART 5: OPERATIONS MANAGEMENT (EXERCISES 9–11)

Exercise A: The Strategic Profit Model

Objectives

1. To study the components of the strategic profit model: profit margin, asset turnover, and financial leverage
2. To demonstrate how varying total assets and total liabilities affects net worth, net sales, and net profit
3. To compute profit margin, asset turnover, financial leverage, and the strategic profit model from total assets, total liabilities, net worth, net sales, and net profit figures
4. To classify profit margin, asset turnover, financial leverage, and strategic profit model results from poor to excellent

Key Terms and Concepts

strategic profit model	**asset turnover**
profit margin	**financial leverage**

Explanation of Exercise

As a retailing consultant, you use the strategic profit model to evaluate ongoing retailers for possible purchase by major conglomerates. This exercise lets you vary total assets and liabilities; the computer program automatically computes net worth (total assets − total liabilities), net sales, and net profit (from a pre-set computer simulation). The computer program then evaluates these ratios: profit margin (PM), asset turnover (AT), financial leverage (FL), and the strategic profit model (SPM) from poor to excellent.

The up and down arrow keys are used to choose the value to change (total assets or total liabilities), which is then highlighted. The right and left arrow keys are used to change the level of total assets and total liabilities; the right arrow key raises the value by $50,000, and the left arrow key lowers the value by $50,000. You can vary total assets from $50,000 to $450,000 and total liabilities from $50,000 to $450,000 in $50,000 intervals.

The exercise is keyed to pages 373–374 in the text.

Questions/Assignments

1. Determine the cutoff points for excellent, good, fair, and poor performance for each ratio: profit margin, asset turnover, financial leverage, and the strategic profit model. Explain the answers.
2. Present several ways in which a firm could improve its performance on the asset turnover and profit margin components of the strategic profit model.
3. How could a retailer increase its financial leverage ratio?
4. Describe the pros and cons of improving a firm's return on net worth through increased financial leverage.

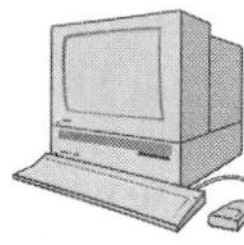

Exercise B: Key Business Ratios

Objectives

1. To study five key business ratios: quick ratio, current ratio, collection period, assets to net sales ratio, and accounts payable to net sales
2. To demonstrate how changes in sales, assets, and liabilities affect each key business ratio
3. To contrast a profit-and-loss statement and a balance sheet

Key Terms and Concepts

quick ratio	**collection period**
current ratio	**assets to net sales**
	accounts payable to sales

Explanation of Exercise

As the owner of Donna's Gift Shop, you are very concerned about your firm's financial position. Net sales and selected items from the firm's balance sheet are presented in this exercise. The decisions you make as to the sales levels and the amount of selected assets and liabilities affect the firm's financial position. Some values in this exercise (total current assets, total current liabilities, total liabilities, and net worth) are calculated by the computer.

The up and down arrow keys are used to choose the value to change, which is then highlighted. New amounts within acceptable ranges can be entered for each highlighted factor. You can vary net sales from $100,000 to $300,000, cash on hand from

$10,000 to $20,000, inventory from $15,000 to $40,000, accounts receivable from $0 to $15,000, payroll expense payable from $0 to $15,000, taxes payable from $0 to $15,000, accounts payable from $5,000 to $40,000, and short-term loans from $0 to $20,000. Each item can be altered in increments of $1,000.

Do not use $ and commas when entering values. For example, enter $150,000 as '150000'.

The exercise is keyed to pages 374–376 in the text.

Questions/Assignments

1. Determine the key business ratios under three different scenarios regarding sales, accounts receivable, and payroll expenses payable. All other inputs should be the same for the three scenarios. Explain your assumptions and the resulting ratios.
2. What are the pros and cons of a high quick ratio and a high current ratio?
3. How does a balance sheet differ from a profit-and-loss statement?
4. Are the assumptions used in this exercise realistic? Explain your answer.

Exercise C: Budgeting and Cash Flow Management

Objectives

1. To study the amount and timing of revenues received versus the amount and timing of expenditures during a specific time period
2. To show the impact of changes in monthly sales on cash flow
3. To demonstrate the difference between a profit-and-loss statement and cash flow analysis

Key Terms and Concepts

budgeting	**incremental budgeting**
zero-based budgeting	**cash flow**

Explanation of Exercise

As the operations manager for an independent retailer, you are quite involved with budgeting and cash flow management. Monthly profit-and-loss and cash flow statements for the months of January, February, and March are presented in this exercise. The decisions you make as to the sales levels in each of these months affect the firm's cash flow; all other values in this exercise are calculated by the computer.

Left and right arrow keys are used to choose the month whose sales are to be changed, which is highlighted. Monthly sales go from $25,000 to $160,000. Sales can be entered in $1,000 increments by typing an amount and pressing the return key. Do not use $ and commas in dollar values. Because all data are in $000, enter $51,000 as '51'.

These assumptions are made in cash flow projections: (1) The owner gets a $10,000 bonus in January. (2) The cost of goods sold is 53 per cent of sales. (3) Because some sales are on credit, one-half of net sales in a month are from the prior month's transactions and one-half are from transactions in the current month. (4) December sales were $165,000. (5) The cost of goods sold is paid in the following month. (6) Operating expenses (such as salaries and rent) are paid in the month incurred. (7) Interest on loans is due the month following the loan. (8) Interest is paid at the annual rate of 11 per cent when cumulative cash flow is negative. Interest is earned at an annual rate of 5 per cent when cumulative cash flow is positive.

The exercise is keyed to pages 376–383 in the text.

Questions/Assignments

1. Differentiate between a profit and loss statement and cash flow analysis. Explain what happens to profits and cash flow when monthly sales are $50,000, $100,000, and $150,000.

2. At a sales level of $75,000 for each month, compare the cash flows for January, February, and March. Discuss why the differences occur.
3. How can the retailer in this exercise improve its cash flow? Be specific.
4. Are the assumptions used in this exercise realistic? Explain your answer.

PART 6: FINANCIAL MERCHANDISE MANAGEMENT (EXERCISES 12–13)

Exercise A: The Retail Method of Accounting

Objectives

1. To illustrate the retail method of accounting and the cost complement
2. To show the impact of changes in net purchases (at cost), additional markup, transportation charges, sales, markdowns, employee discounts, and stock shortages on the computation of the ending retail book value of inventory
3. To demonstrate how the adjusted book value of inventory is determined
4. To consider the complexity of the retail method

Key Terms and Concepts

retail method of accounting	**stock shortages and overages**
cost complement	**adjusted book value of inventory**
deductions from retail value	**ending inventory value**

Explanation of Exercise

As a retail buyer for Quality Furniture store, you recognize that calculating the cost complement and ending inventory value are important aspects of the retail method of accounting. Overall, there are three steps in this process: (1) calculating the cost complement; (2) calculating deductions from the retail value; and (3) converting retail value to cost. This exercise allows you to vary net purchases (at cost), additional markup, transportation charges, sales, markdowns, employee discounts, and stock shortages and to see their effect on ending inventory value. The computer program automatically computes the cost complement and inventory value.

The up and down arrow keys are used to choose the value to change, which is highlighted. New amounts can then be entered. You can vary net purchases (at cost) from $25,000 to $75,000; additional markup from $0 to $7,500; transportation charges from $500 to $4,000; quarterly sales from $40,000 to $130,000; markdowns from $1,000 to $6,000; employee discounts from $1,000 to $3,000; and stock shortages from 1 per cent to 5 per cent of sales. These levels can be chosen in $1,000 increments; stock shortages must be in 1 per cent increments. Do not use $ and commas in entering dollar values or decimals for markup data. For example, enter $50,000 as '50000' and 3 per cent as '3'.

The exercise is keyed to pages 470–474 in the text.

Questions/Assignments

1. Find the cost complement for four different sets of data for beginning inventory (at cost and at retail), net purchases (at cost and at retail), additional markup, and transportation charges. Explain your answers.
2. Determine the ending book value at cost for four different sets of data for net purchases, additional markup, transportation charges, sales, markdowns, employee discounts, and stock shortages. Why do your answers differ?
3. Explain how stock shortages are computed using the retail method of accounting. What are the pros and cons of this procedure?
4. What is the reason for calculating the ending book value at cost in the computation of the open-to-buy figure?

Exercise B: Open-to-Buy

Objectives

1. To demonstrate how open-to-buy is computed
2. To show the effects of planned sales, planned reductions, planned end-of-month stock, and planned beginning-of-month stock on planned purchases
3. To study the difference between planned purchases and open-to-buy at retail
4. To illustrate the conversion of open-to-buy at retail to open-to-buy at cost using the cost complement

Key Terms and Concepts

planned purchases at retail	**open-to-buy at retail**
planned purchases at cost	**open-to-buy at cost**

Explanation of Exercise

As a retail buyer for an apparel store chain, you need to continuously update information on planned sales, planned reductions, planned end-of-month stock, and purchase commitments to determine your open-to-buy position. This computer program uses a cost complement of .65 in converting open-to-buy at retail to open-to-buy at cost.

The value to be changed is highlighted by moving the arrow keys. The new amount can then be entered. Acceptable inputs are planned sales, from $15,000 to $50,000; planned reductions, from $0 to $5,500; planned end-of-month stock, from $12,000 to $55,000; and purchase commitments, from $7,000 to $22,000. The computer will warn you if purchase commitments exceed your planned purchases. Each input can be entered in increments of $1. Do not use $ and commas in entering dollar values. For example, enter $22,500 as '22500'.

The exercise is keyed to pages 483–484 in the text.

Questions/Assignments

1. Determine the open-to-buy at cost for four different sets of data for planned sales, planned reductions, end-of-month stock, and purchase commitments. Discuss the differences in your answers. What is the significance of each answer for a store merchandise manager?
2. What are the roles of planned end-of-month stock and beginning-of-month stock in determining open-to-buy levels? Explain your answer.
3. What are the pros and cons of adhering strictly to open-to-buy amounts when making purchases?
4. What would happen to the open-to-buy at cost figure in this exercise if the cost complement was changed to .75? To .45?

PART 7: PROMOTIONAL PLANNING (EXERCISE 14)

Objectives

1. To demonstrate how quarterly promotional budgets for daily newspapers, sales promotion, and personal selling may be used
2. To show the impact of promotional expenditures in a daily newspaper, sales promotion, and personal selling on quarterly sales and quarterly profits
3. To consider the need for a promotion plan that represents a balanced promotional mix, reflects seasonality, has minimum expenditures in each of various media, and avoids overly drastic shifts in expenditures

Key Terms and Concepts

retail promotion
advertising
sales promotion
personal selling
all-you-can-afford method
incremental method
competitive parity method
percentage-of-sales technique
objective-and-task method

Explanation of Exercise

As the retail promotion director, you have been asked to plan your firm's quarterly expenditures on a daily newspaper, sales promotion, and personal selling during four periods. Quarterly and total sales are calculated by a computer simulation. Profit calculations are based on a 30 per cent gross margin and fixed costs of $300,000 in quarters 1 and 3, $500,000 in quarter 2, and $600,000 in quarter 4:

Quarter 1 profit = (Quarter 1 sales × .30) – ($300,000 + Promotional costs)
Quarter 2 profit = (Quarter 2 sales × .30) – ($500,000 + Promotional costs)
Quarter 3 profit = (Quarter 3 sales × .30) – ($300,000 + Promotional costs)
Quarter 4 profit = (Quarter 4 sales × .30) – ($600,000 + Promotional costs)

These are some of the important characteristics for each form of promotion used by the firm:

1. Daily Newspaper—Net cost (after cooperative allowances) is $1,000 per page; circulation is 100,000; and waste circulation is 40 per cent of total circulation.
2. Sales Promotion—Average cost per event is $10,000; expenses also include in-store materials, the cost of photography, and press releases.
3. Personal Selling—Includes those selling costs above the minimum level; full-time personnel salaries average $15,000; part-time personnel costs average $6.00 per hour.

The media expenditure value to be changed is chosen by using the arrow keys. The value is then highlighted. Acceptable amounts for the media are as follows: daily newspapers, from $0 to $100,000 per quarter; sales promotion, from $0 to $150,000 per quarter; and personal selling, from $0 to $200,000 per quarter. Amounts can be chosen in increments of $1,000. The maximum yearly budget for all media cannot exceed $300,000. Do not use $ and commas in entering dollar values. Because all data are in $000, enter $40,000 as '40'.

Vary your expenditures by promotion type and time, and see the impact on quarterly sales and profits.

The exercise is keyed to pages 597–605 in the text.

Questions/Assignments

1. What is the ideal relationship among daily newspapers, sales promotion, and personal selling for a full-service specialty store? A full-line discount store? Why?
2. At what promotional expenditure levels for the daily newspaper, sales promotion, and personal selling does the firm maximize yearly profits in this exercise? Explain your answer.
3. Why aren't profits maximized at the $300,000 promotional expenditure level? What does this signify for retailers in general?
4. Is this exercise realistic? Explain your answer.

PART 8: SALES OPPORTUNITY GRID (EXERCISE 15)

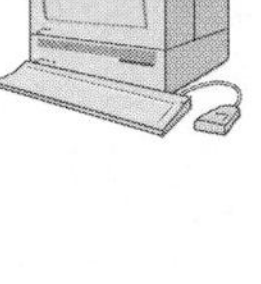

Objectives

1. To illustrate the use of a sales opportunity grid
2. To demonstrate how retail price, floor space used, operating costs, and total yearly sales estimates in units affect gross and net profit estimates at various time periods
3. To compare the shelf-space allocation of two competing brands using a variety of criteria

Key Terms and Concepts

opportunity analysis **sales opportunity grid**

Explanation of Exercise

As store manager for an independent supermarket, you use the sales opportunity grid to evaluate the profitability of both established and new brands. In this exercise, you can vary the price, floor space used, operating costs, and yearly sales estimates for two brands of tuna fish (one established, the other new). The computer program presents the sales opportunity grid and calculates relevant data for the first month, the first six months, and the first year.

The arrow keys are used to pick the value to change, which is highlighted. New amounts can then be entered. Acceptable amounts are: retail price, from $1.00 to $1.60; floor space used, from 5 to 12 square feet; operating costs, from $.05 to $.15 per unit; and total yearly sales estimates in units, from 1,800 to 3,600 for each brand of tuna fish. The amounts can be entered in these increments for each brand: retail price—1 cent, floor space—1 square foot, operating costs—1 cent, and yearly sales estimate—1 unit.

Enter retail price and operating costs as decimals; do not use $. Do not use commas in entering yearly sales estimates. For example, enter a retail price of $1.07 as '1.07', an operating cost of $.10 as '.10', and an annual unit sales estimate of 2,500 as '2500'.

The exercise is keyed to pages 650–654 in the text.

Questions/Assignments

1. Compute net profit during the first year for brands A and B using four sets of data for retail price, floor space needed, operating costs, and annual sales estimates (in units). Explain the differences in your answers.
2. Which brand of tuna fish would offer the best long-run profit potential for the supermarket? Why? What other factors should be considered?
3. Under what conditions would you allocate space to the brand with a smaller net profit estimate for the first year? Why?
4. What is the difference between a sales opportunity grid and a sales-productivity ratio that allocates store space on the basis of sales per square foot?

SUPERCO: A Retail Simulation

SUPERCO is a simulation that depicts a supermarket retailer with two departments: food and nonfood. Through *SUPERCO,* you can make semimonthly decisions with regard to the number of advertising pages, the number of sale items, the quantity of goods purchased, and the markup for each department. In addition, you must consider the number of centralized cashiers needed to serve the two departments. The decisions made affect the sales revenues, advertising expenses, general overhead expenses, and net profit before tax.

After each period's decisions are entered, the simulation program generates a profit-and-loss statement that breaks out sales, expenses, and profitability by department. You can also access charts depicting the store's performance—a strategy comparison graph that contrasts the current period's sales and profit with the previous period's (after the second period). One year equals 24 periods.

FEATURES

These are among the features of *SUPERCO*:

- It is an especially easy-to-use retail simulation. You should be able to learn the decision rules in a relatively short time.
- "Learning by doing" is encouraged.
- You can better develop your skills in running a retail business by being sensitive to seasonality, coordinating ordering and sales, and analyzing financial statements and graphs.
- It can be used as either a simulation or as a series of exercises. As a simulation, students or student teams would compete against each other for a defined time. As an exercise, you would be asked to determine relationships among retail inputs such as markups, the number of sale items, sales, and profits.
- After you have entered your store name and class section, *SUPERCO* will automatically list this information on each screen. All screens can be printed by pressing the [Print Screen] key.

HOW TO USE THE SUPERCO SOFTWARE

If you are using a two floppy-disk system, insert the DOS diskette in drive A and turn on the computer. At the "A>" (the A prompt), remove the DOS diskette, insert your *Retail Management Software* diskette, type "CD SUPERCO" (without the quote marks), and press the return key. When "A>\SUPERCO" (the A SUPERCO directory prompt) next shows up on the screen, type "SUPER" (without the quote marks) and press the return key. The computer will do the rest.

If you are using a computer with a hard drive, turn on the computer and at the "C>" (the C prompt), type "CD SUPERCO" (without the quote marks) and press the return key. When "C>\SUPERCO" (the C SUPERCO directory prompt) next shows up on the screen, type "SUPER" (without the quote marks) and press the return key. The computer will do the rest.

Each subsequent time you want to use the program, turn on the computer and repeat the preceding directions, depending on your computer's configuration.

For class submission purposes, be sure that you enter your own name (or your team name) when prompted by the simulation. Your name will then appear on each page that you hand in to your professor.

These are the basic directions for the use of *SUPERCO*:

(1) The initial *SUPERCO* screen will automatically blend into a copyright notice. The program will then ask you for your name and class section. Enter your last name first. If your team has chosen a company name, this should be entered instead of any individual person's name. Next, enter your course and section number. You can make corrections by answering [N] and then pressing [Enter] to the question: "Is this correct?" If the information is correct, answer [Y] to that question and press [Enter]. The Data Manipulation Operation screen now appears.

(2) Once you move into the *SUPERCO* simulation from the name entry screen, context-sensitive help messages can be accessed by pressing the [F1] key.

Some messages occupy multiple screens. For those messages, you will be instructed to use the [PgDn] or [PgUp] keys to access additional information. To exit a help screen, press any key. When you press the [F1] key twice, a Master Help screen menu is available. It shows all of the topics for which information is provided. Arrow keys (either up, down, right, or left) may be used to select any topic. Pressing the [Enter] key will then access a chosen help screen. After you read the help screen(s), pressing any key will return you to the previous screen with which you were working.

(3) On the Data Manipulation Screen, you can change any or all of these variables: advertising pages, the number of sale items, the quantity of goods purchased, the number of cashiers, and markup. The acceptable limits for each of these variables are:

	Food	Nonfood
Advertising Pages	0– 8	0– 8
Number of Sale Items	0– 40	0– 40
Purchased Goods (in $000s)	10–200	10–200
Markup (%)	10– 80	10– 80

The limit for the number of cashiers is 4–14; this is a centralized decision as the same cashiers and support people ring up both food and nonfood products.

Although the default values are the same for both foods and nonfoods, each department responds differently to changes in the retail mix. In entering your decisions, bear in mind that:

(a) The cost of an ad page is $350 per period for the food department and $350 per period for the nonfood department. You cannot place fractional page ads (such as one-half page).

(b) Sale items increase volume but negatively affect your profit margins.

(c) The purchased goods quantity in this exercise is listed in thousands ($000) of dollars. Each student or team begins the first period with $150,000 in food and $65,000 in nonfood items in starting inventory. You can order between $10,000 and $200,000 per period for food and between $10,000 and $200,000 per period for nonfoods. Your wholesaler apportions orders to reflect sales by SKU.

(d) You must plan to have ample quantities of goods on hand. Goods must be purchased one period in advance of their sale. A stockout will reduce your sales in the affected period. However, overordering will increase your general overhead costs and reduce your inventory turnover. The inventory turnover will be affected by your retail strategy. Note: You do not make decision entries on the Data Manipulation Screen for the starting inventory; it is automatically adjusted by the computer program.

(e) Inventory is calculated on a cost basis. Ending inventory for each department at cost equals the department's beginning inventory (at cost) + the department's purchases for the period (at cost) − the department's cost of goods sold for the period. Note: Purchase amounts only appear on the Data Manipulation Operation screen.

(f) Inventory carrying costs (for interest, storage, insurance, and spoilage) are 4.5 per cent of the food department's beginning inventory value per period and 3.0 per cent of the nonfood department's beginning inventory value. For example, the inventory carrying costs for the first period equal $150,000 × .045 = $6,750 for food and $65,000 × .03 = $1,950 for nonfood items. These costs are added to general overhead costs.

(g) General overhead costs are $12,000 per period (excluding inventory carrying costs). Two-thirds of the general overhead costs ($8,000) are charged to the food department during each period; one-third ($4,000) are charged to the nonfood department. *Total* general overhead costs also reflect the actual inventory carrying costs noted in (f) for each department. Thus, the total overhead costs for the first period, at the default values, are $14,750 ($8,000 + $6,750) for the food department and $5,950 ($4,000 + $1,950) for the nonfood department.

(h) Increases in advertising expenditures and inventory levels will raise sales levels, but they involve higher costs. Beyond certain levels, increases in advertising and inventory will have little effect on sales.

(i) The costs for cashiers and support persons are $750 per person for each period. Two-thirds of these costs are charged to the food department and one-third are charged to the nonfood department. The quantity of personnel must be sufficient to handle the number of customers expected.

(j) The supermarket business is extremely seasonal. Seasonality also affects each department differently. You will need to carefully study the seasonality among foods and nonfoods to insure that your performance will be acceptable.

(4) When enacting changes in retailing-mix values, simply move the cursor (by using the arrow keys), highlight the variable you want to change, select a new value (within the acceptable range), and press the [Enter] key. Repeat this procedure for each retailing-mix variable that is to be revised for both the food and nonfood departments. An entry made in error can be amended by simply retyping your decision according to the instructions just noted. If you realize your mistake before the [Enter] key is pressed, the incorrect entry can be erased by using either the [backspace] or [left arrow] key.

(5) After you have entered all of your retail firm's strategy modifications onto the Data Manipulation Operation screen, press "R" to operate the simulation program and generate your projected results. A Profit & Loss Summary screen will automatically appear. This screen breaks out sales, costs (cost of goods sold, advertising, cashier cost, and general overhead expense) and financial performance (profitability, inventory turnover, and sales per cashier) for each department for the current and previous periods. Inventory turnover is computed as (Cost of goods sold × 24)/[(Beginning inventory + Ending inventory)/2]. Multiplying the cost of goods sold by 24 annualizes this figure.

(6) Pressing any key (the first time that you run the simulation in any period) will move the program to the next screen, which depicts the Year-to-Date Profit & Loss Summary Screen. Years 1 and 2 are shown (with Year 1 on the left).

(7) After the first period is saved, a Strategy Comparison Screen will appear. This graph contrasts sales and profits with the previous period.

(8) Pressing any key will return you to the Data Manipulation Operation screen. That screen will show the prior entries for your firm.

(9) To quit the program and/or reset/save values, type "Q" when the Data Manipulation Operation screen appears. A Quit with Options screen will appear automatically:

(a) If you are sharing the program disk with other students or teams, press "R" every time you want to exit the program. This will erase your team name and the values you have entered. In this way, no one else can see your decisions. After pressing "R", you will be asked to confirm your decision by pressing "Y".

(b) If you have the exclusive use of a student program disk throughout the semester, press "S" every time you want to exit the program. This command will permanently save your decisions, which will automatically appear when you reboot the program.

(c) Should you want to continue the simulation after resetting or saving values, type "C".

(d) You can quit the simulation and return to DOS by pressing "Q". Once you exit the program, reboot the computer by simultaneously pressing the [Ctrl], [Alt], and [Del] keys—or turn the computer off.

(10) Any screen of *SUPERCO* can be printed by pressing the [Print Screen] key when the screen is viewed on your monitor.

A SPECIFIC SUPERCO EXERCISE

In this section, we provide a specific *SUPERCO* exercise so that you may learn more about this software and apply several of the retailing concepts that you have been studying.

For questions 1 and 2, use these values for advertising pages, number of sale items, and markup:

	Food	Nonfood
Advertising Pages	4	4
Number of Sale Items	10	10
Markup (%)	20	50

Set the number of cashiers and support personnel at 6; and set purchased goods at $200 (000) to help prevent a stockout. After running the simulation for each period, be sure to quit (by pressing "Q"), save your results (by pressing "S"), and continue the simulation (by pressing "C"). Make sure that you have saved your results properly by verifying that the period has changed.

For questions 3 to 6, systematically change one variable at a time (such as markup) and enter your decisions for at least 12 semimonthly periods. Be sure that you ultimately manipulate each variable in this way.

Answer these questions about your market and your store:

1. Describe the seasonality of the market for foods. Be sure to Quit (by pressing "Q"), save your results (by pressing "S"), and continue the simulation (by pressing "C"). Make sure that you have saved your results properly by verifying that the semimonthly period has advanced.
2. Describe the seasonality of the market for nonfoods. Be sure to Quit (by pressing "Q"), save your results (by pressing "S"), and continue the simulation (by pressing "C"). Make sure that you have saved your results properly by verifying that the semimonthly period has advanced.
3. Which department is the most price sensitive? Explain your answer.
4. How does the number of sale items during a semimonthly period affect the period's sales revenues?
5. Explain how the number of cashiers affects sales in each department.
6. What is the optimal number of cashiers? Explain your answer.

Appliance Data Base: A Customer and Inventory Management Data Base

Appliance Data Base is a complied data-base management program that has been applied to an appliance service business. Through *Appliance Data Base*, you can create and maintain both an up-to-date inventory system and a customer data base.

The inventory management program allows you to develop and use a data base to keep track of a firm's inventory-on-hand without having to do a physical count. This application also signals you when a particular item falls below a target level. The customer data base enables you to generate a mailing list, track the frequency of patronage by customers, keep a record of service calls, and monitor which customers have had problems in settling their accounts. Both data-base programs let you print written reports that enable you to better manage the appliance service business.

FEATURES

These are among the features of *Appliance Data Base*:

- It is especially easy to use. The program generates on-screen prompts. Little knowledge of computers and no knowledge of data-base programs is required to run these applications.
- You can better develop your skills in running a retail business through being sensitive to the uses of properly organized information and reports.
- It can be used as either an exercise in which students enter and interpret information and/or as an exercise wherein students evaluate the usefulness of the program for an appliance service business.
- After you have entered your name and class section, *Appliance Data Base* will automatically list your name and class section on each screen. All screens in *Appliance Data Base* can be printed by pressing the [Print Screen] key.

HOW TO USE APPLIANCE DATA-BASE SOFTWARE

If you are using a two floppy-disk system, insert the DOS diskette in drive A and turn on the computer. At the "A>" (the A prompt), remove the DOS diskette, insert your *Retail Management Software* diskette, type "CD APPLDATA" without the quote marks), and press the return key. When "A>\APPLDATA" (the A APPLDATA directory prompt) next shows up on the screen, type "MAIN" (without the quote marks) and press the return key. The computer will do the rest.

If you are using a computer with a hard drive, turn on the computer and at the "C>" (the C prompt), type "CD APPLDATA" (without the quote marks) and press the return key. When "C>\APPLDATA" (the C APPLDATA directory prompt) next shows up on the screen, type "MAIN" (without the quote marks) and press the return key. The computer will do the rest.

Each subsequent time you want to use the program, turn on the computer and repeat the preceding directions, depending on your computer's configuration.

For class submission purposes, be sure that you enter your own name (or your team name) when prompted by the program. Your name will then appear on each of the reports that you hand in to your professor.

Note: Information has already been stored in both the inventory data base and the customer data base. This information may be accessed by following the instructions that appear next—in particular, point 7 in the inventory management section and point 4 in the customer data-base section.

Inventory Management

These are the basic directions for the first-time use of the inventory management portion of *Appliance Data Base*:

(1) The initial screen will automatically blend into a copyright notice. The first time you use the program, press 2 so you may enter your name and class section. Enter your last name first. If your team has chosen a company name, this should be entered instead of any individual person's name. Next, enter your course and section number. Finally, press 1 to access the program. The Main Menu screen now appears. Note: If you are using your own disk, you just press 1 on subsequent uses of the software.

(2) To start the Inventory Management application, select option 1 (INVENTORY) from the Main Menu. The Inventory Management main menu will then appear. When you start using the inventory management program, you will need to enter all the items that you would like to track. The following procedure sets up the date-base record with the necessary fields. First, select option 3

(Add/ Remove/ Change Item) from the Inventory Management main menu. Second, select option 1 (Add New Item to Inventory) from the Maintenance menu. Third, input information into the data entry form on a product's part name, model number, vendor, beginning inventory level, and target on hand inventory level. After typing the requested information for a given field, press the [Enter] or arrow keys to move to the next field. Prior to pressing the [Enter] key on the target on hand inventory field, you can correct any entry by moving the arrow keys to the appropriate field and typing the correct entry.

(3) To record the reduction in inventory-on-hand for an item, select option 1 (Record Items Used) from the Inventory Management main menu. The screen will then show the model numbers of all the different items that have been entered into the data base. To reduce the book inventory for a given item, type its model number and press [Enter]. The data-base program will then generate information about the item and ask you to enter the number of units you have used. After the information has been entered, the status of the item will be updated and displayed. Press any key to return to the Inventory Management main menu.

(4) To record a purchase, select option 2 (Record Items Purchased) from the Inventory Management main menu. Once again, the model numbers of all items will be displayed. Type in the number for the item that you have purchased and press [Enter]. The program will generate information about the item and ask you to enter the number of items purchased and the price paid per unit. After information has been entered, the status of the item will be updated and displayed. Press any key to return to the Inventory Management main menu.

(5) If you want to remove an item from your inventory list or modify its characteristics, select option 3 (Add/ Remove/ Change Item) from the Inventory Management main menu. To delete an item, select option 2 (Remove Item from Inventory) from the Maintenance menu. To modify an item's description, select option 3 (Edit Inventory Item) from the Maintenance menu. Then, use the up and down arrow keys to enter the field you wish to correct, type in the corrected entry, and press the [Ctrl] and [End] keys simultaneously to save the changes.

(6) At the end of each year, it is important that book inventory be reconciled with the physical inventory-on-hand. By selecting option 3 (Add/ Remove/ Change Item) from the Inventory Management main menu and then selecting option 4 (Print Year End Report and Setup for New Year), you can print an end-of-year inventory report. The report lists how many units of each item were purchased during the past year and how many units of each item were used during the past year. Besides printing the end-of-year inventory report, this procedure initializes certain fields, such as setting ending inventory as starting inventory. A warning will be displayed and you will be asked to confirm the procedure

(7) The entire inventory-on-hand or individual items can be displayed on the computer screen. First, select option 4 (Display Inventory) from the Inventory Management main menu. Then, choose what form of display you would like (1) Display Entire Inventory, (2) Display One Item, or (3) Display Items Below Target) from the Print menu. The Display Items Below Target screen will indicate those items for which the inventory-on-hand level is below the target level sought, thus signaling a potential out-of-stock situation.

(8) To print a listing of inventory items, select option 5 (Print Inventory) from the Inventory Management main menu. Then, choose the information you would like printed from among the options (1) Print Items Below Target, (2) Print Entire Inventory, or (3) Print Part Numbers And Descriptions from the Print menu.

(9) To quit the inventory management data base, select 9 on the Inventory Management main menu. This will return you to the Main Menu. Select 9 to quit the data base and to return to DOS.

Customer Data Base

These are the basic directions for the first-time use of the customer data-base portion of *Appliance Data Base*:

(1) The initial *Appliance Data Base* screen will automatically blend into a copyright notice. The first time you use the program, press 2 so you may enter your name and class section. Enter your last name first. If your team has chosen a company name, this should be entered instead of any individual person's name. Next, enter your course and section number. Finally, press 1 to access the program. The Main Menu screen now appears. Note: If you are using your own disk, you just press 1 on subsequent uses of the software.

(2) To start the Customer Data Base, select option "2" (CUSTOMER) from the Main Menu. The Customer main menu will now be displayed.

(3) To add a new customer into the data base, select option 1 (Add New Customer) from the Customer main menu. Enter all the information in the appropriate fields (customer's last name, first name, address, phone number, and directions). You can move from field to field by pressing the [Enter] or the arrow keys. You can use the up and down arrow keys to correct a typing error prior to pressing the [Enter] key on the last line. Move the [Enter] key to the last line to terminate this operation.

(4) You can print a listing of the existing customers in your data base by selecting option 4 (Print Customer List) from the Customer main menu; and a list of customers with their names, addresses, and service call history will be printed.

(5) To record a service call to an existing customer, select option 2 (Record Visit to Existing Customer) from the Customer main menu. You will be asked to enter the customer's last name (spelling is important). The program will then search the data base and display information about the first customer it finds matching the last name entered. You will be asked if this is the customer you had mind. If you respond yes, you will be asked to enter information about the most recent visit. If you respond no, the program will continue to search for another customer with the same last name. If no more matches are found, check to make sure the last name was entered correctly. When you have found the customer of interest, the program will display information about the last five service calls to this customer. After this information is displayed, you will be asked to enter information regarding the new visit. While entering the information, you can move from field to field by using the [Enter] or arrow keys. The new information will be stored in the data base once the form of payment has been entered. After the new information has been entered, the program will display the last five visits again. This time the most recent visit, will be the one just entered.

(6) If you discover an error in a customer's record or if you just want to amend a customer's record, enter option 3 (Edit Customer Information) from the Customer main menu. You will be asked to enter the customer's last name; then, the program will search the data base for the first customer with a matching last name and display enough information to determine if this is the customer you had in mind. If not, it will search for the next customer with a matching last name. When you have located the customer you had in mind, the program will ask if you want to edit customer information or visit information. Customer information involves the name, address, and phone number. Visit information is the service-call data.

(7) You can display customer information by selecting option 5 from the Customer main menu.

(8) To remove a customer from your data base, select option 6 (Delete a Customer from the Data Base) on the Customer main menu screen. By responding to prompts, you can remove one or more names and the related service call information stored with each name.

A SPECIFIC APPLIANCE DATA-BASE EXERCISE

In this section, we provide a specific *Appliance Data Base* exercise so that you may learn more about this software and apply several of the retail concepts you have been studying.

Questions 1 to 3 relate to the inventory management data-base exercise. Questions 4 to 6 are directed towards the customer data-base exercise:

1. For the inventory management data base,
   a. add a new item to your inventory.
   b. edit the description of this item to reflect a change in price.
   c. display the inventory record for this item.

   Print each of these screens.
2. Develop a policy for determining the target units on hand for each replacement part. Assume that your van can stock 200 different parts, that the cost of capital is 10 per cent, that the cost of a repairperson going to a parts store is $20 per visit, and that the cost of a repairperson revisiting a customer is $20.
3. Assess the inventory management data-base program in terms of ease of use, the quality of management reports, and the applicability for a service retailer. Develop specific recommendations to improve this program.
4. For the customer data base,
   a. add a new customer to the customer data base.
   b. record a visit to an existing customer.
   c. change visit information to an existing customer.
   d. display customer information.

   Print each of these screens.
5. Explain how the information contained in this program can be used to
   a. assess the firm's overall customer service levels.
   b. evaluate specific repairpersons.
   c. reactivate dormant accounts.
   d. generate mailing lists for special promotions.
6. Assess the customer data-base program in terms of ease of use, the quality of management reports, and the applicability for a service retailer. Develop specific recommendations to improve this program.

Glossary

Addition to Retail Percentage Measures a price rise as a percentage of original price:

$$\text{Addition to retail percentage} = \frac{\text{New price} - \text{Original price}}{\text{Original price}}$$

Additional Markup An increase in retail price after—and in addition to—the original markup; it is used when demand is unexpectedly high or when costs are rising.

Additional Markup Percentage Looks at total dollar additional markups as a percentage of net sales:

$$\text{Additional markup percentage} = \frac{\text{Total dollar additional markups}}{\text{Net sales (in \$)}}$$

Administered Pricing Occurs when a retailer seeks consumer patronage on the basis of a distinctive retailing mix. If strong differentiation can be reached, a firm can control the prices it charges.

Advertising Any paid, nonpersonal communication transmitted through out-of-store mass media by an identified sponsor.

Affinity Exists when the various stores at a given location complement, blend, and cooperate with one another, and each benefits from the others' presence.

Agate Line Used in newspaper advertising; there are 14 agate lines to an inch of space, one column wide.

All-You-Can-Afford Method A promotional budgeting technique in which a retailer first allocates funds for every element of the retail strategy mix except promotion. Any funds left over are placed into a promotional budget.

Analog Model A computer site-selection tool in which potential sales are estimated based on existing store revenues in similar areas, the competition at the prospective location, expected market shares at that location, and the size and density of the location's primary trading area.

Ancillary Customer Services Extra elements that enhance a retail strategy mix. They do not have to be provided.

Application Blank Provides data on an applicant's education, experience, health, reasons for leaving previous jobs, organizational memberships, hobbies, and references.

Asset Turnover A performance measure based on a retailer's net sales and total assets. It is equal to net sales divided by total assets.

Assets Any items a retailer owns that have a monetary value.

Assortment Display An interior display in which a retailer exhibits a wide range of merchandise for the customer. It may be open or closed.

Atmosphere The physical characteristics of a store that are used to develop an image and to draw customers.

Attitudes (Opinions) The positive, neutral, or negative feelings a person has about the economy, politics, goods, services, institutions, and so on.

Audit Form Lists the area(s) to be examined and the exact data required in evaluating each area.

Automatic Markdown Plan Controls the amount and timing of markdowns on the basis of the length of time merchandise remains in stock.

Automatic Reordering System Orders merchandise when stock-on-hand reaches a pre-determined reorder point. An automatic reorder can be generated by a computer on the basis of a perpetual inventory system and reorder point calculations.

Bait Advertising An illegal practice whereby a retailer lures a customer by advertising goods and services at very low prices; then, once the customer contacts the retailer, he or she is told the good/service of interest is out of stock or of inferior quality. A salesperson tries to convince the customer to purchase a better, more expensive substitute that is available. The retailer has no intention of selling the advertised item.

Bait-and-Switch Advertising *See* Bait Advertising.

Balance Sheet Itemizes a retailer's assets, liabilities, and net worth at a specific point in time; it is based on the principle that assets equal liabilities plus net worth.

Balanced Tenancy Occurs when stores in a planned shopping center complement each other in the quality and variety of product offerings. The kind and number of stores are linked to the needs of the population.

Basic Stock List Specifies the inventory level, color, brand, style category, size, package, and so on for every staple item carried by the retailer.

Basic Stock Method An inventory-level planning tool wherein a retailer carries more items than it expects to sell over a given period:

Basic stock = Average monthly stock at retail − Average monthly sales

Battle of the Brands When retailers and manufacturers compete for the shelf space allocated to various brands and for control over the location of displays.

Bifurcated Retailing Denotes the decline of the middle market in retailing as both mass merchandising and positioned retailing become more popular.

Book Inventory System Keeps a running total of the value of all inventory on hand at cost at a given time. This is done by regularly recording purchases and adding them to existing inventory value; sales transactions are then subtracted to arrive at the new current inventory value (all at cost).

Bottom-Up Approach to Space Management Exists when planning starts at the individual product level and then proceeds to the category, total store, and overall company levels.

Bottom-Up Budgeting Requires lower-level executives to develop budget requests for their departments; these requests are then assembled, and an overall companywide budget is designed.

Box (Limited-Line) Store A food-based discounter that focuses on a small selection of items, moderate hours of operation, few services, and limited national brands.

BPI *See* Buying Power Index.

Budgeting Outlines a retailer's planned expenditures for a given time period based on its expected performance.

Bundled Pricing Involves a retailer providing a number of services for one basic price.

Business Format Franchising An arrangement in which the franchisee receives assistance on site location, quality control, accounting systems, startup practices, management training, and responding to problems—in addition to the right to sell goods and services.

Buying Power Index (BPI) A measure of a geographic area's market characteristics, expressed as:

0.5 (the area's percentage of U.S. effective buying income)
+0.3 (the area's percentage of U.S. retail sales)
+0.2 (the area's percentage of U.S. population)

Canned Sales Presentation A memorized, repetitive speech given to all customers interested in a particular item.

Capital Expenditures Retail expenditures that are long-term investments in fixed assets.

Case Display Employed to exhibit heavier, bulkier items than racks hold.

Cash Flow Relates the amount and timing of revenues received to the amount and timing of expenditures made during a specific time period.

Category Killer Store An especially large specialty store featuring an enormous selection in its product category and relatively low prices.

Category Management A technique that some retailers, particularly supermarkets, are beginning to use to improve shelf-space productivity.

CBD *See* Central Business District.

Census of Population Supplies a wide range of demographic data for all U.S. cities and surrounding vicinities. Data are organized on a geographic basis.

Central Business District (CBD) The hub of retailing in a city. It is the largest shopping area in that city and is synonymous with the term "downtown." The CBD exists where there is the greatest concentration of office buildings and retail stores.

Centralized Buying Organization Occurs when a retailer has all purchase decisions emanating from one office.

Chain Multiple retail units under common ownership that engage in some level of centralized (or coordinated) purchasing and decision making.

Channel Control Occurs when one member of a distribution channel can dominate the decisions made in that channel via the power it possesses.

Channel of Distribution Comprises all of the businesses and people involved in the physical movement and transfer of ownership of goods and services from producer to consumer.

Class Consciousness The extent to which a person desires and pursues social status.

Classification Merchandising Allows firms to obtain more financial data by subdividing each specified department into further categories for related types of merchandise.

COD (Collect on Delivery) Lets a customer have a product delivered to him or her before paying for it.

Cognitive Dissonance Doubt that occurs after a purchase is made, which can be alleviated by customer after-care, money-back guarantees, and realistic sales presentations and advertising campaigns.

Collect on Delivery *See* COD.

Combination Store Unites supermarket and general merchandise sales in one facility, with general merchandise typically accounting for 25 to 40 per cent of total store sales.

Commercial Cue A message sponsored by a retailer, a manufacturer, a wholesaler, or some other seller.

Community Shopping Center A moderate-sized, planned shopping site with a branch department store, a variety store, and/or a category killer store, in addition to several smaller stores. From 20,000 to 100,000 people, who live or work within 10 to 20 minutes of the center, are served by this type of retail location.

Company Audit Specialist An internal employee whose prime job is the retail audit.

Company Department Manager [Auditor] An internal employee whose prime responsibility is operations management, but who may be asked to participate in the retail audit.

Comparative Advertising Messages comparing a retailer's offerings with those of competitors.

Compensation Includes both direct monetary payments (such as salaries, commissions, and bonuses) and indirect payments (such as paid vacations, health and life insurance benefits, and retirement plans).

Competition-Oriented Pricing An approach in which a retailer uses competitors' prices as a guide rather than demand or cost factors.

Competitive Advantage The distinct competency of a retailer relative to its competitors.

Competitive Advertisement Has persuasion as its goal.

Competitive Parity Method A promotional budgeting technique by which a retailer's budget is raised or lowered on the basis of competitors' actions.

Competitive Pricing A strategy whereby a service retailer sets its prices on the basis of the prices charged by competitors.

Computerized Checkout Enables retailers to efficiently process transactions and maintain strict control over inventory. In a UPC-based system, cashiers manually ring up sales or pass items over or past optical scanners. Computerized registers instantly record and display sales, customers are given detailed receipts, and all inventory data are stored in the computer's memory bank.

Conglomerchant *See* Diversified Retailer.

Consignment Purchase Items not paid for by retailer until they are sold. The retailer can return unsold merchandise. Title is not taken by the retailer until the final sale is completed.

Constrained Decision Making Excludes franchisees from or limits their involvement in the strategic planning process.

Consumer Behavior The process by which people decide whether, what, when, where, how, from whom, and how often to purchase goods and services.

Consumer Cooperative A retail firm owned by its customer members. A group of consumers invests, receives stock, elects officers, manages operations, and shares the profits or savings that accrue.

Consumer Decision Process The stages a consumer goes through in buying a good or service: stimulus, problem awareness, information search, evaluation of alternatives, purchase, and post-purchase behavior. Demographics and life-style factors affect this decision process.

Consumerism Involves the activities of government, business, and independent organizations that are designed to protect individuals from practices that infringe upon their rights as consumers.

Contingency Pricing An arrangement whereby the retailer does not receive payment from the customer until after a service is performed. Payment is contingent on the service's being satisfactory.

Control The phase in the evaluation of a firm's strategy and tactics in which a semiannual or annual review of the firm should occur.

Control Units Merchandise categories for which data are gathered.

Controllable Variables Those aspects of business that the retailer can directly affect (such as store hours and sales personnel).

Convenience Store A food-oriented retailer that is well located, is open long hours, and carries a moderate number of items. It is small, has average to above-average prices, and average atmosphere and customer services.

Conventional Supermarket A departmentalized food store that emphasizes a wide range of food and related products; sales of general merchandise are rather limited.

Cooperative Advertising Occurs when a manufacturer or wholesaler and a retailer, or two or more retailers, share advertising costs.

Cooperative Buying The procedure used when a group of independent retailers gets together to make large purchases from a single supplier.

Corporation A retail firm that is formally incorporated under state law. It is a legal entity apart from individual officers (or stockholders).

Cost Complement The average relationship of cost to retail value for all merchandise available for sale during a given time period.

Cost Method of Accounting Requires the retailer's cost of every item to be recorded on an accounting sheet and/or coded on a price tag or merchandise container. During a physical inventory, every item's cost must be ascertained, the quantity of every item in stock counted, and the total inventory value at cost calculated.

Cost of Goods Sold The amount a retailer has paid to acquire the merchandise that is sold during a given time period. It equals the cost of merchandise available for sale minus the cost value of ending inventory.

Cost-Oriented Pricing An approach in which a retailer sets a price floor, the minimum price acceptable to the firm so it can reach a specified profit goal. A retailer usually computes merchandise and retail operating costs and adds a profit margin to these figures.

Cost-Plus Pricing Occurs when a retailer adds a desired profit margin to merchandise or service cost to arrive at a selling price.

Credit Management Involves the policies and practices retailers follow in receiving payments from their customers.

Cross-Training Enables personnel to learn tasks associated with more than one job.

Culture A distinctive heritage shared by a group of people. It influences the importance of family, work, education, and other concepts by passing on a series of beliefs, norms, and customs.

Curving (Free-Flowing) Traffic Flow Presents displays and aisles in a free-flowing pattern.

Customary Pricing A pricing strategy whereby a retailer sets prices for goods or services and seeks to maintain them for an extended time.

Customer Services The identifiable, but sometimes intangible, acts of a retailer in conjunction with the basic goods and services it sells.

Customer Space The area for shoppers to lounge, try on clothing, eat, park, and so on.

Cut Case An inexpensive display, in which merchandise is left in the original carton.

Data Analysis The stage in the research process which assesses secondary and/or primary data and relates it to a defined issue or problem.

Data-Base Management The procedure used to gather, integrate, apply, and store information related to specific subject areas. It is a key element in a retail information system.

Days Supply Equals the number of days of supply of an item that is on the shelf; it is a similar measure to inventory turnover.

Dead Areas Awkward spaces where normal displays cannot be set up.

Dealer Brands *See* Private Brands.

Debit Transfer System A computerized system whereby the purchase price of a good or service is automatically and immediately deducted from a consumer's bank account and entered into a retailer's account.

Decentralized Buying Organization Allows purchase decisions to be made locally or regionally.

Deferred Billing Lets regular charge customers make purchases and not pay for them for several months, with no interest charge.

Demand-Oriented Pricing An approach by which a retailer sets prices based on consumer desires. It determines the price range acceptable to the target market.

Demographics Objective and quantifiable population data that are easily identifiable and measurable.

Department Store A large retail unit with an extensive assortment (width and depth) of goods and services that is organized into separate departments for purposes of buying, promotion, customer service, and control.

Depth of Assortment Refers to the variety in any one goods/service category with which a retailer is involved.

Destination Store A retail unit where merchandise selection and presentation, pricing, or other unique features act as a magnet for customers.

Direct Marketing A form of retailing in which a customer is first exposed to a good or service through a nonpersonal medium and then orders by mail or telephone—sometimes, by computer.

Direct Product Profitability (DPP) Calculated when a retailer determines the profitability of each category or unit of merchandise it sells by computing adjusted per-unit gross margin and assigning direct product costs for expense categories such as warehousing, transportation, handling, and selling. It equals an item's gross profit less its direct retailing costs.

Direct Selling Includes both personal contact with consumers in their homes (and other nonstore locations such as offices) and telephone solicitations that are initiated by a retailer.

Discretionary Income Money left over after paying taxes and buying necessities.

Disguised Audit One in which a retailer's employees are not aware that an audit is taking place.

Disguised Survey One in which the respondent is not told the real purpose of a research study.

Distributed Advertising Effort Employed by retailers that promote constantly throughout the year.

Diversification The way in which retailers become active in business outside their normal operations—and add distinctly different goods and/or service categories.

Diversified Retailer A multiline merchandising firm under central ownership.

Diversionary Pricing A practice used by deceptive retailers. A low price is stated for one or a few items (emphasized in promotion) to give the illusion that all of the firm's prices are low.

Dollar Control Involves planning and monitoring a retailer's financial investment in merchandise over a stated time period.

Downsizing Exists when unprofitable stores are closed or divisions are sold off by retailers dissatisfied with their performance.

DPP *See* Direct Product Profitability.

Dual Vertical Marketing System Involves firms engaged in more than one type of distribution arrangement. This enables those firms to appeal to different consumers, increase sales volume, share some of their costs, and maintain a good degree of control over their strategy.

Dump Bin A case display that houses piles of sale clothing, marked-down books, or other products.

Ease of Entry Occurs for retailers due to low capital requirements and no, or relatively simple, licensing provisions.

EBI *See* Effective Buying Income.

Economic Base Refers to an area's industrial and commercial structure—the firms and industries that residents need to earn a living.

Economic Order Quantity (EOQ) The quantity per order (in units) that minimizes the total costs of processing orders and holding inventory:

$$EOQ = \sqrt{\frac{2DS}{IC}}$$

where

EOQ = Economic order quantity (in units)
D = Annual demand (in units)
S = Costs to place an order (in dollars)
I = Percentage of annual carrying cost to unit cost
C = Unit cost of an item (in dollars)

ECR *See* Efficient Consumer Response.

EDI *See* Electronic Data Interchange.

Editor & Publisher Market Guide Provides a lot of economic base data for cities on a yearly basis. It also has statistics on population size and total households by city.

EDLP *See* Everyday Low Pricing.

Effective Buying Income (EBI) Personal income (wages, salaries, interest, dividends, profits, rental income, and pension income) minus federal, state, and local taxes and nontax payments (such as personal contributions for social security insurance).

Efficient Consumer Response (ECR) A form of logistics management through which supermarkets are incorporating aspects of quick response inventory planning, electronic data interchange, and logistics planning.

Elasticity of Demand *See* Price Elasticity of Demand.

Electronic Article Surveillance Involves attaching specially designed tags or labels to products.

Electronic Banking Involves the use of automatic teller machines (ATMs) and the instant processing of retail purchases.

Electronic Data Interchange (EDI) Lets retailers and suppliers regularly exchange information via their computers with regard to inventory levels, delivery times, unit sales, and so on, of particular items.

Electronic Point-of-Sale System Performs all the tasks of a computerized checkout and also verifies check and charge transactions, provides instantaneous sales reports, monitors and changes prices, sends intra- and interstore messages, evaluates personnel and profitability, and stores information.

Employee Empowerment A method of improving customer service in which workers have discretion to do what they believe is necessary—within reason—to satisfy the customer, even if this means bending some rules.

Ensemble Display An interior display whereby coordinated merchandise is grouped and displayed together.

EOQ *See* Economic Order Quantity.

Equal Store Organization Centralizes the buying function. The branches become sales units with equal operational status.

Ethics Lets a retailer act in a trustworthy, fair, honest, and respectful manner with each of its constituencies.

Evaluation of Alternatives The stage in the decision process where a consumer selects one good or service to buy from a list of alternatives.

Everyday Low Pricing (EDLP) A version of customary pricing, whereby a retailer strives to sell all of its goods and services at consistently low prices throughout the selling season.

Exclusive Distribution Takes place when suppliers enter into agreements with one or a few retailers that designate the latter as the only companies in specified geographic areas that are allowed to carry certain brands and/or product lines.

Experiment A type of research in which one or more elements of a retail strategy mix are manipulated under controlled conditions.

Extended Decision Making Occurs when a consumer makes full use of the decision process, usually for expensive, complex goods and services.

Extensive Media Coverage An approach whereby ads reach many people but with relatively low frequency.

External Secondary Data Available from sources outside a firm.

Factory Outlet A manufacturer-owned store selling that firm's closeouts, discontinued merchandise, irregulars, canceled orders, and, sometimes, in-season, first-quality merchandise.

Fair Trade Protects smaller and full-service retailers against discounters by requiring uniform retail prices. Fair trade is now banned in the United States.

Family Two or more related persons living together.

Family Life Cycle Describes how a traditional family evolves from bachelorhood to children to solitary retirement.

Feedback Signals or cues as to the success or failure of part of a retail strategy.

FIFO Method Logically assumes old merchandise is sold first, while newer items remain in inventory. It matches the inventory level with the current cost structure.

Financial Leverage A performance measure based on the relationship between a retailer's total assets and net worth. It is equal to total assets divided by net worth.

Financial Merchandise Management Occurs when a retailer specifies exactly which products (goods and services) are purchased, when products are purchased, and how many products are purchased.

Financial Resources Funds needed for a retailer to operate. They must cover both business and personal living expenses.

Fixed Pricing Exists when a government branch has some degree of control and retailers must conform to a stated price structure.

Flat Organization A firm with a large number of subordinates reporting to one supervisor.

Flea Market Has many retail vendors offering a range of products at discount prices in plain surroundings. Many flea markets are located in nontraditional sites not normally associated with retailing.

Flexible Pricing A strategy that allows consumers to bargain over selling prices; consumers who are good at bargaining obtain lower prices than those who are not.

Floor-Ready Merchandise Items that are received at the store in condition to be put right on display with no preparation by retail workers.

Food-Based Superstore A retailer that is larger and more diversified than a conventional supermarket but usually smaller and less diversified than a combination store. It caters to consumers' complete grocery needs and enables them to buy fill-in general merchandise.

Formal Buying Organization Views the merchandise-buying function as a distinct retail task; a separate department is set up.

Franchising A contractual arrangement between a franchisor (that may be a manufacturer, a wholesaler, or a service sponsor) and a retail franchisee, that allows the franchisee to conduct a given form of business under an established name and according to a given pattern of business.

Free-Flowing Traffic Flow *See* Curving Traffic Flow.

Frequency Measures the average number of times each person who is reached is exposed to company ads during a given time period.

Fringe Trading Area Includes the customers not found in primary and secondary trading areas. These are the most widely dispersed customers.

Full-Line Discount Store A type of department store characterized by (1) a broad merchandise assortment; (2) centralized checkout service; (3) merchandise normally sold via self-service with minimal assistance; (4) no catalog order service; (5) private-brand nondurable goods and well-known manufacturer-brand durable goods; (6) hard goods accounting for 60 per cent of merchandise sold; (7) a relatively inexpensive building, equipment, and fixtures; and (8) less stress on credit sales than in full-service stores.

Fully Integrated Vertical Marketing System Exists when a single firm performs all production and distribution functions without the aid of any other firms.

Functional Classification Divides jobs among functional areas such as sales promotion, buying, and store operations so that expert knowledge is utilized.

Functional Product Groupings Categorize and display a store's merchandise by common end uses.

Generic Brands No-frills goods stocked by some retailers. They usually receive secondary shelf locations, have little or no promotion support, are sometimes of less overall quality than other brands, are stocked in limited assortments, and have plain packages.

Geographic Classification Divides jobs by area so that personnel in multiunit stores are adapted to local conditions.

Geographic Information Systems (GIS) Combine digitized mapping with key locational data to graphically depict such trading-area characteristics as the demographic attributes of the population, data on customer purchases, and listings of current, proposed, and competitor locations.

GIS *See* Geographic Information Systems.

GMROI *See* Gross Margin Return on Investment.

Goal-Oriented Job Description Enumerates a position's basic tasks, the relationship of each job to overall goals, the interdependence of positions, and information flows.

Goods Retailing Focuses on the sale of tangible (physical) products.

Goods/Service Category A retail firm's line of business.

Graduated Lease Calls for precise rent increases over a specified period of time.

Gravity Model A computer site-selection model based on the premise that people are drawn to stores that are closer and more attractive than competitors'.

Gray Market Goods Generally brand-name products purchased in foreign markets or goods transshipped from other retailers. They are often sold at low prices by unauthorized dealers.

Gridiron Traffic Flow *See* Straight Traffic Flow.

Gross Margin The difference between net sales and the total cost of goods sold. Also known as Gross Profit.

Gross Margin Return on Investment (GMROI) Shows the relationship between total dollar operating profits and the average inventory investment (at cost) by combining profitability and sales-to-stock measures:

$$\text{GMROI} = \frac{\text{Gross margin in dollars}}{\text{Net sales}} \times \frac{\text{Net sales}}{\text{Average inventory at cost}} = \frac{\text{Gross margin in dollars}}{\text{Average inventory at cost}}$$

Gross Profit The difference between net sales and the cost of goods sold. Also known as Gross Margin.

Gross Profit Per Linear Foot of Shelf Space Equals annual gross profit divided by the total linear footage devoted to the product category.

Herzberg's Theory Specifies that factors involved in producing job satisfaction and motivation (satisfiers) differ from those leading to job dissatisfaction (dissatisfiers).

Hidden Assets Depreciated assets, such as office buildings and shopping centers, that are reflected on a retailer's balance sheet at low values relative to their actual worth.

Hierarchy of Authority Outlines the job relationships within a company by describing the reporting relationships among employees. Coordination and control are provided through this hierarchy.

Hierarchy-of-Effects Model The sequence of steps a consumer goes through, in reacting to promotion, which leads him or her from awareness to knowledge to liking to preference to conviction to a purchase.

Horizontal Cooperative-Advertising Agreement Enables two or more retailers (usually small, situated together, or franchisees of the same company) to share an advertisement.

Horizontal Price Fixing Involves agreements among manufacturers, among wholesalers, or among retailers to set prices. Such agreements are illegal, regardless of how "reasonable" resultant prices may be.

Horizontal Retail Audit An analysis of a retailer's overall performance, from organizational mission to goals to customer satisfaction to strategy mix and its implementation in an integrated, consistent way.

Household One or more persons occupying a housing unit, whether related or not.

Household Life Cycle Incorporates the life stages of both family and nonfamily households.

Huff's Law of Shopper Attraction Delineates trading areas on the basis of the product assortment carried at various shopping locations, travel time from the consumer's home to alternative shopping locations, and the sensitivity of the kind of shopping to travel time. It is expressed as:

$$Pij = \frac{\dfrac{Sj}{(Tij)^{\lambda}}}{\sum_{j=1}^{n} \dfrac{Sj}{(Tij)}}$$

where

Pij = Probability of a consumer's traveling from home i to shopping location j

Sj = Square footage of selling space in shopping location j expected to be devoted to a particular product category

Tij = Travel time from consumer's home i to shopping location j

λ = A parameter used to estimate the effect of travel time on different kinds of shopping trips

n = Number of different shopping locations

Human Resource Management Involves the recruitment, selection, training, compensation, and supervision of personnel in a manner consistent with a retailer's organization structure and strategy mix.

Human Resource Management Process Consists of these interrelated personnel activities: recruitment, selection, training, compensation, and supervision. The goals are to obtain, develop, and retain employees.

Image Refers to how a given retailer is perceived by consumers and others.

Implementation The stage in the research process during which recommendations are put into practice.

Importance of the Purchase Affects the amount of time a person will spend in making a decision and the range of alternatives considered.

Impulse Purchases Occur when consumers purchase products and/or brands they had not planned to buy before entering a store, reading a mail-order catalog, seeing a TV shopping show, and so on.

Income Statement *See* Profit-and-Loss Statement.

Incremental Budgeting The process whereby a firm uses current and past budgets as guides and adds to or subtracts from these budgets to arrive at the coming period's expenditures.

Incremental Method A promotional budgeting technique by which a percentage is either added to or subtracted from this year's budget to determine next year's budget.

Independent A retailer that owns only one retail unit.

Independent Vertical Marketing System Consists of three levels of independently owned businesses: manufacturers, wholesalers, and retailers. It is the leading form of vertical marketing system.

Informal Buying Organization Does not view merchandising as a distinct retail function; existing personnel handle both merchandising and other retail functions.

Information Search Consists of two parts: determining alternative goods or services that will solve the problem at hand and ascertaining the characteristics of each alternative. Search may be internal or external.

Initial Markup (at Retail) Based on the original retail value assigned to merchandise less the costs of the merchandise, expressed as a percentage of the original retail price. This may be expressed as:

$$\text{Initial markup percentage (at retail)} = \frac{\begin{array}{c}\text{Planned retail operating expenses}\\ + \text{ Planned profit} + \text{Planned retail reductions}\end{array}}{\text{Planned net sales} + \text{Planned retail reductions}}$$

Inside Buying Organization Staffed by a retailer's own personnel; merchandise decisions are made by permanent employees of the firm.

Institutional Advertisement Strives to keep the retailer's name before the public without emphasizing the sale of goods or services.

Intensive Distribution Takes place when suppliers sell via as many retailers as possible. This arrangement usually maximizes suppliers' sales; and it lets retailers offer many different brands and product versions.

Intensive Media Coverage An approach whereby ads are placed in selected media and repeated frequently.

Internal Secondary Data Available within a company.

Inventory Management Involves a retailer seeking to acquire and maintain a proper merchandise assortment while ordering, shipping, handling, and other related costs are kept in check.

Inventory Shrinkage Involves employee theft, customer shoplifting, and vendor theft (mostly short shipping).

Inventory Turnover The number of times during a given period, usually one year, that the average inventory on hand is sold.

Isolated Store A freestanding retail outlet located on either a highway or a street. There are no adjacent retailers with which this type of store shares traffic.

Issue (Problem) Definition A step in the marketing research process that involves a clear statement of the topic to be studied.

Item Price Removal A practice whereby prices are marked only on shelves or signs and not on individual items. This practice is banned in several states and local communities.

Job Analysis Consists of gathering information about each job's functions and requirements: duties, responsibilities, aptitude, interest, education, experience, and physical condition.

Job Motivation The drive in people to attain work-related goals.

Job Standardization Makes the tasks of personnel with similar positions in different departments, such as cashiers and stockpersons in clothing and candy departments, relatively uniform.

Key Business Ratios May be used to measure a retailer's success or failure in reaching particular performance standards.

Law of Demand States that consumers usually purchase more units at low prices than at high prices.

Layaway Plan Lets any customer give a retailer a deposit to hold a product. When the customer completes payment, he or she takes the item.

LBO *See* Leveraged Buyout.

Leader Pricing Occurs when a retailer advertises and sells key items in its goods/service assortment at less than usual profit margins. The goal is to increase customer traffic for the retailer in the hope of selling regularly priced goods and services in addition to the specially priced items.

Leased Department A department in a store—usually a department, discount, or specialty store—that is rented to an outside party.

Leveraged Buyout (LBO) An ownership change that is mostly financed by loans from banks, investors, and others.

Liabilities Any financial obligations a retailer incurs in operating a business.

Life-Styles The ways in which individual consumers and families (households) live and spend time and money.

LIFO Method Assumes new merchandise is sold first, while older stock items remain in inventory. It matches current sales with the current cost structure.

Limited Decision Making Occurs when a consumer uses each of the steps in the purchase process but does not need to spend a great deal of time on all of them.

Limited-Line Store *See* Box Store.

Logistics The total process of moving goods from a manufacturer to a customer in the most timely and cost-efficient manner possible.

Loss Leaders Items priced below cost to attract more customer traffic. Loss leaders are restricted by state minimum-price laws.

Maintained Markup (at Retail) Based on the actual prices received for merchandise sold during a time period less merchandise cost, expressed as a percentage:

$$\text{Maintained markup (at retail)} = \frac{\text{Actual retail operating expenses} + \text{Actual profit}}{\text{Actual net sales}}$$

or

$$\frac{\text{Average selling price} - \text{Merchandise cost}}{\text{Average selling price}}$$

Maintenance-Increase-Recoupment Lease Has a provision allowing for increases in rent if a property owner's taxes, heating bills, insurance, or other expenses rise beyond a certain point.

Manufacturer (National) Brands Produced and controlled by the manufacturers. They are usually well known, are supported by manufacturer advertising, are somewhat pre-sold to consumers, require limited retailer investment, and often represent maximum product quality to consumers.

Mapping A technique to evaluate the trading area of a store by determining the distances people are likely to travel to get to the store, the population density of the geographic area surrounding the store, and the travel patterns and times from various locations. A map is then drawn showing these factors.

Markdown A reduction from selling price to meet the lower price of another retailer, adapt to inventory overstocking, clear out shopworn items, reduce assortments of odds and ends, and increase customer traffic.

Markdown Control Evaluates the number of markdowns, their proportion of sales, and their causes.

Markdown Percentage The total dollar markdown as a percentage of net sales (in dollars):

$$\text{Markdown percentage} = \frac{\text{Total dollar markdown}}{\text{Net sales (in \$)}}$$

Market Penetration A pricing strategy in which a retailer seeks to capture large sales by setting low prices and selling a high unit volume.

Market Pricing Occurs in a competitive environment characterized by retailers pricing similarly to each other. Firms have little control over price. Demand for specific retailers is weak enough so a number of customers would switch to a competitor if prices are raised much.

Market Segment A specific group of consumers.

Market-Segment Product Groupings Place various products appealing to a given target market together.

Market Skimming A pricing strategy wherein a firm charges premium prices and attracts customers less concerned with price than service, assortment, and status.

Marketing Research in Retailing Entails collecting and analyzing information related to specific issues or problems facing a retailer.

Marketing Research Process Embodies a series of activities: defining the issue or problem to be studied, examining secondary data, generating primary data (if needed), analyzing data, making recommendations, and implementing findings.

Markup The difference between merchandise costs and retail selling price.

Markup Percentage (at Cost) The difference between retail price and merchandise cost expressed as a percentage of merchandise cost:

$$\text{Markup percentage (at cost)} = \frac{\text{Retail selling price} - \text{Merchandise cost}}{\text{Merchandise cost}}$$

Markup Percentage (at Retail) The difference between retail price and merchandise cost expressed as a percentage of retail price:

$$\text{Markup percentage (at retail)} = \frac{\text{Retail selling price} - \text{Merchandise cost}}{\text{Retail selling price}}$$

Markup Pricing A form of cost-oriented pricing in which a retailer sets prices by adding per-unit merchandise costs, operating expenses, and desired profit.

Marquee A sign used to display a store's name and/or logo.

Mass Market A broad spectrum of consumers.

Mass Merchandising A positioning approach involving retailers that present a discount or value-oriented image, handle several merchandise lines, and have large store facilities.

Massed Advertising Effort Used by retailers that promote mostly in one or two seasons.

Mazur Plan Divides all retail tasks into four functional areas: merchandising, publicity, store management, and accounting and control.

Megamall An enormous planned shopping center with 1 million+ square feet of retail space, multiple anchor stores, up to several hundred specialty stores, food courts, and entertainment facilities.

Membership Club Appeals to price-conscious consumers, who must be members to shop. It straddles the line between wholesaling and retailing.

Memorandum Purchase Occurs when items are not paid for by the retailer until they are sold. The retailer can return unsold merchandise. However, it takes title on delivery and is responsible for damages.

Merchandise Available for Sale Equals beginning inventory, purchases, and transportation charges.

Merchandise Buying and Handling Process Consists of an integrated and systematic sequence of steps from establishing a buying organization through regular re-evaluation.

Merchandise Space The area where nondisplayed items are kept in stock or inventory.

Merchandising The activities involved in acquiring particular goods and/or services and making them available at the places, times, and prices and in the quantity that will enable a retailer to reach its goals.

Mergers Involve the combination of separately owned retail firms.

Micro-Merchandising A strategy that lets a firm adjust shelf-space allocations to respond to customer and other local market differences.

Milline Rate Represents the cost to a retailer of one agate line of advertising per million circulation:

$$\text{Milline rate (newspaper efficiency)} = \frac{\text{Cost per agate line} \times 1{,}000{,}000}{\text{Circulation}}$$

Minimum-Price Laws State regulations preventing retailers from selling certain merchandise for less than its cost plus a fixed percentage to cover overhead. These laws restrict predatory pricing and loss leaders.

Model Stock Approach Method of determining the amount of floor space necessary to carry and display a proper assortment of merchandise.

Model Stock Plan The planned composition of fashion goods, which reflects the mix of merchandise available based on expected sales. The model stock plan indicates product lines, colors, and size distributions.

Monthly Payment Credit Account Requires the customer to pay for a purchase in equal monthly installments. Interest is usually charged.

Monthly Sales Index A measure of sales seasonality that is computed by dividing each month's actual sales by average monthly sales and then multiplying the results by 100.

Mother Hen with Branch Store Chickens Organization Exists when headquarters executives oversee and operate the branches. This works well when there are few branches and the buying preferences of branch customers are similar to those of the main store's customers.

Motives The reasons for consumers' behavior.

Multidimensional Scaling A statistical technique that allows attitudinal data to be collected for several attributes in a manner that allows data analysis to produce a single overall rating of a retailer.

Multiple Segments Two or more distinct consumer groups.

Multiple-Unit Pricing A policy whereby a retailer offers discounts to customers who buy in quantity.

Multistage Approach Divides the major pricing elements into six successive steps, with each placing limits on those that follow: selecting a target market, choosing a retail image, outlining the retail strategy mix, selecting a broad price policy, selecting a price strategy, and choosing specific prices.

National Brands *See* Manufacturer Brands.

NBD *See* Neighborhood Business District.

Need-Satisfaction Approach A sales technique based on the principle that each customer has different wants and that the sales presentation should be geared to the demands of the individual customer.

Negotiated Contract Requires that the retailer and the supplier carefully negotiate all aspects of the purchase.

Negotiated Pricing Occurs when a retailer works out pricing arrangements with individual customers.

Neighborhood Business District (NBD) An unplanned shopping area that appeals to the convenience-shopping and service needs of a single residential area. The leading retailer is typically a supermarket, a large drugstore, or a variety store and it is situated on the major street(s) of its residential area.

Neighborhood Shopping Center A planned shopping facility with the largest store being a supermarket and/or drugstore. It serves 3,000 to 50,000 people within 15 minutes' driving time (often less than 10 minutes).

Net Lease Calls for all maintenance expenses, such as heating, electricity, insurance, and interior repair, to be paid by the retailer—which is responsible for the satisfactory quality of these items.

Net Profit Equals gross profit minus retail operating expenses.

Net Profit Before Taxes The profit earned after all costs have been deducted.

Net Profit Margin A performance measure based on a retailer's net profit and net sales. It is equal to net profit divided by net sales.

Net Sales The revenues received by a retailer during a given time period after deducting customer returns, markdowns, and employee discounts.

Net Worth Computed as a retailer's assets minus its liabilities.

Never-Out List Used if a firm plans stock levels for best-sellers. Items accounting for high sales volume are stocked in a manner that ensures they are always available.

Nondisguised Audit One in which a retailer's employees are aware that an audit is being conducted.

Nondisguised Survey A technique in which the respondent is told the real purpose of a research study.

Nongoods Services The area of service retailing in which intangible personal services (rather than goods) are offered to consumers—who experience the services rather than possess them.

Nonprobability Sample An approach in which stores, products, or customers are chosen by the researcher—based on judgment or convenience.

Nonstore Retailing Utilizes strategy mixes that are not store-based to reach consumers and complete transactions. It is conducted through vending machines, direct selling, and direct marketing.

Objective-and-Task Method A promotional budgeting technique by which a retailer clearly defines its promotional goals and then determines the size of the budget needed to satisfy these objectives.

Objectives The goals, long- and short-run, that a retailer hopes to reach. Goals can involve sales, profit, satisfaction of publics, and image.

Observation A form of research in which present behavior or the results of past behavior are observed and recorded. It can be human or mechanical.

Odd Pricing A strategy in which retail prices are set at levels below even-dollar values, such as $0.49, $4.95, and $199.00.

Off-Price Chain Features brand-name apparel and accessories, footwear, linens, fabrics, cosmetics, and/or housewares and sells them at everyday low prices in an efficient, limited-service environment.

Off-Retail Markdown Percentage The markdown for each item or category of items as a percentage of original retail price:

$$\text{Off-retail markdown percentage} = \frac{\text{Original price} - \text{New price}}{\text{Original price}}$$

One-Hundred Per Cent Location The optimum site for a particular store. A location classified as 100 per cent for one retailer may be less than optimal for another.

One-Price Policy A strategy wherein a retailer charges the same price to all people seeking to purchase an item under similar conditions.

Open Credit Account Requires the consumer to pay his or her bill in full when it is due.

Open-to-Buy The difference between the planned purchases and purchase commitments already made by a buyer for a given time period, often a month. It is what the buyer has left to spend at any point in a month.

Operating Expenditures The short-term selling and administrative costs of running a business.

Operating Expenses The cost of running a retail business.

Operations Management The efficient and effective implementation of the policies and tasks necessary to satisfy a firm's customers, employees, and management (and stockholders, if a publicly owned company).

Opinions *See* Attitudes.

Opportunities The marketplace openings that exist because other retailers have not yet capitalized on them.

Opportunity Costs Involve foregoing possible benefits that may occur if a retailer could make expenditures in another opportunity rather than the one chosen.

Option Credit Account A form of revolving account that allows partial payments. No interest is assessed if the consumer pays the bill in full when it is due.

Order-Getting Salesperson Active in informing and persuading customers, and with closing sales. This is a true "sales" employee.

Order Lead Time The time span from the date an order is placed by a retailer to the date merchandise is ready for sale (received, price-marked, and put on the selling floor).

Order-Taking Salesperson Involved in routine clerical and sales functions, such as setting up displays, placing inventory on the shelves, answering simple questions, filling orders, and ringing up sales.

Organization Chart Graphically displays the hierarchical relationships within a firm.

Organizational Mission A retailer's understanding of its role in the business system. It is reflected in the firm's attitudes to customers, employees, competitors, government, and others.

Outshopping When a person goes out of his or her hometown to shop.

Outside Auditor A retail consultant that performs an audit.

Outside Buying Organization A company or person external to the retailer that is hired to fulfill the buying function, usually for a fee.

Overstored Trading Area A geographic area with so many stores selling a specific good or service that some retailers will be unable to earn an adequate profit.

Owned-Goods Services The area of service retailing in which goods owned by consumers are repaired, improved, or maintained.

Parasite Store An outlet that does not create its own traffic and that has no real trading area of its own.

Partially Integrated Vertical Marketing System Involves two independently owned businesses along a channel that perform all production and distribution functions without the aid of a third. For example, a manufacturer and retailer may complete transactions and shipping, storing, and other distribution functions without an independently owned wholesaler.

Partnership An unincorporated retail firm owned by two or more persons, each of whom has a financial interest.

Perceived Risk The level of risk a consumer believes exists regarding the purchase of a specific good or service from a specific retailer, whether or not that belief is factually correct.

Percentage Income Statement *See* Percentage Profit-and-Loss Statement.

Percentage Lease Stipulates that rent is related to a retailer's sales or profits.

Percentage-of-Sales Method A promotional budgeting technique whereby a retailer ties its promotion budget to sales revenue.

Percentage Profit-and-Loss (Income) Statement Summarizes a retailer's revenues and expenses for a specific period of time, with data expressed as per cents of net sales.

Percentage Variation Method An inventory-level planning method wherein the beginning-of-month planned inventory level during any month differs from the planned average monthly stock by only half of that month's variation from estimated average monthly sales. Under this method:

Beginning-of-month planned inventory level (at retail) =

Planned average monthly stock at retail
× 1/2 [1 + (Estimated monthly sales/ Estimated average monthly sales)]

Performance Measures The criteria used to assess retailer effectiveness. They include total sales, average sales per store, sales by goods/service category, sales per square foot, gross margins, gross margin return on investment, operating income, inventory turnover, markdown percentages, employee turnover, financial ratios, and profitability.

Perpetual Inventory System *See* Book Inventory System.

Perpetual-Inventory Unit-Control System Keeps a running total of the number of units handled by a retailer via ongoing record-keeping entries that adjust for sales, returns, transfers to other departments or stores, receipt of merchandise shipments, and other transactions. It can be maintained manually, use merchandise tags that are processed by computers, or rely on point-of-sale devices such as optical scanning equipment.

Personal Abilities The aptitude, education, and experience needed for success in different types of retailing.

Personal Selling Involves oral communication with one or more prospective consumers for the purpose of making sales.

Personality The sum total of an individual's traits, which make that individual unique.

Personnel Space The area required for employees for changing clothes, lunch and coffee breaks, and restrooms.

Physical Drive A stimulus that occurs when one or more of a person's physical senses are affected.

Physical Inventory System Involves an actual counting of merchandise. A retailer using the cost method of inventory valuation and relying on a physical inventory system can derive its gross profit only as often as it does a complete physical inventory.

Pioneer Advertisement Has awareness as a goal and offers information (usually on a new firm or location).

Planned Shopping Center Consists of a group of architecturally unified commercial establishments built on a site that is centrally owned or managed, designed and operated as a unit, based on balanced tenancy, and surrounded by parking facilities.

Planogram A visual (graphical) representation of the space to be allocated to selling, merchandise, personnel, and customers—as well as to product categories.

PMs A manufacturer's payments for retail salespeople selling that manufacturer's brand. PMs are in addition to the compensation received from the retailer.

Point of Indifference The geographic breaking point between two cities (communities), so that the trading area of each can be determined. At this point, consumers would be indifferent to shopping at either area.

Point-of-Purchase (POP) Display An interior display providing consumers with information, adding to store atmosphere, and serving a substantial promotional role.

Positioned Retailing A strategy whereby retailers identify customer segments and develop unique strategies to address the desires of them.

Positioning Enables a retailer to determine how consumers perceive the firm (its image) relative to its retail category and its competitors.

Post-Purchase Behavior Further purchases and/or re-evaluation based on a purchase.

Poverty of Time Occurs when greater striving for financial security leads to less rather than more free time, since the alternatives competing for consumers' time rise considerably.

Power Center A shopping site with (a) a half-dozen or so category killer stores and a mix of smaller stores or (b) several complementary stores specializing in one product category.

Power Retailer The status reached by a company that is dominant in some aspect of its strategy. Consumers view the company as distinctive enough to become loyal to it and go out of their way to shop there.

Pre-training An indoctrination on the history and policies of the retailer and a job orientation on the hours, compensation, chain of command, and job duties.

Predatory Pricing Involves big retailers that attempt to destroy competition by selling goods and services at extremely low prices, which causes small retailers to go out of business. The practice is restricted by federal and state laws.

Prestige Pricing Assumes that consumers will not buy goods and services at prices considered too low.

Price Adjustments Let retailers use price as an adaptive mechanism. Markdowns and additional markups may be needed in adapting to such factors as competition, seasonality, demand patterns, merchandise costs, and pilferage.

Price Elasticity of Demand Relates to the sensitivity of buyers to price changes in terms of the quantities they will purchase:

$$\text{Elasticity} = \frac{\dfrac{\text{Quantity 1} - \text{Quantity 2}}{\text{Quantity 1} + \text{Quantity 2}}}{\dfrac{\text{Price 1} - \text{Price 2}}{\text{Price 1} + \text{Price 2}}}$$

Price Guarantees Protect retailers against possible price declines. If a retailer cannot sell an item at a given price, the manufacturer pays it the difference between planned retail and actual retail selling prices.

Price Line Classifications Enable retail sales, inventories, and purchases to be analyzed by retail price category.

Price Lining A practice whereby retailers sell items at a limited range of price points, with each price point representing a distinct level of quality.

Price-Lining Strategy Used by service retailers that provide a wide selection of services. A range of prices is matched to service levels.

Price-Quality Association The concept stating that many consumers feel high prices connote high quality and low prices connote low quality.

Price War A situation in a very competitive environment whereby various retailers continually lower prices below regular amounts and sometimes below merchandise costs to attract consumers.

Primary Customer Services Those considered basic ingredients in the retail strategy mix; they must be provided.

Primary Data Collected to address the specific issue or problem under study. These data can be gathered internally or externally via surveys, observations, experiments, and simulation.

Primary Trading Area Encompasses 50 to 80 per cent of a store's customers. It is the geographic area closest to a store and has the highest density of customers to population and the highest per-capita sales.

Private (Dealer) Brands Contain names designated by wholesalers or retailers, are more profitable to retailers, are better controlled by retailers, are not sold by competing retailers, are less expensive for consumers, and lead to customer loyalty to retailers.

Prize Money *See* PMs.

Probability (Random) Sample An approach whereby every store, product, or customer has an equal or known chance of being chosen for study.

Problem Awareness The stage in the decision process where the consumer recognizes that the good or service under consideration may solve a problem of shortage or unfulfilled desire.

Problem Definition *See* Issue Definition.

Product Classification Divides jobs on a goods or service basis.

Product Life Cycle Shows the expected behavior of a good or service over its life. The traditional cycle has four stages: introduction, growth, maturity, and decline.

Product/Trademark Franchising An arrangement in which franchised dealers acquire the identities of their suppliers by agreeing to sell the latter's products and/or operate under suppliers' names.

Productivity The efficiency with which a retail strategy is carried out.

Profit-and-Loss (Income) Statement Represents a summary of a retailer's revenues and expenses over a particular period of time, usually on a monthly, quarterly, and/or yearly basis.

Profitability Objectives Involve a minimum level of profits during a designated time period, usually a year. They may be expressed in dollars or as a percentage of sales.

Promotional Money *See* PMs.

Prototype Stores Occur with an operations strategy that requires various outlets in a chain to conform to relatively uniform construction, layout, and operations standards.

Psychological Pricing Involves consumer perceptions of retail prices.

Publicity Any nonpersonal communication transmitted through mass media where the time or space provided by the media is not paid for and where there is no identified commercial sponsor.

Purchase Act The exchange of money or a promise to pay for the ownership or use of a good or service. Purchase variables include the place of purchase, terms, and availability of merchandise.

Purchase-Motivation Product Groupings Appeal to a person's urge to buy a product and the time he or she is willing to spend in shopping.

Push Money *See* PMs.

QR Inventory Planning *See* Quick Response Inventory Planning.

Quick Response (QR) Inventory Planning Enables a retailer to reduce the amount of inventory it keeps on hand by ordering more frequently and in lower quantity.

Rack Display An interior display that neatly hangs and presents products.

Random Sample *See* Probability Sample.

Rationalized Retailing A strategy involving a high degree of centralized management control combined with rigorous operating procedures for every phase of business.

Reach Refers to the number of distinct people who are exposed to a retailer's ads during a specified time period.

Real Income Household income after adjusting for inflation.

Recognition of Shortage Occurs when a consumer discovers that a good or service may need to be repurchased.

Recognition of Unfulfilled Desire Occurs when a consumer becomes aware of a good or service that has not been purchased before—or a retailer that has not been patronized before.

Recommendations The stage in the research process during which the alternative approach to best solve a problem or issue is presented.

Recruitment The activity whereby a retailer generates a list of job applicants.

Reference Groups Influence people's thoughts and/or behavior. There are aspirational, membership, and dissociative groups.

Regional Shopping Center A large, planned shopping location that appeals to a geographically dispersed market. It has at least one or two full-sized department stores and 50 to 150 or more smaller retailers. The market for this center is 100,000+ people who live or work up to 30 minutes' driving time from the center.

Regression Model A computer site-selection model that develops a series of mathematical equations showing the association between potential store sales and various independent variables at each location under consideration.

Reilly's Law of Retail Gravitation A means of trading area delineation that establishes a point of indifference between two cities or communities so that the trading area of each can be determined. The law may be expressed algebraically as

$$Dab = \frac{d}{1 + \sqrt{\frac{Pb}{Pa}}}$$

where

Dab = Limit of city A's trading area, measured in miles along the road to city B

d = Distance in miles along a major roadway between cities A and B

Pa = Population of city A

Pb = Population of city B

Relationship Retailing Exists when retailers seek to establish and maintain long-term bonds with customers, rather than act as if each sales transaction is a completely new encounter with them.

Reminder Advertisement Geared to loyal customers and emphasizes the attributes that have made a retailer successful.

Rented-Goods Services The area of service retailing in which consumers lease and use goods for specified periods of time.

Reorder Point The stock level at which new orders must be placed:

Reorder point = (Usage rate × Lead time) + Safety stock

Resident Buying Office An inside or outside buying organization that is usually situated in an important merchandise center (source of supply) and provides valuable information and contacts.

Retail Audit The systematic examination and evaluation of a firm's total retailing effort or some specific aspect of it. Its purpose is to study what a retailer is presently doing, to appraise how well the retailer is performing, and to make recommendations for future actions.

Retail Balance The mix of stores in a district or shopping center.

Retail Catalog Showroom An operation where the consumer selects merchandise from a catalog and shops at a warehouse-style setting. Some goods are stored out of the shopper's reach.

Retail Conglomerate *See* Diversified Retailer.

Retail Information System Anticipates the information needs of retail managers; collects, organizes, and stores relevant data on a continuous basis; and directs the flow of information to the proper retail decision makers.

Retail Institution Refers to the basic format or structure of a business. Institutions can be classified by ownership, store-based retail strategy mix, nonstore-based retail strategy mix, and service versus goods retail strategy mix.

Retail Life Cycle A theory asserting that institutions—like the goods and services they sell—pass through identifiable cycles with four stages: innovation, accelerated development, maturity, and decline.

Retail Method of Accounting A way by which the closing inventory value is determined by calculating the average relationship between the cost and retail values of merchandise available for sale during the period.

Retail Organization How a firm structures and assigns tasks (functions), policies, resources, authority, responsibilities, and rewards in order to efficiently and effectively satisfy the needs of its target market, employees, and management.

Retail Performance Index Encompasses five-year trends in revenue growth and profit growth, and a six-year average return on assets.

Retail Promotion Any communication by a retailer that informs, persuades, and/or reminds the target market about any aspect of that firm.

Retail Reductions Represent the difference between beginning inventory plus purchases during the period and sales plus ending inventory. They should encompass anticipated markdowns, employee and other discounts, and stock shortages.

Retail Strategy The overall plan guiding a retail firm. It has an influence on the firm's business activities and its response to market forces, such as competition and the economy.

Retailing Consists of those business activities involved in the sale of goods and services to consumers for their personal, family, or household use.

Retailing Concept Bases planning on these elements: customer orientation, coordinated effort, and goal orientation.

Retailing Effectiveness Checklist Enables a firm to systematically assess its preparedness for the future.

Return on Assets (ROA) A performance ratio based on a retailer's net sales, net profit, and total assets:

$$\text{Return on assets} = \frac{\text{Net profit}}{\text{Net sales}} \times \frac{\text{Net sales}}{\text{Total assets}} = \frac{\text{Net profit}}{\text{Total assets}}$$

Return on Inventory Investment Equals annual gross profit divided by average inventory at cost.

Return on Net Worth (RONW) A performance ratio based on a retailer's net profit, net sales, total assets, and net worth:

$$\text{Return on net worth} = \frac{\text{Net profit}}{\text{Net sales}} \times \frac{\text{Net sales}}{\text{Total assets}} \times \frac{\text{Total assets}}{\text{Net worth}}$$

Revolving Credit Account Allows a customer to charge items and be billed monthly on the basis of the outstanding cumulative balance.

Risk-Minimization Retailing A strategy that reduces both initial investment costs and the ongoing costs of operations.

ROA *See* Return on Assets.

Robinson-Patman Act Prohibits manufacturers and wholesalers from discrimination in price or sales terms among retailers purchasing products of "like quality," if the effect is to injure competition.

RONW *See* Return on Net Worth.

Routine Decision Making Takes place when a consumer buys out of habit and skips steps in the purchase process.

Safety Stock The extra inventory kept on hand to protect against out-of-stock conditions due to unexpected demand and delays in delivery.

Sale-Leaseback The practice of retailers building new stores and selling them to real-estate investors, who lease the property back to the retailers on a long-term basis.

Sales Forecasting Enables a retailer to estimate expected future revenues for a given time period.

Sales Objectives Concerned with the volume of goods and services sold by a retailer, such as growth, stability, and/or market share.

Sales Opportunity Grid Rates the promise of new goods, services, and/or store outlets across a variety of criteria.

Sales Per Linear Foot of Shelf Space Equals annual sales divided by the total linear footage devoted to the product category.

Sales-Productivity Ratio Method for assigning floor space on the basis of sales or profit per foot.

Sales Promotion The paid marketing communication activities—other than advertising, publicity, and personal selling—that stimulate consumer purchases and dealer effectiveness.

Satisfaction of Publics' Objectives Concerned with stockholders, consumers, suppliers, employees, and the government.

Saturated Trading Area A geographic area having the proper amount of retail facilities to satisfy the needs of its population for a specific good or service, as well as to enable retailers to prosper.

SBD *See* Secondary Business District.

Scrambled Merchandising Occurs if a retailer adds goods and services that are unrelated to each other and to its original business.

Secondary Business District (SBD) An unplanned shopping area in a city or town that is usually bounded by the intersection of two major streets. It has at least a junior department store, a variety store, and/or some larger specialty stores—in addition to many smaller stores.

Secondary Data Have already been gathered for purposes other than to address the issue or problem currently under study.

Secondary Trading Area A geographic area containing an additional 20 to 25 per cent of a store's customers. It is located outside the primary trading area.

Selective Distribution Takes place if suppliers sell via a moderate number of retailers. This lets suppliers have higher sales than possible in exclusive distribution and lets retailers carry some competing brands.

Self-Fulfillment A life-style concept whereby people express their growing sense of uniqueness through goods and services purchases.

Selling Against the Brand The practice of retailers carrying manufacturers' brands and placing high prices on them so rival brands (such as private-label merchandise) can be sold more easily.

Selling Space The area set aside for displays of merchandise, interactions between salespeople and customers, demonstrations, and so on.

Semantic Differential A disguised or nondisguised survey technique, whereby a respondent is asked to rate one or more retailers on several criteria; each criterion is evaluated along a bipolar adjective scale.

Separate Store Organization Treats each branch as a separate store with its own buying responsibilities. Customer needs are identified quickly, but duplication by managers in the main store and the branches is possible.

Service Blueprint Systematically lists all the service functions to be performed and the average time required for each one to be completed.

Service Retailing Involves transactions between companies or individuals and final consumers where the consumers do not purchase or acquire ownership of tangible products. It encompasses rented goods, owned goods, and nongoods.

SERVQUAL Allows retailers to assess the quality of their service offerings by asking customers to react to a series of statements in five areas of performance: tangibles, reliability, responsiveness, assurance, and empathy.

Simulation A type of experiment whereby a computer-based program is used to manipulate the elements of a retail strategy mix rather than test them in a real setting.

Single-Source Data Collection Occurs when a research firm develops a sample of consumer households, determines the demographic and life-style backgrounds of those households via surveys, observes television viewing behavior via in-home cable hookups to the firm's computers, and monitors shopping behavior by having people make purchases in designated stores.

Situation Analysis The candid evaluation of the opportunities and potential problems facing a prospective or existing retailer.

Social Class An informal ranking of people in a culture based on their income, occupation, education, dwelling, and other factors.

Social Cue A signal communicated by talking with friends, fellow employees, and so on. It comes from an interpersonal, noncommercial source.

Social Performance Refers to how well a person does his or her roles as worker, citizen, parent, consumer, and so on.

Social Responsibility Occurs when a retailer acts in the best interests of society—as well as itself. The firm then strives to balance corporate citizenship with a fair level of profits.

Sole Proprietorship An unincorporated retail firm owned by one person.

Sorting Process Involves the retailer's collecting an assortment of goods and services from various sources and offering them to customers.

Specialty Store An outlet that concentrates on selling one goods or service line.

Standard Merchandise Classification A detailed list of common merchandise-reporting categories devised by the National Retail Federation. Its use lets retailers compare their financial data with industry averages.

Standardization A strategy of directly applying a domestic market retail strategy to foreign markets.

Stimulus A cue (social or commercial) or a drive (physical) meant to motivate or arouse a person to act.

Stock-Counting System A unit control system that determines the number of units on hand at regular intervals by actual counting. It records inventory on hand, purchases, sales volume, and shortages during specified periods.

Stock Overage The amount by which a physical inventory value exceeds the book inventory figures. This may be due to errors in conducting a physical inventory or in maintaining a book inventory.

Stock Shortage The amount by which a book inventory figure exceeds a physical ending inventory. This is due to such factors as pilferage, bookkeeping errors, and overshipments not billed to customers.

Stock-to-Sales Method An inventory-level planning technique wherein a retailer wants to maintain a specified ratio of goods-on-hand to sales.

Stock Turnover Represents the number of times during a specific period, usually one year, that the average inventory on hand is sold. Stock turnover can be computed in units or dollars (at retail or cost):

$$\text{Annual rate of stock turnover (in units)} = \frac{\text{Number of units sold during year}}{\text{Average inventory on hand (in units)}}$$

$$\text{Annual rate of stock turnover (in retail dollars)} = \frac{\text{Net yearly sales}}{\text{Average inventory on hand (at retail)}}$$

$$\text{Annual rate of stock turnover (at cost)} = \frac{\text{Cost of goods sold during the year}}{\text{Average inventory on hand (at cost)}}$$

Storability Product Groupings Classify and display products requiring special handling and storage together.

Store Loyalty Exists when a consumer regularly patronizes a particular retailer that he or she knows, likes, and trusts.

Store Maintenance Encompasses all of the activities involved in managing the retailer's physical facilities.

Storefront The total physical exterior of a store. It includes the marquee, entrances, windows, lighting, and construction materials.

Straight Lease Requires the retailer to pay a fixed dollar amount per month over the life of a lease. It is the simplest, most direct lease.

Straight (Gridiron) Traffic Flow Presents displays and aisles in a rectangular or gridiron pattern.

Strategic Approach Concentrates on planning for and adapting to a complex, changing environment.

Strategic Profit Model Expresses the mathematical relationship among net profit margin, asset turnover, and financial leverage. It can be used in planning or controlling a retailer's asset management.

Strategy Mix A firm's particular combination of store location, operating procedures, goods/services offered, pricing tactics, store atmosphere and customer services, and promotional methods.

String An unplanned shopping area comprising a group of retail stores, often with similar or compatible product lines, located along a street or highway.

Supercenter A special type of combination store that blends an economy supermarket with a discount department store.

Supermarket A self-service food store with grocery, meat, and produce departments and minimum annual sales of $2 million. This retail category includes conventional supermarkets, food-based superstores, combination stores, box (limited-line) stores, and warehouse stores.

Supervision The manner of providing a job environment that encourages employee accomplishment.

Survey A research technique whereby information is systematically gathered from respondents by communicating with them.

Survey of Buying Power Reports current demographic data on metropolitan areas, cities, and states. It also provides such information as total annual retail sales by area, annual retail sales for specific product categories, annual effective buying income, and 5-year population and retail sales projections.

Tactics Actions that encompass a retailer's daily and short-term operations.

Tall Organization A format with several levels of managers. It leads to close supervision and fewer employees reporting to each manager.

Target Market The customer group that a retailer seeks to attract and satisfy.

Terms of Occupancy Include ownership versus leasing, the type of lease, operations and maintenance costs, taxes, zoning restrictions, and voluntary regulations.

Theme-Setting Display An interior display that shows a product offering in a thematic manner and lets a retailer portray a specific atmosphere or mood.

Theory X A traditional view of motivation that assumes employees must be closely supervised and controlled.

Theory Y A more modern view of motivation that assumes employees can use self-management and be delegated authority.

Theory Z An emerging view that assumes employees can be given a more participatory role in defining their jobs and sharing some decision making with management.

Threats Environmental and/or marketplace factors that can adversely affect retailers if they do not react to them.

TIGER Computer Tapes Comprise a computer-readable data base that contains digital descriptions of geographic areas (such as area boundaries and codes, latitude and longitude coordinates, and address ranges).

Time Demands The time a person needs to spend operating a business. It is influenced both by consumer demand and needs and by the owner's or manager's ability to automate operations or delegate activities to others.

Time Utilization Refers to the types of activities in which a person is involved and the amount of time allocated to them.

Top-Down Approach to Space Management Exists when a retailer starts with its total available store space (by store and for the overall firm, if a chain), divides it into categories, and then works on in-store layouts.

Top-Down Budgeting Places financial decisions with top management. Their decisions are then communicated down the line to succeeding levels of managers.

Total Retail Experience Consists of all the elements in a retail offering that encourage or inhibit consumers during their contact with a given retailer.

Trading Area The geographic area containing the customers of a particular firm or group of firms for specific goods or services.

Trading Area Overlap Occurs when the trading areas of stores in different locations encroach upon one another. In the overlap area, the same customers are served by both stores.

Traditional Department Store A department store where merchandise quality ranges from average to quite good, pricing is moderate to above average, and customer service levels of help range from medium to high.

Traditional Job Description Contains each position's title, supervisory relationships, committee assignments, and the specific roles and tasks to be performed on an ongoing basis.

Training Programs Used to teach new (and existing) personnel how best to perform their jobs or how to improve themselves.

Transfer of Title When ownership changes from supplier to buyer.

Trickle-Across Theory States that within any social class, there are innovative customers who act as opinion leaders.

Trickle-Down Theory States that a fashion passes from the upper to the lower social classes via three vertical stages: distinctive, emulation, and economic emulation.

Unbundled Pricing Involves a retailer's charging separate prices for each service provided.

Uncontrollable Variables Those aspects of business to which the retailer must adapt (such as competition, the economy, and laws).

Understored Trading Area A geographic area having too few stores selling a specific good or service to satisfy the needs of its population.

Uniform Contract Involves terms that are standard or have already been agreed on, and the order is handled in a routine manner.

Unit Control Relates to the quantities of merchandise a retailer handles during a stated time period.

Unit Pricing A practice required by various states, whereby retailers (mostly food stores) must express price in terms of both the total price of an item and its price per unit of measure.

Universal Product Code (UPC) A classification for coding data onto products via a series of thick and thin vertical lines. The technology lets retailers record information instantly on a product's model number, size, color, and other factors when an item is sold; and transmit the data to a computer that monitors unit sales, inventory levels, and other factors. The UPC is not readable by humans.

Unplanned Business District A retail location where two or more stores are situated together or (in close proximity) in such a manner that the total arrangement or mix of stores in the district is not the result of prior long-range planning.

UPC *See* Universal Product Code.

Usage Rate Average sales per day, in units, of merchandise.

Value Pricing Occurs when prices are set on the basis of fair value for both the service provider and the consumer.

Variable Markup Policy A strategy whereby a retailer designedly varies markups by merchandise category.

Variable Pricing A pricing strategy wherein a retailer alters its prices to coincide with fluctuations in costs or consumer demand.

Variety Store An establishment selling a wide assortment of inexpensive and popularly priced goods and services, such as stationery, gift items, women's accessories, health and beauty aids, light hardware, toys, housewares, confectionary items, and shoe repair.

Vending Machine A retailing format that involves the coin- or card-operated dispensing of goods and services. It eliminates the use of sales personnel and allows for around-the-clock sales.

Vertical Cooperative-Advertising Agreement Enables a manufacturer and a retailer or a wholesaler and a retailer to share an advertisement.

Vertical Marketing System Comprises all the levels of independently owned businesses along a channel of distribution. Goods and services are normally distributed through one of three types of systems: independent, partially integrated, and fully integrated.

Vertical Price Fixing Occurs when manufacturers or wholesalers are able to control the retail prices of their goods and services.

Vertical Retail Audit An in-depth analysis of a retail firm's performance in one area of its strategy mix or operations.

Video-Ordering System Can be in-store or in-home based. In an in-store system, a consumer orders merchandise by entering data into a self-prompting, computerized video-display monitor. The order is processed by the computer, and the consumer goes to a checkout area to pick up and pay for it. An in-home video-ordering system may rely on television programming, interactive computer programming, and merchandise catalogs.

Visual Inspection System A unit control system that uses stock cards to monitor inventory levels.

Want Book A notebook in which store employees record items desired by customers but unstocked or out of stock.

Want Slip A slip on which store employees record requested merchandise that are unstocked or out of stock.

Warehouse Store A discounter offering a moderate number of food items in a no-frills setting.

Weeks' Supply Method An inventory-level planning method wherein beginning inventory is equal to several weeks' expected sales. It assumes the inventory carried is in direct proportion to sales. Under this method:

Beginning-of-month planned inventory level (at retail)	=	Average weekly sales × Number of weeks to be stocked

Weighted Application Blank A form whereby criteria that best correlate with job success are given more weight than others. After weighted scores are given to all job applicants, a minimum total score can be used as a cutoff point for hiring.

Wheel of Retailing A theory stating that retail innovators often first appear as low-price operators with a low-cost structure and low profit-margin requirements. Over time, these innovators upgrade the products they carry and improve store facilities and customer services. They then become vulnerable to new discounters with lower cost structures.

Width of Assortment Refers to the number of distinct goods/service categories with which a retailer is involved.

Word-of-Mouth Communication Occurs when one consumer talks to others.

Yield Management Pricing Used when a service retailer determines the combination of prices that yield the highest level of revenues for a given time period.

Zero-Based Budgeting The practice followed when a firm starts each new budget from scratch and outlines the expenditures needed to reach its goals during that period. All costs must be justified each time a budget is done.

Name Index

Subject Index

An asterisk (*) before a term indicates Glossary entry.

The Use of Computerized Scanning Equipment by Independent Supermarkets

Annual Store Sales Volume	Percentage of Supermarkets Scanning
$2–$4 million	51
$4–$6 million	82
$6–$8 million	92
$8–$12 million	92
$12–$20 million	95
$20 + million	100

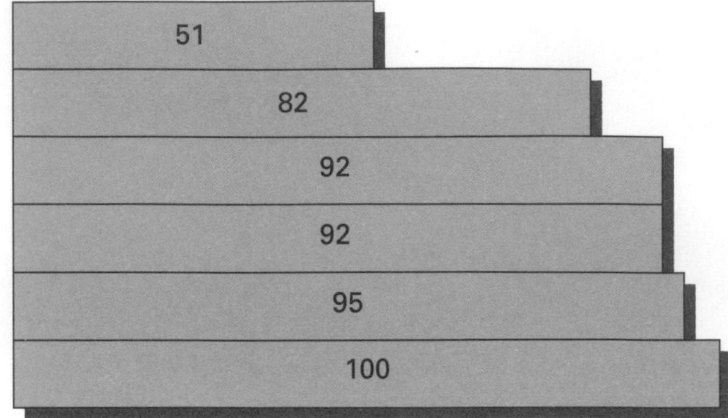

Source: "61st Annual Report of the Grocery Industry," *Progressive Grocer* (April 1994), p. 62.

Typical Compensation Ranges for Personnel in Selected Retailing Positions

Position	Compensation Range
Store management trainee	$17,000–$25,000 +
Assistant buyer	$17,000–$35,000 +
Department manager	$17,000–$35,000 +
Store manager	$17,000–$75,000 +
Buyer	$24,000–$70,000 +
Security director	$32,000–$70,000 +
Senior human resources executive	$33,000–$140,000 +
Market research director	$35,000–$75,000 +
Divisional merchandise manager	$42,000–$85,000 +
Senior advertising executive	$42,000–$110,000 +
Operations director	$47,000–$90,000 +
General merchandise manager	$47,000–$125,000 +
Senior financial executive	$63,000–$200,000 +
Senior merchandising executive	$75,000–$250,000 +
President	$150,000–$800,000 +
Chairman of the board	$150,000–$10,000,000 +

Source: Compiled by the authors from various sources.